MW00769851

University Casebook Series

EDITORIAL BOARD

DAVID L. SHAPIRO
DIRECTING EDITOR
Professor of Law, Harvard University

EDWARD L. BARRETT, Jr.
Professor of Law Emeritus, University of California, Davis

ROBERT C. CLARK
Dean of the School of Law, Harvard University

DANIEL A. FARBER
Professor of Law, University of Minnesota

OWEN M. FISS
Professor of Law, Yale Law School

GERALD GUNTHER
Professor of Law, Stanford University

THOMAS H. JACKSON
President, University of Rochester

HERMA HILL KAY
Dean of the School of Law, University of California, Berkeley

HAROLD HONGJU KOH
Professor of Law, Yale Law School

ROBERT L. RABIN
Professor of Law, Stanford University

CAROL M. ROSE
Professor of Law, Yale Law School

CASS R. SUNSTEIN
Professor of Law, University of Chicago

CASES AND MATERIALS

ON

THE INTERNATIONAL LEGAL SYSTEM

FOURTH EDITION

By

COVEY T. OLIVER
Ferdinand Wakeman Hubbell Professor of Law Emeritus
University of Pennsylvania

EDWIN B. FIRMAGE
Samuel D. Thurman Professor of Law
University of Utah College of Law

CHRISTOPHER L. BLAKESLEY
J.Y. Sanders Professor of Law
Louisiana State University Law Center

RICHARD F. SCOTT
Professor of International Law
American University of Paris

SHARON A. WILLIAMS
Professor of International Law
Osgoode Hall Law School, York University

Westbury, New York
THE FOUNDATION PRESS, INC.
1995

COPYRIGHT © 1973, 1981, 1988 THE FOUNDATION PRESS, INC.

COPYRIGHT © 1995 By THE FOUNDATION PRESS, INC.

615 Merrick Ave.
Westbury, N.Y. 11590–6607
(516) 832–6950

All rights reserved
Printed in the United States of America

Library of Congress Cataloging-in-Publication Data

Cases and materials on the international legal system / by Covey T.
Oliver . . . [et al.]. — 4th ed.
    p.   cm. — (University casebook series)
  Rev. ed. of: Cases and materials on the international legal system
/ by Joseph Modeste Sweeney, Covey T. Oliver, Noyes E. Leech. 3rd
ed. 1988.
  Includes index.
  ISBN 1–56662–135–6
  1. International law—Cases.   2. International and municipal law—
United States—Cases.   I. Oliver, Covey T., 1913–   .
II. Sweeney, Joseph M.   Cases and materials on the international
legal system.   III. Series.
JX68.S88   1994
341—dc20   94–10640

TEXT IS PRINTED ON 10% POST
CONSUMER RECYCLED PAPER

PRINTED WITH
SOY INK

Dedicated to our spouses:
Barbara H. Oliver, Suzy E. Blakesley,
Lorraine L. Scott, and Robert W. Cosman.

*

PREFACE TO THE FOURTH EDITION

The Third Edition of THE INTERNATIONAL LEGAL SYSTEM went to press in August, 1988. Since then, quite recently, molar changes almost entirely unforeseen have occurred, altering the planetary societal environment that had developed after World War II. During the period covered by the first three editions of this work [1972–1988] major conditioning factors bearing on the status, effectiveness and growth of world legal order included Doomsday-like dangers of mass destruction, seemingly unbridgeable ideological conflicts between groups of nation–states, particularly the superpowers; and the division of the world between "Rich Nations — Poor Nations."

Perhaps the most significant, positive, legal development in this period was the rise of human rights as a law-involving development, albeit this being a partial and uncertain one. Unmet challenges included gridlock in the United Nations, resulting from the effect of the Cold War on the use of the veto power in the Security Council and the domination of the General Assembly by underdeveloped, often defensive and perturbed, countries. Judicial resolution of legal issues between states by the World Court was sporadic and halting; and a decade or so into the period the United States withdrew as defendant from an aggression complaint after it lost the first (jurisdictional) round, specifically impugning, in the process, the integrity of the Court itself. Despite the negative factors, however, scholarly attention to and student participation in "international legal studies" grew robustly, including oceans, atmosphere and space law; international trade, investment and financial law; international crime law; the legal philosophy of international law; "peace-keeping" by United Nations forces; and, as already mentioned, human rights.

Today, legal norms, principles, and structures are being subjected to stresses that may alter materially some of the contours of planetary legal order. Among these stressed areas are the territorial reach of state authority, individual and group human rights, access to and sharing of planetary resources, protection of the physical environment of a small planet, evermore heavily populated; and equilibrium between ethnicity and statehood. This edition gives attention to such areas, including an entirely new part on Environmental Law. We continue to draw cases and materials from other legal systems than that of the United States where we deem them useful. But the majority of users will remain American and we must continue to deal with some aspects of the foreign affairs law of the United States, such as the American way with treaties, immunity of foreign sovereignties, and separation of powers within the Federal triad.

Professors Leech and Sweeney, two of the originating editors, have chosen for personal reasons not to continue with this one; but their solid contributions to the earlier books continue to influence the tone and style of this edition, especially as to the encouragement of student interest and involvement.

The focus described in the Preface to the First Edition and continued in the Second and Third has been well-received by both students and teachers. We of the Fourth Edition have tried to keep the "feel" of the earlier versions, despite the environment of change and new dimensions described above. We are highly pleased to have for this book Professor Sharon A. Williams, a colleague from Canada. Her association will assuredly bring new perspectives, worldwide as well as neighborly and hemispheric. Also, Professor Richard F. Scott, who teaches at Paris (France), and Christopher L. Blakesley who teaches International Criminal and "Civil Law" courses in Louisiana, one of the two United States "civil law" jurisdictions, and who often teaches and publishes in Europe, will ensure continuation of the linkages to European outlooks heretofore provided by Professor Sweeney. Edwin B. Firmage brings special expertise in U.S. Constitutional Law and its combination with International Law, human rights, and foreign affairs.

COVEY T. OLIVER
EDWIN B. FIRMAGE
CHRISTOPHER L. BLAKESLEY
RICHARD F. SCOTT
SHARON A. WILLIAMS

December 19, 1994

TABLE OF CONTENTS

TABLE OF CONTENTS

xix

TABLE OF CONTENTS

TABLE OF CONTENTS

TABLE OF CONTENTS

TABLE OF ABBREVIATIONS

The following are abbreviations that have been used by the editors in their citations to principal cases and major materials and in their notes.

A.B.A.J. ....American Bar Association Journal
A.C. ....Law Report series [British], House of Lords
ADIZ..................................Air Defense Identification Zone
All E.R. ....All England Law Reports [1936–date]
A.J.I.L. ....American Journal of International Law
A.S.I.L..............................American Society of International Law
ANCOM ....Andean Common Market
Ann.Dig. ....Annual Digest and Reports of International Law
                Cases [title of Int'l Law Reports prior to 1953]
Brit.Y.B.Int'l L. ....British Yearbook of International Law
C.A. ....Law Report series, Court of Appeal
CACM ....Central American Common Market
C.F.R. ....Code of Federal Regulations
Cal.2d ....California Reports, Second Series
CCH Trade Cases...........Trade Regulation Reporter
                [Commerce Clearing House]
Ch. ....Law Report series, Chancery [1891–date]
Common Mkt.L.R. ....Common Market Law Reports
C.M.A................................Court of Military Appeals Reports
C.-M.Rep. ....Court-Martial Reports
Cr.Cas.Res. ....Law Report series, Crown Cases Reserved
                [1865–1875]
D. ....Recueil Dalloz, [French Reporter]
Dall....................................Dallas, United States Supreme Court Reports
DEWIZ.............................Distant Early Warning Identification Zone
E.C. ....European Community
E.Comm.Ct.J.Rep...........European Community Court of Justice Reports
ECOSOC Off.Rec. ....United Nations Economic and Social Council,
                Official Records
EEC...................................European Economic Community
EFTA.................................European Free Trade Association
F.2d ....Federal Reporter, Second Series [1924–date]
F.R.D. ....Federal Rules Decisions
F.Supp. ....Federal Supplement
FCN....................................Friendship, Commerce and Navigation Treaties
FM ....Department of the Army Field Manual
Ga. ....Georgia Supreme Court Reports
G.A.Res. ....General Assembly Resolution
GATT ....General Agreement on Tariffs and Trade
GSP....................................Generalized System of Preference
Harv.Int'l L.J. ....Harvard International Law Journal
IATA..................................International Air Transport Association

ICI	Imperial Chemical Industries, Ltd.
I.C.A.O.	International Civil Aviation Organization
I.C.J.Rep.	International Court of Justice Reports
ICSID	International Center for Settlement of Investment Disputes
Ill.Rev.Stat.	Illinois Revised Statutes
I.L.O.Off.Bull.	International Labour Office, Official Bulletin
Int'l & Comp.L.Q.	International and Comparative Law Quarterly
I.L.M.	International Legal Materials
Int'l L.Rep.	International Law Reports
IMT	International Military Tribunal
K.B.	Law Report series, Kings Bench
LAFTA	Latin American Free Trade Association
L.Ed.2d	Lawyer's Editors, Second Series, United States Supreme Court Reporter
MFN	Most favored nation
M.I.T.I.	Ministry of International Trade and Industry
N.Y.Misc.2d	New York Miscellaneous, Second Series, [1955–date]
MNEs	Multinational enterprises
NATO	North Atlantic Treaty Organization
N.E.	North Eastern Reporter [1885–1936]
N.Y.	New York Reports
N.Y.S.2d	New York Supplement, Second Series [1937–date]
OECD	Organization for Economic Cooperation and Development
OPIC	Overseas Private Investment Corporation
P.	Law Report series, Probate, Divorce and Admiralty
P.2d	Pacific Reporter, Second Series
Pas.	Pasicrisie [Belgian Reporter]
P.C.I.J.	Permanent Court of International Justice
Q.B.	Law Report series, Queen's Bench
SALT I	Strategic Arms Limitation Talks I
S.Ct.	Supreme Court Reporter [U.S., 1882–date]
Sirey	Sirey, Recueil Général des Lois et des Arrêts [France]
S.E.	Southeastern Reporter
So.2d	Southern Reporter, Second Series [1941–date]
So.African L.Rep.	South African Law Reports
Stat.	Statutes at Large, United States
T.I.A.S.	Treaties and Other International Acts Series
U.N.Conf.Int'l Org.	United Nations Conference on International Organization [San Francisco Conference]
UNCITRAL	United Nations Commission on International Trade Law
UNCTAD	United Nations Conference on Trade and Development

TABLE OF ABBREVIATIONS

*

ACKNOWLEDGMENTS

We would like to acknowledge our indebtedness to the following authors, publishers and organizations for giving us permission to reprint excerpts from the books, periodicals and other documents indicated in parentheses:

Agence France Presse (excerpt from World's Smallest States at Risk over Environment);

Alfred A. Knopf, Inc., New York (excerpt from Morgenthau, Politics Among Nations);

American Association of the International Commission of Jurists (excerpt from Human Rights in United States and United Kingdom Foreign Policy);

American Institute of Aeronautics & Astronautics (excerpts from Proceedings of the Twenty-sixth Colloquium on the Law of Outer Space);

American Law Institute (excerpts from 1965 Restatement of the Law);

American Law Institute (excerpts from 1987 Restatement of the Law);

American Society of International Law (excerpt from American Society of International Law Newsletter);

American Society of International Law (excerpt from Cossman, Reform, Revolution, or Retrenchment? International Human Rights in the Post-Cold War Era);

American Society of International Law (excerpt from Koskenniemi, The Future of Statehood);

American Society of International Law (excerpts from American Journal of International Law);

American Society of International Law (excerpts from American Society of International Law, Environmental Law Interest Group Newsletter);

American Society of International Law (excerpts from International Legal Materials);

American Society of International Law (excerpts from Proceedings, 77th Annual Meeting, American Society of International Law);

American Society of International Law and Bruno Ristau (excerpt from International Legal Materials);

American University Journal of International Law and Policy (excerpt from American University Journal of International Law and Policy);

Associated Press (excerpt from The San Francisco Chronicle);

Bellhaven Press (excerpt from Environmental Protection and the Law of War);

ACKNOWLEDGMENTS

Buchheit and Yale University Press (excerpt from Buchheit, Secession: The Legitimacy of Self-Determination);

Burroughs & Co., Ltd., Canada (excerpt from Western Weekly Report);

Butterworth's, Canada, Ltd. (excerpts from Williams and De Mestral, An Introduction to International Law);

Butterworth's , London (excerpt from All E.R.);

Butterworth's, London (excerpt from Introduction to International Law);

Carnegie Endowment for International Peace (excerpts from Carnegie Endowment);

Case Western Reserve Journal of International Law (excerpt from Case Western Reserve Journal of International Law);

Columbia Journal Trans. Law (excerpt from Columbia Journal Trans. Law);

Columbia University Press (excerpt from Friedmann and Beguin, Joint International Business Ventures in Developing Countries);

Council for Ocean Law (excerpt from Oceans Policy News);

Council on Foreign Relations, Inc. (excerpts from Campbell, The United States in World Affairs);

Detroit-Mercy Law Review and Louis Rene Beres (excerpt from After the Gulf War: Iraq, Genocide and International Law);

E. Lauterpacht and Grotuis Publications, Inc., England (excerpt from Annotated Digest);

Editions du Centre National de la Recherche Scientifique, Paris (excerpt from Repertoire de la Pratique Francaise en Matiere de Droit International Public);

Editions Techniques, Paris (excerpts from Journal du Droit International);

Editor of the International Law Reports (excerpts form Annotated Digest);

Editor of the International Law Reports (excerpts from International Law Reports);

Editoriale Scientifica, Naples (excerpts from Italian Yearbook of International Law);

Elinore Ostrom, Simon & Sauster, and Prentice-Hall Publishers (excerpt from Ostrom, Governing the Commons);

European Law Centre, London (excerpts from Common Market Law Reports);

Fletcher Forum of World Affairs (excerpt from Fletcher Forum of World Affairs);

ACKNOWLEDGMENTS

Fordham International Law Journal (excerpt from Fordham International Law Journal);

George Mason Law Review (excerpt from Firmage, Rogue Presidents);

Georgia Journal of International and Comparative Law (excerpts from Georgia Journal of International and Comparative Law);

Georgia University Law Review (excerpt from Georgia University Law Review);

Harvard Human Rights Journal (excerpt from Harvard Human Rights Journal);

Harvard International Law Journal Association (excerpts from Harvard Journal of International Law);

Houston Journal of International Law (excerpt from Houston Journal of International Law);

Indian Society of International Law (excerpts from Indian Journal of International Law);

Institute and Centre of Air and Space Law, McGill University (excerpt from Annals of Air and Space Law);

Instituto Interamericano de Drechos Humanos, Costa Rica (excerpt from Human Rights, Sustainable Development and the Environment);

International Bar Association (excerpt from International Business Lawyer);

International Bar Association (excerpt from International Newsletter of Committee F of the Section of Business Law of the International Bar Association);

International Bureau of Fiscal Documentation, Amsterdam (excerpts from European Taxation);

International Commission of Jurists, Switzerland (excerpt from Review of the International Commission of Jurists);

International Committee of the Red Cross (excerpt from 1991 Annual Report of the International Committee of the Red Cross);

International Enforcement Law Reporter (excerpt from International Enforcement Law Reporter);

Johns Hopkins University Press, Law and Civil War in the Modern World (J.Moore, ed., 1974) (excerpt from E.Firmage, on Wars of National Liberation);

Johns Hopkins University Press, The International Law of Civil War (Falk ed. 1971) (excerpt from E.Firmage, Summary and Interpretation);

Joseph W. Bishop, Jr. (excerpt from Bishop, Justice Under Fire);

Journal of Commerce (excerpt from The Journal of Commerce);

ACKNOWLEDGMENTS

Julius Stone and Wm. W. Gaunt & Sons, Inc., Florida (excerpt from Stone, Legal Controls of International Conflict);

Kluwer Academic Publishers, The Netherlands (excerpt from The Structure and Process of International Law: Essays in Legal Philosophy, Doctrine, and Theory);

l'Institut Henri Dunant (excerpt from Durand, From Sarajevo to Hiroshima);

Kluwer Law & Tax Publishers (excerpts from The European Community Law – Making Machine and Litigating European Community Law);

Lawyers Alliance for Nuclear Arms Control (excerpt from Smith, Foreword to Sherr, A Legal Analysis of the "New Interpretation" of the Anti-Ballistic Missile Treaty);

Le Monde (excerpt from The Second National Apology in the Rainbow Warrior Affair);

Loyola Louisiana Law Review (excerpt from Loyola Louisiana Law Review);

Martinus Nijhoff (excerpt from Experts Group on Environmental Law of the World Commission on Environment and Development IX);

Martinus Nijhoff (excerpts from Experts Group on Environmental Law of the World Commission on Environment and Development, Environmental Protection and Sustainable Development, Legal Principles and Recommendations, Elements for a Draft Convention);

Martinus Nijhoff (excerpts from Kwiatkowska & Soons, Transboundary Movements and Disposal of Hazardous Wastes in International Law);

Martinus Nijhoff (excerpts from Schachter, International Law in Theory and Practice 11);

Max Planck Institute for Comparative Public Law and International Law, Heidelberg (excerpts from International Symposium on Judicial Settlement of International Disputes);

Michigan Journal of International Law (excerpts from Michigan Journal of International Law);

Michigan Journal of International Law and Karen Engel (excerpt from Engel, International Human Rights and Feminism: When Discourses Meet);

Michigan Law Review (excerpt from Michigan Law Review);

Morton A. Kaplan and John Wiley & Sons (excerpt from Kaplan and Katzenbach, The Political Foundations of International Law);

N.P. Engel, Publisher, Virginia (excerpt from Human Rights Law Journal);

New York University Journal of International Law and Policy (excerpt from New York University Journal of International Law and Policy);

ACKNOWLEDGMENTS

Oceana Publications, New York (excerpt from Studies in International Adjudication);

Oxford University Press (excerpt from Birnie and Boyle, International Law and the Environment);

Oxford University Press (excerpt from Brownlie, Principles of Public International Law 698);

Oxford University Press (excerpt from World Commission on Environment and Development);

Oxford University Press (excerpts from Brownlie, International Law 4);

P. Loomis, R. Grant, and the North-Holland Publishing Company (excerpts from Journal of Comparative Corporate Law and Securities Regulation);

Pocket Star Books and Bob Woodward (excerpt from Woodward, The Commanders);

Prentice-Hall, New Jersey (excerpt from Bennett, International Organizations: Principles and Issues);

Princeton University Press (excerpt from DeVisscher, Theory and Reality in Public International Law);

Princeton University Press (excerpt from Patterson, Discrimination in International Trade, the Policy Issues);

Quadrangle Books, Inc, New York (excerpt from Taylor, Nuremberg and Vietnam);

Ruth Wedgwood and the Bar of the City of New York (excerpt from Report for the Association of the Bar of the City of New York's Committee on International Arms Control and Security Affairs & the Committee on International Law, the Use of Armed Force in International Affairs: The Case of Panama, in the Record of the Association of the Bar of the City of New York);

Schulthess Polygraphischer Verlag AG, Zurich (excerpt from Annuaire Suisse De Droit International);

Sharon A. Williams (excerpt from Williams, The International and National Protection of Cultural Property: A Comparative Study);

Sijthoff & Nordhoff International Publishers, The Netherlands (excerpt from Seyersted, United Nations Forces in the Law of Peace and War);

South Dakota Law Review (excerpt from South Dakota Law Review);

Stanford Law Review (excerpt from Stanford Law Review);

Stevens & Sons, Ltd., (excerpt from Law Quarterly Review);

Stevens & Sons, Ltd., London (excerpt from McNair, The Law of the Air 4);

ACKNOWLEDGMENTS

Stevens & Sons, Ltd., London (excerpts from O'Connell, International Law);

T.M.C. Asser Instituut, The Hague (excerpts from Netherlands Yearbook of International Law);

Texas International Law Journal (excerpt from Texas International Law Journal);

The Incorporated Council of Law Reporting for England and Wales, London (excerpt from W.L.R.);

The Incorporated Council of Law Reporting for England and Wales, London (excerpts from the Queen's Bench);

The Incorporated Council of Law Reporting for England and Wales, London (excerpts from the King's Bench);

The Incorporated Council of Law Reporting of England and Wales, London (excerpt from A.C.);

The Macmillan Company, New York (excerpt from Schwartz, A Commentary on the Constitution of the United States: The Powers of Government);

The Office for Official Publications; European Communities, Luxembourg (excerpts from Louis, The Community Legal Order);

Third World Quarterly (excerpt from Third World Quarterly);

Transnational Publishers, Inc. (excerpt from Brunee, Acid Rain and Ozone Layer Depletion: International Law and Regulation);

Transnational Publishers, Inc. (excerpt from Kiss and Shelton, International Environmental Law);

Transnational Publishers, Inc. and Edith Brown Weiss (excerpts from Weiss, In Fairness to Future Generations);

United Nations (excerpt from United Nations Handbook on the Pacific Settlement of Disputes Between States 55);

United Nations University Press, Japan (excerpts from Environmental Change and International Law);

University of Illinois Press (excerpts from Wormuth and Firmage, To Chain the Dog of War);

University of Indiana Law Journal and Fred Rothman & Co. (excerpt from Delbruck, A Fresh Look at Humanitarian Intervention under the Authority of the United Nations);

University of Pennsylvania Press (excerpt from Human Rights in Cross-Cultural Perspectives);

University of Pittsburgh Law Review (excerpt from University of Pittsburgh Law Review);

ACKNOWLEDGMENTS

Virginia Journal of International Law (excerpt from Virginia Journal of International Law);

Virginia Journal of International Law (excerpts from Virginia Journal of International Law);

Wash. and Lee Law Review and J.H. Jackson (excerpt from Jackson, World Trade Rules and Environmental Policies: Congruence or Conflict?);

Wisconsin Law Review (excerpt from Wisconsin Law Review);

Yale Journal of International Law (excerpt from Yale Journal of International Law);

Yale University Press (excerpt from H. Koh, The National Security Constitution);

We would also like to thank our colleagues: John S. Baker, Jr.; Chancellor Winston R. Day; John Devlin; Karen L. Engle; Lee W. Hargrave; Alain A. Levasseur; Ileana N. Porras; George W. Pugh; Katherine S. Spaht; Symeon C. Symeonides; John Valérie White; Judge Tran van Linh; George D. Jacobsen; Madeline H. Hebert; Charlotte Melius; our research assistants: Fred Burmester; Heidi Buchi; Christina Fletcher; Aline Aucoin; and our staff colleagues: Gladys H. Dreher; Susan Sarnataro; Delia Dupré; and Barbara Catrow; Laurie T. Knight.

*

TABLE OF CASES

Principal cases are in italic type. Non-principal cases are in roman type. References are to Pages.

1

CASES AND MATERIALS

ON

THE INTERNATIONAL LEGAL SYSTEM

*

Chapter 1

APPLICATION OF THE LAW OF THE INTERNATIONAL SYSTEM

---

1. *The nature of international law.* This book begins with a sketch of the structure of the present legal order of the planet. Along with many others, we think there is such an order, albeit less intricate and possibly less assuredly applicable than internal law in those modern states where there is a reasonably high correlation between the rules and what happens.

We could have begun with such classic introductory devices as: (a) Is international law law? (b) What is law anyway? (c) Can there be law if there is no supranational authority to impose it? We believe that the student will be better able to deal with these questions after some

1

exposure to the subject matter that is the corpus juris of what is called international public law, transnational law, and foreign affairs law and dealt with as such by lawyers all over the world, whether in advocacy, consultative or decision making roles.

The more jurisprudential materials are in our Chapter 18. Some may prefer to take them earlier. Even so, we think Chapter 1 should be taken first.

The law we study is not adequate to manage planetary affairs even now. A major purpose of a law school course in this area is to draw attention to the urgent need for the growth of order beyond the rules that have developed in the West, along with the national state system, over the past half millenium. We must do the best we can with what is currently available.

Chapter 1 is analytically descriptive of the system. It also introduces some of the major operational challenges, viz: (a) universality, (b) effectiveness, (c) state dissent from binding effect, (d) limitations of the arbitral-adjudicatory process as a means of resolving conflicts.

2. *Traditional sources of international law.* The subject is complex, but there is no attempt to treat it here in depth. It is presented merely in outline; its components can be discussed in detail wherever suitable in the book. See, for example, Chapter 4, The Law of the Sea, with its extensive discussion of the nature of customary international law and its relationship to treaty law. The sole purpose of this note is to introduce the subject.

Article 38 of the Statute of the International Court of Justice:

1. The Court, whose function is to decide in accordance with international law such disputes as are submitted to it, shall apply:

a. international conventions, whether general or particular, establishing rules expressly recognized by the contesting states;

b. international custom, as evidence of a general practice accepted as law;

c. the general principles of law recognized by civilized nations;

d. subject to the provisions of Article 59, judicial decisions and the teachings of the most highly qualified publicists of the various nations, as subsidiary means for the determination of rules of law.

* * *

This hierarchy of legal authority is *"civilian"* or continental in nature. International conventions, like legislation or the code in *civilian* jurisdictions, international custom, and general principles of law, are all binding or primary authority. Judicial decisions and teachings of the most highly qualified publicists, or doctrine, are persuasive authority. The latter, essentially are to be used to prove the existence of custom. This is the same as in *civilian* domestic systems. Take, for example, the Civil Code of Louisiana, which originally was adopted from the French *Projet* or Digest for their *Code Napoléon*:

Art. 1: The sources of law are legislation and custom.

Art. 2: Legislation is the solemn expression of legislative will.

Art. 3: Custom results from practice repeated for a long time and generally accepted as having acquired the force of law. Custom may not abrogate legislation.

Art. 4: When no rule for a particular situation can be derived from legislation or custom, the court is bound to proceed according to equity. To decide equitably, resort is made to justice.

Or note the Iraqi Code, which follows essentially the same hierarchy of authority, adding general principles of Islam:

§ 1: The Code governs all questions of law which come within the letter or spirit of any of its provisions.

§ 2: If the Code does not furnish an applicable provision, the court shall decide in accordance with customary law, and failing that, in accordance with those *principles of Muslim law* (Shari'a) which are most in keeping with the provisions of this Code, without being bound by any particular school of jurisprudence, and, failing that, in accordance with the principles of equity.

§ 3: In all of this, the Court shall be guided by judicial decisions and by the principles of jurisprudence in Iraq and in foreign countries whose laws are similar to those of Iraq.

Thus, to understand international law properly, to be able to negotiate, litigate, or even to communicate effectively in the arena of international law, it is necessary to understand that its origin and discipline, its philosophical context, and the mindset of most of its practitioners is "civilian" or a variation on that theme.

Questions

How does this hierarchy of sources compare to that in "common law" systems? What is the only binding authority? Will the nature of the sources of international law make a difference in how you will research, negotiate, or litigate a legal problem? Where will you look to find evidence of authoritative sources such as Custom and General Principles? Keep these issues in mind as you study.

3. **International Custom.**

Custom is also analyzed in chapter 4, infra.

BROWNLIE, INTERNATIONAL LAW 4 (4th ed., 1990)*

Definition. Article 38 refers to "international custom, as evidence of a general practice accepted as law", and Brierly remarks that "what is sought for is a general recognition among States of a certain practice as obligatory". Although occasionally the terms are used interchangeably, "custom" and "usage" are terms of art and have different meanings.

* Reprinted with the permission of the Oxford University Press.

A usage is a general practice which does not reflect a legal obligation, and examples are ceremonial salutes at sea and the practice of exempting diplomatic vehicles from parking prohibitions.

Evidence. The material sources which establish custom are numerous and include the following: diplomatic correspondence, policy statements, press releases, the opinions of official legal advisers, official manuals on legal questions, e.g. manuals of military law, executive decisions and practices, orders to naval forces etc., comments by governments on drafts produced by the International Law Commission, state legislation, international and national judicial decisions, recitals in treaties and other international instruments, a pattern of treaties in the same form, the practice of international organs, and resolutions relating to legal questions in the United Nations General Assembly. Obviously the value of these sources varies and much depends on the circumstances.

The elements of custom

(a) Duration. Provided the consistency and generality of a practice are proved, no particular duration is required: the passage of time will be a part of the evidence of generality and consistency. A long practice is not necessary, and rules relating to airspace and the continental shelf have emerged from fairly quick maturing of practice. The International Court does not emphasize the time element as such in its practice.

(b) Uniformity, consistency of the practice. This is very much a matter of appreciation and a tribunal will have considerable freedom of determination in many cases. Complete uniformity is not required, but substantial uniformity is, and thus in the Fisheries case [19] the Court refused to accept the existence of a ten-mile rule for bays.

(c) Opinio juris et necessitatis. The Statute of the International Court refers to "a general practice *accepted as law*". Brierly speaks of recognition by states of a certain practice "as obligatory", and Hudson requires a "conception that the practice is required by, or consistent with, prevailing international law". Some writers do not consider this psychological element to be a requirement for the formation of custom, but it is in fact a necessary ingredient. The sense of legal obligation, as opposed to motives of courtesy, fairness, or morality, is real enough, and the practice of states recognizes a distinction between obligation and usage. Proof, and especially the incidence of the burden of proof [are the most difficult problems].

In terms of the practice of the International Court of Justice—which provides a general guide to the nature of the problem—there are two methods of approach. In many cases the Court is willing to assume the existence of an *opinio juris* on the basis of evidence of a general practice, or a consensus in the literature, or the previous determinations of the Court or other international tribunals. However, in a significant minor-

---

19. ICJ Reports (1951), 116 at 131. See also the Genocide case, ibid. 25: "In fact, the examples of objections made to reserva- tions appear to be too rare in international practice to have given rise to such a rule."

ity of cases the Court has adopted a more rigorous approach and has called for more positive evidence of the recognition of the validity of the rules in question in the practice of states. The choice of approach appears to depend upon the nature of the issues (that is, the state of the law may be a primary point in contention), and the discretion of the Court.

* * *

The persistent objector. The way in which custom resolves itself into a question of special relations is illustrated by the rule that a state may contract out of a custom in the process of formation. Evidence of objection must be clear and there is probably a presumption of acceptance which is to be rebutted. Whatever the theoretical underpinnings of the principle, it is well recognized by international tribunals, and in the practice of states. Given the majoritarian tendency of international relations the principle is likely to have increased prominence.

The subsequent objector. In the Fisheries case [*infra,* ch. 4] part of the Norwegian argument was that certain rules were not rules of general international law, and, even if they were, they did not bind Norway, which had "consistently and unequivocally manifested a refusal to accept them". The United Kingdom admitted the general principle of the Norwegian argument [but denied] that, as a matter of fact, Norway had consistently and unequivocally manifested a refusal to accept the rules. Thus the United Kingdom regarded the question as one of persistent objection. The Court did not deal with the issue in this way, however, and the *ratio* in this respect was that Norway had departed from the alleged rules, if they existed, *and other states had acquiesced* in this practice. But the Court is not [clear] about the role of acquiescence in validating a subsequent contracting out of rules. [The] problem of change in a customary regime [is problematic]. Presumably, if a substantial number of states assert a new rule, the momentum of increased defection, complemented by acquiescence, may result in a new rule, as in the case of the law on the continental shelf. [*See* ch. 4, *infra.*] If the process is slow and neither the new rule nor the old have a majority of adherents then the consequence is a network of special relations based on opposability, acquiescence, and historic title.

Proof of custom. In principle a court is presumed to know the law and may apply a custom even if it has not been expressly pleaded. In practice the proponent of a custom has a burden of proof, the nature of which will vary according to the subject-matter and the form of the pleadings. Thus in the Lotus case [*infra,* ch. 3] the Court spoke of the plaintiff's burden in respect of a general custom. Where a "local or regional custom" is alleged, the proponent "must prove that this custom is established in such a manner that it has become binding on the other Party".

SCHACHTER, INTERNATIONAL LAW IN
THEORY AND PRACTICE 11 (1991) *

Does it follow * * * that a particular State may reject the system and opt out of it? In a speculative way, one may conceive of a régime in control of a territory resting its claim to authority solely on its naked power (or perhaps on assertion of religious authority) without a claim of rights under international law as such. Whether the exercise of authority in such cases would be acquiesced in by other States is an empirical matter. In practice, no State in the contemporary period has attempted to reject the system as a whole. However, on occasion, representatives of newly independent States asserted in the 1960s that they could not be bound by a system of law in whose creation they had no opportunity to participate. However, this sweeping assertion did not in fact preclude their explicit or implicit claim of rights of territorial integrity and political independence (and other basic rights) under international law. The acceptance of international law was a necessary implication of their assertion of sovereign equality and their claim to be treated as a State. In actuality, the claim that they could not be bound by the rules to which they had not assented was aimed at specific customary law rules (such as those in State responsibility), and not at the whole body of customary law.

* * *

The leading pronouncements by the Court appear in the judgment in the Asylum case:

The party which relies on a custom * * * must prove that this custom is established in such a manner that it has become binding on the other party * * * that the rule invoked * * * is in accordance with a constant and uniform usage practised by the States in question, and that this usage is the expression of a right appertaining to the State granting asylum and a duty incumbent on the territorial State. This follows from Article 38 of the Statute of the Court, which refers to international custom "as evidence of a general practice accepted as law".

* * *

(c) *Generality of the practice.* This is an aspect which complements that of consistency. Certainly universality is not required, but the real problem is to determine the value of abstention from protest by a substantial number of states in face of a practice followed by some others. Silence may denote either tacit agreement or a simple lack of interest in the issue. It may be that the Court in the Lotus case misjudged the consequences of absence of protest and also the significance of fairly general abstention from prosecutions by states other than the flag state. In the Fisheries Jurisdiction case * * * the International Court referred to the extension of a fishery zone up to a twelve-mile limit "which appears now to be generally accepted" and to "an increasing and widespread acceptance of the concept of preferential rights for coastal states" in a situation of special dependence on coastal fisheries.

* Reprinted with the permission of Martinus Nihoff.

[Another] * * * proposition constitutes the "strongest" use of voluntarist theory. It would allow a State to reject the application of a customary rule to it simply on the ground that it was contrary to the State's present will. No State, to my knowledge, has openly espoused that position. It would amount to a denial of customary law and it is most unlikely that any State would be prepared to take that position. However, a State may seek to avoid submitting to a rule by adopting a more moderate form of consensualism and asserting that it had manifested its objection in the past or that its lack of explicit consent taken together with similar lack of acceptances by other States has been enough to defeat the application of the rule as universally binding. This would be similar to the argument West Germany successfully maintained in the *North Sea Continental Shelf* case in denying the application of the equidistant line as a mandatory rule of law. The issue in a case of this kind would turn on the facts and the requirements as to the degree of generality, consistency of practice and extent of *opinio juris*. In making such assessments, underlying attitudes as to the importance of the "will" of States are likely to play a role, even if they are not articulated. * * *

Voluntarism in a somewhat different guise can also be found when a State objects to a rule on the ground that it is incompatible with a vital interest of the State. In such case, the recalcitrant State rests not simply on its will per se but on a superior norm of self-interest that is said to prevail over law. An example well known in the United States was the statement of the former Secretary of State, Dean Acheson, at the time of the Cuban missile case that the "quarantine" imposed by the United States could not be dealt with as a legal issue since international law "does not deal with questions of ultimate power" and "the survival of States is not a matter of law". The statement has been taken to mean that a State may decide for itself whether its "ultimate power" or survival are at stake and, if so, to disregard the law. This view, it should be noted, is not the same as reliance on the legal right of self-defence. It is a claim that the State's will, if based on a vital State interest, must prevail over law. The position in effect denies the applicability of the law to critical issues particularly involving the right to use force.

4. *Actions of International Organizations as sources of law.*

BROWNLIE, PRINCIPLES OF PUBLIC INTERNATIONAL LAW 698 (4th ed., 1990) *

The varied roles played by organizations may be distinguished as follows:

(a) Sponsorship of treaty-making. The United Nations has convoked diplomatic conferences for the purposes of drafting and opening for signature important multilateral treaties, as for example the four Conventions on the Law of the Sea of 1958. The constituent instrument of an organization may contain provisions giving the organization an initiating power, and streamlining the procedure, in respect of amendments to the instrument.

* Reprinted with the permission of the Oxford University Press.

(b) Forums for state practice. Statements on legal questions by governments through their representatives in organs and committees of organs provide evidence of customary law. So it is also with the voting on resolutions concerned with legal matters. * * *

(c) Prescriptive resolutions. A resolution not in itself binding may prescribe principles of international law and be merely declaratory. However, the mere formulation of principles may elucidate and develop the customary law. When a resolution of the General Assembly touches on subjects dealt with in the United Nations Charter, it may be regarded as an authoritative interpretation of the Charter: obvious examples are the Universal Declaration of Human Rights and the Declaration on the Granting of Independence to Colonial Countries and Peoples contained in resolutions of the General Assembly. Resolutions on new legal problems provide a means of corralling and defining the quickly growing practice of states, while remaining hortatory in form.

(d) Channels for expert opinion. Organizations often establish bodies of legal experts in connection with projects for the codification or progressive development of the law, the most important being the International Law Commission of the United Nations General Assembly, and, like governments, organizations have a staff of legal advisers from whom proceed expert and highly influential opinions.

(e) Decisions of organs with judicial functions. Clearly decisions of judicial organs, such as the Court of Justice of the European Communities, may contribute to the development of the law of treaties, principles of interpretation, and general international law. The specialized function of such bodies may of course limit their contribution to the latter.

(f) The practice of political organs. Political organs, and particularly the General Assembly and Security Council of the United Nations, make numerous recommendations and decisions relating to specific issues, which involve the application of general international law, or, where there is no identity of the two, the provisions of the Charter or some other constituent instrument. Such practice provides evidence of the state of the law and also of the meaning of texts, and has considerable legal significance. However, as with the practice of states, the nature of the particular decision and the extent to which legal matters were considered must be examined before much legal weight is given to the decision. Furthermore, to give legal significance to an omission of an organ to condemn is hazardous in the extreme, since this omission turns often on the political attitude of the majority in the organ concerned. Moreover, many jurists regard the decisions of political organs in terms of the arithmetic of voting, the decisions being taken to represent the views of n states in the majority and their cogency being roughly on a scale n majority divided by n minority states. Obviously states cannot by their control of numbers of international organizations raise in some sense the value of their state practice by reference to the "practice of organizations".

In certain instances a consistent and uniform interpretation by members of an organ placed upon a persistent practice, for example, in matters of voting, adopted *by that organ* will be opposable to *all* members provided that there is substantial evidence of general acceptance by members of the organization. On this basis in its Advisory Opinion in the *Namibia case* the International Court rejected the South African argument that the key Security Council resolution was invalid since two permanent members had abstained. The consistent practice of the members of the Security Council had been to interpret such abstention as not constituting a bar to the adoption of resolutions in spite of the provisions of Article 27, paragraph 3, of the Charter which refer to the "concurring votes" of the permanent members.

(g) Powers of legislation delegated to organizations. In certain instances states have delegated important law-making powers to organizations. Thus the High Authority of the European Coal and Steel Community may make decisions and regulations which are legally effective within the legal system of member states. Other forms of delegation exist involving various procedures for acceptance of the regulations by members. Some organs, for example the World Health Assembly of WHO or the Council of ICAO may make regulations by majority decision, leaving states to contract out by express rejection or by entering reservations.

(h) External practice of organizations. Organizations may make agreements with member and non-member states and with other organizations, and may present international claims and make official pronouncements on issues affecting them. Subject to what has been said above about the need for care in evaluating acts of political organs, the practice of organizations provides evidence of the law.

(i) Internal law-making. Organizations have considerable autonomy in making rules on internal matters such as procedure and the relations of the organization and its staff. Resolutions of organs of the United Nations on questions of procedure create internal law for members. * * The United Nations has developed a code of staff regulations and rules governing the conditions of service of its officials, and the General Assembly has established a United Nations Administrative Tribunal to adjudicate upon applications alleging non-observance of employment contracts of staff members of the Secretariat.

———

5. ***Decision ex aequo et bono.*** Article 38–2 of the Statute of the International Court of Justice specifies that the court may decide a case ex aequo et bono—i.e. according to what is just and good—if the parties so agree. In addition, states referring a dispute to an arbitral tribunal frequently provide in the *compromis*—i.e. the agreement to submit to arbitration—whether the tribunal shall decide according to rules of international law or ex aequo et bono. Does *ex aequo et bono* mean to decide equitably? Equity does not have the specialized meaning it has in the common law system, but expresses concepts of justice, reason, and fairness. As in the case of decisions ex aequo et bono, equity empowers the tribunal to decide without regard to technical legal rights. The decision to choose one or another basis may depend on whether the dispute is of a non-legal nature. Another perception of "equity" is that

it already (a priori) forms a part of *all* law; each word is informed with
equity. For a useful and extensive analysis of international practice, see
Sohn, The Function of International Arbitration Today, [1963] 1 Acade-
mie de Droit International, Recueil des Cours 1, 41.

Questions

1. If one wished to prove that a given U.N. Resolution was *"law"*
or binding authority, what would one have to argue? What types of
evidence would you have to muster? Is it ever binding of itself? If so,
under what circumstances or upon what argument?

2. Do U.N. Resolutions ever function like treaties? If so, would
they be like legislation in the domestic arena? Would this be a good or a
bad thing? See discussion of this issue in Chapter 2, § B.

3. Is to decide *ex aequo et bono* to decide equitably? If not, what is
the exact difference?

4. What is the nature of Equity in the international law hierarchy
of sources? Is it a body of maxims or rules as in so-called "law of
equity" in common law jurisdictions?

One should compare how the common law and the "law of equity"
developed in the common law world, with the law/equity dichotomy (or
lack thereof) in the *civilian* world. That study will show that there is an
aspect of *equity* in the continental sense of the term that forms part of
custom and informs *all* international law. This understanding is necessary for any common–law trained international lawyer to understand the
frame of reference or analytical approach of a "Civil Law" trained judge
(on the ICJ, or other court) or counter-part lawyer.

SECTION A. APPLICATION WITHIN NATIONAL LEGAL SYSTEMS

---

1. RULES OF CUSTOMARY INTERNATIONAL LAW NOT IN CONFLICT WITH DOMESTIC LAW

THE PAQUETE HABANA
THE LOLA

United States Supreme Court, 1900.
175 U.S. 677, 20 S.Ct. 290, 44 L.Ed. 320.

Mr. Justice GRAY delivered the opinion of the court.

These are two appeals from decrees of the District Court of the
United States for the Southern District of Florida, condemning two
fishing vessels and their cargoes as prize of war.

Each vessel was a fishing smack, running in and out of Havana, and
regularly engaged in fishing on the coast of Cuba; sailed under the

Spanish flag; was owned by a Spanish subject of Cuban birth, living in the city of Havana; was commanded by a subject of Spain also residing in Havana * * *. Her cargo consisted of fresh fish, caught by her crew from the sea, put on board as they were caught, and kept and sold alive. Until stopped by the blockading squadron, she had no knowledge of the existence of the war, or of any blockade. She had no arms or ammunition on board, and made no attempt to run the blockade after she knew of its existence, nor any resistance at the time of the capture.

* * *

Both the fishing vessels were brought by their captors into Key West. A libel for the condemnation of each vessel and her cargo as prize of war was there filed * * * a claim was interposed by her master, on behalf of himself and the other members of the crew, and of her owner; evidence was taken, showing the facts above stated; and on May 30, 1898, a final decree of condemnation and sale was entered, "the court not being satisfied that as a matter of law, without any ordinance, treaty or proclamation, fishing vessels of this class are exempt from seizure."

Each vessel was thereupon sold by auction; the Paquete Habana for the sum of $490; and the Lola for the sum of $800. * * *

* * *

We are then brought to the consideration of the question whether, upon the facts appearing in these records, the fishing smacks were subject to capture by the armed vessels of the United States during the recent war with Spain.

By an ancient usage among civilized nations, beginning centuries ago, and gradually ripening into a rule of international law, coast fishing vessels, pursuing their vocation of catching and bringing in fresh fish, have been recognized as exempt, with their cargoes and crews, from capture as prize of war.

This doctrine, however, has been earnestly contested at the bar; and no complete collection of the instances illustrating it is to be found, so far as we are aware, in a single published work, although many are referred to and discussed by the writers on international law, notably in 2 Ortolan, Règles Internationales et Diplomatie de la Mer, (4th ed.); in 4 Calvo, Droit International, (5th ed.); in De Boeck, Propriété Privée Ennemie sous Pavillon Ennemi; and in Hall, International Law, (4th ed.). It is therefore worth the while to trace the history of the rule, from the earliest accessible sources, through the increasing recognition of it, with occasional setbacks, to what we may now justly consider as its final establishment in our own country and generally throughout the civilized world.

[The court then proceeds to trace the history of the rule through an extensive examination of inconsistent state practice, beginning with the issuance of orders by Henry IV to his admirals in 1403 and 1406.]

Since the English orders in council of 1806 and 1810 * * * in favor of fishing vessels employed in catching and bringing to market fresh fish, no instance has been found in which the exemption from capture of private coast fishing vessels, honestly pursuing their peaceful industry, has been denied by England, or by any other nation. And the Empire of Japan, (the last State admitted into the rank of civilized nations,) by an ordinance promulgated at the beginning of its war with China in August, 1894, established prize courts, and ordained that "the following enemy's vessels are exempt from detention"—including in the exemption "boats engaged in coast fisheries," as well as "ships engaged exclusively on a voyage of scientific discovery, philanthropy or religious mission."

International law is part of our law, and must be ascertained and administered by the courts of justice of appropriate jurisdiction, as often as questions of right depending upon it are duly presented for their determination. For this purpose, where there is no treaty, and no controlling executive or legislative act or judicial decision, resort must be had to the customs and usages of civilized nations; and, as evidence of these, to the works of jurists and commentators, who by years of labor, research and experience, have made themselves peculiarly well acquainted with the subjects of which they treat. Such works are resorted to by judicial tribunals, not for the speculations of their authors concerning what the law ought to be, but for trustworthy evidence of what the law really is. Hilton v. Guyot, 159 U.S. 113, 163, 164, 214, 215.

* * *

This review of the precedents and authorities on the subject appears to us abundantly to demonstrate that at the present day, by the general consent of the civilized nations of the world, and independently of any express treaty or other public act, it is an established rule of international law, founded on considerations of humanity to a poor and industrious order of men, and of the mutual convenience of belligerent States, that coast fishing vessels, with their implements and supplies, cargoes and crews, unarmed, and honestly pursuing their peaceful calling of catching and bringing in fresh fish, are exempt from capture as prize of war.

The exemption, of course, does not apply to coast fishermen or their vessels, if employed for a warlike purpose, or in such a way as to give aid or information to the enemy; nor when military or naval operations create a necessity to which all private interests must give way.

Nor has the exemption been extended to ships or vessels employed on the high sea in taking whales or seals, or cod or other fish which are not brought fresh to market, but are salted or otherwise cured and made a regular article of commerce.

This rule of international law is one which prize courts, administering the law of nations, are bound to take judicial notice of, and to give effect to, in the absence of any treaty or other public act of their own government in relation to the matter.

* * *

The United States [position] during the recent war with Spain was quite in accord with the rule of international law, now generally recognized by civilized nations, in regard to coast fishing vessels.

On April 21, 1898, the Secretary of the Navy gave instructions to Admiral Sampson commanding the North Atlantic Squadron, to "immediately institute a blockade of the north coast of Cuba, extending from Cardenas on the east to Bahia Honda on the west." The blockade was immediately instituted accordingly. On April 22, the President issued a proclamation, declaring that the United States had instituted and would maintain that blockade, "in pursuance of the laws of the United States, and the law of nations applicable to such cases." And by the act of Congress of April 25, 1898, c. 189, it was declared that the war between the United States and Spain existed on that day, and had existed since and including April 21.

On April 26, 1898, the President issued another proclamation, which, after reciting the existence of the war, as declared by Congress, contained this further recital: "It being desirable that such war should be conducted upon principles in harmony with the present views of nations and sanctioned by their recent practice." This recital was followed by specific declarations of certain rules for the conduct of the war by sea, making no mention of fishing vessels. But the proclamation clearly manifests the general policy of the Government to conduct the war in accordance with the principles of international law * * *.

* * *

Upon the facts proved in either case, it is the duty of this court, sitting as the highest prize court of the United States, and administering the law of nations, to declare and adjudge that the capture was unlawful, and without probable cause; and it is therefore, in each case,

Ordered, that the decree of the District Court be reversed, and the proceeds of the sale of the vessel, together with the proceeds of any sale of her cargo, be restored to the claimant, with damages and costs.

[Dissenting opinion of Mr. Chief Justice Fuller, with whom concurred Mr. Justice Harlan and Mr. Justice McKenna, omitted.]

——————

TRENDTEX TRADING CORPORATION
v. CENTRAL BANK OF NIGERIA

England, Queen's Bench, 1977.
[1977] 1 Q.B. 529, 553–554.*

[The issue was whether the bank was entitled to sovereign immunity i.e., whether it was immune from suit in the courts of England.

At the time the suit was brought, the applicable rule of customary international law did not require the court to grant the immunity. Lord Denning discussed the manner in which this rule of international law became part of the law of England. A portion of his opinion follows.]

* * *

———

* Reprinted by permission of the Incorporated Council of Law Reporting for England and Wales, London.

A fundamental question arises. * * * What is the place of international law in our English law? One school of thought holds to the doctrine of *incorporation*. It says that the rules of international law are incorporated into English law automatically and considered to be part of English law unless they are in conflict with an Act of Parliament. The other school of thought holds to the doctrine of *transformation*. It says that the rules of international law are not to be considered as part of English law except in so far as they have been already adopted and made part of our law by the decisions of the judges, or by Act of Parliament, or long established custom. The difference is vital when you are faced with a change in the rules of international law. Under the doctrine of incorporation, when the rules of international law change, our English law changes with them. But, under the doctrine of transformation, the English law does not change. It is bound by precedent. It is bound down to those rules of international law which have been accepted and adopted in the past. It cannot develop as international law develops.

(i) The doctrine of incorporation. The doctrine of incorporation goes back to 1737 in Buvot v. Barbut [sic] (1736) 3 Burr. 1481 in which Lord Talbot L.C. (who was highly esteemed) made a declaration which was taken down by young William Murray (who was of counsel in the case) and adopted by him in 1764 when he was Lord Mansfield C.J. in Triquet v. Bath (1764) 3 Burr. 1478:

> Lord Talbot declared a clear opinion—"That the law of nations in its full extent was part of the law of England. * * *

That doctrine was accepted, not only by Lord Mansfield himself, but also by Sir William Blackstone, and [numerous] other great names.

* * *

(iii) Which is correct? * * * I now believe that the doctrine of incorporation is correct. Otherwise I do not see that our courts could ever recognise a change in the rules of international law. It is certain that international law does change. I would use of international law the words which Galileo used of the earth: "But it does move." International law does change: and the courts have applied the changes without the aid of any Act of Parliament. * * *

(iv) Conclusion on this point. Seeing that the rules of international law have changed—and do change—and that the courts have given effect to the changes without any Act of Parliament, it follows to my mind inexorably that the rules of international law, as existing from time to time, do form part of our English law. It follows, too, that a decision of this court—as to what was the ruling of international law 50 or 60 years ago—is not binding on this court today. International law knows no rule of stare decisis. * * *

* * *

PRACTICES OF NATIONAL COURTS

It may be impossible, to find a national legal system which arbitrarily refuses to apply rules of customary international law not in conflict with domestic law. The main issue in this section is not whether courts in national legal systems give effect to such rules, but how they go about it. The two preceding cases are illustrative.

———

Notes & Questions 1. *Where there is no constitutional provision directing courts to apply rules of customary international law.* In common law states, courts usually justify their application of customary law by stating that international law is part of the law of the land. The simplicity of the proposition is deceptive, for if it were accepted as literally true, courts would need only to determine whether there was an applicable rule of customary international law and apply it so long as they found an applicable rule not in conflict with domestic law. Yet this is not quite the way the courts proceeded in the cases set forth above. Did the court apply international law? Domestic law? Both?

In The Paquete Habana, the court determined the applicable rule of customary international law only after ascertaining that there was no applicable rule of domestic law already established by previous executive or legislative act or judicial decision. *Why was the court concerned with the possibility that a rule of domestic law might be available? And why would a nation be determined to apply a rule of customary international law until it had been transformed into a rule of domestic law?*

In "civil law" jurisdictions, if there is no constitutional provision commanding the application of customary international law, the courts often show the same proclivity as common law courts to search for an applicable rule of domestic law. Illustrative of this propensity is the decision in *the Immunity Case,* Yugoslavia, Supreme Court of the People's Republic of Croatia, 86 Journal de Droit International 525 (1959). As in the Trendtex case, the issue was sovereign immunity, i.e., whether a foreign state could claim immunity from suit. The court found the foreign state was entitled to immunity by a rule of customary international law. But it also found there was a rule of domestic law which provided immunity for the foreign state and gave judgment accordingly.

Suppose that in the Yugoslav case, the court had found there was no applicable rule of domestic law. Would it have applied the rule of customary international law as the rule of decision? Did the Supreme Court of the United States apply a rule of customary international law as the rule of decision in The Paquete Habana? In these two cases, did the Yugoslav and the American courts follow identical theories concerning the relationship of customary international law to domestic law? Do these theories differ from the theory implicit in the opinion of Lord Denning in the Trendtex case?

   2. **Provisions in constitutions.** National constitutions may provide a legal basis for the application of rules of customary international
law. Among those a number of modest formulations provide (or contain
language to the effect) that "The State shall endeavour to * * * foster
respect for international law and treaty obligations in the dealings of
organized peoples with one another" Article 51(c) of the Constitution of
India (VIII Blaustein and Flanz, Constitutions of the Countries of the
World, India, at 65 (1990)).[a] Comparable provisions are found in the
constitutions of a number of countries, including Bulgaria Article 24(1)
(Id., III at 91 (1992)), Nepal Article 26(15) (Id., XII at 37 (1992)),
Namibia Article 96(d) (Id., XI at 50 (1990)), The Netherlands Article 90
(Id., XII at 23 (1990)), the Russian Federation draft Constitution of
February 21, 1991, Article 11(1) (Id., XIX Supp. 3 at 10 (1991) and Sri
Lanka Article 27(15)) (Id., XVII at 24 (1989)).

   Stronger terms of acceptance of international law are found in other
national constitutions, including those of Ireland, Article 29(3) (Id., VIII
at 55 (1988)). Paraguay Article 143 (Id., XIV at 25 (1993)) and Romania
Article 10 (Id., XV at 6 (1992)). For example, Article 29(3) of the
Constitution of Ireland provides: "Ireland accepts the generally recognized principles of international law as its rule of conduct in its relations
with other States."

   Whether a broadly worded constitutional provision justifies application of customary international law depends on past practice. French
courts have traditionally given effect to such rules and for this reason
some argue that the preamble to the French Constitution of 1946 merely
acknowledged the fact: "The French Republic, faithful to its tradition,
abides by the rules of international law." 2 Peaslee, Constitutions of
Nations 7 (2d ed. 1956). The provision was incorporated by reference in
the 1958 Constitution of the Fifth French Republic. It has been contended by a French author that the provision is not only unnecessary but
also dangerous, because it might put into question the inherent power of
French courts to apply rules of international law. Rousseau, Droit
International Public 14 (Précis Dalloz, 5th ed. 1970). Compare Article
55 of the French Constitution of 1958 which provides specifically for the
binding force of qualified treaties and agreements—but not for customary international law. These have a status *superior* to that of laws, a
result for customary law regretted by one French author. Dupuy, *Droit
International Public* 304 (Précis Dalloz, 1992); but see Carreau, *Droit
International Public* 57 (3rd ed. 1991). The Hungarian Constitution of
1949 as amended in 1989, is exceptional in providing in Chapter 1, sec. 7
that: "The legal system of the Republic of Hungary accepts the generally recognized rules of international law, and furthermore, it shall ensure
the agreement between the accepted international legal obligations and
domestic statutes." Id. Vol. VII at 2 (1990).

   a. Subsequent references in this chapter   section on the particular country. The
to Blaustein and Flanz are made with "Id."   identification of that section is apparent
followed by the volume number in roman   from the context and is not repeated in the
and the page and date. The page number   citation.
refers to the removable Blaustein and Flanz

Some constitutions provide a basis for applying rules of customary international law by declaring specifically that international law is part of the law of the land. Thus Article 2(3) of the Constitution of the Philippines states: "The Philippines * * * adopts the generally accepted principles of international law as part of the law of the land." (Id., XIV at 68 (1985)). The Austrian Constitution states in Article 9: "[t]he generally recognized principles of International Law are valid parts of the Federal Law." (Id., I at 29 (1985)). Article 25 of the German Constitution provides: "The general rules of public international law shall be an integrated part of federal law." (Id., VI at 91 (1991)). Does this mean that custom is automatically integrated or must something be done to integrate it?

German Basic Law (Constitution) incorporates international law directly. Thus, for example, decisions of the European Court of Human Rights and customary international law are a direct source of law in German domestic law. See further development of this theme in Chapter 10 (Human Rights) and Chapter 14 (International Agreements), *infra*. A very few constitutions go further and contemplate not only the application of rules of customary international law but also the possibility of conflict between such rules and rules of domestic law and indicate the manner in which the conflict should be resolved.

------

2. RULES OF DOMESTIC LAW IN CONFLICT WITH CUSTOMARY INTERNATIONAL LAW

In a case which decided issues relating to criminal law (selling and distributing illegal whisky some 19 miles off the U.S. shore) and jurisdiction, the U.S. District Court for Connecticut held that, while the U.S. Congress could pass a law that both extended criminal jurisdiction beyond U.S. territory and which violated international law, this particular statute did extend jurisdiction beyond U.S. territory, but did not extend it far enough to cover defendants' conduct. It noted the *presumption* that the U.S. Congress intends to follow international law. *The Over the Top; Schroeder v. Bissell,* 5 F.2d 838 (D.C.Conn.1925). *What would be the domestic result if the off-loading happened to be within U.S. territory? What would be the result under international law?*

ATTORNEY–GENERAL OF ISRAEL v. EICHMANN

Israel, District Court of Jerusalem, 1961.
36 Int'l L.Rep. 5, 24 (1968).*

[Adolf Eichman was tried in Israel under a law punishing Nazis and their collaborators for crimes against the Jewish people committed in Germany during World War II. His counsel argued that, under applicable rules of customary international law, the court had no jurisdiction to try him for crimes committed outside Israel when neither the law, nor Israel, yet existed. He also argued that Israel law was in conflict with international law.]

The argument that Israel law is in conflict with international law and that it cannot vest jurisdiction in this Court, raises the preliminary question of the validity of international law in Israel and whether, in the event of conflict, it is to be preferred to the law of the land. The law in force in Israel resembles that in force in England in this regard. * * *

As to the question of the incorporation of the principles of international law in the national law [of Israel] we rely on Blackstone, Commentaries on the Laws of England (Book IV, Chap. 5):

In England * * * the law of nations * * * is * * * adopted in its full extent by the common law, and it is held to be a part of the law of the land * * * without which it must cease to be a part of the civilized world.

The same applies to other countries, such as the United States of America, France, Belgium and Switzerland, where the usages of international law have been recognized as part of the national law.

* * *

With respect to statutory law, Justice Agranat said in High Court:

B. It is a well-known maxim that a municipal statute should— except where its contents require a different interpretation—be interpreted in accordance with the rules of public international law.

And in Criminal Appeal No. 5/51 Mr. Justice Sussman said (p. 1065):

It is a well-known rule that in interpreting a statute the Court will as far as possible try to avoid a conflict between the municipal law and the obligations incumbent on the State by virtue of international law. But this is only one of the canons of interpretation. That is to say, where we are dealing not with the Common Law but with a written statute which expresses the will of the legislator, then the Court must carry out the will of the legislator without considering if there exists a contradiction between the statute and international law * * *. Furthermore, the Courts here derive their jurisdiction from municipal law and not from international law.

Our jurisdiction to try this case is based on the Nazi and Nazi Collaborators (Punishment) Law, an enacted Law the provisions of which are unequivocal. The Court has to give effect to a law of the

---

* Reprinted with the permission of the Editor of the International Law Reports.

Knesset, and we cannot entertain the contention that this Law conflicts with the principles of international law. For this reason alone counsel's first submission must be rejected.

We have, however, also considered the sources of international law, including the numerous authorities cited by learned defence counsel in his basic written brief upon which he based his oral pleadings, and by the learned Attorney–General in his comprehensive oral pleadings, and have failed to find any foundation for the contention that Israel law is in conflict with the principles of international law. On the contrary, we have reached the conclusion that the Law in question conforms to the best traditions of the law of nations.

* * *

Note: U.S. v. Alvarez–Machain, 112 S.Ct. 2188 (1992), held that the abduction by U.S. agents of a doctor who allegedly assisted in the torture and murder of DEA agend Kiki Camarina, was not a violation of the extradition treaty between the U.S. and Mexico and, hence, did not require the defendant's release. The opinion is presented in Ch. 3, *infra.*

PRACTICES OF NATIONAL COURTS

1. ***Where there is no constitutional provision directing courts to give precedence to rules of customary international law.*** Absent a constitutional provision commanding precedence, the courts of national legal systems frequently assert that they must give effect to their domestic law if it is in clear conflict with customary international law. Should a court resolve the conflict in such manner, the state to which it belongs would be in violation of international law. Thus, in the United States an act of Congress supersedes an inconsistent rule of customary international law, but that "does not relieve the United States of its international obligation or of the consequences of a violation of that obligation." Section 115(1)(b) of Restatement of the Law Third, The Foreign Relations Law of the United States (1987).[b]

Actually courts in national legal systems are rarely confronted with the necessity of resolving the conflict by giving precedence to their domestic law. English courts, for example, make it a point of stating that they would give effect to the will of parliament if its legislation were in clear conflict with customary international law, but this is no more than "a deferential nod to Cerberus before by-passing him." 1 O'Con-

----

b. From here on cited as the 1987 Restatement, while Restatement of the Law Second, The Foreign Relations Law of the United States (1965) is cited as the 1965 Restatement.

nell, International Law 57 (2d ed. 1970). Similarly, a Norwegian scholar characterizes the conflicts between domestic law and international law, including customary international law, as relating to "pathological cases" and that, "clear conflict situations are rare. * * * [S]carcely one has been brought before the Norwegian Supreme Court * * *." Smith, International Law in Norwegian Courts, 12 Scandinavian Studies in Law 1968, at 153, 160 (1968).

The main reason for the rarity of the conflict is that courts can avoid it by construction of the rule of domestic law involved.

2. **Provisions in constitutions.** Article 10 of the Italian Constitution states: "Italy's legal system conforms with the generally recognized principles of international law." Conformity between the two, according to the Supreme Court of Italy, means that rules of municipal law which are contrary to customary international law "must be eliminated." Re Martinez, Italy, Court of Cassation, 1959, 28 Int'l L.Rep. 170 (1963).

Article 28(1) of the Greek Constitution of 1975 declares that "the generally recognized rules of international law * * * * '* * * shall be an integral part of domestic Greek law and shall prevail over any contrary provision of law.' Id., VII at 26 (1988). The 1991 Constitution of Slovenia provides in Article 8, that "[l]aws and other regulations must be in accordance with the generally valid principles of international law. * * *" (Id., XVI at 2 (1992)).

---

3. RULES OF DOMESTIC LAW IN CONFLICT WITH INTERNATIONAL AGREEMENTS

A conflict between domestic law and an international agreement may arise in either of two ways. First, the agreement may be in conflict with a rule of domestic law already in effect at the time the international agreement becomes binding. Second, a rule of domestic law may come into effect after the agreement has become binding and be in conflict with it. In either case, a state would be in violation of international law if it gave effect to the conflicting rule of domestic law, for it cannot invoke its contrary domestic law as justification for its failure to abide by international agreement or customary international law.

1. **International agreement in conflict with constitutional provision.** If an international agreement is in conflict with the constitution of the national legal system, domestic law prevails, unless the constitution provides otherwise. In United States law, the last in time prevails only with regard to legislation. See Chapter 14 infra. The international rule would not apply in Chile (see *Skrabs v. Krieger* (portions of the opinions are in Ch. 12, on consular immunities). Neither would it be internally operative in Mexico. *In re Vera*, Supreme Court, 1948, [1948] Ann.Dig. 328 (No. 114). The Court of Appeal for East Africa at Nairobi takes the same position. Criminal Appeal No. 156 of 1969, 9 ILM 561 (1970). Article 182 of the 1987 Constitution of

Nicaragua provides that any treaties that "oppose it or alter its dispositions shall have no value." Id., Vol. XIII at 33 (1987)). Paraguay Constitution of 1992, Article 137 provides for "preeminence" of the Constitution over international treaties, conventions and agreements. (Id., XIV at 24 (1993)).

The constitutions of some national systems made provision for resolving conflicts between the constitution and an international agreement. Thus the 1987 Netherlands Constitution provides in Article 91.3 that, "[a]ny provisions of a treaty that conflict with the Constitution or which lead to conflicts with it may be approved by the Chambers of the States General only if at least two-thirds of the votes cast are in favor." (Id., XII at 23 (1990)). The 1978 Spanish Constitution provides in Article 95.1 that "[t]he conclusion of an international treaty which contains stipulations contrary to the Constitution shall require a prior constitutional revision." (Id., XVII at 63 (1991)).

Article 54 of the French Constitution of 1958 provides that if the Constitutional Council should declare that an international agreement contains a clause contrary to the Constitution, the authorization of the legislature "to ratify or approve this commitment may be given only after amendment of the Constitution." * * * (Id., VI at 39 (1988)). The application of this procedure is described in Carreau, *Droit International* 57–58 (3rd ed., 1991), where the author notes as well that this "French model" was adopted in many constitutions in French speaking African countries. In 1992, the French Conseil Constitutional determined that the Maastricht Treaty on European Union contained provisions contrary to the French Constitution, which resulted in the requirement that the Constitution be amended as provided in Article 54 before Maastricht could be ratified or approved. (See Kokott, French Case Note, 86 A.J.I.L. 824 (1992)).

2. *International agreement in conflict with legislation.* Where the conflict is between an international agreement and anterior legislation, courts usually resolve a conflict in favor of the international agreement, but usually do not take the position that the agreement is intrinsically superior to existing legislation. Instead, they treat it as equal in rank with the legislation and apply the rule of construction that, as between anterior and posterior laws in conflict, the one later in time prevails.

In the United States, the equality in rank of treaties and acts of Congress is provided by Article VI, Clause 2, of the Constitution. Since neither is superior, the one later in time prevails. Hence, a self-executing treaty, i.e. one whose provisions are directly applicable as rules of domestic law without the need of implementation by an act of Congress, supersedes the provisions of prior and inconsistent federal legislation. Should the treaty not be self-executing, its provisions, once enacted into rules of domestic law by act of Congress, also supersede the provisions of prior and inconsistent federal legislation. On these and other aspects of the internal effect of international agreements of the United States, see Chapter 14.

The *United States Supreme Court's position is illustrative:* "[we have] repeatedly taken the position that an Act of Congress * * * is on a full parity with a treaty, and that when a statute which is subsequent in time is inconsistent with a treaty, the statute to the extent of conflict renders the treaty null." *Reid v. Covert,* 354 U.S. 1, 18 (1957). In recent years, the courts of some other national legal systems have shown a willingness to give more weight to international agreements in conflict with subsequent domestic law than might be expected under the doctrine of precedence for the one later in time. The matter is discussed in the following decision.

3. ***Decisions of the French Conseil d'Etat.*** The *Avocet Genéral* argued without success that the terms of the Treaty of Rome should apply without reference to Article 55 of the Treaty. Why would he argue that the Constitutional provision that incorporates treaties is not necessary. After the *Jacques Vabre* Case, 16 Comm.Mkt.L.Rptr. 336 (1975), 14 years passed before the *Conseil d'Etat,* the highest administrative judicial body in France, decided that it had jurisdiction to review the compatibility of a later statute with a treaty applicable to France. In the latter case, the claim of conflict between the Treaty of Rome and later French legislation on elections to the European Parliament was rejected. *Arrêt* M. Nicolo, of October 20, 1989 *La documentation Française, Jurisprudence du Conseil d'Etat 1989* 57 (1990). *See, Riesenfeld,* 84 Am.J.Int.L. 765 (1990). The distinction between private law and administrative law in France is discussed below in Chapter 7, Immunities of States and International Organizations. Following *Nicolo,* the *Conseil d'Etat* has since found such jurisdiction in a case involving a prior Regulation of the European Economic Community in the agriculture sector and invalidated the challenged French measure (*Arrêt Boisdet,* September 24, 1990, *La documentation Française, Jurisprudence du Conseil d'Etat 1990* 44 (1991)). In another case, the European Convention for the Protection of Human Rights and Fundamental Freedoms (1950) was invoked unsuccessfully in a challenge to measures authorizing the marketing of the abortion pill *RU* 486. *Arrêt Confederation national des associations familiales catholiques.* Id. at 58. The *Conseil d'Etat* found in the latter case that the Universal Declaration of Human Rights (1948) was not included in the category of treaties or agreements to which Article 55 of the French Constitution of 1958 applies. *Why not?*

4. ***Parliamentary sovereignty in the United Kingdom.*** When the United Kingdom became a member of the European Economic Community, it enacted legislation which Lord Denning construed as conferring priority to the treaty over subsequent acts of Parliament inconsistent with it. He said:

* * *

> That priority is given by our own law. It is given by the European Communities Act 1972 itself. Community law is now part of our law: and whenever there is any inconsistency, Community law has priority. It is not supplanting English law. It is part of our law which overrides any other part which is inconsistent with it. Macarthys Ltd. v. Smith, England, Court of Appeal, 1981, [1981] Q.B. 180, 200.

At an earlier stage of the same litigation, Lord Denning also said:

I pause here, however, to make one observation on a constitutional point. Thus far I have assumed that our Parliament, whenever it passes legislation, intends to fulfil its obligations under the Treaty. If the time should come when our Parliament deliberately passes an Act with the intention of repudiating the Treaty or any provision in it or intentionally of acting inconsistently with it and says so in express terms then I should have thought that it would be the duty of our courts to follow the statute of our Parliament. I do not however envisage any such situation. As I said in Blackburn v. Attorney–General: "But if Parliament should do so, then I say we will consider that event when it happens." Unless there is such an intentional and express repudiation of the Treaty, it is our duty to give priority to the Treaty. * * * Id.

More [recently] however, and in a quite different context involving the insolvency of the International Tin Council, Lord Templeman said:

These appeals raise a short question of construction of the plain words of a statutory instrument. The trial judges (Staughton, J. and Millett, J.) and the Court of Appeal (Kerr, Nourse and Ralph Gibson, L.JJ.) rightly decided this question in favour of the respondents. Losing the construction argument, the appellants put forward alternative submissions which are unsustainable. Those submissions, if accepted, would involve a breach of the British constitution and an invasion by the judiciary of the functions of the Government and of Parliament. The Government may negotiate, conclude, construe, observe, breach, repudiate or terminate a treaty. Parliament may alter the laws of the United Kingdom. The courts must enforce those laws; judges have no power to grant specific performance of a treaty or to award damages against a sovereign state for breach of a treaty or to invent laws or misconstrue legislation in order to enforce a treaty.

A treaty is a contract between the governments of two or more sovereign states. International law regulates the relations between sovereign states and determines the validity, the interpretation and the enforcement of treaties. A treaty to which Her Majesty's Government is a party does not alter the laws of the United Kingdom. A treaty may be incorporated into and alter the laws of the United Kingdom by means of legislation. Except to the extent that a treaty becomes incorporated into the laws of the United Kingdom by statute, the courts of the United Kingdom have no power to enforce treaty rights and obligations at the behest of a sovereign government or at the behest of a private individual. * * * Australia and New Zealand Banking Group Ltd., et al. v. Commonwealth of Australia and 23 Others, etc., House of Lords [1989] 3 W.L.R. 969; 29 I.L.M. 670 (1990).

------

5. ***Primacy of international agreement in Switzerland.***
Switzerland's highest court holds that an international agreement pre-

vails over subsequent and inconsistent domestic law. *Thareau v. Ministère Public Fédéral,* 1974, 31 Ann. Suisse Dr. Int'l 204 (1975).

Some constitutional provisions which apparently give primacy to treaties over domestic legislation are not altogether clear about whether subsequent as well as prior legislation is trumped by the treaty. Article 5(4) of the Bulgarian Constitution of 1991, for example, provides that qualified international treaties "are part of the country's internal laws. They take precedence over conflicting domestic legislation." *See* Blaustein and Flanz; Vol. III at 88. *See also* 2 of the Constitutional Law No. 23 (January 9, 1991) of the Czech and Slovak Federative Republic (Id., V at 1), and Articles 7(3), 138(b) and 139(1) of the Draft proposed by former President Havel (Id., V at 41), as well as the Rumanian Constitution of 1991 which states in Article 11.2 that "The treaties ratified by Parliament, according to law, are part of domestic law." (Id., XV at 6) and for Paraguay Article 137 (Id., XIV at 24 (1993)) and Article 94 of the Netherlands Constitution of 1987 (Id., XII at 24.)

A number of constitutions have directly addressed the problem of treaty conflict with subsequent legislation. Article 96.1 of the Spanish Constitution of 1978 states that "[v]alidly concluded international treaties once officially published in Spain shall constitute part of the internal (legal) order. Their provisions may only be abolished, modified or suspended in the manner provided for in the treaties themselves or in accord with general norms of international law." (Id., XVII at 63). Similarly, see Article 134 of the Croation Constitution of 1990 (Id., IV at 64). The 1991 Constitution of Slovenia provides in Article 8 that "[l]aws and other regulations must be in accordance with the generally valid principles of international law and with international contracts to which Slovenia is bound." (Id., XVI at 2).

According to Article 28(1) of the Greek Constitution of 1975, "international conventions * * * shall prevail over any contrary provision of law." See Roucounas, Le Droit International dans la Constitution de la Grèce du 9 Juin 1975, 29 Revue Hellénique du Droit International 63, 65 (1976), where the author asserts that the article gives primacy to the treaty over both anterior and posterior domestic laws.

Questions: What if a treaty is inconsistent with U.S. federal law? How do you reconcile the American "last in time" doctrine, which favors subsequent Congressional legislation, with Article 27 of the Vienna Convention on the Law of Treaties (in the Doc. Supp.) which provides in part that "[a] party may not invoke the provisions of its internal law as justification for its failure to perform a treaty"?

How do you think courts in the United Kingdom would resolve the problem of legislation in conflict with a subsequent treaty?

What are the domestic and international consequences of the rule? What do the foregoing materials teach us about the overall relationship between domestic law and international law?. Are they two different systems? Or only one, of which each is an integral part? These questions foreshadow the theoretical question of dualism v. monism, taken up infra, in Chapter 18, Section B.

Are the approaches to international law of Mr. Justice Gray in the Paquette Habana and of Chief Justice Rehnquist in *Alvarez–Machain* compatible? Read the brief excerpts from Mr. Justice Story in *The Schooner La Jeune Eugenie* and from Chief Justice Marshall in *The Antelope,* presented in the introduction to Chapter 18; consider how each Justice would likely approach the two cases.

---

4. DOMESTIC ACTION TO CONFORM WITH INTERNATIONAL LAW

LEGAL ADVISERS TO GOVERNMENT DEPARTMENTS

Organization of legal advisory services on international law. Ministries of foreign affairs in most nations have a "Legal Adviser" including a major legal staff. Other governmental departments also have international attorneys. In the early days of the United States, the legal issues arising in the conduct of its foreign affairs were often handled by the Secretaries of State themselves. They proved to be able lawyers. Eventually, legal affairs in the Department of State became a specialized function and is now vested in the Office of the Legal Adviser. The role of the adviser on international law matters is a demanding one, sometimes precarious, as shown in the material below.

THE ROLE OF THE LEGAL ADVISER OF THE DEPARTMENT OF STATE

A REPORT OF THE JOINT COMMITTEE ESTABLISHED BY THE AMERICAN SOCIETY OF INTERNATIONAL LAW AND THE AMERICAN BRANCH OF THE INTERNATIONAL LAW ASSOCIATION

85 Am.J.Int'l L. 358 (1991).*

* * *

* * * The position of Legal Adviser is established by statute. The Legal Adviser is appointed by the President, by and with the advice and consent of the Senate, and heads an office at present comprising some 100 government attorney-advisers. The Legal Adviser is responsible for furnishing legal advice on all problems, domestic and international, which arise in the course of the work of the Department of State. Thus, the Legal Adviser's responsibilities generally correspond to those of General Counsel of other Executive Branch agencies. In this capacity, the Legal Adviser and attorneys of that office are involved in many

* Reprinted by permission, American Society of International Law.

aspects of formulating and implementing the foreign policy of the United States. More particularly, they have special responsibilities regarding the handling of international legal issues arising in the conduct of U.S. foreign relations, as well as for promoting respect for and the development of international law and institutions as a fundamental element of U.S. foreign policy.

* * *

II. Compliance With International Law

The U.S., like most countries, generally complies with its international treaty and customary law obligations. But, as is the case with almost every other country, problems of compliance occasionally arise, particularly in situations where international norms appear to conflict with what are perceived as national security or other vital national interests. It is in regard to these situations that the role of the Legal Adviser is of particular interest.

Whether the United States has complied with international law in any given case is * * * a matter for individual scrutiny and study. Lawyers often divide in their views as do governments. It is pertinent to recall that in recent years the United States has taken a number of actions that have been widely questioned on legal grounds both within the United States and by foreign governments in international bodies. Examples of such actions include the U.S. military operation in Grenada, mining of Nicaraguan harbors and armed support for the "contras," bombing of Libya, forcing down of the Egyptian airliner carrying the *Achille Lauro* terrorists, failure to pay UN contributions, reinterpretation of the ABM Treaty, rejection of the World Court's judgment in the *Nicaragua* case, assertion of the right to seize fugitives from a foreign state's territory without the foreign government's consent, and the invasion of Panama. In addition to these publicized actions, many other situations have arisen of a specialized character in regard to which the legality of U.S. actions under international law has been questioned. [See also] international trade, tax treaties, and the law of the sea. * * *

* * *

III. The Legal Adviser's Special Role Regarding U.S. Participation in the International Legal System

As counsel to the Secretary of State and Department of State, the Legal Adviser's responsibilities involve not only the usual business of a general counsel to a major Executive Branch department, but also responsibility for matters relating to U.S. participation in the international legal system.

First, unlike most other lawyers, the Legal Adviser operates within the framework of two separate legal systems. Thus, the Legal Adviser must consider the consequences of legal advice, and of U.S. government decisions and actions based on that advice, not only on the national legal system but also on the international legal system.

Second, the Legal Adviser's "client"—the U.S. government—is one of some 160 or so nations that constitute the international society and through their actions and interactions make international law. This means that, in contrast to most other lawyers, the Legal Adviser's advice may significantly affect the content and integrity of international rules and institutions. If legal advisers did no more than provide legal rationalizations of their government's political actions, the international legal system would be the elaborate charade that some detractors of international law consider it to be.

Third, in contrast to the situation of most other government and private lawyers, the Legal Adviser's advice is subject to only relatively weak external checks. Most lawyers operate solely within a domestic legal system in which their legal advice is subject to judicial or other impartial review; they know that, if they assert legal positions beyond appropriate limits, there is ultimately a "backstop" of judicial or other institutional checks to restrain potential abuse of the legal process and to safeguard the integrity of the legal system. The advice given by the Legal Adviser, on the other hand, is not usually subject to definitive review by international courts or other international institutions.

* * *

IV. *The Conflict Between the Legal Adviser's Different Responsibilities*

As the U.S. government official primarily responsible for ensuring that the U.S. complies with its international obligations, the Legal Adviser must be in a position to present an objective analysis of any questions of international law arising in the formulation and conduct of U.S. foreign policy, and to tell the Secretary of State and other policy-making officials if their proposed actions or policies may violate international law. On the other hand, the Legal Adviser is usually a political appointee, and is also expected to act as adviser to the Secretary of State, and sometimes as advocate for Administration policies.

It seems clear that these two roles contain the seeds of conflict.

Thus, the Legal Adviser's first responsibility is to tell the Secretary of State and Administration candidly and objectively what existing law is or requires in a given situation. Every lawyer owes this duty to his or her client. As indicated, unless the Secretary and other policy officials are given competent, objective and honest advice as to the legal consequences of proposed actions and decisions, they cannot make informed and intelligent foreign policy judgments or properly balance the national interests involved; indeed, the success of a decision or policy may depend on its compliance with international law. [T]he Legal Adviser can, and often should, accompany an objective legal analysis with concrete suggestions as to how particular policy objectives can be achieved in a manner consistent with international law and U.S. obligations. It is also desirable that, in dealing with particular cases, the Legal Adviser seek to further the long-range international law objectives of the United States.

However, once the Secretary or other responsible officials decide upon a particular policy, the nature of the Legal Adviser's role changes. Some Committee members believe that, even if the decision reached is contrary to what the Legal Adviser believes is the better view, the Legal Adviser, like other attorneys with respect to their clients, can properly serve as the Secretary's advocate and make the best case possible in support of the Administration's position—at least so long as the arguments presented are in good faith and legally responsible. Of course, if the Legal Adviser believes that a situation involves an important issue of conscience or professional or personal ethics, the Legal Adviser may be unwilling to participate further in the matter and, in an extreme case, may wish to resign.

* * *

V.   *The Role of the Legal Adviser vis-à-vis Other U.S. Government Attorneys*

The Committee discussed how the Legal Adviser's role in providing legal advice concerning international legal issues compares with that of other government attorneys, such as the Attorney General, Legal Counsel of the Department of Justice, Legal Adviser to the National Security Council, General Counsels of other Executive Branch agencies, and Congressional staff counsel.

* * *

XI.   *Recommendations*

The Committee recommends that the American Society of International Law and American Branch of the International Law Association recommend and support the following proposals:

1.   The President should take appropriate action: (a) to recognize and provide for the primary responsibility of the Legal Adviser of the Department of State (in consultation, where appropriate, with the Attorney General of the United States) with respect to participation of the United States in the international legal system and the giving of advice on international legal issues; and (b) establishing effective mechanisms for the coordination of such activities or legal advice relating to international legal matters within the government, through interagency committee or otherwise, recognizing the general responsibility of the Legal Adviser.

2.   The President and Congress should take appropriate action to raise the status of the position of the Legal Adviser of the Department of State to a level equivalent to that of Under Secretary of State.

3.   The President and Secretary of State, in considering the qualifications of candidates for Legal Adviser of the Department of State, should give substantial weight to the desirability of prior experience and standing in the field of international law.

4.   The Secretary of State should ensure within the Department of State that the Legal Adviser shall participate at an early stage regarding the making of all policy decisions that involve a question of international law.

* * *

Note: See also, Cassese, The Role of Legal Advisors in Ensuring that Foreign Policy Conforms to International Legal Standards, 14 Mich.J.Int'l L. 139 (1992).

UNITED STATES: DEPARTMENT OF DEFENSE REPORT TO CONGRESS ON THE CONDUCT OF THE PERSIAN GULF WAR—APPENDIX ON THE ROLE OF THE LAW OF WAR, 31 I.L.M. 612 (1992)

THE ROLE OF THE LAW OF WAR

"Decisions were impacted by legal considerations at every level, [the law of war] proved invaluable in the decision-making process." General Colin Powell, Chairman, Joint Chiefs of Staff

* * *

ROLE OF LEGAL ADVISERS

The Office of General Counsel of the Department of Defense (DOD), as the chief DOD legal office, provided advice to the Secretary of Defense, the Deputy Secretary of Defense, the Under Secretary of Defense for Policy, other senior advisers to the Secretary and to the various components of the Defense legal community on all matters relating to Operations Desert Shield and Desert Storm, including the law of war. For example, the Secretary of Defense tasked the General Counsel to review and opine on such diverse issues as the means of collecting and obligating for defense purposes contributions from third countries; the Wars Powers Resolution; DOD targeting policies; the rules of engagement; the rules pertinent to maritime interception operations; issues relating to the treatment of prisoners of war; sensitive intelligence and special access matters; and similar matters of the highest priority to the Secretary and DOD. In addition, military judge advocates and civilian attorneys with international law expertise provided advice on the law of war and other legal issues at every level of command in all phases of Operations Desert Shield and Desert Storm. Particular attention was given to the review of target lists to ensure the consistency of targets selected for attack with United States law of war obligations.

In Count von Moltke, Letters from Freya,[1] the author was a descendent of the family of Bismarck's field marshal. A member of the Foreign Division of the German Military Intelligence Service (*Abwehr*) under Admiral Canaris and a legal advisor to the Supreme Command of the Armed Forces (Oberkommando der Wehrmacht OKW) during World War

1. Count Von Moltke, Letters from Freya 1939–1945, at 132 and 258 (trans., Beate Ruhm von Oppen, 1990).

II, he had written numerous illuminating letters to his wife Freya. [He was later convicted of attempting to change the Reich's Constitution by force and was executed in January, 1945.] His letters portray some of the problems faced by a conscientious government legal adviser:

On April 29, 1941, from Berlin, Count von Moltke wrote of a tremendous row on matters of principle, concerning the defense of one Schmitz in Belgrade. Von Moltke had played his way into the foreground on this case and, thus, was going to be told to report to Canaris on the subject. Von Moltke was happy about being able to report to Canaris, because he would be able to force Canaris to face the serious issues of policy that the case represented. Von Moltke would be able to force Canaris to make a decision, rather than avoiding it, as the latter would have liked to do. Von Moltke stated:

> "I certainly shall treat [the issues] exclusively as matters of principle and shall see what happens. I'll be alone with Canaris, so that his only possible reason for dissimulation would be one that lies in me. I can only hope that I'll have a good day. My basic theme is this: what is right and lawful is good for the people, what is international law is good for the conduct of the war. * * * Perhaps I'll be thrown out. If not, my position will be firmer."

On April 30, Count von Moltke wrote that his discussion with Canaris had lasted an hour. He felt that it had been "thoroughly satisfactory." He said that he had left no doubt about his views and "[Canaris] completely agreed with me," although nothing was decided in the meeting. Von Moltke at least was happy to have "learned" where Canaris stood and hoped that the process would move forward properly.

On November 3, 1942, Von Moltke wrote that he had just had a "decisive exchange" with Bürkner. Bürkner had been refusing to sign a paper that "mattered a great deal" to Von Moltke. The two had argued about the "justification for an undiluted murder." Order by the Führer.[2] During the argument, Von Moltke stated to Bürkner:

> You see, Herr Admiral, the difference between us is that I can't argue about such questions. As long as I recognize imperatives that cannot be repealed by any Führer Order and that must be followed against a Führer Order, I cannot let such things pass, because for me the difference between good and evil, justice and injustice exists *a priori.* It is not subject to considerations of expediency or argument.

After that vigorous and courageous statement, Bürkner "signed without demur." Von Moltke found it interesting to see how "such people can be swayed to the right side by a resolute stand." It is also interesting to note that, poignantly, Von Moltke was eventually executed because of his courage and his resolute stands. *See also, and more*

---

2. The "Order" referred to was undoubtedly the infamous "*Commando Order*" of October 18, 1942, which had recently come to the notice of the Abwehr. Hitler's order was made in light of the Allied commando and sabotage operations, becoming more frequent in Africa and in the Western theater. He ordered that all participants were to be killed and not to be taken prisoner. Even those one or two who were taken to be interrogated first, they, too, were to be shot immediately afterwards."

broadly on this subject, Detlev Vagts, *International Law in the Third Reich,* 84 Am.J.Int'l L. 661 (1990).

———

EXECUTIVE OPPOSITION TO PROPOSED LEGISLATION VIOLATIVE OF INTERNATIONAL LAW

LETTER FROM THE U.S. SECRETARY OF THE TREASURY TO THE CHAIRMAN OF THE SENATE FINANCE COMMITTEE APRIL 7, 1986

25 International Legal Materials 760 (1986).*

* * *

Certain provisions of the tax reform legislation recently passed by the House of Representatives and now under consideration by the Senate conflict with U.S. obligations under existing tax treaties. In some instances, the intention to override treaties is made explicit, either in the Bill or in the committee report. As you are aware, under our Constitutional system a later enacted statute takes precedence over a pre-existing treaty where that is the manifest intent of the Congress. * * * This administration strongly opposes treaty overrides in tax reform legislation. * * *

* * *

I urge that you not enact treaty override provisions as part of tax reform legislation and that you reaffirm in the accompanying committee reports the U.S. commitment to honor its outstanding treaty obligations. Bilateral negotiation, not unilateral override, is the appropriate way to deal with treaty abuses. In the long run, such an approach will best serve the interests of the United States in the international marketplace.

* * *

———

Relative success. On July 31, 1986, the Secretary of the Treasury also wrote to the Chairman of the House Ways and Means Committee concerning the tax reform provisions in conflict with tax treaties of the United States, and emphasized again the opposition of the executive to them. An official of the Treasury Department later claimed success in obtaining deletion in the final bill of many, but not all, of the treaty overrides. The remaining discrepancies between the legislation and the treaties would thus become a matter of diplomatic negotiations.

* Reprinted with the permission of the American Society of International Law from material published at 25 I.L.M. 760 under the title "United States: Letter of the Secretary of the Treasury Concerning Opposition to Tax Reform Legislation That Overrides Bilateral Tax Treaties."

Legislative override. In 1989 the OECD Committee on Fiscal Affaires made a report on this subject as respects tax treaty override by national legislation. It made its Report to the Council of OECD, where 24 member states from the traditional market economy countries of North America, Western Europe and the Far East are represented. In acting on the Committee's Report, the OECD Council's Recommendation, adopted by consensus, included the following:

RECOMMENDATION OF THE COUNCIL
Concerning Tax Treaty Override
(adopted by the Council at its 717th session of 2nd October, 1989)

* * *

Considering that double taxation conventions contribute to the removal of obstacles to the free movement of goods, services, capital and manpower between Member countries of the OECD and that the network of conventions brings certainty into international tax matters:

Considering that such certainty has been called into question, and to some extent undermined, by the enactment of legislation which is intended to nullify unilaterally the application of international treaty obligations:

Considering that bilateral or multilateral consultations are the first course of action in dealing with problems arising from conflicts between domestic legislation and treaty provisions:

I.   RECOMMENDS Member countries:

    1.   To undertake promptly bilateral or multilateral consultations to address problems connected with tax treaty provisions, whether arising in their own country or raised by countries with which they have tax treaties:

    2.   To avoid enacting legislation which is intended to have effects in clear contradiction to international treaty obligations.

II.   INSTRUCTS the Committee on Fiscal Affairs to follow developments in this area and to bring to the attention of the Council any action which would constitute a material breach of Member countries' international treaty obligations.

INFERRED LEGISLATIVE INTENT NOT TO VIOLATE INTERNATIONAL LAW

1987 RESTATEMENT, SECTION 115 *

Comment *a.*

* * * It is assumed that Congress does not intend to repudiate an international obligation * * * by nullifying a rule of international

* Copyright 1987 by the American Law Institute. Reprinted with permission.

law or an international agreement * * * or by making it impossible for the United States to carry out its obligations. * * * Therefore, when an act of Congress and an international agreement or a rule of customary law relate to the same subject, the courts, regulatory agencies, and the Executive Branch will endeavor to construe them so as to give effect to both. The courts do not favor a repudiation of an international obligation by implication and require clear indication that Congress, in enacting legislation, intended to supersede the earlier agreement or other international obligation. The fact that an act of Congress does not expressly exclude matters inconsistent with international law or a United States agreement does not necessarily imply a Congressional purpose to supersede [those obligations].

STANDING INSTRUCTIONS FOR ADMINISTRATION AND IMPLEMENTATION OF INTERNATIONAL LAW

In the services of the Government of the United States such as the Armed Forces, the Coast Guard, the Foreign Service and the Immigration and Naturalization Service, standing instructions are issued to officers who, because of their position or mission, may have to handle situations susceptible of creating serious international repercussions. The instructions may anticipate some specific situations and spell out procedures for meeting them in conformity with international law. With respect to situations which cannot be specifically anticipated, the instructions usually call for referral to higher authority and eventually the Department of State. * * *

* * * The issuance of standing instructions to services for insuring national action in conformity with international law is a practice followed in many national systems.

DEPARTMENT OF DEFENSE DIRECTIVE NO. 5100.77 JULY 9, 1977

SUBJECT: DOD Law of War Program

References: (a) DOD Directive 5100.77, "DOD Program for the Implementation of the Law of War (Short Title: DOD Law of War Program)," November 5, 1974 (hereby canceled).

     * * *

A. *REISSUANCE AND PURPOSE*

This Directive reissues reference (a) and provides policy guidance and assignment responsibilities within the Department of Defense for a program to ensure compliance with the law of war.

     * * *

C. POLICY

It is the policy of the Department of Defense to ensure that:

1. The law of war and the obligations of the U.S. Government under that law are observed and enforced by the U.S. Armed Forces.

2. A program, designed to prevent violations of the law of war, is implemented by the U.S. Armed Forces.

3. Alleged violations of the law of war, whether committed by or against U.S. or enemy personnel, are promptly reported, thoroughly investigated, and, where appropriate, remedied by corrective action.

* * *

D. DEFINITION AND EXCLUSION

1. The law of war encompasses all international law with respect to the conduct of armed conflict, binding on the United States or its individual citizens, either in international treaties and agreements to which the United States is a party, or applicable as customary international law.

* * *

(d) Geneva Convention for the Amelioration of the Condition of the Wounded and Sick in Armed Forces in the Field, August 12, 1949.

(e) Geneva Convention for Amelioration of the Condition of the Wounded, Sick and Shipwrecked Members of Armed Forces at Sea, August 12, 1949.

(f) Geneva Convention Relative to the Treatment of Prisoners of War, August 12, 1949.

(g) Geneva Convention Relative to the Protection of Civilian Persons in Time of War, August 12, 1949.

(h) Hague Convention No. IV Respecting the Laws and Customs of War on Land, October 18, 1907.

* * *

UNITED STATES NAVY REGULATIONS SUBPART F—COMMANDERS IN CHIEF AND OTHER COMMANDERS

Code of Federal Regulations, 32 C.F.R. 700.605 (1974).

§ 700.605 Observance of international law.

At all times a commander shall observe, and require his command to observe, the principles of international law. Where necessary to fulfillment of this responsibility, a departure from other provisions of Navy Regulations is authorized.

See Reisman and Leitzau, Moving International Law from Theory to Practice: The Role of Military Manuals in Effectuating the Law of

Armed Conflict, in 64 International Law Studies, The Law of Naval Operations 1 (1991); U.S. Dept. of the Navy, The Commander's Handbook on the Law of Naval Operations NWP–9 (Washington, 1987).

UNITED STATES, DEPARTMENT OF STATE GUIDELINES ON PROTECTION OF FOREIGN MISSIONS

22 C.F.R. § 2a.1 (1987).

§ 2a.1 Purpose.

(a) The purpose of these guidelines is to establish a program, under which the Department can review and promote coordination between federal, state and local security authorities in the protection of foreign missions in the United States, and can assist in the provision of protective services for such missions. State and local governments of the United States will continue to have the primary responsibility for law enforcement within their respective jurisdictions. This program does not establish any legal entitlement to assistance either for a foreign mission or for any state or local government or authority. The Bureau of Diplomatic Security will maximize available federal assistance through coordination of programs and through limited federal financial assistance by contract or reimbursement for certain protective services in cases of extraordinary protective need, to the extent funds are available therefore.

(b) This program will assist the United States to carry out its international obligations relating to the protection of foreign diplomatic and consular and international organization personnel and premises in the United States under the Vienna Convention on Diplomatic Relations, the Vienna Convention on Consular Relations, the Convention on the Prevention and Punishment of Crimes Against Internationally Protected Persons, Including Diplomatic Agents, the Convention to Prevent and Punish Acts of Terrorism, international agreements relating to organizations such as the United Nations Headquarters Agreement, and other applicable multilateral and bilateral agreements and provisions of international law.

(c) The program will include the following—(1) Foreign Missions, generally—Extraordinary protective services may be provided directly through the Department of State, or by reimbursement for services to state and local governments or contract; (2) Missions to International Organizations—Extraordinary protective services may be provided by reimbursement to State or local officials, to missions to certain international organizations, such as the United Nations, under title 3 of the U.S.Code, 202 and 208.

(d) The provisions of these guidelines may be applied to protective assistance under both paragraph (a) and (b) of this section unless otherwise stated therein or separate standards or criteria are required by applicable law. Supplementary guidelines may be issued by the Department of State from time to time in order to implement these guidelines in particular jurisdictions. This part is authorized by the Foreign Missions Act of 1982, the Foreign Missions Amendments Act of 1983 and Executive Order No. 12478.

For the administration of diplomatic privileges and immunities in the United States, see chapter 7, infra, including excerpts from the State Department's Guidelines for Law Enforcement Officers.

———

NATIONAL APOLOGY FOR VIOLATION OF INTERNATIONAL LAW

RULING OF THE SECRETARY–GENERAL OF THE UNITED NATIONS ON THE RAINBOW WARRIOR AFFAIR BETWEEN FRANCE AND NEW ZEALAND, JULY 6, 1986

26 International Legal Materials 1346 (1987).*

[On July 10, 1985, the Rainbow Warrior was sunk in Auckland harbor, New Zealand, as a result of extensive damage caused by explosives. A Dutch crewman drowned. The ship was owned by the Greenpeace organization and used by it in its campaign against French nuclear tests in the Pacific. Two agents of the French secret service were arrested in New Zealand, prosecuted and sentenced to prison for the crimes. In a communique issued September 22, 1985, the Prime Minister of France acknowledged that the Rainbow Warrior had been sunk by the two agents acting on instructions from higher authority.

On the same date, the French Minister for External Affairs indicated that France was prepared to undertake reparations for the consequences of its action and enter into negotiations for this purpose with New Zealand. Having failed to reach an agreement, the parties referred the affair to the Secretary–General of the United Nations and agreed to abide by his ruling. He invited them to submit written statements of their positions. The parties' positions and the ruling of the Secretary–General, follow].

* * *

Memorandum of the Government of New Zealand

Reparations Sought by New Zealand

New Zealand seeks redress as follows:

(A) Apology

The Government of New Zealand is entitled, in accordance with international law, to a formal and unqualified apology for the violation of its sovereignty and its rights under international law.

* * *

* Reprinted with the permission of the American Society of International Law.

Memorandum of the Government of France

Reparations Sought by New Zealand

A. Apologies

The violation of New Zealand territory by France did not in itself cause any material damage to New Zealand. It may, [however], be admitted that it has caused it moral damage which, according to international law, may be compensated by the offer of regrets and apologies.

The Government of New Zealand requests the French Government to offer it apologies. The French Government is prepared to make compensation * * * for the moral damage suffered by New Zealand and the French Prime Minister is ready, therefore, to address to the New Zealand Prime Minister a formal and unconditional letter of apology for the attack carried out on 10 July 1985.

* * *

Ruling of the Secretary General

1. Apology

New Zealand seeks an apology. France is prepared to give one. My ruling is that the Prime Minister of France should convey to the Prime Minister of New Zealand a formal and unqualified apology for the attack, contrary to international law, on the "Rainbow Warrior" by French service agents which took place on 10 July 1985.

* * *

———

Other reparations. Among other reparations, New Zealand sought compensation for the violation of its sovereignty and all the costs, including the costs of investigation, incurred as a direct result of the incident. The Secretary–General ruled that the French Government should pay $7 million to the Government of New Zealand "as compensation for all the damage it has suffered." As to the death of the crewman, New Zealand did not have standing to claim compensation on behalf of his family, because he was not one of its nationals, but wanted to make sure the French Government made appropriate arrangements. The French Government did so. As to the sinking of the Rainbow Warrior, the French Government agreed with the Greenpeace organization to submit the issue of damages suffered to an arbitral tribunal. On October 2, 1987, the tribunal awarded Greenpeace the sum of $8,159,-000. *Le Monde,* Dimanche 5 Octobre 1987, at 16. (Editors' translation).

———

THE SECOND NATIONAL APOLOGY IN THE
RAINBOW WARRIOR AFFAIR [a*]

[The *Rainbow Warrior Affair* did not end there. A second arbitration took place and an apology was made. The two French officers (known in France as the "false couple Turinge")] * * * had been sentenced to ten years in prison by a New Zealand court. This term was reduced to a minimum period of three years following an agreement between the Secretary–General of the United Nations and the two governments, on the condition that the term be served at the French military base at Hao in the Pacific to which they were purposely transferred. They were forbidden to leave their place of forced residence for any reason except by agreement between the two parties.

In contravention of that condition, France, in which the political majority in Parliament had changed in the meantime, decided to repatriate Major Mafart, invoking his state of health, and then Captain Prieur in May, 1988, because she was pregnant and her father was ill. These successive decisions displeased the New Zealand Government, which appealed to international law complaining of France's non-respect of engagements.

The Tribunal rendered a condemnation of pure form against France, noting that in evacuating Major Mafart from Hao, the French Republic did not violate its obligations to New Zealand, because his health condition required it.

On the other hand, the court held that France had violated those obligations in not ordering the return of the officer to the atoll after his treatment. Regarding Captain Prieur, France violated its obligations on three successive occasions: [1] in not seeking in good-faith to obtain the agreement of New Zealand for her departure from the island; [2] in evacuating her in May 1988; [3] and finally in not returning her to the atoll. The Tribunal found, however, that the obligations to maintain the two officers on the island were extinguished on 22 July, 1989 (end of the minimal period of three years). Therefore, the Tribunal could not accept New Zealand's application requesting it to order the two officers returned to the island. All considered, the judgement against France for violations of its obligations to New Zealand "constitutes, in view of the circumstances, adequate reparation for the juridical and moral prejudice suffered by New Zealand." Rousseau, Chroniques des Faits Internationaux, 94 Rev.Gen. de Droit Int'l 1069 (1990).[b]

[Ultimately France and New Zealand reconciled].

SECTION B. APPLICATION IN
DIPLOMATIC PRACTICE

CHARTER OF THE UNITED NATIONS

Article 33.

1. The parties to any dispute, the continuance of which is likely to endanger the maintenance of international peace and security, shall,

---

a. Translations by the editors.
* Reprinted by permission, *Le Monde.*

b. The arbitration award is reported at 82 Int'l.L.Rep. 500 (1990).

first of all, seek a solution by negotiation, enquiry, mediation, conciliation, arbitration, judicial settlement, resort to regional agencies or arrangements, or other peaceful means of their own choice.

DIPLOMATIC REPRESENTATIONS

Diplomatic practice.   The primary means of resolving claims asserted under international law by one state against another is diplomatic correspondence.   It is the everyday working method of the international system for settling legal disputes.   Centuries of practice attest to its effectiveness.   Hence correspondence recording the diplomatic negotiations of states in settling their legal claims is a vast and valuable repository of information on the application of international law.

A note of caution is in order.   The assertion of a claim under international law by one state against another is a contentious statement.   The diplomatic presentation of its claim is the state's partisan position, a one-sided view of the facts and the law applicable to them.   In some cases, the claim may be exactly stated and incontrovertible on both facts and law.   In many more cases, however, the defending state questions either or both.   Not until the parties have achieved mutual agreement as to both can it be said they have recognized a particular rule of international law as applicable to the particular case, although a claim based upon a stated legal proposition, even if not agreed by the other party, should constitute a recognition of the proposition by the claimant state.   Some agreements may be fully based on compromise, *not law.*

Thus the totality of the relevant diplomatic exchanges has to be considered before any conclusion can be reached regarding the rule of international law applied to the resolution of a claim.   Moreover, it must be kept in mind that the resolution of a claim by diplomatic negotiation may turn in the end, not on considerations of international law, but partly or entirely on political, economic and other empirical factors. Diplomatic representations often are made not only by formal correspondence but also by other direct communications of representatives meeting in Foreign Offices or Embassies and increasingly by press, television and radio announcements or even "leaks."

Digests of International Law published in the United States contain, inter alia, a great deal of diplomatic correspondence on issues of international law.   They are valuable tools for the international lawyer. The Moore Digest of 1906 was followed by that of Hackworth in 1940. Between 1963 and 1972 fifteen volumes of Whiteman's Digest of International Law were published.   Since 1973, updated volumes of the Digest have also been published as The Digest of the Foreign Relations of the

United States. They are published yearly and updated in the American Journal of International Law. Other Digests published from 20 to 25 years after the events, frequently throw light on legal issues involved in originally highly classified documents.

Foreign Digests: Information on diplomatic practice relating to international law is also becoming increasingly available in other states. It may be provided by specialized publications such as the British Digest of International Law, the Réportoire de la Pratique Française en Matière de Droit International Public and the Prassi Italiana di Diritto Internazionale. More often a national journal of international law will reserve a section for periodic reports on national diplomatic practice. Journals so doing include: the American Journal of International Law; the Annuaire Francais de Droit International; the Annuaire Suisse de Droit International; the Australian Yearbook of International Law; the Canadian Yearbook of International Law; the Indian Journal of International Law; the Italian Yearbook of International Law; the Japanese Annual of International Law; the Netherlands Yearbook of International Law; the Revue Belge de Droit International; the Malaya Law Review.

Commissions of inquiry. For a description of arrangements for commissions of inquiry, their structure and function, see Chapter 16, *infra* and the United Nations Handbook on the Pacific Settlement of Disputes Between States 24–33 (N.Y., 1992). * * *

Commissions for conciliation. A feature of some international conventions is the provision of commissions for conciliation to which parties can resort for an amicable solution of their disputes, either in place of or prior to submission of the dispute to arbitration or to adjudication. Among the conventions in the Documentary Supplement see, e.g., the following: Article 42 of the International Covenant on Civil and Political Rights, Article 12 of the International Convention on the Elimination of all Forms of Racial Discrimination, Article 66 of the Vienna Convention on the Law of Treaties, Article III of the Optional Protocol to the Vienna Convention on Diplomatic Relations, Article IV of the Optional Protocol to the 1958 Conventions on the Law of the Sea. Historically, few disputes have been brought before conciliation commissions.

SECTION C.   APPLICATION IN INTERNATIONAL TRIBUNALS

---

1.   THE INTERNATIONAL COURT OF JUSTICE

The first world court. In 1920, the Council of the League of Nations appointed an Advisory Committee of Jurists to prepare a draft for the establishment of the Permanent Court of International Justice contemplated in Article 14 of the Covenant. Though the United States had refused to become a member of the League, Elihu Root, American lawyer and statesman, was one of the ten jurists chosen for the task, with James Brown Scott, a widely recognized authority on international law, serving as his adviser. The names of both were closely associated with the efforts made by the United States at the Second Hague Peace Conference of 1907 to create such a court.

THE ORIGINAL DREAM

Permanent Court of International Justice, Advisory Committee of Jurists,
Procès–Verbaux of the Proceedings of the Committee, June 16–July
24, 1920, at 2, 3, 5, 7, 11, 693, 727 (1920).

Speech delivered by M. le Jonkheer van Karnebeek.

[After reviewing the accomplishments and the failures of the two Hague Peace Conferences, the speaker made this statement.] Gentlemen, events have not been able to arrest the onward march of ideas. The League of Nations has taken up again the thread which for a long time seemed abandoned, and has entrusted to you the task of assisting it, by your advice, to formulate the important decisions to be taken in the near future. The grandeur of this task is apparent when, above the conflict of interests and passions of mankind, is seen the guiding star of the noble idea of governing the future by the laws of justice. In a world which has passed through one of the greatest trials which history has ever known, in an international society shaken to its foundations, and almost at the end of its resources, the work of justice which is to be carried on in this Palace appears like an awakening, like a promise of moral reconstruction, like the message of a better future worthy of the League of Nations.

Speech delivered by M. Léon Bourgeois.

* * *

I have come here * * * in the name of the Council of the League of Nations. * * * A Memorandum by the Secretary–General has set out for you * * * the principal questions which you will have to resolve. * * *

* * *

From the start, however, some points will appear to you to be already certainly obtained. The Court of Justice must be a true Permanent Court. It is not simply a question of arbitrators chosen on a particular occasion, in the case of conflict, by the interested parties; it is a small number of judges sitting constantly and receiving a mandate the duration of which will enable the establishment of a real jurisprudence, who will administer justice. This permanence is a symbol. It will be a seat raised in the midst of the nations, where judges are always present, to whom can always be brought the appeal of the weak and to whom protests against the violation of right can be addressed. * * *

* * *

You are about * * * to give life to the judicial power of humanity. * * *

* * *

————

1. ***The use of the Permanent Court of International Justice.*** The obstacle to the use of the court turned out to be less the lack of compulsory jurisdiction in the statute creating it than the reluctance of states to settle their disputes by judicial means. Between 1920 and 1939, some 41 states accepted at one time or another the compulsory jurisdiction of the court through the optional clause. This was a large number, being about four-fifths of the 52 states which became members of the League of Nations in 1920. Yet the court gave dispositive judgments in only 18 instances, according to André Gros, French judge on the International Court of Justice. Twice it held that it had no jurisdiction and in nine instances the cases were discontinued. A Propos de Cinquante Années de Justice Internationale, 76 Revue Gén. de Dr. Int. Pub. 5, 6 (1972).

During the same period, however, the court gave 27 advisory opinions, all at the request of the Council of the League. Opponents of the court in the United States were very much concerned that it should be empowered to give such opinions. When the Senate considered giving its advice and consent to the United States becoming a party to the statute of the court, a resolution that the Senate discussed, but did not pass, contained a reservation virtually ensuring to the United States a veto power over the whole advisory jurisdiction of the court.

The United States did not become a party to the statute. Opposition to the court in the Senate could not be surmounted from 1920 to 1935, the date of the final negative vote on advice and consent.

2. ***Dissolution of the first court and creation of its successor.*** After winding up some unfinished business in the fall of 1945, the surviving members of the court submitted their resignation to the Secretary General of the League of Nations on January 1, 1946. The Assembly of the League thereupon resolved that the Permanent Court of International Justice was for all purposes to be regarded as dissolved. See Rosenne, Documents on the International Court of Justice 491–493 (1979).

Its successor, the International Court of Justice, was brought into being by the Charter of the United Nations. The Statute of the I.C.J., which is essentially the same as that of its predecessor, is in the Documentary Supplement. In early 1994, the composition of the Court was as follows:

————

	Order of precedence	Country	Date of expiry of Term of Office
President	M. Bedjaoui	Algeria	5 February 1997
Vice–President	S.M. Schwebel	United States	5 February 1997
Judges	S. Oda	Japan	5 February 1994
	R. Ago	Italy	5 February 1997
	N.K. Tarassov	USSR	5 February 1997
	Sir R. Jennings	United Kingdom	5 February 2000
	G. Guillaume	France	5 February 2000
	M. Shahabuddeen	Guyana	5 February 1997
	A. Aguilar Mawdsley	Venezuela	5 February 2000
	C.G. Weeramantry	Sri Lanka	5 February 2000
	R. Ranjeva	Madagascar	5 February 2000
	C.A. Fleischhauer	Germany	5 February 2003
	A.G. Koroma	Sierra Leone	5 February 2003
	S. Juiyong	China	5 February 2003
	G. Herczegh	Hungary	5 February 2003

Source: International Court of Justice.

JURISDICTION BY CONSENT

United Nations, Handbook on the Pacific Settlement of Disputes Between States 70 (1992).

* * *

(a) *Jurisdiction, competence and initiation of the process*

202.   Settlement of international disputes by international courts is subject to State acceptance of jurisdiction over such disputes.[187]   This recognition may be expressed by way of a special agreement between the States parties (*compromis*) conferring jurisdiction upon a court in a particular dispute, or by a compromissory clause providing for an agreed or unilateral reference of a dispute to a court, or by other means.   In the event of a dispute as to whether a court has jurisdiction, the matter is settled by the decision of the court.[188]   For example, the court may rule on questions of competence or other substantive preliminary objections that can be raised by a respondent State.[189]   Issues relating to procedural preliminary objections under the rule of exhaustion of local remedies are also heard.

(i) *Special agreement*

203.   Article 36, paragraph 1, of the Statute of the International Court of Justice provides that the "jurisdiction of the Court comprises

---

187. For cases in which the International Court of Justice found that it could not accept jurisdiction because the opposing party did not recognize its jurisdiction, see *I.C.J. Yearbook 1987–1988*, p. 51, note 1.

188. ICJ Statute, Article 36, paragraph 6.

189. Objections to jurisdiction have been taken in the International Court of Justice on several grounds, such as: (a) that the instrument conferring jurisdiction is no longer in force; see, e.g., Temple of Preah Vihear (Cambodia v. Thailand), I.C.J. Reports 1961, p. 17; or not applicable (e.g., Aerial Incident of 10 March 1953 (United States v. Czechoslovakia), I.C.J. Reports

1956, p. 6); or the dispute is excluded by virtue of a reservation to the instrument (Military and Paramilitary Activities in and against Nicaragua (Nicaragua v. United States), I.C.J. Reports 1984, p. 392); or (b) that the dispute is not admissible for reasons of jus standi (e.g., South West Africa (Ethiopia v. South Africa, Liberia v. South Africa), I.C.J. Reports 1962, p. 319); or non-exhaustion of local remedies (e.g., Interhandel (Switzerland v. United States), I.C.J. Reports 1957, p. 105); or non-existence of dispute (e.g., Rights of Passage over Indian territory (Portugal v. India), I.C.J. Reports 1957, p. 125).

all cases which the parties refer to it", which is done normally by way of notification to the Registry of a special agreement (*compromis*) concluded by the parties for that purpose. The Special Agreement of 23 May 1976 concerning the Delimitation of the Continental Shelf (Libya/Malta), for example, provides:

"The Government of the Republic of Malta and the Government of the Libyan Arab Republic agree to recourse to the International Court of Justice as follows:

"*Article I,*

"The Court is requested to decide the following questions:

"What principles and rules of international law are applicable to the delimitation of the area of the continental shelf which appertains to the Republic of Malta and the area of continental shelf which appertains to the Libyan Arab Republic and how in practice such principles and rules can be applied by the two parties in this particular case in order that they may without difficulty delimit such areas by an agreement * * *."

204. By asking the Court to indicate also how, in practice, such principles and rules can be applied in the case, the Libya/Malta *compromis* went further than what had been requested in a special agreement on another delimitation case referred to the Court. In the *North Sea Continental Shelf* cases the special agreement in 1967 between Denmark and [the Federal Republic of] Germany, like the special agreement of the same date between the Netherlands and Germany, contained the provision set out below, requesting the Court to do no more than to rule on the principles applicable to the delimitation as between the Parties:

"(1) The International Court of Justice is requested to *decide* the following question: What principles and rules of international law are applicable to the delimitation as between the Parties of the areas of the continental shelf in the North Sea which appertain to each of them beyond the partial boundary determined by the above-mentioned Convention of 9 June 1965.

"(2) The Governments of the Kingdom of Denmark and of the Federal Republic of Germany shall delimit the continental shelf in the North Sea as between their countries by agreement in pursuance of the decision requested from the International Court of Justice."

(ii) *Compromissory clause in treaties*

205. Article 36, paragraph 1, of the Statute * * * provides also that the jurisdiction * * * comprises "all matters specially provided for * * * in treaties and conventions in force". There are numerous treaties containing such a compromissory clause, some of which provide for unilateral reference of all or certain categories of disputes to the International Court of Justice. At the global level, for example, under the General Act for the Pacific Settlement of International Disputes of 26 September 1928 and 28 April 1949 all legal disputes are subject to

compulsory adjudication by the Court, unless the parties agree to submit them to arbitration or conciliation. * * *

206. At the regional level, * * * the European Convention for the Peaceful Settlement of Disputes of 29 April 1957, * * * provides for the submission of all international legal disputes to the International Court of Justice.

(iii) *Other means of conferring jurisdiction*

207. * * * States parties to the Statute of the [International Court of Justice] have the option of making a declaration under Article 36, paragraph 2, of the Statute by which they accept in advance the jurisdiction of the Court "in all legal disputes concerning (*a*) the interpretation of a treaty; (*b*) any question of international law; (*c*) the existence of any fact which, if established, would constitute a breach of an international obligation; (*d*) the nature or extent of the reparation to be made for the breach of an international obligation". States are bound by this declaration only with respect to States which have also made such a declaration. The declaration may be made unconditionally or on condition of reciprocity on the part of several or certain States, or for a certain time. Optional clauses of compulsory jurisdiction also exist with respect to the European Court of Human Rights and the Inter–American Court of Human Rights.

208. By contrast, other treaties establishing an international court automatically confer jurisdiction to that court with respect to its scope of activities. The States parties do not need and do not have the option to make a declaration of acceptance of the compulsory jurisdiction of that court. Thus, by becoming a party to the Treaties establishing the European Communities, member States automatically subject themselves to the jurisdiction of the Court of Justice of the European Communities for disputes connected with the application and interpretation of the Treaties. States parties to the 1982 United Nations Convention on the Law of the Sea *ipso facto* accept the compulsory jurisdiction of various forums for the settlement of law of the sea disputes.[202] However, under the Convention, States parties have to make a declaration on the choice of the forum for judicial settlement established thereunder.[203]

(iv) *Initiation of process*

209. Contentious proceedings before international courts are instituted either unilaterally by one of the parties to a dispute or jointly by the parties, depending upon the terms of the relevant agreement in force

---

202. These forums are: (*a*) the International Tribunal for the Law of the Sea; (*b*) the International Court of Justice; (*c*) an arbitral tribunal constituted under the relevant provisions (annex VII) of the 1982 Convention; (*d*) a special arbitral tribunal constituted under the relevant provisions (annex VIII) of the 1982 Convention.

203. Articles 286 and 287.

between them.[204] Thus, if under the agreement the parties have accepted the compulsory jurisdiction of the International Court of Justice in respect of the dispute, then proceedings may be instituted unilaterally by the applicant State. In the absence of such a prior acceptance, however, proceedings can only be brought before international courts on the basis of the mutual consent of the parties.

210. The procedure for instituting contentious proceedings is defined in the basic statute of the respective international courts. The Statute of the International Court of Justice provides under Article 40 as follows:

> "1. Cases are brought before the Court, as the case may be, either by the notification of the special agreement or by a written application addressed to the Registrar. In either case the subject of the dispute and the parties shall be indicated.

> "2. The Registrar shall forthwith communicate the application to all concerned.

> "3. He shall also notify the Members of the United Nations through the Secretary–General, and also any other States entitled to appear before the Court."

* * *

(v) *Advisory opinions*

212. International courts may be empowered to give an advisory opinion on a legal question relating to an existing international dispute between States referred to them by an international entity. The opinion does not bind the requesting entity, or any other body, or any State. Nevertheless, procedure in advisory cases, as in contentious cases, involves elaborate written and oral proceedings in accordance with the predetermined rules of the court in question, and as such advisory opinions could assume the character of judicial pronouncements which, while not binding, might entail practical consequences * * *.

———

Acceptance of the Jurisdiction of the Court. By mid–1991 the jurisdiction of the court had been accepted in over 250 international agreements, but only 51 states had made declarations accepting the Court's jurisdiction under the optional clause. Jurisdiction for advisory opinions, provided in Article 96 of the Charter, is conferred case by case by request of the competent organ of the United Nations or of the Agency entitled to make the request.

———

204. In some regional courts, cases may be brought to them by entities other than States (e.g., the European Commission of Human Rights with respect to the European Court of Human Rights; the Council or the Commission with respect to the Court of Justice of the European Communities; the Inter–American Commission on Human Rights with respect to the Inter–American Court of Human Rights) or even by individuals (e.g., the Court of Justice of the European Communities). * * *

EXAMPLES OF DECLARATIONS UNDER ARTICLE 36(2) OF THE STATUTE OF THE INTERNATIONAL COURT OF JUSTICE

NICARAGUA

International Court of Justice, Yearbook 1990–1991 at 93 (1992) [Translation from French]

On behalf of the Republic of Nicaragua I recognize as compulsory unconditionally the jurisdiction of the Permanent Court of International Justice. Geneva, 24 September 1929. (Signed) T.F. MEDINA.

UNITED STATES OF AMERICA

International Court of Justice, Yearbook 1984–1985, at 99 (1985)

I, Harry S. Truman, President of the United States of America, declare on behalf of the United States of America, under Article 36, paragraph 2, of the Statute of the International Court of Justice, and in accordance with the Resolution of 2 August 1946 of the Senate of the United States of America (two-thirds of the Senators present concurring therein), that the United States of America recognizes as compulsory ipso facto and without special agreement, in relation to any other State accepting the same obligation, the jurisdiction of the International Court of Justice in all legal disputes hereafter arising concerning

(a) the interpretation of a treaty;

(b) any question of international law;

(c) the existence of any fact which, if established, would constitute a breach of an international obligation;

(d) the nature or extent of the reparation to be made for the breach of an international obligation;

Provided, that this declaration shall not apply to

(a) disputes the solution of which the parties shall entrust to other tribunals by virtue of agreements already in existence or which may be concluded in the future; or

(b) disputes with regard to matters which are essentially within the domestic jurisdiction of the United States of America as determined by the United States of America; or

(c) disputes arising under a multilateral treaty, unless (1) all parties to the treaty affected by the decision are also parties to the case before the Court, or (2) the United States of America specially agrees to jurisdiction; and

Provided further, that this declaration shall remain in force for a period of five years and thereafter until the expiration of six months after notice may be given to terminate this declaration.

Done at Washington this fourteenth day of August 1946.

(Signed) HARRY S. TRUMAN.

[The declaration was terminated on October 7, 1985. See *infra* pp. 64 et seq.]

———

The self-judging reservation. Of the 51 states subject, on July 31, 1991, to the compulsory jurisdiction of the court by virtue of a declaration of acceptance, more than half attached reservations substantially limiting the scope of the jurisdiction. While the reservations cover a wide variety of matters, many exclude matters within the domestic jurisdiction of the signatory. In some cases, the reservations exclude matters which, by international law, are essentially within its domestic jurisdiction. But in other cases—see, for example, the reservation devised by the United States, the so-called Connally Amendment, *supra*—the signatory reserves to itself the power to determine what is a matter or dispute within its domestic jurisdiction.

———

CASE OF CERTAIN NORWEGIAN LOANS (FRANCE v. NORWAY)

International Court of Justice, 1957.
[1957] I.C.J.Rep. 9.

[Legislation in Norway permitted payment of Norwegian loans in Bank of Norway notes instead of gold. The French Government espoused the claims of French nationals who held the Norwegian bonds and desired payment in gold. The French Government asserted to the Norwegian Government "that it would not seem that a unilateral decision can be relied upon as against foreign creditors." The Norwegian Government rejected French proposals to submit the matter to a mixed commission of economic and financial experts, to arbitration or to the International Court of Justice, maintaining that the claims of bondholders involved solely the interpretation and application of Norwegian law and that the bondholders should sue in the Norwegian courts.

The French Government referred the matter to the International Court of Justice.]

* * *

The Application [of France] expressly refers to Article 36, paragraph 2, of the Statute of the Court and to the acceptance of the compulsory jurisdiction of the Court by Norway on November 16th, 1946, and by France on March 1st, 1949. The Norwegian Declaration reads:

> I declare on behalf of the Norwegian Government that Norway recognizes as compulsory ipso facto and without special agreement, in relation to any other State accepting the same obligation, that is to say, on condition of reciprocity, the jurisdiction of the International Court of Justice in conformity with Article 36, paragraph 2, of the Statute of the Court, for a period of ten years as from 3rd October 1946.

The French Declaration reads:

> On behalf of * * * the French Republic, and subject to ratification, I declare that I recognize as compulsory ipso facto and without special agreement, in relation to any other State accepting the same obligation, that is on condition of reciprocity, the jurisdiction of the International Court of Justice, in conformity with Article 36, paragraph 2, of the Statute of the said Court, for all disputes which may arise in respect of facts or situations subsequent to the ratification of the present declaration, with the exception of those with regard to which the parties may have agreed or may agree to have recourse to another method of peaceful settlement.

> This declaration does not apply to differences relating to matters which are essentially within the national jurisdiction as understood by the Government of the French Republic.

> * * *

After presenting the first ground of its first Preliminary Objection on the basis that the loan contracts are governed by municipal law, the Norwegian Government continues in its Preliminary Objections:

> There can be no possible doubt on this point. If, however, there should still be some doubt, the Norwegian Government would rely upon the reservations made by the French Government in its Declaration of March 1st, 1949. By virtue of the principle of reciprocity, which is embodied in Article 36, paragraph 2, of the Statute of the Court and which has been clearly expressed in the Norwegian Declaration of November 16th, 1946, the Norwegian Government cannot be bound, vis-à-vis the French Government, by undertakings which are either broader or stricter than those given by the latter Government.

> * * *

It will be recalled that the French Declaration accepting the compulsory jurisdiction of the Court contains the following reservation:

> This declaration does not apply to differences relating to matters which are essentially within the national jurisdiction as understood by the Government of the French Republic.

In [Norway's] Preliminary Objections it is stated:

> The Norwegian Government did not insert any such reservation in its own Declaration. But it has the right to rely upon the restrictions placed by France upon her own undertakings.

> Convinced that the dispute which has been brought before the Court by the Application of July 6th, 1955, is within the domestic jurisdiction, the Norwegian Government considers itself fully entitled to rely on this right. Accordingly, it requests the Court to decline, on grounds that it lacks jurisdiction, the function which the French Government would have it assume.

In considering this ground of the Objection the Court notes in the first place that the present case has been brought before it on the basis of Article 36, paragraph 2, of the Statute and of the corresponding

Declarations of acceptance of compulsory jurisdiction; that in the present case the jurisdiction of the Court depends upon the Declarations made by the Parties in accordance with Article 36, paragraph 2, of the Statute on condition of reciprocity; and that, since two unilateral declarations are involved, such jurisdiction is conferred upon the Court only to the extent to which the Declarations coincide in conferring it. A comparison between the two Declarations shows that the French Declaration accepts the Court's jurisdiction within narrower limits than the Norwegian Declaration; consequently, the common will of the Parties, which is the basis of the Court's jurisdiction, exists within these narrower limits indicated by the French reservation. * * *

France has limited her acceptance of the compulsory jurisdiction of the Court by excluding beforehand disputes "relating to matters which are essentially within the national jurisdiction as understood by the Government of the French Republic". In accordance with the condition of reciprocity to which acceptance of the compulsory jurisdiction is made subject in both Declarations and which is provided for in Article 36, paragraph 3, of the Statute, Norway, equally with France, is entitled to except from the compulsory jurisdiction of the Court disputes understood by Norway to be essentially within its national jurisdiction.

* * *

For these reasons,

The COURT, by twelve votes to three, finds that it is without jurisdiction to adjudicate upon the dispute which has been brought before it by the Application of the government of the French Republic * * *.

* * *

Separate Opinion of Judge Sir HERSCH LAUTERPACHT

* * * I consider that as the French Declaration of Acceptance excludes from the jurisdiction of the Court "matters which are essentially within the national jurisdiction as understood by the Government of the French Republic"—the emphasis being here on the words "as understood by the Government of the French Republic"—it is for the reason of that latter qualification an instrument incapable of producing legal effects before this Court and of establishing its jurisdiction. * * *

* * * [T]he first reason for that view is that that particular part of the acceptance of the Optional Clause on the part of the French Republic is contrary to the Statute of the Court. In the reservation in question [France] says in effect: If a Government brings an application before the Court in reliance on the French acceptance of the jurisdiction of the Court and if the Government of France maintains that the Court has no jurisdiction on the ground that the subject-matter of the dispute is essentially within the domestic jurisdiction of France, then the Court has no power to decide upon that particular allegation; it must accept as binding the French understanding of the legal position on the subject.

If that type of reservation is valid, then the Court is not in the position to exercise the power conferred upon it—in fact, the duty imposed upon it—under paragraph 6 of Article 36 of its Statute. That paragraph provides that "in the event of a dispute as to whether the Court has jurisdiction, the matter shall be settled by a decision of the Court". The French reservation lays down that if, with regard to that particular question, there is a dispute between the Parties as to whether the Court has jurisdiction, the matter shall be settled by a decision of the French Government. The French reservation is thus not only contrary to one of the most fundamental principles of international—and national—jurisprudence according to which it is within the inherent power of a tribunal to interpret the text establishing its jurisdiction. It is also contrary to a clear specific provision of the Statute of the Court as well as to the general Articles 1 and 92 of the Statute and of the Charter, respectively, which require the Court to function in accordance with its Statute.

Now what is the result of the fact that a reservation or part of it is contrary to the provisions of the Statute of the Court? The result is that that reservation or that part of it is invalid. * * *

      * * *

My conclusion is therefore that, having regard to the reservation relating to matters which are essentially within domestic jurisdiction as understood by the French Republic, the French Declaration of Acceptance is invalid for the reason:

(1) That it is contrary to the Statute of the Court;

(2) That it is incapable of giving rise to a legal obligation inasmuch as it claims, and effectively secures, the right of unilateral determination of the extent and of the existence of the obligation of judicial settlement with regard to a comprehensive and indefinite category of disputes covering potentially most disputes which may come before the Court;

(3) That the particular qualification of the reservation in question forms an essential part of the Acceptance and that it is not possible to treat it as invalid and at the same time to maintain the validity of the reservation to which it is attached or of the Acceptance as a whole.

Accordingly, * * * the entire French Declaration of Acceptance must be treated as devoid of legal effect and as incapable of providing a basis for the jurisdiction of the Court. It is for that reason that * * * the Court has no jurisdiction over the dispute. The majority of the Court has reached the same result by acting upon the "automatic reservation" and the French Declaration of Acceptance—both of which I consider to be invalid. However, as the Court has expressly stated that, having regard to the circumstances before it, its Judgment does not pre-judge the major issue involved, I feel that a Separate Opinion—as distinguished from a Dissenting Opinion—meets the requirement of the case.

[A declaration, a separate opinion and dissenting opinions omitted.]

———

1. *Problems.*

a. Suppose the Norwegian declaration had been unconditional rather than reciprocal? Would the court have reached a different result? Consider paragraph (3) of Article 36 of the statute of the court and the following commentary in Waldock, Decline of the Optional Clause, 32 Brit.Y.B.Int'l L. 1955–6, at 244, 255 (1957):

> Paragraph 3 of Article 36 * * * provides that a declaration may be made "unconditionally or on condition of reciprocity on the part of several or certain States or for a certain time". This paragraph does not relate to "reciprocity". It simply authorizes States to accept compulsory jurisdiction under the Optional Clause for limited periods, and to make their liability to jurisdiction conditional on compulsory jurisdiction having been also accepted by a particular number of other States or by particular named States. The reference in paragraph 3 to a "condition of reciprocity on the part of several or certain States" is, indeed, a legacy from a special preoccupation of the Brazilian delegate, M. Fernandez, in the 1920 Committee of Jurists. Brazil considered it impolitic to venture on a unilateral acceptance of compulsory jurisdiction unless some at least of the Great Powers did likewise. Accordingly, M. Fernandez proposed the following formula for the Optional Clause:

>> They may adhere unconditionally or conditionally to the Article providing for compulsory jurisdiction *a possible condition* being reciprocity on the part of a certain number of Members or, again, if a number of Members including such and such specified Members.

> Although M. Fernandez's version of the Optional Clause itself was dropped in favour of the one which now appears in the Statute, the "condition of reciprocity" on the part of several or certain States was included in paragraph 3 in order to satisfy him. Afterwards Brazil did in fact make her declaration subject to a condition of reciprocity on the part of two, at least, of the Great Powers, but she is the only State to have resorted to this form of condition. Such a condition, as will be appreciated, is not really a "condition of reciprocity" but rather a condition that the declaration is not to be in force unless and until a certain number of States or certain named States have accepted compulsory jurisdiction under the Optional Clause.

b. If France were a respondent and pleaded its reservation in an effort to oust the court of jurisdiction, what result? What if the matter before the Court involved a question of treaty interpretation and the applicant state (plaintiff) argued that the French Government could not lawfully understand the matter to be "essentially within the national jurisdiction" of France? What was the position of the parties in the Norwegian Loans case as to the validity of the French reservation?

c. The Nuclear Test Ban Treaty contains the following provision:

> Each Party shall in exercising its national sovereignty have the right to withdraw from the Treaty if it decides that extraordinary

events, related to the subject matter of this Treaty, have jeopardized the supreme interests of its country.

What effect does this clause have on the jurisdiction of the International Court of Justice to decide what is meant by the words "extraordinary events"?

2. *The United States reservation of matters within its domestic jurisdiction.* In the Interhandel case (Switzerland v. United States), [1959] I.C.J.Rep. 6, Switzerland asked the court to declare that the United States was under an obligation to restore assets of the International (Swiss) company. Interhandel owned most of the shares of General Aniline and Film Corporation (GAF); almost all of these shares had been appropriated by the United States during World War II under the Trading With the Enemy Act, on the ground that General Aniline's shares in reality belonged to I.G. Farben, a German company, or that GAF was controlled by that company. Among the preliminary objections raised by the United States was that the court was "without jurisdiction to entertain the Application of the Swiss Government, for the reason that the sale or disposition by the Government of the shares of the GAF which have been vested as enemy property 'has been determined by the United States of America, pursuant to paragraph (b) of the Conditions attached to this country's acceptance of this Court's jurisdiction, to be a matter essentially within the domestic jurisdiction of this country.' "

The court did not rule upon this objection, but upheld a different preliminary objection and thereby held that the Application of the Swiss Government was inadmissible because Switzerland had not exhausted the local remedies available to it in the United States courts.

Judge Sir Hersch Lauterpacht filed a separate opinion in which he reiterated the views he had expressed about the self judging reservation in the Case of Certain Norwegian Loans.

CASE CONCERNING MILITARY AND PARAMILITARY ACTIVITIES IN AND AGAINST NICARAGUA (NICARAGUA v. UNITED STATES OF AMERICA)

International Court of Justice, 1984.
[1984] I.C.J.Rep. 392.

[On April 9, 1984, the Government of Nicaragua filed an application instituting proceedings against the United States with respect to its military and paramilitary activities in Nicaragua.

On April 6, 1984, i.e. three days before the filing, the Secretary of State of the United States sent to the Secretary–General of the United Nations the letter which follows.]

* * *

I have the honor on behalf of the Government of the United States of America to refer to the Declaration of my Government of

August 26, 1946, concerning the acceptance by the United States of America of the compulsory jurisdiction of the International Court of Justice, and to state that the aforesaid Declaration shall not apply to disputes with any Central American state or arising out of or related to events in Central America, any of which disputes shall be settled in such manner as the parties to them may agree.

Notwithstanding the terms of the aforesaid Declaration, this *proviso* shall take effect immediately and shall remain in force for two years, so as to foster the continuing regional dispute settlement process which seeks a negotiated solution to the interrelated political, economic and security problems of Central America.

* * * 23 International Legal Materials 670 (1984).

[The United States appeared and pleaded that the court lacked jurisdiction relying, inter alia, on its letter of April 6, 1984, and on proviso (c) of its reservations to its acceptance of the compulsory jurisdiction of the court. See the text of the declaration supra p. 47.

By eleven votes to five, the court held that it had jurisdiction to entertain the application of Nicaragua on the basis of Article 36, paragraphs 2 and 5 of the I.C.J. Statute. It rejected the United States' arguments based on the letter of April 6, 1984, in the language which follows.]

57. The terms of the 1984 notification, introducing substantial changes in the United States Declaration of Acceptance of 1946, have been quoted above; they constitute an important element for the development of the Court's reasoning. The 1984 notification has two salient aspects: on the one hand it states that the 1946 Declaration of acceptance shall not apply to disputes with any Central American State or arising out of or related to events in Central America; on the other hand it states that it is to take effect immediately, notwithstanding the terms of the 1946 Declaration, and is to remain in force for two years.

* * *

59. Declarations of acceptance of the compulsory jurisdiction of the Court are facultative, unilateral engagements, that States are absolutely free to make or not to make. In making the declaration a State is equally free either to do so unconditionally and without limit of time for its duration, or to qualify it with conditions or reservations. In particular, it may limit its effect to disputes arising after a certain date; or it may specify how long the declaration itself shall remain in force, or what notice (if any) will be required to terminate it. However, the unilateral nature of declarations does not signify that the State making the declaration is free to amend the scope and the contents of its solemn commitments as it pleases. * * *

60. In fact, the declarations, even though they are unilateral acts, establish a series of bilateral engagements with other States accepting the same obligation of compulsory jurisdiction, in which the conditions, reservations and time-limit clauses are taken into consideration. In the establishment of this network of engagements, which constitutes the Optional–Clause system, the principle of good faith plays an important

role: the Court has emphasized the need in international relations for respect for good faith and confidence in particularly unambiguous terms. * * *

61. The most important question relating to the effect of the 1984 notification is whether the United States was free to disregard the clause of six months' notice which, freely and by its own choice, it had appended to its 1946 Declaration. In so doing the United States entered into an obligation which is binding upon it vis-à-vis other States parties to the Optional–Clause system. Although the United States retained the right to modify the contents of the 1946 Declaration or to terminate it, a power which is inherent in any unilateral act of a State, it has, nevertheless assumed an inescapable obligation towards other States accepting the Optional Clause, by stating formally and solemnly that any such change should take effect only after six months have elapsed as from the date of notice.

62. The United States has argued that the Nicaraguan 1929 Declaration, being of undefined duration, is liable to immediate termination, without previous notice, and that therefore Nicaragua has not accepted "the same obligation" as itself for the purposes of Article 36, paragraph 2, and consequently may not rely on the six months' notice proviso against the United States. The Court does not however consider that this argument entitles the United States validly to act in non-application of the time-limit proviso included in the 1946 Declaration. The notion of reciprocity is concerned with the scope and substance of the commitments entered into, including reservations, and not with the formal conditions of their creation, duration or extinction. It appears clearly that reciprocity cannot be invoked in order to excuse departure from the terms of a State's own declaration, whatever its scope, limitations or conditions. As the Court observed in the Interhandel case:

> "Reciprocity enables the State which has made the wider acceptance of the jurisdiction of the Court to rely upon the reservations to the acceptance laid down by the other party. There the effect of reciprocity ends. It cannot justify a State, in this instance, the United States, in relying upon a restriction which the other party, Switzerland, has not included in its own Declaration." * * *

The maintenance in force of the United States Declaration for six months after notice of termination is a positive undertaking, flowing from the time-limit clause, but the Nicaraguan Declaration contains no express restriction at all. It is therefore clear that the United States is not in a position to invoke reciprocity as a basis for its action in making the 1984 notification which purported to modify the content of the 1946 Declaration. On the contrary it is Nicaragua that can invoke the six months' notice against the United States—not of course on the basis of reciprocity, but because it is an undertaking which is an integral part of the instrument that contains it.

* * *

65. In sum, the six months' notice clause forms an important integral part of the United States Declaration and it is a condition that must be complied with in case of either termination or modification. Consequently, the 1984 notification, in the present case, cannot override the obligation of the United States to submit to the compulsory jurisdiction * * * vis-à-vis Nicaragua, a State accepting the same obligation.

* * *

[The court then rejected United States' arguments based on proviso (c) of its reservations, i.e. the so-called multilateral treaty (Vandenberg) reservation, in the language which follows.]

* * *

72. The multilateral treaty reservation in the United States Declaration has some obscure aspects, which have been the subject of comment since its making in 1946. There are two interpretations of the need for the presence of the parties to the multilateral treaties concerned in the proceedings before the Court as a condition for the validity of the acceptance of the compulsory jurisdiction by the United States. It is not clear whether what are "affected", according to the terms of the proviso, are the treaties themselves or the parties to them. Similar reservations to be found in certain other declarations of acceptance, such as those of India, El Salvador and the Philippines, refer clearly to "all parties" to the treaties. The phrase "all parties to the treaty affected by the decision" is at the centre of the present doubts. The United States interprets the reservation in the present case as referring to the States parties affected by the decision of the Court, merely mentioning the alternative interpretation, whereby it is the treaty which is "affected", so that all parties to the treaty would have to be before the Court, as "an *a fortiori* case". This latter interpretation need not therefore be considered. The argument of the United States relates specifically to El Salvador, Honduras and Costa Rica, the neighbour States of Nicaragua, which allegedly would be affected by the decision of the Court.

73. It may * * * be noted that the multilateral treaty reservation could not bar adjudication by the Court of all Nicaragua's claims, because Nicaragua * * * does not confine those claims only to violations of the four multilateral conventions referred to above (paragraph 68). On the contrary, Nicaragua invokes a number of principles of customary and general international law that, according to the Application, have been violated by the United States. The Court cannot dismiss the claims of Nicaragua under principles of customary and general international law, simply because such principles have been enshrined in the texts of the conventions relied upon by Nicaragua. The fact that the above-mentioned principles, recognized as such, have been codified or embodied in multilateral conventions does not mean that they cease to exist and to apply as principles of customary law, even as regards countries that are parties to such conventions. Principles such as those of the non-use of force, non-intervention, respect for the independence

and territorial integrity of States, and the freedom of navigation, continue to be binding as part of customary international law, despite the operation of provisions of conventional law in which they have been incorporated. Therefore, since the claim before the Court in this case is not confined to violation of the multilateral conventional provisions invoked, it would not in any event be barred by the multilateral treaty reservation in the United States 1946 Declaration.

* * *

75. The United States Declaration uses the word "affected", without making it clear who is to determine whether the States referred to are, or are not, affected. The States themselves would have the choice of either instituting proceedings or intervening for the protection of their interests, in so far as these are not already protected by Article 59 of the Statute. As for the Court, it is only when the general lines of the judgment to be given become clear that the States "affected" could be identified. By way of example we may take the hypothesis that if the Court were to decide to reject the Application of Nicaragua on the facts, there would be no third State's claim to be affected. Certainly the determination of the States "affected" could not be left to the parties but must be made by the Court.

76. At any rate, this is a question concerning matters of substance relating to the merits of the case: obviously the question of what States may be "affected" by the decision on the merits is not in itself a jurisdictional problem. The present phase of examination of jurisdictional questions was opened by the Court itself by its Order of 10 May 1984, not by a formal preliminary objection submitted by the United States; but it is appropriate to consider the grounds put forward by the United States for alleged lack of jurisdiction in the light of the procedural provisions for such objections. That being so, and since the procedural technique formerly available of joinder of preliminary objections to the merits has been done away with since the 1972 revision of the Rules of Court, the Court has no choice but to avail itself of Article 79, paragraph 7, of the present Rules of Court, and declare that the objection based on the multilateral treaty reservation of the United States Declaration of Acceptance does not possess, in the circumstances of the case, an exclusively preliminary character, and that consequently it does not constitute an obstacle for the Court to entertain the proceedings instituted by Nicaragua under the Application of 9 April 1984.

* * *

[The United States thereupon withdrew, as discussed infra, p. 63.]

UNITED STATES LETTER TO THE REGISTRAR OF
THE INTERNATIONAL COURT OF JUSTICE

31 I.L.M. 105 (1992).*

United States Department of State, The Legal Adviser, Washington D.C.

September 25, 1991

Mr. Eduardo Valencia–Ospina
Registrar
International Court of Justice
The Hague
The Netherlands

Sir,

On behalf of the Government of the United States, I have the honor to refer to your letter of September 12, 1991, concerning a letter from the Agent of Nicaragua in the case of Nicaragua v. United States of America informing the Court that the Government of Nicaragua does not wish to go on with these proceedings and providing the United States with an opportunity to state whether it opposes the discontinuance of the proceedings.

Taking into account the agreement of the United States and Nicaragua to take steps to enhance their friendship and mutual cooperation, including the renunciation by Nicaragua of all further right of action based on the aforementioned case, the United States welcomes the Nicaraguan request for discontinuance of the proceedings.

The United States takes this action without prejudice to its long-standing view that the Court is without jurisdiction to entertain the dispute and that the Nicaraguan Application of April 9, 1984 is inadmissible. Accept, Sir, the assurances of my highest consideration.

Sincerely,

Edwin D. Williamson

––––––

The Order removing the case from the list was made on 26 September, 1991. I.C.J. Reports 1991, 47; 31 I.L.M. 103 (1992).

––––––

JURISDICTION CONFERRED BY PROVISIONS
OF INTERNATIONAL AGREEMENTS

1. *The use of the International Court of Justice.* The Yearbook of the International Court of Justice supplies a list of cases filed to date. The list is in the Documentary Supplement.

* Reprinted by permission, American Society of International Law.

CASE CONCERNING QUESTIONS OF INTERPRETATION AND AP-PLICATION OF THE 1971 MONTREAL CONVENTION ARISING FROM THE AERIAL INCIDENT AT LOCKERBIE

(Libyan Arab Jamahiriya v. United States of America)

REQUEST FOR THE INDICATION OF PROVISIONAL MEASURES

International Court of Justice (1992).
[1992] I.C.J. Rep. 231; 31 I.L.M. 662.

[This was an application by Libya alleging a breach by the United States of the Montreal Convention. The Court denied Libya's request for an indication of interim measures pending a determination of the case. Excerpts from the Order follow.]

22. Article 14, paragraph 1, of the Montreal Convention, relied on by Libya as basis of jurisdiction in the case, reads as follows:

"Any dispute between two or more Contracting States concerning the interpretation or application of this Convention which cannot be settled through negotiation, shall, at the request of one of them, be submitted to arbitration. If within six months of the date of the request for arbitration the Parties are unable to agree on the organization of the arbitration, any one of those Parties may refer the dispute to the International Court of Justice by request in conformity with the Statute of the Court";

23. * * * In its Application, Libya states that a dispute exists between Libya and the United States as to the interpretation or application of the Montreal Convention; that it has not been possible to settle this dispute by negotiation; that a request by Libya to the United States for arbitration of the dispute has been rejected by the United States, and that the Parties have been unable to agree on the organization of such an arbitration; and that in the light of the urgency of rectifying the continuing violations by the United States of the Montreal Convention and the United States refusal to enter into arbitration, the Court has jurisdiction to hear Libya's claims arising under the Montreal Convention; whereas, in its request for the indication of provisional measures, Libya submitted that the Court's jurisdiction in the case was prima facie established under the Montreal Convention; and whereas in the course of the oral proceedings, Libya confirmed those views and further contended that the various conditions laid down by Article 14, paragraph 1, of the Montreal Convention had been fulfilled, including the requirement related to the six-month period;

25. * * * In the oral proceedings the United States contended that the requested provisional measures should not be indicated because Libya had not presented a prima facie case that the provisions of the Montreal Convention provide a possible basis for jurisdiction inasmuch as the six-month period prescribed by Article 14, paragraph 1, of the Convention had not yet expired when Libya's Application was filed; and that Libya had not established that the United States had refused to arbitrate;

45. * * * To pronounce on the present request for provisional measures, the Court is not called upon to determine any of the other questions which have been raised before it in the present proceedings, including the question of its jurisdiction to entertain the merits of the case; and whereas the decision given in these proceedings in no way prejudges any such question, and leaves unaffected the rights of the Government of Libya and the Government of the United States to submit arguments in respect of any of these questions;

46. For these reasons, THE COURT, by eleven votes to five,

Finds that the circumstances of the case are not such as to require the exercise of its power under Article 41 of the Statute to indicate provisional measures.

* * *

DECLARATION OF ACTING PRESIDENT ODA

* * *

The Respondent asked that the Court should decline to indicate provisional measures on the ground that the Court lacked jurisdiction in this case, since the requirements of Article 14, paragraph 1, of the Montreal Convention had not been fulfilled. However, through the Court's jurisprudence it is established that, if the Court appears prima facie to possess jurisdiction, it may (if it thinks fit) indicate provisional measures, and this rule has always been interpreted most generously in favour of the applicant, lest a denial be needlessly prejudicial to the continuation of the case. Thus the possibility of indicating provisional measures may be denied *in limine* only in a case where the lack of jurisdiction is so obvious as to require no further examination of the existence of jurisdiction in a later phase.

* * * There does not seem to exist any convincing ground for asserting that the Court's jurisdiction is obviously lacking. The Respondent's argument whereby the Court's jurisdiction is denied through the non-lapse of the six-month period would appear too legalistic, if one were to find that no room remained to negotiate on the organization of arbitration in the face of a categorical denial of the possibility of an arbitration.

* * *

DISSENTING OPINION OF JUDGE WEERAMANTRY

* * *

Article 14(1) of the Montreal Convention is the foundation of the Court's jurisdiction to entertain this application. It stipulates a six-month period from the date of request for arbitration within which if parties are unable to agree on the organization of the arbitration, any one of them may refer a dispute to the International Court.

The Respondents have contended that the pre-conditions to the jurisdiction of this Court have not been satisfied inasmuch as there is no "dispute" within the meaning of Article 14(1) and that, in any event, the stipulated six-month period has not elapsed.

At the present stage of proceedings it is inappropriate to give a narrow or restrictive meaning to the word "dispute". I am satisfied prima facie that there is a substantial dispute between the Parties, for Libya relies on the rule of customary international law, *aut dedere aut judicare,* as the governing principle which entitles it to try its own citizens in the absence of an extradition treaty, while the Respondent demands the surrender of the two suspects. Libya declares that it will try them and has invited the Respondent to send its officials and lawyers to observe the trial, arguing that it is thus satisfying its obligations under the Treaty. The Respondent demands that the suspects be tried in its own courts. Libya contends that its domestic law forbids the surrender of its citizens for trial elsewhere and that the Respondent's demand is an infringement of its sovereignty. The Respondent denies that this is a valid excuse for not surrendering them. All of this in my view amounts prima facie at any rate to a dispute, thus satisfying one of the prerequisites of Article 14(1).

The Respondent's further contention, which is a more substantial one, is that the letter in which Libya first mentioned arbitration was dated 18 January and this case was instituted on 3 March, well before six months had elapsed. It contends therefore that an essential prerequisite to the invocation of the Court's jurisdiction has not been satisfied. This may well be a correct statement of the legal position.

At the same time, there is another view that is plausible and is certainly arguable. That is, that where a party has in anticipation indicated that it will not consider itself bound by mediation or negotiation, the insistence by that party on a waiting period specified as a prerequisite before the matter is taken to the International Court could defeat the purposes of such a provision. Material has been placed before us to the effect that the United States had stated to the Security Council that this was not a difference of approach that could be mediated or negotiated and that the Security Council must not be distracted by Libyan attempts to convert this issue of international peace and security into one of bilateral differences. In other words, the argument placed before us was one of anticipatory repudiation of a consensual obligation.

The question of law before us is this: if, in a hypothetical case, a party refuses negotiation, can such party insist on the six-month period of delay before the matter is brought to this Court? Such insistence can well be a roadblock in the path of a party seeking relief from this Court. The provision can then be construed to mean that a party is free to use other methods than conciliation during this six-month period. Such a construction could well be a negation of the purposes and principles of such a provision, as was cogently stated by Judge Ago in his separate opinion in the Preliminary Objections phase of the case concerning *Military and Paramilitary Activities in and against Nicaragua:*

> "I am in fact convinced that prior resort to diplomatic negotiations cannot constitute an absolute requirement, to be satisfied even when the hopelessness of expecting any negotiations to succeed is clear

from the state of relations between the parties, and there is no warrant for using it as a ground for delaying the opening of arbitral or judicial proceedings when provision for recourse to them exists."

The general principle * * * in that passage is even more pointedly formulated in the context of a specified waiting period such as is stipulated in the Montreal Convention. It can be plausibly argued that there is no purpose in allowing a party who has repudiated conciliation to argue for the rejection of an application on grounds of its non-compliance with procedures which it has itself rejected. A period of freedom from conciliatory and judicial processes would thus be given to the party repudiating, leaving it at liberty to pursue other non-conciliatory procedures, while its opponent is required to stand by without help or remedy.

Such a construction of the Article fits also within theories of interpretation which emphasize that treaty provisions must be so interpreted as not to render nugatory their object and purpose. One cannot without further consideration conclude whether one or the other view should prevail. They both have much to be said for them and we are in a situation where we can only say that the view that the six-month period in Article 14(1) does not constitute an absolute prohibition is at least an arguable one.

The recitals in the Court's Order in the *Nuclear Tests* cases also bear out this provisional approach to jurisdiction:

> "13. Whereas on a request for provisional measures the Court need not, before indicating them, finally satisfy itself that it has jurisdiction on the merits of the case, and yet ought not to indicate such measures unless the provisions invoked by the Applicant appear, prima facie, to afford a basis on which the jurisdiction of the Court might be founded;

> * * *

> 17. Whereas the material submitted to the Court leads it to the conclusion, at the present stage of the proceedings, that the provisions invoked by the Applicant appear, prima facie, to afford a basis on which the jurisdiction of the Court might be founded; and whereas the Court will accordingly proceed to examine the Applicant's request for the indication of interim measures of protection;"

* * * I would hold that the circumstances invoked by the Applicant appear, prima facie, to afford a basis on which the jurisdiction of the Court might be founded. If, after the issue of such provisional measures, it appears at a later stage or at the stage of consideration of the merits that the Court has no jurisdiction, the provisional measures would immediately cease to have effect.

Granted this conclusion in regard to the Court's jurisdiction under Article 14 of the Montreal Convention, the next major question is whether Security Council resolutions 731 (1992) and 748 (1992) present obstacles to the Court's consideration of this matter. * * *

* * *

U.S. WITHDRAWAL FROM THE PROCEEDINGS
INITIATED BY NICARAGUA IN THE ICJ

United States Department of State Bulletin, March 1985, p. 64.

Statement, Jan. 18, 1985

The United States has consistently taken the position that the proceedings initiated by Nicaragua in the International Court of Justice (ICJ) are a misuse of the Court for political purposes and that the Court lacks jurisdiction and competence over such a case. The Court's decision of November 26, 1984, finding that it has jurisdiction, is contrary to law and fact. With great reluctance, the United States has decided not to participate in further proceedings in this case.

* * *

The conflict in Central America, * * * is an inherently political problem that is not appropriate for judicial resolution. The conflict will be solved only by political and diplomatic means—not through a judicial tribunal. The ICJ was never intended to resolve issues of collective security and self-defense and is patently unsuited for such a role. Unlike domestic courts, the World Court has jurisdiction only to the extent that nation-states have consented to it. When the United States accepted the Court's compulsory jurisdiction in 1946, it certainly never conceived of such a role for the Court in such controversies. Nicaragua's suit against the United States—which includes an absurd demand for hundreds of millions of dollars in reparations—is a blatant misuse of the Court for political and propaganda purposes.

As one of the foremost supporters of the ICJ, the United States is one of only 44 of 159 member states of the United Nations that [ever] accepted the Court's compulsory jurisdiction. * * * The vast majority of these 44 states have attached to their acceptance reservations that substantially limit its scope. Along with the United Kingdom, the United States is one of only two permanent members of the UN Security Council that have accepted that jurisdiction. And of the 16 judges now claiming to sit in judgment on the United States in this case, 11 are from countries that do not accept the Court's compulsory jurisdiction.

Few if any other countries * * * would have appeared at all in a case such as this which they considered to be improperly brought. Nevertheless, out of its traditional respect for the rule of law, the United States has participated fully in the Court's proceedings thus far, to present its view that the Court does not have jurisdiction * * * in this case.

* * *

On November 26, 1984, the Court decided—in spite of the overwhelming evidence before it—that it does have jurisdiction over Nicaragua's claims and that it will proceed to a full hearing on the merits.
* * *

This decision is erroneous as a matter of law and is based on a misreading and distortion of the evidence and precedent.

* * *

[After stating some reasons for this assertion, the Department continued]: For these reasons, we are forced to conclude that our continued participation in this case could not be justified.

* * *

———

Questions. Does it really show respect for the rule of law to argue lack of jurisdiction and, having lost on that issue, to refuse to proceed on the merits? Does it show respect for the court to label its decision "erroneous as a matter of law" and "based on a misreading and distortion of the evidence"? It should be noted in this connection that by combining the votes on the various grounds of decision, the court eventually held it had jurisdiction by fifteen votes in favor and one vote against, the dissenting voice being that of the judge from the United States.

———

U.S. TERMINATES ACCEPTANCE OF ICJ COMPULSORY JURISDICTION

United States Department of State Bulletin, January 1986, p. 67.

Secretary's Letter to UN Secretary General, Oct. 7, 1985.

* * *

I have the honor on behalf of the Government of the United States of America to refer to the declaration of my Government of 26 August 1946, as modified by my note of 6 April 1984, concerning the acceptance by the United States of America of the compulsory jurisdiction of the International Court of Justice, and to state that the aforesaid declaration is hereby terminated, with effect six months from the date hereof.

* * *

Legal Adviser Soafer Statement, Dec. 4, 1985.[2]

* * *

Our experience in the case instituted against the United States by Nicaragua in April 1984 provided the chief motivation for the Administration's review of our acceptance of the Court's compulsory jurisdiction.

* * *

We recognized, first of all, that the hopes originally placed in compulsory jurisdiction by the architects of the Court's Statute have

2. Made before the Senate Foreign Relations Committee.

never been realized and will not be realized in the foreseeable future. We had hoped that widespread acceptance of compulsory jurisdiction and its successful employment in actual cases would increase confidence in judicial settlement of international disputes and, thus, eventually lead to its universal acceptance.

* * *

Compulsory jurisdiction cases have not been the principal part of the Court's overall jurisprudence. Of some 50 contentious cases between 1946 and the end of 1983, 22 were based on the Court's compulsory jurisdiction, of which only five resulted in final judgment on the merits. The last case decided under the Court's compulsory jurisdiction, the Temple of Preah Vihear, was completed in 1962. In the remaining 17 cases, objections to the Court's jurisdiction were sustained in 13; four were dismissed on other grounds.

Another consideration we weighed is the fact that, although we have tried seven times, we have never been able successfully to bring a state before the Court. We have been barred from achieving this result not only by the fact that few other states accept compulsory jurisdiction but also by the principle of reciprocity as applied to our 1946 declaration. * * *

[The Legal Adviser discussed the Connally Amendment.]

On a more general level, other countries, the international legal community, and, indeed, the executive branch have severely criticized the "self-judging" nature of the Connally reservation. Some commentators even argue that the Connally reservation made the 1946 declaration a legal nullity because of its wholly unilateral and potentially limitless character. Certainly, that reservation has undercut the example the United States tried to set for other countries by its acceptance of compulsory jurisdiction.

For these reasons we have never been able successfully to bring another state before the Court on the basis of our acceptance of compulsory jurisdiction. On the other hand, we have been sued under it three times: by France in the Rights of Nationals of the United States in Morocco case in 1950–1952; by Switzerland in the Interhandel case in 1957–1959; and, finally, by Nicaragua last year.

The terms of our acceptance of compulsory jurisdiction contain an additional weakness. Nothing in it prevents another state from depositing an acceptance of compulsory jurisdiction solely for the purpose of bringing suit against the United States and, thereafter, withdrawing its acceptance to avoid being sued by anyone in any other matter. Students of the Court long have recognized that this "sitting duck" or "hit-and-run" problem is one of the principal disadvantages to the system of compulsory jurisdiction under Article 36(2). It places the minority of states that have accepted compulsory jurisdiction at the mercy of the majority that have not.

The Court's composition also is a source of institutional weakness. At present, 9 of 15 judges come from states that do not accept compulsory jurisdiction; most of these states have never used the Court at all.

Judges are elected by the General Assembly and Security Council, frequently after intense electioneering. One reasonably may expect at least some judges to be sensitive to the impact of their decisions on their standing with the UN majority. Whereas in 1945 the United Nations had some 50 members, most which were aligned with the United States and shared its views regarding world order, there are now 160 members. A great many of these cannot be counted on to share our view of the original constitutional conception of the UN Charter, particularly with regard to the special position of the permanent members of the Security Council in the maintenance of international peace and security. This same majority often opposes the United States on important international questions.

None of the weaknesses deriving from the Court's composition and our 1946 declaration is new. We have hitherto endured them on the assumption that the respect states owed to the Court and the Court's own scrupulous adherence to its judicial role would insulate us from abuses of the Court's process for political or propaganda ends. The Nicaragua case showed that it would be unrealistic to continue to rely on that assumption.

　　　* * *

　　　―――――

Questions. Is the analysis of the Legal Adviser sound? Has the compulsory jurisdiction of the court been an historical failure?

For a statement denying that it was a failure, see U.S. Decision to Withdraw from the International Court of Justice, Hearing before the Subcommittee on Human Rights and International Organizations of the House Committee on Foreign Affairs, 99th Cong., 1st Sess. 92–109 (1986) (statement of Burns H. Weston and Bessie D. Murray for the Independent Commission on Respect for International Law).

Another scholar recently reached the pessimistic conclusion about its future set forth below.

　　　―――――

ADVISORY OPINIONS

APPLICABILITY OF THE OBLIGATION TO ARBITRATE UNDER SECTION 21 OF THE UNITED NATIONS HEADQUARTERS AGREEMENT OF 26 JUNE 1947

ADVISORY OPINION OF 26 APRIL 1988

International Court of Justice, 1988

I.C.J. Reports 1988, p. 12

1. The question upon which the advisory opinion of the Court has been asked was contained in resolution 42/229B of the United Nations General Assembly, adopted on 2 March 1988. * * *

"The General Assembly,

* * *

Decides, in accordance with Article 96 of the Charter of the United Nations, to request the International Court of Justice, in pursuance of Article 65 of the Statute of the Court, for an advisory opinion on the following question, taking into account the time constraint:

'In the light of facts reflected in the reports of the Secretary–General, is the United States of America, as a party to the Agreement between the United Nations and the United States regarding the Headquarters of the United Nations, under an obligation to enter into arbitration in accordance with section 21 of the Agreement?' "

* * *

7. The question upon which the opinion of the Court has been requested is whether the United States of America (hereafter referred to as "the United States"), as a party to the United Nations Headquarters Agreement, is under an obligation to enter into arbitration. The Headquarters Agreement of 26 June 1947 came into force in accordance with its terms on 21 November 1947 by exchange of letters between the Secretary–General and the United States Permanent Representative. The Agreement was registered the same day with the United Nations Secretariat, in accordance with Article 102 of the Charter. In section 21, paragraph *(a)*, it provides as follows:

"Any dispute between the United Nations and the United States concerning the interpretation or application of this agreement or of any supplemental agreement, which is not settled by negotiation or other agreed mode of settlement, shall be referred for final decision to a tribunal of three arbitrators, one to be named by the Secretary–General, one to be named by the Secretary of State of the United States, and the third to be chosen by the two, or, if they should fail to agree upon a third, then by the President of the International Court of Justice."

There is no question but that the Headquarters Agreement is a treaty in force binding the parties thereto. What the Court has therefore to determine, in order to answer the question put to it, is whether there exists a dispute between the United Nations and the United States of the kind contemplated by section 21 of the Agreement. For this purpose the Court will first set out the sequence of events, preceding the adoption of [the] resolutions * * * which led first the Secretary–General and subsequently the General Assembly * * * to conclude that such a dispute existed.

* * *

8. The events in question centred round the Permanent Observer Mission of the Palestine Liberation Organization (referred to hereafter as "the PLO") to the United Nations in New York. The PLO has enjoyed in relation to the United Nations the status of an observer since 1974, the Organization was invited to "participate in the sessions and

the work of the General Assembly in the capacity of observer". Following this invitation, the PLO established an Observer Mission in 1974, and maintains an office, entitled office of the PLO Observer Mission at 115 East 65th Street, in New York City, outside the United Nations Headquarters District. Recognized observers are listed as such in official United Nations publications: the PLO appears in such publications in a category of "organizations which have received a standing invitation from the General Assembly to participate in the sessions and the work of the General Assembly as observers".

* * *

* * * Section 11 of the Headquarters Agreement provides that

"The federal, state or local authorities of the United States shall not impose any impediments to transit to or from the headquarters district of: (1) representatives of Members * * * or the families of such representatives * * *; * * * (5) other persons invited to the headquarters district by the United Nations * * * on official business * * *."

Section 12 provides that, "[T]he provisions of section 11 shall be applicable irrespective of the relations existing between the Governments of the persons referred to in that section and the Government of the United States."

Section 13 provides (*inter alia*) that, "[L]aws and regulations in force in the United States regarding the entry of aliens shall not be applied in such manner as to interfere with the privileges referred to in section 11."

* * *

23. The question put to the Court is expressed to concern a possible obligation of the United States, "In the light of [the] facts reflected in the reports of the Secretary–General, that is to say in the light of the facts which had been reported to the General Assembly at the time at which it took its decision to request an opinion. The Court does not however consider that the General Assembly, in employing this form of words, has requested it to reply to the question put on the basis solely of these facts, and to close its eyes to subsequent events of possible relevance to, or capable of throwing light on, that question. The Court will therefore set out here the developments in the affair subsequent to the adoption of resolution 42/229B.

* * *

24. On 11 March 1988 the Acting Permanent Representative of the United States to the United Nations wrote to the Secretary–General, referring to General Assembly resolutions 42/229A and 42/229B and stating as follows:

"I wish to inform you that the Attorney General of the United States has determined that he is required by the Anti–Terrorism Act of 1987 to close the office of the Palestine Liberation Organization Observer Mission to the United Nations in New York, irrespective of any obligations the United States may have under the Agreement between the United Nations and the United States regarding the Headquarters of the United Nations. If the PLO does not comply with the Act, the Attorney General will initiate legal action to close the PLO Observer Mission on or about March 21, 1988, the effective date of the Act. This course of action will allow the orderly enforcement of the Act. The United States will not take other actions to close the Observer Mission pending a decision in such litigation. Under the circumstances, the United States believes that submission of this matter to arbitration would not serve a useful purpose."

This letter was delivered by hand to the Secretary–General by the Acting Permanent Representative of the United States. * * * On receiving the letter, the Secretary–General protested to the Acting Permanent Representative and stated that the decision taken by the United States Government as outlined in the letter was a clear violation of the Headquarters Agreement between the United Nations and the United States.

* * *

[The Court examined the requirements of Section 21 and found that they were satisfied.]

57. The Court must therefore conclude that the United States is bound to respect the obligation to have recourse to arbitration under section 21 of the Headquarters Agreement. The fact remains however that, as the Court has already observed, the United States has declared (letter from the Permanent Representative, 11 March 1988) that its measures against the PLO Observer Mission were taken "irrespective of any obligations the United States may have under the [Headquarters] Agreement". If it were necessary to interpret that statement as intended to refer not only to the substantive obligations laid down in, for example, sections 11, 12 and 13, but also to the obligation to arbitrate provided for in section 21, this conclusion would remain intact. It would be sufficient to recall the fundamental principle of international law that international law prevails over domestic law. This principle was endorsed by judicial decision as long ago as the arbitral award of 14 September 1872 in the *Alabama* case between Great Britain and the United States, and has frequently been recalled since, for example in the case concerning the *Greco–Bulgarian "Communities"* in which the Permanent Court of International Justice laid it down that

"it is a generally accepted principle of international law that in the relations between Powers who are contracting Parties to a treaty, the provisions of municipal law cannot prevail over those of the treaty" (*P.C.I.J., Series B, No. 17,* p. 32).

* * *

58. For these reasons,

THE COURT,

Unanimously,

Is of the opinion that the United States of America, as a party to the Agreement between the United Nations and the United States of America regarding the Headquarters of the United Nations of 26 June 1947, is under an obligation, in accordance with section 21 of that Agreement, to enter into arbitration for the settlement of the dispute between itself and the United Nations.

Notes & Questions

1. For further developments in the United States concerning the effort to close the PLO Observer Mission, *see* United States v. Palestine Liberation Organization, 695 F.Supp. 1456 (S.D.N.Y.1988) in which the U.S. government's motion for an injunction closing the P.L.O. office was denied and the PLO's motion to dismiss was granted. Thereafter, "[t]he United States Department of Justice announced on August 29, 1988, that the Administration would not appeal the decision rendered by the U.S. District Court for the Southern District of New York, permitting the P.L.O. to maintain its mission in New York to the United Nations * * *. The Administration based its decision on foreign policy considerations. Specifically, the State Department expressed concern that the closure of the mission would violate the U.S. obligations as the host country under the United Nations Headquarters Agreement".

2. How would you characterize the status of I.C.J. advisory opinions? Are these opinions obligatory, and if so, in what sense and on whom? Or are they merely hortatory but to be taken into account? Are they any more or less binding than other decisions of the I.C.J.? *See* U.N. Charter Article 96 and I.C.J. Statute Articles 65–68. Compare Charter Article 94 which makes I.C.J. decisions in contentious cases binding on the parties. Does Statute Article 38 affect your analysis?

3. What procedures might be employed to make advisory opinions formally binding in the sense of Charter Article 94 as applied to contentious cases? What would be the effect of an agreement providing that "[t]he opinion of the Court shall be accepted as decisive by the parties"? *See* in the Documentary Supplement, Section 30 of the Convention on the Privileges and Immunities of the United Nations.

4. Parties authorized to request advisory opinions under Charter Article 94 are limited to 6 U.N. organs and 12 Agencies. (I.C.J. Yearbook 1990–1991, 60 (1991). Should it be expanded to include the Secretary–General and even other public international organizations not directly affiliated with the United Nations, such as the Council of Europe, OECD, NATO, the OAS? How might that be done in formal terms?

5. For use of the advisory opinion procedure in a case of actual dispute without the consent of the state concerned, see Applicability of Article VI, Section 22 on the Convention on the Privileges and Immunities of the United Nations, Advisory Opinion, I.C.J. Reports 1989, p. 177;

29 I.L.M. 100 (1990). Does that suggest a possible means for expanding the role of the I.C.J.?

THE SECRETARY–GENERAL'S VIEWS

UNITED NATIONS: REPORT OF THE SECRETARY–GENERAL ON AN AGENDA FOR PEACE—PREVENTIVE DIPLOMACY, PEACEMAKING AND PEACE–KEEPING

U.N. Doc. A/47/277, S/24111, June 17, 1992, 31 I.L.M. 953 (1992).

The World Court

38. The docket of the International Court of Justice has grown fuller but it remains an under-used resource for the peaceful adjudication of disputes. Greater reliance on the Court would be an important contribution to United Nations peacemaking. In this connection, I call attention to the power of the Security Council under Articles 36 and 37 of the Charter to recommend to Member States the submission of a dispute to the International Court of Justice, arbitration or other dispute-settlement mechanisms. I recommend that the Secretary–General be authorized, pursuant to Article 96, paragraph 2, of the Charter, to take advantage of the advisory competence of the Court and that other United Nations organs that already enjoy such authorization turn to the Court more frequently for advisory opinions.

39. I recommend the following steps to reinforce the role of the International Court of Justice:

(a) All Member States should accept the general jurisdiction of the International Court under Article 36 of its Statute, without any reservation, before the end of the United Nations Decade of International Law in the year 2000. In instances where domestic structures prevent this, States should agree bilaterally or multilaterally to a comprehensive list of matters they are willing to submit to the Court and should withdraw their reservations to its jurisdiction in the dispute settlement clauses of multilateral treaties;

(b) When submission of a dispute to the full Court is not practical, the Chambers jurisdiction should be used;

(c) States should support the Trust Fund established to assist countries unable to afford the cost involved in bringing a dispute to the Court, and such countries should take full advantage of the Fund in order to resolve their disputes.

OTHER INTERNATIONAL COURTS

The function of the Court of Justice of the European Union is to serve, not world-wide, but the special purposes of the constituent communities—i.e., the European Economic Community, the European Coal and Steel Community, and the European Atomic Energy Community— the members including Belgium, Denmark, France, Greece, Ireland, Italy, Luxembourg, the Netherlands, Portugal, Spain, the United Kingdom and Germany.

The court is vested with compulsory jurisdiction over questions arising under the treaties creating the constituent communities. Though states members may in principle sue one another, in practice they have been reluctant to do so and have resorted to negotiation when confronted with a highly divisive treaty issue.

While the parties to cases before the International Court of Justice are limited to states, the parties entitled to appear before the Court of Justice of the European Union include individuals, firms and institutions of the community as well as states. Moreover, courts of the E.U. member states, even lower courts, may request the Court of Justice to give rulings on the interpretation and validity of community laws. While encouraging such requests, the court has been cautious in the exercise of this jurisdiction. Thus, in interpreting a point of community law, it will refuse to pass on the compatibility of the national law involved and leave the requesting court to decide whether its national law is or is not compatible with its interpretation.

The Court of Justice of the European Union has been, on the whole, a successful institution. Its success is especially surprising in view of the strong, sometimes fierce, historical opposition in the member states to any form of judicial review. In the case before the supreme court of France *supra* p. 22, its procureur général was alluding to this traditional opposition when he stated, in praise of the Court of Justice for its role in the development of community law, that it had avoided "the reefs of government by the judiciary."

While the International Court of Justice and the European Court of Justice are perhaps the best known international tribunals applying international law to disputes between states, there are a number of lesser known universal, regional or functional institutions which can also be considered to perform as courts of international law. They include the European Court of Human Rights, the Inter–American Court of Human Rights, the International Tribunal for the Law of the Sea and its Sea–Bed Disputes Chamber (when established), the OECD European Nuclear Energy Tribunal, the Benelux Court of Justice, the European Tribunal on state immunities, the Tribunal of OAPEC, the Tribunal of the Western European Union, the Court of Justice of the Cartagena Agreement (Andean Pact), the Administrative Tribunals of the U.N., I.L.O., World Bank, OAS, OECD, Council of Europe and other specialized tribunals. See Philip and de Cara, Nature et Evolution de la Juridiction Internationale, in La Juridiction Internationale Permanente—Colloque de Lyon 3, 13 (Paris, 1987); United Nations, Handbook on the Pacific Settlement of Disputes 69 (1992).

———

Note: The Ad Hoc Tribunal for Crimes Against Humanitarian Law in the Former Yugoslavia is presented in Chapter 10, infra. See Blakesley, *Obstacles to the Creation of a Permanent International War Crimes Tribunal,* 18 Fletch.For.Wld.Aff'rs 77 (1994).

---

2. INTERNATIONAL ARBITRATION

UNITED NATIONS HANDBOOK ON THE PACIFIC SETTLEMENT OF DISPUTES BETWEEN STATES 55 (1992) *

168. The 1899 and 1907 Hague Conventions for the Pacific Settlement of International Disputes described the object of international arbitration as the settlement of disputes between States by judges chosen by the parties themselves and on the basis of respect for law. They further provided that recourse to the procedure implied submission in good faith to the award of the tribunal. Accordingly, one of the basic characteristics of arbitration is that it is a procedure which results in binding decisions upon the parties to the dispute.

169. The power to render binding decisions is, therefore, a characteristic which arbitration shares with the method of judicial settlement by international courts whose judgements are not only binding but also, as in the case of the International Court of Justice, final and without appeal, as indicated in article 60 of the I.C.J. Statute. For this reason, arbitration and judicial settlement are both usually referred to as compulsory means of settlement of disputes.

170. However, while both arbitration and judicial settlement are similar in that respect, the two methods of settlement are nevertheless structurally different from each other. Arbitration, in general, is constituted by mutual consent of the States parties to a specific dispute where such parties retain considerable control over the process through the power of appointing arbitrators of their own choice. By contrast, judicial settlement relies upon pre-constituted international courts or tribunals, the composition of which is not to the same extent subject to control by the parties to the dispute.

* * *

(a) *Types of arbitration agreements*

174. Consent of the parties to arbitration may be expressed prior to or after the occurrence of a dispute. Parties may agree to submit all or special categories of future disputes to arbitration. Such commitment may be made in multilateral or bilateral treaties entirely devoted to the peaceful settlement of disputes.[116] A more common method is by inclu-

---

* Reprinted with the permission of the United Nations.

116. One of the well-known multilateral general dispute settlement agreements is

sion of a compromissory clause in a treaty, by which parties agree to submit all or part of their future disputes regarding that treaty to arbitration. Parties may also agree to go to arbitration by a special agreement or a *compromis* after the occurrence of a dispute.

* * *

CARON, THE NATURE OF THE IRAN–UNITED STATES CLAIMS TRIBUNAL AND THE EVOLVING STRUCTURE OF INTERNATIONAL DISPUTE RESOLUTION

84 Am.J.Int'l L. 104 (1990). *

The Iran–United States Claims Tribunal [1] has been called "the most significant arbitral body in history"; its awards, "a gold mine of information for perceptive lawyers." In a recent international commercial arbitration, however, an arbitrator reportedly stated that decisions of the Tribunal, although on point, were not persuasive because the Tribunal, after all, involves a special type of arbitration. This arbitrator is not alone. A lecturer at the Hague Academy of International Law, speaking on international commercial arbitration, reportedly did not refer to the Tribunal's jurisprudence because he did not find it relevant to his work

the Hague Convention for the Pacific Settlement of International Disputes of 18 October 1907. It was one of the more successful first attempts to design a multilateral convention aimed specifically at proposing a variety of means and procedures for the peaceful settlement of disputes. The Convention establishes a system of arbitration for which new agencies were created. The most important part of the Convention was devoted to the organization and the operation of the Permanent Court of Arbitration. The Permanent Court was created with the object of facilitating an immediate recourse to arbitration of international disputes which could not be settled by diplomacy.

The Revised General Act for the Pacific Settlement of International Disputes of 1949 is another important multilateral general dispute settlement agreement. Chapter III is devoted to arbitration. The chapter provides a system for the establishment of the tribunal, including the mode of appointment and number of arbitrators, the cases of vacancies and so forth. Under article 21 of the Revised General Act the parties may agree to a different mode of establishing the tribunal. See United Nations, *Treaty Series,* vol. 71, p. 101.

An example of a bilateral treaty wholly devoted to the peaceful settlement of disputes is the Treaty for Conciliation, Judicial Settlement and Arbitration (with annexes)

between the United Kingdom of Great Britain and Northern Ireland and Switzerland, signed at London on 7 July 1965. Chapter IV of the Treaty is devoted to arbitration. It sets out the number of arbitrators, their nationality and their appointment. It also deals with the question of vacancy and the scope of the competence of the arbitration tribunal. The annex to this Treaty contains recommended rules of procedure for the arbitration tribunal that the parties may wish to choose. Under article 15 of the Treaty the parties may agree to a different mode of establishment of the arbitral tribunal. * * *

* Reprinted with the permission of the American Society of International Law.

1. The Iran–United States Claims Tribunal was established in 1981 pursuant to the Declaration of the Government of the Democratic and Popular Republic of Algeria (hereinafter General Declaration) and the Declaration of the Government of the Democratic and Popular Republic of Algeria concerning the Settlement of Claims by the Government of the United States of America and the Government of the Islamic Republic of Iran (hereinafter Claims Settlement Declaration), collectively referred to as the Algiers Accords. For the text of the Accords, see 1 Iran–United States Claims Tribunal Reports [hereinafter Iran–U.S. C.T.R.] 3 (1981–2), 75 AJIL 418 (1981).

for the same reason. Viewed as a gigantic experiment in international dispute resolution rather than merely a claims settlement device for this particular group of disputes, the Tribunal thus appears (at least to some) to yield decisions of unclear precedential value. Millions of dollars have been spent on its operation and hundreds of awards rendered, yet an apparently not uncommon perception is that the work of this, in some respects unique, institution is not applicable elsewhere.

In one sense, the doubt about the relevance of the Tribunal's work reflects a more fundamental uncertainty about the proper place of the Tribunal and its work within traditional categories of international dispute resolution. Like any truly nagging question, that fundamental uncertainty comes to be phrased in various ways. A phrasing frequently used by scholars inquires into the "nature" of the Tribunal. The assumption apparently underlying this question is that there are basically two distinct types of international arbitration: interstate arbitration such as the *Beagle Channel* arbitration between Chile and Argentina (sometimes referred to here as public international arbitration); and international commercial arbitration such as proceedings between private companies before the International Chamber of Commerce (ICC) (sometimes more broadly referred to here as private international arbitration). Practitioners often regard the inquiry into the nature of the process as irrelevant to lawyering until it is pointed out that many practical questions, such as the enforceability of an award and the ability to challenge an award, turn upon the answer.

* * *

Interstate Arbitration

The internal world of interstate arbitration typically is created and defined by treaty. The agreement to arbitrate and (where applicable) the treaty establishing the responsible institution are the most relevant treaties. The external world may be of little significance for two reasons. So far as the relationship of the customary international legal system to the arbitration is concerned, the international lawmaking capability of the parties may lead to a merging of the internal/external models. The models can collapse into one because states by their agreements both define the internal world of the arbitration *and* modify the applicable international law. In this sense, international law leaves the structuring and conduct of the arbitration entirely in the control of the parties. Consequently, the prime question is whether by their agreement to arbitrate the state parties intend to adopt, supplement or, instead, replace entirely the customary international law that governs such processes. Many agreements to ad hoc arbitration are quite brief and are intended to rest upon the pertinent customary international practice. Even a brief agreement, however, may raise the question whether aspects of customary practice have been displaced.

II.   The Legal System Supervising the Iran-U.S. Claims Tribunal

One of the most innovative and intellectually satisfying aspects of the Algiers Accords is that they establish for the Iran–United States Claims Tribunal a rather complete internal world. There is little need for the parties to request assistance from powers external to the Tribunal. The UNCITRAL Arbitration Rules provide for an appointing authority to resolve disputes between the parties over the composition of the Tribunal. More importantly, the Algiers Accords established a fund, the Security Account, with a portion of the Iranian assets that the United States had frozen. With the Algerian Government acting as escrow agent for the Security Account pursuant to the Tribunal's instructions, the Security Account assures the availability of funds to satisfy most awards of the Tribunal.

* * *

Another factor in analyzing the Tribunal's relationship to the external legal world is the Tribunal's three primary jurisdictional grants. It must be asked whether the legal system supervising the arbitral process before the Tribunal is a function of the particular basis of jurisdiction. First, the Tribunal may hear "claims of nationals of the United States against Iran and claims of nationals of Iran against the United States" (claims of nationals). Second, the Tribunal has jurisdiction over "official claims of the United States and Iran against each other arising out of [certain] contractual arrangements between them" (official claims). Third, the Tribunal may hear disputes between Iran and the United States concerning the interpretation or performance of any provision of the General Declaration or the interpretation or application of the Claims Settlement Declaration (interpretive disputes). * * *

* * *

IV. CONCLUSION

The arbitral proceedings before the Iran–United States Claims Tribunal involving claims of nationals are governed by the legal system of the Netherlands. This conclusion does not sit easily with the prevailing tendency to think that the proceedings of a tribunal formed by treaty to resolve a crisis between two countries are an interstate process not subject to interference by municipal legal orders. The tension between this conclusion and intuition is all the more striking, as the support for the former is extensive, if not overwhelming. The prevailing tendency nonetheless persists because it rests upon a categorical distinction between public and private international dispute resolution that in the past reflected practice quite faithfully. This distinction, however, no longer adequately describes the variations in international dispute resolution. The inadequacy of the distinction is problematic particularly for the interpreters of treaties because it may lead them unconsciously to force the innovative features of a treaty into the pigeonholes of the past. Thus, unconscious reliance upon this distinction should be replaced with a case-by-case examination of the mechanism the parties intended to create. Where this is done, innovation through treaty is protected, and a means for the development of international organization preserved.

The desire to innovate is driven by the perception that existing mechanisms do not fulfill the needs of the parties. To the parties, the various mechanisms are not separate doctrines but, rather, alternatives that should be measured against their needs. In this way, the parties' needs fuel the evolution of these mechanisms. Two particularly important dimensions to international dispute resolution in which innovation has occurred are the means of reviewing the validity of the result and the means of gaining enforcement of the result. The emergence of specific machinery such as the Tribunal and ICSID, and the increasing incidence of transnational litigation involving states and international commercial arbitration with state parties—all concurrent with an arguably decreasing need to rely on diplomatic protection—indicate that the various private, state and interstate mechanisms for the resolution of international disputes should not be viewed as operating in isolation, but as competing with, and evolving in response to, one another. To be sure, this evolving system is not the result of a master plan; rather, it is the Darwinian consequence of numerous separate demands. * * *

TREATY BETWEEN THE UNITED STATES AND THE RUSSIAN FEDERATION CONCERNING THE ENCOURAGEMENT AND RECIPROCAL PROTECTION OF INVESTMENT, APRIL 3, 1992, 31 I.L.M. 794 (1992).*

Article VII [a]

1. Any dispute between the Parties concerning the interpretation or application of the Treaty which is not resolved through consultations or other diplomatic channels, shall be submitted, upon the request of either Party, to an arbitral tribunal for binding decision in accordance with the applicable rules of international law. In the absence of an agreement by the Parties to the contrary, the UNCITRAL Rules, except to the extent modified by the Parties, shall govern.

2. Within two months of receipt of a request, each Party shall appoint an arbitrator. The two arbitrators shall select a third arbitrator as Chairman, who is a national of a third State. The UNCITRAL Rules for appointing members of three member panels shall apply to the appointment of the arbitral panel, except that the appointing authority referenced in those rules shall be the Secretary–General of the Permanent Court of Arbitration.

---

* Reprinted with the permission of the American Society of International Law.

a. Arbitration between a state party and a national or company of the other party is provided in Article VI. Arbitration of certain international law questions is provided in Article 5 of the Investment Incentive Agreement between the United States and the Russian Federation, April 3, 1992, 31 I.L.M. 777 (1992).

3.   Unless otherwise agreed, all submissions shall be made and all hearings shall be completed within six months of the date of selection of the third arbitrator, and the Tribunal shall render its decisions within two months of the date of the final submissions or the date of the closing of the hearings, whichever is later.

4.   Expenses of the Chairman, the other arbitrators, and other costs of the proceedings shall be paid for equally by the Parties. The Tribunal may, however, at its discretion, direct that a higher proportion of the costs be paid by one of the Parties.

3.   COMPLIANCE WITH DECISIONS OF INTERNATIONAL TRIBUNALS
JUDGMENTS OF THE WORLD COURT
Anand, Studies in International Adjudication 274–275 (1969) *

* * * [T]he history of international adjudication since 1945 * * * clearly demonstrates that the execution of international judicial awards is not [a] negligible problem. There have been several cases, if not of open defiance, at least of disregard of the decisions of an international court. In the present tension-ridden, polarized world society, where even a small dispute can develop into a nuclear catastrophe, it may not be as prudent to use force to compel a State—even a small and weak State—to adhere to such a judgment as it was, perhaps, in earlier times. Albania can disregard the judgment in the Corfu Channel case with impunity. Haya de la Torre had to remain a virtual prisoner in the Colombian Embassy for almost three years after the Court's final decision. Thailand took upon itself to declare, though for a brief period, that it would not abide by an adverse decision; and it ultimately accepted the decision only under protest and with a reservation attached to its acceptance. Also, * * * none of these cases involved the vital interests of a nation. In any event, these cases do demonstrate that countries do not always accept an adverse decision.

* * * Advisory opinions of the International Court of Justice also have been disregarded at times. * * * In practice the * * * General Assembly, as well as other international organs which have requested advisory opinions, always have approved the opinions of the Court and have tried to adapt their future actions to accord with the advice given. Despite this formal approval of the opinions, however, several opinions of the Court have remained absolutely ineffective. Thus the Court's opinions in the Conditions of Admission of a State to Membership in the United Nations, the Interpretation of Peace Treaties (First Phase), and the International Status of South–West Africa case were conveniently disregarded by the States concerned. Non-acceptance of the opinion in the Certain Expenses case led to a crisis in the United Nations. Also, the order made by the Court in the Anglo–Iranian Oil Company case,

* Reprinted by permission of Oceana Publications, Dobbs Ferry, New York.

indicating certain provisional measures for the preservation of the rights of the parties, was never accepted by Iran.

* * *

———

1. ***Judgment concerning the release of American hostages in Teheran.*** The decision, which appears in Chapter 12, *infra,* ordered Iran to release the hostages immediately and make reparation to the United States in a form and amount to be settled, if necessary, by a subsequent procedure before the court. It was dated May 24, 1980.

The release of the hostages was eventually secured by the Declarations of January 19, 1981. In paragraph 11 of the first declaration, the United States agreed to withdraw promptly "all claims now pending before the International Court of Justice."

2. ***Role of the United Nations.*** Article 94 of the United Nations Charter provides:

> 1. Each Member of the United Nations undertakes to comply with the decision of the International Court of Justice in any case to which it is a party.

> 2. If any party to a case fails to perform the obligations incumbent upon it under a judgment rendered by the Court, the other party may have recourse to the Security Council, which may, if it deems necessary, make recommendations or decide upon measures to be taken to give effect to the judgment.

The Security Council * * * has never decided upon measures to be taken "to give effect to the judgment." Questions as yet undecided include the following: Does the Security Council have power under the Charter to order a state to comply with a judgment? Can the Security Council direct or authorize the use of force to enforce such an order? Is the council limited, in its use of force to enforce a judgment of the court, to those situations in which non-performance of an order of the court can be considered a threat to the peace, breach of the peace, or act of aggression under Article 39 of the Charter of the United Nations?

3. ***Awards of arbitral tribunals.*** The effectiveness of the awards of international arbitral tribunals depends upon the willingness of states to abide by their agreements to be bound by such awards. "It is a striking fact that states have seldom refused to carry out or abide by the decisions of international tribunals. * * * In the vast majority of instances in which positive action has been required, execution has followed as a matter of course." Hudson, International Tribunals 129 (1944). The statement is still generally valid today.

In some instances, however, disputes over the award have delayed final compliance or settlement for years.

———

THE CHAMIZAL BOUNDARY DISPUTE

49 United States Department of State Bulletin 199 (1963).

Department Statement, July 18

The Presidents of the United States and Mexico announced today their agreement to conclude a convention for the settlement of the Chamizal boundary dispute. The recommended terms of settlement which the Presidents have approved were submitted to them in identical memoranda by the Department of State and the Mexican Ministry of Foreign Relations. According to the terms of the recommended settlement, the United States would transfer to Mexico 437 acres in the vicinity of El Paso, Texas. Conclusion of the convention will be a final step in the resolution of this controversy, which has been earnestly sought by every United States administration since 1910.

An international arbitral commission awarded to Mexico in 1911 an undeterminable part of the Chamizal zone in El Paso, Texas. The area of the zone then totaled approximately 598 acres. The Mexican claim was based on a shift in the channel of the Rio Grande. The United States Government, which had disputed the claim, rejected the award on several grounds,[a] but in the understanding that the Governments of the two countries could proceed at once to settle their differences through diplomatic channels. Since 1911 the controversy has been a major problem in relations between the two countries. Every United States administration beginning with that of President Taft has attempted to resolve it in a mutually satisfactory manner. Proposals for a settlement have varied. * * * In June 1962 President López Mateos urged that a further attempt be made, and President Kennedy agreed. The two Presidents instructed their respective executive agencies to recommend a complete solution which, without prejudice to the juridical positions of the two Governments, would take into account the entire history of the tract. They recognized that any mutually acceptable settlement would affect many people in the city of El Paso and agreed that respect for the rights and interests of the people affected on both sides of the border should be a principal consideration in reaching a solution. The recommended settlement follows generally the solution set forth in the international arbitral award of 1911.

* * *

---

a. Carlston, The Process of International Arbitration 153 (1946).

SECTION D. APPLICATION IN THE UNITED NATIONS

UNITED NATIONS SECURITY COUNCIL RESOLUTIONS ON THE PERSIAN GULF CRISIS

(IRAQ–KUWAIT) (1990–1991).

In the course of the 1990–1991 Persian Gulf Crisis, the Security Council adopted a number of measures applying international law to Iraq or creating legal obligations on states in relation to Iraq. In each case the Council acted under Chapter VII of the United Nations Charter in which Article 39 empowers the Council to "decide" on measures contained in the excerpts set forth below. Charter Article 25 provides that "Members of the United Nations agree to accept and carry out the decisions of the Security Council in accordance with the present Charter". Iraq was a member of the United Nations at all relevant times. Examples of portions of those measures are presented in the Documentary Supplement and analyzed in Chapter 16.

In the course of 1989 the United Nations initiated the "United Nations Decade of International Law" for the period 1990–1999 (A/RES/44/23 of December 17, 1989) covering a broad and ambitious range of development activities. Detailed programmes of activities were established by the General Assembly for 1990–1992 in A/RES/45/53 of December 9, 1991 and for 1993–1994 in A/RES/47/32 of December 21, 1992.

Chapter 2

THE STRUCTURE OF THE INTERNATIONAL LEGAL SYSTEM: STATES, INTERNATIONAL ORGANIZATIONS, OTHER ENTITIES, AND NON–STATE GROUPS

SECTION A. STATES AND STATEHOOD: THE AURA OF SOVEREIGNTY

1. *Nomenclature, Standing, and Role of States.* In the international legal system the terms "nations," "peoples," "states," and "nation-states" are used interchangeably and somewhat imprecisely, from a socio-anthropological standpoint, to refer to the legally-organized political power-structures that are the highest authority in a country, i.e., states. These entities have long been, and still are, the major structural units of the legal-political order of the planet. Historically, the imprecision noted above goes back to ancient usages, to the times when emperors and kings really ruled their peoples, or nations. States inherited the aura of sovereignty from them. Sovereignty is the sine qua non of statehood: there is no higher earthly authority. States are not often composed of one people, but are still the supreme authority over the inhabitants of their territories. They are legally endowed with

independence, equality, and the capacity to deal with other states, whether in war or peace. For centuries, states have been the recognized actors in the international legal system, where living persons as such have had no standing, except through their states. In classical theory, states are the "subjects" of "inter-state" law that they make for themselves, either by accepted custom or by specific agreements. We still call it "inter*national* law," and it is too late to change that; but most states rule over more than one race or nationality.

States traditionally, therefore, have had the virtually exclusive role in the evolution of the international legal system. Some scholars recently have seen international law as almost entirely the product of the Western World, having entered its "modern" stage at the end of the Thirty Years War, via the treaties made at Westphalia, in 1648, when sovereign equality moved from a few key monarchies, the Holy Roman Empire, and the Holy See, to a number of newly-independent states. See Gross, The Peace of Westphalia, 1648–1948, 42 Am.J.Intl.Law 20 (1948); Falk, *The Interplay of Westphalia and Charter Conceptions of International Legal Order,* essay in International Law: A Contemporary Perspective 116 (1985).

It may be that civilization is moving now into an era in which states are not the only subjects of international law and are no longer entirely sovereign. These notions will be studied throughout. Nonetheless, statehood is still highly relevant subject-matter in the study of the international legal system. We focus on that in this chapter.

———

2. *The Elements of Statehood.* The definition of state in Section 201 of the 1987 Restatement may be useful: " * * * an entity which has a defined territory and permanent population, under the control of its own government, and which engages in, or has the capacity to engage in, formal relations with other such entities." This definition does not make reference to any central legal process by which those facts are to be determined. The lack of a central legal process for this purpose stands in contrast to domestic legal systems in which legal entities such as corporations are created by explicitly required legal processes. Frequently municipal law requires issuance of a charter or certificate of incorporation by an official after the applicants have satisfied minimum factual criteria set forth in the relevant statute. A corporation thus, can be defined as an entity that has been created by compliance with that statutorily prescribed process. No such legal process exists in the case of the formation of entities called states.

The nearest international law analogues are (a) the process by which new members are admitted to the United Nations and (b) the phenomenon known as recognition in the international system. These analogues are imperfect. Admission to the United Nations is not automatically accorded to every entity that meets the factual criteria for statehood, since Article 4 of the Charter lays down additional criteria. As for the process of recognition, (i) there is no central recognizing authority, for each state in the international community makes its own unilateral determination to recognize a new state (or a new government of an existing state) and (ii) there is some disagreement among legal theorists on the question whether the fact of recognition by other states is one of the minimum facts necessary for a new state to come into existence, is merely a neutral acknowledgment of an historical fact, i.e., that a new state has come into existence, or is purely political. The question of recognition will be explored in Section B, *infra.*

The relevant "factual prerequisites" to statehood are: territory, population, government and engagement or capacity to engage, in foreign relations—what normal legal consequences follow from establishment of these facts? Some of these consequences can be gleaned from an examination of the charters of international organizations. Extracts from the United Nations Charter, the Statute of the International Court of Justice, the Charter of the Organization of American States and the Vienna Conventions on the Law of Treaties and on Diplomatic Relations and cases, which are set out below.

In the Doc. Supps, see, the Study Declaration on Principles of International Law Concerning Friendly Relations and Cooperation among States, adopted by the General Assembly in 1970. Note the emphasis on independence, territorial inviolability and equality. Now turn to the United Nations Charter in the Doc. Supp. and Study articles 2, 3, 4, 32, and 35.

STATUTE OF THE INTERNATIONAL COURT OF JUSTICE

Article 34–1. Only states may be parties in cases before the Court.

Now consider Articles 1, 4, 9, 12, 18, 19, and 20, of the **Charter of the Organization of American States** also in the Doc. Supp.

VIENNA CONVENTION ON THE LAW OF TREATIES

Adopted May 22, 1969; opened for Signature May 23, 1969 by the U.N. Conference on the Law of Treaties. (U.N.Doc. A/CONF. 39/27), p. 289.

Article 1

Scope of the present Convention

The present Convention applies to treaties between States.

VIENNA CONVENTION ON DIPLOMATIC RELATIONS OF APRIL 18, 1961

500 U.N.T.S. 95.

Article 48

The present Convention shall be open for signature by all States Members of the United Nations or of any of the specialized agencies or Parties to the Statute of the International Court of Justice, and by any other State invited by the General Assembly of the United Nations to become a Party to the Convention * * *.

———

Minimum facts for statehood not clearly present. It is easy enough to identify entities of long standing as states and to concede that whatever one normally believes to be the rights and duties of states inheres in those entities. France is a state, without doubt, and has the normal rights and duties of a state. The same can be said for most of the members of the United Nations.

But cases may arise when evidence of the factual criteria to support a finding of statehood are either not clearly discernible, or when parties to a controversy take differing views on the existence or non-existence of the facts, or when essential facts clearly do not exist. What, then, are the rights and duties of such an entity? For example, as a result of political compromise it was agreed at the founding of the United Nations that two of the federal states of the Union of Soviet Socialist Republics would be admitted to the United Nations as members: Byelorussian Soviet Socialist Republic and Ukranian Soviet Socialist Republic. The founders of the United Nations agreed to this compromise, even though these units of the USSR did not freely engage in international relations with the rest of the world.

Thus political entities which did not satisfy the minimum factual criteria for statehood were treated, at least for purposes of membership in the United Nations, as though they were states. *Did they thereby become states*? This is not just an abstract question. Rather, the lawyer is presented with the concrete issue: whether such an entity, not fully meeting the factual criteria for statehood, will or will not have a given legal right and obligation normally accorded to states, this attribute to be identified as problems arise. Under international law, were the Byelorussian Soviet Socialist Republic and the Ukranian Socialist Soviet Republic proper parties to treaties? Is such an entity protected by the provisions of Article 2(4) of the United Nations Charter, prohibiting the use of force against states? Does such an entity enjoy the inherent right of self defense referred to in Article 51 of the Charter? Are such questions to be answered by first determining whether these entities are states, or by analysis of the purposes to be served by according these entities in the particular case the particular attribute of statehood in question? If the latter question is the appropriate one, the subsidiary processes of inquiry may be enormously complex.

Acceleration of changes in the roster of states: In the last edition of this book, we called attention to entities accepted as states that had or have somewhat unusual characteristics, such as the Holy See, Namibia, the two Koreas, and the two Germanies; to continued United States recognition of Estonia, Latvia, and Lithuania, although they were administered by the Soviet Union as internal sub-entities. We also considered the "mini-state" phenomenon. The change since 1988, is astounding! Namibia's statehood is no longer clouded. The three Baltic states are free again. The two Germanies are one. Czechoslovakia split peaceably into two states. The Soviet Union has become the Russian Federation, with some unusual characteristics for some of its internal units. Ukraine is an independent state, as is former Byelorussia, the two one-time second and third UN votes of the USSR; and a number of new states now exist in former territories of the USSR. The former Yugoslavia is sanguinously fracturing into five, six, or more states. There is some expectation that Cyprus may become one again. At least one African state (Somalia) may be in a state of *debellatio* (complete disappearance of effective internal order). Will Liberia survive as a state? More former colonial territories have become states, some of them "micro"-ministates. Indonesia has swallowed a smaller state. Old embassies are re-opened in Washington for the diplomatic missions of newly-revived states; housing is feverishly sought for completely new states. Recognition has become virtually routine. Similar situations prevail in other capitals, especially those of the major European countries and Japan. Questions abound. It is not possible to estimate at this time what additional diplomatic representation a small or relatively poor state can afford, for example, will Bolivia send an Ambassador and staff to the State of Georgia? Can Mini-state X afford representation at one or more of the three headquarters of the United Nations Organization? What about membership, representation, and voting power of Ubekistan at the World Bank and the International Monetary Fund?

Might it be anticipated that the current "inflation" of statehood will alter, in some particulars, the status of statehood itself? Will the Pig's utterance in Orwell's ANIMAL FARM become ineluctably true as to states? In *In re Citizenship of X,* reported by Stefan Riesenfeld, in 77, Am.J.Int'l L. 160 (1983), a German citizen took possession of an abandoned former anti-aircraft platform, 8 nautical miles off the southern coast of the United Kingdom. The platform was "taken over" by one Major R.B., who proclaimed it the Duchy of Sealand. He promulgated a constitution and became *Roy of Sealand.* At the point of litigation, 106 persons occupied the "Duchy." The Administrative Court of Cologne, Germany held that the Duchy of Sealand was not a state. To constitute a state, territory, population, and government must exist. At least two of these were missing in Sealand: territory must be natural, not artificial; and the population must be "bonded" by living a common life.[1]

---

1. The attempts to create "Atlantis" on Triumph Reef, United States v. Ray, 423 F.2d 16 (5th Cir.1970), and "Abalonia" and "Taluga" on Cortes Bank, are discussed in Stang, Wet Land: The Unavailable Resource of the Outer Continental Shelf, 2 J.L. & Econ. 153 (1968).

Question. Was the ruling on the character of territory requisite to statehood based on law? What other characteristics might have been considered? Distance from a mainland or natural island? Permanence of the installation? What of a permanent undersea colony on the ocean floor? Or a space station? Should that question await technological developments and population growth by the year 2488?

Statehood in United Nations practice. Denial of United Nations membership to a political entity is at best ambiguous on the question of statehood, since Article 4 of the Charter opens membership to states that meet other criteria besides statehood. In addition, since admission is not automatic but requires affirmative action by two political bodies, the Security Council and the General Assembly, reasons for non-admission can be both numerous and unspecified.

When an entity is admitted to membership in the United Nations before meeting the standard minimum criteria for statehood as defined by international law, is one to assume that the members have acted illegally or, at least, outside the law? Or are the members saying that the purposes of the Charter may be fulfilled when an entity is well on the way to meeting those criteria and that it is thus a state as that term is used in Article 4 of the Charter?

Qualitative factors as elements of statehood? The generally accepted definition of statehood does not include qualitative factors, except as they may be subsumed under the rubric of capacity to engage in formal relations with other states. Should the size of an entity's territory be a factor? The size of its population? Its gross national product? Its ability to survive without foreign aid? Such factors have not been considered relevant in international law. Statehood is a question of fact; a question of power. If an aggregation of people claim that they are independent and *can get away with it,* international law recognizes that fact. There are many reasons why a people may wish to separate from a particular state. *See,* inter alia, the Declaration of Independence of the United States. The means of cessation are various: force of arms; force of public opinion (a major factor in the rise to statehood of former colonial peoples); agreement due to their own lack of economic or militarily strategic value to any other state.

Newly independent states want the dignity, prestige and overt recognition of their independence that flow from United Nations membership. Not surprisingly, the major powers sometimes chafe at the notion that a vote in the organization by a member with a population of less than 100,000 is as significant as that of China with its population of over one billion. However, the so-called "mini-state" problem is less significant than a decade ago, as one has become habituated to the phenomenon.

PROBLEMS IN THE APPLICATION OF
THE CONCEPT OF STATEHOOD

Notes & Questions.   In the Arantzazu Mendi Case, House of Lords [1939] A.C. 256, during the Spanish Civil War, Lord Atkin of the British House of Lords pronounced that, "the Nationalist Government of Spain at the date of the writ was a foreign sovereign State." Were there, then, two governments of the single territory known as Spain? Or was that territory divided into two territories, each with its own government? Was it necessary for the court to find that the Nationalist Government was a state to reach the result in the case?

————

THE CASE OF KOREA IN THE UNITED NATIONS

United Nations Security Council, Off.Rec., V, No. 24, Aug. 3, 1950; No. 27,
Aug. 10, 1950; No. 28, Aug. 11, 1950; No. 31, Aug. 22, 1950; No. 36, Sept. 1, 1950.

[Korea had existed independently and as a single entity for centuries prior to falling under Japanese rule in 1905; it was still under Japanese rule during the Second World War. Allied leaders had first planned to place Korea under a trusteeship after the war, but these plans fell through. As a military matter, Korea was divided at the 38th parallel in 1945, when Japanese troops surrendered to the USSR north of that parallel and to the United States in the south.

The United Nations addressed itself to Korean independence but no way could be found to provide a single government for all Korea. In 1948, elections were held in the south under United Nations supervision and the United Nations General Assembly adopted a resolution declaring that "there has been established a lawful government (the Government of the Republic of Korea) having effective control and jurisdiction over the part of Korea where the Temporary Commission was able to observe and consult and in which the great majority of the people of all Korea reside; that this Government is based on elections which were a valid expression of the free will of the electorate of that part of Korea and which were observed by the Temporary Commission; and that this is the only such Government in Korea." Also in that year, a Democratic People's Republic of Korea was proclaimed by a Supreme People's Assembly. The Republic claimed jurisdiction over all Korea. Elections to the assembly were not observed by the United Nations.

The USSR and the United States announced withdrawal of forces from Korea in 1948 and 1949. The United Nations was informed that the North Koreans had invaded South Korea on June 25, 1950. The Security Council met; the Russians were not present, since they had left the council some months earlier over the refusal of the council to oust the Nationalist Chinese in favor of the Communist Chinese. In a series of resolutions the council recommended "that the members of the United Nations furnish such assistance to the Republic of Korea as may be necessary to repel the armed attack and to restore international peace and security in the area," recommended that the members provide forces to a unified command under the United States, requested the United States to designate the commander and authorized the "use of the United Nations flag in the course of operations against North Korean forces concurrently with the flags of the various nations participating." [a]

The USSR entered into the debate on the Korean question for the first time when it returned to the council on August 1, 1950, with Mr. Malik then taking his turn in the chair.] * * *

The President (translated from Russian):

[the rest of the debate over Korea is in Chapter 16].

Commentary and questions. The foregoing extracts, are but a small trickle in the torrent of words emanating from the Security Council during the debate. * * * The formal issues before the council were the matters of agenda and invitation of representatives. The more pervasive and substantive issue was the question of the military operation of the United Nations, although this was not explicitly indicated by draft resolutions. * * * What was the relevance of the arguments on Korean statehood on the formal issues of agenda and representation? On the issues of the legality of the United Nations military operations? Analytically Korea could be characterized as one state or two states. Or as no state. Is such characterization the beginning or the end of the inquiry? If the legal problem before the council is not to be phrased as is Korea a single state?, then what is the problem? By what legal criteria should it be solved?

---

3. *The Territorial Element in Statehood*

Acquisition of land territory. The existence of a state is conditioned upon its occupation of a defined area. Territory often correlates with the other organic requirements for statehood: the requirement of a defined population and the requirement of a government in control of it.

Historically, competition for the acquisition of land territory has been a main feature of the rise of the nation state and the source of bitter and violent conflicts as well. Conquest was a common and legally recognized form of acquisition of title to territory, and this mode of establishing a right to permanent occupation of a defined area is not extinct, though it occurs much less frequently than it used to. Peaceful means of title acquisition, such as purchase, prescription, and, as to water boundaries, accretion (but not avulsion) also developed. Usually any state-to-state land transfer is eventually formalized by international agreement providing for cession. Discovery, once a major means of land acquisition, is no longer possible for lack of land to discover. All known

a. These events are more fully described in Higgins, United Nations Peacekeeping, 1946–67, II Asia 153 (1970); Sohn, Cases and Materials on United Nations Law (2d ed. 1967).

land is owned by one state or another, except for the Antarctic continent. The Arctic is, as it is said in Russian, "the Northern Frozen Ocean". "Territory" in "Outer Space" is another issue considered in chapter 5.

Antarctica, once subject to various claims, including discovery and sectorial longitudinal projections, is immunized from national territorial claims by an "internationalizing" agreement, the *Antarctic Treaty* of December 1, 1959, 12 U.S.T. 794, 402 U.N.T.S. 71. It entered into force on June 23, 1961, upon the deposit of ratifications by all the signatory states: Argentina, Australia, Belgium, Chile, France, Japan, New Zealand, Norway, Union of South Africa, Union of Soviet Socialist Republics, United Kingdom and the United States.

The intent of the treaty is to ensure that Antarctica shall be used exclusively for peaceful purposes and not become the object of international discord. It is to promote freedom of and international cooperation in scientific investigation in the area. Article 4 provides that nothing in the treaty shall be interpreted as a renunciation of asserted rights of sovereignty or bases for claims of sovereignty by the parties, or prejudice their recognition or non-recognition of claims by other states. It further states that the acts or activities of the parties taking place in Antarctica shall not constitute a basis for asserting, supporting or denying claims of sovereignty in the area or creating rights of sovereignty therein.

As to the maritime territory of states, see Chapter 4, and as to their airspace above their land and maritime territory, see Chapter 5.

Territorial boundaries. Over the centuries, many contests between states concerning territorial questions have been over the location of land boundaries delimiting their respective areas of sovereignty. Even when allocations of territory have been agreed upon by two or more states, there still remains the actual boundary demarcation problem.

In parts of the earth where allocations of territory have been stable for a long time, and descriptions and demarcations of boundaries made long ago, there are still portions of boundaries involving small areas, in controversy. The issue may be resolved by litigation before the International Court of Justice, as in the *Case Concerning Sovereignty over Certain Frontier Land,* (Belgium v. Netherlands), [1959] I.C.J.Rep. 209. Or it may be resolved by some other settlement, as in the Italian Peace Treaty of February 10, 1948, where provisions were made for changes in the Franco–Italian boundary. A border issue was also involved in the case before the International Court of Justice concerning the *Temple of Preah Vihear* (Cambodia v. Thailand), [1962] I.C.J.Rep. 6. Hostilities over a border question broke out between India and Pakistan in 1965 and the issue was submitted to arbitration. Rann of Kutch Arbitration, 1968, VII International Legal Materials 633 (1968). The People's Republic of China and India have been embroiled over the years in border disputes which flare up occasionally into limited hostilities. Recent news has included an old boundary dispute which caused the armed conflict between Iraq and Iran beginning in 1980, and between Iraq and Kuwait resulting in the Persian Gulf War. See Chapters 16 and 17.

It would be pointless to try to derive specific international law principles from boundary cases because the issues nearly always come down to a matter of interpretation of agreements. There is an exception to this, however, when the boundary between two states is a navigable river. In such a case, the location of the boundary is the *thalweg,* i.e. the middle of the channel of navigation. See the 1965 Restatement, Section 12. The same section also states that when the boundary between two states is a non-navigable river or lake, its location is in the middle of the river or lake. For the settlement of the *Chamizal Boundary Dispute* between the United States and Mexico, which involved the Rio Grande, see Chapter 1.

Newly independent states. Since World War II, the breaking-up of colonial empires has accelerated. As a result, a substantial number of independent states have come into being which previously were dependent territories of a colonial power or were subjected in various degrees to administrative control by another state, e.g., mandates or trusteeships. The emergence of new states has created difficult problems of succession, including those concerning succession to treaties dealing with territorial boundaries.

At its 1972 Session, the International Law Commission adopted *Draft Articles* on the Succession of States in Respect of Treaties. II Yearbook of the International Law Commission 1972, at 223. Part V of the draft is entitled: Boundary Regimes or Other Territorial Regimes Established by a Treaty. It consists of two articles.

Article 29 provides: Boundary regimes

A succession of States shall not as such affect:

(a) a boundary established by a treaty; or

(b) obligations and rights established by a treaty and relating to the regime of a boundary.

The commentary on this article states in part:

There was general agreement in the Commission upon the basic principle that a succession of States does not, as such, affect a boundary or a boundary regime established by treaty. Having regard to the various considerations mentioned * * * and to the trend of modern opinion on the matter, the Commission concluded that it should formulate the rule not in terms of the treaty itself but of a boundary established by a treaty and of a boundary regime so established. Accordingly, article 29 provides that a succession of States shall not as such affect: (a) a boundary established by a treaty; or (b) obligations and rights established by a treaty and relating to the regime of a boundary. In accepting this formulation the Commission underlined the purely negative character of the rule, which goes no further than to deny that any succession of States simply by reason of its occurrence affects a boundary established by a treaty or a boundary regime so established. As already pointed out (in paragraph 16), it leaves untouched any legal ground that may exist for challenging the boundary, such as self-determination or the invalidity of the treaty, just as it also leaves untouched any legal ground of defence to such a challenge. The Commission was also agreed that this negative rule must apply equally to any boundary regime established by a treaty, whether the same treaty as established the boundary or a separate treaty.

Article 30 Other territorial regimes

1. A succession of States shall not as such affect:

(a) obligations relating to the use of a particular territory, or to restrictions upon its use, established by a treaty specifically for the benefit of a particular territory of a foreign State and considered as attaching to the territories in question;

(b) rights established by a treaty specifically for the benefit of a particular territory and relating to the use, or to restrictions upon the use of a particular territory of a foreign State and considered as attaching to the territories in question.

2. A succession of States shall not as such affect:

(a) obligations relating to the use of a particular territory, or to restrictions upon its use, established by a treaty specifically for the benefit of a group of States or of all States and considered as attaching to that territory;

(b) rights established by a treaty specifically for the benefit of a group of States or of all States and relating to the use of a particular territory, or to restrictions upon its use, and considered as attaching to that territory.

This article is intended to deal with situations in which the predecessor state granted to another state by treaty certain rights in the territory such as lease of a port in perpetuity, operation of commercial aircraft for certain bases, rights of navigation on rivers or canals, and rights to use water resources.

The commentary states in part:

Some further precedents of one kind or another might be examined, but it is doubtful whether they would throw any clearer light on the difficult question of territorial treaties. Running through the precedents and the opinions of writers are strong indications of a belief that certain treaties attach a regime to territory which continues to bind it in the hands of any successor State. Not infrequently other elements enter into the picture, such as an allegation of fundamental change of circumstances or the allegedly limited competence of the predecessor State, and the successor State in fact claims to be free of the obligation to respect the regime. Nevertheless, the indications of the general acceptance of such a principle remain. At the same time, neither the precedents nor the opinions of writers give clear guidance as to the criteria for determining when this principle operates. The evidence does not, however, suggest that this category of treaties should embrace a very wide range of so-called territorial treaties. On the contrary, this category seems to be limited to cases where a State by a treaty grants a right to use territory, or to restrict its own use of territory, which is intended to attach to territory of a foreign State or, alternatively, to be for the benefit of a group of States or of all States generally. There must in short be something in the nature of a territorial regime.

Draft article 30 restricts the devolution by succession of the types of rights involved to those situations where the right either benefits the particular territory of another state and attaches to it, or benefits a group of states or all states. Can you see why? What would happen to the lease of a port in perpetuity, or to a right to operate commercial aircraft from bases in the territory, under draft article 30?

At its 1974 session, The International Law Commission modified Articles 29 and 30 of the draft by replacing, in both, the word "shall" with the word "does," deleting in Article 30 the adverb "specifically," and replacing in Article 30 the words "a particular territory" with "any territory." I YB.Int'l L.Comm. 1974, at 261. They were in that form, but renumbered 11 and 12 respectively, when the United Nations Conference on Succession of States in Respect of Treaties adopted the draft as a convention on the subject on August 22, 1978. 17 ILM 1488 (1978).

Rights over territory short of title. A state may cede to another a portion of its territory, just as a person may pass title to his property in private law. But just as rights in property may be created in private law which fall short of title, so it is in international law with respect to the territory of a state. Thus a state may lease to another a portion of its territory for a term of years. The convention between the United States and Panama of November 18, 1903, granted to the United States in perpetuity the use, occupation and control of a ten-mile strip of Panamanian territory for the purpose of constructing and operating a ship canal, and in this zone the United States exercised all the rights it "would possess and exercise if it were the sovereign of the territory" to the entire exclusion of the exercise by Panama of any such sovereign rights. For the termination of the convention, see Chapter 13.

The trusteeship system set up under Articles 75–91 (in Doc. Supp.) of the Charter of the United Nations presents obvious analogies to the institution of the trust in the common law. It does not follow, however, that a state holding a territory in trusteeship is vested with title to it as a trustee is usually vested with title to the trust at common law. The common core of the concept which underlies the system of trusteeship under the Charter of the United Nations and the preceding systems of mandates under the League of Nations is the vesting of power of control in the mandatary and the trustee for the benefit of the people in the territory under mandate or trusteeship. The most absolute power of control available, i.e. title to or sovereignty over the territory, is not given to the mandatary or the trustee state, though of course the scope of the power is very broad.

* * *

SECTION B.   RECOGNITION OF STATES AND THEIR GOVERNMENTS

---

1. THE EFFECT OF NON-RECOGNITION IN JUDICIAL PROCEEDINGS

Decline of Recognition Doctrine.   In previous editions of this book, what is now a small subdivision of this chapter was carried as a Chapter.   It is now clear that issues about recognition of states and governments are not currently or foreseeably an active area of concern. Books, traditionally, differentiated recognition of states and of governments.   Then, they worry over the question whether acts of recognition by other states (through their governments, of course) are essential to the existence of the recognition-seeking state or not.   They consider whether an unrecognized regime has standing to represent the state, in a range of roles from diplomacy to litigation in domestic courts.

Further, as to governments, recognition policies of various states have been categorized either based on the facts of governmental capacity (recognition de facto) or on acting-state preferences, from morality to ideology.   Wryly, in older times, the human rights record of the government under appraisal was not a factor in recognition.   Today, as large numbers of new states arise, recognition of states is, as a legal-political matter, usually resolved by the state's admission to the United Nations Organization, under Charter provisions.   However, it continues to be accepted that United Nations membership is not a requirement for recognition.

In the past few years more states have shifted their foreign policies away from recognition of "unacceptable" new governments toward a unilateral decision simply on whether or not to maintain or accept diplomatic relationships with the new government (and, perforce, with the state it represents).   Ordinary governmental changes, as through elections, do not raise recognition problems.   This shift eliminates an assumption of older recognition doctrine: that "de-recognition" was not possible unless the bases for recognition had changed.   Traditional notions of recognition are obsolete.   But, any state is free to choose whether it wishes to maintain diplomatic relations with another.   The shift described is an after-death triumph for a one-time foreign minister of Mexico (Estrada), whose contention was that even revolutionary changes of government should not require re-recognition, but only foreign relations adjustments.   The present recognition practice of the United States in this area has been called a "modified" Estrada Doctrine.

The 1987 RESTATEMENT is useful.   See §§ 202–206.   It asserts that other states have an affirmative obligation not to recognize an entity or a government that has come to power as a result of a threat or use of armed force in violation of the U.N. Charter.   It cites Articles 2(4), 25 and 51 of the Charter and the Security Council action as to the situation in Rhodesia before the establishment of the State of Zimbabwe.

As of mid-summer, 1993, the situation in Bosnia–Hertzegovina had not clearly become one of recognition or non-recognition of states or governments for United Nations purposes but one of acceptance or non-acceptance of transfers of territory in relationship to use of force to control such territory.

———

CASES INVOLVING NON–RECOGNITION IN DOMESTIC JUDICIAL PROCEEDINGS

———

By far the majority of legal issues concerning recognition and non-recognition have arisen in domestic courts. The classic issue has been: in the absence of diplomatic recognition of a state or of a regime by the pertinent department or branch of the forum state government, may such entity or regime be treated by domestic courts as having juridical existence? The courts of a forum state may be incapable of acting at all. Or, the courts might feel that the characterizations of parties as state entities or as governments should be made by the diplomatic branch. The courts, however, might make such decisions for themselves. If so, what law would they apply? International? Principles of law common to the world's major legal systems? Judicial notice? Analogies to the private law of entities such as corporations?

Regarding Sovereign Immunity

———

The case in the Cour de Cassation: In upholding the decision of the court of appeal, the Court of Cassation stressed the existence of commercial and other relations between France and the Democratic Republic of Vietnam. Court of Cassation, 1971, 99 Journal du Droit International 267 (1972). At the time, immunity from execution was the rule in French courts. The rule has changed since. See supra, Chapter 7.

Denial of access to courts to the Soviet government in other legal systems. Access to courts was denied to the non-recognized Soviet government in a number of states. *See, R.S.F.S.R. v. Cibrario,* 235 N.Y. 255, 139 N.E. 259 (1923). Thus the non-recognized Soviet government was refused the right to sue in Soviet Government v. Ericsson, Sweden, Supreme Court, 1921, [1919–1922] Ann.Dig. 54 (No. 30). The outcome was the same in Societé Despa v. USSR, Belgium, Court of Appeal of Liège, 1931, Pasicrisie II, 108 (1931). In USSR v. Luxembourg and Saar Company, Luxembourg, Tribunal of Commerce of Luxembourg, 1935, Sirey, IV, 26 (1936), the USSR was allowed to sue but on the ground it had been impliedly recognized by Luxembourg and hence the bar against bringing the suit had been removed.

Access to court permitted in some legal systems. In some states, however, the unrecognized regime has been allowed to sue. Commercial Representation of the USSR v. Levant Red Sea Coal Co., Egypt, Tribunal of Alexandria, 1933, 62 J.Dr. Int'l 199 (1935); Republic of the South Moluccas v. Netherlands New Guinea, Netherlands, District Court of the Hague, 1954, 21 Int'l L.Rep. 48 (1957).

———

Access to courts in the United States for corporations created by an unrecognized government. The policy to deny an unrecognized government access to courts does not extend to corporations or its assignee owned by the unrecognized government. *See* 1987 Restatement, Comment *a* to Section 205 and Reporters' Note 1 to that section setting forth United States cases in point.

———

1. **No legal change until 1979.** Richard M. Nixon re-established political relations with the People's Republic of China, having begun to indicate a shift in the United States position early in his first administration. But it was not until 1979 that diplomatic relations between the United States and Beijing were formally established by the Joint Communiqué on the Establishment of Diplomatic Relations between the United States of America and the People's Republic of China, January 1, 1979, U.S. Dept. of State Bull., January 1979, pp. 25–26, in which each of the parties agreed to recognize the other, a formula that the People's Republic had insisted upon with other well-recognized states, such as the United Kingdom and France, when these, some years earlier, shifted relations from Taiwan to Beijing. Agreements were concluded—and became effective at signature on January 31, 1979,—concerning: Consular Relations, 30 U.S.T. 17; Cultural Relations, 30 U.S.T. 26; and Scientific Cooperation, 30 U.S.T. 35.

On May 11, 1979 an Agreement on the Settlement of Claims was signed (effective at signature). 30 U.S.T. 19. The United States waived the nationalization claims of itself and its nationals for takings on or after October 1, 1949, for a lump sum payment of $80.5 million, the United States to be solely responsible for its distribution among claimants. The People's Republic waived claims arising from the blocking of Chinese assets after December 17, 1950; and the United States agreed to unblock these assets and further agreed [Art. II(b)] " * * * that prior to unblocking * * * it will notify the holders of blocked assets which the records of the Government of the United States indicate are held in the name of residents of the PRC that the Government of the PRC requests * * * not be transferred or withdrawn without its consent."

An Agreement on Trade Relations came into force on February 1, 1980, 31 U.S.T. 4651.

The President also "derecognized" the regime on Taiwan as the government of China and invoked the termination clause in the Mutual

Defense Treaty with Taiwan. As to the former, see Unger (the last American ambassador to Taiwan), Derecognition Worked, Foreign Policy No. 36,105 (Fall 1979). The termination of the mutual defense treaty resulted in the litigation considered in Chapter 15.

So-called retroactive effect of recognition. In Haile Selassie v. Cable and Wireless, Ltd. (No. 2), England, Court of Appeal, 1938, [1939] Ch. 182, the dethroned emperor of Ethiopia claimed he was entitled to the payment of sums admittedly due by the company under a contract with Ethiopia. The company argued he had no title to sue, because the Government of Italy had defeated him in war and was now the Government of Ethiopia.

The lower court held for the emperor, on the ground that His Majesty's Government, while recognizing the Government of Italy as the government de facto of Ethiopia, recognized Haile Selassie as the de jure emperor of Ethiopia. By the time the case came on appeal, however, His Majesty's Government no longer recognized Selassie as the de jure emperor of Ethiopia and so recognized instead the king of Italy. Hence the king of Italy was entitled by succession to the public property of the state of Ethiopia.

The appellate court also held that the right of succession was to *be dated back* to the date of the king of Italy's recognition as the de facto sovereign of Ethiopia, i.e. December 1936. Accordingly, the court said, the right to sue became vested in the king of Italy in December 1936, i.e., before the date of issue of the writ in the action.

Giving retroactive effect to recognition is troublesome. Suppose that the decision below in favor of the dethroned emperor had become final and the sums of money involved had been paid to him. Suppose further that the next day the king of Italy had been recognized by the British government as the de jure sovereign of Ethiopia. If the Court of Appeal meant literally what it said in stating that, for the purpose of succession to property, recognition was retroactive to the time of recognition of the king of Italy as de facto sovereign of Ethiopia, what would be the result? Would the king of Italy be entitled to funds that a person had previously paid to the emperor of Ethiopia?

One can argue that, in any event, the king of Italy would not sue the emperor of Ethiopia in the British courts because the issue would be moot based on sovereign immunity. But this defense can be avoided. Consider the case of Gdynia Ameryka Linie v. Boguslawski, [1953] A.C. 11, which involved the Polish government in exile in London and the Lublin regime in Poland. A department of the Polish government in exile agreed on behalf of the Polish shipping companies it controlled in England to give severance pay to the seamen of Polish vessels. The British government recognized the Lublin government. Next some of the crew sued one of the Polish shipping companies for the severance pay. The company argued that the recognition of the Lublin government retroactively invalidated all the acts of the former government in exile. The defense was rejected and the result can be explained by pointing out that the British government had specified it recognized the Lublin Government only *after* midnight July 5–6, 1945. Hence, the

British government had specified that its recognition had no retroactive effect. Suppose the British government had not been so careful, and assume further the Polish government in London had paid the severance pay before recognition. Does it follow that the Lublin government could claim the payment was invalid?

A great deal of confusion has arisen in both the British courts and the courts of the United States over the meaning of so-called retroactivity. Whatever the rationale advanced, the result of the decisions in the United States and the United Kingdom is that rights acquired or obligations incurred by the previously recognized government are not denied effect as a result of the recognition of the successor government. The question then is whether it is proper to speak at all of retroactivity, as the courts do, or whether it would be better to accept the fact that, in the kind of situations presented in the cases appearing in this subsection, there is neither need nor justification for doing so.

In the kind of situations involved in these cases, the government of a state continues to recognize a government of another state which has lost control of all or a major part of its territory. Even so, the dispossessed government still has some matters under its effective control so long as other governments continue to recognize it. What this often means is that the United States had the choice of continuing the Nationalist government in effective control of the funds or else shifting the effective control of the funds to the People's Republic by the simple process of recognizing it.

Yet the issue created by talk of retroactivity is false. A nation is not under a legal duty to recognize a successor regime even though the latter occupies the territory at stake. The nation has a right to maintain the government they recognize in effective control of matters still within the former's jurisdiction, such as funds in its banks.

In this kind of situation, the effect of recognition is clean cut. One day the emperor of Ethiopia is entitled to the funds due the state of Ethiopia, and the next day the government of Italy is. One day he can sue in the name of his state and the next day cannot. There is no question of invalidating his act and much less of invalidating the continuing recognition given him by the state in which he has taken refuge. In short there is no issue of retroactivity.

The issue is somewhat different, however, when a newly recognized government presents itself in the courts of the state which has recognized it and discarded, so to speak, the previous government. Though yesterday the king of Italy was told he could not claim "Ethiopian" funds because he was not recognized as its government, today, because of the act of recognition, he cannot be turned down. But what if he should rely for his claim on some act he previously took in the territory of Ethiopia, in which he was in effective control, and long before he was recognized? May he not be treated as if he were the recognized government at the time of his de facto control?

The answer, of course, is no. The newly recognized government cannot be considered as if it were in a vacuum—sometimes of many years duration—between the time it acquired effective control of territory and population and the time the fact was formally acknowledged by way of the act of recognition. Its prior de facto control cannot now be denied. In this sense, the act of recognition may be labeled as having a retroactive effect. It operates to suppress the defense of non-recognition with respect to past as well as future occurrences.

This is not to say, however, that all acts previously done, or which may be done in the future, by a newly recognized government will be given effect by the recognizing state. It simply means that whatever legal rules would be operative aside from non-recognition come into effect at recognition.

Regarding the Lawmaking Authority
of Unrecognized Governments

A. M. LUTHER v. JAMES SAGOR & CO.

England, Court of Appeal, 1921.
[1921] 3 K.B. 532, 539.*

BANKES, L.J. The action was brought to establish the plaintiff company's right to a quantity of veneer or plywood which had been imported by the defendants from Russia. The plaintiffs' case was that they are a Russian company having a factory or mill at Staraja Russia in Russia for the manufacture of veneer or plywood, and that in the year 1919 the so-called Republican Government of Russia without any right or title to do so seized all the stock at their mill and subsequently purported to sell the quantity in dispute in this action to the defendants. The plaintiffs contended that the so-called Republican Government had no existence as a government, that it had never been recognized by His Majesty's Government, and that the seizure of their goods was pure robbery. As an alternative they contended that the decree of the so-called government nationalizing all factories, as a result of which their goods were seized, is not a decree which the Courts of this country would recognize.

The answer of the defendants was two-fold. In the first place they contended that the Republican Government which had passed the decree nationalizing all factories was the de facto Government of Russia at the time, and had been recognized by His Majesty's Government as such, and that the decree was one to which the Courts of this country could not refuse recognition. Secondly they contended that the plaintiff company was an Estonian and not a Russian company * * *. Roche, J. decided the two main points in the plaintiffs' favour. Upon the evidence which was before the * * * judge I think that his decision was quite right. As the case was presented in the Court below the appellants

* Reprinted with the permission of The Incorporated Council of Law Reporting for England and Wales, London.

relied on certain letters from the Foreign Office as establishing that His Majesty's Government had recognized the Soviet Government as the de facto Government of Russia. The principal letters are referred to by the learned judge in his judgment. He took the view that the letters relied on did not establish the appellants' contention. * * * I entirely agree.

In this Court the appellants asked leave to adduce further evidence, and as the respondents raised no objection, the evidence was given. It consisted of two letters from the Foreign Office dated respectively April 20 and 22, 1921. The first is in reply to a letter dated April 12, which the appellants' solicitors wrote to the Under Secretary of State for Foreign Affairs, asking for a "Certificate for production to the Court of Appeal that the Government of the Russian Socialist Federal Soviet Republic is recognized by His Majesty's Government as the de facto Government of Russia." To this request a reply was received dated April 20, 1921, in these terms: "I am directed by Earl Curzon of Kedleston to refer to your letter of April 12, asking for information as to the relations between His Majesty's Government and the Soviet Government of Russia. (2.) I am to inform you that His Majesty's Government recognize the Soviet Government as the de facto Government of Russia." The letter of April 22 is in reply to a request for information whether His Majesty's Government recognized the Provisional Government of Russia, and as to the period of its duration, and the extent of its jurisdiction. The answer contains (inter alia) the statement that the Provisional Government came into power on March 14, 1917, that it was recognized by His Majesty's Government as the then existing Government of Russia, and that the Constituent Assembly remained in session until December 13, 1917, when it was dispersed by the Soviet authorities. The statement contained in the letter of April 20 is accepted by the respondents' counsel as the proper and sufficient proof of the recognition of the Soviet Government as the de facto Government of Russia.

* * *

* * * [U]pon the construction which I place upon the communication of the Foreign Office to which I have referred, this Court must treat the Soviet Government, which the Government of this country has now recognized as the de facto Government of Russia, as having commenced its existence at a date anterior to any date material to the dispute between the parties to this appeal.

An attempt was made by the respondents' counsel to draw a distinction between the effect of a recognition of a government as a de facto government and the effect of a recognition of a government as a government de jure, and to say that the latter form of recognition might relate back to acts of state of a date earlier than the date of recognition, whereas the former could not. Wheaton quoting from Mountague Bernard states the distinction between a de jure and a de facto government thus (1): "A de jure government is one which, in the opinion of the person using the phrase, ought to possess the powers of sovereignty, though at the time it may be deprived of them. A de facto government is one which is really in possession of them, although the possession may be wrongful or precarious." For some purposes no doubt a distinction can be drawn between the effect of the recognition by a sovereign state of the one form of government or of the other, but for the present purpose in my opinion no distinction can be drawn. The Government of this country having, to use the language just quoted, recognized the Soviet Government as the Government really in possession of the powers of sovereignty in Russia, the acts of that Government must be treated by the Courts of this country with all the respect due to the acts of a duly recognized foreign sovereign state.

* * *

Since writing this judgment a further communication from the Foreign Office dated May 4, 1921, has been supplied by the respondents' solicitors to the members of the Court, and to the appellants' solicitors. The communication was made to a firm of solicitors interested in some other litigation. In the communication the writer states that he is instructed to state that His Majesty's Government recognize the Soviet Government of Russia as the de facto Government of that country as from March 16, 1921. I have ascertained that the words "as from" should be read "as on." So read the communication adds nothing to the information already before the Court and I need not refer to it further.

[Other opinions omitted.]

————

Decisions in other legal systems concerning the law-making authority of the Soviet government. Effect was denied to law-making acts of the Soviet Government done in its own territory by a number of courts outside the common law system in cases where they would otherwise have determined the issue by applying their rules of private international law, i.e. conflict of laws. The exclusive reliance on non-recognition as a ground for refusing effect to the act involved has led on occasion to peculiar results.

Lhoest–Siniawskaia v. Officer de l'Etat Civil de Liège, Belgium, Tribunal Civil of Liège, 1929, 56 J.Dr.Int'l 1158 (1929), involved an action to compel the registrar to record an act of marriage established in Russia in 1919. In view of the non-recognition of the USSR by Belgium, there was no Russian official whose act could be recognized as valid in Belgium and in any case the signatures on the document were not certified. In Krimtchansky v. Officer de l'Etat Civil of Belgium, Tribunal Civil of Liège, 1929, 56 J.Dr.Int'l 1159 (1929), the action was to compel the registrar to accept a document as evidence of a divorce in Russia in 1928 so that the plaintiff could get a marriage license. The document had been recorded in Odessa. But since Belgium did not recognize the government of the USSR, the document, quite apart from other defects, could not be recognized as a valid act by a Russian official.

An heir claimed the money deposited in a bank account by the deceased in Hamarvy v. Credit Lyonnais, Egypt, Tribunal of Alexandria, 1925, 52 J.Dr.Int'l 475 (1925). Proof of his identity as heir depended on a certification by the appropriate Russian authorities. Since Egypt did not recognize the USSR, however, the proof would have to be furnished by consuls from the former Russian Government who were still in Egypt. In Decision No. 5641, Greece, Tribunal of Athens, 1924, 52 J.Dr.Int'l 1111 (1925), a will was given effect though contrary to Soviet law which would normally govern, on the ground that, since Greece did not recognize the government of the Soviet Union, it would be contrary to the public order to give effect to Soviet law.

There were cases of Russian companies whose directors in France could not, as a practical matter, comply with the Russian law in force prior to the taking of power by the Soviet government. Still that law controlled, rather than that of the unrecognized regime, and the directors were to follow it as much as feasible and otherwise do the best they could under the circumstances. Vlasto v. Banque Russo Asiatique, France, Tribunal of Commerce of the Seine, 1922, 50 J. Dr. Int'l 933 (1923); Shramchenko v. Tcheloff, France, Tribunal of Commerce of Marseille, 1920, 51 J. Dr. Int'l 141 (1924). A similar type of issue and ruling was also involved in Katsikis v. Societá Fati Svoroni di Pallone, Italy, Tribunal of Genoa, 1923, 50 J. Dr. Int'l 1021 (1923).

[Later] however, French courts appear to have shifted their position. Stroganoff–Scherbatoff v. Bensimon, Tribunal of General Jurisdiction of the Seine, 1966, 56 Rev. Critique du Dr. Int'l Privé 120 (1967), involved the following facts. By laws of succession of 1817 and 1847, Lieutenant Stroganoff became owner of certain properties. In 1918, the Soviet government abolished the legislation under which he had title to them, took some of the art objects, and sold them in Berlin to the defendant company. A nephew of Stroganoff claimed as heir the objects involved.

Part of the issue turned on whether the art objects continued to be immovables under the Russian laws of 1817 and 1847 or became movables by the Soviet law of 1918. The court said that the non-recognition of the Soviet government did not entitle French courts to disregard Soviet legislation on succession enacted before recognition of the Soviet government by France. It went on to apply the appropriate choice of law rules and found that Lieutenant Stroganoff lost possession of the objects in 1918 and hence the thirty year prescription (i.e. statute of limitations) had run long before the plaintiff brought his action. The decision was eventually upheld by the Court of Cassation, 1973, 101 J.Dr.Int'l 859 (1974).

Non–Recognition Distinguished From Severance of Diplomatic Relations

BANCO NACIONAL DE CUBA v. SABBATINO
United States Supreme Court, 1964.
376 U.S. 398, 84 S.Ct. 923, 11 L.Ed.2d 804.

Banco Nacional, an instrumentality of the Cuban government, brought an action in the Federal District Court for the Southern District of New York alleging conversion of bills of lading representing sugar previously expropriated by the Cuban government; the action seeks recovery of proceeds from the sale of the sugar. At the outset several procedural questions were presented to the court, one of which was dealt with when Mr. Justice HARLAN delivered the opinion of the court, as follows.]

* * *

It is first contended that this petitioner, an instrumentality of the Cuban Government, should be denied access to American courts because Cuba is an unfriendly power and does not permit nationals of this country to obtain relief in its courts. * * * If the courts of this country should be closed to the government of a foreign state, the underlying reason is one of national policy transcending the interests of the parties to the action, and this Court should give effect to that policy sua sponte even at this stage of the litigation.

Under principles of comity governing this country's relations with other nations, sovereign states are allowed to sue in the courts of the United States * * *. [P]rior to some recent lower court cases which have questioned the right of instrumentalities of the Cuban Government to sue in our courts, the privilege of suit has been denied only to governments at war with the United States * * *.

Respondents, pointing to the severance of diplomatic relations, commercial embargo, and freezing of Cuban assets in this country, contend that relations between the United States and Cuba manifest such animosity that unfriendliness is clear, and that the courts should be closed to the Cuban Government. We do not agree. This Court would hardly be competent to undertake assessments of varying degrees of friendliness or its absence, and, lacking some definite touchstone for determination, we are constrained to consider any relationship, short of war, with a recognized sovereign power as embracing the privilege of resorting to United States courts. Although the severance of diplomatic relations is an overt act with objective significance in the dealings of sovereign states, we are unwilling to say that it should inevitably result in the withdrawal of the privilege of bringing suit. Severance may take place for any number of political reasons, its duration is unpredictable, and whatever expression of animosity it may imply does not approach that implicit in a declaration of war.

It is perhaps true that nonrecognition of a government in certain circumstances may reflect no greater unfriendliness than the severance of diplomatic relations with a recognized government, but the refusal to recognize has a unique legal aspect. It signifies this country's unwillingness to acknowledge that the government in question speaks as the sovereign authority for the territory it purports to control * * *. Political recognition is exclusively a function of the Executive. The possible incongruity of judicial "recognition," by permitting suit, of a government not recognized by the Executive is completely absent when merely diplomatic relations are broken.

* * *

———

2. INTERNATIONAL LEGAL EFFECT OF NATIONAL RECOGNITION POLICIES

INTERNATIONAL LEGAL PROBLEMS RELATED TO RECOGNITION

Withdrawal of recognition and tacit derecognition. The basis of recognition is cognition or perception. There is an inherent illogic when one later attempts to say, when no change has intervened, What we said we saw we now say we no longer see. Withdrawal of the recognition of states, moreover, would involve doctrinal problems about the *declaratory* versus the *constitutive* theory of the recognition of states. Some states, including the United States, have viewpoints on record that do not exclude the possibility that the recognition of a regime as a government can be withdrawn; see the 1965 Restatement Section 96, and especially Reporters' Note 1. When it recognized the People's Republic of China as the government of all the territory of the state of China the United States derecognized the regime on Taiwan as the government of even a part of the territory (Taiwan) of the state of China. What is United States cognition of the regime on Taiwan following the resumption of relations with a government on the mainland? The Joint Communiqué states that "the people of the United States will maintain cultural, commercial, and other unofficial relations with the people of Taiwan." A Presidential memorandum, *Relations with the People on Taiwan,* December 30, 1978 provides that all programs with the people of Taiwan will be carried out through "an unofficial instrumentality in corporate form, to be identified shortly." The 1979 Taiwan Relations Act, 22 USC § 3301 et seq., identifies this instrumentality as The American Institute of Taiwan, 22 USC § 3305. Section 4 of the Public Law, 22 USC § 3303, provides very interestingly for the continuation in legal effect so far as the United States is concerned "of laws of the United States with respect to Taiwan." Congressional oversight of the act is provided, 22 USC § 3313. For detail as to the institute, consult 22 USC §§ 3306 through 3312, and 3315.

In October, 1980, an arrangement as to immunities for the United States personnel of the American Institute was concluded with the regime on Taiwan. It is discussed in the following material.

———

Notes & Questions. In view of the unofficial relations maintained with Taiwan by so many states, should it be considered to be a state, although perhaps a state a bit different from the usual? Why should not that be possible? Are there not entities, such as the Holy See, which do not meet the requirements expected of a state in the traditional sense? According to Reporters' Note 8 to Section 201 of the 1987 Restatement, the authorities on Taiwan do not even claim that it is a state. See

International Agreements and U.S.–Taiwan Relations, 22 Harv. I.L.J. 451 (1981).

3. RECOGNITION OF BELLIGERENCY AND OF INSURGENCY

REPORTERS' NOTES TO SECTION 94 OF THE 1965 RESTATEMENT *

1. ***Recognition of belligerency.*** Recognition of belligerency by a state is an act by which the state, in issuing a declaration of neutrality, asserts that it (a) is neutral in an armed conflict, (b) assumes certain neutral duties toward the parties to the conflict and (c) has certain rights with respect to trade between its nationals and persons within the territory of the belligerency subject to the rules of international law regarding visitation, search, contraband, blockade and prize. Recognition of belligerency for an otherwise unrecognized entity or regime may arise from a declaration of neutrality by another state as between a constitutional government and rebels in a civil war. This occurred in the American Civil War when Great Britain recognized the belligerency of the Confederacy, declared its neutrality and claimed neutral trading rights. It is well-established, as in that instance, that recognition of a rebel's belligerency does not have the effect, standing alone, of committing the second state to treat the rebel regime as the government or the rebel entity (if one is claimed to have come into existence) as a state.

2. ***Recognition of insurgency.*** In customary practice, recognition of insurgency has considerably less legal significance than recognition of belligerency. Historically, the object of recognition of insurgency by non-contending states was to obtain for rebels carrying on organized military operations the protections given by international law. Recognition of insurgency has often been the first official notice that other states have taken of the eventual possible success of a revolutionary regime.

The more recent tendency has been to rely on ad hoc assurances in revolutionary situations that the basic principles underlying the rules of warfare will be respected. * * *

4. PEOPLE AND STATES; WILL PEOPLE BECOME DIRECT "SUBJECTS" OF THE INTERNATIONAL LEGAL SYSTEM?

Of course, a few types of bad people are already direct subjects of international law, such as pirates and (somewhat less directly) airplane hijackers, convicted war criminals and some terrorists. But even these, as you will come to see in later chapters, are reached often through states that are given jurisdiction over them by international law. Direct governance of people by non-state institutions is very rare, the Nuremburg War Crimes Trials (See Chapter 11) being a "quasi-instance," (e.g., the victor states created an "international" tribunal, which they administered). The *Ad Hoc Tribunal for the Crimes Against Humanity in the former Yugoslavia* is another. On the other hand, the presence of

* Copyright 1965 by the American Law Institute. Reprinted with permission.

United Nations Forces in various troubled areas of 1991–94 comes nearer to direct UN action, despite the authorizing resolutions of the Security Council, which, in a broad way curb state autonomy. The proposed *ad hoc* international criminal tribunal for the former Yugoslavia also depends on states "agreeing" via the Security Council. On the whole, direct governance of peoples seems still a function of states, not international organizations.

Possible beginnings of law-making activity in the international arena by individuals or groups, as such, not states, is seen in the positive activism by those individuals or groups in support of new rules and doctrines of governance by international organizations. Non–Governmental Organizations (NGOs) that attach themselves to various United Nations appendages and to other international agencies and entities, are prime examples.

To a considerable degree the development of international people-based influences may be put into effect through the willingness of states to delegate, rather than surrender, their powers to international institutions. Such delegations, once made, may never be retracted, because the people of states will not want them to be.

SECTION C. OTHER STRUCTURES AND ELEMENTS OF THE INTERNATIONAL SYSTEM

1. INTERNATIONAL ORGANIZATIONS AND THE UNITED NATIONS SYSTEM: A COLLECTIVE BUT "SOFTER" SOVEREIGNTY?

Although the keystone of the international system in operation remains the "sovereign" state, seen close-up in the preceding Section, possible competitors over the past hundred years or so have been visible on or over the horizon. Has the development and recent integration of the United Nations system and other intergovernmental organizations caused the disintegration of sovereignty? Have competitors to state sovereignty arrived? If not, do they have a reasonable prospect of arriving in the foreseeable future? To consider those questions, you need to look at some of the defining legal characteristics of international organizations, especially those which have a generally world-wide or "universal" membership of states and which exercise powers and functions more or less in parallel to states. We focus primarily on the United Nations system in which are found sixteen organizations in addition to the U.N. itself, qualified under Article 57 of the Charter as Specialized Agencies. These include:

International Labor Organization (ILO)

Food and Agriculture Organization (FAO)

United Nations Educational, Scientific and Cultural Organization (UNESCO)

World Health Organization (WHO)

World Bank: International Bank for Reconstruction and Development (IBRD)

International Development Association (IDA)

International Finance Corporation (IFC)

International Monetary Fund (IMF)

International Civil Aviation Organization (ICAO)

Universal Postal Union (UPU)

International Telecommunication Union (ITU)

World Meteorological Organization (WMO)

International Maritime Organization (IMO)

World Intellectual Property Organization (WIPO)

International Fund for Agricultural Development (IFAD)

United Nations Industrial Development Organization (UNIDO).

Although the United Nations and each of its specialized agencies is legally independent in accordance with its respective constituent treaty, those organizations have many parallel structural and operational elements and coordinate their activities on a regular and systematic basis.

Other organizations operate outside of the United Nations system. Some are universal, others regional or functional. These include the General Agreement on Tariffs and Trade (GATT) and its expected successor, the World Trade Organization (W.T.O.), International Atomic Energy Agency (IAEA), North Atlantic Treaty Organizations (NATO), Organization for Economic Co-operation and Development (OECD), Council of Europe, International Energy Agency (IEA), Organization of Petroleum Exporting Countries (OPEC), Organization of American States (OAS), Organization of African Unity (OAU) and Western European Union (WEU), to mention only a few of the several hundred existing international organizations (I.O.s) in this category. The European Community (European Union) as a "regional economic integration organization," has quite extensive powers making it perhaps *sui generis.*

The international organizations are sometimes referred to as "public international organizations" or "intergovernmental organizations" to distinguish them from *Non–Governmental Organizations (NGOs)* which are also important actors in the international system as you will see in Subsection 2 below. NGOs are normally established under and are governed by a national legal system rather than international law. The international organizations considered in this Subsection are established under and pursuant to international law, in each case by a treaty, to which the Vienna Convention on the Law of Treaties applies (see Article 5; the text is found in the Documentary Supplement).

International organizations are not yet properly characterized as "states". I.O.s have no territory as such but hold private titles of ownership or rights under leases to the real property they occupy at their headquarters or other locations. Organizations also lack populations in the sense that states are populated with individual human beings and various forms of domestic entities made subject to the states' clearly sovereign powers. Organizations, however, do have constituent states as members and do exercise certain powers with respect to them.

They have Secretariats which correspond broadly to national civil services and are subject to institutional command. Organizations do enjoy international legal personality as required for the full and effective exercise of their functions. The comparison becomes blurred, however, when we look at the criterion of a "government" exercising independent (or "sovereign") control over the "population" and having effective power to engage in foreign relations. Some institutional elements analogous to government are present in international organizations, and they do carry out "foreign relations" in the regular use of diplomatic forms and in entering into binding treaty relations. In the U.N. system (as well as in other organizations) there are internal bodies fulfilling legislative-like functions, notably the U.N. Security Council and the General Assembly, but they are subject to the limitations set forth in the United Nations Charter. There is an "executive" in the Secretary–General and the Secretariat, again with limited although potentially far reaching powers and functions. There is also a judicial "branch", in the form of the International Court of Justice, but with the limitations on jurisdiction taken up in Chapter 1. Are the elements of statehood present in more than merely a formal or theoretical legal sense.

a. *Legal Personality.* Perhaps a threshold question is whether the U.N. enjoys the capacity to act as an institution in its own name through the device of international legal personality. Functional legal personality is provided clearly in Article 104 of the Charter: "in the territory of each of its Members," but the Charter is silent about the territory of non-Members and sheds little direct light on the question of the U.N.'s capacity to pursue international claims as states may do on behalf of themselves and their nationals. These questions were presented in one of the earliest advisory cases brought to the International Court of Justice. In reaching its conclusions favorable to United Nations powers, the Court considered some of the broader issues of the function and nature of the United Nations. *See,* the *Reparations Case,* below at p. 111.

If the United Nations enjoys sufficient international legal personality to pursue an international claim, the Organization also enjoys under the applicable texts the capacity to enter into contracts, to acquire and dispose of immovable property and movable property as well as to institute legal proceedings (see Section 1 of the Convention on the Privileges and Immunities of the United Nations, in the Documentary Supplement). On the international level, these are powers analogous to those of states which in fact enjoy more legal status than legal personality and capacity. Under the international law doctrine of sovereign immunity taken up in Chapter 7, states also enjoy effective immunity from the jurisdiction of other states. The United Nations and other organizations enjoy immunities similar in most respects to those applicable to states, perhaps even more expansive. *See,* Ch. 7, § B. Moreover, a House of Lords ruling emphasized that an international organization is not regarded as merely an unincorporated association of states in which the member states would be exposed to liability for debts of the organization in case of its insolvency; in Australia and New Zealand Banking Group Ltd. et al. v. Commonwealth of Australia and 23 others, [1989];

29 I.L.M. 670 (1990), the House of Lords rejected claims that the member states of the International Tin Council should be liable for the unsatisfied debts of the Council. Does this suggest an analogy with states?

Another question is whether, as legal entities separate from their member states, organizations are empowered to enter into international treaties. They do so regularly under powers specifically provided in their respective constituent treaties or inferred from Article 104 of the U.N. Charter, and similar provisions for other organizations. The treaty power is now clearly recognized in the Vienna Convention on the Law of Treaties Between States and International Organizations or Between International Organizations (25 I.L.M. 543 (1986); see Report of the International Law Commission on the Work of its Thirty-fourth Session, ORGA 34th Sess.Supp. No. 10, A/37/10). Is the treaty power another line of analogy?

b. *Legislative power.* The United Nations' legislative power may also be compared to that of states, but here the differences are perhaps more striking. Chapter 16, below considers the several legislative measures adopted by the Security Council during the Persian Gulf Crisis. When framed in obligatory terms, those decisions are binding on the states to which they are addressed (Charter Articles 2.2 and 25), and may be acted upon as applicable to non-Members as well (Article 2.6). Are those institutional arrangements indicia of "government?"

But what about the effect of United Nations decisions on individuals? Are embargo decisions, for example, binding upon the individuals and companies in the member states? How does that compare with national legislative powers? Where does sovereignty lie with respect to embargo decisions? How may they be enforced? Viewing them from Saddam Hussein's perspective at the close of Desert Storm, would you expect him to have a different response from yours? From that of Presidents Bush or Clinton?

Is the U.N. a "Super–Legislature"? Would you consider it wise to have the U.N. be a Super–Legislature?

One other way of looking at legislative powers in the U.N. is that decisions are often made *by* the members and *for* the members themselves. These decisions are often made quite independently of the U.N. in the treaty process or by international custom. In acting through the U.N., rather than by direct diplomacy, have nations not merely changed place and procedure? At times that might be true, but would it be true when one third of the Members is outvoted in the General Assembly? Nine members of the Security Council, including the five permanent members, can legally bind the entire membership in the neighborhood of 180 states. Some non-members can be compelled to comply. Do these situations affect your assessment of the possible "sovereignty" of the United Nations? When a member or non-member refuses to comply and the U.N. does nothing, does that mean that the decision was non-binding?

c. *Executive power.* In the United Nations, the executive power is divided between the Secretary–General and the member states themselves. The powers of the Secretary–General as provided in Chapter XV of the Charter are largely dependant upon actions of the Security Council and the General Assembly. Enforcement actions are adopted by the Security Council under Chapter VII on Action with Respect to Threats to the Peace, Breaches of the Peace and Acts of Aggression, (or possibly by the General Assembly under the Uniting for Peace Resolution), and are carried out by the Member States with quite far-reaching and powerful consequences, as will be seen in Chapter 16 below. In enforcement actions, the most consequential of all organization activities, there has always been a prior political decision to be taken. That carries the obvious advantage in a decentralized sanction system of requiring that the political will exists for the decision to be implemented but also the clear disadvantage of risking failure to take the decision and the loss of enforcement and deterrence when the political will is weak or entirely absent. How does this element of "government" compare to its national counterpart?

d. ***Judicial Institutions.*** International judicial institutions have been described in some detail in Chapter 1. Jurisdiction over responding parties and access by international organizations present some of the major difficulties. How would you compare the ICJ with a national sovereign's judicial jurisdiction over disputing citizens or institutions on the domestic scene? Organizations themselves suffer a serious infirmity with respect to contentious cases, by virtue of denial of their access to the Court under Article 36 of the Court's Statute, which admits only States. While the U.N. and Specialized Agencies are generally afforded access in *advisory* cases (only), even that avenue is shut off for other organizations, such as the Council of Europe, NATO, OECD and all others outside of the U.N. system. Action under Charter Article 94.2 to enforce an ICJ judgment requires a prior political decision in the Security Council. How does that compare to the enforcement of domestic court judgments under national sovereignties? Can the U.N. create an International Criminal Court? A War Crimes Tribunal? If so, by what authority? *See* discussion in Chapter 11.

e. ***Compulsory Funding.*** The organizations in the United Nations system are largely dependent upon the member states for financing of their operations; however, the decisions on budget levels and funding are made by the competent organ in each case. For the U.N. itself, the rules are contained in Article 17 of the Charter along lines which established the pattern for most other organizations both within and without the U.N. system. Article 17 provides that the General Assembly shall consider and approve the budget of the Organization. The expenses of the Organization shall be borne by the Members as apportioned by the General Assembly. The General Assembly shall consider and approve any financial and budgetary arrangements with specialized agencies referred to in Article 57 and shall examine the administrative budgets of such specialized agencies with a view to making recommendations to the agencies concerned.

United Nations funding consists of assessed contributions of the members, voluntary contributions and income from sales and services. In adopting the budgets and fixing the assessed contributions of members, the General Assembly acts by a two-thirds majority of the members present and voting (Article 18.2), with each member having one vote irrespective of its share in the financing. The Assembly's powers are stated in terms which make it clear that these decisions are legally binding on *all* of the members, including those in opposition. (See the International Court of Justice opinion in *Certain Expenses of the United Nations* (Advisory Opinion), infra at p. 1226, in which the Court answered in the affirmative the question: "Do the expenditures authorized in General Assembly resolutions * * * relating to the United Nations operations in the Congo * * * and the expenditures authorized in General Assembly resolutions * * * relating to the operations of the United Nations Emergency Force * * * constitute 'expenses of the Organizations' within the meaning of Article 17, paragraph 2, of the Charter of the United Nations?")

––––––––––

What does the foregoing tell us about whether the U.N.'s sovereignty is "hard", "soft" or non-existent?

––––––––––

Note: In 1949, the International Court of Justice, in an advisory opinion, that the U.N. has capacity to bring a claim for reparations for injuries suffered by an agent of the U.N. in the performance of his duties. Reparation for Injuries Suffered in the Service of the United Nations, [1949] I.C.J.Rep. 174. The International Court of Justice noted:

> Upon examination of the character of the functions entrusted to the Organization and of the nature of the missions of its agents, it becomes clear that the capacity of the Organization to exercise a measure of functional protection of its agents arises by necessary intendment out of the Charter.

> The obligations entered into by States to enable the agents of the Organization to perform their duties are undertaken not in the interest of the agents, but in that of the Organization. When it claims redress for a breach of these obligations, the Organization is invoking its own right, the right that the obligations due to it should be respected. In claiming reparation based on the injury suffered by its agent, the Organization does not represent the agent, but is asserting its own right, the right to secure respect for undertakings entered into towards the Organization.

> Having regard to the foregoing, * * * and to the undeniable right of the Organization to demand that its Members shall fulfil the obligations entered into by them in the interest of the good working of the Organization, the Court is of the opinion that, in the case of a breach of these obligations, the Organization has the capacity to claim adequate reparation, and that in assessing this reparation it is

authorized to include the damage suffered by the victim or by persons entitled through him.

The question remains whether the Organization has "the capacity to bring an international claim against the responsible de jure or de facto government with a view to obtaining the reparation due in respect of the damage caused (a) to the United Nations, (b) to the victim or to persons entitled through him" when the defendant State is not a member.

In considering this aspect it is necessary to keep in mind the reasons which have led the Court to give an affirmative answer to it when the defendant State is a Member of the Organization. It has now been established that the Organization has capacity to bring claims on the international plane, and that it possesses a right of functional protection in respect of its agents. Here again the Court is authorized to assume that the damage suffered involves the responsibility of a State, and it is not called upon to express an opinion upon the various ways in which that responsibility might be engaged. Accordingly the question is whether the Organization has capacity to bring a claim against the defendant State to recover reparation in respect of that damage or whether, on the contrary, the defendant State, not being a member, is justified in raising the objection that the Organization lacks the capacity to bring an international claim. On this point, the Court's opinion is that fifty States, representing the vast majority of the members of the international community, had the power, in conformity with international law, to bring into being an entity possessing a legal personality and the objective characteristics of an organization.

---

2. *Regional Economic Integration Organization*

Now broaden the focus of your analysis beyond states and the U.N. System to include the European Union (EU) as well. The EU provides an additional comparison point. It more importantly, qualifies as a major and innovative international organization in itself. The EU is so advanced in many respects over conventional international organizations in structure, powers and operations that it is sometimes seen as establishing an entirely new category of international institution designated as a "regional economic integration organization," with the emphasis clearly on "integration".

The Maastricht Treaty of European Union establishes what appears to be a single international entity, although for many legal purposes the three underlying European Communities will continue to exist. The three Communities are the familiar European Coal and Steel Community (ECSC), the European Atomic Energy Community (Euratom) and the European Economic Community (EEC), each created under its own treaty. The institutional components of the three Communities have been integrated into the single set of operational institutions analyzed in the following materials.

You will note that the European Union's functions extend far beyond those normally conferred upon traditional international organizations like the United Nations and its specialized agencies which are essentially intergovernmental *cooperative* organizations. In cooperative organizations, governments are normally not bound legally without their consent, given either by formal agreement or by consent to be bound as a party to international agreements developed under the auspices of the organizations (but compare the powers of the Security Council under Chapter VII of the United Nations Charter). More dramatically, the EU's institutions have received extensive powers to establish and enforce legislation binding legally not only upon the Member States but also upon individuals and other entities, and not always with each Member State's specific consent. When the EU legislates in that fashion, it is clearly more than a "cooperative international institution." The EU then acts as an ***integrated supranational*** body much like the central government of a federation. For further background on these points, see Hartley, The Foundations of European Community Law 3–7 (2nd Ed., 1988).

As you study the EU materials below, consider the differences between the competences of United Nations type organizations and those of the EU. In your view, would some of the operational problems of the United Nations become more manageable if EU-like powers were conferred upon it? Where does sovereignty lie now under the EU system? Do EU powers suggest future directions for more traditional international organizations? Do you see serious political problems in moving in that direction?

EUROPEAN COMMUNITY LAW AFTER 1992
THE EUROPEAN COMMUNITY LAW-MAKING MACHINE,* 3 (1993)

Ralph H. Folsom

The European Community has been creating law at a dazzling speed. It is almost impossible to function as a lawyer on EC matters without an understanding of the Community's law-making institutions and procedures. Once these are understood, attorneys and others can seek to influence the development of Community law in ways which reflect the interests of their clients. For example, major amendments to the Treaty of Rome were undertaken in the Single European Act (SEA) which became effective in 1987. The Single European Act envisions the adoption by the end of 1992 of 282 new legislative acts designed to fully integrate the Common Market. As of 1991, proposals for all of these measures have been drafted by the Commission and roughly three-quarters of them adopted by the Council. Implementation at the national level has proceeded much more slowly and is of concern. Italy and Greece appear particularly behind schedule. Denmark and the United Kingdom rank first on implementation of 1992 legislation.

* Reprinted with the permission of Kluwer Law & Tax Publishers.

The treaties of the three European communities (the ECSC, the EEC and Euratom) as amended are the "primary" sources of Community law. The EC treaties have had a common set of institutions since 1967. These are the Council of Ministers, the Commission, the Parliament and the Court of Justice (to which the Court of First Instance was attached in 1989). These institutions, supplemented by national legislatures, courts and tribunals, have been busy generating a remarkably vast and complex body of "secondary" Community law. Regarding legislation, some of this law is adopted directly at the EC level, but much of it is enacted by national governments under the "direction" of the Community. Similarly, some (and the most important) of the secondary case law of the EC is created by decisions of the European Court of Justice or Court of First Instance, but much development of Community law also occurs in the national courts acting in many instances with "advisory rulings" from the Court of Justice. Community secondary law also includes international obligations, often undertaken through "mixed" EC and national negotiations and ratifications.

The starting point for a basic understanding of Community lawmaking is the Treaty of Rome. This treaty is premised upon the idea of a Community government of limited or derived powers (*compétence d'attribution*). That is to say, the Treaty does not convey a general power to create Community law. Community lawmaking is either specifically authorized (including the many authorizations found in the 1987 Single European Act amendments to the Treaty of Rome) or dependent upon the terms of Article 235. That Article permits action if "necessary to attain, in the course of the operation of the common market, one of the objectives of the Community and this Treaty has not provided the necessary powers." Article 235 has been used rather extensively, and in ways which suggest that there are relatively few limits upon what the Community can legislate or negotiate by way of international agreements once a political consensus has been reached to move forward. For example, Article 235 was widely used as the legal basis of the Community's environmental programs well prior to the Single European Act amendments that specifically authorize Community action in this field. Furthermore, the Court of Justice has slowly been fashioning a doctrine of *implied* powers under the Treaty of Rome, most notably concerning the Community's external relations' powers. Although variations do occur from treaty to treaty, the Community's legislative, administrative and judicial processes are generally similar. * * *

* * *

The European Parliament (first called the Assembly in the treaties) was originally composed of representatives appointed by Member State governments. In other words, the people's representation was indirect, although the members of the European Parliament (MEPs) had to be serving in their national parliaments. Since 1979, universal suffrage is employed to directly elect the 518 representatives of the citizens of the Community to their Parliament. There are 81 MEPs from Britain, Germany, France and Italy, 60 from Spain, 25 from Holland, 24 from Belgium, Greece and Portugal, 16 from Denmark, 15 from Ireland and 6 from Luxembourg. These numbers correspond roughly to the populations of each country except united Germany. MEPs serve 5-year terms, and are presently divided into transnational political groups.

* * *

With direct elections, the impetus toward greater Parliamentary input into the legislative process has magnified. Traditionally, the Parliament has a right to be consulted and to give an "Opinion" as part of the Community's legislative process. That Opinion is not binding upon the Commission or Council, but it can prove increasingly awkward if it is disregarded. * * *

Left unanswered is just exactly how long Parliament may delay giving an Opinion. If the Council amends the Commission's legislative proposal substantively, the Parliament has the right to be consulted and issue a second Opinion. Since 1977, a "conciliation procedure" may be used whenever the Council departs from an Opinion of the Parliament on proposed legislation of importance to the Community's income or expenses. This procedure was instituted by a Joint Declaration of the Parliament, Council and Commission.

An important step forward towards democratic governance of the Community was taken in the Single European Act of 1987. Article 149 of the Treaty of Rome creates a "cooperation procedure" which gives the Parliament more of a voice on selected legislation. * * * Basically, when the Treaty requires adherence to this procedure, the Parliament may reject or seek to amend the Council's "common position" on a legislative proposal from the Commission. The formation of a common position by qualified majority vote in the Council of Ministers and use of the cooperation procedure is not needed if on the traditional "first reading" the Council decides to follow the Opinion of Parliament on the legislative proposal. Since this does not often happen, the "second reading" commences with the communication of the common position by the Council to the Parliament. If Parliament fails to act within three months, the Council may adopt the proposal into law. If the Parliament rejects the common position, the legislation may still be adopted by a unanimous vote in [sic] the Council.

* * *

LITIGATING EUROPEAN COMMUNITY LAW,* 29 (1993)

Ralph H. Folsom

There has been an explosive growth in litigation of European Community law. The bulk of this growth has taken place in national courts and tribunals. These bodies are vested with wide (but not final) authority to resolve EC legal issues. For example, contracts disputes can raise a host of Community law questions. Is an exclusive dealing distribution con-

* Reprinted with the permission of Kluwer Law & Tax Publishers.

tract enforceable as a matter of competition law? Can goods to which a sales contract applies be freely traded in the Common Market? Is payment for sales across borders protected by EC law? Does an employment contract fail to provide equal pay for equal work? Can employees be terminated because of their nationality? May patent licensing agreements contain grant-back clauses? Can franchisees be limited to certain geographic markets? What joint ventures can be established for research and development purposes?

Administrative decisions present another fertile field of EC law litigation. When can customs officers seize goods in transit between Member States? When can they collect money in such situations? When can immigrations authorities keep workers from other EC states out? When can they deport them? When can professional licensing boards deny the applications of citizens of Community nations? Can national authorities deny EC nationals the right to establish a restaurant? Can they require residency or work permits? What about the families of all these persons? What about pensions, social security, health insurance and other job-related benefits for resident EC workers? These listings only scratch the surface of EC law litigation in national courts and tribunals.

LOUIS, THE COMMUNITY LEGAL ORDER 44–49

(2nd ed., by J.D. Louis, 1990).*

* * *

22. Itself a creature of the law and dependent on the law for its effectiveness, the legal order of the European Community is also, as we have seen, a major source of law. It has highly developed machinery for producing legislation and also for enforcing the law it creates through a judicial authority.

Unlike international courts of the traditional kind such as the International Court of Justice, the Court of Justice of the European Communities automatically has jurisdiction in the cases where the Treaties so provide; it is not necessary for the Member State concerned first to submit to that jurisdiction. Its jurisdiction is mandatory simply by virtue of the entry into force of the Treaties. It should also be noted that the Court of Justice is accessible not only to the Member States and the EC institutions but also (to varying extents in the different Treaties) [1] to companies and individuals. Finally, judgments of the Court

----

* Reproduced from THE COMMUNITY LEGAL ORDER (2nd ed. 1990, by J.V. Louis) by permission of the publisher, The Office for Official Publications, European Communities, L–2895 Luxembourg.

1. For example, coal and steel firms can ask the Court to annul decisions of the High Authority (Commission) in a larger number of cases than can private firms or individuals under the EEC or Euratom Treaties: see the second paragraph of Article 33 of the ECSC Treaty and the second paragraph of Article 173 of the EEC Treaty. Under the EEC and Euratom Treaties, firms and individuals cannot challenge regulations.

imposing fines or daily default penalties[2] on firms are enforceable without an enforcement order from a national court; the national authority responsible for enforcement merely has the right to check the authenticity of the judgment.

A central judicial authority is essential in any integration process. The transfers of control which integration involves require some guarantee for the member countries that both the supranational institutions and their partner countries are playing by the rules. If the central institutions could overstep the limits of their authority, a transfer of sovereignty would be unacceptable. Similarly, it would be difficult for a member country to comply with the rules laid down by the central institutions unless it were sure that the rules were being applied uniformly by all the other members.

The Court of Justice thus performs a vital function, that of assuring observance of the law in the interpretation and application of the European Treaties (Article 164 of the EEC Treaty, Article 136 of the Euratom Treaty and Article 31 of the Coal and Steel Treaty). The description of the office of Advocate General, who is required, 'acting with complete impartiality and independence, to make, in open court, reasoned submissions on cases brought before the Court of Justice' (second paragraph of Article 166, EEC Treaty), is a good illustration of the task of the whole Court.

23. The Court, now composed of 13 judges assisted by six Advocates General (Articles 17 and 18 of the 1985 Act of Accession of Spain and Portugal), has three main functions.[3]

It reviews the legality, under the Community's constitution and under existing Community legislation, of acts of the EC institutions, when Member States, other Community institutions or companies and individuals bring an action before it directly for that purpose and when the issue arises in another dispute that has been referred to it. It determines in a particular case whether Member States are fulfilling their obligations under the Community's constitution and its legislation.

Finally, it decides questions of the interpretation of Community law or of the validity of acts of the Community institutions referred to it by national courts.

24. In its *judicial review* function, the Court can be likened to a constitutional court when it determines the conformity with Community law of legislation passed by the Council. On the other hand, when reviewing the legality of decisions of the Commission addressed to individuals its role is more like that of an administrative court. Since a Community institution can act illegally by omission as well as by commission, the Treaties also provide for a right of action by other EC institutions, Member States or, in more limited circumstances, individu-

---

2. As when the Court varies a Commission decision fining a firm for violations of the competition rules, for example.

3. It is not possible to describe here all the different types of action that can be brought before the Court. An important type of action that is omitted here concerns claims for damages for injury suffered as a result of acts of the Community or its staff.

als for a declaration by the Court that the Council or Commission has failed to act when it was obliged to do so.

27. The Court of Justice differs from an international court of the traditional kind also in the aims it serves, its role and its relations with national courts. While the Court of Justice is not a federal court that is hierarchically above the individual state courts, the importance of its role in determining the legality of state or EC measures, its direct relations with national courts, and the access to it enjoyed by private individuals do make the Court into the central judicial authority of a community of nations engaged in a process of integration.

* * *

* * * Charged with interpreting the law and determining the validity of Community legislation, the Court has no power to overturn decisions of national courts that are contrary to Community law or to say how Community law applies to the facts of a particular case. It is not a court of appeal. Nor, as already noted, does it have all the powers of a typical federal court. In this respect its status is not free of ambiguity, because in its relations with the Member States and the EC institutions it is necessarily looking more and more like a court of the federal type.

* * *

Question: What now can be said about sovereignty and the European Union? Professor Louis' views on this subject follow.

LOUIS, THE COMMUNITY LEGAL ORDER
11 (2nd ed., 1990).*

* * *

4. The law of the European Community is, in the truest sense of the term, a legal order, that is to say, an "organized and structured system of legal rules, with its own sources, and its own institutions and procedures for making, interpreting and enforcing those rules".[1]

... The main features of Community law that give it its character of a legal order, a body of law that is "at once hierarchical and autonomous", and establish its uniqueness [include] the direct effect and the primacy of Community law, [each rightly regarded as pillars of the Community legal order].

Section 1.   The transfer of sovereignty

5. The basis of the Community legal order is a transfer of decision-making to common institutions and a corresponding limitation of the

---

* Reproduced from THE COMMUNITY LEGAL ORDER (2nd ed. 1990) by permission of the Office for Official Publications, European Communities, L–2895 Luxembourg.

1. G. Isaac, Droit communautaire général, Paris (Masson), 1983, p. 111.

areas of decision-making remaining with the individual Member States. This fundamental fact, the transfer of national sovereignty to the Community, has been stated in many judgments both of the European Court of Justice and of national courts. It is worth quoting from some.

One of the most forceful statements is found in the judgment of the Court of Justice of 15 July 1964 in Costa v ENEL,[3] whose influence on national supreme courts has been considerable. There the Court said:

"By contrast with ordinary international treaties, the EEC Treaty has created its own legal system which, on the entry into force of the Treaty, became an integral part of the legal systems of the Member States and which their courts are bound to apply.

By creating a Community of unlimited duration, having its own institutions, its own personality, its own legal capacity and capacity of representation on the international plane and, more particularly, real powers stemming from a limitation of sovereignty or a transfer of powers from the States to the Community, the Member States have limited their sovereign rights, albeit within limited fields, and have thus created a body of law which binds both their nationals and themselves."

In this judgment the Court harked back to the very origins of the European unification movement after the Second World War. The Hague Congress held on 7 to 10 May 1948 had declared in a political resolution that "the time has come for the nations of Europe to transfer certain of their sovereign rights in order henceforward to exercise those rights jointly, and so to coordinate and develop their resources".

No significance may be attached to the fact that the Court referred to sovereignty only being "limited", not "transferred" as advocated by the Hague Congress.

The artificiality of such a distinction is clear from the following passage in a later judgment:

"The States have thus conferred on the Community institutions power to take measures fixing the levy such as those which form the subject-matter of Regulation No 22, thus submitting their sovereign rights to a corresponding limitation. More particularly, to the extent to which this concerns fiscal sovereignty, such a result is perfectly in accordance with the system of the Treaty."

The granting to the Community of power to tax imports of agricultural products had taken this power away from the Member States, thereby limiting the total extent of their sovereignty.

* * *

The surrender of sovereignty is final as long as the Community continues in existence, barring a duly enacted amendment of the Community's constitution, the Treaties.

6. The notion of sovereignty to which the Court is referring is clearly not the traditional abstract, indeed semi-metaphysical, view of sovereignty developed by philosophers from Bodin, through Hobbes and

3. Case 6/64 [1964] ECR 585, at p. 593.

others, to Hegel, which lies behind the nineteenth century view of the State. On that view, sovereignty is indivisible and inalienable.

A new concept of sovereignty, consistent with sovereignty being divisible, is apparent in the Hague declaration. Under this approach, partial transfers of sovereignty are feasible. But transfers of sovereignty are not to be seen in a quantitative sense like surrendering pieces of territory. Rather, certain powers are vested in the Community and from that vesting of powers and the Community's exercise of them it must be determined which of the two, Member State or Community, has jurisdiction over a particular matter. In appropriate cases jurisdiction may be shared or the Member States may be delegated certain subordinate tasks.

The view of sovereignty as something divisible is fundamental to the idea of any process of integration in which sovereignty is said to be altered, pooled or exercised collectively.

* * *

8. The corollary of the "division of sovereignty" is the direct effect and primacy of Community law. As the German Federal Constitutional Court pointed out in an order made on 9 June 1971, the lawful delegation of powers necessarily entails the recognition that the acts adopted by the new holder of the powers have direct effect in domestic law and prevail over contrary national law. These principles have repeatedly been emphasized by the Court of Justice. * * *

9. The idea of a division of sovereignty inevitably brings to mind the federal model. However, the analogy with a federal system should not be pressed too far. The relationship between the Community and national powers is different from that in a federation. The Treaties establishing the Community do not, unlike many federal constitutions, assign jurisdiction over whole fields of activity to the Community institutions, and as a rule it is not when jurisdiction is transferred, but only when it is exercised, that the Member States lose their authority to take action contrary to the centrally agreed rules.

The EEC Treaty—and especially its provisions on specific policies, such as agriculture, transport and overseas trade—sets a framework of tasks that the central institutions are to perform in pursuance of the Treaty's general goals and the particular objectives of individual chapters of it, and in accordance with a prescribed procedure. It is the performance of these duties that ousts the jurisdiction of the Member States.

* * *

———

Questions: Do you agree with Professor Louis' reasoning and conclusions about European Union sovereignty? Applying his reasoning to the United Nations would you give the same response? Why? Why not?

3. *NGOs, Other Entities and Individuals.*

A. BENNETT, INTERNATIONAL ORGANIZATIONS: PRINCIPLES AND ISSUES 250–257 (5th Ed., 1991) *

The constant change in world relations affects individuals, states, businesses, and organizations—domestic or international, public or private. Better transportation and communication link people, ideas, and commodities across national borders to a degree never before possible.

These changes force states and international organizations to adjust their policies and operations in order to maintain their relevance in international relations. Nongovernmental organizations in business, labor, and many other fields encroach upon states' prerogatives and escape government control. Often the network of contracts and transactions among nongovernmental actors threatens to undermine state sovereignty in important areas and questions the adequacy of the state-centric model of international relations.

* * *

Transnational or nongovernmental international organizations may be divided into two broad categories. One is the nonprofit organizations, of which there are approximately 4,500. The other category is the multinational business enterprise organized for profit, the number of which varies from 400 to 1,500 depending on the definition of how widespread the activities of such an enterprise must be in order to qualify as multinational.

* * *

* * * International nonprofit organizations are also proliferating at an unprecedented rate since 1945, and the possibilities for political influence multiply as improved transportation and communications increase the facilities for linking members and groups across national boundaries. Complex interactions are encouraged by close working relationships between intergovernmental organizations, such as the United Nations or its specialized agencies, and nongovernmental organizations. Nongovernmental organizations not only enjoy consultative status with intergovernmental organizations but frequently enter into working relationships with them for the attainment of commonly shared goals. The distinction between public and private functions becomes blurred in this as well as in numerous other areas.

* * *

* * * International nongovernmental organizations have been created in almost every conceivable field of human concern, from religion to transport and from art to science.

Nongovernmental organizations do not operate in a vacuum hermetically sealed off from each other or from governments and intergovernmental organizations. One of the major purposes of focusing greater attention on the study of nongovernmental actors is to assess the

---

* Reprinted with the permission of Prentice–Hall.

interactions between them and governments so that the political process may be examined in its fullest dimensions. Knowledge of the importance of these interactions is at an elementary stage, but preliminary investigations indicate a complex pattern of relationships warranting further study.

One indication of the interaction between NGOs and intergovernmental organizations is the provision for consultative status of NGOs with United Nations agencies. The most sought-after consultative status is granted by the Economic and Social Council. The breadth of ECOSOC's mandate explains the large number of NGOs that have been granted consultative status, including more than 800 organizations divided into three categories according to the extent of their involvement in ECOSOC's program. All the specialized agencies except the Universal Postal Union and the financial group also enter into consultative agreements with NGOs. The number of NGOs that have such a relationship varies from fifteen organizations for the World Meteorological Organization to more than 540 for UNESCO. The United Nations Children's Fund, the United Nations Conference on Trade and Development, and the International Atomic Energy Agency also grant consultative status to substantial numbers of NGOs.

The relationships between United Nations agencies and hundreds of NGOs demonstrate the impossibility of effectively separating public from private organizations.

* * *

THE INTERNATIONAL RED CROSS

INTERNATIONAL RED CROSS HANDBOOK
17, 421–422 (12th Ed., 1983).

STATUTES OF THE INTERNATIONAL COMMITTEE OF THE RED CROSS
(Adopted on 21 June 1973, revised on 6 December 1973, 1 May 1974, 14 September 1977 and 29 April 1982)

The relevant portions of the Handbook and Statutes are in the Documentary Supplement.

DURAND, FROM SARAJEVO TO HIROSHIMA *
654 (1984).

* * *

Thus, we have followed the ICRC's activities step by step from the Tripolitania War to the end of the Second World War and its aftermath.

---

* Reprinted with the permission, *l'Institut Henri Dunant.*

During those thirty-five years, we have seen the ICRC in action in fifteen wars, at least nine of which were international. In order, they were: the Tripolitania War (1911), the first Balkan War (1912) and the second Balkan War (1913), the First World War (1914–1918), the Russian Revolution and civil war (1917–1920), the revolution in Hungary (1919), the civil war in Upper Silesia (1921), the Greek–Turkish conflict (1922), the civil war in Ireland (1922), the Rif War (1924), the Sino–Japanese War (1932), the war in the Gran Chaco (1932), the war in Abyssinia (1935), the Spanish Civil War (1936–1939) and the Second World War (1939–1945). The list shows how the wars succeeded each other without a break: no sooner had fighting ceased in one than another conflict appeared to take its place. Only between 1925 and 1931 was there a kind of lull in belligerence, at least in overt belligerence. It was, as we have seen, during just this period that the Powers were attempting to preserve the peace or to mitigate the evils of war through international agreements. But this in no way meant that the world was at peace. Asia remained a prey to sporadic disturbances, while independence movements were springing up in the colonies and mandated territories with, in 1927, the growth of revolutionary troubles in China. The same year saw the start of revolt against colonial power in Indonesia, while in 1929 clashes broke out in India and the mandated part of Palestine; in 1930 there was a general uprising in French Indo–China. None of these disturbances, however, entailed action by the ICRC. According to the attitude at the time, they were internal troubles, and it is unlikely that any colonial or mandatory Power would have been willing to accept action by the International Committee in territory under its control. The only conflict of the colonial type in which the ICRC offered its services during this period was the Rif War—but that could have been described as military operations conducted by belligerents each of which held part of the disputed territory.

Yet it was precisely this type of conflict—wars of independence or liberation—which were to require the intervention of the ICRC from 1945 onwards. The widening of the Committee's field of action, which has been discussed in this account, was to continue. Immediately after the First World War, we saw the ICRC move from declared international wars to civil wars; after the Second, and before the repatriation of prisoners of war had been completed, it was in action, and was to be so with increasing frequency, in wars of independence and liberation. In 1945 war broke out in Vietnam bringing thirty years of conflict. The partition of India ... in 1948 resulted in a long period of violence and troubles. The British mandate in Palestine ended the same year and there began a conflict whose repercussions are still not at an end. In all these situations, the ICRC offered its services and, when they were accepted, conducted protection operations in circumstances new to it. During the same period it provided help, chiefly in the form of relief, in the civil war in Paraguay and Greece.

Finally, in the sphere of humanitarian law, the immediate post-war period was characterized by the revision or drafting of what became the 1949 Geneva Conventions; for the Conventions of 1907 and 1929, though they had provided a solid basis for the work of the International

Committee in many ways, needed their provisions strengthening and supplementing to cover the changes in warfare and the appearance of new types of conflict and their principles adapting to cases of armed conflict not international in character. The time had come to meet the wishes of the 1929 Diplomatic Conference by extending the protection of the Conventions to civilians. In the last years of the war the ICRC had already analysed its experience and collected a large number of documents on the subject. As soon as the war was over, it held several conferences of experts: in 1946 it convened the preliminary conference of National Red Cross Societies and in 1947 the Conference of Government Experts. On the basis of the work done by these meetings, the ICRC presented to the Seventeenth International Red Cross Conference in Stockholm in 1948 the drafts of four new or revised Conventions, the final texts of which were established by the Diplomatic Conference convened by the Swiss Federal Council and held in Geneva from 21 April to 12 August 1949. The four Geneva Conventions of 12 August 1949 were: the Convention for the Amelioration of the Condition of the Wounded and Sick in Armed Forces in the Field, the Convention for the Amelioration of the Condition of Wounded, Sick and Shipwrecked Members of Armed Forces at Sea, the Convention relative to the Treatment of Prisoners of War, and the Convention relative to the Protection of Civilian Persons in Time of War.

* * *

1991 ANNUAL REPORT OF THE INTERNATIONAL COMMITTEE OF THE RED CROSS 6–10 (1992) *

LEGAL BASES

In law, the work of the ICRC is based upon the Geneva Conventions and their Additional Protocols, the Statutes of the International Red Cross and Red Crescent Movement, and the resolutions adopted by International Conferences of the Red Cross and Red Crescent.

It was at the prompting of the ICRC that governments adopted the first Geneva Convention in 1864. In the years since, the ICRC, with the support of the entire Movement, has put constant pressure on governments to adapt international humanitarian law to changing circumstances, especially developments in the means and methods of warfare, in order to provide more effective protection and assistance for the victims of armed conflicts.

Today almost all States are bound by the four Geneva Conventions of 12 August 1949, which, in times of armed conflict, protect wounded, sick and shipwrecked members of the armed forces, prisoners of war and civilians.

Two Protocols additional to these Conventions were adopted on 8 June 1977. They are intended mainly to reaffirm and develop the

* Reprinted with the permission of the International Committee of the Red Cross.

humanitarian rules governing the conduct of hostilities (Protocol I) and to extend the body of humanitarian law applicable in non-international armed conflicts (Protocol II). Almost two-thirds of the world's States are now bound by the Protocols.

The legal bases of any action undertaken by the ICRC may be summed up as follows:

☐ In the four Geneva Conventions of 1949 and Additional Protocol I, the international community gave the ICRC a mandate in the event of *international armed conflict*. In particular, the ICRC has the right to visit prisoners of war and civilian internees. The Conventions also confer on the ICRC a broad right of initiative.

☐ In situations of *armed conflict which are not international in character,* the ICRC also has a right of initiative recognized by the States and enshrined in the four Geneva Conventions.

☐ In the event of *internal disturbances and tension,* and in any other situation which warrants humanitarian action, the ICRC has a right of humanitarian initiative which is recognized in the Statutes of the International Red Cross and Red Crescent Movement and allows it to offer its services to governments without that offer constituting interference in the internal affairs of the State.

Activities for people deprived of their freedom

By virtue of the Geneva Conventions of 1949 and their Additional Protocols of 1977, the ICRC visits persons deprived of their freedom in international armed conflicts (prisoners of war within the meaning of Article 4 of the Third Convention and Article 44 of Protocol I) and persons protected under the Fourth Convention (civilian internees, persons arrested by the Occupying Power and penal-law detainees in enemy hands).

In the event of a non-international armed conflict, covered by Article 3 common to the four Geneva Conventions of 1949 and Protocol II of 1977, the ICRC concerns itself with persons deprived of their freedom in connection with the conflict (combatants of government or armed opposition forces captured by the enemy, civilians arrested or tried by the government or the rebels because of their support, active or not, real or not, for the opposing forces).

In situations of internal disturbances and tension, which are not covered by international humanitarian law, the ICRC has a statutory right of initiative entitling it to offer its services to visit people arrested for political or security reasons.

The purpose of ICRC visits is purely humanitarian; ICRC delegates observe the material and psychological conditions of detention and the treatment accorded to detainees, provide them with relief supplies if required (medicines, clothing, toilet articles) and ask the authorities to take any steps deemed necessary to improve the detainees' treatment.

ICRC visits to places of detention, whether pursuant to the Geneva Conventions or outside the field of application of international humanitarian law, are carried out according to specific criteria. Its delegates must be allowed to see all the detainees and talk freely to them without witnesses, to have access to all premises used for detention and to repeat their visits, and must be provided with a list of the persons to be visited (or be permitted to draw up a such a list during the visit).

Before and after these visits, discussions at various levels are held with the people in charge of the detention centres. Confidential reports are then drawn up. In the case of international armed conflicts, these reports are sent to both the Detaining Power and the Power of Origin of the prisoners of war, while in other cases they are sent only to the detaining authorities.

These confidential reports are not intended for publication. The ICRC confines itself to releasing the number and names of the places visited, the dates of the visits and the number of people seen. It does not express an opinion on the grounds for detention and does not publicly comment on the material conditions or treatment it observes. If a government should publish incomplete or inaccurate versions of ICRC reports, the ICRC reserves the right to publish and circulate them in full.

Central Tracing Agency

The ICRC's first small information offices came into being during and after the Franco–Prussian war of 1870–71. The subsequent central information agencies set up by it during the two World Wars were huge in comparison. The latest, the Central Tracing Agency, today makes extensive use of computers. It is represented in the field by some 60 specialized delegates posted to 27 delegations. At its Geneva headquarters, over 80 staff members work on card files—a mute record of the many families torn apart by past and present conflicts. Sixty million such cards have been established since 1914, including, for example, the 500,000 cards bearing names of Indo–Chinese refugees or displaced persons compiled since 1979.

On the basis of the ICRC's obligations under the Geneva Conventions and its right of humanitarian initiative, the Agency's main tasks are as follows:

☐ to obtain, centralize and, where necessary, forward any information that might help to identify the people in whose behalf the ICRC works;

☐ to maintain the exchange of family correspondence when the usual means of communication have been disrupted;

☐ to trace persons reported missing or whose families have had no news of them;

☐ to arrange for transfers and repatriations and to reunite separated families;

☐ to issue, for a limited period and a single journey, "ICRC travel documents" to persons without identity papers;

☐ to issue captivity, hospitalization or death certificates for former detainees, prisoners of war or their rightful claimants.

The forwarding of family messages, tracing activities and family reunifications are often carried out in conjunction with the National Red Cross and Red Crescent Societies. The Central Tracing Agency, which acts as technical adviser to those Societies, organizes training courses, some of which are regional in nature.

* * *

Dissemination of international humanitarian law and of the Movement's principles and ideals

The dissemination of knowledge of international humanitarian law is primarily the responsibility of the States which undertook to make this law known and respected and to ensure respect for it when they became parties to the 1949 Geneva Conventions and to their two Additional Protocols of 1977.

The ICRC bases its dissemination activities on the primary responsibility conferred upon it in this connection by the Statutes of the International Red Cross and Red Crescent Movement, which stipulate that:

The role of the International Committee, in accordance with its Statutes, is in particular:

— to maintain and disseminate the Fundamental Principles of the Movement, namely humanity, impartiality, neutrality, independence, voluntary service, unity and universality;

— to work for the understanding and dissemination of knowledge of international humanitarian law applicable in armed conflicts and to prepare any development thereof.[1]

Assisted in this task by the National Red Cross and Red Crescent Societies and by their International Federation, the ICRC has focused on training disseminators. In particular, it helps train national instructors within the armed forces and dissemination officers within the National Societies.

Certain target groups have also been the object of particular attention. They are government and academic circles, youth, and the media.

The adoption of the Additional Protocols in 1977 represented a decisive step towards greater awareness of the importance of dissemination.[2]

Since then, innumerable activities have been undertaken every year throughout the world to spread knowledge of international humanitarian law and the Movement's principles, ideals and work. The aims of these dissemination efforts are:

☐ to limit the suffering caused by armed conflicts and situations of disturbances and tension through improved knowledge of and greater respect for international humanitarian law;

---

1. Statutes of the International Red Cross and Red Crescent Movement, Art. 5, paras. (a) and (g).

2. Resolution 21—Diplomatic Conference, 1974–1977.

☐ to ensure the security of humanitarian operations and the safety of Red Cross and Red Crescent personnel so that the victims can be helped;

☐ to strengthen the identity and image of the Movement, to contribute to its unity through greater awareness and understanding of its principles, history, workings and activities;

☐ to foster the propagation of a spirit of peace.

Today's combatants are all too often ignorant of the rules of international humanitarian law. By the same token, journalists and the public tend to become aware of humanitarian law and its applications only in the wake of tragedy.

To be respected, international humanitarian law must be known. To be supported and accepted, the activities of the Red Cross and Red Crescent must be understood.

Civilians are frequently unaware of their rights and their obligations with regard to international humanitarian law. When they benefit from the protection and assistance of the Movement, they should be better informed as to the mandate, role and ethical considerations which govern Red Cross and Red Crescent work.

* * *

The Gulf war had a significant impact on all the ICRC's operational activities in 1991, both at headquarters and in the field. Not since the Second World War had the institution had to find such enormous resources, in terms of staff, funds, food aid, medical relief and logistic support, in such a short space of time. In facing this challenge, the ICRC enjoyed the backing of the entire International Red Cross and Red Crescent Movement.

Hostilities in the Gulf must nevertheless not be allowed to overshadow other situations which also mobilized the institution in many areas of the world, including elsewhere in the Middle East and in Asia, where protracted conflicts continued; on the African continent, where needs remained an urgent priority during the year; or even in Europe, where far-reaching political change gave rise to mounting humanitarian needs. In contrast, the Latin American continent in general evolved in 1991 towards a more peaceful situation, thereby significantly improving the living conditions of people hitherto affected by conflicts or insecurity and enabling the ICRC to scale down its activities there.

In 1991, the ICRC had 49 delegations and regional delegations worldwide, employing on average over 720 delegates, 190 staff from National Red Cross and Red Crescent Societies and nearly 4,800 local employees.

Activities for people deprived of their freedom

ICRC delegates conducted more than 8,000 visits in nearly 2,000 places of detention in 49 countries (prisoner-of-war camps, civilian and military prisons, centres run by police forces), and saw nearly 154,000 persons deprived of their freedom (prisoners of war, security detainees, civilian internees).

The Gulf conflict resulted in a significant expansion in detention-related activities. The number of detainees visited by delegates in the Middle East and North Africa rose sharply to around 113,000 (as against 84,000 in 1990). Major developments in Africa enabled the ICRC virtually to double the number of visits conducted (564 as against 245 the previous year), its delegates having gained access to more detention centres in a greater number of countries and, for the first time, to provisional places of detention (police stations, military barracks). In Asia, too, the ICRC was granted access to new categories of detainees (in particular in Afghanistan and Indonesia), while the political upheavals and conflicts in Europe, chiefly affecting the Balkans, prompted the institution to initiate visits to detention centres in two countries (Albania and Yugoslavia).

Central Tracing Agency

There was also a rise in Tracing Agency work owing to the Gulf conflict. The number of staff assigned to tracing-related tasks in Geneva had to be doubled during a period of five months so as to register around 80,000 prisoners of war and civilian internees. Throughout the world, the Tracing Agency processed more than 72,300 requests concerning people presumed missing, forwarded nearly 420,000 messages between separated family members and issued more than 6,400 travel documents (enabling people who no longer had any identity papers to travel to a host country).

* * *

**OPEN LETTER TO PRESIDENT CLINTON
FROM ASIL PRESIDENT [a] ***

ASIL Newsletter, January–February 1 (1993).

December 17, 1992

To the President–Elect of the United States

Dear President–Elect Clinton:

On January 20 you will become the first President of the United States to assume office since the end of the Cold War ushered in a changed world order. I urge you to dedicate your Administration to the rule of law in relations between nations.

------

a. The ASIL is the American Society of International Law. Similarly influential scholarly groups have been organized in the United Kingdom (British Institute of International and Comparative Law), France (Société française pour le Droit International) and in other countries.

* Reprinted with the permission of the American Society of International Law.

In 1945, the United States led the victorious Allies in establishing a new world order, represented by the United Nations Charter and the UN Organization, and dedicated to international peace and security and to the rule of law. The Cold War frustrated the realization of that world order, and the rule of law was sometimes sacrificed—even by the United States—to perceived needs of national security.

I believe that the changed world order provides a fresh opportunity for the United States to help realize its goals of half a century ago. To that end, I call upon you:

1. To seize the earliest opportunity to declare that international peace and security and the rule of law will be the pillars of U.S. foreign policy.

2. In order to make that commitment specific and credible, to commit the United States to pursue the following policies and to take the following measures:

a. The United States will respect the territorial integrity and political independence of other states as required by the UN Charter. The United States will not send military forces into other countries except by invitation, or pursuant to its international obligations, as, for example, under the North Atlantic Treaty, or under the authority of the UN, as in Iraq and Somalia.

b. U.S. officials will not enter the territory of any other state without the consent of its government for any official purpose. In particular, they will not abduct persons in other countries for trial in the United States.

c. The United States will pay its outstanding dues to the United Nations and will pay its dues promptly in the future. It will support efforts by the UN to maintain international peace and security. It will negotiate agreements with the UN Security Council to make forces available, as required by the UN Charter (Article 43) and authorized by Congress.

d. The United States will deposit a new declaration accepting again the compulsory jurisdiction of the International Court of Justice.

e. The United States will honor its treaty obligations scrupulously. In particular, it will honor its undertaking under the Protocol on the Status of Refugees: U.S. officials will not send any bona fide refugee back to any country where his/her life or freedom would be threatened. U.S. officials will not keep any person in prolonged detention solely because he/she has not been lawfully admitted and no other country is willing to receive him/her. The United States will immediately reconsider its Haitian Interdiction Program.

f. The Executive Branch will urge Congress to enact legislation to carry out the provisions of the Convention Against Torture and of the International Covenant on Civil and Political Rights, which the U.S. has ratified, including provisions to which the United States entered reservations that were not required by the Constitution. The Executive Branch will urge the Senate to consent to ratification of the other human rights agreements signed by President Carter for the United States, i.e., the

Covenant on Economic, Social and Cultural Rights, the Convention on the Elimination of All Forms of Racial Discrimination, and the American Convention on Human Rights. The Executive Branch will request the Senate to consent also to the Optional Protocol to the Covenant on Civil and Political Rights and to the Convention on the Elimination of All Forms of Discrimination Against Women and the Convention on the Rights of the Child.

3. The rule of law implies not only respect for existing law but establishing new norms and institutions to bring order into important inter-state relations. I urge in particular that the United States:

— enter promptly into negotiations to remove the obstacles to general adherence to the 1982 UN Convention on the Law of the Sea

— take the lead to establish an effective international law for the environment, including a biodiversity treaty and a global warming treaty

— pursue negotiations towards agreement to prevent the further proliferation of nuclear weapons and to limit sharply commerce in weapons generally.

The rule of law is essential to national and international prosperity. It is in the national interest of all states, not least the United States. On behalf of the American Society of International Law, I express the hope that your Administration will be known, deservedly, as the Rule of Law Administration.

Respectfully yours,
Louis Henkin

_____

INDIVIDUALS

Systematic and comprehensive treatment of individuals in relation to other actors in the international system is found below in Chapters 10 (Human Rights) and 11 (Individual Responsibility).

_____

The European System, pursuant to the Council of Europe and its Commission on Human Rights, France seems to provide individuals more opportunity for access. Is this good? What does it suggest about Europe? About the separate nations in Europe? About future directions of the legal system?

_____

Chapter 3
JURISDICTION

ALLOCATION OF JURISDICTION IN
THE INTERNATIONAL SYSTEM

INTRODUCTION.

1. ***Meaning of Jurisdiction: General.*** Jurisdiction may be defined as the authority to effect and affect legal interests—to prescribe rules of law (legislative or prescriptive jurisdiction), to adjudicate legal questions, and to compel or induce compliance (enforcement jurisdiction). Neither international law nor domestic law can have any real, direct or immediate impact on a legal personality, unless legislative, adjudicative, or enforcement jurisdiction obtains. Jurisdiction is the means to make law functional.

2. ***Jurisdiction in national legal systems.*** The term jurisdiction, is also common to national legal systems. In the United States, for example, we speak of federal jurisdiction contrasted with jurisdiction of the states of the Union. We do so because under our domestic law—the Constitution in this instance—certain categories of persons, events or places are subject to federal law and others to the law of the several states.

The concept of jurisdiction is also commonly used in national legal systems to allocate the judicial function to different courts. Many nations place limits upon the categories of persons, events or places with which particular courts may deal. Thus we may find that certain courts have jurisdiction over civil matters, some over commercial, and others over criminal matters. In some states the civil courts are specialized, each having jurisdiction over certain civil matters but not others. Often jurisdiction of different criminal courts is determined by the level of gravity of the offense. There are states where jurisdiction over litigation between individuals and the government is vested in a system of administrative courts, separate and distinct from other civil courts.

3. ***Jurisdiction in the international legal system.*** Jurisdiction, in the international legal system, refers to the authority of the state as a whole and not of its constituent units or political subdivisions. The United States is a federation and France is not. Whether an alien is tried by a court of New York State or by a federal court, or whether in France he is tried by a court in Paris or Marseilles, does not create an international issue of jurisdiction. The jurisdictional question in the international system is whether the United States in the one case, or France in the other, is entitled to try the alien, and not where or by what court in either state.

In the international legal system, the term jurisdiction expresses a concept similar to that in national legal systems. When we speak of the jurisdiction of a state in the international system, we mean the state is entitled under international law to subject certain categories of persons, events or places to its rules of law. The rules of international law determining whether a state has jurisdiction over a particular person, event or place, are often different from those used in a national legal system.

The international legal system is not concerned with the allocation by a state of jurisdiction among its branches of government. In a national legal system, the making of legal rules might be vested in a legislature and their enforcement vested in the executive or judicial branch. But this division of functions is not always so clear cut. The House of Lords in the United Kingdom has legislative functions and also functions as a law court. In turn a court of law in a national legal system may not have been instructed by its legislature to apply a particular rule and may have to articulate one of its own devising before it can resolve the legal problem before it. Or the executive may be empowered to make legal rules. International law does not determine which branch of government should do what.

Accordingly it is advisable, if not necessary, to discuss the jurisdiction of states under international law in terms which are neutral in terms of the organs of government exercising the jurisdiction. In the international legal system, however, there may be newly emerging issues of separation of powers. For example, recent activity by the Security Council in relation to the Gulf War, Somalia, and Bosnia may suggest that the Council is exercising executive, legislative, and judicial powers. We will consider these issues below and in chapter 16.

4. ***Jurisdiction to prescribe, to adjudicate, and to enforce.*** The term jurisdiction is often used imprecisely. A sharp distinction between rule-making and rule-enforcing jurisdiction is essential to effective analysis. First, the state prescribes a rule, which is to say that either by act of the legislature, decree of the executive, administrative regulation, or decision of a court, it declares a principle or legal norm. Second, the state enforces the rule. That is, it extradites, arrests, subpoenas witnesses and documents, tries and punishes for violation of the rule, or enters a judgment in vindication of the rule. Enforcement jurisdiction may be refined further, by separating out jurisdiction to adjudicate; the state's judiciary decides questions of law and fact and metes out the punishment or remedy it deems appropriate and called for by the law. Indeed, jurisdiction to adjudicate is not always a species of jurisdiction to enforce.

A state normally has jurisdiction to prescribe rules of domestic law governing conduct taking place physically within its territory. At the other extreme no state has jurisdiction to prescribe rules of domestic law governing all conduct of everyone everywhere in the world. A state normally also has jurisdiction to adjudicate issues which arise within its prescriptive jurisdiction, and to enforce within its own territory the rules of law it has properly prescribed. A state does not have jurisdiction to enforce, if it does not have jurisdiction to prescribe. A state may not legally without permission, send its police and courts outside its borders to arrest, prosecute and punish people even for murders committed within its territory.

This chapter examines some of the bases which are accepted in the international legal system as adequate foundations for a state's prescriptive and enforcement jurisdiction. The chapter is introductory only;

jurisdictional issues will be presented in greater complexity in subsequent chapters.

5. ***The legal consequences of lack of jurisdiction.*** Under the domestic law of states these consequences are frequently different from those in the international legal system. Should a court purport to convict an alien of a crime when it lacks jurisdiction to do so under the domestic law of a state, the consequence usually will be the release of that person from imprisonment. Yet should the trial be in violation of international law rules of jurisdiction, there may be no legal consequence under the domestic law of the state involved, i.e. the person may remain in prison. On the other hand, international law provides the state of nationality of the alien victim a claim against the offending state.

6. ***Jurisdiction, vel non, not always dispositive.*** Be careful not to read too much into the term jurisdiction. To say that a state has acted outside its jurisdiction suggests an immediate legal consequence. But to say that it has acted within its jurisdiction may be only the first step in analysis. A state is considered to owe special obligations of fair treatment to aliens who are within their territory. For example, the United States is required by international law to give a fair trial to any alien arrested here. Failure to provide the alien with a fair trial gives the state of his nationality a claim against the United States, even though the United States, in trying the alien at all, acted within its rights under international rules of jurisdiction.

7. For detailed analysis of Jurisdiction, see Blakesley, Terrorism, Drugs, International Law, and the Protection of Human Liberty Chs. 2 and 3 (1992).

SECTION A. JURISDICTION TO PRESCRIBE RULES OF LAW GOVERNING CONDUCT

---

1. SUBJECTIVE TERRITORIALITY: CONDUCT WITHIN THE TERRITORY

Subjective Territoriality obtains when an element of the offense occurs within the State.

---

1. ***Meaning of conduct.*** Jurisdiction triggering conduct within the territory encompasses many forms of human behavior. Employment within the territory is conduct which a state has jurisdiction to control. The same with marriage, the acquisition of property, the disposition of wealth, the conclusion of contracts, the commission of torts, and other consequences or relationships of a private nature.

2. ***Conduct having effect outside the territory.*** Often, conduct within the territory has its effect exclusively therein. There are situa-

tions, however, where the effect of conduct within the territory takes place outside of it. Whether the effect occurs within or without the territory, the state where the "conduct" occurs has jurisdiction to prescribe rules of law dealing with it. The state in whose territory the effect may also have jurisdiction. The jurisdiction of that state is called objective territoriality. It does not affect the jurisdiction of the state where the conduct occurs.

The state in which the conduct takes place may even treat its effect outside its territory as criminal, even though it is not criminal in the affected state. Austria Supreme Court, 1972, 101 J. Dr. Int'l 632 (1974). Two Austrians assembled, arranged, and caused an illustrated book to be published by a West German publishing house. They were charged in Austria with pornography. They argued that they had committed no crime because the charges of pornography against them in West Germany had been dismissed and their illustrations were accepted there as modern art. The Austrian court rejected the argument and, though predicating jurisdiction on the ground they were Austrians, indicated that their conduct in Austria was also a basis for making their conduct criminal even though it was not punishable in Germany.

3. ***Conduct partly within and partly without the territory.*** In some situations, the conduct may consist of a series of acts, some taking place within the territory and some elsewhere. This was the *Denunciation to the Enemy Case,* Netherlands Court of Cassation, 1958, 88 Journal du Droit International 893 (1961):[a]

> Benders, an employee of the Twentsche Bank, revealed to the German authorities in 1936 that the Spier brothers, Jews of German nationality, had, contrary to the legislation then in force in Germany, placed a considerable fortune in safety in the Twentsche Bank in the Netherlands. By * * * imprisoning one of the Spier brothers and the wife of the other the German authorities were able to constrain them to return the fortune to Germany, after which, naturally under a cloak of legitimacy, it was almost entirely confiscated. The heirs sued Benders and the Bank.

> .   What is the law governing Benders' unlawful act? In order to carry out his * * * design, he went just beyond the Netherlands frontier, to make contact in Germany with Oberzollrat Kinzel of Dusseldorf. The interview consummating this betrayal, which netted 10,000 deniers for Benders, therefore took place in Germany. Was Germany therefore the locus delicti and German law for that reason applicable? The Court of Appeal of Amsterdam rightly thought that this was a little too easy. The execution of the design, the Court said, began by the compilation of documents in the offices of the Bank in the Netherlands; the infamous act was directed against a fortune in the Netherlands, while it was at the same time calculated to injure the Bank in the Netherlands. "In the light of all these facts", notes, the Court, "Benders' act took place to such

a. English text in the Journal. Reprinted with the permission of Editions Techniques, S.A., Paris.

an extent in the Netherlands that the Tribunal was fully justified in subjecting it to Netherlands law."

4. Thus, when at least one constituent element of an offense constituting [a crime] occurs within a state's territory, that state has jurisdiction based on the subjective territoriality theory. See, e.g. French Code de Procédure Pénale article 693, which provides that an offense is considered to have been committed in France when "an act characterizing one of its elements is accomplished in France." Virtually all countries utilize this principle. Even if all of the other elements of an offense (say theft) occur abroad, if one material element occurs within the state (receipt of the stolen property), it will provide jurisdiction. See, e.g. R. v. Nel, South Africa Supreme Court, App.Div. 1953, 20 Int'l L.Rptr. 192 (1957). What state would have jurisdiction in a case in which a defendant triggers a computer in one state to modify a program in another state which automatically transfers money from an account in still another state to an account in still another? Would they all have jurisdiction? For the crime of conspiracy which is culminated abroad, like in some of the cases which we will consider below, the offense is considered to have been committed in any state in which any one of the elements occurred.

5. ***Problem.*** Would the result be the same in a complicated securities fraud case, where the standard for fraud differed in the two states? Would it make a difference if the case were: (a) criminal? (b) civil?

---

2. OBJECTIVE TERRITORIALITY—CONDUCT OUTSIDE THE TERRITORY CAUSING EFFECT WITHIN

THE CUTTING CASE LETTER, SECRETARY OF STATE TO UNITED STATES AMBASSADOR TO MEXICO

[1887] Foreign Relations of the United States 751 (1888).
Department of State, Washington, November 1, 1887.

SIR: On the 19th of July, 1886, the minister of the United States at the City of Mexico was instructed to demand of the Mexican Government the release of A.K. Cutting, a citizen of the United States, then imprisoned at Paso del Norte, where he had been incarcerated since the 23rd of the preceding month on a charge of libel alleged to have been published by him in Texas.

The case was first brought to the notice of the Department by Mr. Brigham, consul of the United States at Paso del Norte, who, in a dispatch dated the 1st July, 1886, reported that Mr. Cutting had been arrested and imprisoned for the publication in Texas, in the United States, of an alleged libel against a citizen of Mexico. Accompanying the consul's dispatch were affidavits substantiating his statements. * * *

* * * It is sufficient here to state, as was set forth at the time of the demand, that the ground upon which Mr. Cutting's release was demanded was that the judicial tribunals of Mexico were not competent under the rules of international law to try a citizen of the United States for an offense committed and consummated in his own country, merely because the person offended happened to be a Mexican. * * *

* * * Not only was this claim, which is defined in Article 186 of the Mexican penal code, defended and enforced by Judge Zubia, before whom the case of Mr. Cutting was tried, and whose decision was affirmed by the supreme court of Chihuahua * * *, but the claim was defended and justified by the Mexican Government in communications to this Department, emanating both from the Mexican minister at this capital and from the department of foreign affairs in the City of Mexico.

The statement of the consul at Paso del Norte that Mr. Cutting was arrested on the charge of the publication in Texas of an alleged libel against a Mexican is fully sustained by the opinion of Judge Zubia. It is stated that on the 22nd of June, 1886, "the plaintiff enlarged the accusation, stating that although the newspaper, the El Paso Sunday Herald, is published in Texas, Mr. Cutting had had circulated a great number in this town (Paso del Norte) and in the interior of the Republic, it having been read by more than three persons, for which reason an order had been issued to seize the copies which were still in the office of the said Cutting." The conclusive inference from this statement is that the charge upon which the warrant of arrest was issued was the publication of the alleged libel in Texas. * * * It appears, however, that the claim made in Article 186 of the Mexican penal code was actually enforced in the case in question as a distinct and original ground of prosecution. The decision of Judge Zubia was framed in the alternative, and it was held that, even supposing the defamation arose solely from the publication of the alleged libel in the El Paso (Texas) Sunday Herald, Article 186 of the Mexican penal code provided for punishment in that case; Judge Zubia saying that it did not belong to the judge to examine the principle laid down in that article but to apply it fully, it being the law in force in the State of Chihuahua. It nowhere appears that the Texas publication was ever circulated in Mexico so as to constitute the crime of defamation under the Mexican law. As has been seen, this was not a part of the original charge on which the warrant for Mr. Cutting's arrest was issued; and while it is stated in Judge Zubia's decision that an order was issued for the seizure of copies of the Texas paper which might be found in the office of Mr. Cutting in Paso del Norte, it nowhere appears from that decision that any copies were actually found in that place or elsewhere in Mexico.

But, however this may be, this Government is still compelled to deny what it denied on the 19th of July, 1886, and what the Mexican Government has since executively and judicially maintained, that a citizen of the United States can be held under the rules of international law to answer in Mexico for an offense committed in the United States, simply because the object of that offense happens to be a citizen of Mexico. * * *

* * *

As to the question of international law, I am unable to discover any principle upon which the assumption of jurisdiction made in Article 186 of the Mexican penal code can be justified. There is no principle better settled than that the penal laws of a country have no extraterritorial force. Each state may, it is true, provide for the punishment of its own citizens for acts committed by them outside of its territory; but this makes the penal law a personal statute, and while it may give rise to inconvenience and injustice in many cases, it is a matter in which no other Government has the right to interfere. To say, however, that the penal laws of a country can bind foreigners and regulate their conduct, either in their own or any other foreign country, is to assert a jurisdiction over such countries and to impair their independence. Such is the consensus of opinion of the leading authorities on international law at the present day * * *. There being then no principle of international law which justifies such a pretension, any assertion of it must rest, as an exception to the rule, either upon the general concurrence of nations or upon express conventions. Such a concurrence in respect to the claim made in Article 186 of the Mexican penal code can not be found in the legislation of the present day. Though formerly asserted by a number of minor states, it has now been generally abandoned, and may be regarded as almost obsolete.

* * *

It has constantly been laid down in the United States as a rule of action, that citizens of the United States can not be held answerable in foreign countries for offenses which were wholly committed and consummated either in their own country or in other countries not subject to the jurisdiction of the punishing state. When a citizen of the United States commits in his own country a violation of its laws, it is his right to be tried under and in accordance with those laws, and in accordance with the fundamental guaranties of the Federal Constitution in respect to criminal trials in every part of the United States.

To say that he may be tried in another country for his offense, simply because its object happens to be a citizen of that country, would be to assert that foreigners coming to the United States bring hither the penal laws of the country from which they come, and thus subject citizens of the United States in their own country to an indefinite criminal responsibility. Such a pretension can never be admitted. * * *

* * *

You are therefore instructed to say to the Mexican Government, not only that an indemnity should be paid to Mr. Cutting for his arrest and detention in Mexico on the charge of publishing a libel in the United States against a Mexican, but also, in the interests of good neighborhood and future amity, that the statute proposing to confer such extraterritorial jurisdiction should, as containing a claim invasive of the independent sovereignty of a neighboring and friendly state, be repealed. * * *

* * *

T.F. BAYARD.

Query: Consider the spirit of this language again after you read the Alvarez–Machain Case, *infra* at p. 195.

————

THE S.S. "LOTUS" (FRANCE v. TURKEY)

Permanent Court of International Justice, 1927.
P.C.I.J., Ser. A, No. 10.

* * *

By a special agreement signed at Geneva on October 12th, 1926, between the Governments of the French and Turkish Republics * * *, [France and Turkey] have submitted to the Permanent Court of International Justice the question of jurisdiction which has arisen between them following upon the collision which occurred on August 2nd, 1926, between the steamships Boz–Kourt and Lotus.

According to the special agreement, the Court has to decide the following questions:

> (1) Has Turkey, contrary to Article 15 of the Convention of Lausanne of July 24th, 1923, respecting conditions of residence and business and jurisdiction, acted in conflict with the principles of international law—and if so, what principles—by instituting, following the collision which occurred on August 2nd, 1926, on the high seas between the French steamer Lotus and the Turkish steamer Boz–Kourt and upon the arrival of the French steamer at Constantinople—as well as against the captain of the Turkish steamship— joint criminal proceedings in pursuance of Turkish law against M. Demons, officer of the watch on board the Lotus at the time of the collision, in consequence of the loss of the Boz–Kourt having involved the death of eight Turkish sailors and passengers?

* * *

On August 2nd, 1926, just before midnight, a collision occurred between the French mail steamer Lotus, proceeding to Constantinople, and the Turkish collier Boz–Kourt, between five and six nautical miles to the north of Cape Sigri (Mitylene). The Boz–Kourt, which was cut in two, sank, and eight Turkish nationals who were on board perished. After having done everything possible to succour the shipwrecked persons, of whom ten were able to be saved, the Lotus continued on its course to Constantinople, where it arrived on August 3rd.

At the time of the collision, the officer of the watch on board the Lotus was Monsieur Demons, a French citizen, lieutenant in the merchant service and first officer of the ship, whilst the movements of the

Boz–Kourt were directed by its captain, Hassan Bey, who was one of those saved from the wreck.

* * *

On August 5th, Lieutenant Demons was requested by the Turkish authorities to go ashore to give evidence. The examination, the length of which incidentally resulted in delaying the departure of the Lotus, led to the placing under arrest of Lieutenant Demons—without previous notice being given to the French Consul–General—and Hassan Bey, amongst others. This arrest, which has been characterized by the Turkish Agent as arrest pending trial (arrestation préventive), was effected in order to ensure that the criminal prosecution instituted against the two officers, on a charge of manslaughter, by the Public Prosecutor of Stamboul, on the complaint of the families of the victims of the collision, should follow its normal course.

The case was first heard by the Criminal Court of Stamboul on August 28th. * * * Lieutenant Demons submitted that the Turkish Courts had no jurisdiction; the Court, however, overruled his objection. * * *

On September 15th, the Criminal Court delivered its judgment, the terms of which have not been communicated to the Court by the Parties. It is, however, common ground, that it sentenced Lieutenant Demons to eighty days' imprisonment and a fine of twenty-two pounds, Hassan Bey being sentenced to a slightly more severe penalty.

* * *

The action of the Turkish judicial authorities with regard to Lieutenant Demons at once gave rise to many diplomatic representations and other steps on the part of the French Government or its representatives in Turkey, either protesting against the arrest of Lieutenant Demons or demanding his release, or with a view to obtaining the transfer of the case from the Turkish Courts to the French Courts.

As a result of these representations, the Government of the Turkish Republic declared on September 2nd, 1926, that "it would have no objection to the reference of the conflict of jurisdiction to the Court at The Hague". The French Government having, on the 6th of the same month, given "its full consent to the proposed solution", the two Governments appointed their plenipotentiaries with a view to the drawing up of the special agreement to be submitted to the Court; this special agreement was signed at Geneva on October 12th, 1926, * * *.

* * *

I

Before approaching the consideration of the principles of international law contrary to which Turkey is alleged to have acted—thereby infringing the terms of Article 15 of the Convention of Lausanne of July 24th, 1923, respecting conditions of residence and business and jurisdiction—, it is necessary to define, in the light of the written and oral proceedings, the position resulting from the special agreement. * * *

1.   The collision which occurred * * *, between the S.S. Lotus, flying the French flag, and the S.S. Boz–Kourt, flying the Turkish flag, took place on the high seas: the territorial jurisdiction of any State other than France and Turkey therefore does not enter into account.

2.   The violation, if any, of the principles of international law would have consisted in the taking of criminal proceedings against Lieutenant Demons.   It is not therefore a question relating to any particular step in these proceedings—such as his being put to trial, his arrest, his detention pending trial or the judgment given by the Criminal Court of Stamboul—but of the very fact of the Turkish Courts exercising criminal jurisdiction.   That is why the arguments put forward by the Parties in both phases of the proceedings relate exclusively to the question whether Turkey has or has not, according to the principles of international law, jurisdiction to prosecute in this case.

The discussions have borne exclusively upon the question whether criminal jurisdiction does or does not exist in this case.

3.   The prosecution was instituted because the loss of the Boz–Kourt involved the death of eight Turkish sailors and passengers.   * * * It is * * * a case of prosecution for involuntary manslaughter.   * * * There is no doubt that [the death of the victims] may be regarded as the direct outcome of the collision, and the French Government has not contended that this relation of cause and effect cannot exist.

* * *

5.   The prosecution was instituted in pursuance of Turkish legislation.   * * *

Article 6 of the Turkish Penal Code, * * * runs as follows:

> [Translation] Any foreigner who, apart from the cases contemplated by Article 4, commits an offence abroad to the prejudice of Turkey or of a Turkish subject, for which offence Turkish law prescribes a penalty involving loss of freedom for a minimum period of not less than one year, shall be punished in accordance with the Turkish Penal Code provided that he is arrested in Turkey.   * * *

* * *

Even if the Court must hold that the Turkish authorities had seen fit to base the prosecution of Lieutenant Demons upon the above-mentioned Article 6, the question submitted to the Court is not whether that article is compatible with the principles of international law; it is more general.   The Court is asked to state whether or not the principles of international law prevent Turkey from instituting criminal proceedings against Lieutenant Demons under Turkish law.   Neither the conformity of Article 6 in itself with the principles of international law nor the application of that article by the Turkish authorities constitutes the point at issue; it is the very fact of the institution of proceedings which is held by France to be contrary to those principles.   * * *

II

Having determined the position resulting from the terms of the special agreement, the Court must now ascertain which were the principles of international law that the prosecution of Lieutenant Demons could conceivably be said to contravene.

It is Article 15 of the Convention of Lausanne of July 24th, 1923, respecting conditions of residence and business and jurisdiction, which refers the contracting Parties to the principles of international law as regards the delimitation of their respective jurisdiction.

This clause is as follows:

> Subject to the provisions of Article 16, all questions of jurisdiction shall, as between Turkey and the other contracting Powers, be decided in accordance with the principles of international law.

* * * In these circumstances it is impossible—except in pursuance of a definite stipulation—to construe the expression "principles of international law" otherwise than as meaning the principles which are in force between all independent nations and which therefore apply equally to all the contracting Parties.

* * *

III

* * * The French Government contends that the Turkish Courts, * * * to have jurisdiction, should be able to point to some title to jurisdiction recognized by international law in favour of Turkey. * * * The Turkish Government takes the view that Article 15 allows Turkey jurisdiction whenever such jurisdiction does not * * * conflict with a principle of international law.

* * *

International law governs relations between independent States. The rules of law binding upon States therefore emanate from their own free will as expressed in conventions or by usages generally accepted as expressing principles of law and established in order to regulate the relations between these co-existing independent communities or with a view to the achievement of common aims. Restrictions upon the independence of States cannot therefore be presumed.

Now the first and foremost restriction imposed by international law upon a State is that—failing the existence of a permissive rule to the contrary—it may not exercise its power in any form in the territory of another State. In this sense jurisdiction is certainly territorial; it cannot be exercised by a State outside its territory except by virtue of a permissive rule derived from international custom or from a convention.

It does not, however, follow that international law prohibits a State from exercising jurisdiction in its own territory, in respect of any case which relates to acts which have taken place abroad, and in which it cannot rely on some permissive rule of international law. Such a view would only be tenable if international law contained a general prohibition to States to extend the application of their laws and the jurisdiction of their courts to persons, property and acts outside their territory, and if, as an exception to this general prohibition, it allowed States to do so in certain specific cases.   But this is certainly not the case under international law as it stands at present.   Far from laying down a general prohibition to the effect that States may not extend the application of their laws and the jurisdiction of their courts to persons, property and acts outside their territory, it leaves them in this respect a wide measure of discretion which is only limited in certain cases by prohibitive rules; as regards other cases, every State remains free to adopt the principles which it regards as best and most suitable.

This discretion left to States by international law explains the great variety of rules which they have been able to adopt without objections or complaints on the part of other States; it is * * * to remedy the difficulties resulting from such variety that efforts have been made for many years past, both in Europe and America, to prepare conventions the effect of which would be precisely to limit the discretion at present left to States in this respect by international law, thus making good the existing lacunae in respect of jurisdiction or removing the conflicting jurisdictions arising from the diversity of the principles * * * [in] various States.

In these circumstances, all that can be required of a State is that it should not overstep the limits which international law places upon its jurisdiction; within these limits, its title to exercise jurisdiction rests in its sovereignty.   It follows from the foregoing that the contention of the French Government to the effect that Turkey must in each case be able to cite a rule of international law authorizing her to exercise jurisdiction, is opposed to the generally accepted international law to which Article 15 of the Convention of Lausanne refers.   * * *

* * *

The Court therefore must * * * ascertain whether * * * there exists a rule of international law limiting the freedom of States to extend the criminal jurisdiction of their courts to a situation uniting the circumstances of the present case.

IV

The Court will now proceed to ascertain whether general international law, to which Article 15 of the Convention of Lausanne refers, contains a rule prohibiting Turkey from prosecuting Lieutenant Demons.

For this purpose, it will in the first place examine the value of the arguments advanced by the French Government, without however omitting to take into account other possible aspects of the problem, which might show the existence of a restrictive rule applicable in this case.

The arguments advanced by the French Government [include]:

(1) International law does not allow a State to take proceedings with regard to offences committed by foreigners abroad, simply by reason of the nationality of the victim; and such is the situation in the present

case because the offence must be regarded as having been committed on board the French vessel.

* * *

As regards the first argument, the Court * * * [recalls] that its examination is strictly confined to the specific situation in the present case, for it is only in regard to this situation that its decision is asked for.

* * * The characteristic features of the situation of fact are as follows: there has been a collision on the high seas between two vessels flying different flags, on one of which was one of the persons alleged to be guilty of the offence, whilst the victims were on board the other.

This being so, the Court does not think it necessary to consider the contention that a State cannot punish offences committed abroad by a foreigner simply by reason of the nationality of the victim. For this contention only relates to the case where the nationality of the victim is the only criterion on which the criminal jurisdiction of the State is based. Even if that argument were correct generally speaking—and in regard to this the Court reserves its opinion—it could only be used in the present case if international law forbade Turkey to take into consideration the fact that the offence produced its effects on the Turkish vessel and consequently in a place assimilated to Turkish territory in which the application of Turkish criminal law cannot be challenged, even in regard to offences committed there by foreigners. But no such rule of international law exists. No argument has come to the knowledge of the Court from which it could be deduced that States recognize themselves to be under an obligation towards each other only to have regard to the place where the author of the offence happens to be at the time of the offence. On the contrary, it is certain that the courts of many countries, even of countries which have given their criminal legislation a strictly territorial character, interpret criminal law in the sense that offences, the authors of which at the moment of commission are in the territory of another State, are nevertheless to be regarded as having been committed in the national territory, if one of the constituent elements of the offence, and more especially its effects, have taken place there. French courts have, in regard to a variety of situations, given decisions sanctioning this way of interpreting the territorial principle. Again, the Court does not know of any cases in which governments have protested against the fact that the criminal law of some country contained a rule to this effect or that the courts of a country construed their criminal law in this sense. Consequently, once it is admitted that the effects of the offence were produced on the Turkish vessel, it becomes impossible to hold that there is a rule of international law which prohibits Turkey from prosecuting Lieutenant Demons because of the fact that the author of the offence was on board the French ship. Since, as has already been observed, the special agreement does not deal with the provision of Turkish law under which the prosecution was instituted, but only with the question whether the prosecution should be regarded as contrary to the principles of international law, there is no reason preventing the Court from confining itself to observing that, in this case, a prosecution may also be justified from the point of view of the so-called territorial principle.

* * * The fact that the judicial authorities may have committed an error in their choice of the legal provision applicable to the particular case and compatible with international law only concerns municipal law and can only affect international law in so far as a treaty provision enters into account, or the possibility of a denial of justice arises.

* * *

The offence for which Lieutenant Demons appears to have been prosecuted was an act—of negligence or imprudence—having its origin on board the Lotus, whilst its effects made themselves felt on board the Boz–Kourt. These two elements are, legally, entirely inseparable, so much so that their separation renders the offence nonexistent. Neither the exclusive jurisdiction of either State, nor the limitations of the jurisdiction of either State, nor the limitations of the jurisdiction of each to the occurrences which took place on the respective ships would appear calculated to satisfy the requirements of justice and effectively to protect the interests of the two States. It is only natural that each should be able to exercise jurisdiction and to do so in respect of the incident as a whole. It is therefore a case of concurrent jurisdiction.

* * *

For These Reasons, the COURT, having heard both Parties, gives, by the President's casting vote—the votes being equally divided—, judgment to the effect

(1) that, following the collision which occurred on August 2nd, 1926, on the high seas between the French steamship Lotus and the Turkish steamship Boz–Kourt, and upon the arrival of the French ship at Stamboul, and in consequence of the loss of the Boz–Kourt having involved the death of eight Turkish nationals, Turkey, by instituting criminal proceedings in pursuance of Turkish law against Lieutenant Demons, officer of the watch on board the Lotus at the time of the collision, has not acted in conflict with the principles of international law, contrary to Article 15 of the Convention of Lausanne of July 24th, 1923, respecting conditions of residence and business and jurisdiction;

* * *

[Separate and dissenting opinions omitted.]

---

1. **Question.** Does the *Lotus* decision state (a) a rule of jurisdiction in international law or (b) the legal consequences of the lack of a rule of international law?

2. **Current rule as to prosecution for high seas collision.** Article 11 of the 1958 Convention on the High Seas and Article 97 of the United Nations Convention on the Law of the Sea, both provide:

In the event of a collision * * * concerning a ship on the high seas, involving the penal or disciplinary responsibility of the master or of any person in the service of the ship, no penal or disciplinary proceedings may be instituted against such persons except before the judicial or administrative authorities either of the flag state or of the state of which such person is a national. [The text of both conventions is in the Doc. Supp.]

The grand old *Alcoa case* developed the classic aspects of the effects doctrine. Consider *Alcoa* and, what is perhaps its European counterpart, *Wood Pulp Cartel*, which follow: For more on this and its further development, see our section on resolution of jurisdictional conflicts, infra at p. 224.

UNITED STATES v. ALUMINUM CO. OF AMERICA

United States Court of Appeals, Second Circuit, 1945.
148 F.2d 416, 442.

[This was a prosecution for violation of the Sherman Act. One of the defendants was Aluminum Limited, a Canadian corporation formed to take over properties of the Aluminum Company of America outside the United States. Not quite half of each company's shares were owned by the same group of individuals. The court was concerned about the participation of each company in a foreign cartel, called the Alliance. The court concluded that the American company, Alcoa, was not a party to the Alliance and "did not join in any violation of § 1 of the Act, so far as concerned foreign commerce." Judge Learned Hand opines:]

Whether "Limited" itself violated that section depends upon the character of the "Alliance." It was a Swiss corporation, created in pursuance of an agreement entered into on July 3, 1931, the signatories to which were a French corporation, two German, one Swiss, a British, and "Limited." The original agreement, or "cartel," provided for the formation of a corporation in Switzerland which should issue shares, to be taken up by the signatories. This corporation was from time to time to fix a quota of production for each share, and each shareholder was to be limited to the quantity measured by the number of shares it held, but was free to sell at any price it chose. The corporation fixed a price every year at which it would take off any shareholder's hands any part of its quota which it did not sell. No shareholder was to "buy, borrow, fabricate or sell" aluminum produced by anyone not a shareholder except with the consent of the board of governors, but that must not be "unreasonably withheld." * * *

The agreement of 1936 abandoned the system of unconditional quotas, and substituted a system of royalties. Each shareholder was to have a fixed free quota for every share it held, but as its production exceeded the sum of its quotas, it was to pay a royalty, graduated progressively in proportion to the excess; and these royalties the "Alliance" divided among the shareholders in proportion to their shares. This agreement—unlike the first—did not contain an express promise that the "Alliance" would buy any undisposed of stocks at a fixed price, although perhaps [part of the agreement] may have impliedly recognized such an obligation. Probably during the two years in which the shareholders operated under this agreement, that question did not arise for the demand for aluminum was very active. Nevertheless, we understand from "Limited's" answer to an interrogatory that the last price fixed under the agreement of 1931 was understood to remain in force. Although this agreement, like its predecessor, was silent as to imports into the United States, when that question arose during its preparation, as it did, all the shareholders agreed that such imports should be included in the quotas. The German companies were exempted from royalties—for obvious reasons—and that, it would seem, for practical purposes put them out of the "cartel" for the future, for it was scarcely possible that a German producer would be unable to dispose of all its production, at least within any future period that would be provided for. The shareholders continued this agreement unchanged until the end of March, 1938, by which time it had become plain that, at least for the time being, it was no longer of service to anyone. Nothing was, however, done to end it, although the German shareholders of course became enemies of the French, British and Canadian shareholders in 1939. The "Alliance" itself has apparently never been dissolved; and indeed it appeared on the "Proclaimed List of Blocked Nationals" of September 13, 1944.

Did either the agreement of 1931 or that of 1936 violate § 1 of the Act? The answer does not depend upon whether we shall recognize as a source of liability a liability imposed by another state. * * * We are concerned only with whether Congress chose to attach liability to the conduct outside the United States of persons not in allegiance to it. That being so, the only question open is whether Congress intended to impose the liability, and whether our own Constitution permitted it to do so: as a court of the United States, we cannot look beyond our own law. Nevertheless, it is quite true that we are not to read general words, such as those in this Act, without regard to the limitations customarily observed by nations upon the exercise of their powers; limitations which generally correspond to those fixed by the "Conflict of Laws." We should not impute to Congress an intent to punish all whom its courts can catch, for conduct which has no consequences within the United States. American Banana Co. v. United Fruit Co.; United States v. Bowman; Blackmer v. United States; on the other hand, *it is settled law*—as "Limited" itself agrees—*that any state may impose liabilities, even upon persons not within its allegiance, for conduct outside its borders that has consequences within its borders which the state reprehends*;[a] and these liabilities other states will ordinarily recognize. Strassheim v. Daily. * * * It may be be argued that this Act extends further. Two situations are possible. There may be agreements made beyond our borders not intended to affect imports, which do affect them, or which affect exports. Almost any limitation of the supply of goods in Europe, for example, or in South America, may have repercussions in the United States if there is trade between the two. Yet when one considers the international complications likely to arise from an effort in this country to treat such agreements as unlawful, it is safe to assume that Congress certainly did not intend the Act to cover them. Such agreements may on the other hand intend to include imports into the United

---

a. Emphasis supplied by the editors.

States, and yet it may appear that they have had no effect upon them. That situation might be thought to fall within the doctrine that intent may be a substitute for performance in the case of a contract made within the United States; or it might be thought to fall within the doctrine that a statute should not be interpreted to cover acts abroad which have no consequence here. We shall not choose between these alternatives; but for argument we shall assume that the Act does not cover agreements, even though intended to affect imports or exports, unless its performance is shown actually to have had some effect upon them. Where both conditions are satisfied, the situation certainly falls within such decisions as United States v. Pacific & Artic R. & Navigation Co.; Thomsen v. Cayser; and United States v. Sisal Sales Corporation (United States v. Nord Deutcher Lloyd, illustrates the same conception in another field.) * * *

Both agreements would clearly have been unlawful, had they been made within the United States; and it follows from what we have just said that both were unlawful, though made abroad, if they were intended to affect imports and did affect them. Since the shareholders almost at once agreed that the agreement of 1931 should not cover imports, we may ignore it and confine our discussion to that of 1936: indeed that we should have to do anyway, since it superseded the earlier agreement. The judge found that it was not the purpose of the agreement to "suppress or restrain the exportation of aluminum to the United States for sale in competition with Alcoa." By that we understand that he meant that the agreement was not specifically directed to "Alcoa," because it only applied generally to the production of the shareholders. If he meant that it was not expected that the general restriction upon production would have an effect upon imports, we cannot agree, for the change made in 1936 was deliberate and was expressly made to accomplish just that. It would have been an idle gesture, unless the shareholders had supposed that it would, or at least might, have that effect. The first of the conditions which we mentioned was therefore satisfied; the intent was to set up a quota system for imports.

The judge also found that the 1936 agreement did not "materially affect the * * * foreign trade or commerce of the United States"; apparently because the imported ingot was greater in 1936 and 1937 than in earlier years. We cannot accept this finding, based as it was upon the fact that, in 1936, 1937 and the first quarter of 1938, the gross imports of ingot increased. It by no means follows from such an increase that the agreement did not restrict imports; and incidentally it so happens that in those years such inference as is possible at all, leads to the opposite conclusion. It is true that the average imports— including "Alcoa's"—for the years 1932–1935 inclusive were about 15 million pounds, and that for 1936, 1937 and one-fourth of 1938 they were about 33 million pounds; but the average domestic ingot manufacture in the first period was about 96 million and in the second about 262 million; so that the proportion of imports to domestic ingot was about 15.6 per cent for the first period and about 12.6 per cent for the second. We do not mean to infer from this that the quota system of 1936 did in fact restrain imports, as these figures might suggest; but we do mean that nothing is to be inferred from the gross increase of imports. We shall dispose of the matter therefore upon the assumption that, although the shareholders intended to restrict imports, it does not appear whether in fact they did so. Upon our hypothesis the plaintiff would therefore fail, if it carried the burden of proof upon this issue as upon others. We think, however, that, after the intent to affect imports was proved, the burden of proof shifted to "Limited." In the first place a depressant upon production which applies generally may be assumed, ceteris paribus, to distribute its effect evenly upon all markets. Again, when the parties took the trouble specifically to make the depressant apply to a given market, there is reason to suppose that they expected that it would have some effect, which it could have only by lessening what would otherwise have been imported. If the motive they introduced was overbalanced in all instances by motives which induced the shareholders to import, if the United States market became so attractive that the royalties did not count at all and their expectations were in fact defeated, they to whom the facts were more accessible than to the plaintiff ought to prove it, for a prima facie case had been made. Moreover, there is an especial propriety in demanding this of "Limited," because it was "Limited" which procured the inclusion in the agreement of 1936 of imports in the quotas.

There remains only the question whether this assumed restriction had any influence upon prices * * *. To that Socony–Vacuum Oil Co. v. United States, *supra*, is an entire answer. * * * The underlying doctrine was that all factors which contribute to determine prices, must be kept free to operate unhampered by agreements. For these reasons we think that the agreement of 1936 violated § 1 of the Act.

* * *

———

1. *Why was a circuit court decision this important?* This case has the theoretical standing of a Supreme Court decision, because it was decided on certification and transfer from the Supreme Court for lack of a quorum of qualified justices. The Supreme Court has decided other antitrust cases along similar lines: United States v. Sisal Sales Corp., 274 U.S. 268 (1927); United States v. Holophane Co., 352 U.S. 903 (1956) (per curiam affirmance of lower court order under the Sherman Act requiring the defendants to compete actively in foreign markets); Continental Ore Co. v. Union Carbide & Carbon Corp., 370 U.S. 690 (1962). In the 1911 dissolution of the American Tobacco Trust in United States v. American Tobacco Co., 221 U.S. 106 (1910), the decree ran to the British–American Tobacco Company, a United Kingdom company.

2. *The economic effects doctrine and antitrust jurisdictional conflicts.* The U.S. and other nations have traditionally tried to exclude economic impacts within state territory resulting from conduct outside. The rationale is that such effects, unlike bullets and poisoned chocolates, are not palpable. Today, however, the prevailing view in the

developed world (with little or no views from the other) is that foreign economic activity is within a state's prescriptive jurisdiction if it produces discernibly significant economic damage to the state's interests. Both the 1965 and 1987 Restatements take this position as a matter of customary international law. National legislation explicitly linked to recognition of the effects doctrine exists in Germany and seems implicit in the economic regulatory laws of some other states. The economic effects doctrine is recognized and asserted by the Commission (executive) of the European Community (European Union). It was the basis of decision by the European Community Court of Justice in Beguelin *Import Co. v. G.L. Import Export SA,* 11 Comm.Mkt.L.Rep. 81. The *Avocat–Général* of the Court of Justice recommended, not long after this decision, in the Dyestuffs *Cartel case* against Imperial Chemicals Industries, that cartels located outside the Community be reached under the effects doctrine, but the Court chose to apply Community antitrust law on the ground that such external parent companies had wholly-owned subsidiaries within the Community. Imperial Chemical Industries Ltd. v. E.C. Commission, 11 Comm.Mkt.L.R. 557 (1972). Most expert opinion traditionally regarded the Beguelin precedent as unaffected by the Dyestuffs decision, in as much as the British, then not in the Community, were so strongly opposed to the application of Community law to Imperial Chemicals Industries under the effects doctrine. The Court therefore, was considered to have been induced to reach its result on the corporate control ground. The European approach was "updated" in the "Wood Pulp" case, *infra.* The materials that follow *infra* in this deal with the roles of courts as to clashes of states' interests in antitrust situations. National legislative, diplomatic, and treaty-making activities have not been significant.

3. *Interesting recent scholarship on extraterritorial jurisdiction and Antitrust, includes the following:* Deanna Conn, Assessing the Impact of Preferential Trade Agreements and New Rules of Origin on the Extraterritorial Application of Antitrust Law to International Mergers, 93 Colum.L.Rev. 119 (1993); Waller, A Unified Theory of Transnational Procedure, 26 Cornell Int'l L.J. 101 (1993) (good brief overview of the "current doctrinal mess in which the courts have required the endless repetition of the same or similar balancing tests for most of the important procedural and jurisdictional issues in transnational litigation"); Born, A Reappraisal of the Extraterritorial Reach of U.S. Law, 24 Law & Pol'y Int'l Bus. 1 (1992) (excellent, long, involved article tracing the historical evolution of extraterritorial jurisdiction, applying the thesis of liberalization of extraterritoriality through abandonment of the territorial presumption); Weintraub, The Extraterritorial Application of Antitrust and Securities Laws: An Inquiry Into the Utility of a "Choice-of-Law" Approach, 70 Tex.L.Rev. 1799 (1992) (excellent article, a bit heavy on the American vision of the "interest approach," but applying "choice-of-law" and notions of comity); Alford, The Extraterritorial Application of Antitrust Laws: The United States and the European Community Approaches, 33 Va.J.Int'l L. 1 (1992); Friedberg, The Convergence of Law in an Era of Political Integration: *Wood Pulp and Alcoa Effects Doctrine,* 52 U.Pitt.L.Rev. 289 (1991).

*Have the Europeans embraced the effects theory in the antitrust arena?
See what you think of their approach in the Wood Pulp case, which
follows.* First read the argument of the *Avocat–Général*.

RE WOOD PULP CARTEL, A. AHLSTRÖM OSAKEYHTIÖ AND OTHERS v. COMMISSION OF THE EUROPEAN COMMUNITIES

Concerted practices between undertakings established in non-member countries affecting selling prices to purchasers established in the Community

Joined Cases, Nos. 89, 104, 114, 116, 117, and 125–129/85 [1988] E.C.R. 5193

Opinion of M. Avocat–Général Darmon

(Delivered 25 May 1988).
[1988] E.C.R. 5214.

Mr. President,
Members of the Court,

* * *

1. * * * the issue [relates to] of the Community's jurisdiction to apply the competition rules of the Treaty to undertakings in non-member countries. * * *

* * *

3. It is the basis on which the Commission relied in its contested decision in order to establish its jurisdiction—namely the location of the effects—which is challenged by the applicants and disapproved of by the United Kingdom. Whatever its position on this matter may have been in other contexts and even if, as some have been at pains to point out, the Commission has tended in its documents to rely at times on the location of the effects and at other times on the location of the anti-competitive conduct, it seems to me that it must be on the basis of the former that the issue of Community jurisdiction is decided.

4. In that respect, I differ with the United Kingdom, which has asked the Court to resolve this dispute by holding that this case involves the exercise of territorial jurisdiction, which is accepted both by Community law and by international law.

5. The opponents of the effects doctrine have sought to make out their case against it on the basis of arguments derived from both Community law and international law. Thus the objection to the Commission's decision is that neither Community law nor international law authorizes the application of the Community competition rules to undertakings established outside the Community solely by reason of the effects produced within the Community.

I—The effects doctrine in the light of Community law

7. * * * [T]he challenge to the Community's jurisdiction to apply its competition rules to undertakings established outside the Community

rests on two considerations. In the first place, it is said that there is nothing in the wording of Article 85 of the Treaty to allow it to be extended to cover undertakings outside the Community solely by reason of anti-competitive effects produced within the territory of the Community. Secondly, it is suggested that the case-law of the Court can be construed as rejecting the effects doctrine. * * * I will advise the Court to uphold neither of those objections.

(1) *The wording of Article 85*

8. The wording of Article 85 of the Treaty offers general support for the proposition that Community competition law is applicable, by its very essence, whenever anti-competitive effects have been produced within the territory of the Community. The effect on trade between Member States constitutes the demarcating criterion between Community jurisdiction and national jurisdiction in the matter. It is agreements, decisions and concerted practices which have as their object or effect the prevention, restriction or distortion of competition within the common market that are prohibited and declared incompatible with the Treaty.

9. * * * The vast majority of academic writers take the view that it is neither the nationality nor the geographical location of the undertaking but the location of the anti-competitive effect which constitutes the criterion for the application of Community competition law.

     * * *

(2) *Principles laid down by the Court in its case-law*

11. Although the Court has not, in its decisions to date, formally upheld the effects doctrine with regard to the application of competition law to undertakings outside the Community, that does not imply that it rejects the doctrine.

12. The cases most frequently cited in this connection are the so-called 'Dyestuffs' cases. In its judgments of 14 July 1972, although Mr. Advocate General Mayras had suggested that the Court adopt the criterion of the effects, albeit the qualified effects, in order to establish the Community's jurisdiction over undertakings outside its territory, the Court preferred to base such jurisdiction on the unity of the undertaking. But that certainly does not mean that the location of the effects would not constitute a sufficient basis for jurisdiction. * * *

13. Nor is it possible to infer from the Court's judgments in that field conclusive arguments in favour of the effects doctrine, even though some of those judgments contain statements which may go some way towards supporting it. * * *.

14. In other words, the case-law * * * is not conclusive either for or against the effects doctrine as the criterion for the applicability of Community law to undertakings situated outside the Community.

     * * *

II—The effects doctrine in the light of international law

19. The two undisputed bases on which State jurisdiction is founded under international law are *territoriality* and *nationality*. The former

confers jurisdiction on the State in which the person or the goods in question are situated or the event in question took place. The latter confers jurisdiction over nationals of the State concerned.

20. Territoriality itself has given rise to two distinct principles of jurisdiction:

(i) *subjective* territoriality, which permits a State to deal with acts which originated within its territory, even though they were completed abroad,

(ii) *objective* territoriality, which, conversely, permits a State to deal with acts which originated abroad but which were completed, at least in part, within its own territory.

21. The principle of objective territoriality has played a decisive role in the extension of national jurisdiction in the field of competition. From it is derived the effects doctrine, which, in order to deal with the effects in question, confers jurisdiction upon a State even if the conduct which produced them did not take place within its territory.

22. Is the location of effects doctrine, as a basis for jurisdiction, consistent with the rules of international law? In order to answer that question, it is necessary first of all to consider the very nature of international law. Is it law which confers powers, so that a State seeking to exercise its jurisdiction must establish the existence of a permissive rule of international law? Or is it, on the contrary, a law which respects all the powers of the State—a corollary of sovereignty— and merely sets certain limits to the exercise of such sovereignty which, in the absence of prohibitive rules, remains intact?

23. Academic * * * discussion has revolved essentially around the significance and scope of the *Lotus* judgment, delivered on 7 September 1927 by the Permanent Court of International Justice. That judgment, adopted by the President's casting vote, states in particular that international law does not prohibit a State:

> from exercising jurisdiction in its own territory, in respect of any case which relates to acts which have taken place abroad, and in which it cannot rely on some permissive rule of international law. Such a view would only be tenable if international law contained a general prohibition to States to extend the application of their laws and the jurisdiction of their courts to persons, property and acts outside their territory, and if, as an exception to this general prohibition, it allowed States to do so in certain specific cases. But this is certainly not the case under international law as it stands at present. Far from laying down a general prohibition to the effect that States may not extend the application of their laws and the jurisdiction of their courts to persons, property and acts outside their territory, it leaves them in this respect a wide measure of discretion which is only limited in certain cases by prohibitive rules; as regards other cases, every State remains free to adopt the principle which it regards as best and most suitable. * * *

The full force of that statement becomes apparent if it is read in conjunction with the Permanent Court's declaration that 'international law governs relations between independent States' and that 'restrictions upon the independence of States cannot therefore be presumed'.

* * *

25.   Another passage in the *Lotus* judgment has been relied upon by certain writers * * * to limit its scope with regard to recognition of the effects doctrine as a basis for State jurisdiction.   The Permanent Court pointed out that even the courts of countries which have a strictly territorial conception of their criminal legislation interpret it in such a way as to include within its scope offences, even if committed abroad, if 'one of the constituent elements of the offence, and more especially its effects' have taken place within the national territory.   The Permanent Court goes on to point out * * * that, in that case, the act and its effects 'are, legally, entirely inseparable', which has led certain writers to argue that only circumstances of that kind permit a State to exercise its jurisdiction by virtue of the principle of objective territoriality.

26.   However, on the assumption that the Permanent Court wished, in so doing, to circumscribe the jurisdiction of the State based on objective territoriality to cases in which the effect produced within its territory was itself a constituent element of the offence, that would have no bearing on the application of the Community competition rules to undertakings established outside the Community.   It should be recalled that Article 85 of the Treaty prohibits any agreements, decisions—and concerted practices which have as their effect 'the prevention, restriction or distortion of competition within the common market'.   Is not such an effect necessarily a constituent element of the offence?   That was the view taken by Mr. Advocate General Mayras when he stated that 'in competition law the effect of the offence is in fact one of its constituent elements and probably even the essential element'.

27.   Accordingly, even though, for other reasons, the question has been asked 'is the Lotus still sailing', there would appear to be no doubt that the principle thus laid down, which has admittedly been criticized by academic writers but has not so far been contradicted by international case-law, permits the conclusion to be drawn that consideration of the location of the effects as the basis of a State's jurisdiction is in conformity with the rules of international law.   And what is thus permissible for States must necessarily also be permissible for the Community, as a subject of international law, where the jurisdiction of the Community has been substituted for that of the Member States.

28.   The jurisdiction thus conferred is 'jurisdiction to prescribe'.   It cannot be understood as constituting 'jurisdiction to enforce', which is the 'power of a State to give effect to a general rule or an individual decision by means of substantive implementing measures which may include even coercion by the authorities'.   That opinion is widely shared by those academic writers who accept that the effects doctrine may constitute a basis for the assertion of jurisdiction by the State.   Moreover, it is essentially against measures taken pursuant to enforcement jurisdiction that some 20 countries have adopted so-called 'blocking statutes'.   But the question * * * whether the power to impose a fine

comes within the scope of prescriptive jurisdiction or enforcement jurisdiction.

* * *

IV—Suggested jurisdictional criteria

47. The difficulties encountered in this area illustrate clearly that territoriality, as a connecting factor, does not make it possible to resolve all the problems connected with the scale and nature of contemporary international trade. According to Professor Mann, an inflexible territoriality principle is no longer suited to the modern world. The same view is taken by Professor Prosper Weil.

* * *

48. This assessment has led different writers to devise different criteria for the extraterritorial application of laws. Sir Robert Jennings, for example, considers that under international law a State is entitled to exercise extraterritorial jurisdiction where its legitimate interests are concerned but that it may not abuse that right. There is abuse where the exercise of extraterritorial jurisdiction constitutes interference with the exercise of the local territorial jurisdiction. * * * Advocating that jurisdiction should be based on 'closeness of connection', Professor Mann considers 'that a State has (legislative) jurisdiction, if its contact with a given set of facts is so close, so substantial, so direct, so weighty, that legislation in respect of them is in harmony with international law and its various aspects (including the practice of States, the principles of non-interference and reciprocity and the demands of interdependence)'.

* * * A mere political, economic, commercial or social interest does not constitute a close connection. In the case, more particularly, of the law of competition, he considers that the effect, whether intended, foreseeable or, a fortiori, unanticipated, cannot establish a connection of that kind.

49. Other writers suggest that the jurisdiction of the State in which 'the primary effect' of the act is felt should be recognized. To determine whether the effect is primary or secondary, it is necessary to take a twofold factor into consideration: is the effect produced within the State concerned more direct and more substantial than the effect produced in other States. It is suggested that that approach permits jurisdiction to be exercised only by States having a legitimate interest therein. * * * [I]nternational law does not preclude concurrent jurisdiction. * * * [A]ccording to some writers, the development of customary international law leads to the emergence of certain specific limitations on the extraterritorial exercise of a State's jurisdiction. Thus, international law would prohibit the extraterritorial application of domestic law where it might give rise to conflicting obligations, or provoke conflicts of jurisdiction.

50. * * * Those * * * concerns are, for the most part, taken into account by the adoption of the criterion of qualified effect. That criterion, which does not conflict with any prohibitive rule of interna-

tional law, has gained wide acceptance in the practice of States. [I]t is, on objective grounds, particularly appropriate in view of the specific nature of competition law, as a law designed to regulate market conditions and safeguard 'ordre public' in the economic context. It is on the basis of those considerations and of the criteria of international law that it is necessary to define the characteristics of an effect whose location justifies the assertion of prescriptive jurisdiction over undertakings established outside the Community.

* * *

52. According to the substantive provisions of Community law, the restriction of competition must be 'perceptible' or 'appreciable'. The adverse affect on competition may be either direct or indirect and objectively or reasonably foreseeable. Those are the characteristics of the effect envisaged as a constituent element of interference with freedom of competition within the Community.

53. * * * Not all of those characteristics have to be adopted if the effect is taken as the criterion of extraterritorial jurisdiction. The most important reservation in that regard concerns indirect effect. * * * [M]r. Advocate General Mayras suggested, in his Opinion in the 'Dyestuffs' cases, the adoption of the criterion of the direct and immediate, reasonably foreseeable and substantial effect, I agree with that solution and, for the reasons which he sets forth, I would adopt his analysis:

'Surely the Commission would be disarmed if, faced with a concerted practice, the initiative for which was taken and the responsibility for which was assumed exclusively by undertakings outside the common market, it was deprived of the power to take any decision against them? This would also mean giving up a way of defending the common market and one necessary for bringing about the major objectives of the European Economic Community.'

* * *

55. Admittedly, in its observations, the United Kingdom, referring to the aide-mémoire of 20 October 1969 which it submitted to the Commission regarding the 'Dyestuffs' cases, has maintained that the territorial basis alone can justify the Community's assertion of jurisdiction in these cases. It therefore considers that the principle laid down in the 'Dyestuffs' cases must apply not only to subsidiaries but also to other intermediate establishments, situated within the Community, whose conduct within the Community has had an anti-competitive effect there. In those circumstances, according to the United Kingdom, it is merely the exercise of territorial jurisdiction which is involved.

56. In the light of all the foregoing considerations, I do not believe that I can advise the Court to take that approach. Moreover, the applicants deny that there is a territorial connection with the Community such as to enable it to assume jurisdiction over them. They claim that any conduct which may be attributed to them took place outside the Community. The applicants add that their various representatives acted independently and that none of those representatives' activities may be imputed to the applicants. Be that as it may, it serves no purpose * * *

to enter into a discussion on the nature of the legal relationship between the applicant companies and their various establishments within the Community.

57.   * * * There is no rule of international law which is capable of being relied upon against the criterion of the direct, substantial and foreseeable effect. Nor does the concept of international comity, in view of its uncertain scope, militate against that criterion. * * *

58.   In the absence of any such prohibitive rule and in the light of widespread State practice, I would therefore propose that in view of its appropriateness to the field of competition, it be adopted as a criterion for the jurisdiction of the Community.

* * *

RE WOOD PULP CARTEL, A AHLSTRÖM OSAKEYHTIÖ & OTHERS v. COMMISSION OF THE EUROPEAN COMMUNITIES

Joined Cases, Nos. 89, 104, 114, 116, 117, and 125–129/85 [1988] E.C.R. 5193

* * *

1.   By applications * * * wood pulp producers and two associations of wood pulp producers, all having their registered offices outside the Community, brought an action under the second paragraph of Article 173 of the EEC Treaty for the annulment of Decision IV/29.725 of 19 December 1984, * * * in which the Commission had established that they had committed infringements of Article 85 of the Treaty and imposed fines on them.

2.   The alleged infringements consisted of: concertation between those producers on prices announced each quarter to customers in the Community and on actual transaction prices charged to such customers * * * [and]; price recommendations addressed to its members by the Pulp, Paper and Paperboard Export Association of the United States (formerly named Kraft Export Association and hereinafter referred to as 'KEA'), an association of a number of United States producers. * * *

3.   In paragraph 79 of the contested decision the Commission set out the grounds which in its view justify the Community's jurisdiction to apply Article 85 of the Treaty to the concertation in question. It stated first that all the addresses of the decision were either exporting directly to purchasers within the Community or were doing business within the Community through branches, subsidiaries, agencies or other establishments in the Community. It further pointed out that the concertation applied to the vast majority of the sales of those undertakings to and in the Community. Finally it stated that two-thirds of total shipments and 60% of consumption of the product in question in the Community had been affected by such concertation. The Commission concluded that: 'The effect of the agreements and practices on prices announced and/or charged to customers and on resale of pulp within the EEC was therefore not only substantial but intended, and was the primary and direct result of the agreements and practices.'

* * *

6. All the applicants which have made submissions regarding jurisdiction maintain * * * that by applying the competition rules of the Treaty to them the Commission has misconstrued the territorial scope of Article 85. They note that in its judgment of 14 July 1972, * * * the Court did not adopt the 'effects doctrine' but emphasized that the case involved conduct restricting competition within the common market because of the activities of subsidiaries which could be imputed to the parent companies. The applicants add that even if there is a basis in Community law for applying Article 85 to them, the action of applying the rule interpreted in that way would be contrary to public international law which precludes any claim by the Community to regulate conduct restricting competition adopted outside the territory of the Community merely by reason of the economic repercussions which that conduct produces within the Community.

7. The applicants which are members of the KEA further submit that the application of Community competition rules to them is contrary to public international law in so far as it is in breach of the principle of non-interference. They maintain that in this case the application of Article 85 harmed the interest of the United States in promoting exports by United States undertakings as recognized in the Webb Pomerene Act of 1918 under which export associations, like the KEA, are exempt from United States anti-trust laws.

* * *

Incorrect assessment of the territorial scope of Article 85 of the Treaty and incompatibility of the decision with public international law.

(a) *The individual undertakings*

11. * * * Infringement of Article 85 of the Treaty itself: * * * [That] provision prohibits all agreements between undertakings and concerted practices which may affect trade between Member States and which have as their object or effect the restriction of competition within the common market.

12. * * * The main sources of supply of wood pulp are outside the Community, in Canada, the United States, Sweden and Finland and that the market therefore has global dimensions. Where wood pulp producers established in those countries sell directly to purchasers established in the Community and engage in price competition to win orders from those customers, that constitutes competition within the common market.

13. It follows that where those producers concert on the prices to be charged to their customers in the Community and put that concertation into effect by selling at prices which are actually coordinated, they are taking part in concertation which has the object and effect of restricting competition within the common market within the meaning of Article 85 of the Treaty.

14. Accordingly, it must be concluded that by applying the competition rules in the Treaty in the circumstances of this case to undertakings whose registered offices are situated outside the Community, the Com-

mission has not made an incorrect assessment of the territorial scope of Article 85.

15.   The applicants have submitted that the decision is incompatible with public international law on the grounds that the application of the competition rules in this case was founded exclusively on the economic repercussions within the common market of conduct restricting competition which was adopted outside the Community.

16.   * * * An infringement of Article 85, such as the conclusion of an agreement which has had the effect of restricting competition within the common market, consists of conduct made up of two elements, the formation of the agreement, decision or concerted practice and the implementation thereof.   If the applicability of prohibitions laid down under competition law were made to depend on the place where the agreement, decision or concerted practice was formed, the result would obviously be to give undertakings an easy means of evading those prohibitions.   The decisive factor is therefore the place where it is implemented.

17.   The producers in this case implemented their pricing agreement within the common market.   It is immaterial in that respect whether or not they had recourse to subsidiaries, agents, sub-agents, or branches within the Community in order to make their contacts with purchasers within the Community.

18.   Accordingly the Community's jurisdiction to apply its competition rules to such conduct is covered by the *territoriality* principle as universally recognized in public international law.

19.   As regards the argument based on the infringement of the principle of non-interference, the applicants who are members of KEA have referred to a rule according to which where two States have jurisdiction to lay down and enforce rules and the effect of those rules is that a person finds himself subject to contradictory orders as to the conduct he must adopt, each State is obliged to exercise its jurisdiction with *moderation*.   The applicants have concluded that by disregarding that rule in applying its competition rules the Community has infringed the principle of non-interference.

20.   There is no need to enquire into the existence in international law of such a rule since it suffices to observe that the conditions for its application are in any event not satisfied.   There is not, in this case, any contradiction between the conduct required by the United States and that required by the Community since the Webb Pomerene Act merely exempts the conclusion of export cartels from the application of United States anti-trust laws but does not require such cartels to be concluded.

21.   * * * [F]urther * * * the United States authorities raised no objections regarding any conflict of jurisdiction when consulted by the Commission pursuant to OECD Council Recommendation of 25 October 1979 concerning cooperation between member countries on restrictive business practices affecting international trade (*Acts of the organization*, Vol. 19, p. 376).

22. As regards the argument relating to disregard of international comity, it suffices to observe that it amounts to calling in question the Community's *jurisdiction* to apply its competition rules to conduct such as that found to exist in this case and that, as such, that argument has already been rejected.

23. Accordingly [we hold] that the Commission's decision is not contrary to Article 85 of the Treaty or to the rules of public international law. * * *

       * * *

On those grounds,

THE COURT, before giving judgment on all the applicants' submissions, hereby: Rejects the submission relating to the incorrect assessment of the territorial scope of Article 85 of the Treaty and the incompatibility of Commission Decision IV/29.725 of 19 December 1984 with public international law. * * *

       * * *

Notes & Questions: U.S. Courts have attempted to infuse moderation into their antitrust decisions, but the Clinton administration appears to be reasserting extraterritorial pressure. These cases are presented *infra* in § E.

1. Did the European Court of Justice adopt an *effects* theory in antitrust? Does the decision remind you of the *Alcoa case,* supra? Do you think that U.S. Companies appreciated this decision? Can you distinguish the effects of the conduct in this case from the conduct itself? Could the Court? If some of the *"conduct"* took place within the Community, would that make a difference? If so, on what theory?

2. Did the European Court attempt to *"moderate"* its decision by balancing interests? For discussion of the issue of moderation and balancing, see, the material around the *Timberlane case,* which we present in the last section of this Chapter, § E (on resolving conflicts of jurisdiction). The OECD has enacted a code relating to anti-competitive practices and has issued related recommendations * * *.

3. The classic example of the *objective territoriality* or effects theory is presented in European coursebooks: Defendant shoots a gun in Italy, injuring a person in France. The injured person runs to Switzerland, where he succumbs to his wounds [Merle & Vitu, *Droit Pénal (6th ed. 1988).* A significant effect or the result of an offense must occur in the territory of a state for this basis of jurisdiction to obtain.

4. ***Conduct outside the territory producing an intangible effect within the territory.*** Under customary international law are the following cases distinguishable as to the legitimacy of the application of State B's Law?

In State A, X and Y conspire to and do send poisoned chocolates into State B with the intention that Z, the addressee, eat them and die. This happens. State B has X and Y before its courts on indictment for murder. X and Y are nationals of State A, and State A objects on the ground that international law does not authorize State B to apply its law. *Result?*

The same states and the same parties, except that in State A, X and Y conspire to and do perpetrate a stock fraud by mail on Z in State B. State B has X and Y before its courts on indictment for embezzlement. X and Y are nationals of State A. State A objects on the ground that international law does not authorize State B to apply its law of fraudulent stock offers to X and Y. *Result?*

The same states and the same parties, except that in State A, X and Y agree to divide world markets, allocate and restrict production, and fix prices for commodities as to which, between them, they have a dominant world position. In State B this agreement is assumed to have the effect of reducing State B's exports of the commodity and of increasing its imports, at higher prices, thus reducing its favorable balance of trade. State B has X and Y before its courts on indictment under its antitrust law. State A objects on these grounds: (a) same as in cases 1 and 2; (b) that economic effects cannot be likened to shooting bullets or sending poisoned chocolates across frontiers; (c) that no measurement of adverse effect is possible; (d) that A and B did not intend any injury to State B or its nationals but only to achieve their profit maximization objectives.

Would it make any difference as to any of State A's arguments if the suit in State B had been private litigation by B nationals in the same commodity trade who claim injury and seek recovery under a treble damages provision in the antitrust law of State B?

The above hypothetical cases review the law and pose many of the major variables in a continuing debate on the role and rule of customary international law as to the extent to which a state may prescribe the legal consequences of economic conduct outside the territory by non-nationals that is objectionable to the state. Detailed consideration of the reach of antitrust laws of the United States is in § 3.a. of this chapter.

5. *Illustrations of the effects doctrine in national courts.*

German cartel law. On July 27, 1957, the Federal Republic of Germany enacted an Act Against Restraints of Competition, Gesetz gegen Wettbewerbsbeschränkungen, usually cited as GWB. An English translation of it appears in 1 *Guide to Legislation on Restrictive Business Practices,* Germany 1.0, 1 (1964), published by the Organization for Economic Cooperation and Development (OECD). Section 98(2) of the cartel law provides: "This Act shall apply to all restraints of competition which have effect in the area in which this Act applies, even if they result from acts done outside such area."

Mobarik Ali Ahmed v. The State of Bombay, India, Supreme Court, 1957, 24 Int'l L.Rep. 156 (1961). The defendant, a Pakistani, was before the courts of India, and was convicted of *"cheating"*, an offense under § 420 of the Indian Penal Code. The accused, while in Karachi, Pakistan, fraudulently induced an Indian in Bombay to part with a substantial sum of money. The supreme court affirmed the conviction, as against the defendant's contention that he " * * * is a Pakistani national who during the entire period of the [alleged] commission of the offense never stepped into India * * * and cannot be tried by an Indian Court." The supreme court cited the Lotus case in support of the objective territorial principle.

Regina v. Baxter, United Kingdom, Court of Appeal, 1971, [1972] 1 Q.B. 1, 8. The defendant was charged with attempting to obtain property by deception. He had posted from Northern Ireland to football promoters in England false claims that he had correctly forecast the outcome of games on a certain day and was entitled to payment. His false representations were detected when the letters arrived in England. The court held the attempt to obtain money by deception occurred at the moment of discovery, i.e. when the letters arrived in England. The court noted that its decision was in accord with an early American case, *Simpson v. State,* 17 S.E. 984 (1893), in which a bullet having been fired from South Carolina, missing the man at whom it was aimed in Georgia. The Supreme Court of Georgia held that Georgia had prescriptive jurisdiction over the attempted murder.

Beausir, France, Court of Cassation, 1977, 82 Rev.Gén. Dr. Int'l Pub. 1171 (1978). A Belgian industrialist in Belgium polluted, by chemical discharges, a river flowing from Belgium to France. He was charged under a provision of French law prohibiting the discharge of any substance which destroys fish or adversely affects its food supply, its reproduction or its quality for eating. It was enough, said the court, that the effect upon the biological milieu required for the life of the fish had taken place in France.

6. *Illustration of the effects doctrine in an international court.* Handelswerkerij G.J. Bier and Stiching Reinwater (The Reinwater Foundation) v. Mines de Potasse d'Alsace S.A., Court of Justice of the European Communities, 1976, [1977] 1 Common Mkt. L.R. 284. The plaintiff, in the business of nursery gardening in the Netherlands, used water from the Rhine for irrigation. It had a high salinity content so required expensive treatment before it could be used. The Reinwater Foundation, created to improve the quality of the water of the Rhine, joined Bier in a tort action against a French company whose works in Alsace discharged large quantities of industrial wastes into the Rhine, considerably augmenting its salinity. The lower Dutch court held that it had no jurisdiction because the event causing the damage had taken place in France. The event, therefore, was not covered by Article 3 of the European Convention of September 27, 1968, on Jurisdiction and Enforcement of Judgments which provided that jurisdiction belongs to "the place where the harmful event occurred." The court of appeal asked the European Court of Justice for an interpretation of the operative words in the convention.

The Avocat Général, advising the Court, reviewed the judicial practice of the several members of the Community whose legislation contained similar or identical provisions, including Germany, France, Italy,

Belgium, the United Kingdom and Denmark. He concluded that the practice suggested: jurisdiction obtained in the place where the act was committed or in the place where the damage occurred. Upon his recommendation, the Court ruled that the "place where the harmful event occurred" in the convention was intended to cover both. Hence the plaintiff could sue in either nation. Thereupon the Dutch court of appeal held that the Court below had jurisdiction over the suit for pollution originating in France and causing damage in the Netherlands. 81 Rev. Gén. Dr. Int'l Pub. 1186 (1977).

1965 RESTATEMENT, SECTION 18 *

JURISDICTION TO PRESCRIBE WITH RESPECT TO EFFECT WITHIN TERRITORY

A state has jurisdiction to prescribe a rule of law attaching legal consequences to conduct that occurs outside its territory and causes an effect within its territory, if either

(a) the conduct and its effect are generally recognized as constituent elements of a crime or tort under the law of states that have reasonably developed legal systems, or

(b)(i) the conduct and its effect are constituent elements of activity to which the rule applies; (ii) the effect within the territory is substantial; (iii) it occurs as a direct and foreseeable result of the conduct outside the territory; and (iv) the rule is not inconsistent with the principles of justice generally recognized by states that have reasonably developed legal systems.

1987 RESTATEMENT, SECTION 402

BASES OF JURISDICTION TO PRESCRIBE *

Subject to § 403, a state has jurisdiction to prescribe law with respect to

(c) conduct outside its territory that has or is intended to have substantial effect within its territory;

Justice Holmes notes, in the most commonly cited decision in American Supreme Court jurisprudence on the objective territoriality theory, Strassheim v. Daily, 221 U.S. 280 (1911): "[a]cts done outside a jurisdiction, but *intended to produce and producing* detrimental effects within it, justify a state in punishing a cause of the harm as if he had

---

* Copyright 1965 by the American Law Institute. Reprinted with their permission.   * Reprinted with the permission of the American Law Institute.

been present at the effect, if the state should succeed in getting him within its power." It is clear from Justice Holmes's opinion and from historical precedent that the objective territorial theory is not designed to apply when parties merely intend to cause an effect within a state, but fail to do so. A significant effect or the result of the offense must actually occur within the state's territory. Lately, however, many federal courts in the United States (and the Restatement 3rd) have applied it to thwarted extraterritorial conspiracies, even though no effect ever occurs on the territory (territoriality beyond territory). The courts confused the substantive elements of the federal crime of conspiracy, which requires no overt act, with the jurisdictional prerequisite (an effect occurring on the territory). The courts "reasoned" that, since no overt act was required for the offense, jurisdiction obtained on the basis of the effects theory, as long at there had been an intent to have such an effect. *Is this a correct interpretation or application?*

Recently, the courts have taken to using the various bases of jurisdiction, including the subjective and objective territoriality theories, as factors establishing a nexus for jurisdiction. See *U.S. v. Juda, infra* at p. 173.

---

3. NATIONALITY THEORY: ACTIVE, ASCRIBED AND PASSIVE PERSONALITY *

ACTIVE PERSONALITY (*personalité active*)

The nationality principle with regard to individuals. The nationality of individuals is a well established basis of jurisdiction to prescribe. It permits the state of a person's nationality to prescribe rules of conduct even for nationals outside its territory. This stems from the old Roman Law notion that one's law travels with him. Nationality jurisdiction is important to *"Civil Law"* jurisdictions. In fact, it and the concomitant prohibition to extradite one's nationals is often enshrined in their Constitutions. Many *"Civil Law"* nations go so far as to provide that virtually all offenses committed by nationals abroad are punishable. Their reasoning is that their national sovereign pride and honor is tainted when their nationals commit offenses abroad. They want the authority to control their nationals and to ensure that their laws and reputation are respected. They also want their system of justice to apply, which they deem more appropriately and fairly applied to their nationals. Thus, they refuse to extradite, but will prosecute their nationals who commit extraterritorial crime.

The passive personality principle, presented on p. 168, infra, is a related old Roman Law notion. It was adopted, developed further and

* Copyright 1987 by the American Law Institute. Reprinted with the permission of the American Law Institute.

became widespread during the European Middle Ages. It provides that the state of the *victim's* nationality has jurisdiction. German criminalists of the 19th century promoted the notion of *Realsystem,* which combined *passive personality with active personality* (nationality) jurisdiction and the *protective principle (presented below, at pp. 169–173).* *Realsystem* emphasized the role of the state's duty to protect its dignity and security (which were infringed when a national committed a crime or was the victim of a crime). The state's sovereignty depended on its ability to control its nationals and to protect them. * * * The United States does not refuse to extradite its nationals nor does it have the same tradition of asserting nationality jurisdiction. There are many laws, however, which do utilize the nationality connection. Some nationality jurisdiction cases follow.

A Dutch national "is liable to prosecution in Holland for an offense committed abroad, which is punishable under Dutch law and which is also punishable under the law of the country where the offense was committed." *Public Prosecutor v. Y.,* 24 Int'l L.Rep. 264, 265 (1961). In *X v. Public Prosecutor,* Neth. Dist. Court of Middelburg, Ct. App., the Hague, 1952, 19 Int'l Law Rptr. 226 (1957) the defendant was a national of the Netherlands. She lost her nationality by marriage, then committed a criminal offense, outside the Netherlands, for which she was prosecuted and convicted in the state where it was committed. Upon the dissolution of her marriage, she automatically recovered her former Dutch nationality. She was then prosecuted for the same offense in the Netherlands. It was held that the previous prosecution abroad did not preclude a new prosecution in Holland, though it might mitigate the punishment. She could not object to the prosecution on the ground that she had lost her nationality at the time the offense was committed. Any alien committing an offense abroad could be prosecuted if and when such person subsequently became a citizen of the Netherlands. A number of states will not prosecute their nationals again if they were previously prosecuted for an offense committed outside the territory. * * *

ASCRIBED NATIONALITY

1. *General principle.* It is well established that a state may ascribe its nationality to corporations, vessels or aircraft. Their nationality, like that of individuals, then becomes a basis of jurisdiction to prescribe. The scope of the jurisdiction to prescribe thus created is not the same, however, as the scope of the jurisdiction based on the nationality of the individual. It differs as among corporations, or other legal entities, vessels, aircraft and military services—which also have the nationality of their state.

2. *Application to vessels, aircraft and military services.* Prescriptive jurisdiction of a state based upon the nationality of individuals is limited in its effectiveness because the rules prescribed on this basis can be enforced only by action taken in the territory. Prescriptive jurisdiction based on the nationality of vessels, aircraft and military

services, however, does not suffer from the same limitation. Jurisdiction to enforce rules prescribed on this basis accompanies the vessels, aircraft or military services wherever they go, although the exercise of the enforcement jurisdiction is limited by rules of international law when they are in the territory of another state.

This jurisdiction extends, moreover, to persons aboard the vessels or aircraft, as well as to members of the military services, regardless of the nationality of the individuals involved. In *The Queen v. Anderson,* [1868] L.R. 1 Cr.Cas.Res. 161, an American seaman was convicted of manslaughter on a British vessel which was in the Garonne River in France, some 45 miles upstream. While France had concurrent jurisdiction on the basis of territory, it did not exercise it. The court held that the defendant was subject to British law and hence the conviction was valid. Was this a matter of nationality or territorial jurisdiction?

3. *Application to corporations.* Suppose a corporation organized in a foreign state, and doing all its business there, is a subsidiary of a United States corporation. May the United States use its prescriptive jurisdiction to compel the corporation into ordering its subsidiary to act in violation of the law of the foreign state?

4. In 1982, a U.S. federal court approved a Commerce Department plan to penalize a U.S. Company *Dresser Industries,* for refusing to comply with the "Reagan" sanctions (*Export Administration Act of 1979*) for supplying equipment to the Siberian pipeline. *Dresser's offense* was to refuse to order its French subsidiary to defy a French Government order to deliver the self-same equipment. It was also reported in the press that *Dresser and Dresser France* would be placed on a "denial list," which would prevent *Dresser France* from having any commercial dealings with the United States. Criminal sanctions were also available for both companies.

Dresser France had argued that it would be subject to criminal penalties in France if it complied with President Reagan's demands. **Was the French Government's order to Dresser France that it had to ship the equipment legal? Under whose law?** The U.S. Department of Justice refused to concede that this was "valid under French law." *Dresser France* is a wholly owned French Corporation, operating in France, under French Law, although it is a subsidiary of Dresser U.S. The Europeans, including France, registered serious protests, arguing that the U.S. should not be able to extend its jurisdiction to such circumstances. *See, N.Y. Times, Aug. 25, 1982, p. 1.*

———

Questions. Is it true, as maintained by a Justice Department official, that France could not validly exercise jurisdiction over Dresser France? Does the United States really have jurisdiction to order Dresser France not to ship the compressors? Is the answer different in international as compared to domestic law?

———

PASSIVE PERSONALITY

In the *Cutting case,* supra page 137, the United States objected to the prosecution by Mexico of an American national "merely because the person offended happened to be a Mexican." The Mexicans asserted the passive personality theory of jurisdiction, which has traditionally been anathema to United States law and practice. Passive personality jurisdiction proscribes conduct that injures that state's nationals. In Europe, this basis of jurisdiction is again on the ascendancy. It began in ancient Rome and was revitalized in medieval Europe, when it was widespread on the Continent, especially in Italy. Its rationale was, and is, that because criminal law has as its essential object to protect public and private interests (private ones implicate the public), the victim's national law and justice had the best appreciation of just what protection ought to be afforded. Passive personality jurisdiction went into desuetude during the heyday of positivism in the 19th Century, until it rebounded in the mid–20th century.

The United States now could be said to apply the passive personality principle under the option provided in Article 5 of the International Convention Against the Taking of Hostages of December 17, 1979 and the Omnibus Terrorism Prevention Act. This is not really a wholesale use of the passive personality principle, as it requires the protection of *national* interests in addition to the violence against a national. This is really more like the protective principle and is appropriate. Terrorism virtually by definition threatens national security or important governmental functions. Thus, jurisdiction is really based on a combination of the passive personality and the protective principles. The Terrorism Act provides jurisdiction, without the benefit of an international convention, over terrorist acts of violence abroad against United States nationals. See Subsection 6; and the Omnibus Diplomatic Security and Anti–Terrorism Act of 1986 [Ch. 113A, added to 18 U.S.C. § 2331]. See full discussion in Blakesley, Terrorism, Drugs * * * supra at 132–134, 136–37.

In the *Lotus case,* supra p. 140, France argued before the Permanent Court of International Justice that "international law does not allow a State to [proceed against] offences committed by foreigners abroad, simply by reason of the nationality of the victim." The court did not decide whether France was correct in so contending. Since then, however, France has enacted legislation based on passive nationality—*Code de Procédure Pénale*, Article 689, paragraph 1. During the drafting of the International Convention Against the Taking of Hostages, took the lead in proposing the adoption of the passive nationality principle in Article 5 of the Convention.

4. PROTECTIVE PRINCIPLE: EXTRATERRITORIAL CONDUCT AFFECTING IMPORTANT STATE INTERESTS

UNITED STATES v. PIZZARUSSO

United States Court of Appeals, Second Circuit, 1968.
388 F.2d 8.

MEDINA, Circuit Judge. This case is of interest because it brings before this Court for the first time the question of the jurisdiction of the District Court to indict and convict a foreign citizen of the crime of knowingly making a false statement under oath in a visa application to an American consular official located in a foreign country, in violation of 18 U.S.C. Section 1546.[1] Supreme Court cases give some guidance but none of them passes on this question directly.[2]

The indictment charges that Pizzarusso wilfully made under oath a number of false statements in her "Application for Immigrant Visa And Alien Registration" at the American Consulate, Montreal, Canada. * * * Although at all times pertinent to this case she was a citizen of Canada, she was taken into custody in the Southern District of New York. * * *

Upon the issuance of the visa and by its use Mrs. Pizzarusso immediately entered the territory of the United States, but this fact is not alleged in the indictment nor required by the terms of the statute, nor is it material, as we find the crime was complete when the false statements were made to an American consular official in Montreal. * * *

The evidence to sustain the charge is so overwhelming that we shall not pause to discuss it. Indeed, the only contention made on this appeal is that the District Court lacked jurisdiction to indict appellant and convict her of the crime alleged. As we find no lack of jurisdiction, we affirm the judgment. Our reasons follow.

* * *

International law has recognized, in varying degrees, five bases of jurisdiction with respect to the enforcement of the criminal law. * * * Thus both the territoriality and nationality principles, under which jurisdiction is determined by either the situs of the crime or the nationality of the accused, are universally accepted. The third basis, the protective principle, covers the instant case. By virtue of this theory a state "has jurisdiction to prescribe a rule of law attaching legal consequences to conduct outside its territory that threatens its security as a state or the operation of its governmental functions, provided the conduct is generally recognized as a crime under the law of states that have reasonably developed legal systems." * * *

---

1. Fraud and misuse of visas, permits and other entry documents. * * *

2. United States v. Bowman, 260 U.S. 94 (1922), cited by appellee as authority for upholding jurisdiction in the instant case is distinguishable as that case involved imposition of criminal liability on United States citizens for acts committed abroad.

Traditionally, the United States has relied primarily upon the territoriality and nationality principles, * * * and judges have often been reluctant to ascribe extraterritorial effect to statutes. * * * Our courts have developed what has come to be termed the objective territorial principle as a means of expanding the power to control activities detrimental to the state. This principle has been aptly defined by Mr. Justice Holmes in Strassheim v. Daily. "Acts done outside a jurisdiction, but intended to produce and producing detrimental effects within it, justify a state in punishing the cause of the harm as if he had been present at the effect * * *." * * * Underlying this principle is the theory that the "detrimental effects" constitute an element of the offense and since they occur within the country, jurisdiction is properly invoked under the territorial principle. * * *

However, the objective territorial principle is quite distinct from the protective theory. Under the latter, all the elements of the crime occur in the foreign country and jurisdiction exists because these actions have a "potentially adverse effect" upon security or governmental functions, and there need not be any actual effect in the country as would be required under the objective territorial principle. Courts have often failed to perceive this distinction. Thus, the Ninth Circuit, in upholding a conviction under a factual situation similar to the one in the instant case, relied on the protective theory, but still felt constrained to say that jurisdiction rested partially on the adverse effect produced as a result of the alien's entry into the United States. The Ninth Circuit also cited Strassheim and Aluminum Company of America as support for its decision. With all due deference to our brothers of the Ninth Circuit, however, we think this reliance is unwarranted. A violation of 18 U.S.C.A. Section 1546 is complete at the time the alien perjures himself in the foreign country. It may be possible that the particular criminal sanctions of Section 1546 will never be enforced unless the defendant enters the country, but entry is not an element of the statutory offense. Were the statute re-drafted and entry made a part of the crime we would then be presented with a clear case of jurisdiction under the objective territorial principle.

Statutes imposing criminal liability on aliens for committing perjury in United States Consulates in foreign countries have been in existence for over one hundred years * * *. Only one court has ever held that the United States did not have jurisdiction to proceed against an alien under the legislation governing this case. United States v. Baker, 136 F.Supp. 546 (S.D.N.Y.1955). In Baker it was conceded that there was authority for deporting an alien for making perjurious statements to a United States Consul, United States ex rel. Majka v. Palmer, 67 F.2d 146 (7th Cir.1933), but the court thought the imposition of criminal sanctions was "far different" from deportation and dismissed the indictment. We would have sustained jurisdiction in Baker had the case been before us, and in this view we are apparently joined by the judge who decided Baker, since he presided over the instant case in the court below.

Affirmed.

1. *Distinction between the territorial and protective principles.*

The objective and subjective territorial principles are species of territoriality, but the protective principle is an exception to it. While the objective and subjective territorial theories require a territorial nexus (*objective*—an effect; *subjective*—an element of the offense) the protective principle provides jurisdiction over offenses committed *wholly* outside the forum state's territory, but only when the offense poses a danger of causing or causes an adverse effect on a state's security, integrity, sovereignty, or other important governmental function. Any offense designed to intimidate, influence, or to extort some concession from the state or to threaten its security or sovereignty, for example terrorism, will be covered by the protective principle. The focus of the protective principle is the nature of the interest that is or may be injured, rather than the place of the harm or the place of the conduct. This distinction was clearly indicated in United States v. Pizzarusso, *supra.* The protective principle is the only accepted theory that allows jurisdiction over conduct that poses a *potential* threat to certain interests or functions of the asserting state, but it is *limited* to recognized and limited interests or functions. With very few exceptions, national penal codes recognize this principle and its limitation.

2. *Distinction between the protective principle and passive personality.*

The language of early drafts of the Omnibus Anti–Terrorism Act of 1986 [noted above] was too broad as it aimed at creating jurisdiction over terrorism committed extraterritorially against Americans. It covered any criminal violence against United States nationals. Ultimately, Congress attempted to make the Act apply strictly to terrorist violence, by noting: 'No prosecution for any offense described in this section shall be undertaken by the United States except on written certification of the Attorney General or the highest ranking subordinate * * * with responsibility for criminal prosecutions that, in the judgment of the certifying official, such *offense was intended to coerce, intimidate, or retaliate against a government or a civilian population.*' What do you think about the executive branch's role in this? Is the Attorney General's decision that the conduct was designed to coerce, etc., a substantive element of the offense?

Rosalyn Higgins notes, in her *General Course on Public International Law:* International Law and the Avoidance, Containment and Resolution of Disputes, [1991–V] Recueil Des Cours 100–104:

> * * * we must also admit that in recent years there has been a revived interest in invoking the passive personality principle. This has occurred against the background of the explosion of international terrorism. * * *

> Accordingly, other States with a direct legal interest in the events and a strong political belief in the need to combat terrorism have sought to identify a possible basis for asserting jurisdiction

themselves.   The United States and France provide interesting examples.

* * *

[The U.S. Terrorist Prosecution Act of 1985, and the Omnibus Diplomatic Security and Antiterrorism Act of 1986 seek] [196] * * * to establish a passive personality basis of jurisdiction.   However, it would seem that the assertion of jurisdiction is still intended to be limited to offences that would commonly be described as "terrorist" offences. There appears to be no intention to assert jurisdiction (notwithstanding the broad wording of the Act), where, for example, Americans abroad are the victims of bar room violence or robberies.   * * *

Thus the passive personality principle is invoked by the United States, but only in relation to terrorist-type offences.   The confinement of a passive personality claim to terrorist-type cases points to a constellation of facts which touches on a State's sovereignty and the security of its citizens in relation thereto.   It has been pointed out that this "triggers the protective principle.   Thus, there is no need to call upon the more controversial and less accepted passive personality theory."

In France too [199] traditional hostility to the passive personality principle has been overtaken by more recent legislation based on this principle.   Once again, it has been explained by those responsible for such legislation that its invocation is intended to be restricted to cases involving national security.

3.   *Expansion of protective principle in the United States.* The court in Pizzarusso held the principle to be applicable because the conduct of aliens abroad had a "*potentially* adverse effect" upon an important governmental function.   The alternative would have been to hold that an effect in the territory had taken place when the aliens entered the United States.   Had the court adopted this position, it would have reflected a traditional attitude towards the protective principle, for little use had been made of it in the United States in the past.   A manifestation of this traditional attitude can be found in legislation on counterfeiting: it has been a federal offense to counterfeit foreign currency in the United States, but not a federal offense to counterfeit United States currency abroad.

The expanding use of the protective principle is consistent with an international practice of long standing.   The 1987 Restatement reflects this practice.   It provides in § 403 that a state has jurisdiction to prescribe with respect to "conduct outside its territory by persons not its nationals that is directed against the security of the state or against a limited class of other state interests."

196. 18 USC § 2331 (1986). For commentary, see C. Blakesley, "Jurisdictional Issues and Conflicts of Jurisdiction" in Legal Responses to International Terrorism, US Procedural Aspects (ed. Bassiouni) 1988, 131–181. Blakesley criticizes generally the attempts to extend the reach of US jurisdiction; and specifically the US Restatement as contrary to international legal principles. Ibid., fn. 26.

199. This aspect is very well explained in Blakesley, *supra,* at 172–177. * * *

4. Dangers inherent in the protective principle, which can be abused because it is susceptible of practically unlimited expansion. Is the limitation on protective principle jurisdiction artificial? Does limiting it to conduct abroad that threatens certain narrowly defined interests including security and the integrity of its governmental operations (e.g. visa fraud, counterfeiting), really protect against abuse?

5. COMBINATION OF BASES: JURISDICTION, THE CONSTITUTION & THE REQUIREMENT OF A NEXUS

UNITED STATES v. JUDA

United States District Court, Northern District of California, 1992.
797 F.Supp. 774.

* * *

LEGGE, District Judge.

Defendants have filed motions which present issues about unsettled areas of law; that is, the constitutional authority of the United States to investigate, intercept and prosecute drug activities occurring outside the United States. The six defendants in this case were on board a [stateless] vessel, the Malekula, headed from Southeast Asia to Canada. As a result of extensive international cooperation and investigative work, Malekula was intercepted in international waters off the coast of Canada by a United States Coast Guard ship. Defendants' vessel was loaded with hashish. When Malekula was intercepted by the Coast Guard, it was set on fire—allegedly by one of the defendants. Defendants abandoned the vessel and were rescued by the Coast Guard; the Coast Guard also retrieved some of the cargo of hashish.

Defendants were arrested and this indictment was brought against them * * *. All six * * * are charged with violations of 46 U.S.C.App. § 1903(a) (persons on board a vessel possessing a controlled substance with intent to distribute), and 46 U.S.C.App. § 1903(j) (conspiracy to commit that offense).

* * *

[The more substantial ground for the motion to dismiss is whether it is] a violation of due process for the United States to prosecute defendants since they were on a vessel in international waters headed for a foreign country? Defendants contend that the due process clause * * * requires a nexus between their activities and the United States, and that the required nexus must be that the hashish be destined for the United States.

A.

Several decisions in this circuit, including a decision of this court, have considered variations on this issue. United States v. Aikins, 923 F.2d 650 (9th Cir.1990); United States v. Davis, 905 F.2d 245 (9th Cir.1990); United States v. Peterson, 812 F.2d 486 (9th Cir.1987);

United States v. Biermann, 678 F.Supp. 1437 (N.D.Cal.1988). A brief discussion of the development of the law by these cases is necessary to the conclusions which this court states below. In United States v. Peterson, the Ninth Circuit discussed the so-called protective principle of jurisdiction, as a constitutional basis for exercising jurisdiction over defendants in international waters without any showing of an actual effect on the United States. In reliance on the discussion in Peterson, this court in United States v. Biermann, considered the defendants' arguments regarding nexus, but concluded that a showing of nexus was not required because jurisdiction could constitutionally be exercised under the protective principle * * *. However, in United States v. Davis, the appeal of the Biermann case, the Ninth Circuit held that due process required a nexus. And the court found nexus primarily from evidence of the intention of the defendants to bring the drugs into the United States. In United States v. Aikins, this circuit followed Davis, reaffirmed the requirement of a nexus, and found nexus because the marijuana was destined for the United States * * *.

* * * Based upon the Davis court's discussion, this court concludes that the circuit has rejected the protective principle discussed in Peterson and Biermann as being an independent ground for jurisdiction, and instead requires a constitutionally sufficient nexus.

Article I, Section VIII, clause 10 of the constitution [sic] does give congress the power to "define and punish * * * felonies on the high seas." And by enacting Section 1903(a), congress exercised that power and intended that the United States' drug laws apply in international waters. However, in order for Section 1903 to be applied to a particular vessel or a particular defendant, the decisions of this * * * circuit require a nexus between the defendant and the United States.

B.

The government seeks to avoid the requirement of nexus on the ground that Malekula was a "*stateless*" vessel. The government argues that occupants of stateless vessels may be prosecuted by any country, without any requirement of nexus with the prosecuting country.

There is some authority for the government's argument that nexus is not required between a *stateless vessel* and the country seeking to exercise jurisdiction. In United States v. Rubies, 612 F.2d 397, 403 (9th Cir.1979), the Ninth Circuit said, "with regard to stateless vessels, no question of comity nor of any breach of international law can arise, if there is no state under whose flag the vessel sails." *However, that decision only goes so far. That is, the court was discussing comity and rules of international law; it was not considering the requirements of the United States Constitution.* Even if stateless vessels are ones as to which the United States owes no obligations to another country, that does not mean that persons on those vessels do not have the protection of the constitution in a prosecution by the United States.

Decisions of other circuits have noted that distinction. The Eleventh Circuit stated that there need not be a nexus between a stateless vessel and the country seeking to exercise its jurisdiction. However, the issue of due process under the United States Constitution was not raised. In United States v. Alvarez–Mena, 765 F.2d 1259 (5th Cir.1985), the Fifth Circuit held that no nexus was required by statute or international law. The court discussed only international law and congressional intent, and noted that there was no basis for a claim of due process violation in that case. The Second Circuit held that no nexus was required for the assertion of jurisdiction over a stateless vessel under international law. That court recognized that congress has the power to legislate in excess of the jurisdiction defined by international law. When Congress changed former 21 U.S.C. § 955a into the present 46 U.S.C. § 1903, it added a provision that the failure to comply with international law should not divest a court of jurisdiction. Section 1903(d). But the court also noted that a federal court would not be bound to follow that congressional direction if "this would violate the due process clause of the Fifth Amendment." And in United States v. Howard–Arias, * * * the statutes [applied] "to the extent permitted by the due process clause of the Fifth Amendment." In summary, the above cases dealt only with principles of statutory construction and international law. They were not decisions on the extent that United States criminal laws can be applied as a matter of due process.

In contrast, the holdings of the Ninth Circuit in Davis and Aikins, and perhaps in Peterson, were not limited to international law considerations. Those decisions were constitutional in nature; that is, defining the constitutionally permissible scope of acts of congress over international waters.

* * * This court * * * concludes that the constitutional requirement of nexus applies to stateless vessels. While such vessels may have no rights to object to jurisdiction under international law, the due process clause of the Fifth Amendment, as interpreted by the Ninth Circuit, requires a sufficient nexus between defendants and the United States for the United States to prosecute them. * * *

C.

* * * What is the nexus that is required? In the *Davis* and *Aikins cases,* the drugs were bound for the United States and the court of appeals determined that was a sufficient nexus. However that nexus is absent in this case. The declarations, including those of defendants and the United States, demonstrate that the drugs were bound for Canada. There is no substantial evidence that the drugs were destined, even ultimately, for the United States. If the only permissible nexus is that the drugs be destined for the United States, there is an absence of nexus in this case. Can there be connections between defendants and the United States, other than the intended destination of the drugs, which are a constitutionally sufficient nexus? The reported decisions do not offer much guidance on what nexus is sufficient * * *.

This court concludes that the * * * connections between the United States and defendants and their vessel are a sufficient nexus to support the constitutional application of United States laws. The contacts with the United States were substantial, and indeed it appears that the transaction was essentially organized in the United States. The basic requirements for a constitutional exercise of jurisdiction are minimal contacts meeting a basic test of fairness. See also, International Shoe Co. v. Washington (exercise of personal jurisdiction over defendant consistent with due process requires minimum contacts with territory of forum such that maintenance of suit does not offend traditional notions of fair play and substantial justice). * * * The required contacts are present in this case.

A case could be hypothesized where it would be unfair to prosecute a United States citizen, in the United States and under United States law, for something done entirely overseas. But this is not that case. The offense involved, the international importation of narcotics, is not just a creature of United States law or an offense peculiar to only a few countries. It is unlawful in virtually all countries. The constitution does not require that the United States be a safe haven for the planning of international crimes, just so long as the crime itself does not have a direct impact on the United States * * *.

D.

* * * Separate consideration must be given to defendant Manuel Avila, who is not a citizen of the United States or a resident alien. He is a citizen of the Philippines, was recruited for the voyage in southeast Asia, and has no other connection with the United States evident from the record. This court concludes that the United States may not constitutionally exercise jurisdiction over him.

The language of the statute would appear to encompass Avila. Section 1903(a) makes it unlawful for "any person" who is "on board a vessel subject to the jurisdiction of the United States" to possess a controlled substance with the intent to distribute it. And Section 1903(c) includes as a "vessel subject to the jurisdiction of the United States" a vessel "without nationality." Malekula was a stateless vessel. However, the issue is whether the statute can constitutionally be applied to Avila. There is little reported authority bearing on this issue. See U.S. v. Yunis, 681 F.Supp. 896 (D.D.C.1988), aff'd 924 F.2d 1086 (D.C.Cir.1991); United States v. Georgescu, 723 F.Supp. 912 (E.D.N.Y. 1989). As stated, he had no connections with the United States other than being on the vessel. The offense which he committed occurred between southeast Asia and the international waters off of Canada. And there is insufficient evidence that any of the drugs were destined, even ultimately, for the United States. This court therefore believes that there is not a constitutionally sufficient nexus for the United States to exercise jurisdiction over him.

* * *

Questions: What was the jurisdictional basis applied by the court? Did it reject the traditional bases of jurisdiction? Was statelessness of the vessel relevant to jurisdiction? If so, how? Did the court confuse in personam with subject matter jurisdiction? Was there any discussion of subject matter jurisdiction? Do they overlap in this arena? Does the Constitution interrelate them in these circumstances? What does the court intend by its discussion of due process? Traditionally, U.S. courts applied a fairly relaxed due process scrutiny in relation to jurisdiction over defendants on stateless vessels on the high seas. Is the traditional distinction between registered and stateless vessels meaningful from a constitutional standpoint? From the point of view of international law? What was the *"nexus "* which the court saw as allowing jurisdiction in *Juda?* What traditional theory of jurisdiction obtains when one or more of the parties commit elements of an offense within a state's territory? Does the court consider that to be a sufficient nexus? With regard to the non-U.S. nationals, did the court consider whether they were involved in a conspiracy, the elements of which occurred in U.S. territory? What do you make of the statement that "compliance with international law does not determine whether the United States may apply the act to [defendant's] conduct"? What does that mean? Do the traditional international law bases of jurisdiction play a role in relation to the establishment of a nexus?

In the referenced cases relating to non-stateless ships, what role did the flag-ship government play? The traditional rule for registered vessels is that permission is required from the government of registry before boarding and seizure are legal. *See, e.g., U.S. v. Wright–Barker,* 784 F.2d 161, 167–70, 175–76 (3d Cir.1986); *U.S. v. Rasheed,* 802 F.Supp. 312 (D.Hawaii 1992), and the other cases cited in *Juda.*

6. JURISDICTION BASED ON UNIVERSAL INTEREST

1. *Crimes of universal interest.* International law provides for prescriptive jurisdiction over certain offenses even though the offense was not committed on its territory, did not cause an effect on its territory, was not committed by a national, and did not otherwise come within its jurisdiction to prescribe. These are offenses that are condemned by virtually all national domestic law, are seen as violative of international law. They trigger an obligation to extradite or to prosecute the accused. *See, Demjanjuk v. Petrovsky,* 776 F.2d 571, 581–82 (6th Cir.1985), *infra,* Ch. 11 (explicitly recognizing the universality principle).

The most ancient crime of universal interest is piracy, which is considered in Chapter 4, infra. It became a universal crime under customary international law because it was in the common interest of maritime states to preserve freedom of navigation. Since its development, several other crimes may also have become recognized as being within the universality theory. Such recognition may have begun as a non-derogable general principle recognized by all nations (*jus cogens*), or in customary international law for some of these crimes, but it is now usually embodied in international agreements. These agreements must be consulted to determine under what circumstances and to what extent a state may participate in the repression of the particular crime. Some of the crimes involved are:

> Acts of violence against diplomats, see Chapter 12; Genocide, see Chapters 10 & 17; Hijacking, see Chapter 5; Sabotage of civil aircraft, see Chapter 5; Slave trade, see in the Documentary Supplement Articles 13 and 22 of the 1958 Convention on the

High Seas and Articles 99 and 110 of the Convention on the Law of the Sea; Apartheid; War crimes, see Chapters 11, 17.

2. *Is terrorism a crime of universal interest?* Despite the increase in the number of acts of terrorism in recent years, it is still a matter of controversy whether it is a crime within the universality theory.

————

1987 RESTATEMENT, SECTION 404 *

UNIVERSAL JURISDICTION TO DEFINE
AND PUNISH CERTAIN OFFENSES

A state has jurisdiction to define and prescribe punishment for certain offenses recognized by the community of nations as of universal concern, such as piracy, slave trade, attacks on or hijacking of aircraft, genocide, war crimes, and *perhaps certain acts of terrorism,* even where none of the bases of jurisdiction indicated in § 402 is present.

* * *

————

7.   EXTRATERRITORIAL ACTS OF TERRORISM: WHAT BASIS OF JURISDICTION?

A.   *What is Terrorism?*

There is no agreement on a definition of terrorism. Some experts argue that the core of terrorism is "the use or threat of violence, a method of combat or a strategy to achieve certain goals, that its aim is to induce a state of fear in the victim, that it is ruthless and does not conform to humanitarian norms, and that publicity is an essential factor in terrorist strategy." Laqueur, *Reflections on Terrorism,* 65 For. Aff. at 86, 88 (1986). Is this definition sufficient for some and not for other purposes? Is it too vague? What are its elements? How do you define them? What is the difference between war and this definition? Isn't all warfare ruthless? Doesn't war always aim at creating fear in the enemy? If the conduct does not conform to humanitarian norms, is it a war crime, or terrorism, or both? Will universal jurisdiction appropriately cover the conduct proscribed by Laqueur's definition? Could a person be prosecuted based on it? This is no easy problem.

One of the difficulties in defining terrorism is that there is no universal concept: one's definition has meaning and impact only on the basis of and in the context of the purpose for which it is being put. An anthropologist sees it one way, a political scientist another, a politician another and an international lawyer another, a prosecutor or defense attorney yet another. Moreover, the tendency has been for the definition to be appropriated by propagandists who claim to be presenting a

* Copyright 1987 by the American Law Institute. Reprinted with permission.

legal definition, but who are often presenting a defense of their own conduct and wholesale condemnation of that of their enemies.

If one really is looking for a legal definition of terrorism, if one really wishes to justify the use of force to stop it or to prosecute its perpetrators, one must have specific, explicit elements which may be proved by evidence (e.g. an actus reus and the mens rea). We will consider it in detail in Chapter 17 (States and the Use of Force) and in Chapter 11 (Individual Responsibility).

B. *Jurisdiction.*

Terrorism can be conducted on land, at sea, or in the air. This subsection deals with acts of terrorism taking place on land. Terrorism at sea, such as the taking over of a ship, see Chapter 4. Terrorism in the air, such as the hijacking of a plane is in Chapter 5. The threat of violence by a terrorist may begin in one zone and continue in another. Acts of terrorism can also be directed to a particular class of persons, such as diplomats. See Chapter 12.

Terrorism on land is subject to the jurisdiction of the state in whose territory the acts are committed. Could any other state have jurisdiction? Jurisdiction covers acts of terrorism directed at individuals, those intended to affect the conduct of the government of the state in whose territory the acts take place, and those committed in the territory with the intention of affecting the conduct of the government of another state. What basis of jurisdiction to prescribe empowers a state with respect to acts of terrorism committed by aliens outside its territory with the intention of affecting the conduct of its government?

U.S. v. YUNIS

United States District Court, District of Columbia, 1988.
681 F.Supp. 896.

* * *

In the original multi-count indictment, * * * the United States charged Fawaz Yunis, a resident and citizen of Lebanon, for his alleged involvement in the hijacking of a Jordanian civilian aircraft in the Middle East.

Defendant's counsel has moved to dismiss the indictment on grounds that this Court lacks subject matter jurisdiction under general principles of international law * * * [and] provisions of the United States Code. The motion is predicated on grounds that the Jordanian aircraft never flew over United States airspace and had no contact whatsoever with United States territory. Without such connection, Yunis' * * * counsel argues that this Court has no basis for asserting either subject matter or personal jurisdiction. In analyzing whether physical contact with the United States is necessary to proceed with the indictment, the Court first reviews the events surrounding the hijacking.

The Court also examines various principles of international law to determine whether they afford grounds for exercising jurisdiction over defendant. Lastly, two relevant statutes, the Hostage Taking Act, 18 U.S.C. § 1203, and the several discrete provisions invoked under the Destruction of Aircraft Act, 18 U.S.C. §§ 82(a) and (b) [also referred to as The Aircraft Piracy Act] are examined to determine whether they apply to offenses committed overseas.[1]

* * *

[T]he Court concludes that consistent with reputable and generally accepted treatises and international law principles, there are sufficient grounds for asserting both subject matter and personal jurisdiction. Further, the Hostage Taking Act and Section 32(b) of the Aircraft Piracy Act impose liability for offenses allegedly committed by defendant. However, for the reasons explained more fully below, the Court concludes that Section 32(a) of the Aircraft Piracy Act does not apply. The alleged offenses thereunder have no connection whatsoever to United States territory.

I.

BACKGROUND

This criminal proceeding and indictment arise from the hijacking of a Jordanian civil aircraft. There is no dispute that the only nexus to the United States was the presence of several American nationals on board the flight. The airplane was registered in Jordan, flew the Jordanian flag and never landed on American soil or flew over American airspace.

* * *

* * * Its flightpath was limited to an area within and around the Mediterranean Sea. Based on the absence of any nexus to United States territory, Yunis has moved to dismiss the entire indictment, arguing that no United States federal court has jurisdiction to prosecute a foreign national for crimes committed in foreign airspace and on foreign soil. *He further claims that the presence of the American nationals on board the aircraft is an insufficient basis for exercising jurisdiction under principles of international law.* [emphasis added]

* * * [T]hreshold inquiries: whether * * * there is a basis for jurisdiction under international law, and if so, whether Congress intended to and had authority to extend jurisdiction of our federal courts over criminal offenses and events * * * committed and occurred overseas and out of the territorial jurisdiction of such courts.

---

1. Section 32(a) covers offenses committed on aircraft having some physical nexus to the United States, either operating in "the special aircraft jurisdiction" or in "overseas or foreign air commerce." Section 32(b) authorizes jurisdiction over offenses committed entirely in foreign airspace if the "offender is later found" in the United States.

II.

ANALYSIS

A. JURISDICTION UNDER INTERNATIONAL LAW

The parties agree that there are five traditional bases of jurisdiction over extra-territorial crimes under international law: *Territorial; National; Protective; Universal; Passive personal.*

These general principles were developed in 1935 by a Harvard Research Project in an effort to codify principles of jurisdiction under international law. Most courts, including our Court of Appeals, have adopted the Harvard Research designations on jurisdiction.

* * *

The Universal and the Passive Personal principle appear to offer potential bases for asserting jurisdiction over the hostage-taking and aircraft piracy charges against Yunis. However, his counsel argues that the Universal principle is not applicable because neither hostage-taking nor aircraft piracy are heinous crimes encompassed by the doctrine. He urges further, that the United States does not recognize Passive Personal as a legitimate source of jurisdiction. The government flatly disagrees and maintains that jurisdiction is appropriate under both.

1. *Universal Principle*

The Universal principle recognizes that certain offenses are so heinous and so widely condemned that "any state if it captures the offender may prosecute and punish that person on behalf of the world community regardless of the nationality of the offender or victim or where the crime was committed." M. Bassiouini, II International Criminal Law, Ch. 6 at 298 (ed. 1986). The crucial question for purposes of defendant's motion is how crimes are classified as "heinous" and whether aircraft piracy and hostage taking fit into this category.

Those crimes that are condemned by the world community and subject to prosecution under the Universal principal [sic] are often a matter of international conventions or treaties. See Demjanjuk v. Petrovsky (treaty against genocide signed by a significant number of states made that crime heinous; therefore, Israel had proper [universal] jurisdiction over a nazi war criminal. * * *

Both offenses are the subject of international agreements. A majority of states in the world community including Lebanon, have signed three treaties condemning aircraft piracy: The Tokyo Convention, The Hague Convention, and The Montreal Convention. The Hague and Montreal Conventions explicitly rely on the principle of Universal jurisdiction in mandating that all states "take such measures as may be necessary to establish its jurisdiction over the offences * * * where the alleged offender is present in its territory." Hague Convention Art. 4 §2; Montreal Convention Art. 5 §2. Further, those treaties direct that all "contracting states * * * of which the alleged offender is found, * * * shall, be obliged, *without exception whatsoever and whether or not the offense was committed in its territory,* to submit the case to its competent authorities for the purpose of prosecution." These two provisions together demonstrate the international community's strong commitment to punish aircraft hijackers irrespective of where the hijacking occurred.

The global community has adopted the International Convention for the Taking of Hostages, an agreement which condemns and criminalizes the offense of hostage taking. Like the conventions denouncing aircraft piracy, this treaty requires signatory states to prosecute any alleged offenders "present in its territory."

In light of the global efforts to punish aircraft piracy and hostage taking, international legal scholars unanimously agree that these crimes fit within the category of heinous crimes for purposes of asserting universal jurisdiction. See * * * Blakesley, United States Jurisdiction over Extraterritorial Crime, 73 J. of Crim.L. & Criminology (1982).

Our Circuit has cited the Restatement with approval and determined that the Universal principle, standing alone, provides sufficient basis for asserting jurisdiction over an alleged offender. "The premise of universal jurisdiction is that a state 'may exercise jurisdiction to define and punish certain offenses recognized by the community of nations as of universal concern,' * * * even where no other recognized basis of jurisdiction is present." Therefore, under recognized principles of international law, and the law of this Circuit, there is clear authority to assert jurisdiction over Yunis for the offenses of aircraft piracy and hostage taking.

2. *Passive Personal Principle*

This principle authorizes states to assert jurisdiction over offenses committed against their citizens abroad. It recognizes that each state has a legitimate interest in protecting the safety of its citizens when they journey outside national boundaries. Because American nationals were on board the Jordanian aircraft, the government contends that the Court may exercise jurisdiction over Yunis under this principle. Defendant argues that this theory of jurisdiction is neither recognized by the international community nor the United States and is an insufficient basis for sustaining jurisdiction over Yunis.

Although many international legal scholars agree that the principle is the most controversial of the five sources of jurisdiction, they also agree that the international community recognizes its legitimacy. Most accept that "the extraterritorial reach of a law premised upon the * * * principle would not be in doubt as a matter of international law." * * * More importantly, the international community explicitly approved of the principle as a basis for asserting jurisdiction over hostage takers. The Hostage Taking Convention set forth certain mandatory sources of jurisdiction. But it also gave each signatory country discretion to exercise extraterritorial jurisdiction when the offense was committed "with respect to a hostage who is a national of that state if that state considers it appropriate." Art. 5(a)(d). Therefore, even if there are doubts regarding the international community's acceptance, there can be no doubt concerning the application of this principle to the offense of hostage taking, an offense for which Yunis is charged. * * *

Defendant's counsel correctly notes that the Passive Personal principle traditionally has been an anathema to United States lawmakers.[8]
But his reliance on the Restatement (Revised) of Foreign Relations Laws
for the claim that the United States can never invoke the principle is
misplaced. In the past, the United States has protested any assertion of
such jurisdiction for fear that it could lead to indefinite criminal liability
for its own citizens. This objection was based on the belief that
foreigners visiting the United States should comply with our laws and
should not be permitted to carry their laws with them. Otherwise
Americans would face criminal prosecutions for actions unknown to
them as illegal. However, in the most recent draft of the Restatement,
the authors noted that the theory "has been increasingly accepted when
applied to terrorist and other organized attacks on a state's nationals by
reason of their nationality, or to assassinations of a state's ambassadors,
or government officials." Restatement (Revised) § 402, comment g
* * * The authors retreated from their wholesale rejection of the
principle, recognizing that perpetrators of crimes unanimously condemned by members of the international community, should be aware of
the illegality of their actions. Therefore, qualified application of the
doctrine to serious and universally condemned crimes will not raise the
specter of unlimited and unexpected criminal liability.

This case does not present the first time that the United States has
invoked the principle to assert jurisdiction over a hijacker who seized an
American hostage on foreign soil. The government relied on this very
principle when it sought extradition of Muhammed Abbas Zaiden, the
leader of the terrorists who hijacked the Achille Lauro vessel in Egyptian
waters and subsequently killed Leon Klinghoffer, an American citizen.
As here, the only connection to the United States was Klinghoffer's
American citizenship. Based on that link, an arrest warrant was issued
charging Abbas with hostage taking, conspiracy and piracy.

Thus the Universal and Passive Personality principles, together,
provide ample grounds for this Court to assert jurisdiction over Yunis.
In fact, reliance on both strengthens the basis for asserting jurisdiction.
Not only is the United States acting on behalf of the world community to
punish alleged offenders of crimes that threaten the very foundations of
world order, but the United States has its own interest in protecting its
nationals.

B. JURISDICTION UNDER DOMESTIC LAW

Even if there is authority to assert jurisdiction over Yunis under
International law, defendant's counsel argues that the Court has no
jurisdiction under domestic law. He contends that Congress neither had
the power nor the intention to authorize jurisdiction over the offenses of
hostage taking and aircraft piracy committed "half way around the
world".

But defendant's argument fails to recognize the power of the Congress to legislate overseas and to define and punish offenses committed

---

8. However, defendant improperly relies
on United States v. Layton, 509 F.Supp.
212, 215 (N.D.Cal.1981) for the proposition
that the United States categorically rejects
this principle.

on foreign soil. Article I, section 8, Clause 11 of the Constitution gives Congress the power to "define and punish Piracies and Felonies committed on the High Seas and Offenses against the Law of Nations." As explained, *supra,* * * * both hostage taking and aircraft piracy have been defined as offenses against the law of nations.

The reliance that Yunis' counsel places on United States v. Bowman, to argue that Congress has no power to extend jurisdiction outside its territorial boundaries, is misplaced. *Bowman* stands for the contrary proposition. Indeed, it is routinely quoted for the holding that "there is no constitutional bar to the extraterritorial application of penal laws." * * *

A more accurate interpretation of *Bowman* and its progeny is that Congress has the power to punish crimes committed overseas but it must evince such an intent with clarity. "If punishment * * * is extended to include those [acts] committed outside of the strict territorial jurisdiction, it is natural for Congress to say so in the statute and failure to do so will negate the purpose of Congress in this regard."

The two statutes under which the defendant was indicted, the Hostage Taking Act and the Aircraft Piracy Act, were part of a three bill package enacted by Congress in 1984 aimed at combating the rise of terrorism. Both were promulgated to extend jurisdiction over extraterritorial crimes and satisfy the country's obligations as a party to various international conventions. Because of the newness of the statutes, no court has been called upon to analyze the scope of the jurisdictional provisions. Therefore, the Court must rely on the recognized tools of statutory interpretation, the language of the statute along with the statutory history, to evaluate whether these provisions apply to the particular offenses charged in this indictment.

1. *Hostage Taking Act, 18 U.S.C. 1203*

This statute imposes liability on any individual who takes an American national hostage irrespective of where the seizure occurs. Congress wrote the jurisdictional reach of the statute in clear and unambiguous language. Subsection (b)(1) provides that a defendant is properly chargeable for offenses occurring outside the United States if *any one* of the following circumstances exists:

(A) the offender or the person seized or detained is a national of the United States;

(B) the offender is found in the United States; or

(C) the governmental organization sought to be compelled is the Government of the United States.

Congress enacted the Hostage Taking Act to meet its obligations as a signatory state to the Hostage Taking Convention, *supra.* Article 5 of that treaty required signatory states to extend jurisdiction over hijacking committed outside the United States when the offender was a citizen of the states, or "present" in the state. It also provided states with the discretion to assert jurisdiction when their nationals were taken hostage. Congress' voluntary decision to adopt this permissive basis of jurisdiction underscores its intent to exercise broad jurisdiction over any offender who threatens American nationals. Therefore, the plain language of the statute coupled with its legislative history and purpose clearly support a finding that Congress intended to assert extraterritorial jurisdiction over offenders such as Yunis who allegedly seized Americans hostage in foreign territory.

2. *Destruction of Aircraft Act, 18 U.S.C. 32*

(a.) *Application of 32(b):* jurisdiction over offenders later "found" in the United States.

This provision expressly extends jurisdiction over an alleged saboteur who commits offenses against an aircraft located in foreign airspace and has no other nexus to the United States other than that he or she "is later found in the United States." 18 U.S.C. 32(b)(4). Defendant was charged with violating these provisions, in the superceding indictment of October 1, 1987 that was filed after Yunis was arrested and flown to this country aboard a naval plane.

Defendant's counsel argues that his client was not "found" in the United States within the meaning of the statute. He purports that the word "found" only pertains to individuals who voluntarily entered the United States and were later discovered by the government; the term was never envisioned to apply to defendants forcibly abducted and brought to the United States. Yunis did not voluntarily enter the country. To the contrary, he was lured through efforts and stratagem of FBI agents to international waters off the coast of Cyprus, where he was arrested and forcibly brought to the United States. Therefore, counsel argues that the government's forcible kidnapping of Yunis obviates any jurisdiction under this statute. In response, the government states that the term "found" is neither defined in the statute nor explained in the legislative history. Indeed, the statute neither precludes nor approves the extension of jurisdiction over offenders who have been brought to this country by force. However, the government urges that the legislative history and purpose behind the statute support asserting jurisdiction over the defendant.

Defendant's attempt to limit the Court's jurisdiction is unavailing. Once a defendant is brought within the jurisdiction of the Court he is subject to prosecution for all federal offenses. Yunis was seized for alleged violation of the hostage taking statute. Physical presence in United States territory is not a necessary element for exercising subject matter jurisdiction over that offense. Only after he stepped onto American soil was the defendant charged with aircraft piracy. Indeed, once he was within the boundaries of the United States, the government was obligated by statute and the Montreal Convention to prosecute him for destroying the aircraft. As discussed earlier, both the Hague Convention and the Montreal Convention require all contracting states to exercise jurisdiction over individuals charged with seizing control of an aircraft. Any state that secures custody of the alleged hijackers is obligated to prosecute or extradite them.[20]

  (b.) *Application of 32(a):* jurisdiction over aircraft in "overseas or foreign air commerce".

  This provision imposes liability on individuals who damage and destroy an aircraft and/or perform acts of violence against passengers on board a civil aircraft that operates in "overseas or foreign air commerce." Yunis has been charged specifically in Count I with conspiracy to hijack and destroy an aircraft; Count III with destroying a civil aircraft; Count IV with placing a destructive device on a civil aircraft; and in Count V with performing acts of violence against passengers of a civil aircraft. * * *

  The 32(a) provision does not become operative unless the aircraft flies in "overseas or foreign air commerce." Defendant contends that the terms "overseas air commerce" and "foreign air commerce" require some nexus to the United States. Because the ALIA flight never landed on or even flew over American air space, he urges the Court to dismiss these counts. In turn, the government argues that Congress intended to regulate air commerce broadly and impose liability against alleged perpetrators of aircraft piracy irregardless of where the offense took place or which country operated the aircraft.

  The Court agrees that Counts III, IV, and V must be dismissed. Section (a) of this provision is applicable only to aircraft operating in "interstate, overseas or foreign air commerce." The definitional provision of the Act, 18 U.S.C. § 31, relies on the "meaning ascribed to those terms in the Federal Aviation Act of 1958, as amended." That statute provides:

  "interstate air commerce, overseas air commerce, and foreign air commerce respectively, mean the carriage by aircraft of persons * * * or the operation or navigation of aircraft in the conduct or furtherance of a business or vocation, in commerce between, respectively,—

   (a) a place in any State of the United States * * * through the airspace over any place outside thereof; or between places in the same Territory or possession of the United States,

   (b) a place in any State of the United States and any place in a Territory or possession of the United States; and

   (c) a place in the United States and any place outside thereof whether such commerce moves wholly by aircraft or partly by aircraft and partly by other forms of transportation."

49 U.S.C. § 1301(23).

  By focusing solely on the passengers and their connection to United States soil no matter how remote, the government's definition makes almost every aircraft subject to regulation by the United States. Airline

---

  20. See, Blakesley, Jurisdiction as Legal Protection against Terrorism, 19 Conn. L.Rev. 895, 918 (1987).

companies operating exclusively overseas which wanted to avoid such regulation would be forced to research the travel history of every potential passenger and then exclude any person who had ever traveled to the United States.

When exposed to its core, the government's extreme interpretation is rejected. Neither the courts nor the United States Department of Transportation ("DOT"), the agency in charge of administering the Act, have ever adopted the government's broad, open-ended definition. Indeed, the agency has expressly rejected the mirror image of the interpretation urged by the government here.

Based on the above, Counts III, IV and V of the indictment must be dismissed. Dismissal of those Counts also requires dismissal of the corresponding sections of Count I; ¶ 4b, c, & d, charging the defendant with violations under 18 U.S.C. § 32(a). However, the remaining section of the conspiracy count, ¶ 4a, charging defendant with violations under 18 U.S.C. §§ 1203 and 2 shall stand.

ORDERED

That defendant's Motion to Dismiss the Indictment and to Dismiss the Defendant from the Jurisdiction of the Court is granted as to that portion of Count I as stated above and Counts III, IV, and V charging defendant with violation of 18 U.S.C. § 32(a). The Motion to Dismiss as to the remainder * * * is denied.

————

Questions: What theories of jurisdiction were applied by the court? Was it correctly applied? What connection did Yunis's crime really have with the United States? What do you think of the argument that once Yunis was in the United States, although abducted, the U.S. was obligated to prosecute? In Yunis, FBI agents arrested Yunis aboard a Cypriot vessel on the high seas. Should the flag-state have exclusive enforcement jurisdiction on board? Was permission obtained? Does the FBI have legal authority to conduct such action within a foreign jurisdiction? Under U.S. law? International law?

Is prescriptive jurisdiction over conduct perpetrated by a Lebanese national against Jordanian aircraft in the Middle East? Does such expansive prescription risk putting U.S. nationals travelling abroad in danger? Terrorists and drug traffickers ought to be apprehended and prosecuted, but do you see a danger in establishing a precedent or domestic policy allowing abduction and harsh treatment to obtain incriminating evidence? Could American nationals ever be put in a situation where these tactics could be used against them? If so, do you think that our governmental protestations will ring true? Were not at least some of the hostages in the Middle–East held under a pretext sounding similar to this? The Attorney General in the Reagan Administration "authorized FBI agents to arrest defendants anywhere, including Foreign territory." Immediately after this, the Iranian Government issued the previously noted order, providing for the arrest of U.S. nationals anywhere.

The Attorney General said Yunis would be prosecuted under laws enacted by Congress in 1984 and 1986 that provide for a life sentence for hostage taking. The Attorney General insisted that law enforcement officials had legal authority to seize Yunis and transport him to the United States under a hostage-taking law enacted by Congress in 1984. The statute provides jurisdiction over offenses committed outside the United States when American nationals are among those taken hostage. A senior Justice Department official said Yunis is a "full-time employee of the Amal militia and works for Nabih Berri." Berri has been Lebanon's justice minister and the leader of Amal, Lebanon's largest Shiite organization. Berri offered to help mediate the release of American hostages and served as an intermediary in the resolution of another hijacking—that of Trans World Airlines Flight 847 in June 1985. In that incident, Robert Stethem, a U.S. Navy diver, who was among the passengers, was killed by a hijacker [while the plane was on the ground]. A man accused of being one of the hijackers, Mohammed Ali Hamadei, was arrested in Germany and was convicted of murder and kidnapping. Germany rejected American appeals to extradite Hamadei to the United States. *Chronicle*, Sept. 18, 1987, p. 1.

The Law on Hostage Taking Abroad under the Law of the United States, 18 U.S.C. 1203, is in the Documentary Supplement.

1. *Problems concerning jurisdiction to prescribe with respect to hostage taking abroad.* 18 U.S.C. § 1203 is based on Article 5 of the International Convention Against the Taking of Hostages to which the United States became a party on January 6, 1985. The text of the Convention is in the Doc. Supp. The preamble specifies that "all acts of taking of hostages" are "manifestations of international terrorism." The Yunis prosecution was presumably based on the prescription in Section 1203(b)(1)(A) which makes hostage taking an offense against the United States if the "person seized or detained is a national of or found in the United States." This provision is based in turn on Article 5(d) of the Convention, which provides that a state may exercise jurisdiction to prescribe with respect to the offender when the hostage is one of its nationals "if that state considers it appropriate."

Lebanon was not a party to the Convention at the time of the capture. Is this relevant to the issue of whether the United States had jurisdiction under the Convention? What would be the basis of U.S. jurisdiction under customary international law? Could it be predicated on one or more of the bases of jurisdiction discussed in this chapter? A ground of jurisdiction separate from the nationality of the hostage is provided in Article 5, 1(c) of the Convention and Section 1203(b)(1)(C) of Title 18 in the United States Code. According to these provisions, the United States would have jurisdiction over the terrorist if he had taken the passengers hostage to compel the United States "to do or abstain from doing any act." The hostage taking in this instance was directed to compelling the members of the Arab League to cancel a resolution just adopted by it. Should this fact be considered in deciding whether the United States was vested with jurisdiction? Does the fact that only four Americans were among the passengers taken hostage weigh against concluding that the United States was vested with jurisdiction?

2. *Jurisdiction to prescribe with respect to the killing of an American national.* In a separate incident an American national was killed during a hijacking. The passengers were being held on the ground when the killing took place. The issues of jurisdiction arising in this situation are presented in the materials which follow.

———

"OMNIBUS ANTI–TERRORISM ACT" TERRORIST ACTS OF VIOLENCE ABROAD AGAINST UNITED STATES NATIONALS: LAW OF THE UNITED STATES

18 U.S.C. 2331.

(a) HOMICIDE.—Whoever kills a national of the United States, while such national is outside the United States, shall—

(1) if the killing is a murder as defined in section 1111(a) of this title, be fined under this title or imprisoned for any term of years or for life, or both so fined and so imprisoned;

(2) if the killing is a voluntary manslaughter as defined in section 1112(a) of this title, be fined under this title or imprisoned not more than ten years, or both; and

(3) if the killing is an involuntary manslaughter as defined in section 1112(a) of this title, be fined under this title or imprisoned not more than three years, or both.

(b) ATTEMPT OR CONSPIRACY WITH RESPECT TO HOMICIDE.—Whoever outside the United States attempts to kill, or engages in a conspiracy to kill, a national of the United States shall [be subject to listed penalties.]

(c) OTHER CONDUCT.—Whoever outside the United States engages in physical violence—

(1) with intent to cause serious bodily injury to a national of the United States; or

(2) with the result that serious bodily injury is caused to a national of the United States;

shall be fined under this title or imprisoned not more than five years, or both.

* * *

(e) LIMITATION ON PROSECUTION.—No prosecution for any offense described in this section shall be undertaken by the United States except on written certification of the Attorney General or the highest ranking subordinate of the Attorney General with responsibility for criminal prosecutions that, in the judgment of the certifying official, such offense was intended to coerce, intimidate, or retaliate against a government or a civilian population.

* * *

1. ***Problem concerning jurisdiction to prescribe with respect to terrorist acts of violence abroad against United States nationals.*** 18 U.S.C. § 2331 is not based on an international convention. Is there basis under customary international law for this exercise of jurisdiction to prescribe? What would it be?

The Legal Adviser of the Department of State appeared before the Senate Judiciary Committee. His prepared statement asserted the "proposed extension of jurisdiction is both warranted by reality and logic, and consistent with international law." He argued "there is no compelling reason why the seizure of a private U.S. citizen abroad as a hostage should be a U.S. federal crime but the terrorist murder of that same U.S. citizen should not." He endorsed the view of a member of the subcommittee that the principle of protective jurisdiction could be extended to the type of offenses covered by the legislation.

Query: Why was ¶ (e) of the Act included? Is it a substantive rule of law and an element of an offense? Is it a special type of violence against U.S. citizens that triggers this jurisdiction? What sort of violence counts? Would heavy bombardment of a U.S. military unit engaged in military action (such as in Somalia or Bosnia–Herzegovina) constitute terroristic violence pursuant to the Act? The intent of the bombardment would likely be to intimidate the U.S. into quitting the fight. Would the law apply?

2. ***Resolution on international terrorism in the United Nations.*** On December 9, 1985, the General Assembly adopted Resolution 40/61 concerning measures to prevent international terrorism. It is reproduced in 25 ILM 239 (1986). It "unequivocally condemns, as criminal, all acts, methods and practices of terrorism wherever and by whomever committed." Did this create a normative rule making any act of terrorism a crime under international law, thus justifying the enactment of 18 U.S.C. § 2331? If such was the intent, why does the preamble to the resolution state that the General Assembly reaffirms "the inalienable right to self-determination and independence of all peoples under colonial and racist regimes" and upholds "the legitimacy of their struggle, in particular the struggle of national liberation movements"?

3. ***Regional conventions dealing with terrorism.*** The member states of the Council of Europe elected to deal with acts of terrorism by removing from the "political exception to extradition" offenses such as the taking of hostages and acts of violence against the life or physical integrity of a person. The text of the European convention is in 15 International Legal Materials 1272 (1976). The United States was a party with several Latin American states to a Convention to Prevent and Punish the Acts of Terrorism Taking the Form of Crimes Against Persons and Related Extortion That Are of International Significance. 27 U.S.T. 3949 (1976).

———

8. THE PRINCIPLE OF REASONABLENESS

Recent U.S. judicial decisions have expanded the traditional bases of jurisdiction to proscribe thwarted extraterritorial narcotics conspiracies, even when no element of the offense (or any effect) has occurred in U.S. territory. The Restatement (Third)'s *"Rule of Reasonableness "* endorses this expansion. The rule of reasonableness provides that even where an appropriate basis for jurisdiction exists, assertion of jurisdiction will not be appropriate, if such assertion is unreasonable or exorbitant. U.S. courts have utilized this rule in conjunction to expanding the territoriality theories of jurisdiction, deciding, themselves, whether their assertion of jurisdiction is exorbitant or unreasonable. Thus, even when a narcotics conspiracy has occurred totally abroad, but evidence exists that the intent was to violate U.S. law and territory, the objective territoriality theory has been held to apply. Jurisdiction, however, will not be asserted if it will violate a significant interest of another state or is otherwise exorbitant. Do you see any theoretical and practical problems with this approach?

SECTION B. JURISDICTION TO PRESCRIBE CHOICE OF LAW RULES

1. *Enforcement of choice of law rules.* A defendant bought the diamond necklace in New York City without paying for it. The courts in New York have jurisdiction to prescribe a rule of law governing a transaction that took place in its territory. The "purchaser" was a Mexican national, and the courts of Mexico have jurisdiction to prescribe based upon the nationality of Tuduri. Spain's courts took jurisdiction when Plaintiff sued Defendant (a Spanish domiciliary). Does Spain's jurisdiction to prescribe justify the exercise by its courts of jurisdiction to adjudicate? *Winston v. Tuduri,* 34 ILR 49 (1967).

The answer is that a state may make a choice of law. Thus, the Spanish court must decide whether to apply New York or Mexican law *for the settlement of claims* between persons—nationals or aliens— present in the territory or for the resolution of claims asserted against property located in the territory, even though it otherwise has no jurisdiction to prescribe substantive rules of law with respect to the persons involved or the property in issue. This is within the realm of conflicts of law also known as private international law. Such rules will guide the Spanish court in choosing between the three sets of laws that it could conceivably enforce, i.e. the law of New York, Mexican law, or possibly Spanish law. The problem of choice of law is more complex.

2. *Treatment of subject in the 1987 Restatement.**

* Copyright 1987 by the American Law Institute. Reprinted with the permission of the American Law Institute.

§ 401, Categories of Jurisdiction

Under international law, a state is subject to limitations on

(1) jurisdiction to prescribe, i.e., to make its law applicable to the activities, relations, or status of persons, or the interests of persons in things, whether by legislation, by executive act or order, by administrative rule or regulation, or by determination of a court;

(2) jurisdiction to adjudicate, i.e., to subject persons or things to the process of its courts or administrative tribunals, whether in civil or in criminal proceedings, whether or not the state is a party to the proceedings;

(3) jurisdiction to enforce, i.e., to induce or compel compliance or punish noncompliance with its laws or regulations, whether through the courts or by use of executive, administrative, police, or other non-judicial action.

Interest analysis in conflict of laws and Section 40 of the 1965 Restatement as a requirement of international public law. In the early 1960's, Section 40 was presented to and approved by the American Law Institute as an emerging principle of customary international law that ought to be recognized. The section provides as a requirement of international public law that courts, administrative tribunals and similar agencies within a state should, under certain circumstances, recognize that international law requires a good faith effort to accommodate the different laws of one or more states to a transnational economic problem, even though nothing in the national law of the forum authorizes specifically any moderation of the impact of the forum rule that otherwise would apply.

Interest analysis, originally developed by the late Professor Brainerd Currie as a process for choosing the applicable rule of law in a private law case involving the law of two (or more) law-making entities, directed a court always to apply the rule of the forum state if that state had any governmental interest in the outcome of the case, even if there were a true conflict in the sense that another state also had a governmental interest in the application of its rule to produce a different outcome. The effect of this position was that true conflicts could never be resolved by a single principle applicable regardless of where the case was brought. Forum shopping would thus clearly be encouraged. In time the interest analysis approach was modified by Professor Currie to provide that the court responsible for the choice of law operation should act, as to foreign law, in a restrained and enlightened manner. By the end of the decade the interest analysis approach to choice of law in private international law had evolved in America toward the position earlier taken as to public law by Section 40 of the 1965 Restatement.

Although the American Law Institute was formulating a new Restatement of Conflict of Laws in the same decade, this work did not follow the interest analysis approach in either its original or its modified versions. See, however, Restatement, Second, Conflict of Laws, § 6.

See, Symeon Symeonides, Revolution and Counter–Revolution in American Conflicts of Law: Is There a Middle Ground? 46 Ohio St.L.J. 549 (1985); Symeon Symeonides, Choice of Law in the American Courts, 1993: A Preliminary View, 42 A.J.Comp.L. 701 (1994).

SECTION C. JURISDICTION TO ENFORCE RULES OF LAW

---

1. DEPENDENCE OF JURISDICTION TO ENFORCE UPON JURISDICTION TO PRESCRIBE

ARRET FORNAGE

France, Court of Cassation, 1873.
84 Journal du Palais 299 (1873).[a]

[The accused was prosecuted for grand larceny committed in Switzerland. In accordance with French procedure, the indictment was presented to a court whose function was to decide whether the evidence was sufficient to support prosecution and which criminal court had jurisdiction to try the case. It found sufficient evidence for prosecution and decided the case should be tried by the Court of Assizes. From this decision, the accused could have appealed to the Court of Cassation, i.e. the supreme court, but failed to do so.

At trial, he objected he could not be prosecuted in the French courts for a crime committed in a foreign country. * * *

The appeal was heard by the Criminal Section of the Court of Cassation and decided in accord with the arguments presented by a conseiller rapporteur, i.e. a member of the court appointed to make recommendations, and those presented by the avocat général. The conseiller rapporteur conceded the ruling of the Court of Assizes was in accord with the precedents established by the Court of Cassation, but went on to make the argument which appears below.]

Is it not possible also to say that, in the case presented to you, there are considerations of a superior nature justifying an exception to the general rule? The only basis for the right to punish is sovereignty, which dies at the border. If French law allows the prosecution of French nationals for crimes or offenses committed in a foreign country, it is because criminal law applies both on a territorial and personal basis. A French national, even abroad, still remains a citizen of his country and as such remains subject to French law, which has power over him as soon as he comes back to France. But [without an exceptional basis,] the law itself cannot give French courts the power to try foreign nationals for crimes or offenses committed outside French territory; such exorbitant jurisdiction, whose basis could neither be territorial nor personal, would constitute a violation of international law, a breach of the sovereignty of other states. There [are a limited number of] exceptions to this rule of international law. When, [for example,] a foreign

a. Translation by the editors.

national has committed, even abroad, a crime against the security of the state, he can be prosecuted, tried and punished in France. [This exception] is based on the right of self-defense [others may be based on universality or passive personality. Apart from these, which are very limited], foreign nationals can only be prosecuted by the courts of their own country for acts committed outside the territory. * * * The Court of Assizes, by punishing this act, would commit an abuse of power; it would usurp a right of sovereignty belonging to a foreign power. Would it not be contrary to all principles of justice to force the judges into knowingly becoming guilty of an arbitrary act, a violation of international law? * * * [The Court of Assizes] must examine the evidence presented by the accused in support of his claims and declare itself without jurisdiction if it finds that he is an alien and the act of which he is accused has been committed outside French territory.

Indeed, French justice has jurisdiction only to try French nationals for crimes committed by them outside the territory * * *; it has no jurisdiction over aliens; so the question of nationality must be decided beforehand; for the right of jurisdiction depends upon the resolution of the question. The ruling which is challenged appears to me to have overlooked those fundamental principles.

* * * [I]t is a general principle that * * * jurisdiction, however broad it may be, cannot extend to crimes committed outside the territory by aliens who, in respect to those acts, are not punishable in French courts. * * * [T]his lack of jurisdiction in this regard is absolute, permanent; it can be cured neither by the silence nor by the consent of the accused; it continues to exist at all levels * * * [and the indicting court] cannot give the Court of Assizes a right it does not itself possess, to try acts which do not come under the jurisdiction of French law. * * * [R]aymond Fornage was sent to the Court of Assizes of Haute–Savoie and accused of having committed grand larceny in the Canton of Valais (Switzerland); before the trial began, he presented arguments to the effect that the court was without jurisdiction * * * the Court of Assizes wrongly applied * * * [the law]; and by ordering the trial to proceed without deciding the motion based on nationality * * * disregarded the rights of the defendant.

––––––

1. ***Relevance of the Lotus Case.*** The Reporters' Note to the section refers to the Lotus Case, supra. Why is it relevant?

2. ***Treatment of subject in 1987 Restatement.*** Comment *a* to Section 431 states: "Under international law, a state may not exercise authority to enforce law that it has no jurisdiction to prescribe."

––––––

2. EXCLUSIVE CHARACTER OF JURISDICTION TO ENFORCE WITHIN THE TERRITORY

THE SCHOONER EXCHANGE v. McFADDON

United States Supreme Court, 1812.
11 U.S. (7 Cranch) 116, 136, 3 L.Ed. 287.

MARSHALL, C.J.   * * *

  * * *

The jurisdiction of the nation within its own territory is necessarily exclusive and absolute. It is susceptible of no limitation not imposed by itself. Any restriction upon it, deriving validity from an external source, would imply a diminution of its sovereignty to the extent of the restriction, and an investment of that sovereignty to the same extent in that power which could impose such restriction.

  * * *

———

UNITED STATES v. ALVAREZ–MACHAIN

United States Supreme Court, 1992.
504 U.S. ___, 112 S.Ct. 2188, 119 L.Ed.2d 441.

THE CHIEF JUSTICE delivered the opinion of the Court. The issue in this case is whether a criminal defendant, abducted to the United States from a nation with which it has an extradition treaty, thereby acquires a defense to the jurisdiction of this country's courts. We hold that he does not, and that he may be tried in federal district court for violations of the criminal law of the United States.

Respondent, Alvarez–Machain, is a citizen and resident of Mexico. He was indicted for participating in the kidnap and murder of United States Drug Enforcement Administration (DEA) special agent Enrique Camarena–Salazar and a Mexican pilot working with Camarena, Alfredo Zavala–Avelar. The DEA believes that respondent, a medical doctor, participated in the murder by prolonging agent Camarena's life so that others could further torture and interrogate him. On April 2, 1990, respondent was forcibly kidnapped from his medical office in Guadalajara, Mexico, to be flown by private plane to El Paso, Texas, where he was arrested by DEA officials. The District Court concluded that DEA agents were responsible for respondent's abduction, although they were not personally involved in it. United States v. Caro–Quintero, 745 F.Supp. 599, 602–604, 609 (DC Cal.1990).[2]

Respondent moved to dismiss the indictment, claiming that his abduction constituted outrageous governmental conduct, and that the

---

2. Apparently, DEA officials had attempted to gain respondent's presence in the United States through informal negotiations with Mexican officials, but were unsuccessful. DEA officials then, through a contact in Mexico, offered to pay a reward and expenses in return for the delivery of respondent to the United States. United States v. Caro–Quintero.

District Court lacked jurisdiction to try him because he was abducted in violation of the Extradition Treaty between the United States and Mexico. Extradition Treaty, May 4, 1978, [1979] United States–United Mexican States (Extradition Treaty or Treaty). The District Court rejected the outrageous governmental conduct claim, but held that it lacked jurisdiction to try respondent because his abduction violated the Extradition Treaty. The district court discharged respondent and ordered that he be repatriated to Mexico.

The Court of Appeals affirmed the dismissal of the indictment and the repatriation of respondent, relying on its decision in United States v. Verdugo–Urquidez. In Verdugo, the Court of Appeals held that the forcible abduction of a Mexican national with the authorization or participation of the United States violated the Extradition Treaty between the United States and Mexico.[3] Although the Treaty does not expressly prohibit such abductions, the Court of Appeals held that the "purpose" of the Treaty was violated by a forcible abduction, * * * which, along with a formal protest by the offended nation, would give a defendant the right to invoke the Treaty violation to defeat jurisdiction of the district court to try him. The Court of Appeals further held that the proper remedy for such a violation would be dismissal of the indictment and repatriation of the defendant to Mexico.

In the instant case, the Court of Appeals affirmed the district court's finding that the United States had authorized the abduction of respondent, and that letters from the Mexican government to the United States government served as an official protest of the Treaty violation. Therefore, the Court of Appeals ordered that the indictment against respondent be dismissed and that respondent be repatriated to Mexico * * *. We granted certiorari * * * and now reverse.

Although we have never before addressed the precise issue raised, * * *, we have previously considered proceedings in claimed violation of an extradition treaty, and proceedings against a defendant brought before a court by means of a forcible abduction. We addressed the former issue in United States v. Rauscher, 119 U.S. 407 (1886); more precisely, the issue of whether the Webster–Ashburton Treaty of 1842, which governed extraditions between England and the United States, prohibited the prosecution of defendant Rauscher for a crime other than the crime for which he had been extradited. Whether this prohibition, known as the doctrine of specialty, was an intended part of the Treaty had been disputed between the two nations for some time. Justice Miller delivered the opinion of the Court, which carefully examined the terms and history of the Treaty; the practice of nations in regards to extradition treaties; the case law from the states; and the writings of commentators, and reached the following conclusion:

> "[A] person who has been brought within the jurisdiction of the court *by virtue of proceedings under an extradition treaty,* can only be tried for one of the offenses described in that treaty, and for the

3. Verdugo–Urquidez was also indicted for the murder of agent Camarena. In an earlier decision, we held that the 4th Amendment did not apply to a search by United States agents of Verdugo–Urquidez' home in Mexico. U.S. v. Verdugo–Urquidez, 494 U.S. 259 (1990).

offence with which he is charged in the proceedings for his extradition, until a reasonable time and opportunity have been given him, after his release or trial upon such charge, to return to the country from whose asylum he had been forcibly taken under those proceedings." Id., at 430 (emphasis added).

In addition, Justice Miller's opinion noted that any doubt as to this interpretation was put to rest by two federal statutes which imposed the doctrine of specialty upon extradition treaties to which the United States was a party * * *. Unlike the case before us today, the defendant in Rauscher had been brought to the United States by way of an extradition treaty; there was no issue of a forcible abduction.

In Ker v. Illinois, 119 U.S. 436 (1886), also written by Justice Miller and decided the same day as Rauscher, we addressed the issue of a defendant brought before the court by way of a forcible abduction. Ker had been tried and convicted in an Illinois court for larceny; his presence before the court was procured by means of forcible abduction from Peru. A messenger was sent to Lima with the proper warrant to demand Ker by virtue of the extradition treaty between Peru and the United States. The messenger, however, disdained reliance on the treaty processes, and instead forcibly kidnapped Ker and brought him to the United States. We distinguished Ker's case from Rauscher, on the basis that Ker was not brought into the United States by virtue of the extradition treaty between the United States and Peru, and rejected Ker's argument that he had a right under the extradition treaty to be returned to this country only in accordance with its terms. We rejected Ker's due process argument more broadly, holding in line with "the highest authorities" that "such forcible abduction is no sufficient reason why the party should not answer when brought within the jurisdiction of the court which has the right to try him for such an offence, and presents no valid objection to his trial in such court." * * *.

In Frisbie v. Collins, 342 U.S. 519 * * * (1952), we applied the rule in Ker to a case in which the defendant had been kidnapped in Chicago by Michigan officers and brought to trial in Michigan. We upheld the conviction over objections based on the due process clause and the Federal Kidnapping Act and stated:

> "This Court has never departed from the [Ker] rule, that the power of a court to try a person for crime is not impaired by the fact that he had been brought within the court's jurisdiction by reason of a 'forcible abduction.' No persuasive reasons are now presented to justify overruling this line of cases. They rest on the sound basis that due process of law is satisfied when one present in court is convicted of crime after having been fairly apprized of the charges against him and after a fair trial in accordance with constitutional procedural safeguards. There is nothing in the Constitution that requires a court to permit a guilty person rightfully convicted to escape justice because he was brought to trial against his will."

The only differences between Ker and the present case are that Ker was decided on the premise that there was no governmental involvement in the abduction, * * * and Peru, from which Ker was abducted, did not object to his prosecution. Respondent finds these differences to be dispositive, as did the Court of Appeals in Verdugo, * * *, contending that they show that respondent's prosecution, like the prosecution of Rauscher, violates the implied terms of a valid extradition treaty. The Government * * * argues that Rauscher stands as an "exception" to the rule in Ker only when an extradition treaty is invoked, and the terms of the treaty prove that its breach will limit the jurisdiction of a court * * *. Therefore, our first inquiry must be whether the abduction of respondent from Mexico violated the extradition treaty between the United States and Mexico. If we conclude that the Treaty does not prohibit respondent's abduction, the rule in Ker applies, and the court need not inquire as to how respondent came before it.

In construing a treaty, as in construing a statute, we first look to its terms to determine its meaning. * * * The Treaty says nothing about the obligations of the United States and Mexico to refrain from forcible abductions of people from the territory of the other nation, or the consequences under the Treaty if such an abduction occurs. * * *

More critical to respondent's argument is Article 9 of the Treaty:

"1. Neither Contracting Party shall be bound to deliver up its own nationals, but the executive authority of the requested Party shall, if not prevented by the laws of that Party, have the power to deliver them up if, in its discretion, it be deemed proper to do so.

"2. If extradition is not granted pursuant to paragraph 1 of this Article, the requested Party shall submit the case to its competent authorities for the purpose of prosecution, proved that Party has jurisdiction over the offense."

According to respondent, Article 9 embodies the terms of the bargain which the United States struck: if the United States wishes to prosecute a Mexican national, it may request that individual's extradition. Upon a request from the United States, Mexico may either extradite the individual, or submit the case to the proper authorities for prosecution in Mexico. In this way, respondent reasons, each nation preserved its right to choose whether its nationals would be tried in its own courts or by the courts of the other nation. This preservation of rights would be frustrated if either nation were free to abduct nationals of the other nation for the purposes of prosecution. More broadly, respondent reasons, as did the Court of Appeals, that all the processes and restrictions on the obligation to extradite established by the Treaty would make no sense if either nation were free to resort to forcible kidnapping to gain the presence of an individual for prosecution in a manner not contemplated by the Treaty. * * *

We do not read the Treaty in such a fashion. Article 9 does not purport to specify the only way in which one country may gain custody of a national of the other country for the purposes of prosecution. In the absence of an extradition treaty, nations are under no obligation to surrender those in their country to foreign authorities for prosecution. Rauscher, * * * Factor v. Laubenheimer, 290 U.S. 276, 287 (1933) * * *. Extradition treaties exist so as to impose mutual obligations to surrender individuals in certain defined sets of circumstances, following established procedures * * *. The Treaty provides a mechanism which would not otherwise exist, requiring, under certain circumstances, the United States and Mexico to extradite individuals to the other country, and establishing the procedures to be followed when the Treaty is invoked.

The history of negotiation and practice under the Treaty also fails to show that abductions outside of the Treaty constitute a violation of the Treaty. As the Solicitor General notes, the Mexican government was made aware, as early as 1906, of the Ker doctrine, and the United States' position that it applied to forcible abductions made outside of the terms of the United States–Mexico Extradition Treaty.[11] Nonetheless, the current version of the Treaty, signed in 1978, does not attempt to establish a rule that would in any way curtail the effect of Ker. Moreover, although language which would grant individuals exactly the right sought by respondent had been considered and drafted as early as 1935 by a prominent group of legal scholars sponsored by the faculty of Harvard Law School, no such clause appears in the current treaty.*

Thus, the language of the Treaty, in the context of its history, does not support the proposition that the Treaty prohibits abductions outside of its terms. The remaining question, therefore, is whether the Treaty should be interpreted so as to include an implied term prohibiting prosecution where the defendant's presence is obtained by means other than those established by the Treaty. See Valentine, 299 U.S., at 17 ("Strictly the question is not whether there had been a uniform practical construction denying the power, but whether the power had been so clearly recognized that the grant should be implied").

Respondent contends that the Treaty must be interpreted against the backdrop of customary international law, and that international abductions are "so clearly prohibited in international law" that there was no reason to include such a clause in the Treaty itself * * *. The international censure of international abductions is further evinced, according to respondent, by the United Nations Charter and the Charter of the Organization of American States. * * * Respondent does not argue that these sources of international law prove an independent basis for the right respondent asserts not to be tried in the United States, but rather that they should inform the interpretation of the Treaty terms.

---

11. In correspondence between the United States and Mexico growing out of the 1905 Martinez incident, in which a Mexican national was abducted from Mexico and brought to the United States for trial, the Mexican charge wrote to the Secretary of State protesting that as Martinez' arrest was made outside of the procedures established in the extradition treaty, "the action pending against the man can not rest [on] any legal foundation." * * * The Secretary of State responded that the exact issue raised by the Martinez incident had been decided by Ker, and that the remedy open to the Mexican government, namely a request to the United States for extradition of Martinez' abductor had been granted by the United States * * *. Respondent and the Court of Appeals stress a statement made in 1881 by Secretary of State James Blaine to the governor of Texas to the effect that the extradition treaty in its form at that time did not authorize unconsented to abductions from Mexico. * * * This misses the mark, however, for the Government's argument is not that the Treaty authorizes the abduction of respondent; but that the Treaty does not prohibit the abduction.

Editors' note: The U.S. and Mexico signed, in spring 1994, a treaty supplement, which now explicitly prohibits such abductions.

The Court of Appeals deemed it essential, * * * for the individual defendant to assert a right under the Treaty, that the affected foreign government had registered a protest * * *. Respondent agrees that the right exercised by the individual is derivative of the nation's right under the Treaty, since nations are authorized, notwithstanding the terms of an extradition treaty, to voluntarily render an individual to the other country on terms completely outside of those proved in the Treaty. The formal protest * * * ensures that the "offended" nation actually objects to the abduction and has not in some way voluntarily rendered the individual for prosecution. Thus the Extradition Treaty only prohibits gaining the defendant's presence by means other than those set forth in the Treaty when the nation from which the defendant was abducted objects.

This argument seems to us inconsistent with the remainder of respondent's argument. The Extradition Treaty has the force of law, and if, as respondent asserts, it is self-executing, it would appear that a court must enforce it on behalf of an individual regardless of the offensiveness of the practice of one nation to the other nation. In Rauscher, the Court noted that Great Britain had taken the position in other cases that the Webster–Ashburton Treaty included the doctrine of specialty, but no importance was attached to whether or not Great Britain had protested the prosecution of Rauscher for the crime of cruel and unusual punishment as opposed to murder.

More fundamentally, the difficulty with the support respondent garners from international law is that none of it relates to the practice of nations in relation to extradition treaties. In Rauscher, we implied a term in the Webster–Ashburton Treaty because of the practice of nations with regard to extradition treaties. In the instant case, respondent would imply terms in the Extradition Treaty from the practice of nations with regards to international law more generally.[14] Respondent would have us find that the Treaty acts as a prohibition against a violation of the general principle of international law that one government may not "exercise its police power in the territory of another state." * * * There are many actions which could be taken by a nation that would violate this principle, including waging war, but it cannot seriously be contended an invasion óf the United States by Mexico would violate the terms of the Extradition Treaty between the two nations.

In sum, to infer from this Treaty and its terms that it prohibits all means of gaining the presence of an individual outside of its terms goes beyond established precedent and practice * * *. The general principles cited by respondent simply fail to persuade us that we should imply in

14. Similarly, the Court of Appeals in Verdugo reasoned that international abductions violate the "purpose" of the Treaty, stating that "[t]he requirements extradition treaties impose constitute a means of safeguarding the sovereignty of the signatory nations, as well as ensuring the fair treatment of individuals." * * * The ambitious purpose ascribed to the Treaty by the Court of Appeals, we believe, places a greater burden on its language and history than they can logically bear. In a broad sense, most international agreements have the common purpose of safeguarding the sovereignty of signatory nations, in that they seek to further peaceful relations between nations. This, however, does not mean that the violation of any principle of international law constitutes a violation of this particular Treaty.

the United States–Mexico Extradition Treaty a term prohibiting international abductions.

Respondent and his *amici* may be correct that respondent's abduction was "shocking," * * *, and that it may be in violation of general international law principles. Mexico has protested the abduction of respondent through diplomatic notes * * *, and the decision of whether respondent should be returned to Mexico, as a matter outside of the Treaty, is a matter for the Executive Branch. [*The Mexican Government has requested the extradition of two individuals who allegedly participated in the abduction from Mexico*]. We conclude, however, that respondent's abduction was not in violation of the Extradition Treaty between the United States and Mexico, and therefore the rule of Ker v. Illinois is fully applicable to this case. The fact of respondent's forcible abduction does not therefore prohibit his trial in a court in the United States for violations of the criminal laws of the United States * * *.

Justice STEVENS, with whom Justice BLACKMUN and Justice O'CONNOR join, dissenting.

* * * The case is unique for several reasons. It does not involve an ordinary abduction by a private kidnaper, or bounty hunter, as in Ker v. Illinois, [supra]; nor does it involve the apprehension of an American fugitive who committed a crime in one State and sought asylum in another, as in Frisbie v. Collins, [supra]. Rather, it involves this country's abduction of another country's citizen; it also involves a violation of the territorial integrity of that other country, with which this country has signed an extradition treaty.

A Mexican citizen was kidnapped in Mexico and charged with a crime committed in Mexico; his offense allegedly violated both Mexican and American law. Mexico has formally demanded on at least two separate occasions that he be returned to Mexico and has represented that he will be prosecuted and punished for his alleged offense. It is clear that Mexico's demand must be honored if this official abduction violated the 1978 Extradition Treaty between the United States and Mexico. In my opinion, a fair reading of the treaty in light of our decision in [U.S. v. Rauscher] * * *, and applicable principles of international law, leads inexorably to the conclusion that the District Court, U.S. v. Caro–Quintero [supra], and the Court of Appeals for the Ninth Circuit, [supra] (per curiam), correctly construed that instrument.

* * *

I

The Extradition Treaty with Mexico is a comprehensive document * * *. The parties announced their purpose in the preamble: The two Governments desire "to cooperate more closely in the fight against crime and, to this end, to mutually render better assistance in matters of extradition." From the preamble, through the description of the parties' obligations with respect to offenses committed within as well as beyond the territory of a requesting party, the delineation of the procedures and evidentiary requirements for extradition, the special provisions for political offenses and capital punishment, and other details, the

Treaty appears to have been designed to cover the entire subject of extradition. Thus, Article 22, entitled "Scope of Application" states that the "Treaty shall apply to offenses specified in Article 2 committed before and after this Treaty enters into force," and Article 2 directs that "[e]xtradition shall take place, subject to this Treaty, for willful acts which fall within any of [the extraditable offenses listed in] the clauses of the Appendix." Moreover, as noted by the Court * * *, Article 9 expressly proves that neither Contracting Party is bound to deliver up its own nationals, although it may do so in its discretion, but if it does not do so, it "shall submit the case to its competent authorities for purposes of prosecution."

Petitioner's claim that the Treaty is not exclusive, but permits forcible governmental kidnaping, would transform these, and other, provisions into little more than verbiage. For example, provisions requiring "sufficient" evidence to grant extradition (Art. 3), withholding extradition for political or military offenses (Art. 5), withholding extradition when the person sought has already been tried (Art. 6), withholding extradition when the statute of limitations for the crime has lapsed (Art. 7), and granting the requested State discretion to refuse to extradite an individual who would face the death penalty in the requesting country (Art. 8), would serve little purpose if the requesting country could simply kidnap the person. As the Court of Appeals for the Ninth Circuit recognized in a related case, "[e]ach of these provisions would be utterly frustrated if a kidnapping were held to be a permissible course of governmental conduct." United States v. Verdugo–Urquidez, [supra]. In addition, all of these provisions "only make sense if they are understood as requiring each treaty signatory to comply with those procedures whenever it wishes to obtain jurisdiction over an individual who is located in another treaty nation." Id., at 1351.

It is true, as the Court notes, that there is no express promise by either party to refrain from forcible abductions in the territory of the other Nation * * *. Relying on that omission, the Court, in effect, concludes that the Treaty merely creates an optional method of obtaining jurisdiction over alleged offenders, and that the parties silently reserved the right to resort to self help whenever they deem force more expeditious than legal process. If the United States, for example, thought it more expedient to torture or simply to execute a person rather than to attempt extradition, these options would be equally available because they, too, were not explicitly prohibited by the Treaty. That, however, is a highly improbable interpretation of a consensual agreement, which on its face appears to have been intended to set forth comprehensive and exclusive rules concerning the subject of extradition. In my opinion, "the manifest scope and object of the treaty itself," plainly imply a mutual undertaking to respect the territorial integrity of the other contracting party. That opinion is confirmed by a consideration of the "legal context" in which the Treaty was negotiated * * *.

II

In Rauscher, the Court construed an extradition treaty that was far less comprehensive than the 1978 Treaty with Mexico. The 1842 Treaty with Great Britain determined the boundary between the United States and Canada, proved for the suppression of the African slave trade, and also contained one paragraph authorizing the extradition of fugitives "in certain cases." In Article X, each Nation agreed to "deliver up to justice all persons" properly charged with any one of seven specific crimes, including murder. * * *. After Rauscher had been extradited for murder, he was charged with the lesser offense of inflicting cruel and unusual punishment on a member of the crew of a vessel on the high seas. Although the treaty did not purport to place any limit on the jurisdiction of the demanding State after acquiring custody of the fugitive, this Court held that he could not be tried for any offense other than murder. Thus, the treaty constituted the exclusive means by which the United States could obtain jurisdiction over a defendant within the territorial jurisdiction of Great Britain.

The Court noted that the Treaty included several specific provisions, such as the crimes for which one could be extradited, the process by which the extradition was to be carried out, and even the evidence that was to be produced, and concluded that "the fair purpose of the treaty is, that the person shall be delivered up to be tried for that offence and for no other." Id., at 423 * * *. The Court reasoned that it did not make sense for the Treaty to prove such specifics only to have the person "pas[s] into the hands of the country which charges him with the offence, free from all the positive requirements and just implications of the Treaty under which the transfer of his person takes place." Id., at 421, * * *. To interpret the Treaty in a contrary way would mean that a country could request extradition of a person for one of the seven crimes covered by the Treaty, and then try the person for another crime, such as a political crime, which was clearly not covered by the Treaty; this result, the Court concluded, was clearly contrary to the intent of the parties and the purpose of the Treaty.

Rejecting an argument that the sole purpose of Article X was to prove a procedure for the transfer of an individual from the jurisdiction of one sovereign to another, the Court stated:

> "No such view of solemn public treaties between the great nations of the earth can be sustained by a tribunal called upon to give judicial construction to them.

> "The opposite view has been attempted to be maintained in this country upon the ground that there is no express limitation in the treaty of the right of the country in which the offence was committed to try the person for the crime alone for which he was extradited, and that once being within the jurisdiction of that country, no matter by what contrivance or fraud or by what pretence of establishing a charge proved for by the extradition treaty he may have been brought within the jurisdiction, he is, when here, liable to be tried for any offence against the laws as though arrested here originally. This proposition of the absence of express restriction in the treaty of the right to try him for other offenses than that for which he was extradited, is met by the manifest scope and object of the treaty itself." Id., at 422. * * *

Thus, the Extradition Treaty, as understood in the context of cases that have addressed similar issues, suffices to protect the defendant from prosecution despite the absence of any express language in the Treaty itself purporting to limit this Nation's power to prosecute a defendant over whom it had lawfully acquired jurisdiction.

Although the Court's conclusion in Rauscher was supported by a number of judicial precedents, the holdings in these cases were not nearly as uniform as the consensus of international opinion that condemns one Nation's violation of the territorial integrity of a friendly neighbor.[21] It is shocking that a party to an extradition treaty might believe that it has secretly reserved the right to make seizures of citizens in the other party's territory. Justice Story found it shocking enough that the United States would attempt to justify an American seizure of a foreign vessel in a Spanish port:

> "But, even supposing, for a moment, that our laws had required an entry of the Apollon, in her transit, does it follow, that the power to arrest her was meant to be given, after she had passed into the exclusive territory of a foreign nation? We think not. *It would be monstrous* to suppose that our revenue officers were authorized to enter into foreign ports and territories, for the purpose of seizing vessels which had offended against our laws. It cannot be presumed that Congress would voluntarily justify such a clear violation of the laws of nations." The Apollon, 9 Wheat. 362, 370–371 (1824) (emphasis added).[22]

The law of Nations, as understood by Justice Story in 1824, has not changed. Thus, a leading treatise explains: "A State must not perform acts of sovereignty in the territory of another State."

"* * *

---

21. When Abraham Sofaer, Legal Adviser of the State Department, was questioned at a congressional hearing, he resisted the notion that such seizures were acceptable: " 'Can you imagine us going into Paris and seizing some person we regard as a terrorist * * *? [H]ow would we feel if some foreign nation—let us take the United Kingdom— came over here and seized some terrorist suspect in New York City, or Boston, or Philadelphia, * * * because we refused through the normal channels of international, legal communications, to extradite that individual?' " Bill To Authorize Prosecution of Terrorists and Others Who Attack U.S. Government Employees and Citizens Abroad: Hearing before the Subcommittee on Security and Terrorism of the Senate Committee on the Judiciary, 99th Cong., 1st Sess., 63 (1985).

22. Justice Story's opinion continued: "The arrest of the offending vessel must, therefore, be restrained to places where our jurisdiction is complete, to our own waters, or to the ocean, the common highway of all nations. It is said, that there is a revenue jurisdiction, which is distinct from the ordinary maritime jurisdiction over waters within the range of a common shot from our shores. And the provisions in the Collection Act of 1799, which authorize a visitation of vessels within four leagues of our coasts, are referred to in proof of the assertion. But where is that right of visitation to be exercised? In a foreign territory, in the exclusive jurisdiction of another sovereign? Certainly not; for the very terms of the act confine it to the ocean, where all nations have a common right, and exercise a common sovereignty. And over what vessels is this right of visitation to be exercised? By the very words of the act, over our own vessels, and over foreign vessels bound to our ports, and over no others. To have gone beyond this, would have been an usurpation of exclusive sovereignty on the ocean, and an exercise of an universal right of search, a right which has never yet been acknowledged by other nations, and would be resisted by none with more pertinacity than by the American." The Apollon, 9 Wheat., at 371–373.

"It is * * * a breach of International Law for a State to send its agents to the territory of another State to apprehend persons accused of having committed a crime. Apart from other satisfaction, the first duty of the offending State is to hand over the person in question to the State in whose territory he was apprehended." 1 Oppenheim's International Law 295, and n. 1 (H. Lauterpacht 8th ed. 1955). Commenting on the precise issue raised by this case, the chief reporter for the American Law Institute's Restatement of Foreign Relations used language reminiscent of Justice Story's characterization of an official seizure in a foreign jurisdiction as "monstrous:"

When done without consent of the foreign government, abducting a person from a foreign country is a gross violation of international law and gross disrespect for a norm high in the opinion of mankind. It is a blatant violation of the territorial integrity of another state; it eviscerates the extradition system (established by a comprehensive network of treaties involving virtually all states).

In the Rauscher case, the legal background that supported the decision to imply a covenant not to prosecute for an offense different from that for which extradition had been granted was far less clear than the rule against invading the territorial integrity of a treaty partner that supports Mexico's position in this case. If Rauscher was correctly decided—and I am convinced that it was—its rationale clearly dictates a comparable result in this case.

III

A critical flaw pervades the Court's entire opinion. It fails to differentiate between the conduct of private citizens, which does not violate any treaty obligation, and conduct expressly authorized by the Executive Branch of the Government, which unquestionably constitutes a flagrant violation of international law, and in my opinion, also constitutes a breach of our treaty obligations. Thus, at the outset, the Court states the issue as "whether a criminal defendant, abducted to the United States from a nation with which it has an extradition treaty, thereby acquires a defense to the jurisdiction of this country's courts." * * * That, of course, is the question decided in Ker v. Illinois, supra; it is not, however, the question presented for decision today.

* * * The Court's admittedly "shocking" disdain for customary and conventional international law principles, * * * is thus entirely unsupported by case law and commentary.

IV

As the Court observes at the outset of its opinion, there is reason to believe that respondent participated in an especially brutal murder of an American law enforcement agent. That fact, if true, may explain the Executive's intense interest in punishing respondent in our courts. Such an explanation, however, proves no justification for disregarding the Rule of Law that this Court has a duty to uphold. That the Executive may wish to reinterpret the Treaty to allow for an action that the Treaty in no way authorizes should not influence this Court's interpretation. Indeed, the desire for revenge exerts "a kind of hydraulic pressure * * * before which even well settled principles of law will bend," Northern Securities Co. v. United States, 193 U.S. 197, * * * (1904) (Holmes, J., dissenting), but it is precisely at such moments that we should remember and be guided by our duty "to render judgment evenly and dispassionately according to law, as each is given understanding to ascertain and apply it." United States v. Mine Workers, 330 U.S. 258, * * * (1947) (Rutledge, J., dissenting). The way that we perform that duty in a case of this kind sets an example that other tribunals in other countries are sure to emulate.

The significance of this Court's precedents is illustrated by a recent decision of the Court of Appeal of the Republic of South Africa. Based largely on its understanding of the import of this Court's cases—including our decision in Ker v. Illinois—that court held that the prosecution of a defendant kidnaped by agents of South Africa in another country must be dismissed. S v. Ebrahim, S.Afr.L.Rep. (Apr.–June 1991). The Court of Appeal of South Africa—indeed, I suspect most courts throughout the civilized world will be deeply disturbed by the "monstrous" decision the Court announces today. For every Nation that has an interest in preserving the Rule of Law is affected, directly or indirectly, by a decision of this character. As Thomas Paine warned, an "avidity to punish is always dangerous to liberty" because it leads a Nation "to stretch, to misinterpret, and to misapply even the best of laws." To counter that tendency, he reminds us: "He that would make his own liberty secure must guard even his enemy from oppression; for if he violates this duty he establishes a precedent that will reach to himself."

I respectfully dissent.

————

Notes, Questions, & Critique: For discussion of Alvarez–Machain, see 86 AJIL 811 (No. 4) (1992) (comment by Jacques Semmelman); and Due Process, International Law, and Jurisdiction Over Criminal Defendant's Abducted Extraterritorially, 30 Colum.J.Transnat'l L. 513 (1992); Michael Glennon, State–Sponsored Abduction: *A Comment on U.S. v. Alvarez–Machain,* 86 AJIL 746 (1992); LeBlanc, United States v. Alvarez–Machain and the Status of International Law in American Courts 53 La.L.Rev. 1411 (1993); Jacques MacChesney & Anthony D'Amato, International Law Anthology 246 (1993); Malvina Halberstam, In Defense of the Supreme Court Decision in Alvarez–Machain, 86 AJIL 736 (1992). *Note* that U.S. and Mexico have negotiated and are about to sign in April, 1994, a new extradition treaty, which will specify explicitly that extradition is the sole means of obtaining custody for prosecution. See, Minerva Cruz, Roberto Villereal & Carlos Velasco, *Oued listo el tratado de extradition y será signado a más tardar en abril:* Tello, El Universal (Mexico City) Feb. 20, 1994, at p. 31, col. 1; 10 Int'l Enf.L.Rptr. 51 (Feb.1994).

The decision notes that the extradition treaty does not explicitly prohibit abduction. Is the defendant's argument that the treaty implicitly does so a strong one? What do you think of Justice Stevens' point in dissent that the extradition treaty also does not prohibit the use of torture or the commission of murder by authorities? Does this mean that those acts are allowed under the treaty? Also, is not extradition premised on the notion that nations are sovereign and must agree to any foreign enforcement of law within their territory? Isn't that the very reason for which extradition treaties are necessary?

Defendant's more important argument seems to be that customary international law prohibits official abduction and requires repatriation. Was this issue before the Court? Do you think that the Court gratuitously disparaged customary international law as a source of law for decision in the case? The Court did concede that abduction "may be in violation of general international law principles * * * the decision of whether respondent should be returned to Mexico, as a matter outside of the Treaty, is a matter for the Executive branch." *Is this point correct under the Constitution? If so, is it wise? Should the judiciary have any role at all in the arena of returning fugitives? See discussion in Chapters 11, 17, and 14 on the Political Question Doctrine and other issues related to the separation and sharing of powers under the Constitution.*

The Decision places Americans in Danger: Does the *Alvarez–Machain* decision signal a danger that some potential evils of which Thomas Paine warned (see Stevens' dissent) have not disappeared? Does the "legalization" of abductions such as this put the "rule of law" at risk? While not many countries will send their troops or agents to abduct Americans on our soil, the decision does *render Americans travelling abroad more vulnerable.* Does it make American business people, government agents or tourists vulnerable to similar abuses? How credible will our protests be if other nations or groups abduct, prosecute, convict, and punish? Do you think that we will be willing to go to war over the abduction of our nationals? What does past practice indicate?

Follow-up:

In U.S. v. Toscanino, the Second Circuit Court of Appeals distinguished Ker and Frisbie by noting that the defendant had been forcibly abducted in violation of principles of international law, evidenced by the Charters of the U.N. and the O.A.S. In 1975, the Second Circuit held that "[for] a defendant * * * to interpose the violation of [the U.N. and O.A.S. Charters] as a defense to a criminal prosecution," an official state protest by a state whose sovereignty was violated by the abduction would be required. [U.S. ex rel. Lujan v. Gengler]. Alvarez–Machain, along with Matta–Ballesteros, 697 F.Supp. 1040, 1041–42 (S.D.Ill.1988)(7th Cir.1990), manifest the reality in the United States that, while forcible abduction of a person from a foreign country violates international law, the defendant is provided little, if any, recourse.

Dr. Alvarez-Machain has now sued the U.S. Government and the individuals involved in his abduction and alleged torture. Abduction abroad of fugitives by U.S. authorities is illegal under international law and can lead to civil penalties or criminal prosecution in the offended nation. Jurisdiction to prosecute the abductee, however, apparently, is not impaired. A minor exception to immunity has been developed in cases where the fugitive is able to prove not only abduction, but torture or other circumstances which make the capture and return egregious.

The Mexican Government has requested the extradition of two individuals it suspects of abducting Alvarez in Mexico. "[I]t is shocking that a party to an extradition treaty might believe [is now held legitimately to believe] that it has secretly reserved the right to make seizures of citizens in the other party's territory" (dissent in *Alvarez*). Indignation over the alleged conduct of the fugitive and the enthusiasm for the "war on drugs," pervades the rationale of this decision. The dissent notes, "[a]s the Court observes at the outset of its opinion, there is reason to believe that respondent participated in an especially brutal murder of an American law enforcement agent. That fact, if true, may explain the Executive's intense interest in punishing respondent in our courts. Such an explanation, however, provides no justification for disregarding the Rule of Law that this Court has a duty to uphold." Do you agree? The U.S. is party to 16 bilateral M.L.A.T.'s (Mutual Legal Assistance Treaties) with Mexico, Panama, Uruguay, and some nations of the Caribbean, among others. The Alvarez-Machain Case, raises serious doubt about the vitality of these Treaties, especially with countries in Latin America. The same could be true of other cooperative ventures, such as prisoner transfers and even extradition. Canada, in its *amicus brief* began with the warning: "[t]he issues presented in this case could have a profound effect on Canada–USA extradition relations." The U.S. and Mexico have now completed renegotiation of their extradition treaty, rendering abduction a violation.

The judge in the U.S. ultimately dismissed the case against Alvarez for want of evidence. See, Seth Mydans, Judge Clears Mexican in Agent's Killing, N.Y. Times, A12, Dec. 15, 1992. The U.S. Government refused to honor Mexico's request for the extradition of those allegedly involved in the Alvarez abduction, although it was kidnapping. Instead, reports are that the U.S. paid $2.7 million to various prosecution witnesses. Payments are Detailed in Case of Slain Drug Agent, NY Times, Nov. 8, 1992, at A12. Mexico and other nations as well have made it clear that they view such conduct as a crime. President Clinton pledged that the U.S. will not abduct anyone else from Mexico during negotiations modifying the U.S.–Mexico Extradition Treaty. MacChesney & D'Amato, Anthology, supra at 246.

The Court's Vision of Jus Cogens: *Do you think that the Court believes that a returned fugitive has standing to raise protections or interests pursuant to human rights or other treaties (even if they are self-executing) and custom?*

Standing to object to kidnapping: In Ker v. Illinois, 119 U.S. 436 (1886), the defendant was kidnapped in Peru by Illinois officials, but the court held the mode of his arrest was not a constitutional ground for objection to his trial. The defendant appeared to be a national of the United States, but the court did not discuss the bearing, if any, of his nationality in holding he had no standing to object to his unlawful arrest. In Frisbie v. Collins, the court relied on its decision in Ker, holding that a defendant arrested in Illinois by officers from Michigan similarly had no constitutional ground for objecting to his trial.

The U.S. is not alone: Colonel Argoud, a French national notorious for his opposition to General de Gaulle's policies of independence for Algeria, was sought for prosecution by the French authorities but found refuge in West Germany. He was kidnapped there by "persons unknown" and found tied up in a truck in Paris after an anonymous phone call. The French court ruled that, in the absence of an objection by the Federal Republic of Germany, no international law issue was before it. In argument before the court, and in the prior proceedings, much was made by the prosecution of applicable precedents in Anglo–Saxon countries; *i.e., Ker-Frisbie.* In re Argoud, France, Court of Cassation, 1964, 45 Int'l L.Rep. 90 (1972).

The kidnapping of the accused on Argentine territory by Israeli agents did raise an international law issue, in contrast to the Argoud case, but Eichmann was not given standing to raise it in the Israeli courts. The issue was treated as a matter only between Israel and Argentina and was disposed of by the agreement between the two states to consider the incident closed. Attorney General of Israel v. Eichmann, supra, Chapter 1, p. 18.

BUSER, THE JAFFE CASE AND THE USE OF INTERNATIONAL KIDNAPPING AS AN ALTERNATIVE TO EXTRADITION

14 Georgia Journal of International and Comparative Law 357 (1984).*

* * *

The history of bounty hunters in the United States dates from the period of the Old West. In 1872 the Supreme Court * * * recognized that the surety of a person released on bail could appoint someone to pursue a bail jumper and return the bail jumper to the jurisdiction to appear before the court, but only if the bail jumper was located within the territory of the United States. Bounty hunters, however, also had the powers of de facto deputies; they could ride after, capture, and return to the sheriff fugitives from the law. In asserting jurisdiction over fugitives apprehended and returned by bounty hunters, courts use the Ker–Frisbie rule which states that a court may claim jurisdiction over a criminal defendant without regard to the means by which he was brought before the court. The Ker–Frisbie rule follows the ancient Roman maxim male captus, bene detenum, which translates: an illegal apprehension does not preclude jurisdiction. Bounty hunting has declined and is limited today mainly to apprehending bail jumpers.

* * *

Sidney Jaffe was a Florida land developer who in 1980, was engaged in the sale of newly created subdivisions. He ran into difficulties,

* Reprinted with the permission of the Georgia Journal of International and Comparative Law.

however, and was arrested on charges of violating Florida's new Land Sales Act. Bail was posted for Jaffe by a professional bonding company, and he was released from jail. Jaffe fled to Toronto, obtained Canadian citizenship, and failed to appear for his preliminary hearing in Florida. Faced with losing its investment, the company applied to the state Attorney General for the commencement of extradition proceedings.

The extradition proceedings advanced slowly, and the bonding company feared it would have to forfeit its bond. There were also some questions as to whether land sale violation charges were extraditable under the 1971 Treaty. The bonding company, therefore, commissioned one of its agents, Daniel Kear, to abduct Jaffe from his Toronto home. Kear enlisted the aid of Timm Johnsen, a professional bounty hunter.

Kear and Johnsen went to Toronto to retrieve Jaffe. Posing as a policeman, Johnsen approached Jaffe after the latter's morning jog to ask him a few questions. Jaffe was * * * thrown in the back of a rented car and driven to the border, after which he was flown back to Florida. Upon his arrival in Florida, Jaffe was arrested for jumping bail and was incarcerated. He was convicted * * * on twenty-eight counts of illegal land sales and was sentenced to thirty years in prison. * * *

The Canadian government was infuriated by the abduction of Jaffe. As Argentina had done during the Eichmann incident, Canada complained that its national sovereignty had been violated. Federal officials in the United States also sought Jaffe's release, a request refused by Florida authorities. Florida cited an 1872 Supreme Court decision which held that a bondsman or his agent could pursue and return the bail jumper to the jurisdiction to appear before the court. Canadian authorities then requested the extradition of Kear and Johnsen to stand trial on kidnapping charges. The two have been extradited to Canada and are free on bond pending trial for Jaffe's kidnapping.

* * *

1. ***Note on the Jaffe case.*** Canada sought the extradition of Kear, one of the Florida bounty-hunters, to be prosecuted for kidnapping. The extradition request was approved and Judge Murnaghan, of the Fourth Circuit Court of Appeals affirmed the District Court's denial of defendant's writ of habeas corpus, noting:

"... Presumably congratulating himself on the outcome [the abduction], Kear no doubt was rudely jolted to learn that Canadian authorities took a very jaundiced view of his behavior. Canada has sought to extradite Kear ... claiming violation of a statute which makes it a crime to kidnap a person with the intent to send or transport the person kidnapped out of Canada against his will ...

"In sum, circumstances justifying extradition have been established. The denial of a writ of habeas corpus by the district court accordingly was proper. The Canadian court may listen sympathetically to Kear as he seeks to portray himself as someone cought in a complexity of intricate international law beyond his imagination or comprehension. The fact that his cohort Johnsen may have posed as a member of the Ontario police force might make things a bit awkward, but in all events the matter is one of defense or mitigation to be raised in the Canadian courts. It is not a grounds [sic] for refusing to honor the Canadian request for extradition." Kear v. Hilton, 699 F.2d 181, 182, 185 (4th Cir.1983).

Kear and his partner Johnsen were convicted in Canada of kidnapping. Jaffe was convicted and sentenced to consecutive jail terms totalling 145 years in prison. His conviction for fraud was overturned after he had served two years. He was later paroled on the charge of absconding. Jaffe returned to Canada and the latter has steadfastly refused to extradite him on refiled fraud charges. See, Abramovsky, Transfer of Penal Sanctions Treaties: An Engangered Species?, 24 Vand.J.Trans'l L. 449, n. 104 (1991).

2. *Law enforcement extraterritorial efforts.* In many cases, the violation of a state's sovereignty in its territory arises from overzealous behavior at or near the border on the part of low echelon law enforcement authorities. Instead of becoming causes célèbres, they are usually resolved more quietly by bureaucratic action.

Ronald Anderson, an American citizen and a conscientious objector during the hostilities in Vietnam, was living in British Columbia. While attempting to cross the border in order to visit his mother in the state of Washington, he was seized by American customs officers. A number of witnesses, and a photograph by a reporter, established that he had been seized by the American customs officers on the Canadian side. Following a protest by the Canadian Ministry for Foreign Affairs, the U.S. military authorities returned him to Canada. 79 Rev. Gen. de Dr. Int'l. Pub. 462 (1975).

A Swiss, implicated in charges of drug trafficking, crossed into France when her fiancé was arrested. The Swiss judge's clerk in charge of the case went to the woman's residence in France and convinced her to return to Geneva, where she was promptly arrested. In reporting her release the *Chronique des Faits Internationaux* noted that a French clerk or a French judge would have been severely punished for such conduct. 78 Rev. Gen. de Dr. Int'l. Pub. 1158 (1974).

3. *Other acts.* An inspector from the Spanish police was arrested in 1975 upon entering the French territory carrying a hand gun. He stated he had come to do some shopping and had forgotten to leave the gun home. He was given a suspended sentence of two months in prison. 80 Rev. Gen. Dr. Int'l. Pub. 248 (1976).

At an airport in Switzerland, two agents of the Italian Secret Service were keeping under surveillance an Italian national wanted by Italy for espionage. They were taking photographs of people and taking down the registration plates of automobiles. They were arrested and prosecution was begun even though the Italian Government presented its excuses through diplomatic channels. 89 Rev. Gen. de Dr. Int'l. Pub. 460 (1985).

4. *Rescue raids.* On April 24, 1980, the United States flew into Iran a military force whose objective was the rescue of the American nationals held hostage in Teheran. The raid was not successful. The

hijacking of planes, with large numbers of passengers aboard, has also led in recent years to several rescue raids prompting claims of violation of territorial sovereignty. For a discussion of rescue raids, see infra, Chapter 17.

Service in criminal cases. In Service of Summons in Criminal Case, Austria, Supreme Court, 1961, 38 Int'l L.Rep. 133 (1969), a German national was tried in absentia in Austria and convicted. The summons had been served by mail. The court held the trial was null and void, because the service was a violation of international law. For international judicial or mutual assistance generally, see the excellent treatise by Bruno Ristau and Mike Abbell, International Judicial Assistance (Civil & Commercial) & (Criminal) (6 vols. 1990) (revised yearly).

Distinction between service of notice and service of compulsory process. In Federal Trade Commission v. Compagnie de Saint–Gobain–Pont–á–Mousson, 636 F.2d 1300 (D.C.Cir.1980), the commission sent to the defendant in France by registered mail an investigatory subpoena ordering the production of documents under threat of penalties. The court found that the service was improper under the Federal Trade Commission Act, "as construed * * * in conformity with general principles of international law." The court drew a distinction between service of notice and service of a subpoena, stating the first was informational in nature and thus relatively benign, while the second, especially when served upon a foreign subject on foreign soil, was an exercise of sovereignty in another nation's territory and as such a violation of international law.

UNITED STATES: REVISED FEDERAL RULES OF CIVIL PROCEDURE BEARING ON TRANSNATIONAL LITIGATION *

[December 1, 1993] Cite as 33 I.L.M. 550 (1994) (See Doc.Supp.)

Introductory Note by Bruno A. Ristau

For almost sixty years, the laws governing the practice and procedure in the federal courts of the United States have been enacted in a

---

* [The Introductory Note was prepared for International Legal Materials by Bruno A. Ristau, Ristau & Abbell, and member of the I.L.M. Editorial Advisory Committee, reprinted by permission, American Society of International Law and Bruno Ristau.

[The Federal Rules of Civil Procedure for Rules 4, 26, and 28 are reproduced from U.S. Congress, House, Committee on the Judiciary, Federal Rules of Civil Procedure, 103rd Cong., 1st Sess., 1993, Committee Print, pp. 1–6, 29–36 and 38. The Notes of the Advisory Committee following each rule are reproduced from Title 28 U.S.C.A. 1993 Supplement, pp. 7–14 and pp. 28–36.

[Reports on the Operation of the Hague Service Convention by the Permanent Bu-

rather unique manner: speaking in the broadest terms, until 1938, federal courts followed (with exceptions) the local procedural laws of the states in which they sat. In that year, the Congress of the United States passed a "Rules Enabling Act" (since amended on numerous occasions), authorizing the Supreme Court of the United States to prescribe general rules of practice and procedure and rules of evidence for suits in United States District Courts (federal courts of first instance) and United States Courts of Appeals (federal courts of second instance). The Enabling Act prescribed that such rules shall not restrict, enlarge or modify any substantive rights—an area in which Congress alone can legislate. The Supreme Court must transmit any proposed new rule to the Congress by May 1 of the year in which the rule is to become effective, and Congress has until December 1 of that year to modify or reject the proposed new rule. If Congress takes no action, the new rule becomes part of the federal procedural law.

On December 1, 1993, numerous revisions and amendments to the Federal Rules of Civil Procedure (F.R.Civ.P.) came into force. Of particular interest to the foreign or international practitioner are those provisions incorporated in the revised Rule 4, F.R.Civ.P., that deal with service of process abroad, and the amendments to Rules 26 and 28, F.R.Civ.P., regarding the taking of evidence abroad. These revisions and amendments highlight for the first time the availability of the procedures set forth in the several procedural conventions that the United States has ratified since 1969, such as the Hague Service Convention [4 I.L.M. 341 (1965)], the Hague Evidence Convention [8 I.L.M. 37 (1969)] and the Inter–American Letters Rogatory Convention [14 I.L.M. 339 (1975)] with additional Protocol [18 I.L.M. 1238 (1979)].

See the relevant Rules in the Documentary Supplement.

RULES OF CIVIL PROCEDURE
FOR THE
UNITED STATES DISTRICT COURTS [1]

Effective September 16, 1938, as amended to December 1, 1993.

II.　COMMENCEMENT OF ACTION; SERVICE OF PROCESS, PLEADINGS, MOTIONS, AND ORDERS

* * *

Rule 4.　Summons

(f) SERVICE UPON INDIVIDUALS IN A FOREIGN COUNTRY. Unless otherwise provided by federal law, service upon an individual from whom a waiver

reau of the Hague Conference and by the U.S. Delegation appear at 17 I.L.M. 312 (1978). Reports on the Operation of the Hague Evidence Convention by the U.S. Delegation and by the Permanent Bureau of the Hague Conference appear at 17 I.L.M. 1417 (1978). The Special Commission Report on the Operation of the Hague Service and Evidence Conventions appears at 28 I.L.M. 1556, 1563–69 (1989).]

1. Title amended December 29, 1948, effective October 20, 1949.

has not been obtained and filed, other than an infant or an incompetent person, may be effected in a place not within any judicial district of the United States:

(1) by any internationally agreed means reasonably calculated to give notice, such as those means authorized by the Hague Convention on the Service Abroad of Judicial and Extrajudicial Documents; or

(2) if there is no internationally agreed means of service or the applicable international agreement allows other means of service, provided that service is reasonably calculated to give notice:

(A) in the manner prescribed by the law of the foreign country for service in that country in an action in any of its courts of general jurisdiction; or

(B) as directed by the foreign authority in response to a letter rogatory or letter of request; or

(C) unless prohibited by the law of the foreign country, by

(i) delivery to the individual personally of a copy of the summons and the complaint; or

(ii) any form of mail requiring a signed receipt, to be addressed and dispatched by the clerk of the court to the party to be served; or

(3) by other means not prohibited by international agreement as may be directed by the court.

(2) in a place not within any judicial district of the United States in any manner prescribed for individuals by subdivision (f) except personal delivery as provided in paragraph (2)(C)(i) thereof.

(i) SERVICE UPON THE UNITED STATES, AND ITS AGENCIES, CORPORATIONS, OR OFFICERS.

(As added Apr. 22, 1993, eff. Dec. 1, 1993.)

NOTES OF ADVISORY COMMITTEE ON RULES
1993 AMENDMENT

Subdivision (f). This subdivision provides for service on individuals who are in a foreign country, replacing the former subdivision (i) that was added to Rule 4 in 1963. Reflecting the pattern of Rule 4 in incorporating state law limitations on the exercise of jurisdiction over persons, the former subdivision (i) limited service outside the United States to cases in which extraterritorial service was authorized by state or federal law. The new rule eliminates the requirement of explicit authorization. On occasion, service in a foreign country was held to be improper for lack of statutory authority. E.g., Martens v. Winder, 341 F.2d 197 (9th Cir.), cert. denied, 382 U.S. 937 (1965). This authority, however, was found to exist by implication. E.g., SEC v. VTR, Inc., 39 F.R.D. 19 (S.D.N.Y.1966). Given the substantial increase in the number of international transactions and events that are the subject of litigation in federal courts, it is appropriate to infer a general legislative authority to effect service on defendants in a foreign country.

A secondary effect of this provision for foreign service of a federal summons is to facilitate the use of federal long-arm law in actions brought to enforce the federal law against defendants who cannot be served under any state law but who can be constitutionally subjected to the jurisdiction of the federal court. Such a provision is set forth in paragraph (2) of subdivision (k) of this rule, applicable only to persons not subject to the territorial jurisdiction of any particular state.

Paragraph (1) gives effect to the Hague Convention on the Service Abroad of Judicial and Extrajudicial Documents, which entered into force for the United States on February 10, 1969. See 28 U.S.C.A., Fed.R.Civ.P. 4 (Supp.1986). This Convention is an important means of dealing with problems of service in a foreign country. See generally 1 B. Ristau, International Judicial Assistance §§ 4–1–1 to 4–5–2 (1990). Use of the Convention procedures, when available, is mandatory if documents must be transmitted abroad to effect service. See Volkswagenwerk Aktiengesellschaft v. Schlunk, 486 U.S. 694 (1988) (noting that voluntary use of these procedures may be desirable even when service could constitutionally be effected in another manner); J. Weis, The Federal Rules and the Hague Conventions: Concerns of Conformity and Comity, 50 U.Pitt.L.Rev. 903 (1989). Therefore, this paragraph provides that, when service is to be effected outside a judicial district of the United States, the methods of service appropriate under an applicable treaty shall be employed if available and if the treaty so requires.

The Hague Convention furnishes safeguards against the abridgment of rights of parties through inadequate notice. Article 15 provides for verification of actual notice or a demonstration that process was served by a method prescribed by the internal laws of the foreign state before a default judgment may be entered. Article 16 of the Convention also enables the judge to extend the time for appeal after judgment if the defendant shows a lack of adequate notice either to defend or to appeal the judgment, or has disclosed a prima facie case on the merits.

The Hague Convention does not specify a time within which a foreign country's Central Authority must effect service, but Article 15 does provide that alternate methods may be used if a Central Authority does not respond within six months. Generally, a Central Authority can be expected to respond much more quickly than that limit might permit, but there have been occasions when the signatory state was dilatory or refused to cooperate for substantive reasons. In such cases, resort may be had to the provision set forth in subdivision (f)(3).

Two minor changes in the text reflect the Hague Convention. First, the term "letter of request" has been added. Although these words are synonymous with "letter rogatory," "letter of request" is preferred in modern usage. The provision should not be interpreted to authorize use of a letter of request when there is in fact no treaty obligation on the receiving country to honor such a request from this country or when the United States does not extend diplomatic recognition to the foreign nation. Second, the passage formerly found in subdivision (i)(1)(B), "when service in either case is reasonably calculated to give actual notice," has been relocated.

Paragraph (2) provides alternative methods for use when internationally agreed methods are not intended to be exclusive, or where there is no international agreement applicable. It contains most of the language formerly set forth in subdivision (i) of the rule. Service by methods that would violate foreign law is not generally authorized. Subparagraphs (A) and (B) prescribe the more appropriate methods for conforming to local practice or using a local authority. Subparagraph (C) prescribes other methods authorized by the former rule.

Paragraph (3) authorizes the court to approve other methods of service not prohibited by international agreements. The Hague Convention, for example, authorizes special forms of service in cases of urgency if convention methods will not permit service within the time required by the circumstances. Other circumstances that might justify the use of additional methods include the failure of the foreign country's Central Authority to effect service within the six-month period provided by the Convention, or the refusal of the Central Authority to serve a complaint seeking punitive damages or to enforce the anti-trust laws of the United States. In such cases, the court may direct a special method of service not explicitly authorized by international agreement if not prohibited by the agreement. Inasmuch as our Constitution requires that reasonable notice be given, an earnest effort should be made to devise a method of communication that is consistent with due process and minimizes offense to foreign law. A court may in some instances specially authorize use of ordinary mail. Cf. Levin v. Ruby Trading Corp., 248 F.Supp. 537 (S.D.N.Y.1965).

SECTION D. EXTRADITION AND OTHER MEASURES OF COOPERATION

International extradition is the legal mechanism whereby sovereign nations render fugitives to the justice of other sovereign nations. It is a judicial process in most countries, although some consider it to be administrative. U.S. law requires a treaty; comity will not suffice for delivery. Most other nations utilize extradition treaties, but will extradite on the basis of comity, pursuant to their domestic extradition law. Nations, being sovereign, by definition must agree to the rendition of a fugitive. Any exercise of legal process on the territory of another nation, abduction in lieu of extradition for example, violates the sovereignty of the nation from which the fugitive was taken and violates international law. Extradition is appropriate when there is sufficient evidence (probable cause) to allow a judge to believe the fugitive committed the extraditable offense.

General Note: The United States Government has utilized the "War on Drugs" to accommodate significant expansion of jurisdictional principles. While enforcement and prescriptive jurisdiction has been extended vigorously abroad, the Supreme Court has decided that the Constitution, at least the Warrant Clause of the 4th Amendment, stays home. The infamous torture and execution-style murder of DEA agent Enrique Camarena–Salazar and his pilot, gave rise to the abduction of Verdugo–Urquidez and of Alvarez-Machain. In addition, the DEA conducted warrantless searches.

In ***U.S. v. Verdugo–Urquidez***, 494 U.S. 259 (1990), noted above, the U.S. Supreme Court decided that the phrase ***"the people"*** in the 4th Amendment (and the 1st, 2nd, 9th and 10th Amendments) "refers to a class of persons who are part of a national community or who have otherwise developed sufficient connection with this community to be considered part of that community * * *." At least some of the 4th Amendment was held not to apply to the home, office, effects, or person of a foreign national abducted in Mexico and turned over to U.S. authority to be prosecuted. The exclusionary rule was held not to apply to exclude evidence obtained without a warrant and pursuant to conduct that would be an unlawful search under the 4th Amendment if it occurred to "people" under the Constitution. A plurality of the Court, including the Chief Justice, and Justices O'Connor, Scalia, and White, suggested that the rest of the Fourth Amendment does not apply as well. Thus, the requirement of probable cause and that a search be conducted reasonably do not apply. As Ruth Wedgewood notes, the " 'water's edge' rule for the Fourth Amendment, except for citizens and resident aliens, stems from the plurality's sense that U.S. action abroad must be governed by necessity, a sense more familiar to war than to peace * * *." Ruth Wedgewood, Verdugo-Urquidez Analysis, 84 AJIL 747, 752 (1990).

Similarly, in *E.E.O.C. v. Arabian American Oil Company,* 111 S.Ct. 1227 (1991), the U.S. Supreme Court held that Title VII of the Civil Rights Act of 1964, 42 U.S.C. §§ 2000a–2000h–6, does not apply to the practices of U.S. Companies employing U.S. citizens abroad. It held that, since the Act did not specifically and explicitly apply Title VII extraterritorially, the Legislature did not intend to do so. The Court relied on its, "long-standing principle * * * 'that legislation of Congress, unless a contrary intent appears, is meant to apply only within the territorial jurisdiction of the United States.'" Note also, however, that a 1991 amendment to the above-mentioned Civil Rights Act overturned The Aramco Case. "With respect to employment in a *foreign country,*" it redefined "employee" under the Act to include "an individual who is a citizen of the United States." 42 U.S.C. § 2000e (1964), as amended (1991) (emphasis ours).

This geographical requirement is in turn the weakness of the system. Once an individual commits an offense in the territory of a state, but manages to get beyond its frontiers, he is, in the absence of appropriate arrangements, beyond the reach of the power of the state. The state, powerful as it may be as the sole legitimate depositary of power in its territory, is now helpless (relatively speaking, since *Alvarez*). As a result, we find states otherwise highly dedicated to the rule of law in effect sponsoring—under the Latin motto male captus, bene detenum—kidnapping and other illegal practices which deliver the offender back into their power. The Alvarez–Machain case, supra, is now a classic example of this tendency.

The legal option is extradition. The United States currently has more than 90 treaties of extradition in force. See the Doc. Supp. Extradition treaties, therefore, palliate the inherent weakness of the system. Each state determines for itself the procedures under which it will extradite a person charged by another state with being a fugitive. The so-called political offense exception, is a provision in practically every extradition treaty allowing each party not to grant extradition if the offense is deemed to be one of a political character. The **political offense exception** is explored in the cases and materials which follow.

THE STATE v. SCHUMANN

Ghana, Court of Appeal of Accra, 1966.
39 Int'l L.Rep. 433 (1970).*

[The Government of the Federal Republic of Germany requested the Government of Ghana to extradite Dr. Horst Schumann on a charge of murder. The specific acts for the charge were the killing from 1939 to 1941 of more than 30,000 patients in mental establishments within two concentration camps in Germany and the killing from 1942 to 1944 of a large number of Jews at Auschwitz in the course of experiments with

* Reprinted with the permission of the
Editor of the International Law Reports.

mass sterilization. At the time the request for extradition was made, Schumann was employed by the government as a medical officer.]

* * *

Counsel for the State submitted that the principles relating to an offence of a political character have been examined and enunciated in the English cases of Re Meunier [1894] 2 Q.B.D. 415, Re Castioni [1891] 1 Q.B.D. 149; and R. v. Governor of Brixton Prison, Ex parte Kolczynski [1955] 1 All E.R. 35, and that none of the facts stated in the appellant's evidence fell within these principles. In the cases of Re Meunier and Re Castioni, the principle is stated that to constitute an offence of a political nature there must be some political disturbance or upheaval or there must be some physical struggle between two opposing political parties for the mastery of the government of the country, and that the crime in question must have been committed in furtherance of that disturbance or struggle. The principle was extended in the Kolczynski case to cover "offences committed in association with a political object (e.g., anti-Communism) or with a view to avoiding political persecution or prosecution for political defaults" * * *.

It is clear beyond argument that the appellant's case is not covered by these principles. It is not his case that the poor helpless lunatics at the Munsungen Asylum or the Jews at Auschwitz had rebelled against the Nazi ideology and had thereby created some form of political disturbance which needed quelling, nor indeed does he claim to have committed the offence charged with a view to avoiding political persecution or prosecution.

[CRABBE, J.A., amplified somewhat the holding in Kolczynski]: * * * It seems to have been established by Kolczynski's case that an act committed solely on the ground of fear of prosecution for a political offence or of political persecution will be sufficient to give the crime a political colouring, if such fear led immediately or directly to the commission of the crime for which extradition is sought. There must exist a direct connexion of the criminal act with a political object.

[LASSEY conceded the killings were done "in circumstances which were not entirely without political significance" and stated]:

The crucial question here is this: In those circumstances is it necessary to widen the scope or meaning of these magic words, "of a political character", if only for reasons of humanity? I desire to answer this by saying that to determine the political character of the particular offence so as to make it not extraditable there must necessarily be present at the time of the commission of the particular crime some element of organized or violent opposition or resistance to the execution of the planned policy of the ruling political party and the offence must be committed in the conflict which might result between the opposing parties. In this context any such offence committed either by the agents of the ruling political party seeking to carry out their principal's orders or by the agents of those who dislike or resist the carrying into effect of the particular political policy may be brought under the category of an offence "of a political nature or character" and therefore excusable in extradition proceedings. * * *

* * *

In my view neither the helpless lunatics in the mental institution at "Munsungen" nor the Jews in "Auschwitz" appeared to have offered any organized resistance to the Nazi Party in Germany * * *.

––––––––

RE BRESSANO

Argentina, Camara Federal de la Capital, 1965.
40 Int'l L.Rep. 219 (1975).*

The Facts.—Peru requested the extradition of Hugo M. Bressano on charges of bank robbery and assault committed in the Miraflores branch of the Credit Bank of Peru. * * * The Court of first instance refused extradition on the ground that the offences constituted common crimes connected with a political offence and hence were not extraditable * * *. On appeal to the Federal Court of the Capital (Buenos Aires).

Held: that extradition must be granted * * *. [A portion of the opinion appears below.]

Even if we accept the contention that the motive for the principal offence was to provide funds for the support of a programme of training of groups in guerrilla warfare to be directed against the existing political, social and economic order in Peru, and with the ultimate objective of directing this subversive activity against other Latin–American States, we cannot agree that this argument affords a valid reason for treating the offence in question as a political offence, thereby enabling the perpetrators to enjoy protection in any country in which they might seek asylum.

[The court held that, even if it were not established as positive law that the doctrine of political offense presupposed the existence of a democratic state, offenses as preparation for guerrilla warfare on an international scale did not qualify as political in any case.]

––––––––

Note: The political offense exception is one of the more controversial aspects of extradition law today. Paradoxically, it is one of the most universally accepted, yet strongly contested rules of international law. Virtually all domestic extradition laws and international treaties contain the exception. It remains heatedly contested because it is sometimes invoked by those who have participated in wanton violence or violence against innocent people (terrorism). Further, the criteria for meeting the exception are disputed; it has been difficult for courts to discern whether given conduct is covered by the exception.

* Reprinted with the permission of the Editor of the International Law Reports.

Despite its universality, no extradition treaty and virtually no legislative act has attempted to define "political offense" or "offense of a political character." Thus, courts have had to provide the guidelines for determining whether particular conduct falls within the exception. The term "political offense" has been characterized as referring not to a well-determined criminal transaction which can be specified in terms of a moral and mental element, but as a "descriptive label" to be considered vis-à-vis otherwise extraditable offenses. This view of the political offense exception provides insight into the courts' various approaches to its application.

Three basic types of conduct have been found to be political offenses: first, *"purely political offenses"* such as treason, sedition, or espionage. There is no problem with the application of the exception in the context of so-called "purely political offenses." Second, the exception may apply to *"offenses of a political character,"* or common crimes like burglary or homicide when committed in particular circumstances. Third, the exception may apply when the extradition was requested for a political purpose.

"Offenses of a political character" are difficult. Nations have attempted to resolve the difficulty by applying several specific approaches or tests incorporated by their judiciaries. These include: the political motivation test; the injured rights theory; the model of connexity; the political incidence or disturbance test; and several mixed approaches (combining the political incidence, connexity, and motivation tests).

"The Political Motivation Approach." has been applied on a few occasions by French and U.S. judiciaries. However, as Judge Sofaer suggests, the judiciaries in France, Switzerland, and the U.S. have now clearly rejected the political motivation test. French courts appear now to follow a *"predominance proportionality theory."* This test applies both subjective and objective criteria to determine whether a given offense is of sufficient political character to warrant exception from extradition. The test was refined in the *Ockert case* where a Swiss court defined political offenses, as those "acts which have the character of an ordinary crime appearing on the list of the extraditable offenses, but which, because of the attendant circumstances, in particular because of the *motive* and the *object*, are of a predominantly political complexion." In 1961, a Swiss Federal Tribunal further refined the definition so that even when the motive is largely political, the means employed must be virtually the *only* means available to accomplish the end pursued. In *Ktir,* the Swiss court granted a French extradition request for a French national who was a member of the Algerian F.L.N., who had been charged with the murder of an F.L.N. brother. The court required that the motives inspiring the acts must all indicate that the acts were predominantly political in character: " * * * the act [must be] inspired by political passion, [it must be] committed either in the framework of a struggle for power or for the purpose of escaping a dictatorial authority, and [must be] directly and closely related to the political purpose. Further, * * * the damage caused [must] be proportionate to the result sought, in other words, * * * the interests at stake should be sufficiently

important to excuse, if not justify, the infringement of private legal rights." Extremely serious offenses, such as murder, will rarely succeed in being excepted from extradition; they are required to meet the "ultima ratio" standard—the act must constitute the only means to accomplish the political end sought.

Political Incidence Approach: In 1891, a British judge ruled that political offenses are those which are "incidental to and form a part of political disturbances." This objective approach focuses on the act, without attention to the author's motivation. U.S. and British decisions adopted this approach. For example, in 1894, a U.S. federal district court held the political offense exception applied to government agents seeking to suppress an uprising, as well as to the rebels, in "any offense committed in the course of or furthering of civil war, insurrection, or political commotion." In a 1959 dictum, the District Court for the Southern District of California provided: "Generally speaking it is an offense against the government itself or incident to political uprisings * * * The crime must be incidental to and form a part of political disturbances; it must be in furtherance of one side or another in a bona fide struggle for political power." The criminal conduct must be "closely identified with" or committed "incidental to," "in the course of," and "in furtherance of" the political uprising. The "incidental to component is not satisfied by 'any connection, however feeble, between a common crime and a political disturbance.' * * * The act must be causally or ideologically related to the uprising." See, Quinn v. Robinson, 783 F.2d 776, 797, 798, 202 (9th Cir.1986). Generally, the "disturbance" or "uprising" must have a "reasonable possibility of success."

A Better Test: More recently, U.S. courts have begun to apply another test denying the exception to those who intentionally or indiscriminately attack innocent civilians, regardless of the motivation or whether it is committed incident to a political upheaval. ·This is a much better test, especially if it is based on a self-defense and laws of armed conflict model. There should be no political offense exception applied to attacks on innocent civilians. With regard to offenses relating to insurrections or internal wars (the political incidence approach), the French Extradition Law applies the exception, unless the conduct "constitute[s] acts of odious barbarism and vandalism prohibited by the laws of war, and only when the civil war has ended."

Injured Rights Test: Other nations have adopted an objective *"injured rights"* theory. The *Gatti* Case required the criminal action to be directed against the state's political organization: " * * * [t]he fact that the reasons of sentiment which prompted the offender to commit the offense belong to the realm of politics does not itself create a political offense. The offense does not derive its political character from the motive of the offender but from the nature of the rights it injures."

Another objective approach is the **model of connexity,** wherein the crime is considered a political offense based on its connection to a purely political offense. Thus, a person who assists a spy to escape would fit within this definition of the political offense exception. This has applied even when the accused perpetrator is a son, daughter, spouse, or friend.

Many nations apply the political offense exception *when officials believe the extradition request was politically motivated.* The French Extradition Law, for example, provides that extradition will be denied "when the crime or the offense has a political character or when it results from circumstances indicating that the extradition is requested with a political purpose."

French commentators have noted that the purpose of the political offense exception is to avoid prosecution based on a moral flaw. After a civil war, those extradited would not necessarily be criminals, but vanquished partisans of a cause. French tribunals have become sensitive to this and refuse extradition in cases like those of the Spanish Republicans, sought by the Franco regime after the Spanish Civil War, on the ground that their offenses were of a political character.

The Political Offense exception generally does not apply to counterfeiting, even for political ends, and for many forms of terrorism. The famous *"clause belge"* allows extradition for the murder of the head of state or anyone in his family. Extradition is also allowed for offenses falling within the French term *"infraction sociale,"* as it relates to the *"doctrine de gravité."* This term represents those offenses directed against the social structure, rather than the government per se.

Exceptions to the defense have developed over the years and have been called the *"**humanitarian exceptions**"* to the political offense clause. Certain offenses will not be excepted from extradition. These include the offenses of "barbarous or wanton violence", and crimes aimed at civilians rather than the military opposition are not to be exempted from extradition. Thus, the judiciaries of most countries have developed sufficient standards for distinguishing a political offense from terrorism. The political offense exception is important, because it often functions as a repository for human rights protections. It could be limited, if human rights protections were placed directly into extradition treaties. Adopted from Blakesley, Terrorism, Drugs, *supra* at 263–270 (footnotes omitted).

The U.S.-U.K. Treaty. In a major shift of extradition policy, the United States entered into a treaty with the United Kingdom to narrow the scope of the political offense exception contained in their extradition treaty of June 8, 1972. The Supplementary Treaty provides that certain offenses shall *not* be regarded as being of a political character. Murder, manslaughter, kidnapping, the taking of a hostage, offenses relating to explosives and offenses relating to firearms and ammunition can not be political offenses. The text of the supplementary treaty is in the Doc. Supp. It entered into force December 23, 1986. The Supplementary Treaty has been variously praised and attacked. *Does it deprive the courts of their rightful jurisdiction to decide whether an offense is of a political character?* Is there a "liberty interest" involved in an extradition hearing?

SECTION E.   REDUCTION AND RESOLUTION OF JURISDICTIONAL CONFLICTS STATES

1.   SITUATIONS THAT CREATE CONFLICTS OF JURISDICTION

What happens when more than one state has a basis of jurisdiction under international law and seek to exercise it? The simplest solution is a successful attack on the validity of an asserted claim to jurisdiction, but that solution, while often possible in jurisdiction-to-enforce situations, is rarely possible in situations involving jurisdiction-to-prescribe. Why?

The extension of the bases of prescriptive jurisdiction presented heretofore in this Chapter, have not come easily to states on opposite sides of an issue. Out of contention, customary international law has developed some ad hoc arrangements among states as to the allocation of primary jurisdiction. Some of these arrangements take the form of international agreements of substantial technical content, such as bilateral and multilateral treaties for the elimination of double taxation of income. These arrangements are limited. The anti-double taxation treaties, for example, usually are resorted to, not when State A asserts jurisdiction and denies it entirely to State B, but where both states have a basis of jurisdiction which the other acknowledges. In such cases the resolution of a conflict of jurisdiction is essentially a re-allocation of exclusive authority to act by mutual agreement. The agreements themselves usually refer to this process as the designation of one of the states as having "primary" jurisdiction.

Conflicts of jurisdiction can also arise regarding jurisdiction to enforce. The international legal community is accustomed to courts trying conflicts of law cases that include significant foreign elements but do not involve governmental values or interests that have been cast into legal rules by a state, such as tax law, business regulation, and the like. Conflicts of law focuses on the rights of the private parties before a forum. Courts by their actions in such cases usually do not raise questions involving conflict of public law, although occasionally they do. See, Laker case, infra, p. 262. The United States and some other states are now making arrangements for high seas boarding in suspected narcotics-carrying cases on the basis of specific, case-to-case, prior clearance with the flag state. Such arrangements call for "waiver" of a right to complain as to an excess of jurisdiction to enforce.

States heavily involved in international finance, banking, and securities regulation are opening the way to jurisdictional cooperation as to stock fraud, misuse of "insider knowledge", and other types of essentially criminal manipulations. Even Switzerland, that mountain fortress of bank secrecy, has come to moderate its once rigidly territorial exclusivity in deference to the interests of other states on behalf of investors entitled to their help or protection. So far, States have reduced or resolved jurisdictional conflicts, with only indirect assistance from international organizations and agencies. Some European states already see it as such, see e.g., *discussion of German and other European law in* Blakesley & Lagodny, Finding Harmony Amidst Disagreement Over Extradition, Jurisdiction, the Role of Human Rights, and Issues of Extraterritoriality Under International Criminal Law, 24 Vand.J.Trans'l L. 1 (1991); Blakesley & Lagodny, Competing National Criminal Laws: Network or Jungle, in Principles and Procedures for a New Transnational Criminal Law, (Max–Planck Institute for Foreign and International Criminal Law, Freiburg, Germany, 1992).

----

2. ARRANGEMENTS FOR RESOLUTION OF CONFLICTS OF JURISDICTION

(a) *International Arrangements and Agreements to Avoid Multiple Taxation*

Ask yourself the following questions as you read the cases in this section: *What are courts doing?* Are they (i) applying principles linked to customary international law, such as balancing of interests or applying rules of reasonableness; (ii) exercising a national judicial power to moderate or reduce the reach of national legislation? And as to each of the above, on what sources of support are the courts relying? Are they giving what you consider due weight to any one or more of the following: international opinio juris, their national legislatures and foreign affairs agencies, and the hardships of the conflicting demands of various legal systems if one or more of such systems are not denied exercise of jurisdiction?

An illustrative tax treaty is in the Documentary Supplement.

Networks of bilateral tax treaties. The United States has long been active in negotiating bilateral tax treaties. As the following case shows, Italy and Germany have also. What else, if anything, does the following case teach? What if a multipartite tax-allocating convention to which the United States, Germany and Italy were parties had existed: same lesson?

1. It is curious that, as between the states of the Union, the interstate compact approach to the reduction or avoidance of multistate death and income taxation has been so little used. Some degree of uniformity of treatment of resident and nonresident income exists in the various state income tax laws, and there is a practice of informal consultation between state taxing authorities as to both death and income taxes. The threat of multistate taxation within the United States became greater when the United States Supreme Court abandoned the view that substantive due process of law limited jurisdiction to tax in particular instances to a single state among a number of states having tax contacts. The problem of multistate tax claims tends to

become more serious as rates rise. What should happen internationally? *See,* Dec. of Fed.Tax.Ct.Ger. 12 Eur.Tax.II. 36 (1971).

2. ***Relationship among states' interests as to taxation.*** If any one of several states having bases of jurisdiction to tax exercises its jurisdiction to the fullest or disregards the tax expectations of another, the tax source is apt to be affected to the fiscal detriment of one, some, or all the states involved. A standard complaint of developing countries in Latin America against the United States is that the latter uses very extensively its jurisdiction to tax business income on the basis of nationality, even when the sourced income being taxed is elsewhere. The complaint is not based on jurisdictional grounds but on the practical effect of high United States taxes on the ability of the source state to impose higher rates. Do you find this plausible?

3. ***Tax credits.*** A number of states, including the United States, allow varying degrees of reduction of the domestic business income tax because of taxes paid elsewhere on the same income. In some instances tax credit systems supplement tax-allocating international agreements. In others such credits are the only relief available. United States tax law requires the foreign tax paid to have been an income tax under United States criteria. Difficult issues naturally result.

———

(b) *International Arrangements and Agreements as to Jurisdiction in Regard to Visiting Foreign Military Forces*

Persons in the armed services may fail in the performance of their military duties, and they may make mistakes or misbehave when off duty and amidst the civilian community. Or they may deviate from the performance of their official duty while on a mission off post, with resultant injury to someone who is not a member of the military. In general, the problems of conflicts of jurisdiction that arise when a state receives within its territory an organized military unit of a friendly state, usually an ally, are like those that arise between the military and civilian authorities in the environs of any domestic military installation. For some types of conduct, all agree that the military person should be responsible only to the law of his military unit. At the opposite extreme, all agree that in other instances he should be treated like anyone else within the civilian jurisdiction in which he has acted. As experience with friendly foreign forces present at the invitation of the territorial state has accumulated, principles have been worked out for the allocation of primary jurisdiction to one or the other of the states concerned. As the following cases show, applications of the rules of allocation may present problems inherently more difficult than the drafting of the rules themselves. Behind the immediate problem there may be issues involving a protected human right, against double jeopardy, or denial of the defenses of prior acquittal or prior conviction.

———

WHITLEY v. AITCHISON

France, Court of Cassation, 1958.
26 Int'l L.Rep. 196 (1963).*

Facts: Article VII(3)(b) of the N.A.T.O. Status of Forces Agreement [S.O.F.A.], provides that in the case of offences not arising out of acts done in the performance of the official duty of a member of a visiting force, "the authorities of the receiving State shall have the primary right to exercise jurisdiction". Subparagraph (c) of the same paragraph provides that "if the State having the primary right decides not to exercise jurisdiction, it shall notify the authorities of the other State as soon as practicable * * *." Article VII(8) * * * provides:

> Where an accused has been tried by the authorities of one Contracting Party and has been acquitted, or has been convicted and is serving, or has served, his sentence or has been pardoned, he may not be tried again for the same offence within the same territory by the authorities of another Contracting Party.

On November 25, 1953, the appellant, a major of the United States Air Force stationed in France under the provisions of the North Atlantic Treaty, was driving his car at high speed along a road within the judicial district of the French town of Corbeil. He was carrying as a passenger one Aitchison, an officer in the Royal Canadian Air Force. As subsequently found, the applicant drove negligently and as a result of his driving the car crashed and Aitchison was killed. It was also found that when driving the car the appellant was not acting in the performance of his official duty; and in accordance with Article VII(3)(b) of the Agreement of June 19, 1951, the primary right of jurisdiction was vested in the French courts. The United States military authorities requested the French authorities to waive their primary right of jurisdiction, and this request was approved by the French Ministry of Justice and the Prosecutor of the Court of Corbeil. The French authorities duly notified the United States military authorities in accordance with Article VII(3)(c) of the Agreement that they had decided not to exercise jurisdiction.

Notwithstanding the waiver of their primary right of jurisdiction by the French authorities * * * the widow of Aitchison (the respondent herein) instituted proceedings against the appellant for damages as *partie civile,* as is customary under French law in connection with criminal proceedings. At that time the United States military authorities had not yet made any decision as to the manner in which they intended to proceed against the appellant in the exercise of the right of jurisdiction granted to them by the French authorities, but subsequently they decided not to take any action against the appellant.

The appellant objected to the jurisdiction of the French court on the ground that the waiver by the French authorities of their primary right of jurisdiction was irrevocable, and that the right once waived could not be revived by the decision of the United States authorities not to prosecute. The Court of Corbeil overruled the objection and held itself

* Reprinted with the permission of the Editor of the International Law Reports.

competent to adjudicate the respondent's claim for damages. The Paris Court of Appeal dismissed the appellant's appeal against that decision.[1]

On further appeal to the Court de Cassation,

Held: (i) that the appeal must be allowed. Once the French authorities had waived their right to primary jurisdiction and notified United States military authorities of the waiver, their right to exercise jurisdiction was incapable of being revived, notwithstanding that the United States military authorities decided not to prosecute.

(ii) Even though under French municipal law a prosecutor cannot definitively waive the right to prosecute, the Agreement, in accordance with Article 26 of the French Constitution of October 27, 1946, must take precedence and as, according to the Agreement, a right of primary jurisdiction once waived cannot be revived, the French courts were no longer competent. [A portion of the opinion of the court appears below.]

* * * The notice of appeal alleges a violation of Articles VII(3)(c) and XX(3) of the N.A.T.O., S.O.F.A., promulgated by Decree dated October 13, 1952; a violation of Articles 26 et seq. of the Constitution of October 27, 1946; of Articles 3 and 182 of the Code of Criminal Procedure; and of Article 7 of the Law of April 20, 1810. It is contended that the judgment under appeal, notwithstanding the waiver of the right of primary jurisdiction by the Minister of Justice as well as by the Prosecutor of the Court of Corbeil, in favour of the United States authorities, wrongly considered the Magistrates' Court of Corbeil entitled to deal with the civil action and the criminal prosecution. The Court of Corbeil, it is said, took this view on the ground that a waiver by the authorities of the country entitled to the right of primary jurisdiction is neither irrevocable nor unconditional, and that in order to be final and irrevocable and generally binding, a waiver must be subject to the requirement of the existence of a judgment against the accused. As long as such a judgment has not come into existence the victim, according to the view expressed by the lower courts, cannot be deprived of his right to bring proceedings in the criminal courts with a view to obtaining damages for the injury sustained. Neither the Minister of Justice nor the Public Prosecutor, according to this view, is in full control of the criminal proceedings, and they cannot waive these because such waiver would have no legal effect and could not, in any event, deprive the claimant (*partie civile*) of his own rights which the law confers on him.

If the host State which has the right of primary jurisdiction decides to waive this right, there arises a genuine lack of competence for the benefit of the other State which is not entitled to the right of primary jurisdiction. The State which has waived its right can no longer exercise jurisdiction unless the State which benefits from the waiver decides not to exercise jurisdiction and notifies the State which has waived its right. *International conventions have the force of law even if they conflict with municipal law,* and they must be applied instead of the latter where occasion demands. The provisions of the North Atlantic Treaty neces-

---

1. The judgment of the Court of Appeal of Paris is reported in International Law Reports, 1956, p. 255.

sarily imply that it is the Public Prosecutor's department which is entitled to waive the right of primary jurisdiction, and that when the right has been waived the French courts are no longer competent, notwithstanding that according to French municipal law the Public Prosecutor cannot waive the right to institute criminal proceedings. The victim of the criminal offence, who can always bring his claim before the civil courts, cannot question a renunciation of competence which has been made for reasons of international courtesy.

Article VII(3)(c) of the Agreement of June 19, 1951, between the Parties to N.A.T.O., as published in the Decree dated October 11, 1952, provides:

> If the State having the primary right decides not to exercise jurisdiction, it shall notify the authorities of the other State as soon as practicable. Authorities of the State having primary right shall give sympathetic consideration to a request from the authorities of the other State for a waiver of its right in cases where that other State considers such waiver to be of particular importance.

Where, in accordance with this provision, the authorities of the State which has the right of primary jurisdiction have, at the request of the other State, waived that right, their decision is final, and the criminal courts of the State concerned can no longer exercise jurisdiction over facts in respect of which there has been a waiver. There is no need to enquire whether the State in whose favour the right has been waived has exercised jurisdiction through its own courts. The only exception to this would be the case where the State which has been granted the right to exercise jurisdiction by the State in which the primary right was vested, expressly informs the latter that it does not wish to exercise jurisdiction and leaves the matter to the judicial authorities of the other Contracting Party.

Article 26 of the Constitution of October 27, 1946, provides that international treaties duly ratified and published have the force of law even if they conflict with French municipal law. After the death of Aitchison, the latter's widow instituted proceedings against Whitley before the criminal court of Corbeil–Essonnes, alleging involuntary homicide committed against her husband while Whitley was not acting in the performance of his official duties. That Court, in arriving at a finding that the subsidiary civil action (*action de la partie civile*) was subject to the jurisdiction, held that if before the institution of these proceedings the Minister of Justice and the Public Prosecutor of Corbeil–Essonnes agreed, at the request of the United States authorities and in accordance with the [N.A.T.O., S.O.F.A.], to waive the right of primary jurisdiction, this did not imply a waiver of the right subsequently to exercise jurisdiction if, as in this case, the alleged offender has not been tried by the judicial authorities of his home State, because the Agreement itself contemplates the case of an accused who has not been tried in the home State and of an accused who, though convicted, has not served his sentence—unless there has been an amnesty.

The appealed judgment has misinterpreted the Agreement of June 19, 1951, and violated the provisions referred to in the notice of appeal, because it arrived at its finding notwithstanding the absence of any express declaration by the home State that it waived its right to exercise jurisdiction, which jurisdiction had been recognized by France when that country agreed not to exercise its primary right of jurisdiction. The judgment of the Court of Appeal of Paris is therefore reversed, and there is no need for remand.

* * *

WILSON, SECRETARY OF DEFENSE v. GIRARD

United States Supreme Court, 1957.
354 U.S. 524, 77 S.Ct. 1409, 1 L.Ed. 1544.

PER CURIAM. Japan and the United States became involved in a controversy whether the respondent Girard should be tried by a Japanese court for causing the death of a Japanese woman. * * *

Girard, a Specialist Third Class in the United States Army, was engaged on January 30, 1957, with members of his cavalry regiment in a small unit exercise at Camp Weir range area, Japan. Japanese civilians were present in the area, retrieving expended cartridge cases. Girard and another Specialist Third Class were ordered to guard a machine gun and some items of clothing that had been left nearby. Girard had a grenade launcher on his rifle. He placed an expended 30–caliber cartridge case in the grenade launcher and projected it by firing a blank. The expended cartridge case penetrated the back of a Japanese woman gathering expended cartridge cases and caused her death.

The United States ultimately notified Japan that Girard would be delivered to the Japanese authorities for trial. Thereafter, Japan indicted him for causing death by wounding. Girard sought a writ of habeas corpus in the United States District Court for the District of Columbia. The writ was denied, but Girard was granted declaratory relief and an injunction against his delivery to the Japanese authorities. The petitioners appealed to the Court of Appeals for the District of Columbia, and, without awaiting action by that court on the appeal, invoked the jurisdiction of this Court under 28 U.S.C.A. § 1254(1). Girard filed a cross-petition for certiorari to review the denial of the writ of habeas corpus.

Note on the Girard case. What should the result be? The decision of the American military authorities to turn Girard over to Japanese justice, once the authorities admitted in an official statement that " * * * This was upheld by the U.S. Supreme Court, after it reversed District Court injunction against his delivery to Japan. Girard's action in firing empty shell cases from a rifle grenade launcher was not authorized * * * ", was sharply criticized in some quarters in the United States; and there was great interest in the action brought in the

United States on Girard's behalf. A professor of international law on temporary duty in the Department of Justice, was speeding into Washington on a Sunday to work on the government's side of the case before the Supreme Court. The traffic policeman was skeptical both as to Sunday work and haste, until told that the professor was working on the Girard case. Then, tearing up the ticket, the policeman exclaimed: "Get on in there and get that boy out, ya hear?" Girard was convicted in Japan of bodily injury resulting in death. He served a comparatively light sentence without further attention from the public.

(c) *International Arrangements and Agreements as to Conflicting State Demands Based on Nationality or Allegiance*

States may make demands for service of various kinds on the basis of jurisdiction over nationals or the existence of obligations arising from allegiance; see Ch. 9. Such demands conflict when more than one state considers itself entitled to demand service of the person on nationality or related grounds, as in cases of demands for military service. When the United States had compulsory military service (the draft) it sought by international agreements to eliminate or lower the risk that a person might have to serve in more than one military system.

3. CONFLICTS OF JURISDICTION AS TO THE APPLICATION OF ECONOMIC REGULATIONS

----

1. *Question.* In the situations dealt with in this Section, primary jurisdiction-allocating international arrangements are rare, compared to Section A situations. Consider as you go along why this is so.

2. *Multiplicities of state regulatory interests.* In the one-world atmosphere of contemporary economic and business activity, unavoidably, the governmental interests of various states and of at least one association of states, the European Union, became involved over a wide range of conduct. Further, the application of the objective territorial principle to economic effects potentially enlarges the scope of conflict.

Resolution is difficult because the easy-to-formulate allocation devices considered in the preceding sections are not relevant. Ideally, what is needed is some way of quantifying state regulatory interests, and of leaving regulation to the law-making authority with the most preponderant interest. But how are such interests to be determined and what is the authority of the law-applier in a state to disregard its law?

Neither law as rules nor law as method is settled. Perhaps methods for the partial resolution of conflicts that we shall consider below might be thought to justify a conclusion that reciprocal judicial deference, moderation, equity and comity are not reliable enough and that conflict should be reduced by the adoption of new rules. But what rules? Rules to narrow the bases of national jurisdiction? Or new rules that would replace the welter of national restraints about jurisdiction, such as the reasonable-unreasonable exercise test of the 1987 Restatement?

3. ***Areas of economic activity involved.*** The problems of conflicts involving regulatory policy in the field of anticompetitive practices (restrictive business practices and practices tending toward market domination and monopoly) are the ones that have been the most fully considered. Thus, in the cases to follow you will study, first, the problems of reach of law, including both those related to investigative preliminaries and those related to actual imposition of a particular law. Then we direct your attention to various approaches to resolutions of those problems through one moderating device or another. We follow the antitrust presentation with one involving the reach of national regulation of securities transactions. Of course, environmental law and other arenas are important and are considered in their pertinent chapter.

(a) *Antitrust*

Hypothetical case to illustrate the differences among antitrust laws. Assume that all the law enforcement authorities involved in the hypothetical case below know and can prove that the producers of 95% of the world supply of a certain basic hard mineral, some thirty corporations that are nationals of ten countries, conform to a pattern in which each national market is left to the companies organized there. Further, total production by all the companies is adjusted to total demand in such a way as to keep prices stable and relatively high. However, it is not possible to prove that the thirty companies have made any contractual arrangement to these ends. (This is a classic antitrust problem; concerted action to allocate markets and to control price by restricting production of a single product.)

The Facts:

a. In some of the ten countries even a contractual cartel arrangement would not violate any law; and, indeed, a breach of such a contract would be actionable.

b. In the United States the concerted action would violate the Sherman Act, even if it did not result in market dominance, i.e., a per se violation. Moreover, the sanctions would include invalidation of the contract, criminal prosecution, equitable enforcement by imprisonment or fines for civil contempt, or treble damages to injured competitors outside the cartel arrangement.

c. In Germany the supreme court has held that the cartel law does not reach concerted actions where there is no contract.

d. In the United States and in Germany an antitrust violation under national law, if otherwise actionable, exists if the companies' conduct, wherever it took place, has economic effects within the territories of these states.

e. But in Germany, unlike the United States, criminal and civil contempt sanctions would not lie; the fine is the major sanction.

Questions.

Now, suppose that by coincidence antitrust proceedings are brought in each legal system except those in category (a). In the United States proceeding, to the shock of the Europeans, there is a criminal count against the executives of the companies in the cartel, only a few of which can be personally served. Also, in the United States, foreign corporations that cannot otherwise be served with process in the proceedings are served through companies organized in the United States as subsidiaries of the foreign companies but which, the United States claims, are really the parent companies and control the foreign companies. The United States also demands of the corporations so served that they produce for an American grand jury the books and records kept abroad by the ostensible foreign parent company.

What results if:

a. A state in category (a) objects under customary international law to every aspect of the United States proceeding, insofar as its citizens and companies organized under its law are concerned. What do you think the legal counts in a diplomatic protest would be? What is the proper legal response of the Department of State?

b. The ambassador of the United States to the European Union, acting on the instruction of his government, asks the European Commission not to proceed with its case against the cartel, as the matter is being prepared for trial in the United States, the world's largest consumer of the mineral involved. What is a proper response of the commission to the ambassador?

c. The commission grants an exception under Article 85–3 of the Treaty of Rome which permits the commission to exempt from sanction cartels that are found to contribute to improved production, distribution, or technical or economic progress, or, more simply, cartels deemed "good." (In the United States antitrust law there are no "good" cartels.) The United States thereafter proceeds to final judgment against all members of the cartel that can be served in the United States, and the commission protests to the American ambassador. What is a proper legal and policy response from him?

d. Is there any better way to deal with these conflicts of regulatory law? What is it?

The U.S. approach to antitrust regulation does not aim at the attainment of a prohibition of a specified level of concentration, but attacks cartelization at the margins (i.e., incremental restraints of trade). *See,* Stephan, Wallace, and Roin, International Business & Economics: Law & Policy 515 (1993). Moreover, antitrust provides a fine study of the differing approaches to regulation in the U.S. vs. that in continental systems: most U.S. antitrust law is based on judicial decision, not on any precise, systematic, or even coherent, statutory rules. Thus, both the content and scope of the law has varied enormously over time. *Id.*

We studied the *"effects"* theory of jurisdiction above. The history of antitrust law in the United States began with the leading case, *American Banana, supra,* where territoriality was held by Justice Holmes to be literal and very restrictive. The concept of what was *"conduct within a territory"* expanded and undermined *American Banana,* as well as provided expanded jurisdiction over crime and tort of all sorts. We saw how *The ALCOA case, supra,* held, in 1945, that a totally extraterritorial anticompetitive conspiracy came within U.S. prescriptive jurisdiction, if the conspirators intended to cause an effect on U.S. commerce. U.S. antitrust law since *ALCOA* has been a reaction to that case, either attempting to provide content to or to create exceptions to the *ALCOA* effects test. *Id.,* at 517.

The OECD has promulgated a model code on anticompetitive practices and has recommended cooperative measures to be taken by businesses. None of this provides any substantive rules of competition or even adopts a policy. Would it be wise to do so? Periodically, the U.S. judiciary has attempted to promote moderation in their antitrust decisions.

CCH, Common Market Reporter, is a useful source in English of the antitrust laws.

THE SHERMAN ACT [a]

15 U.S.C. §§ 1–2.

Sec. 1. Every contract, combination in the form of trust or otherwise, or conspiracy, in restraint of trade or commerce among the several States, or with foreign nations, is [hereby] declared to be illegal * * *.

Sec. 2. Every person who shall monopolize, or attempt to monopolize, or combine or conspire with any other person or persons, to monopolize any part of the trade or commerce among the several States, or with foreign nations shall be deemed guilty of a misdemeanor * * *.

[To the declarations of invalidity and the criminal penalties provided above, the United States antitrust laws contain as sanctions the *use of injunctions, with the corresponding power to punish for civil contempt, and treble damages* for injured private parties. European antitrust laws in many instances provide only for fines; such is the case with the provisions against restraints of trade (Article 85) and monopoly power misused (Article 86) of the Treaty of Rome, which establishes the European Economic Community.]

---

a. The original and still basic federal antitrust law, later supplemented by legislation such as the Clayton Act, the Federal Trade Commission Act, and the Robinson–Patman Act.

The Nylon Spinners cases. DuPont invented nylon and, as is customary, patented its invention in all—or certainly all industrial countries—including the United Kingdom. The patent for exploitation of the British market was transferred to Imperial Chemicals Industries (ICI). The United States Department of Justice charged that this transfer was one item in an arrangement whereby the large United States chemical company and the British corporation had pooled their patents and divided the [markets of the] world between them. ICI was properly served in the United States. It unsuccessfully contended before the United States court that British patent law and policy favored such territorial divisions in patent cases, i.e., that British patent rights should prevail over American antitrust laws, even as to the pooling of patents, the nylon patent in Britain being legally a British patent. The trial judge ordered the dissolution of the pool and directed ICI by an affirmative decree in equity to open the British nylon patent to all wishing to use the patent on payment of standard royalties.

In its decree ordering ICI to open the British nylon patent to non-exclusive licensing, the United States District Court had recognized that " * * * substantial legal questions * * * " might be raised as to the effectiveness of this direction in Great Britain and that " * * * the effectiveness of the exercise * * * depends upon the recognition * * * given to our judgment as a matter of comity by the courts of the foreign sovereign which has granted the patents * * * " [*U.S. v. Imperial Chemical Industries, Ltd.,* 105 F.Supp. 215, 229 (S.D.N.Y.1952).] Despite the deferential non-assertiveness of the American judge, the various British jurists involved in a specific performance suit by Nylon Spinners against ICI (to prevent opening the patent to all qualified users) exhibited degrees of reserve, from coolness to mild toleration, as to the action of the American court. Compare the statements of Upjohn, J., Evershed, M.R., and Denning, L.J. in Nylon Spinners, Ltd. v. Imperial Chemicals Industries, Ltd., [1953] Ch. 19, Court of Appeal, 1952, at an interlocutory stage. In the end, specific performance of the exclusive licensing agreement was ordered, under the English law of contracts, despite the American decree. In due course ICI took over and liquidated Nylon Spinners.

Questions. ICI (the American antitrust proceeding) is an instance in which an American trial judge wrote moderation into the reach of antitrust decree. What do you think might have led him to this? What, at this stage, would you consider possible bases for judicial restraint? Judge Cashin's decree in U.S. v. The Watchmakers of Switzerland Information Center, Inc., 1965 CCH Trade Cases ¶ 71,352 (S.D.N.Y. 1965) did the same thing and brought an end to official Swiss objections to the antitrust suit.

Statutory systems impeding antitrust enforcement transnationally: a précis on non-cooperation and clawback statutes.
Even though antitrust laws no longer exist only in the U.S. and some American judges have unilaterally moderated the transnational reach of their antitrust decrees, a number of European states have passed legislation designed to restrain, handicap, or prevent antitrust action by another state. The United Kingdom pioneered in 1980 legislation restricting the national enforcement of multiple damage antitrust judgments rendered abroad and running to private parties under antitrust laws giving private parties causes of action for antitrust injury to them. The Sherman Act contains a treble damages provision for the benefit of private parties. Along with criminal liability and civil contempt in equity, these provisions have long been objectionable features of American antitrust law as seen by Western Europeans. The treble damages provision became particularly controversial in Britain, Canada, and Australia after its use in the 1970's when Westinghouse sued a prominent British mining company as an alleged participant in a multinational cartel charged with controlling the price and production of uranium oxide ("yellowcake", the primary fuel source of the atomic age). The Protection of Trading Interests Act, 1980, c. 11, contains a sweeping interdiction of the enforcement in the United Kingdom of foreign treble damage judgments. It reinforces this with a "clawback" provision, under which the losing British defendant in the foreign antitrust judgment is given a British cause of action against the original plaintiff for the difference between any multiple damage recovery in a third country and a purely compensatory amount considered fair in Britain. Further, the Act provides for the enforcement in Britain, on a basis of reciprocal treatment, of clawback judgments in other countries. This permits the expansion of effective opposition to multiple damage antitrust judgments. See, generally, Lowe, Blocking Extraterritorial Jurisdiction: the British Protection of Trading Interests Act, 1980, 75 Am. J. Int'l L. 257 (1981).

In addition to what Parliament has done, the British courts have, in recent times, used injunctions against antitrust suits outside the United Kingdom, as in Laker v. Sabena Airlines, et al. For a useful survey of recent developments, see Born, Recent British Responses to the Extraterritorial Application of United States Law: The Midland Bank Decision and Retaliatory Legislation Involving Unitary Taxation, 26 Va.J. Int'l L. 91 (1985).

Perspective on Timberlane I and II. In its two dealings with the same suit, the United States Court of Appeals for the Ninth Circuit first developed for the trial court a test (Timberlane I) and then reviewed (Timberlane II) the trial court's application of a judicial test for determining whether United States or Honduras antitrust law should govern in a treble damage suit. While the Timberlane decisions are on antitrust issues, the methodology developed has potentially wider application. There are interesting comparisons possible between the Timberlane cases and fairly contemporaneous activity of the Court of Appeals for the Second and Third Circuits in the securities regulation cases, *infra.* The Timberlane decisions have been widely cited.

[In these two cases Timberlane Lumber Company, a California corporation, sued Bank of America and one of its United States subsidiaries under the Sherman Antitrust Act for treble damages, claiming that the defendants, acting through a Bank of America branch bank in Honduras, conspired with certain [authorities] in Honduras to impede and frustrate Timberlane's foreign investment in a lumber mill in Honduras through such acts as preventing Timberlane from getting title documents to the mill, interference with the operation of the mill, and engineering the false imprisonment under Honduran authority of Timberlane's manager for Honduran operations. The Court of Appeals in Timberlane I held the act of state defense inapplicable, laid down a three factor balancing procedure for the trial court to use in deciding the applicable antitrust law, and remanded the case. The trial court's subsequent finding against Timberlane was affirmed in Timberlane II, but the trial court was "corrected" as to its use of the balancing test, now referred to as a seven-factor test.]

TIMBERLANE LUMBER CO. v. BANK OF AMERICA, N.T. AND S.A.

United States Court of Appeals, Ninth Circuit, 1976.
549 F.2d 597.

CHOY, Circuit Judge.

* * *

The act of state doctrine demonstrates that the judiciary is sometimes cognizant of the possible foreign implications of its action. Similar awareness should be extended to the general problems of extraterritoriality. Such acuity is especially required in private suits, like this one, for in these cases there is no opportunity for the executive branch to weigh the foreign relations impact, nor any statement implicit in the filing of the suit that that consideration has been outweighed.

What we prefer is an evaluation and balancing of the relevant considerations in each case—in the words of Kingman Brewster, a "jurisdictional rule of reason." * * *

The elements to be weighed include the degree of conflict with foreign law or policy, the nationality or allegiance of the parties and the locations or principal places of business of corporations, the extent to which enforcement by either state can be expected to achieve compliance, the relative significance of effects on the United States as compared with those elsewhere, the extent to which there is explicit purpose to harm or affect American commerce, the foreseeability of such effect, and the relative importance to the violations charged of conduct within the United States as compared with conduct abroad. A court evaluating these factors should identify the potential degree of conflict if American authority is asserted. A difference in law or policy is one likely sore spot, though one which may not always be present. Nationality is another; though foreign governments may have some concern for the treatment of American citizens and business residing there, they primarily care about their own nationals. Having assessed the conflict, the court should then determine whether in the face of it the contacts and interests of the United States are sufficient to support the exercise of extraterritorial jurisdiction.[34]

We conclude, then, that the problem should be approached in three parts: Does the alleged restraint affect, or was it intended to affect, the foreign commerce of the United States? Is it of such a type and magnitude so as to be cognizable as a violation of the Sherman Act? As a matter of international comity and fairness, should the extraterritorial jurisdiction of the United States be asserted to cover it? The district court's judgment found only that the restraint involved in the instant suit did not produce a direct and substantial effect on American foreign commerce. That holding does not satisfy any of these inquiries.

The Sherman Act is not limited to trade restraints which have both a direct and substantial effect on our foreign commerce. Timberlane has alleged that the complained of activities were intended to, and did, affect the export of lumber from Honduras to the United States—the flow of United States foreign commerce, and as such they are within the jurisdiction of the federal courts under the Sherman Act. Moreover, the magnitude of the effect alleged would appear to be sufficient to state a claim. The comity question is more complicated. From Timberlane's complaint it is evident that there are grounds for concern as to at least a few of the defendants, for some are identified as foreign citizens: Laureano Gutierrez Falla, Michael Casanova and the Casanova firms, of Honduras, and Patrick Byrne, of Canada. Moreover, it is clear that most of the activity took place in Honduras, though the conspiracy may have been directed from San Francisco, and that the most direct economic effect was probably on Honduras. However, there has been no indication of any conflict with the law or policy of the Honduran government, nor any comprehensive analysis of the relative connections and interests of Honduras and the United States. Under these circumstances, the dismissal * * * cannot be sustained on jurisdictional grounds.

34. In requiring district courts to assess the conflicting contacts and interests of those nations involved, we do not thereby assign them the same task which the "act of state" doctrine prohibits them from undertaking. As the quotation from comment *d.* to § 41 of the Restatement, Second, Foreign Relations Law of the United States (1965), makes clear, there is an important distinction between examining the validity of the "public interests" which are involved in a sovereign policy decision amounting to an "act of state" and evaluating the relative "interests" which each state may have "in providing the means of adjudicating disputes or claims that arise within its territory." Our "jurisdictional rule of reason" does not in any way require the court to question the "validity" of "foreign law or policy." Rather, the legitimacy of each nation's interests is assumed. It is merely the relative involvement and concern of each state with the suit at hand that is to be evaluated in determining whether extraterritorial jurisdiction should be exercised by American courts as a matter of comity and fairness.

We * * * vacate the dismissal and remand the Timberlane action.

* * *

TIMBERLANE LUMBER CO. v. BANK OF AMERICA, N.T. AND S.A.

United States Court of Appeals, Ninth Circuit, 1984.
749 F.2d 1378.[a]

SNEED, Circuit Judge.

* * *

B. Timberlane I's "jurisdictional rule of reason."

* * *

1. "Does the alleged restraint affect, or was it intended to affect, the foreign commerce of the United States?"

The first part of Timberlane I's analysis requires "that there be *some* effect—actual or intended—on American foreign commerce before the federal courts may legitimately exercise subject matter jurisdiction under [the antitrust] statutes." On appeal, Bank of America does not deny that Timberlane has met this requirement. "[B]y alleging the ability and willingness to supply cognizable markets with lumber that they allege would have been competitive with that already in the marketplace, they have satisfied this prong of the Circuit's test."

2. "Is it of such a type and magnitude so as to be cognizable as a violation of the Sherman Act?"

Under the second part of Timberlane I's analysis, "a greater showing of burden or restraint may be necessary to demonstrate that the effect is sufficiently large to present a cognizable injury to the plaintiffs and, therefore, a civil *violation* of the antitrust laws." Courts and commentators, however, have had difficulty identifying the nature and extent of proof required to satisfy this part of the inquiry. It has been suggested that Timberlane I requires a showing of a "direct and substantial" effect on the foreign commerce of the United States. In fact, however, no such showing is necessary. The only issue under the second part of the inquiry is whether the magnitude of the effect identified in the first part of the test rises to the level of a civil antitrust violation, i.e., conduct that has a direct and substantial anticompetitive effect. * * * Timberlane I's requirement that the allegation state a claim under the antitrust laws, however, "is a 'practical, case-by-case economic judgment,' not one based on 'abstract or mechanistic formulae,' * * * and * * * the barrier raised is not very high."

In this case Timberlane alleges that Bank of America conspired with its Honduran subsidiaries to prevent Timberlane from milling lumber in Honduras and exporting it to the United States. Our review of the

a. Cert. denied, 472 U.S. 1032.

complaint reveals that Timberlane has alleged an injury that would state a claim under the antitrust laws against Bank of America. Thus, it satisfies the second part of the analysis.

3. "As a matter of international comity and fairness, should the extraterritorial jurisdiction of the United States be asserted to cover it?"

Under the third part of Timberlane I's analysis, the district court must determine "whether the interests of, and links to, the United States—including the magnitude of the effect on American foreign commerce—are sufficiently strong, vis-a-vis those of other nations, to justify an assertion of extraterritorial authority." This determination requires that a district court consider seven factors. The district court here found that the undisputed facts required that jurisdiction not be exercised in this case. We agree. * * * [E]ach factor will be examined.

a. *"The degree of conflict with foreign law or policy"*

We must determine whether the extraterritorial enforcement of United States antitrust laws creates an actual or potential conflict with the laws and policies of other nations. Timberlane argues that no conflict exists between United States and Honduran law. We disagree. The application of United States antitrust law in this case creates a potential conflict with the Honduran government's effort to foster a particular type of business climate.

Although Honduras does not have antitrust laws as such, it does have definite policies concerning the character of its commercial climate. To promote economic development and efficiency within its relatively undeveloped economy, the Honduran Constitution and Commercial Code guarantee freedom of action. *The Code specifically condemns any laws prohibiting agreements (even among competitors) to restrict or divide commercial activity. Under Honduran law, competitors may agree to allocate geographic or market territories, to restrict price or output, to cut off the source of raw materials, or to limit credit financing to obtain enterprises as long as the contracting parties are not de facto monopolists.*[b] It appears that Honduran law intimately regulates private commercial activity in that country. Honduran law also promotes agreements that improve the competitive position of domestic industries in world markets by promoting efficiency and economies of scale.

On balance, we believe that the enforcement of United States antitrust laws in this case would lead to a significant conflict with Honduran law and policy. This conflict, unless outweighed by other factors in the comity analysis, is itself a sufficient reason to decline the exercise of jurisdiction over this dispute.

b. *"The nationality or allegiance of the parties and the locations of principal places of business of corporations"*

Next we should consider the citizenship of the parties and witnesses involved in the alleged illegal conduct. In this case, with only one exception, all of the named parties are United States nationals. But it is

---

b. Emphasis supplied. Editor's note: What kind of an anti-trust policy is this?

also true that "[a]ll of the crucial percipient witnesses to the incidents were either Honduran citizens or residents." We believe, therefore, that the citizenship of the parties weighs slightly in favor of the exercise of jurisdiction.

c. *"The extent to which enforcement by either state can be expected to achieve compliance"*

The weighing of this factor yields no clear answer. Of course, any judgment against Bank of America could easily be enforced in a United States court. Whether such a judgment could be enforced as easily in Honduras is less certain. We believe that the enforcement factor tips slightly in favor of the assertion of jurisdiction in this case.

d. *"The relative significance of effects on the United States as compared with those elsewhere"*

A more definitive answer emerges when we compare the effect of the alleged illegal conduct on the foreign commerce of the United States with its effect abroad. The insignificance of the effect on the foreign commerce of the United States when compared with the substantial effect in Honduras suggests federal jurisdiction should not be exercised.

A comparison of Honduran lumber imports to both United States imports and total United States lumber consumption is instructive. During the years 1970 through 1972, the amount of lumber imported from Honduras expressed as a percentage of total United States lumber imports was as follows: [figures presented]

Clearly, Honduran imports have only a minuscule effect on United States lumber markets.

Second, a comparison of the specific submarkets of "Pine Lumber Dressed" and "Pine Lumber Rough" in no way helps Timberlane's case. Honduran imports of both "Pine Lumber" and "Pine Lumber NES Rough" expressed as a percentage of total pine lumber imports were as follows: [figures presented]

Again, these figures represent only an insignificant part of the pine lumber import market. And although we do not have the relevant statistics, we believe that Honduran imports represent an insubstantial part of total United States pine lumber consumption.

The actual effect of Timberlane's potential operations on United States foreign commerce is, therefore, insubstantial, even in the narrow pine lumber market. In comparison, the effects of its activity on the considerably smaller Honduran lumber markets would have been much greater. The bank's actions also affect several other aspects of the Honduran economy such as the number of jobs, the amount of foreign exchange and taxes, and the internal competitive market. We believe that the relative significance of effects in this case weighs strongly against the exercise of jurisdiction.

e. *"The extent to which there is explicit purpose to harm or affect American commerce"*

We should also consider whether the defendant's actions were intended to harm or affect the commerce of the United States. Our review of the record reveals that Bank of America's acts were directed primarily towards securing a greater return on its investment. Its actions were consistent with Honduran customs and practices. Timberlane has not demonstrated that Bank of America had any particular interest in affecting United States commerce.

f. *"The forseeability of such effect"*

A court should also consider whether, at the time of the alleged illegal behavior, the defendant should have forseen an effect on the foreign commerce of the United States. Aside from the fact that American commerce has not been substantially affected, Timberlane has not shown that Bank of America should have foreseen the consequences of its actions. Bank of America simply enforced its mortgage in an attempt to recoup its investment. The effects of this action were merely part of the inevitable consequences that flow from attempting to salvage something from a failing business enterprise. We do not believe that a reasonable investor would have foreseen the minimal effect that has occurred here. This weighs against the exercise of jurisdiction.

g. *"The relative importance to the violations charged of conduct within the United States as compared with conduct abroad"*

Finally, a court should consider the location of the alleged illegal conduct to assess the appropriateness of the exercise of extraterritorial jurisdiction. In this case both parties agree that virtually all of the illegal activity occurred in Honduras. This factor clearly weighs against the exercise of jurisdiction.

h. *Resolving the Seven Factor Test*

It follows that all but two of the factors in Timberlane I's comity analysis indicate that we should refuse to exercise jurisdiction over this antitrust case. The potential for conflict with Honduran economic policy and commercial law is great. The effect on the foreign commerce of the United States is minimal. The evidence of intent to harm American commerce is altogether lacking. The forseeability of the anticompetitive consequences of the allegedly illegal actions is slight. Most of the conduct that must be examined occurred abroad. The factors that favor jurisdiction are the citizenship of the parties and, to a slight extent, the enforcement effectiveness of United States law. We do not believe that this is enough to justify the exercise of federal jurisdiction over this case.

* * *

Questions about the Timberlane Cases.

1. In United States v. Sisal Sales Corp., 274 U.S. 268 (1927), the government won where a conspiracy-collusion activity with powerful figures in Mexico was charged against an American company, to the detriment of another American interest. What would the Timberlane court have done if the case against the Bank of America had been brought by the Department of Justice or the Federal Trade Commission? Is a non-governmental treble damages antitrust suit not entitled to the same weight as a government suit in the application of the seven-factor calculus of Timberlane II? If not, why not?

2. In the Aluminum Co. case Judge L. Hand, citing inter alia the Banana case, wrote: " * * * We should not impute to Congress an intent to punish all whom its courts can catch, for conduct which has no consequences within the United States * * * ". In Timberlane can it be said there are no consequences within the United States? Or does the Court of Appeals decide that regardless of such consequences the balance in favor of the Honduran anti-antitrust law must prevail?

Alternatively, is the Ninth Circuit acting to resolve a potential conflict of antitrust laws by limiting the previously declared reach of the Sherman Act? If so, did the court act in conformity with the standard of the ALCOA case as to the application of the effects doctrine?

3. In both of its Timberlane opinions the court stressed that a principle of reasonableness as to reach of antitrust law is "jurisdictional". What is the significance of this position? What does "jurisdictional" mean in this context? Does it mean that there is no jurisdiction to prescribe an unreasonable reach? If it does, why bother with the rules as to prescriptive jurisdiction? What is unreasonable? Who decides? What does it have to do with reason? If you were European, would you trust a U.S. court's decision on what is "reasonable?" The 1987 Restatement finesses the issues by differentiating between a base of jurisdiction (which either exists or does not exist) and a legitimate exercise of a [base] of jurisdiction, which depends on the existence of reasonableness. See, 403(1) and Reporters' Notes 1–4. Do Timberlane and the 1987 Restatement use "jurisdictional" in the same sense, i.e., as a principle of moderation? Is it necessary or desirable to state a principle of moderation as "jurisdictional"?

4. The litigation scenarios in American Banana (1909) and Timberlane (1976, 1984) are startlingly similar: a smaller American company sues a giant American company in a Central American country, under the Sherman Act, for manipulation detrimental to the plaintiff's business in that country. The Sherman Act is held not to protect the

plaintiff in either case. Look again at the portion of Timberlane II put
in italics on page 240. Is the court raising an anti-antitrust act in
Honduras above the policy level of the long-standing American law
against unfair competitive practices between American concerns? Or is
it stressing that the Honduran law deals only with the misuse of
monopoly power and that the exclusion of unfair competition from the
Honduran law should be respected under a principle of moderation?
Have you any guess as to the intensity with which the governments that
have come and gone in Honduras enforce Honduran competition policy?
As to their impartiality? If no act of state is involved (so held), why
should Honduran law govern the suit in Timberlane, other than on the
basis used in American Banana? How would the Ninth Circuit decide a
replay of the 1909 case?

5. Suppose that in Timberlane the suit against the Bank of America had been brought by the receiver of Timberlane Lumber Company on
the basis of a provable contention that the episode in Honduras had
resulted in bankruptcy. Same result? What is the status of Timberlane
after *Hartford Ins. v. California* infra at pp. 246, et seq.?

AMERICAN BANANA CO. v. UNITED FRUIT CO.

United States Supreme Court, 1909.
213 U.S. 347, 29 S.Ct. 511, 53 L.Ed. 826.

[In the earlier editions of this book this case was carried immediately before the Aluminum Company decision, to show that the strictly
territorial construction of the Sherman Act in it did not survive. We
place its fact situation and outcome before you now for comparisons with
the facts and outcomes in Timberlane I and II.]

* * * The plaintiff is an Alabama corporation, organized in 1904.
The defendant is a New Jersey corporation, organized in 1899. Long
before the plaintiff was formed, the defendant, with intent to prevent
competition and to control and monopolize the banana trade, bought the
property and business of several of its previous competitors, with provision against their resuming the trade, made contracts with others,
including a majority of the most important, regulating the quantity to be
purchased and the price to be paid, and acquired a controlling amount of
stock in still others. For the same purpose it organized a selling
company, of which it held the stock, that by agreement sold at fixed
prices all the bananas of the combining parties. By this and other
means it did monopolize and restrain the trade and maintained unreasonable prices. The defendant being in this ominous attitude, one
McConnell in 1903 started a banana plantation in Panama, then part of
the United States of Colombia, and began to build a railway (which
would afford his only means of export), both in accordance with the laws
of the United States of Colombia. He was notified by the defendant that
he must either combine or stop. Two months later, it is believed at the
defendant's instigation, the governor of Panama recommended to his
national government that Costa Rica be allowed to administer the
territory through which the railroad was to run, and this although that
territory had been awarded to Colombia under an arbitration agreed to

by treaty. The defendant, and afterwards, in September, the government of Costa Rica, it is believed by the inducement of the defendant, interfered with McConnell. In November, 1903, Panama revolted and became an independent republic, declaring its boundary to be that settled by the award. In June, 1904, the plaintiff bought out McConnell and went on with the work, as it had a right to do under the laws of Panama. But in July, Costa Rican soldiers and officials, instigated by the defendant, seized a part of the plantation and a cargo of supplies and have held them ever since, and stopped the construction and operation of the plantation and railway. In August one Astua, by ex parte proceedings, got a judgment from a Costa Rican court, declaring the plantation to be his, although, it is alleged, the proceedings were not within the jurisdiction of Costa Rica, and were contrary to its laws and void. Agents of the defendant then bought the lands from Astua. The plaintiff has tried to induce the government of Costa Rica to withdraw its soldiers and also has tried to persuade the United States to interfere, but has been thwarted in both by the defendant and has failed. The government of Costa Rica remained in possession down to the bringing of the suit.

As a result of the defendant's acts the plaintiff has been deprived of the use of the plantation, and the railway, the plantation and supplies have been injured. The defendant also, by outbidding, has driven purchasers out of the market and has compelled producers to come to its terms, and it has prevented the plaintiff from buying for export and sale. This is the substantial damage alleged. * * * It is contended, however, that, even if the main argument fails and the defendant is held not to be answerable for acts depending on the cooperation of the government of Costa Rica for their effect, a wrongful conspiracy resulting in driving the plaintiff out of business is to be gathered from the complaint and that it was entitled to go to trial upon that.

[The court affirmed the dismissal of the complaint as not setting forth a cause of action. Justice Holmes wrote for the Court:]

* * * It is obvious that, however stated, the plaintiff's case depends on several rather startling propositions. In the first place the acts causing the damage were done, so far as appears, outside the jurisdiction of the United States and within that of other states. It is surprising to hear it argued that they were governed by the act of Congress.

* * *

* * * The general and almost universal rule is that the character of an act as lawful or unlawful must be determined wholly by the law of the country where the act is done. * * *

* * *

For another jurisdiction, if it should happen to lay hold of the actor, to treat him according to its own notions rather than those of the place where he did the acts, not only would be unjust, but would be an interference with the authority of another sovereign, contrary to the

comity of nations, which the other state concerned justly might resent.
* * *

    * * *

The foregoing considerations would lead in case of doubt to a construction of any statute as intended to be confined in its operation and effect to the territorial limits over which the lawmaker has general and legitimate power. "All legislation is prima facie territorial." * * * Words having universal scope, such as "Every contract in restraint of trade," "Every person who shall monopolize," etc., will be taken as a matter of course to mean only every one subject to such legislation, not all that the legislator subsequently may be able to catch. In the case of the present statute the improbability of the United States attempting to make acts done in Panama or Costa Rica criminal is obvious, yet the law begins by making criminal the acts for which it gives a right to sue. We think it entirely plain that what the defendant did in Panama or Costa Rica is not within the scope of the statute so far as the present suit is concerned. * * *

More Comments and questions. Obviously, certain groups have sought to direct attention to the alleged harmful effects of the reach of American antitrust laws on American economic activities abroad. To what extent does the statement of the Department of Justice suggest that moderation may be jurisdictional? Suppose the United States should abandon the use of the effects doctrine in antitrust cases, either outright or by casting the balance against application. What assurance would American business have that the antitrust laws elsewhere, such as those of Germany or the European Union would not apply, either because of presence within the territory through controlled subsidiaries or the effects doctrine?

Symeonides, Choice of Law in the American Courts in 1993 (and in the Six Previous Years)

42 A.J.Comp.L. 701, 716–718; 714–716; 718–719 (1993).
(some footnotes eliminated, some modified) *

Supreme Court Decisions: Extraterritorial Reach of American Statutes

Hartford Fire Insurance Company v. California, 125 L.Ed.2d 612 (1993), involved the extraterritorial application of the Sherman Act. Defendants, London reinsurers of American insurers were accused of conspiring with American insurers to limit coverage of certain pollution risks in North America and generally to adversely affect the insurance market in the United States. Supported by the British Government

---

* Printed with the permission of Symeon Symeonides and the American J. Comp.L.

appearing as amicus, defendants argued that their London conduct was perfectly consistent with British law and policy; applying the Act to that conduct would conflict significantly with British law and the comprehensive regulatory regime provided by it for the London reinsurance market; and, consequently, the District Court should have declined to exercise its jurisdiction under the principle of international comity.

In an opinion by Justice Souter, the Court held that, since the defendant's London activities were meant to produce and did in fact produce substantial effect in the United States, the Sherman Act applied to them. To the defendant's comity argument, the Court responded by saying that: "even assuming that in a proper case a court may decline to exercise Sherman Act jurisdiction over foreign conduct * * *, international comity would not counsel against exercising jurisdiction"[1] in a case such as this one which did not present a "true conflict" between American and foreign law. The fact that conduct is lawful in the foreign state will not, of itself, bar application of the United States antitrust laws, "even where the foreign state has a strong policy to permit or encourage such conduct."[2] Since the defendants did not claim that British law required them to act in a way that is prohibited by American law, or that their compliance with the laws of both countries was otherwise impossible, there was no conflict and the defendants were perfectly capable of complying with both laws.

Justice Scalia, who dissented from this part of the opinion, found this assertion of no true conflict between American and British law to be a "breathtakingly broad proposition, which * * * will bring the Sherman Act and other laws into sharp and unnecessary conflict with the legitimate interests of other countries—particularly our closest trading partners." He said that, in the sense in which the term "conflict" is generally understood in the field of conflicts of laws, there is clearly a conflict whenever applicable foreign and domestic law provide different substantive rules of decision to govern the parties' dispute, and that in such a case a conflict-of-laws analysis is necessary. Justice Scalia distinguished between adjudicatory jurisdiction and legislative or prescriptive jurisdiction. He agreed with the majority that the district court unquestionably did have adjudicatory jurisdiction, and that Congress did possess legislative jurisdiction to regulate the defendants' London activity. However, the question was whether Congress had actually done so, which in turn depended on how one delineates the extraterritorial reach of the Sherman Act. In such delineation, Scalia said, one should keep in mind that, even when the presumption against extraterritoriality is overcome, an act of Congress ought not to be construed in a way that violates the principles of international law, including "international comity," which is a traditional component of choice-of-law theory. Relying on section 403 of the Restatement (Third) of Foreign Relations Law, Scalia concluded that an interpretation of the Sherman Act that would make it applicable to defendant's London activities would be "unreason-

---

1. 125 L.Ed.2d at 640.

2. Id. (citing Restatement (Third) Foreign Relations Law § 415, Comment j).

able." [3] He pointed out that the defendants' activity took place primarily in the United Kingdom, and that the defendants are British corporations having their principal place of business or residence outside the United States. Great Britain has established a comprehensive regulatory scheme governing the London reinsurance markets, and clearly has a heavy "interest in regulating the activity." [4] * * *

Other recent cases on prescriptive jurisdiction: The United States Supreme Court rendered two decisions dealing with the extraterritorial reach of Federal statutes in 1993.[15] Because these cases are often handled as cases of statutory construction, many conflicts scholars tend to consider them not to be conflicts cases in the traditional sense. Yet, defining the spatial operation of laws by ascertaining their intended reach is one of the oldest ways of resolving conflicts problems. In any event, these cases are important, if only because they are decided by the Supreme Court.

Smith v. United States [16] involves the application of the Federal Tort Claims Act (FTCA) in Antarctica, a "sovereignless region without civil tort law of its own." [17] Section 1346(b) of the Act waives the sovereign immunity of the United States for certain torts committed by federal employees "under circumstances where the United States, if a private person, would be liable to the claimant in accordance with the law of the place where the act or omission occurred." [18] However, section 2680(k) exempts from the scope of the Act "[a]ny claim arising in a foreign country." The question in Smith was whether Antarctica is a "foreign country" within the meaning of the last quoted section.[19]

The plaintiff argued that the purpose of the foreign-country exception was to insulate the United States from tort liability imposed pursuant to foreign law. Because Antarctica has no law of its own, and since the United States does not recognize the validity of other nations' claims to Antarctica, plaintiff argued, "conventional choice-of-law rules control and require the application of Oregon law, the law of her domicile." Thus, the rationale for the foreign-country exception would not be compromised by the exercise of jurisdiction here, since the United States would not be subject to liability under the law of a foreign nation.

In an eight-to-one opinion authored by Chief Justice Rehnquist, the Court rejected the plaintiff's arguments and held that Antarctica is a

---

3. Id. at 653–54. "I think it unimaginable that an assertion of legislative jurisdiction by the United States would be considered reasonable, and therefore it is inappropriate to assume, in the absence of statutory indication to the contrary, that Congress has made such an assertion." Id. at 654.

4. Id. at 653.

15. For similar cases at the state level, see D'Agostino v. Johnson & Johnson, Inc., 133 N.J. 516, 628 A.2d 305 (1993) and Peterson v. Deloite & Touche, 1993 U.S.Dist.Lexis 10274 (N.D.Ill.1993).

16. 113 S.Ct. 1178 (1993).

17. 122 L.Ed.2d at 552.

18. 28 U.S.C. § 1346(b).

19. Smith was a wrongful death action against the U.S. filed by the surviving spouse of an American citizen who worked as a carpenter in Antarctica, for a construction company under contract to the National Science Foundation, an agency of the United States. Smith fell in a crevasse when he walked off the marked route to walk across a snow field. Petitioner alleged that the U.S. was negligent in failing to provide adequate warning of the dangers posed by crevasses in areas beyond the marked paths.

"foreign country" within the meaning of section 2680(k) and thus it is excluded from the coverage of the FTCA. Quoting from Richards v. United States,[20] the Court said, if it were otherwise, then § 1346(b) "would instruct courts to look to the law of a place that has no law in order to determine the liability of the United States—surely a bizarre result." The Court also rejected plaintiff's argument of applying the law of the plaintiff's domicile, Oregon, since "her cause of action is [not] based on acts or omissions occurring in Oregon." Finally, quoting from EEOC v. Arabian American Oil Co.,[23] and speaking of the "the common-sense notion that Congress generally legislates with domestic concerns in mind" and "against the backdrop of the presumption against extraterritoriality," the Court concluded that its construction of the FTCA was consistent with "the presumption against extraterritorial application of U.S. statutes [which] requires that any lingering doubt regarding the reach of the FTCA be resolved against its encompassing torts committed in Antarctica" [122 L.Ed.2d at 555–56], "a desolate and extraordinarily dangerous land." Id.

In a dissenting opinion, Justice Stevens criticized the majority for its "parsimonious construction of the FTCA's 'sweeping' waiver of sovereign immunity" and for reading the Act "through the opaque green eye-shade of the cloistered bookkeeper." In his opinion, the word "foreign country" connotes a "territory subject to the sovereignty of another nation," and not a "sovereignless region" like Antarctica, the high seas, or the outer space. The fact that Antarctica is sovereignless does not mean that it has no law. "The relevant substantive law in this case is the law of the State of Oregon, where petitioner resides." Quoting from Justice Holmes in American Banana Co. v. United Fruit Co. supra, Justice Stevens thought that Oregon, the forum State, had "a substantial interest in applying its civil tort law to a case involving the allegedly wrongful death of the spouse of one of its residents."[29]

In the New Jersey case D'Agostino v. Johnson & Johnson, Inc.,[30] the allegedly wrongful conduct had taken place in New Jersey and had its impact in Switzerland. Executives of a New Jersey corporation allegedly "orchestrated" the retaliatory firing of an American citizen employed by their wholly owned Swiss subsidiary for refusing to bribe Swiss officials regulating the licensing of pharmaceuticals in Switzerland. If true, this conduct would be in direct violation of the Federal Corrupt Practices Act (FCPA) which was "incorporated" into New Jersey law by New Jersey cases. Under Swiss law, the alleged bribes would be considered "consulting fees" and would be lawful, and so would the employee's firing.

---

20. 369 U.S. 1, 9 (1962) ("Congress has expressly stated that the Government's liability is to be determined by the application of a particular law, the law of the place where the act or omission occurred * * *").

23. 499 U.S. 244 (1991) ("It is a long-standing principle of American law 'that legislation of Congress, unless a contrary intent appears, is meant to apply only within the territorial jurisdiction of the United States.' ").

29. 122 L.Ed.2d at 562. For a 1993 case involving application of the FTCA within the United States, see Pietrantonio v. United States, 827 F.Supp. 458 (W.D.Mich.1993) (decided under Wisconsin's Leflar's approach and applying Michigan law to a medical malpractice committed in a Wisconsin VA hospital against a Michigan veteran).

30. 133 N.J. 516, 628 A.2d 305 (1993).

In an important unanimous opinion applying interest analysis,[31] the New Jersey Supreme Court held that New Jersey's interests in deterring wrongful conduct in New Jersey "outweigh the Swiss interest in the at-will employment relationship that would not seek to deter such conduct through its civil law." Although the fired employee was at all times a resident of Switzerland and had signed in that country an at-will employment contract containing a choice of Swiss law, and although Switzerland has an interest in regulating the employment relationship between a Swiss company and a Swiss resident, that country did "not have an interest in condoning corporate bribery orchestrated beyond its boundaries." Distinguishing this case from other cases in which New Jersey deferred to the policies of the state of the employment relationship,[34] the court emphasized that "this case is not about regulating just Swiss employment relationships. It is as much about regulating the conduct of parent companies in New Jersey that engage in corrupt practices through subsidiary employees." This was "not exporting New Jersey employment law so much as applying New Jersey domestic policy * * * to a domestic company." Because of New Jersey's position as a "worldwide leader in the pharmaceutical markets, [t]he effect of commercial bribery abroad has a potential effect on New Jersey and the health and welfare of its citizens." The strength of New Jersey's commitment to deterring commercial bribery, coupled with the "extensive New Jersey contacts," suggests a "strong public interest in this case. Any opposing interest involving extraterritoriality does not outweigh this forum's interests in preventing bribery, which could have a negative impact on public health and safety in New Jersey." * * *

(b) *Securities Regulation, Including Fraudulent Sales and Insider Trading*

Stage of development of the problem. Federal regulatory initiative to put aside caveat emptor in securities trading became nationally significant in the United States in 1933. American securities regulation is still much farther advanced than in any other country, but the beginnings of such regulation are now developing elsewhere. As to conflicts between regulatory systems, the situation that now partially exists as to antitrust is not replicated. Thus the major international problems in the securities area have been about the reach of the American regulatory system. Progress is being made toward international cooperation with the United States as to stock fraud and insider trading. This has been especially significant as between the United States and Switzerland, which has been willing to relax its bank secrecy law and policy where otherwise it would protect serious crime and other grave antisocial conduct. The materials that follow show courts in America coping with the proper reach of American law in the securities regulation field. As with similar judicial efforts in antitrust, the principles being developed have broader

31. After completing its interest analysis, the court observed that "this case has aspects of both tort and contract law * * * [and] as such, it does not fit easily within any of the conventional rubrics for choice of law." 628 A.2d at 320. Perhaps because of this, the court felt the need to validate its conclusions through the application of the Restatement Second which would produce the same result. Id. at 320–21.

34. See, e.g., Eger v. E.I. du Pont de Nemours Co., 110 N.J. 133, 539 A.2d 1213 (1988).

potential applicability as general methodologies for the reduction or elimination of conflicts of jurisdiction.

Notes & Queries: *Hartford,* therefore, seems to have settled the difficult issues of how much deference U.S. courts ought to give to legitimate foreign sovereignty interests in the arena of extraterritorial application of U.S. antitrust law. It equates extraterritorial and internal infringements and renders them to the same fate, except in the rare instance of a foreign interest actually being faced with a foreign command actually in conflict with a U.S. counter-command. *Did Hartford, thus, repudiate the judicial rule of reason? Are comity and interest balancing dead? Is this a good or a bad thing?*

SECURITIES AND EXCHANGE COMMISSION v. KASSER

United States Court of Appeals, Third Circuit, 1977.
548 F.2d 109.

ADAMS, Circuit Judge.

The central issue * * * is whether the Securities and Exchange Commission (SEC) may invoke the jurisdiction of the federal courts over defendants who have allegedly engaged in fraudulent conduct within the United States, when the sole victim is a foreign corporation and when the purported fraud had little, if any, impact within this country.

* * *

Basically, the SEC avers that the defendants engaged in a scheme to defraud and make misrepresentations to the Manitoba Development Fund ("Fund") * * * [.] * * *

The SEC brought this action in the New Jersey district court, alleging that the defendants, individual and corporate, violated various antifraud provisions of the Securities Act of 1933 and the Securities Exchange Act of 1934. It sought injunctions against any further violations as well as ancillary relief. However, the district court dismissed the complaint with prejudice, holding that it lacked subject-matter jurisdiction over the alleged fraud. The SEC then filed the present appeal in this Court.

Since we believe that a district court does have jurisdiction in an SEC suit for injunctive relief under the federal securities laws, given circumstances such as are presented here, we reverse and remand.

* * *

Although this case presents a relatively new legal problem, several opinions already have addressed similar matters. They, and their underlying principles, suggest that the position of the district court was too restrictive and that jurisdiction should vest.

Just recently, this Court in Straub v. Vaisman & Co., considered the jurisdictional aspects of transnational securities fraud. There, an American broker-dealer engaged in fraudulent sales of securities to nonresident foreigners. A unanimous panel of this Court found jurisdiction under the 1933 and 1934 Acts. Speaking for the panel, Judge Weis posited that "[c]onduct within the United States is alone sufficient from a jurisdictional standpoint to apply the federal [securities] statutes * * *."

It could be argued that Straub differs somewhat from the case at hand. The stock in the Straub fraud was traded on an American OTC exchange, unlike the securities here which were not so traded. Frequently, trading on an exchange has helped to undergird findings of jurisdiction in other transnational fraud cases. Where a stock exchange is involved, courts have found sufficient impact in the United States to sustain jurisdiction. In addition, there may have been slightly more conduct in the United States in Straub than in the present case, for Judge Weis said that the panel was "not here faced with a predominantly foreign transaction." Despite these possible variations, however, Straub indicates that jurisdiction does exist in this case. This is so because Judge Weis flatly proclaimed that conduct in this country, standing alone, is enough for jurisdiction to attach under the federal securities laws.

Perhaps the leading opinions which have delved into the problem of jurisdiction in transnational securities fraud cases are IIT v. Vencap, Ltd. and Bersch v. Drexel Firestone, Inc.—Second Circuit decisions written by Judge Friendly. Of these two cases, IIT is more supportive of subject-matter jurisdiction here. In IIT, the alleged securities fraud arose out of negotiations outside the United States. These negotiations led to the sale in the Bahamas of preferred stock in Vencap, a Bahamian corporation whose shares were not traded on any American exchange, to IIT, a Luxembourg investment trust. While the Second Circuit intimated that the defendants may well have engaged in sufficient conduct in this country to justify subject-matter jurisdiction under the Securities Acts, the Court nonetheless remanded for additional findings as to the extent and nature of the intranational fraudulent activities. Even so, IIT is quite pertinent to the present appeal.

In suggesting that jurisdiction might exist in IIT, Judge Friendly made several asseverations which are very damaging to the position of defendants here. He expressly noted that there was "little factual support for the view that [defendants'] activities had a significant *effect* in the United States * * *." Despite the absence of impact within the United States, Judge Friendly declared that jurisdiction still could exist. In so doing, he essentially rejected the position taken by the defendants in the case before us, i.e., that substantial or even some impact in this country is a prerequisite to jurisdiction over extraterritorial securities transactions.

As critical as may be the rejection of an "effect" requirement is the following declaration in IIT:

We do not think Congress intended to allow the United States to be used as a base for manufacturing fraudulent security devices for export, even when these are peddled only to foreigners. * * * it is hard to believe Congress meant to prohibit the SEC from policing [such] activities within this country * * *.

While the defendants in the present appeal contend that such language constitutes dicta, it sets forth a sound proposition, and one which we now adopt.

The federal securities laws, in our view, do grant jurisdiction in transnational securities cases where at least some activity designed to further a fraudulent scheme occurs within this country. There is nothing in § 10(b) or its companion anti-fraud provisions to thwart their application to fraudulent transactions when the actual focus of the harm is outside the territorial limits of the United States. Indeed, by their own terms, the anti-fraud laws suggest that such application is proper. The securities acts expressly apply to "foreign commerce," thereby evincing a Congressional intent for a broad jurisdictional scope for the 1933 and 1934 Acts. Moreover, § 10(b) and its related provisions seem to be largely concerned with conduct, having no requirement that accomplishment of the attempted fraud be a precondition to statutory liability.

We are, like the IIT court, skeptical that Congress wished to preclude all SEC suits for injunctive relief where the victim of a fraudulent scheme happens to be foreign or where there was insubstantial impact on the United States. Consequently, we decline to immunize, for strictly jurisdictional reasons, defendants who unleash from this country a pervasive scheme to defraud a foreign corporation. This would appear to be especially appropriate where the corporation is owned by a foreign governmental subdivision of a neighboring nation.

The IIT court did narrow its decision somewhat by saying: "Our ruling on this basis of jurisdiction is limited to the perpetration of fraudulent acts themselves and does not extend to mere preparatory activities or the failure to prevent fraudulent acts where the bulk of the activities were performed in foreign countries * * *."

* * * In our view, the conduct of the defendants here cannot be deemed to be "mere[ly] preparatory" to fraudulent acts committed outside this country, for it was much more substantial than the United States-based activities in IIT. It thus would appear that IIT supports jurisdiction over this SEC suit, which is primarily for injunctive relief.

      * * *

In sum, the prior pronouncements of this Court and those of the Second Circuit, a court with especial expertise in matters pertaining to securities, lend great support for a holding of jurisdiction here. Straub, IIT and, to a lesser extent, Bersch together indicate that such a ruling is the appropriate one. While those cases diverge somewhat from the factual setting present here, the differences do not, in our view, militate against reinstatement of the SEC's complaint seeking injunctive and ancillary relief.

III.

From a policy perspective, and it should be recognized that this case in a large measure calls for a policy decision, we believe that there are sound rationales for asserting jurisdiction. First, to deny such jurisdiction may embolden those who wish to defraud foreign securities purchasers or sellers to use the United States as a base of operations. By sustaining the decision of the district court as to the lack of jurisdiction, we would, in effect, create a haven for such defrauders and manipulators. We are reluctant to conclude that Congress intended to allow the United States to become a "Barbary Coast," as it were, harboring international securities "pirates."

Also, we are concerned that a holding of no jurisdiction might induce reciprocal responses on the part of other nations. Some countries might decline to act against individuals and corporations seeking to transport securities frauds to the United States. Such parties may well be outside the ambit of the power of our courts. For foreign nations to adopt the position that the defendants are urging this Court to take would enable defrauders beyond the reach of our courts to escape with impunity. By finding jurisdiction here, we may encourage other nations to take appropriate steps against parties who seek to perpetrate frauds in the United States. Accordingly, our inclination towards finding jurisdiction is bolstered by the prospect of reciprocal action against fraudulent schemes aimed at the United States from foreign sources.

As a final policy justification for asserting jurisdiction here, we register the opinion that the antifraud provisions of the 1933 and 1934 Acts were designed to insure high standards of conduct in securities transactions within this country in addition to protecting domestic markets and investors from the effects of fraud. By reviving the complaint in this case, this Court will enhance the ability of the SEC to police vigorously the conduct of securities dealings within the United States. Such a result would appear to comport with the basic purposes of the federal statutes.

* * *

---

4. WHAT IS TO BE DONE WHEN EXPLICIT CONFLICTS OF JURISDICTION TO PRESCRIBE EXIST?

Where two or more states have made prescriptive rules to govern conduct or situations and the states concerned have not agreed on jurisdictional primacy among themselves, and no state moderates its reach unilaterally, how, if at all, are these direct conflicts to be resolved? This subsection considers a problem not yet resolved. In the absence of transfer of regulatory authority from national to international agencies, it can reasonably be foreseen that the areas in which national regulatory interests directly conflict will expand. Why?

(a) *International Legal Requirements as to Resolution? The Attempts in the 1965 and 1987 Restatements*

UNITED STATES OF AMERICA v. FIRST NATIONAL CITY BANK

United States Court of Appeals, Second Circuit, 1968.
396 F.2d 897.

KAUFMAN, Circuit Judge. The issue presented on this appeal is of considerable importance to American banks with branches or offices in foreign jurisdictions. We are called upon to decide whether a domestic bank may refuse to comply with a valid Grand Jury subpoena duces tecum requiring the production of documents in the possession of a foreign branch of the bank on the ground that compliance would subject it to civil liability under the law of the foreign state.

* * *

On March 7, 1968, First National City Bank of New York [Citibank] was served with a subpoena duces tecum in connection with a federal Grand Jury investigation of certain alleged violations of the antitrust laws by several of its customers. The subpoena required the production of documents located in the bank's offices in New York City and Frankfurt, Germany, relating to any transaction in the name of (or for the benefit of) its customers C.F. Boehringer & Soehme, G.m.b.H., a German corporation, and Boehringer Mannheim Corporation, a New York corporation [referred to jointly hereinafter as "Boehringer"]. Citibank complied with the subpoena insofar as it called for the production of material located in New York but failed to produce or divulge any documents reposited in Frankfurt. Indeed, the bank even refused to inquire or determine whether any relevant papers were overseas. Instead, William T. Loveland, Citibank's vice-president responsible for the decision to defy the subpoena, appeared before the Grand Jury and asserted that the bank's action was justified because compliance would subject Citibank to civil liability and economic loss in Germany.

* * *

The basic legal question confronting us is not a total stranger to this Court. With the growing interdependence of world trade and the increased mobility of persons and companies, the need arises not infrequently, whether related to civil or criminal proceedings, for the production of evidence located in foreign jurisdictions. It is no longer open to doubt that a federal court has the power to require the production of documents located in foreign countries if the court has in personam jurisdiction of the person in possession or control of the material. See, e.g., First National City Bank of New York v. Internal Revenue Service etc., 271 F.2d 616 (2d Cir.1959), cert. denied. Thus, the task before us, as Citibank concedes, is not one of defining power but of developing rules governing the proper exercise of power. The difficulty arises, of course, when the country in which the documents are located has its own rules and policies dealing with the production and disclosure of business information—a circumstance not uncommon. This problem is particularly acute where the documents are sought by an arm of a foreign

government. The complexities of the world being what they are, it is not surprising to discover nations having diametrically opposed positions with respect to the disclosure of a wide range of information. It is not too difficult, therefore, to empathize with the party or witness subject to the jurisdiction of two sovereigns and confronted with conflicting commands. For an example of a comparable dilemma resulting from the application of the antitrust laws, see British Nylon Spinners Ltd., supra
* * *.

In any event, under the principles of international law, "A state having jurisdiction to prescribe or enforce a rule of law is not precluded from exercising its jurisdiction *solely* because such exercise requires a person to engage in conduct subjecting him to liability under the law of another state having jurisdiction with respect to that conduct." Restatement (2d), § 39(1) (1965) (emphasis supplied). It is not asking too much however, to expect that each nation should make an effort to minimize the potential conflict flowing from their joint concern with the prescribed behavior. Id. at § 39(2). Where, as here, the burden of resolution ultimately falls upon the federal courts, the difficulties are manifold because the courts must take care not to impinge upon the prerogatives and responsibilities of the political branches of the government in the extremely sensitive and delicate area of foreign affairs. Mechanical or overbroad rules of thumb are of little value; what is required is a careful balancing of the interests involved and a precise understanding of the facts and circumstances of the particular case.

With these principles in mind, we turn to the specific issues presented by this appeal. Citibank concedes, as it must, that compliance with the subpoena does not require the violation of the criminal law of a foreign power, as in Societe Internationale etc. v. Rogers, 357 U.S. 197 (1958) (discovery under the Federal Rules of Civil Procedure); Ings v. Ferguson, 282 F.2d 149, 152 (2d Cir.1960), or risk the imposition of sanctions that are the substantial equivalent of criminal penalties, as in Application of Chase Manhattan Bank, 297 F.2d 611, 613 (2d Cir.1962), or even conflict with the public policy of a foreign state as expressed in legislation, compare Restatement, supra, § 39, Reporters' Notes at p. 113. Instead, all that remains, as we see it, is a possible prospective civil liability flowing from an implied contractual obligation between Citibank and its customers that, we are informed, is considered implicit in the bank's license to do business in Germany.

But, the government urges vigorously, that to be excused from compliance with an order of a federal court, a witness, such as Citibank must show that following compliance it will suffer criminal liability in the foreign country. We would be reluctant to hold, however, that the mere absence of criminal sanctions abroad necessarily mandates obedience to a subpoena. Such a rule would show scant respect for international comity; and, if this principle is valid, a court of one country should make an effort to minimize possible conflict between its orders and the law of a foreign state affected by its decision. The vital national interests of a foreign nation, especially in matters relating to economic affairs, can be expressed in ways other than through the criminal law. For example, it could not be questioned that, insofar as a court of the

United States is concerned, a statement or directive by the Bundesbank (the central bank of Germany) or some other organ of government, expresses the public policy of Germany and should be given appropriate weight. Equally important is the fact that a sharp dichotomy between criminal and civil penalties is an imprecise means of measuring the hardship for requiring compliance with a subpoena. * * * It would be a gross fiction to contend that if the Bundesbank were to revoke the license of Citibank for a violation of bank secrecy the impact would be less catastrophic than having to pay an insignificant fine because the revocation is theoretically not "equivalent to a misdemeanor" or criminal sanction. We are not required to decide whether penalties must be under the "criminal law" to provide a legally sufficient reason for noncompliance with a subpoena; but, it would seem unreal to let all hang on whether the label "criminal" were attached to the sanction and to disregard all other factors. In any event, even were we to assume arguendo that in appropriate circumstances civil penalties or liabilities would suffice, we hold that Citibank has failed to provide an adequate justification for its disobedience of the subpoena.

In evaluating Citibank's contention that compliance should be excused because of the alleged conflict between the order of the court below and German law, we are aided materially by the rationale of the recent Restatement (2d), § 40:

> Where two states have jurisdiction to prescribe and enforce rules of law and the rules they may prescribe require inconsistent conduct upon the part of a person, each state is required by international law to consider, in good faith, moderating the exercise of its enforcement jurisdiction, in the light of such factors as
>
> (a) vital national interests of each of the states,
>
> (b) the extent and the nature of the hardship that inconsistent enforcement actions would impose upon the person,
>
> (c) the extent to which the required conduct is to take place in the territory of the other state,
>
> (d) the nationality of the person, and
>
> (e) the extent to which enforcement by action of either state can reasonably be expected to achieve compliance with the rule prescribed by that state.

In the instant case, the obvious, albeit troublesome, requirement for us is to balance the national interests of the United States and Germany and to give appropriate weight to the hardship, if any, Citibank will suffer.

The important interest of the United States in the enforcement of the subpoena warrants little discussion. The federal Grand Jury before which Citibank was summoned is conducting a criminal investigation of alleged violations of the antitrust laws. These laws have long been considered cornerstones of this nation's economic policies, have been vigorously enforced and the subject of frequent interpretation by our Supreme Court. We would have great reluctance, therefore, to countenance any device that would place relevant information beyond the reach

of this duly impaneled Grand Jury or impede or delay its proceedings.
* * *

We examine the importance of bank secrecy within the framework of
German public policy with full recognition that it is often a subtle and
difficult undertaking to determine the nature and scope of the law of a
foreign jurisdiction. There is little merit, however, in Citibank's suggestion that the mere existence of a bank secrecy doctrine requires us to
accept on its face the bank's assertion that compliance with the subpoena would violate an important public policy of Germany. * * * While
we certainly do not intend to deprecate the importance of bank secrecy
in the German scheme of things, neither can we blind ourselves to the
doctrine's severe limitations as disclosed by the expert testimony. We
have already made the assumption that the absence of criminal sanctions
is not the whole answer to or finally determinative of the problem. But,
it is surely of considerable significance that Germany considers bank
secrecy simply a privilege that can be waived by the customer and is
content to leave the matter of enforcement to the vagaries of private
litigation. Indeed, bank secrecy is not even required by statute. See
Restatement, supra, § 40, comment (c): "A state will be less likely to
refrain from exercising its jurisdiction when the consequence of obedience to its order will be a civil liability abroad." See also Restatement,
supra, § 39, Reporters' Notes at p. 113.

Moreover, Section 300 of the Criminal Code of Germany provides
that:

> Anybody who without authority discloses the secrets of another,
> shall be punished by imprisonment for a term not to exceed six
> months or by a fine, if the secret was intrusted or became known to
> him in his capacity as a
>
> > (1) Physician, dentist, pharmacist [and similar professions]
> >
> > (2) Attorney, patent attorney, notary public, defense counsel,
> auditor, Certified Public Accountant, or tax consultant.

It is not of little significance that a German court has noted, "The fact
that bank secrecy has not been included in the penal protection of
Section 300 of the Criminal Code must lead to the conclusion that the
legislature did not value the public interest in bank secrecy as highly as
it did the duty of secrecy of doctors and attorneys." District Court of
Frankfurt (1953). Further, Section 53 of the German Code of Criminal
Procedure grants the right of refusal to testify to a number of persons,
ranging from clergymen and mid-wives to publishers and printers;
again, reference to bankers is conspicuously absent. It would be anomalous if Citibank, deprived of any right to assert bank secrecy in a
criminal investigation conducted in Germany, could—in the absence of
statutes imposing greater limitations upon foreign governments, cf. First
National City Bank of New York v. Internal Revenue Service etc., supra,
271 F.2d at 619–620—benefit from German bank secrecy in a criminal
investigation in the United States.

In addition, it is noteworthy that neither the Department of State
nor the German Government has expressed any view on this case or

indicated that, under the circumstances present here, enforcement of the subpoena would violate German public policy or embarrass German–American relations. * * * We are fully aware that when foreign governments, including Germany, have considered their vital national interests threatened, they have not hesitated to make known their objections to the enforcement of a subpoena to the issuing court. * * * So far as appears, both the United States and German governments have voiced no opposition to Citibank's production of the subpoenaed records.

We turn now to the nature and extent of the alleged hardships to which Citibank would be subjected if it complied with the subpoena. It advances two grounds on which it will suffer injury. First, it states that it will be subjected to economic reprisals by Boehringer and will lose foreign business that will harm it and the economic interests of the United States. It paints a dismal picture of foreign companies boycotting American banks for fear that their business records will be subject to the scrutiny of our courts. A partial answer is that the protection of the foreign economic interests of the United States must be left to the appropriate departments of our government, especially since the government is the moving litigant in these proceedings. Moreover, and not without importance, is the fact that the alleged economic reprisals are of doubtful legal relevance in light of the Supreme Court's rejection of a similar argument in First National City Bank (Omar), (dissenting opinion of Justice Harlan), and this Court's decision in First National Bank of New York v. Internal Revenue Service, etc., supra; and the factual underpinning for this claim is quite feeble considering Citibank's overseas growth following the decision in First National City Bank (Omar), supra.

Second, Citibank complains that it will be subjected to civil liability in a suit by Boehringer. The importance of the possible financial loss Citibank might suffer as a result of such a suit must be viewed in light of Loveland's statement that: "[W]e were not concerned with this isolated case and what one individual might do. The importance [sic], I believe, is the effect that it would have on our operations all over the world * * *." We have already rejected the contention that Citibank's alleged loss of business abroad is a sound justification for disobedience of the subpoena. In any event, Judge Pollack concluded that risk of civil damages was slight and speculative, and we agree. The chance that Boehringer will suffer compensable damages is quite remote and Citibank appears to have a number of valid defenses if it is sued, both under the terms of the contract and principles of German civil law. In addition, as we have noted, German courts are given wide latitude in determining whether to award any damages even in the face of liability. In the unlikely event that Boehringer were to sue Citibank, we cannot believe that Boehringer's adamant refusal to apply for a readily available injunction will pass unnoticed by the Court.

Finally, additional factors support our conclusion that the district judge was correct in citing Citibank and Loveland for civil contempt. As noted above, Citibank has failed to produce or segregate documents or records which reflect the bank's own work product. And, the expert testimony indicated that disclosure of such material would not violate any policy of bank secrecy. Moreover, one of the companies being investigated by the Grand Jury—Boehringer Mannheim Corporation—is incorporated in New York. Whatever one may think of requiring disclosure of records of a German corporation reposited in a bank in Germany, surely an American corporation cannot insulate itself from a federal Grand Jury investigation by entering into a contract with an American bank abroad requiring bank secrecy. Compare Restatement, supra, § 40, Comment (c). If indeed Citibank might suffer civil liability under German law in such circumstances, it must confront the choice mentioned in First National City Bank of New York v. Internal Revenue Service etc., supra,—the need to "surrender to one sovereign or the other the privileges received therefrom" or, alternatively a willingness to accept the consequences.

Since the life of the Grand Jury is rapidly drawing to a close, we direct that the mandate issue forthwith but that it be stayed for a period of seven days from the date of the filing of this opinion to permit Citibank, if it so chooses, to apply to the Supreme Court or a Justice thereof for a further stay or other relief.

Affirmed.

———

1987 RESTATEMENT, SECTION 403 *

LIMITATIONS ON EXERCISE OF JURISDICTION TO PRESCRIBE

(1) Even when one of the bases for jurisdiction * * * is present, a state may not exercise jurisdiction to prescribe law with respect to a person or activity having connections with another state when the exercise of such jurisdiction is unreasonable.

(2) Whether exercise of jurisdiction over a person or activity is unreasonable is determined by evaluating all relevant factors, including, where appropriate:

(a) the link of the activity to the territory of the regulating state, i.e., the extent to which the activity takes place within the territory, or has substantial, direct, and foreseeable effect upon or in the territory;

(b) the connections, such as nationality, residence, or economic activity, between the regulating state and the person principally responsible for the activity to be regulated, or between that state and those whom the regulation is designed to protect;

(c) the character of the activity to be regulated, the importance of regulation to the regulating state, the extent to which other states regulate such activities, and the degree to which the desirability of such regulation is generally accepted;

* Copyright 1987 by the American Law Institute. Reprinted with the permission of the American Law Institute.

(d) the existence of justified expectations that might be protected or hurt by the regulation;

(e) the importance of the regulation to the international political, legal, or economic system;

(f) the extent to which the regulation is consistent with the traditions of the international system;

(g) the extent to which another state may have an interest in regulating the activity; and

(h) the likelihood of conflict with regulation by another state.

(3) When it would not be unreasonable for each of two states to exercise jurisdiction over a person or activity, but the prescriptions by the two states are in conflict, each state has an obligation to evaluate its own as well as the other state's interest in exercising jurisdiction, in light of all the relevant factors, [including those set out in] [a] Subsection (2); a state should defer to the other state if that state's interest is clearly greater.

Comment:

a. Reasonableness in international law and practice. The principle that an exercise of jurisdiction on one of the bases indicated in § 402 is nonetheless unlawful if it is unreasonable is established in United States law, and has emerged as a principle of international law as well. There is wide international consensus that jurisdiction to prescribe is subject to legal restraints, implicit in a system of nation-states, and that the links of territoriality or nationality, while generally necessary, are not in all instances sufficient conditions for the exercise of such jurisdiction. Legislatures and administrative agencies, in the United States and in other states, have generally refrained from exercising jurisdiction where it would be unreasonable to do so, and courts have usually interpreted broad general language in statutes as not intended to apply in circumstances where application of the statute would be unreasonable. See Comment *g.*

Some U.S. courts have applied the principle of reasonableness as a requirement of comity, that term being understood not merely as a matter of discretion but reflecting a sense of obligation among states. But as a rule of international law, the principle set forth in this section applies regardless of the state of relations between the state exercising jurisdiction and another state whose interests may be affected. While the term "comity" is sometimes understood to incorporate a requirement of reciprocity, this section does not depend on any finding that another state would exercise its jurisdiction to the same extent, though some elements of reciprocity may be relevant in evaluating the factors listed in Subsection (2). See Reporters' Note 5.

* * *

---

a. The editors of the casebook have supplied in the brackets language apparently missing in the text of Section 403.

(b) *National Limits on Comity and Unilateral Moderation*

LAKER AIRWAYS LTD. v. SABENA, BELGIAN WORLD AIRLINES & KLM ROYAL DUTCH AIRLINES

United States Court of Appeals, District of Columbia Circuit, 1984.
731 F.2d 909.

WILKEY, Circuit Judge.

We review today the limits of a federal court's power to conserve its adjudicatory authority over a case properly filed with the court when, instead of actively raising all defensive claims in the federal court, the named defendants initiate suits in foreign tribunals for the sole purpose of terminating the federal court's adjudication of the litigation. Three months after Laker Airways, Ltd. ("Laker") filed an antitrust action in United States District Court for the District of Columbia against several defendants, including domestic, British, and other foreign airlines, the foreign airlines filed suits in the High Court of Justice of the United Kingdom seeking an injunction forbidding Laker from prosecuting its American antitrust action against the foreign defendants. After the High Court of Justice entered interim injunctions against Laker, the Court of Appeal issued a permanent injunction ordering Laker to take action to dismiss its suit against the British airlines. In the meantime, Laker responded by requesting injunctive relief in the United States District Court, arguing that a restraining order was necessary to prevent the remaining American defendants and the additional foreign defendants Laker had named in a subsequent antitrust claim from duplicating the foreign defendants' successful request for an English injunction compelling Laker to dismiss its suit against the defendants.

If these defendants had been permitted to file foreign injunctive actions, the United States District Court would have been effectively stripped of control over the claims—based on United States law—which it was in the process of adjudicating. Faced with no alternative but acquiescence in the termination of this jurisdiction by a foreign court's order, United States District Judge Harold H. Greene granted Laker's motion for a preliminary injunction restraining the remaining defendants from taking part in the foreign action designed to prevent the district court from hearing Laker's antitrust claims.

* * *

* * * Although the flash point of the controversy has been the antisuit injunctions, the real powder keg is the strongly mandated legislative policies which each national court is bound to implement. Thus, it is unlikely that the underlying controversy would be defused regardless of the action we take today.

Because the principles of comity and concurrent jurisdiction clearly authorize the use of a defensive preliminary injunction designed to permit the United States claim to go forward free of foreign interference, we affirm the decision of the district court.

* * *

Laker's potential competitors allegedly resisted the entry of this new carrier, delaying the commencement of Laker's novel economy service for several years. However, by 1977 Laker obtained the necessary authorizations from the United States and British governments and inaugurated its low cost transatlantic airline service between London and New York.

* * *

* * * [S]everal airlines allegedly conspired to set even lower predatory prices. In October 1981 Pan American Airlines, Trans World Airlines, and British Airways dropped their fares for their full service flights to equal those charged by Laker for its no-frills service. They also allegedly paid high secret commissions to travel agents to divert potential customers from Laker. These activities further restricted Laker's income, exacerbating its perilous economic condition. At IATA meetings in December 1981 at Geneva, Switzerland, and in January 1982 at Hollywood, Florida, the IATA airlines allegedly laid plans to fix higher fares in the spring and summer of 1982 after Laker had been driven out of business.

* * *

[A British court issued] * * * an injunction prohibiting Laker from taking any action *in United States courts* to redress an alleged violation by the defendants *of United States antitrust laws.* The writs specifically sought to compel Laker to dismiss its suit against the foreign defendants * * * and to prohibit Laker from instituting any other proceedings in any non-English forum to redress any alleged violation of English or other laws prohibiting intentional or unlawful commercial injury.

The substantive basis for the requested relief was the alleged inapplicability of United States antitrust laws under the Bermuda II Treaty and the British Protection of Trading Interests Act. Shortly thereafter Justice Parker issued an interlocutory injunction preventing Laker from taking any action in the United States courts or elsewhere to interfere with the proceedings the defendants were commencing in the High Court. * * *

* * *

In a judgment read by Justice Parker on 20 May 1983, the High Court of Justice held that the injunctive relief requested by the British airlines was not justified and terminated claims for relief filed by British Caledonian and British Airways. Justice Parker held that the application of American antitrust laws to companies carrying on business in the United States was not contrary to British sovereignty or the terms of the Bermuda II Treaty, at least while the dormant terms of the British Protection of Trading Interests Act had not been invoked. The judgment did recognize that a determination by the English Secretary of State that Britain's trading interests were negatively implicated by the United States antitrust action could change the result. *However, at this point, before any intervention by the British Executive, the British court was willing to hold that Laker could not be prohibited from proceeding*

with its antitrust claims against British Airways and British Caledonian.
The original interim injunctions were maintained pending an appeal to
the Court of Appeal by British Airways and British Caledonian.

The complexion of the controversy changed dramatically the next
month when the British Government invoked the provisions of the
British Protection of Trading Interests Act ("Act"). Upon a determination that measures taken to regulate international trade outside the
United Kingdom "threaten to damage the trading interests of the United
Kingdom," the Act authorizes the English Secretary of State to require
that any person conducting business in the United Kingdom disobey all
foreign orders and cease all compliance with the foreign judicial or
regulatory provisions designated by the Secretary of State. The Act
authorizes the Secretary of State to prevent United Kingdom courts
from complying with requests for document production issued by foreign
tribunals, and forbids enforcement of treble damage awards or antitrust
judgments specified by the Secretary of State. On 27 June 1983 the
Secretary of State for Trade and Industry cited his powers under the Act
and issued an order and general directions prohibiting persons who carry
on business in the United Kingdom, with the exception of American air
carriers designated under the Bermuda II Treaty, from complying with
"United States antitrust measures" in the district court arising out of
any (1) "agreement or arrangement (whether legally enforceable or not)
to which a UK designated airline is a party," or (2) "any act done by a
UK designated airline" that relates to the provision of air carriage under
the Bermuda II Treaty.

   * * *

On 26 July 1983 the Court of Appeal announced its judgment that
the order and directions were well within the power of the Secretary of
State to issue, and hence valid. * * *

[The battle of injunctions continued.]

Supported by amici curiae Swissair and Lufthansa, KLM and Sabena
challenge the United States District Court's preliminary injunction on
appeal to this court. They claim that the injunction was unnecessary to
protect the district court's jurisdiction and violates their right to take
part in the "parallel" actions commenced in the English courts. Denial
of this opportunity, they assert, flouts international principles of comity.
Moreover, they charge that the district court ignored Britain's "paramount right" to apply British law to Laker, which is a British subject.
Appellants and amici request that we overturn the district court's
injunction as a clear abuse of discretion.

II. ANALYSIS

This appeal is the direct result of a clash between two governments
asserting jurisdiction to prescribe law over a single series of transactions.
The district court's injunction is defended by Laker as necessary to
protect the court's jurisdiction. If there is no justification for the court's
exercise of jurisdiction, the injunctive relief should necessarily fail.
Similarly, if the United Kingdom courts would lack jurisdiction over a
claim filed by Sabena and KLM, the district court should be under no

obligation to defer to the actions of those foreign tribunals. A true conflict arises only if the national jurisdictions overlap. We must therefore begin our analysis with a review of the recognized bases supporting prescriptive jurisdiction, and then examine whether the alleged facts of this case satisfy those requirements.

* * *

* * * [To] a large extent the conflict of jurisdiction is one generated by the political branches of the governments. There is simply no room for accommodation here if the courts of each country faithfully carry out the laws which they are entrusted to enforce. The Master of the Rolls expressed hope that "the courts of the two countries will ... never be in conflict. The conflict, if there be conflict, will be purely one between the laws of the two countries, for which neither court is responsible." We echo that hope.

2. Judicial Interest Balancing

Even as the political branches of the respective countries have set in motion the legislative policies which have collided in this litigation, they have deprived courts of the ability meaningfully to resolve the problem. The American and English courts are obligated to attempt to reconcile two contradictory laws, each supported by recognized prescriptive jurisdiction, one of which is specifically designed to cancel out the other.

The suggestion has been made that this court should engage in some form of interest balancing, permitting only a "reasonable" assertion of prescriptive jurisdiction to be implemented. However, this approach is unsuitable when courts are forced to choose between a domestic law which is designed to protect domestic interests, and a foreign law which is calculated to thwart the implementation of the domestic law in order to protect foreign interests allegedly threatened by the objectives of the domestic law. Interest balancing in this context is hobbled by two primary problems: (1) there are substantial limitations on the court's ability to conduct a neutral balancing of the competing interests, and (2) the adoption of interest balancing is unlikely to achieve its goal of promoting international comity.

a. Defects in the Balancing Process

Most proposals for interest balancing consist of a long list of national contacts to be evaluated and weighed against those of the foreign country. These interests may be relevant to the desirability of allocating jurisdiction to a particular national forum. However, their usefulness breaks down when a court is faced with the task of selecting one forum's prescriptive jurisdiction over that of another.

Many of the contacts to be balanced are already evaluated when assessing the existence of a sufficient basis for exercising prescriptive jurisdiction. Other factors, such as "the extent to which another state may have an interest in regulating the activity," and "the likelihood of conflict with regulation by other states" are essentially neutral in deciding between competing assertions of jurisdiction. Pursuing these inquiries only leads to the obvious conclusion that jurisdiction could be exercised or that there is a conflict, but does not suggest the best avenue of conflict resolution. These types of factors are not useful in resolving the controversy.

Those contacts which do purport to provide a basis for distinguishing between competing bases of jurisdiction, and which are thus crucial to the balancing process, generally incorporate purely political factors which the court is neither qualified to evaluate comparatively nor capable of properly balancing. One such proposed consideration is "the degree to which the *desirability of such regulation* [of restrictive practices] is *generally accepted.*" We doubt whether the legitimacy of an exercise of jurisdiction should be measured by the substantive content of the prescribed law. Moreover, although more and more states are following the United States in regulating restrictive practices, and even exercising jurisdiction based on effects within territory, *the differing English and American assessment of the desirability of antitrust law is at the core of the conflict. An English or American court cannot refuse to enforce a law its political branches have already determined is desirable and necessary.*

The court is also handicapped in any evaluation of "the existence of *justified* expectations that might be protected or hurt by the regulation in question." In this litigation, whether the reliance of Laker and its creditors on United States antitrust laws is justified depends upon whether one accepts the desirability of United States antitrust law. Whether the defendants could justifiably have relied on the inapplicability of United States law to their conduct alleged to have caused substantial effects in the United States is based on the same impermissible inquiry. The desirability of applying ambiguous legislation to a particular transaction may imply the presence or absence of legislative intent. However, once a decision is made that the political branches intended to rely on a legitimate base of prescriptive jurisdiction to regulate activities affecting foreign commerce within the domestic forum, the desirability of the law is no longer an issue for the courts.

* * *

Given the inherent limitations of the Judiciary, which must weigh these issues in the limited context of adversarial litigation, we seriously doubt whether we could adequately chart the competing problems and priorities that inevitably define the scope of any nation's interest in a legislated remedy. This court is ill-equipped to "balance the vital national interests of the United States and the [United Kingdom] to determine which interests predominate." When one state exercises its jurisdiction and another, in protection of its own interests, attempts to quash the first exercise of jurisdiction "it is simply impossible to judicially 'balance' these totally contradictory and mutually negating actions."

Besides the difficulty of properly weighing the crucial elements of any interest balancing formula, one other defect in the balancing process prompts our reluctance to adopt this analysis in the context of preservation of jurisdiction. Procedurally, this kind of balancing would be difficult, since it would ordinarily involve drawn-out discovery and requests for submissions by political branches. There was no time for this process in the present case. Either jurisdiction was protected or it was lost. It is unlikely that the employment of a hasty and poorly informed balancing process would have materially aided the district court's evaluation of the exigencies and equities of Laker's request for relief.

b. Promotion of International Comity

We might be more willing to tackle the problems associated with the balancing of competing, mutually inconsistent national interests if we could be assured that our efforts would strengthen the bonds of international comity. However, the usefulness and wisdom of interest balancing to assess the most "reasonable" exercise of prescriptive jurisdiction has not been affirmatively demonstrated. This approach has not gained more than a temporary foothold in domestic law. Courts are increasingly refusing to adopt the approach. Scholarly criticism has intensified.[154] Additionally, there is no evidence that interest balancing represents a rule of international law. Thus, there is no mandatory rule requiring its adoption here, since Congress cannot be said to have implicitly legislated subject to these international constraints.[155]

If promotion of international comity is measured by the number of times United States jurisdiction has been declined under the "reasonableness" interest balancing approach, then it has been a failure. Implementation of this analysis has not resulted in a significant number of conflict resolutions favoring a foreign jurisdiction. A pragmatic assessment of those decisions adopting an interest balancing approach indicates none where United States jurisdiction was declined when there was more than a de minimis United States interest. Most cases in which use of the process was advocated arose before a direct conflict occurred when the balancing could be employed without impairing the court's jurisdiction to determine jurisdiction.[157] When push comes to shove, the domestic forum is rarely unseated.

Despite the real obligation of courts to apply international law and foster comity, domestic courts do not sit as internationally constituted tribunals. Domestic courts are created by national constitutions and statutes to enforce primarily national laws. The courts of most developed countries follow international law only to the extent it is not

---

154. See, e.g., Maier, Interest Balancing and Extraterritorial Jurisdiction, 31 Am. J.Comp.L. 579 (1983); Grippando, Declining to Exercise Extraterritorial Antitrust Jurisdiction on Grounds of International Comity: An Illegitimate Extension of the Judicial Abstention Doctrine, 23 Va.J.Int'l L. 394 (1983); Kadish, Comity and the International Application of the Sherman Act: Encouraging Courts to Enter the Political Arena, 4 N.W.J.Int'l L. & Bus. 130 (1982); Rahl, International Application of American Antitrust Laws: Issues and Proposals, 2 N.W.J.Int'l & Bus. 336, 362–64 (1980). Cf. Juenger, Conflict of Laws: A Critique of Interest Analysis, 32 Am.J.Comp.L. 1 (1984).

155. Congress is presumed to legislate within the constraints of international law, unless it expressly manifests a contrary intent. Natural Resources Defense Council v. Nuclear Regulatory Comm'n, 647 F.2d 1345, 1357 (D.C.Cir.1981); Federal Trade Comm'n v. Compagnie de Saint–Gobain–Pont–a–Mousson, 636 F.2d 1300, 1315 (D.C.Cir.1980); See Restatement (Third) § 134, supra note 21; Restatement (Second) § 3(3)....

157. See, e.g., Wells Fargo & Co. v. Wells Fargo Express Co., 556 F.2d 406 (9th Cir.1977); Timberlane Lumber Co. v. Bank of America, 549 F.2d 597 (9th Cir.1976); Mannington Mills, Inc. v. Congoleum Corp., 595 F.2d 1287 (3d Cir.1979).

overridden by national law.[160]   Thus, courts inherently find it difficult
neutrally to balance competing foreign interests.   When there is any
doubt, national interests will tend to be favored over foreign interests.
This partially explains why there have been few times when courts have
found foreign interests to prevail.

* * *

The decision of the District Court is therefore affirmed.

STARR, Circuit Judge, dissenting: It is with reluctance that I am
constrained to dissent, for there is much in the majority's thorough
opinion with which I fully agree.   The majority's opinion demonstrates
persuasively that the jurisdictional basis for Laker's action in the United
States District Court is firmly established under settled principles of
United States and international law.   Judge Wilkey's scholarly analysis
further demonstrates that it is not at all unusual for a court vested with
jurisdiction to issue appropriate orders to vindicate that jurisdiction,
even when such orders arrest the prosecution of actions in the courts of
another sovereign.

But it is my judgment that principles of comity among the courts of
the international community counsel strongly against the injunction in
the form issued here.

* * *

* * * By its terms, the District Court's order quite literally forbids
the foreign airlines from entering any court in the world, including
courts of their own respective nations, to contest Laker's right to
maintain the instant action.   This approach, fashioned under the strain
of critical moments when it reasonably appeared to the learned trial
judge that jurisdiction over important defendants might irrevocably be
lost, is simply too broad to sustain, in light of the countervailing
considerations of comity among nations.

Thus, I would favor vacating the present injunction and remanding
the case to the District Court for consideration of narrowing its order.

* * *

I would further suggest that in the exercise of its sound discretion
the District Court invite the Executive to present the views of the United
States.   Those views might well have an important bearing upon the
extent of the sovereign interests of the United States, if any, in this
action.

* * *

Questions.

1.   Does the majority opinion base itself upon the essential unwork-
ability of interest balancing or upon the inappropriateness of the exercise
of this function by the American judiciary in cases where the Congress

---

160. See J. Sweeney, C. Oliver & N.
Leech, The International Legal System 14–
23 (1981).

has prescribed the applicable rule in such a way as to make it clear that conflicting foreign prescriptions should be disregarded?

2. What of dissenting Judge Starr's suggestion in the last paragraph?

---

5. OTHER LINES OF SOLUTION?

(a) *Reducing or Eliminating Differences in Substantive Law*

An interesting question arises whether, as nations move toward the specific regulation of the same types of private economic activity, the differences in their approaches, remedies and tolerations will exacerbate or relieve conflicts of jurisdiction. From one point of view, that of achieving the general objective of social control of particular types of economic conduct, it does not seem to make much difference which set of rules actually gets applied. But administrators and legislators in nation states as well as in the European Union proceed in economic matters from localized senses of mission. Thus the increased number of potentially applicable sets of rules may threaten the effective conduct of transnational business enterprise and create a common need for some system of rationalization or harmonization of regulatory principles. In the period 1948–52, roughly, the first major effort to create a set of international rules for restrictive trade practices and monopoly, the Havana Charter of the aborted International Trade Organization failed through lack of sufficient agreement among states). Later efforts for the creation of new, positive, universal law in this sector has been slight so far. But perhaps circumstances are changing, due both to the increased array of particularistic regulatory systems and the growth of multinational enterprise.

Efforts toward the unification of private law continue, by either conventions or undertakings to enact parallel legislation, and the work of the relatively new United Nations Commission on International Trade Law (UNCITRAL) is having an impact. Its Convention on the International Sale of Goods, to which the United States is a party, has entered into force.

Short of detailed uniform codifications or shifts from national to international administration, international limitations upon the maximum reaches of national laws may develop, thus reducing conflict through narrowing bases of jurisdiction in certain instances. Is it possible, in certain instances, that a human right not to be bedeviled by the conflicting demands of different legal systems might develop? However, it must be admitted that the further multiplication of bases of jurisdiction as to crime may result from the threat of transnational terrorism. See *supra,* pp. 168; 171–173; 178–193.

(b) *Administrative Accommodation and Beyond*

Remarkable progress in cooperation short of formal international agreements, has been made, on a basis of mutual interests and reciprocity, between the regulatory authorities of several countries, such as between the Swiss Confederation, the United States, and other countries, as to tax evasion, narcotics traffic, the voting of corporate proxies, bank secrecy related to suspected criminal conduct, and the like. Such arrangements do not usually allocate primary exercise as between concurrent bases of jurisdiction, as in the cases of taxation, status of forces, and military service conventions, but they do reduce significantly disputes about jurisdiction. Is it possible that ignoring jurisdictional issues and working together around them may become a major alternative solution? See Chapter 15, pp. 1107–1171, for developments along this line.

Beyond this, can a plausible case be made that both the law of state jurisdiction and the law of resolution or reduction of conflicts of jurisdiction have been over-developed by lawyers—or even that the so-called rules of law about jurisdiction are really only marker buoys for diplomacy?

———

Chapter 4

A VIEW FROM THE BRIDGE: SEA LAW
IN HISTORICAL PERSPECTIVE

The term "Law of the Sea" is used here as international lawyers usually use it, to refer to the rules of law, increasingly from positive law sources, that govern the rights and duties of states as to the exercise of jurisdiction and the pursuit of benefits in, on, under, and even over, this watery planet's waters. In a broader, historical sense the term also covers the private law of vessel ownership and management, carriage of goods by sea, rules of the maritime road, maritime torts such as collisions at sea, maritime liens, salvage, and processes in special courts that apply the general law maritime, called courts of Admiralty. Maritime law has a very long history, beginning as customary law over 5,000 years ago, passing through various partial codification in different lands, and existing in the United States today as a mixture of customary law and national statutes applied exclusively by federal judges without juries. The Admiralty or private law side of the law of the sea remains essentially national, rather than international (as by codification in treaties) but nonetheless, remarkably uniform as between various national legal systems.

SECTION A. CODIFICATION OF THE LAW OF THE SEA

---

1. THE UNITED NATIONS CONVENTION ON THE LAW OF THE SEA

Historical background. Navigation, fishing and extraction of minerals take place on or under the sea. For centuries, there has been an ongoing struggle over whether these activities can be engaged in freely by all almost anywhere in the sea or whether states can carve out areas of the sea for their exclusive use and control.

Attempts at resolving the issue by codification of the law of the sea began as early as 1930 at a conference of some 40 states held at The Hague under the auspices of the League of Nations, but it was not successful.

More than 80 states participated in the 1958 Geneva conference on the law of the sea and produced four conventions codifying portions of the customary law and creating new law in some cases. Three of these are still carried in the Documentary Supplement, because, as we shall explain later, they may still contain some law of the United States. They are:

1. Convention on the Territorial Sea and the Contiguous Zone, which entered into force on September 10, 1964; as of August 19, 1993, 47 states were parties to this convention; [a]

2. Convention on the High Seas, which entered into force on September 30, 1962; as of August 19, 1993, 59 states were parties to this convention; and

3. Convention on the Continental Shelf, which entered into force on June 10, 1964; as of August 19, 1993, 54 states were parties to this convention.

The fourth, Convention on Fishing and Conservation of the Living Resources of the High Seas, is not included. The text of this convention is in 17 U.S.T. 138, 559 U.N.T.S. 285.

After a second conference on the law of the sea failed in 1960 to agree on the breadth of the territorial sea, the General Assembly of the United Nations convened a third conference in 1973. After eleven sessions, it adopted the United Nations Convention on the Law of the Sea of December 10, 1982. The text is in the Documentary Supplement.

---

a. U.S. Treaties in Force [and thus the U.S. State Department] lists 47 as of Aug. 19, 1993. Senegal has also ratified the Treaty, but there was a denunciation by Great Britain. Thus, the U.S. lists 47, and others may list 48 parties.

The convention will go into effect one year after its ratification by 60 parties. This happened in late 1994.

The sixtieth state having acceded (Article 308[1]), the Convention came into force in 1994. But no member of the Group of Seven (the major developed countries) has yet become a party. However, as we close this revision, there are efforts afoot by the United States and some other states to delineate areas for exclusive exploitation of deep sea bed resources, despite the "common heritage of mankind" concept of Article 136 and the provisions that follow in Section 2 of Part XI (*The Area*). This new development might possibly involve some interpretative problems as between the "no reservations or exceptions" provision of Article 3 and the Articles on "amendment" (312–316). According to the Secretary–General, " * * * Practically all the states [that have become parties] are developing states. The industrialized states have expressed dissatisfaction with some of the terms of Part XI of the Convention and this * * * led them to refrain from ratifying or acceding to the Convention, particularly in view of the World economic situation that has changed fundamentally since the early 1980s * * *." U.N. Doc. 47/5/93. Just what does the statement as to "fundamental change" imply? Does it contemplate economic, geo-political, or some other type of change? The Secretary–General's report also states that: * * * of the states that have established their consent to be bound, 26 are African, 11 Asian, 13 Latin–American–Carribbean. Only two European states have ratified, Iceland (June 21, 1985) and former Yugoslavia (as of May 5, 1986). No Group-of-Seven [G–7] country or member of the European Community has consented to become a party.

The question arises: *Why have so few states ratified or acceded? Could the following be a reason?* Article 309 forbids all reservations or exceptions to the Convention unless expressly permitted in particular articles as to that article. But see Article 310, on declarations and statements made at ratification, and Articles 312 and 313, on amendments proposed by parties to the Convention. *Why were reservations prohibited?* Consider this question again when studying Reservations to Treaties in Chapter 13. As we shall see later in this Chapter, the Reagan Administration, while rejecting the Convention as a whole, declared it to be the best exposition of international law of a customary nature relating to the delineations of national and international areas of the oceans, a matter of obvious concern to a naval power. *Does this instance of having cake and eating it too explain the attitudes of some other non-signatory [so far] states?*

Refusal of the United States to sign the convention. On July 9, 1982, President Reagan announced that the United States would not sign the Convention. Statement by the President, 18 Weekly Compilation of Presidential Documents 887 (July 12, 1982). The main reason for the decision was the opposition of the United States to the portion establishing a deep seabed mining regime. This regime and the objections to it of the United States, are considered *supra* and in Section E of this chapter.

Nevertheless, the United States claims it is entitled to the benefit of most of the provisions in other portions of the convention because, in its view, the provisions to which the U.S. agrees do not state new rules of law but, instead, only restate rules of customary international law. James L. Malone, Assistant Secretary of State for Oceans and International Environmental and Scientific Affairs, defended the claim in a speech. Excerpts follow.

MALONE, FREEDOM AND OPPORTUNITIES: FOUNDATION FOR A DYNAMIC OCEANS POLICY

United States Department of State Bulletin, December 1984, p. 76.

* * *

Recognizing that the peaceful uses of the world's oceans and the management and conservation of marine resources remain a matter of fundamental concern—as well as a potential source of boundless opportunity—to all maritime states, President Reagan set forth on March 10, 1983, the principles upon which the United States would base its future oceans policy * * *.

In order to fully grasp and appreciate that policy, however, a key principle underlying it—namely, that the nonseabed sections of the treaty reflect customary law in distinction to those prescribing the mining regime—must be understood.

Of paramount importance in assigning the proper meaning to the various sections of the LOS Convention is the need to recognize that unlike all former oceans-related conventions, UNCLOS III does two things: it codifies existing law and prescribes new law. The attempt was made to both set out present and developing law in familiar areas in light of circumstances since 1958 as well as to provide new regimes for unregulated activities. Navigation rights, as seen in the very wording of the LOS Convention articles on navigation, were frequently drawn from the 1958 Geneva Conventions on the Territorial Sea and Contiguous Zone and that on the High Seas, which embodied customary law as it had developed to that time. As such, it is void of merit to argue that only parties to the LOS Convention enjoy customary international legal rights of longstanding status.

Similarly, it is without legal foundation to maintain, on the basis of the so-called contractual theory, that the convention is a package and that for a non-party all rights are lost if a state does not become a party to it. Absent a peremptory norm to the contrary, customary rights of sovereign states remain inviolate and cannot otherwise be denied. I do not subscribe to the views of critics of the U.S. position who accuse nonsignatories of "picking and choosing" among sections of the convention. The "package deal" concept was, it must be remembered, nothing more than a procedural device, based on a December 1973 "gentleman's agreement" and designed to further the achievement of consensus. As such, the concept died upon the conclusion of the LOS negotiations. It has no continuing merit whatever.

States certainly are free to continue to apply customary international law and ignore *de novo* prescriptive provisions which have neither been tried nor admitted by wide practice to be a source of recognized international law.

It is the position of the United States then that, despite its shortcomings, the Law of the Sea Convention does reflect a successful effort to articulate and codify existing rules of maritime law and actual state practice with respect to the traditional uses of the oceans, such as navigation and overflight. Indeed, the United States believes that most of the provisions of the treaty, apart from the seabed mining text in part XI, fairly balance the interests of all states and are fully consistent with norms of customary international law. Hence, it is prepared to accept and act in accordance with these provisions on a reciprocal basis.

But, since the seabed mining portions of the convention establish wholly new law and new obligations, which are contractual in nature and not part of customary international law, the provisions will be binding only on parties to the convention and, then, only when and if it enters into force. The provisions in part XI of the convention are predicated on the establishment of a new international organization, the International Seabed Resource Authority, and on the acceptance by parties of that organization's jurisdiction and of their own obligation to act in accordance with its mandates. Such obligations must be willingly assumed by states and cannot be thrust upon them. The United States does not and will not accept them and is not bound by them.

In nonseabed areas, however, as I have said, the United States does recognize the existence of an international law of the sea entirely independent of—though reflected in—the Law of the Sea Convention and based upon accepted principles of customary international law. The United States will continue to honor those principles and will assert its rights consistent with those principles on a global basis.

* * *

Customary international law and treaty law. The position of the United States raises fundamental questions about the nature of customary international law and its relationship to treaty law. *Can it be argued, for example, that the whole of the United Nations Convention on the Law of the Sea, including provisions on deep seabed mining, is declaratory of customary international law?* Consider the following.

ANAND, U.N. CONVENTION ON THE LAW OF THE SEA AND THE UNITED STATES

24 Indian Journal of International Law 153, 154, 163–164, 184–187, 188, 190–191, 193 (1984).*

* * *

On April 30, 1982, after nine years of intense, arduous, sometimes bitter and protracted negotiations, the Third United Nations Conference on the Law of the Sea adopted what has been called "a comprehensive constitution for the Oceans", a Convention which was said to be "the most significant international agreement since the Charter of the United Nations," providing a legal regime for nearly 70 per cent of the earth's surface. Largely put together through compromises and consensus in a conference which was in session for 93 weeks from the time it opened in December 1973 until it concluded its substantive work in September 1982, it was the largest conference in history in which 157 countries participated and 11 delegations attended as observers.

Following the consensus procedure all through its deliberations requiring all delegations to make efforts, in good faith, to accommodate the interests of others, resisting the temptation of putting substantive proposals to the vote, the Conference in the end was forced to adopt the Convention, on the insistence of the United States, by a vote of 130 in favour to 4 against (Israel, Turkey, United States and Venezuela), with 17 abstentions which included the Soviet Union and its allies and a few West European industrialized countries like Germany, Italy, Luxembourg, Netherlands, Spain and the United Kingdom. Based on numerous "mini-packages"—balanced compromises on at least 25 different contested subjects and issues ranging from seabed production to marine scientific research in offshore waters negotiated in different negotiating fora—the Convention was accepted in the end as "a package" and "an integral whole." It was for this reason that, as President of the Conference, Dr. Tommy Koh explained,

> * * * the Convention does not provide for reservations. It is therefore not possible for States to pick what they like and disregard what they do not like. In International law, as in domestic law, rights and duties go hand in hand. It is, therefore, legally impermissible to claim rights under the Convention without being willing to assume the correlative duties.

He added: "Let no nation put asunder this landmark achievement of the international community."

* * *

Seabed Beyond the Limits of National Jurisdiction

While the international society, almost for the first time in history, came to agree on a large part of international law of the sea, and UNCLOS–III, despite its cumbersome and time-consuming rules of procedure, settled most of the issues which in the beginning seemed

* Reprinted by permission of the Indian Society of International Law.

unsolvable, one issue which threatened the disintegration of the entire conference was the mining of the deep seabed manganese nodules. It is important to note that although there were sharp disagreements amongst states about the structure and powers of an international seabed authority that must be established to control and manage the deep seabed and its resources, the acceptance of the area as "common heritage of mankind" which could not be appropriated by any state and must be explored and exploited for the benefit of mankind as a whole, was unquestioned. This principle, iterated and reiterated by the General Assembly in numerous resolutions, not only symbolized the interests and aspirations of the developing countries, but had been endorsed by all the developed countries, including the United States. As early as 1966, President Johnson wanted to "ensure that the deep seas and the ocean bottoms are, and remain, the legacy of all human beings." In 1970, President Nixon, renouncing all sovereign rights to the seabed and its resources and announcing the American policy to help establish an international machinery to administer the licensing of exploration and exploitation of the resources of the seabed, declared:

> The International Seabed Area would be *the common heritage of mankind* and no state could exercise sovereignty or sovereign rights over this area or its resources.

Presidents Ford and Carter recognized these principles without any question and enthusiastically participated at the UNCLOS–III to develop an international regime to govern seabed mining activities. Even after the United States got frustrated with the slow progress in the UNCLOS–III and decided to enact an interim legislation for the exploration and exploitation of deep seabed resources to prod the conference to expedite its work, it acknowledged the commitment of the United States to the 1970 UN Declaration. Sections 7 and 8 of the U.S. Deep Seabed Hard Minerals Resources Act of 1980 stated:

> (7) On December 17, 1970, the United States supported (by affirmative vote) General Assembly Resolution 2749 (XXV) declaring inter alia the principle that the mineral resources of the deep seabed are the common heritage of mankind, with the expectation that this principle would be legally defined under the terms of a comprehensive international Law of the Sea Treaty yet to be agreed upon.

> (8) It is in the national interest of the United States and other nations to encourage a widely acceptable Law of the Sea Treaty, which will provide a new legal order for the oceans covering a broad range of ocean interests, including exploration for and commercial recovery of hard mineral resources of the deep seabed.

* * *

[Having asserted that the United States originally subscribed to the "common heritage principle," the author later argues that emerging principles of customary international law are binding on states which fail to object to them from the outset. He begins with an analysis of the growth of customary international law in state practice, which includes most of the analysis of custom and is presented in chapter 1.]

* * *

Treaty Custom Dichotomy

Another significant * * * custom-creating process is through "generalizable provisions in bilateral and multilateral treaties (which) generate customary rules of law binding upon all states". * * *

Although a codifying treaty normally presupposes a fair amount of established customary law which it seeks to codify, a treaty which breaks entirely new ground may stimulate the crystalization of customary rules binding even on non-parties to the treaty. * * *

The 1969 Vienna Convention on the Law of Treaties * * * clearly recognized this phenomenon. After dealing with the pacta tertiis problem in Articles 34 to 37, Article 38 states that:

> Nothing in Articles 34 to 37 precludes a rule set forth in a treaty from becoming binding upon a third state as a customary rule of international law, recognized as such.

* * *

* * * [S]trong dissent to a treaty by a small number of states, or even a single powerful and influential state, whose interests are directly affected, especially if they have consistently and openly maintained their dissent, would distract from the authority of the treaty and adversely affect the emergence of customary law on the subject. However, the dissent of certain states may be ineffective if there is general acceptance of a practice "as law", or the dissentient states have not made their views heard until the rule has in practice crystallized and become firmly established, or the dissent relates to some fundamental principle. * * * [W]hile a state may acquire an exceptional position with regard to some general rule of customary law, there is no such right for the state to isolate itself from the impact of a fundamental principle. In other words, it is submitted that no state can evade a treaty or the operation of a principle which has emerged as jus cogens, or avoid the operation of a rule or rules which are so bound up with the essential nature of a concept of international law, which has become universally binding, that they cannot be excluded without denying the existence of the concept. * * * For this situation, when a treaty seeks to codify a general fundamental norm and effects the sudden acceleration of usage the position of dissenting states which are in a small minority may be made more difficult. *In the normal course of inter-state relations, the state which declines to accept an emerging rule of general law has to object to its application to itself, consistently and openly, from the time when the rule begins to crystallize.* [Italics supplied] But if the dissenting state itself has been a party to the emergence and acceptance of a general norm of international law sought to be codified, it cannot decline its acceptance by refusing to sign and ratify the treaty and may find it difficult to resist the application of the general rule to its own interests at a subsequent stage.

* * *

* * * [T]he basic tenets of the "common heritage" principle have come to be universally accepted, and have become jus cogens. The traditional law can never be interpreted to permit the exclusive exploitation of hundreds of miles of a seabed mining site for extended periods of time by any nation or its nationals. Acceptance of the Convention by a vast majority of states with abstentation [sic] by a few industrialized Western Powers which did not oppose it, can be said to have created a strong presumption in favour of an emergent custom which even the strongest Power on earth cannot violate except at a considerable cost and without being challenged.

* * *

Effect of the United Nations Convention on the Geneva Conventions of 1958.

UPDATE ON THE LAW OF THE SEA CONVENTION

The sixtieth state having acceded (Article 308(1)), the Convention came into force in 1994. But no member of the Group of Seven (the major developed countries) has yet become a party. However, as we close this revision, there are efforts afoot, by the United States and some other states, to delineate areas for exclusive exploitation of deep sea bed resources, despite the "common heritage of mankind" concept of Article 136 and the provisions that follow in Section 2 of Part XI (The Area). This new development might possibly involve some interpretative problems as between the "no reservations or exceptions" provision of Article 309 and the Articles on "amendment" (312–316).

During the first half of 1994, negotiations under U.N. auspices resulted in an "Agreement" adopted by the General Assembly, July 28, 1994 (UNGA Resolution A/RES/48/263), under which the United States and the other developed countries here found it possible to accept the entire Convention, including Part XI. In his report to the President of the United States (upon which the President based a Message to the Senate, proposing Senate approval of the entire Convention) the Secretary of State wrote:

"... The legally binding changes set forth in the Agreement meet the objections of the United States to Part XI of the Convention. The United States and all other major industrialized states have signed the Agreement."

* * *

This Agreement amounts to an interesting _"end-run"_ around the _"No Reservations"_ Article to the Convention. The January, 1995 issue of the American Journal of International Law will analyze the defacto modifications and moderations of the deep sea mining portion of the Convention that the agreement is expected to produce. These effects, in turn, make approval of the Convention as a whole quite likely in 1995.

* * *

After this book was in page proofs, the U.S. signed a treaty entitled, *"Agreement Relating to the Implementation of Part XI of the 1982 U.N. Convention on the Law of the Sea, of December 10, 1982.* See, Cong. Record., June 30, 1994, Vol. 140, No. 86, p. S8095. This new treaty modifies the implementation of Part XI of the Convention, relating to mineral resources of the high seas. The October 1994 issue of the American Journal of International Law focuses on this recent development, in its *Law of the Sea Forum: The 1994 Agreement on Implementation of Part XI of the Convention on the Law of the Sea.* It will include: Bernard Oxman, *The 1994 Agreement and the Convention;* Louis Sohn, *International Law Implications of the 1994 Agreement;* and Jonathan Charney, *Provisional Application of the 1994 Agreement.*

Would its provisions prevail over corresponding and inconsistent provisions of the Geneva Conventions of 1958, to which the United States is a party? *Does the following material answer the question?*

1987 RESTATEMENT, INTRODUCTORY NOTE TO PART V, THE LAW OF THE SEA *

* * * [M]any * * * provisions of the Convention follow closely provisions in the 1958 conventions * * * which largely restated customary law as of that time. Other provisions in the LOS Convention set forth rules that, if not law in 1958, became customary law since that time, as they were accepted at the Conference by consensus and have influenced, and came to reflect, the practice of states. * * * In particular, in March 1983 President Reagan proclaimed a 200–nautical-mile exclusive economic zone for the United States and issued a policy statement in which the United States in effect agreed to accept the substantive provisions of the Convention, other than those dealing with deep sea-bed mining, in relation to all states that do so with respect to the United States. Thus, by express or tacit agreement accompanied by consistent practice, the United States, and states generally, have accepted the substantive provisions of the Convention, other than those addressing deep sea-bed mining, as statements of customary law binding upon them apart from the Convention. * * * In a few instances, however, there is disagreement whether a provision of the Convention reflects customary law. * * * Some provisions of the Convention, notably those accepting particular arrangements for settling disputes, clearly

* Copyright 1987, by the American Law Institute. Reprinted with the permission of the American Law Institute.

are not customary law and have not been accepted by express or tacit agreement.

————

More Questions about the U.S. Position:

The Clinton Administration has just undone Star Wars; will it "reverse" President Reagan on the LOS Convention, if it ever gets around to considering the matter? Should it? Why or why not? Have you any intermediate ideas as to what should be done by the United States Government?

————

2.   THE CONVENTION AND THE
PRACTICE OF STATES

EXTENT OF MARITIME ZONES UNDER THE
UNITED NATIONS CONVENTION

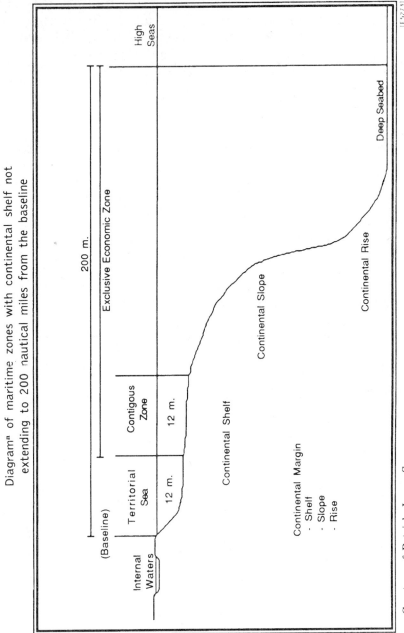

Diagram[a] of maritime zones with continental shelf not extending to 200 nautical miles from the baseline

a. Courtesy of Patrick James Sweeney.

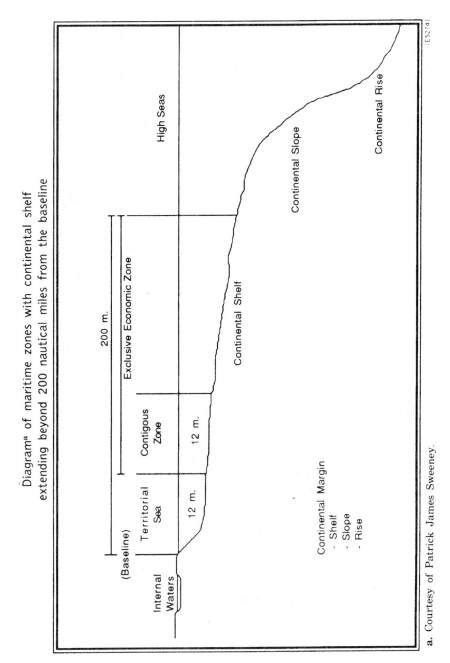

Diagram[a] of maritime zones with continental shelf extending beyond 200 nautical miles from the baseline

a. Courtesy of Patrick James Sweeney.

**EXTENT OF MARITIME ZONES ESTABLISHED
BY NATIONAL LEGISLATION**

U.N. Office of the Special Representative of the Secretary–General for the Law
of the Sea, Law of the Sea Bulletin No. 2, March 1985, p. 1

One of the most important consequences of the Third United Nations Conference on the Law of the Sea was the acceleration of the process of revision of national laws undertaken by Governments, in particular those laws regulating the nature and breadth of maritime areas subject to sovereignty or national jurisdiction. Since the beginning of deliberations, several States have amended their maritime legislation in order to reflect the new trends and concepts that were emerging in the Conference; this is evidenced, inter alia, by the fact that 54 States have since 1974 adopted laws establishing an exclusive economic zone * * *. This important development was recognized by the Secretary–General of the United Nations at the closing session of the Conference in these terms: "In order to affirm that international law is now irrevocably transformed so far as the seas are concerned, we need not wait for the process of ratification to begin."

The Office of the Special Representative for the Law of the Sea considered that it might be useful for governments and bodies of the United Nations system to have quick and convenient access to updated information on the status of national legislation concerning maritime zones around the world. This information may be of assistance to States in their process of ratification of the Convention on the Law of the Sea and for the adjustment of their legislation to it. For this purpose, this Office has prepared the present issue of the Law of the Sea Bulletin Series containing a tabulation of national legislation establishing the breadth and régimes governing maritime zones over which coastal States exercise their sovereignty or jurisdiction (territorial sea, contiguous zone, exclusive economic zone, fishery zone, continental shelf and others). * * *

The following terms and symbols are used in the tables of this Bulletin:

TS	Territorial Sea
CZ	Contiguous Zone
EEZ	Exclusive Economic Zone
Fish	Fishery Zone
CSh	Continental Shelf
Other	Other zones
f	Fathom (1 f = 1.83 metres)
m	Metres
EXP	Exploitability
CM	Outer edge of the Continental Margin

The extensive tables as to national actions taken carried in the previous edition are no longer carried, as they are otherwise readily available from the source cited.

SUMMARY TABLE OF EXTENT OF MARITIME ZONES

TERRITORIAL SEA

Breadth (nautical miles)	Number of States	Breadth (nautical miles)	Number of States
3	18	12	84
4	2	15	1
6	5	20	1
		30	2

Breadth (nautical miles)	Number of States
35	1
50	3
70	1
100	1
150	1
200	13

FISHERY ZONE

Breadth (nautical miles)	Number of States
12	1
25	1
50	1
200	23

CONTIGUOUS ZONE

Breadth (nautical miles)	Number of States
3	1
12	2
18	5
24	13

CONTINENTAL SHELF

Criteria	Number of States
Depth (100 fathoms)	1
Depth (200 metres)	1
Exploitability	1
Depth (200 metres) plus exploitability	51
Breadth (150 nautical miles)	1
Breadth (200 nautical miles)	3
Outer edge of the continental margin or breadth of 200 nautical miles	16

EXCLUSIVE ECONOMIC ZONE

Breadth (nautical miles)	Number of States
150	1
200	54

SECTION B.   CONTROL OF NATIONAL VESSELS

Source Note: the material in Section B. blends some older customary and treaty law with influences from the 1982 Law of the Sea Convention.

———

1.   NATIONALITY OF VESSELS

PUBLIC MINISTRY v. MOGENS GLISTRUP

Denmark, Maritime and Commercial Court, 1967.
95 Journal du Droit International 979 (1968).[a]

A vessel belonging to a Danish corporation and registered in Denmark and flying the Danish flag, was bareboat chartered[b] to an American company which used it in Nigerian waters.   While the vessel was under charter, it had a crew which did not meet the conditions of the Danish Act on the Manning of Ships of 1965.   According to paragraph 1, the act applies to all Danish vessels.   The director of the American corporation had interpreted this provision as applying only to vessels under actual Danish control.

The court held however that the act applied to all Danish vessels even when bareboat chartered.   The law of the flag controls.   Otherwise, said the court, a vessel flying the Danish flag could escape all legislation or public control [of Denmark].

a. Translation by the editors. Reprinted by permission of Editions Techniques, S.A., Paris.

b. Leased without provision of officers or crew by the owner.

Even though Denmark has not ratified the Geneva Convention on the High Seas, the rule in Article 5 of the convention which makes the nationality of vessels depend upon the existence of a genuine link between the state and vessel flying its flag, must be considered without any question to be a part of public international law. The decision [therefore] seems to be perfectly in accord with the principle expressed in that article: genuine link means that the state effectively exercises its jurisdiction and its control * * *.

---

1. *Genuine link in Article 5 of the 1958 Convention on the High Seas.* The article provides, in Paragraph 1:

Each state shall fix the conditions for the grant of its nationality to ships, for the registration of ships in its territory, and for the right to fly its flag. Ships have the nationality of the state whose flag they are entitled to fly. There must exist a genuine link between the state and the ship; in particular, the state must effectively exercise its jurisdiction and control in administrative, technical and social matters over ships flying its flag.

What is the function of the genuine link? Consider in connection with this question the statement made before the United States Senate Committee on Foreign Relations by Mr. Arthur H. Dean, the head of the delegation of the United States at the 1958 Geneva Conference. He said:

The International Law Commission did not decide upon a definition of the term "genuine link." This article as originally drafted by the Commission would have authorized other states to determine whether there was a "genuine link" between a ship and the flag state for purposes of recognition of the nationality of the ship.

It was felt by some states attending the Conference on the Law of the Sea that the term "genuine link" could, depending upon how it were defined, limit the discretion of a state to decide which ships it would permit to fly its flag. Some states, which felt their flag vessels were at a competitive disadvantage with vessels sailing under the flags of other states, such as Panama and Liberia, were anxious to adopt a definition which states like [the latter] could not meet.

By a vote of 30 states, including the United States, against 15 states for, and 17 states abstaining, a provision was eliminated which would have enabled states other than the flag state to withhold recognition of the national character of a ship if they considered that there was no "genuine link" between the state and the ship.

Thus, under the Convention on the High Seas, it is for each state to determine how it shall exercise jurisdiction and control in administrative, technical and social matters over ships flying its flag. The "genuine link" requirement need not have any effect upon the practice of registering American built or owned vessels in such countries as Panama or Liberia. The existence of a "genuine link" between the state and the ship is not a condition of recognition of the nationality of a ship; that is, no state can claim the right to determine unilaterally that no genuine link exists between a ship and the flag state. * * * Excerpt from Executive Report No. 5— Law of the Sea Conventions, 106 Cong.Rec. 11189, 11190 (1960). *This topic is covered in chapter 9, as to persons, and chapter 3 as to jurisdiction.*

2. *Flags of convenience and the United Nations Convention on the Law of the Sea.* The attempt made at the 1958 Geneva Conference to frame an effective genuine link requirement was intended to curb the use of flags of convenience. The term refers, broadly speaking, to vessels operating under the flags of states that do not require the owners to be nationals or long term residents. The practice, also called open registry, means that such states are seldom directly concerned with the management of the vessels and, in some cases, show little interest in regulating their operation. The opportunity is thereby created for less scrupulous owners to run substandard vessels with inadequate equipment or incompetent crews.

It is well known that substandard vessels and incompetent crews can also be found in fleets from certain states with closed registries. Nevertheless, much of the pressure for the adoption of regulations was generated in recent years by spectacular oil spills from wrecked or sinking tankers flying flags of convenience and the publicity given thereafter to the lack of competence of the crew, the inadequacy of the equipment aboard and the faulty design of the vessel.

The United Nations Convention on the Law of the Sea does not deal directly with the definition of genuine link. Instead, its provisions specify in detail the duties incumbent upon a state in order effectively to exercise jurisdiction and control over its flag vessels. These provisions require the state to take measures regarding: the construction, equipment and seaworthiness of vessels; the manning of vessels, labour conditions and the training of crews; and the use of signals, the maintenance of communications and the prevention of collisions. See Article 94 of the convention in the Documentary Supplement.

The convention does not go so far as to strip from a vessel the nationality of the flag state in the event the flag state fails to take such measures. Section 6 of Article 94 provides only the following recourse:

> A State which has clear grounds to believe that proper jurisdiction and control with respect to a ship have not been exercised may report the facts to the flag State. Upon receiving such a report, the flag State shall investigate the matter and, if appropriate, take any action necessary to remedy the situation.

The problem of defining the genuine link which should exist between a vessel and the state whose flag it flies was considered in a conference called especially to deal with it pursuant to a resolution of the

General Assembly of the United Nations. The conference adopted on
February 7, 1986 the convention set forth in part below.

THE UNITED NATIONS CONVENTION ON CONDITIONS
FOR REGISTRATION OF SHIPS

U.N. Office of the Special Representative of the Secretary–General for the Law
of the Sea, Law of the Sea Bulletin No. 7, April 1986, pp. 87, 93, is in the
Documentary Supplement. Please analyze articles 7, 8, and 9.

Entry into force of the convention. It was open for signature from
May 1, 1986 to April 30, 1987 and will go into effect when ratified by 40
states whose combined tonnage amounts to at least 25 per cent of the
world registered tonnage. Statistics on world registered tonnage are
available in the Law of the Sea Bulletin, No. 7, April 1986, p. 103,
published by the U.N. Office of the Special Representative of the
Secretary–General for the Law of the Sea. They reflect the importance
of flags of convenience in world shipping.

Rounded off to the millionth ton, the world registered tonnage—
vessels of 500 gross tons and above—is 384,000,000 tons. The two states
best known as suppliers of flags of convenience, Liberia and Panama
account for more than 25 per cent of the world tonnage between them.
The tonnage given for the Bahamas, for Cyprus, and for Singapore, also
reflect the fact that they are important suppliers of flags of convenience.

The United States is reputed to be the largest beneficiary of flags of
convenience. The statistics bear this out. The economic pressure
generated by the use of flags of convenience has led to the curious
practice described in the following material.

SPAIN, FINLAND JOINING RUSH TO FORM
FLAGS OF CONVENIENCE

The Journal of Commerce, November 18, 1986, p. 1.*

Spain and Finland have joined the growing list of European nations
seeking to establish domestic flags of convenience to try to halt or even
reverse the exodus of shipowners from their national flags.

Luxembourg also is keen to include a shipping register in its drive to
expand its financial services sector.

The Spanish government is mulling a proposal to turn the Canary
Islands into an offshore registry for the country's hard-pressed shipowners. Authorities on the Aland Islands, midway between Finland and
Sweden, are seeking special status to attract Finnish ships sailing under
foreign flags.

The proposed Canary Islands registry is part of a package designed
to help Spanish shipowners, who have accumulated debts of about $1.5

---

* Reprinted by permission of the Journal
of Commerce.

billion. Eighty companies are likely to move their operations to the Canaries, bringing about 360 of the country's 580 ships, according to the Spanish Maritime Institute.

The semi-autonomous administration of the Aland Islands is seeking changes in Finland's constitution that would allow a more favorable fiscal and labor regime to attract the 40% of the national fleet registered overseas.

Fifteen Finnish ships have switched flags this year to Panama, Cyprus and the Cayman Islands.

Several European countries have already set up offshore registries to compete with Liberia and Panama. * * *

Norway, whose shipowners are deserting in droves to flags of convenience, pioneered the concept of an offshore flag earlier this year with a plan to establish a registry on the Svalbard Islands in the Spitzbergen archipelago. Shipowners would enjoy the same benefits there as they would in Panama or Liberia.

Other maritime nations quickly followed suit. British owners are transferring the registry of their ships to the Isle of Man, the small self-governing island in the Irish Sea, while French owners are hoisting their flag on the Kerguelen Islands in the Antarctic.

The new registries are "flags with a flag," allowing shipowners to reap the financial benefits of offshore operation while remaining under the sovereignty of their national registries.

Time is running out for European nations to halt shrinkage of their fleets. Last year Norway's flag fleet dwindled by 10 million deadweight tons to a record low of 16.9 million dwt. The exodus is accelerating, with the flag losing 67 ships of almost 5 million deadweight tons in the first nine months of the year.

Norwegian-owned tonnage under foreign flags is now equal to the size of the domestic fleet.

At the end of this year the size of the British-flag fleet will be smaller than that of the flagged-out fleet controlled by U.K.-registered companies, according to the General Council of British Shipping.

More than 50 vessels have left the West German fleet this year, with Cyprus the favored location. About 45% of the German-owned fleet is operating under foreign flags and the figure is rising fast.

Several national fleets could disappear within the next few years as shipowners seek cover from falling freight rates, rising labor costs and intensified low-cost competition from the Far East.

West European shipowners, especially bulk operators, cannot afford to compete with Asian lines employing cheaper crews. The annual wage bill for a 10,000–ton U.K.-crewed ship is about $1 million, twice that of a Hong Kong-registered vessel crewed by Asians.

    * * *

1. Reflagging of Kuwaiti tankers as United States vessels. A
foreign vessel may qualify for registry in the United States, and fly the
American flag, if its ownership is transferred to a person or entity of
American nationality, as for example, a Delaware corporation, and it
meets a number of technical requirements as to design, construction and
other such matters. See Section 2101 and following of Title 46 of the
United States Code. Should the vessel not meet these requirements, it
may still qualify for registry in the United States if the President directs
they be waived because the needs of foreign commerce so require. See
Section 3101 of the same title.

In the case of the Kuwaiti tankers, however, the authority to waive
the requirements was provided by Article 27 of the Act of December 27,
1950, Ch. 1155, § 1, 64 Stat. 1120. It empowers the Secretary of
Defense to direct the waiver in the interests of national defense.

***2. Use of flags of convenience by the former USSR and the
Peoples Republic of China.*** In February of 1977, the People's Republic of China was reported as having placed some 80 of its merchant
vessels under the Panamanian flag, thereby following the example of the
former USSR which long before that had placed about one hundred of its
merchant vessels under the same flag. 81 Revue Générale de Droit
International Public 1120 (1977). What benefits do you suppose were
derived by these nations from the use of flags of convenience? This was
ironic, given their earlier vigorous attacks upon the employment of flags
of convenience as economic colonialism.

2. JURISDICTION OVER VESSELS

Discussion and analysis of jurisdiction in general, including issues of
jurisdiction over vessels and on the High Seas is found in Chapter 3.

THE PEOPLE v. ROBERT J. THOMAS
Eire, Supreme Court, 1954.
22 Int'l L.Rep. 295 (1958).*

The Facts. The accused was convicted of the manslaughter of one
Humphries. The accused and Humphries were travelling together on
the Irish ship Munster, from Liverpool to Dublin. They had both been
drinking, when, some 15 miles out from the Welsh coast, about midnight, there was a fight in which Humphries went overboard and was
lost. Thomas was not an Irish citizen.

There was an appeal on the ground, first, of alleged lack of evidence,
and secondly on the ground that the Court had no jurisdiction to try an
offence of manslaughter on an Irish ship where the death did not occur
on board the ship, or within the jurisdiction.

* Reprinted with the permission of the
Editor of the International Law Reports.

Held (affirming the Court of Criminal Appeal): that the appeal failed on both grounds.

* * * The next ground of appeal is that there was no jurisdiction in the Central Criminal Court to try the appellant for manslaughter as the death did not occur on board the ship and so was not within the jurisdiction of the Court.   It is clear that the Central Criminal Court has all the jurisdiction formerly exercised by the Admiral and later exercised by the Commissioners of Oyer and Terminer appointed to exercise the Admiralty jurisdiction in criminal cases.   This was not contested.   Mr. Bell [counsel for the accused] contended that the jurisdiction was confined to the trial of persons committing offences on board an Irish ship on the high seas where such offences were committed and completed on the ship.   Manslaughter, Mr. Bell says, is a complex crime consisting of two essential ingredients.   The first is some unlawful act or culpable neglect, which causes the death, and the second is the fact of death itself. The death admittedly did not take place on the ship.   The crime, therefore, according to the argument, not being completed on board the ship was not committed within the jurisdiction.   Mr. Bell referred at length to the case of The Queen v. Keyn.   Keyn, a foreigner, was in command of a foreign ship which ran into a British ship within three miles of the English shore and sank her.   A passenger on board the English ship was drowned.   The facts were such as would in English law amount to manslaughter.   On his being indicted for that offence in the Central Criminal Court the jury found Keyn guilty.   Counsel for the prisoner objected that the Court had no jurisdiction.   Pollock B., the trial Judge, stated a case on the point for the opinion of the Court for Crown Cases Reserved.   The majority * * * held that as the offence was not committed on a British ship there was no jurisdiction to try the prisoner, even though the ship at the time of the occurrence was within what has become known as the "three-mile limit."

* * *

Applying these observations, the contention on behalf of the appellant is that since the death took place, if at all, in the water, the crime was not complete upon the Irish ship and therefore no crime in fact or in law took place on the ship, and it follows that the jurisdiction of the Central Criminal Court which is confined in its admiralty jurisdiction to trying cases of crimes committed in Irish ships is not brought into operation.   If the argument is correct it would appear that there is no jurisdiction in any Court of this country to try either a citizen or foreigner on an Irish ship who by culpable negligence or design throws another overboard with the result that death occurs in the water.

* * *

It will be convenient in discussing the matter of the Admiral's jurisdiction to consider it from two aspects.   First, what jurisdiction the Admiral had as regards the place where the crime was committed, and, secondly, in respect of what persons that jurisdiction operated.

* * *

* * * It is sufficient to say that it is clear law that the jurisdiction extends to a foreigner on an Irish ship.

It being undoubted that crimes committed by foreigners on board British or Irish ships are cognizable by British or Irish Courts, as the case may be, without any statute, is there anything in the origins or the legal theory giving rise to this rule of law to indicate that whatever jurisdiction attaches is limited to the punishment of a crime begun and completed on board the ship, as distinct from a crime completed by the death taking place in the water surrounding the ship?

The basis of the jurisdiction is the right of the country to which the ships belong to control the conduct of those on board from the point of good order and the prevention of crime by virtue of the protection afforded to such persons while sailing in such ship. In The Queen v. Anderson, Blackburn, J., says: "There are a vast number of cases which decide that when a ship is sailing on the high seas and bearing the flag of a particular nation, the ship forms a part of that nation's country, and all persons on board of her may be considered as within the jurisdiction of that nation whose flag is flying on the ship, in the same manner as if they were within the territory of that nation." Coke says: "Protectio trahit subjectionem et subjectio protectionem." Lord Coleridge in The Queen v. Carr, says: "The true principle is, that a person who comes on board a British ship where English law is reigning, places himself under the protection of the British flag, and as a correlative, if he thus becomes entitled to our law's protection, he becomes amenable to its jurisdiction, and liable to the punishment it inflicts upon those who there infringe its requirements." He adds that there is no distinction to be drawn between a member of the crew and a passenger.

* * *

The verdict of manslaughter in this case involved a finding of fact that Humphries is dead. The evidence points only to a death by drowning on the high seas. The other ingredient of the crime, the act or omission causing the death, occurred on board the M.V. "Munster", an Irish ship. Thus the event leading to the death also took place upon the high seas. The two elements necessary to give jurisdiction were thus both present. The crime was committed on the high seas and the appellant was at the time of its commission on an Irish ship. The appellant was, therefore, properly triable in the Central Criminal Court.

The appeal in so far as it was based on want of jurisdiction also fails.

———

Question. Consider the discussion by the court of The Queen v. Keyn in which it was held that "as the offense was not committed on a British ship there was no jurisdiction to try the prisoner, even though the ship at the time of the occurrence was within what has become known as the three-mile limit." *Was this a statement of a rule of* *international law?* See discussion of territorial jurisdiction in chapter 3, supra.

RE BIANCHI

Argentina, Cámara Nacional Especial, 1957.
24 Int'l L.Rep. 173 (1961).*

The Facts. The appellant, Gerónimo C. Bianchi, a member of the crew of the R.T., a ship of Argentine registry, was charged with the commission of a theft on board the ship while it was anchored in the harbour of Río de Janeiro, Brazil. In the absence of any action in the matter by Brazilian authorities, charges were brought against Bianchi in Argentina. It was unsuccessfully argued for the defendant that the Argentine court lacked jurisdiction over an offence which had been committed in foreign territorial waters. On appeal,

Held: that the judgment appealed from must be affirmed. Where local authorities did not take jurisdiction over an offence committed on board a ship anchored in foreign territorial waters, jurisdiction reverted to the courts of the State of registry of the ship.

* * * [I]n the trial Court, an inquiry was made into a theft which was allegedly committed on board the R.T., a ship of Argentine registry, while it was at anchor in the port of Río de Janeiro. Article 1, para. 1, of the Penal Code provides that [it] is applicable to offences committed in places subject to the national jurisdiction. According to the rules of public international law, which have not been reproduced for obvious reasons in the said Article but which are none the less binding upon Argentine courts, offences committed on board a private ship fall within the jurisdiction of the courts of the flag State if the ship is on the high seas, and fall within the jurisdiction of a foreign State only in the event that such offences have been committed while the ship is in the territorial waters of that other State.

This latter principle is not an absolute rule, however, for if the foreign State does not choose to exercise its right to institute proceedings because it considers that the act has not affected the community at large or the peace of the port (as maintained in French and Italian doctrine) [a], the flag State may then assert full authority over the ship for the purpose of restoring order and discipline on board or protecting the rights of the passengers. We may reasonably conclude with regard to the case before us, given the fact that the preliminary hearing was apparently held "en route", that the Brazilian authorities had relinquished jurisdiction over the alleged offence, so that this offence then became subject to the jurisdiction of the Argentine courts. As this

---

* Reprinted with the permission of the Editor of the International Law Reports.

a. But see infra the Wildenhus's case and the peace of the port doctrine, according to which the exercise of jurisdiction by the flag state is not contingent upon the decision of the territorial state not to exercise jurisdiction.

reasoning accords with the judgment of the trial Court * * * regarding the case, the judgment under appeal is affirmed.

————

SPECIAL MARITIME AND TERRITORIAL JURISDICTION OF THE UNITED STATES

18 U.S.C. § 7.

The term "special maritime and territorial jurisdiction of the United States", as used in this title, includes:

(1) The high seas, any other waters within the admiralty and maritime jurisdiction of the United States and out of the jurisdiction of any particular State [of the United States], and any vessel belonging in whole or in part to the United States, or any citizen thereof, or to any corporation created by or under the laws of the United States, or of any State, Territory, District, or possession thereof, when such vessel is within the admiralty and maritime jurisdiction of the United States and out of the jurisdiction of any particular State.

(2) Any vessel registered, licensed, or enrolled under the laws of the United States, and being on a voyage upon the waters of any of the Great Lakes, or any of the waters connecting them, or upon the Saint Lawrence River where the same constitutes the International Boundary Line.

* * *

————

1. *Crimes included in special maritime jurisdiction of the United States.* Title 18 of the United States Code defines as criminal a number of acts that are performed within the special maritime jurisdiction of the United States: Sections 113, assaults; 114, maiming; 661, theft; 662, receiving stolen goods; 1111, murder; 1112, manslaughter; 1113, attempt to commit murder or manslaughter; 2031, rape; 2032, statutory rape; 2111, robbery. (See, also Title 49, Section 1472(k), dealing with these same crimes when committed within the "special *aircraft* jurisdiction of the United States." This jurisdiction is discussed in Chapter 5.)

2. *Vessels included in special maritime jurisdiction of the United States.* In civil matters involving vessels on the high seas such as collision and salvage, the United States as well as other states apply the rules of maritime law to foreign flag vessels as well as to vessels sailing under their national flag. The general law maritime is not itself a part of international law. Rather, it is a body of rules reflecting the universal interest of states in achieving a substantial degree of uniformity in the handling of civil claims arising on the high seas. In the application of such rules, each state may use its own understanding or domestic version of the rules without subjecting itself thereby to a claim under international law by another state.

But would it be valid under international law for the United States to apply rules of criminal law under Section 7 of Title 18 to vessels owned by United States citizens or corporations if the vessels were registered under a foreign flag?

For more discussion of Jurisdiction on the High Seas and otherwise on vessels, see also Chapter 3, *supra*.

U.S. v. AIKINS

United States Court of Appeal Ninth Circuit, 1991.
923 F.2d 650 (9th Cir.1991).

* * *

Before CANBY, NOONAN and RYMER, Circuit Judges.

NOONAN, Circuit Judge:

George Aikins, Manuel Angulo–Castillo, Roberto Cayasso–Schellett, Lai Chai Hai, Anastacio Henry–Barnard, Roosevelt Rodney, Eusebio Samudio–Jiminez, and William Snyder were convicted of possessing with intent to distribute 21,000 pounds of marijuana on the high seas on February 19, 1988 and of distributing a separate 14,000 pounds of marijuana on the high seas on February 17, 1988, all in violation of the Maritime Drug Enforcement Act, 46 U.S.C.App. § 1903(a). We reverse their convictions and remand for a new trial.

FACTS

The facts are well set out by Judge Takasugi in the district court and with minor editorial revisions are restated here:

> During an ongoing undercover investigation of marijuana trafficking/importation, approximately two weeks preceding the seizure in this case, an undercover United States Customs agent was solicited by a marijuana trafficker to off-load a large quantity of marijuana from a mother ship located on the high seas southeast of the Hawaiian Islands. The undercover agent agreed to provide a vessel to off-load marijuana from the mother ship and transport the substance to the Bay Area of Northern California as directed by the trafficker.

> A plan was developed among members of United States Customs, Drug Enforcement Administration and the United States Coast Guard whereby a crew of federal agents, posing as marijuana traffickers, would rendezvous with the mother ship and off-load the marijuana. The plan included the United States Coast Guard cutter *Mallow*'s following the undercover off-load vessel at a safe distance and remaining in radio contact with the off-load vessel.

On February 16 and 17, 1988, the undercover vessel rendez-voused with the mother ship approximately 600–800 miles southeast of the Hawaiian Islands. The mother ship was identified as the *Christina M,* a Panamanian coastal freighter bearing a Panamanian flag. After off-loading to a capacity of approximately 14,000 pounds of marijuana from the *Christina M,* the undercover agents were able to ascertain that the Panamanian freighter still had a large quantity of marijuana remaining aboard. All identification, registry and description of the *Christina M* were relayed by radio from the undercover crew to the *Mallow.*

Thereafter, the government contends that on February 18, 1988, U.S. Coast Guard officials on the *Mallow* sought and received permission from Panamanian officials "to the enforcement of United States law by the United States against the individuals found aboard the *M/V Christina M.*" The *Christina M* was not then proceeding toward the United States.

On February 19, 1988, some 48 hours after the previous off-loading operation by the undercover vessel, the *Mallow* closed within visual distance of the *Christina M.* Lt. Commander Christian Bohner, Commanding Officer of the *Mallow,* identified the *Mallow* as a United States Coast Guard vessel and requested permission to board the *Christina M.* Defendant Augustus Rodney, Captain of *Christina M,* initially refused Bohner's request. Bohner then indicated to Rodney that the Coast Guard had permission of the Panamanian authorities to board and search the *Christina M* and that he, Bohner, had "other means" to stop the *Christina M.* Rodney relented and the *Christina M* made no effort to flee.

Shortly thereafter, without a search or arrest warrant or any efforts to secure same, the Coast Guard personnel from *Mallow* boarded the *Christina M* for the express purpose of searching the freighter for marijuana. A strong odor of marijuana was immediately apparent to all members of the boarding party, except for one who was stuffy. They found in excess of 21,000 pounds of marijuana in the aft hold. Although no other cargo was found, other than the bales of marijuana, documents and other personal effects were found and seized from the living quarters assigned to the crew. Rodney and his crew of seven men were arrested. The *Mallow* possessed radio equipment capable of communicating with a magistrate in Hawaii or the mainland. Captain Rodney and the seven crew members were arrested and subsequently indicted.

* * *

2. The Search and Seizure of the *Christina M.*

The defendants raise the protection of the Fourth Amendment in objection to the Coast Guard's search and seizure of the vessel. The Fourth Amendment was not "understood by contemporaries of the Framers to apply to activities of the United States directed against aliens in foreign territory or in international waters." United States v. Verdu-go–Urquidez. The Fourth Amendment does not apply to a search of aliens conducted in foreign territory. Id. The Fourth Amendment does not apply to the search of non-resident aliens on a ship in international waters. United States v. Davis. All but one of the defendants here was an alien to whom the guarantees of the Fourth Amendment do not apply. William Snyder, who is an American citizen, has no standing to challenge the search of the *Christina M,* "it being well settled that the crew has no legitimate expectation of privacy in the cargo hold of a vessel." United States v. Peterson.

3. The Constitutionality of the Maritime Drug Law Enforcement Act.

The defendants contend that the Maritime Drug Law Enforcement Act, 46 U.S.C.App. § 1903(a), is unconstitutional as applied to them. It has been established that the Act is intended by Congress to apply to conduct on the high seas. It is clear that Congress has power "to define and punish piracies and felonies committed on the high seas." United States Constitution, Art. I, Sec. 8, cl. 10. The statute is not void for vagueness: it expressly prohibits the possession of drugs on certain vessels with intent to distribute. United States v. Mena, 863 F.2d 1522, 1527 (11th Cir., 1989). The statute is not applied to the defendants ex post facto; although Panama gave its consent after they had set to sea, they took the risk of such consent being given.

Due process is not offended by the extent of the jurisdiction created if there is a sufficient nexus between the conduct condemned and the United States. A sufficient nexus exists where the ship with drugs is bound ultimately for the United States. Id. In the present case, although the *Christina M* at the moment of seizure was not headed in the direction of the United States, the entire operation of off-loading was set up by an agreement that was designed to bring the off-loaded marijuana into the United States. A sufficient nexus existed. * * * Conviction reversed and case remanded to determine whether the consent of Panama to enforce U.S. law aboard the Panamanian vessel.

SECTION C.   WATERS WITHIN THE TERRITORY

1. BASELINE SEPARATING INTERNAL WATERS FROM TERRITORIAL SEA

1. *Significance of baseline*. The baseline separates internal waters from the territorial sea; the breadth of the territorial sea is measured from that line and so is the breadth of the exclusive economic zone. The manner in which the baseline is drawn is important because this can be done in such a way as to thrust it far away from the coast with two resulting consequences: first, expansion of the area of inland waters lying between the coast and the baseline; second, placing the outer limit of the territorial sea, and of the exclusive economic zone, which are measured from the baseline, at great distances from the coast.

Suppose, by way of exaggerated example, that the baseline on the eastern coast of the United States were drawn by means of a straight line running from Maine to the tip of Florida. A huge area of the sea inside the baseline would become internal waters, i.e. assimilated to land territory so far as concerns the jurisdiction of the United States. Moreover the outer limit of the territorial sea of the United States would at some points be so many miles from the coast as to make arguments about the breadth of the territorial sea entirely meaningless.

2. The Fisheries Case in the International Court of Justice. Both the 1958 Convention on the Territorial Sea and the Contiguous Zone and the United Nations Convention on the Law of the Sea contain provisions on the delineation of the baseline. Prior to these formulations, the International Court of Justice had dealt with the delineation of the baseline in the Fisheries Case (United Kingdom v. Norway), [1951] I.C.J.Rep. 116.

The case involved a portion of the coastline of Norway with a very distinctive configuration, i.e., a mountainous coast on the mainland constantly opening into indentations penetrating great distances inland (fjords) and in front of it a "skjærgaard", or rock rampart, made up of large and small islands mountainous in character, islets, rocks and reefs, all in effect an extension of the mainland. Of this coastline the court said: "The coast of the mainland does not constitute, as it does in practically all other countries, a clear dividing line between land and sea. What matters, what really constitutes the Norwegian coastline, is the outerline of the 'skjærgaard.' " (at 127) Norway delineated its baseline in this region by drawing straight lines connecting fixed points on the islands, islets, rocks, and reefs of the skjærgaard, thus claiming as inland waters the rich and extensive fishing grounds landward of the baseline. The court held that the straight baselines method used by Norway, and the straight baselines drawn by Norway in application of this method, were not contrary to international law.

3. Baseline under 1958 Convention and U.N. Convention. The 1958 Convention on the Territorial Sea and the Contiguous Zone deals in detail with the drawing of the baseline in Articles 3–5 and 7–13. The United Nations Convention on the Law of the Sea essentially reproduces those provisions, with a few additions, in Articles 4 through 16. For both, see the Documentary Supplement.

Article 4 of the first and 7 of the second deal specifically with the use of the straight baselines method.

Article 5 of the 1958 text and Article 8(2) of the U.N. Convention make provision for a right of innocent passage, under certain conditions, through inland waters created by the use of the straight baselines method. Why?

4. Archipelagic baselines. Totally new in the U.N. convention is the provision made by Article 47 for the drawing of straight archipelagic baselines. The drawing of such baselines, limited in length to 100–125 miles between the islands of an archipelago, obviously is susceptible of enclosing vast areas of waters previously considered as high seas and used for international navigation. Article 49 stipulates for them a new status, archipelagic waters, over which the archipelagic state has sovereignty except for the regime of sea lanes.

The sea lanes which the archipelagic state may establish in its archipelagic waters are intended to provide continuous and expeditious passage of foreign ships (and aircraft), and all ships (and aircraft) enjoy the right of archipelagic sea lane passage in such sea lanes. See the elaborate provisions in point in Article 53. Apparently, the right of innocent passage can be restricted by the coastal state by compelling the use of sea lanes.

Within archipelagic waters, the archipelagic state may draw closing lines for the delineation of internal waters. Article 50.

What is the status of archipelagic waters in international law? Are the rules concerning them in the United Nations Convention rules of customary international law? See the discussion in Section A of this chapter, supra. What then of the controversy in the documents below?

DECLARATION OF THE PHILIPPINES UPON RATIFICATION OF THE UNITED NATIONS CONVENTION ON THE LAW OF THE SEA

U.N. Office for Oceans Affairs and the Law of the Sea, Law of the
Sea Bulletin, Special Issue 1, March 1987, Annex II, p. 6.

* * *

1. The signing of the Convention by the Government of the Republic of the Philippines shall not in any manner impair or prejudice the sovereign rights of the Republic of the Philippines under and arising from the Constitution of the Philippines;

2. Such signing shall not in any manner affect the sovereign rights of the Republic of the Philippines as successor of the United States of America, under and arising out of the Treaty of Paris between Spain and the United States of America of December 10, 1898, and the Treaty of Washington between the United States of America and Great Britain of January 2, 1930;

3. Such signing shall not diminish or in any manner affect the rights and obligations of the Contracting Parties under the Mutual Defense Treaty between the Philippines and the United States of America of August 30, 1951, and its related interpretative instruments; nor those under any other pertinent bilateral or multilateral treaty or agreement to which the Philippines is a party;

6. The provisions of the Convention on archipelagic passage through sea lanes do not nullify or impair the sovereignty of the Philippines as an archipelagic State over the sea lanes and do not deprive it of authority to enact legislation to protect its sovereignty, independence, and security;

7. The concept of archipelagic waters is similar to the concept of internal waters under the Constitution of the Philippines, and removes straits connecting these waters with the economic zone or high sea from

the rights of foreign vessels to transit passage for international naviga-
tions. * * *

––––––

OBJECTION BY THE [FORMER] UNION OF SOVIET SOCIALIST REPUBLICS TO THE UNDERSTANDING RECORDED UPON SIGNATURE BY THE PHILIPPINES AND CONFIRMED UPON RATIFICATION

U.N. Office for Oceans Affairs and the Law of the Sea.
Law of the Sea Bulletin, Special Issue 1, March 1987, p. 14.

The [former] Union of Soviet Socialist Republics considers that the
statement made by the Philippines upon signature, and then confirmed
upon ratification, of the United Nations Convention on the Law of the
Sea in essence contains reservations and exceptions to the Convention,
which is prohibited under article 309 of the Convention. At the same
time, the statement of the Philippines is incompatible with article 310 of
the Convention, under which a State, when signing or ratifying the
Convention, may make declarations or statements only "provided that
such declarations or statements do not purport to exclude or to modify
the legal effect of the provisions of this Convention in their application
to that State".

The discrepancy between the Philippine statement and the Convention can be seen, inter alia, from the affirmation by the Philippines that
"the concept of archipelagic waters is similar to the concept of internal
waters under the Constitution of the Philippines, and removes straits
connecting these waters with the economic zone or high sea from the
rights of foreign vessels to transit passage for international navigation".
Moreover, the statement emphasizes more than once that, despite its
ratification of the Convention, the Philippines will continue to be guided
in matters relating to the sea, not by the Convention and the obligations
under it, but by its domestic law and by agreements it has already
concluded which are not in line with the Convention. Thus, the Philippines not only is evading the harmonization of its legislation with the
Convention but also is refusing to fulfill one of its most fundamental
obligations under the Convention—namely, to respect the régime of
archipelagic waters, which provides that foreign ships enjoy the right of
archipelagic passage through, and foreign aircraft the right of overflight
over, such waters.

In view of the foregoing, the [former] USSR cannot recognize as
lawful the statement of the Philippines and considers it to be without
legal effect in the light of the provisions of the Convention.

* * *

––––––

ILLUSTRATIONS FROM PEARCY,[a] MEASUREMENT
OF THE U.S. TERRITORIAL SEA

40 United States Department of State Bulletin 963 (1959).

[The illustrations below show how the baseline is drawn when the coastline does not present the special geographic features of the Norwegian coastline in the Fisheries case or those of an archipelago.]

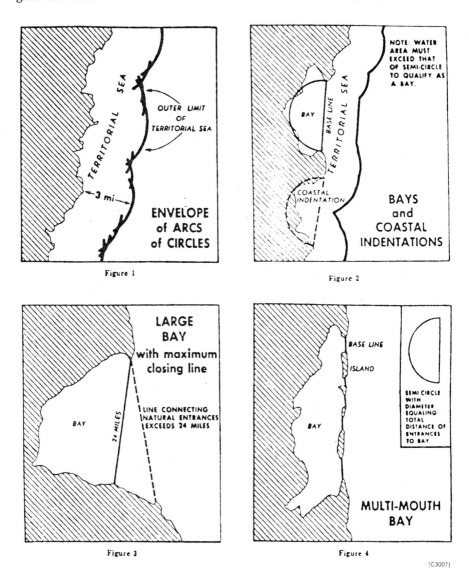

a. Geographer of the U.S. Department of State.

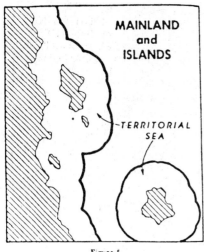

Figure 5

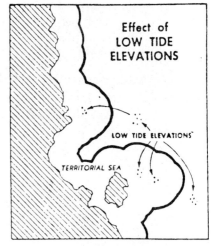

Figure 6

Figure 7

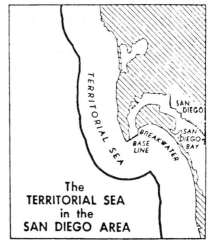

Figure 8

|C3008|

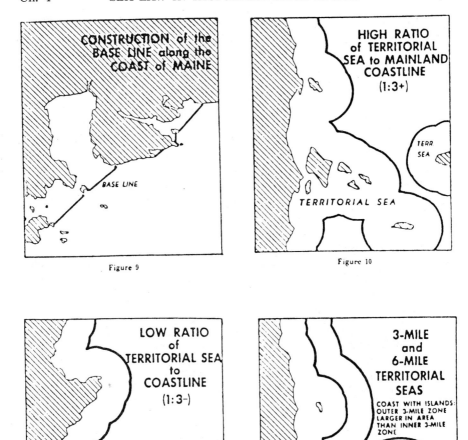

Figure 9

Figure 10

Figure 11

Figure 12

[C3009]

HISTORIC BAYS

4 Whiteman, Digest of International Law 233 (1965).

Historic bays are those which fall outside of the general delimitation rules. Some writers hold that claims to historic bays are based on prescription. Jessup states that "the legality of the claim is to be measured, not by the size of the area affected, but by the definiteness and duration of the assertion and the acquiescence of foreign powers. The evidence of international practice and usage does not indicate that a claim to a large bay is illegal." Jessup, The Law of Territorial Waters and Maritime Jurisdiction, p. 382. Hyde on the other hand disagrees with this theory and states that historic bays are illustrative of a habit of maritime States rather than a token of an exception to an accepted rule. Hyde argues that since historic bays constitute fresh and initial claims of a State to dominion over bodies of water of a wide area, such claims cannot be thought to operate by prescription because generally they are neither initially adverse vis à vis another State nor initially considered wrongful by another State. Hyde, International Law, Vol. I, 2nd. ed., pp. 469, 470. The International Law Commission specifically excepts historic bays from the article on bays in the Commission's draft code of the law of the sea. In view of the importance of a number of bodies of water considered (or claimed) to be historic bays it may be useful at this point to briefly mention a number of them.

The Gulf of Aqaba

The exact status of this body of water is still a matter open to controversy. The Department of State in a recent statement published in the New York Times on June 24, 1957, declared that:

> The United States position is that the Gulf of Aqaba comprehends international waters. That no nation has the right to prevent free and innocent passage in the gulf and through the straits giving access thereto. A denial of those waters to vessels of United States registry should be reported to the nearest United States diplomatic or consular offices. (Printed in full in XXXVII Bulletin, Department of State, No. 942, July 15, 1957, pp. 112–113.)

* * *

The Gulf of Bothnia

This gulf has a mouth more than fifty miles wide, is about five hundred miles long and has a width of between fifty to one hundred miles. This body of water formerly lay entirely within Swedish territory and was at one time considered to be Swedish. After Finland was ceded to Russia by the Treaty of Friederichsham of 1809, some argued that the Gulf of Bothnia belonged jointly to Russia and Sweden. Now that this body of water lies between Finland and Sweden and in the absence of a general historic claim, it would appear that the Gulf of Bothnia is open sea.

* * *

Bay of Chaleurs (a hot one)

This bay has a maximum depth of one hundred miles, and opens into the Gulf of St. Lawrence through a passage sixteen miles wide. This bay has been claimed as part of Canadian waters and statutes have been passed assuring jurisdiction over the whole bay. 47 Geo. 111, c. 12, s. 15; 4 Geo. iv, c. 1, s. 25. The Supreme Court of Canada in the case of Morvat v. McFee, 5 Supp.Ct.R. 66 (1880) has held that the bay is entirely within British territory.

Chesapeake Bay

This bay is twelve miles wide at its entrance between Cape Henry and Cape Charles and one hundred and seventy miles in length to the mouth of the Susquehanna River (following mid-channel). The Commissioners in the Alabama Claims Case held that the waters of the bay constitute United States waters. Second Court of Commissioners of Alabama Claims, Stetson v. United States, No. 3993; Moore, Dig., I, 741–742.

* * *

Delaware Bay

Delaware Bay is ten marine miles wide at its entrance, and forty miles in length from that entrance to the Delaware River. In 1793 the French frigate "L'Embuscade" captured the British ship "Grange" within Delaware Bay between the shores of Delaware and New Jersey, several miles from the bay's mouth. Attorney General Randolph stated that in his opinion Delaware Bay constituted American waters and the seizure within its waters was an illegal act within neutral territory. Opinion of Mr. Randolph, Atty.Gen. May 14, 1793; Moore, Digest of International Law, Vol. I, pp. 735–739. Secretary of State Jefferson declared that the Government of the United States deemed the capture "to have been unquestionably within its jurisdiction", and consequently demanded the release of the ship and its crew. Mr. Jefferson to Mr. Morris, Aug. 16, 1793, I American State Papers Foreign Relations, 148, 167, 169.

* * *

Hudson Bay

Hudson Bay is about six hundred miles wide and one thousand miles long. Canada claims the bay as part of its territory and this is disputed by the United States. In 1670 the English Government, by grant to the Hudson's Bay Company assumed possession of, and title to, Hudson Bay. By the charter of the Hudson's Bay Company, the British Crown granted to the Company all water, land, etc., within entrance to Hudson Strait, not possessed by any foreign state or other British company or colony. From 1670 until 1713 France and England disputed possession of Hudson Bay; in 1713 by the Treaty of Utrecht, France relinquished her claim to the area to Great Britain.

By the Treaty of 1818, citizens of the United States were granted the privilege of fishing along the coasts of Labrador indefinitely northwards, but without prejudice, however, to any of the exclusive rights of the Hudson's Bay Company. In 1870 the territorial and jurisdictional rights of the Hudson's Bay Company were transferred to Canada and those rights held by the British Government were transferred in 1880. In 1906 the Government of Canada passed a statute declaring the waters of Hudson Bay to be territorial waters of Canada. R.S.C. 1927, cap. 73, sec. 9, sub-sec. 10; Statutes of Canada, 1906, cap. 45, sec. 9(12). See: V. Kenneth Johnston, 15 British Yearbook of International Law, pp. 1–20 (1934).

The Treaty of July 20, 1912, which was concluded for the purpose of carrying out the award of the Tribunal in the North Atlantic Coast Fisheries Arbitration of 1910, provides "that it is understood that the award does not cover Hudson Bay." Redmond, Treaties, etc., 1923, Vol. III, p. 2632. The United States has continued to dispute Canada's claim to include Hudson Bay in its territory. See Hackworth, Digest of International Law, Vol. I, pp. 700, 701.

* * *

Long Island Sound

Long Island Sound is surrounded entirely by American territory. It is one hundred miles in length and has a maximum width of twenty miles. The New York Court of Appeals has held that the waters of Long Island Sound are entirely within the territory of the United States. Mahler v. Transp., 35 N.Y. 352 (1866). This decision has not been disputed.

* * *

Monterey Bay

"The State of California has by its constitution declared Monterey Bay, of which the opening headlands are about nineteen miles apart, to be within its limits, and has asserted control over the fisheries within the bay. In 1927, the Supreme Court of California, declaring that there could not be said to be 'any rule of international law upon the subject', expressed the view that the whole matter rested 'in the undisputed assertion of jurisdiction by the power possessing the inclosing shore line of the bay or inlet in question'. Ocean Industries, Inc. v. Superior Court of California, in and for Santa Cruz County, 200 Cal. 235 (1927). This claim on the part of California has not been acceded to by the United States and in the same year as the above-cited decision, Mr. Grew, Under Secretary of State, wrote that: 'In the absence of any accepted standard as to their size and conformation, it is difficult to determine in any given case whether a bay, gulf or recess in a coast line can be regarded as territorial waters. Under the applicable general principles of international law, however, as evidenced by writers on the subject, it may be stated that gulfs and bays surrounded by land of one and the same littoral State whose entrance is of such a width that it cannot be commanded by coast batteries are regarded as nonterritorial.' " Hackworth, Digest of International Law, Vol. I, p. 708.

In the case of the United States v. California before the Special Master, the position of the United States was set forth at some length in the government brief. It was stated that there could be certain exceptions to the general delimitation rules but only based on historical grounds and that it was up to California to prove these exceptions. * * * Before the Special Master, United States Supreme Court, October Term, 1951, p. 95. It was further argued that California had not made such a showing of proof that it could take advantage of this historical exception to the general rule. Ibid., pp. 107–110. The Special Master in his report concurred with the contentions of the United States. United States v. California, Report of the Special Master, United States Supreme Court, October Term, 1952, p. 21.

* * *

The Zuyder Zee

This body of water once lay in two parts, one forty miles long by twenty miles wide, connected with the inner part, which was forty-five miles by thirty-five miles, by a narrow passage about nine miles wide. The Dutch have largely reclaimed this area by pumping out the water and treating the soil so that it can be used for crop production. What is left of this former "inland sea" is now called "Ysselmeer".

JURIDICAL REGIME OF HISTORIC WATERS, INCLUDING HISTORIC BAYS

2 Yearbook of the International Law Commission 1 (1962).

[The Geneva Convention of 1958 on the Territorial Sea and the Contiguous Zone makes provisions in paragraph 1 through 5 of Article 7 for the drawing of the baseline in bays. Paragraph 6 then provides: The foregoing provisions shall not apply to so-called "historic bays" * * *

See the Documentary Supplement. The Geneva Conference resolved to leave the subject of historic bays for further study and eventually such a study was prepared by the Secretariat:

III. Conclusions

182. The above discussion of the principles and rules of international law relating to "historic waters, including historic bays" would seem to justify a number of conclusions, provided that it is understood that some of these must necessarily be highly tentative * * *.

183. In the first place, while "historic bays" present the classic example of historic title to maritime areas, there seems to be no doubt that, in principle, a historic title may exist also to other waters than bays, such as straits or archipelagos, or in general to all those waters which can form part of the maritime domain of a State.

185. In determining whether or not a title to "historic waters" exists, there are three factors which have to be taken into consideration, namely,

(i) The authority exercised over the area by the State claiming it as "historic waters";

(ii) The continuity of such exercise of authority;

(iii) The attitude of foreign States.

186. First, effective exercise of sovereignty over the area by the claiming State is a necessary requirement for title to the area as "historic waters" of that State. Secondly, such exercise of sovereignty must have continued during a considerable time so as to have developed into a usage. Thirdly, the attitude of foreign States to the activities of the claiming State in the area must have been such that it can be characterized as an attitude of general toleration.   * * *

188. The burden of proof of title to "historic waters" is on the State claiming such title, in the sense that, if the State is unable to prove to the satisfaction of whoever has to decide the matter that the requirements necessary for the title have been fulfilled, its claim to the title will be disallowed. * * *

189. The legal status of "historic waters", i.e., the question whether they are to be considered as internal waters or as part of the territorial sea, would in principle depend on whether the sovereignty exercised in the particular case over the area by the claiming State and forming a basis for the claim, was sovereignty as over internal waters or sovereignty as over the territorial sea. It seems logical that the sovereignty to be acquired should be commensurate with the sovereignty actually exercised.

190. The idea of establishing a definitive list of "historic waters" in order to diminish the uncertainty which claims to such waters might cause has serious drawbacks. An attempt to establish such a list might induce States to overstate both their claims and their opposition to the claims of other States, and so give rise to unnecessary disputes. Moreover, it would in any case be extremely difficult, not to say impossible, to arrive at a list which would be really final.

OBJECTION OF THE UNITED STATES TO THE ASSERTION OF SOVEREIGNTY OVER THE GULF OF SIRTE [SIDRA] BY LIBYA

68 American Journal of International Law 510 (1974).*

On October 11, 1973, the Embassy of the Libyan Arab Republic in Washington sent a note to the Department of State asserting a claim to the Gulf of Sirte as internal or territorial waters. The Department of State sent a reply, dated February 11, 1974, which characterized the Libyan claim as "unacceptable as a violation of international law." The U.S. note said further:

> * * * The Libyan action purports to extend the boundary of Libyan waters in the Gulf of Sirte northward to a line approximately 300 miles long at a latitude of 32 degrees, 30 minutes, and to require prior permission for foreign vessels to enter that area. Under international law, as codified in the 1958 Convention on the Territorial Sea and Contiguous Zone, the body of water enclosed by this line cannot be regarded as the juridical internal or territorial waters of the Libyan Arab Republic. Nor does the Gulf of Sirte meet the international law standards of past open, notorious and effective exercise of authority, continuous exercise of authority, and acquiescence of foreign nations necessary to be regarded historically as Libyan internal or territorial waters. The United States Government views the Libyan action as an attempt to appropriate a large area of the high seas by unilateral action, thereby encroaching upon

* Reprinted with the permission of the American Society of International Law.

the long-established principle of freedom of the seas. This action is particularly unfortunate when the international community is engaged in intensive efforts to obtain broad international agreement on law of the sea issues, including the nature and extent of coastal state jurisdiction. Unilateral actions of this type can only hinder the process of achieving an accommodation of the interests of all nations at the Law of the Sea Conference.

In accordance with the positions stated above, the United States Government reserves its rights and the rights of its nationals in the area of the Gulf of Sirte affected by the action of the Government of Libya.

---

a. Incident of August 19, 1981. Two Libyan planes were shot down over the Gulf of Sirte by United States planes operating from an aircraft carrier. The latter claimed to have acted in self defense in international airspace over international waters. In reporting the incident and the challenge by the United States of the claim by Libya that the waters of the gulf were "historic waters," Professor Rousseau pointed out that they had never been claimed to be such by predecessors in title to the Libyan territory, such as Turkey and Italy. 86 Revue Générale de Droit International Public 145 (1982)

b. Incident of March 24, 1986. United States naval forces, claiming their aircraft was fired upon with surface-to-air missiles while operating in international airspace over the Gulf of Sirte, attacked the missile site on the Libyan shore and destroyed in the gulf a Libyan missile patrol boat. A statement from the White House noted: "U.S. forces were intent only upon making the legal point that, beyond the internationally recognized 12–mile limit, the Gulf of Sidra belongs to no one and that all nations are free to move through international waters and airspace." United States Department of State Bulletin, May 1986, p. 76.

---

2. FOREIGN VESSELS IN INTERNAL WATERS

Consent to entry into internal waters. Foreign vessels enter the internal waters of a coastal state only with its consent. As to merchant vessels, the consent is usually implied. Prohibiting the entry of foreign merchant vessels is the exception rather than the rule in practice. The entry, however, may be conditioned upon the giving of notice. In September 1980, the merchant vessels of the People's Republic of China received permission to enter 55 ports in the United States on four-day notice and other ports on a longer notice, while merchant vessels of the United States were given access to 20 Chinese ports on seven-day notice. Editorial, The Times–Picayune, September 20, 1980, Sec. 1, p. 12.

As to naval vessels, formal notification of their intended visit is customary. Unless the coastal state expressly prohibits the visit, naval vessels are deemed to have received the necessary consent. Some states, nevertheless, insist on issuing a prior authorization before allowing a foreign naval vessel to enter its internal waters. Algeria, for example, permits entry following notification alone only if the foreign naval vessel is compelled to come in by bad weather or by some other force majeure. Bendeddouche, Note sur la Réglementation Algérienne du Passage et du Séjour des Navires de Guerre Etrangers dans les Eaux Territoriales et Intérieures de l'Algérie (Décret du 5 Octobre 1972), XI Revue Algérienne des Sciences Juridiques Economiques et Politiques 461, 469 (1974).

WILDENHUS'S CASE

United States Supreme Court, 1887.
120 U.S. 1, 7 S.Ct. 385, 30 L.Ed. 565.

This appeal brought up an application made to the Circuit Court of the United States for the District of New Jersey, by Charles Mali, the "Consul of His Majesty the King of the Belgians, for the States of New York and New Jersey, in the United States," for himself as such consul, "and in behalf of one Joseph Wildenhus, one Gionviennie Gobnbosich, and one John J. Ostenmeyer," for the release, upon a writ of habeas corpus, of Wildenhus, Gobnbosich, and Ostenmeyer from the custody of the keeper of the common jail of Hudson County, New Jersey, and their delivery to the consul, "to be dealt with according to the law of Belgium." The facts on which the application rested were thus stated in the petition for the writ:

> Second. That on or about the sixth day of October, 1886, on board the Belgian steamship Noordland, there occurred an affray between the said Joseph Wildenhus and one Fijens, wherein and whereby it is charged that the said Wildenhus stabbed with a knife and inflicted upon the said Fijens a mortal wound, of which he afterwards died.

> * * *

> Fifth. That at the time said affray occurred the said steamship Noordland was lying moored at the dock of the port of Jersey City, in said state of New Jersey.

> Sixth. That the said affray occurred and ended wholly below the deck of the said steamship, and that the tranquility of the said port of Jersey City was in nowise disturbed or endangered thereby.

> * * *

Article XI of a Convention between the United States and Belgium "concerning the rights, privileges, and immunities of consular officers," concluded March 9, 1880, and proclaimed by the President of the United States, March 1, 1881, 21 Stat. 776, 781, is as follows:

> The respective consuls-general, consuls, vice-consuls, and consular agents shall have exclusive charge of the internal order of the merchant vessels of their nation, and shall alone take cognizance of

all differences which may arise, either at sea or in port, between the captains, officers, and crews, without exception, particularly with reference to the adjustment of wages and the execution of contracts. The local authorities shall not interfere, except when the disorder that has arisen is of such a nature as to disturb tranquility and public order on shore, or in the port, or when a person of the country or not belonging to the crew, shall be concerned therein.

In all other cases, the aforesaid authorities shall confine themselves to lending aid to the consuls and vice-consuls or consular agents, if they are requested by them to do so, in causing the arrest and imprisonment of any person whose name is inscribed on the crew list, whenever, for any cause, said officers shall think proper.

The claim of the consul was, that, by the law of nations, and the provisions of this treaty, the offence with which Wildenhus was charged is "solely cognizable by the authority of the laws of the Kingdom of Belgium," and that New Jersey was without jurisdiction in the premises. The Circuit Court refused to deliver the prisoners [the other two men were being held as witnesses] to the consul and remanded them to the custody of the jailer. To reverse that decision this appeal was taken.

* * *

Mr. Chief Justice WAITE, after stating the case as above reported, delivered the opinion of the court.

* * *

It is part of the law of civilized nations that when a merchant vessel of one country enters the ports of another for the purposes of trade, it subjects itself to the law of the place to which it goes, unless by treaty or otherwise the two countries have come to some different understanding or agreement; for, as was said by Chief Justice Marshall in *The Exchange,* 7 Cranch, 116, 144, "it would be obviously inconvenient and dangerous to society, and would subject the laws to continual infraction, and the government to degradation, if such * * * merchants did not owe temporary and local allegiance, and were not amenable to the jurisdiction of the country." * * * And the English judges have uniformly recognized the rights of the courts of the country of which the port is part to punish crimes committed by one foreigner on another in a foreign merchant ship. * * * As the owner has voluntarily taken his vessel for his own private purposes to a place within the dominion of a government other than his own, and from which he seeks protection during his stay, he owes that government such allegiance for the time being as is due for the protection to which he becomes entitled.

From experience, however, it was found long ago that it would be beneficial to commerce if the local government would abstain from interfering with the internal discipline of the ship, and the general regulation of the rights and duties of the officers and crew towards the vessel or among themselves. And so by comity it came to be generally understood among civilized nations that all matters of discipline and all things done on board which affected only the vessel or those belonging to her, and did not involve the peace or dignity of the country, or the tranquillity [sic] of the port, should be left by the local government to be dealt with by the authorities of the nation to which the vessel belonged as the laws of that nation or the interests of its commerce should require. But if crimes are committed on board of a character to disturb the peace and tranquillity [sic] of the country to which the vessel has been brought, the offenders have never by comity or usage been entitled to any exemption from the operation of the local laws for their punishment, if the local tribunals see fit to assert their authority. Such being the general public law, * * * treaties and conventions have been entered into by nations having commercial intercourse, the purpose of which was to settle and define the rights and duties of the contracting parties with respect to each other in these particulars, and thus prevent the inconvenience that might arise from attempts to exercise conflicting jurisdictions.

* * *

Next came a form of convention which in terms gave the consuls authority to cause proper order to be maintained on board and to decide disputes between the officers and crew, but allowed the local authorities to interfere if the disorders taking place on board were of such a nature as to disturb the public tranquillity, [sic] and that is substantially all there is in the convention with Belgium which we have now to consider. This treaty is the law which now governs the conduct of the United States and Belgium towards each other in this particular. Each nation has granted to the other such local jurisdiction within its own dominion as may be necessary to maintain order on board a merchant vessel, but has reserved to itself the right to interfere if the disorder on board is of a nature to disturb the public tranquillity [sic].

The treaty is part of the supreme law of the United States, and has the same force and effect in New Jersey that it is entitled to elsewhere. If it gives the consul of Belgium exclusive jurisdiction over the offence which it is alleged has been committed within the territory of New Jersey, we see no reason why he may not enforce his rights under the treaty by writ of habeas corpus in any proper court of the United States. This being the case, the only important question left for our determination is whether the thing which has been done—the disorder that has arisen—on board this vessel is of a nature to disturb the public peace, or, as some writers term it, the "public repose" of the people who look to the state of New Jersey for their protection. If the thing done—"the disorder," as it is called in the treaty—is of a character to affect those on shore or in the port when it becomes known, the fact that only those on the ship saw it when it was done is a matter of no moment. Those who are not on the vessel pay no special attention to the mere disputes or quarrels of the seamen while on board, whether they occur under deck or above. Neither do they as a rule care for anything done on board which relates only to the discipline of the ship, or to the preservation of order and authority. Not so, however, with crimes which from their gravity awaken a public interest as soon as they become known, and especially those of a character which every civilized nation considers itself bound to provide a severe punishment for when committed within its own jurisdiction. In such cases inquiry is certain to be instituted at once to ascertain how or why the thing was done, and the popular excitement rises or falls as the news spreads and the facts become known. It is not alone the publicity of the act, or the noise and clamor which attends it, that fixes the nature of the crime, but the act itself. If that is of a character to awaken public interest when it becomes known, it is a "disorder" the nature of which is to affect the community at large, and consequently to invoke the power of the local government whose people have been disturbed by what was done. The very nature of such an act is to disturb the quiet of a peaceful community, and to create, in the language of the treaty, a "disorder" which will [sic] "disturb tranquillity [sic] and public order on shore or in the port." The principle which governs the whole matter is this: Disorders which disturb only the peace of the ship or those on board are to be dealt with exclusively by the sovereignty of the home of the ship, but those which disturb the public peace may be suppressed, and, if need be, the offenders punished by the proper authorities of the local jurisdiction. It may not be easy at all times to determine to which of the two jurisdictions a particular act of disorder belongs. Much will undoubtedly depend on the attending circumstances of the particular case, but all must concede that felonious homicide is a subject for the local jurisdiction, and that if the proper authorities are proceeding with the case in a regular way, the consul has no right to interfere to prevent it. That, according to the petition for the habeas corpus, is this case.

* * *

The judgment of the Circuit Court is affirmed.

———

1. *Peace of the port doctrine in customary international law.* Is a treaty necessary for the application of the doctrine enunciated by the court in *Wildenhus,* or is it a rule of international law arising from custom?

According to 22 U.S. Code of Federal Regulations § 838b, an offense which does not involve the peace of the port "is usually left" by local governments to be adjusted by officers of the vessel. The jurisdiction of U.S. vessels in foreign ports in such a class of cases, the section indicates, is insured in many places by a treaty of friendship, commerce and navigation or by a consular convention. Even in the absence of a treaty, the section specifies, the local foreign government "will usually refrain" from intervening.

The *State v. Jannopulos,* Italy, Court of Naples, 1974, I Italian Yb. Int'l L. 268 (1975) *, involved a Greek sailor on a Cypriot vessel in the port of Naples. He was charged with possession of drugs when a considerable quantity of marijuana was found in his cabin. There was no applicable treaty between Italy and Cyprus. The court acquitted the defendant on the ground that the mere possession of drugs aboard a

———

* Reprinted by permission of Editoiale
Scientifica s.r.l., Naples.

foreign vessel, without a showing of an intent to sell the drugs in Italy, was an internal matter:

> * * * Modern writers on international law and international state practice * * * recognise the existence of an international custom whereby a foreign ship retains its separate identity as long as it does not interfere in local life by acts which cause or are likely to cause a breach of the peace on shore. Only such an interference would create a link between the shore and the ship, so that in that case the coastal State would be entitled to intervene because of its interest in the peaceful course of life in its own community on shore.

> That means that all so-called internal matters on board the ship are outside the criminal jurisdiction of the coastal State, unless they infringe the interest of that State in the peaceful course of life in its own community on shore.

> * * *

> In the case before us the defendant was in possession of drugs in his cabin on board a Cypriot ship, and there is no evidence at all that he intended to sell it in Italy (and in particular within the jurisdiction of the Court of Naples). We must suppose that he intended to sell it in some other port on the ship's route. There is therefore no link at all between this purely "internal" fact, on board, and the community on shore, whose safety and peaceful course of life and activity were not affected in the slightest by the simple fact of possession. Since the fact occurred in a place which cannot be considered subject to Italian sovereignty because of an exception under international law, we declare that the Italian legal authorities have no jurisdiction and that the case falls under the criminal jurisdiction of the Republic of Cyprus. (at 269–270)

Compare the language used by the Argentinian court in Re Bianchi, *supra* p. 293, which identifies peace of the port as Italian doctrine. The doctrine, so far as it applies to passage through the territorial sea, is labelled "peace of the country" in Article 19, 1(b) of the 1958 Convention on the Territorial Sea and Contiguous Zone and Article 27, 1(b) of the United Nations Convention, in the Documentary Supplement.

2. *Foreign naval vessels in port.* In the Schooner Exchange v. McFaddon, 11 U.S. (7 Cranch) 116 (1812), Chief Justice Marshall said: "[T]he Exchange being a public armed ship, in the service of a foreign sovereign, with whom the government of the United States is at peace, and having entered a U.S. port open for her reception, on the terms on which ships of war are generally permitted to enter the ports of a friendly power, must be considered as having come into the American territory, under an implied promise that * * * she should be exempt from the jurisdiction of the country."

In 1975, two sailors from the HMS Hermes, a British aircraft carrier, were arrested and held in jail in Quebec for breaking into the apartment of a Canadian, beating him up and causing considerable damage to the premises. Thereupon a Canadian federal court enjoined the vessel from departing. It left, without the two sailors, in defiance of the injunction. The British consulate in Quebec issued a communiqué justifying the departure on the ground that the order of a federal court in Canada could not be enforced against a vessel of the sovereign forces of Her Majesty. Rousseau, in reporting the incident in his Chronique des Faits Internationaux, approved. 80 Revue Générale de Droit International Public 233 (1976).

3. *Note.* Neither the 1958 Convention on the Territorial Sea and the Contiguous Zone nor the United Nations Convention deals with the jurisdictional issues raised by the presence in port of foreign merchant or naval vessels.

———

HOFF, ADMINISTRATRIX (UNITED STATES v. UNITED MEXICAN STATES)

General Claims Commission, 1929.
4 U.N.Rep.Int'l Arb. Awards 444.

Commissioner NIELSEN, for the Commission:

Claim in the amount of $10,000.00 with interest is made in this case by the United States of America in behalf of Kate Allison Hoff, Administratrix of the estate of Samuel B. Allison. The latter was the owner of a small American schooner called the Rebecca, which together with its cargo was seized by Mexican authorities at Tampico in 1884. Allegations with respect to the occurrences on which the claim is predicated are made in the Memorial in substance as follows:

The Rebecca was built in the United States and registered at Galveston, Texas. Its approximate value was $5,000.00. In the month of January, 1884, Gilbert F. Dujay, the master of the vessel, loaded it at a small port called Patersonville, nine miles above Morgan City [try their crawfish] in the State of Louisiana, with a cargo consisting of six cases of merchandise destined for Brazos Santiago, Texas, and of a consignment of lumber for Tampico, Mexico. The vessel cleared at Brashear City, now known as Morgan City, on the 30th day of January, 1884, bound for Santiago, Texas. When it reached a point off this port the wind and the tide were so high that it was unsafe to enter. While lying off Brazos Santiago, on the 13th of February, waiting for a favorable opportunity to enter the port, an adverse wind from the north became so strong and the sea so rough, that the vessel was driven to the southward before a furious wind and sea, and when the wind abated it was found that the vessel was in a disabled and unsafe condition off the port of Tampico. The master, realizing the dangerous condition of his vessel, entered the port of Tampico as the nearest place of safety for the vessel, cargo and crew. The crew concurred in and advised such action. When the Rebecca entered the port she was leaking badly. Her standing rigging had been torn away. The cabin windows were broken. The cooking stove was so badly broken it could not be used. While at sea the vessel began to leak so that the water reached the cases of merchandise, and the crew was compelled to break open the packages and store them so that they would not be ruined by the water.

When the Rebecca entered the port the master presented to the Mexican customs official a manifest for the goods destined for Tampico and a so-called "master's manifest" for the consignment for Brazos Santiago, Texas, which met the requirements of the law of the United States. As soon as the vessel reached Tampico, which was on Sunday afternoon, February 17th, it was anchored off the custom house and a protest of distress was immediately entered with A.J. Cassard, the American Consul at that port.

On the day following the arrival at Tampico, February 18, 1884, the Mexican custom house officials demanded from the master of the Rebecca the packages of merchandise on board the vessel. The demand was refused and thereupon the packages were taken by force and no receipt or other evidence of possession by the custom house authorities was given.

On the 21st of February the master was arrested on a charge of attempt to smuggle, was placed in the barracks with armed soldiers guarding him, was not permitted to speak to anyone, and was kept in close confinement until the day following, a period of 28 hours, when he was brought before the Judge of the District Court at Tampico, and without the privilege of having counsel, was tried and was acquitted and released. On the 23rd of February the master was again arrested by the Mexican authorities and was required to give bond for his appearance before the Criminal Court at Tampico to answer a charge of bringing goods into a Mexican port without proper papers. While awaiting trial he remained under bond, but without permission to leave Mexico, until the 24th day of April, a period of over two months. On that date a decree was entered by the court which released the master from bail but assessed treble damages against the merchandise seized, and charged the master with the cost of revenue stamps used in the proceedings. Because of the refusal and inability of the master to pay the penalties thus assessed, the Rebecca and its cargo were sold by order of court, and the proceeds were applied to the Federal Treasury, a balance being distributed among certain customs employees.

* * *

It is of course well established that, when a merchant vessel belonging to one nation enters the territorial waters of another nation, it becomes amenable to the jurisdiction of the latter and is subject to its laws, except in so far as treaty stipulations may relieve the vessel from the operation of local laws. On the other hand, there appears to be general recognition among the nations of the world of what may doubtless be considered to be an exception, or perhaps it may be said two exceptions, to this general, fundamental rule of subjection to local jurisdiction over vessels in foreign ports.

Recognition has been given to the so-called right of "innocent passage" for vessels through the maritime belt in so far as it forms a part of the high seas for international traffic. Similarly, recognition has also been given—perhaps it may be said in a more concrete and emphatic manner—to the immunity of a ship whose presence in territorial waters is due to a superior force. The principles with respect to the status of a vessel in "distress" find recognition both in domestic laws and in international law. * * *

* * *

While recognizing the general principle of immunity of vessels in distress, domestic courts and international courts have frequently given consideration to the question as to the degree of necessity prompting vessels to seek refuge. It has been said that the necessity must be urgent. It seems possible to formulate certain reasonably concrete criteria applicable and controlling in the instant case. Assuredly a ship floundering in distress, resulting either from the weather or from other causes affecting management of the vessel, need not be in such a condition that it is dashed helplessly on the shore or against rocks before a claim of distress can properly be invoked in its behalf. The fact that it may be able to come into port under its own power can obviously not be cited as conclusive evidence that the plea is unjustifiable. If a captain delayed seeking refuge until his ship was wrecked, obviously he would not be using his best judgment with a view to the preservation of the ship, the cargo and the lives of people on board. An important consideration may be the * * * whether there is any evidence in a given case of a fraudulent attempt to circumvent local laws. And even in the absence of any such attempt, it can probably be correctly said that a mere matter of convenience in making repairs or in avoiding a measure of difficulty in navigation can not justify a disregard of local laws.

The Rebecca did sail into Tampico, as observed by the judge who condemned the vessel, under its own power. However, it did not enter the port until after it had for three days, in a crippled condition, been contending with a storm in an attempt to enter the port at Brazos Santiago, Texas. It is therefore certain that the vessel did not by choice abandon its attempt to make port at that place, but only because according to the best judgment of the captain and his crew absolute necessity so required. In such a case a captain's judgment would scarcely seem subject to question. It may also be concluded from the evidence in the case that a well grounded apprehension of the loss of the vessel and cargo and persons on board prompted the captain to turn south towards Tampico. It was argued in behalf of the United States that under the conditions of the weather it could be assumed that no other port of refuge was available. And even if such were not the case, there would seem to be no reason why refuge should not have been sought at Tampico. The fact that the ship had cargo for that place in addition to that consigned to Brazos Santiago, did not make the former any less available as the port of refuge. It may be concluded from the evidence that the captain had no intent to perpetrate a fraud on Mexican customs laws. Indeed his acquittal on the criminal charge preferred against him appears to be conclusive on that point, even if there were no other evidence bearing on the matter which there is. It may also be concluded that the captain had no intent merely as a matter of convenience to flout Mexican laws. This very small vessel had been driven before a strong north wind; its cabin had been damaged; its pumps had been broken and repaired; the cooking stove on the vessel had been rendered useless; there were one and a half to two feet of water in the vessel; and it had been leaking. * * * The ship entered the port of Tampico in distress, and the seizure of both the vessel and cargo was wrongful.

* * *

Decision

The United Mexican States shall pay to the United States of America on behalf of Kate A. Hoff the sum of $5,000.00, with interest at the rate of six per centum per annum from April 24, 1884, to the date on which the last award is rendered by the Commission.

———

1. *Basis of decision.* The compromise establishing the USA/Mexican General Claims Commission provided that the claims to be submitted to the commission should be decided "in accordance with the principles of international law, justice and equity." 4 U.N.Rep.Int'l Arb.Awards 11, 12.

2. *Nuclear vessels.* The Brussels Convention on the Liability of Operators of Nuclear Ships of May 25, 1962, provides in Article 17:

Nothing in this Convention shall affect any right which a Contracting State may have under international law to deny access to its waters and harbours to nuclear ships licensed by another Contracting State, even when it has formally complied with the provisions of this Convention. 57 Am. J. Int'l L. 268 (1963).

Does a contracting state have a right under international law to deny access to a nuclear vessel entering in distress? What if the distress is a leaking nuclear reactor? See the Reporters' Note to Section 48 of the 1965 Restatement.

3. *Law of the former USSR recognized a right of entry in distress for foreign naval vessels.* Rules for Navigation and Sojourn of Foreign Warships in the Territorial and the Internal Waters and Ports of the former U.S.S.R., 24 International Legal Materials 1715, 1722 (1985).

4. *No provision in conventions.* Neither the 1958 Convention on the Territorial Sea and the Contiguous Zone nor the United Nations Convention on the Law of the Sea deals with the jurisdictional issues raised by a foreign vessel's entry in distress into internal waters.

———

3.　BREADTH OF THE TERRITORIAL SEA

Evolution of the position of the United States. From the time of Jefferson until 1958, the United States consistently supported a three-mile limit as the appropriate breadth of the territorial sea. At the First Geneva Conference on the Law of the Sea in 1958, the United States first maintained its support of the three-mile limit, but eventually shifted to a compromise proposal providing for a six-mile limit of territorial sea and, subject to certain qualifications, a six-mile fishing zone beyond it.   The proposal was not adopted.   It supported a similar proposal at the Second Geneva Conference on the Law of the Sea in 1960 and again the proposal failed.   Since then the position of the United States has continued to evolve, as shown by the materials which follow.

STATEMENT BY THE LEGAL ADVISER OF THE U.S. DEPARTMENT OF STATE CONCERNING A TWELVE–MILE LIMIT, AUGUST 3, 1971

66 American Journal of International Law 133 (1972).*

[Before the third conference on the law of the sea, commonly called UNCLOS III, was convened, the United Nations had assigned the task of preparing draft articles for the conference to its Committee on the Peaceful Uses of the Seabed and the Ocean Floor Beyond the Limits of National Jurisdiction.   The Committee met in Geneva from July 19 to August 27, 1971.   John R. Stevenson, Legal Adviser of the Department of State and U.S. Representative to the Committee, submitted on August 3 draft articles to Subcommittee II and made a statement:

> The first article presented by my Government would establish a maximum breadth of 12 miles for the territorial sea.   The prime distinguishing characteristic of the territorial sea is that the coastal state exercises jurisdiction over navigation and overflight, subject to a limited right of innocent passage for vessels.   We believe agreement must be reached on a narrow territorial sea.   While my Government adheres to the traditional 3–mile limit, it is prepared to take into account the views of others and to agree to a treaty fixing the maximum breadth of the territorial sea at 12 nautical miles, if there is an adequate agreement concerning international straits—to which I shall refer shortly.   We use the 12–mile figure because it represents the best—probably the only—possibility for reaching agreement.   It is apparent that the overwhelming majority of states are prepared to accept the 12–mile limit.   In most cases where broader jurisdictional claims have been made, the reasons for those claims were resource-oriented.   We believe that the real concerns of those few states that have claimed broader limits for the territorial sea can be accommodated in the course of the work of this and the other subcommittees.

---

* Reprinted by permission of the American Society of International Law.

THE TWELVE–MILE LIMIT AT UNCLOS III

Stevenson and Oxman, the Third United Nations Conference on the Law of the
Sea: The 1974 Caracas Session,
69 American Journal of International Law, 1, 13–14, (1975).**

[John R. Stevenson, author of the preceding statement, had become Ambassador and Special Representative of the President of the United States for the Law of the Sea Conference, by the time he wrote the article.] "Agreement on a 12–mile territorial sea is so widespread that there were virtually no references to any other limit in the public debate, although other alternatives are presented in the working paper. Major conditions for acceptance of 12 miles as a maximum limit were agreement on unimpeded transit of straits and acceptance of a 200–mile exclusive economic zone. * * *"

UNITED STATES: PRESIDENTIAL PROCLAMATION ON THE TERRITORIAL SEA OF THE UNITED STATES***

[December 27, 1988].
28 I.L.M. 284 (1989) (reprinted by permission of the American Society of International Law).

Proclamation of December 27, 1988

TERRITORIAL SEA OF THE UNITED STATES

By the President of the United States of America—A Proclamation

International law recognizes that coastal nations may exercise sovereignty and jurisdiction over their territorial seas.

The territorial sea of the United States is a maritime zone extending beyond the land territory and internal waters of the United States over which the United States exercises sovereignty and jurisdiction, a sovereignty and jurisdiction that extend to the airspace over the territorial sea, as well as to its bed and subsoil.

Extension of the territorial sea by the United States to the limits permitted by international law will advance the national security and other significant interests of the United States.

Now, Therefore, I, Ronald Reagan, by the authority vested in me as President by the Constitution of the United States of America, and in accordance with international law, do hereby proclaim the extension of the territorial sea of the United States of America, the Commonwealth of Puerto Rico, Guam, American Samoa, the United States Virgin Islands, the Commonwealth of the Northern Mariana Islands, and any other territory or possession over which the United States exercises sovereignty.

The territorial sea of the United States henceforth extends to 12 nautical miles from the baselines of the United States determined in accordance with international law.

** Reprinted by permission of the American Society of International Law.

*** [Reproduced from U.S. Weekly Compilation of Presidential Documents, Volume 24, Number 52 (January 2, 1989), p. 1661. The 1982 United Nations Convention on the Law of the Sea as in Doc.Supp.].

In accordance with international law, as reflected in the applicable provisions of the 1982 United Nations Convention on the Law of the Sea, within the territorial sea of the United States, the ships of all countries enjoy the right of innocent passage and the ships and aircraft of all countries enjoy the right of transit passage through international straits.

Nothing in this Proclamation:

(a) extends or otherwise alters existing Federal or State law or any jurisdiction, rights, legal interests, or obligations derived therefrom; or

(b) impairs the determination, in accordance with international law, of any maritime boundary of the United States with a foreign jurisdiction.

In Witness Whereof, I have hereunto set my hand this twenty-seventh day of December, in the year of our Lord nineteen hundred and eighty-eight, and of the Independence of the United States of America the two hundred and thirteenth.

/s/ Ronald Reagan

4.　FOREIGN VESSELS IN THE TERRITORIAL SEA
CORFU CHANNEL CASE (UNITED KINGDOM v. ALBANIA)

International Court of Justice, 1949.
[1949] I.C.J.Rep. 4, 28.

[On May 5, 1946, British cruisers were fired upon by an Albanian battery while passing through the Corfu Channel, which, on that date, was clear of minefields. "The government of the United Kingdom protested on the ground that innocent passage through straits was a right recognized by international law. The government of Albania answered that neither foreign naval vessels, nor foreign merchant vessels, had a right under international law to pass through Albanian territorial waters without prior notification to, and permission of, the Albanian authorities."

On October 22, 1946, a squadron of British naval vessels proceeded through the Corfu Channel without the permission of the Albanian authorities and in the passage two destroyers were heavily damaged by mines, with loss of life.

By special agreement, the parties submitted questions to the International Court of Justice, one of which was whether the acts of the Royal Navy on October 22, 1946, violated the sovereignty of Albania.

The court dealt with the question as follows:]

The Court will now consider the Albanian contention that the United Kingdom Government violated Albanian sovereignty by sending the warships through this Strait without the previous authorization of the Albanian Government.

It is, in the opinion of the Court, generally recognized and in accordance with international custom that states in time of peace have a right to send their warships through straits used for international navigation between two parts of the high seas without the previous authorization of a coastal state, provided that the passage is innocent. Unless otherwise prescribed in an international convention, there is no right for a coastal state to prohibit such passage through straits in time of peace.

The Albanian Government does not dispute that the North Corfu Channel is a strait in the geographical sense; but it denies that this Channel belongs to the class of international highways through which a right of passage exists, on the grounds that it is only of secondary Nations Convention on the Law of the Sea deals with it in Articles 17–32. [For both texts, see the Documentary Supplement.]

Some of the articles in the United Nations Convention deal with matters not covered in the 1958 text. Article 21, for example, is new in providing a list of the matters with respect to which a coastal state may enact laws and regulations applicable to foreign vessels in innocent passage. So is Article 22, which specifies a coastal state may establish sea lanes and traffic separation schemes in the territorial sea and lists the factors it must take into account in so doing. Article 23 is also new in dealing with foreign nuclear-powered vessels and vessels carrying nuclear or other dangerous substances.

Other articles incorporate principles already in the 1958 text, but expand them by elaborating their meaning or application in great detail. Such is the case with Article 19. It repeats paragraph 4 of Article 14 in the 1958 text: "Passage is innocent so long as it is not prejudicial to the peace, good order or security of the coastal state." Then it goes on to give a list of 12 activities which will render the passage prejudicial if engaged in by a foreign vessel in the territorial sea.

The net effect of such additions and expansions may be to give coastal states more control over foreign vessels in innocent passage than granted in the 1958 Convention.

––––––––

ANAND, TRANSIT PASSAGE AND OVERFLIGHT IN INTERNATIONAL STRAITS

26 Indian Journal of International Law 72, 91–95 (1986).*

* * *

The United States representative said in Sub-committee of the Seabed Committee that "in addition to the importance of sea navigation for their international trade, many states depended upon air and sea mobility in order to exercise their inherent right of individual and collective self-defence". He pointed out that "the security of the United States and its allies depended to a very large extent on the freedom of

* Reprinted by permission of the Indian
Society of International Law.

navigation and on the overflight of the high seas. More extensive territorial seas, without the right to free transit of straits, would threaten that security". The United States maintained that the invulnerability of its nuclear missile submarines (SSBNs)—currently the Polaris/Poseidon fleet—and hence their indispensable role in an adequate second strike force depended on their right to pass through straits submerged and unannounced. In the U.S. view, the right of free transit through straits was "an indispensable adjunct to the freedom of navigation and that of overflight on the high seas themselves". Moreover, the regime of innocent passage provided for in the 1958 Convention on the Territorial Sea was "inadequate when applied to international straits" because it was a subjective standard subject to abuse. Some states, he said, had in fact claimed that certain types of passage—by nuclear-powered ships and super tankers—should be considered as non-innocent per se.

The United States made it clear time and again that it would not accept any extension of the territorial sea from three miles to twelve miles unless the right of *free passage* through international straits was accepted. It demanded freedom of unobstructed passage for warships, including nuclear submarines, on the surface or submerged, without notification and irrespective of mission. Further, it wanted freedom of civilian and military flights through the superjacent airspace. All these rights were claimed not only in those straits that were wider than six miles and were supposed to have, at least theoretically, a corridor of high seas in their midst, but in *all straits irrespective of their breadth or importance.*

The United States was willing to accept and "observe reasonable traffic safety and marine pollution regulations"; regulations that were "consistent with the basic right of transit". The safety standards to be applied in straits, however, should be established by international agreement and should not be unilaterally imposed by the coastal state.

As to the free transit of aircraft, the United States stated that civil aircraft already enjoyed transit rights over national territory of other states, under the Convention on International Civil Aviation and the International Air Service Transit Agreement. But such rights were not available to state aircraft. The United States demanded a right of free transit for all aircraft over straits, but also stated that such aircraft need not be routed over the strait itself but, at the coastal state's discretion, could be directed through "suitable corridors over land areas".

The United States was supported on this issue not only by the western maritime powers, like the United Kingdom, France, West Germany and others but also by the Soviet Union and Communist bloc countries which also insisted that the limited right of "innocent passage" was not sufficient and "had never been and could never be applied to such straits as those of Gibraltar, Dover, Malacca, Singapore and Babel-Mandeb, where freedom of navigation had always been enjoyed." In accordance with these views on 25 July 1972, the Soviet Union proposed "Draft Articles on Straits used for International Navigation".

Although "the coastal state should be given appropriate guarantees of its security and protection against pollution of the waters of its adjacent straits", the Soviet Union, like the United States, was absolutely convinced that "the concept of innocent passage could not be accepted as applying to the principal straits used for international navigation because it was too widely interpreted as a concept giving, so to speak, the last word to the coastal state or states concerned". Refusal to recognize the principle of free passage would mean, according to the Soviet Union, "establishing the domination of only 12 to 15 states adjacent to straits over the passage of vessels of some 130 states of the world". * * *

* * *

Despite all the misgivings and apprehensions of the smaller coastal and strait states * * *, the maritime powers were not prepared to give up their demands. Both the superpowers and their allies left no one in doubt that "unless unimpeded passage on, over and under straits used for international navigation was conceded to all commercial vessels and warships, including submarines, there was simply no possibility of coming to an agreement on the subject of national jurisdiction. * * *

* * * As finally adopted, the Convention provides for a guaranteed non-suspendable transit passage through straits and archipelagic waters, subject only to the power of the coastal state to make certain rules related to navigational safety, pollution, and fishing. For the first time, the Convention provides separate regimes for "innocent passage" through territorial sea, laid down in Part II, Section 3 (Articles 17 to 32), and "Transit Passage," through International Straits, laid down in Part III, Section 2 (Articles 37 to 44), and Section 3 (Article 45), the latter applicable only to special straits. The right of transit passage applies to "straits which are used for international navigation between one part of the high sea or an exclusive economic zone and another part of the high seas or an exclusive economic zone" [Article 37]. But transit passage does not apply to:

(1) Straits formed by an island of a state bordering the strait and its mainland if there exists seaward of the island a route through the high seas or through an EEZ of similar convenience with respect to navigational and hydrographical characteristics [Article 38(1)].

(2) Straits used for international navigation between one area of the high seas or an EEZ and the territorial sea of a foreign state [Article 45(1)(b)].

For these two categories the right of "innocent passage" is deemed sufficient which however cannot be suspended [Article 45(2)].

Transit passage is defined as: "the exercise in accordance with this part of the freedom of navigation and overflight solely for the purpose of continuous and expeditious transit of the strait between one part of the high seas or an EEZ and another part of the high seas or an EEZ. However, the requirement of continuous and expeditious transit does not preclude passage through the strait for the purpose of entering, leaving or returning from a state bordering the strait, subject to the conditions of entry to that state [Art. 38(2)]."

Article 39 lays down the duties of ships and aircraft while exercising the right of transit passage, such as, to (1) proceed without delay through or over the strait; (2) refrain from use of force against the sovereignty, integrity or independence of the bordering states, or in any manner in violation of the principles of international law; (3) refrain from any activities other than those incidental to their normal modes of continuous and expeditious transit unless rendered necessary by force majeure or by distress.

* * *

World straits.   There are at least 120 straits in the world 24 miles in width, or less.   Thus the universal adoption of 12 miles as the breadth of the territorial sea would place the waters in all such straits under the national jurisdiction of bordering states, subject only to a right of innocent passage.   Transit through many of these straits is not important for international traffic, but transit through certain of them is essential for international maritime commerce and crucial for global deployment of naval power.

In preparation for the 1958 Geneva Conference on the Law of the Sea, the Secretariat of the United Nations made a study of straits constituting routes for international traffic which would be affected should 12 miles become the breadth of the territorial sea.   The study listed 33.   I United Nations Conference on the Law of the Sea 114 (1958).

The Office of the Geographer of the United States Department of State has issued a chart entitled World Straits Affected by a 12 Mile Territorial Sea on which there appears the notation: "Capitalization used to denote major straits from other and minor straits."   From this notation, Pirtle infers that the straits whose names are in capitals are of strategic significance to the security of the United States.   Transit Rights and U.S. Security Interests in International Straits: The "Straits Debate" Revisited, 5 Ocean Development and International Law 477, 488 (1978).   These straits include some straits not listed in the United Nations study.[a]

---

a. The United Nations study lists the following straits: Bab el Mandeb, Gibraltar, Zanzibar Channel, The Serpent's Mouth, The Dragon's Mouth, St. Lucia Channel, Strait between St. Lucia and St. Vincent, Dominica Channel, Straits between Dominica and Guadeloupe, Magellan, Juan de Fuca, Chosen, Hainan, Palk, Malacca, Ombae, Soenda, San Bernardino, Surigao, Hormuz, St. George's Channel (Bismarck Archipelago), Cook, Foveaux, Kaiwi Channel, Dover, Canal de Menorca, Messina, Bonifa-

cio, The Dardanelles, Sea of Marmara and the Bosphorus, Kithera, Carphatos, The Sound and Singapore Strait.

Pirtle lists the 16 straits of strategic importance to the United States as follows: West Korean, Malacca, Sunca, Lombok, Ombae, West Bering, Juan de Fuca, Old Bahamas Channel, Dominica Channel, Martinique Channel, St. Lucia Channel, St. Vincent Passage, Gibraltar, Bab el Mandeb, Hormuz.

PUBLIC PROSECUTOR v. KAIRISMAA

Sweden, Court of Appeal of Svea, 1960.
Supreme Court, 1960.
32 Int'l L.Rep. 117 (1966).*

The Facts. Kairismaa, a Finnish citizen, was charged before the City Court of Stockholm with, inter alia, obtaining a loan of 1,000 Swedish crowns from another Finnish citizen, Stjernvall, superintendent on the Finnish ship the Bore II, by fraudulently alleging that he needed the money immediately for a business transaction concerning an automobile and that he would repay it later the same day. The Public Prosecutor alleged that the crime had been committed within Swedish territorial waters. The City Court having found the defendant guilty, he appealed. Referring to the fact that the ship was Finnish, that both he himself and Stjernvall were Finnish citizens, and claiming that the transaction had taken place while the Bore II was outside Swedish territorial waters, the defendant urged the Appeal Court to reject the present part of the charge.

Held (by the Court of Appeal of Svea): that the appeal must fail and the judgment of the Court below must be confirmed. [The Court said:]

> * * * It has been made clear [however], chiefly by the evidence given by Stjernvall before the City Court, that the transaction had taken place after the ship's entry into the Stockholm archipelago. As the Bore II—which plies in regular passenger traffic between Stockholm and Helsinki—thus at the time when the act was committed was in Swedish territorial waters, the Court of Appeal finds that the act shall be deemed to have taken place within the country. Under Chapter 1, Article 2, paragraph 1, of the Penal Code, a Swedish Court is consequently competent to consider the present part of the charge.

Kairismaa applied for permission to appeal to the Supreme Court and urged that Court to reject the charge. * * *

* * *

Kairismaa also contended that it was not clear from the reasons given by the Court of Appeal for its judgment whether the present charge could be brought in Sweden on the sole ground that, at the time when the crime was committed, the ship was in Swedish territorial waters, or whether a second condition was required, namely, that the ship be plying in regular traffic between a Swedish and a foreign port. * * * It was true that the principle applied by the Court of Appeal had been expressed earlier, in cases concerning crimes by Swedish citizens. * * * It was much more natural, however, to consider a crime committed against an alien on a foreign ship within Swedish territorial waters as a matter of Swedish concern when committed by a Swede than when it was committed by an alien. * * *

* Reprinted with the permission of the Editor of the International Law Reports.

Held (by the Supreme Court): that the application for permission to appeal must be rejected. The Court found no reason to alter the decision of the City Court. Accordingly, the judgment of the Court of Appeal must be affirmed.

———

1. *Amendment of Swedish law subsequent to decision.* The decision appears to have been the cause of an amendment to the Swedish code of criminal law which went into effect on January 1, 1965. Under this amendment, special permission from the executive is required before prosecution is initiated for an offense committed by an alien aboard a foreign vessel in Swedish territory and affecting another alien or alien interests. The amendment is reported in a note at the end of a comment on the case by Eek, Chronique de Jurisprudence Suédoise Relative au Droit International Privé 1960–1964, 93 Journal du Droit International 410 (1965–1966).

2. *Jurisdiction over merchant vessels in innocent passage under 1958 Convention and U.N. Convention.* As to criminal jurisdiction, see in the Documentary Supplement Article 19 of the 1958 Convention on the Territorial Sea and the Contiguous Zone and Article 27 of the United Nations Convention on the Law of the Sea. As to civil jurisdiction, see Article 20 of the former and Article 28 of the latter.

———

SECTION D. WATERS BEYOND THE TERRITORIAL SEA

———

1. FREEDOM OF NAVIGATION

———

THE PRINCIPLE
NEGROPONTE,[a] WHO WILL PROTECT THE FREEDOM OF THE SEAS?

United States Department of State, Bureau of Public Affairs,
Current Policy No. 855.

* * *

The world's oceans are vital to mankind in diverse ways. We are just beginning to understand their environmental significance. We have always used their fishery resources. We have begun to learn how to exploit some of their other resources. And through the centuries the world's oceans have been essential as waterways, and now airways, necessary to preserve the peace and to move world trade and commerce.

The freedom of use of the world's marine waters is what we mean by the freedom of the seas. It is perhaps our oldest customary international law doctrine.

———

a. At the time—July 21, 1986—he gave the speech, John D. Negroponte was the Assistant Secretary of State for Oceans and International Environmental and Scientific Affairs, in the U.S. Department of State.

The freedom of the seas was not given to mankind. It was won—won through scholarly and legal debate and in naval engagements. Over the years, the freedom of the seas has undergone some changes and refinements. Its exercise has become geographically compressed; its composition has been broken into fragments, and some of those have been lost. So, today, when we speak of the freedom of the seas, we mean, primarily, the freedom of movement on the world's seas and oceans by navies and maritime commerce: the freedom to navigate and to fly from one continent to another over broad expanses; the freedom to navigate and to fly from one sea to another through even the narrowest of straits.

Without the freedom of the seas, the world would be a different place. Maritime commerce as we know it would not exist. The global balance of power would be unalterably shifted.

* * *

AGREEMENT ALLOWING U.S. AUTHORITIES TO SEIZE BRITISH FLAG VESSELS OUTSIDE THE TERRITORIAL SEA AND CONTIGUOUS ZONE

21 International Legal Materials 439 (1982).*

Foreign and Commonwealth Office
London SW.1A 2AH, 13 November 1981

His Excellency
The Honourable
John J. Louis Jr.
Embassy of the United States of
America

Your Excellency,

I have the honour to refer to the recent discussions between representatives of our two Governments concerning the desire of the authorities of the United States to take more effective measures to suppress the unlawful importation of cannabis and other narcotic drugs into the United States.

Bearing in mind the special nature of this problem and having regard to the need for international co-operation in suppressing the illicit traffic in narcotic drugs, which is recognised in the Single Convention on Narcotic Drugs of 1961, I have the honour to propose the following:

1. The Government of the United Kingdom of Great Britain and Northern Ireland agree that they will not object to the boarding by the authorities of the United States, outside the limits of the territorial sea

---

* Reprinted by permission of the American Society of International Law from material published at 21 I.L.M. 439 under the title "United Kingdom: Letters to U.S. Concerning Measures to Suppress the Unlawful Importation of Narcotic Drugs into the United States."

and contiguous zone of the United States and within the areas described in paragraph 9 below, of private vessels under the British flag in any case in which those authorities reasonably believe that the vessel has on board a cargo of drugs for importation into the United States in violation of the laws of the United States.

2. On boarding the vessel the authorities of the United States may address enquiries to those on board, examine the ship's papers and take such other measures as are necessary to establish the place of registration of the vessel. When these measures suggest that an offence against the laws of the United States relative to the importation of narcotic drugs is being committed, the Government of the United Kingdom agree that they will not object to the authorities of the United States instituting a search of the vessel.

3. If the authorities of the United States then believe that an offence against the laws referred to in paragraph 2 above is being committed, the Government of the United Kingdom agree that they will not object to the vessel being seized and taken into a United States port.

4. The Government of the United Kingdom may, within 14 days of the vessel's entry into port, object to the continued exercise of United States jurisdiction over the vessel for purposes of the laws referred to in paragraph 2 above, and the Government of the United States shall thereupon release the vessel without charge. The Government of the United States shall not institute forfeiture proceedings before the end of the period allowed for objection.

5. The Government of the United Kingdom may, within 30 days of the vessel's entry into port, object to the prosecution of any United Kingdom national found on board the vessel, and the Government of the United States shall thereupon release such person. The Government of the United Kingdom agree that they will not otherwise object to the prosecution of any person found on board the vessel.

6. Any action by the authorities of the United States shall be taken in accordance with this Agreement and United States law.

7. In any case where a vessel under the British flag is boarded the authorities of the United States shall promptly inform the authorities of the United Kingdom of the action taken and shall keep them fully informed of any subsequent developments.

8. If any loss or injury is suffered as a result of any action taken by the United States in contravention of these arrangements or any improper or unreasonable action taken by the United States pursuant thereto, representatives of the two Governments shall meet at the request of either to decide any question relating to compensation. Representatives of the two Governments shall in any case meet from time to time to review the working of these arrangements.

9. The areas referred to in paragraph 1 above comprise the Gulf of Mexico, the Caribbean Sea, that portion of the Atlantic Ocean West of longitude 55° West and South of latitude 30° North and all other areas within 150 miles of the Atlantic coast of the United States.

10. I have the honour to suggest that if the foregoing proposals are acceptable to the Government of the United States, this Note and Your Excellency's confirmatory reply shall constitute an Agreement between the Government of the United Kingdom of Great Britain and Northern Ireland and the Government of the United States which shall enter into force on the date of your reply. It may be terminated by either Government on one month's notice but will continue to remain effective in respect of any proceedings based on action taken during its validity.

Accept, Excellency, the renewed assurance of my highest consideration. (For the Secretary of State)

———

Status of vessels on the high seas under 1958 Convention and U.N. Convention. Article 6 of the 1958 Convention on the High Seas and Article 92 of the United Nations Convention on the Law of the Sea both provide that vessels on the high seas are under the exclusive jurisdiction of the state of their flag.

———

Solution to pirate broadcasting in Article 109 of U.N. Convention in Doc. Supp. which allows arrest of individuals and seize vessels engaged in pirate broadcasting.

———

THE CONTIGUOUS ZONE
IN RE MARTINEZ

Italy, Court of Cassation, 1959.
28 Int'l L.Rep. 170 (1963).*

The Facts. [Article 2 of the Italian Maritime Code fixed the limit of territorial waters at six miles from the coast. Article 33 of the Customs Law of September 25, 1940, on the other hand, provide[d] that Italy shall be entitled to exercise jurisdiction over a further six-mile zone for the purpose of preventing and punishing smuggling along the Italian coast. This latter zone is referred to as the "zone of vigilance" (contiguous zone).] The appellants, who were foreign nationals, were convicted of smuggling in the following circumstances: while their vessel was at a distance of nine miles from the coast, warning shots were fired, and upon these shots being ignored the vessel was pursued and ultimately captured at a distance of 54 miles from the coast. The appellants appealed their conviction and contended that Article 24 of the Geneva Convention of 1958 on the Territorial Sea and the Contiguous Zone was declaratory of existing customary international law and accordingly a coastal State, while entitled to prevent customs offences from being

———

* Reprinted with the permission of the
Editor of the International Law Reports.

committed in the contiguous zone, was not entitled to exercise jurisdiction and inflict punishment in respect of such offences; that jurisdiction could only be exercised if an offence had actually been committed within the territorial sea, and therefore Article 33 of the Customs Law was contrary to Article 10 of the Italian Constitution, which provided that Italian law must be consistent with international law. * * *

[Article 24 provides in part:

1. In a zone of the high seas contiguous to its territorial sea, the coastal state may exercise the control necessary to:

(a) Prevent infringement of its customs, fiscal, immigration or sanitary regulations within its territory or territorial sea;

(b) Punish infringement of the above regulations committed within its territory or territorial sea.]

Held: that the appeal must be dismissed: * * *

The contention that Article 33 of the Customs Law is contrary to the Constitution is misconceived and has been rejected by the judgment under appeal. It is undoubtedly true that the rule laid down in Article 10 of the Constitution, according to which Italian law must comply with generally recognized rules of international law, ensures the compatibility of Italian municipal law with international law, viz., with the duties imposed upon the State by international law, so that rules of municipal law which are contrary to international law must be eliminated. However, in order for this to be so, it is necessary for the rules of international law to be generally recognized, and it is admitted on behalf of the defendants that the Geneva Convention, which has been signed by Italy, is not yet in force.

It is not true that Article 24 of the Convention constitutes a customary rule of international law governing the delimitation of the territorial sea in the sense that the sovereignty of the coastal State is limited to the territorial sea itself, without being capable of being extended over the contiguous zone when smuggling has occurred in the latter and not in the territorial sea. No such rule can be said to have been generally accepted in international law. In substance custom is a manifestation of social life which hardens by means of constant and uniform repetition of certain acts on the part of States or individuals, extending over a period of time, to which municipal law attributes legal relevance. In the international field this presupposes the existence of a substantive element, namely, the constant repetition of certain rules of conduct between States, and a psychological element, namely, the conviction that such conduct is obligatory for everybody, so that others can insist upon it, and which does not depend on purely subjective judgment. Only then can custom be a source of law equal to municipal law.

* * *

It is contended on behalf of the defendants that the [International Law] Commission was set up for the progressive development and codification of international law, and that when preparing the report on which the Convention is based it investigated substantially the rules of customary international law. This, it is argued, shows that these rules existed prior to codification, which was merely intended to lay down in codified form what was already custom. Hence the wording of the rule contained in Article 24 of the Convention, which is said to be a faithful reproduction of a pre-existing customary rule which as such is generally recognized and must be considered, by virtue of Article 10 of the Constitution, as having been automatically incorporated in Italian law, and which must not be contrary to the rule laid down in that article.

* * * [T]his rule cannot be said to be a generally recognized rule of customary international law because the rule relating to the width of the territorial sea is still under discussion between States. States apply different rules according to their respective municipal laws, which fact in itself precludes recognition of any pre-existing custom in the matter. In fact, although the Conference on the Law of the Sea was successful in defining a number of rules governing the matter under discussion, it left unsolved the problem of the width of the territorial sea, as can be seen from the preparatory work of the Conference. The disagreement was due to different contrasting views put forward by participating States, one group being in favour of the three-mile limit for territorial waters, as in the past, another holding the opposite view and applying various criteria to the actual width of the territorial sea, without affirming a right to twelve miles. Although various proposals were put forward to reconcile the opposing wishes of States, no positive solution was found. Accordingly, * * * the rule contained in Article 24 of the Convention existed previously as a generally recognized customary rule when the conditions surrounding the delimitation of the territorial sea and the contiguous zone were very different from those contained in that article and when agreement could not be reached. * * *

In fact, not all States have accepted the three-mile limit, which in the past represented a compromise between States: Norway and Sweden have fixed the limit of their territorial sea at four miles; Spain, Portugal, Yugoslavia, Italy and other countries at six, while Bulgaria, the Soviet Union, Communist China, Egypt, Ethiopia, Rumania and Guatemala have fixed it at twelve miles, and Chile and other countries at two hundred. Italy, on the other hand, has not accepted the limit of the contiguous zone in the form in which it is expressed in Article 24. The rules of municipal law of coastal States have therefore remained in force. In Italy it is the rule laid down in Article 33 of the Customs Law, which cannot be said to be contrary to Article 10 of the Constitution. It follows that the offence of smuggling committed in the zone of vigilance, the so-called contiguous zone, is punishable in Italy, and that the arrest of a foreign national is lawful by Article 137 of the Customs Law. Equally lawful is the pursuit of a foreign vessel. * * *

The appellants contend that as Article 2 of the Maritime Code fixes the limit of the territorial sea at six miles from the coast and provides that this is without prejudice to various legal provisions which are to apply in specific cases, the only purpose of the Code was to lay down a six-mile limit for the territorial sea, reserving the right to extend the limit for specific purposes other than sovereignty, and less extensive than the latter. Accordingly, the zone of vigilance provided for by

Article 33 of the Customs Law as being between six and twelve miles is not the territorial sea but merely an area of the sea which is subject to control for the purpose of prevention only and not punishment. Although in theory it may seem as if in the contiguous zone only police and preventive measures may be taken, because this zone forms part of the open sea rather than the territorial sea, a different view must be taken when one considers that the draft code of the Institute of International Law on the contiguous zone clearly recognizes the right to exercise jurisdiction. The International Law Commission, in its 1953 report was decidedly in favour of acknowledging the right to exercise jurisdiction, while in its 1951 draft it merely referred to preventive measures.

* * *

1. *Contraband outside the customs zone.* A British vessel transferred contraband goods to an Italian vessel outside the Italian 12 mile customs zone. An Italian coast guard crew boarded the British vessel on the high seas and arrested its crew. The Supreme Court of Italy ordered the release of the British crew on the ground that a state cannot exercise its jurisdiction over foreign vessels on the high seas, save in the exceptional case of hot pursuit. Re McSporran et al.; SS Sito, Court of Cassation, 1957, 89 J. de Dr. Int'l. 229 (1962).

2. *Contiguous zone under 1958 Convention and U.N. Convention.* Article 33 of the United Nations Convention reproduces verbatim Article 24 of the 1958 Convention on the Territorial Sea and the Contiguous Zone, except that it extends the breadth of the contiguous zone to 24 miles from the baseline, instead of the 12 miles provided in the 1958 Convention.

HOT PURSUIT
RE PULOS AND OTHERS

Italy, Tribunal of Naples, 1976.
3 Italian Yearbook of International Law 282, 286 (1977).*

* * * On 11 November 1976 the vessel "Olimpios Hermes", flying the Greek flag, left the port of Antwerp carrying 25,000 cartons of cigarettes. * * * The voyage was regular until the Straits of Gibraltar were navigated after which, from 16 November there is no further entry in the log-book or the radio-telephone journal: the vessel was surprised on the morning of 29 November 1976 off the coast of the island of Ischia, 27 miles at 220 degrees from Punta Imperatore (this is clear from the file), that is on the high seas, surrounded by some 20 motor-boats whilst another 12 motor-boats were further away and nearer the land which was some 15 miles distant.

* Reprinted by permission of Editoriale Scientifica, s.r.l., Naples.

* * * It must be held established that one of the said motor-boats was carrying from the "Olimpios Hermes" 80 cartons of cigarettes (it should have taken 100 cartons but evidently the arrival of the Guardia di Finanza interrupted the operation).

* * * It is also clear from the file that after the motor-boat had taken on board the said cigarettes it fled despite the orders of the servicemen to stop; however, pursued without interruption first by helicopters and then by coastguards and the patrol boat of the Guardia di Finanza, it sailed initially towards the coast, returning, however, amongst the other motor-boats which were still in the vicinity of the vessel, and endeavoured, by reckless manoeuvres entailing a risk of collision, to hinder the pursuing craft and finally turned again towards the coast; it was captured in territorial waters (10 miles at 220 degrees from Punta Imperatore, Ischia) after the discharge of 70 rounds from light machine guns, some of which damaged the driving gear of the two 350 HP engines of the motor-boat. Thereafter the naval unit notified the capture of the motor-boat in territorial waters to the coastguard vessels Guglielmi and Di Sessa which were lying near the "Olimpios Hermes"; the latter was slowly moving away in a south-south-west direction and the coastguards called upon it to stop by visual and auditory signals and ultimately by hailing; when this proved fruitless the "Olimpios Hermes" was boarded 28 miles at 220 degrees from Punta Imperatore, that is on the high seas, the remainder of the cargo of cigarettes was seized and the persons on board the vessel were arrested. It was subsequently established that the contraband cigarettes carried by the "Olimpios Hermes", part of which had already been unloaded and part of which was about to be unloaded whilst on the high seas to the motor-boats for transshipment to the coast, had been sold in advance in Naples by a person or persons unknown to the prosecution.

* * * To that extent, since it is clear from the file that the police operation against the motor-boat which was captured, concerned an Italian-registered craft, with Italian nationals on board and moreover ended in Italian territorial waters following the said commission of the crime of smuggling 800 kg of foreign cigarettes, it merely remains to consider the lawfulness of that operation since the defence for the accused contests this point because, so far as the "Olimpios Hermes" is concerned, it constitutes the seizure of a foreign vessel on the high seas.

Italian criminal legislation covers all persons, apart from exceptions concerning so-called immunity, whether nationals or foreign, who are on the territory of the state (Art. 3, para. 1, c.p.), that is the territory of the Republic of Italy and accordingly all other places subject to the sovereignty thereof, including Italian vessels or aircraft wherever they may be, apart from exceptions created by international law (Art. 4, para. 2, c.p.). The sovereign right of the State covers the territorial waters up to 12 miles from the coast * * *.

Beyond the territorial waters lies the open sea or high seas. It is precisely the absence of State sovereignty over the area of sea lying beyond the territorial waters which creates the principle of the freedom of such seas which, as it is expressed in Article 2 of the Geneva

Convention of 29 April 1958 on the High Seas, are open "to all nations" * * * and are guaranteed for the use of all States (for navigation, use of the resources and any other freedom acknowledged by the general principles of international law).

Upon this is based the further principle of international law, whether customary or conventional—Art. 6 of the said Geneva Convention—, which has also been adopted in municipal legislation (in the case of Italy in Art. 4 c.p. and Art. 4 c. nav.) whereby ships sailing on high seas come under the exclusive jurisdiction of the State whose flag they fly, save in exceptional cases expressly provided for in international law. Naturally the principle of freedom of the high seas is not without its limits since it is subject to derogations and restrictions on the basis of international customary law and international agreements. * * *

[The court said one limit was the right of a state to repress smuggling and the mother ship had engaged in smuggling through the use of small boats to take the cigarettes ashore.]

The other (specific) limit to the principle in question is that concerning the right of pursuit whereby the coastal State may pursue and seize on the high seas foreign civil vessels which are guilty of infringements of its legislation on internal waters or territorial waters. It must be held that this right is established first of all on the basis of international customary law, as is clear from its usual application in international disputes (in which the disputes were chiefly settled on the basis of the conduct of the State concerned in the exercise of that right) or in the replies given in this connexion by States in the course of the travaux préparatoires for the Hague Codification Conference of 1930; these States, by providing unanimously an affirmative answer to the questions drawn up by the League of Nations and arriving easily at agreement on the wording of Art. II of Appendix No. I to the Report of the second Commission which was systematizing the right, merely noted the existence of that custom for the purpose of establishing its details, prescribing limits to prevent abuses of it.

The same conclusions were reached in substance by the Geneva Conference on the High Seas which repeated at Art. 23 the old principles whilst extending their scope (by providing in the contiguous zone for pursuit by aircraft, that the ship or aircraft need not also be in territorial waters, that the ship or aircraft undertaking the arrest need not be that which initiated the pursuit where boats are operating as a team). In sum it may be stated that with regard to the right of pursuit, Art. 23 of the Geneva Convention, whilst going beyond the scope of the Codification Conference of 1930, is nevertheless narrower than the rules of the relevant customary international law where no specific limits are laid down, which indicates that States are tending to return to a broad conception of the right in order to provide better protection for their national interests which are increasingly threatened by well-trained and highly organised groups of criminals.

The said Art. 23 in fact lays down that foreign civil vessels may be arrested on the high seas if the following conditions are met:

(1) The laws and regulations of the coastal state were infringed;

(2) The vessel itself, or one of its boats, or other craft working as a team and using the said vessel as a mother ship was within the internal waters, territorial waters or the contiguous zone;

(3) Pursuit, begun in territorial waters or the contiguous zone and continued on the high seas, was uninterrupted, although the pursuing craft may have changed;

(4) Visual or auditory signals, which can be seen or heard, conveying an order to halt were given;

(5) Pursuit was given by warships or military aircraft, or other ships or aircraft on government service especially authorized to that effect.

With regard to the first condition it has been established above that there was an infringement of the customs legislation of the coastal State, Italy. The foreign vessel stationed itself near the boundary of the Italian territorial waters, following the sale in advance in Naples of the entire cargo of foreign cigarettes with which it was laden, and supplied those cigarettes to the numerous motor-boats which came from the coast to which they transshipped the cigarettes, in breach of customs legislation, until the arrival of the Guardia di Finanza cut short the unloading.

With regard to the second condition it is established that the vessel was supplying from its cargo the said motor-boats which, drawn up in a queue and in groups alongside the vessel (as is clear from the photographs taken from the helicopters), transshipped, or intended to transship, to the shore to the purchasers. The foreign vessel accordingly acted as the mother ship to those boats by furnishing the latter with the relevant materials, that is the cigarettes, which the boats took to the destination and then returned for more until the vessel was completely unloaded. * * * It may be inferred from the foregoing that those boats operated as a team with the vessel. The whole unloading and subsequent transshipment to the coast, organised by a buyer and sellers unknown, by their agents and by the person in charge of the vessel, with the assistance of the skippers of the motor-boats shows clearly that all those persons acted in concert for the same purpose namely to convey the cigarettes to the shore in breach of Italian customs legislation. This constitutes working as a team and in pursuance of the rule in question the situation is the same as if the vessel itself had entered the territory of the State in order to unload the cigarettes. * * *

With regard to the third condition it has already been shown that after the pursuit of the motor-boat, which carried over into and terminated in the territorial waters, the other craft of the Guardia di Finanza immediately began continuous pursuit of the foreign vessel which soon terminated in the seizure of the vessel on the high seas through which it had been slowly proceeding. It is quite clear that no relevance in the present case can attach to the fact that pursuit of the motor-boat began on the high seas (it nevertheless continued in the territorial waters where it also terminated) in that, since the boat in question was Italian, pursuit and any capture which took place on the high seas was entirely lawful. Accordingly, commencement of pursuit in the territorial waters constituted the precise circumstance permitting the pursuers to hold that they had obtained fulfilment of the condition for "extending" the right of pursuit to the foreign vessel on the high seas.

With regard to the fourth and fifth conditions it has been shown that they were fully complied with since visual and auditory signals were given to halt and the pursuit was carried out by the military craft of the Guardia di Finanza. * * *

---

1. *Hot pursuit under 1958 Convention and U.N. Convention.* The provisions of Article 23 of the Geneva Convention on the High Seas are extended mutatis mutandis by Article 111 of the United Nations Convention to violations in the exclusive economic zone or on the continental shelf.

2. *Use of force in hot pursuit.* In 1977 a local union in Nantes, France, opposed the departure of a merchant vessel flying the Panamanian flag in a dispute over the wages paid the crew. It sailed down the estuary of the Loire river and to sea without taking a pilot aboard as required by law. The pursuit was begun by a small boat of the customs service and taken up by a submarine chaser. After ordering it to stop and firing warning shots, the submarine chaser fired machine gun bursts in the hull above the water, which were ignored. Thereupon the submarine chaser "deeming the infraction not serious enough to risk sinking the vessel," gave up the pursuit and the vessel escaped to the high seas. 81 Revue Générale de Droit International Public 1161–1162 (1977). Compare the case of *The I'm Alone, infra.*

RIGHT OF APPROACH AND VISIT
RIGHT OF APPROACH
4 Whiteman, Digest of International Law 667 (1965).

The right of any ship to fly a particular flag must obviously be subject to verification by proper authority, and from this it follows that warships have a general right to verify the nationality of any merchant ship which they may meet on the high seas. This "right of approach" (*vérification du pavillon* or *reconnaissance*) is the only qualification under customary law of the general principle which forbids any interference in time of peace with ships of another nationality upon the high seas. Any other act of interference (apart from the repression of piracy) must be justified under powers conferred by treaty. Provided that the merchant vessel responds by showing her flag the captain of the warship is not justified in boarding her or taking any further action, unless there is reasonable ground for suspecting that she is engaged in piracy or some other improper activity. In the absence of good cause for suspicion his government may have to accept substantial responsibility for any interference. If the vessel approached shows a foreign flag even suspicious conduct will not justify active interference except in those cases, such as slave trading, where it is authorized by treaty. Otherwise the captain should merely report the incident to superior authority so that further action, if deemed necessary, may be taken through diplomatic channels.

In the past the question of the right of approach has been the subject of some controversy and has occasionally given rise to friction. Under modern conditions the general use of wireless and other developments have made the matter one of very small importance. Smith, The Law and Custom of the Sea (1959) 64–65.

———

Right of visit under 1958 Convention and U.N. Convention. See in the Documentary Supplement Article 22 of the 1958 Convention on the High Seas and Article 110 of the United Nations Convention on the Law of the Sea.

Note on Naval Incidents In and Near Territorial Waters

Naval people have a natural and understandable professional interest in getting in as close as feasible under the circumstances to the shoreside and operating bases of other naval powers. In modern times this interest has been whetted by the development of electronic and other sensing gear. This professional interest is served by the development of clear and widely-accepted rules about foreign naval presence in particular offshore zones, especially that of the territorial sea. All naval powers, including the United States, welcomed the specificity of the 1982 United Nations Convention in this regard, considering the earlier uncertainties resulting from differing views as to the width of the territorial sea. But navies will be navies and, perhaps, sometimes, enter or traverse a foreign territorial sea for reasons that do not appeal to the landside state or come absolutely within the privileges of innocent passage.

The former Soviet Union in a sense responded to its ship's treatment by the U.S. Navy in the incident reported above when in 1988 two small Soviet naval units deliberately bumped two American naval vessels, a cruiser and a destroyer, which had entered Soviet territorial waters in the Black Sea. There was a bit of hull damage; but the Americans left, claiming innocent passage, while the Soviets implied illicit intelligence-gathering and asserted a closed Black Sea. Under the 1982 Convention, the Americans would have been in violation of Article 19 if they had been doing anything specified in paragraph 2 thereof, and if the Convention were in effect and both the USSR and the United States parties thereto. *Mutatis mutandis,* the USSR could not close the Black Sea legally.

Question : Article 19(92)(c) of the Convention is known as the "Pueblo Clause." Why?

For further analysis and useful citations, see Butler, Innocent Passage and the 1982 Convention: The Influence of Soviet Law and Policy, 81 Am.J.Intl.L. 331 (1987).

Question : Assume both Russia and the United States are parties to the Convention and it is in effect. The Executive Officer of the American cruiser in Russian territorial waters is an ardent fisherman and wets a line whilst traversing. What is the legal situation if the Russians should come along-side and order departure?

Questions : What if members of the crew of the U.S. cruiser were ogling bathers on Black Sea beaches, (a) by *"naked"* eyepower; (b) with binoculars? Or, (e) photographing them with telescopic lenses? *Americans are aware, even those who might not have read anything by Tom Clancy, that our coasts have been (are?) observed from offshore, outside the 12 mile limit, and even targeted for nuclear weapons. Have we any legal remedies? If not, should we propose a convention against "offshore eaves-dropping", out to, say 500 to 1000 nautical miles? Why or why not?*

PIRACY

PIRATES RAID SHIP LEASED TO U.S. NAVY

The San Francisco Chronicle, January 31, 1985, p. 1.**

By the Associated Press. A band of pirates boarded an American cargo ship leased to the Navy as it passed through the Strait of Malacca on Tuesday, tying up the ship's master and making off with $19,471 from the ship's safe, the Pentagon said yesterday.

The attack occurred at night off the coast of Indonesia as the Falcon Countess was traveling from Bahrain to Guam, according to the Military Sealift Command. No one was injured, and the ship continued on its route. The assault by the six pirates, who were reported to have been armed with knives and bayonets and traveling in a speedboat, is the second in two years involving a Navy-chartered ship in the Strait of Malacca. The Sealift Arctic was boarded by pirates on Jan. 10, 1983, prompting the Navy to issue instructions calling for guards to be posted when traveling through the area.

The Military Sealift Command said guards had been posted on the Falcon Countess, but their special watch "had just ended as the ship was leaving the 'pirate zone.' "

According to the command, piracy attacks in the area have become almost routine since 1981 and most commercial oil tankers traversing the strait have begun posting guards as well.

The Falcon Countess was traveling at 13 knots at the time of the attack, according to the Pentagon. The pirates apparently used bamboo poles with hooks to climb from their boat onto the ship's stern.

The pirates then rifled the ship's safe, taking $19,471, and threatened and tied up the master, * * *

** Reprinted by permission of the Associated Press.

The ship is chartered to the Military Sealift Command * * *, and was transporting jet fuel and diesel oil under Navy contract.

———

The Achille Lauro Affair. Five Palestinian passengers boarded the Achille Lauro, an Italian cruise liner, while it was in Genoa. On October 7, 1985, they seized the vessel as it proceeded from Alexandria to Port Said. Claiming to be members of the Palestine Liberation Organization, they threatened to kill some of the approximately 450 persons—crew and passengers—aboard unless Israel released fifty Palestinians it held in prison. Israel refused to negotiate. On October 9, Egypt arranged the removal of the terrorists, whereupon it was learned the latter had killed one of the passengers, an American national, Leon Klinghoffer. All these events and their aftermath, including the interception by U.S. military aircraft of a civilian plane believed to be carrying the terrorists, were reported at length by the media. It is discussed further in Chapter 17, infra.

On October 16, the Attorney General of the United States announced the terrorists were being charged with a number of crimes, including piracy. See 24 International Legal Materials 1555 (1985).

Article 15 of the 1958 Convention on the High Seas and Article 101 of the United Nations Convention on the Law of the Sea, both provide:

Piracy consists of the following acts:

(1) Any illegal acts of violence, detention, or any act of depredation, committed for private ends by the crew or the passengers of a private ship * * *, and directed:

(a) On the high seas, against another ship * * *, or against persons or property on board such ship * * *

See the full text, as well as other provisions on piracy, in the two conventions, which appear in the Documentary Supplement.

On the basis of the facts stated above and the law in the documents, was the charge of piracy justified? If so, what is the point of the proposed convention discussed in the material which follows? If not, what could be done?

———

DRAFT CONVENTION ON SUPPRESSION OF
UNLAWFUL ACTS AGAINST VESSELS

Oceans Policy News, December 1986, p. 5.*

A draft convention on "Suppression of Unlawful Acts Against the Safety of Maritime Navigation" was endorsed in principle by the IMO's [a] Council at its 57th session held November 10–14 in London. The

———

* Reprinted by permission of the Council Ocean Law.   **a.** International Maritime Organization.

Council voted to create an ad hoc preparatory commission to discuss the convention further. Submitted to the IMO at the end of September by the governments of Austria, Egypt, and Italy, the draft convention calls upon nations to apply unconditionally the principle *"either to punish or extradite, without exception and without delay"* certain unlawful acts against maritime navigation. The agreement would define offenses to which nations are so committed to include, among others, those involving "seizing of a vessel by force or threat of force or by any other form of intimidation," and those involving "performing or threatening to perform an act of violence against a person on board a ship if that act is likely to endanger the safety of navigation." It also addresses the question of jurisdiction over the offenses by establishing "relevant connecting factors." Jurisdiction would be recognized in: the flag state of the seized vessel; the state in whose territorial sea or archipelagic waters the offense takes place; the state of citizenship or residence of the offender; and the state whose nationals have been seized, threatened, injured, or killed.

The Italian delegate, Professor Luigi Bravo, emphasized the need for such a convention: "[T]he seizure of the S.S. Achille Lauro has demonstrated the existence of a dangerous gap in existing international legislation. In fact, while three universal conventions deal with the safety of air navigation and other conventions of the same type focus on different forms of terrorism, the safety of maritime navigation is not covered by any similar international instrument."

Note: An excellent study of the Law of Piracy is available in Alfred P. Rubin's comprehensive work, THE LAW OF PIRACY (Naval War College 1988); see also the fine article, William R. Casto's, *The Origins of Federal Admiralty Jurisdiction in an Age of Privateers, Smugglers, and Pirates,* 37 Am.J.Leg.Hist. (1993).

---

2. THE EXCLUSIVE ECONOMIC ZONE

UNITED STATES: PROCLAMATION OF AN EXCLUSIVE ECONOMIC ZONE

22 International Legal Materials 461 (1983).*

THE WHITE HOUSE
Office of the Press Secretary fact sheet, March 10, 1983
UNITED STATES OCEANS POLICY

Today the President announced new guidelines for U.S. oceans policy and proclaimed an Exclusive Economic Zone (EEZ) for the United States. This follows his consideration of a senior interagency review of these matters.

* Reprinted by permission of the American Society of International Law.

The EEZ Proclamation confirms U.S. sovereign rights and control over the living and non-living natural resources of the seabed, subsoil and superjacent waters beyond the territorial sea but within 200 nautical miles of the United States coasts. This will include, in particular, new rights over all minerals (such as nodules and sulphide deposits) in the zone that are not on the continental shelf but are within 200 nautical miles. Deposits of polymetallic sulphides and cobalt/manganese crusts in these areas have only been recently discovered and are years away from being commercially recoverable. But they could be a major future source of strategic and other minerals important to the U.S. economy and security.

The EEZ applies to waters adjacent to the United States, the Commonwealth of Puerto Rico, the Commonwealth of the Northern Mariana Islands (consistent with the Covenant and UN Trusteeship Agreement), and United States overseas territories and possessions. The total area encompassed by the EEZ has been estimated to exceed two million square nautical miles.

The President's statement makes clear that the proclamation does not change existing policies with respect to the outer continental shelf and fisheries within the U.S. zone.

Since President Truman proclaimed U.S. jurisdiction and control over the adjacent continental shelf in 1945, the U.S. has asserted sovereign rights for the purpose of exploration and exploitation of the resources of the continental shelf. Fundamental supplementary legislation, the Outer Continental Shelf Lands Act, was passed by Congress in 1953. The President's proclamation today incorporates existing jurisdiction over the continental shelf.

Since 1976 the United States has exercised management and conservation authority over fisheries resources (with the exception of highly migratory species of tuna) within 200 nautical miles of the coasts, under the Magnuson Fishery Conservation and Management Act. The U.S. neither recognizes nor asserts jurisdiction over highly migratory species of tuna. Such species are best managed by international agreements with concerned countries. In addition to confirming the United States sovereign rights over mineral deposits beyond the continental shelf but within 200 nautical miles, the Proclamation bolsters U.S. authority over the living resources of the zone.

The United States has also exercised certain other types of jurisdiction beyond the territorial sea in accordance with international law. This includes, for example, jurisdiction relating to pollution control under the Clean Water Act of 1977 and other laws.

The President has decided not to assert jurisdiction over marine scientific research in the U.S. EEZ. This is consistent with the U.S. interest in promoting maximum freedom for such research. The Department of State will take steps to facilitate access by U.S. scientists to foreign EEZ's under reasonable conditions.

The concept of the EEZ is already recognized in international law and the President's Proclamation is consistent with existing international law. Over 50 countries have proclaimed some form of EEZ; some of these are consistent with international law and others are not.

The concept of an EEZ was developed further in the recently concluded Law of the Sea negotiations and is reflected in that Convention. The EEZ is a maritime area in which the coastal state may exercise certain limited powers as recognized under international law. The EEZ is not the same as the concept of the territorial sea, and is beyond the territorial jurisdiction of any coastal state.

The President's proclamation confirms that, without prejudice to the rights and jurisdiction of the United States in its EEZ, all nations will continue to enjoy non-resource related freedoms of the high seas beyond the U.S. territorial sea and within the U.S. EEZ. This means that the freedom of navigation and overflight and other internationally lawful uses of the sea will remain the same within the zone as they are beyond it.

The President has also established clear guidelines for United States oceans policy by stating that the United States is prepared to accept and act in accordance with international law as reflected in the results of the Law of the Sea Convention that relate to traditional uses of the oceans, such as navigation and overflight. The United States is willing to respect the maritime claims of others, including economic zones, that are consistent with international law as reflected in the Convention, if U.S. rights and freedoms in such areas under international law are respected by the coastal state.

The President has not changed the breadth of the United States territorial sea. It remains at 3 nautical miles. The United States will respect only those territorial sea claims of others in excess of 3 nautical miles, to a maximum of 12 nautical miles, which accord to the U.S. its full rights under international law in the territorial sea.

Unimpeded commercial and military navigation and overflight are critical to the national interest of the United States. The United States will continue to act to ensure the retention of the necessary rights and freedoms.

By proclaiming today a U.S. EEZ and announcing other oceans policy guidelines, the President has demonstrated his commitment to the protection and promotion of U.S. maritime interests in a manner consistent with international law.

United States Oceans Policy
Statement by the President.
March 10, 1983

The United States has long been a leader in developing customary and conventional law of the sea. Our objectives have consistently been to provide a legal order that will, among other things, facilitate peaceful, international uses of the oceans and provide for equitable and effective management and conservation of marine resources. The United States also recognizes that all nations have an interest in these issues.

Last July I announced that the United States will not sign the United Nations Law of the Sea Convention that was opened for signature on December 10. We have taken this step because several major problems in the Convention's deep seabed mining provisions are contrary to the interests and principles of industrialized nations and would not help attain the aspirations of developing countries.

The United States does not stand alone in those concerns. Some important allies and friends have not signed the convention. Even some signatory states have raised concerns about these problems.

However, the convention also contains provisions with respect to traditional uses of the oceans which generally confirm existing maritime law and practice and fairly balance the interests of all states.

Today I am announcing three decisions to promote and protect the oceans interests of the United States in a manner consistent with those fair and balanced results in the Convention and international law.

First, the United States is prepared to accept and act in accordance with the balance of interests relating to traditional uses of the oceans—such as navigation and overflight. In this respect, the United States will recognize the rights of other states in the waters off their coasts, as reflected in the Convention, so long as the rights and freedoms of the United States and others under international law are recognized by such coastal states.

Second, the United States will exercise and assert its navigation and overflight rights and freedoms on a worldwide basis in a manner that is consistent with the balance of interests reflected in the convention. The United States will not, however, acquiesce in unilateral acts of other states designed to restrict the rights and freedoms of the international community in navigation and overflight and other related high seas uses.

Third, I am proclaiming today an Exclusive Economic Zone in which the United States will exercise sovereign rights in living and nonliving resources within 200 nautical miles of its coast. This will provide United States jurisdiction for mineral resources out to 200 nautical miles that are not on the continental shelf. Recently discovered deposits there could be an important future source of strategic minerals.

Within this Zone all nations will continue to enjoy the high seas rights and freedoms that are not resource related, including the freedoms of navigation and overflight. My proclamation does not change existing United States policies concerning the continental shelf, marine mammals, and fisheries, including highly migratory species of tuna which are not subject to United States jurisdiction. The United States will continue efforts to achieve international agreements for the effective management of these species. The proclamation also reinforces this government's policy of promoting the United States fishing industry.

While international law provides for a right of jurisdiction over marine scientific research within such a zone, the proclamation does not assert this right. I have elected not to do so because of the United

States interest in encouraging marine scientific research and avoiding any unnecessary burdens. The United States will nevertheless recognize the right of other coastal states to exercise jurisdiction over marine scientific research within 200 nautical miles of their coasts, if that jurisdiction is exercised reasonably in a manner consistent with international law.

The Exclusive Economic Zone established today will also enable the United States to take limited additional steps to protect the marine environment. In this connection, the United States will continue to work through the International Maritime Organization and other appropriate international organizations to develop uniform international measures for the protection of the marine environment while imposing no unreasonable burdens on commercial shipping.

The policy decisions I am announcing today will not affect the application of existing United States law concerning the high seas or existing authorities of any United States Government agency.

In addition to the above policy steps, the United States will continue to work with other countries to develop a regime, free of unnecessary political and economic restraints, for mining deep seabed minerals beyond national jurisdiction. Deep seabed mining remains a lawful exercise of the freedom of the high seas open to all nations. The United States will continue to allow its firms to explore for and, when the market permits, exploit these resources.

The administration looks forward to working with the Congress on legislation to implement these new policies.

SECTION E. ALLOCATION OF THE RESOURCES OF THE SEABED

---

1. THE CONTINENTAL SHELF

1. Evolution of the doctrine of the continental shelf. President Truman proclaimed on September 28, 1945, that "the natural resources of the subsoil and sea bed of the continental shelf beneath the high seas but contiguous to the coasts of the United States" were regarded by the United States as appertaining to it and "subject to its jurisdiction and control." Thereafter, claims to the resources of the continental shelf were made by a large number of other states. Only thirteen years after the presidential proclamation, the Convention on the Continental Shelf was signed. As of January 1, 1980, 53 states were parties to it. The ready acceptance of the new basis of jurisdiction illustrates the capacity of international law to adapt and change very rapidly when the international community so demands.

After this book was in page proofs, the U.S. signed a treaty entitled, *"Agreement Relating to the Implementation of Part XI of the 1982 U.N. Convention on the Law of the Sea, of December 10, 1982."* This new treaty modifies the implementation of Part XI of the Convention, relating to mineral resources of the high seas. The October 1994 issue of the American Journal of International Law focuses on this recent development in its *Law of the Sea Forum: The 1994 Agreement on Implementation of Part XI of the Convention on the Law of the Sea.* It will include: Bernard Oxman, *The 1994 Agreement and the Convention;* Louis Sohn, *International Law Implications of the 1994 Agreement;* and Jonathan Charney, *Provisional Application of the 1994 Agreement.*

2. *Division of the resources of the continental shelf between the States and the federal government.* In the Submerged Lands Act of May 22, 1953, 67 Stat. 29, the States of the United States were granted rights to the lands which are part of the continental shelf of the United States up to three nautical miles from the coast on the Atlantic and Pacific Oceans, and up to nine nautical miles in the Gulf of Mexico if the states involved could establish an historical claim to such distance. Beyond those limits, the federal government controls the resources of the continental shelf. Outer Continental Shelf Lands Act of August 7, 1953, 67 Stat. 462. The division of the resources does not create an issue of international law, however. The issue is one of domestic law, as illustrated in the following case.

UNITED STATES v. FLORIDA

United States Supreme Court, 1976.
425 U.S. 791, 96 S.Ct. 1840, 48 L.Ed.2d 388.

DECREE

The joint motion for entry of a decree is granted.

For the purpose of giving effect to the decision and opinion of this Court announced in this case on March 17, 1975, 420 U.S. 531, and to the Supplemental Report of the Special Master filed January 26, 1976, it is Ordered, Adjudged, and Decreed as Follows:

As against the State of Florida, the United States is entitled to all the lands, minerals, and other natural resources underlying the Atlantic Ocean more than 3 geographic miles seaward from the coastline of that State and extending seaward to the edge of the Continental Shelf, and the State of Florida is not entitled to any interest in such lands, minerals, and resources. As used in this decree, the term "coastline" means the line of ordinary low water along that portion of the coast which is in direct contact with the open sea and the line marking the seaward limit of inland waters, as determined under the Convention on the Territorial Sea and the Contiguous Zone, 15 U.S.T. (Pt. 2) 1606.

As against the United States, the State of Florida is entitled to all the lands, minerals, and other natural resources underlying the Atlantic Ocean extending seaward from its coastline for a distance of 3 geographic miles, and the United States is not entitled, as against the State of Florida, to any interest in such lands, minerals, or resources, with the exceptions provided by Section 5 of the Submerged Lands Act, 43 U.S.C. § 1313.

As against the State of Florida, the United States is entitled to all the lands, minerals and other natural resources underlying the Gulf of Mexico more than 3 marine leagues from the coastline of that State; the State of Florida is not entitled to any interest in such lands, minerals, and resources. Where the historic coastline of the State of Florida is landward of its coastline, the United States is additionally entitled, as against the State of Florida, to all the lands, minerals, and other natural resources underlying the Gulf of Mexico more than 3 marine leagues from the State's historic coastline (but not less than 3 geographic miles from its coastline), and the State of Florida is not entitled to any interest in such lands, minerals, and resources. As used in this decree, the term "historic coastline" refers to the coastline as it existed in 1868, as to be determined by the parties.

As against the United States, the State of Florida is entitled to all the lands, minerals, and other natural resources underlying the Gulf of Mexico extending seaward for a distance of 3 marine leagues from its coastline or its historic coastline, whichever is landward, but for not less than 3 geographic miles from its coastline; the United States is not entitled, as against the State of Florida, to any interest in such lands, minerals, or resources, with the exceptions provided by Section 5 of the Submerged Lands Act, 43 U.S.C. § 1313.

For the purpose of this decree, the Gulf of Mexico lies to the north and west, and the Atlantic Ocean to the south and east, of a line that begins at a point on the northern coast of the island of Cuba in 83° west longitude, and extends thence to the northward along that meridian of longitude to 24°35′ north latitude, thence eastward along that parallel of latitude through Rebecca Shoal and the Quicksands Shoal to the Marquesas Keys, and thence through the Florida Keys to the mainland at the eastern end of Florida Bay, the line so running that the narrow waters within the Dry Tortugas Islands, the Marquesas Keys, and the Florida Keys, and between the Florida Keys and the mainland, are within the Gulf of Mexico.

There is no historic bay on the coast of the State of Florida. There are no inland waters within Florida Bay, or within the Dry Tortugas Islands, the Marquesas Keys, and the lower Florida Keys (from Money Key to Key West), the closing lines of which affect the right of either the United States or the State of Florida under this decree.

Jurisdiction is reserved by this Court to entertain such further proceedings, enter such orders and issue such writs as may from time to time be deemed necessary or advisable to give proper force and effect to this decree.

ODECO (OCEAN DRILLING AND EXPLORATION CO.) v. TORAO ODA, SUPERINTENDENT OF SHIBA REVENUE OFFICE

Japan, District Court of Tokyo, 1982;
27 Japanese Annual of International Law 148 (1984).[a]

TEXT OF JUDGMENT

1. All of the plaintiff's claims are dismissed.
2. The cost of the action shall be borne by the plaintiff.

* * *

Summary: The plaintiff of the case is a company incorporated under the laws of Panama. From 1971 to 1973, the company undertook exploring activities of the seabed outside the territorial sea of Japan under a contract concluded with a Japanese and an American company. Taxes were levied by the Revenue Office on the income derived from the boring activities of the seabed for the years 1971, 1972 and 1973. The company did not file final income tax returns by reason that the seabed outside the territorial sea does not fall within the "enforcement area" as defined in the Japanese Corporation Tax Law. The State authorities rejected this view.

* * *

OPINION OF THE COURT

* * *

When a foreign corporation like the plaintiff has the "income accruing from domestic areas" defined in Article 138 of the Corporation Tax Law, it is under obligation to pay corporation taxes [Article 4(2) of the same Law]. The range of taxable incomes includes the kinds of income accruing from domestic areas enumerated in each paragraph of Article 141 of the same Law and is determined in accordance with the kinds of foreign corporation enumerated in each paragraph of the same Article [Article 9 of the same Law]. The defendant contends that the plaintiff's incomes from the drilling activities concerned correspond to the "income derived from activities within the domestic areas" defined as one of the incomes accruing from domestic areas in Article 138(1) of the Corporation Tax Law; that the plaintiff corresponds to a "foreign corporation which engages in other activities within the domestic areas for more than one year" defined in Article 141(2) of the same Law; and that the plaintiff is under obligation to pay corporation taxes in respect to the income derived from the drilling activities concerned among its income in each business year. On the other hand, the plaintiff contends

---

a. Original in Japanese. Translation into English by the editorial staff of The Japanese Annual of International Law. Re-printed with the permission of the International Law Association of Japan.

that the region where the plaintiff engaged in the drilling activities concerned is outside the territorial sea of Japan; that Japan's right to impose taxes does not extend over such a region; that the effect of the Corporation Tax Law does not extend, either; and that the region does not correspond to the "domestic areas" defined in the same Law.

And so, in the first place, the question is whether Japan's right to impose taxes extends over the region where the drilling activities were performed. The defendant contends that the region is outside the territorial sea of Japan but it is part of Japan's continental shelf, and that Japan has sovereign rights over the continental shelf by virtue of customary international law, whereby Japan can exercise a right to impose taxes in the region concerned. The Court must examine the existence and contents of customary international law in relation to the continental shelf.

According to the evidence [omitted], with regard to the existence and contents of customary international law concerning the continental shelf at the time of 1971 to 1973, the following facts can be recognized:

A. Harry S. Truman, President of the United States, proclaimed "the Policy of the United States of America with regard to the Natural Resources of the Subsoil and Seabed of the Continental Shelf" on September 28, 1945. This Proclamation read as follows:

* * *

Now therefore, I, Harry S. Truman, President of the United States of America, do hereby proclaim the following policy of the United States of America with respect to the natural resources of the subsoil and seabed of the continental shelf.

Having concern for the urgency of conserving and prudently utilizing its natural resources, the Government of the United States regards the natural resources of the subsoil and seabed of the continental shelf beneath the high seas but contiguous to the coasts of the United States as appertaining to the United States, subject to its jurisdiction and control. In cases where the continental shelf extends to the shores of another state, or is shared with an adjacent state, the boundary shall be determined by the United States and the state concerned in accordance with equitable principles. The character as high seas of the waters above the continental shelf and the right to their free and unimpeded navigation are in no way thus affected.

Although the scope of the continental shelf is not defined in this proclamation itself, it was thought, according to the statement reported in the newspapers, that it extends to where the depth of the superjacent waters is 100 fathoms (approximately 200 meters).

The Truman Proclamation awakened the states to the possibility of a right over the resources beneath the seabed of the high seas and initiated the formulation of international law with regard to the continental shelf. Following the Truman Proclamation, a great number of states made proclamations or legislation concerning the continental shelf, but their contents were not uniform.

B. Under these circumstances the U.N. International Law Commission (I.L.C.) embarked in 1949 on the codification of rules of the high seas. Within that framework, it discussed draft articles on the continental shelf from 1950 to 1956. In 1956 it adopted draft conventions on the law of the seas and submitted them to the United Nations. Article 68 of the draft convention provides that the coastal state may exercise over the continental shelf sovereign rights for the purpose of exploring it and exploiting its natural resources. As to the meaning of natural resources, the attitude of the I.L.C. changed. According to the understanding of the I.L.C. in 1951, natural resources, no doubt, were limited to the mineral resources. In the fourth report (1953) by Francois, special rapporteur, which was the basis of the deliberation of the I.L.C., the words "natural resources" were replaced by the words "mineral resources." In the session of 1953, however, the opinion was put forward that the living resources belonging to sedentary species should be regarded as part of the resources in the continental shelf, and this opinion was supported by the majority of the I.L.C. Eventually, the I.L.C. concluded that the natural resources in the continental shelf should include the living organisms belonging to sedentary species.

C. The United Nations, having discussed the draft on the Law of Sea that the I.L.C. had proposed, and according to the recommendation of the commission, decided by resolution on February 24, 1957 to convene the Conference on the Law of Sea and to provide for the result in a proper treaty or other documents. The conference was convened on February 24, 1958 at the European headquarters of the U.N., and the Convention on the Continental Shelf was adopted by 57 votes to three (Japan, West Germany, and Belgium) with eight abstentions. This Convention was signed by 46 states and came into effect on June 10, 1964 by the ratification or accession of 22 states. As of March 15, 1969, the number of the states that ratified or acceded to the convention was 39. Japan has neither ratified nor acceded to the convention. The provisions of the Convention on the Continental Shelf are as follows.

[The court quotes Articles 1, 2, 3 and 12 of the convention.]

Japan, West Germany, and Belgium criticized the system of the continental shelf itself in the conference, but the basic idea that the coastal state has monopolistic rights for the development of resources of the area called continental shelf was approved by most of the states; this gained a position which could no longer change. But an agreement about the nature of the rights the coastal state has and the scope of the resources involved in the continental shelf system could never be easily reached. The argument about the nature of the rights * * * never [left] in much doubt that the coastal state could monopolize the development of the continental shelf. Getting into actual problems, the subject of warmest debate was what particular resources the coastal state should have the monopoly to develop.

The European states such as Sweden, Norway, Greece, Spain, Denmark, and Italy insisted that these should be limited to mineral resources. At the other end of the debate, Latin American states, Iceland, and Indonesia insisted, although this insistence was virtually neglected, that the resources should include deep-sea fishes and species living in the bottom of the sea. A compromise proposal of the six states, Australia, Ceylon, Malaya, India, Norway, and the United Kingdom eventually became the text of Article 2, paragraph 4 of the adopted convention * * *. France, in its accession on June 14, 1965, made an interpretative declaration: "France considers that the crustacea except for the crab called barnade are excluded for living organisms belonging to sedentary species."

[Japan objected to the inclusion in "natural resources" of living organisms belonging to sedentary species, because of its fishermen's long established practice of recovering oysters—for pearls—on the continental shelf of other states such as Australia.

France's objections were based on the interest of its fishermen in lobsters off the coast of Brazil.]

D.   The International Court of Justice made the following judgment on the so-called North Sea Continental Shelf Case, February 20, 1969.

    * * * [This] is the most fundamental of all the rules of law relating to the continental shelf, enshrined in the 1958 Geneva Convention,—namely that the rights of the coastal State in respect of the area of continental shelf that constitutes a natural prolongation of its land territory into and under the sea exist *ipso facto* and *ab initio*, by virtue of its sovereignty over the land, and as an extension of it in an exercise of sovereign rights for the purpose of exploring the seabed and exploiting its natural resources. In short, there is here an inherent right. In order to exercise it, no special legal process has to be gone through, nor have any special legal acts to be performed. Its existence can be declared (and many States have done this) but does not need to be constituted. To echo the language of the Geneva Convention, it is "exclusive" in the sense that if the coastal State does not choose to explore or exploit the areas of shelf appertaining to it, that is its own affair, but no one else may do so without its express consent.

    More fundamental than the notion of proximity appears to be the principle of the natural prolongation or continuation of the land territory or domain, or land sovereignty of that State. There are various ways of formulating this principle, but the underlying idea, namely of an extension of something already possessed, is the same, and it is this idea of extension which is, in the Court's opinion, determinant. Submarine areas do not really appertain to the coastal State because * * * they are near it. They are near it of course; but this would not suffice to confer title, * * * What confers the ipso jure title which international law attributes to the coastal State in respect of its continental shelf, is the fact that the submarine areas concerned may be deemed to be actually part of the territory over which the coastal State already has dominion,—in the sense that, although covered with water, they are a prolongation or continuation of that territory, an extension of it under the sea.

    * * * [S]peaking generally, it is a characteristic of purely conventional rules and obligations that, in regard to them, some faculty

of making unilateral reservations may, within certain limits, be admitted, * * * whereas this cannot be so in the case of general or customary law rules and obligations which, by their very nature, must have equal force for all the members of the international community, and cannot therefore be the subject of any right of unilateral exclusion exercisable at will by any one of them in its own favor. Consequently, it is to be expected when, for whatever reasons, rules or obligations of this order are embodied, or are intended to be reflected in certain provisions of a convention, such provisions will figure amongst those in respect of which a right of unilateral reservation is not conferred, or is excluded. This expectation is, in principle, fulfilled by Article 12 of the Geneva Continental Shelf Convention "other than to Article 1 to 3 inclusive"—these three Articles being the ones which, it is clear, were then regarded as reflecting, or as crystallizing, received or at least emergent rules of customary international law relative to the continental shelf, amongst them the question of the seaward extent of the shelf; the kind of the natural resources to which these relate; and the preservation intact of the legal status as high seas of the waters over the shelf, and the legal status of the superjacent air-space.

E.   As was mentioned above, in spite of the claim of rights of each country to its continental shelf, which the Truman Proclamation had led, followed by discussions in the International Law Commission of the United Nations, the international law on the continental shelf has been formed gradually. The adoption of the Convention on the Continental Shelf in the Conference on the Law of Sea and the subsequent practice of states (Judge Lachs states in his dissenting opinion in the judgment of the North Sea Continental Shelf Case of the ICJ, it is noteworthy that about seventy states are now engaged in the exploration and development of the continental shelf areas) make the basic idea of the continental shelf incorporated in Articles 1 through 3 of the Convention on the Continental Shelf into rules-of-custom international law. The existence of the customary international law was affirmed by the judgment on the North Sea Continental Shelf Case of the ICJ.

But it cannot be said that all of the provisions of Articles 1 through 3 have become rules-of-custom international law. The judgment of the ICJ states: "These three provisions were at that time clearly regarded to reflect or embody the received or appearing rules on customary international law relating to the continental shelf." It does not state that all these three Articles are rules already received as customary international law. Article 2, paragraph 4 of the Convention includes "living organisms belonging to sedentary species" in the resources whose development the coastal state can monopolize, but, as is stated above, this point met a division in opinions in the U.N. International Law Committee and the Committee on the Law of Sea. * * * It was only the result of the compromise between the states in the Conference on the Law of Sea that living organisms belonging to sedentary species were incorporated into resources of the continental shelf.

In addition, * * * France made an interpretative declaration that "France thinks that the crustacea except for the crab called barnade are excluded from living organisms belonging to sedentary species," and from these facts, the very concept of "living organisms belonging to sedentary species" itself allows various interpretations and is not necessarily clear. Accordingly, it is a rule legislated by the Convention on the Continental Shelf and cannot be said to be a rule-of-custom international law that the coastal state can monopolize the capture of living organisms belonging to sedentary species. And there is no document attesting that that rule has, after the conclusion of the convention, grown into customary international law. On the other hand, the rules incorporated in Articles 1–3, except for the resources of sedentary species, are the basic system of the continental shelf and can be seen by the time of the judgment on the North Sea Continental Shelf Case of the ICJ, February 1969, at the latest to have become customary international law.

F.   Accordingly, in the years * * * [involved in this case,] Japan could exercise its sovereign rights for exploring and developing the mineral resources of the Japanese continental shelf, (the continental shelf contiguous to the Japanese coast but outside the territorial seas of Japan) as a warrant of customary international law, even if Japan has not acceded to the convention. The nature and content of the sovereign rights are as follows.

1.   The territorial sovereignty of a state is a right to exercise governmental functions toward the territorial area belonging to the state (territory, territorial sea, and territorial air) generally and exclusively, and for the purpose of realizing the aims that state fixes in its disposition. The sovereign rights to the continental shelf are extensions of the territorial sovereignty to the area of the bottom of the high seas, but the reason it is called sovereign rights and not sovereignty is based on the fact that these rights are limited by the purpose of exploring (exploring the continental shelf itself when the varied resources are not yet known) and developing (mining the already known resources); and furthermore they cannot affect any status of the superjacent waters as high seas or that of the air space above those waters or high air, except to the extent necessary to the realization of this purpose. But the sovereign rights to the continental shelf include all the sovereign rights necessary to the exploration and development of the mineral resources of the continental shelf or relate to it—that is, legislative, executive, and judicial powers. Namely, they are limited by the purpose, but have a complete nature in the scope of the purpose mentioned above, comprehensive and exclusive, and are not different from sovereignty.

2.   Accordingly, the sovereign rights to the continental shelf include, ipso facto, the right of taxation which is a side of the sovereignty. That is, the sovereign rights to the continental shelf is extension of the territorial sovereignty as long as its subject is the exploration or development of mineral resources or related activities, and it exercises jurisdiction over these activities as a domestic withheld income. Furthermore, the services by the contract are also included in the scope of the above-mentioned purpose as long as they are related to the exploration or development of mineral resources in the continental shelf, and taxes are imposed as those within the territorial jurisdiction as long as the services are done on the continental shelf.

3. The sovereign rights to the continental shelf are based on the idea of extension of the territorial sovereignty to the sea bottom area under high seas, which is an inherent right of a state and independent to neither an effective or ideal preoccupation nor an express declaration. Accordingly, the exercise of the sovereign rights need neither express declaration by the state in advance, nor special legal processes or acts.

* * *

Problem. Under the United Nations Convention on the Law of the Sea, the continental shelf of a state extends to the outer edge of the continental margin. The outer edge of the margin may fall short of 200 miles or extend beyond it. When the outer edge of the continental margin does extend beyond 200 miles, the outer limit of the continental shelf of a state is 350 miles from the baseline or 100 miles from the 2,500 metre isobath. See Article 76(1), (4) and (5).

The outer edge of the continental margin off the coast of the United States does not extend beyond 200 miles in some areas. The rights of the United States in those areas are based on customary international law, according to the presidential proclamation on the exclusive economic zone of March 10, 1983. But in some areas, the outer edge of the continental margin extends beyond 200 miles. What rights may the United States claim—if any—in the segment of the shelf extending between 200 miles and 350 miles from the baseline or 100 miles from the 2,500 metre isobath?

In view of its broad rejection of those provisions of the convention not reflecting customary international law, is the United States precluded from claiming rights in that segment of the shelf? Could it take the position that Article 76 of the convention expresses, as to that segment, customary international law? If it did take that position, what of the requirement in Article 82 that states engaged in the production of minerals in that segment make certain payments to an international fund set aside for the benefit of developing states? Could the United States claim the rights only if it made the payments?

2. MINERAL RESOURCES BEYOND NATIONAL JURISDICTION

Technological advances induce quest for law as to mineral resources under the high seas. As we have noted above, the U.S. and other major nations are currently active in promoting the declaration, distribution and exploration of deep seabed resources, despite UNCLOS "common heritage of mankind language." For most of the modern era, conflicts of national interest did not arise as to the extraction of substances from the waters, bed, and subsoil of what once were called the high seas but now must be more exactly characterized as areas beyond national jurisdiction.

By analogy to high seas fishing, anyone could take natural materials from these waters; and even the fixing of installations by mooring and otherwise was considered not to be illegal per se.

By the 1960s, technologies for the drilling for oil and gas in very deep water and collection and lifting from the seabed of polymetallic nodules became feasible. These technological developments coincided in a general way with increasing need everywhere for liquid hydrocarbons and deficiencies in national production by some states, particularly highly industrialized states such as the United States, of highly strategic alloy metals contained in the seabed nodules, viz., manganese, cobalt, and nickle. Copper and iron (usually in highly attractive ferromanganese compounds) are also found in nodular form. Nodules vary in metallic composition and content from place to place. The quantities are immense, and the areas of concentration are vast.

It was the developed states, particularly the United States in its private sector, that brought about the improvements in technology that have made extraction of the substances referred to feasible. These states also have capabilities for mobilizing the capital such operations will require. The less well developed states, faced with disappointments as to expectations for rapid growth and in an environment of a widening gap—rather than a narrowing one—between rich countries and poor countries, viewed with apprehension the prospect that the planet's last source of natural wealth not already appropriated would be denied to them through preemption by states able to take the lead in exploitation.

In the developed states, the profit motive in the private sector (reflected, of course, in national politics) and a security interest in the public sector created pressures for action to use the new technology on an individual state basis. But in these same states, a prudent concern for national image, the verdict of history, and the broader national interest in world stability supported the search for means to achieve equitable sharing of the new resources on the basis of respective needs and national contributions.

In 1968 a private international consortium, without leave of any state, claimed exclusive rights to the extraction of seabed brine from a large area in the Red Sea, asserting that no licensing authority existed anywhere. See Nanda, Some Legal Questions on the Peaceful Uses of Ocean Space, 9 Va.J.Int'l L. 343, 384 (1969). Other plans to act unilaterally were announced and received publicity. The basic issues came rapidly to the attention of various segments of the United Nations, the Senate Committee on Foreign Relations, and legal writers.

Collins, Mineral Exploitation of the Seabed: Problems, Progress, and Alternatives, 12 Natural Resources Lawyer 599, at 636 (1979) *, describes what has come to be recognized as a key development:

> * * * August 17, 1967, was the date on which the seabed question was born. On that date Malta's United Nations ambassador, Arvid Pardo, proposed that an item entitled "Declaration and

* Reprinted by permission of the Section on Natural Resources Law of the American Bar Association.

Treaty Concerning the Reservation Exclusively for Peaceful Purposes of the Seabed and of the Ocean Floor Underlying the Seas Beyond the Limits of Present National Jurisdiction and the Use of their Resources in the Interests of Mankind" be added to the agenda of the General Assembly. It was Dr. Pardo's subsequent speech to the General Assembly that set off the explosion of international interest in the formation of a regime to exploit the seabed not then under national jurisdiction. Pardo * * * mesmerized many United Nations delegations from developing countries with his assertions that the vast, readily exploitable mineral wealth of the seabed could quickly redress the inequities of economic development * * *.

The Pardo proposal contained the following essential points:

—that the ocean floor and its resources * * * are to be considered the common property of mankind;

—that they are not subject to national appropriation;

—that they must be used for peaceful purposes only;

—that the resources should be developed cooperatively, not competitively, and particularly for the benefit of developing nations; and

—that an international regime should be created, within the framework of the United Nations or emanating from the United Nations, to guarantee these principles and plan for the development of common ocean resources.

The initiative just described set in train a long process of negotiations at UNCLOS III. On the one hand the less well developed states made determined efforts to vest exclusive rights of exploitation of seabed resources beyond national jurisdiction in an international authority so organized they could dominate it by taking full advantage of their number. On the other hand the developed states, while willing to accommodate to the principles stated above, resisted the creation of an international authority not responsive to their interests even though the successful operation of the authority would depend on technology and risk capital they alone could provide.

In some quarters in developed states, the free enterprise system as to mining was seen as imperiled by the insistence of the developing states that structured international controls be provided for all significant activities in the seabed area beyond national jurisdiction. Concern about national security in relation to supplies of scarce substances was prominent in developed states. Some states, mainly developing ones, are producers on land of vital metals also found on the ocean floor in nodules. These feared damage to markets and price structure from additional production of these metals from the new source and wished to have such production controllable in support of their interests, or, alternatively, guaranteed commodity price support systems for their production of the metals concerned.

The seabed beyond national jurisdiction is named "The Area" in the Convention on the Law of the Sea and Articles 133–191 of Part XI of the convention are devoted to organizing the exploitation of its resources which are declared in Article 136 to be "the common heritage of mankind."

The Authority set up to function in the Area consists of an Assembly, Articles 159–160, a Council which is the executive body of the seabed authority, Articles 161–165, a Secretariat, Articles 166–169, and an Enterprise, Article 170, which is to carry out the activities in the Area, including the transportation, processing and marketing of minerals recovered from the Area. In this Authority, however, the conflicting state interests sketched above are not harmonized. Structurally, and in the statements of principle, the convention favors the views of the developing states.

NOTE OF JANUARY 13, 1986, FROM THE UNITED STATES MISSION TO THE UNITED NATIONS ADDRESSED TO THE SECRETARY–GENERAL OF THE UNITED NATIONS

U.N. Office of the Special Representative of the Secretary–General for the
Law of the Sea, Law of the Sea Bulletin No. 7, April 1986, p. 74.

The Government of the United States wishes to provide the United Nations with the attached notices published in the Federal Register of the United States, which provide public notice of the issuance, by the National Oceanic and Atmospheric Administration, United States Department of Commerce, of four licences authorizing deep seabed hard mineral resource exploration in specified areas of the east-central Pacific Ocean * * *. Included in the Federal Register notices are the geographical coordinates of the deep seabed areas within which deep seabed hard mineral exploration has been authorized.

These licences were issued pursuant to the Deep Seabed Hard Mineral Resources Act. In accordance with section 102(b)(2) of that Act, these licences are exclusive as against "any other United States citizen or any citizen, national or government agency of, or any legal entity organized or existing under the laws of, any reciprocating State". Reciprocating States are those States designated as such in accordance with section 118 of the Act.

The Government of the United States also calls attention to section 3(a) of the Act, which states:

By the enactment of the Act, the United States:

(1) Exercises jurisdiction over United States citizens and vessels, and foreign persons and vessels otherwise subject to its jurisdiction, in the exercise of the high seas freedom to engage in exploration for, and commercial recovery of, hard mineral resources of the deep seabed in accordance with generally accepted principles of international law recognized by the United States; but

(2) Does not thereby assert sovereignty or sovereign or exclusive rights or jurisdiction over, or the ownership of, any areas or resources in the deep seabed.

In addition to confirming for the United Nations, and through it its Member States, the existence of licences for exploration of the hard mineral resources of the deep sea-bed, the Government of the United States takes this opportunity to state that, in view of the international legal obligation of all States to avoid unreasonable interference with the interests of other States in their exercise of the freedoms of the high seas, the Government of the United States stands ready to consult on this subject with any other Government. The Government of the United States also notes that it has been informed by representatives of the recipients of United States licences that they also are prepared to discuss the subject of avoidance of interference of activities with any other entity engaged in such activities in the areas within which their deep seabed hard mineral exploration has been authorized.

The Government of the United States requests that this note, and the attached Federal Register notices, be circulated by the United Nations as part of the next Law of the Sea Bulletin prepared by the Office of the Special Representative of the Secretary–General for the Law of the Sea.

Note: The United States position is based on the contention that deep sea mining is governed by customary law about the "freedom of the seas". Suppose the Third Law of the Sea Convention comes into force for sixty states, not including the United States? What then?

———

NOTE ON THE "COMMON HERITAGE OF MANKIND" DOCTRINE

The concept that no state can acquire an exclusive right to use of certain areas, deposits, or other things of value, because they belong to all mankind has been advanced in regard to orbits in space, mineralized areas of the Moon and other celestial bodies, and the Antarctic continent. But nowhere else has this doctrine been as firmly asserted and as elaborately surrounded with specific regulatory structure and rules of sharing as in regard to minerals of the deep beds under "high seas" waters, in Part XI of the 1982 United Nations Convention on the Law of the Sea. It is our recommendation that this Part in the Documentary Supplement be scanned, and the following provisions appraised: Sections 137, 140, 149, 150, 151, 156, 159, 161, 162, 163, 164, 165, 166, 170, 171, 174, and 187. The array is astoundingly elaborate and predictably very costly to administer.

The ethical concept of a common heritage fits in a general way with the long-held view that the high seas are not subject to exclusive appropriations by any state, even though certain structures built in high seas waters have been respected as the property of the erecting state if reasonably compatible with general use of the area. *Does "common heritage" in Part XI go beyond this to create a common economic right? Look at Section 140 again.*

This apogee of planetary sharing developed in a period when the less well developed countries of the world were more insistent, through the General Assembly, than they have been recently about equality in the rights and duties of states. And the drive was fanned, as to Part XI, by great expectations as to immense wealth at the bottom of the deep seas. A decade later, not much mining is going on, even though the Convention is not yet in effect. Will it ever be? If "Yes", will it be with or without Part XI?

———

Chapter 5

LAW OF AIRSPACE, OUTER SPACE
AND CELESTIAL BODIES

Section A. Airspace.
      1. Aerial Transit.
      2. Offenses Aboard Aircraft.
      General Offenses.
      Hijacking.
      Sabotage.
      Extradition and Aircraft Offenses.
Section B. Outer Space.
      Round-up on Other Legal Aspects of the Use of Space.
Section C. Celestial Bodies.

OVERVIEW

The century now closing saw the rise of the technologies of both airflight and spaceflight, each of them inducing the evolution of new legal principles. Such principles regarding airspace and its utilization have become relatively stabilized. After a flurry linked to the orbital flight of Sputnik 1 in 1957, which produced a few, generalized international agreements, much activity in the United Nations General Assembly of a proto-law nature, and considerable additions to scholarly legal literature, space law is essentially in a holding pattern.

Flight operations of powered, steerable aircraft, both lighter-than-air and heavier-than-air, developed in the First World War along the military lines of aerial observation, combat, and bombing, especially of cities. Such usages remain uncontrolled by restrictive norms of warfare. Between the two world wars, commercial aviation began, grew, and came under a number of legal controls, national and international. Virtually all of this law, the subject of a recognized and active legal specialty, is positive, rather than customary, in its origins. Air law, unlike much of sea law, is not consuetudinarian. Significantly, for instance, a "high seas" freedom for aerial transit, though put forward by early scholars, did not survive the Zeppelin bombing raids on London. The only free airspace today is that above the high seas. And, as we shall see, that freedom narrows as national airspace is approached.

In the course of its relatively brief and partial development, space law has had to deal with the problems of where space begins; for what purpose or purposes; sharing of advantages, such as orbits and substances from celestial bodies; liability for space debris; and the use of space for military operations. Space law as a specialty is still mainly in the hands of scholars and national and international officials. However, communications law has developed a practitioner specialty related to satellite ownership, financing, control, launching, and utilization.

———

SECTION A. AIRSPACE

———

1. AERIAL TRANSIT

DRAFT CONVENTION, REGIME OF AEROSTATS AND WIRELESS TELEGRAPHY (1906)

21 Annuaire de l'Institut de Droit International 293, 327 (1907).[a]

Mr. Fauchille, rapporteur, * * * summarizes the main conclusions:

* * *

The fundamental difficulty * * * concerns the nature of airspace and the rights of states in the atmosphere. How can this question be solved? It must be defined. The atmosphere can be divided into three zones. Above 5000 meters [there is] a zone where breathing is impossible and where balloons cannot penetrate. Close to earth, [is] a zone [which is] subject to appropriation through building up to, at present, a height of 330 meters since the highest construction today, the Eiffel Tower, is 300 meters high and the highest telegraphic masts reach 30 meters. But even in that situation, airspace is subject to appropriation by the state. What is state property is not airspace but the constructions in the airspace. Thus, it is only in that airspace from the ground up, where there are no constructions, and up to 5000 meters, that there exists a [third] zone whose [legal] regime must be determined. *5000 m* *330 m*

Two absolute theories have been advanced.

In one * * * airspace is completely free in all its zones, be it for aerial navigation or for radio telegraphy. In the other, the subjacent state has a right of property or sovereignty in airspace within a limit, according to one view, * * * [equivalent] to the range of a cannon, or according to another view, * * * within limits to be determined by an international agreement similar to the one proposed by the Netherlands in 1895 for territorial waters.

The first system does not take into account the dangers for states in the matter of espionage, especially, and the operation of radio telegraphy, [which would result] from the passage of aerostats at low altitude. [In the second], the range of a cannon varies widely and may attain, it is said, a range of 4800 meters, it would follow that aerial navigation would in fact become impossible. * * * [To the extent] the second system involves determining the rights of the subjacent state by international agreement, the determination, has no rational basis and would be arbitrary. [A single observation] applies both aspects of this second

---

a. Translation by the editors. The text in the Annuaire is a summary minute of what the rapporteur said rather than the verbatim transcript of his statement.

system: Airspace, by its very nature, is not susceptible of appropriation or subjection to sovereignty.

The rapporteur proposes, accordingly, a combination of two uncontested principles: (1) airspace is not susceptible of appropriation or subjection to sovereignty, and therefore is free; (2) a state has a right of self-preservation and of self-defense to guaranty the essential elements of its existence, both in a material sense and as a legal person. Hence this formula: airspace is free, subject to the right of self-preservation and self-defense of the subjacent state.

Two consequences follow from the proposal:

(1) What is the most serious danger from aerostats? Espionage. What form does this danger take? Photography. But useful photography of a country's fortifications can be made only at an altitude of less than 1500 meters. Thus, under 1500 meters, the navigation of aerostats should be forbidden.

(2) What is today the most serious problem for wireless telegraphy? It is the possibility of interference with telephone communications and ordinary telegraphy.

* * * [The following text was adopted by the Institute.]

Article 1. Airspace is free. States have in it, in time of peace or in time of war, only the rights necessary for their self-preservation.

* * *

FROM THEORY TO TREATY LAW

McNair, The Law of the Air 4 (Kerr & Evans, 3d ed. 1964).*

* * * Until after the war of 1914–18 the only aspects of aerial navigation which had engaged the serious attention of English lawyers, and, indeed, of [most] lawyers, were the rules of public international law and of the Conflict of Laws which ought to govern it. * * *

It was generally admitted that the airspace was free [over the high seas]. * * *

(1) *That the airspace is free, subject only to the rights of states required in the interests of their self-preservation.* This theory, which will always be associated with the name of its champion, Fauchille, was adopted by the Institute of International Law in 1906. * * *

(2) The second theory was that *upon the analogy of the maritime belt or territorial waters there is over the land and waters of each state a lower zone of territorial airspace, and a higher, and unlimited, zone of free airspace.*

(3) The third theory was *that a state has complete sovereignty in its superincumbent airspace to an unlimited height,* thus applying the *cujus est solum* maxim in its crude form.

---

* Reprinted with the permission of Stevens & Sons, Ltd., London.

(4) The fourth theory was the third *with the addition of a servitude of innocent passage for foreign non-military aircraft,* akin to the right of innocent passage of merchant ships through territorial waters.

The war of 1914–18 brought about a realisation of the importance of aerial navigation and of its potential danger to the subjacent state and its inhabitants. It is therefore not surprising to find now the almost universal adoption by international treaty and by national legislation of the theory of complete sovereignty (No. (3) above), subject to a mutual, carefully safeguarded, and easily determinable treaty right of free entry and passage for the non-military aircraft of foreign countries.

Thus the first Article of the Paris Convention of 1919 [read]: "The High Contracting Parties recognise that every Power has complete and exclusive sovereignty over the air space above its territory.

> For the purpose of the present Convention the territory of a State shall be understood as including the national territory, both that of the Mother Country and of the Colonies, and the territorial waters adjacent thereto."

* * *

GOEDHUIS, CIVIL AVIATION AFTER THE WAR

36 American Journal of International Law 596, 605 (1942).*

The * * * accelerated speed of change in the last thirty years has been such that, politically, air navigation has already passed through many of the phases which it took sea navigation centuries to span.

As to air navigation, * * * in 1910 the states were preoccupied only with guaranteeing the safety of their territory; the necessity of permitting other states to navigate freely to and over their territory was recognized to the fullest extent where this freedom did not affect the security of the state. The period 1910–1919 can thus be compared with that period in the history of shipping in which the adjacent seas were appropriated primarily to secure the land from invasion.

In 1919 the first consideration was still the security of the states, but the study of the minutes of the meetings held by the Aëronautical Commission of the Peace Conference reveals the fact that some small clouds were already appearing on the horizon of the free sky. In the minds of some of the delegates the idea took shape to use the power of the state over the air to protect its own air navigation against foreign competition. As in shipping, the pretensions to the appropriation of the sea and the power to restrict foreign sea commerce grew in proportion to the increase of the direct profits to be expected from them, so in aviation the pretensions to unrestricted sovereignty—not in doctrine but in

* Reprinted with the permission of the
American Society of International Law.

practice—grew in proportion to the development of aviation during the period from 1919 to 1929. * * *

* * *

INTERNATIONAL AIR TRANSPORT AND FOREIGN POLICY

Campbell, The United States in World Affairs, 1947–1948, 276, at 280 (1948).**

* * *

The present concern of the United States with foreign air policy questions is of comparatively recent origin. The United States participated in the drafting but later failed to ratify the Convention Relating to the Regulation of Aerial Navigation, signed at Paris in 1919 and later accepted by most European nations. It signed and ratified the Pan American Convention on Commercial Aviation concluded at Havana in 1928, but this convention had little practical effect since it was almost ignored even by the few nations which had accepted it.

* * *

Even before the outbreak of the second World War, the United States had entered into intergovernmental negotiations for the establishment of international air services. The transatlantic route discussions with Great Britain, Canada and Ireland in 1935–1937 and an exchange of notes with France in 1939 paved the way for the inauguration of Pan American Airways' service to Great Britain and to France a few months before the outbreak of war. During the war U.S. flag international air transport increased beyond any possible prior contemplation. Part of the enormous amount of flying was conducted directly by commercial air carriers, part by such air carriers acting on government account, and a large part by the Army Air Transport Command and the Naval Air Transport Services. The routes used were expanded where the war effort required by informal arrangements made between the United States and its allies. But the very informality of the wartime expansion made it more than clear that urgent and important foreign policy problems would be involved in stabilizing the general international air transport position when the war ended, particularly if the routes desired by the United States were to be put into operation.

* * *

Toward the end of the war it was clear that the great changes which had taken place called for some measure of international agreement beyond the prewar pattern. Faced with the certain reorganization of world air transport that would follow the termination of hostilities, the United States consulted with various foreign nations, particularly Great Britain, and, as a result of such negotiations, invited its allies and the

** Copyright, Council on Foreign Relations, Inc. 1948. Reprinted with permission.

neutral powers to an International Civil Aviation Conference at Chicago in November 1944.

The Chicago conference was by far the most important ever held dealing with international civil aviation. It provided a forum for foreign air policy discussions such as had never existed before. * * *

* * *

At the conclusion of the conference, three executive agreements and one formal convention were opened for signature. The United States signed all four. Through the executive branch of the government, it later formally accepted the executive agreements, and, through the formal constitutional procedure, duly ratified the convention.

* * *

Under the terms of the Chicago convention, agreement was reached on certain questions of major importance affecting world aviation. The agreed principles included the following: acceptance of airspace sovereignty as in the Paris convention of 1919 and the Havana convention of 1928; authority without further permit for aircraft of contracting states not engaged in international air service to fly non-stop across the territory of other contracting states and to make stops for non-traffic purposes, with the provision that such aircraft may take on or discharge passengers, cargo or mail "subject to the right of any state where such embarkation or discharge takes place to impose such regulations, conditions or limitations as it may consider desirable"; provisions that no scheduled international air service may be operated over or into the territory of a contracting state except by special permission; that any contracting state may refuse permission to aircraft of other contracting states to carry cabotage traffic (i.e., traffic from one point to another within the same country); that contracting states may set up prohibited areas for reasons of military necessity or public safety; that aircraft shall have the nationality of the state in which they are registered; that contracting states will adopt all practicable measures to facilitate navigation between their territories; that contracting states, so far as practicable, will install and provide air navigation facilities for international air navigation; that all aircraft shall carry certain documents and be equipped (including radio equipment) in the manner set out in the convention; that each contracting state may designate routes to be followed and airports to be used by any international air service within its territory; that the convention should supersede the Paris and Havana conventions; and that the formation of an International Civil Aviation Organization should be undertaken.

* * *

The convention made no provision, however, for the general automatic or other grant of the privilege of regular scheduled air services of one contracting state to fly over or into the territory of other contracting states, or the terms under which such services should or could be organized and operated. On this question hinged the long discussions and futile compromise efforts of the conference. Basically divergent foreign policy views were involved.

Australia and New Zealand proposed the establishment of an international air transport authority which would be responsible for the operation of air services on international trunk routes and which would own the aircraft and ancillary equipment employed on these routes. Canada proposed the organization of an international authority to fix routes, frequencies, capacity and rates applicable to international air services and to issue permits to international civil aviation operators much as the Civil Aeronautics Board does in the United States for U.S. flag operators. Great Britain also favored such an authority with power to allocate operating frequencies and capacity and to fix rates. The United States opposed these suggestions, favoring instead a wide exchange of transit privileges by which scheduled services of any contracting state could fly over or land for refueling or other technical purposes in the territory of another contracting state. The transit privileges (the right to fly over, or to land for technical purposes) are sometimes called the first and second freedoms, and the transport privileges (the right to carry traffic to another contracting state, bring back traffic from such state, or to carry traffic between another contracting state and other states) are referred to as the third, fourth and fifth freedoms.

The Australian and New Zealand position found little support. Many efforts were made to find a compromise between the British insistence on some type of economic regulation which they deemed necessary to assure "order in the air" and the American opposition to any prior allocation of frequencies or capacity, or to any other form of international economic regulation of the growing United States air transport services. Various automatic and semi-automatic formulas were suggested, but without result. In the absence of general agreement on economic regulation of scheduled services, the transit and transport agreements were drafted separately, apart from the convention. Both were supported by the United States. The Transit Agreement covered the first and second freedoms, and, in addition, authorized any nation flown over to require the international operator to land and offer reasonable commercial services. The Transport Agreement covered all five freedoms, including both transit and commercial privileges. * * *

* * *

Thus by the close of the war, the foreign air policy of the United States, so far as it could be determined from the position of the executive branch of the government, had taken definite shape. * * *

* * *

THE CHICAGO CONVENTION: EXCERPTS
61 Stat. 1180, 15 U.N.T.S. 295.

[The convention is applicable only to civil (not state) aircraft.]

See articles 1, 2, 5, 6, 17, in the Documentary Supplement.

1. *I.C.A.O.* The convention creates the International Civil Aviation Organization, an intergovernmental organization the objectives of which are to "develop the principles and techniques of international air navigation and to foster the planning and development of international air transport." The convention entered into force for the United States on April 4.

2. *The International Air Services Transit Agreement.* The United States became a party in 1945. 59 Stat. 1693; 84 U.N.T.S. 389. Article 1, Section 1, provides the so-called "two freedoms" for scheduled air services:

> Each contracting State grants to the other contracting States the following freedoms of the air in respect of scheduled international air services:
>
> (1) The privilege to fly across its territory without landing;
>
> (2) The privilege to land for non-traffic purposes.

> The privileges of this section shall not be applicable with respect to airports utilized for military purposes to the exclusion of any scheduled international air services. In areas of active hostilities or of military occupation, and in time of war along the supply routes leading to such areas, the exercise of such privileges shall be subject to the approval of the competent military authorities.

3. *The International Air Transport Agreement.* The United States became a party in 1945. So few states became parties to this agreement that the United States withdrew as a party in 1947. Article 1, Section 1, provides the so-called "five freedoms" for scheduled air service: Each contracting State grants to the other contracting States the following freedoms of the air in respect of scheduled international air services:

(1) The privilege to fly across its territory without landing;

(2) The privilege to land for non-traffic purposes;

(3) The privilege to put down passengers, mail and cargo taken on in the territory of the State whose nationality the aircraft possesses;

(4) The privilege to take on passengers, mail and cargo destined for the territory of the State whose [aircraft's] nationality;

(5) The privilege to take on passengers, mail and cargo destined for the territory of any other contracting State and the privilege to put down passengers, mail and cargo coming from any such territory.

With respect to the privileges specified under paragraphs (3), (4) and (5) of this Section, the undertaking of each contracting State relates only to through services on a route constituting a reasonably direct line out from and back to the homeland of the State [of the aircraft's] nationality.

4. *Scheduled air services.* The package of agreements emanating from the Chicago conference thus did not include a multilateral agreement of wide acceptance sufficient to deal with the question of scheduled air service. To provide the authorizations and permissions foreshadowed in Article 6 of the Chicago Convention, states entered into a vast network (or cobweb) of bilateral agreements, covering routes, types of traffic and volume of traffic (capacity), as well as a variety of administrative and legal matters of concern to the airline industry. See Lissitzyn, Bilateral Agreements on Air Transport, 30 J. of Air L. & Commerce 248 (1964); Hill, Bermuda II: The British Revolution of 1976, 44 J. of Air L. & Commerce 111 (1978). Following the Chicago conference, rates were set for many years by conference machinery established by the International Air Transport Association (IATA), a private association of airlines, sometimes referred to as a cartel. With the onset of airline industry deregulation in the United States in the late 70s and the removal of IATA's antitrust immunity, IATA's ratemaking function ceased. Schwartz, Flynn & First, Free Enterprise and Economic Organization: Government Regulation 625 (6th ed. 1985).

POWERS CASE

Union of Soviet Socialist Republics, Supreme Court Military Collegium, 1960.
30 Int'l L.Rep. 69 (1966).*

* * * On May 1, 1960, at 5 hours 36 minutes, Moscow time, a military unit of the Soviet anti-aircraft defence in the area of the city of Kirovabad, the Tajik S.S.R., at an altitude of 20,000 metres, unattainable for planes of the civil air fleet, spotted an unknown aircraft violating the State frontier of the U.S.S.R.

The military units of the Soviet anti-aircraft defence vigilantly followed the behaviour of the plane as it flew over major industrial centres and important objectives, and only when the intruder plane had penetrated 2,000 kilometres into Soviet territory and the evil purpose of the flight, fraught with disastrous consequences for world peace in an age of thermonuclear weapons, became absolutely obvious, a battery of ground-to-air missiles brought the aggressor plane down in the area of Sverdlovsk at 8 hours 53 minutes as ordered by the Soviet Government.

The pilot of the plane bailed out and was apprehended upon landing. On interrogation, he gave his name as Francis Gary Powers, citizen of the United States of America. Examination of the wreckage of the plane which had been brought down showed that it was of American make, specially designed for high altitude flights and fitted with various equipment for espionage reconnaissance tasks.

* Reprinted with the permission of the Editor of the International Law Reports.

In view of this, the pilot Powers was arrested and committed for trial on charges of espionage against the Soviet Union.

During the court hearings, the defendant Powers testified in detail about his espionage activity and the circumstances connected with the violation of Soviet air space on May 1, 1960.

* * *

On the night of April 30, 1960, Colonel Shelton gave Powers the assignment to fly over the territory of the Soviet Union at an altitude of 20,000 metres along the following course: Peshawar, the Aral Sea, Sverdlovsk, Kirov, Archangel, Murmansk, and to land in Norway, at Bodoe airport, with which Powers familiarized himself back in 1958.

Flying over Soviet territory, Powers, on Shelton's orders, was to switch on at definite points his special equipment for aerial photography and the registration of the operation of Soviet anti-aircraft defence radar stations. Powers was to give special attention to two spots—in one of them American intelligence suspected the presence of missile launching ramps and in the other a particularly important defence objective.

The material evidence of the case and his testimony has established that Powers fulfilled the criminal mission given him.

Having taken off from Peshawar airport in Pakistan, Powers flew over the territory of Afghanistan and for more than 2,000 kilometres over the Soviet Union in accordance with the established course. Besides Powers' testimony, this is confirmed by the American flight map discovered in the debris of the U–2 plane and submitted to the Court, bearing the route plotted out by Major Dulak, navigator of the detachment "Ten–Ten", and also notes and signs made by Powers, who marked down on this map several important defence objectives of the Soviet Union he had spotted from the plane.

Throughout the flight, to the very moment the plane was shot down, Powers switched on his special intelligence equipment, photographed important defence objectives and recorded signals of the country's anti-aircraft radar installations. The development of the rescued aerial photography films established that defendant Powers photographed from the U–2 plane industrial and military objectives of the Soviet Union— plants, depots, oil storage facilities, communication routes, railway bridges and stations, electric transmission lines, aerodromes, the location of troops and military equipment.

The numerous photos of the Soviet Union's territory, taken by defendant Powers from an altitude of 20,000 metres, in possession of the Military Collegium of the U.S.S.R. Supreme Court, make it possible to determine the nature of industrial establishments, the design of railway bridges, the number and type of aircraft on the airfields, the nature and purpose of military material.

Powers tape-recorded impulses of certain [USSR] radar stations with a view to detecting the country's anti-aircraft defence system.

According to the conclusion of experts, the information collected by defendant Powers during his flight in Soviet air space on May 1, 1960, constitutes a State and military secret of the Soviet Union, which is specially guarded by law.

* * *

Thus, the court hearings have established definitely that the Lockheed U–2 reconnaissance aircraft belonged to the United States Air Force and that defendant Powers was a secret agent of the Central Intelligence Agency of the United States of America.

Powers was an obedient executor of the perfidious designs of the Central Intelligence Agency of the United States of America, carried out with the consent of the American Government.

Powers himself admitted that he realized when intruding into the air space of the Soviet Union that he was violating the national sovereignty of the U.S.S.R. and flying over its territory on an espionage mission, whose main purpose consisted of detecting and marking down missile launching sites.

* * *

Article 2 [of the Law on Criminal Responsibility for State Crimes]:

Espionage

The giving away, theft or collection with the intention of conveying to a foreign Power, a foreign organization, or their agents, of information constituting a State or military secret, as well as the giving away or collection on the instructions of foreign intelligence agencies of other information to be used against the interests of the U.S.S.R., if the espionage is committed by a foreigner or by a stateless person—is punishable by deprivation of liberty for a period of from seven to fifteen years with confiscation of property, or by death and confiscation of property.

* * * [T]he Military Collegium of the U.S.S.R. Supreme Court takes into account that the intrusion of the American military intelligence plane constitutes a criminal breach of a generally recognized principle of international law, which establishes the exclusive sovereignty of every State over the air space above its territory. This principle, laid down by the Paris Convention of October 13, 1919, for the regulation of aerial navigation, and several other subsequent international agreements, is proclaimed in the national legislations of different States, including the Soviet Union and the United States of America.

Violation of this sacred and immutable principle of international relations creates in the present conditions a direct menace to universal peace and international security.

At the present level of military technology, when certain States possess atomic and hydrogen weapons, as well as the means of delivering them quickly to targets, the flight of a military intelligence plane over Soviet territory could have directly preceded a military attack. This danger is the more possible in conditions when the United States of America, as stated by American generals, constantly keeps bomber patrols in the air, always ready to drop bombs on earlier marked-out targets of the Soviet Union.

Under these conditions the aggressive act of the United States of America, carried out on May 1 of this year by defendant Powers, created a threat to universal peace.

* * *

Having examined the materials of the case, material and other evidence and expert findings, and having heard the testimony of the defendant and the witnesses, the speeches of the State Prosecutor and of the Defence Counsel, and also the last plea of the defendant, the Military Collegium of the U.S.S.R. Supreme Court holds established that defendant Powers was for a long time an active secret agent of the United States Central Intelligence Agency, directly fulfilling espionage missions of this agency against the Soviet Union; and that on May 1, 1960, with the knowledge of the Government of the United States of America, in a specially equipped U–2 intelligence plane, he intruded into Soviet air space and with the help of special radio-technical and photographic equipment collected information of strategical importance, which constitutes a State and Military secret of the Soviet State, thereby committing a grave crime covered by Article 2 of the Soviet Union's Law "On Criminal Responsibility for State Crimes".

At the same time, weighing all the circumstances of the given case in the deep conviction that they are inter-related, taking into account Powers' sincere confession of his guilt and his sincere repentance, proceeding from the principles of socialist humaneness, and guided by Articles 319 and 320 of the Code of Criminal Procedure of the Russian Federation, the Military Collegium of the U.S.S.R. Supreme Court

Sentences: Francis Gary Powers, on the strength of Article 2 of the U.S.S.R. Law "On Criminal Responsibility for State Crimes", to ten years' confinement with the first three years to be served in prison.

* * *

———

1. *Reprise on Powers, the Lockheed U–2 aircraft, and aerial surveillance.* Much still has to come out about spying-by-aircraft during the Cold War period. We know that Powers was not the only American pilot downed; also, that the Lockheed U–2 was a marvel of specialty design for observation operations above 60,000 feet. (Note in the Soviet Report on the Powers Case that the interception by a surface-to-air missile was at 20,000 meters * * * "unattainable for planes in the civilian air fleet * * *." Civil? What about the Soviet military air fleet?)

The U–2 operation was run by the Central Intelligence Agency, not the Air Force or the Defence Intelligence Agency, from friendly bases. Information now beginning to come out of Russia indicates downings of Americans other than Powers and begins to throw light on Soviet operations of a similar nature. So far no American interceptions of Soviet surveillance aircraft have been reported.

Powers was exchanged at the classic spy-exchange bridge into East Berlin for Col. Rudolf Abel, a brilliant Soviet spymaster who had operated for years from a photography shop in Brooklyn. Powers died in Los Angeles, while engaged in an aerial journalism mission. He wrote no book.

President Eisenhower's early evasion of the above Soviet report was almost immediately blown, whereupon he reiterated his call for an "Open Skies" policy, originally made in 1955.

Aerial surveillance during the Cuban Missile Crisis was of great importance to President Kennedy and his emergency staff, but the degree to which it was by aircraft or by low-orbit satellite has not been made public.

2. *Sanctions against aircraft entering airspace.* Does the fact that a state has jurisdiction to prescribe law governing an event mean that it has freedom of choice in the methods used to exercise that jurisdiction? Does a state have a right to shoot down any plane that enters its airspace? In 1955, an El Al Israel Airlines Ltd. commercial airplane, with passengers aboard, entered the airspace of Bulgaria for some unknown reason. Bulgarian fighter aircraft fired at the plane; it exploded in flight and crashed in Bulgarian territory. All 58 persons aboard were killed, including American and British passengers. Proceedings were instituted against Bulgaria in the International Court of Justice by Israel, the United States and the United Kingdom, protesting the inhuman and excessive use of force by the Bulgarians, the lack of adequate warning, the failure of Bulgaria to recognize the right of entry in distress. The cases did not proceed to the merits because of Bulgaria's having failed to consent to the jurisdiction of the Court. 9 Whiteman, Digest of International Law 326–340 (1963).

3. *Excessive use of force: analogies from the law of the sea.* **The I'm Alone,** 1935, 3 U.N.Rep.Int'l Arb. Awards 1609 involved a dispute between Canada and the United States arising out of the sinking of a Canadian rum-running vessel. A convention between the United States and Great Britain permitted search and seizure by the United States of British vessels suspected of liquor smuggling if the vessels were found close to, though outside, United States territorial waters. The hot pursuit of the *I'm Alone* ended 200 miles away from the Louisiana coast in the Gulf of Mexico. The commanding officer of the pursuing American coast guard cutter ordered the *I'm Alone* to stop and informed the commander of the *I'm Alone* that it would be sunk unless it stopped. After warning shots were fired, the United States vessel put enough shots into the hull of the *I'm Alone* to sink her. Commissioners appointed to report on this event stated:

> * * * The question is whether, in the circumstances, the Government of the United States was legally justified in sinking the I'm Alone.

The answer given to this question is as follows:—

> On the assumptions stated in the question, the United States might, consistently with the Convention, use necessary and reason-

able force for the purpose of effecting the objects of boarding, searching, seizing and bringing into port the suspected vessel; and if sinking should occur incidentally, as a result of the exercise of necessary and reasonable force for such purpose, the pursuing vessel might be entirely blameless. But the Commissioners think that, in the circumstances stated in paragraph eight of the Answer, the admittedly intentional sinking of the suspected vessel was not justified by anything in the Convention.

* * *

The *I'm Alone* was sunk on the 22nd day of March, 1929, on the high seas, in the Gulf of Mexico, by the United States revenue cutter Dexter. By their interim report the Commissioners found that the sinking of the vessel was not justified by anything in the Convention. The Commissioners now add that it could not be justified by any principle of international law.

Are there special risks associated with aircraft that require peremptory use of destructive force?

A PROPOSED OPEN SKIES TREATY; A POST–COLD WAR INITIATIVE

There is, pending advice and consent in the United States Senate, a proposed Open Skies Treaty whose negotiation was initiated by the United States, on the basis of a concept announced by President Eisenhower in 1955. Senate action approved this Treaty on August 6, 1993. Salient provisions of the Treaty are in the Documentary Supplement. Hearings were conducted in the Foreign Relations Committee on this Treaty in which officials from the Joint Chiefs of Staff, the Departments of State and Defense, and the Arms Control and Disarmament Agency testified in its favor.

In essence the Treaty provides for states' acceptance of unarmed, short-notice overflights of each others' territories for general observation related to confidence-and-security-building knowledge of each other's offensive and defensive installations. Signers of the Treaty, subject to ratification or accession, include the 16 NATO countries, the East European members of the former Warsaw Pact, Russia and at least four other successor states of the former Soviet Union, and the former Czechoslovakian state, now divided, with both new states intending to re-acknowledge signature and seek ratifications.

Various overflight arrangements of interest to particular states have been declared, and the data from any overflight by any participating country is to be made available by purchase to any and all treaty parties.

QUESTION: Is it likely that this Treaty, if it comes into force, will significantly reduce the dangers of air disasters such as those that immediately follow? Why or why not?

DESTRUCTION OF KOREAN AIR LINES BOEING 747 OVER SEA OF JAPAN, 31 AUGUST 1983

REPORT OF INVESTIGATION BY SECRETARY GENERAL OF CIVIL AVIATION ORGANIZATION (DECEMBER 1983)

23 International Legal Materials 867 (1984).*

SUMMARY OF FINDINGS AND CONCLUSIONS

On 31 August 1983, a Korean Air Lines Boeing 747, designated KE007, departed John F. Kennedy International Airport, New York, United States, on a one-stop scheduled flight for Kimpo International Airport, Seoul, Republic of Korea. The en-route stop occurred at Anchorage International Airport, Alaska. At Anchorage, the aircraft was refuelled, serviced for the remainder of the flight to Seoul, and, in accordance with the standing company practice, the flight and cabin crews were changed.

The flight departed at the planned estimated time of departure (ETD) which, in keeping with the standard Korean Air Lines' procedure, was separately calculated for each flight of KE007. The ETD at Anchorage was planned so that its arrival in Seoul was at its scheduled arrival time of 0600 (local time) or as close thereto as possible. The actual departure time of 1300 hours on 31 August should have resulted in an on-time arrival of KE007 at Seoul had the flight been completed successfully and fully in accordance with its filed flight plan.

On departing Anchorage, the flight had 269 persons on board consisting of three flight crew members, twenty cabin attendants, six crew employees of KAL being repositioned to Seoul for duty assignments and 240 passengers.

Soon after its departure from Anchorage, KE007 began deviating to the right (north) of its assigned direct route to Bethel. This deviation resulted in a progressively ever greater lateral displacement to the right of its planned route which, ultimately, resulted in its penetration of adjacent high seas airspace in flight information regions (FIRs) operated by the Union of Soviet Socialist Republics (USSR), as well as of sovereign USSR airspace overlying portions of the Kamchatka Peninsula and Sakhalin Island and their surrounding territorial waters.

No evidence was found * * * to indicate that the flight crew of KE007 was, at any time, aware of the flight's deviation from its planned route in spite of the fact that it continued along the same general off-track flight path for some five hours and twenty-six minutes.

At about 1820 hours when it was in the vicinity of Sakhalin Island, USSR, the flight was intercepted by military aircraft operated by the USSR. At 1827 hours, the aircraft was hit by at least one of two air-to-air missiles fired from one of the USSR interceptor aircraft whose pilot

* Reprinted with the permission of the American Society of International Law from materials published in 23 I.L.M. 864–937 under the general title "International Civil Organization: Action with Regard to the Downing of the Korean Air Lines Aircraft."

had been directed by his ground command and control unit to terminate the flight of KE007.

As a direct result of the missile attack, KE007 crashed and sank into the Sea of Japan southwest of Sakhalin Island. There were no survivors among the passengers, flight crew and cabin attendants. Only fragmentary pieces of the aircraft and a small number of items of personal property have been salvaged to-date. Most of this debris apparently was either dislodged as a result of impact forces at the time the aircraft struck the water or subsequently floated to the surface where they were dispersed by tidal currents.

The search and rescue and salvage efforts of the several interested ICAO Contracting States have now been suspended or terminated completely after more than two months of sustained effort.

Due to the absence or unavailability of: 1) surviving crew members with whom discussions might have taken place; 2) some of the communications which might have shed light on the reasons for KE007's major course deviation; 3) indications of flight crew awareness of their being off track; 4) indication that the crew of KE007 knew they were the subject of interception activity; 5) a record of communications emanating from ground intercept control units; 6) vital flight instrumentation, communications and avionics equipment from the wreckage of KE007 and, finally; 7) the flight data and the cockpit voice recorders from KE007, the investigative effort was compelled to proceed on the basis of limited hard evidence and facts, circumstantial evidence, assumptions and calculations and to base some of its key findings on postulated and then simulated, most-likely scenarios of what may have transpired.

Several potentialities for KE007's straying off track were ultimately discarded by this ICAO investigation as being too unlikely to warrant further consideration. They are:

a) unlawful interference;

b) crew incapacitation;

c) deliberate crew action associated with fuel savings incentives; and

d) extensive cockpit avionics/navigation systems failures or malfunctions.

In light of the information in the second paragraph above concerning the revised ETD of KE007 which should have resulted in an "on-time" arrival at Seoul, the investigation did not consider further the hypothesis considered by the USSR Accident Investigation Commission that there was a deliberate delay in KE007's departure from Anchorage and a premeditated deviation from the flight plan route for intelligence gathering purposes.

As the investigation proceeded, many postulations were heard and considered as to how and why KE007 strayed so far off track. It was possible to narrow the number of plausible explanations to three, each of which were amenable to study, analysis, testing and verification through simulation or sophisticated calculation methodologies. They are:

1) That the crew inadvertently flew virtually the entire flight on a constant magnetic heading (in the "heading mode") due to its unawareness of the fact that "heading" had been selected as the mode of navigation rather than "inertial navigation system" (INS). In such a situation, with the INS system activated although not controlling flight navigation, the crew would have been provided with regular indications of INS waypoint passages at or near the flight plan estimates for such passages and could, therefore, have been under the impression they were navigating in the INS mode.

2) That an undetected 10 degree longitudinal error was made in inserting the "present position" coordinates of the Anchorage gate position into one or more of the INS units on board the aircraft. Such an entry mistake could be made by a single "finger error" in entering more than 100 digits and letters that would be needed to fully load a single INS unit at the outset of the flight.

3) That at some point a crew member inserted the Seoul (destination) coordinates into the INS steering unit as a waypoint merely to obtain an indication of the direct distance to Seoul. In so doing, rather than using the "remote ranging" capability of the INS, he erroneously entered the present position to Seoul as a directed track change. Such an inadvertent action would produce the information desired but also cause the aircraft to take up the direct, great circle track to Seoul bypassing all other waypoints which, in the early stages of the flight would result in a change in heading, which would easily remain undetected.

After a simulation study which included four flights, three of which were of four to five and one half hours in duration, the scenarios in 1) and 2) presented possible explanations for the straying to the right of track by KE007 virtually from the beginning of its ill-fated flight. Each of the scenarios assumes a considerable degree of lack of alertness and attentiveness on the part of the entire flight crew but not to a degree that is unknown in international civil aviation.

Concerning the interception and associated identification, signalling and communications the investigation found the following:

1) Interceptions of KE007 were attempted by USSR military interceptor aircraft, over Kamchatka Peninsula and in the vicinity of Sakhalin Island.

2) The USSR authorities assumed that KE007 was an "intelligence" aircraft and, therefore, they did not make exhaustive efforts to identify the aircraft through in-flight visual observations.

3) KE007's climb from FL 330 to FL 350 during the time of the last interception, a few minutes before its flight was terminated, was interpreted as being an evasive action thus fur-

ther supporting the presumption that it was an "intelligence" aircraft.

4) ICAO was not provided any radar recordings, recorded communications or transcripts associated with the first intercept attempt or for the ground-to-interceptor portion of the second attempt, therefore, it was not possible to fully assess the comprehensiveness or otherwise of the application of intercept procedures, signalling and communications.

5) In the absence of any indication that the flight crew of KE007 was aware of the two interception attempts, it was concluded that they were not.

PRELIMINARY INFORMATION ON PROGRESS OF THE USSR INVESTIGATION INTO THE ACCIDENT TO A SOUTH KOREAN AEROPLANE ON 1 SEPTEMBER 1983

23 International Legal Materials 910 (1984).*

1.1 General information

On the night of 1 September 1983, at 05.30 Kamchatka time (20.30 Moscow summer time on 31 August 1983), an unknown aeroplane violated the State frontier of the Union of Soviet Socialist Republics and penetrated deep into USSR airspace. The intruder aeroplane spent about 2 hours over the Kamchatka Peninsula, the area of the Okhotsk Sea and the Island of Sakhalin.

Interception procedures were executed within USSR airspace, over the Kamchatka Peninsula, by aircraft of the USSR Air Defence Command (PVO) in accordance with the established USSR regulations, for the purpose of compelling the aeroplane to land on USSR territory. The intruder aeroplane did not comply with the demands of the interceptors but continued flying in the direction of the Sea of Okhotsk.

In the course of the intruder aircraft's onward flight in Soviet airspace over the Island of Sakhalin the regulatory USSR interception procedures were executed once more. In view of the refusal of the intruder aircraft to comply with the demands of the USSR anti-aircraft defence forces to land on USSR territory, the flight was terminated in Soviet airspace over USSR territory—above the Pravda housing project in the southwest part of Sakhalin Island—on 1 September 1983 at 06.24 Sakhalin time (22.24 Moscow time on 31 August 1983).

On 1 September—10 hours after the termination of the intruder aircraft's flight—the USSR received an official request from the United States for information concerning a South Korean aeroplane which "according to the information of American tracking stations, has lost its way in the area of Sakhalin".

It thus became known from foreign sources that the sovereignty of the USSR, the rules of Soviet and international law and the Standards of

* Reprinted with the permission of the American Society of International Law.

the International Civil Aviation Organization (ICAO) had been violated by an aircraft registered in South Korea. No official confirmation of this has been communicated to the Soviet side by South Korea.

* * *

CONCLUSIONS

1. The investigation of the violation of the State frontier of the USSR and deep penetration of USSR airspace by the intruder aeroplane in the areas of Kamchatka and South Sakhalin on the night of 31 August/1 September has brought to light numerous breaches of Soviet law, and specifically of the Air Code of the USSR and the Law on the State Frontier of the USSR, and violations of the terms of the 1944 Chicago Convention, Annexes 2 and 10 and the rules promulgated in AIP USSR and the requirements of ICAO air navigation documents.

2. [T]hat the intruder aeroplane belonged to a South Korean airline was received by the Soviet authorities from foreign sources only after its flight had been terminated by the Air Defence Command.

3. It has been established that the flight of the South Korean aeroplane over Soviet territory was conducted with prior intent.

This is confirmed by the following:

a) a deviation from track of more than 500 km far exceeds the permissible navigational errors for this type of aeroplane;

b) the indications of the airborne radar equipment made it possible for the crew to be aware of the fact that they were crossing the Kamchatka Peninsula and Island of Sakhalin, which was clearly inconsistent with the plan to fly on airway R20;

c) the ATS units of the United States and Japan, notwithstanding the absence of the South Korean aeroplane from its prescribed track for over 3 hours in their controlled airspace, took no steps to return the aeroplane to that track;

d) the flight crew of the intruder aeroplane did not respond to the series of actions taken by the Soviet Air Defence forces to attract the attention of the South Korean aeroplane to the fact that it was being intercepted and oblige it to land;

e) the deviation of the * * * aeroplane from the international airway was such that its flight took place over strategically important Soviet centres in the Far East and coincided with a stepped-up operation by United States intelligence forces in this area.

4. The South Korean aeroplane was engaged in a preplanned intelligence-gathering and provocative mission.

5. The actions of the Soviet anti-aircraft defence interceptors were conducted in strict conformity with current Soviet legislation and the provisions set out in AIP USSR. The intruder aeroplane ignored the actions of the intercepting fighters and altered its heading, altitude and flight speed, which proves that the crew was in full control of the flight. In view of the complete refusal of the intruder aeroplane to obey the

instructions given by the Air Defence aircraft, the intruder aeroplane's flight was terminated on orders from the ground.

6.   The ATC services of the United States and Japan, which were responsible for providing navigational support to the South Korean aeroplane on flight KAL 007 along the Anchorage–Tokyo airway, did not utilize the possibilities open to them of detecting and forestalling such a glaring deviation by the aeroplane.

Chairman of the Accident Investigation Commission, A.I. Okhonsky

-----

REVIEW OF SECRETARY–GENERAL'S REPORT BY THE AIR NAVIGATION COMMISSION OF THE ICAO

23 International Legal Materials 924 (1984).*

* * *

4.4   Although the preliminary information provided by the USSR in Appendix F to C–WP/7764 is that the actions of the USSR intercepting aircraft were conducted in strict conformity with the interception procedures promulgated in the USSR AIP, which are essentially in line with the ICAO procedures, the transcript in Appendix D to C–WP/7764 of air-ground communications between the intercepting aircraft and intercept control units gives no clear indication that the intercepting aircraft had taken up a position "within view of the pilot of the intercepted aircraft" or "to enable the pilot of the latter aircraft to see the visual signals given" as recommended in Attachment A to Annex 2.   This has been highlighted because the Commission realizes that many factors have to be considered in assessing the ideal position for an interceptor to be seen by the pilot of the civil aircraft.   Therefore, it is of paramount importance for the interceptor aircraft to ensure that it attracts the attention of the pilot-in-command of the civil aircraft.

4.5   The Air Navigation Commission is unable to establish the exact cause for the significant deviation from tract.   The magnitude of the diversion cannot be explained, particularly as the aircraft was equipped with navigation equipment which should have enabled the crew to adhere to its track.   It has to be understood that operators have extensive ab-initio and recurrent training programmes to train pilots in the use of self-contained navigation aids.   This is the case also for Korean Air Lines.

* * *

5.   Conclusions

5.1   During the technical review of the Secretary General's report as contained in C–WP/7764, the Air Navigation Commission has not attempted to offer any firm conclusions regarding the various aspects of the incident, because the information presented to the Commission in relation to the total period of flight KE007 was incomplete and some of

* Reprinted with the permission of the American Society of International Law.

the information received by ICAO had differences which could not be cleared up. Furthermore, the Commission found it difficult to validate and endorse the conclusions connected with the scenarios postulated in the Secretary General's report because any one of them contained some points which could not be explained satisfactorily.

5.2 The Commission noted that the evaluations and simulations conducted did not include an extensive evaluation of INS equipment malfunctions or other failures involving significant track deviations which have occurred in the past and is of the opinion that study of this subject should be pursued.

* * *

RESOLUTION ADOPTED BY THE COUNCIL
OF THE ICAO, MARCH 6, 1984

23 International Legal Materials 937 (1984).*

THE COUNCIL,

1) RECALLING the resolutions adopted and the decisions taken on 16 September 1983 at the Extraordinary Session of the ICAO Council and endorsed by the 24th Session of the ICAO Assembly in October 1983 as well as the Council Resolution of 13 December 1983, relating to the destruction of a Korean Air Lines civil aircraft on 1 September 1983 by Soviet military aircraft;

2) HAVING CONSIDERED the report of the investigation by the Secretary General and the subsequent technical review by the Air Navigation Commission;

3) RECOGNIZING that, although this investigation was unable, because of lack of necessary data, to determine conclusively the precise cause for the serious deviation of some 500 kilometers from its flight plan route by the Korean aircraft into the airspace above the territory under the sovereignty of the Soviet Union, no evidence was found to indicate that the deviation was premeditated or that the crew was at any time aware of the flight's deviation;

4) REAFFIRMING that, whatever the circumstances which, according to the Secretary General's report, may have caused the aircraft to stray off its flight plan route, such use of armed force constitutes a violation of international law, and invokes generally recognized legal consequences;

5) RECOGNIZING that such use of armed force is a grave threat to the safety of international civil aviation, and is incompatible with the norms governing international behavior and with the rules, Standards and Recommended Practices enshrined in the Chicago

---

* Reprinted with the permission of the American Society of International Law.

Convention and its Annexes and with elementary considerations of humanity;

6) EXPRESSING its continuing sympathy with the families bereaved in this tragic incident;

1) CONDEMNS the use of armed force which resulted in the destruction of the Korean airliner and the tragic loss of 269 lives;

2) DEEPLY DEPLORES the Soviet failure to cooperate in the search and rescue efforts of other involved States and the Soviet failure to cooperate with the ICAO investigation of the incident by refusing to accept the visit of the investigation team appointed by the Secretary General and by failing so far to provide the Secretary General with information relevant to the investigation;

3) URGES all Contracting States to cooperate fully in the work of examining and adopting an amendment to the Chicago Convention at the 25th Session (Extraordinary) of the ICAO Assembly and in the improvement of measures for preventing a recurrence of this type of tragedy.

————

Reaction to the destruction of KAL Flight 007. The United States presented notes to the Soviet Union demanding compensation for the attack on the airliner. The Soviet Union refused to accept the notes. 78 Am.J. Int'l L. 213 (1984). Similar notes were presented by Australia, Canada, Japan, Malaysia, the Philippines, Thailand, the United Kingdom and (through the United States) Korea. 22 International Legal Materials 1190 (1983). Public controversy over the affair highlighted one question: did the Soviets know they were attacking a civilian airliner or did they mistakenly believe that the aircraft was a military reconnaissance plane? See Hersh, "The Target is Destroyed" (1986).

————

NORTH PACIFIC ROUTE SYSTEM: EMERGENCY COMMUNICATIONS
80 American Journal of International Law 152 (1986).*

By a trilateral exchange of notes at Tokyo on October 8, 1985 among American Ambassador Mike Mansfield, Soviet Ambassador to Japan Pyotr Abrasimov and Japanese Minister of Foreign Affairs Shintaro Abe, the United States of America, the Union of Soviet Socialist Republics and Japan brought into force arrangements to enhance the safety of flights over the North Pacific Route System. These arrangements were set out in a memorandum of understanding signed by representatives of the three Governments at Tokyo on July 29, 1985. The trilateral exchange confirmed the memorandum, which provides for a new communications network among the parties' respective air control centers at

* Reprinted with the permission of the American Society of International Law.

Anchorage, Tokyo and Khabarovsk in order to coordinate actions to assist a civil aircraft in an emergency.

Recognizing the complete and exclusive sovereignty of each state over the airspace above its territory, the memorandum designates the area control centers (ACCS) at Anchorage, Tokyo and Khabarovsk as points of contact among the parties' respective air traffic control services, with the center at Tokyo the principal point of contact. Contact among the three air traffic control services is to be conducted on a priority basis. To achieve coordination of their actions, the area control centers at Anchorage and Tokyo will initiate communication with the Khabarovsk area control center to provide all available information regarding a civil aircraft assigned to a North Pacific route when they are aware of its possible entry into a Soviet flight information region (FIR). When necessary, the area control center at Khabarovsk will initiate communication with the Tokyo and Anchorage area control centers to exchange information about an unidentified aircraft appearing in a Soviet flight information region. To the extent available, the following will be exchanged: information provided by the appropriate area control center that the situation has occurred; data on the type of aircraft; its radio call sign, transponder code, nationality, operator, location, altitude, and speed; the time and type of the event; the pilot's intentions if known; actions taken and assistance requested; information to the responsible search and rescue agencies. The communication facilities between the Anchorage, Tokyo and Khabarovsk area control centers are to be available on a round-the-clock basis.

A new dedicated direct speech circuit, using the currently existing telephone cable, is to be established between the Tokyo and Khabarovsk area control centers. The existing high-frequency speech circuit between the Sapporo (Japan) and Khabarovsk area control centers, connected by domestic telephone channel to the Tokyo area control center, is to be used as a backup to the direct speech circuit.

KAL–007 Black Boxes Retrieved by the USSR

Russian President Yeltsin announced in October, 1992 that the Soviets had retrieved the downed aircraft's flight recorders from the depths of the Sea of Japan. The bearing of this source of possible information on what really happened is not yet clear.

---

1. *Beyond trespass: espionage as a state offense.* Issues other than technical trespass of Soviet airspace were involved in the U–2 incident (and claimed by the Soviets to be involved in the KAL case). The criminal charge against Powers in the Soviet Union was of espionage as defined in the domestic law of that state.[a] In the tradition of the

a. Compare 18 United States Code § 796, with respect to photography of military installations from aircraft.

international spy, fictional and real, the espionage agent is "out in the cold" all by himself. He expects to be disowned if caught. And the conventional practice of states is not overtly to charge another state with espionage but to counter-attack in kind, in what Dean Acheson once called "the underworld of international relations." In the U-2 case, however, although Powers was caught and prosecuted under Soviet law, the USSR openly charged the United States with responsibility, calling for condemnation by the Security Council of the United Nations of the aggressive acts of the United States. President Eisenhower responded with the unprecedented admission that the United States was responsible for Powers' flight, justifying it " 'to obtain information now concealed behind the iron curtain' in order to lessen the danger of surprise attack on the free world * * *." Wright, Legal Aspects of the U-2 Incident, 54 Am.J.Int'l L. 836, 838 (1960).

Are there, therefore, issues of espionage at the international level? That is, is the law of espionage purely domestic, directed at the individual only, or is there state responsibility to the state spied upon? In view of the practices of states over centuries, it is not possible to find a consentio juris that spying per se is an offense under customary law. Has it become so under the United Nations Charter, either as to (a) conventional espionage through the penetration of the state's ground frontier, or (b) aerial espionage through the penetration of airspace? See Article 2(4). Also, espionage is a purely political offense, exempting alleged perpetrators from extradition.

2. *Identification zones.* The United States has established air defense identification zones (ADIZ) and a distant early warning identification zone (DEWIZ) in areas of the airspace over the high seas adjacent to its coasts. Similar zones have been established by some other states. Aircraft operating in or penetrating such zones are subject to requirements with respect to filing flight plans; pilots of aircraft entering the United States through an ADIZ or a DEWIZ are required to report positions. 14 C.F.R., Part 99. Since these zones extend seaward several hundreds of miles, do they entail a violation of international law respecting the jurisdiction of the United States over airspace? Can the United States lawfully prescribe rules regulating activity in these zones on the ground that obedience to the rules is a condition to entry into the territory of the United States? *See*, Comment *e* to Section 21, and the 1987 Restatement, Reporters' Note 2 to Section 521.

The Air Tragedy at Lockerbie, Scotland

The destruction of Pan–Am 103, Dec. 21, 1988, with loss of all passengers and crew due to the explosion of an infernal machine placed aboard it at Frankfurt, possibly by persons protected from extradition by Libya, will be considered under *Sabotage* in the next sub-division of this Chapter, *Offensives Aboard Aircraft.* One question may be posed now: If it should be shown that the saboteurs and/or the baggage handlers at Frankfurt were the agents of the State of Libya, does an international claim against Libya in the *Pan–Am Case* differ from a possible claim against Russia as the successor to the Soviet State for the KAL–007 loss? Or, in the usage of some scholars: Are the délits of the two states, if both are involved, the same or different? Explain.

―――

Where to Draw the Line between the International Public Law of Airspace and Transnational Air Transport Private Law

Previously we have alluded to differences in the origins and natures of sea law as to what is public international law and what is not. See Chapter 4. The problem as to air law is more complex, chiefly because almost all of air law is of treaty origin, insofar as over-borders operations are concerned. Because of its treaty origins, should all of air law be presented in public international law studybooks? In this book we have decided that the Chicago Convention and its progeny, bilateral civil aviation route and passenger-handling agreements, should be presented here, because of the very large direct involvement of state interests, including territorial airspace. But we think the Warsaw Convention and its progeny in international agreement form, dealing with liabilities of contractual commercial carriers to passengers, baggage and cargo, belong elsewhere. Hence, we present only a brief summary of an intensely litigated area of private claims against carriers and insurers, that of the Warsaw Convention and its modifications.

―――

International Aircarrier Liability to Passengers, "Offenses" in a Nutshell

Establishing tort liability (or is it contractual?) of a common carrier is difficult enough on the ground and within a single jurisdiction. It is much more difficult in the case of civil aviation operations among states, because of the ways in which aircraft losses happen and the widely different treatment of liabilities for losses in diverse legal systems, especially as between common law and civil law jurisdictions. The operative heart of the Warsaw Convention of 1925–29 should be printed on your ticket if you fly abroad, in at least 10–point type.

But if the print is smaller or you lose the ticket stub, the Convention still applies. It limits death or injury claims to $75,000, without proof of fault, or, in some American states, $58,000 exclusive of legal fees and costs. There are also baggage loss limitations. A comparative law scholar will instantly see the relationship of this scheme to the civil law limits on tort recovery for personal injury. Not unnaturally, common law lawyers and judges are not wildly enthusiastic about such a system, but then they begin to think of the difficulties of proving fault of the flight crew and the ground management of an air-carrier. Recent disasters such as KAL–007 have "pushed the envelope" in American tort jurisprudence a bit, but the courts have held firm in favor of the Convention's application as against technical and constitutional-level attacks. Of perhaps only minor consolation is the provision in the

Convention that removes the recovery limitation if wilful misconduct on the part of the aircarrier can be proved. The international air traveler is well advised to insure himself up to any amount he wishes or can afford, above the difficult to avoid Warsaw Convention capped recovery.

Questions for a Torts Class or a Beer Hall:

1. Would the Warsaw Convention scheme be better for automobile passengers than mandatory no-fault auto insurance?

2. Would the Warsaw Convention scheme be better than trying to enforce adequate auto insurance policy injury liability limits, say, in California?

2.　OFFENSES ABOARD AIRCRAFT

GENERAL OFFENSES
SILBERWACHT v. ATTORNEY–GENERAL

Israel, District Court of Tel Aviv, 1953.
20 Int'l L.Rep. 153 (1957).*

The Facts. This was an appeal from a decision of the Magistrate's Court convicting the appellant of smuggling and of being in possession of smuggled goods. The appellant was employed at Lydda Airport where there existed a clandestine organization for purchasing tinned food from South African airmen and bringing it on to the market without customs examination and payment of customs duty. By section 2 of the Customs Ordinance smuggling is defined as:

> Any importation, exportation, carriage coastwise or over the land frontiers, or attempted importation, exportation, carriage coastwise or over the land frontiers, of goods, with intent to defraud the revenue or to evade any prohibition of, restriction on, or regulations as to, the importation, exportation, carriage coastwise or over the land frontiers of any goods; and "smuggle" and "smuggled goods" have corresponding meanings.

One of the grounds of appeal was that when the tins were removed from the aircraft by the aircrew they had already been smuggled by the South African crew and were therefore smuggled goods, so that the appellant could not be convicted of smuggling.

Held: that the appeal must be admitted and the conviction dismissed. [A portion of the opinion of the court appears below.]

* * * This ground of appeal raises several important questions of public international law * * *. The question whether the removal of the goods from the aircraft (which, it seems, was a South African aircraft, although it is not clear whether it was privately owned or a State aircraft) constitutes their importation into Israel, or whether the goods entered Israel at the moment when the aircraft entered Israel, is

----

* Reprinted with the permission of the Editor of The International Law Reports.

connected with the question whether an aircraft has to be regarded as foreign territory. Although the rule is nowhere explicitly laid down, it seems that the law of Israel presupposes that the law governing territorial sovereignty (from the point of view of jurisdiction) is similar to the concept of ownership of land, and includes authority not only over the surface of the land but also down to its depth and also in the skies above jusque ad coelum. The general opinion in public international law is similar. See Article I of the Chicago Air Agreement of 1944. * * *

* * *

* * * [E]ven if South Africa has jurisdiction over acts performed in her aircraft in accordance with South African laws regarding the air and regarding jurisdiction (assuming that the existence of extraterritorial laws of that character is not contrary to international law and the public policy of Israel)—nevertheless the foreign aircraft is not foreign territory. The result, therefore, is that the act of smuggling came to an end when the pilot imported the tins into Israel with the intention of defrauding the customs. The act of smuggling did not commence at the moment when the tins were removed from the aircraft since they were already within Israel. * * *

Judge Avissar, dissenting, said: "As to the smuggling, it seems to me to make no difference to the appellant whether the pilot who landed at Lydda Airport with the tinned goods on board and intending to smuggle them was guilty of an offence or not. * * * When the appellant received the goods from the aircraft and removed them from Lydda Airport without paying customs—as has been proved to have occurred—he committed the offence. The position of a person who receives goods from an aircraft at an airport cannot be any different from the position of a person who receives goods from a ship within the territorial waters of the country and imports them by smuggling. At all events, such a person is to be considered as an importer in the sense of the definition of smuggling contained in section 2 of the Customs Ordinance; and why should any discrimination be made in favour of the man who commits the smuggling by receiving the goods from an aircraft which has landed at an airport? * * *"

———

Problem. A South African commercial aircraft is making a nonstop transit through the airspace of Israel on a flight to Turkey at an altitude of 30,000 feet. No Israeli nationals are on board the plane. A passenger in the plane assaults a stewardess. Both are South African nationals. If the passenger subsequently travels to Tel Aviv, and is arrested and tried there for assault, does South Africa have any basis for complaint under international law?

———

CHUMNEY v. NIXON

United States Court of Appeals, Sixth Circuit, 1980.
615 F.2d 389.

EDWARDS, Chief Judge.

Plaintiffs-appellants Chumney, man and wife, appeal from dismissal of their complaint. The District Judge before whom this matter was argued, after considerable deliberation, granted defendants-appellees' motions to dismiss. He reached his final conclusion on motion to reconsider or rehear his dismissal, at which point he held that "the claims could not be said to arise under this criminal statute." The statute referred to, 18 U.S.C. § 113, is a criminal statute which provides penalties for personal assaults on any aircraft within the special aircraft jurisdiction of the United States.

This is a strange case on the alleged facts. It is also a difficult one as far as legal concepts are concerned.

THE ALLEGATIONS OF FACT

The facts alleged which may be digested from plaintiffs' complaint and amendments thereto, are as follows.

Chumney claims that, while he and his wife were returning from a Memphis, Tennessee, Shrine Temple charter flight to Rio de Janeiro, a physical assault on him by defendant Nixon, the mayor of Shelby County, Tennessee, and the other individual defendants, broke some of his teeth and resulted in other serious, possibly permanent injuries. At the time of the assault, the complaint alleges that the aircraft was approximately 2½ hours out of Rio de Janeiro en route to Memphis, Tennessee. At oral argument, the parties appeared to agree that at the time concerned, the aircraft was at 29,000 feet over the Brazilian jungle. Judicial notice of a world map strongly suggests that plaintiffs' pleading should be so construed.

The motivation for this assault is alleged by Chumney to have originated in the fact that Nixon had once been sheriff of Shelby County and that Chumney, as a lawyer, had represented one of Nixon's deputies who had been fired by Nixon and had succeeded in getting him ordered replaced on the job.

There are sundry other interesting facts alleged in the background of this involved case, such as that Mr. and Mrs. Chumney were using this charter flight for their honeymoon following their recent marriage, that the Chumneys were seated next to an unnamed man (who did not participate in this assault) whose "body odor" was highly offensive to the Chumneys and they were much offended by having to continue to sit near him, which complaint they had made known to the individual defendants who were officers of the Shrine Temple and that, as alleged by the complaint, Braniff Airlines served quantities of liquor to everybody concerned, including both the plaintiffs and the individual defendants, and failed to prevent the assault.

THE LEGAL ISSUES

It is plaintiffs' contention that the individual defendants named as having participated in the assault clearly violated 18 U.S.C. § 113(d) and that their actions did damage which exceeded $10,000. They assert that their complaint arose under the laws of the United States as a civil action under 28 U.S.C. § 1331(a), the federal question jurisdictional statute. * * *

Plaintiffs in their tendered amended complaint assert that the United States District Court for the Western District of Tennessee, Western Division, has federal question jurisdiction under 28 U.S.C. § 1331 (1976) because defendants violated 18 U.S.C. § 113 (1976) which statute punishes assaults within the maritime and territorial jurisdiction of the United States. They claim the cited statute is made specifically applicable to the current fact problem by 49 U.S.C. § 1472(k)(1) (1976) pertaining to the special aircraft jurisdiction of the United States.

The federal question statute 28 U.S.C. § 1331(a) which plaintiffs rely upon reads:

> (a) The district courts shall have original jurisdiction of all civil actions wherein the matter in controversy exceeds the sum or value of $10,000, exclusive of interest and costs, and arises under the Constitution, laws, or treaties of the United States.

18 U.S.C. § 113 reads:

> Whoever, within the special maritime and territorial jurisdiction of the United States, is guilty of an assault shall be punished as follows:
>
>   * * *
>
> (d) Assault by striking, beating, or wounding, by fine of * * * or imprisonment for not more than six months, or both.
>
> (e) Simple assault, by fine * * * or imprisonment for not more than three months, or both.
>
> (f) Assault resulting in serious bodily injury, by fine * * * or imprisonment for not more than ten years, or both.

The applicability of 18 U.S.C. § 113 is established by the following statutory provisions:

18 U.S.C. § 7 reads:

> The term "special maritime and territorial jurisdiction of the United States", as used in this title [18 U.S.C. § 1 et seq.] includes:
>
>   * * *
>
> (5) Any aircraft belonging in whole or in part to the United States, or any citizen thereof, or to any corporation created by or under the laws of the United States, or any State, Territory, district, or possession thereof, while such aircraft is in flight over the high seas, or over any other waters within the admiralty and maritime jurisdiction of the United States and out of the jurisdiction of any particular State.

49 U.S.C. § 1472(k)(1) reads:

(k)(1) Whoever, while aboard an aircraft within the special aircraft jurisdiction of the United States, commits an act which, if committed within the special maritime and territorial jurisdiction of the United States, as defined in section 7 of Title 18, would be in violation of section 113, 114, 661, 662, 1111, 1112, 1113, 2031, 2032, or 2111 of such Title 18 shall be punished as provided therein.

Finally, 49 U.S.C. § 1301(34)(d)(i) reads:

(34) The term "special aircraft jurisdiction of the United States" includes—

* * *

(d) any other aircraft outside the United States—

(i) that has its next scheduled destination or last point of departure in the United States, if that aircraft next actually lands in the United States; [a]

We believe that these statutes clearly indicate that the Congress of the United States has undertaken to apply federal law to American (and other) aircraft while such aircraft are en route from an airport in the United States or are returning from a foreign country directly to an airport in the United States. The nature of 18 U.S.C. § 113 is that of a criminal statute designed to protect law abiding passengers on such an aircraft from either simple or felonious assault. The sanctions created by § 113 and made applicable to the subject circumstances by 49 U.S.C. §§ 1472(k)(1) and 1301(34)(d) are, however, purely criminal sanctions.

This leaves for our resolution the following question: Are plaintiffs entitled to a civil cause of action for damages against defendants which is derived from the federal criminal statutes described above and over which the federal courts would have jurisdiction under 28 U.S.C. § 1331(a)? The answer is anything but easy to come by. The District Judge accurately defined the question and answered it in the negative. Although it is certainly a close question, we disagree.

* * *

In our instant case, each plaintiff is clearly "one of the class for whose especial benefit" the statutes here involved were created. We find no specific language in the legislative history of the statutes previously cited which shows specific intent to create a civil remedy or which prohibits inference of such intent. It is clear to us that Congress has taken care in comprehensive legislation to protect the safety of passengers flying on United States airlines or flying on aircraft intended to land at United States airports or on aircraft bound for foreign lands after departure from an airport in the United States. A clear-cut purpose has been defined in federal legislation and the federal courts have been given specific jurisdiction to impose criminal penalties against those who commit simple or felonious assaults on aircrafts under the conditions described above. A civil action for damages would certainly

---

a. The definition now appears as paragraph 38 of 49 U.S.C. § 1301.

be consistent with the over-all congressional purpose and we believe should be inferred therefrom.

Indeed the existence or nonexistence of a civil cause of action in this case may create a legal precedent which will affect other possible fact situations (aircraft kidnapping or terrorism) some of which may well cry out for more than the criminal remedy.

Finally, the maintenance of civil peace on airlines flying to and from the United States and foreign lands is clearly a topic of federal, not state, significance. The State of Tennessee has not legislated on this subject and we believe that most state courts would be loath to reach for jurisdiction over the results of an altercation which occurred at 29,000 feet over the Brazilian jungle. This problem is certainly not one "traditionally relegated to the state courts."

It seems to this court to be an appropriate step under the legal doctrines which we have outlined above to approve a civil cause of action for damages derived from criminal statutes which plaintiffs alleged were violated in this case.

We recognize, of course, that when and if this case is finally tried, it may result in a swearing match between individuals, all of whom are now alleged to have been under some influence of liquor, and that sorting out who hit whom first may appear to be a task more appropriate for a police court than a federal district court.[1]

As to the portions of the complaint seeking damages from the individual defendants, the judgment of the District Court is reversed and the case is remanded for further proceedings consistent with this opinion.

* * *

———

1. *Questions.* What basis of jurisdiction under international law supports the United States federal prosecution in the Chumney case?

Should the result in the Chumney case have been different if the airline had been Brazilian? If the individuals involved had also been Brazilian nationals? In particular: (a) Would the assault have been covered by the statutes in those cases? (b) Would Brazil have a basis for complaint against the United States if the defendants had been convicted in those cases?

2. *The accretion of legislative bases of jurisdiction.* As the world has grown smaller and technological progress has produced more interactions between the United States and the rest of the Planet, Congress has acted to expand federal jurisdiction on a piecemeal basis. Title 18 United States Code defines as criminal a number of acts that are performed within the special maritime and territorial jurisdiction of the

---

1. Indeed, the district judge was of a view that the action could be maintained appropriately in the state court since all parties involved were residents of Memphis, Tennessee.

United States. In United States v. Cordova, 89 F.Supp. 298 (E.D.N.Y. 1950), the court found no federal jurisdiction with respect to assaults by a passenger on an American airplane flying over the Atlantic Ocean between Puerto Rico and New York. At that time, federal jurisdiction extended to specified crimes committed *upon* the high seas. The court held that this word could not be extended to include the airspace *over* the high seas. Shortly after the Cordova decision, in 1952, the definition of special maritime and territorial jurisdiction of the United States was expanded by the addition of paragraph (5) of 18 United States Code § 7, quoted in the Chumney case. Still later, in 1970, Congress expanded jurisdiction over Title 18 criminal acts (i.e., the acts listed at p. 294) to include those acts when committed within the special aircraft jurisdiction of the United States, now defined in 49 United States Code § 1301(38) (quoted in part in the Chumney case). Responding again to the rush of technology, Congress added space flight to the special maritime and territorial jurisdiction in 1981. In 1984 it added "Any place outside the jurisdiction of any nation with respect to an offense by or against a national of the United States."

————

HIJACKING

A passenger in a commercial airplane threatens to explode a bomb which, he says, is in a handbag he is carrying. The pilot diverts the flight of the plane to a destination demanded by the passenger. The passenger leaves the plane at that destination and the plane is flown to its original destination.

Even in this simple example there may be a number of problems of domestic and international law. The plane may be registered in the United States or in some other country. The passenger may hijack the plane on the ground in New York, or while it is over the Atlantic on its way to London, or while it is on the ground in London. The hijacker may be a United States national, or the national of another state. He may or may not eventually return to the United States and thus be subject to its enforcement jurisdiction. The United States may ask the government of the foreign state in which the hijacker is located to return him to the United States by extradition proceedings. The government of a state to which the hijacker has fled may decide to try him even though that state has had no connection with the event other than having become a place of refuge.

————

1. *International Conventions.*

The Tokyo Convention (Convention on Offenses and Certain Other Acts Committed on Board Aircraft, 20 U.S.T. 2941; Documentary Supplement) was drafted under the auspices of the International Civil Aviation Organization and signed in 1963. It entered into force for the

United States on December 4, 1969; 143 states were parties to the convention on January 1, 1992.

The convention is concerned broadly with the question of crimes on board aircraft in flight, on the surface of the high seas or any other area outside the jurisdiction of a nation state. A special purpose of the convention is to provide that there be no lapse of jurisdiction with respect to such crimes. To that end Article 3(1) provides that at least one state shall have jurisdiction: "The State of registration of the aircraft is competent to exercise jurisdiction over offenses and acts committed on board." This jurisdiction is not exclusive, however. The convention deals in detail with the powers of the aircraft commander to "off-load" and to restrain offenders or suspected offenders.

Article 11 deals specifically with hijacking, but in a limited way. It merely requires states parties to the convention to restore control of a hijacked airplane to the lawful commander or to preserve his control. The provision for extradition is relatively weak. Article 16 specifies that, for purposes of extradition, offenses on the aircraft shall be treated as though they had been committed not only in the place in which they occurred but also in the territory of the state of registration of the aircraft. However, the article states that it does not create an obligation to grant extradition.

The Hague Convention (Convention for the Suppression of Unlawful Seizure of Aircraft, 22 U.S.T. 1641, Documentary Supplement) was also the product of the work of the ICAO. It was approved at a diplomatic conference at The Hague in 1970 and entered into force for the United States on October 14, 1971. 148 states were parties to the Convention on January 1, 1993. In contrast to the Tokyo Convention, the Hague Convention is directed narrowly to the question of hijacking. Its major provisions create universal jurisdiction for the prosecution of hijackers and impose an obligation on the states either to prosecute the hijacker or to extradite him. See in particular Article 4, requiring the state to take jurisdiction over hijacking offenses. Jurisdiction is recognized for hijacking offenses that take place on board aircraft having connections with the state, i.e., the craft is registered there (or leased to someone located there) or the craft lands in the state with the offender still on board. The innovative thrust of this article is that it provides for universal jurisdiction, i.e. in the case where the offender is present in the state's territory. In this latter case the state is required to prosecute or extradite the hijacker. See Article 7.

Article 8 sets forth a strong provision with respect to extradition: a hijacking offense is deemed to be included as an extraditable offense in existing extradition treaties and is to be included in future extradition treaties. Under this article, if a hijacker is found in the United States (after hijacking a British airplane en route from London to South Africa and landing it in Libya), is arrested but escapes to Italy, can the United States demand his extradition from Italy? Look also at the United States—Italy extradition treaty in the Documentary Supplement.

2. *French legislation.* France deposited its ratification to the Hague Convention on September 18, 1972. The following legislation, Law 72–623,[a] was enacted July 5, 1972:

Art. L. 121–7. French courts have jurisdiction over any infraction committed aboard an airplane registered in France. They have jurisdiction as well over any crime or tort committed against such plane outside of the French territory.

Art. L. 121–8. French courts have jurisdiction with respect to a crime or a tort committed aboard a plane which is not registered in France when the author or the victim has French nationality, when the plane lands in France after the commission of the crime or tort, or when the infraction was committed aboard a plane which is rented without crew to a person who has his principal place of establishment or, if there be none, his permanent residence in France.

Moreover, in case a plane is forced off its course [i.e. hijacked] which is not registered in France, French courts have jurisdiction over the infraction and over every other act of violence against the passengers or the crew done by the person alleged to have forced the plane off its course in the commission of [literally, in direct relationship to] the offense, when the person is found in France. 92 Gazette du Palais (Legislation) 360 (1972).

Does the French legislation grant jurisdiction to French courts with respect to any crime or tort committed on any airplane, anywhere in the world, whether or not the plane is registered in France, whether or not it lands in France after the commission of the act—so long as the victim is French? Is this grant of jurisdiction provided by the convention? Is it consistent with international law?

3. *United States legislation.* Even before the United States became a party to the Hague Convention, it was a crime to commit aircraft piracy (i.e., "any seizure or exercise of control, by force or violence or threat of force or violence and with wrongful intent, of an aircraft within the special aircraft jurisdiction of the United States"), 49 U.S.C. § 1472. After becoming a party to the convention, the United States enacted legislation to broaden its definition of special aircraft jurisdiction to take account particularly of Subsections (b) and (c) of Section 1 of Article 4 of the convention. 49 U.S.C. § 1301(38). In implementation of Article 4(2) of the convention the United States added Section 1472 to Title 49 of the United States Code, criminalizing a hijacking offense outside the special aircraft jurisdiction of the United States if the offender is afterward found in the United States.

4. *Problem.* A hijacker is found in the United States and is prosecuted there. The aircraft is registered in Israel and never had contact with the United States. The hijacker is a national of State Z, a country in the Middle East, but State Z is not a party to the convention. Has the United States violated the rights of State Z? Can the United States justify its assertion of jurisdiction by claiming that its anti-hijacking legislation is an implementation not only of the Hague Conven-

---

a. Translation by the editors.

tion's grant of jurisdiction but also of jurisdiction that is recognized by the customary international law of piracy? See p. 339 with respect to the law of piracy as it has developed in the maritime context. A peculiar problem arises when analogy to classic piracy is attempted, since only one aircraft is involved in the event.

5. *Hijacking as piracy.* Some stress that piracy refers to an assault upon one vessel and its passengers, crew and cargo by criminal elements from another vessel. Thus, it has been argued that an infiltration and assault not involving another vessel is not piracy jure gentium. In one instance, infiltrators from within the vessel who took control of it for purposes of making a political demonstration and killed the watch officer and wounded several of the crew, were not treated as pirates by the state to which they surrendered nor claimed as such by any other state. See the *Santa Maria,* 4 Whiteman, Digest of International Law 665 (1965). On the other hand, the 1985 seizure of an Italian liner by infiltration, followed by murder of a passenger, has been claimed to be piracy jure gentium, or otherwise reachable by the state of the nationality of the victim, as well as by the state of the nationality of the vessel. See the Achille Lauro, 24 International Legal Materials 1509 (1985).

Although some states for political reasons have resisted a general principle that all acts of terrorism should be punished on the universal basis of jurisdiction, if not on any other, the net of punishment somewhere appears to be closing on terrorists and hijackers, either by the expansion of the universality principle or other bases.

––––––

SABOTAGE

The Sabotage Convention—Convention for the Suppression of Unlawful Acts Against the Safety of Civil Aviation—was adopted by a Conference on International Air Law at Montreal in 1971. 24 U.S.T. 564. The text is in the Documentary Supplement. It entered into force in the United States on January 26, 1973. Its scope was described by the head of the United States delegation:

> Although this convention is similar to the Hijacking Convention in many respects, it is significantly distinct: It does not, basically, require states to define any new offenses—it covers acts which already are common crimes; it does not, for the most part, establish new crimes to fall within the extradition process—most of the acts already are extraditable crimes. These were important elements of the Hijacking Convention. It might be said that states could punish offenders or extradite them without this convention.

> What this convention does is to impose an obligation on states *requiring* them to prosecute or extradite offenders. It serves as a warning to any person who contemplates such acts that the international community has responded with unanimity to condemn such acts. In this respect it is like the Hijacking Convention.

And in an important respect this convention does more than the Hijacking Convention. It covers acts against aircraft in a state's domestic service, even when the acts take place wholly within that same state, if the offender escapes to another state. While this element is not critical for the Hijacking Convention, it is crucial for the effectiveness of the convention we have concluded, because of the possibility that offenders may escape before they are discovered. This convention declares that no one who sabotages a civil aircraft— whether in domestic or international service—no one who places a bomb on board such an aircraft, no evildoer who commits violence aboard such an aircraft in flight, no criminal of this character shall ever find sanctuary anywhere in the world, no matter how deviously he may seek to evade retribution for his deeds. The parties to this convention have declared that this despicable criminal shall be pursued without respite. 65 U.S.Dept.State Bull. 464 (1971).

EXTRADITION AND AIRCRAFT OFFENSES

1. *The prosecute or extradite principle.* While there were earlier uses of this principle in regard to terrorism, such as in a 1936 League of Nations treaty, it quickly became a standard legal and political response when modern terrorism began to exploit the vulnerability of the passenger airplane, resulting in the international conventions examined in this Chapter. Terrorism and hijacking conventions still suffer from a disinclination of some states to accept their obligations. Even when accepted, there may be other problems as to their effectiveness, including: (i) unsuccessful prosecution in the first state, leading to acquittal or the dropping of charges; (ii) contradictions between the prosecute or extradite undertaking and pre-existing bilateral general extradition treaties, especially as to the specification of extraditable offenses; (iii) the legal competence of the requesting state under its own law (or possibly under international law) to try the accused criminally; and (iv) the factor of the nationality or allegiance of the person sought to be extradited. By far the major problem for extradition in the context of modern terrorism has been in regard to an asserted political offense exception to extradition. At its most difficult, the problem involves good people using illegal means such as aircraft hijacking to escape from "tyranny." (It also arises when underground resistance movements use terrorism as a means to political ends, themselves not necessarily reprehensible.) It has been claimed as a privilege even by terrorists whose means and ends have both been reprehensible. At the present time the decision on the applicability of the political offense exception lies with the authorities in the state of which extradition has been requested, unless the states parties to an extradition agreement mutually provide otherwise, as in the United States–United Kingdom agreement, discussed in Chapter 3.

2. *Extradition under the Hague Convention.* Article 8(1) of the Hague Convention provides, in effect, for the automatic amendment of extradition treaties to add hijacking to the list of extraditable crimes.

What, then, of the individual who seeks to escape from a country which refuses to allow him to emigrate by hijacking a plane in the domestic air service of that country and requiring the pilot to fly the plane to a country of refuge? If the underlying extradition treaty provides for the usual exception for offenses of a political character, can the requested state consider that hijacking under those circumstances is such a crime? Do the hijacking conventions eliminate it as a political offense? If it does so consider it and refuses to extradite, the obligation to prosecute, under Article 7 of the Hague Convention, comes into play. What does the obligation to prosecute mean?

A CASE OF REFUSAL TO EXTRADITE

McDowell, Digest of United States Practice in International Law 1975, at 168
(1976).

On April 14, 1975, the Chambre d'accusation of the Cour d'appel of Paris refused a request of the United States for extradition of Willie Roger Holder and Mary Katherine Kerkow for trial in the United States on aircraft hijacking charges. The refusal was based on the fugitives' allegations of political motive. They had been indicted in June 1972 in both New York and California in connection with the 1972 hijacking of a flight between Los Angeles and Seattle, followed by a forced landing in San Francisco, a stop for refueling in New York, and a forced flight to Algeria.

In support of its request for extradition, the United States had submitted to the French Foreign Ministry and to the Justice Ministry the following memorandum of law, dated April 3, 1975:

Memorandum of Law

* * *

The fugitives, Holder and Kerkow, have been indicted for the crimes of aircraft piracy, kidnapping and extortion, which are extraditable offenses under Article II of the Extradition Treaty between the United States and France, of January 6, 1909, as amended by the supplementary convention of February 12, 1970. Thus, France has a treaty obligation to surrender these fugitives for prosecution in the United States, unless the case comes within the terms of the exemption established in Article VI for political offenses. Article VI provides: Extradition shall not be granted in any of the following circumstances:

* * *

4. If the offense for which the individual's extradition is requested is of a political character, or if he proves that the requisition for his surrender has, in fact, been made with a view to try or punish him for an offense of a political character. If any question arises as to whether a case comes within the provisions of this

subparagraph, the authorities of the government on which the requisition is made shall decide.

* * *

Under this provision the requested state determines whether a crime is of a political character. However, the determination does not involve an exercise of discretion. It is a legal determination as to whether a treaty obligation exists on the facts of the particular case. No allegation has been made in this case, nor could it be sustained, that the United States requests the surrender of these fugitives in order to punish them for any offense other than the common crimes for which extradition is requested. Therefore, the sole question for the court is whether the crimes charged constitute offenses of a "political character" in the legal sense of Article VI.

Although the treaty does not prescribe a specific definition of offenses of a "political character" there is considerable jurisprudence and international extradition practice which establish the parameters of this concept. Offenses "of a political character" include traditional political crimes such as sedition and treason. The concept may also include common crimes which are clearly connected with offenses of a political character under special circumstances which have been defined by the tribunals of states and international practice.

There are numerous decisions holding that ordinary common crimes cannot be considered offenses of a political character unless they occur in the context of a civil war, rebellion or similar political disturbance. * * * [See chapters 3 and 11.]

Although political offenses have been found by tribunals in some other circumstances—usually involving compelling human considerations—it is well established that political motive alone does not give a common crime the character of a political offense.

* * *

In this case the fugitives were not engaged in any attempt to overthrow the Government of the United States or in any other political offense with which their crime could be connected. There is no evidence and no allegation that they belonged to any political group or had engaged in any political activities in the past. There is no allegation that the fugitives were subject to political persecution or harassment of any kind. The defense bases its claim of political offense exclusively on the alleged motive of the defendants to have the hijacked aircraft fly to Hanoi. The only evidence on this point is that the defendant Holder asked that the first plane fly to Hanoi and did not persist in that request when he was provided a second aircraft with the capacity to do so. His references to Angela Davis at the outset of the flight and to Eldridge Cleaver near the destination at Algiers evidence a confused mixture of vague and ill-defined motives. There is no precedent and no basis for construing the criminal activity of these fugitives as an offense of a political character.

Aircraft piracy is a serious, common crime which threatens the lives of innocent persons, disrupts international civil aviation, and causes tensions in international relations. It is an offense against the human rights of passengers and crew, and against the public order of all states. As such, it has been repeatedly condemned by the Security Council, the * * * General Assembly and the International Civil Aviation Organization in solemn resolutions supported by France and the United States. The General Assembly resolution of November 25, 1970, "condemns, without exception whatsoever, all acts of aircraft hijacking" and "calls upon states to take all appropriate measures to deter, prevent or suppress such acts within their jurisdiction * * *." The Hague Convention for the Suppression of Unlawful Seizure of Aircraft, signed December 16, 1970, to which France and the United States are party, provides for the extradition or prosecution of the perpetrators of such crimes.

While there are cases in years past in which states held a particular hijacking to be a political offense where the persons involved were fleeing from tyranny and faced severe political persecution if they were returned, the danger inherent in the increasing incidence of aircraft hijacking in more recent years has alarmed the entire international community and given grounds for a presumption that aircraft hijacking is a most serious common crime regardless of the circumstances. Moreover, there is wide recognition in the international community that cases of aircraft hijacking involving extortion or actual injury to passengers or crew represent an aggravated form of the offense which requires punishment as a common crime. * * *

In this case there is no suggestion that the fugitives were subject to any political persecution or needed the transportation to leave the country; they did threaten the lives of passengers and crew to extort $500,000 from the airline. This extortion contradicts any notion of idealism or of "political character" in this case.

It is recognized that extradition is the most effective deterrent to the crime of aircraft hijacking. Surrender of these fugitives for prosecution in the United States will contribute to such deterrence and thus protect lives and the interests of France as well as those of the United States. Refusal of extradition on the specious grounds that this crime is an offense of a political character would appear to condone hijacking and could contribute to repetition of such crimes to the danger of the entire international community.

[End of Memorandum of Law.]

On July 7, 1975, the United States Embassy at Paris delivered to the Acting Legal Adviser in the French Foreign Ministry a note with respect to the French refusal of extradition and the applicability of the U.S.–French extradition convention, as supplemented (TS 561; TIAS 7075; 22 UST 407). The substantive portion of the note follows:

* * *

The Embassy notes that the decision of the Chambre d'accusation regarding the question of extradition is final and that in accordance with the Convention for the Suppression of Unlawful Seizure of Aircraft, signed at The Hague on December 16, 1970, a case has been opened against the accused at the Parquet de Paris on charges of the illegal seizure of an aircraft and restraint of hostages under threat. The Embassy trusts that these proceedings will result, in the event the accused are found guilty, in the application of the penalty which is proportionate to the seriousness of the crime and which will further the purposes of the Hague Convention to deter aircraft hijacking.

The interested officials of the United States Government have now had the opportunity to review the decision of the Chambre d'accusation on the request for extradition made by the United States, and this Embassy has been instructed to bring to the attention of the Foreign Ministry the serious concern of the United States Government over the rejection of its extradition request.

In the view of the United States Government the decision of the French Government in this case to deny extradition on the sole grounds of an alleged political motivation for the crime is inconsistent with France's obligations under the Treaty of Extradition between the United States of America and the Republic of France of January 6, 1909, as amended by the supplementary convention signed at Paris on February 12, 1970. * * *

Although the treaty does not prescribe a specific definition of an offense of a "political character," and international practice is somewhat varied, the considerable jurisprudence and * * * cases in this field clearly establish that mere political motive is not sufficient to characterize a serious common crime as a political offense. * * *

* * *

A strong case can be made that serious crimes such as aircraft hijacking are so dangerous to human life and so inimical to international order that they should not be regarded as "political offenses" regardless of the circumstances. Even if it is assumed that there are special circumstances in which an act of hijacking may be considered to have a political character, it is an extreme position to argue that the mere plea of political motive is sufficient to establish the political nature of the offense. * * *

The effect of the decision by the Cour d'appel is to construe hijacking as a "political offense" in any case in which a political motive is alleged, even where large sums of money are extorted under the threat of murder of the passengers and crew. The effect of the decision in this case, if it were followed by other states, would be virtually to eliminate extradition as a remedy in hijacking cases, and by suppressing the most effective deterrent to aircraft hijacking, would encourage the commission of more such crimes in the future.

* * *

1. *Subsequent conviction.* On June 13, 1980, Willie Holder received a suspended five-year prison sentence for the hijacking. His companion left France earlier and was to be tried in absentia. The New York Times, June 15, 1980, Sec. A, p. 8.

2. *Question.* There are quite a few cases involving hijackers from states behind the former Iron Curtain, such as Poland and Czechoslovakia, in which the authorities of the state where they landed—Denmark, Austria, Western Germany—denied the requests for extradition and gave these hijackers light sentences when they tried them. See 76 Revue Générale de Droit International Pub. 484, 509 (1972) and Vol. 82 at 1083 (1978). Would the Department of State protest these denials of extradition on the ground that mere political motive is not sufficient to characterize hijacking as a political offense? Should it? And if, as the Department of State says, a strong case can be made that hijacking is so dangerous to human life it should not be regarded as a political offense regardless of the circumstances, how do you explain its immediate denial of extradition when two persons from Eastern Germany hijacked a Polish plane and forced it to land at Tempelhof airport, in the American zone of Berlin? 83 Rev. Gén. de Dr. Int'l Pub. 480 (1979).

3. *Deterrence.* Speaking to the United Nations General Assembly in 1977 in support of a resolution calling upon states not only to adopt the anti-hijacking conventions but also to take steps to improve security arrangements at airports and by airlines, the United States Representative, Congressman Lester L. Wolff, made the following observation:

> One might ask whether the sorts of actions which this resolution envisages will really have much impact on hijacking. The answer to any such questions can only be an emphatic yes. I would cite in this connection the experience of the United States in its successful effort against hijacking domestically. In 1969, prior to the establishment of security measures, designed to prevent incidents of this type, there were 40 attempts to hijack U.S. civilian aircraft, 33 of which were successful. In 1973, the first full year after stringent security procedures were made mandatory for all U.S. airports, the number of such incidents fell to two. In 1976 as well, there were only two incidents. These figures speak for themselves.

> Looking at the current situation on a worldwide basis, we find that the number of hijacking incidents is once again on the rise and that lax security procedures at airports have been responsible for most of them. The figures are striking. Of the 28 airline hijackings thus far this year—as opposed to 16 during all of 1976—20 can be attributed to failures in passenger screening procedures. Since 1973 there have been no hijackings in the United States which resulted from a failure to detect guns and other weapons during the screening process. I might point out that the United States has been and continues to be willing to share its experience in this area with other interested countries. For instance, the United States has offered to share its screening procedures, equipment, and testing measures

with other countries, and thus far 36 countries have taken advantage of this offer.

In calling upon the competent specialized U.N. agency, ICAO, to develop additional measures to increase international civil aviation security, the resolution we have adopted clears the way for new initiatives in that respected and impartial Organization. Among the steps which we believe ICAO should take are the following:

(1) Strengthening of the current ICAO standard on passenger screening to require specifically the screening of all passengers and all carry-on baggage for all airline flights, both foreign and domestic;

(2) Elevation of certain ICAO recommended practices dealing with security to the status of standards, including: (a) provision of law enforcement support for aviation security and (b) provision of security for aircraft under hijacking or sabotage threat; and

(3) Continuing emphasis by ICAO on universal adherence to and ratification of The Hague (hijacking) and Montreal (sabotage) conventions. Such action would effectively eliminate safe havens for aviation criminals. U.S. Dept. of State Bull., 1978, p. 54.

4. *Self help.* The rescue of hijacked airplane passengers is considered in Chapter 17 from the standpoint of territorial intervention by the rescuing state. Such rescue efforts, which are unilateral remedies for unlawful activity, must satisfy international legal requirements of necessity and proportionality, and must also conform to United Nations Charter obligations. See the 1987 Restatement, Section 905.

5. *On Extradition and Hijacking* generally, and other acts of terrorism in the air, see Christopher L. Blakesley, Terrorism, supra at pp. 84–100, 129, 146, 202–215.

————

Subsequent proceedings in the Nuclear Tests Cases. Despite the court's order for interim measures of protection, France continued to conduct tests during the summer months of 1973 and 1974. The court held hearings on the question of its jurisdiction, France not participating, see supra, Chapter 1. Thereafter the court took note of a number of public declarations by the French government, including a communiqué issued by the President of France stating that "in view of the stage reached in carrying out the French nuclear defence programme France will be in a position to pass on to the stage of underground explosions as soon as the series of tests planned for this summer is completed." The court read these unilateral acts as creating a legally binding obligation on the part of France to cease testing in the atmosphere in the South Pacific. Since the court concluded that Australia's objective in this proceeding was to obtain termination of French atmospheric nuclear tests in the South Pacific, it found, by a vote of nine to six "that the claim of Australia no longer has any object and that the court is therefore not called upon to give a decision thereon." [1974] I.C.J.

Reports 253. The same result was reached in the New Zealand proceedings. Id. at 457.

———

SECTION B.   OUTER SPACE [b]

———

Theories about airspace and outer space delimitation.   Speakers at the Twenty-sixth Colloquium on the Law of Outer Space, sponsored by the International Institute of Space Law, October, 1983, addressed the question of the boundary between airspace and outer space. Two views are set forth below.

———

ROSENFIELD, SOME THOUGHTS ON THE DISTINCTION BETWEEN AIR SPACE AND OUTER SPACE

Proceedings of the Twenty-sixth Colloquium on the Law of Outer Space
93–94 (1984).*

* * *

In researching this question I went back through all of the previous twenty-five colloquia. To my surprise I found that this question was on the first colloquium, and it has appeared on almost every subsequent colloquium since that time. During the first colloquium the question was addressed by Andrew Haley of the United States who supported a scientific approach, the Von Karman line; [a] by Luig de Gonzaga Bevilacqua of Brazil, who advocated a theory that the boundary should depend on the nature of the craft involved, namely the altitude to which a specific craft remained dependent on the atmosphere; John Cobb Cooper who suggested several different possibilities without selecting between them. His list included: the height to which a craft can proceed while using aerodynamic lift; the height at which a satellite would go into orbit; the Von Karman line theory; the height at which no atmosphere

———

b. We believe the term "outer space" to be a bit antiquated, but we use it here, because it signals the question about lines, borders, or limits between sectoral airspace above territory and what lies immediately beyond. But, surely, one would not refer to the void between Earth and Sol's nearest neighbor as "outer space"!

———

* Reprinted with the permission of the American Institute of Aeronautics & Astronautics.

a. "[The Von Karman line] accepts the basic concept of aerodynamic lift but argues that such lift need not be the only 'support' and that present law could be interpreted as extending sovereignty up to the point where any aerodynamic lift is available. For an object traveling at 25,000 feet per second, that line is said to be about 275,000 feet from the earth's surface. * * * [I]t would * * * vary with atmospheric conditions and with design changes and other factors affecting the flight of objects." Lipson and Katzenbach, The Law of Outer Space 12 (1961).

exists (estimated to be about 1000 miles); a nation's sovereignty extends without limit above its territory; and, the height to which a state may exercise "effective control". Finally, Robert Jastrow of the United States advocated the lowest point at which a vehicle could orbit the earth, estimated at approximately 100 miles.

It is surprising to me to note that even the arguments have changed very little over the years. It is particularly surprising when it is recalled that this first meeting was in 1958, shortly after the first artificial earth satellite was placed in orbit, but ten years prior to the first legal space treaty. The early arguments were more technical and more theoretical emphasizing, inter alia, the Von Karman line, the point where gravity ceases, the layers of the atmosphere or the maximum altitude of flight. However the foundation for today's arguments were also being laid. Functionalism, use of an arbitrary height, a free zone between air space and outer space—these are not ideas developed in the 1970's and 1980's. They were also being suggested in the earliest meeting of the 1950's.

* * *

It may be that the real problem is that there does not seem to be a problem. A part of the solution has been the functional approach of the outer space treaties. Any problems that have come up have been solved through the functionalism of the existing treaties. The result is that there is in fact no problem to be resolved.

———

DANILENKO, THE BOUNDARY BETWEEN AIR SPACE AND OUTER SPACE IN MODERN INTERNATIONAL LAW

Proceedings of the Twenty-sixth Colloquium on the Law of Outer Space
71, 73 (1984).*

* * *

The evaluation of the current practice of states leads to the formulation of the rule of conduct which is observed by all states of the international community. In their mutual relations all states observe the rule according to which space objects in orbit, including the orbit with the technically lowest perigee achieved by any satellite so far placed in orbit, are within the sphere of application of the principle of freedom of outer space. This means that the sovereignty of underlying states does not extend at least over limits outlined by lowest perigees of earth-orbiting satellites. Thus according to established international practice the lower limit of outer space and the upper limit of national air space at present are broadly defined by the lowest altitudes at which the satellites can be maintained and used in orbit in an unpowered flight (100(± 10) km above sea-level).

The practice of states constituting the rule of international law which establishes the boundary between air space and outer space meets

* Reprinted by permission of the American Institute of Aeronautics & Astronau-   tics.

the requirements of generality, consistency, uniformity and continues over the period of time of more than 25 years. * * *

* * *

The recognition or acceptance of customary rules of conduct by which air space and outer space are demarcated as a rule of international law on the part of space powers was primarily manifested through their actual space activities connected with the launching and operation of space objects. These activities amounted to an implied legal claim to the right to carry out the exploration and use of outer space at various altitudes over the territories of subjacent states. At the same time the acting states recognized the right of other states of the international community to carry out similar activities over their territories. At least one of the space powers—the Soviet Union—has expressly recognized the existence of "an international legal custom" defining the boundary between air space and outer space on the basis of the criterion of the lowest perigee of orbiting satellite, i.e. at a height of approximately 100–110 km above sea-level. The acceptance of the established practice on the part of non-space powers was primarily manifested through their passive conduct expressing consent to the legal claims of space powers. Tacit consent of states who are not as yet capable of launching and operating space objects is evidenced by absence of protests based on the principle of state sovereignty against the space activities at the lowest altitudes over their territorial air space. * * *

* * *

DEFINITION AND DELIMITATION OF OUTER SPACE
Summary Report of a Discussion in the Legal Sub–Committee of the United Nations
Committee on the Peaceful Uses of Outer Space, March–April 1984.
21 UN Chronicle No. 4, p. 32 (1984).

Where does outer space begin? Does it have a physical boundary by which States could stake claim to areas above them? What problems would ensue from establishing legal definitions and boundaries?

The Legal Sub–Committee established a working group to deal with the problems of definition and delimitation of outer space and the character and use of the geostationary orbit. The working group, on a proposal of its Chairman, agreed on separate consideration of the two subjects. However, it felt time should also be allotted to consider the item as a whole.

Some countries maintained that a definition and delimitation of outer space was necessary and wanted a multilateral agreement, open to all States, to establish a specific altitude as the upper limit of air space. Related questions are whether outer space should be considered as beginning where air space ends; and at what altitude air space should be regarded as ending.

A number of nations favouring a "spatial definition" supported the Soviet proposal that the boundary between outer space and air space be at an altitude not exceeding 110 kms above sea level. Provision could be made for that to be changed in the future, by international agreement, should circumstances make it necessary, according to the proposal.

In the debate, the Soviet Union said delimitation and definition of outer space was needed to guarantee effectively a reliable legal basis for new spheres of space activity and to guarantee that the study and use of space would be carried out in the interests of all States. The problem of defining the boundary between the two types of space was important. That boundary was the limit of the height of the application of State sovereignty. Definition of the boundary was a means of establishing the area for applying international air and space law.

Bulgaria said the absence of a boundary between air and outer space opened the door to countless violations of State sovereignty. The absence of a clearly defined limit would compel States whose security would be threatened to enact measures to prevent such violation.

India said outer space should be defined and delimited because of the existence of different legal régimes for air and outer space. There was a need to provide a clear area for applying existing outer space law and facilitating the further development of that law to determine the upper limit of State sovereignty, to safeguard the security of national air space and prevent disputes between States.

Hungary said as there were two law régimes, of outer space and of air space, there could well be situations in the future which would raise the question as to which applied. Explicit definitions of outer space and air space were technically possible.

Nigeria said a definition was needed as a requirement for the full exercise of State sovereignty. Czechoslovakia said delimitation of space was important to preserve it for activities of a peaceful nature only.

Some States, while favouring the "spatial definition" approach, did not agree with the proposed altitude for the demarcation between air space and outer space. Kenya, for example, had some reservations regarding setting a specific distance in terms of delimiting outer space, as it seemed arbitrary. A definition of air space would be possible only after outer space had been defined.

Other delegations stated that: there was no present scientific basis for defining and delimiting outer space or for placing the boundary at any particular altitude; the development and application of the law of outer space had proceeded satisfactorily without such a definition or delimitation; and it would be unreasonable to adopt an arbitrary definition or delimitation which could give rise to difficulties and impede the development of space technology.

The United States said the establishment of a demarcation between outer space and air space in advance of a genuine and practical need for doing so would be an inherently arbitrary exercise having unforeseeable and almost certainly detrimental consequences for future outer space activities.

The United Kingdom said it was premature to define outer space, and was not convinced of the need for such a definition. The Netherlands said to draw a boundary between outer space and air space at a certain altitude was not only unnecessary but undesirable, as it could create problems that did not now exist.

Italy said a rigid and general delimitation of outer space did not meet the scientific criteria or respond to practical and functional criteria. A number of space agreements had been formulated without such a definition. A rigid definition would create major problems for certain smaller States in contradiction of the principle of free access to space activity.

Brazil said any definition could not be separated from the scientific knowledge available. The drawing of an arbitrary line to divide outer space and air space was always a possibility, but other approaches, such as spatial or functional, could be taken.

Some delegations considered that as the positions of delegations had not moved closer over many years, the Sub–Committee should, without prejudice to its future work on the question of the definition and delimitation of outer space, concern itself with such matters as the definition of "space objects" and "space activities". Others felt a consensus on the definition of a "space object" would be more difficult to achieve than on a definition and delimitation of outer space.

France said a definition of space objects or space activities would make possible a definition of the basic legal concepts for outer space law and determine all implications of a future definition of outer space.

Bulgaria said the Sub–Committee could not attribute privileges to space objects if it were to base its work on definition of space objects and activities. Violation of air space by a space object rather than an aircraft represented the same danger to States as overflight by aircraft.

Launching and landing of space objects. Members of the Committee on the Peaceful Uses of Outer Space expressed views, similar to those summarized above, at its 1986 session. Among matters discussed was a Soviet proposal for a "multilateral agreement establishing the beginning of outer space at an altitude not exceeding 110 kilometres above sea level and allowing for innocent passage, at lower altitudes, through the airspace of one State of another State's space object for the purpose of reaching orbit or returning to Earth. It was noted during the discussion that the particular altitude of demarcation was open to negotiation." 23 UN Chronicle No. 4 (1986), p. 86.

The editors of the Third Edition of this book asked the General Counsel of NASA (National Aeronautics and Space Administration): "Is it the practice of NASA to procure the permission of a state through whose airspace a space vehicle may pass on launching or landing? If so, how is airspace defined for the purpose of determining whether permission is needed?"

General Counsel John E. O'Brien response, on June 18, 1986 follows:

Regarding your question, it should be noted that there is no boundary between air space and outer space that has been endorsed by the world community. For a number of years, the question of where air space ends and outer space begins has been on the agenda of the Legal Subcommittee of the U.N. Committee on the Peaceful Uses of Outer Space. It is the position of the United States that there is a gray area between air space and outer space which does not permit us to agree that an arbitrary boundary should be set between these two areas.

While experimental airplanes have flown to about 50 miles, there is no clarity as to where air space ends. Due to this circumstance, it has not been necessary for the United States to obtain the permission of a State through whose air space a space vehicle may pass during launching or landing. We do not know of any instance where on launching or landing a space vehicle has clearly been passing through the air space of another state. If a space vehicle were clearly passing through the air space of another State, on launching or landing, we would, of course, notify that State and obtain its permission if it were determined that such permission were required.

You should be aware that a practice has evolved over the past twenty-five years which permits a space vehicle, upon launching or landing, to pass over other States. As far as I know, there has been no protest by any State in this area.

As of May 1993, the above summary of NASA practice and nonobjection thereto by other states seemingly still holds. Is it possible that a legal principle governing tolerated foreign airspace passage in climb-to-orbit, free movement in "outer" space, and tolerated re-entry through foreign airspace is evolving or has evolved? Does it matter, in this regard, whether the vehicle is winged, so that it flies through airspace after it drops out of "outer space"? Would you analogize launch and re-entry tolerations in airspace above national territory to innocent passage and port-entry in the Law of the Sea? On the other hand, is an American shuttle-craft an airplane when in glide path, under aerodynamic lift? Should a flight plan be filed with an ADIZ[a] county transited whilst approaching landing in the United States?

Suppose the shuttle takes on a few passengers-for-pay. Would the Warsaw Convention apply to losses, (a) on launch before orbit; (b) to airlift glidepath after re-entry?

---

a. Aircraft Defense Identification Zone regulations, which require a flight plan to be filed prior to take-off on a flight that is planned to come within certain distances from a state so requiring. * * *

MISHRA and PAVLASEK, ON THE LACK OF PHYSICAL BASES FOR DEFINING A BOUNDARY BETWEEN AIR SPACE AND OUTER SPACE

7 Annals of Air and Space Law 399, 412 (1982).*

* * *

The objective of this statement has been to examine physical factors which might be considered as bases for the definition of a boundary between air space and outer space. For this purpose, pertinent physical phenomena and their practical applications were considered under the following groupings or "regimes": 1. "State of Matter". 2. "Gravitational Field", 3. "Electromagnetic", 4. "Geometrical/Geographical", 5. "Biological/Environmental" and 6. "Technological".

In the ongoing "legal debate" of the past, since "space activities" started, it appears that two basic seemingly different types of arguments have been advanced for the definition of a boundary, which may appear to be contradictory. These are characterizable as the "physical boundary" versus the "functional boundary" arguments. * * * From a physical world point of view there is *no real difference* between these two! The "Physical Boundary" hypothesis considers the possibility of a physical *condition* whereas the "Functional Boundary" approach concerns the use of physical means towards a particular *application*. Both of these are "physical" and there is thus no fundamental difference, there is merely a change in vantage point and perspective!

It is the conclusion of this statement that there in fact exist no physical bases which might be used as a sound and absolute reason for defining a boundary between air space and outer space. In examining the first five regimes enumerated above it is clear that there exists no definite physical condition which can be described as a boundary. Furthermore, an overview of the technological applications shows equally well that there are no useful "functional" boundaries either. In fact the examination simply confirms the obvious, namely that the planet earth is only a minor component of, but forms an indivisible integral part of the universe. It does so both materially and in terms of the "physical laws" by which its existence is governed. The "indivisibility principle" is fundamental and cannot be altered regardless of human desires or imaginings to do so.

The consequences of this conclusion to the problem of defining a boundary between air space and outer space are quite clear. The notion of a "boundary" is simply a humanly conceived constraint, possibly a matter of convenience or a means of controlling conflicting human objectives. The definition must therefore be sought in human terms. In terms of human experience this means that such a definition is an act of willful desire, an arbitrary decision and the answer must be achieved through well known processes of human decision making in such cases. Such decisions may be achieved on social, cultural, economic, historical and political grounds as an act of collective will, through negotiated

* Reprinted by permission of the Institute and Centre of Air and Space Law, McGill University.

agreement or, regrettably even the use of force. Since such a decision will have no physical foundation it will benefit from an inherently flexible definition with a built in possibility of subsequent revision or even ultimate abolishment, as the human perspective of the problem evolves in the future.

Any attempt however to make use of physical arguments to define a boundary will be contrived, artificial, illusory and therefore intellectually unsound—even if temporarily expedient as a masking of the human urge for imagining a boundary.

----

* * *

1. *International conventions.* Several international conventions address the legal problems of space.

The Outer Space Treaty (Treaty on Principles Governing the Activities of States in the Exploration and Use of Outer Space, Including the Moon and Other Celestial Bodies), 18 U.S.T. 2410, 610 U.N.T.S. 205— see the Documentary Supplement—entered into force for the United States on October 10, 1967. The following articles are suggestive of the generality of its provisions:

Article I

The exploration and use of outer space, including the moon and other celestial bodies, shall be carried out for the benefit and in the interests of all countries, irrespective of their degree of economic or scientific development, and shall be the province of all mankind.

Outer space, including the moon and other celestial bodies, shall be free for exploration and use by all States without discrimination of any kind, on a basis of equality and in accordance with international law, and there shall be free access to all areas of celestial bodies.

There shall be freedom of scientific investigation in outer space, including the moon and other celestial bodies, and States shall facilitate and encourage international co-operation in such investigation.

Article III

States Parties to the Treaty shall carry on activities in the exploration and use of outer space, including the moon and other celestial bodies, in accordance with international law, including the Charter of the United Nations, in the interest of maintaining international peace and security and promoting international cooperation and understanding.

In analyzing this treaty, which purports to set general principles, the following questions should be addressed:

i. Has the treaty made any change in the law that would be applicable without the treaty? Another way of putting this question is: is a non-party to the treaty freer than a party to do as it wishes in outer space and, if so, in what respects?

ii. Are enough facts known about space to justify a state's committing itself at this stage of technological development to the principles enunciated in the treaty? How can a state protect its interests if startling new facts are discovered about outer space in the future?

The Agreement on the Rescue of Astronauts, the Return of Astronauts, and the Return of Objects Launched Into Outer Space, 19 U.S.T. 7570, entered into force for the United States on December 3, 1968. 88 states were parties on January 1, 1987, and 88 parties still in 1992.

The Convention on International Liability for Damage Caused by Space Objects—see the Documentary Supplement—entered into force for the United States on October 9, 1973. 82 states were parties on January 1, 1992. The convention provides that the launching state shall be liable for damage caused by its space object absolutely in some cases, or for its fault in others. A claims procedure involves a Claims Commission, whose decision shall be binding if the parties have so agreed or whose award shall be recommendatory "which the parties shall consider in good faith." (Article XIX). The legal principles to be applied in determining compensation are particularly interesting:

Article XII

The compensation which the launching State shall be liable to pay for damage under this Convention shall be determined in accordance with international law and the principles of justice and equity, in order to provide such reparation in respect of the damage as will restore the person, natural or juridical, State or international organization on whose behalf the claim is presented to the condition which would have existed if the damage had not occurred.

Convention on Registration of Objects Launched into Outer Space, entered into force for the United States on September 15, 1976. 28 U.S.T. 695.

2. *Work on new conventions at the United Nations.* The committee on the Peaceful Uses of Outer Space has for a number of years worked on the drafting of agreements relating to remote sensing of the environment of the earth from outer space, the definition and/or delimitation of outer space (see p. 404 and questions relating to the geostationary orbit). The progress of the Outer Space Committee is reported from time to time in the UN Chronicle (e.g. 23 UN Chronicle No. 4, 1986, p. 84).

a. *Remote sensing.* Satellites orbiting the earth can collect photographic information about military affairs, such as troop concentrations, military installations, naval movements and missile emplacements. Remote sensing of the earth also produces vast quantities of information of a non-military nature, useful in such matters as weather prediction, maritime navigation, geological exploration, estimating agricultural crops, monitoring the growth of deserts, surveying natural disasters and map-making, to mention only a few uses.

Some countries have objected to being observed from outer space without their consent, but the more recent concerns have dealt with access to the non-military information that is being gathered by the few countries that have the capacity to conduct remote sensing operations.

In December 1986, the United Nations General Assembly adopted a resolution setting forth fifteen principles on remote sensing, recommended by the Committee on Peaceful Uses of Outer Space and its Legal Sub–Committee. Principle XII deals with the right of observed states to have access to primary and processed data and to analyzed information concerning their territory. The principle provides that such access shall be made available on a non-discriminatory basis and at reasonable cost.

b. *The geostationary orbit.* Communications satellites are put into orbit directly above the equator at a distance of 22,300 miles above the earth. The speed of the satellite in orbit is synchronized to that of the earth so that a satellite appears to be located permanently in a particular, stationary spot above the earth. Certain states located at the equator have claimed special territorial rights with respect to the space occupied by the orbiting satellites, but the consensus of the remainder of states appears to be to reject that claim. It is generally considered that the geostationary orbit falls within outer space under the terms of the Outer Space Treaty and thus, under Article I, is free for use by all states. So many satellites have been placed in geostationary orbit that developing states have voiced concern that the orbit will become saturated with satellites by developed states, including the United States and the USSR, so as to preclude the use of the orbit by other states when their technology has developed. The matter has been a frequent subject of contention in the UN Committee on Peaceful Uses of Outer Space. At the 1985 World Administrative Radio Conference sponsored by the International Telecommunications Union, one hundred twelve nations made a beginning on meeting the concerns of all states in the use of the orbit, as described below.

STAPLE, THE NEW WORLD SATELLITE ORDER:
A REPORT FROM GENEVA

80 American Journal of International Law 699, 700 (1986).*

* * *

The Geneva satellite congress, known as the 1985 World Administrative Radio Conference on Space WARC, was held under the auspices of the International Telecommunication Union (ITU). As the specialized United Nations agency responsible for coordinating use of the world's radio spectrum and setting international telecommunications standards, the ITU plays a central role in global communications. The new world satellite plan that emerged from the conference guarantees all countries at least one satellite orbital position and an associated block of

* Reprinted with the permission of the
American Society of International Law.

radio frequencies to meet their basic communications needs. A second conference session in 1988 is scheduled to implement the plan, which will then be revised roughly every 10 years.

Space WARC also provisionally decided to rewrite the ITU's rules, known as Radio Regulations, that spell out the procedures for countries in coordinating the radio frequencies and orbital positions used by their satellites. The revised rules will establish a new multilateral planning process to ensure that new entrants to the world's satellite club are more equitably accommodated. This process will be used by countries to access most of the satellite radio spectrum, only a modest portion of which was earmarked for the country-by-country plan.

The new global plan adopted by the WARC nevertheless represents a marked departure from the existing legal regime. Since the early days of the space race, the United States and other countries with the technical know-how and financial resources to place communication satellites into orbit generally have had their choice of orbital positions and frequency blocks. This system of "first come, first served" (sometimes labeled "squatters' rights") has been bitterly resented by many developing countries whose satellite plans have only recently come to fruition. In its place, these countries have long argued for the kind of a priori plan tentatively approved by the 1985 WARC.

> * * *

Military uses of outer space. Article IV of the Outer Space Treaty provides that the parties "undertake not to place in orbit around the Earth any objects carrying nuclear weapons or any other kinds of weapons of mass destruction, install such weapons on celestial bodies, or station such weapons in outer space in any other manner." See the Documentary Supplement. Despite this commitment, already made, the Soviet Union has proposed a draft treaty on the prohibition of stationing of weapons of any kind in outer space. It has also proposed a treaty on the prohibition of the use of force in outer space and from outer space with regard to the earth. To what extent would a treaty on the latter subject place limits on states not already provided by the United Nations Charter or by customary international law? Although Article 2(4) of the Charter limits a state's use of force generally, Article 51 expressly preserves the right of self defense. See Chapter 17.

The most current international controversy on the military use of space involves the use of anti-satellite weaponry, in particular on the interpretation of the 1972 Anti–Ballistic Missile Treaty between the United States and the Soviet Union. The question whether the United States is free under that treaty to deploy anti-satellite devices under its Strategic Defense Initiative (popularly called Star Wars) involves a question of treaty interpretation which is posed in Chapter 13.

ROUND–UP ON OTHER LEGAL ASPECTS
OF THE USE OF SPACE

1.　A very useful source book in this field is Cristol, Space Law: Past, Present and Future (Kluwer, 1991), especially *Part I, Where We Have Been and Where We Are.*

2.　The common heritage of mankind concept, dealt with heretofore in regard to deep sea mining, Part XI of the 1982 Law of the Sea Convention, is linked (in various phrasings) to the space treaties carried in the Documentary Supplement. So far, however, the concept has not been sought to be applied to space law with the rigor, detail, and structure of that not-yet-in-force treaty. Note that the so-called "Moon Treaty" (Doc.Supp.) is in force with very few participants, not including the United States, the former USSR, or the Russian Federation, the only two states so far that have, by different means, brought anything back from the Moon. Activity on the Moon does not seem to be on the "take action" agenda of any "space power"; but, suppose, there should be a flurry of interest in the extraction of very valuable or security-important substances from the Moon, would we see a replay of Part XI of the Law of the Sea Convention?

3.　*The problem of geosynchronous (or geostationary) orbits:* Satellites orbiting in equatorial regions at altitudes essentially equal to the circumference of the Earth can be arranged so as to "accompany" the planet in its revolution on its own axis. Such positions give great advantages as to optical observation, signals projection and detection ("remote sensing"); and communications, including radio frequencies and new light-beam technologies. In the 1970's a group of equatorial states, led by Colombia, made a determined effort in the United Nations and elsewhere to assert sovereign claims of an essentially territorial nature to the areas of such orbits. They failed. Meanwhile, the International Telecommunications Union (ITU), a specialized agency under Articles 57 and 63 of the Charter, has managed to "keep the peace" as to utilizations of the limited number of orbital paths available. For the prospects of possibly greater demand for use, see Gleick, *The Telephone Transformed—Into Almost Everything,* New York Times Magazine (May 16, 1993).

4.　*Radio and Television Broadcasting from Space.* Technical problems of electronic interference (which usually are manageable) aside, what if a state feels invaded, culturally, socially, or even politically, by broadcasts from space vehicles by another state? Are such broadcasts legally distinguishable from broadcasts beamed from land, vessels, or aircraft? Is the problem different from, say, broadcasts from vessels or aircraft operating within the territorial jurisdiction of the target state? Why or why not? Is there a legal right of a state and its people "to be let alone" from foreign broadcasts intentionally and specifically directed toward it and them, regardless of source? There is virtually no "hard" (or real?) law in this area. Diplomacy, retaliation, and getting along are the main resorts of offended states. Efforts at "soft law" through

General Assembly Resolutions have not fared well even when limited to obligations to inform, consult, and, inferentially, receive prior consent.

A question for a first course in international law: should the source of the objectionable broadcast be in and of itself, a key variable as to the claimed "rights" of the objecting state and the assertion liability of the "state of the broadcast"? Suppose an objecting state should criminalize all unauthorized (by it) broadcasts heard or seeable in its territory, from whatever source emanating, then sit back and wait for the broadcasters to be (a) found in or (b) hauled into its territory? Should "source" of a satellite in space or on the ground in the sending state be crucial?

Actually, so far, most of the transitional problems involving broadcasting have been the simple over-lapping of signals areas, such as in national sectors along the Canadian, United States and Mexican borders, and in Europe. Propaganda broadcasting by radio was at its height during World War II and the Cold War. Some can still be heard between Castro's Cuba and the United States. (Television seems not to have lent itself as well to direct and unadorned propaganda.)

5. Telecommunications law is a well-developed specialty practice, both nationally and transnationally.

6. *Remote Sensing.* Space satellites, mainly un-manned, have an extensive use in observing, measuring, classifying, and otherwise appraising aspects and characteristics of the planet Earth and its atmosphere, including weather. As is to be expected, states that are more observed than observing of others develop a degree of sensitivity and even concern. Tensions are reduced by the degree to which states with developed sensing capabilities share the results of their observances with other states. See, generally, Christol, Space Law, op. cit. sup., pp. 73–95. "Soft law" through a unanimous Resolution of the General Assembly in 1986 (A–41/65) has linked the sharing of remote sensing results to the "Space Activities Treaty of 1967". Sensing by the United States purports to comply with this and other re-assuring principles. The United States sensing operation was privatized in 1985, on a subsidized basis which, it is assumed by us, is not excessively costly to foreign and other users of the sensed data. One has to assume, however, that observations from space of a military intelligence nature take place and are classified, rather than shared, in view of the secrecy with which certain satellites for military use are launched.

SECTION C.   CELESTIAL BODIES

---

1. *The Outer Space Treaty.* Article II of the treaty provides: "Outer space, including the moon and other celestial bodies, is not subject to national appropriation by claim of sovereignty, by means of use or occupation, or by any other means."

Suppose that a state discovers a particularly rare and valuable mineral on the moon, which it is able to mine cheaply with manned or unmanned equipment. Does the treaty prohibit that state from exploiting the moon's resources for its own exclusive benefit? Can the state set up a base over which it has exclusive control so as to prevent another state from exploiting resources within that base? See Article XII.

What law governs the state, not a party to the treaty (or one that has withdrawn pursuant to Article XVI) that wishes to claim a portion of the moon as its territory? Do the principles relating to the acquisition of territory on the surface of the earth apply? If so, what facts would support a claim that a state has lawfully acquired a portion of the moon as its territory? [a]

2. *The Moon Treaty.* In Dec. 1979, the General Assembly adopted an Agreement Governing the Activities of States on the Moon and other Celestial Bodies. Although the treaty came into force on July 11, 1984, it has very few adherents. Only 8 states were parties to the treaty on Jan. 1, 1993. Developed states parties include France, Austria and the Netherlands, but not the United States or the Soviet Union.

The text of the treaty is set forth in the Documentary Supplement. Article 3 of the Treaty prohibits any threat or use of force or any other hostile act or threat of hostile act on the moon, which France stated upon signature to be only a reaffirmation of the principle of prohibition of use of force which states are obligated to observe under the provisions of the Charter of the United Nations. In Article 11(2) the treaty reiterates the prohibition against national appropriation set forth in the Outer Space Treaty.

A striking feature of the treaty is its declaration that the moon and its natural resources are the common heritage of mankind (Article 11). (Compare the provisions of the Treaty on the Law of the Sea adopting the same concept with respect to the seabed and ocean floor and subsoil beyond the limits of national jurisdiction. Article 136.)

In addition to provisions dealing with notice of activities undertaken on the moon (and other celestial bodies), freedom of scientific investigation, and protection of the moon's environmental balance, the agreement looks ahead to an eventual partial internationalization of the moon. Article 11 provides:

> States Parties to this Agreement hereby undertake to establish an international regime, including appropriate procedures, to govern the exploitation of the natural resources of the moon as such exploitation is about to become feasible. * * *

One of the main purposes of such an international regime is:

> An equitable sharing by all States Parties in the benefits derived from those resources, whereby the interests and needs of the

---

a. Of some utility in the analysis of the legal problems of celestial bodies is a study of Antarctica. See the Antarctic Treaty, 12 U.S.T. 794, 402 U.N.T.S. 71, which entered into force for the United States on June 23, 1961; 42 states were parties as of January 1, 1993. The treaty is briefly discussed in Chapter 11. The text of the treaty and bibliographic references are also in Lay and Taubenfeld, The Law Relating to Activities of Man in Space 59–62 (1970).

developing countries, as well as the efforts of those countries which have contributed either directly or indirectly to the exploration of the moon, shall be given special consideration.

To what extent does the treaty inhibit commercial exploitation of the moon's resources by a state party? Does the agreement provide for a moratorium on such exploitation prior to the establishment of the projected international regime? These questions were the subject of debate in the United States. See the Committee Print on the Agreement prepared for the Committee on Commerce, Science, and Transportation, United States Senate, 96th Cong., 2d Sess., Parts 1 and 2 (May 1980), p. 57, and Part 3 (Aug. 1980), pp. 311, 331.

———

3. *What About Space Stations?* From the movies we are familiar enough with them. Remember the stop at the space station in *2001: A Space Odyssey?* The scene was not unlike coming aboard a United States Navy ship-of-the-line, except that there was no quarter-deck to salute and liquor was served. The Moon launch in 2001 was from the Space Station. Of course, the hugeness of the movie station, more like a city than a mere vessel, contrasts with the modest size of the only station now in space, Russia's *Mir*. In fact, it is difficult to distinguish *Mir* from a mere shuttle, except that *Mir* cannot fly back to Earth but is doomed to burn on re-entry and probably drop debris. The legal literature on space stations is rather iffy and vague, as is to be expected, given their virtually negative state of development and inability to maintain orbit or flight control on re-entry. But, *Mir* has stayed "up" longer than any American shuttle has ever remained in space, thus tending, perhaps, to induce considering a space station as a short-life artificial satellite with people aboard, thus giving rise to questions that would not be relevant as to an un-manned remote-sensing vehicle or a TV repeater. At least one scholar worries about whether the state of the nationality of a space station has any priority of claim as to its orbit, once it drops and has to be replaced. Stay tuned.

4. *The Unmet Problems of Space Debris.* The problem of debris within space was highlighted at mid-summer, 1993, when an American shuttle crew had to take evasive action to avoid collision. There is a lot of trash in orbit and so far nothing has been done about it. The old 1950s treaty on liability for objects falling from space has not been made the basis for liability claims so far.

Chapter 6

INTERNATIONAL PROTECTION
OF THE ENVIRONMENT

---

1. *The development of international environmental law and emerging principles.* The last twenty-one years since the 1972 Stockholm Conference on the Human Environment has evidenced the increasing international and national concern for environmental protection. There has been a growing realization that the ecosystem is complex and interrelated and the approach to combat environmental harm must also be interrelated and integrated among states.

This Chapter begins with an analysis of the early beginnings of the international legal protection of the environment as exemplified in the trilogy of cases, the Trail Smelter Arbitration, the Corfu Channel and the Lake Lanoux Arbitration, which can be regarded as the jurisprudential backing for the 1972 Stockholm Declaration. It then goes on to survey the treatment given to particular areas of environmental concern such as, *inter alia,* transboundary air pollution and acid rain, the ozone

417

layer, climate change, marine pollution and protection of endangered species.   The Rio Declaration on Environment and Development and Agenda 21 will also be discussed.   The second part of the Chapter addresses emerging international law principles such as sustainable development, inter-generational equity and environmental rights as human rights.   The aim here is to give the reader a sense of the new imperatives that are called for to strengthen the legal framework, increase international cooperation and protect the environment for future generations.

2.   ***Environmental issues and the world community.***   The balancing of environmental issues and development present the world community with a unique challenge, as they involve not only conflicting interests but also the interdependence of environmental, economic, political, social and security issues.   A cross-sectoral integrated approach is called for.

WHAT ON EARTH'S THE MATTER?
THE RIO CONFERENCE
UNESCO Sources, No. 37, May 1992, 7–8.

The degradation of the planet's environment is accelerating.   It has been estimated that 10 to 20 million hectares of forest—an area five times the size of Belgium—are destroyed each year, while another six million hectares of arable land turn into desert.   Whole species vanish and ecosystems are destroyed at a dizzying pace, shrinking the earth's genetic capital before when we have even explored all of its resources.

For the first time in history, human deeds have an impact that goes beyond local boundaries and encompasses the globe: witness, for example, climatic changes caused by the greenhouse effect.   And such changes could well prove irreversible.

The human factors accounting for the worsening of our environment are known.   Foremost among them are the world's demographic explosion—the population of the Third World will have quadrupled between 1950 and 2025—the damaging consequences of global manufacturing and consumerism, and the inability of our existing forms of government and social practices to resolve such problems.   These human factors are all linked; unsustainable development and the environmental crisis are but two sides of the same coin.

The physical phenomena involved, be they local or worldwide, are increasingly understood by scientists.   Today, these phenomena can be forecast with enough accuracy to set the alarm bells ringing.   Changing climatic patterns, for example, could lead to rising temperatures and sea levels which, in turn would modify the agricultural potential of entire regions, submerge hundreds of thousands of square kilometers of coastal areas—where three-quarters of the world's population live today—and disrupt, maybe ruin, the lives of millions.

* * *

Humanity is therefore living with a paradox: it is certain that apathy or sporadic and incoherent explosions of activity, will lead us to catastrophe, yet this certainty does not rid us of our impotence and paralysis. This paradox, at the heart of the environmental crisis, is so acute that it can't be explained by circumstantial factors, such as lack of funds, but rather by structural problems.

If paralysis stems from ignorance of the accumulating risks, the environmental crisis then reveals tremendous inefficiency in research methods and/or communication of knowledge.

Environmental problems completely ignore borders, whether they be between nations or scientific disciplines; interdisciplinary approaches, involving not only natural sciences but also social sciences, and cooperation among communities of scientists throughout the world are the only way that environmental research can leap ahead.

* * *

E. BROWN WEISS, GLOBAL ENVIRONMENTAL CHANGE AND INTERNATIONAL LAW: THE INTRODUCTORY FRAMEWORK

in E. Brown Weiss (ed.)
Environmental Change and International Law, 3–7 (1992) (footnotes omitted).*

International law has been based on the relationship between independent states that exercise exclusive national sovereignty over their territories. Global change is altering this vision by causing states to realize that they are locked together in sharing the use of a common global environment. While human activities have always contributed to environmental change, it is only within the last half of this century that their effects have become global and serious, and in many cases irreversible. This has led to a growing awareness that the interests of human- ✓ kind must constrain the interests of individual states. Moreover, actors other than states have become essential to managing global environmental change. These developments are leading to a fundamental shift in the paradigm of international law that is evolving in the international environmental field.

* * * Concern among primarily industrialized countries about the serious risk of environmental harm to countries around the world motivated states to convene the 1972 Conference on the Human Environment, the first world conference on the environment.

By 1970 the world population had more than doubled since the beginning of the century (from 1.6 to 3.4 billion), industrial processes were generating unprecedented amounts of pollutants, and in some countries popular concern for the environment had sky-rocketed. The United States, for example, had passed its first piece of national environmental legislation, the National Environmental Policy Act of 1969. USA

* © (1992) by the United Nations University, all rights reserved. Reprinted with the permission of United Nations University Press, Japan.

At the time of the Stockholm Conference countries were deeply divided over the issue of whether environmental protection and economic development were compatible. The conceptual breakthrough that provided the paradigm for joining these two important goals emerged from a meeting of experts held in Founex, Switzerland, just prior to the Stockholm Conference. Today countries recognize that sound economic development must be environmentally sustainable and are concerned about how to do this. They realize that we need to substantially increase the living standards of the poor in a manner that is environmentally sustainable. The issue in 1992 that divides countries is an equity one: how to finance environmentally sustainable economic development for present and future generations.

Today, 20 years after the Stockholm Conference, countries are concerned with global environmental problems that were either not yet identified or barely addressed. These include acid precipitation, ozone depletion, climate change, hazardous waste disposal, loss of biological diversity, and forest degradation and loss and land-based sources of marine pollution.

The trends in population, resource consumption, and environmental degradation that caused such concern in the early 1970s have continued, or accelerated, while our capacity to address them has increased at a slower rate, albeit arguably more rapidly than for some other problems.

Population growth, resource consumption, and technological development continue to be primary catalysts for global environmental change. By 1990, world population had reached 5.3 billion, more than triple than in 1900 and almost 2 billion more than in 1970. Current estimates are that world population will reach at least 8.5 billion by the year 2025. The bulk of population growth is projected to be in the developing world.

The link between population growth and environmental degradation is complex and not well understood, as reflected in the several competing schools of thought on the issues. However, a larger population generally translates into greater demands on the Earth's resources. As has been demonstrated, population size that exceeds local carrying capacity of the ecosystems can cause soil depletion, deforestation, and desertification. If we multiply projected population increases by the substantially higher standard of living that equity requires for impoverished communities today and for future populations, the potential demands on the environment in the decades ahead are dramatic.

Since 1968, the world's consumption of energy has grown. Overall, the total energy requirements of industrialized countries have increased almost 30 per cent from 1970 to 1988, although this masks two periods of decline after the oil-price shocks. The rate of increase in energy consumption in the developing countries has declined, but remains high. Most of the world's energy continues to come from burning fossil fuels, whose general by-products are a primary contributor to global warming. Annual emissions of carbon dioxide from fossil fuels more than doubled from 1960 to 1988.

In addition, the release of ozone-depleting chloro-fluorocarbons (e.g. CFC–11 and CFC–12), which were virtually non-existent prior to World War II, has risen from 35 million kilograms in 1950, to 506 million kilograms in 1970, and to 707 million kilograms by 1988. Fortunately, countries have now agreed to phase out their production and consumption by the year 2000, and likely sooner. Human-caused emissions of trace metals have followed a similar growth pattern.

Agriculture demands and practices have also raised important environmental concerns. Irrigated crop land, which accounts for about 17 per cent of the world's crop land and one-third of the global harvest, is being eroded by waterlogging and made less productive by salinization (the cumulative build-up of salts left by evaporation of irrigation water). Deforestation, loss of biological diversity, and soil erosion have significantly increased.

Fresh water continues to be a critical resource. In addition to the well-documented water-quality problems of surface waters, new concern has emerged over groundwater resources. Contamination results from the disposal of wastes, both hazardous and non-hazardous, and from the seepage of chemicals such as pesticides and fertilizers into the aquifers. Pesticides, whose use has doubled in the US since 1961, have created groundwater contamination problems in 40 of the 50 US states. Pesticides are used worldwide, with an over–$18–billion market in 1987, and their use is frequently unregulated or not well monitored. The agricultural use of chemicals has also grown dramatically, leading to increased run-off and contamination of lakes, streams, and groundwater. While the open oceans remain relatively undisturbed by humankind's activities, the oceans' coastal zones, the most biologically productive areas, are under severe pressure from population growth and development activities. In addition, there is evidence that we may be reaching the limits of the seas' natural productive capacity. The average annual catch of marine fisheries (79 million metric tons for 1987) are at or near estimates of their sustainable yield (between 62 and 96 million metric tons per year).

In the past, pollution and environmental degradation have operated largely on the local level and hence their effects have been isolated in impact. Given the increasingly global scale of environmental degradation and the ever-increasing volume of pollutants entering the environment, however, their effects are now being felt on regional and global levels. In addition, the scope and irreversible nature of some global changes reach through time to affect the well-being of future generations.

PLOMAN, GLOBAL LEARNING: CONCEPT AND APPLICATIONS

in E. Brown Weiss (ed.) Environmental Change and International
Law 459, 476–478 (1992) (footnotes omitted).*

Concerns about the environment are not new. Yet only in recent years have ecological crises reached such pervasive, disruptive, and potentially disastrous levels that "suddenly the world itself has become a world issue." Thus, today's environmental problems are closely inter-linked, planetary in scale, and, literally, deadly serious.

However, more important than another list of issues is the interlink-age of environmental problems, particularly what they all amount to in the aggregate. The Brundtland Commission has aptly used the image of our earth seen from space as an entry point when it said, "From space we see a small and fragile ball, dominated not by human activity and edifices, but by a pattern of clouds, oceans, greenery, and soil. Humani-ty's inability to fit its doings into that pattern is fundamentally changing planetary systems. Many such changes are accompanied by life-threat-ening hazards. This new reality, from which there is no escape, must be recognized—and managed."

* * * Social unrest due to environmental degradation, resource depletion, and social injustice have already occurred in various countries. Analysts also foresee that if present trends continue unchecked, environ-mental problems might well become major reasons for international conflict, and even war. In the coming decades such problems will range from squabbles over mineral deposits and other natural resources to controversies over unilateral decisions in one country that will affect situations in other countries (transborder pollution, downstream effects of effluents, deforestation, over-fishing, and destruction of habitat).

In fact, analysts have pointed out that comparisons to the environ-mental changes now under way can only be found by going back millions of years in earth's history; the situation is thus totally outside of any human experience. As a result, learning how to cope with these changes is, and will continue to be, a new and difficult experience.

The reluctant and/or partial recognition of this new reality has already led to some action. Despite often bitter scientific and sociopoliti-cal controversy in this area, the ecological crises have reached such a level that the scientific community has merged and agreed on a number of scientific projects on a global scale.

There have also been some surprisingly rapid intergovernmental agreements on specific problems such as the Vienna Ozone Treaty and its Montreal Protocol, as well as a series of high-level meetings. Howev-er, in addition to the difficulties in getting even limited agreements accepted and implemented, voices are already raised in concern that what has been done is not enough and often too late. In general, the agreements are attacking symptoms rather than causes.

    * © 1992, by the United Nations Univer-   the permission of United Nations Universi-
sity, all rights reserved. Reprinted with   ty Press, Japan.

Even though the reality of the situation is only partly perceived and accepted even less so, it has led to a new look at the causes, trends, and phenomena that make current measures appear inadequate, insufficient, and sometimes frivolous. It would be easy to find some examples of these newly perceived issues that hint at the kind of changes that are required. However, it is more important to recognize the interlinkage between development, population, and environment. Far from being antagonistic to development, environmental protection is an irreplaceable partner to development. Environment and development are now seen as opposite sides of the same coin.

* * * In summary, what is required is a change in thinking, and changes in the way things are done and organized. While little has so far been said about the global learning that is required, it is obvious that the learning dimension will be crucial if we are to achieve:

— the necessary integration of population, environment, and development policies;

— growth beyond such immature attitudes as growth for growth's sake or hiding behind "technological fixes";

— economic stability by rethinking our economies;

— a change in attitudes towards nature and the interrelationship between man and nature.

SECTION A. THE DEVELOPMENT OF INTERNATIONAL ENVIRONMENTAL LAW

1. FOUNDATION IN EARLY RULES OF PUBLIC INTERNATIONAL LAW

SHARON A. WILLIAMS & A.L.C. DE MESTRAL, AN INTRODUCTION TO INTERNATIONAL LAW

267–269 (2d ed., 1987) (footnotes omitted).*

* * *

The term transboundary pollution encompasses environmental pollution from many sources. The connecting factor is that the phrase is used to denote "pollution" that emanates from the territory of one state and causes injury, actual or prospective in another state. It is clear that pollution does not respect international boundaries. Hazardous air pollution may be produced in one state and cause damage within the borders of another state. Environmental pollution may be caused by chemicals such as sulphur dioxide (SO_2) and oxides of nitrogen (NOx) being put into the air in state X and along with other products being vented upwards, especially by tall stacks, undergoing complex chemical reactions high in the atmosphere and then circulating with the air

---

* Published by Butterworths Canada, Ltd., reprinted with their permission.

masses, with the end result that after perhaps travelling hundreds or even thousands of miles, acid precipitation falls in state Y. Smoke and fumes may be blown from one state to another. Hazardous liquid and solid wastes may be discharged onto the land and into inland waters causing damage to health and property in another state. This may be of particular danger where two states share a common drainage basin. Oil pollution and effluent waste disposal may cause damage to the maritime environment offshore. Other methods of possible injury could include: thermal pollution; radiation of the atmosphere; nuclear emissions into the atmosphere; disturbance of the oxygen-carbon dioxide balance and the nitrogen cycle and by the use of pesticides, defoliants and other chemicals harmful to people and to the environment that surrounds them.

* * * Due to the novelty of this subject, the law is still very much in the process of development. There are glaring gaps in the law and the fundamental principles underlying the law are not always easy to discern. Any analysis of international environmental law must begin with existing rules of international law. Thus, the fundamental rules of sovereignty, territorial integrity, state responsibility, and maritime jurisdiction, however inappropriate, provide the basic framework within which the law has developed, but it is also true that many of the rules of international law which are slowly emerging contain much that is different in content and purpose from traditional international law.

The process of development of international environmental law has been rapid and complex. As one might expect with a new body of law, the United Nations and other international organizations such as the United Nations Environment Program (U.N.E.P.) and the International Maritime Organization (I.M.O.) have played an important role. Nongovernmental organizations such as the International Law Association and the International Council on Environmental Law have also contributed. International conferences have played a conspicuous part: in particular the United Nations Conference on the Human Environment, held at Stockholm in 1972, marked a watershed in the development of international environmental law. Also of great importance was the Third United Nations Conference on the Law of the Sea culminating in the 1982 Convention on the Law of the Sea. Treaty law has been a most important source of law both for specific areas such as marine pollution and for the development of general principles. Bilateral and regional state practice has also begun to follow a number of significant patterns concerning such issues as transboundary water pollution or marine pollution. Unilateral state action such as the adoption of the *Arctic Waters Pollution Prevention Act* by Canada in 1970 has also been a significant, albeit controversial, source of law.

———

TRAIL SMELTER ARBITRATION (UNITED STATES v. CANADA)

Arbitral Tribunal, 1941.
3 U.N.Rep.Int'l Arb. Awards 1905, 1907 (1949).
Convention for Settlement of Difficulties Arising
From Operation of Smelter at Trail, B.C.

* * *

Article III

The Tribunal shall finally decide the questions, hereinafter referred to as "the Questions", set forth hereunder, namely:

(1) Whether damage caused by the Trail Smelter in the State of Washington has occurred since the first day of January, 1932, and, if so, what indemnity should be paid therefor?

(2) In the event of the answer to the first part of the preceding Question being in the affirmative, whether the Trail Smelter should be required to refrain from causing damage in the State of Washington in the future, and if so, to what extent?

(3) In the light of the answer to the preceding Question, what measures or régime, if any, should be adopted or maintained by the Trail Smelter?

(4) What indemnity or compensation, if any, should be paid on account of any decision or decisions rendered by the Tribunal pursuant to the next two preceding Questions?

Article IV

The Tribunal shall apply the law and practice followed in dealing with cognate questions in the United States as well as international law and practice, and shall give consideration to the desire of the high contracting parties to reach a solution just to all parties concerned.

* * *

DECISION

Reported on March 11, 1941, to the Government of the United States
of America and to the Government of the Dominion of Canada,
Under the Convention Signed April 15, 1935.

* * *

On April 16, 1938, the Tribunal reported its "final decision" on Question No. 1, as well as its temporary decisions on Questions No. 2 and No. 3, and provided for a temporary régime thereunder. The decision reported on April 16, 1938, will be referred to hereinafter as the "previous decision".

* * *

In conclusion (end of Part Two of the previous decision), the Tribunal answered Question No. 1 as follows:

Damage caused by the Trail Smelter in the State of Washington has occurred since the first day of January, 1932, and up to October

1, 1937, and the indemnity to be paid therefor is seventy-eight thousand dollars ($78,000), and is to be complete and final indemnity and compensation for all damage which occurred between such dates. * * *

* * *

In 1896, a smelter was started under American auspices near the locality known as Trail, B.C. In 1906, the Consolidated Mining and Smelting Company of Canada, Limited, obtained a charter of incorporation from the Canadian authorities, and that company acquired the smelter plant at Trail as it then existed. Since that time, the Canadian company, without interruption, has operated the Smelter, and from time to time has greatly added to the plant until it has become one of the best and largest equipped smelting plants on the American continent. In 1925 and 1927, two stacks of the plant were erected to 409 feet in height and the Smelter greatly increased its daily smelting of zinc and lead ores. This increased production resulted in more sulphur dioxide fumes and higher concentrations being emitted into the air. In 1916, about 5,000 tons of sulphur per month were emitted; in 1924, about 4,700 tons; in 1926, about 9,000 tons—an amount which rose near to 10,000 tons per month in 1930. In other words, about 300–350 tons of sulphur were being emitted daily in 1930. (It is to be noted that one ton of sulphur is substantially the equivalent of two tons of sulphur dioxide or SO_2.)

From 1925, at least, to 1937, damage occurred in the State of Washington, resulting from the sulphur dioxide emitted from the Trail Smelter as stated in the previous decision.

* * *

The second question under Article III of the Convention is as follows:

> In the event of the answer to the first part of the preceding question being in the affirmative, whether the Trail Smelter should be required to refrain from causing damage in the State of Washington in the future and, if so, to what extent?

Damage has occurred since January 1, 1932, as fully set forth in the previous decision. To that extent, the first part of the preceding question has thus been answered in the affirmative.

* * *

The first problem which arises is whether the question should be answered on the basis of the law followed in the United States or on the basis of international law. The Tribunal, however, finds that this problem need not be solved here as the law followed in the United States in dealing with the quasi-sovereign rights of the States of the Union, in the matter of air pollution, whilst more definite, is in conformity with the general rules of international law.

Particularly in reaching its conclusions as regards this question as well as the next, the Tribunal has given consideration to the desire of the high contracting parties "to reach a solution just to all parties concerned".

As Professor Eagleton puts it (Responsibility of States in International Law, 1928, p. 80): "A State owes at all times a duty to protect other States against injurious acts by individuals from within its jurisdiction." A great number of such general pronouncements by leading authorities concerning the duty of a State to respect other States and their territory have been presented to the Tribunal. These and many others have been carefully examined. International decisions, in various matters, from the Alabama case onward, and also earlier ones, are based on the same general principle, and, indeed, this principle, as such, has not been questioned by Canada. But the real difficulty often arises rather when it comes to determine what, pro subjecta materia, is deemed to constitute an injurious act.

A case concerning, as the present one does, territorial relations, decided by the Federal Court of Switzerland between the Cantons of Soleure and Argovia, may serve to illustrate the relativity of the rule. Soleure brought a suit against her sister State to enjoin use of a shooting establishment which endangered her territory. The court, in granting the injunction, said: "This right (sovereignty) excludes * * * not only the usurpation and exercise of sovereign rights (of another State) * * * but also an actual encroachment which might prejudice the natural use of the territory and the free movement of its inhabitants." As a result of the decision, Argovia made plans for the improvement of the existing installations. These, however, were considered as insufficient protection by Soleure. The Canton of Argovia then moved the Federal Court to decree that the shooting be again permitted after completion of the projected improvements. This motion was granted. "The demand of the Government of Soleure", said the court, "that all endangerment be absolutely abolished apparently goes too far." The court found that all risk whatever had not been eliminated, as the region was flat and absolutely safe shooting ranges were only found in mountain valleys; that there was a federal duty for the communes to provide facilities for military target practice and that "no more precautions may be demanded for shooting ranges near the boundaries of two Cantons than are required for shooting ranges in the interior of a Canton".

No case of air pollution dealt with by an international tribunal has been brought to the attention of the Tribunal nor does the Tribunal know of any such case. The nearest analogy is that of water pollution. But, here also, no decision of an international tribunal has been cited or has been found.

There are, however, as regards both air pollution and water pollution, certain decisions of the Supreme Court of the United States which may legitimately be taken as a guide in this field of international law, for it is reasonable to follow by analogy, in international cases, precedents established by that court in dealing with controversies between States of the Union or with other controversies concerning the quasi-sovereign rights of such States, where no contrary rule prevails in international law and no reason for rejecting such precedents can be adduced from the limitations of sovereignty inherent in the Constitution of the United States.

In the suit of Missouri v. Illinois (200 U.S. 496, 521) concerning the pollution, within the boundaries of Illinois, of the Illinois River, an affluent of the Mississippi flowing into the latter where it forms the boundary between that State and Missouri, an injunction was refused. "Before this court ought to intervene", said the court, "the case should be of serious magnitude, clearly and fully proved, and the principle to be applied should be one which the court is prepared deliberately to maintain against all considerations on the other side. (See Kansas v. Colorado, 185 U.S. 125.)" The court found that the practice complained of was general along the shores of the Mississippi River at that time, that it was followed by Missouri itself and that thus a standard was set up by the defendant which the claimant was entitled to invoke.

* * *

In the more recent suit of New York against New Jersey (256 U.S. 296, 309), concerning the pollution of New York Bay, the injunction was also refused for lack of proof * * *. What is true between States of the Union is, at least, equally true concerning the relations between the United States and the Dominion of Canada.

In another recent case concerning water pollution (283 U.S. 473), the complainant was successful. The City of New York was enjoined, at the request of the State of New Jersey, to desist, within a reasonable time limit, from the practice of disposing of sewage by dumping it into the sea, a practice which was injurious to the coastal waters of New Jersey in the vicinity of her bathing resorts.

In the matter of air pollution itself, the leading decisions are those of the Supreme Court of Georgia v. Tennessee Copper Company and Ducktown Sulphur, Copper and Iron Company, Ltd. Although dealing with a suit against private companies, the decisions were on questions cognate to those here at issue. Georgia stated that it had in vain sought relief from Tennessee, on whose territory the smelters were located, and the court defined the nature of the suit by saying: "This is a suit by a State for an injury to it in its capacity of quasi-sovereign. In that capacity, the State has an interest independent of and behind the titles of its citizens, in all the earth and air within its domain."

On the question whether an injunction should be granted, the court said (206 U.S. 230):

> It (the State) has the last word as to whether its mountains shall be stripped of their forests and its inhabitants shall breathe pure air. * * * It is not lightly to be presumed to give up quasi-sovereign rights for pay and * * * if that be its choice, it may insist that an infraction of them shall be stopped. This court has not quite the same freedom to balance the harm that will be done by an injunction against that of which the plaintiff complains, that it would have in deciding between two subjects of a single political power. Without excluding the considerations that equity always takes into account * * * it is a fair and reasonable demand on the

part of a sovereign that the air over its territory should not be polluted on a great scale by sulphurous acid gas, that the forests on its mountains, be they better or worse, and whatever domestic destruction they may have suffered, should not be further destroyed or threatened by the act of persons beyond its control, that the crops and orchards on its hills should not be endangered from the same source. * * * Whether Georgia, by insisting upon this claim, is doing more harm than good to her own citizens, is for her to determine. The possible disaster to those outside the State must be accepted as a consequence of her standing upon her extreme rights.

Later on, however, when the court actually framed an injunction, in the case of the Ducktown Company (237 U.S. 474, 477) (an agreement on the basis of an annual compensation was reached with the most important of the two smelters, the Tennessee Copper Company), they did not go beyond a decree "adequate to diminish materially the present probability of damage to its (Georgia's) citizens".

* * *

The Tribunal, therefore, finds that the above decisions, taken as a whole, constitute an adequate basis for its conclusions, namely, that, under the principles of international law, as well as of the law of the United States, no State has the right to use or permit the use of its territory in such a manner as to cause injury by fumes in or to the territory of another or the properties or persons therein, when the case is of serious consequence and the injury is established by clear and convincing evidence.

The decisions of the Supreme Court of the United States which are the basis of these conclusions are decisions in equity and a solution inspired by them, together with the regime hereinafter prescribed, will, in the opinion of the Tribunal, be "just to all parties concerned", as long, at least, as the present conditions in the Columbia River Valley continue to prevail.

Considering the circumstances of the case, the Tribunal holds that the Dominion of Canada is responsible in international law for the conduct of the Trail Smelter. Apart from the undertakings in the Convention, it is, therefore, the duty of the Government of Canada to see to it that this conduct should be in conformity with the obligation of the Dominion under international law as herein determined.

The Tribunal, therefore, answers Question No. 2: (2) So long as the present conditions in the Columbia River Valley prevail, the Trail Smelter shall be required to refrain from causing any damage through fumes in the State of Washington; the damage herein referred to and its extent being such as would be recoverable under the decisions of the courts of the United States in suits between private individuals. The indemnity for such damage should be fixed in such manner as the Governments, acting under Article XI of the Convention should agree upon.

The third question under Article III of the Convention is as follows: "In the light of the answer to the preceding question, what measures or régime, if any, should be adopted and maintained by the Trail Smelter?"

Answering this question in the light of the preceding one, since the Tribunal has, in its previous decision, found that damage caused by the Trail Smelter has occurred in the State of Washington since January 1, 1932, and since the Tribunal is of opinion that damage may occur in the future unless the operations of the Smelter shall be subject to some control, in order to avoid damage occurring, the Tribunal now decides that a régime or measure of control shall be applied to the operations of the Smelter and shall remain in full force unless and until modified in accordance with the provisions hereinafter set forth. * * *

* * *

1. *Jurisdiction to legislate with respect to air pollution.* Does either the State of Washington or the United States have jurisdiction to prescribe laws regulating the pollution of Washington or United States airspace by Canadian polluters?

2. *Applicable law.* Heretofore in Chapter 5 the law governing events occurring in airspace has been domestic law and the inquiry has been whether or not a state has jurisdiction to prescribe the relevant rule. In what respect does the Trail Smelter case present a different problem? What is the source of the governing rule?

Why is Canada held responsible in this case? By what standard is its conduct measured? Does international law impose an obligation on Canada only after a showing of historical injury, or would a showing of potential injury be sufficient? For a discussion of the implications of the Trail Smelter case for situations in which modern technological developments threaten the environment (e.g., weather modification), see Kirgis, Technological Challenge to the Shared Environment: United States Practice, 66 Am.J.Int'l L. 290 (1972).

CORFU CHANNEL CASE (MERITS) (UNITED KINGDOM v. ALBANIA)

International Court of Justice 1949.
[1949] I.C.J. Rep. 4.

[During transit of the Corfu Channel within the territorial sea of Albania two British warships were damaged heavily by mines. Following this two other British warships mine-swept the Corfu Channel. From the international environmental law perspective the Court's pronouncement on the question of Albanian responsibility and liability to compensate for damage and loss of life caused by the explosions occurring in its waters is of relevance.]

THE COURT:

* * * It is clear that knowledge of the minelaying cannot be imputed to the Albanian Government by reason merely of the fact that a minefield discovered in Albanian territorial waters caused the explosions of which the British ships were the victims. It is true, as international practice shows, that a State on whose territory or in whose waters an act contrary to international law has occurred, may be called upon to give an explanation. It is also true that that State cannot evade such a request by limiting itself to a reply that it is ignorant of the circumstances of the act and of its authors * * *. [I]t cannot be concluded from the mere fact of the control exercised by a State over its territory and waters that that State necessarily knew, or ought to have known, of any unlawful act perpetrated therein, nor yet that it necessarily knew, or should have known, the authors. This fact, by itself and apart from other circumstances, neither involves *prima facie* responsibility nor shifts the burden of proof.

On the other hand, the fact of this exclusive territorial control exercised by a State within its frontiers has a bearing upon the methods of proof available to establish the knowledge of that State as to such events. By reason of this exclusive control, the other State, the victim of a breach of international law, is often unable to furnish direct proof of facts giving rise to responsibility. Such a state should be allowed a more liberal recourse to inferences of fact and circumstantial evidence. This indirect evidence is admitted in all systems of law, and its use is recognized by international decisions. It must be regarded as of special weight when it is based on a series of facts linked together and leading logically to a single conclusion.

The court must examine therefore whether it has been established by means of indirect evidence that Albania has knowledge of minelaying in her territorial waters independently of any connivance on her part in this operation. The proof may be drawn from inferences of fact, provided that they leave no room for reasonable doubt * * *.

From all the facts and observations * * * the Court draws the conclusion that the laying of the minefield which caused the explosions * * * could not have been accomplished without the knowledge of the Albanian Government. * * *

[It is] every State's obligation not to allow knowingly its territory to be used for acts contrary to the rights of other States. * * *

LAKE LANOUX ARBITRATION (FRANCE v. SPAIN)
12 U.N. Rep. Int'l Arb. Awards 281 (1957).

[Spain objected to a French proposal to use Lake Lanoux for hydroelectric purposes, in that it would interfere with the flow of boundary waters contrary to an 1866 bilateral treaty. The arbitral tribunal first found for France, that its development scheme would not breach the bilateral treaty. In doing so it made an important finding concerning liability for environmental harm. The Tribunal then considered what conduct was expected of France in its relations with Spain over the project and Spain's contention that prior agreement of both States was needed.]

THE TRIBUNAL: * * *

One might have attacked this conclusion [that the French plans were not in breach of the treaty] in several different ways.

It could have been argued that the works would bring about an ultimate pollution of the waters of the Carol or that the returned waters would have a chemical composition or temperature or some other characteristic which could injure Spanish interests. Spain could then have claimed that her rights had been impaired in violation of the Additional Act. Neither in the *dossier* nor in the pleadings in this case is there any trace of such an allegation.

[As to the Spanish contention that its agreement with the French scheme was necessary, the Tribunal said:]

* * * To admit that jurisdiction in a certain field can no longer be exercised except on the condition of, or by way of, an agreement between two States, is to place an essential restriction on the sovereignty of a State, and such restriction could only be admitted if there were clear and convincing evidence. Without doubt, international practice does reveal some special cases in which this hypothesis has become reality; thus, sometimes two States exercise conjointly jurisdiction over certain territories (joint ownership, *co-imperium,* or *condominium*); likewise, in certain international arrangements, the representatives of States exercise conjointly a certain jurisdiction in the name of those States or in the name of organizations. But these cases are exceptional, and international judicial decisions are slow to recognize their existence, especially when they impair the territorial sovereignty of a State, as would be the case in the present matter.

In effect, in order to appreciate in its essence the necessity for prior agreement, one must envisage the hypothesis in which the interested States cannot reach agreement. In such case, it must be admitted that the State which is normally competent has lost its right to act alone as a result of the unconditional and arbitrary opposition of another State. This amounts to admitting a "right of assent", a "right of veto", which at the discretion of one State paralyses the exercise of the territorial jurisdiction of another.

That is why international practice prefers to resort to less extreme solutions by confining itself to obliging the States to seek, by preliminary negotiations, terms for an agreement, without subordinating the exercise of their competences to the conclusion of such an agreement. Thus, one speaks, although often inaccurately, of the "obligation of negotiating an agreement". In reality, the engagements thus undertaken by States take very diverse forms and have a scope which varies according to the manner in which they are defined and according to the procedures intended for their execution; but the reality of the obligations thus undertaken is incontestable and sanctions can be applied in the event, for example, of an unjustified breaking off of the discussions, abnormal delays, disregard of the agreed procedures, systematic refusals to take into consideration adverse proposals of interests, and, more generally, in cases of violation of the rules of good faith.

* * * States are today perfectly conscious of the importance of the conflicting interests brought into play by the industrial use of international rivers, and of the necessity to reconcile them by mutual concessions. The only way to arrive at such compromises of interests is to conclude agreements on an increasingly comprehensive basis. International practice reflects the conviction that States ought to strive to conclude such agreements: there would thus appear to be an obligation to accept in good faith all communications and contracts which could, by a broad comparison of interests and by reciprocal good will, provide States with the best conditions for concluding agreements. This point will be referred to again later on, when enquiring what obligations rest on France and Spain in connection with the contracts and the communications preceding the putting in hand of a scheme such as that relating to Lake Lanoux.

But international practice does not so far permit more than the following conclusion: the rule that States may utilize the hydraulic power of international watercourses only on condition of a *prior* agreement between the interested States cannot be established as a custom, even less as a general principle of law. * * *

The * * * question is to determine the method by which these interests can be safeguarded. If that method necessarily involves communications, it cannot be confined to purely formal requirements, such as taking note of complaints, protests or representations made by the downstream State. The Tribunal is of the opinion that, according to the rules of good faith, the upstream State is under the obligation to take into consideration the various interests involved, to seek to give them every satisfaction compatible with the pursuit of its own interests, and to show that in this regard it is genuinely concerned to reconcile the interests of the other riparian State with its own. * * *

As a matter of form, the upstream State has, procedurally, a right of initiative; it is not obliged to associate the downstream State in the elaboration of its schemes. If, in the course of discussions, the downstream State submits schemes to it, the upstream State must examine them, but it has the right to give preference to the solution contained in its own scheme provided that it takes into consideration in a reasonable manner the interests of the downstream State.

* * * In the case of Lake Lanoux, France has maintained to the end the solution which consists in diverting the waters of the Carol to the Ariege with full restitution. By making this choice France is only making use of a right; the development works of Lake Lanoux are on French territory, the financing of and the responsibility for the enterprise fall upon France, and France alone is the judge of works of public utility which are to be executed on her own territory, save for the provisions of Articles 9 and 10 of the Additional Act, which, however, the French scheme does not infringe.

On her side, Spain cannot invoke a right to insist on a development of Lake Lanoux based on the needs of Spanish agriculture. In effect, if

France were to renounce all of the works envisaged on her territory, Spain could not demand that other works in conformity with her wishes should be carried out. Therefore, she can only urge her interests in order to obtain, within the framework of the scheme decided upon by France, terms which reasonably safeguard them.

It remains to be established whether this requirement has been fulfilled * * *.

When one examines the question of whether France, either in the course of the dealings or in her proposals, has taken Spanish interests into sufficient consideration, it must be stressed how closely linked together are the obligation to take into consideration, in the course of negotiations, adverse interests and the obligation to give a reasonable place to these interests in the solution finally adopted. A State which has conducted negotiations with understanding and good faith * * * is not relieved from giving a reasonable place to adverse interests in the solution it adopts simply because the conversations have been interrupted, even though owing to the intransigence of its partner. Conversely, in determining the manner in which a scheme has taken into consideration the interests involved, the way in which negotiations have developed, the total number of the interests which have been presented, the price which each Party was ready to pay to have those interests safeguarded, are all essential factors in establishing * * * the merits of that scheme.

[In conclusion, the Tribunal was of the view that France had sufficiently involved Spain in the preparations of the project.]

DECLARATION OF THE UNITED NATIONS CONFERENCE ON THE HUMAN ENVIRONMENT

U.N. Document A/CONF. 48/14 and Corr. 1.
11 International Legal Materials 1416 (1972), in the Doc. Supp.

COLLOQUY

Proceedings, 77th Annual Meeting, American Society of International Law 433–34 (1983).*

CHRISTIAN HERTER: * * * In terms of the Trail Smelter case and the precedent it set for the development of Principle 21, has there been any comparable case since the Trail Smelter? If not, why not?

* * *

Professor HANDL: In response to why there has not been a second Trail Smelter case, the answer perhaps is related to why there has been a decline in the amount of international adjudication. Today, there seems to be a reluctance on the part of most states to submit to international adjudication coupled with a tendency of states to negotiate and arbitrate informally. I also think that we are seeing a movement toward the adoption of soft norms, reflecting a sense of soft responsibility on the part of states for international matters. On the other hand, it can be argued that Principle 21 is widely accepted by states as customary

* Reprinted with the permission of the
American Society of International Law.

international law and that it is no longer contested. However, Principle 21 has a different impact today, a different application from what it originally had in the Trail Smelter context.

————

As of July, 1993, the International Court of Justice is deliberating two cases, those concerning Certain Phosphate Lands in Nauru (Nauru v. Australia) and the Gabcikovo–Nagymaros Project (Hungary/Slovakia) with important implications for international law on matters relating to the environment.[1] Their outcome should be interesting.

STATE RESPONSIBILITY AND THE STANDARD OF FAULT

SHARON A. WILLIAMS, PUBLIC INTERNATIONAL LAW GOVERNING TRANSBOUNDARY POLLUTION,

International Business Lawyer, 243, 244–245 (1984) (footnotes omitted).*

Of particular relevance and difficulty is the question of liability and on what basis is it to be determined. Is it to be based on subjective fault criteria, objective fault criteria or strict or absolute liability? According to many writers it is the objective fault or responsibility principle that has been followed by states in their practice, by arbitral tribunals and by the International Court of Justice. It follows that if in the area of transboundary pollution fault should play a part, it should only be in the objective sense.

It has been suggested that the use of strict liability may be still de lege ferenda. However, there is some support for it at the present time. It can be argued that in the Corfu Channel case and in the Trail Smelter Arbitration fault of no kind was established. Likewise, in the Gut–Dam Arbitration [between Canada and the U.S.] the tribunal was not interested in fault or knowledge of prospective injuries by Canada. Canada was held liable. This decision, however, is of less value when it is added that Canada had accepted the obligation of compensation payment in advance. In the Lac Lanoux arbitration between France and Spain, fault on the part of France was not a requirement. The matter is not addressed in the Stockholm Declaration of June 16th, 1972. It has been argued that this might negate any requirement for the establishment of fault. Further, some O.E.C.D. states have argued that a system of strict liability should be introduced in all cases of transboundary pollution, regardless of any safeguard measures that have been taken.

On this basis, it can be argued that strict liability may become, in the not too distant future, the accepted norm re liability in customary international law. This argument is justified if the aforementioned arbitral decisions, declarations and statements by governments can be seen to indicate the required state practice and opinio juris necessary to form a rule of customary international law.

1. ICJ unofficial communique for immediate release, No. 93/20 (July 19, 1993).

* Reprinted with the permission of the International Bar Association.

It is impossible to designate any similar status to the absolute liability theory. There is no indication through any of the forms of state practice or judicial or arbitral decisions that would allow the supposition that this theory is presently or is imminently on the verge of crystallizing into a role of customary international law. Unless states agreed to such a rule of liability in an international agreement, the notion of absolute liability does not appear to merit practical consideration.

In international law the effect of a finding of state responsibility is that the state found responsible to another must make reparation. The usual type of reparation for a wrongful act or omission is an indemnity that corresponds to the damage suffered. In the context of damage caused by transboundary pollution restitution in the majority of cases would not be a possibility. It is impossible to re-establish the situation as it existed prior to the delinquent act and hence to wipe out the consequences of the illegality. Therefore compensation in monetary terms and formal apologies, statements of consideration or intent for the future might be in order. It has been suggested by one author that international tribunals may impose injunctions to restrain pollution activities in the future. Also the International Court of Justice may grant interim measures to prevent further damage ensuing during the conduct of an action before it.

F. ORREGO VICUÑA, STATE RESPONSIBILITY, LIABILITY AND REMEDIAL MEASURES UNDER INTERNATIONAL LAW: NEW CRITERIA FOR ENVIRONMENTAL PROTECTION

in E. Brown Weiss (ed.), Environmental Change and International
Law 124, 134–135, 138–140 (1992) (footnotes omitted).*

* * * [T]he fact that international law has been exploring more stringent forms of responsibility is, in and of itself, indicative of the sense of change that is taking place. The most significant of these changes is the introduction of the concept of absolute and strict liability. Delinking the adverse effects of a given hazardous or dangerous activity from the element of *culpa* of the state or operator incorporates the test of "objective" responsibility as opposed to the "subjective" criteria of traditional international law. Still more stringent criteria have been emerging lately, particularly as concerns the idea of holding a state responsible for damage ensuing from given activities irrespective of whether it took all necessary measures to prevent injury. The result is that responsibility will attach in spite of due diligence having been observed. Liability for acts not prohibited by international law is another major development * * *.

* * * [T]he International Law Commission has made the point that material damage would not be an essential element in the case of responsibility for wrongful acts. The attribution of the conduct to the state and the breach of an international obligation would suffice to invoke responsibility. Under traditional international law, however, the

* © 1992 by the United Nations University, all rights reserved. Reprinted with the   permission of United Nations University Press, Japan.

violation of the obligation would be sufficient to engage responsibility, which means that the old rules are very helpful indeed to broaden the scope of the law at present. On the other hand, when the international liability is for acts not prohibited by international law, material damage would be the essential basis of compensation, resulting in the paradox that, on this point, the new rules are more restrictive than the old.

Although the seriousness of the damage is another issue where the practice is not entirely uniform, certain gravity is, without a doubt, required. This requirement, however, is qualified by two considerations that relate to the evolving state of international law. First, given the emphasis on preventive measures characterizing present environmental law, the adoption of all necessary preventive and remedial measures even where no injury has occurred is beginning to emerge as a new type of obligation. Second, as mentioned in the *Restatement of the Law (Third),* when pollution is caused by substances that are highly dangerous to human life and health, there is no need to prove a significant impact or injury, thereby altering rather dramatically the traditional standards of international law. Examples of this trend are blacklisting of hazardous products and abnormally dangerous activities like the launching of space objects.

* * * International liability for acts not prohibited by international law involves a rather stringent form of responsibility-liability, which in turn has a strong impact on the nature and extent of remedial measures in the field. It follows that the debate about the present state of international law on this point has been most lively.

First, it should be noted that the much discussed decision of the International Law Commission in 1976, referred to above (which lists among international crimes those relating to the breach of an international obligation of essential importance for the safeguarding and preservation of the human environment), has to be understood more as an expression of concern in line with the Stockholm Conference than as a radical departure in terms of the consequences attached to the breach of such an obligation.

The work of the International Law Commission on "International Liability" reveals a cautious approach to the state of international law on the matter. On the one hand the separation of liability for acts not prohibited by international law from State Responsibility is indicative of the policy of attaching a legal consequence—liability—even to international lawful activities, yet on the other hand State Responsibility could well apply to extra-hazardous operations, thus also attaching a legal consequence to activities that are not, *per se,* unlawful. In this regard the remedial aspect of the law would not be different under either approach. What is of importance is that international law is accepting legal consequences for a variety of activities that may result in an adverse impact upon the environment.

The "compound 'primary' obligation" identified by the International Law Commission in its schematic outline on "international liability" refers to four basic duties: prevent, inform, negotiate, and repair. The emphasis is on preventive measures as well as the new obligation to notify and consult. However, it is surprising that the failure to comply with the first three duties mentioned is not regarded as wrongful and, consequently, no action can be brought against such failure; only the failure to make reparations is ultimately identified with a wrongful act and, hence, engages the State's responsibility.

It follows that from the perspective of the International Law Commission, there is really not much difference between international liability and state responsibility, since the ultimate test of wrongfulness in both lies in the failure to make a reparation. While it is true that under international liability the initial activity can be lawful and under state responsibility normally it will be unlawful (although neither excludes both lawful and unlawful activities), the two are equated in terms of the end result.

It has been rightly observed that one consequence of the International Law Commission approach could "allow a state to persist in an unlawful act even without the consent of the injured state, as long as the acting state pays monetary reparations to the injured state." In the field of environmental protection this result would be utterly unacceptable and self-defeating, which is why there has been an emphasis on both preventive measures and new developments that require that pollution be terminated and allow all states to bring actions to this effect.

Although there has also been debate about whether the *Trail Smelter* decision involved, in addition to its pioneering invocation of international liability, an element of international responsibility given that a wrongful act had been committed, it is quite clear that the effect of the decision never would have allowed the harmful activity to persist. As noted above it ordered the smelter to "refrain" from such activity and put in place a regime for the control of emissions. This result is in line with the emerging consensus that international law ought to provide adequate protection of the environment.

Another element of the debate prompted by the International Law Commission's work is the method of determining reparation. The schematic outline favours the method of reparation determined by a "balance-of-interests" test, which takes into account the shared expectations of the states involved, a number of principles and factors, and the extent to which the duties to prevent, inform, and negotiate have been complied with. This approach offers the advantage of introducing an element of flexibility that allows the weighing of the different circumstances of the case, but, on the other hand, it involves greater subjectivity. The alternative test of strict liability is in a sense more objective, because the harmful result will be separated from the intention of the state and even from the fact of having discharged the relevant duties. Again this last approach is more in line with the needs of environmental protection.

———

COSMOS 954 CLAIM (CANADA v. U.S.S.R.)

18 International Legal Materials 899 (1979).*

[The satellite Cosmos 954 was placed in orbit in space by the U.S.S.R. on September 18, 1977. The Secretary–General of the United Nations was officially informed. The satellite had on board a nuclear reactor that worked on uranium enriched with isotope of uranium 235. On January 24, 1978 Cosmos 954 re-entered the earth's atmosphere and intruded into Canada's air space. Debris from the satellite was found on Canadian territory, specifically in the Northwest Territories, Alberta and Saskatchewan. The Canadian Armed Forces and the Canadian Atomic Energy Control Board immediately began to locate, recover, remove and test the debris and to clean up the sites where it had landed. The total cost of these operations which were conducted in two phases in 1978 was approximately 14 million dollars. Canada claimed 6 million dollars from the U.S.S.R. The following extract is taken from Canada's Statement of Claim.] "On behalf of CANADA: * * *

(a) International Agreements

15.   Under Article II of the Convention on International Liability for Damage Caused by Space Objects, hereinafter referred to as the Convention, "A launching State shall be absolutely liable to pay compensation for damage caused by its space object on the surface of the earth * * *." The Union of Soviet Socialist Republics, as the launching State of the Cosmos 954 satellite, has an absolute liability to pay compensation to Canada for the damage caused by this satellite. The deposit of hazardous radioactive debris from the satellite throughout a large area of Canadian territory, and the presence of that debris in the environment rendering part of Canada's territory unfit for use, constituted "damage to property" within the meaning of the Convention.

16.   The intrusion into Canadian air space of a satellite carrying on board a nuclear reactor and the break-up of the satellite over Canadian territory created a clear and immediate apprehension of damage, including nuclear damage, to persons and property in Canada. The Government of the Union of Soviet Socialist Republics failed to give the Government of Canada prior notification of the imminent re-entry of the nuclear powered satellite and failed to provide timely and complete answers to the Canadian questions of January 24, 1978 concerning the satellite. It thus failed to minimize the deleterious results of the intrusion of the satellite into Canadian air space.

17.   Under general principles of international law, Canada had a duty to take the necessary measures to prevent and reduce the harmful consequences of the damage and thereby to mitigate damages. Thus, with respect to the debris, it was necessary for Canada to undertake without delay operations of search, recovery, removal, testing and clean-up. * * * Article VI of the Convention imposes on the claimant State a

*Reprinted with the permission of the American Society of International Law.

duty to observe reasonable standards of care with respect to damage caused by a space object.

18.   * * * Costs included by Canada * * * were incurred solely as a consequence of the intrusion into Canadian air space and the deposit on Canadian territory of hazardous radioactive debris from the satellite.

19.   In respect of compensation for damage caused by space objects, the Convention provides for " * * * such reparation in respect of the damage as will restore * * * [the claimant State] to the condition which would have existed if the damage had not occurred" (Article XII).   In accordance with its Preamble, the Convention seeks to ensure " * * * the prompt payment * * * of a full and equitable measure of compensation to victims of such damage" * * *.   Canada's claim includes only those costs which were incurred in order to restore Canada to the condition which would have existed if the damage inflicted by the Cosmos 954 satellite had not occurred.   The Convention also provides that "The compensation which the launching State shall be liable to pay for damage under this Convention shall be determined in accordance with international law and the principles of justice and equity * * * " (Article XII).   In calculating the compensation claimed, Canada has applied the relevant criteria established by general principles of international law and has limited the costs included in its claim to those costs that are reasonable, proximately caused by the intrusion of the satellite and deposit of debris and capable of being calculated with a reasonable degree of certainty.

20.   The liability of the [U.S.S.R.] * * * for damage caused by the satellite is also founded in Article VII of the Treaty on Principles Governing the Activities of States in the Exploration and Use of Outer Space, including the Moon and Other Celestial Bodies, done in 1967, and to which both Canada and the [U.S.S.R.] * * * are parties.   This liability places an obligation on the [U.S.S.R.] * * * to compensate Canada in accordance with international law for the consequences of the intrusion of the satellite into Canadian air space and the deposit on Canadian territory of hazardous radioactive debris from the satellite.

. (b) General Principles of International Law

21.   The intrusion of the Cosmos 954 satellite into Canada's air space and the deposit on Canadian Territory of hazardous radioactive debris from the satellite constitutes a violation of Canada's sovereignty. * * * International precedents recognize that a violation of sovereignty gives rise to an obligation to pay compensation.

22.   The standard of absolute liability for space activities, in particular activities involving the use of nuclear energy, is considered to have become a general principle of international law.   * * * The principle of absolute liability applies to fields of activities having in common a high degree of risk.   It is repeated in numerous international agreements and is one of "the general principles of law recognized by civilized nations" (Article 38 of the Statute of the International Court of Justice).   Accord-

ingly, this principle has been accepted as a general principle of international law."

––––––

1. ***Cosmos 954 Settlement.*** In February, June and November 1980 negotiations took place between Canada and the U.S.S.R. The result was a three million dollar settlement in the form of a Protocol signed by the Canadian Ambassador and the Soviet Deputy Minister of Foreign Affairs. It did not acknowledge liability formally.

2. ***Territorial sovereignty versus common interest.*** The crux of the international environmental debate is whether a state being sovereign, may carry out, or permit to be carried out, hazardous activities in its territory that are injurious to the environment. Can other states complain, even if they have not suffered actual injury? Is the obligation to protect the environment owed *erga omnes,* because of the common interest of humanity in its well-being? Note the recognition of this by the International Court of Justice in the Barcelona Traction case [1970] I.C.J.Rep. 4, when the Court stated that:

> [A]n essential distinction should be drawn between the obligations of a State towards the international community as a whole, and those arising vis-à-vis another State in the field of diplomatic protection. By their very nature the former are the concern of all states. In view of the importance of the rights involved, all states can be held to have a legal interest in their protection; they are obligations *erga omnes.*

The 1992 Report of the International Law Commission on the Work of its Forty–Fourth Session on the topic of state responsibility had this to say on the question of differently injured states, U.N. GAOR 47th Sess. Supp. No. 10 (A/47/10) 93–95:

> The violation of obligations arising, for example, under rules concerning disarmament, promotion of and respect for human rights and environmental protection, termed *"erga omnes* obligations", simultaneously injured the subjective rights of all the States bound by the norm, whether or not they were specifically affected * * *. The Special Rapporteur * * * arrived at the conclusion that the distinction between "directly" and "indirectly" injured States did not hold water and that the differing situations were distinguished by the nature or the extent of the injury. * * * It must therefore be determined to what extent each of those States was, on the one hand, entitled to claim cessation, restitution in kind, pecuniary compensation, satisfaction and/or guarantees of non-repetition, and, on the other hand, entitled to resort to sanctions or countermeasures.

These questions go to the heart of the problem, in that under the traditional customary international law rules of state responsibility discussed in Chapter 10(A), a state is only responsible for damage caused resulting from an illegal activity. Also, the jurisprudence on state responsibility has concerned for the most part injuries to aliens occurring within the territory of the respondent state. (See Handl, Territorial Sovereignty and the Problem of Transnational Pollution, 69 Am.J.Int'l L. 50 (1975).) Can these traditional rules be extended to and cope with transnational ecosystem damage and the threat thereof?

Note: The principle of imputability is important in determining state responsibility. Would a state be able to plead a domestic law or lack of same in defence of any environmental claims made against it by other states? See the *Free Zones case,* P.C.I.J.Ser. A/B, No. 46, 167 (1932). When cross-border pollution or other environmental harm occurs does state responsibility arise when no action is taken either to prosecute the alleged perpetrators or to give access to remedies to the victims?

3. **The standard of fault.** There has been a great deal of discussion as to the appropriate standard to be applied in transnational environmental cases. Is it to be based on fault, or strict or absolute liability irrespective of fault? In the absence of a specific treaty obligation such as illustrated above in the Cosmos 954 claim under, *inter alia,* the 1972 Convention on International Liability for Damage Caused by Space Objects, 24 U.S.T. 2389, T.I.A.S. No. 7762, it is doubtful that customary international law has gone this far. The cases reproduced above would seem to indicate this.

4. **Sic utere tuo, ut non alienum laedas.** Apart from and in addition to the rules of customary international law that may be applied to environmental protection are certain general principles of law such as that expressed in this latin maxim, meaning "use your property so as not to injure that of another". This fundamental principle may be seen as equivalent to the general principle of "good neighbourliness" which is specifically recognized in Article 74 of the U.N. Charter and may be said to fall under Article 38(1)(c) of the Statute of the International Court of Justice. It may be said to have been the underlying principle in the Trail Smelter case considered earlier in this section. It is also reflected in Article X of the International Law Association's Helsinki Rules on the Uses of Waters of International Rivers, referred to infra. (See S.A. Williams, Public International Law Governing Transboundary Pollution, International Business Lawyer 243, 249 (June 1984)).

5. **Causal link.** It is a general principle accepted by states that there must be a causal link between the conduct and the injury. On account of the nature of environmental pollution this can be problematic in that a great distance may separate the source of the pollution from the locus of the injury. Another factor is the time between the emission of the pollutants and the injury and thus the possibility of intervening causes that may be argued to have broken the chain of causation.

6. **Stockholm Declaration.** This Declaration was adopted at the 1972 U.N. Conference on the Human Environment by acclamation. There were 113 states present. Although not a treaty but a declaration, it represents a basic charter of environmental protection and its principles are reflected in, *inter alia,* Article 30 of the Charter of Economic Rights and Duties of States, U.N.G.A.Res. 3281 (XXI) December 12, 1974, 29 U.N. GAOR Supp. (No. 31) 50, U.N.Doc. A/9631 (1974), Articles

192–194 of the 1982 Law of the Sea Convention, U.N.Doc. A/CONF. 62/122 (1982), the OECD Principles Concerning Transfrontier Pollution, Council Rec. C(74) 224, 14 Int'l Leg.Mat. 242 (1975), the 1979 ECE Convention on Long Range Transboundary Pollution, Preamble, T.I.A.S. 10541, the 1985 Vienna Convention for the Protection of the Ozone Layer, Preamble, 26 Int'l Leg.Mat. 1516 (1987), the 1991 Canada–United States Air Quality Agreement, Preamble, 30 Int'l Leg.Mat. 678 (1991), the 1992 United Nations Framework Convention on Climate Change, Preamble, 31 Int'l Leg.Mat. 851 (1992), the 1992 United Nations Convention on Biodiversity, Article 3, 31 Int'l Leg.Mat. 822 (1992), the Statement of Principles for a Global Consensus on the Management, Conservation and Sustainable Development of all Types of Forests, 31 Int'l Leg.Mat. 818 (1992), and the 1992 Rio Declaration on Environment and Development, 31 Int'l Leg.Mat. 874 (1992). In the Nuclear Tests Cases, [1974] I.C.J.Rep. 253, 457, it was argued by Australia and New Zealand that it reflected the attitude of the international community.

The 1972 Declaration was accompanied by 109 recommendations. The U.N. General Assembly endorsed these recommendations and in December 1972 created the United Nations Environmental Programme (UNEP), headquartered in Nairobi, Kenya, to carry them out. See UNGA Res. 2997/27, UN GAOR, 27th Sess. Supp. (No 30) 43, UN Doc. No. A/8730 (1972) and Petsonk, The Role of the United Nations Environmental Programme (UNEP) in the Development of International Environmental Law, 5 Am.U.J.Int.L. & Pol. 351 (1990). In 1991 the U.N. Convention on Environmental Impact Assessment in a Transboundary Context was signed, 30 Int'l Leg.Mat. 809 (1991). This Convention provides, *inter alia,* for an assessment procedure that must be undertaken for any activity that is proposed that falls within Appendix I that is likely to cause significant adverse transboundary impact. There are provisions for notification and consultation of affected states parties and the public in those states.

7. *The 1987 Restatement.* See Section 601, which obligates states to take "such measures as may be necessary, to the extent practicable under the circumstances" with respect to the environment of other states and imposes responsibility for significant injury resulting from violation of this obligation. Comment *d* to this section makes an additional observation: "However, even if it has taken the necessary and practicable measures, a state is responsible where injury results from a discharge of highly dangerous substances (radioactive, toxic, etc.), or from abnormally dangerous activities (e.g. launching of space satellites)."

DRAFT CODE OF CRIMES AGAINST THE PEACE AND SECURITY OF MANKIND

REPORT OF THE INTERNATIONAL LAW COMMISSION ON THE WORK OF ITS 44TH SESSION, 29 APRIL–19 JULY, 1991

UN GAOR 46th Session Supp. No. 10 (A/46/10), 198, 275–276.
In the Doc. Supp.

Work of the International Law Commission. The ILC has been working on the Draft Code of Crimes (formerly called Offences) since

1949, following its establishment by the U.N. General Assembly in 1947 by U.N.G.A.Res. 174(II), U.N.Doc. A/519, 105–10 (1947). For a history of the Draft Code of Crimes see L. Gross, Some Observations on the Draft Code of Offences Against the Peace and Security of Mankind, 13 Is. Yearbook Human Rights 9 (1983); S.A. Williams, The Draft Code of Offences Against the Peace and Security of Mankind, in M.C. Bassiouni (ed.) International Criminal Law (1985), vol. I, 109 and M.C. Bassiouni, The History of the Draft Code of Crimes Against the Peace and Security of Mankind, 27 Is.L.Rev. 247 (1993).

Note: Draft Article 19(3)(d) of the ILC's Draft Articles on State Responsibility, mentioned in the commentary to Draft Article 26 of the Code of Crimes, provides that "a serious breach of an international obligation of essential importance for the safeguarding and preservation of the human environment" is an international crime. It should be noted that the term "international crime" as it is used there according to the Commission means international wrongs that are serious in the extreme and for which there is state responsibility. Although the designation sounds confusing, it must not be thought to entail incrimination of states or individuals. (See [1976] Y.B.I.L.C. 11, 109, 119). In its 1994 Report, the ILC has re-opened discussion on this issue (*see* UN-GAOR 49th Sess. Supp. No. 10 (A/49/10), 327. For its work on state responsibility the Commission decided to separate the concepts of international responsibility and international liability. The former deals with the consequences of prohibited or wrongful activity, while the concept of liability entails the harmful consequences of lawful activity. A significant distinction between the two is that, although a state may be obligated (liable) to pay compensation for harm caused by lawful activity, the underlying activity as such (e.g., the maintenance of a nuclear power station) need not be stopped. The separation of the two concepts has created analytical problems. The work on state responsibility and liability has occupied the Commission for many years. (See Handl, Liability as an Obligation Established By a Primary Rule of International Law, 16 Netherlands Yb. Int'l L. 49 (1985).)

The work of the ILC on international consequences of acts not prohibited by international law has been ongoing since 1978. (See Handl, State Liability for Accidental Harm by Private Persons, 74 Am.J.Int'l.L. 525 (1980); Boyle, State Responsibility and International Liability for Injurious Consequences of Acts Not Prohibited by International Law: A Necessary Distinction, 39 Int. & Comp.L.Q. 1 (1990)).

2. TRANSBOUNDARY AIR POLLUTION AND ACID RAIN

In 1991, the United States and Canada entered an agreement dealing with the problems of transboundary air pollution and acid rain between the two countries. This agreement delineated specific objectives for air quality; assessment, notification and mitigation of proposed activities, actions and projects; and provided for a dispute settlement mechanism and the establishment of a Bilateral Air Quality Commission.

A portion of the Agreement between Canada and the United States on Air Quality, 30 Int'l Leg. Mat. 676 is in the Doc. Supplement.

1. ***Acid rain.*** A joint United States—Canada Research Consultation Group on Long–Range Transport of Air Pollutants concluded in 1979: "The transport of air pollutants over distances of hundreds to thousands of kilometers is taking place in eastern North America. The [group] has identified acidic precipitation as the problem of greatest common concern at the present time. Acidic precipitation is primarily the result of sulfur dioxide and oxides of nitrogen emissions which are transformed as they are transported by the atmosphere. The most recent estimates of sulphur dioxide emissions are 25.7 million metric tons for the United States and 5.0 million metric tons for Canada." The group found that these emissions crossed the border between the two countries. While noting that the greater part of each country's pollutants was caused by its own emissions, it reported that more acid rain was being sent to Canada by the United States.

It took fifty years after the decision in the Trail Smelter arbitration for the United States and Canada to negotiate an air quality agreement requiring specific government controls on industries causing cross-frontier deposits of acid rain. Although the Canadian government had pushed for such controls, in particular with respect to industries in the Ohio Valley burning coal with high sulphur content, the United States government had hesitated pending more research. Such agreements as were entered into dealt with research, monitoring, notification and exchange of information. See, e.g., Memorandum of Intent Concerning Transboundary Air Pollution, August 5, 1980, 32 UST 2521, TIAS 9856. (Note J. Brunée, Acid Rain and Ozone Layer Depletion: International Law and Regulation (1988) and C. Flinterman, B. Kwiatkowska and J. Lammers (eds.) Transboundary Pollution (1986).)

The United States and Canada are parties to the Convention on Long–Range Transboundary Air Pollution of 1979 (in force March 16, 1983), TIAS 10541, 18 Int'l Leg.Mat. 1442 (1979), to which states from both eastern and western Europe are parties, and to the 1985 and 1988 Protocols to that Convention on reduction of sulphur dioxide and nitrogen oxide emissions respectively. See 27 Int'l Leg.Mat. 707 (1988) and 28 Int'l Leg.Mat. 214 (1989). The emphasis of the Convention is on research and the exchange of information, and there are few real obligations concerning emission limitations and liability. (See Fraenkel, the Convention on Long–Range Transboundary Air Pollution: Meeting the Challenge of International Cooperation, 30 Harvard Int.L.J. 447 (1989)). A third protocol on the Control of Emissions of Volatile Organic Compounds or their Transboundary Fluxes has been signed by Canada and the United States but has not yet entered into force. See 31 Int'l Leg.Mat. 573 (1992).

2. ***Specific objectives of the 1991 Air Quality Agreement.*** Annex 1 requires that the United States: 1) reduce its annual sulphur dioxide emissions by approximately 10 million tons from 1980 levels by the year 2000; 2) achieve a permanent national emission cap of 8.95 million tons of sulphur dioxide per year for electric utilities by the year

2010; 3) promulgate new or revised standards or such other action under the Clean Air Act as the Administrator of the Environmental Protection Agency deems appropriate aimed at sulphur dioxide emissions from industrial sources in the event that annual sulphur dioxide emissions from industrial sources may reasonably be expected to exceed 5.6 million tons and 4) concerning nitrogen oxides with a view to reducing total annual emissions by approximately 2 million tons from 1980 emission levels, the implementation of stated nitrogen oxide programs. The requirements for Canada under Annex 1 are: 1) the reduction of sulphur dioxide emissions in the seven easternmost provinces to 2.3 million tonnes (metric) per year by 1994 and the achievement of a cap on sulphur dioxide emissions in the seven easternmost provinces at 2.3 million tonnes per year from 1995 through December 31, 1999; 2) achievement of a permanent national emissions cap of 3.2 million tonnes per year by 2000; 3) as an interim requirement the reduction by 2000 of annual national emissions of nitrogen oxides from stationary sources by 10,000 tonnes below the year 2000 forecast of 970,000 tonnes, and by January 1, 1995, the development of further annual national emission reduction requirements from stationary sources to be achieved by 2000 and/or 2005, and 4) the implementation of a more stringent mobile source nitrogen oxides control program for gasoline and diesel powered vehicles and engines.

3. *The International Joint Commission (IJC).* This body was established pursuant to Article VII of the 1909 Boundary Waters Treaty, 1909 T.S. No. 548, 12 Bevans 319, between the United States and Great Britain acting then on behalf of Canada. Its purpose is to aid in the prevention and settlement of disputes over the uses of boundary waters. Article IV provides that the boundary waters "shall not be polluted on either side to the injury of health or property on the other". It is noteworthy that pursuant to Article IX that the IJC must examine, report and make recommendations upon the request of either one of the governments, on any difference between the two states or their inhabitants along the common border. There have been many references under this Article. There are arbitral powers, where both states consent under Article X. So far, this has not been used. The 1991 Air Quality Agreement, augments the activities of the IJC in the air pollution field.

4. *Reciprocal Access.* In response to Principle 22 of the Stockholm Declaration, the American and Canadian Bar Associations, the National Conference of Commissioners on Uniform State Laws and the Uniform Law Conference of Canada recommended legal procedures to compensate victims of transboundary pollution through litigation. This would enable out of jurisdiction victims to have standing to sue in the courts of the jurisdiction where the pollution is situated. Based upon reciprocity, the victim would only have such court access if both the state or province of the victim and alleged polluter have such legislation. Under United States federal legislation, in the form of the Clean Water Act, 33 U.S.C. §§ 1251–1376 and the Clean Air Act, 42 U.S.C. §§ 7401–7642, there can be the participation of a foreign state, on the basis of reciprocity, in hearings held for the revision of a state implementation plan, for the purposes of eliminating adverse consequences for that

foreign state. Note also the 1980 Comprehensive Environmental Response, Compensation and Liability Act, 42 U.S.C. § 9601.

5. ***Proposed European Union (EU) action.*** The EU Commission in Brussels proposed in September 1993 far reaching measures for an integrated approach to the control of air, water and land pollution from large industrial plants. New industries would be expected to introduce the latest technology to reduce pollution, while older plants would have until 2005 to clean up and comply. The Commission proposes a licensing procedure based on admissable levels of pollutants for each individual sector. However, although existing national controls would be coordinated, the twelve member states would still set their own emission limits within EU margins. Heavy industries would have to submit themselves for pollution inspection by national authorities before being granted a license to operate. The draft Directive also provides for the public to scrutinize member states' control measures.

3.   TRANSBOUNDARY NUCLEAR DAMAGE

The Three Mile Island warning and the 1986 Chernobyl disaster have brought home a realization that nuclear accidents can result in pollution in a form and of an intensity beyond levels previously contemplated. What should be the international legal reaction to this newly recognized fact? A multilateral convention that does no more than restate recognized obligations under existing customary international law will not go far to address the problem. The threat of an international obligation to pay reparations for past injuries probably does not provide any greater deterrence on a state than does concern for the safety of the state's own citizens (and rulers). Conventions finely-tailored to specific aspects of the problem are more promising. On September 26, 1986, the International Atomic Energy Agency opened for signature two such conventions: a Convention on Early Notification of a Nuclear Accident and a Convention on Assistance in the Case of a Nuclear Accident or Radiological Emergency, 25 I.L.M. 1370 and 1377 (1986). (See P. Sands, Chernobyl: Law and Communication (1988) and G. Handl, Transboundary Nuclear Accidents: The Post–Chernobyl Multilateral Legislative Agenda, 15 Ecology L.Q. 203 (1988)).

The Treaty Banning Nuclear Weapon Tests in the Atmosphere, in Outer Space and Under Water, 14 U.S.C. 1313, 480 U.N.T.S. 43, Doc. Supplement, entered into force for the United States on October 10, 1963. The preamble to the treaty recites that the parties desired "to put an end to the contamination of man's environment by radioactive substances." There were 120 parties to the treaty on January 1, 1993.

Concerning civil liability the 1960 Paris Convention, 8 E.Y.B. 203, 55 A.J.I.L. 1082, drafted by the O.E.C.D. addresses transboundary nuclear accidents within the Western European member states. The 1963 Vienna Convention, 1063 U.N.T.S. 265, 2 I.L.M. 727 is similar but global in scope. The United States is not a party. (See P. Birnie and A. Boyle, International Law and the Environment, 371 (1992)).

NUCLEAR TESTS (AUSTRALIA v. FRANCE), INTERIM PROTECTION, ORDER OF 22 JUNE 1973

International Court of Justice, 1973.
[1973] I.C.J. Reports 99.[a]

The International Court of Justice,

* * *

Having regard to the Application by Australia filed in the Registry of the Court on 9 May 1973, instituting proceedings against France in respect of a dispute concerning the holding of atmospheric tests of nuclear weapons by the French Government in the Pacific Ocean, and asking the Court to adjudge and declare that the carrying out of further atmospheric nuclear weapon tests in the South Pacific Ocean is not consistent with applicable rules of international law, and to order that the French Republic shall not carry out any further such tests,

Makes the following Order:

1. Having regard to the request * * * whereby the Government of Australia * * * asks the Court to indicate, pending the final decision in the case brought before it by the Application of the same date, the following interim measures of protection: "The provisional measures should be that the French Government should desist from any further atmospheric nuclear tests pending the judgment of the Court in this case;" * * *

* * *

6. Whereas by a letter dated 16 May 1973 from the Ambassador of France to the Netherlands, handed by him to the Registrar the same day, the French Government stated that it considered that the Court was manifestly not competent in the case and that it could not accept the Court's jurisdiction, and that accordingly the French Government did not intend to appoint an agent, and requested the Court to remove the case from its list;

* * *

13. Whereas on a request for provisional measures the Court need not, before indicating them, finally satisfy itself that it has jurisdiction on the merits of the case, and yet ought not to indicate such measures unless the provisions invoked by the Applicant appear, prima facie, to afford a basis on which the jurisdiction of the Court might be founded;

* * *

17. Whereas the material submitted to the Court leads it to the conclusion, at the present stage of the proceedings, that the provisions invoked by the Applicant appear, prima facie, to afford a basis on which the jurisdiction of the Court might be founded; * * *.

* * *

a. Parallel proceedings were instituted by New Zealand. [1973] I.C.J. Reports 135.

22. Whereas the claims formulated by the Government of Australia in its Application are as follows:

(i) The right of Australia and its people, in common with other States and their peoples, to be free from atmospheric nuclear weapon tests by any country is and will be violated;

(ii) The deposit of radio-active fall-out on the territory of Australia and its dispersion in Australia's airspace without Australia's consent:

(a) violates Australian sovereignty over its territory;

(b) impairs Australia's independent right to determine what acts shall take place within its territory and in particular whether Australia and its people shall be exposed to radiation from artificial sources;

(iii) the interference with ships and aircraft on the high seas and in the superjacent airspace, and the pollution of the high seas by radioactive fall-out, constitute infringements of the freedom of the high seas;

* * *

25. Whereas the Government of Australia alleges, inter alia, that a series of atmospheric nuclear tests have been carried out by the French Government in the Pacific during the period from 1966 to 1972, including the explosion of several hydrogen bombs and a number of devices of high and medium power; that during recent months there has been a growing body of reports, not denied by the French Government, to the effect that the French Government is planning to carry out a further series of atmospheric nuclear tests in the Pacific in 1973; that this series of tests may extend to 1975 and even beyond that date; that in diplomatic correspondence and in discussions earlier in the present year the French Government would not agree to cease nuclear testing in the atmosphere in the Pacific and would not supply Australia with any information as to the dates of its proposed tests or the expected size and yield of its explosions; and that in a statement made in the French Parliament on 2 May 1973 the French Government indicated that, regardless of the protests made by Australia and other countries, it did not envisage any cancellation or modification of the programme of nuclear testing as originally planned;

* * *

27. Whereas the Government of Australia also alleges that the atmospheric nuclear explosions carried out by France in the Pacific have caused wide-spread radio-active fall-out on Australian territory and elsewhere in the southern hemisphere, have given rise to measurable concentrations of radio-nuclides in foodstuffs and in man, and have resulted in additional radiation doses to persons living in that hemisphere and in Australia in particular; that any radio-active material deposited on Australian territory will be potentially dangerous to Australia and its people and any injury caused thereby would be irreparable; that the conduct of French nuclear tests in the atmosphere creates

anxiety and concern among the Australian people; that any effects of the French nuclear tests upon the resources of the sea or the conditions of the environment can never be undone and would be irremediable by any payment of damages; and any infringement by France of the rights of Australia and her people to freedom of movement over the high seas and superjacent airspace cannot be undone;

28. Whereas the French Government, in a diplomatic Note dated 7 February 1973 and addressed to the Government of Australia, the text of which was annexed to the Application in the present case, called attention to Reports of the Australian National Radiation Advisory Committee from 1967 to 1972, which all concluded that the fall-out from the French tests did not constitute a danger to the health of the Australian population; whereas in the said Note the French Government further expressed its conviction that in the absence of ascertained damage attributable to its nuclear experiments, they did not violate any rule of international law, and that, if the infraction of the law was alleged to consist in a violation of a legal norm concerning the threshold of atomic pollution which should not be crossed, it was hard to see what was the precise rule on which Australia relied;

29. Whereas for the purpose of the present proceedings it suffices to observe that the information submitted to the Court, including Reports of the United Nations Scientific Committee on the Effects of Atomic Radiation between 1958 and 1972, does not exclude the possibility that damage to Australia might be shown to be caused by the deposit on Australian territory of radio-active fall-out resulting from such tests and to be irreparable;

* * *

33. Whereas the decision given in the present proceedings in no way prejudges the question of the jurisdiction of the Court to deal with the merits of the case, or any questions relating to the admissibility of the Application, or relating to the merits themselves, and leaves unaffected the right of the French Government to submit arguments in respect of those questions;

* * *

Accordingly, The COURT, Indicates, by 8 votes to 6, pending its final decision in the proceedings instituted on 9 May 1973 by Australia against France, the following provisional measures: The Governments of Australia and France should each of them ensure that no action of any kind is taken which might aggravate or extend the dispute submitted to the Court or prejudice the rights of the other Party in respect of the carrying out of whatever decision the Court may render in the case; and, in particular, the French Government should avoid nuclear tests causing the deposit of radio-active fall-out on Australian territory; * * *

[Declarations and dissenting opinions omitted.]

Subsequent proceedings in the Nuclear Tests Cases. Despite the court's order for interim measures of protection, France continued to conduct tests during the summer months of 1973 and 1974. The court held hearings on the question of its jurisdiction, France not participating. Thereafter the court took note of a number of public declarations by the French government, including a communiqué issued by the President of France stating that "in view of the stage reached in carrying out the French nuclear defence programme France will be in a position to pass on to the stage of underground explosions as soon as the series of tests planned for this summer is completed." The court read these unilateral acts as creating a legally binding obligation on the part of France to cease testing in the atmosphere in the South Pacific. Since the court concluded that Australia's objective in this proceeding was to obtain termination of French atmospheric nuclear tests in the South Pacific, it found, by a vote of nine to six "that the claim of Australia no longer has any object and that the court is therefore not called upon to give a decision thereon." [1974] I.C.J. Reports 253. The same result was reached in the New Zealand proceedings. Id. at 457.

---

4. PROTECTING THE OZONE LAYER

The ozone layer is a protective screen that filters ultraviolet radiation and thus protects the earth from over-exposure. It is estimated that approximately ninety per cent of all the atmospheric ozone is to be found in the stratosphere. (*See* J. Brunée, Acid Rain and Ozone Layer Depletion: International Law and Regulation, 35 (1988)). The balance of the ozone layer has been undermined by industrial and human actions, whereby deterioration is caused by chemicals, especially chlorofluorocarbons (CFCs), but also by methane, nitrogen oxides and halons. CFCs are used in many consumer goods such as refrigerators, air conditioners, aerosol cans, solvents and styro-foam. It is not known exactly how the chemicals are transported into the stratosphere. The impact of this ozone layer depletion is that more harmful rays of UV–B have increased and global scale effects will result on human health and in fact on the whole eco-system with some variations based on latitude, unless the situation is rapidly ameliorated. (*See, Id.,* 43). There is also the relation between ozone layer depletion and climate change, otherwise commonly known as the "greenhouse effect", in that ozone absorbs and then emits what is termed "thermally significant terrestrial infrared radiation". (See A. Gallagher, The New Montreal Protocol and the Future of International Law for Protection of the Global Environment, 14 Houston J.Int.L. 267, 274–277 (1992)). The two are linked because the gases CO_2, methane, N_2O, CFC 11 and 12 are among the major greenhouse gases and are also responsible for ozone layer deterioration. In 1985 the Vienna Convention for the Protection of the Ozone Layer, 26 ILM 1516 (1987), became the first multilateral convention to deal with this dangerous problem. It came into force on September 22, 1988. However, as with the ECE Long Range Transboundary Air Pollution

Convention considered earlier in section A.2 of this Chapter, it is only a framework for cooperation, with no real substantive obligations. The aim was, and has been since, to adopt protocols or amendments to existing protocols that deal with specific obligations. The 1987 Montreal Protocol, which entered into force on January 1, 1989, 26 ILM 1541 (1987) and London Adjustments thereto of 1990, 30 ILM 537 (1991), that are reproduced in the Doc. Supplement, are part of that process. In 1992 a further meeting in Copenhagen produced other adjustments and amendments to the Montreal Protocol. See 32 ILM 874 (1993).

GLOBAL OZONE TRENDS

A. GALLAGHER, THE "NEW" MONTREAL PROTOCOL AND THE FUTURE OF INTERNATIONAL LAW FOR PROTECTION OF THE GLOBAL ENVIRONMENT

14 Houston Journal of International Law 267, 274–277 (1992) (footnotes omitted).*

Despite several decades of observation and the utilization of increasingly sophisticated equipment, scientists have found it difficult to accurately measure past changes in global ozone. Considerable natural variations, due, *inter alia,* to cyclical changes in atmospheric motion and solar activity, have hindered efforts to assess net ozone losses. In 1986, the National Aeronautical Space Administration (NASA), in conjunction with other national and international organizations, including the World Meteorological Association (WMO) and the United Nations Environment Programme (UNEP), conducted a major review and re-analysis of all available data relating to atmospheric ozone concentrations. A final report from NASA and the Ozone Trends Panel was released in 1988, and included results from the NASA-backed Airborne Antarctic Ozone Experiment conducted the previous year. The Panel, after adjusting measurements to allow for natural geophysical variability, detected small but statistically significant changes in both total column ozone and its vertical distribution between 1979 and 1986. The Panel concluded that such changes may well be due to the increased abundance of atmospheric trace gases—primarily CFCs.

Of far greater magnitude were the levels of stratospheric ozone depletion measured over Antarctica during the 1987 Experiment. The springtime "hole" has been observed since the early eighties, each year growing progressively deeper, despite what appeared to be explicable turnarounds in 1986 and 1988. Some think the unique winter/spring Antarctic meteorology permits the creation of an isolated air-mass (polar vortex) with temperatures sufficiently cold to perturb the critical composition of the upper atmosphere. Within this vortex, the anthropogenically influenced processes by which ozone is destroyed are hastened and intensified.

In 1989, NASA launched another expedition, this time an investigation of the winter Arctic stratosphere. The expedition's final report revealed that the chemistry responsible for Antarctic ozone depletion was also present in the atmosphere above the North Pole. The Arctic

* Reprinted with the permission of the Houston J. Int'l L.

ozone layer, it appears, is "primed for destruction." Parallel investigations conducted by a Canadian research team using specially filled balloons confirmed the NASA group's findings.

Rapid advances in the field of polar atmospheric photochemistry helped explain the large decreases in Antarctic ozone and confirmed the existence of Arctic conditions indicating potential for a similar level of destruction. What remains unclear is whether this phenomena forebodes ozone thinning elsewhere in the stratosphere, whether the processes responsible could be important at other latitudes, and whether a hemispheric depletion of ozone is possible through dilution of the wider layer.

The search for answers to these questions is becoming increasingly urgent. The 1990 springtime hole over Antarctica was far deeper and persisted for considerably longer than expected. In April 1991 NASA completed analysis of data collected by its total ozone mapping satellite over a period of eleven years and seven months. The Agency confirmed that ozone depletion in the northern hemisphere is occurring between two and five times faster than previously predicted by theoretical models and is extending further away from the polar regions.

5. CLIMATE CHANGE AND THE PRECAUTIONARY PRINCIPLE

J. BRUNÉE, ACID RAIN AND OZONE LAYER DEPLETION: INTERNATIONAL LAW AND REGULATION

47 (1988) (footnotes omitted).*

* * * The Earth's temperature depends on the amounts of sunlight coming in, in relation to the amounts which are reflected back into space. This reflection is prevented by the [greenhouse] gases [CO_2, methane, N_2O, CFC 11 and 12 and tropospheric ozone] which have the effect of a screen and retain heat comparable to a greenhouse. With concentrations of these gases rising at current levels, global temperatures could rise between 1.5° C by the middle of the next century. However, noticeable changes may occur within the next decade * * *.

The consequences would, of course, be immense: climate zones could shift and impair global agriculture and food supplies, sea levels could rise between 20 and 140 meters due to thermal expansion and melting of glaciers and polar ice, human health could be directly affected, at least in an adaption period.

Because of the immense impact of CO_2 emissions and the difficulty of controlling them (they occur necessarily in every combustion process), the greenhouse effect might be an even more pressing problem than the depletion of the ozone layer. Some scientists consider global warming to be inevitable and suggest that even now we begin preparations of countries and economies for climatical, geographical, and social changes.

---

* Reprinted with the permission of Transnational Publishers Inc.

Convention on Climate Change. On June 5, 1992, the United Nations Framework Convention on Climate Change was opened for signature, at the U.N. Conference on Environment and Development. No reservations to this Convention are allowed. See the Doc. Supp. for the Convention and related U.N. General Assembly resolutions. Two of the most important portions of these documents are reproduced below. (See also D. Bodansky, Scientific Uncertainty and the Precautionary Principle, 33(7) Environment 4 (1991) and J. Cameron & J. Abouchar, The Precautionary Principle: A Fundamental of Law and Policy for the Protection of the Global Environment, 14 B.C. Int'l & Comp.L.Rev. 1 (1991)).

FRAMEWORK CONVENTION ON CLIMATE CHANGE PRINCIPLES
U.N. Doc. A/AC 237/18 (Pt. II) Add. 1; 31 International Legal Materials 851 (1992).*

* * *

3. Parties should take precautionary measures to anticipate, prevent or minimize the causes of climate change and mitigate its adverse effects. Where there are threats of serious or irreversible damage, lack of full scientific certainty should not be used as a reason for postponing such measures, taking into account that policies and measures to deal with climate change should be cost-effective so as to ensure global benefits at the lowest possible cost. To achieve this, such policies and measures should take into account different socio-economic contexts, be comprehensive, cover all relevant sources, sinks and reservoirs of greenhouse gases and adaptation, and comprise all economic sectors. Efforts to address climate change may be carried out cooperatively. * * *

RIO DECLARATION ON ENVIRONMENT AND DEVELOPMENT
June 13, 1992; A/CONF. 151/5/Rev. 1, 31 International Legal Materials 874 (1992).**

Principle 15
In order to protect the environment, the precautionary approach shall be widely applied by States according to their capabilities. Where there are threats of serious or irreversible damage, lack of full scientific certainty shall not be used as a reason for postponing cost-effective measures to prevent environmental degradation.

Non-binding Declarations. On March 11, 1989, a non-binding declaration was signed at the Hague, the Netherlands, by twenty-four state leaders. It called for a new approach to dealing with matters pertaining to the atmosphere through new principles of international law being developed and new international institutional authority. (See 28 ILM 1308 (1989)). Note also the 1989 Malé Declaration on Global Warming and Sea Level Rise by so-called "small states" and the 1989

---

* Reprinted with the permission of the American Society of International Law.   ** Reprinted with the permission of the American Society of International Law.

Noordwijk Declaration on Atmospheric Pollution and Climate Change made by the 67 state representatives, the Commission of the European Communities and ten international organizations. (See M. Molitor (ed.) International Environmental Law: Primary Materials (1991)). The 1990 Ministerial Declaration of the Second World Climate Conference, attended by representatives of 137 states, amongst other things urged developed states to limit non-Montreal Protocol greenhouse gases and called for a framework convention on climate change. (See G. Handl (ed.) 1 Yb. Int'l Env.L. 473 (1990)).

6. INTERNATIONAL RIVERS, LAKES AND DRAINAGE BASINS

Environmental protection of international rivers, lakes and drainage basins, including groundwater as well as surface water is fundamental. However, here we are not only talking about protection from pollution, but also of water quantity issues. Reference should be made to the International Law Association's Helsinki Rules on the Uses and Waters of International Rivers and the Montreal Rules on Water Pollution in an International Drainage Basin and to the International Law Commission's Draft Articles on the Law of the Non–Navigational Uses of International Watercourses, contained in the Documentary Supplement.

EQUITABLE UTILIZATION OR PARTICIPATION

SHARON A. WILLIAMS, PUBLIC INTERNATIONAL LAW AND WATER QUANTITY MANAGEMENT IN A COMMON DRAINAGE BASIN: THE GREAT LAKES

18 Case Western Reserve Journal of International Law 155, 165–168 (1986)
(footnotes omitted).*

This theory of equitable utilization, currently described as equitable participation is clearly accepted by States and can be designated today as a rule of customary international law.

This theory was the basis for "equitable apportionment" in the case of Kansas v. Colorado [206 U.S. 46 (1907)] and was adopted as "equitable utilization" by the Helsinki Rules on the Uses of the Waters of International Rivers adopted by the International Law Association in 1966. The phrase "equitable participation" can be found in the draft articles on the Law of the Non–Navigational Uses of International Watercourses adopted by the International Law Commission.

* * * Under these rules, basin states include all states whose territories contribute to the international drainage basin, whether or not they are "riparian" states. Thus, it is recognized in the Helsinki Rules (which although not a binding agreement between states, but rather a document produced by a non-governmental organization seeks to state

* Reprinted with the permission of Case West.J.Int'l L.

the rules of customary international law) that underground waters may contribute to an international drainage basin. Article IV is illustrative of the key principle of the Rules, which is that every basin state in an international drainage basin has the right to reasonable use and an equitable share of the waters of the basin. The Rules reject outright the "Harmon Doctrine" of unlimited sovereignty. This rejection is based on state practice. A basin state is obligated to look to the rights and needs of other states and each is entitled to an equitable share. This latter concept is to provide the maximum benefit to each basin state from the waters in question, along with a minimum of detriment.

The determination of what is a reasonable and equitable share is to be determined "in the light of all the relevant factors in each particular case." [Article V of the Helsinki Rules] Naturally, rights which are "equal in kind and correlative with those" of co-basin states will not necessarily mean that the share in the uses of waters are identical. This will depend upon the weight given to relevant factors. The rules consider the reasonable uses of international drainage basins.

Each of * * * [the factors listed in Article V of the Helsinki Rules are] deemed relevant must "aid in the determination or satisfaction of the social and economic needs of co-basin states." Consider the following scenario: In the case of a common drainage basin where state A, the lower "co-basin" state, uses the waters for irrigation purposes but state B, the upper "co-basin" state, wants to produce hydroelectric power from the shared waters, the question arises as to whose use is preeminent. The two uses are * * * partially at odds as the storage period for the hydroelectric power may overlap with the growing season of crops in state A when the water is needed for nourishment. A number of elements [are] crucial to a resolution of this dilemma. State A has always used the inundation method of irrigation. An objective study indicates that the use of the water of the basin for hydroelectric purposes would be more valuable than irrigation methods. The dam would allow flow control of seasonal flooding and economically speaking would in the long term result in reasonable agricultural productivity. However, it would not be as high as that before the dam was built. Even though the population of state A for many centuries depended upon the agriculture in the basin area of state A, this is not now the case. Alternative sources for food are present, but not enough to completely rule out the need for the old produce area. A survey in state A indicates that there are substantial underground waters in state A. The new hydroelectric production from the basin would benefit several hundred thousand people in state B. Power obtained from other resources would cost much more.

The following factors, based on Article V would appear relevant: (1) an existing reasonable use; (2) the relative dependence on the waters; (3) the population; (4) the climatic and weather conditions; (5) alternative sources of food in state B; (6) inefficient utilization of water in state B; and (7) the financial status of the two co-basin states.

An analysis of this situation would probably show that although state A has an existing reasonable use, irrigation, the other competing factors militate for some modification of that use. State A has other sources of food and is using an antiquated method of irrigation which could be replaced with a system that wastes less of the basin's water. This replacement would be within state A's economic capacity. The potential use of the water for hydroelectric purposes is very valuable. A balancing here of all the factors would lead to a conclusion that modification of A's utilization and accommodation of state B's is desirable.

Reconciliation of the problem between states A and B would seem to lie in state A either changing its system of irrigation for a more water-efficient method, using alternate food supplies, using its underground water, or any combination of all of these options. However, state B might be required to help bear the costs involved in developing, for example, the new system of irrigation, or alternative food supplies. Compensation might be required should state A have to abandon any permanent installations or parts thereof.

If no combination of the above suggested solutions is agreeable to both states, then one of the uses, existing irrigation or new hydroelectric power will prevail with the other use being impaired or stopped. At that juncture, the state deprived of its use would undoubtedly seek compensation. Basin states therefore must share the waters equitably. * * *

———

1. ***Common Interest.*** The equitable utilization principle is an excellent example of the recognition of common interest in a shared resource. The international concern with fresh water pollution resulted in the inclusion of Articles IX–XI in the International Law Association's Helsinki Rules, reproduced in the Doc. Supp. The definition of "water pollution" contained in Article IX is very broad and should be contrasted with Principle 6 of the 1972 Stockholm Declaration. (See J. Lipper, Equitable Utilization, in A.H. Garretson et al., The Law of International Drainage Basins, 15 (1967) and G. Handl, Balancing of Interests and International Liability for the Pollution of International Watercourses: Customary Principles of Law Revisited, 13 Can. Yb. Int'l L. 156 (1975).

2. ***Harmon Doctrine.*** This is the most extreme view of plenary jurisdiction. Stemming from a dispute in 1895 over the right of the United States to divert water from the Upper Rio Grande, at a point where that river was completely within United States territory, the doctrine was named after U.S. Attorney General Judson Harmon who in a legal opinion to the Secretary of State of the United States, 21 Op.Att'y Gen. 274, 281 (1895), stated that absolute sovereignty within its territory is a fundamental principle of international law. The International Law Association took the view in 1966 that this doctrine, as it pertained to international rivers, had never had a wide acceptance. (See Austin, Canadian–United States Practice and Theory Respecting the International Law of International Rivers: A Study of the History and Influence of the Harmon Doctrine, 37 Can. Bar Rev. 393 (1959)).

3. ***The Work of the International Law Commission.*** The Commission recently completed its first reading of the Draft Articles on

the topic of the Law of Non–Navigational Uses of International Water-courses. Comments were requested from governments by January 1993. Note that the Draft Articles provide a framework that states may modify and adjust as between themselves to suit the particular uses and characteristics of a certain international watercourse. (See S. McCaffrey, The Law of International Watercourses—The ILC Completes its Draft Articles, 22 Env.L. & Pol. 1 (1992)).

4. *Canada–United States Great Lakes Cooperation.* The Great Lakes system had become extremely polluted by 1970 from many sources including industrial and urban usages and maritime vessel wastes. A study and report that revealed this convincingly was produced by the International Joint Commission (IJC), a body set up in 1909 by the Boundary Waters Treaty, U.S.T.S. 548, between the United States and Great Britain, on behalf of Canada, for the purpose of helping the settlement of and preventing disputes over the use of boundary waters. Article IV of the 1909 Treaty declares that the boundary waters "shall not be polluted on either side to the injury of health or property on the other". It did not, however, give to the IJC a specific mandate with respect to pollution. Over the years, the IJC has assisted in resolving mostly navigation and water diversion matters, but it seems that its major impact was the Report on the polluted state of Lakes Erie and Ontario, as well as the international section of the St. Lawrence River. This led to the 1978 Canada–United States Great Lakes Water Quality Agreement, 30 U.S.T.S., TIAS 9257, which superceded the earlier 1972 Agreement. This does not abrogate Article IV of the 1909 Treaty, but rather supplements it. The Agreement seeks to provide for more effective cooperative actions to restore and enhance water quality in the Great Lakes basin ecosystem, by adopting common objectives and implementing cooperative programs and measures. The purpose, as laid out in Article II is to restore and maintain through a maximum effort, the chemical, physical and biological integrity of the waters of the basin. Key to this Agreement and the manner in which it supercedes the previous 1972 Agreement is that it is not only dealing with the boundary waters within the Great Lakes system itself, but also with the elimination or reduction of the discharge of pollutants into the basin ecosystem. Article I(g) defines this ecosystem as "the interacting components of air, land, water and living organisms, including man, within the drainage basin of the St. Lawrence River at or upstream from the point at which this river becomes the international boundary between Canada and the United States". The IJC under Article VII shall assist, *inter alia,* in the implementation of the Agreement through collation, analysis and dissemination of data, tendering of advice and recommendations to the parties and their component states and provinces, coordination of joint activities and such investigations as the parties may refer to it. In discharging these responsibilities the IJC may under the powers given to it in the Agreement and by domestic legislation passed pursuant thereto conduct public hearings and compel the testimony of witnesses and the production of documents. (See S.A. Williams, Public International Law and Water Quantity Management in a Common Drainage Basin: The Great Lakes, 18 Case W.Res.J.Int.L. 155 (1986); E. Brown Weiss, New

Directions for the Great Lakes Water Quality Agreement: A Commentary, 65 Chic.–Kent L.Rev. 375 (1989)).

In 1985 the Great Lakes states and the Canadian provinces of Ontario and Quebec signed the Great Lakes Charter. This provides for ongoing consultation and management of the Great Lakes ecosystem. As the component entities of both federal states do not have treaty-making capacity, what status does this "Charter" have? (See Great Lakes Governors Task Force on Water Diversion and Great Lakes Institutions, Final Report and Recommendations—A Report to the Governors and Premiers of the Great Lakes States and Provinces (1985)).

WATER QUANTITY

In emphasizing the problems of pollution, water quantity issues cannot be overlooked. The Great Lakes basin is a case on point, being the largest single fresh water resource in the world shared by Canada and the United States. Questions are raised concerning diversion of some of the water out of the basin to help solve drought problems in the west.

SHARON A. WILLIAMS, PUBLIC INTERNATIONAL LAW AND WATER QUANTITY MANAGEMENT IN A COMMON DRAINAGE BASIN: THE GREAT LAKES BASIN

18 Case Western Reserve Journal of International Law 155, 178–179 (1986)
(footnotes omitted).*

The Boundary Waters Treaty of 1909 signed by Great Britain (on behalf of Canada) and the United States is still the most important bilateral treaty on the subject of management of the shared fresh water resource between the two states today.

The preamble to the Treaty details its purpose as being:

[t]o prevent disputes regarding the use of boundary waters and to settle all questions which are now pending between the United States and the Dominion of Canada involving the rights, obligations, or interests of either in relation to the other or to the inhabitants of the other, along their common frontier, and to make provision for the adjustment and settlement of all such questions as may hereafter arise * * *.

The preliminary article defines boundary waters as the waters that stretch from main shore to main shore of the lakes, rivers and connecting waterways through which the international boundary passes. It does not include tributary waters which "in their natural channels would flow into such lakes, rivers or waterways * * *" or waters

---

* Reprinted with the permission of Case West.J.Int'l L.

flowing from such. The Treaty provides in Article II that the purpose enunciated in the preamble was to be achieved by granting parties injured by one state's use or diversion of the tributary waters the same legal remedies as if the injury took place in the country where such diversion or use occurred. Secondly, the Treaty sets up a joint commission, known as the International Joint Commission, with the requirement that the Commission give approval before uses, obstructions or diversions, temporary or permanent, of boundary waters that affect the natural level or flow of the waters take place. The International Joint Commission was given the power to examine, report and make recommendations.

Under Articles III and IV the International Joint Commission has a quasi-judicial role in that it may approve or disapprove of any use, obstruction or diversion of boundary waters or waters that flow from boundary waters or in waters at a lower level than the boundary in rivers that flow across the boundary, if such would have the effect of raising the water level on the other side of the boundary, unless agreed to by the states' parties.

Conditions of approval may be imposed. Such a condition could be, for example, that injured parties be compensated.

Under Article IX the Commission has an investigative and advisory role. It may examine and report on any questions that are referred to it by either the United States or Canada. It may then follow up with conclusions and recommendations. Although, the two states could act alone in referring a matter to the Commission, this has not occurred in practice. The reports made are not considered "as decisions of the questions or matters so submitted either on the facts or the law, and shall in no way have the character of an arbitral award." Where both parties consent, the Commission may act as an arbitration panel with a binding power of decision.

The Commission is given the authority by Article XII to employ technical staff, such as engineers and clerical assistants, to conduct open hearings, take evidence on oath, compel the attendance of witnesses and adopt rules of procedure that are in accordance with justice and equity.

Trends before the Commission indicate that although originally the majority of its cases concerned approval under Article III and Article IV, in recent years it has been dealing with references under Article IX.

The Commission takes note of Canadian and United States statutes but has never considered itself bound by them. It has not applied the doctrine of stare decisis.

The Commission has had success in the area of adjudication and advisory opinions. However, it does have some drawbacks, notably that it is confined by the 1909 Treaty itself and by the appointment of its Commissioners by the two governments. The United States and Canada can limit the references made to the Commission. Having said this, practice seems to show that the Commissioners have handled matters with neutrality * * *.

This being said, it must be realized that in the context of a proposed large scale water diversion into or out of the Great Lakes, the national ties of the six Commissioners might well come to the fore. Should either state propose such a project and the other strenuously object, it would remain to be seen whether the International Joint Commission is as impartial as its record appears to indicate.

The Global Environmental Monitoring System. Global deterioration of water quality and quantity has been pinpointed as the key to sustainable development in the twenty-first century, for more than a third of the developing countries. The Water Quality Program of the Global Environmental Monitoring System (GEMS), a U.N. program coordinated by UNEP and the central part of the U.N.'s Earthwatch program, is the first international program to address global freshwater quality issues using a worldwide network of monitoring stations of surface and ground-water. GEMS/Water has 57 participating countries. It played the pivotal role in developing the freshwater chapter of Agenda 21.

7.   THE MARINE ENVIRONMENT

Marine pollution has caused great concern for several decades. Under the auspices of the International Maritime Organization (IMO), formerly called the International Maritime Consultative Organization (IMCO), the United Nations Environmental Program (UNEP) and regional organizations, many conventions have been adopted dealing with, *inter alia,* design and construction of ships, oil pollution damage, a compensation fund and the dumping of wastes at sea. See, the 1954 International Convention for the Prevention of Pollution of the Sea by Oil (OILPOL) 12 U.S.T.S. 2989; TIAS 4900; the 1973 International Convention for the Prevention of Pollution from Ships (MARPOL), 12 ILM 1319 (1973) and 17 ILM 546 (1979); the 1990 International Convention on Oil Pollution Readiness, Response and Cooperation, 30 ILM 735 (1991); the 1969 Convention on Civil Liability for Oil Pollution Damage, 9 ILM 45 (1970); 1976 Protocol, 16 ILM 617 (1977), 1984 Protocol, Misc. No. 8 (1986), Cmnd. 9927 and 1992 Protocol, IMO Doc. LEG/CONF. 9/15 (1992); the 1971 International Convention on the Establishment of a Fund for Compensation for Oil Pollution Damage, 11 ILM 284 (1972), 1976 Protocol, 16 ILM 621, 1984 Protocol, 23 ILM 195 (1984) and 1992 Protocol, IMO Doc. LEG/CONF. 9/16 (1992); the 1976 London Convention on Civil Liability for Oil Pollution Damage Resulting From Exploration for and Exploitation of Seabed Mineral Resources, 16 ILM 1450 (1977), and the 1972 Convention on the Prevention of Marine Pollution by Dumping of Wastes and Other Matter, 26 U.S.T.S. 2403, TIAS 8165, 11 ILM 1291 (1972). Intervention Against Maritime Casualties is provided for in the 1969 Convention Relating to Intervention on the High Seas in Cases of Oil Pollution Casualties, 26 U.S.T. 765, T.I.A.S. No. 8068, 9 ILM 25 (1970) and the Protocol Relating to Intervention on the High Seas in Cases of Pollution by Substances Other Than Oil, TIAS 10561, 13 ILM 605 (1974).

Regional agreements dealing with the maritime environment include the 1974 Helsinki Convention on the Protection of the Marine Environment of the Baltic Sea Area, 13 ILM 546 (1974); the 1976 Barcelona Convention for the Protection of the Mediterranean Sea Against Pollution and its Protocols of 1976 and 1980, 15 ILM 290, 300 and 306 (1976), and 19 ILM 869 (1980); the 1978 Kuwait Regional Convention for Cooperation on the Protection of the Marine Environment from Pollution and Protocol, 17 ILM 511 and 526; the 1981 Abidjan Convention for Cooperation in the Protection and Development of the Marine and Coastal Environment of the West and Central African Region and Protocol, 20 ILM 746 and 756 (1981); the 1983 Cartenega Convention for the Protection and Development of the Marine Environment of the Wider Caribbean Region and Its Protocols, TIAS 11085, 22 ILM 227 and 240 (1983) and the 1986 Noumea Convention for the Protection of the National Resources and Environment of the South Pacific Region and Protocols, 26 ILM 38 and 58 (1987). The most recent agreement, the 1992 Paris Convention for the Protection of the Marine Environment of the North–East Atlantic, 32 ILM 1072 (1993), seeks to coordinate protection of the North–East Atlantic. Until it comes into force the 1972 Oslo Convention for the Prevention of Marine Pollution by Dumping from Ships and Aircraft, 11 ILM 262 (1972) and the 1974 Paris Convention for the Prevention of Marine Pollution from Land Based Sources and Protocol, 13 ILM 352 (1974), 27 ILM 625 (1988), remain in force. The 1992 Bucharest Convention on the Protection of the Black Sea Against Pollution and Its Protocols on Protection of the Black Sea Marine Environment Against Pollution from Land Based Sources, on Cooperation in Combatting Pollution of the Black Sea Environment by Oil and Other Harmful Substances in Emergency Situations and on the Protection of the Black Sea Marine Environment Against Pollution By Dumping, is not yet in force, 32 ILM 1110, 1122, 1127 and 1129 (1993).

The efficacy of the above Conventions has been frustrated to a great extent by lack of ratification and lack of consequent necessary domestic implementation. Enforcement mechanisms are also missing. At the 1992 United Nations Conference on Environment and Development in Rio de Janeiro emphasis was laid on the crucial need for such full participation.

———

THE 1982 UNITED NATIONS CONVENTION
ON THE LAW OF THE SEA

SHARON A. WILLIAMS AND A.L.C. DE MESTRAL, AN
INTRODUCTION TO INTERNATIONAL LAW

280–281 (2nd ed. 1987) (footnotes omitted).*

The most ambitious attempt to protect the marine environment is to be found in the provisions of the 1982 Convention on the Law of the Sea. At the onset of negotiations, Canada, among other states, in a working paper presented to the Seabed Committee [U.N.Doc. A/AC 138/S.C. III/L. 26, August 18, 1972, 733] and Draft Articles [U.N.Doc. A/AC 138/S. III/L. 28, March 8, 1973, 762] called for treaty provisions which would provide a comprehensive framework for the conclusion of a complete network of treaties dealing with all aspects of marine pollution. This approach is reflected in the 1982 Convention, Part XII which [now that it is in force, since November 1994] will have the effect of committing all states parties to taking measures, nationally and internationally, to prevent pollution from the principal sources of marine pollution: land, sea, continental shelf and atmospheric. States parties will be under an obligation to conclude international conventions dealing with the different manifestations of pollution of the marine environment or to take measures at least as effective as "generally accepted international standards". Failure to live up to such minimum international standards will constitute a violation of the Law of the Sea Convention and in appropriate circumstances will give rise to state responsibility.

The Convention contains general provisions committing states to protect the marine environment from pollution from all sources and prohibiting the transfer of pollution from one area to another. The text also provides for global and regional cooperation, notification of other states in the event of imminent or actual damage, the preparation of joint contingency plans, environmental monitoring and assessment of data, and technical assistance. The subsequent articles will have the effect of committing states to develop national and international rules on pollution from land-based sources, seabed activities, and ocean dumping. Complementary articles deal with enforcement of these rules. Articles 211 and 217 to 236 deal with pollution caused by ships. Traditional flag state obligations are somewhat strengthened. Most noteworthy are the new rules allowing limited jurisdiction to "coastal" and "port" states to enforce international rules and standards against foreign ships in strictly defined circumstances. Of great interest to Canada is article 234 allowing coastal states broad jurisdiction to adopt and enforce their own rules for the prevention, reduction and control of marine pollution from ships in "ice-covered areas" within the limits of the exclusive economic zone. This authority shall have due regard to navigation.

Perhaps the most significant development of the Convention is the duty set out in article 194(2) not to "cause damage by pollution to other states and their environment" which, coupled with article 235 on liabili-

* Published by Butterworths Canada, Ltd., reprinted with their permission.

ty and responsibility, will make states liable for damages attributable to natural or juridical persons under their jurisdiction and responsible to ensure prompt and adequate recourse against persons under their jurisdiction who cause pollution affecting other states or their nationals. Failure to respect this obligation or other international treaty obligations will make the state responsible liable to compensate the injured party. States' parties are obligated to cooperate also in the development of criteria and procedures for payment of adequate compensation, such as compulsory insurance or compensation funds. It remains to be seen whether this approach to state responsibility and liability for pollution damage will be adopted more generally in international environmental law for other forms of pollution damage. Evidence that the 1982 Convention may afford a model for other areas can be seen in the work of U.N.E.P. on shared natural resources and the even more recent work of the U.N.E.P. Committee on International Environmental Law. It is also noteworthy that the Convention is already complemented by a number of important regional conventions dealing with pollution of the marine environment.

F. ORREGO VICUÑA, STATE RESPONSIBILITY, LIABILITY, AND REMEDIAL MEASURES UNDER INTERNATIONAL LAW: NEW CRITERIA FOR ENVIRONMENTAL PROTECTION

in E. Brown Weiss (ed.), Environmental Change and International Law, 124, 144–147 (1992) (footnotes omitted).*

The 1982 Convention on the Law of the Sea and related treaties have significantly developed the rules of international law applicable to the preservation of the marine environment and illustrate the evolution of state responsibility. In point of fact, states are under the obligation to ensure that activities under their jurisdiction or control "are so conducted as not to cause damage by pollution to other States and their environment" and that any pollution arising from such activities "does not spread beyond the areas where they exercise sovereign rights." The activities included in this obligation are those undertaken both by the state and by entities of a private nature under state jurisdiction and control. It is also quite apparent that this provision covers not only transboundary effects of pollution but also harm to areas beyond national jurisdiction. In other words, the global scale of environmental effects is incorporated into this particular regime.

This regime encompasses all sources of pollution, a further indication of the broadening concern and scope of international law. In addition, a broad definition of pollution of the marine environment is included in this and other treaty regimes as an expression of the very same concern. Important IMO and related conventions have developed a well-structured normative regime dealing with specific questions of marine pollution particularly in terms of oil pollution, discharge and dumping of waste, and safety at sea.

In light of this more advanced regime, it follows quite naturally that international law has accepted holding a state responsible for pollution

* © 1992, U.N. University, all rights reserved. Reprinted with their permission.

injuries resulting from a violation of its obligations in this field.   Although the primary obligation to enforce the law is bestowed upon the flag state of the ships concerned, other states are not prevented from taking the necessary preventive or remedial actions.   In addition to the powers allocated to the coastal state and the port state in given instances, there is the most important right of intervention on the high seas, which is ultimately related to a measure of self-help under international law.   The obligation to notify is also prominent in this field.   These developments of course do not prejudice the rules dealing specifically with issues such as the environmental consequences of seabed-mining operations, cooperation in emergencies, or the protection of fragile ecosystems.

Remedial measures have also evolved significantly in the area of the law of the sea.   In addition to recourse to the general remedies provided for under international law, coastal and port states can participate actively by detaining and investigating ships and by instituting proceedings.

1. *The 1982 Law of the Sea Convention.*   This Convention which is reproduced in the Documentary Supplement, was the product of the Third United Nations Law of the Sea Conference (UNCLOS III).   Part XII, dealing with the protection and preservation of the marine environment seeks to balance the interests of coastal states and flag states.   National jurisdiction to control is moderated by the reference to "generally accepted international law rules".   (See generally A. Timagenis, International Control of Pollution (1980) and P. Sand, Marine Environmental Law in the U.N. Environmental Program: An Emergent Eco–Regime (1989)).

2. *Ice covered areas.*   Article 234 of the 1982 Law of the Sea Convention which gives coastal states extensive jurisdiction over such areas is of special importance to states such as Canada which border the extensive ecologically fragile Arctic.   Do you think that this Article affirms the unilateral action taken by Canada when it enacted in 1970 the Arctic Waters Pollution Prevention Act, R.S.C. 1985, c. A–12, whereby it provided for regulation of shipping within one hundred nautical miles of land into the Arctic?   The United States strongly protested against this legislation.   Note that in 1988 Canada and the United States entered into an Agreement on Cooperation in the Arctic, 1988 Can.T.S. No. 29, T.I.A.S. 11565 in which they agreed to seek permission of the other before sending icebreaking ships into the Arctic areas under their respective territorial jurisdictions.   (*See* R. Bilder, The Canadian Arctic Waters Pollution Prevention Act: New Stresses on the Law of the Sea, 69 Mich.L.Rev. 1 (1970–71) and L. Henkin, Anti–Pollution: Does Canada Make or Break International Laws?, 65 AJIL 131 (1971)).   It is interesting to observe more recent action concerning Arctic environmental protection, in the form of official meetings between the eight Arctic states, Canada, Denmark, Finland, Iceland, Norway, Sweden, the former U.S.S.R. and the United States.   With the assistance of observers from

other governments, as well as international governmental and non-governmental organizations, in 1991 an Arctic Environmental Protection Strategy was developed. The Arctic states are committed to international cooperation to ensure environmental protection in the region and its sustainable and equitable development, while protecting the cultures of indigenous peoples. *See* 30 ILM 1624 (1991).

Note the Convention on the Regulation of Antarctic Mineral Resource Activities, 27 ILM 868 (1988), especially Article 4 that provides that mineral resource activity is pre-conditioned by a judgment that it is environmentally safe and also the 1959 Antarctica Treaty, 19 ILM 860 (1980) and the 1991 Protocol on Environmental Protection to the Antarctic Treaty, 30 ILM 1455 (1991). (See L. Pineschi, The Antarctic Treaty System and General Rules of International Environmental law, in Francioni and Scovazzi (eds.) International Law of Antarctica, 187 (1987) and A. Watts, International Law and the Antarctic Treaty System (1992).)

8.   THE WORLD CULTURAL AND NATURAL HERITAGE

SHARON A. WILLIAMS, THE INTERNATIONAL AND NATIONAL PROTECTION OF CULTURAL PROPERTY: A COMPARATIVE STUDY

173–174 (1978) (footnotes omitted).*

The 1972 UNESCO Convention [for the Protection of the World Cultural and Natural Heritage, 11 Int'l Leg.Mat. 1358 (1972), which entered into force on December 17, 1975, and is reproduced in the Documentary Supplement] * * * reiterates the concept that parts of the cultural heritage are of outstanding interest and therefore need to be preserved as part of the "world heritage of mankind as a whole". It is stated that in view of the magnitude and gravity of the dangers caused to the world cultural and natural heritage, by traditional decay as well as the new dangers of the changing social and economic conditions which aggravate the situation with a more formidable phenomenon of damage and destruction, it is incumbent upon the international community as a whole to participate in the protection of the cultural and natural heritage of outstanding value, by the granting of collective assistance, which will serve as a complement to the action taken by the states concerned. * * * Whilst the parties fully respect the sovereignty of the states on whose territory the cultural and natural heritage is situated, and without prejudice to property rights provided by national legislation, they recognize that such heritage constitutes a world heritage for whose protection it is the duty of the international community as a whole to co-operate. For the purpose of the Convention, the term international protection is to be understood to mean the establishment of a system of international co-operation and assistance designed to support states in their efforts to conserve and identify their heritage. The Convention establishes an Intergovernmental Committee [World Heritage Commit-

* Reprinted with the permission of Sharon A. Williams.

tee] to ensure proper functioning of the terms of the Convention and "World Heritage Fund" whose purpose is to support the protection of the world cultural and natural heritage of outstanding value.

———

1. ***World Heritage List.*** The 1972 Convention, which the United States is a party to, 27 U.N.T.S. 37; T.I.A.S. 8226, also sets up a World Heritage List. Under Article 11(1), it is provided that every state party shall submit to the World Heritage Committee an inventory of property forming part of the natural and cultural heritage, situated in its territory and suitable for inclusion in the list. The United States has listed, for example, the Grand Canyon. It is further provided in Article 11(4) that the Committee shall establish and keep up to date a List of World Heritage in Danger. This list may only contain property forming the part of the cultural and natural heritage that is threatened by, *inter alia,* serious and specific dangers, such as the threat of disappearance caused by accelerated deterioration, large-scale public or private projects or rapid urban or tourist development projects; destruction caused by changes in the use or ownership of land; the outbreak of or the threat of armed conflict and other calamities, serious fires, earthquakes, landslides, floods and so on.

2. ***Obligations under the 1972 UNESCO Convention.*** In Commonwealth of Australia v. State of Tasmania (1983), 46 A.L.R. 625 (H.C.) it was held that Articles 4 and 5 of the 1972 Convention imposed legal obligations upon Australia to protect a World Heritage listed site, the listed wilderness parks in Tasmania. See also State of Queensland v. Commonwealth of Australia (1989), 86 A.L.R. 519 and Richardson v. Forestry Commission (1988), 164 C.L.R. 261.

9. PROTECTION OF WETLANDS
A. KISS AND D. SHELTON, INTERNATIONAL ENVIRONMENTAL LAW
249 (1991) (footnotes omitted).*

* * * *The Convention on Wetlands of International Importance* was the first treaty based on the idea that the habitat of endangered species should be the focus of protection. One of the first major conservation treaties, it is relatively simple in its structure. It is based on recognition that wetlands are among the most productive sources of ecological support on earth, acting as habitat for myriad species and as flood control regions.

The preamble affirms that wetlands constitute a resource of great economic, cultural, scientific and recreational value, the loss of which would be irreparable. Wetlands are defined in Article 1 as being areas of marsh, fen, peatland or water, whether natural or artificial, permanent or temporary, with water that is static or flowing, fresh, brackish or salt,

* Reprinted with the permission of Transnational Publishers, Inc.

including areas of marine water whose depth does not exceed six meters at low tide. Waterfowl, whose protection was the purpose of this convention, are defined as birds ecologically dependent on wetlands.

The original objective of the Convention was to protect the habitat of waterfowl. However, its importance has outstripped that objective as the ecological importance of wetlands has become recognized, particularly their role in supporting marine life. Unfortunately, during recent decades drainage operations and drought, as well as landfill, have considerably reduced the extent of wetlands.

Note: Refer to the Convention in the Documentary Supplement and also S. Lyster, International Wildlife Law (1985).

10. PROTECTION OF FORESTS

The 1992 United Nations Conference on Environment and Development at Rio adopted a non-binding statement of principles on the protection of forests. In the lead-up time to the 1992 Rio Conference the possibility of adoption of a convention at the conference on point was rejected. See the Resulting Statement of Principles for a Global Consensus on the Management, Conservation and Sustainable Development of All Types of Forests, UN Doc. A/CONF. 151/6/Rev. 1; 31 ILM 818 (1992), reproduced in the Documentary Supplement.

EARTH SUMMIT IN FOCUS

No. 5, February 1992, U.N. Department of Public Information, DP1/1198–92173.

Saving the Forests:

Forging a Global Compact

Reconciling the need to preserve the Earth's remaining forests with the needs of countries to exploit their forests as economic resources is one of the most challenging tasks on the agenda of the United Nations Conference on Environment and Development, known as the Earth Summit.

* * *

Conflicting Interests

The divergence of views on the forestry issue is not surprising. Trees mean different things to different people: it is tempting to claim that others "do not see the forest for the trees".

- To many indigenous peoples, forests are home. They have lived in the forests for thousands of years, making little impact on them, but they fear for their way of life.

- To farmers and ranchers, forests are obstacles that must be burned and cleared to provide new lands; to loggers, they provide jobs and income.

- To more than two billion people in developing countries who lack other options, forests are an essential source of fuel for cooking.

- To Government leaders, forests are sovereign resources which countries have the right to exploit.

Developing countries in particular—desperate to provide basic necessities for their people and to earn foreign exchange to pay their debts—are under great economic pressure to exploit or clear their forests. They are also under increasing pressure from environmentalists and Northern Governments to preserve tropical forests, both as wildlife habitats and to counter global warming.

But developing countries question why they should bear the economic burden for solving a problem created largely by pollution in the North: most greenhouse gases are caused by the burning of fossil fuels in industrialized countries.

These conflicting views, especially those between the Northern industrialized nations and Southern developing countries, surfaced clearly during early preparations for the Earth Summit. The North's focus on tropical forests has been met with the South's requirement that the global forest—including that which has been cut in the North in the past—be considered.

Fuel for the North's Wealth

The industrialized countries began clearing their forests in the 6th century. Some 32–35 per cent of temperate forests have been lost since pre-agricultural times, compared with about 15–20 per cent of old-growth tropical forests. Three quarters of Europe (not counting the former Soviet Union) was probably covered by forest; about 50 per cent of the original cover has been cleared.

More than a quarter of all forests growing in the United States in the 17th century had been felled before programmes to replant trees began during this century. However, newly planted trees cannot fully replace old-growth forests in the ecological balance. During the 1980s, the last of the virgin timberlands were being cleared at the rate of 24,000 hectares per year, and the Government is under pressure to open up public land in the Northwest to logging interests. One out of every four logs is exported—much of it to Japan to build homes.

In Canada, * * * called the "Brazil of the North", over seven million hectares of forest were burned in 1989; some two million hectares are burned in an average year. In New Zealand, settled as late as 1840, the islands have been almost cleared of forests to create land for the sheep and cattle grazing on which the wealth of the country has been built.

Jobs or Trees: The Economic Dilemma

Many people make their livelihood from cutting down trees. Global-ly, logging is an $85–billion–a–year industry. Some 3.4 billion cubic metres of wood are taken from the Earth's forests each year, half of it from the United States, Canada and the former Soviet Union. Roughly 50 per cent is used for fuel, and the other half for lumber, paper and other wood products. By 2030, world-wide annual demand is expected to grow from today's 1.7 billion cubic metres to between 2 and 2.6 billion cubic metres.

The wealth derived from logging feeds into the economic life of countries as a basis for jobs and growth. Developing countries want the chance to exploit their natural resources—as industrialized countries have done—to generate the income sorely needed to provide food, education, health care and other basics for their peoples. Nearly all of the timber produced by developing countries is exported to earn much-needed foreign exchange.

However, once the trees are felled, jobs disappear; neither the environment nor the economic life of the community is protected. The critical question is the sustainable management of forests. Without it there will eventually be no jobs.

In the past, forests have been treated as never-ending resources. Nations have taken turns supplying the world's lumber needs. These countries have often been left with widespread land erosion and result-ing human suffering. Damage to the floodplain of India and Bangladesh along the Ganges, caused largely by massive deforestation, exceeds $1 billion annually.

A Wider View of Values

The value of forests [is often] described in narrow economic terms, as an exploitable resource. However, in recent years a wider view has emerged of the varied functions forests serve, many of which have far-reaching economic and social implications. Increasingly, forests are seen:

- as homes for indigenous peoples.

- as "sinks" for converting carbon dioxide through photosynthesis into the oxygen needed to keep us alive.

- as protection for watersheds. Forests help prevent avalanches, floods, landslides and mud-flows, and protect hydroelectric power plants, irrigation and municipal water supplies.

- as wildlife habitats for a rich diversity of species of plant, animal and insect life. Tropical forests are believed to be home to more than half the species on earth, including medicinal plants and food crops. Fallen leaves are a primary source of humus, the topsoil which sustains plant life.

- as key players in maintaining crucial ecological balances, such as the annual cycle of sediments and flood water needed for the production of rice to feed hundreds of millions of people.

- as recreation areas.

- as fuel used daily by some two billion people in developing countries. Half the annual forest harvest is for fuel. Where forests are degraded, women must walk farther to find cooking fuel; but in some areas, there is no wood at all. By 2000, the fuel-wood deficit could reach 960 million cubic metres a year, the energy equivalent of $30 billion worth of oil annually.

Converging Forces Cause Alarm

Today's situation is made urgent by the rate at which forests are being lost, the increased burning of fossil fuels and the contribution of forest-burning to climate change.

Studies suggest that in the last 20 years, human activity has cleared as much of the Earth's forest cover as was previously cleared in all of history. In 1980, the Food and Agriculture Organization of the United Nations (FAO), in cooperation with the United Nations Environment Programme and the UN Economic Commission for Europe, conducted a comprehensive survey of world forests.

Ten years ago forests covered an estimated 3.6 billion hectares or 36 million square kilometres—27.6 per cent of the planet's total land area (excluding Greenland and Antarctica). Deforestation of tropical forests was estimated to be 11.4 million hectares per year. Shifting agriculture was responsible for about 45 per cent of the deforestation. Ranching, colonization, permanent cash-crop agriculture and over-exploitation for fuelwood were other causes.

FAO's 1990 data paints a bleak picture of the last decade. Boreal (northern) forest cover is relatively stable, but total forest area in the tropical regions has decreased by some 200 million hectares. For the 76 countries which contain 79 per cent of the world's tropical forests, the annual deforestation rate is as high as 16.8 million hectares. Except where there is little forest left, deforestation has accelerated throughout the tropics.

A related problem is widespread degradation of forests, which is more gradual and difficult to detect than clearing or burning. It is caused by selective cutting of the most valuable trees, overexploitation for fuel, excessive hunting and grazing, air pollution, repeated fires and war. It is often accompanied by degradation of the soil and of plant and animal life.

The Link to Global Warming

While forests are diminishing at an alarming rate, the use of fossil fuels stands to increase dramatically—a combination projected to accelerate global warming and other climate change. Industrialized nations are currently the primary source of air pollution from the use of fossil fuels, but it is expected that the rate of energy consumption in some developing nations will be twice that of industrialized nations from now to the year 2000.

Every country consumes energy at a faster rate at the beginning of its industrial growth than it does in later stages. Peoples in developing countries seek to raise their standard of living and own the same appliances and automobiles enjoyed by peoples in the North. Unless they are technically and financially assisted to use fuels more efficiently and to make a transition to alternative, "environmentally cleaner" technologies, they will not be able to avoid creating the same pollution— on a far more massive scale—than has been produced by countries in the industrialized world.

The effects of forest burning also are directly linked to global warming. The Earth's forests store 450 billion metric tons of carbon, much of it gathered from carbon dioxide found in air pollution. When burned, forests release carbon dioxide. Forest burning is the second largest source of greenhouse gases, after the use of fossil fuels.

Sustainable Forest Development

To sustain the forests while maintaining economic development, people will have to change the way they view forests. Experts point to three phases: in the first, the forest is viewed as an unlimited resource. Its destruction may be promoted by encouraging agricultural expansion. In the second phase, destruction of the forest may cause concern that leads to the institution of controls. In the third phase, attempts are made to re-create the forest.

Reforestation (replanting areas that once were forests) and afforestation (planting new forests) have been under way in some parts of the world for centuries. Between the 17th and 19th centuries, practices in Japan shifted from unregulated deforestation, which produced landslides and a wood supply shortage, to afforestation.

The United States began deforestation in the 1600s to provide timber, firewood and new lands for grazing and farming. In the 1930s, for the first time, forest land began to re-expand. Deforestation began in Europe in the 6th century; a wood shortage developed and, beginning in the 19th century, the process was reversed.

Now, although deforestation rates are soaring, satellites and other technology make it possible to inventory and plan for reforestation projects on a regional and global scale. Regional and international organizations and businesses are playing an expanded role. * * *

Many nations are now taking steps to change destructive practices. Parts of Scandinavia, Canada and the former USSR are carrying out sustainable management practices. More than 60 countries have agreed to prepare national forestry programmes under the Tropical Forestry Action Plan, launched in 1985 by FAO. Logging in the tropics has not traditionally had sustainability as a goal. Typically, only 10 to 20 per cent of the trees are harvested, but up to half are destroyed in the logging process. The soil is so disturbed that the forest does not regenerate and becomes degraded. Simply changing logging techniques would be a significant step.

Although plantation forests can play an important role, many species will need protected native habitats if they are to survive. The setting aside of selected forests is already under way. Recently, Bolivia has launched a five-year ecological moratorium, temporarily suspending logging concessions. Guyana has set aside 360,000 hectares of tropical forest for conservation and research. India and Viet Nam have launched conservation efforts.

Public policy and trade are also being used as tools to encourage sustainable forestry practices. Brazil has modified its incentives for cattle ranching, which encouraged clearing the Amazon. Germany, the United Kingdom and the Netherlands have placed special restrictions and controls on the use and imports of tropical timber, although such regulations have been sharply criticized by some developing countries as unfair trade practices.

Work is also beginning at the grass-roots level. In many cultures women have the responsibility for food- and fuel-gathering and have a keen insight into the importance of forests. The Greenbelt Movement in Kenya, a women's organization, has planted millions of trees for food and fodder and raised awareness of the forest issue. Projects like this can help prevent degraded forests from becoming deserts.

Governments and a variety of local and international organizations have identified sustainable forestry practices as a priority. The process of understanding the problem, establishing plans to fix it and finding the resources to apply to the task has at least begun. The debate and negotiations taking place as part of the Earth Summit preparations, and the set of forestry principles that are expected to be adopted in Rio, will undoubtedly make a major contribution to that process.

THE INTERNATIONAL TROPICAL TIMBER AGREEMENT
UNCTAD, DOC.TO/TIMBER/II (Geneva, 18 November 1983).

A. Objectives and Achievements
The objectives of the ITTA are to promote the management of tropical forests on a sustainable basis and to provide a framework for co-operation between producing and consuming member states in the tropical timber industry. The expansion of tropical timber production by producing member states will promote the economic development of producing countries through increased export earnings. The ITTA aims to encourage the planning of tropical timber reforestation and the establishment of forest management in order to achieve a sustainable utilisation and conservation of tropical forests, both as an economic resource and an important factor in maintaining ecological balance in the regions concerned. Although the ITTA was first drafted as a commodity agreement, the final version adopted in 1983 was a comprehensive agreement to govern development [of] the tropical timber industry in the context of environmental implications and the impact on the economies of producing regions. The Agreement entered into force on 1 April 1985. The operational activities under the ITTA began in November 1987, after the establishment of the Secretariat in Yokohama, Japan.

The membership of the International Tropical Timber Organisation ("ITTO") set up by the ITTA is categorized into producers and consumers of tropical timber. Almost all producers are developing countries, situated in the tropical belts of Africa, Asia and Latin America. The consuming countries are mainly developed countries in Europe, North America and the Far East.

Since almost all tropical timber producing countries are Parties, the potential importance of the ITTA and related instruments on the ecological balance is on a global level. The establishment of methods to manage tropical timber resources as renewable economic resources is essential to sustained economic improvement for much of the world's population, as well as to halting the environmental damage caused by rapid deforestation.

About half of the Parties involved in drafting the ITTA were developing countries. The ITTA recognises that financial and technical assistance to developing producer countries is a prerequisite of long term planning and forestry management. Studies, projects and guidelines under the ITTA are therefore undertaken conscious of the needs of developing countries, and in particular the necessity to integrate policies of economic development into measures to improve forestry management. The ITTA provisions on projects incorporate the needs of producer countries for technological transfer, training and investment. Thus the ITTA projects represent a conduit of external financial aid and know-how.

There are a few developing countries, such as China, Nepal and Egypt, amongst tropical timber consumer members of ITTO. Hence the ITTA makes provision for developing importing members whose interests are adversely affected by measures taken under the ITTA to apply for appropriate differential and remedial measures. On the other hand, all Contracting States must make an assessed contribution to the annual budget to cover the administrative costs of administering and supervising the implementation and operations of the ITTA; and must bear the expenses of their own delegations to the Sessions of the International Tropical Timber Council (ITTC) and its Permanent Committees, working parties, etc.

The ITTA states that the Council should review the world tropical timber situation annually with regard to trade economic, ecological and environmental aspects. Each year the Council must publish an annual report on its activities. In addition, reports on tropical timber issues are produced as part of ITTA project activity.

An Action Plan has been published as a result of the 9th Session of the Council in November 1990. This summarises activities envisaged under the ITTA so far and identifies priority areas for programme development and project work. According to the Action Plan, the central objectives of the ITTA are yet to be achieved on any significant scale. The Action Plan underscores the consensus for the continuing depletion of the tropical forest base. Long-term management and forest policies are not being implemented. The key aim of the ITTA—a sustainable management of the resource base for the supply of wood raw material and other non-wood forest services and goods—is not being achieved because of socio-economic factors leading to deforestation and forest degradation. A prime objective of ITTO is the expansion of forest estates to produce timber for processing within the producer countries, as opposed to exporting timber as unprocessed raw material. However, export of logs by producer countries still dominates. The Action Plan identifies the obstacles to economic development concurrent with environmental preservation as lack of investment in the timber processing industries in producer countries; lack of skill in operating harvesting equipment; and technical constraints due to the expense of forestry research and a breakdown in R & D co-operation.

On the other hand, the ITTO appears to have set up reasonably effective methods of monitoring the tropical timber position. The ITTO also seems to have been quite successful as an inter-governmental organisation responsible for co-ordinating research and project activity by international organisations and NGOs. Furthermore, the ITTO has succeeded in achieving almost comprehensive membership among producing and consuming countries. This has contributed significantly to enhancing the forum for consultation and co-operation between governments, conservations, NGOs and timber trade associations. Nonetheless, the Action Plan concludes that the opportunities to conserve and utilise the world's tropical forest will remain illusive if the level of human and financial resources committed to it remains insufficient.

B. Participation

Membership is open to any state which produces or consumes tropical timber. Current membership is 48, including 22 producers and 26 consumers. Article 43 prohibits reservations.

Beyond contributions to the administrative budget and to ITTO secretariat, producer Governments' visibility and participation in the substantive work of ITTO could be further enhanced.

The ITTA places heavy emphasis on the means needed in order to achieve its ends (i.e. conservation alongside economic utilisation of the world's tropical forests). The ITTA recognises that such goals can only be achieved by planned development in the producing regions. This requires technical, educational and financial assistance to these regions as well as the promotion of trade and R & D in tropical timber. The incentive for participation by developing countries lies in the opportunity to benefit from financial, trade, investment and technological assistance and co-operation. However, while it is clear that the ITTA intends to facilitate implementation by developing countries, the human and financial resources devoted to this assistance are totally insufficient for the scale of the problems. The ITTA does provide in general terms for collaboration in technological transfer, training, research and market intelligence.

It seems that the very high level of membership among developing countries is due to the opportunity to benefit from financial, technical and scientific assistance, while it is likely that participation among developed countries, representing most of the consumers of tropical timber, has been influenced by pressure from media, public opinion, Parliaments and NGO's in the current international atmosphere of concern for the role of tropical forests in the global environmental and development crisis.

C. Implementation

The provisions of Article 37 requiring a minimum package of ratifications, economically balanced between producer and consumer countries, delayed entry into force beyond the planned date of 1 October 1984 to 1 April 1985. However, several Governments opted for earlier provisional application (Article 36).

The ITTA itself only imposes obligations of a broad nature. The three ITTA duties for member countries are to pay the contributions to the Administrative Account, and (in the case of developed consumer members particularly) to the special account for projects; to provide data on tropical timber requested by the Council; and to use their best endeavours to co-operate to promote the attainment of the ITTA objectives. Members are obliged to accept decisions taken by the Council.

In December 1990 the Council adopted the "ITTO Guidelines for the Sustainable Management of Natural Tropical Forests" as an international reference standard, in the form of principles, to guide the development of more detailed national guidelines. Thus the legal implementation and enforcement of practical measures are left to member countries themselves, and are therefore subject to the economic and political pressures on law-makers in member states (principally producer countries). A competitive market price for timber (tending towards the marginal cost of production omitting costs of replacement) generally means that renewal of forest resources is not economically feasible.

The assessment of compliance by Parties with ITTA principles is the responsibility of the Council and permanent Committees. Emphasis is placed on monitoring and review of ITTO projects and the programme set up by the Action Plan. An expert Committee has been established for the technical assessment of project proposals. On the other hand, the Committee on Market Intelligence appears to have been fairly effective in obtaining information on the tropical timber market. It is also mandated to assist member countries to improve their own statistical services.

An example of assessment of implementation by ITTO itself rather than by national governments is the ITTO mission to Sarawak, Malaysia in 1989.

The ITTO has not succeeded in enforcing the obligation on members to contribute to its resources. Producer states have paid less than two-thirds of their assessed contributions to the administrative budget, and consumers have also fallen short.

The development and environmental aspects of ITTO's remit (which are inextricably inter-dependent) do not appear yet to have achieved any measurable progress. Timber-dependent producer economies have felt no significant improvements yet. On the other hand, ITTA has been effective as a trade agreement in providing improved market information. Detailed assessments of project proposals are carried out by the appropriate permanent Committee in pre-project studies. These are outlined in the ITTO Project Cycle. Parties are expected to report data on timber imports and exports, as a basis for the ITTO annual assessment of the world tropical timber situation. For 1990, data were received from 24 consuming countries and 15 producing countries.

The ITTA provides that any complaint that a member has failed to fulfil its obligations under the ITTA, or any dispute on the application of the ITTA shall be referred to the Council for decision. It appears that ITTO is unlikely to pursue non-compliance in member states (primarily meaning producer countries) because of the political impossibility of ensuring compliance by Governments concerned.

The main cause of failure to achieve the ITTA's objectives for development and environmental protection is the failure to provide adequate financial resources to make sustained timber exploitation economically viable. * * * even otherwise achievable levels of efficiency in timber use (for example, stemming from modern harvesting techniques), are being missed through inadequate technology or scientific know-how.

Public awareness of the danger to tropical timber forests, and the linked economic problems of the producing nations, has been raised by publicity from media and Non-governmental Organizations. This has raised pressure on the Governments of democratic developed countries to act to improve the situation. However, NGOs seem to have concluded that public opinion in developed economies is a better target for mobilization and near-term change than the long-term institution-building in which ITT now is engaged.

* * *

E. Operation, review and adjustment

The ITTA established the International Tropical Timber Organisation, which functions through the International Tropical Timber Council and three permanent Committees. The Committees are:

(a) Committee on Economic Information and Market Intelligence;

(b) Committee on Reforestation and Forest Management;

(c) Committee on Forest Industry.

The operational activities of the Council and the permanent Committees fall into two basic categories. The first category consists of the formulation and implementation of projects in research and development, market intelligence, processing, reforestation. The second category consists of monitoring commercial activity in tropical timber; reviewing the future need of the trade and assistance provided for production; and encouraging transfer of know-how and technology.

In 1989 the ITTO administrative budget was $2.54 million. In 1990, this rose to $2.8 million and in 1991 was $3.1 million. This is financed by contributions from all member States in proportion to their votes on the International Tropical Timber Council (ITTC). * * *

The Council is the governing body of the Organization. Its work consists of formulation of overall policies, approving the programme of work for the Organization, allocating funds for its implementation and undertaking an annual review and assessment of the tropical timber market and economy. Funding of project activities is from the Common

Fund for Commodities; relevant regional and international financial institutions; and voluntary contributions from members and interested organizations. Generally target contributions from donor members are made at the bi-annual sessions of the Council. However, direct funding of ITTO's projects from the multilateral Common Fund has been delayed due to the late start-up of the operations of the Fund. Projects are proposed by member States, often with the technical advice of the Secretariat. Almost three quarters of the total US $44 million so far of project and pre-project funding has been provided by Japan. The idea is to persuade consumer States and their importing industries to contribute to ITTO as a gesture of commitment and political goodwill towards achieving sustainable use and conservation of tropical forests. This has not yet been achieved on a significant scale, except in the case of Japan.

Producer States are the intended beneficiaries of the three main ITTA programmes (i.e. market intelligence; reforestation and forest management; and further processing by developing countries), although market information may be of use to all parties in the timber trade. There is no provision in the ITTA to assist developing countries in bearing the expense of sending delegates to meetings and working parties, in order to play a more pro-active role in directing ITTO policies. Consumer States play an important role as donors supporting ITTO projects.

The ITTA envisages that policy should be based on scientific advice, and all projects must be expertly assessed before approval. For this purpose, the ITTA provides that the ITTO should, as far as possible, utilize facilities and expertise provided by existing national and international agencies and NGOs, and should collaborate with such organizations in research and data collection. It also allows the ITTO to use funds offered to it from these organizations. Any such organizations may request formally to be invited to meetings of the Council as observers. ITTO thus accepts earmarked funds to advance bilateral agendas whilst still pursuing its own multilateral theme.

The ITTA is subject to periodic extension or renewal by the Parties. A mechanism for amending the ITTA, involving the approval of at least two thirds of producing members and two thirds of consuming members is provided in Article 38. The intent of the drafters of the ITTA was to leave the Parties free to decide on any changes at any time it so decides. Further extension of the ITTA has been decided twice in 1989 and 1991, for two consecutive periods of extension 1990–1992 and 1992–1994.

F. Codification programming

At the initiative of FAO, the Secretary–General of the UNCED convened an *ad hoc* meeting of heads of UN agencies and the ITTO in March 1991 to explore possibilities of instituting periodic consultations among the relevant Secretariats in order to co-ordinate current negotiations on legal instruments for climate change and biodiversity and a possible consensus on forests. ITTO participated together with FAO, UNESCO, WMO, UNEP, UN/DIEC and the Intergovernmental Negotiating Committees concerned.

11. ENDANGERED SPECIES

A. KISS AND D. SHELTON, INTERNATIONAL ENVIRONMENTAL LAW

257–258 (1991) (footnotes omitted).*

* * * Unlike the prior conventions, the *Convention on International Trade in Endangered Species of Wild Fauna and Flora (CITES)*, is not based on a spatial concept of protection, but on a given activity relating to wildlife: international trade. One of the most powerful motives for the exploitation of plant and animal species is income production, especially in poor countries lacking other major resources. Certain products derived from wildlife species, such as the rhinoceros horn, which is powdered for use as a medicine or stimulant, ivory, tortoise shell, and fur skins, can command high prices and attract hunters, traders and poachers. It is estimated that near the end of the 1960s, five to ten million crocodile skins were traded on the international market. In 1972, the record year, the exports of ivory from Kenya reached 150 tons. To counter trade in animals, plants and their derivatives, to eliminate this source of income, quotas or duties may be imposed. However, no measure of this type can be truly effective without international cooperation between exporting, transit, and importing states. The major framework in this regard is CITES, the most complete treaty at present on trade in endangered species, to which the majority of states in the world are parties.

———

1. *Lacunae in the Convention.* It is apparent from the Convention on International Trade in Endangered Species, 27 U.S.T.S. 1087; T.I.A.S. 8249, reproduced in the Documentary Supplement, that there are a number of exemptions from the imposed permit system, such as for what is called a "pre-Convention" specimen, and those that are categorized as "personal or household effects". The recent controversy over the trade in ivory is illustrative. In 1979 the African elephant was moved from Appendix II to Appendix I to stop the ivory trade that was killing great numbers of the animal. Some states parties to the Convention argued that ivory stockpiled in their states before their adherence to the Convention were "pre-Convention" specimens. The second gap that the elephant case indicates is that of the allowance of specific reservations to the Convention which both ivory-producing and consuming states used. Another problem is that the Convention only applies to species that fall within its Article I definition and thus does not go so far as to protect endangered species not being traded in, but in danger because of habitat destruction. (See Sands and Bedecarre, Convention on International Trade in Endangered Species: The Role of Public Interest Non–Governmental Organizations in Ensuring the Effective Enforcement of the Ivory Trade Ban, 17 Boston Coll.Env.Aff.L.Rev. 799 (1990) and M. Glenon, Has International Law Failed the Elephant, 84 Am.J.Int.L. 1 (1990)).

* Reprinted with the permission of Transnational Pub. Inc.

2. ***Migratory species.*** The Bonn Convention on the Conservation of Migratory Species of Wild Animals, 19 ILM 15 (1980) deals with the obligations of states whose territories are part of the range of such wild animals. Appendix I deals with wild animals in danger of extinction. The United States is not a party to this Convention. Note also the Convention for the Regulation of Whaling, 3 Bevans 26, 155 L.N.T.S.; International Convention for the Regulation of Whaling, 161 U.N.T.S. 72, and 1956 Protocol, 10 U.S.T.S. 952, 338 U.N.T.S. 366; the 1973 Agreement on the Conservation of Polar Bears, 27 U.S.T.S. 3918; T.I.A.S. 8409; the 1972 Convention for the Conservation of Antarctic Seals, 29 U.N.T.S. 441; T.I.A.S. 8826 and most recently in order to prevent the killing of dolphins and porpoises, the 1989 Convention for the Prohibition of Fishing with Long Driftnets in the South Pacific, which entered into force for the United States on February 28, 1992 and Protocols, 29 ILM 1453 (1990).

Canada and the United States have several bilateral treaties on point. They are firstly, the 1916 Convention for the Protection of Migratory Birds, 12 Bevans 375. This Convention does not protect the habitat of migratory birds, but addresses protection from killing and nest despoilation. Second, there is the 1987 Agreement on the Conservation of the Porcupine Caribou Herd with annex, T.I.A.S. 11259, which provides for conservation and habitat. It should be noted that this agreement recognizes the traditional rights of aboriginal peoples to harvest subject to the need to establish bilateral cooperative mechanisms to coordinate conservation. Third, there is an informal mechanism in the 1988 North American Waterfowl Management Plan for the protection of migratory species. (See R. Osterwoldt, Implementation and Enforcement Issues in the Protection of Migratory Species—Two Case Studies: Waterfowl in North America, Seals in Europe, 29 Nat.Res.J. 1017 (1989)).

12. BIOLOGICAL DIVERSITY

Refer to the 1992 Convention on Biological Diversity contained in the Doc. Supp. No reservations may be made to this Convention, which was adopted in Nairobi, by the Intergovernmental Negotiating Committee in May 1992. It was signed by 154 states at the United Nations Conference on Environment and Development. Thirty ratifications are necessary to bring it into force. The United States did not sign.

AMERICAN SOCIETY OF INTERNATIONAL LAW, ENVIRONMENTAL LAW INTEREST GROUP NEWSLETTER
Vol. 3(1), 2 (1992).*

The Convention is directed at the conservation and sustainable use of biological diversity, the fair and equitable sharing of the benefits arising out [of] its utilization, and the regulation of biotechnology. The

* Reprinted with the permission of the American Society of International Law.

Convention stresses national measures to conserve biodiversity and does not require the development of international lists of threatened species and areas of biological importance, as some countries had urged. Under the Convention:

- Parties are required to develop national plans or programs for the conservation and sustainable use of biological diversity, and to integrate, as far as possible and as appropriate, the conservation and sustainable use of biological diversity into their relevant sectoral and cross-sectoral plans, programs and policies.

- Access to and transfer of technology "shall be provided and/or facilitated under fair and favourable terms, including on concessional and preferential terms where mutually agreed." Patented technologies shall be transferred "on terms which recognize and are consistent with the adequate and effective protection of intellectual property rights." The Parties shall cooperate to ensure that intellectual property rights are "supportive of and do not run counter to" the Convention's objectives.

- Contracting Parties are required to take "all practicable measures to promote and advance [the source country's] priority access on a fair and equitable basis * * * to the results and benefits arising from biotechnologics based upon genetic resources provided by [it]." Access shall be on mutually agreed terms.

- Developed country Parties shall provide "new and additional financial resources to enable developing country Parties to meet the agreed full incremental costs * * * of implementing measures which fulfil the obligations" of the Convention and are agreed between a developing country Party and the Convention's financial mechanism.

- The financial mechanism shall operate under the "authority and guidance of, and be accountable to" the Conference of the Parties. Provided it has been "fully restructured," the GEF will serve as the financial mechanism on an interim basis, until the first meeting of the Conference of the Parties.

While many Western countries expressed reservations about the Convention, all but the US ended up signing. In declining to sign the Convention, the United States said that the text was "seriously flawed," and identified three areas of concern: the provision on intellectual property rights; the funding provisions, which the US said would establish a different role for the Global Environment Facility than agreed at the April GEF Participants Meeting * * * and the biotechnology provisions.

R. FRYE, UNCLE SAM AND UNCED: A UNITED STATES PERSPECTIVE ON THE EARTH SUMMIT

International Newsletter of Committee F of the Section of Business
Law of the International Bar Association 5 (1993).*

Biodiversity Convention

The Framework Convention on Biological Diversity is a good example of the competing interests of developed and developing nations. As *Newsweek* magazine commented: "While few delegates know a fungus from a mold, they do know the most important thing about biodiversity: the rich North needs, the poor South has it." Maintaining biodiversity, a wide range and assortment of plants, helps to provide protection against pests and disease and is vital for the breeding of improved crop varieties. Under the terms of the Biodiversity Convention, its contracting parties agree to pursue "conservation of biological diversity, the sustainable use of its components and the fair and equitable sharing of the benefits arising out of the utilization of genetic resources * * *."

The US refused to sign the Biodiversity Convention because of concern about its effect on intellectual property rights. Advocates of the Convention offer that, while it does call for transfer of technology to developing countries which provide genetic resources, it is only on mutually agreed terms. Critics of the Biodiversity Convention, however, suggest that the convention might have been acceptable to the United States had the staff "stuck to [the] subject of preserving species." Unsure how the Biodiversity Convention might affect their property rights, private biotechnology companies may elect to reduce investment in potentially affected businesses where they may later be required to surrender technology or pay royalties to other countries.

13. ENVIRONMENTAL PROTECTION AND INTERNATIONAL TRADE

The relationship between environmental protection and international trade cannot today be ignored. The liberalization of international trade exemplified by the General Agreement on Tariffs and Trade (GATT), 61 Stat. (5), (6), T.I.A.S. 1700, 4 Bevans 639, the 1987 Free Trade Agreement, between Canada and the United States with exchanges of letters, 27 ILM 293 (1988), and the 1992 North American Free Trade Agreement, between Canada, Mexico and the United States, envision this by providing that domestic measures intended to protect the environment must in turn comply with international trade law. If they fail, they may be classified as an unlawful restriction on trade.

---

* Reprinted with the permission of the
International Bar Association.

J.H. JACKSON, WORLD TRADE RULES AND ENVIRONMENTAL POLICIES: CONGRUENCE OR CONFLICT?

49 Wash.Lee L.Rev. 1227–1230, 1242–1245, 1255–1259 (1992) (footnotes omitted).**

Proposition 1: Protection of the environment has become exceedingly important, and promises to be more important for the benefit of future generations. Protecting the environment involves rules of international cooperation, sanction, or both, so that some government actions to enhance environmental protection will not be undermined by the actions of other governments. Sometimes such rules involve trade restricting measures.

Proposition 2: Trade liberalization is important for enhancing world economic welfare and for providing a greater opportunity for billions of individuals to lead satisfying lives. Measures that restrict trade often will decrease the achievement of this goal.

These two propositions state the opposing policy objectives that currently pose important and difficult dilemmas for governments. This type of "policy discord" is not unique; there are many similar policy discords, at both the national and the international levels, that governments must confront. Indeed, there is some evidence that environmental policy and trade policy are complementary, at least in the sense that increasing world welfare can lead to citizen demands and governmental actions to improve protection for the environment. The poorest nations in the world cannot afford such protection, but as welfare increases protection becomes more affordable.

An unfortunate development in public and interest group attention to trade and the environment is the appearance of hostility between proponents of the two different propositions stated above. The hostility is misplaced because both groups will need the assistance and cooperation of the other group in order to accomplish their respective policy objectives. Of course, some of this tension is typical of political systems. Political participants often seek to achieve opposing objectives and goals. Each side may endorse legitimate goals, but when the goals clash, accommodation is necessary.

To some extent, the conflicts between the trade liberalization proponents and the environmental protection proponents derive from a certain "difference in cultures" between the trade policy experts and the environmental policy experts. Oddly enough, even when operating within the framework of the same society, these different "policy cultures" have developed different attitudes and perceptions of the political and policy processes, and these different outlooks create misunderstandings and conflict between the groups.

These problems are part of a broader trend of international economic relations that is posing a number of perplexing and troublesome situations for statesmen and policy leaders. Part of the difficulty inevitably results from the growth of international economic interdependence. Such interdependence increases trade in both products and services across national borders and brings many benefits to participating countries. International interdependence also results in efficiencies and economies of scale that can raise world welfare (but not necessarily

** Reprinted with the permission of Wash. & Lee Law Review and J.H. Jackson.

everyone's welfare, because some groups will be required to adjust in the face of increased competition).   This trend towards increased international economic interdependence requires a different sort of attitude towards government regulation.   Within a nation, government regulations in such areas as consumer protection, competition policy, prudential measures (of banking and financial institutions), health and welfare (for example, alcohol and abortion control), and human rights (for example, prohibiting discrimination), are all designed by governments to promote worthy policies that sometimes clash with market oriented economic policies.   When economic interdependence moves a number of these issues to the international scene, they become (at least in today's defective international system) much more difficult to manage.   The circumstances and the broader scope of the international system create in many contexts (not just those concerning environmental policies) a series of problems and questions including:

— General questions of effectiveness of national "sovereignty" in the face of a need to cooperate with other countries to avoid some aspects of the "prisoners dilemma" or "free rider" problems. Unless there is cooperation, individual countries can profit from the efforts of other countries without contributing to those efforts, but in the longer run all may suffer;

— Perplexing questions of how new international rules should be made, questions that often involve voting procedures;

— General questions of the appropriateness and degree to which national sovereignty will submit to international dispute settlement procedures to resolve differences on various policy matters;

— Problems of a single national sovereign using the extraterritorial reach of its regulation (sometimes termed unilateralism) to impose its will on the actions of other nations, or the citizens of other nations;

— Significant legitimate differences of view between nations as to economic structure, level of economic development, forms of government, appropriate role of government in economic activities, etc. Developing countries, for example, will have different views than on many "trade-off" matters, with developing countries generally arguing that environmental regulations unfairly restrain their economic development. They note that rich countries have benefitted from decades or centuries of freedom from environmental protection rules, and that even today the rich countries are responsible for most of the world's pollution. Furthermore, poor countries argue that the imposition of environmental regulations threatens their economies with stagnation and populations with starvation.

All these circumstances and arguments occur in the context of a relatively chaotic and unstructured international system, which in many ways has not evolved adequately to keep up with the implications of growing international economic interdependence.

* * *

The term "environmental policies" is defined very broadly. * * * It includes, for example, measures relating to health or health risks. The phrases "trade policies" and "trade liberalization" also are defined broadly to include not only trade in goods, but also trade in services.

* * *

THE PROCESS–PRODUCT PROBLEM: THE TUNA DOLPHIN CASE & THE GLOBAL COMMONS QUESTIONS

An important conceptual "difficulty" of GATT is the so-called process-product characteristic problem, which relates closely to the Article XX exceptions and also to the national treatment obligations and other provisions of GATT. This issue is central to the so-called tuna/dolphin case and needs to be explained.

Suppose an importing country wishes to prohibit the sale of domestic or imported automobiles that emit more pollutants in their exhaust than permitted by a specified standard. Subject to the discussion in Part II, there seems to be little difficulty with this regulation. It relates to the characteristics of the product itself. If the product itself is polluting, then on a nondiscriminatory basis the government may prohibit its sale (or also prohibit its importation, as a measure to prohibit sale).

Suppose, on the other hand, that the government feels that an automobile plant in a foreign country is operated in such a way that it poses substantial hazards to human health, possibly through dangers of accidents from the machinery, pollutants or unduly high temperatures in the factory. On an apparently nondiscriminatory basis, the government may wish to impose a prohibition on the sale of domestic or imported automobiles that are produced in factories with certain characteristics. However, in this case it should be noted that the imported automobiles themselves are perfectly appropriate and do not have dangerous or polluting characteristics. Thus, the target of the importing country's regulation is the production "process." The key question under the GATT/MTO system is whether the importing country is justified either under national treatment rules of nondiscrimination, or the exceptions of Article XX (which do not require strict national treatment nondiscrimination as was discussed above). Trade policy experts are concerned that if a nation is allowed to use the process characteristic as the basis for trade restrictive measures, then the result would be to open a pandora's box of problems that could open large loopholes in the GATT. The following are some hypothetical illustrations of potential "process" problems further down the road.

— An importing country prohibits the sale of radios, whether domestic or imported, that are produced by workers who are paid less than a minimum amount of wages specified by the importing country. This minimum amount might be the importing country's own minimum wage, or it might be an amount considerably less but still substantial (in deference to poor countries).

— An importing country that prohibits women from working in certain types of manufacturing plants also prohibits the importation of goods produced in similar plants that utilize women employees.

— An importing country that specifies a weekly religious holiday, for example, Saturday or Sunday, prohibits the importation of goods produced by work on the specified religious holiday.

— An importing country has strong political interests regarding the threat to marine mammals from certain fishing practices on the high seas, and thus prohibits the sale of products from both its domestic fishing industry and from foreign fishing if the products come from countries that permit the destructive fishing practices.

Obviously the tuna/dolphin case relates to these issues. Although the GATT panel report is not entirely clear on this matter, it seems fair to say that there were two important objections to the U.S. embargo on the importation of tuna. First, there is the question of "eco-imperialism," where one nation unilaterally imposes its fishing standards (albeit for environmental purposes) on other nations in the world without their consent or participation in the development of the standard. Second, there is the problem that the import embargo is inconsistent with the GATT rules unless there is some GATT exception that would permit the embargo. That exception relates to the "process-product" interpretation problem and therefore also to the problem in the national treatment rule (Article III) and the general exceptions of GATT (Article XX).

The approach in the GATT system so far has given great weight to this slippery slope concern, and thus tilted towards interpreting both the Article III (including some Article XI questions) and the Article XX exceptions to apply to the product standards and to life and health within the importing country, but not to extend these concepts and exceptions to "processes" outside the territorial limits of jurisdiction. The alternative which threatens to create the great loop hole is a serious worry. The theories of comparative advantage which drive the policy of liberal trade, suggest that differences among nations are an important reason for trade. These can be differences of natural resources, as well as differences of cultural and population characteristics such as education, training, investment, and environment. To allow an exception to GATT to permit some governments to unilaterally impose standards on production processes as a condition of importation would substantially undermine these policy objectives of trade liberalization. On the other hand, trade sanctions, which include embargoes, are a very attractive and potentially useful means of providing enforcement of international cooperatively developed standards, including environmental standards.

Thus, there is an important trade-off that the GATT must face. It is not adequate, in this writer's view, for the GATT simply to say that trade should never be used as a sanction for environmental (or human rights, or anti-prison labor) purposes. There are already a number of situations in which the GATT has at least tolerated, if not explicitly accepted, trade sanction type activity for what is perceived to be valid overriding international objectives. What are the implications of this problem? To this writer, it seems clear that the GATT/MTO system must give specific and significant attention to this trade-off in order to provide for exceptions for environmental purposes. The exceptions should have well-established boundaries so as to prevent them from being used as excuses for a variety of protectionist devices or unilateral social welfare concerns. Possibly these exceptions should be limited to the situation where governments are protecting matters that occur within their territorial jurisdiction.

It may be feasible to develop an explicit exception in the GATT/MTO system, possibly by the waiver process which is reasonably efficient for a certain list of specified broad-based multilateral treaties. One of the concerns expressed about the tuna/dolphin case in GATT is the implications that it might have for the so-called "Montreal Protocol" concerning chlorofluorocarbons (CFCs) and the danger to the Earth's ozone layer. The Montreal Protocol provides a potential future authorization of trade sanction measures against even nonsignatories for processes, not produce characteristics, that violate the norms of the treaty. If the current rules of the GATT are interpreted to exclude exceptions for the process situation, the Montreal Protocol Measures, except as among the signatories to the Montreal Protocol, would be contrary to GATT obligations. It may take some time and study to develop the precise wording of an appropriate amendment or treaty exception for the GATT/MTO system for these environmental treaty cases, but in the short run for a limited period of years, it could be efficient to use a GATT waiver to clarify the issue as to specifically named treaties.

In all likelihood, there are a sufficient number of signatories to the Montreal Protocol that are also GATT members so that a GATT waiver authorizing the trade measures contemplated in the Montreal Protocol could be adopted. Adoption of a waiver requires approval by two-thirds vote of the GATT contracting parties. But at the same time, it might be wise to go a few steps further and include in such a waiver several other specified treaties. Obviously the waiver can also be amended in the future to add more specifically named treaties.

Even under such a waiver approach, there are still some important policy and treaty drafting questions that must be faced. For example, should the exception to the GATT be worded to apply only to the mandatory trade measures required by the specified environmental treaties? Or should it also be extended to those measures that are deemed discretionary but "authorized" by the environmental treaties? Or, would the GATT waiver even go one step further and authorize GATT members to take trade measures unilaterally to help enforce the substantive environmental norms contained in the environmental treaties, even when such environmental treaties do not have trade measures or sanctions indicated in their treaty texts?

* * *

The discussions of this paper cover only the tip of the iceberg regarding the problematic relationship between world trade system policies and environmental policies. But in the light of those discussions, what can we say about the relationship of two policy sets? Are they congruent or conflicting? The answer obviously is a bit of both.

In the broader long term perspective there would seem to be a great deal of congruence. Some of that congruence derives from the economic and welfare enhancement of trade liberalization policies. Such welfare enhancement can in turn lead to enhancement of environmental policy objectives, as mentioned at the outset of this paper.

On the other hand, it is clear that the world trade policies and environmental policies do provide a certain amount of conflict. This conflict is not substantially different from a number of other areas where governmental policies have to accommodate conflicting aims and goals of the policy makers and their constituents. Thus, to some degree it is a question of where the line will be drawn, or how the compromises will be made. In that sense, institutions obviously become very important because the decision making process can tilt the decision results. If the world trade rules are pushed to their limit, for example, free trade with no exceptions for problems raised by environmental policies and actions effecting environments, clearly the trade rules will cause damage to environmental objectives. Likewise, if the environmental policies are pushed to their limit at the expense of the trading rules, so that governments will find it convenient and easy to set up a variety of restrictive trade measures, in some cases under the excuse of environmental policies, world trade will suffer.

Furthermore, * * * the "cultures" of the two policy communities: that of trade, and that of environment, differ in important ways. The trade policy experts have tended, over decades and perhaps centuries, to operate more under the practices of international diplomacy, which often means secrecy, negotiation, compromise, and to some extent behind the scenes catering to a variety of special economic interests. In addition, at the international level, because there is no over-arching "sovereign leader," the processes are slow, faltering, and lend themselves to lowest common denominator results, or to diplomatic negotiations that agree to language without real agreement on substance.

The environmental policy groups, perhaps partly because they primarily operate on the national scene, have become used to using the processes of publicity and lobbying pressure on Congress or Parliaments, to which they have considerable access. There is, thus, a much broader sense of "participation" in the processes, which the international processes have not yet accommodated. Furthermore, the environmental policy groups, like many other groups working on the domestic level, have a sense of power achieved through successes in the legislative and public discussion processes. They feel somewhat frustrated with the international processes because those are sufficiently different to pose puzzling obstacles to the achievement of environmental goals.

This difference in culture is not inevitably permanent, and indeed the international processes need to accommodate more transparency and participation. * * * As more and more decisions that effect firms, citizens, and other groups, are made at the international level, it will be necessary for the international decision making process to accommodate the goals of transparency, adequate expertise, and participation in the advocacy and rule making procedures.

To some extent, the rhetoric of some environmental policy advocates has been the rhetoric of antagonism to international organizations and procedures altogether. This, I suggest, is not constructive. The notion that the United States, for example, can, or should impose unilaterally its environmental views and standards on other parts of the world, without any constraint from international rules or international dispute settlement procedures, is not likely to be a viable approach in the longer run. This means that in some cases when the United States submits (as it must, partly so as to reciprocally get other countries to submit) to international dispute settlement procedures, it will sometimes lose, and find itself obliged to alter its own domestic policy preferences. This has already been the case, and the United States has a mixed record of compliance with GATT rulings, although for a large powerful nation that record is not too bad.

Apart from these longer run and institutional issues, there are matters that can be undertaken jointly by the trade and environmental policy communities, in the context of the GATT/MTO system. * * * [T]here seem to be two groups of actions that would be called for, the near term, and the longer term.

Focusing first on the near term actions: it seems feasible for the international trading system to accommodate some of the following actions or goals:

    1) Greater transparency both in the rule making and in the dispute settlement procedures of the trading system. This would call for more participation, greater opportunity for policy advocacy inputs, and for more openness in terms of publication of the relevant documents faster and in a way more accessible to interested parties;

    2) Greater access to participation in the processes,

    3) Some clarification is needed about the degree to which the international process will be allowed to intrude upon the scope of decision making of national and sub-national governments. For example, the "scope of review" of international GATT/MTO panels over national government regulatory decisions concerning environment needs to be better defined. This is not an easy question, and it will not be solved quickly, but there probably needs to be some near term accommodation through interpretive notes or otherwise in the Dunkel Draft texts, for example. Some of the NAFTA text approach can be a useful example; and

    4) Finally, there will have to be some near-term rule accommodation by the GATT, by which I mean some adjustments or changes in those rules through one or another of the techniques for changing GATT rules (probably focusing on the waiver procedure) to establish a reasonably clear set of exceptions for certain multilateral environmental treaty provisions that call for trade action that would otherwise be inconsistent with the GATT/MTO rules.

Looking at the longer term, it is clear that there is a substantial agenda that must be addressed with regard to the intersection and potential clash of trade policies and environmental policies. The GATT/MTO system must develop mechanisms, including working parties and negotiations, to address these, and they will take time. The long term agenda includes the following actions and goals:

1) The subsidies area will need substantial study and some kind of rule alteration to accommodate the respective interest;

2) Some type of more permanent exception will be needed either as an amendment or waiver embellishment of the Article XX exceptions of the GATT system, or possibly in the context of the national treatment rules. This can build upon the short term rule alterations (for example, by waiver) mentioned above, with particular reference to the process-product characteristic question, so as to accommodate the broadly agreed international environmental policy provisions, such as those now contained in some treaties;

3) Undoubtedly the GATT/MTO dispute settlement procedure will continue to evolve, in the light of experience. Even if near term provision is made for policy advocacy inputs from environmental policy experts, as time goes on and experience is obtained, there will need to be further adjustments in that procedure, possibly with some added limitations on the scope of review of international panels over domestic national environmental provisions; and

4) In particular, some clarification [is needed] about the rules and exceptions to accommodate national government unilateral imposition of environmentally justified rules that require or provide incentive for a higher standard of environmental protection than that for which the international community is able to develop a consensus.

It would be tragic if increased antagonism between the two policy groups occurred in such a way that the essential policy goals of both groups would be damaged unnecessarily. Hopefully, with some of the clarifications of the policies outlined in this paper, combined with some of the institutional measures suggested, such antagonism can be largely avoided, or creatively channeled to promote a constructive accommodation of the discordant policy objectives.

GENERAL AGREEMENT ON TARIFFS AND TRADE: DISPUTE SETTLEMENT PANEL REPORT ON UNITED STATES RESTRICTIONS ON IMPORTS OF TUNA

30 International Legal Materials 1594 (1991) (footnotes omitted).*

* * *   1.1. On 5 November 1990, Mexico requested consultations with the United States concerning restrictions on imports of tuna. These consultations were held on 19 December 1990. On 25 January

* Reprinted with the permission of the American Society of International Law.

1991, Mexico requested the Contracting Parties to establish a panel under Article XXIII:2 to examine the matter as the sixty-day period for consultations had expired without a mutually satisfactory adjustment having been reached. On 6 February 1991 the Council agreed to establish the Panel and authorized its Chairman to designate the chairman and members of the Panel in consultation with the parties concerned. At that meeting of the Council, Australia, Canada, Chile, Colombia, Costa Rica, the European Communities, India, Indonesia, Japan, Korea, New Zealand, Nicaragua, Norway, Peru, the Philippines, Senegal, Singapore, Tanzania, Thailand, Tunisia and Venezuela reserved their rights, to be heard by the panel and to make written submissions.

1.2.   On 12 March 1991, the Council was informed that the Panel would have the following composition:

> Chairman: Mr. András Szepesi
> Members: Mr. Rudolph Ramsauer; Mr. Elbio Rosselli

As the parties had not agreed otherwise within twenty days from the establishment of the Panel, standard terms of reference apply, as follows:

> 'To examine, in the light of the relevant GATT provisions, the matter referred to the CONTRACTING PARTIES by Mexico in document DS21/1 and to make such findings as will assist the CONTRACTING PARTIES in making the recommendations or in giving the rulings provided for in Article XXIII:2.'.

1.3.   The Panel held meetings with the parties to the dispute on 14 and 15 May and 17 June 1991. Australia, the European Communities, Indonesia, Japan, Korea, the Philippines, Senegal, Thailand and Venezuela made oral presentations to the Panel on 15 May, and Canada and Norway submitted their separate views in writing. The Panel submitted its conclusions to the parties on 16 August 1991.

2.   *Factual Aspects*

Purse-seine fishing of tuna

2.1.   The last three decades have seen the deployment of tuna fishing technology based on the "purse-seine" net in many areas of the world. A fishing vessel using this technique locates a school of fish and sends out a motorboat (a "seine skiff") to hold one end of the purse-seine net. The vessel motors around the perimeter of the school of fish, unfurling the net and encircling the fish, and the seine skiff then attaches its end of the net to the fishing vessel. The fishing vessel then purses the net by winching in a cable at the bottom edge of the net, and draws in the top cables of the net to gather its entire contents.

2.2.   Studies monitoring direct and indirect catch levels have shown that fish and dolphins are found together in a number of areas around the world and that this may lead to incidental taking of dolphins during fishing operations. In the Eastern Tropical Pacific Ocean (ETP), a particular association between dolphins and tuna has long been observed, such that fishermen locate schools of underwater tuna by finding and chasing dolphins on the ocean surface and intentionally encircling them with nets to catch the tuna underneath. This type of association has not been observed in other areas of the world; consequently,

intentional encirclement of dolphins with purse-seine nets is used as a
tuna fishing technique only in the Eastern Tropical Pacific Ocean.
When dolphins and tuna together have been surrounded by purse-seine
nets, it is possible to reduce or eliminate the catch of dolphins through
using certain procedures.   * * *

Marine Mammal Protection Act of the United States (Measures on Imports from Mexico)

2.3.   The Marine Mammal Protection Act of 1972, as revised
(MMPA) [86 Stat. 1027 (1972), as amended, notably by 102 Stat. 4755
(1988) and most recently by 104 Stat. 4467 (1990); codified in part at 16
U.S.C. 1361ff], [generally prohibits] "taking" (harassment, hunting,
capture, killing or attempt thereof) and importation into the United
States of marine mammals, except where an exception is explicitly
authorized.   Its stated goal is that the incidental kill or serious injury of
marine mammals in the course of commercial fishing be reduced to
insignificant levels approaching zero.   The MMPA contains special provisions applicable to tuna caught in the ETP, defined as the area of the
Pacific Ocean bounded by 40 degrees north latitude, 40 degrees south
latitude, 160 degrees west longitude, and the coasts of North, Central
and South America.   These provisions govern the taking of marine
mammals incidental to harvesting of yellowfin tuna in the ETP, as well
as importation of yellowfin tuna and tuna products harvested in the
ETP.   The MMPA is enforced by the National Marine Fisheries Service
(NMFS) of the National Oceanic and Atmospheric Administration
(NOAA) of the Department of Commerce, except for its provisions
regarding importation which are enforced by the United States Customs
Service under the Department of the Treasury.   * * *

2.5.   Section 101(a)(2) of the MMPA * * * states that "The Secretary of Treasury shall ban the importation of commercial fish or products from fish which have been caught with commercial fishing technology which results in the incidental kill or incidental serious injury of
ocean mammals in excess of United States standards".   This prohibition
is mandatory.   Special ETP provisions in section 101(a)(2)(B) provide
that importation of yellowfin tuna harvested with purse-seine nets in the
ETP and products therefrom is prohibited unless the Secretary of
Commerce finds that (i) the government of the harvesting country has a
program regulating taking of marine mammals that is comparable to
that of the United States, and (ii) the average rate of incidental taking of
marine mammals by vessels of the harvesting nation is comparable to
the average rate of such taking by United States vessels.   The Secretary
need not act unless a harvesting country requests a finding.   If it does,
the burden is on that country to prove through documentary evidence
that its regulatory regime and taking rates are comparable.   If the data
show that they are, the Secretary must make a positive finding.

2.6.   The provisions for ETP yellowfin tuna in section 101(a)(2)(B)
of the MMPA provide special prerequisites for a positive finding on
comparability of a harvesting country's regulatory regime and incidental
taking rates.   The regulatory regime must include the same prohibitions
as are applicable under United States rules to United States vessels.

The average incidental taking rate (in terms of dolphins killed each time the purse-seine nets are set) for that country's tuna fleet must not exceed 1.25 times the average taking rate of United States vessels in the same period.   Also, the share of Eastern spinner dolphin and coastal spotted dolphin relative to total incidental takings of dolphin during each entire (one-year) fishing season must not exceed 15 per cent and 2 per cent respectively.   NMFS regulations have specified a method of comparing incidental taking rates by calculating the kill per set of the United States tuna fleet as an unweighted average, then weighting this figure for each harvesting country based on differences in mortality by type of dolphin and location of sets;   these regulations have also otherwise implemented the MMPA provisions on importation.

2.7.   On 28 August 1990, the United States Government imposed an embargo, pursuant to a court order, on imports of commercial yellowfin tuna and yellowfin tuna products harvested with purse-seine nets in the ETP until the Secretary of Commerce made positive findings based on documentary evidence of compliance with the MMPA standards.   This action affected Mexico, Venezuela, Vanuatu, Panama and Ecuador.   On 7 September this measure was removed for Mexico, Venezuela and Vanuatu, pursuant to positive Commerce Department findings;   also, Panama and Ecuador later prohibited their fleets from setting on dolphin and were exempted from the embargo.   On 10 October 1990, the United States Government, pursuant to court order, imposed an embargo on imports of such tuna from Mexico until the Secretary made a positive finding based on documentary evidence that the percentage of Eastern spinner dolphins killed by the Mexican fleet over the course of an entire fishing season did not exceed 15 per cent of dolphins killed by it in that period.   An appeals court ordered on 14 November 1990 that the embargo be stayed, but when it lifted the stay on 22 February 1991, the embargo on imports of such tuna from Mexico went into effect.

2.8.   On 3 April 1991, the United States Customs Service issued guidance implementing a further embargo, pursuant to another court order of 26 March, on imports of yellowfin tuna and tuna products harvested in the ETP with purse-seine nets by vessels of Mexico, Venezuela and Vanuatu.   Under this embargo, effective 26 March 1991, the importation of yellowfin tuna, and "light meat" tuna products which can contain yellowfin tuna, under specified Harmonized System tariff headings is prohibited unless the importer provides a declaration that, based on appropriate inquiry and the written evidence in his possession, no yellowfin tuna or tuna products in the shipment were harvested with purse-seines in the ETP by vessels from Mexico, Venezuela or Vanuatu. The importer of such tuna or tuna products is also required to submit the NOAA Form 370–1 "Yellowfin Tuna Certificate of Origin".   Form 370–1 requires the importer to declare the country under whose laws the harvesting vessel operated, which is then deemed to be the country of origin of the tuna.   Over-the-side sales of fish are subject to the same information requirements.   For unprocessed tuna there is no difference between the country of origin for customs purposes and for purposes of the MMPA. The country of origin is the country under whose laws the vessel harvesting the tuna is registered.

2.9. The MMPA also provides that six months after the effective date of an embargo on yellowfin tuna or tuna products, the Secretary of Commerce shall certify this fact to the President. This certification triggers the operation of section 8(a) of the Fishermen's Protective Act of 1967 (22 U.S.C. 1978(a)), also known as the "Pelly Amendment". This provision provides discretionary authority for the President to order a prohibition of imports of fish products "for such duration as the President determines appropriate and to the extent that such prohibition is sanctioned by the General Agreement on Tariffs and Trade".

* * *

3. MAIN ARGUMENTS

Findings and Recommendations Requested by the Parties

3.1. Mexico requested the Panel to find, with respect to the MMPA import prohibition imposed on yellowfin tuna and tuna products from Mexico, that *inter alia*:

(a) the embargo provisions in MMPA section 101(a)(2) as well as relevant provisions of the corresponding regulations were inconsistent with the general prohibition of quantitative restrictions under Article XI; the provisions of MMPA section 101(a)(2)(B) and relevant implementing regulations established discriminatory specific conditions for a specific geographical area, in violation of Article XIII;

(b) once the question of whether or not the United States measures were compatible with Articles XI and XIII has been clarified (i.e. after products could be imported), the conditions of comparison between yellowfin tuna regulation in the United States and in another country provided in the MMPA violated Article III (the conditions referred to being those in MMPA sections 101(a)(2)(B)(I), (II) and (III), and 104(h)(2)(A) and (B), as well as relevant implementing regulations); and

(c) the possible extension of the import prohibition to "all fishery products" from Mexico under the provisions of MMPA section 101(a)(2)(D), the Pelly Amendment and relevant implementing regulations were in violation of Article XI.

3.2. With respect to the "intermediary nations embargo" imposed on importation into the United States of such tuna products from other contracting parties, Mexico requested the Panel to find that MMPA section 101(a)(2)(C) and the relevant implementing regulations were in violation of Article XI and that the possible extension of the import prohibition to "all fishery products" from an "intermediary nation" under the provisions of MMPA section 101(a)(2)(D), the Pelly Amendment and relevant implementing regulations was in violation of Article XI.

3.3. With respect to the Dolphin Protection Consumer Information Act, Mexico requested that the Panel find this legislation was inconsistent with Articles IX and I by virtue of its establishment of discriminatory and unfavourable specific conditions for a specific geographical area.

3.4.   Mexico also requested that the Panel find that none of the measures mentioned in paragraphs 3.1 to 3.3 above were justified under the General Agreement.

3.5.   Mexico suggested that the Panel recommend that the CONTRACTING PARTIES request the United States to bring its measures into conformity with its obligations under the General Agreement.

3.6.   The United States requested the Panel to find that:

(a) the measures imposed under the MMPA with respect to certain domestic yellowfin tuna from Mexico were internal regulations affecting the sale, offering for sale, purchase, transportation, distribution or use of tuna and tuna products consistent with Article III:4; and

(b) even if these measures are not consistent with Article III, they were covered by the exceptions in Article XX(b) and XX(g).

3.7.   The United States further requested that the Panel find, with respect to the MMPA measures prohibiting imports of yellowfin tuna and tuna products from "intermediary nations", that:

(a) the "intermediary nations" measures were also regulations consistent with Article III, and

(b) even if they are not consistent with Article III, these measures were within the scope of Article XX(b), XX(d) and XX(g).

3.8.   The United States further requested that the Panel find, with respect to the Dolphin Protection Consumer Information Act, (a) that these measures were subject not to Article IX but to Articles I and III, and (b) that because the Act discriminated on the basis of the waters in which the tuna is caught, not the origin of the tuna, it was consistent with the requirements of Articles I and III.

3.9.   The United States asked the Panel to reject Mexico's complaint.

* * *

Article XX(b)

3.33.   The United States stated that the MMPA embargo was necessary to protect the life and health of dolphins. No alternative measure was available or had been proposed that could reasonably be expected to achieve the objective of protecting the lives or health of dolphins. Purse-seining for tuna in the ETP meant deliberate encirclement of schools of dolphin with nets. Without efforts to protect them, they would be killed when the tuna was harvested. In order to avoid these needless deaths, the United States had established requirements for tuna production: yellowfin tuna harvested in the ETP using purse-seine nets and imported into the United States must have been produced under a program providing for harvesting methods to reduce dolphin mortality. Furthermore, in the case of vessels other than those of the United States, the resultant mortality had to be no greater per set than

25 per cent more than the average mortality per set for United States vessels during the same period, and the mortality of two stocks especially vulnerable to depletion could not exceed specified per centages of overall mortality. These measures were directly and explicitly to prevent dolphin deaths or severe injury. Accordingly, it was clear that the measures of the United States were necessary to protect animal life or health.

3.34. Mexico responded that the MMPA embargo was not "necessary" in the sense of Article XX, as the lives and health of dolphins could be protected consistently with the General Agreement. Mexico's own dolphin-protection measures had been taken in conformity with the General Agreement, demonstrating that the General Agreement did not oblige its contracting parties to adopt measures contrary to the environment. Indeed, dolphin protection should be carried out not just for purse-seining in the ETP but in all waters of the world, all fishing methods, all fisheries, and all dolphin species. Thus, Mexico had proposed in the Food and Agriculture Organization of the United Nations that an international conference be held to examine the interaction of fisheries and incidental taking of marine mammals. The best way of protecting the lives and health of dolphins was international cooperation among all concerned, not by arbitrary, discriminatory and unilateral trade measures.

3.35. Mexico stated that the text and prior interpretation of Article XX(b) indicated that it referred to protection of the life and health of humans and animals within the territory of the contracting party protecting them. Otherwise, one contracting party could arrogate to itself the right to protect the life or health of humans and animals in international areas or within the territory of other contracting parties. Such a case had never arisen in GATT, was not provided for in the General Agreement, and above all would be contrary to international law.

3.36. The United States responded that a government could prohibit imports of a product in order to protect the life or health of humans, plants or animals outside its jurisdiction. The United States assumed that Mexico shared this view, since Mexico too prohibited the importation of dolphins and dolphin products in order to protect dolphin outside its jurisdiction. In this case, the United States could prohibit imports of tuna produced in a manner resulting in the needless deaths of dolphin outside the jurisdiction of the United States and of any country, since dolphin roam the high seas. The United States noted that under the Convention on International Trade in Endangered Species of Wild Fauna and Flora (CITES), a CITES party was obligated, *inter alia,* to prohibit the importation of products in order to protect endangered species found only outside the jurisdiction of that party.

3.37. Further with regard to Article XX(b), Mexico argued that this provision referred solely to protection of the life or health of humans, animals or plants as a population (for instance in the case of epizootics), and not as separate individuals. If it could be invoked to avoid the death of individual animals as claimed by the United States, then countries could restrict imports of beef to prevent the killing of cows abroad, or prohibit imports of any product of a living organism claiming that the prohibition was aimed at protecting the life of that organism. Moreover, according to Mexico, it was not consistent for the United States to claim the protection of dolphins as separate individuals while at the same time, as in the present case, it was authorizing the incidental kill of up to 20,500 dolphins a year by its own fleet. There was no basis to transform this arbitrarily-determined figure into a benchmark for applying Article XX(b) internationally.

3.38.   Mexico also stated that, if the purpose of the MMPA was to protect dolphins, as the United States claimed, then that legislation, in order to be compatible with the GATT and with its own objectives, should protect all dolphins regardless of the type of fishery, species of dolphin, fishing method used or geographical area, which was not the case under the special and selective provisions of the MMPA on which the embargo was based. The special provisions of the MMPA applied solely to a situation in which a very special combination existed: yellow-fin tuna, associated with certain species of dolphins, fished with purse-seine nets, and caught in the ETP. In this context, Mexico noted that off the Alaskan coast more than 15,000 dolphins were killed each year with drift-nets in squid fishing, with no special provisions to protect them being in place remotely of the kind of those on which the embargo to Mexico was based. Those dolphins were not even counted against the United States general permit for its own fleet (20,500 dolphins per year in the ETP). Similar situations occurred in Georgia and Florida, not to mention other parts of the world. In contrast, Mexico protected all marine mammals with no discrimination by geographical areas, marine mammals species, fishing techniques or fisheries involved. Mexico's protection referred to dolphins as such, not to the way or the place they were incidentally taken.

3.39.   The United States replied that the MMPA did in fact protect all dolphins regardless of the type of fishery, species of dolphin, fishing method used or geographical area. The United States noted that the MMPA prohibited the taking of marine mammals generally.

Article XX(g)

3.40.   The United States further recalled the exception in Article XX(g), for measures "relating to the conservation of exhaustible natural resources if such measures are made effective in conjunction with restrictions on domestic production or consumption". The United States, recalling a previous panel, stated that dolphins were an exhaustible natural resource. Dolphin populations would be unable to sustain themselves if too high a mortality rate persisted. The United States noted that the need to conserve dolphin was recognized internationally, as for example in the work of the Inter–American Tropical Tuna Commission and the United Nations Convention on the Law of the Sea. The Government of Mexico had also agreed with the objective of conserving dolphin. The Marine Mammal Protection Act of 1972, under which the import prohibition was taken, was designed to conserve marine mammals, including dolphin, and the current measures were instituted in response to a complaint by conservation groups.

3.41. The United States also stated that the measures in question were made effective in conjunction with restrictions on domestic production or consumption. The United States had imposed comprehensive restrictions on domestic production practices expressly to conserve dolphin, which restrictions were more stringent than those applied to production by foreign vessels. The United States had since the beginning of its regulation of its tuna industry required certain gear and fishing procedures. Currently, it also prohibited sets on dolphin after sundown, prohibited the use of explosives to herd schools of dolphin, regulated the number of speedboats that could be used in purse-seining operations, required that each vessel carry an observer, and enforced performance standards under which no United States vessel operator could exceed a rate of dolphin mortality set in regulations. Violation of these regulations could result in vessel and cargo seizure. The import prohibition at issue in the current dispute was a natural outgrowth of the restrictions on the domestic production of yellowfin tuna in the ETP. The United States measures were primarily aimed at rendering effective these restrictions on the United States fleet, as restricting United States vessel practices would not ensure the conservation of dolphin if other countries' vessels continued to cause dolphin mortality.

3.42. Finally, the United States stated that Article XX(g) did not specify whether the exhaustible natural resources being conserved must be depleted or threatened, nor was it limited in terms of the location of those natural resources. Moreover, the coverage of Article XX(g) was not limited to certain types of conservation measures. The Contracting Parties had not yet had an opportunity to address these questions of interpretation of the General Agreement.

3.43. Mexico argued in reply first that it was clear from the General Agreement, the preparatory work therefor and the established precedents, that the term "exhaustible natural resources" in Article XX(g) did not include fisheries and fishery products, nor in fact any living being. By definition, exhaustible natural resources were resources which once taken or utilized cannot be renewed: that is, products whose physical or chemical characteristics bring about their destruction or definitive transformation when they are used, such as petroleum, uranium or any other fuel. Living beings, which can reproduce themselves, could not fall within this definition of "exhaustible". Living beings might become extinct as a population, depending on man-made or natural circumstances beyond the control of man (i.e. pollution or urbanization of their habitat, lack of nurseries, variation in climate, epizootics, etc.) but in the case of non-living natural resources, exhaustion occurred simply as a result of exploitation or use of that kind of products. While the panel in 1982 on "United States—Prohibition of Imports of Tuna and Tuna Products from Canada" had noted that both parties in that dispute considered tuna as exhaustible natural resource, this merely recorded an agreement between those two parties which did not necessarily apply to all disputes.

3.44.   Mexico further argued that even if "exhaustible natural resources" were deemed to include living beings, a resource could be considered exhaustible within the meaning of Article XX(g) if and only if the party invoking the provision showed by means of scientific and internationally-recognized data that the resource in question was actually in danger of extinction.   In the present case, the Convention on International Trade in Endangered Species of Wild Fauna and Flora (CITES) did not include in its Appendix I list of species in danger of extinction any of the species of dolphins which the United States was claiming to protect.   According to CITES, the only dolphins in danger of extinction were dolphins of the genus *platanista* (species *Gangetica* and *Minor*), of the species *Lipotes Vexillifer,* of the genus *Sousa* (species *Chimensis* and *Teuszii*) and of the genus *Sotalia* (species *Fluviatilis*); while the only species of dolphin mentioned in the United States Act are *Delphinus Delphis* (common dolphin), *Stenella Attenuata* (spotted dolphin) and *Stenella Longirostris* (spinner dolphin).   The taxonomical difference between the dolphins mentioned in the MMPA and those in danger of extinction according to CITES was so large that there was even not a coincidence at family level.   While the three species of protected dolphins in the ETP also existed in all the world's oceans, the dolphins actually threatened with extinction were to be found only outside the ETP and were not protected by United States legislation even though purse-seining was carried out near them.   Moreover, data of the Inter–American Tropical Tuna Commission (IATTC) and the United States Government showed that the populations of spotted, spinner and common dolphins in the ETP had remained stable and in some cases had tended to increase.   United States authorities (NOAA) had publicly agreed that there was no substantial evidence indicating that dolphin populations in the ETP were threatened with extinction.   Mexico further remarked that the United States regulations would lead fishermen not to fish for the large tuna which were associated with dolphin in the ETP; this would undermine conservation of tuna stocks, since the alternative was to fish the younger, immature tuna that had not yet reproduced.   From the standpoint of both economics and nature, it was more rational to use a renewable resource after it had reproduced rather than before.

3.45.   Nevertheless, Mexico requested that the Panel find in its favour not because the dolphins in question were not in danger of extinction but because the concept itself of "exhaustible natural resource" did not apply to living beings.   The Panel should not broaden a general exception which should be interpreted restrictively.   Moreover, extension of Article XX(g) to living beings would require future interpreters of it to become expert on fishery questions and the law of the sea, which would raise institutional and practical problems and overlap with the competence of other organizations.

3.46.   The United States replied that the text of Article XX(g) referred to "exhaust*ible* natural resources", not to "exhaust*ed* natural resources" or "almost exhausted" natural resources.   Nowhere in Article XX(g) was there a requirement that the exhaustible resources being conserved be threatened with extinction.   This would make no sense; as soon as a species was recovering, the measures to protect or conserve it would no longer be justified under Article XX and the species would then be doomed to a perpetual threat of extinction.   It was also not clear to the United States why, if conservation efforts were needed only when a population was in danger of extinction, Mexico had stated it was undertaking strong conservation efforts with respect to dolphins in the ETP. Furthermore, the United States view was that at current mortality rates of over 2 per cent annually, the population was declining and dolphin stocks would never recover to their pre-fishery levels.   If a party's measures were based on scientific information evaluated using recognized scientific approaches, a dispute settlement panel in the GATT should not substitute its own judgment for that of the contracting party whose measure is challenged.

3.47.   Mexico argued with respect to Article XX(g) that the United States legislation did not fulfil the condition that the measures in question be applied "in conjunction with restrictions on domestic production or consumption".   Firstly, Article XX(g) did not grant rights over extraterritorial natural resources situated in the territory of other contracting parties;   secondly, the embargoed product was not the same as the product sought to be conserved;   and finally, even if so, the United States was not applying restrictions on domestic production or consumption.

3.48.   Mexico stated that the average rates of incidental taking and other MMPA provisions for tuna caught in the ETP represented a unilateral imposition by the United States of extraterritorial restrictions on fishing by other contracting parties in their own economic zones, under the pretext of protecting natural resources located abroad.   The interference implicit in such action was not provided for in GATT Article XX(g).   It was clear from the letter and spirit of Article XX(g) that it referred to imposition of export restrictions by a contracting party to conserve exhaustible natural resources located in its *own* territory; hence the requirements that the measures be accompanied by restrictions on domestic production or consumption, as elements to restore equity and non-discrimination as between nationals and foreigners. Permitting one contracting party to impose trade restrictions to conserve the resources of others would introduce the concept of extraterritoriality into the GATT.   This would threaten all contracting parties, especially when restrictions were established unilaterally and arbitrarily as in the case of the United States MMPA.   The sensitive nature of extraterritoriality and unilaterality had been taken into account in Article XX(h) which provided that even intergovernmental agreements had to conform "to criteria submitted to the CONTRACTING PARTIES and not disapproved by them".

3.49.   The United States replied that there was nothing in Article XX to support assertions that the United States legislation was extraterritorial.   These measures simply specified the products that could be marketed in the territory of the United States.   Trade measures by nature had effects outside a contracting party's territory;   for example, the Note Ad Article III reflected this point in referring to applying a contracting party's requirements at the time or point of importation (that is, before the goods enter that contracting party's customs territory). The conservation objective of these measures motivated and permeated the United States legislation. Without conservation measures, dolphins, a common natural resource, would be exhausted. Without these measures on imports, the restrictions on domestic production would be ineffective at conserving dolphins. Dolphins were highly migratory species that roamed the high seas. The interpretation urged by Mexico would mean that a country must allow access to its market to serve as an incentive to deplete the populations of species that are vital components of the ecosystem. There was a general recognition that countries should not be required to allow this situation. CITES, for example, required a CITES party to restrict imports of specimens of species found only in the territory of another country, in addition to restrictions on listed species found in the high seas or in several countries' territories.

3.50. Mexico went on to note that the United States measures applied to imports of yellowfin *tuna* and yellowfin *tuna products* from Mexico whereas the Article XX(g) claim by the United States sought to justify the measures on the ground of the conservation of *dolphins*. Mexico did not permit its fishermen to intentionally catch dolphins; the issue here was unintentional incidental catching of dolphins in the course of tuna fishing in the ETP. Consequently, the United States was not conserving one resource (dolphins) or two resources (dolphins and tuna) but rather a specific combination of products (tuna/dolphins) located in a specific geographical area (the ETP), which did not correspond to any known trade classification either within or outside GATT. This novel claim was not only contrary to the concept of "like product", but would also raise problems practically impossible to resolve. While the interpretation of "the like product" did vary depending on which provision of the General Agreement was in question, justification of the MMPA's link between measures on tuna and dolphins could be found nowhere in the General Agreement. It was clear from the concept of 'like product' and the GATT background that the product to which the restriction applies must be the same product as that which it is sought to conserve. Mexico recalled a prior panel which had found that a country could not justify under Article XX(g) its prohibition on all tuna imports from another country because the first country's measures restricting domestic production or consumption did not include certain tuna (albacore). If restrictions of the tuna-dolphin type were deemed to be justified under Article XX(g), contracting parties could begin, for example, imposing prohibitions on the import of paper in order to protect the trees used to produce the paper, or on imports of pharmaceuticals to protect the animals used as laboratory test subjects for them.

3.51. Mexico also argued that because the MMPA requirements applied solely to fishing of yellowfin tuna in the ETP, its measures (particularly the quantitative requirements) could not be considered to be "in conjunction with restrictions on domestic production or consumption".

United States law did not impose any restrictions on domestic production or consumption of *tuna* in general or yellowfin tuna in particular; the MMPA only limited incidental *dolphin* mortality for the United States fleet in the ETP, not tuna as such. If the product restricted under Article XX(g) had to be itself subject to domestic production or consumption restrictions, as Mexico had argued, then it was clear that the MMPA failed to meet this requirement.

While the United States did limit incidental mortality of *dolphins,* there was no domestic production or consumption of dolphins either in the United States or in Mexico. The limit on incidental dolphin mortality (20,500 dolphins per year) had been the same before and since the MMPA was amended in 1988 to provide for import embargoes on yellowfin tuna and tuna products, and had no causal connection with the 1988 amendments. Moreover, since the embargo was not on dolphins but on tuna it could not be said to have been taken in conjunction with restrictions on domestic production or consumption.

As for restrictions on *tuna/dolphins,* no such product existed either in nature or in any known tariff nomenclature, and therefore its application within the general exceptions to the General Agreement would exceed the principle that such exceptions must be interpreted restrictively in order to avoid abuses. Even if this hybrid could be considered under Article XX, it would then be necessary to clarify, for instance, who defines it, what its characteristics were, what its scientific basis was, or what the relationship was between the two.

Finally, argued Mexico, even for tuna/dolphins, the restrictions on the United States fleet applied solely to the ETP, not the entire United States fleet. Since the great majority of the United States tuna fleet did its fishing outside the ETP, this meant that the bulk of United States yellowfin tuna production was not actually or legally subject to such restrictions. The only way of ensuring that all domestic production would be subject to the restrictions was to apply them to all the regions of the world. Mexico referred to a 1991 report of the Food and Agriculture Organization on tuna-dolphin interactions, and stated that this report showed such interactions occurred worldwide.

3.52. The United States responded that the United States measures were limited to the ETP because it was only there that the unique linkage between yellowfin tuna and dolphins occurred, so it was only there that the danger to dolphins from commercial tuna fishing existed. To extend the United States production requirements to tuna harvested beyond the ETP would be to impose unnecessary barriers to trade. This would be contrary to the fundamental principles of the General Agreement. The United States noted that Mexico did permit its fishermen to intentionally catch dolphins, which was inherent in setting on dolphins since the dolphins are deliberately encircled by the purse-seine net. The United States further noted that, unlike in numerous other provisions of the General Agreement, the term "like product" was nowhere used in Article XX(g).

* * *

5. *Findings*

A. *Introduction*

5.1. The Panel noted that the issues before it arose essentially from the following facts: the Marine Mammal Protection Act (MMPA) regulates, *inter alia,* the harvesting of tuna by United States fishermen and others who are operating within the jurisdiction of the United States. The MMPA requires that such fishermen use certain fishing techniques to reduce the taking of dolphin incidental to the harvesting of fish. The United States authorities have licensed fishing of yellowfin tuna by United States vessels in the ETP on the condition that the domestic fleet not exceed an incidental taking of 20,500 dolphins per year in the ETP.

5.2. The MMPA also requires that the United States Government ban the importation of commercial fish or products from fish caught with commercial fishing technology which results in the incidental killing or incidental serious injury of ocean mammals in excess of United States standards. Under United States customs law, fish caught by a vessel registered in a country is deemed to originate in that country. As a condition of access to the United States market for the yellowfin tuna or yellowfin tuna products caught by its fleet, each country of registry of vessels fishing yellowfin tuna in the ETP must prove to the satisfaction of the United States authorities that its overall regulatory regime regarding the taking of marine mammals is comparable to that of the United States. To meet this requirement, the country in question must prove that the average rate of incidental taking of marine mammals by its tuna fleet operating in the ETP is not in excess of 1.25 times the average incidental taking rate of United States vessels operating in the ETP during the same period. The exact methods of calculating and comparing these average incidental taking rates have been specified by regulation.

5.3. The MMPA also provides that ninety days after imports of yellowfin tuna and yellowfin tuna products from a country have been prohibited as above, importation of such tuna and tuna products from any "intermediary nation" shall also be prohibited, unless the intermediary nation proves that it too has acted to ban imports of such tuna and tuna products from the country subject to the direct import embargo.

5.4. Six months after either the direct embargo or the "intermediary nations" embargo goes into effect, the United States authorities are required to take action which triggers Section 8 of the Fishermen's Protective Act (the Pelly Amendment). This provision enables the President in his discretion to prohibit imports of all fish or wildlife products from the country in question, "for such duration as the President determines appropriate and to the extent that such prohibition is sanctioned by the General Agreement on Tariffs and Trade."

5.5. Under the MMPA, the United States currently prohibits importation into its customs territory of yellowfin tuna and yellowfin tuna products from Mexico which were caught with purse-seine nets in the ETP. A predecessor embargo was imposed on such tuna and tuna products on 28 August 1990; the embargo in its present form has been in place since 26 March 1991. Since 24 May 1991 the United States has also implemented the "intermediary nations" embargo provisions of the MMPA by prohibiting the importation of yellowfin tuna or yellowfin tuna products from any other country if the tuna was harvested with purse-seine nets in the ETP by vessels of Mexico. If either of these prohibitions is in effect six months after its inception, then as of that date the President will have the discretionary authority under the Pelly Amendment to prohibit imports of all fish products of Mexico or of any "intermediary nation" for such duration as he determines appropriate and to the extent that such action is "sanctioned by the General Agreement".

5.6. The Dolphin Protection Consumer Information Act (DPCIA) provides that when a tuna product exported from or offered for sale in the United States bears the optional label "Dolphin Safe" or any similar label indicating it was fished in a manner not harmful to dolphins, this tuna product may not contain tuna harvested on the high seas by a vessel engaged in driftnet fishing, or harvested in the ETP by a vessel using a purse-seine net unless it is accompanied by documentary evidence showing that the purse-seine net was not intentionally deployed to encircle dolphins. The use of the label "Dolphin Safe" is not a requirement but is voluntary. The labelling provisions of the DPCIA took effect on 28 May 1991.

5.7. The Panel decided to examine successively:

(a) the prohibition of imports of certain yellowfin tuna and certain yellowfin tuna products from Mexico imposed by the United States and the provisions of the MMPA on which it is based;

(b) the prohibition of imports of certain yellowfin tuna and certain yellowfin tuna products from "intermediary nations" imposed by the United States and the provisions of the MMPA on which it is based;

(c) the possible extension of each of these import prohibitions to all fish products from Mexico and the "intermediary nations", under the MMPA and Section 8 of the Fishermen's Protective Act (the Pelly Amendment); and

(d) the application to tuna and tuna products from Mexico of the labelling provisions of the DPCIA, as well as these provisions as such.

In accordance with the established practice, the Panel further decided that it would examine each of the above issues first in the light of the provisions of the General Agreement which Mexico claims to have been violated by the United States and then, if it were to find an inconsistency with any of the provisions invoked by Mexico, in the light of the exceptions in the General Agreement raised by the United States.

* * *

Article XX

General

5.22. The Panel noted that the United States had argued that its direct embargo under the MMPA could be justified under Article XX(b) or Article XX(g), and that Mexico had argued that a contracting party could not simultaneously argue that a measure is compatible with the general rules of the General Agreement and invoke Article XX for that measure. The Panel recalled that previous panels had established that Article XX is a limited and conditional exception from obligations under other provisions of the General Agreement, and not a positive rule establishing obligations in itself. Therefore, the practice of panels has been to interpret Article XX narrowly, to place the burden on the party invoking Article XX to justify its invocation, and not to examine Article XX exceptions unless invoked. Nevertheless, the Panel considered that a party to a dispute could argue in the alternative that Article XX might apply, without this argument constituting *ipso facto* an admission that the measures in question would otherwise be inconsistent with the General Agreement. Indeed, the efficient operation of the dispute settlement process required that such arguments in the alternative be possible.

5.23.   The Panel proceeded to examine whether Article XX(b) or Article XX(g) could justify the MMPA provisions on imports of certain yellowfin tuna and yellowfin tuna products, and the import ban imposed under these provisions. The Panel noted that Article XX provides that:

> "Subject to the requirement that such measures are not applied in a manner which would constitute a means of arbitrary or unjustifiable discrimination between countries where the same conditions prevail, or a disguised restriction on international trade, nothing in this Agreement shall be construed to prevent the adoption or enforcement by any contracting party of measures * * *
>
> (b) necessary to protect human, animal or plant life or health;
> * * *
>
> (g) relating to the conservation of exhaustible natural resources if such measures are made effective in conjunction with restrictions on domestic production or consumption; * * * ".

Article XX(b)

5.24.   The Panel noted that the United States considered the prohibition of imports of certain yellowfin tuna and certain yellowfin tuna products from Mexico, and the provisions of the MMPA on which this prohibition is based, to be justified by Article XX(b) because they served solely the purpose of protecting dolphin life and health and were "necessary" within the meaning of that provision because, in respect of the protection of dolphin life and health outside its jurisdiction, there was no alternative measure reasonably available to the United States to achieve this objective. Mexico considered that Article XX(b) was not applicable to a measure imposed to protect the life or health of animals outside the jurisdiction of the contracting party taking it and that the import prohibition imposed by the United States was not necessary because alternative means consistent with the General Agreement were available to it to protect dolphin lives or health, namely international co-operation between the countries concerned.

5.25. The Panel noted that the basic question raised by these arguments, namely whether Article XX(b) covers measures necessary to protect human, animal or plant life or health outside the jurisdiction of the contracting party taking the measure, is not clearly answered by the text of that provision. It refers to life and health protection generally without expressly limiting that protection to the jurisdiction of the contracting party concerned. The Panel therefore decided to analyze this issue in the light of the drafting history of Article XX(b), the purpose of this provision, and the consequences that the interpretations proposed by the parties would have for the operation of the General Agreement as a whole.

5.26. The Panel noted that the proposal for Article XX(b) dated from the Draft Charter of the International Trade Organization (ITO) proposed by the United States, which stated in Article 32, "Nothing in Chapter IV [on commercial policy] of this Charter shall be construed to prevent the adoption or enforcement by any Member of measures: * * * (b) necessary to protect human, animal or plant life or health". In the New York Draft of the ITO Charter, the preamble had been revised to read as it does at present, and exception (b) read: "For the purpose of protecting human, animal or plant life or health, if corresponding domestic safeguards under similar conditions exist in the importing country". This added proviso reflected concerns regarding the abuse of sanitary regulations by importing countries. Later, Commission A of the Second Session of the Preparatory Committee in Geneva agreed to drop this proviso as unnecessary. Thus, the record indicates that the concerns of the drafters of Article XX(b) focused on the use of sanitary measures to safeguard life or health of humans, animals or plants within the jurisdiction of the importing country.

5.27. The Panel further noted that Article XX(b) allows each contracting party to set its human, animal or plant life or health standards. The conditions set out in Article XX(b) which limit resort to this exception, namely that the measure taken must be "necessary" and not "constitute a means of arbitrary or unjustifiable discrimination or a disguised restriction on international trade", refer to the trade measure requiring justification under Article XX(b), not however to the life or health standard chosen by the contracting party. The Panel recalled the finding of a previous panel that this paragraph of Article XX was intended to allow contracting parties to impose trade restrictive measures inconsistent with the General Agreement to pursue overriding public policy goals to the extent that such inconsistencies were unavoidable. The Panel considered that if the broad interpretation of Article XX(b) suggested by the United States were accepted, each contracting party could unilaterally determine the life or health protection policies from which other contracting parties could not deviate without jeopardizing their rights under the General Agreement. The General Agreement would then no longer constitute a multilateral framework for trade among all contracting parties but would provide legal security only in respect of trade between a limited number of contracting parties with identical internal regulations.

5.28.   The Panel considered that the United States' measures, even if Article XX(b) were interpreted to permit extrajurisdictional protection of life and health, would not meet the requirement of necessity set out in that provision.   The United States had not demonstrated to the Panel— as required of the party invoking an Article XX exception—that it had exhausted all options reasonably available to it to pursue its dolphin protection objectives through measures consistent with the General Agreement, in particular through the negotiation of international cooperative arrangements, which would seem to be desirable in view of the fact that dolphins roam the waters of many states and the high seas. Moreover, even assuming that an import prohibition were the only resort reasonably available to the United States, the particular measure chosen by the United States could in the Panel's view not be considered to be necessary within the meaning of Article XX(b).   The United States linked the maximum incidental dolphin taking rate which Mexico had to meet during a particular period in order to be able to export tuna to the United States to the taking rate actually recorded for United States fishermen during the same period.   Consequently, the Mexican authorities could not know whether, at a given point of time, their policies conformed to the United States' dolphin protection standards.   The Panel considered that a limitation on trade based on such unpredictable conditions could not be regarded as necessary to protect the health or life of dolphins.

5.29.   On the basis of the above considerations, the Panel found that the United States' direct import prohibition imposed on certain yellowfin tuna and certain yellowfin tuna products of Mexico and the provisions of the MMPA under which it is imposed could not be justified under the exception in Article XX(b).

Article XX(g)

5.30.   The Panel proceeded to examine whether the prohibition on imports of certain yellowfin tuna and certain yellowfin tuna products from Mexico and the MMPA provisions under which it was imposed could be justified under the exception in Article XX(g).   The Panel noted that the United States, in invoking Article XX(g) with respect to its direct import prohibition under the MMPA, had argued that the measures taken under the MMPA are measures primarily aimed at the conservation of dolphin, and that the import restrictions on certain tuna and tuna products under the MMPA are "primarily aimed at rendering effective restrictions on domestic production or consumption" of dolphin. The Panel also noted that Mexico had argued that the United States measures were not justified under the exception in Article XX(g) because, *inter alia,* this provision could not be applied extrajurisdictionally.

5.31.   The Panel noted that Article XX(g) required that the measures relating to the conservation of exhaustible natural resources be taken "in conjunction with restrictions on domestic production or consumption".   A previous panel had found that a measure could only be considered to have been taken "in conjunction with" production restrictions "if it was primarily aimed at rendering effective these restrictions".   A country can effectively control the production or consumption of an exhaustible natural resource only to the extent that the production or consumption is under its jurisdiction. This suggests that Article XX(g) was intended to permit contracting parties to take trade measures primarily aimed at rendering effective restrictions on production or consumption within their jurisdiction.

5.32. The Panel further noted that Article XX(g) allows each contracting party to adopt its own conservation policies. The conditions set out in Article XX(g) which limit resort to this exception, namely that the measures taken must be related to the conservation of exhaustible natural resources, and that they not "constitute a means of arbitrary or unjustifiable discrimination * * * or a disguised restriction on international trade" refer to the trade measure requiring justification under Article XX(g), not however to the conservation policies adopted by the contracting party. The Panel considered that if the extrajurisdictional interpretation of Article XX(g) suggested by the United States were accepted, each contracting party could unilaterally determine the conservation policies from which other contracting parties could not deviate without jeopardizing their rights under the General Agreement. The considerations that led the Panel to reject an extrajurisdictional application of Article XX(b) therefore apply also to Article XX(g).

5.33. The Panel did not consider that the United States measures, even if Article XX(g) could be applied extrajurisdictionally, would meet the conditions set out in that provision. A previous panel found that a measure could be considered as "relating to the conservation of exhaustible natural resources" within the meaning of Article XX(g) only if it was primarily aimed at such conservation. The Panel recalled that the United States linked the maximum incidental dolphin-taking rate which Mexico had to meet during a particular period in order to be able to export tuna to the United States to the taking rate actually recorded for United States fishermen during the same period. Consequently, the Mexican authorities could not know whether, at a given point of time, their conservation policies conformed to the United States conservation standards. The Panel considered that a limitation on trade based on such unpredictable conditions could not be regarded as being primarily aimed at the conservation of dolphins.

5.34. On the basis of the above considerations, the Panel found that the United States direct import prohibition on certain yellowfin tuna and certain yellowfin tuna products of Mexico directly imported from Mexico, and the provisions of the MMPA under which it is imposed, could not be justified under Article XX(g).

* * *

6. CONCLUDING REMARKS

6.1. The Panel wished to underline that its task was limited to the examination of this matter "in the light of the relevant GATT provisions", and therefore did not call for a finding on the appropriateness of the United States' and Mexico's conservation policies as such.

6.2. The Panel wished to note the fact, made evident during its consideration of this case, that the provisions of the General Agreement impose few constraints on a contracting party's implementation of domestic environmental policies. The Panel recalled its findings in paragraphs 5.10–5.16 above that under these provisions, a contracting party is free to tax or regulate imported products and like domestic products as long as its taxes or regulations do not discriminate against imported products or afford protection to domestic producers, and a contracting party is also free to tax or regulate domestic production for environmental purposes. As a corollary to these rights, a contracting party may not restrict imports of a product merely because it originates in a country with environmental policies different from its own.

AMERICAN SOCIETY OF INTERNATIONAL LAW ENVIRONMENTAL INTEREST GROUP NEWSLETTER

Vols. 3(1), 6 (1992).*

Turtle/Shrimp Case—On July 16, 1992, U.S. District Judge Vukasin of the Northern District of California dismissed *Earth Island Institute v. Baker*. The case was based on P.L. 101–162, section 609, which calls upon the Executive to negotiate with foreign governments to protect sea turtles and to embargo imports of shrimp and shrimp products from countries whose governments do not maintain programs comparable to the U.S. programs to protect certain species of sea turtles from incidental mortality in the course of shrimp trawl fishing. Earth Island Institute argued that the USG had failed to initiate negotiations and had failed to implement the embargo provisions properly, by limiting the provisions to the Wider Caribbean Region and giving governments in that region a three-year phase-in period. The Court found that (1) the issue of whether Congress can compel the Executive to enter into international negotiations is a non-justiciable political question, and (2) the U.S. Court of International Trade (CIT) has exclusive jurisdiction over the claim relating to the statutorily-mandated trade embargo. The Court did not reach the issue of whether, in light of the Supreme Courts' decision in *Defenders of Wildlife* Earth Island Institute has standing. This case presents similar issues to the "tuna/dolphin" case (*Earth Island Institute v. Mosbacher*) extracted below.

EARTH ISLAND INSTITUTE v. MOSBACHER

929 F.2d 1449 (9th Cir.1991) (footnotes omitted).

OPINION

SCHROEDER, Circuit Judge:

The government appeals from a preliminary injunction entered October 19, 1990, which enjoined the importation of yellowfin tuna from Mexico. The plaintiffs who sought the injunction are the Earth Island Institute, the Marine Mammal Protection Fund and David Brower, environmentalist (collectively termed "Earth Island"), all concerned with the enforcement of the Marine Mammal Protection Act ("MMPA"

* Reprinted with the permission of the American Society of International Law.

or "Act"). Congress amended the MMPA in 1988 to enhance protections for dolphins that were being killed in large numbers as a result of tuna fishing. *See* 16 U.S.C. §§ 1361–1407; *Caribbean Marine Servs. Co. v. Baldrige,* 844 F.2d 668, 670 (9th Cir.1988). The district court granted the injunction because it concluded that the Secretary of Commerce had not made a positive finding, as required by the Act, that Mexico had met the applicable standards regarding the incidental killing of dolphins. We affirm.

Congress enacted the MMPA in 1972 to address, among other problems, the tremendous number of dolphins killed by the purse-seine method of fishing for yellowfin tuna in the eastern tropical Pacific Ocean. For unknown reasons, yellowfin tuna swim below schools of dolphins in that area. Thus, fishing vessels often set their purse-seine nets on dolphins to catch the tuna below. The dolphins are frequently killed or maimed in this process. In the early 1970s, the United States fishing fleet was responsible for the slaughter of over 300,000 dolphins annually. 134 Cong.Rec.S. 16336, 16344–45 (1988).

Although the Act brought about a material reduction in the number of dolphins killed by the United States fleet, dolphin slaughter by foreign nations remained a growing problem. By amendments to the Act in 1984 and 1988, Congress enacted specific standards intended to ensure that foreign tuna fishing fleets would reduce the number of dolphins killed and to protect certain endangered subspecies of dolphins. Such subspecies included the eastern spinner dolphin which is the subject of this lawsuit. The weapon Congress chose to bring about such reductions in killings was a mandatory embargo on the importation of yellowfin tuna to be imposed upon those countries whose fleets failed to meet the standards Congress established.

The statute mandates the Secretary of the Treasury to ban imports of yellowfin tuna products from a foreign nation until the Secretary of Commerce certifies that that nation's incidental kill rate of dolphins is comparable to that of the United States. The statute specifies that the total incidental kill rate of a foreign nation shall not be found comparable unless it is no more than 2.0 times the total incidental kill rate of the United States fleet. 16 U.S.C. § 1371(a)(2)(B)(ii)(II). With respect to the eastern spinner dolphin, the statute additionally provides that the total number of eastern spinner dolphins killed by a foreign fleet cannot exceed fifteen percent of the total number of mammals killed by the fleet of that country. 16 U.S.C. § 1371(a)(2)(B)(ii)(III).

The portion of the statute with which we must be concerned provides as follows: "The Secretary of the Treasury shall ban the importation of commercial fish or products from fish which have been caught with commercial fishing technology which results in the incidental kill or incidental serious injury of ocean mammals in excess of United States standards. For purposes of applying the preceding sentence, the Secretary. * * * "

* * *

(B) in the case of yellowfin tuna harvested with purse-seines in the eastern tropical Pacific Ocean, and products therefrom, to be exported to the United States, shall require that the government of the exporting nation provide documentary evidence that—

* * *

(ii) the average rate of that incidental taking by the vessels of the harvesting nation is comparable to the average rate of incidental taking of marine mammals by United States vessels in the course of such harvesting, except that the Secretary shall not find that the regulatory program, or the average rate of incidental taking by vessels, of a harvesting nation is comparable to that of the United States for purposes of clause (i) or (ii) of this paragraph unless—

* * *

(II) the average rate of the incidental taking by vessels of the harvesting nation is no more than 2.0 times that of United States vessels during the same period by the end of the 1989 fishing season and no more than 1.25 times that of U.S. vessels during the same period by the end of the 1990 fishing season and thereafter;

(III) *the total number of eastern spinner dolphin (Stenella longirostris) incidentally taken by vessels of the harvesting nation during the 1989 and subsequent fishing seasons does not exceed 15 percent of the total number of all marine mammals incidentally taken by such vessels in such year* * * *.

16 U.S.C. § 1371(a)(2) (emphasis supplied). The statute authorizes the National Marine Fisheries Service ("NMFS" or "agency") to promulgate regulations implementing its provisions. 16 U.S.C. §§ 1373 & 1382.

This dispute arises from a NMFS regulation promulgated March 26, 1990. This regulation provides that foreign countries must supply data to the NMFS by July 31 of each year regarding the number of dolphins killed during the previous calendar year. Thus, on July 31, 1990, data was due for 1989. 50 C.F.R. § 216.24(e)(5)(iv). The controversial portion of the regulation is the further provision that if a foreign nation has exceeded the limitations for a given year, and therefore remains under the embargo, the Secretary may nevertheless "reconsider" the embargo and certify compliance with the statute's provisions based upon data for only the first six months following the year the limits were exceeded.

The events giving rise to the preliminary injunction in this appeal are as follows. On June 25, 1990, Earth Island filed its first motion for a preliminary injunction in the federal district court for the Northern District of California. Earth Island sought an "interim" embargo which would enjoin the importation of yellowfin tuna products pending NMFS' issuance of the comparability findings required by the MMPA as to the total number of dolphins killed and the percentage of eastern spinner dolphins killed by foreign fleets fishing for yellowfin tuna. Earth Island argued that, by the plain terms of the MMPA, an embargo was mandatory and the agency could not authorize imports until the requisite comparability findings were made; therefore, it argued, the agency was required to impose an embargo until after the relevant data had been reviewed. The agency countered that it needed several months to compile and analyze data from the previous year and the MMPA did not require it to take action until it had done so.

On August 28, 1990, the district court granted the preliminary injunction, on the ground that the agency had not made the finding required with respect to total kill comparability. On September 6 the government ostensibly imposed the embargo ordered by the district court. The very next day, however, NMFS made the required comparability findings and lifted the embargo for Mexico, despite the fact that Mexico had exceeded the limits for both total dolphins killed and percentage of eastern spinner dolphins killed for 1989. NMFS based its decision to lift the ban on the reconsideration regulation at issue here. On the same day that NMFS determined that Mexico had exceeded the MMPA limits for 1989, it also determined that Mexico was within the limits on killing eastern spinner dolphins for the first six months of 1990. It is difficult to understand how the government could issue a favorable determination in this case in less than two weeks when it had previously argued that it needed at least six months to collect and analyze data from foreign nations.

On September 17, 1990, Earth Island applied for a temporary restraining order banning the import of yellowfin tuna from Mexico. Earth Island argued that NMFS had already found that Mexico had violated the eastern spinner kill comparability requirements for 1989, and that, under the plain language of the statute, the comparability finding for the eastern spinner dolphin limit must be based on an entire year of data.

On October 4, 1990, the district court granted the TRO. The district court held that the regulation allowing "reconsideration" of the 1989 embargo based on only six months of 1990 data violated the language and purpose of the statute and was thus beyond the agency's authority. See *Chevron U.S.A., Inc. v. Natural Resources Defense Council, Inc.,* 467 U.S. 837, 842–43 (1984). The district court held that a year's data were required by the clear language of subsection III: "The Secretary of the Treasury *shall ban* the importation of * * * yellowfin tuna * * * *unless* * * * the total number of eastern spinner dolphins (Stenella longirostris) incidentally taken by vessels of the harvesting nation during the *1989* and subsequent *fishing seasons* does not exceed 15 percent of the total number of all marine mammals incidentally taken by such vessels in *such year.*" Since the comparability finding for eastern spinner dolphins must be based on an entire year of data, and the limit was exceeded for 1989, the most recent year for which data were [sic] available, the court concluded that the embargo required by the 1989 data had to remain in effect until an evaluation of the data for all of 1990 demonstrated that the kills fell within the tolerated limits established by Congress.

On October 19, 1990, the court, at the government's request, converted the TRO into a preliminary injunction, and the government filed this appeal. The government challenges the district court's order on several grounds. The questions presented are essentially questions of law involving interpretation of the MMPA. Because we see no basis for overturning the district court's ruling, we affirm.

The government's primary argument is that the six-month "reconsideration" provision is within the discretion delegated by Congress to the agency for regulatory implementation of the Act. The government points to the deference the courts owe to agencies in matters of statutory interpretation. See, e.g., *Chevron,* 467 U.S. at 844 ("We have long recognized that considerable weight should be accorded to an executive department's construction of a statutory scheme it is entrusted to administer"). The difficulty with this position is that agencies do not have discretion to issue regulations which conflict with statutory language and congressional purpose. *Id.* at 842–43. This regulation clearly does.

The only textual support that the government advances for its position is the absence of any specific prohibition of "reconsideration" upon less than one year's data. The government argues that the lack of any explicit prohibition allows the agency to adopt an interpretation of the MMPA which permits such reconsideration. We reject this argument because the statute does require findings to be based on a full year's data. As the district court recognized, the language of the statute is clear; it requires an embargo unless "the total number of eastern spinner dolphins (Stenella longirostris) incidentally taken by vessels of the harvesting nation *during the 1989 and subsequent fishing seasons* does not exceed 15 percent of the total number of all marine mammals incidentally taken by such vessels *in such year.*"   16 U.S.C. § 1371(a)(2)(B)(ii)(III) (emphasis added); see also Marine Mammal Protection Act Amendments of 1988, S.Rep. No. 592, 100th Cong., 2d Sess. 6 (1988) [hereinafter S.Rep. No. 100–592] (referring to "annual quota" of dolphins killed). In the face of such a clear directive, the regulation in question is invalid.

The government also suggests that regardless of the language used in the statute, the reconsideration provision should be upheld as a matter of policy because it offers an incentive to foreign countries to speed up their efforts to meet the statutory standards. The record in this case belies the existence of any incentive effect. The record demonstrates that the six-month reconsideration allows foreign nations and NMFS to withhold the release of negative findings until they have available a subsequent set of positive findings, as occurred with the 1989–90 data for Mexico. The result in this case was that Mexico, which had exceeded MMPA standards for an entire year, was subject to embargo for less than one day. Under this regulation, foreign nations could thus continually exceed MMPA limits for part of each year, yet never be subject to the ban. Because the reconsideration regulation creates such potential for abuse, and has in fact already been used to circumvent the intent of Congress, we reject the government's argument that the reconsideration regulation offers a more effective incentive to foreign countries to reduce dolphin kill rates.

The agency's contention that it seeks only to provide additional incentives consistent with Congress' intent is further belied by the agency's own record of non-enforcement of congressional directives during the years which preceded the 1988 amendments. In enacting those amendments, Congress expressed its concern that the NMFS was not holding foreign vessels to U.S. dolphin protection standards. The agency's lax record of promulgating and enforcing standards for foreign fleets was alluded to repeatedly in the legislative history. The Senate Committee on Commerce, Science & Transportation pointed out that "[w]hile the U.S. industry has made dramatic improvements since enactment of the MMPA, unregulated tuna fleets of foreign nations now present a far more serious source of porpoise mortality." S.Rep. 100–592 at 7. The Senate Committee also stated:

> While the Committee is disappointed that the interim final regulations implementing the 1984 comparability amendments to the Act were issued only recently, it expects that these new amendments will be incorporated into the final regulations immediately. Recognizing that the foreign fleets harvest 60 percent of the yellowfin tuna in the [eastern Tropical Pacific] but kill 80 percent of the porpoise, the Committee intends these new requirements to reduce the foreign take of marine mammals, similar to those reductions made by the U.S. fleet. Individual members of Congress were more severe in their criticism of NMFS' performance. Senator Hollings, referring to the 1984 amendments, said, "[T]he national marine fisheries service has failed to implement these requirements adequately." According to Senator Adams, "[T]he administration has been inexcusably lax in implementing these laws." There is no basis in the history of the enforcement of the Act for us to conclude that the agency's policies are aimed at more stringent enforcement of Congressional policy.

Because the government's position is at odds with both the language and the purpose of MMPA, and the agency's intended role under it, we affirm the district court's order of October 4. AFFIRMED.

CANADA'S OBJECTIVES MET IN THE NORTH AMERICAN AGREEMENT ON ENVIRONMENTAL CO-OPERATION AND THE NORTH AMERICAN AGREEMENT ON LABOUR CO-OPERATION

Government of Canada, News Release, No. 157, August 13, 1993.

* * * The agreements aim to settle disputes through co-operation. But where countries fail to enforce their labour and environmental laws and do not correct the problem, they may be subject to fines paid into special environmental and labour funds. In Canada, fines will be enforced by domestic courts. The United States and Mexico, on the other hand, will face suspension of NAFTA benefits based on the size of the penalty. This could be in the form of a duty or trade sanction.

* * * The precedent-setting agreements commit all three countries to close and ongoing co-operation on a broad variety of environmental

and labour issues.   These agreements build upon the already strong commitments to work together that were negotiated in the North American Free Trade Agreement (NAFTA).   The NAFTA and the side agreements are scheduled to come into force on January 1, 1994.

The agreements mark the first time that developed nations have pledged to work with a developing country on common environmental and labour goals in conjunction with a trade agreement.   The agreements are based on the premise of domestic enforcement of domestic laws.   The side agreements respect each country's sovereignty as well as provincial jurisdiction.

Canada negotiated the side agreement on environmental co-operation to create a Commission on Environmental Co-operation; strengthen environmental co-operation among Canada, the United States and Mexico; address and resolve disputes; promote sustainable development; and increase co-operation in the development and enforcement of environmental regulations.

The Commission will promote a work plan based on priority areas, including limits on specific pollutants, assessing projects with transboundary implications and reciprocal court access.   As well, the Commission will co-operate with the Free Trade Commission to achieve the environmental goals of the NAFTA.   * * *

----

1. *Endangered species.*   As discussed in Section A.11 international trade in endangered species is governed by the Convention on International Trade in Endangered Species of Wild Fauna and Flora, 993 U.S.T.S. 243.

2. *Hazardous Wastes.*   International trade in hazardous wastes is restricted by the Basel Convention on the Control of Transboundary Movements of Hazardous Wastes and their Disposal, 28 ILM 657 (1989). Note also the 1991 Organization of African Unity Bamako Convention on the Ban of the Import into Africa and the Control of Transboundary Movement and Management of Hazardous Wastes Within Africa, 30 ILM 775 (1991) and the Canada–United States Agreement concerning the Transboundary Movement of Hazardous Waste, T.I.A.S. 11099. (See G. Handl and R. Lutz, Transferring Hazardous Technologies and Substances (1989)).   Also, the Montreal Protocol on Substances that Deplete the Ozone Layer, 26 ILM 1541 (1987), considered in Section A.4, imposes trade restrictions on non-state parties.

14.   THE PROTECTION OF THE ENVIRONMENT IN TIME OF ARMED CONFLICT

The Iraq–Kuwait armed conflict, discussed in Chapter 16 illustrated the use of the environment as a weapon of war, in that intentionally millions of barrels of oil were spilled into the Persian Gulf and hundreds of oil wells were set alight by the Iraqi forces.   Not only have the waters of the Gulf been affected but the atmosphere and the wildlife in the area.

The question that remains is whether international humanitarian law as it exists is sufficient to the task of criminalizing such behaviour or whether a new fifth Geneva convention is necessary. Refer to Protocol I to the four Geneva Conventions 1949, 16 ILM 1391 (1977), and the 1977 Convention on the Prohibition of Military or Any Other Hostile Use of Environmental Modification Techniques, 31 U.S.T.S. 333 (1977) contained in the Documentary Supplement.

ENVIRONMENT AND HUMANITARIAN PROTECTION

A. KISS AND D. SHELTON, INTERNATIONAL ENVIRONMENTAL LAW

29–30 (1991) (footnotes omitted).*

* * * Related to the right to environment are the humanitarian protections afforded during periods of armed conflict. These protections have become increasingly important as technology offers destructive forces of unprecedented scope. In addition, activities hazardous during peacetime become even more so during armed conflict and can seriously affect states not parties to the hostilities. Finally, there is an additional relationship between armed conflict and the environment which must be recognized: growing shortages of natural resources caused by waste and environmental damage in fact may lead to conflict and cause further destruction. Each of these problems is glaringly evident in the recent Persian Gulf conflict.

It is a long-standing principle that "the right of belligerents to adopt means of injuring the enemy is not unlimited." Among the most common norms of humanitarian law are those prohibiting destruction of or damage to forests, orchards, fruit trees or vines, and those forbidding the poisoning of wells, springs, and rivers. More recently, general prohibitions on environmental damage have been enacted. Thus, the 1977 Protocols to the 1949 Geneva Conventions ban employing methods or means of warfare which are intended, or may be expected, to cause wide-spread, long-term and severe damage to the natural environment. Similarly, an Environmental Modification Convention [31 U.S.T. 333, T.I.A.S. 9614, 16 ILM 88 (1977)] adopted in 1977, provides in article 1.1 that each state party undertakes not to engage in military or any other hostile use of environmental modification techniques having widespread, long-lasting or severe effects as the means of destruction, damage or injury to any other state party. Article 2 defines environmental modification techniques as "any technique for changing—through the deliberate manipulation of natural processes—the dynamics, composition or structure of the earth, including its biota, lithosphere, hydrosphere and atmosphere, or of outer space." Finally, the 1981 Inhuman Weapon Convention [19 ILM 1523 (1980)] prohibits making forests or other kinds of plant cover the object of attack by incendiary weapons except when such natural elements are used to cover, conceal or camouflage

* Reprinted with the permission of Transnational Publisher's Inc.

combatants or other military objectives, or are themselves military objectives.

G. PLANT, INTRODUCTION AND ELEMENTS OF A "FIFTH GENEVA" CONVENTION ON THE PROTECTION OF THE ENVIRONMENT IN TIME OF ARMED CONFLICT

in G. Plant (ed.) Environmental Protection and the Law of War, 17–18, 37–42 (1992) (footnotes omitted).*

The common ground on the law of war may be stated as follows:

1. The law of war has been concerned with environmental protection since ancient times at least in the sense of prohibiting wanton destruction of forests, orchards, fruit trees and vines and forbidding the poisoning of wells, springs and rivers.

2. Deliberate and wanton destruction of the environment in circumstances where no legitimate military objective is served is contrary to international law.

3. The principle of proportionality between means and methods employed in an attack and the military objective sought to be attained by it, the prohibition against military operations not directed against legitimate military targets, the prohibition against the destruction of enemy property not imperatively demanded by the necessities of war and other well established principles of customary international law have the indirect effect of protecting the environment in many wartime situations.

4. The Martens Clause, as formulated in its most modern version in Protocol I, reads as follows:

    In cases not covered by this Protocol or by other international agreements, civilians and combatants remain under the protection and authority of the principles of international law derived from established custom, from the principles of humanity and from the dictates of public conscience.

    Thus the customary law of war, in reflecting the modern increase in concern for the environment as one of the dictates of public conscience in the sense understood in that Clause, now includes a requirement to avoid unjustifiable damage to the environment.

5. Violations of Article 23(g) of the Regulations attached to the Hague Convention of 1907 (IV) Respecting the Laws and Customs of War on Land, or of Article 53 of the 1949 Geneva Convention (IV) Relative to the Protection of Civilian Persons in Time of War, which prohibit destruction by an Occupying Power of enemy property not required by military necessity, give rise to civil liability. Wanton destruction is considered a grave breach, for which individual criminal responsibility can be attributed by virtue of Article 147 of the latter Convention.

* Reprinted with the permission of Bellhaven Press.

6. States should ensure the wide dissemination and effective imple-
    mentation of their existing obligations under the law of armed
    conflict as they may be relevant to the protection of the environ-
    ment, as well as proper instruction of the military in their
    application. They should be adequately incorporated into mili-
    tary manuals and rules of engagement, in particular, through
    instructions to military commanders on the planning and prepa-
    ration of military activities.

* * *

The deliberate, massive environmental damage in the recent Gulf
conflict calls for a distinct instrument on the laws of war and the
environment.

It seems desirable to include in this clear statements on the relevant
rules of customary law concerning, *inter alia,* state responsibility and
international criminal law.

It seems desirable in this connection to bring the laws of war up to
date to reflect major developments in international environmental law as
it applies in time of peace.

It also seems desirable to improve existing Geneva and Hague law to
afford greater protection to the environment. It is necessary to establish
a specific threshold of protection.

This calls for a new Convention, rather than a Protocol to the
existing Geneva Conventions, because it essentially marks a new departure within Geneva law.

It is appropriate at this initial juncture to await developments in
disarmament fora and elsewhere before seeking to regulate in such a
new instrument the use or first use of nuclear weapons and other
weapons of mass destruction.

Consideration should be given to the possibility of the establishment
of a rapid response body which could carry out in the environmental
field functions similar to that of the Red Cross/Crescent in the humanitarian field, including acting as a Protecting Power for the Environment.

It will be difficult to define 'environment' for these purposes. The
main problem is to distinguish attacks upon humans and their environment from attacks upon the environment as such, in so far as this is a
meaningful distinction. Similarly it will be difficult to determine the
degree of damage to the environment warranting regulation or prohibition.

* * *

The outrage felt at Iraq's actions alone arguably makes it desirable
for the international community to mark in a new instrument the
concern that in future the need to give protection to the *environment* as
such in time of armed conflict should be *explicitly* catered for, if only in
relation to deliberate environmental damage. This is so even if it is
agreed that Iraq's actions were already proscribed by customary or
treaty norms, since the existing relevant norms do not address them-

selves to the environmental impact of the destruction so much as to the indiscriminate and excessive nature of damage to enemy *property*. Most existing norms which might be construed to apply to environmental damage do not expressly mention the environment.

It is also arguably no longer sufficient to rely on the fact that the environment as such *is* expressly protected in the odd provision in one or two instruments, such as Article 35(3) of Additional Protocol I to the Geneva Conventions (Protocol I), especially when the efficacy of those provisions is seriously in doubt.

In addition, there is growing evidence that the prohibition of actions like those in question either is or is developing into a norm of international criminal law. It seems desirable to state this clearly in an international instrument.

This is not the first time that the environment has been blatantly abused in time of armed conflict, but it is perhaps the first time that the facts have been broadcast on such a wide scale. An unscrupulous leader, moreover, is more likely to have increasing destructive possibilities for causing such harm at his disposal as the world moves to more and more intensive exploitation of natural resources and energy sources.

As regards collateral damage to the environment, two matters might suggest the need, at the very least, to update existing Geneva and Hague law to improve the protection afforded to the environment, notwithstanding that many areas of this body of law were re-examined and improved upon during the decade commencing in 1970. Those improvements, after all, were made largely for humanitarian rather than environment-protection purposes. First, the 1980s and early 1990s have seen the development of new generations of weapons systems, which are available in varying degrees to military establishments worldwide; many of these pose an enhanced threat to the environment either by their very nature or in circumstances where they are used intensively or indiscriminately. Second, those years have also seen an environmentally significant diversification of military options in relation to possible targets, in two senses: that new weapons systems might be taken to make possible (and 'legitimize') precision (or other) attacks against targets which it would formerly have been impracticable, or even unlawful, to attack, in such a way as to increase the risk of damage to the environment; and that the number of targets, such as nuclear-power stations, chemical facilities and high dams, the destruction of which might result in environmental disaster, has grown greatly. The Chernobyl disaster is a sobering indication of the potential effects of a strike against the core of a nuclear reactor in time of armed conflict, when evacuation and other response measures will be even more difficult than they are in peacetime.

This document, therefore, suggests improvements mainly in the Geneva law, but also in the Hague law, which cannot be entirely separated from Geneva law, as is illustrated by Protocol I itself. It calls for a new Convention, rather than a Protocol to the existing Geneva Conventions because it essentially marks a new departure within Geneva law, rather than an improvement upon an existing corpus of law. The author is conscious of the many fora in which the laws of war are dealt with. If it is felt that this document contains too much Hague law, it is suggested that to that extent the regulation of weapons systems might be pursued with a view to environmental protection within the review processes set upon under the various relevant conventions.

It is a trite proposition, too, that both Geneva law and Hague law are in practice closely connected with the law of disarmament. It is, for example, much easier to regulate attacks upon targets or the use of certain weapons in armed conflicts, if those weapons are not being developed, tested or stockpiled or have not already been used in practice by armed forces. Improvement of the Geneva law, moreover, is frequently the first step in movements towards disarmament measures. The author is aware that disarmament negotiations are proceeding in various fora on various types of weapons and does not wish the round table conference to prejudice those negotiations.

It follows that, while nuclear and other weapons of mass destruction, for example, should properly be regulated by any new Geneva law instrument concerning the environment, being obvious examples of weapons which, if used, seriously threaten the environment, it is, in the author's view, appropriate at this initial juncture to await developments elsewhere before seeking to regulate or further regulate in such a new instrument the use or first use of such weapons. This is certainly true of nuclear weapons, which form part of the deterrent forces of a number of states and are stockpiled in vast numbers; disarmament measures are likely to be far more important than Geneva law measures in their case. However, it might be that participants will consider that a provision or provisions concerning chemical, biological and other toxin weapons, the stockpiling of which is much less acceptable among the vast majority of states, should be included in a new instrument.

In this context, too, it is recognized that over-strict attempts to regulate weaponry and targetry in an indirect attempt to induce disarmament raises the danger of bringing the law into disregard, given the capacities of modern weaponry, and to weaken its legal and moral force. It is, therefore, necessary to seek a realistic threshold of regulation. What is clear is that this threshold should be expressed in specific, * * * terms; it must have a real impact, at least sufficient to cover the excesses in the Gulf conflict, and not merely seek to prohibit or regulate weaponry or targetry which in practical terms is unlikely to be used.

A third reason for the consideration of a new instrument governing the laws of war and the environment is the desirability of updating the laws of war to reflect major developments in international environmental law as it applies in time of peace. Changes in state practice and the adoption of a large number of international environmental law instruments since the 1970s have reinforced the establishment or imminent emergence of a number of principles and norms of international law. Few of the international instruments refer expressly to their application in time of armed conflict, and the precise applicability of the norms and principles at such times is not clear. Nevertheless, a number, if not all, of them have potential applications at such time too. They include: the principle that states are responsible for ensuring that activities within their jurisdiction or control do not cause damage to the environment of other states or of areas beyond the limits of national jurisdiction; (possibly) a duty to carry out an environmental impact assessment prior to such activities; requirements of notification of such activities and (possibly) of consultation with affected states; (possibly) the application of the precautionary principle to such activities; and requirements to warn neighbouring states when an injurious transboundary escape in fact takes place. A new 'Geneva' convention could be used to clarify their application in wartime. Even taking into account the difficulties surrounding the practical application of several of these principles and norms in peacetime, their application in time of armed conflict might have useful consequences, especially upon the geographical limitation of the effects of such conflict.

A number of states, inter-governmental and non-governmental organizations have been involved in trying to put out the burning oil-wells and clean up the pollution in the Gulf region following the recent conflict. With all due respect to their valiant efforts and cooperation through existing coordinating structures, the response has been both improvized and delayed by the absence of a neutral body with access to the war zone during the conflict. The possibility of establishing a rapid response body which could also be accepted as a sort of Protecting Power for the Environment and could perhaps carry out other functions parallel to those of the ICRC and/or League of the Red Cross and Red Crescent Societies in the humanitarian field, called perhaps the 'Green Cross/Crescent', ought to be considered.

Finally, the author makes no attempt to define the term 'environment'. Many have failed in this difficult venture. A definition is not, however, a unique problem in this context; it has not always been easy to find a workable distinction between civilians and combatants. A new 'Geneva' Convention would clearly be concerned with: damage to the marine environment as a whole and marine wildlife and habitats in particular; pollution of the atmosphere, destructive climate modification, enhanced global warming and degradation of the ozone layer; and the destruction or degradation of terrestrial fauna and flora and their habitats. It should take an ecosystems approach.

Difficulties will be encountered in defining what amounts to destruction or degradation and what degrees of destruction or degradation warrant regulation or prohibition under a new Convention. Particularly strict protection would be justified, for example, of areas of special vulnerability or importance in aesthetic, evolutionary (biodiversity) or other similar terms.

Perhaps the greatest difficulty, however, is posed by the fact that man and many of his works form part of the environment. It is accordingly very difficult to determine whether or not, for example, attacks on the means of survival of human populations themselves, such as attacks upon agricultural land or harvested forest or attacks which result in the spread of malnutrition or disease among humans as well as animals or plants, should always be considered as attacks upon the environment. If all attacks which cause human suffering were treated as attacks upon the environment for these purposes, the result would be absurdity; a dividing line must be found.

Similar considerations might also be applied to attacks upon culturally important sites and monuments. No provision is included concerning these, because they are already protected by the Hague Convention for the Protection of Cultural Property in the Event of Armed Conflict 1954 and by provisions in Protocol I. If such a provision were added to a new Convention, it would only make sense if it were intended to remove the exception to the prohibition of attacks on such objects on grounds of military necessity.

DRAFT CODE OF CRIMES AGAINST THE PEACE AND SECURITY OF MANKIND

REPORT OF THE INTERNATIONAL LAW COMMISSION ON THE WORK OF ITS 44TH SESSION

29 July–19 July, 1991 U.N. GAOR 46th Session Supp. No. 10 (A/46/10), 198, 268–273.

Article 22
Exceptionally Serious War Crimes

1. An individual who commits or orders the commission of an exceptionally serious war crime shall, on conviction thereof, be sentenced [to * * *].

2. For the purposes of this Code, an exceptionally serious war crime is an exceptionally serious violation of principles and rules of international law applicable in armed conflict consisting of any of the following acts: * * *

> (d) employing methods of means of warfare which are intended or may be expected to cause widespread, long-term and severe damage to the natural environment;

Commentary

(1) This draft article is a compromise between one trend in the Commission towards a general definition of war crimes unaccompanied by a detailed list of crimes and an enumeration of the categories of such crimes, and another trend which, without prejudice to a general definition, was in favour of including as detailed a list as possible of all war crimes covered by the article. The Commission therefore opted for a middle-ground solution which, in the chapeau of paragraph 2 sets out a general definition of war crimes covered by the draft Code, a definition followed by an exhaustive enumeration of the categories of war crimes concerned.

(2) It should be emphasized that the war crimes covered by the draft article are not all war crimes in the traditional sense, nor are they all grave breaches covered by the relevant common articles of the 1949 Geneva Conventions * * * or any of the grave breaches covered by Protocol I Additional to the Geneva Conventions (art. 85). Faithful to the criterion that the draft Code should cover only the most serious

among the most serious of crimes, the Commission therefore selected, on the basis of the criterion of exceptional seriousness, violations of international law applicable in armed conflicts that should be crimes under a code of this nature. Hence, the fact that a particular war crime in the traditional sense under humanitarian law or a grave breach within the meaning of the Geneva Conventions or the Additional Protocol is not covered by the present draft article as a crime against the peace and security of mankind in no way affects the fact that they are crimes under international law applicable in armed conflicts: as the beginning of the chapeau of paragraph 2 clearly indicates, the concept of a war crime enunciated in the article applies only for the purposes of the Code.

(3) A war crime, within the meaning of the draft article, necessarily entails: (a) that the act constituting a crime falls within any one of the six categories in paragraph 2(a) to (f); (b) that the act is a violation of principles and rules of international law applicable in armed conflicts; (c) that the violation is exceptionally serious. It is the combination of these three elements that transforms an act or an omission into a war crime for the purposes of the draft Code.

(4) The expression "violation of principles and rules of international law applicable in armed conflict" is a shorter form of the definition contained in article 2(b) of Protocol I Additional to the Geneva Conventions. In addition, the words "armed conflict" cover not only international armed conflicts within the meaning of article 1, paragraph 4, of Protocol I Additional to the Geneva Conventions but also non-international armed conflicts covered by article 3 common to the four 1949 Geneva Conventions.

(5) The term "exceptionally serious" violation in the chapeau of paragraph 2 * * * indicate[s], as already pointed out above, the specific nature of the war crimes covered by the Code. The seriousness of the violation is marked, to a great extent, by the seriousness of the effects of the violation. * * *

The wording of <u>subparagraph (d)</u>, concerning the employment of methods or means of warfare which are intended or may be expected to cause widespread, long-term and severe damage to the natural environment is taken, word for word, from article 35, paragraph 3, and article 55 of Protocol I Additional to the Geneva Conventions. As to the definition of the concept of natural environment and protected objects deriving from that concept, reference is made to the commentary to article 26 of the draft Code, concerning wilful and severe damage to the environment. It should be noted that, in addition to the provisions in question in Protocol I, the Convention on the Prohibition of Military or Any Other Hostile Use of Environmental Modification Techniques, adopted by the General Assembly on 10 December 1976, prohibits military or any other hostile use of environmental modification techniques having widespread, long-lasting or severe effects, as a means of destruction, damage or injury to another party to the conflict. The Convention covers such techniques as changes in atmospheric conditions (clouds, precipitation, cyclones and tornados), changes in climatic conditions, ocean currents, the state of the ozone layer and the ionosphere, artificial earthquakes and tsunamis and disruption of a region's ecological balance. The subparagraph speaks of widespread, long-term and severe damage. For the interpretation of this expression, reference is made to the commentary to article 26, on wilful and severe damage to the environment. In addition, it should be pointed out that, under the subparagraph, it is a crime not only to employ methods or means of warfare intended to cause the damage mentioned above but also those which may be expected to cause such damage. This latter expression covers cases in which destruction of the natural environment was not the essential aim of the user of such methods or means of warfare, but, aware of the potentially disastrous consequences of such means or methods on the environment, he none the less decided to employ them. One member made a formal reservation on subparagraph (d). * * *

1. ***Convention parties.*** At the time of the Gulf War, Iraq, the United Kingdom and the United States were not parties to Protocol I. Kuwait had acceded to it on January 17, 1985. Kuwait, the United Kingdom and the United States were parties to the Environmental modification Convention, but Iraq was not.

2. ***Security Council action.*** The United Nations Security Council Resolution 687 of 1991, 30 ILM 846 (1991) adopted by 12 votes in favour to 1 (Cuba) against with two abstentions (Ecuador and Yemen) reaffirmed that Iraq was "* * * liable under international law for any direct loss, damage, including environmental damage and the depletion of natural resources, or injury to foreign Governments, nationals and corporations, as a result of Iraq's unlawful invasion and occupation of Kuwait." (G. Plant, Environmental Protection and the Law of War (1992); Joyner and Kirkhope, the Persian Gulf War Oil Spill: Reassessing the Law of Environmental Protection and the Law of Armed Conflict, 24 Case W.Res.J.Int.L. 29 (1992)).

3. ***Work of the International Law Commission.*** Note Article 19(3)(d) of the Draft Articles on State Responsibility and Draft Article 22 of the Draft Code of Crimes Against the Peace and Security of Mankind.

15.   TRANSBOUNDARY MOVEMENT AND DISPOSAL OF HAZARDOUS WASTES

GLOBAL ENVIRONMENTAL INTERDEPENDENCE

MOSTAFA K. TOLBA, PREFACE

in B. Kwiatkowska & A.H.A. Soons (eds.), Transboundary Movements and Disposal of Hazardous Wastes in International Law, XIII–XV (1993) (footnotes omitted).*

* * *

The Basel Convention on the Control of Transboundary Movements of Hazardous Wastes and their Disposal represents new norms, rules and

* Reprinted with the permission of Martinus Nijhoff.

procedures in law governing the movement and disposal of hazardous wastes at [the] national and international level. The instrument represents the intention of the international community to solve a global environmental problem in a collective manner.

Institutionalized international cooperation was needed to address the growing amount of hazardous wastes generation, their transboundary movements and disposal. Precise estimates of world wide hazardous wastes volume are difficult to determine, but range from 300 to 400 million tons or more hazardous wastes generated each year. On average, a country who has a gross domestic product of 1 billion US dollars is likely to have to manage about 35,000 tons of hazardous wastes per year. Approximately 2.2 million tons of hazardous wastes made 100,000 border crossings in Europe in 1983. In the OECD countries, a cargo of hazardous wastes cross a national frontier more than once every five minutes.

* * *

As most hazardous wastes come from industries that are among the most important to the growth and maintenance of a modern industrial society, such as iron and steel, nonferrous or precious metals, and the chemical industry, generation of hazardous wastes would continue to be one of the major consequences of industrial development. And when a "not in my backyard" rejection accompanies the growing industrial development transboundary movements of hazardous wastes—even illegal movements—become a boom industry.

* * *

Incentives of wastes brokers are the price and regulation difference in the disposal of hazardous wastes between developing and developed countries. The problem is particularly acute in Africa, where waste disposal rates are, at highest, $40 per ton while European disposal costs are 4–25 times greater and US costs are 12–36 times greater than those in Africa. The prospect of South–South traffic—as developing countries push towards industrialization—is also likely to develop in the near future.

B. KWIATKOWSKA & A.H.A. SOONS, TRANSBOUNDARY MOVEMENTS & DISPOSAL OF HAZARDOUS WASTES IN INTERNATIONAL LAW

XXII (eds.1993) (footnotes omitted).*

* * *

The problem solving part of the question is of global and regional dimensions, as the TMHW occur both between industrialized states themselves (North–North/West–East) and from these states to developing countries (North–South). Whereas in the OECD context most TMHW take place between member states (some 100,000 such movements occurring in OECD European states and 6,000 in North America annually), the most publicized are exports from the developed to the developing states and, to a lesser extent, also those from West to East

* Reprinted with the permission of Martinus Nijhoff.

European states, both these categories of importing states not possessing environmentally sound waste disposal facilities.

* * *

Instances of the North–South TMHW were provided by incidents involving the *Khian Sea* ship subsequently renamed to the *Felicia* (carrying aboard the US incinerator ash from Philadelphia), the Nigerian *Koko* (port) dump site (wherefrom toxic wastes were subsequently removed aboard the Italian *Karin B* and *Deepsea Carrier* ships), the *Pro Ameriacana* ship (which sailed to the port of Rotterdam with the toxic wastes of Belgian, Danish and Italian origin upon refusal of their acceptance by Brazil), or the presumed instances of dumping of radioactive wastes from France and the Soviet Union in Benin.

* * *

The 1989 Basel Convention/1990 IAEA Code system [the latter deals with radioactive wastes, a lacuna in the Basel Convention] plays * * * a central role in the international regulation of the TMHW.

* * *

The main rules of the Basel Convention provide for: the sovereign right of every state to ban the import of hazardous wastes; the prohibition of export of hazardous wastes if the exporting state has reason to believe that their environmentally sound management and disposal would not be guaranteed in the prospective state of import; the prohibition of the export of hazardous wastes to a group of states belonging to an economic and/or political integration organization, particularly of developing states, which have banned imports of wastes; and the prohibition of export of hazardous wastes to non-parties and imports from non-parties, unless such export/import is in accordance with a specific treaty provided it is not less environmentally sound than the Basel Convention. The exporting state is prohibited from allowing TMHW to commence until it has given written notification (with detailed information) to the importing state in which the wastes will be disposed or recycled and until it has obtained the written consent to receive the wastes from the latter state. In cases when an importing state has given its consent, but disposal cannot be completed in an environmentally sound manner, the state of export has the duty to ensure alternative arrangements, including, if necessary, the re-importation of the wastes for domestic disposal. The optimum solution—which however, appeared so far too far-reaching for the developed states—would be to allow exports only if the wastes were to be handled and disposed in the importing state in no less strict a manner than that required in the exporting state.

The Convention declares illegal the TMHW carried out in contravention of its provisions, qualifying such movements as 'criminal'. It also commits the parties to reduce the generation of hazardous wastes to a minimum and introduces the proximity principle requiring to dispose wastes as close as possible to the source of generation. All state parties are obliged to strengthening their cooperation in order to improve and achieve the environmentally sound waste management. This duty to cooperate is primarily designed to benefit the developing countries, through: information exchange; monitoring the effects of the hazardous waste management on human health and the environment; developing and implementing new, and improving the existing, low-waste technologies; as well as transferring technology and waste management systems.

---

1. ***Work of some of the specialized agencies of the United Nations.*** Since the adoption of the Hazardous Wastes Decision by the Governing Council of UNEP in 1990, Decision 16/30 (No. 6.2.4) UNEP has focused its energy on the development of an International Strategy and an Action Programme for the Environmentally Sound Management of Hazardous Wastes. Note should also be taken of the work of the ECOSOC Committee of Experts on the Transport of Dangerous Goods and the International Maritime Organization (IMO), which seek to harmonize other global agreements with the Basel Convention. See B. Kwiatkowska and A.H.A. Soons, ibid., XL–XLVII. Also see Abrams, Regulating the International Hazardous Waste Trade, 28 Colum.J.Trans.L. 801; Mahalu, The OAU Council of Ministers Resolution on Dumping of Nuclear and Industrial Waste in Africa and the Basel Convention, 2 African J. Int'l & Comp.L. 61 and G. Handl, The 1989 Basel Convention: A Preliminary Assessment, in Proceedings of the Canadian Council on International Law 367 (1989). The 1989 Basel Convention and its Bamaco (O.A.U.) Convention are reproduced in the Documentary Supplement. The United States is not a party to Basel Convention.

2. ***UNCED and the future.*** Subsequent to the adoption of Agenda 21 the Commission on Sustainable Development, discussed infra, has been established. Part of its mandate is to address the problem of hazardous wastes and toxic chemicals.

RIO DECLARATION ON ENVIRONMENT AND DEVELOPMENT

UN Doc. A/CONF. 151/26, vol. I, 8–18 (1992).

Principle 14

States should effectively cooperate to discourage or prevent the relocation and transfer to other States of any activities and substances that cause severe environmental degradation or are found to be harmful to human health.

For a topical discussion of the controversy over the transboundary movement of hazardous wastes see the following extract:

Agence France Presse, August 11, 1993 *

World's Smallest States at Risk Over Environment

NAURU, Aug. 11 (AFP)—A gathering of some of the world's smallest nations ended here Wednesday with a loud plea for global recognition that their survival is at risk through continued environmental degradation. Prime ministers and presidents from 13 small Pacific states, plus Australia and New Zealand, ended their annual South Pacific Forum here with a communique dominated by environmental issues.

* * *

The forum said that another problem, the movement of hazardous industrial waste, could have a disastrous impact on the people and natural resources of the region. "In this context the forum noted that numerous approaches had been made to certain South Pacific Island countries by unscrupulous foreign waste dealers for the importation into, and the treatment within the region of, hazardous and other wastes produced in other countries."

The offending countries were not named in the communique, but previous reports have cited Tonga and the Marshall Islands as willing to store hazardous waste. It called on countries to adopt a London Convention amendment later this year to totally outlaw the dumping of radioactive waste at sea. The forum "expressed its grave concern over the dumping of Russian nuclear wastes into the north Pacific, called for its immediate cessation and called for retrieval of those wastes if feasible and safe."

The forum also reaffirmed "its strong commitment to sustainable development". "The vulnerability of the region to natural disasters, environmental degradation and high population growth underlined the need for careful and sustainable management in order to meet the needs of future generations," the communique said.

* * *

————

1. More opposition on the South Pacific: It was widely reported that a U.S. company's intended storage of large amounts of toxic waste on a volcanic island in Tonga triggered violent opposition by New Zealand and other nearby states. The Tongan government apparently had received an offer of $5 million per year for storing up to 35,000 barrels of waste per year on the actively volcanic island of Niuafo'ou. Reporters claimed that Tonga had referred the company's offer to its environmental experts to help them decide whether to accept the reported deal. Neighboring governments, including New Zealand protested and noted that the region's heads of state had voiced strong concern about such dumping one month prior to the report of the deal. The governments of Western Samoa and Niue expressed vigorous opposition. Niue had just previously rejected an offer to have a toxic waste incinera-

* Reprinted with the permission of Agence France Presse.

tor built on its territory. Environmentalist groups have frequently accused international industrial groups of seeking to dump their waste in areas such as the South Pacific, to avoid dumping it at home. *Reuters Business Report,* Sept. 29, 1993, *Pacific Toxic Waste Proposal Stirs Controversy.*

2. *Regional or global?* It seems that the member states of the OAU were dissatisfied with the 1989 Basel Convention, in that in their view it controlled rather than prohibited the TMHW. As Kwiatkowska and Soons, *supra,* LXXII, suggest the Bamako Convention

"largely duplicates the definitions and principles of the Basel Convention, but it provides for a total ban of imports into Africa of hazardous, including radioactive wastes from non-parties. [It] permits, thus, the intra-African TMHW between its parties and the exports from parties to non-parties (be them developed or non-African developing states). Import from a non-party is deemed illegal and a criminal act. In addition, unlike the Basel Convention, the Bamako Convention prohibits ocean dumping of hazardous wastes, including their incineration at sea and disposal in the seabed and sub-seabed * * *."

3. *The United States and its neighbours.* The United States which is the major exporter of waste in the world has agreements on TMHW with Canada (1986), TIAS 11099 and Mexico (1987), TIAS 11269 which it has been estimated import some 20% and between 74% and 85% of U.S. hazardous wastes respectively. The U.S. position is that they are specific bilateral treaties permitted by the Basel Convention, because they are compatible with its requirements for environmentally sound management of hazardous wastes. See Kwiatkowska and Soons, *ibid.,* LII. However, in the context of the U.S.–Mexico agreement, which is based on prior notification from the U.S. Environmental Protection Agency to the Mexican government of shipments of hazardous wastes to Mexico that have been generated in the United States, the same authors suggest at LXXVI that Mexico has a "lack of capacity to handle and dispose of most hazardous wastes". They suggest that Canada, Mexico and the United States should conclude a regional treaty modelled on the 1991 ECE Convention on Environmental Impact Assessment in a Transboundary Context.

4. *Antarctica.* The 1989 Basel Convention bans the export of hazardous wastes and any other wastes for disposal in Antarctica. The 1991 Madrid Protocol on Environmental Protection, 30 ILM 1455 (1991) which supplements the 1959 Antarctica Treaty, 12 U.S.T. 794, TIAS 4780, deals comprehensively with environmental protection including waste disposal in the fragile ecological setting of Antarctica. Annex III deals with waste disposal and management. The Protocol's emphasis is on the principle that what is brought to Antarctica is taken away See B. Kwiatkowska and A.H.A. Soons (eds.), Transboundary Movements of Hazardous Wastes in International Law LXXXV (1993); Francioni and Scovazzi (eds.) International Law for Antarctica (1987) and Kimball, Antarctica, 1 Yb. Int'l Env.L. 176; and 2 Yb. Int'l L. 190.

SECTION B.   EMERGING INTERNATIONAL LAW PRINCIPLES

1.   NEW IMPERATIVES FOR CO-OPERATION AMONG NATIONS AND INTERNATIONAL LAW

ENVIRONMENTAL PROTECTION AND SUSTAINABLE DEVELOPMENT, LEGAL PRINCIPLES AND RECOMMENDATIONS

JUDGE NAGENDRA SINGH, FOREWARD

in Experts Group on Environmental Law of the World Commission
on Environment and Development IX (1987).*

* * * National boundaries are now so very permeable that traditional distinctions between local, national, and international issues have become blurred.   Policies formerly considered to be exclusively matters of "national concern" now have an impact on the ecological basis of other nations' development and survival.   Conversely, the way in which the policies of certain nations—including economic, trade, monetary, and most sectoral policies—are increasingly tending to reach into the "sovereign" territory of other nations, serves to limit those nations' options in devising national solutions to their "own" problems.   This fast-changing context for national action has introduced new imperatives and new opportunities for international co-operation—and for international law.

The international legal framework needs to be significantly strengthened in support of sustainable development.   Although international law relating to the environment has evolved rapidly since the 1972 Stockholm Conference on the Human Environment, there are still major gaps and deficiencies that must be overcome as part of the transition to sustainable development.   A great deal of the evidence and conclusions presented in the report of the World Commission on Environment and Development [Our Common Future (1987)] calls into question the desirability—or even the feasibility—of maintaining an international system that cannot prevent one or more States from damaging the ecological basis for development and the very prospects for survival of other—or, possibly, all—States.

Both municipal and international law have all too frequently lagged behind events.   Today, legal regimes are being rapidly outdistanced by the accelerating pace and expanding scale of actions affecting the environmental base of development.   Human laws must be reformulated to keep human activities in harmony with the unchanging and universal laws of nature.   There is at the present time an urgent need:

- to strengthen and extend the application of existing laws and international agreements in support of sustainable development;

- to recognize and respect the reciprocal rights and responsibilities of individuals and States regarding sustainable development, and

* Reprinted with the permission of Martinus Nijhoff.

to apply new norms for State and interstate behaviour to enable this to be achieved;

● to reinforce existing methods and develop new procedures for avoiding and resolving disputes on environmental and resource management issues.

2. SUSTAINABLE DEVELOPMENT

P. BIRNIE AND A. BOYLE, INTERNATIONAL LAW AND THE ENVIRONMENT

3–6 (1992) (footnotes omitted).*

ENVIRONMENT AND DEVELOPMENT: WHAT IS "SUSTAINABLE DEVELOPMENT"?

It was perceived at the time of the Stockholm Conference that progress on environmental protection was inextricably linked, especially for developing states, with progress in economic development. The UNCHE declaration recognized this need and provided for it in several of its principles. Problems soon emerged, however, because of the political and economic implications of restricting industrial, agricultural, fisheries, and other developmental activities in order to protect the environment from pollution or to conserve resources, and although they continue to arise for all states they do so in an increasingly acute form for developing countries whose incomes are everywhere declining. Their attempts in the 1970s to create a New International Economic Order based on a Charter of Economic Rights and Duties of states were embodied in the General Assembly resolutions * * * but made no reference to and took little account of the impacts of development on the environment.

In the 1980s, however, strategies were promulgated which, though primarily aimed at environmental protection, did take account of the need for development whilst recognizing that the environment could not in all cases sustain unlimited development. The International Union for Conservation of Nature's World Conservation Strategy adopted in 1980 was premised on sustainable utilization of species and ecosystems. The World Charter for Nature adopted by the General Assembly in 1982 aimed, *inter alia,* at optimal sustainable productivity of all resources coupled with conservation and protection.

In 1987, the World Commission on Environment and Development (WCED) [Our Common Future, 43] synthesized these aims in pointing to the need to ensure 'sustainable development' and to provide mechanisms to increase international co-operation to this end. It defined 'sustainable development' as 'development that meets the needs of the present without compromising the ability of future generations to meet their own needs' and UNEP has since added that it requires 'the maintenance, rational use and enhancement of the natural resource base that underpins ecological resilience and economic growth' and 'implies prog-

* Reprinted with the permission of Oxford University Press.

ress towards international equity [UNEP Governing Council Decision 15/2, May 1989, Annex II, GAOR, 44th Session Supp. No. 25 (A/44/25)].

It follows that goals of economic and social development now have to be defined in all states in terms of sustainability. The role of law in achieving sustainable development has been little discussed but is crucial in regulating use of resources and the biosphere. New concepts are emerging such as the inherent rights or interests of future generations, of equitable utilization, and the 'precautionary principle'. The problem of achieving 'sustainable development' is, however, easier to identify than to solve and is essentially one of negotiating balanced solutions taking account of both developmental and environmental factors in the particular context of the problem at issue, and of the wider environmental impacts of possible solutions. International law cannot provide the answers to this dilemma but it can, in its constitutional role, provide mechanisms for negotiating the necessary accommodations, settling disputes, and supervising implementation of treaties and customs, and in its regulatory, prescriptive role can embody the necessary protective measures and techniques in conventions, codes, and standards, and provide flexible procedures for amending and updating these as required, in the light of technological developments and advances in scientific and other information. * * * Moreover, international law can also be used to secure harmonization and development of national environmental law, facilitate compensation for environmental damage, and provide for offences, penalties and other sanctions to be employed under national law against individuals and companies whose activities are harmful to the environment.

* * * Sustainable development is a seductively simple concept, basic to human survival and [sic] though it cannot yet be said to be a norm of international law. As one leading commentator has pointed out 'it is a notion around which legally significant expectations regarding environmental conduct have begun to crystallize' and which he considers might in time become a peremptory norm of international law (*jus cogens*). [Handl, 1 Yb. Int'l Env.L. 25 (1991).] The problems of its content, however, will remain.

———

THE BRUNDTLAND REPORT

"TOWARDS COMMON ACTION: PROPOSALS FOR INSTITUTIONAL AND LEGAL CHANGE," OUR COMMON FUTURE

World Commission on Environment and Development 308–
311, 312–314, 323–324, 330–333, 334–337 (1987)
(footnotes omitted).*

In the middle of the 20th century, we saw our planet from space for the first time. Historians may eventually find that this vision had a greater impact on thought than did the Copernican revolution of the

* Reprinted with the permission of Oxford University Press.

16th century, which upset humans' self-image by revealing that the Earth is not the centre of the universe. From space, we see a small and fragile ball dominated not by human activity and edifice but by a pattern of clouds, oceans, greenery, and soils. Humanity's inability to fit its activities into that pattern is changing planetary systems fundamentally. Many such changes are accompanied by life-threatening hazards, from environmental degradation to nuclear destruction. These new realities, from which there is no escape, must be recognized—and managed.

The issues we have raised in this report are inevitably of far-reaching importance to the quality of life on earth—indeed, to life itself. We have tried to show how human survival and well-being could depend on success in elevating sustainable development to a global ethic. In doing so, we have called for such major efforts as greater willingness and co-operation to combat international poverty, to maintain peace and enhance security world-wide, and to manage the global commons. We have called for national and international action in respect of population, food, plant and animal species, energy, industry, and urban settlements. The previous chapters have described the policy directions required.

The onus for action lies with no one group of nations. Developing countries face the challenges of desertification, deforestation, and pollution, and endure most of the poverty associated with environmental degradation. The entire human family of nations would suffer from the disappearance of rain forests in the tropics, the loss of plant and animal species, and changes in rainfall patterns. Industrial nations face the challenges of toxic chemicals, toxic wastes, and acidification. All nations may suffer from the releases by industrialized countries of carbon dioxide and of gases that react with the ozone layer, and from any future war fought with the nuclear arsenals controlled by those nations. All nations will also have a role to play in securing peace, in changing trends, and in righting an international economic system that increases rather than decreases inequality, that increases rather than decreases numbers of poor and hungry.

The time has come to break out of past patterns. Attempts to maintain social and ecological stability through old approaches to development and environmental protection will increase instability. Security must be sought through change. The Commission has noted a number of actions that must be taken to reduce risks to survival and to put future development on paths that are sustainable.

Without such reorientation of attitudes and emphasis, little can be achieved. We have no illusions about 'quick-fix' solutions. We have tried to point out some pathways to the future. But there is no substitute for the journey itself, and there is no alternative to the process by which we retain a capacity to respond to the experience it provides. We believe this to hold true in all the areas covered in this report. But the policy changes we have suggested have institutional implications, and it is to these we now turn—emphasizing that they are a complement to, not a substitute for, the wider policy changes for which we call. Nor do they represent definitive solutions, but rather first steps in what will be a continuing process.

In what follows we put forward, in the first place, what are essentially conceptual guidelines for institutions at the national level. We recognize that there are large differences among countries in respect of population size, resources, income level, management capacity, and institutional traditions; only governments themselves can formulate the changes they should make. Moreover, the tools for monitoring and evaluating sustainable development are rudimentary and require further refinement.

We also address, in more specific terms, the question of international institutions. The preceding chapters have major implications for international co-operation and reforms, both economic and legal. The international agencies clearly have an important role in making these changes effective, and we endeavour to set out the institutional implications, especially as regards the United Nations system.

I. THE CHALLENGE FOR INSTITUTIONAL AND LEGAL CHANGE

Shifting the Focus to the Policy Sources

The next few decades are crucial for the future of humanity. Pressures on the planet are now unprecedented and are accelerating at rates and scales new to human experience: a doubling of global population in a few decades, with most of the growth in cities; a five- to tenfold increase in economic activity in less than half a century; and the resulting pressures for growth and changes in agricultural, energy, and industrial systems. Opportunities for more sustainable forms of growth and development are also growing. New technologies and potentially unlimited access to information offer great promise.

Each area of change represents a formidable challenge in its own right, but the fundamental challenge stems from their systemic character. They lock together environment and development, once thought separate; they lock together 'sectors', such as industry and agriculture; and they lock countries together as the effects of national policies and actions spill over national borders. Separate policies and institutions can no longer cope effectively with these interlocked issues. Nor can nations, acting unilaterally.

The integrated and interdependent nature of the new challenges and issues contrasts sharply with the nature of the institutions that exist today. These institutions tend to be independent, fragmented, and working to relatively narrow mandates with closed decision processes. Those responsible for managing natural resources and protecting the environment are institutionally separated from those responsible for managing the economy. The real world of interlocked economic and ecological systems will not change; the policies and institutions concerned must.

This new awareness requires major shifts in the way governments and individuals approach issues of environment, development, and international co-operation. Approaches to environment policy can be broadly characterized in two ways. One, characterized as the 'standard agenda', reflects an approach to environmental policy, laws, and institutions that focuses on environmental effects. The second reflects an approach concentrating on the policies that are the sources of those effects. These two approaches represent distinctively different ways of looking both at the issues and at the institutions to manage them.

The effects-oriented 'standard agenda' has tended to predominate as a result of growing concerns about the dramatic decline in environmental quality that the industrialized world suffered during the 1950s and 1960s. New environmental protection and resource management agencies were added on to the existing institutional structures, and given mainly scientific staffs.

* * *

New Imperatives for International Co-operation

National boundaries have become so porous that traditional distinctions between local, national, and international issues have become blurred. Policies formerly considered to be exclusively matters of 'national concern' now have an impact on the ecological bases of other nations' development and survival. Conversely, the growing reach of some nations' policies—economic, trade, monetary, and most sectoral policies—into the 'sovereign' territory of other nations limits the affected nations' options in devising national solutions to their 'own' problems. This fast-changing context for national action has introduced new imperatives and new opportunities for international co-operation.

The international legal framework must also be significantly strengthened in support of sustainable development. Although international law related to environment has evolved rapidly since the 1972 Stockholm Conference, major gaps and deficiencies must still be overcome as part of the transition to sustainable development. Much of the evidence and conclusions presented in earlier chapters of this report calls into question not just the desirability but even the feasibility of maintaining an international system that cannot prevent one or several states from damaging the ecological basis for development and even the prospects for survival of any other or even all other states.

* * *

II.   PROPOSALS FOR INSTITUTIONAL AND LEGAL CHANGE

The ability to choose policy paths that are sustainable requires that the ecological dimensions of policy be considered at the same time as the economic, trade, energy, agricultural, industrial, and other dimensions— on the same agendas and in the same national and international institutions. That is the chief institutional challenge of the 1990s.

There are significant proposals for institutional and legal change in previous chapters of our report. The Commission's proposals for institutional and legal change at the national, regional, and international levels are embodied in six priority areas:

- getting at the sources,
- dealing with the effects,
- assessing global risks,
- making informed choices,

- providing the legal means, and

- investing in our future.

Together, these priorities represent the main directions for institutional and legal change needed to make the transition to sustainable development. Concerted action is needed under all six.

* * *

Assessing Global Risks

The future—even a sustainable future—will be marked by increasing risk. The risks associated with new technologies are growing. The numbers, scale, frequency, and impact of natural and human-caused disasters are mounting. The risks of irreversible damage to natural systems regionally (for example through acidification, desertification, or deforestation) and globally (through ozone layer depletion or climate change) are becoming significant.

Fortunately, the capacity to monitor and map Earth change and to assess risk is also growing rapidly. Data from remote sensing platforms in space can now be merged with data from conventional land-based sources. Augmented by digital communications and advanced information analysis, photos, mapping, and other techniques, these data can provide up-to-date information on a wide variety of resource, climatic, pollution, and other variables. High-speed data communications technologies, including the personal computer, enable this information to be shared by individuals as well as corporate and governmental users at costs that are steadily falling. Concerted efforts should be made to ensure that all nations gain access to them and the information they provide either directly or through the UNEP Earthwatch and other special programmes.

* * *

Providing the Legal Means

National and international law has traditionally lagged behind events. Today, legal regimes are being rapidly outdistanced by the accelerating pace and expanding scale of impacts on the environmental base of development. Human laws must be reformulated to keep human activities in harmony with the unchanging and universal laws of nature. There is an urgent need:

- to recognize and respect the reciprocal rights and responsibilities of individuals and states regarding sustainable development,

- to establish and apply new norms for state and interstate behaviour to achieve sustainable development,

- to strengthen and extend the application of existing laws and international agreements in support of sustainable development, and

- to reinforce existing methods and develop new procedures for avoiding and resolving environmental disputes.

Recognizing Rights and Responsibilities

Principle 1 of the 1972 Stockholm Declaration said that 'Man has the fundamental right to freedom, equality and adequate conditions of life, in an environment of a quality that permits a life of dignity and well-being'. It further proclaimed the solemn responsibility of governments to protect and improve the environment for both present and future generations. After the Stockholm Conference, several states recognized in their Constitutions or laws the right to an adequate environment and the obligation of the state to protect that environment.

Recognition by states of their responsibility to ensure an adequate environment for present as well as future generations is an important step towards sustainable development. However, progress will also be facilitated by recognition of, for example, the right of individuals to know and have access to current information on the state of the environment and natural resources, the right to be consulted and to participate in decision making on activities likely to have a significant effect on the environment, and the right to legal remedies and redress for those whose health or environment has been or may be seriously affected.

* * *

The enjoyment of any right requires respect for the similar rights of others, and recognition of reciprocal and even joint responsibilities. States have a responsibility towards their own citizens and other states:

- to maintain ecosystems and related ecological processes essential for the functioning of the biosphere;
- to maintain biological diversity by ensuring the survival and promoting the conservation in their natural habitats of all species of flora and fauna;
- to observe the principle of optimum sustainable yield in the exploitation of living natural resources and ecosystems;
- to prevent or abate significant environmental pollution or harm;
- to establish adequate environmental protection standards;
- to undertake or require prior assessments to ensure that major new policies, projects, and technologies contribute to sustainable development; and
- to make all relevant information public without delay in all cases of harmful or potentially harmful releases of pollutants, especially radioactive releases.

It is recommended that governments take appropriate steps to recognize these reciprocal rights and responsibilities. However, the wide variation in national legal systems and practices makes it impossible to propose an approach that would be valid everywhere. Some countries have amended their basic laws or constitution; others are considering the adoption of a special national law or charter setting out the rights and responsibilities of citizens and the state regarding environmental protection and sustainable development. Others may wish to consider the designation of a national council or public representative or 'ombudsman' to represent the interests and rights of present and future generations and act as an environmental watchdog, alerting governments and citizens to any emerging threats.

A Universal Declaration and a Convention on Environmental Protection and Sustainable Development

Building on the 1972 Stockholm Declaration, the 1982 Nairobi Declaration, and many existing international conventions and General Assembly resolutions, there is now a need to consolidate and extend relevant legal principles in a new charter to guide state behaviour in the transition to sustainable development. It would provide the basis for, and be subsequently expanded into, a Convention, setting out the sovereign rights and reciprocal responsibilities of all states on environmental protection and sustainable development. The charter should prescribe new norms for state and interstate behaviour needed to maintain livelihoods and life on our shared planet, including basic norms for prior notification, consultation, and assessment of activities likely to have an impact on neighbouring states or global commons. These could include the obligation to alert and inform neighbouring states in the event of an accident likely to have a harmful impact on their environment. Although a few such norms have evolved in some bilateral and regional arrangements, the lack of wider agreement on such basic rules for interstate behaviour undermines both the sovereignty and economic development potential of each and all states.

We recommend that the General Assembly commit itself to preparing a universal Declaration and later a Convention on environmental protection and sustainable development. A special negotiating group could be established to draft a Declaration text for adoption in 1988. Once it is approved, that group could then proceed to prepare a Convention, based on and extending the principles in the Declaration, with the aim of having an agreed Convention text ready for signature by states within three to five years. To facilitate the early launching of that process the Commission has submitted for consideration by the General Assembly, and as a starting point for the deliberations of the special negotiating group, a number of proposed legal principles embodied in 22 Articles that were prepared by its group of international legal experts. These proposed principles are submitted to assist the General Assembly in its deliberations and have not been approved or considered in detail by the Commission. A summary of the principles and Articles appears as Annex 1 of this report.

* * *

Investing in Our Future

We have endeavoured to show that it makes long-term economic sense to pursue environmentally sound policies. But potentially very large financial outlays will be needed in the short term in such fields as renewable energy development, pollution control equipment, and integrated rural development. Developing countries will need massive assistance for this purpose, and more generally to reduce poverty. Responding to this financial need will be a collective investment in the future.

National Action

Past experience teaches us that these outlays would be good investments. By the late 1960s, when some industrial countries began to mount significant environmental protection programmes, they had already incurred heavy economic costs in the form of damage to human health, property, natural resources, and the environment. After 1970, in order to roll back some of this damage, they saw expenditures on environmental pollution measures alone rise from about 0.3 per cent of GNP in 1970 to somewhere between 1.5 per cent and, in some countries, 2.0 per cent around the end of the decade. Assuming low levels of economic growth in the future, these same countries will probably have to increase expenditures on environmental protection somewhere between 20 to 100 per cent just to maintain current levels of environmental quality.

These figures relate only to expenditures to control environmental pollution. Unfortunately, similar figures are not available on the level of expenditures made to rehabilitate lands and natural habitats, re-establish soil fertility, reforest areas, and undertake other measures to restore the resource base. But they would be substantial.

Nations, industrial and developing, that did not make these investments have paid much more in terms of damage costs to human health, property, natural resources, and the environment. And these costs continue to rise at an accelerating pace. Indeed, countries that have not yet instituted strong programmes now face the need for very large investments. Not only do they need to roll back the first generation of environmental damage, they also need to begin to catch up with the rising incidence of future damage. If they do not, their fundamental capital assets, their environmental resources, will continue to decline.

In strictly economic terms, the benefits of these expenditures have been generally greater than the costs in those countries that have made them. Beyond that, however, many of these countries found that economic, regulatory, and other environmental measures could be applied in ways that would result in innovation by industry. And those companies that did respond innovatively are today often in the forefront of their industry. They have developed new products, new processes, and entire plants that use less water, energy, and other resources per unit of output and are hence more economic and competitive.

Nations that begin to reorient major economic and sectoral policies along the lines proposed in this report can avoid much higher future levels of spending on environmental restoration and curative measures and also enhance their future economic prospects. By making central and sectoral agencies directly responsible for maintaining and enhancing environmental and resource stocks, expenditures for environmental protection and resource management would gradually be built into the budgets of those agencies for measures to prevent damage. The unavoidable costs of environmental and resource management would thus be paid only once.

Developing countries, as stated earlier, need a significant increase in financial support from international sources for environmental restoration, protection, and improvement and to help them through the necessary transition to sustainable development.

International Action

At the global level, there is an extensive institutional capacity to channel this support. This consists of the United Nations and its specialized agencies; the multilateral development banks, notably the World Bank; other multilateral development co-operation organizations, such as those of the European Economic Community; national development assistance agencies, most of whom co-operate within the framework of the Development Assistance Committee of OECD or of the Organization of Petroleum–Exporting Countries; and other international groups, such as the Consultative Group on International Agricultural Research, that play an important role and influence on the quality and nature of development assistance. Together, the development organizations and agencies are responsible for the transfer of about $35 billion of ODA annually to developing countries. In addition, they are the source of most technical assistance and policy advice and support to developing countries.

These organizations and agencies are the principal instruments through which the development partnership between industrial and developing countries operates and, collectively, their influence is substantial and pervasive. It is imperative that they play a leading role in helping developing countries make the transition to sustainable development. Indeed, it is difficult to envisage developing countries making this transition in an effective and timely manner without their full commitment and support.

* * *

III.   A Call For Action

Over the course of this century, the relationship between the human world and the planet that sustains it has undergone a profound change. When the century began, neither human numbers nor technology had the power to radically alter planetary systems. As the century closes, not only do vastly increased human numbers and their activities have that power, but major, unintended changes are occurring in the atmosphere, in soils, in waters, among plants and animals, and in the relationships among all of these. The rate of change is outstripping the ability of scientific disciplines and our current capabilities to assess and advise. It is frustrating the attempts of political and economic institutions, which evolved in a different, more fragmented world, to adapt and cope. It deeply worries many people who are seeking ways to place those concerns on the political agendas.

We have been careful to base our recommendations on the realities of present institutions, on what can and must be accomplished today. But to keep options open for future generations, the present generation must begin now, and begin together, nationally and internationally.

To achieve the needed change in attitudes and reorientation of policies and institutions, the Commission believes that an active follow-up of this report is imperative. It is with this in mind that we call for the UN General Assembly, upon due consideration, to transform this report into a UN Programme of Action on Sustainable Development. Special follow-up conferences could be initiated at the regional level. Within an appropriate period after the presentation of the report to the General Assembly, an international Conference could be convened to review progress made and promote follow-up arrangements that will be needed over time to set benchmarks and to maintain human progress within the guidelines of human needs and natural laws.

The Commissioners came from 21 very different nations. In our discussions, we disagreed often on details and priorities. But despite our widely differing backgrounds and varying national and international responsibilities, we were able to agree to the lines along which institutional change must be drawn. We are unanimous in our conviction that the security, well-being, and very survival of the planet depend on such changes, now.

THE CONCEPT OF SUSTAINABLE DEVELOPMENT

ENVIRONMENTAL PROTECTION AND SUSTAINABLE DEVELOPMENT LEGAL PRINCIPLES AND RECOMMENDATIONS

In his Forward to the *Report of the Experts Group on Environmental Law of the World Commission on Environment and Development*, at xi (1987), Judge Nagendra Singh wrote:

The right to development does, however, have certain limitations inasmuch as it cannot be asserted at the expense of the community or even at the expense of neighbouring States whose prospects may be jeopardized. For example a State cannot, in the name of development, proceed to applications of nuclear energy in such a way as to harm the environment and imperil human life, whether in the immediate neighbourhood or in the surrounding region. In fact, environment and development go together and have to be examined simultaneously in this context. In the process of advocating sustainable development, one has to examine the rights and responsibilities of States, both bilaterally and in relation to the international community as a whole. The need for co-operation among nations has to be viewed in the light of new imperatives. The efforts of the World Commission need to be briefly mentioned here because it makes a major contribution to the concept of development in relation to sustainability. The Commission's emphasis on "Sustainable Development" is vital to the well being of humanity not only today but in the context of future generations.

---

1. *Rio Declaration.* The initial intention had been to adopt an "Earth Charter" at Rio. However, in the end result the 1992 Declara-

tion reproduced in the Documentary Supplement was adopted. It reflects a compromise position between developed and developing states.

2. **Agenda 21.** A non-binding plan of action entitled Agenda 21 was drafted at the Rio Conference in 1992. It is reproduced in part in the Documentary Supplement. It has four sections covering (1) social and economic dimensions; (2) conservation and management of resources for development; (3) strengthening the role of major groups; and (4) means of implementation. The creation of a Commission on Sustainable Development as a subsidiary organ of the United Nations is supported here. See A/CONF. 151. (See N. Robinson, (ed.) Agenda 21 and the UNCED Proceedings, 2 vols. (1992).)

3. **The Commission on Sustainable Development (CSD).** The CSD held its first substantive session in June 1993. This meeting had two major outcomes. First, it confirmed the structure and multitier thematic work plan of the CSD. Second, it was the vehicle for bringing together over forty environment ministers who together with the other participants met at the end of the session for two days to discuss how they could provide support politically for the CSD's goals through concrete governmental and international action. For the agenda of the CSD see the extract by Canada's Ambassador for Environment and Sustainable Development (Vice–Chair of the CSD):

A.H. CAMPEAU, A FOUNDATION FOR SUCCESS: THE FIRST MEETING OF THE UNITED NATIONS COMMISSION ON SUSTAINABLE DEVELOPMENT

in Global Agenda, Canada's Foreign Policy and the Environment 2 (Summer 1993).

* * * [we have] an ambitious agenda based on concrete, focussed activities. For example, two intersessional working groups will meet to consider the challenging financial and technology transfer issues. Each will bring together facts, develop analyses and focus on the practical considerations. In addition to the two working groups, many countries have offered to host meetings on topics relevant to the CSD's short-term work plan, such as fresh water, health, human settlements and waste. * * *

[R]eporting by national governments [is] also [important]. Since the global sustainable development agenda depends as much on regional, national and local initiatives as it does on international ones, this will ensure a good balance of commitment in implementation efforts.

Another important outcome of the meeting was the high degree of North–South co-operation that emerged in the wake of Rio. This is a key element to the success of the global sustainable development agenda.

* * *

As in Rio, one valuable aspect of the work of the CSD was the productive and responsible involvement of non-governmental organizations. They took an active and persuasive approach to issues, underlining the value of their participation. Their involvement has already had an impact on CSD actions and its base of support.

The meeting in New York gave the CSD the tools to fulfil its mandate and demonstrated that the will is there to use those tools effectively. The task is now to take the success to date and translate it into concrete results.

W. GRAF, "SUSTAINABLE IDEOLOGIES AND INTERESTS: BEYOND BRUNDTLAND"

13 Third World Quarterly 553–559 (1992) (footnotes omitted).*

* * *

It is instructive that the 1987 report of the World Commission on Environment and Development (WCED), *Our Common Future* (or Brundtland Report), has hitherto enjoyed a virtually uncritical reception in both the South and North West. Its supporters and advocates range from all the European Green parties to John Major's Conservatives and Helmut Kohl's Christian Democrats; from the organised trade union movement to international business. Its major tenets, notably "sustainable development", have become official policy in numerous international organizations such as the World Bank. And the 1992 Rio "Earth Summit" resounded with the language of the WCED Report, as did the parallel 1992 Global Forum. The well-endowed and highly active Centre for Our Common Future in Geneva is therefore no doubt correct in asserting that, owing to the Report's influence, "national, institutional, economic, industrial and social policy changes are underway on a scale not seen before. The UN, governments, industry, young people, and citizen's groups the world over are debating its conclusions and attempting to put its principles into practice."

Considering that, as I will argue here, the WCED Report is essentially yet another attempt, in the genre of the Pearson (1969) and Brandt (1980 and 1983) Reports, to reassert and rationalise Northern global ideological hegemony, it is surprising that it has so far not invoked the fundamental, explicitly anti-imperialist critiques that they did. This article is a (rather belated) attempt to examine the Brundtland prescriptions from such a perspective.

Northern hegemony

The Brundtland Report, like its predecessors, rationalises and vindicates the ideological hegemony of the classes and interests which are the present beneficiaries of the international economic order. As such it is, as I once wrote of the Brandt Report, a platform for legitimising and preserving the international division of labour. Written by politicians rather than environmentalists, these reports, memoranda and appeals are significant less for their intrinsic theses and analyses than for the hegemonic ideological projects that they represent and the particularist interests that underlie them.

It is the need to universalise these particularist interests that explains both the periodic recurrence of these global reports and their fundamental contradictions. They take what is essentially a dialectical

* Reprinted with the permission of Third World Quarterly.

situation of interrelated and multitiered antagonisms between "North" and "South" and transform it into a 'plural', conflict-free and consensual 'gentlemen's agreement'. The special ideological quality of these expressions of global hegemony is their ability to hold out the prospect of gains for all parties—the 'partners in development' of Pearson, the 'mutual interests' of Brandt, the 'common security' of Palme, the 'sustainable development' of Brundtland—if only they will concede the superiority of the North Western political, economic and social order. All Southern demands and aspirations are thus realisable within the framework of the international *status quo;* and only those countries subscribing to the development strategies of the dominant powers can participate. Those who challenge this order in any substantial way—the communists, the anti-imperialists, the mavericks—are ideologically excluded or at least isolated and marginalised.

Hence these global reports are all addressed to Southern governments and their ruling groups. The poor, the masses, the popular classes, in so far as they are recognized at all, emerge as relatively passive strata whose actions are motivated and channelled by their official leaders and on whose behalf 'reforms' are undertaken and 'initiatives' launched. The poor do not act, but are acted upon. The doers, in this 'reformed international order', are bureaucracies and government agencies, big business and transnational corporations—in short élites in North and South who can agree upon joint interests and policies on a global scale.

For this reason, these reports all parallel the New International Economic Order (NIEO), a term which describes the conglomeration of demands by the official South for certain economic concessions on the part of the official North. Although the NIEO is arguably entirely compatible with the existing structure of North–South relations it also represents a potential longer-term threat to Northern hegemony, in two ways: (i) it does promote Southern solidarity and self-awareness which, in an exceptional situation, could produce an anti-Northern common front; and (ii) its logic ultimately challenges the basic principles governing resource allocations in the international system; in other words it is potentially a negation of the international market in favour of the principle of an authoritative (political) allocation of values. This follows from the South's position in the international political economy: lacking the *economic* power associated with capital accumulation and technology control, the South is attempting, via solidarity in pressing for an NIEO and participation in the more 'democratic' institutions of the world system such as the UN General Assembly, to realise its interests by maximising its *political* power according to the majoritarian principle (principle of sovereign equality).

The generic North Western report thus absorbs and defuses many of the more innocuous NIEO demands (increased aid and lending to the South, more technology transfer, guaranteed commodity prices, etc.) in order to forestall their further development into a Southern agenda for fundamental change. This it achieves, rhetorically, by propounding the North Bloc–South Bloc or rich nations-poor nations dichotomy of international folklore even while attempting to rationalise it away (a) idealistically in terms of altruism and international solidarity, and (b) more concretely in terms of 'mutual interests', 'spaceship earth' or 'our common future'.

A crucial flaw in this line of reasoning, as Frances Stewart has pointed out, is that the analyses and reform proposals that ensure are formulated at an *aggregate,* general and international level, whereas the *operational* interests and concerns of states are enacted at a much more specific and national level. In reality, of course, both North and South are fragmented into differential winners and losers in each individual policy area, for instance in the fields of 'free' trade, TNC codes of conduct, higher prices for raw materials, and so forth. What the North Western reports have in common with the NIEO is that both seek to institutionalise collaboration among sets of transnational élites, the former an essentially defensive action by North Western élites, the latter an offensive by Southern ruling groups aimed at renegotiating the specific terms of their subordination, though of course not at overcoming it. That this observation will hold well into the 1990s is indicated by the April 1990 special session of the UN General Assembly on Development Cooperation which both conceded the existence of acute economic problems in the developing countries and failed to develop a corresponding plan of action; the South Commission (made up of the leaders of the world's 29 poorest countries) then nevertheless continued to promote 'a new phase of the North–South dialogue' and a 'revitalization of international economic cooperation'.

Limits of North Western perspectives

Despite the attempts of both the initial Brandt Report and Brandt II to infuse the North–South 'dialogue' with the motivations of 'mutual interests' and altruism, and despite the related Palme Report's 1983 advocacy of 'common security' and 'common prosperity', the limits of North Western prescriptions for world order became abundantly evident in developments surrounding the global economic crisis of the early 1980s. Falling commodity prices, the oil glut, worsening terms of trade, the emerging debt crisis, and the marginalisation of much of the South ('de-development') showed clearly that the North Western proposals, being neither operational nor socially rooted, could not be implemented. This coincided with an economically temporarily stronger USA, bent, under President Reagan, on a more pronounced anti-South attitude that included cutbacks on [sic] in concessional resource flows, more direct pressure on the UN and other international agencies, and reduced contributions to multilateral financial agencies.

As a result, tendencies toward Southern solidarity again, as in the late 1970s, began to threaten North Western hegemony. At UNCTAD VI in Belgrade in 1983 some basic antagonisms began to show through. Whereas the Southern representatives sought to recharge Southern development along Brandtian lines as a stimulus to the moribund world economy, the North argued that it had itself already begun economic recovery which would, by way of a 'trickle-down' process, benefit the South as well. Northern recovery, abetted by Southern 'structural adjustment' would produce global prosperity. It is not surprising, therefore, that the South Commission subsequently concluded that 'Belgrade not only confirmed the impasse in the North–South dialogue but brought dramatically to light that any shared commitment to it had vanished'.

This, then, was the context in which the WCED was established, in the autumn of 1983, by a UN General Assembly resolution. Typically, it was made up primarily of eminent persons, mainly Northern social and liberal democrats and members of the official South. Twelve of its 23 members were from the South and—for the first time—three members were chosen from the then Soviet-dominated East Europe. Thus the usual broad, supra-national and ostensibly non-partisan representation was assured, this time in an even more globally 'representative' manner—representative, that is, of governments and international institutions. Funding and logistical support were secured from a wide cross-section of national governments, international organisations and private foundations. The Commission was able to establish three large advisory panels on energy, industry and food, to hold hearings in a variety of venues, and to commission more than 75 studies and reports from a plethora of sources.

Environment as empowerment

To return to the question posed at the outset, namely the reasons for the near-universal acceptance of the Brundtland Report and the apparent absence of any fundamental critique of it, one trait in particular stands out. Unlike its predecessors, the WCED submission does not address the core of North–South economic relations head on, as it were; it tempers this dissensus-producing subject by ensconcing it in a specific problem which practically everyone can agree is both urgent and in the common interest: the environment. This linking of ecology with changes in global production and hence the international division of labour is the special genius of the WCED Report; and in so doing it touches on what today are probably the two most important (and interrelated) aspects of the international political economy.

However, WCED does not deal with the inherently *political* nature of these issues, that is, the issues of historical responsibility, the beneficiaries of the international system, and the interests involved, since this would undermine its principal consensus-functions, as described above. Instead, the Report (i) attempts to 'technocratize' these political problems by subsuming them under environmental problems, which in turn allows them to be dealt with as merely technical problems susceptible to 'non-political' treatment, and (ii) indiscriminately aggregates environmental and developmental issues, thus depoliticising both and deflecting attention away from both the conflicting dimension of North–South relations and the developmental alternatives available to the South (South–South cooperation, for instance). With this, WCED effectively submerges the thorny problem of *cui bono* from the existing system of North–South relations under the more immediate and universally palatable goals of a clean environment and material development.

A more critical analysis of what the WCED has to say about 'sustainable development' illustrates these assertions. This oxymoronic coinage, borrowed from the more pragmatically oriented exponents of the post-Schumacher schools, is intended to reconcile the imperatives of growth with the limitations of environmental concern. Sustainable development is memorably defined as ' * * * development that meets the needs of the present without compromising the ability of future generations to meet their own needs.' Since any supra-national programme aspiring to enlist support from the South must focus on 'development', and since Northern support can only be retained if the issues of redistribution and the limits to global production are glossed over, the Brundtland Commissioners resort to 'growth' and 'technological progress' as the motive force of their vision of sustainable development. In this they actually fall short of the steady-state theories of the 1972 Club of Rome's *Limits to Growth* and E.F. Schumacher's 1975 *Small is Beautiful*. Their concept is derivative of the long-discredited modernisation paradigm that assumes that a growing international economy 'diffuses' benefits to all the classes and strata in the world, and that the surest road to modernity for the South is to replicate through emulation historical Northern patterns of growth. The Report proposes a 5 to 10 fold increase in manufacturing output on a global scale—in the face of evidence that present levels are already unacceptably degrading the habitat. It also advocates an increased use of chemical fertilizers and pesticides, and accepts projected population growth to 8.5 billion by the year 2025.

Like the classical authors of modernisation theories, the WCED commissioners essentially 'blame the victims' of the North–South system, namely the world's poor, for the state of the environment. Thus, although the commissioners concede that the industrial countries have already used up much of the world's 'ecological capital', and that the North is already consuming 80% of the world's renewable resources, they see the South as potentially the greatest polluter: 'the industries most heavily reliant on environmental resources and most heavily polluting are growing in the developing world, where there is both more urgency for growth and less capacity to minimize damaging side effects'. In a later article, Brundtland herself confirms the Report's tendency to interpret the *manifestations* of poverty as the major *causes* of environmental degradation: desertification, deforestation, droughts, urbanisation, unemployment, lack of housing and so forth, especially since 'poverty undermines people's capacity to use resources wisely'.

Now poverty, underdevelopment and technical backwardness may well contribute to environmental problems, as the South Commission also concedes. But these are merely symptoms of Northern policies and patterns of growth which have produced the thinning of the ozone layer, the greenhouse effect and nuclear radiation and which entail the dumping of hazardous wastes—all of which exacerbate Southern poverty. The G–77, at its 1987 meetings in London and the Hague, asserted that primary responsibility for environmental damage falls on Northern countries whose own development, industrialisation and scientific-technological advances created the problem in the first place. The Brundtland Commission fails to discuss the role of TNCS who are responsible for so much of the environmental degradation in the South, and this failure is no doubt a principal explanation for the acceptibility of the WCED

Report to ruling groups in the North. Indeed, hundreds of Northern plants have been relocated to the Third World specifically to avoid the costs of higher safety and health standards in the North. Bhopal is merely the most spectacular example.

The (relatively meagre) critical post-Brundtland literature has in fact seized upon this blaming-the-victims syndrome. Taking the Commission to task for its advocacy of agroforestry techniques as a solution to deforestation (caused by the poor), Thijs de la Court argues that deforestation is largely the result of large-scale Northern-centred multinational operations, while the poor are relegated to marginal regions where there is not enough wood to survive. And the South Commission points to the operation of the Northern-dominated international economy (debt burden, falling commodity prices, etc.) as well as Northern patterns of growth and consumption as the reasons why developing countries are compelled to overexploit their resources and accept environmentally damaging arrangements with the North.

The Brundtland Commissioners thus fail to examine the issue of responsibility for environmental degradation in terms of the operation of an international division of labour that increasingly locates the main polluting industries in the South. In any case, if poverty is the cause of global pollution, then it follows that the primary concern of any global strategy aimed at protecting the environment ought to be the elimination of that poverty. But on this, apart from a few nebulous allusions to redistribution, the Brundtland Report is silent.

Taking the point of Northern responsibility somewhat further, Frank Tester writes that frequently it is the North's historical destruction of environmentally sound local knowledge and customary practices, rather than poverty as such, that produces environmental degradation:

> It is not only the imposition of predominantly capitalist economic forms on so-called developing countries which has generated the current fiscal and environmental crisis. It is the culture of capitalism—the introduction to developing countries of Fordism and the possessive individualism which accompanies industrial capitalism— that is responsible for many problems.

It is therefore evident that the 'ecological interdependence among nations,' which the WCED advances, is a sham when viewed in the context of its concept of sustainable development. The environment cannot be the starting point from which to derive coherent prescriptions for global reform; nor is it a mere technical problem soluble by scientific means alone; it is a *function* of the *prior transnational system* of domination and subordination, of empowerment and disempowerment.

Elite not popular participation

If 'sustainable development' thus represents the central organising concept for the WCED's prescription for North–South economic and environmental relations, then the notions of 'multilateralism' and 'interdependence' define its *political* strategy for enacting these relations.

'In the final analysis,' the Commission writes, 'sustainable development must rely on political will.' Despite token references to popular participation, it is clear that the source of this will—and consistent with the modernisation ethos that underlies the Report's prescriptions—is the local élites in the Third World, in collaboration with external élites in the North West. This Report does not advance any feasible means of incorporating the poor people or popular classes into the development process. Rather, practically all its reform proposals involve shoring up and further developing existing international bodies—despite its admission that these bodies are 'at present' dominated by the industrial countries. * * * 'Political (good) will', one infers, will produce a consensus between North and South leading to more equitable representation.

Shorn of the rhetoric of multilateralism and interdependence in which it is couched, this prescription is perhaps the most telling evidence of the Brundtland Report's primary agenda. The ruling institutions of the world system are self-evidently those of the North: OECD, NATO, IMF, EC, World Bank, the UN (with the possible exception of its General Assembly), etc. * * * It is precisely such a countervailing framework that the South lacks, and is attempting to create through, for instance, the Non–Aligned Movement and the NIEO. Decision-making powers in these international agencies are of course concentrated in the hands of the North West. The latter's pre-eminence is based partly on the fact that it created this system in the first place, and partly on the fragmentation of the number and nature of international decision-making institutions and fora which can then be operated in an arbitrary and undemocratic manner. The South, by contrast, finds itself in a pre-made situation and its influence relegated to a few larger (and marginalised) fora such as the UNGA. More and more, this Northern-dominated system is able to impose conformity onto the South in the form of 'structural adjustment', 'conditionality' and, more latterly, 'cross-conditionally' which the South Commissioners term 'a system of international economic apartheid'.

'Multilateralism' in the Brundtlandian scheme of things, amounts to a more rational, more efficient way to ensure North Western hegemony in the world system, while the political 'interdependence' it presupposes turns out to be a means of circumscribing the persistent reality of actual domination and subordination in international relations.

A contradictory paradigm

To conclude, the growing cynicism generated by failed development decades, differential development and de-development in the South, meagre evidence of Northern altruism, and a faltering North–South dialogue mean that, in the 1990s, the *forms* of Northern ideological hegemony must be more subtle, more plausible in order to extend their influence and broaden their support. Certainly the Brundtland Report is more sophisticated and nuanced than any of its predecessors. As shown above, it successfully submerges the crucial North–South issues of historical responsibility and current beneficiaries under a succession of less politically laden but fashionable and well-known concepts such as environmentalism, sustainable development, multilateralism, interdependence and food security. The latter are made into the brunt of the argument—indeed into an ersatz for the real argument—while the former are simply defined or declared away.

However, the resulting ideological construct contains a series of contradictions that run integral to the system of North–South relations:

1. The contradiction between a world economic and political system that require fundamental changes—notably in the status of women, the role of markets and the nature of oppressive political regimes—and a set of prescriptions that, in their effect, entrench and perpetuate the *status quo*.

2. Related to that, the contradiction between the fact that international bodies are dominated by the North West, and the formulation of recommendations that rely on these same bodies to implement the 'multilateral' decisions made.

3. The contradiction between the vital need to 'sustain' the environment, and an underlying ethos of growth, based on unchecked accumulation and consumption, in order to avert the prior problem of redistribution.

4. The contradiction between the consensual, cooperative North–South *dialogue* that the Commissioners assume to exist, and the realities of South–North, as well as intra-North and intra-South, antagonisms that repeatedly produce zero-sum *conflicts*.

5. The contradiction arising from the unfounded assumption that capitalism can be adapted, through the force of reason, to new environmental exigencies, namely 'that it is possible to retain capitalist modes of production while practising a form of moral restraint which recognises the limits of world ecosystems.'

In a sense, albeit a more 'open' and 'liberal' one, therefore, the Brundtland Report is still a product of the Cold War, perhaps the last such report to incorporate this postwar bias. In its consistent advocacy of free trade, its unquestioning support for the international market and its conscious exclusion of collective or socialist solutions, it, like its predecessors, is very much the result of North Western ideological reasoning. To this extent, of course, it is already in large part obsolete. The end of the Cold War, the demise of state-socialism, and the more diverse world capitalist system will challenge and modify the WCED proposals in ways that could scarcely be envisioned in the mid–1980s. Will actual developments bring about a new and less ideologically laden paradigm in North–South relations as well?

RIO ONE YEAR LATER,
UNESCO Sources, No. 47, 7–8 (1993).

* * *

What has this unprecedented event achieved? Texts? Certainly. The *"new world partnership for sustainable development"*, called for in Agenda 21? Undoubtedly. New funding? Not really.

UNCED kicked off a preparatory process, begun in 1989 and placed under the auspices of the General Assembly of the United Nations. From the start, this process was universal. All States in all regions were included. Every organization within the UN system cooperated with the secretariat set up by Maurice Strong. From this point of view, the Rio texts reflect a worldwide consensus on the action necessary to achieve sustainable development.

The two conventions drawn up for Rio, on climate and biodiversity, were signed by 150 nations. The United States, which at the time refused to put its signature to these documents, has recently announced that it will now do so.

* * *

And yet Rio's main actors are divided in their reactions to the results of the efforts made since the conference.

* * *

Some are violently critical. For Warren Lindner from the Geneva-based NGO, the Centre for Our Common Future, *"we have not come very far at all"*. *"Non binding agreements and agendas for action and unenforceable declarations of principles are simply not enough"* he stresses. Even recognizing that Rio saw a *"herculean effort made to convince the global community of the need for change"*, he believes the determination necessary for such change is lacking. *"We clearly lack global and national political leadership in respect of most of the issues addressed in Rio. And this applies to both the North and the South"*.

In fact, the challenge set by Rio requires a veritable revolution in methods of production, lifestyles, government and education. However, revolutions do not happen from one day to the next, or even over the course of one year.

Even Warren Lindner admits that *"we were expecting more from UNCED than it could give"*. *"The state of the world demands radical change. It is not difficult to see that we cannot continue very much longer with the environment in the state it is, with a swelling population and the existing financial imbalance,"* he says. But at the same time, he acknowledges, *"we cannot change the world in 15 days"*.

* * *

The real impact of the texts adopted in Rio will only be felt in the long term. In the meantime, despite the inherent constraints of international organizations, an impressive diplomatic machine has been set up in very short time. The Commission for Sustainable Development was created by the UN General Assembly towards the end of [1992]. * * * States must provide it with information on the measures undertaken to implement Agenda 21; non-governmental organizations will be able to participate, and its deliberations should result in more *"operational"* conclusions than the texts usually prepared by such institutions.

The negotiation committee for the desertification convention has also been established and will meet for the first time in May in Nairobi and should be ready by June next year. A conference on small island states will be held in Barbados, also in 1994, while another on the fishing industry is planned for July in New York.

To a certain extent, Rio has revitalized the dialogue between North–South, setting a new base for discussions, and providing a different ideological context to that of the 1970s. That the industrialized countries join forces with the developing nations to make environmentally rational development a common goal represents a major step forward.

This partnership is not limited to states. It includes NGOs, the private sector, and the scientific community to which the Rio texts constantly refer. The mobilization of the NGOs and their involvement in different conferences and follow-up committees indicates their solid commitment to the process. National commissions for sustainable development, including NGOs, have been set up in several countries such as Canada, throughout Africa and Asia.

The partnership should include a financial dimension, essentially in the form of transfers to the South. From the start of the preparatory negotiations, the subject of resources has been considered as crucially important. This question was, along with the fate of the forests, the last to be dealt with in Rio, and the resulting *"financial packet"* relies on several supports: chapter 33 in Agenda 21, which contains general commitments concerning *"new and additional"* resources, the announcements made by various States during the conference, and the verification that these commitments be met by the Commission of Sustainable Development.

It is difficult to quantify the extra resources generated so far by Rio. No calendar was set for countries to put aside the agreed 0.7 per cent of their GNP for development aid. Rough estimates, however, would indicate that the conference has raised only about one billion dollars in supplementary resources for the South—hardly more than the normal increase in public aid. Even so, external resources are not everything. To have a clearer picture, we would have to evaluate on a national level, how much countries are devoting to the implementation of Agenda 21.

On the basis of initial, admittedly vague commitments, the results are very poor. The fate of two, spectacular announcements made at Rio, serve as revealing examples. The President of the World Bank had proposed an "Earth increment" to the resources of the Bank's International Development Association (IDA). This "increment", amounting to several billion dollars, should have been negotiated by donors during the 10th replenishment of IDA's resources. In fact, the negotiations achieved little more than a renewal, in real terms, of the funds made available at IDA–9.

In the second case, Portugal, in the name of the European Community, announced a four billion dollar plan to finance Agenda 21. Since then, the EEC has been debating how this sum should be divided up between its Member States.

In the coming months, the coffers of the Global Environment Facility managed by the World Bank, UNDP and UNEP, will need topping up, providing another test of the capacity of industrialized countries to turn words into action.

The financial difficulties can, in part, be attributed to budgetary deficits and economic recession in donor countries. However they are also the result of a certain ordering of priorities in these countries, which have chosen to give precedence to other urgent problems such as national unemployment and international peacekeeping.

* * *

Disappointing as they may be, these initial results should not lead to the dismissal of UNCED as an impossible quest. As Gisbert Glaser, Coordinator of UNESCO's environmental programmes points out *"the recession will not last forever"*. *"Agenda 21 has the advantage of being ready to go once the economy turns around."*

His optimism is echoed in the comment often repeated by Maurice Strong that Rio was not just an event, but the launch of a long-term process whose results will be judged in the decades to come.

The scientific community is also thinking along these lines. While the Executive Director of the International Council of Scientific Unions, Julia Marton–Lefêvre, deplores the heavy bureaucracy of international organizations and the barriers that continue to separate them from the non-governmental sector, she is *"not disenchanted"*. *"Rio has forced everyone, even us, the scientists, to think of environment and development as a pair. And that is no small achievement."*

The NGO network is more active than ever and has upped the pressure on governments to ensure that they move in the right direction. The UN Secretary General, and the entire UN family, have made the follow-up to Rio central part of their action.

Further encouragement has come from the new administration in Washington. The announcement that the U.S. would sign the Convention on Biodiversity, review energy taxes and increase foreign aid for environmentally sound projects, indicates a new spirit. * * *

* * *

EUROPEAN COMMUNITY AND SUSTAINABLE DEVELOPMENT

G. BERRISCH, AMERICAN SOCIETY OF INTERNATIONAL LAW ENVIRONMENTAL INTEREST GROUP NEWSLETTER

Vol. 3(1), 3–4 (1992).*

On 18 March 1992, the Commission unveiled the 5th Environmental Programme of the Community, entitled "Towards Sustainability: A European Community Programme of Policy and Action in Relation to the Environment and Sustainable Development." The Commission considers the Programme, which was adopted by the Council on 26 May, as a turning point for the Community. If the task for the Community in

---

* Reprinted with the permission of the American Society of International Law.

the 1980s was to complete the internal market, "the reconciliation of environment and development is one of the principal challenges facing the Community and the world at large in the 1990s." The approach of the Programme differs from previous programmes: it is no longer a merely legislative approach but aims at the involvement and commitment of all sectors of society and business in the process of sustainable development. In order to achieve this objective, the Programme broadens the range of instruments from legislative/regulatory instruments, designed to set fundamental levels of protection for the environment and public health, to three new categories of instruments: (1) market-based instruments aimed at internalizing external environmental costs; (2) horizontal, supporting instruments relating to such matters as scientific research, planning, and improved consumer and producer information; and (3) financial support mechanisms such as LIFE. The Programme explicitly recognizes the responsibility of the Community to help protect the global environment. It is intended to cover the period through the year 2000, but shall be reviewed in 1995; a new feature of the Programme is the inclusion of proposed concrete measures for the main sectors, including in each case the envisaged time frame and actors.

ECONOMIC DEVELOPMENT AND THE ENVIRONMENT
A. KISS AND D. SHELTON, INTERNATIONAL ENVIRONMENTAL LAW
48–50, 54 (1991) (footnotes omitted).*

Developing countries contain more than three-quarters of the world's population, with 90 percent of the estimated population increase during the next quarter-century projected to occur in the urban centers of the world's poorest countries. At the same time, developing countries account for only 30 percent of the world income, with the income gap continuing to widen. Over half the developing countries experienced declines in per capita gross domestic product during the early 1980s, with an overall decline of 10 percent occurring during the decade. In its preamble the Stockholm Declaration recognized that

> [i]n the developing countries most of the environmental problems are caused by underdevelopment. Millions continue to live far below the minimum levels required for health and sanitation. Therefore, the developing countries must direct their effort to development, bearing in mind their priorities and the need to safeguard and improve the environment. For the same purpose, the industrialized countries should make efforts to reduce the gap between themselves and the developing countries * * *.

The Third World view of development as an absolute priority became a problem during preparation for the Stockholm Conference, because initially these states did not favor the idea that the cooperation of all countries was necessary to protect the environment. Environmen-

* Reprinted with the permission of Transnational Publishers, Inc.

tal problems were considered predominately an ailment of rich, industrialized countries. From this perspective, deterioration of the environment was assimilated to industrial pollutants, a perspective that has not disappeared. Even in 1989, the Brasilia Declaration of the Latin American and Caribbean summit asserted that "the seriousness of the environmental problems facing the world today stem mainly from industrialization, consumer and disposal patterns in the developed countries, which are at the root of the rapid wear and tear on natural resources on the planet and the ever increasing introduction of pollutants in the biosphere." At Stockholm, the reaction of developing countries wishing to become industrialized was to ignore the environmental costs. The priorities are reflected in the comment of one Third World representative who exclaimed, "let me die polluted."

A second Third World preoccupation arose from the perception that for industrialized countries development issues were considered as less urgent than and subordinated to efforts to protect the environment. Some feared that funds previously dedicated to development would be diverted to fight environmental deterioration. These fears seemed to be borne out several days before the Stockholm meeting, when the Third United Nations Conference on Trade and Development produced particularly disappointing results on development aid.

These circumstances explain parts of the Stockholm Declaration and Action Plan which reflect the agenda of the Third World. Beginning with the condemnation of apartheid and racial discrimination in Principle 1 of the Declaration, subsequent provisions are dedicated to economic and social development as a condition of environmental protection.

* * *

In principle, the problems which surfaced at Stockholm have been resolved. Third World countries now largely accept the need for world cooperation to safeguard the planet. The Brasilia Declaration which condemns the industrial origin of pollution adds that Latin American and Caribbean countries "are committed to a course of action that will be able to prevent a repetition of the mistakes of those development patterns and their consequences." In practice, Kenya, India and Indonesia have taken a leadership role in environmental matters. Zaire, ten years after Stockholm, initiated the World Charter for Nature in the United Nations General Assembly. Finally, Third World countries have adopted regional environmental treaties and largely ratified the global instruments.

* * *

In developed countries and in international organizations, pressure has been exerted to encourage adoption of measures to assess the environmental impact of development assistance. The World Bank has announced plans to assess environmental threats in the thirty most vulnerable developing countries. A February 1990 UNEP meeting stressed the need for grants, investments, and loans to alleviate the critical need for data collection and analysis in developing countries. OECD has adopted a recommendation concerning an environmental checklist for development assistance, calling on member countries to ensure that for both bilateral and multilateral development assistance, environmental aspects are taken into account in the identification, planning, implementation and evaluation of those development projects which are proposed for funding.

There is growing concern among Third World countries that environmental criteria will become a new factor of "conditionality" influencing development assistance and establishing trade barriers. Such conditions are seen as constraints on development opportunities and national sovereignty as well as attempts to protect markets rather than the environment. As a result, the Amazon Declaration specifically objects to attempts to impose conditions in the allocation of international resources for development. As an alternative, an innovative program has begun in some areas to allow developing countries to pay off part of their external debt by committing themselves to invest such funds in environmental protection. These "debt for nature swaps" have been undertaken by private foundations and commercial banks and have found support in national government policies. Proposals also have been made to the World Bank to forgive outstanding loans in exchange for the implementation of specific conservation programs.

In conclusion, developing countries today generally agree on the necessity of safeguarding the environment and integrating methods to protect it in the development process. On the international level, there remain diverse issues over implementation of environmental norms, but the split over the need for and content of these norms has substantially decreased.

3.   INTER–GENERATIONAL EQUITY

E. BROWN WEISS, IN FAIRNESS TO FUTURE GENERATIONS, CONFERENCE ON HUMAN RIGHTS, PUBLIC FINANCE, AND THE DEVELOPMENT PROCESS

8 American University Journal of International Law and Policy.
19–22 (1992) (footnotes omitted).*

Sustainable development is inherently an *inter* generational question as well as an *intra* generational question. Sustainable development relies on a commitment to equity with future generations. I suggest that this ethical and philosophical commitment acts as a constraint on a natural inclination to take advantage of our temporary control over the earth's resources, and to use them only for our own benefit without careful regard for what we leave to our children and their descendants. This may seem a self-centered philosophy, but it is actually embodied in the logic that controls economic decisions over the use of our resources in day-to-day life.

The recent and valid concern over environmental externalities focuses mainly on the costs that we and our contemporaries must bear when

* Reprinted with the permission of the   tional Law and Policy.
American University Journal of Interna-

we pollute the air, water and soil by industrial expansion, deforestation and other aspects of economic development. Concern over these externalities is intended to ensure that the benefits from a contemplated action exceed its costs and that those who bear its costs are adequately compensated. But in practice the costs and benefits are assessed from the perspective of the present generation.

The discount rate, or in some ways the tyranny of the discount rate, ensures that short-term benefits nearly always outweigh long-term costs. For this reason it is useful to address the issue of sustainability philosophically and legally, as well as from an economic perspective. Sustainability requires that we look at the earth and its resources not only as an investment opportunity, but as a trust passed to us by our ancestors for our benefit, but also to be passed on to our descendants for their use.

This notion conveys both rights and responsibilities. Most importantly, it implies that future generations have rights too. These rights have meaning only if we, the living, respect them, and in this regard, transcend the differences among countries, religions, and cultures.

It is also important, as we discuss the appropriate economic instruments for sustainable economic development, to ensure the effective transfer of rights and responsibilities from one generation to the next. If we safeguard this transfer, then we can develop the economic instruments to ensure the most efficient use of resources to protect these rights and responsibilities. But we may continue to have difficulties until we firmly establish the transfer of rights and responsibilities as an entitlement.

Fortunately, the notion that each generation holds the earth as a trustee or steward for its descendants strikes a deep chord with all cultures, religions and nationalities. Nearly all human traditions recognize that we, the living, are sojourners on earth and temporary stewards of our resources. The theory of intergenerational equity states that we, the human species, hold the natural environment of our planet in common with other species, other people, and with past, present and future generations. As members of the present generation, we are both trustees, in a sense responsible for ensuring its integrity, and beneficiaries, with the right, the entitlement, to use and benefit from it for ourselves.

Two relationships must shape any theory of intergenerational equity in the environmental context. The first is our relationship with our natural system, through which we are intricately linked with other parts of the natural system. The second is our relationship with other generations.

The natural system is not always beneficent. Deserts, glaciers, volcanoes and tsunamis are hostile to humans, but we alone, among all other living creatures, have the capacity to significantly shape our relationship with this system. We can use its resources on a sustainable basis or we can degrade the system, and destroy its integrity. Because of our unique ability to control our environment, we have a special responsibility to care for it.

The second fundamental relationship is that among different generations of people. All generations are linked by the ongoing relationship with the earth. The theory of intergenerational equity states that all generations have an equal place in relation to the natural system, and that there is no basis for preferring past, present or future generations for use of the system. This notion has deep roots in international law. The preamble to the universal declaration of human rights begins:

> Whereas recognition of the inherent dignity and of the equal and inalienable rights of all members of the human family is the foundation of freedom, justice and peace in the world. * * *

The reference to all members of the human family has a temporal dimension which brings all generations within its scope. The reference to equal and inalienable rights affirms the basic equality of such generations in the human family.

Every generation should use the natural system to improve the human condition. But when one generation severely degrades the environment, it violates its intergenerational obligations to care for the natural system. In such cases, other generations may in fact have an obligation to restore the robustness of the system, though not to bear all the costs. Those costs must be distributed across generations; and we possess the tools for doing just that.

The state of the legal framework for distributing these costs is the notion of equality as the norm connecting successive generations in the care and use of the environment. A corollary to this principle is the concept of a partnership between humans and nature, as well as among generations. It is useful to refer to Edmund Burke to fully understand this concept:

> As the ends of such a partnership cannot be obtained in many generations, it becomes a partnership, not only between those who are living but between those who are living, those who are dead, and those who are to be born.

The purpose of this partnership must be to realize and protect the welfare and well-being of every generation in relation to the planet. The integrity of the planet requires proper care of the life support systems of the planet, the ecological processes and the environmental conditions necessary for a healthy human environment.

* * * A future generation would want to inherit the earth and have access to its resources as did prior generations. This requires that each generation leave the planet in no worse condition than it received it, and to provide succeeding generations equitable access to its resources and benefits.

EXPERTS GROUP ON ENVIRONMENTAL LAW OF THE WORLD
COMMISSION ON ENVIRONMENT AND DEVELOPMENT, EN-
VIRONMENTAL PROTECTION AND SUSTAINABLE DEVELOP-
MENT, LEGAL PRINCIPLES AND RECOMMENDATIONS, ELE-
MENTS FOR A DRAFT CONVENTION

42–45 (1987).*

Article 2

Conservation for present and future generations

States shall ensure that the environment and natural resources are
conserved and used for the benefit of present and future generations.

Comment

The present article stipulates that the environment and natural
resources are to serve the needs of both present *and future* generations.
It purports to give effect to the statement in the Preamble of the 1972
UN Declaration on the Human Environment that: "To defend and
improve the human environment for present *and future* generations has
become an imperative goal for mankind * * * " (emphasis added). It
obliges States to manage the environment and natural resources for the
benefit of present generations in such a way that they are held in trust
for future generations.

This implies, in the first place, a basic obligation for States to
conserve options for future generations by maintaining to the maximum
extent possible the diversity of the natural resource base. It requires a
management of natural resources of the environment in such a manner
that they may yield the greatest sustainable benefit to present generations while maintaining their potential to meet the needs and aspirations
of future generations. Conservation of the diversity of the natural
resource base for the benefit of future generations is warranted as the
possibilities to develop substitute products or to improve production
and/or extraction technologies are not unlimited. Or else because future
generations may otherwise only be able to obtain the same benefits at
considerably higher costs.

The second basic obligation for States following from the duty to
hold the natural heritage of mankind in trust for future generations
concerns the prevention or abatement of pollution or other forms of
degradation of natural resources or the environment, which would
reduce the range of uses to which the natural resources or environment
could be put or which would confront future generations with enormous
financial burdens to clean up the environment.

Support for the duty of States to ensure that the natural heritage of
mankind is used and conserved for the benefit of both present and future
generations is to be found in many international instruments.

Thus, Principle 1 of the 1972 UN Declaration on the Human
Environment provides that: "Man * * * bears a solemn responsibility to

* Reprinted with the permission of Martinus Nijhoff.

protect and improve the environment for present and future generations". Principle 2 of the 1972 UN Declaration lays down that: "The
natural resources of the earth including the air, water, land, flora and
fauna and especially representative samples of natural ecosystems must
be safeguarded for the benefit of present and future generations through
careful planning or management, as appropriate." Principle 5 provides
that: "The non-renewable resources of the earth must be employed in
such a way as to guard against the danger of their future exhaustion
* * * ", while Principle 6 states that: "The discharge of toxic substances
or of other substances and the release of heat, in such quantities or
concentrations as to exceed the capacity of the environment to render
them harmless, must be halted in order to ensure that serious or
irreversible damage is not inflicted on ecosystems * * * ".

Numerous references to the need to conserve the natural heritage of
mankind for the benefit of present and future generations also are to be
found (usually in the preamble) in many international agreements
concluded after the adoption of the 1972 UN Declaration on the Human
Environment, e.g., in:

1972 Paris Convention concerning the Protection of World Cultural and
Natural Heritage;

1973 Washington Convention on International Trade in Endangered
Species of Wild Fauna and Flora;

1976 Barcelona Convention for the Mediterranean Sea;

1976 Apia Convention on the Conservation of Nature in the South
Pacific;

1977 Geneva Convention on the Prohibition of Military or Any Other
Hostile Use of Environmental Modification Techniques;

1978 Kuwait Regional Convention;

1979 Berne Convention on the Conservation of European Wildlife and
Natural Habitats;

1979 Bonn Convention on the Conservation of Migratory Species of Wild
Animals;

1983 Cartagena de Indias Convention for the Wider Caribbean Region;
and

1985 ASEAN Agreement on the Conservation of Nature and Natural
Resources.

Reference must also be made to Article 30 of the Charter of
Economic Rights and Duties of States proclaimed in UNGA Resolution
No. 3281; to UNGA Resolution No. 36/7 of 27 October 1981 on the
Historical Responsibility of States for the Preservation of Nature for
Present and Future Generations; and to UNGA Resolution No. 37/7 of
28 October 1982 on the World Charter for Nature.

Although in the preceding observations special emphasis has been
laid on the obligation to conserve natural resources and the environment
for the benefit of *future* generations, one should not forget that such an
obligation also exists for the benefit of *present* generations. The basic

obligation for the benefit of both present and future generations is further elaborated in the following articles.

To the extent that this basic obligation concerns international or transboundary natural resources or environmental interferences, it already may in many respects be deemed to find substantial support in existing general international law.

In this connection it may finally be observed that the conservation or use of the environment and natural resources for the benefit of present and future generations also implies certain restraints for the parties to an international or non-international armed conflict in that they shall abstain from methods or means of warfare which are intended, or may be expected, to cause wide-spread, long-lasting or severe damage to the environment. Support for this idea may, inter alia, be found in the 1977 Geneva Convention on the Prohibition of Military or Any Other Hostile Use of Environmental Modification Techniques.

CORE FEATURES
E. BROWN WEISS, IN FAIRNESS TO FUTURE GENERATIONS
38 (1989).*

First, each generation should be required to conserve the diversity of the natural and cultural resource base, so that it does not unduly restrict the options available to future generations in solving their problems and satisfying their own values, and should also be entitled to diversity comparable to that enjoyed by previous generations. This principle may be called "conservation of options". Second, each generation should be required to maintain the quality of the planet so that it is passed on in no worse condition than the present generation received it, and should be entitled to a quality of the planet comparable to the one enjoyed by previous generations. This is the principle of "conservation of quality". Third, each generation should provide its members with equitable rights of access to the legacy from past generations and should conserve this access for future generations. This is the principle of "conservation of access".

———

1. *Intertemporal Concerns.* Professor Brown Weiss notes in her above-quoted book at 34–38, the intertemporal dimension in international law and the long held tradition of using principles of equity to interpret international documents and reach decisions. In this sense equity is used to mean equitable standards or principles and must be distinguished from equity in the sense of a decision *ex aequo et bono* to which the parties must consent under Article 38(2) of the Statute of the International Court of Justice.

* Reprinted with the permission of Transnational Publishers, Inc., and Edith Brown Weiss.

2. ***Global Commons.***   Should only those areas beyond national jurisdiction such as the deep sea bed, high seas and outer space be considered as the "global commons"?   Brown Weiss is of the view (id., 289) that "the planet is a 'global commons' shared by all generations." (See also E. Brown Weiss, Our Rights and Obligations to Future Generations for the Environment, 84 American Journal of International Law 198 (1990).   Note also A. D'Amato, Do We Owe a Duty to Future Generations to Preserve the Global Environment?   84 AJIL 190 (1990)). Do you think that the environmental concerns dealt with in this Chapter fall under this heading of "global commons" or under that of "shared natural resources" that do not fall exclusively within any one state's jurisdiction, but neither are they the common property of all states? Alternatively, can the principle of the "common heritage" as seen in the 1979 Moon Treaty and in Articles 136 and 137 of the 1982 Law of the Sea Treaty be applied in the international environmental context?

REFLECTIONS ON THE COMMONS
E. OSTROM, GOVERNING THE COMMONS

1–3   (footnotes omitted).*

Hardly a week goes by without a major news story about the threatened destruction of a valuable natural resource.   In June of 1989, for example, a *New York Times* article focused on the problem of overfishing in the Georges Bank about 150 miles off the New England coast.   Catches of cod, flounder, and haddock are now only a quarter of what they were during the 1960s.   Everyone knows that the basic problem is overfishing;   however, those concerned cannot agree how to solve the problem.   Congressional representatives recommend new national legislation, even though the legislation already on the books has been enforced only erratically.   Representatives of the fishers argue that the fishing grounds would not be in such bad shape if the federal government had refrained from its sporadic attempts to regulate the fishery in the past.   The issue in this case—and many others—is how best to limit the use of natural resources so as to ensure their long-term economic viability.   Advocates of central regulation, of privitization, and of regulation by those involved have pressed their policy prescriptions in a variety of different arenas.

Similar situations occur on diverse scales ranging from small neighborhoods to the entire planet.   The issues of how best to govern natural resources used by many individuals in common are no more settled in academia than in the world of politics.   Some scholarly articles about the "tragedy of the commons" recommend that "the state" control most natural resources to prevent their destruction;   others recommend that privatizing those resources will resolve the problem.   What one can observe in the world, however, is that neither the state nor the market is

* Reprinted with the permission of Elinore Ostrom and Simon & Shuster—Prentice–Hall Publishers.

uniformly successful in enabling individuals to sustain long-term, productive use of natural resource systems.

* * *

The tragedy of the commons

Since Garrett Hardin's challenging article in *Science* (1968), the expression "the tragedy of the commons" has come to symbolize the degradation of the environment to be expected whenever many individuals use a scarce resource in common. To illustrate the logical structure of his model, Hardin asks the reader to envision a pasture "open to all." He then examines the structure of this situation from the perspective of a rational herder. Each herder receives a direct benefit from his own animals and suffers delayed costs from the deterioration of the commons when his and others' cattle overgraze. Each herder is motivated to add more and more animals because he receives the direct benefit of his own animals and bears only a share of the costs resulting from overgrazing. Hardin concludes: "Therein is the tragedy. Each man is locked into a system that compels him to increase his herd without limit—in a world that is limited. Ruin is the destination toward which all men rush, each pursuing his own best interest in a society that believes in the freedom of the commons." (Hardin 1968, p. 1,244).

Hardin was not the first to notice the tragedy of the commons. Aristotle long ago observed that "what is common to the greatest number has the least care bestowed upon it. Everyone thinks chiefly of his own, hardly at all of the common interest" (*Politics,* Book II, ch. 3). Hobbes's parable of man in a state of nature is a prototype of the tragedy of the commons: Men seek their own good and end up fighting one another. In 1833, William Forster Lloyd (1977) sketched a theory of the commons that predicted improvident use for property owned in common. More than a decade before Hardin's article, H. Scott Gordon (1954) clearly expounded similar logic in another classic: "The Economic Theory of a Common–Property Research: The Fishery." Gordon described the same dynamic as Hardin:

> There appears then, to be some truth in the conservative dictum that everybody's property is nobody's property. Wealth that is free for all is valued by no one because he who is foolhardy enough to wait for its proper time of use will only find that it has been taken by another * * *. The fish in the sea are valueless to the fisherman, because there is no assurance that they will be there for him tomorrow if they are left behind today. (Gordon 1954, p. 124).

* * *

* * * Standard analyses in modern resource economics conclude that where a number of users have access to a common-pool resource, the total of resource units withdrawn from the resource will be greater than the optimal economic level of withdrawal * * *.

If the only "commons" of importance were a few grazing areas or fisheries, the tragedy of the commons would be of little general interest. That is not the case. Hardin himself used the grazing commons as a metaphor for the general problem of overpopulation. The "tragedy of the commons" has been used to describe such diverse problems as the Sahelian famine of the 1970s, * * * firewood crises throughout the Third World, * * * the problem of acid rain, * * *. Much of the world is dependent on resources that are subject to the possibility of a tragedy of the commons.

———

4. COMMON HERITAGE

P. BIRNIE AND A. BOYLE, INTERNATIONAL LAW AND THE ENVIRONMENT

121–122 (1992) (footnotes omitted).*

* * * [T]here remains the objection that common heritage is still of doubtful legal status following its well-known rejection by the United States and other countries opposed to ratification of the 1982 UNCLOS and the Moon Treaty. Significantly, it was not employed in the Ozone Convention. Some conventions do use the term or others such as the "world heritage of mankind" in their preambles in a horatory sense. But these are better viewed, like the term "common concern", as expressions of the common interest of all states in certain forms of ecological protection, and not as attempts to internationalize ownership of resources. Common heritage is important, however, in providing one of the most developed applications of trusteeship or fiduciary relationship in an environmental context, and in that sense it represents a significant precedent * * *.

———

A. KISS AND D. SHELTON, INTERNATIONAL ENVIRONMENTAL LAW

9–18 (1991) (footnotes omitted).**

* * * According to a UNESCO program entitled "Man and the Biosphere", the term biosphere designates the totality of our environment, that part of the universe in which, as far as we know, all life is concentrated. In fact, it is a very narrow stratum encircling the globe. It comprises the earth and several hundred meters above and under the surface of the earth and oceans.

Lawyers may question whether it is possible to legally protect the entire biosphere, as such. One means of protection derived from familiar juridical techniques would be to confer on it a status similar to legal personality, giving the biosphere a legally recognized existence currently afforded juridical entities such as corporations, trusts and, on the international level, international organizations and trust territories. Al-

---

* Reprinted with the permission of Oxford University Press.

** Reprinted with the permission of Transnational Publishers, Inc.

though such a solution for the entirety of our universe is difficult to imagine, the 1982 Convention on the Law of the Sea moves in this direction by proclaiming the deep seabed and its mineral resources (the Area) to be the common heritage of mankind and investing all humanity with rights and responsibilities over the Area. An implementing international authority is established to act for all humanity. In this way, a sector of the globe is given a juridical status and its representation is simultaneously assured. A similar solution might be possible for the biosphere, although this appears highly unlikely.

In the current state of the law, protection of the environment occurs on the international plane, as it does within national legal systems, by adoption of measures targeting sectors of the biosphere such as air or water, based on their importance or benefit to humans. At the beginning of the 1970s some suggested that the legal personality of certain of these environmental sectors be recognized. However, legal systems have difficulty integrating such solutions because the systems are created by humans to serve human interests. This anthropocentric approach to resources is reflected in one of the fundamental international environmental texts, the 1972 Stockholm Declaration on the Human Environment: "The natural resources of the earth, including the air, water, and flora and fauna and especially representative samples of natural ecosystems, must be safeguarded for the benefit of present and future generations through careful planning or management, as appropriate."

More recently, international instruments increasingly have recognized an intrinsic value in components of the environment. The preamble of the 1979 Bern Convention on the Conservation of European Wildlife and Natural Habitats is particularly significant in this regard: "Recognizing that wild flora and fauna constitute a natural heritage of aesthetic, scientific, cultural, recreational, economic, and intrinsic value that needs to be preserved and handed on to future generations."

The text demonstrates an integrated approach: the common heritage of mankind presents a certain number of qualities important for humanity, but these do not lessen its inherent value. It is possible to go further. The most important text of principles since the Stockholm Declaration, the 1982 World Charter for Nature, proclaimed by the United Nations General Assembly, marks an evolution in this regard and indicates possible limits: "Every form of life is unique, warranting respect regardless of its worth to man and, to accord other organisms such recognition, man must be guided by a moral code of action[.]"

An intrinsic value is thus recognized in the basic elements of the environment, but their protection is governed by moral rather than legal rules. Given the refusal to confer legal status on sectors of the environment and to thus recognize their intrinsic, independent value, it seems that another approach is necessary to establish the purpose of environmental protection. The first phrases of the preamble of the World Charter for Nature set out such an alternative: "Mankind is a part of nature and life depends on the uninterrupted functioning of natural systems which ensure the supply of energy and nutrients[.]"

The intrinsic value of the biosphere is not rejected but is integrated with a recognition that man makes up part of the universe and cannot exist without conservation of the biosphere and the ecosystems which comprise it. In this perspective all sectors of the environment have a value not only in their short-term utility to humans, as the earlier exclusively anthropocentric approach would have it, but also as indispensable elements of an interrelated system which must be protected to ensure human survival. While this ultimate aim of human survival remains anthropocentric, humans are not viewed as apart from or above the natural universe, but as an interlinked and interdependent part of it. It follows that because all parts of the natural web are linked, they must each be protected and conserved. It is in this sense that "intrinsic value" may be understood.

* * * [T]he concept of an interrelated system leads to the conclusion that protection of the biosphere is in the common interest of humanity, a conclusion that has important consequences not only for environmental law, but for all of international law. The "common interest" of humanity is, above all, human survival, which underlies all legal and social systems and may be grounded in a genetic or biological imperative. Inevitably, this interest requires that "humanity" be seen to include not only present but also future generations. In fact, the right of future generations is implicit in all which touches environmental protection and the preservation of natural resources. It also is increasingly explicit in international texts, beginning with Principle 2 of the Stockholm Declaration and Article 4 of the UNESCO World Heritage Convention.

Conservation makes sense only in a temporal perspective; absent this consideration everything could be consumed or wasted in the present and human survival foreclosed. Moreover, the conditions of life for those to come—who will be increasingly numerous for at least the coming decades—should not be less favorable than those . which the present generations have inherited from their predecessors. These include the required conditions for individuals and peoples * * * to lead materially satisfying lives in dignity and liberty.

* * * Toward the end of the 1960s, when international environmental law was born, the term "common heritage of mankind" appeared in international texts, applied by virtue of international instruments relating to the deep seabed and the moon and other celestial bodies. In fact, the common heritage of mankind, a concretization in law of the common interest of humanity, already existed in general terms in regimes such as those governing Antarctica and its seas, the radio frequency spectrum, and the orbit of geostationary satellites, all of which contain obligations of nonappropriation, conservation, and rational use. States freely undertake to respect these obligations without obtaining any immediate advantage. The purpose is to serve more long-term objectives which are in mankind's common interest: to prevent international tensions from creating dangers to the maintenance of peace, to respect and ensure the dignity and fundamental rights and liberties of all humans, and to halt the deterioration and destruction of natural resources. It may be that the common interest of humanity is identifiable precisely where conventions are not based on reciprocity. Of course, in the environmental field

the concept of "common interest" also reflects the physical reality of an indivisible environment, notwithstanding the claims of states to "permanent" sovereignty over natural resources.

* * *

Rules of international environmental law fall into the category of norms adopted in the common interest of humanity. They generally do not bring immediate advantages to contracting states when their objective is to protect species of wild plant and animal life, the oceans, the air, the soil, and the countryside. Even in regard to treaties concluded among a small number of states, reciprocity normally is not the primary purpose of the contracting parties. For example, states upstream on a river are not in the same situation as those downstream. The general direction of winds and ocean currents can substantially affect legal obligations, cut against the equality of the parties, and diminish the importance of reciprocity.

The common interest of humanity also is mentioned, usually in the preamble, among the objectives of several treaties aimed at protecting particular elements of the environment. For example, the 1972 UNESCO Convention concerning the Protection of the World Cultural and Natural Heritage proclaims that, "the deterioration or disappearance of any item of the cultural or natural heritage constitutes a harmful impoverishment of the heritage of all nations of the world."

A veritable profession of faith even more characteristically opens the preamble of the 1979 Bonn Convention on the Conservation of Migratory Species of Wild Animals:

> * * * wild animals in their innumerable forms are an irreplaceable part of the earth's natural system which must be conserved for the good of mankind;

> * * * each generation of man holds the resources of the earth for future generations and has an obligation to ensure that this legacy is conserved and, where utilized, is used wisely[.]

Finally, a regional example can be taken from the 1974 Paris Convention for the Prevention of Marine Pollution from Land–Based Sources:

> "the marine environment and the flora and fauna which it supports are of vital importance to all nations."

Thus, the purpose of international environmental law can be seen as serving the general interest of humanity, its survival and well-being, rather than exchanging reciprocal rights and duties.

Climate as common heritage. Malta initiated a proposal for consideration in the U.N. General Assembly entitled "Conservation of climate as part of the common heritage of mankind". It was not successful. However, the General Assembly recognized that climate change is a "common concern of mankind" in that it is an "essential condition which sustains life on earth." See U.N.G.A.RES. 43/53, Jan. 27, 1989, 28 ILM 1326 (1989).

5. ENVIRONMENTAL RIGHTS AS HUMAN RIGHTS

EXPERTS GROUP ON ENVIRONMENTAL LAW OF THE WORLD COMMISSION ON ENVIRONMENT AND DEVELOPMENT, ENVIRONMENTAL PROTECTION AND SUSTAINABLE DEVELOPMENT, LEGAL PRINCIPLES AND RECOMMENDATIONS, ELEMENTS FOR A DRAFT CONVENTION

38–42 (1987).*

Article 1
Fundamental human right

All human beings have the fundamental right to an environment adequate for their health and well-being.

Comment

This article stipulates the fundamental right of every individual human being to an environment adequate for his health and well-being. The formulation of this fundamental right differs in various respects from that proclaimed in Principle 1 of the 1972 UN Declaration on the Human Environment which provides: "Man has the fundamental right to freedom, equality and adequate conditions of life, in an environment of a quality that permits a life of dignity and well-being * * *." The formulated fundamental right is to be preferred to the one contained in Principle 1 of the 1972 UN Declaration. Firstly, because its *direct* and *immediate* object is the maintenance and/or restoration of an adequate environment. The principle in the 1972 UN Declaration on the contrary has as its direct and immediate object "freedom, equality and adequate conditions of life", putting the requirement of an adequate environment merely in second place. Secondly, the formulated fundamental right refers to the more concrete notion of "health" as an interest to be protected and avoids an explicit reference to the concept of "a life of dignity", which may be deemed to be comprised in the notion of "well-being".

Although the environment to which the fundamental right formulated above relates clearly comprises the environment in which human beings live, it also is intended to comprise those parts of the earth and the surrounding sphere which hold important natural resources for man (e.g. marine waters) or which, when disturbed or degraded, may eventually detrimentally affect areas normally inhabited by man (e.g. rain forests or the ozone layer).

Of course, the requirement that the environment must be "adequate for [human] health and well-being" is extremely vague. In any case both physical and mental health and well-being are to be protected and promoted. The adjective "adequate" makes clear that there are limits to the protection of the environment for the purpose of promoting the health and well-being of human beings. Indeed, those limits may to some extent even be dictated by the need to promote the health or well-

* Reprinted with the permission of Martinus Nijhoff.

being of human beings (e.g. by food production or housing). Apart from that, the determination of the adequacy of the environment for the health and well-being of human beings will depend to a considerable extent on many regional or local factors, such as the nature of the environment concerned, the kind of use made of it, the means at the disposal of the public authorities and the population, and the expectations of the human beings themselves.

The fundamental human right to an adequate environment implies at least the existence of an international obligation on the part of States vis-à-vis other States, if not also vis-à-vis individual human beings, to adequately protect the environment for the benefit of individual human beings (substantive human right) and/or to grant to such individual human beings the procedural legal means necessary to protect their interests in an adequate environment (procedural human right) against infringements by the State or by other entities or persons (e.g. private companies or individuals).

By postulating in Article 1 the fundamental human right to an adequate environment, it is made clear that the obligations of States formulated in the subsequent articles are not merely intended to protect the interests of States *inter se* in maintaining or restoring an adequate environment, but also those of individual human beings irrespective of their nationality. Moreover, Article 2 makes clear that these obligations do not merely exist in the interest of *present* human beings, but also for the benefit of *future* generations.

Article 1 only purports to establish a fundamental right of human beings to an adequate environment vis-à-vis other human beings or entities created by man such as States. In other words the emphasis laid in Article 1 on the protection of the interests of human beings may not be deemed to imply a choice for an anthropocentric approach in environmental questions.

It cannot be said that the fundamental human right to an adequate environment already constitutes a well-established right under present international law. As a matter of fact there are as yet no treaties which provide for a specific human right to an adequate environment. Efforts made within the framework of the Council of Europe during the 1970s to adopt such a human right in an additional protocol to the 1950 European Convention for the Protection of Human Rights and Fundamental Freedoms or through an amendment of the 1961 European Social Charter unfortunately failed to obtain the required support. It is true that the 1974 Nordic Environmental Protection Convention grants inhabitants of a country who are (possibly) detrimentally affected by a (planned) environmentally harmful activity in another country, a right of equal access to and of equal treatment by the administrative or judicial authorities of the latter country. However, this convention does not provide for an *independent* (substantive and/or procedural) right to an adequate environment for the inhabitants of the country of origin of the environmentally harmful activity and consequently neither for the inhabitants of countries (possibly) affected by such an activity. The argument of the absence of an independent right to an adequate environment applies, of course, likewise to all those OECD or other recommendations which recommend the granting of a right of equal access or treatment to individuals (possibly) affected by a transboundary environmental interference.

Certain treaties provide for human rights which may imply a corollary duty not to impair the environment beyond a certain degree. Reference may be made here to the inherent right to life of every human being stated in Article 6(1) of the 1966 UN Covenant on Civil and Political Rights. However, it should be kept in mind that this right can only be invoked when the environmental degradation has reached such an extent that life itself is endangered, so that it must be deemed to be of little use to safeguard a certain *quality* of life. Another limitation is to be found in the last sentence of Article 6(1) which provides that "No one shall be *arbitrarily* deprived of his life." (emphasis added).

Certain provisions in the 1966 UN Covenant on Economic, Social and Cultural Rights are more promising. The States Parties to this covenant recognize in Article 11(1) " * * * the right of everyone to an *adequate standard of living* * * * and to the *continuous improvement of living conditions*" (emphasis added) and in Article 12(1) " * * * the right of everyone to the enjoyment of the *highest attainable standard of physical and mental health* ", the full realization of which is to be achieved, inter alia, by "the improvement of all aspects of *environmental * * * hygiene* " (emphasis added). It is clear that the realization of the right to an adequate standard of living and to the highest attainable standard of physical and mental health may well require the taking of measures to prevent or abate impairment of the environment. However, it should also be borne in mind that, according to the 1966 UN Covenant on Economic, Social and Cultural Rights (see Article 2(1)), the realization of these rights need only be progressively achieved by States which are a party to the covenant "by all appropriate means" and "to the maximum of [their] available resources".

En dehors treaties, some indirect support for a right of human beings to an adequate environment also may be found in everyone's right to life (Article 3) or everyone's right to a standard of living adequate for the health and well-being of himself and of his family (Article 25) which are proclaimed in UNGA Resolution No. 217 of 10 December 1948 adopting the Universal Declaration of Human Rights. Noteworthy, however, also is Article 29(2) which provides that the rights proclaimed in the Universal Declaration may be limited by law "for the purpose of * * * meeting the just requirements of * * * the general welfare in a democratic society". Like the 1966 UN Covenant on Economic, Social and Cultural Rights, the Universal Declaration sets only certain standards of achievement (see the Preamble), but, unlike the 1966 UN Covenant, does not constitute a legally binding instrument for States.

Reference to a specific international human right to an adequate environment is, in fact, only to be found in the above-quoted Principle 1 of the 1972 UN Declaration on the Human Environment. Apart from the fact that the States which adopted the 1972 UN Declaration probably regarded the principle as not legally binding but stating merely a goal to be achieved, there also remains the problem of the clear incompatibility of the proclaimed fundamental human right with the statement in Principle 21 of the 1972 UN Declaration that: "States have, in accordance with the Charter of the United Nations and the principles of international law, the sovereign right to exploit their own resources pursuant to their own environmental policies * * * ". This sovereign right is, in Principle 21, only restricted in case damage is caused to the environment of other States or of areas beyond the limits of national jurisdiction.

The source of many human rights which have eventually found recognition on the international plane is to be found in municipal law. Hence, support for an emerging specific fundamental human right to an adequate environment may possibly be found in national constitutional or other legislation. While there are a fair number of constitutional or other legal provisions which impose a basic duty on the State to protect (certain parts of) the environment, there are only very few provisions which provide for a specific right of individual human beings to an adequate environment (see, e.g., Article 45(1) of the 1978 Constitution of Spain; Article 123 of the 1979 Constitution of Peru; and perhaps Article 71 of the 1976 Polish Constitution) or provide that the State must protect the environment for the benefit of individual human beings. Hence, it is as yet not possible to maintain that there already exists a general principle of (national) law recognized by civilized nations in the sense of Article 38(1)(c) of the Statute of the International Court of Justice which embodies a fundamental human right to an adequate environment.

The fundamental human right laid down in Article 1 therefore remains an ideal which must still be realized.

———

Environmental Rights as Human Rights—differing opinions. From the above extract it can be seen that group of experts of the WCED did not find that there exists at the present time a "fundamental human right to an adequate environment" under international law. Consider the views of the writers extracted below on this issue. See also P. Gormley, Human Rights and Environment: The Need for International Cooperation (1976); P. Gormley, The Legal Obligation of the International Community to Guarantee a Pure and Decent Environment: The Expansion of Human Rights Norms, 3 Georgetown Int'l Env.L.Rev. 85 (1990) and A. Cancado Trindade, The Parallel Evolutions of International Human Rights Protection and of Environmental Protection and the Absence of Restrictions upon the Exercise of Recognized Human Rights, 13 Revista del Instituto Interamericano de Derochos Humanos 35 (1991).

———

A. KISS AND D. SHELTON, INTERNATIONAL ENVIRONMENTAL LAW

21–22, 28–31 (1991) (footnotes omitted).*

The Right to Environment

Just as environmental law derives from the common interest of humanity, so does international recognition of human rights and fundamental freedoms. There is no contradiction between the two concepts. The opening paragraph of the preamble to the Universal Declaration of Human Rights, unanimously proclaimed by the General Assembly of the United Nations on December 10, 1948, underlines a common purpose, stating that, "recognition of the inherent dignity and of the equal and inalienable rights of all members of the human family is the foundation of freedom, justice and peace in the world."

The link between human rights and environmental protection is clearly established by Principle 1 of the Stockholm Declaration: "Man has the fundamental right to freedom, equality and adequate conditions of life, in an environment of a quality that permits a life of dignity and well-being. * * * ."

This formulation stops short of proclaiming a direct right to a healthy environment. Rather, it reaffirms the right to freedom, equality and adequate conditions of life; the requirement of an adequate environment is viewed as a means to achieve the protection of that right. Of course, this approach is true as far as it goes; clearly an environment damaged by pollutants and robbed of all beauty and variety is contrary to adequate conditions of life, just as rupturing the ecosystems endangers physical and mental health.

However, there is value in recognizing an independent right to a safe and healthy environment. First, it reinforces and complements other rights guaranteed to each person. For example, inequalities of economic status are accentuated by environmental harm: the wealthy have available the material means necessary to escape both the air pollution and environmental damage of poor urban areas, and to create for themselves safe and healthy zones, at least until environmental damage becomes too widespread. Recognizing the right to a safe and healthy environment thus can become a means to implement other fundamental human rights.

The concept of a right to environment also is inherent in recognizing the interests of future generations. Immediately after the Stockholm Declaration proclaims that man has the right to live in an environment whose quality permits a life of dignity and well-being, it adds that man has the "solemn responsibility to protect and improve the environment for present and future generations." Economic, social and cultural rights cannot be enjoyed in a world where resources are inadequate due to the waste of irresponsible generations. Thus, the right to environ-

* Reprinted with the permission of Transnational Publishers, Inc.

ment as one form of the expression of human dignity may be seen as a necessary precondition to the realization of other rights in the future.

* * * [I]n 1989, the International Labor Organization adopted a new Convention concerning Indigenous and Tribal Peoples in Independent Countries. [28 ILM 1384 (1989).] This treaty requires that states parties take special measures to safeguard the environment of the peoples concerned. In particular governments must ensure that studies are carried out to assess the environmental impact of planned development activities and take measures, in cooperation with the peoples concerned, to protect and preserve the environment of the territories they inhabit. The Convention also recognizes the importance of traditional activities of indigenous peoples, including hunting, fishing, trapping, and gathering. As discussed below, most international instruments for the protection of wildlife contain exceptions permitting traditional hunting by indigenous populations, even with regard to endangered species. Although there is potential conflict between concerns for maintenance of traditional cultures and protection of endangered wildlife species, such conflict remains theoretical at the present time due to the limitations included in the wildlife treaties and traditional indigenous respect for nature.

* * * United Nations organs responsible for human rights issues have begun to consider the inter-relationship of the environment and human rights. The United Nations Subcommission on the Prevention of Discrimination and Protection of Minorities has adopted several resolutions in this field since 1989. One reaffirms that the movement of toxic and dangerous products endangers basic human rights such as the right to life, the right to live in a sound and healthy environment and the right to health, and calls on UNEP to find global solutions to the problem. Another resolution appointed a special rapporteur to study the environment and its relation to human rights, while affirming "the inextricable relationship between human rights and the environment". The UN Human Rights Commission also adopted a resolution in 1990 in which it stressed the importance of the preservation of life-sustaining ecosystems to the promotion of human rights.

* * * It is possible that in the foreseeable future, the right to conservation of the environment will be incorporated more frequently in obligatory international instruments. Besides its procedural aspects, it carries a temporal perspective which could become fundamental for the enjoyment of all other rights guaranteed to individuals, including the interests of future generations in the safeguarding or conservation of resources.

G. HANDL, HUMAN RIGHTS AND PROTECTION OF THE ENVIRONMENT: A MILDLY "REVISIONIST" VIEW

in A. Cancado Trindade (ed.), Human Rights, Sustainable Development and the Environment. 117–122 (1992) (footnotes omitted).*

The concept of environmental rights as "new" human rights—"third generation", so-called "human needs" or "solidarity" rights—is a relatively old one. So is the debate over whether such entitlements presently are, are about to be, or should be guaranteed in international law. However, the upcoming 1992 United Nations Conference on Environment and Development which presents a potentially unique opportunity to write and refine basic international environmental law for the rest of the century and beyond, has again focused attention on the concept of international environmental human rights.

For example, in September 1990, the Parliamentary Assembly of the Council of Europe adopted Recommendation 1130 (1990) (1) which provides for a human right to "an environment * * * conducive to * * * good health, well-being and full development of the human personality". In October 1991, an ECE Experts Meeting in Oslo adopted a draft Charter on Environmental Rights and Obligations which proclaims among its fundamental principles everybody's "right to an environment adequate for his general health and well-being." This formulation follows closely Principle 1 of a text adopted by the Experts Group on Environmental Law of the World Commission on Environment and Development in 1986. More recently, the meeting of Associations of Environmental Law adopted a "Declaration of Limoges," which, once again, recommends recognition of a "human right to the environment" (recommendation 4). These proposals have been made against the background of an on-going study by the United Nations Human Rights Commission's Sub-commission on [the] Prevention of Discrimination and Protection of Minorities of the problem of the environment and its relation to human rights.

During the meetings of Working Group III of the UNCED Preparatory Committee itself, a number of states submitted proposals for a similar entitlement for inclusion in the Conference's final document on general rights and obligations, the "Earth Charter": the Chairman's consolidated draft—now replaced by a set of draft principles proposed by the Chairman—contained several provisions that emphasized a human right to a "healthy environment."

Support for international environmental human rights thus cuts across a wide spectrum of international public opinion. * * * Increasingly, it is also being claimed that there exists already, or there is about to emerge, a broad generic entitlement to a healthy, decent or otherwise qualified environment. Indeed, often this entitlement is referred to simply as a "human right to the environment"—unqualified.

* Reprinted with the permission of Instituto Interamericano de Drechos Humanos San José, Costa Rica.

The assumption that inspires a significant portion of the public discourse, namely that today the cause of environmental protection is furthered by the postulation of a generic human right to a decent or healthy environment, however, is a problematical one. While it should be self-evident that there is a direct functional relationship between protection of the environment and the promotion of human rights, it is much less obvious that environmental protection ought to be conceptualized in terms of a generic human right. Indeed, the emphasis on such a perspective on the interrelationship of human rights and environmental protection carries significant costs; it reflects a maximalist position that offers little prospect of becoming reality in the near term while its propagation diverts attention and efforts from other more pressing and promising environmental and human rights objectives. In short, a generic international environmental entitlement, both as an already existing and an emerging human rights concept, is a highly questionable proposition.

II.   *Environmental Rights as Human Rights*

A.   *The Right to a Healthy Environment as an Existing or Emerging Human Right*

1.   *The Probative Value of International Practice*
(i) Some Theoretical Observations

At the outset it might be advisable to point out that the international human rights discourse continues to suffer from an unresolved "contradiction between conceptions of human rights as either inherent in human beings by virtue of their humanity or as benevolently granted by the state * * * ". This affects not just the perception of the burden of proof but the very nature of the argument regarding the existence of such rights in general international law. For example, some adherents of a natural law theory of human rights might be apt to view any "just claim" as an existing human right. Most international lawyers, however, are likely to agree that the process of international recognition of human rights evinces overlapping positive and natural law conceptions. They are also likely to insist, notwithstanding the relative dearth of traditional state practice in the sense of international claims and counterclaims involving human rights, on evidence of actual supportive state practice remain[ing] an essential element of any persuasive argument that a given human rights claim is recognized by general international law.

This evidentiary requirement applies firstly, even if we assume that by now states implicitly recognize the United Nations General Assembly's special declaratory authority to determine the human rights nature of claims; and secondly, notwithstanding the possibility that with respect to human rights claims, actual state practice may be less of an essential underpinning of international normativity than [it] would be in * * * other claims contexts. After all, from the perspective of assessing allegedly new customary international legal norms, including human rights norms, deeds speak louder than words: only actual practice endorsing a claimed entitlement may provide a realistic measure of determination to render the prescriptive standard effective. Absent a "credible communication" to that effect, the alleged human rights standard is a mere paper right.

In any event, a diminished evidentiary standard regarding actual practice might be applicable only to human rights that are fundamental or inalienable ones. What can be said with confidence, therefore, is that the more attenuated the natural law basis of an alleged human right, the more important will be support of evidence of its reflection in positive international law, i.e., the practice of states and other relevant transnational actors.

Leaving aside for the moment the problem of its intrinsic relativity, the so-called "right to environment", or the right to a "clean," even to a "healthy environment" would be difficult to conceptualize as an inalienable one, notwithstanding the important objectives it purports to serve. If "inalienability" implies the impermissibility of derogations from the human right concerned, it should be evident why any meaningful environmental entitlement would not qualify: The evolution of environmental protection measures has involved a constant re-ordering of socio-economic priorities, of accomodating, adjusting, or off-setting mutually restrictive, if not exclusive, public policy objectives. Environmental entitlements have been and will continue to be susceptible to restrictions for the sake of other, socio-economic objectives, such as ensuring continued "development" or "saving jobs". In short, since a generic environmental entitlement would not be inalienable, it would not therefore share either a characteristic that is traditionally viewed as a hallmark of "natural" rights. Conceptually, it is instead squarely rooted in positive law.

Those who attempt to make the case for an existing or emerging generic environmental human right, therefore, would have to back up their claims by solid positive legal evidence. Alas, when analyzed in light of this evidentiary standard, the claims concerned are unpersuasive: Thus far, the idea of a generic entitlement—as against "sectoral" environmental rights of individuals—has not found express affirmation in any binding or effective international legal instrument.

6. DEBT FOR NATURE SWAPS
E. BROWN WEISS, IN FAIRNESS TO FUTURE GENERATIONS
157–159 (1989) (footnotes omitted).*

One of the most innovative international financing initiatives operating at the national level is the debt for nature swap, or debt/conservation swap, which is a method of allowing developing countries to pay off a portion of their external debt by committing themselves to protecting their own natural resources. This indirectly facilitates funds for conservation projects, which are scarce. The idea is an extension of the debt/equity conversions employed by a number of heavily indebted States, in which foreign holders of the country's commercial debt are allowed to exchange it for local currency which can then be reinvested in specified domestic commercial and industrial projects.

* Reprinted with the permission of Transnational Publishers, Inc.

The debt/conservation swap can take several forms, depending upon whether the debts are owed to private banks or to multilateral and bilateral lending agencies. If the debts are owed to foreign private banks, there is typically a secondary market where the obligations are bought and sold at only a fraction of their face value, because of the high risk that they may be uncollectible. In a debt/conservation swap, a private party who has bought the obligation at the deeply discounted price, returns it to the issuing government in exchange for the latter's agreeing to undertake a specific conservation program in the indebted country. The first successful transaction involved a private charitable foundation, the Weeden Foundation, which provided money to an environmental organization, Conservation International, to buy deeply discounted Bolivian bonds at 15 cents to the dollar. Bolivia agreed to set aside 3.7 million acres of its tropical forest in exchange for cancellation of the debt, and also agreed to allocate money to the maintenance of the reserve. Other such arrangements are being negotiated by private environmental groups such as the World Wildlife Fund.

These swaps are devices to help countries develop on a sustainable basis rather than by destructive short-term resource exploitation in the hope of keeping up with interest payments. They are in essence a form of development assistance that is conditioned on specific programs of environmental conservation. They require for their effectiveness a source of grant funds or concessional loans, preferably one that constitutes a new source of such finance and is not subtracted from funds now being devoted to development assistance.

Bills have been introduced in the U.S. Congress to provide for favorable tax treatment of the debt cancellation or donation. This is intended to encourage commercial banks to donate the outstanding dollar denominated obligations of certain debtor countries to conservation organizations in return for taking a charitable deduction equal, according to the proposed legislation, to the donor's basis in the debt.

When the developing country has borrowed money not from private banks, but from other states through bilateral or multilateral lending agencies, there is no secondary market where the obligations are discounted to third parties. Proposals have been made to encourage the World Bank to forgive certain outstanding loans to developing countries that agree to implement specific conservation programs. These programs could take many different forms depending on the circumstances of each country.

In 1987 the U.S. Secretary of the Treasury expressed support for the principle of debt forgiveness in return for investment in environmental protection measures. Bills have been before both Houses of Congress to require the Executive Director of the World Bank from the United States to propose a pilot program by which countries with debts held by the Bank might suspend repayment by establishing "conservation easements" to protect endangered parts of tropical forests and wetlands.

At the Fourth World Wilderness Congress in September 1987, a World Conservation Bank was proposed to finance conservation projects and address debt problems in developing countries. The World Commission on Environment and Development has proposed that a special international banking facility or program be established in connection with the World Bank to provide loans or develop joint financing activities for conserving critical habitats or ecosystems. This should extend to activities for conserving the knowledge of traditional peoples about these areas.

AMERICAN SOCIETY OF INTERNATIONAL LAW ENVIRONMENTAL LAW INTEREST GROUP NEWSLETTER

Vol. 3(1), 3 (1992).*

Poland announced the first multilateral debt-for-nature scheme in April. Under the scheme, 10 percent of Poland's debt would be converted into an ecological fund, to be used for projects to reduce transboundary pollution flows, reduce pollution in the Baltic Sea, reduce greenhouse gas emissions, and enhance nature conservation. In 1991, the US said that it would approve the eco-conversion of 10 percent of Poland's $3.5 billion debt.

1. *The World Wildlife Fund for Nature.* This NGO has been an active pioneer in this area of debts-for-nature swaps. In 1987–1988 the WWF entered into debts-for-nature swaps with Costa Rica, Ecuador and the Philippines. What concerns do you think might be raised here by the debtor state concerning sovereignty? (See D. Barrans, Promoting Environmental Protection Through Foreign Debt Exchange Transactions, 24 Cornell Int.L.J. 1 (1991); T. Hamlin, Debt-for-Nature Swaps: A New Strategy for Protecting Environmental Interests in Developing Nations, 16 Ecol.L.Q. 1065 (1989)).

* Reprinted with the permission of the American Society of International Law.

Chapter 7

THE IMMUNITIES OF STATES AND INTERNATIONAL ORGANIZATIONS

SECTION A. THE IMMUNITY OF STATES

1. ABSOLUTE AND RESTRICTIVE PRINCIPLES

Modern doctrines of foreign sovereign immunities are a product of evolving customary international law influenced by new legislation and court decisions including Twentieth Century efforts to develop and codify by the treaty process. Immunity shields a foreign sovereign from the exercise of jurisdiction, principally from the jurisdiction of other states' courts in cases where the sovereign has not given consent to such jurisdiction. It allows a sovereign to act in his nation's best interest without fear that his actions will be subject of adjudication in another state. It also is to ensure that the public property of the foreign state remains available for public purposes, free from the constraints of the forum's powers of attachment and execution. Despite many cases over the past several centuries, the international legal rules on sovereign immunity still are not free from dispute and uncertainty. Immunity can be justified only on the basis of the most compelling considerations of public policy.

The classical formulation of the supporting reasons for sovereign immunity was stated by Chief Justice Marshall in 1812, in the *Schooner Exchange v. McFadden, supra*:

> The world being composed of distinct sovereignties, possessing equal rights and equal independence, whose mutual benefit is promoted by intercourse with each other, and by an interchange of those good offices which humanity dictates and its wants require, all sovereigns have consented to a relaxation in practice, in cases under

certain circumstances, of that absolute and complete jurisdiction within their respective territories which sovereignty confers.

* * *

This full and absolute territorial jurisdiction being alike the attribute of every sovereign, and being incapable of conferring extra-territorial power, would not seem to contemplate foreign sovereigns nor their sovereign rights to its objects. One sovereign being in no respect amenable to another; and being bound by obligations of the highest character not to degrade the dignity of his nation, by placing himself or its sovereign rights within the jurisdiction of another, can be supposed to enter a foreign territory only under an express license, or in confidence that the immunities belonging to his independent sovereign station, though not expressly stipulated, are reserved by implication, and will be extended to him.

This perfect equality and absolute independence of sovereigns, and this common interest impelling them to mutual intercourse, and an interchange of good offices with each other, have given rise to a class of cases in which every sovereign is understood to waive the exercise of a part of that complete exclusive territorial jurisdiction, which has been stated to be the attribute of every nation.

The concept of "perfect equality and absolute independence of sovereigns" arose in the 18th and 19th Centuries. It is not altogether forgotten today. The international system, however, has evolved toward a more realistic and pragmatic vision of the sovereign's status. Theoretically, since the American Revolution, the "people" are generally considered sovereign, rather than the head of State. More realistically, the "sovereign" may be a public trading institution or other subordinate governmental operating entity. Notions of sovereignty, equality and independence have become qualified, if not severely limited. The modern sovereign state's equality and independence are severely constrained in institutions like the U.N. or other international organizations. A sovereign can be subject to the most far-reaching and even humiliating formal condemnations, as occurred with Iraq in the Security Council actions taken in the course of the Persian Gulf Crisis in 1990–1991. Chief Justice Marshall's elegant formulations no longer fit either the appearances or reality of international relations. "Perfect equality" does not exist outside ideal abstraction. It is no wonder that the sovereign immunity doctrine has receded from its most extreme form, "*absolute immunity*" in many (but by no means all) countries. With the "absolute immunity" doctrine now finding only minority support, the system extends to accommodate problems in particular sectors and to find new applications and exceptions.

If the doctrine of equality, concerns about dignity, and avoidance of embarrassment no longer carry their former weight, there remain other considerations which explain the durability of the sovereign immunity doctrine. The judicial branch of government may be, or at least may feel, constrained. Judicial determinations rendered against a friendly foreign state or its sovereign leader can interfere with the conduct of foreign relations. Although this problem is sometimes exaggerated, a serious problem could arise, if a court were to adopt a rule or apply a treaty interpretation at variance with the views of the forum executive, developed in negotiations with another state. Protecting a foreign state from nuisance cases or the abusive use of the courts as a negotiating tool or a "public forum" for political advantage presents another problem. The case for immunity is strong when judicial action may interfere with continuing or future governmental action. Concerns about protecting operations are particularly noteworthy in cases of attachment and execution affecting a foreign government's property situated in the forum state. The materials below cover many of these situations. The foregoing policy concerns may be seen as affecting the outcomes, particularly in view of the continuing uncertainty of the law.

In sum, the case for sovereign immunity, particularly in the traditional absolute sense, has become much more difficult to accommodate in the 20th Century. The practice is not uniform and uncertainty exists among and even within many countries. More erosion of the traditional doctrine may be reasonably foreseen. The former socialist countries of central and eastern Europe, among the last bastions of the absolute principle, may find that, as they move to market economies, they will have the same incentives as in traditional market economy countries to find ways of limiting sovereign immunity. They may adopt the "restrictive principle" which relaxes the immunity for commercial and a number of other specified activities.

ABSOLUTE THEORY OF IMMUNITY

Absolute sovereign immunity was articulated by Chief Justice Marshall in the famous *Schooner Exchange* Case, *quoted above. Cf., Aldona S. v. U.K.,* 90 J.Dr.Int'l 190 (1963) (Pol.S.Ct.1948). Absolute immunity was attacked in the early part of this century, often in cases in which foreign vessels were engaged in maritime commerce. The United States Supreme Court, however, refused to limit the scope of sovereignty, rejecting a District Court's decision below that Italy did not enjoy sovereign immunity. This, although the action related to a proceeding *in rem* to enforce a cargo damage claim against a merchant vessel owned and operated by Italy. "We know of no international usage which regards the maintenance and advancement of the economic welfare of a people in time of peace as any less a public purpose than the maintenance and training of a naval force." *Berizzi Bros. Co. v. S.S. Pesaro,* 271 U.S. 562 (1926).

Some Substantive Exceptions. Forum state policy considerations have led to exceptions. These relate to rights in property situated in the forum state, when acquired by succession or gift, and to rights in immovable property there. These exceptions now appear in section 1605(4) of the United States Foreign Sovereign Immunities Act, set forth in the Documentary Supplement. Another exception precludes sovereign immunity for war crimes. This exception appeared specifically in Article 7 of the Charter of the International Military Tribunal established for the Nuremberg Trials after World War II. A parallel exception was adopted by the United Nations Security Council in S/RES/827 (1993) in which an International Tribunal was established to prosecute crimes against humanity in the former Yugoslavia (see Chapter 11)). Article 7.2 of the Annex to that Resolution provides that: "The official position of any accused person, whether as Head of State or Government or as a responsible Government official, shall not relieve such person of criminal responsibility nor mitigate punishment."

U.N. CONVENTION ON THE LAW OF THE SEA

See documentary supplement, focus especially on articles 30, 31, 32, 95 and 96.

In 1952, the U.S. Department of State indicated that it would follow the "restrictive" theory of sovereign immunity. This was incorporated in the *Foreign Sovereign Immunities Act of 1976*. A period of extensive *state* participation in commercial activity during the 19th century until the 1950's, precipitated the change.

UNITED STATES: LETTER FROM THE ACTING LEGAL ADVISER OF THE DEPARTMENT OF STATE TO THE DEPARTMENT OF JUSTICE, MAY 19, 1952 (THE FAMOUS *"TATE LETTER"*)

26 United States Department of State Bulletin 984 (1952).

MY DEAR MR. ATTORNEY GENERAL:

The Department of State has for some time had under consideration the question whether the practice of the Government in granting immunity from suit to foreign governments made parties defendant in the courts of the United States without their consent should not be changed. The Department has now reached the conclusion that such immunity should no longer be granted in certain types of cases. In view of the obvious interest of your Department in this matter I should like to point out briefly some of the facts which influenced the Department's decision.

A study of the law of sovereign immunity reveals the existence of two conflicting concepts of sovereign immunity, each widely held and firmly established. According to the classical or absolute theory of sovereign immunity, a sovereign cannot, without his consent, be made a respondent in the courts of another sovereign. According to the newer or restrictive theory of sovereign immunity, the immunity of the sovereign is recognized with regard to sovereign or public acts (*jure imperii*) of a state, but not with respect to private acts (*jure gestionis*). There is agreement by proponents of both theories, supported by practice, that sovereign immunity should not be claimed or granted in actions with respect to real property (diplomatic and perhaps consular property excepted) or with respect to the disposition of the property of a deceased person even though a foreign sovereign is the beneficiary.

The classical or virtually absolute theory of sovereign immunity has generally been followed by the courts of the United States, the British Commonwealth, Czechoslovakia, Estonia, and probably Poland.

The decisions of the courts of Brazil, Chile, China, Hungary, Japan, Luxembourg, Norway, and Portugal may be deemed to support the classical theory of immunity if one or at most two old decisions anterior to the development of the restrictive theory may be considered sufficient on which to base a conclusion.

The position of the Netherlands, Sweden, and Argentina is less clear since although immunity has been granted in recent cases coming before the courts of those countries, the facts were such that immunity would have been granted under either the absolute or restrictive theory. However, constant references by the courts of these three countries to the distinction between public and private acts of the state, even though the distinction was not involved in the result of the case, may indicate an intention to leave the way open for a possible application of the restrictive theory of immunity if and when the occasion presents itself.

A trend to the restrictive theory is already evident in the Netherlands where the lower courts have started to apply that theory following a Supreme Court decision to the effect that immunity would have been applicable in the case under consideration under either theory.

The German courts, after a period of hesitation at the end of the nineteenth century have held to the classical theory, but it should be noted that the refusal of the Supreme Court in 1921 to yield to pressure by the lower courts for the newer theory was based on the view that that theory had not yet developed sufficiently to justify a change. In view of the growth of the restrictive theory since that time the German courts might take a different view today.

The newer or restrictive theory of sovereign immunity has always been supported by the courts of Belgium and Italy. It was adopted in turn by the courts of Egypt and of Switzerland. In addition, the courts of France, Austria, and Greece, which were traditionally supporters of the classical theory, reversed their position in the 20's to embrace the restrictive theory. Rumania, Peru, and possibly Denmark also appear to follow this theory.

Furthermore, it should be observed that in most of the countries still following the classical theory there is a school of influential writers favoring the restrictive theory and the views of writers, at least in civil law countries, are a major factor in the development of the law. Moreover, the leanings of the lower courts in civil law countries are more significant in shaping the law than they are in common law countries where the rule of precedent prevails and the trend in these lower courts is to the restrictive theory.

Of related interest to this question is the fact that ten of the thirteen countries which have been classified above as supporters of the classical theory have ratified the Brussels Convention of 1926 under which immunity for government owned merchant vessels is waived. In addition the United States, which is not a party to the Convention, some years ago announced and has since followed, a policy of not claiming immunity for its public owned or operated merchant vessels. Keeping in mind the importance played by cases involving public vessels in the field of sovereign immunity, it is thus noteworthy that these ten countries (Brazil, Chile, Estonia, Germany, Hungary, Netherlands, Norway, Poland, Portugal, Sweden) and the United States have already relinquished by treaty or in practice an important part of the immunity which they claim under the classical theory.

It is thus evident that with the possible exception of the United Kingdom little support has been found except on the part of the Soviet Union and its satellites for continued full acceptance of the absolute theory of sovereign immunity. There are evidences that British authorities are aware of its deficiencies and ready for a change. The reasons which obviously motivate state trading countries in adhering to the theory with perhaps increasing rigidity are most persuasive that the United States should change its policy. Furthermore, the granting of sovereign immunity to foreign governments in the courts of the United States is most inconsistent with the action of the Government of the United States in subjecting itself to suit in these same courts in both contract and tort and with its long established policy of not claiming immunity in foreign jurisdictions for its merchant vessels. Finally, the Department feels that the widespread and increasing practice on the part of governments of engaging in commercial activities makes necessary a practice which will enable persons doing business with them to have their rights determined in the courts. For these reasons it will hereafter be the Department's policy to follow the restrictive theory of sovereign immunity in the consideration of requests of foreign governments for a grant of sovereign immunity.

It is realized that a shift in policy by the executive cannot control the courts but it is felt that the courts are less likely to allow a plea of sovereign immunity where the executive has declined to do so. There have been indications that at least some Justices of the Supreme Court feel that in this matter courts should follow the branch of the Government charged with responsibility for the conduct of foreign relations.

In order that your Department, which is charged with representing the interests of the Government before the courts, may be adequately informed it will be the Department's practice to advise you of all requests by foreign governments for the grant of immunity from suit and of the Department's action thereon.

    Sincerely yours,

    For the Secretary of State:

        JACK B. TATE
        Acting Legal Adviser

  * * *

TESTIMONY OF THE LEGAL ADVISER OF THE DEPARTMENT OF STATE OF THE UNITED STATES ON THE FOREIGN SOVEREIGN IMMUNITIES ACT OF 1976

Hearings on H.R. 11315 before the Subcommittee on Administrative Law and Governmental Relations of the Committee on the Judiciary, House of Representatives, 94th Cong., 2d Sess. 24, 26–27 (1976).

[Monroe Leigh, the Legal Adviser, testified]: The first objective is to vest sovereign immunity decisions exclusively in the courts. The bill would accomplish this by prescribing the standards the courts are to apply in deciding questions of sovereign immunity.

* * * [A]fter a foreign-state defendant raises the defense of sovereign immunity, it has an option: either the foreign state can litigate this legal defense entirely in court, or, as is more usually the case, it can make a formal diplomatic request to have the State Department decide the issue.

If it does the latter, and if the State Department believes that immunity is appropriate, the State Department asks the Department of Justice to file a "suggestion of immunity" with the court hearing the case. Under the Supreme Court's decision in Ex Parte Peru, which was decided in 1943, U.S. courts automatically defer to such suggestions of immunity from the executive branch.

In response to various developments in international law, the State Department in 1952 adopted its so-called *Tate letter*. Prior to the Tate letter, the Department of State, when called on to decide questions of immunity, followed the so-called absolute rule of sovereign immunity: a state was immune from suit irrespective of whether it was engaged in a government or a commercial act.

Under the Tate letter, the Department undertook to decide future sovereign immunity questions in accordance with the international legal principle which I have mentioned and which is known as the "restrictive theory"—namely, that a foreign state's immunity is "restricted" to cases based on its public acts, and does not extend to cases based on its commercial or private acts. The Tate letter was based on a realization that the prior absolute rule of sovereign immunity was no longer consistent with modern international law.

The Tate letter, however, has not been satisfactory. * * * From a legal standpoint, it poses a devil's choice. If the Department follows the Tate letter in a given case, it is in the incongruous position of a political institution trying to apply a legal standard to litigation already before the courts.

On the other hand, if forced to disregard the Tate letter in a given case, the Department is in the self-defeating position of abandoning the very international law principle it elsewhere espouses.

From a diplomatic standpoint, the Tate letter has continued to leave the diplomatic initiative to the foreign state. The foreign state chooses which case it will bring to the State Department and in which case it will try to raise diplomatic considerations.

Leaving the diplomatic initiative in such cases to the foreign state places the United States at a disadvantage. This is particularly true since the United States cannot itself obtain similar advantages in other countries. In virtually every other country in the world, sovereign immunity is a question of international law decided exclusively by the courts and not by institutions concerned with foreign affairs.

For this reason, when we and other foreign states are sued abroad, we realize that international law principles will be applied by the courts and that diplomatic relations will not be called into play.

Moreover, from the standpoint of the private citizen, the current system generates considerable commercial uncertainty. A private party who deals with a foreign government entity cannot be certain of having his day in court to resolve an ordinary legal dispute. He cannot be entirely certain that the ordinary legal dispute will not be artificially raised to the level of a diplomatic problem through the government's intercession with the State Department.

The purpose of sovereign immunity in modern international law is not to protect the sensitivities of 19th–century monarchs or the prerogatives of the 20th–century state. Rather, it is to promote the functioning of all governments by protecting a state from the burden of defending law suits abroad which are based on its public acts.

However, when the foreign state enters the marketplace or when it acts as a private party, there is no justification in modern international law for allowing the foreign state to avoid the economic costs of the agreements which it may breach or the accidents which it may cause.

The law should not permit the foreign state to shift these everyday burdens of the marketplace onto the shoulders of private parties. * * *

———

1. *Foreign Sovereign Immunities Act of 1976.* The act (see Doc. Supp.) went into effect in January 1977. It incorporates the restrictive theory. As the Legal Adviser put it in * * * his testimony: "Under international law today, a foreign state is entitled to sovereign immunity only in the cases based on its 'public' acts. However, where a law suit is based on a commercial transaction or some other 'private' act of the foreign state, the foreign state is not entitled to sovereign immunity. The specific applications of this principle of international law are codified in * * * the proposed bill."

The *fundamental rule* is stated in Sec. 1604: "Subject to existing international agreements to which the United States is a party at the time of enactment of this Act a foreign state shall be immune from the jurisdiction of the courts of the United States and of the States except as provided in sections 1605 to 1607 of this chapter." Under those sections there are nine categories for which exceptions apply to section 1604:

    (1) waiver of immunity

    (2) commercial activity

    (3) rights in property taken in violation of international law

(4) rights in property in the United States acquired by succession or gift or rights in immovable property in the United States

(5) money damage tort actions for personal injuries or death or damage to or loss of property

(6) enforcement of an arbitration agreement made by a foreign state with or for the benefit of a private party, in prescribed situations

(7) maritime liens against a vessel where the lien is based upon commercial activities

(8) foreclosure of a preferred mortgage under the Ship Mortgage Act of 1920

(9) counterclaims

In Verlinden B.V. v. Central Bank of Nigeria, 461 U.S. 480 (1983), the U.S. Supreme Court upheld the constitutional power of Congress to enact the legislation.

––––––

2. *United Kingdom: State Immunity Act of 1978.* The United Kingdom became a signatory to the European Convention on State Immunity on May 16, 1972. That convention also incorporates the restrictive theory. Its text is in 11 International Legal Materials 470 (1972). It entered into force on June 11, 1976. To give effect to the convention, the United Kingdom enacted the State Immunity Act of 1978, found in 17 International Legal Materials 1123 (1978).

The 1987 Restatement noted that nearly all "non-Communist" states now accept the restrictive theory. Comment *a* to Section 451.

––––––

3. *International Agreements.* Movement toward the "restrictive principle" is occurring as a function of a number of treaty provisions in force or under consideration and national legislation and judicial decisions (which may well be moving customary law in that direction by accretion). The first of these is the Brussels Convention of 1926. * * * It applied the restrictive principle to government owned or operated vessels involved in trade. *See also*, the 1982 U.N. Convention on the Law of the Sea provisions on the subject of vessels. The European Convention on State Immunity and Additional Protocol of May 16, 1972 adopted the restrictive principle on a broader basis, including the commercial exception as provided in Article 7.1:

A Contracting state may not claim immunity from the jurisdiction of a court of another Contracting State if it has on the territory of the State of the forum an office, agency, or other establishment through which it engages, in the same manner as a private person, in an industrial, commercial or financial activity, and the proceedings relate to that activity of the office, agency or establishment.

In 1991 the International Law Commission adopted "Draft Articles on Jurisdictional Immunities of States and their Property" (UN A/46/405, 11 September, 1991; 30 I.L.M. 1554, 1565) (in the Documentary Supplement). The Draft Articles contain in Article 5 the following broad provision: "A State enjoys immunity, in respect of itself and its property, from the jurisdiction of the courts of another State subject to the provisions of the present articles." This is qualified by a number of exceptions, including: "express consent" (Article 7); proceedings initiated by the State invoking immunity (Articles 8 & 9); commercial transactions (Article 10); contracts of employment (Article 11); personal injuries and damage to property (Article 12); ownership, possession and use of property (Article 13); intellectual and industrial property (Article 14); participation in companies or other collective bodies (Article 15); ships owned or operated by a State for other than government non-commercial purposes (Article 16); and certain proceedings related to an arbitration to which the State had agreed in writing (Article 17).

State immunity from "measures of constraint" is governed by Articles 18 and 19. These provide for the immunity except in described cases of consent, allocation or earmarking of property for satisfaction of the claim, certain property in use or intended for use by the State for other than government non-commercial purposes. Moreover, specific categories of qualifying property may not be reached. These include property (bank accounts included) "used or intended for use for the purposes of the diplomatic mission of the State" (Article 19).

The discussion of the Draft Articles in the 1991 meeting of the Sixth Committee of the General Assembly, makes it clear that the Draft Articles do not yet attract a consensus. This is due to doctrinal disagreement as well as problems of detail and drafting (see U.N. A/CN.4/L. 456, February 6, 1991). The Draft Articles, nevertheless, currently represent the most advanced efforts to resolve the numerous uncertainties in the sovereign immunity arena.

––––––––

4. *French administrative law concepts.* After the French revolution of 1789, France established two parallel systems of courts: one judicial and the other administrative. For all practical purposes, they are equal in rank. The judicial system essentially was given jurisdiction over disputes between private parties, while the administrative system was given jurisdiction over disputes between private parties and the state. The administrative courts have developed—on a case by case basis—a body of administrative law which has no exact counterpart in England or the United States. This "case law" development has become the basis of administrative law in much of continental Europe and has influenced the administrative law of a number of states elsewhere.

It cannot be entirely an accident that states whose courts led the development of the restrictive theory, or eventually adopted it, are also, in the main, those which adopted or were influenced by French administrative law. For in the French system, a fundamental distinction is drawn between situations where the state exercises its public power, and those where the state acts in its private capacity. In the former, litigation authority belongs to the administrative courts. In the latter, it belongs to the judicial system. The distinction is elementary to civil law lawyers, even though it is subject in its application to exceptions, qualifications and refinements as complex as those surrounding the application of the concept of due process in American courts.

Because of their experience with concepts of administrative law of the French type, the courts, by the turn of the century, of a number of civil law states were intellectually conditioned to engage in a critical analysis of the doctrine of sovereign immunity. They did not take it for granted that all acts of a foreign state were sovereign. The theory worked out to delimit acts of sovereignty entitled to immunity, and separate them from other acts not entitled to immunity, borrows the differentiation from French administrative law and uses it as the basis for determining immunity vel non.

Consider the following application of the distinction between public and private acts.

GEORGES DELAUME, CASE NOTE

SOCIÉTÉ IRANIENNE DU GAZ v. SOCIÉTÉ PIPELINE SERVICE

[NIGC] 80 Revue Critique de Droit International Privé 140 (1991).
French Court of Cassation, May 2, 1990.
85 American Journal of International Law 696 (1991) (reprinted
by permission American Society of Int'l Law).

In 1978 a French company (Pipeline) and the National Iranian Gas Company (NIGC) entered into a contract (governed by Iranian law) for the supply and erection of gas pipeline installations linking certain Iranian cities. Apparently not paid for its services, Pipeline brought an action in France against NIGC. NIGC's plea of immunity was denied by the Court of Appeal of Versailles, whose decision was reversed by the Court of Cassation.

From the decision of the Court of Cassation (which, as usual, is essentially abstract and does not supply detailed information on the facts of the case and the arguments of the parties), it appears that NIGC based its plea of immunity on the consideration that it was intimately linked to the Iranian Government and that its activities relating to gas transmission throughout Iran were intended to meet the needs of a "public service" (*service public*). The court of appeal had considered this line of argument irrelevant because the decisive factor in determining the issue of immunity was the nature of the transaction. In its view, under the French *lex fori*, the transaction fell within the category of a "public work subcontract," which should be characterized as a purely commercial transaction. The Court of Cassation disagreed with that characterization, stating: "Foreign states and instrumentalities acting under the direction or on behalf of states are entitled to immunity from suit not only in regard to governmental acts but also in respect of acts performed in furtherance of a public service." [1]

1. Judgment of May 2, 1990, Cass. civ.
80 Revue Critique De Droit International
Privé [RCDIP] 140, 141.

This decision is surprising. It is contrary to a consistent line of cases in which the Court of Cassation has held that, for the implementation of immunity rules, the relevant factor is the nature of the transaction from which the dispute arises, rather than its purpose.[2] The nature of the transaction has been considered decisive in cases involving both immunity from suit and immunity from execution.

A return to the traditional test is apparent from another decision of the Court of Cassation rendered barely a few weeks after the *NIGC* case. The plaintiff, a British newspaperman, brought suit against the Kuwait News Agency following the agency's decision not to renew his contract. The agency pleaded immunity on the grounds that (1) it was an agency of Kuwait linked to the Ministry of Information; (2) its managing board was appointed by the Government; and (3) the contract of employment had a governmental character since the plaintiff's activities regarding the collection of information were carried out for the exclusive benefit of the Kuwaiti Government and, as such, should be regarded as directly related to the pursuit of a "public service." The plea was denied. Although the decision could have been based on the sole ground that the agency had an independent juridical personality and enjoyed financial autonomy, the Court went further and said that, even if the agency were in effect part of the Kuwaiti Government, the employment contract should be regarded as a commercial act with respect to which there was no immunity from suit.

Under the circumstances, the rationale of the *NIGC* decision is not readily apparent. It may be that the Court of Cassation was influenced by domestic administrative law concepts regarding the respective jurisdictions of the administrative and judicial courts. If that were the case, the *NIGC* decision would be a matter of concern because these concepts are not as clear as would be desirable. To project them into the international arena would inject unwarranted uncertainties into the implementation of immunity rules. Another possibility is that the Court may have been influenced by nonlegal considerations due to the improvement in the political climate between France and Iran. In any event, in light of the *Kuwait News Agency* decision, it is not clear whether the Court intended to signal a change in immunity rules in the *NIGC* case.

Questions: What are the conceptual differences between the approach of the Cour de Cassation in the NIGC and the Kuwait cases as described above? Can they be reconciled? Which would lead to the preferred policy result as you see it? Why?

---

2. France long ago adopted the restrictive theory of sovereign immunity. * * * Under the "purpose" test, an act would be considered sovereign if performed for a public purpose. That test has been criticized on the ground that, literally applied, it would eviscerate the "restrictive" theory of immunity since all acts of the sovereign might be construed as having a public purpose. Victory Transport Inc. v. Comisaria General, 336 F.2d 354 (2d Cir.1964). In the United States, the "nature of the act" test was codified in the Foreign Sovereign Immunities Act of 1976, 28 U.S.C. § 1603(d) (1988).

GENERAL RULE OF IMMUNITY

ARGENTINE REPUBLIC v. AMERADA HESS SHIPPING CORP.

United States Supreme Court, 1989.
488 U.S. 428, 109 S.Ct. 683, 102 L.Ed.2d 818.

Chief Justice REHNQUIST delivered the opinion of the Court.

Two Liberian corporations sued the Argentine Republic in a United States District Court to recover damages for a tort allegedly committed by its armed forces on the high seas in violation of international law. We hold that the District Court correctly dismissed the action, because the Foreign Sovereign Immunities Act of 1976 (FSIA), 28 U.S.C. § 1330 et seq., does not authorize jurisdiction over a foreign state in this situation.

Respondents alleged the following facts in their complaints. Respondent United Carriers, Inc., a Liberian corporation, chartered one of its oil tankers, the Hercules, to respondent Amerada Hess Shipping Corporation, also a Liberian corporation. The contract was executed in New York City. Amerada Hess used the Hercules to transport crude oil from the southern terminus of the Trans–Alaska Pipeline in Valdez, Alaska, around Cape Horn in South America, to the Hess refinery in the United States Virgin Islands. On May 25, 1982, the Hercules began a return voyage, without cargo but fully fueled, from the Virgin Islands to Alaska. At that time, Great Britain and petitioner Argentine Republic were at war over an archipelago of some 200 islands—the Falkland Islands to the British, and the Islas Malvinas to the Argentineans—in the South Atlantic off the Argentine coast. On June 3, United States officials informed the two belligerents of the location of United States vessels and Liberian tankers owned by United States interests then traversing the South Atlantic, including the Hercules, to avoid any attacks on neutral shipping.

By June 8, 1982, after a stop in Brazil, the Hercules was in international waters about 600 nautical miles from Argentina and 500 miles from the Falklands; she was outside the "war zones" designated by Britain and Argentina. At 12:15 Greenwich mean time, the ship's master made a routine report by radio to Argentine officials, providing the ship's name, international call sign, registry, position, course, speed, and voyage description. About 45 minutes later, an Argentine military aircraft began to circle the Hercules. The ship's master repeated his earlier message by radio to Argentine officials, who acknowledged receiving it. Six minutes later, without provocation, another Argentine military plane began to bomb the Hercules; the master immediately hoisted a white flag. A second bombing soon followed, and a third attack came about two hours later, when an Argentine jet struck the ship with an air-to-surface rocket. Disabled but not destroyed, the Hercules reversed course and sailed to Rio de Janeiro, the nearest safe port. At Rio de Janeiro, respondent United Carriers determined that the ship had suffered extensive deck and hull damage, and that an undetonated bomb remained lodged in her No. 2 tank. After an investigation by the

Brazilian Navy, United Carriers decided that it would be too hazardous to remove the undetonated bomb, and on July 20, 1978, the Hercules was scuttled 250 miles off the Brazilian coast. * * *

* * * In the FSIA, Congress added a new chapter 97 to Title 28 of the United States Code, 28 U.S.C. §§ 1602–1611, which is entitled "Jurisdictional Immunities of Foreign States." Section 1604 provides that "[s]ubject to existing international agreements to which the United States [was] a party at the time of the enactment of this Act[,] a foreign state shall be immune from the jurisdiction of the courts of the United States and of the States except as provided in sections 1605 to 1607 of this chapter." The FSIA also added § 1330(a) to Title 28; it provides that "[t]he district courts shall have original jurisdiction without regard to amount in controversy of any nonjury civil action against a foreign state * * * as to any claim for relief in personam with respect to which the foreign state is not entitled to immunity under sections 1605–1607 of this title or under any applicable international agreement." § 1330(a).

We think that the text and structure of the FSIA demonstrate Congress' intention that the FSIA be the sole basis for obtaining jurisdiction over a foreign state in our courts. Section 1604 and § 1330(a) work in tandem: § 1604 bars federal and state courts from exercising jurisdiction when a foreign state *is* entitled to immunity, and § 1330(a) confers jurisdiction on district courts to hear suits brought by United States citizens and by aliens when a foreign state is *not* entitled to immunity. As we said in *Verlinden,* the FSIA "must be applied by the district courts in every action against a foreign sovereign, since subject-matter jurisdiction in any such action depends on the existence of one of the specified exceptions to foreign sovereign immunity." Verlinden B.V. v. Central Bank of Nigeria, 461 U.S. 480, 493 (1983).

The Court of Appeals acknowledged that the FSIA's language and legislative history support the "general rule" that the Act governs the immunity of foreign states in federal court. The Court of Appeals, however, thought that the FSIA's "focus on commercial concerns" and Congress' failure to "repeal" the Alien Tort Statute indicated Congress' intention that federal courts continue to exercise jurisdiction over foreign states in suits alleging violations of international law outside the confines of the FSIA. The Court of Appeals also believed that to construe the FSIA to bar the instant suit would "fly in the face" of Congress' intention that the FSIA be interpreted pursuant to " 'standards recognized under international law.' " Ibid., * * *.

Taking the last of these points first, Congress had violations of international law by foreign states in mind when it enacted the FSIA. For example, the FSIA specifically denies foreign states immunity in suits "in which rights in property taken in violation of international law are in issue." 28 U.S.C. § 1605(a)(3). Congress also rested the FSIA in part on its power under Art. I, § 8, cl. 10, of the Constitution "[t]o define and punish Piracies and Felonies committed on the high Seas, and Offenses against the Law of Nations." From Congress' decision to deny immunity to foreign states in the class of cases just mentioned, we draw the plain implication that immunity is granted in those cases involving alleged violations of international law that do not come within one of the FSIA's exceptions.

As to the other point made by the Court of Appeals, Congress' failure to enact a *pro tanto* repealer of the Alien Tort Statute when it passed the FSIA in 1976 may be explained at least in part by the lack of certainty as to whether the Alien Tort Statute conferred jurisdiction in suits against foreign states. Enacted by the First Congress in 1789, the Alien Tort Statute provides that "[t]he district courts shall have original jurisdiction of any civil action by an alien for a tort only, committed in violation of the law of nations or a treaty of the United States." 28 U.S.C. § 1350. The Court of Appeals did not cite any decision in which a United States court exercised jurisdiction over a foreign state under the Alien Tort Statute, and only one such case has come to our attention—one which was decided after the enactment of the FSIA.

* * * [R]espondents argue that cases were brought under the Alien Tort Statute against foreign states for the unlawful taking of a prize during wartime. The Alien Tort Statute makes no mention of prize jurisdiction, and § 1333(2) now grants federal district courts exclusive jurisdiction over "all proceedings for the condemnation of property taken as a prize." In the Santissima Trinidad, 20 U.S. (7 Wheat.) 283, 353–354, 5 L.Ed. 454 (1822), we held that foreign states were not immune from the jurisdiction of United States courts in prize proceedings. That case, however, was not brought under the Alien Tort Statute but rather as a libel in admiralty. Thus there is a distinctly hypothetical case to the Court of Appeals' reliance on Congress' failure to repeal the Alien Tort Statute, and respondents' arguments in this Court based on the principle of statutory construction that repeals by implication are disfavored.

We think that Congress' failure in the FSIA to enact an express *pro tanto* repealer of the Alien Tort Statute speaks only faintly, if at all, to the issue involved in this case. In light of the comprehensiveness of the statutory scheme in the FSIA, we doubt that even the most meticulous draftsman would have concluded that Congress also needed to amend *pro tanto* the Alien Tort Statute and presumably such other grants of subject-matter jurisdiction in Title 28 as § 1331 (federal question), § 1333 (admiralty), § 1335 (interpleader), § 1337 (commerce and antitrust), and § 1338 (patents, copyrights, and trademarks). Congress provided in § 1602 of the FSIA that "[c]laims of foreign states to immunity should *henceforth* be decided by courts of the United States in conformity with the principles set forth in this chapter," and very likely it thought that should be sufficient. § 1602 (emphasis added); see also H.R.Rep., at 12; S.Rep., at 11 * * * (FSIA "intended to preempt any other State and Federal law (excluding applicable international agreements) for according immunity to foreign sovereigns").

Having determined that the FSIA provides the sole basis for obtaining jurisdiction over a foreign state in federal court, we turn to whether any of the exceptions enumerated in the Act apply here. These exceptions include cases involving the waiver of immunity, § 1605(a)(1), commercial activities occurring in the United States or causing a direct effect in this country, § 1605(a)(2), property expropriated in violation of international law, § 1605(a)(3), real estate, inherited, or gift property located in the United States, § 1605(a)(4), non-commercial torts occurring in the United States, § 1605(a)(5), and maritime liens, § 1605(b). We agree with the District Court that none of the FSIA's exceptions applies on these facts.

Respondents assert that the FSIA exception for noncommercial torts, § 1605(a)(5), is most in point. This provision denies immunity in a case

> "in which money damages are sought against a foreign state for personal injury or death, or damage to or loss of property, occurring in the United States and caused by the tortious act or omission of that foreign state or of any official or employee of that foreign state while acting within the scope of his office or employment." 28 U.S.C. § 1605(a)(5).

Section 1605(a)(5) is limited by its terms, however, to those cases in which the damage to or loss of property occurs *in the United States.* Congress' primary purpose in enacting § 1605(a)(5) was to eliminate a foreign state's immunity for traffic accidents and other torts committed in the United States, for which liability is imposed under domestic tort law. See H.R.Rep., at 14, 20–21. * * *

In this case, the injury to respondents' ship occurred on the high seas some 5,000 miles off the nearest shores of the United States * * *.

   * * *

The result * * * is not altered by the fact that petitioner's alleged tort may have had effects in the United States. Respondents state, for example, that the Hercules was transporting oil intended for use in this country and that the loss of the ship disrupted contractual payments due in New York. Under the commercial activity exception to the FSIA, § 1605(a)(2), a foreign state may be liable for its commercial activities "outside the territory of the United States" having a "direct effect" inside the United States. But the noncommercial tort exception, § 1605(a)(5), upon which respondents rely, makes no mention of "territory outside the United States" or of "direct effects" in the United States. Congress' decision to use explicit language in § 1605(a)(2), and not to do so in § 1605(a)(5), indicates that the exception in § 1605(a)(5) covers only torts occurring within the territorial jurisdiction of the United States. Respondents do not claim that § 1605(a)(2) covers these facts.

We also disagree with respondents' claim that certain international agreements entered into by petitioner and by the United States create an exception to the FSIA here. As noted, the FSIA was adopted "[s]ubject to international agreements to which the United States [was] a party at the time of [its] enactment." § 1604. This exception applies when international agreements "expressly conflic[t]" with the immunity provisions of the FSIA, H.R.Rep., at 17; S.Rep., at 17, hardly the circumstances in this case. Respondents point to the Geneva Convention on the High Seas, Apr. 29, 1958, [1962] 13 U.S.T. 2312, T.I.A.S. No. 5200, and the Pan American Maritime Neutrality Convention, Feb. 20, 1928, 47 Stat. 1989, 1990–1991, T.S. No. 845. These conventions, however, only set forth substantive rules of conduct and state that compensation shall be paid for certain wrongs. They do not create private rights of action for foreign corporations to recover compensation from foreign states in United States courts. Cf. Head Money Cases, 112 U.S. 580, 598–599 (1884); Foster v. Neilson, 27 U.S. (2 Pet.) 253, 314 (1829). Nor do we see how a foreign state can waive its immunity under § 1605(a)(1) by signing an international agreement that contains no mention of a waiver of immunity to suit in United States courts or even the availability of a cause of action in the United States. We find similarly unpersuasive the argument of respondents and *Amicus Curiae* Republic of Liberia that the Treaty of Friendship, Commerce and Navigation, Aug. 8, 1938, United States–Liberia, 54 Stat. 1739, T.S. No. 956, carves out an exception to the FSIA. Article I of this Treaty provides, in pertinent part, that the nationals of the United States and Liberia "shall enjoy freedom of access to the courts of justice of the other on conforming to the local laws." The FSIA is clearly one of the "local laws" to which respondents must "conform" before bringing suit in United States courts.

We hold that the FSIA provides the sole basis for obtaining jurisdiction over a foreign state in the courts of this country, and that none of the enumerated exceptions to the Act applies to the facts of this case. The judgment of the Court of Appeals is therefore

REVERSED.

Questions: Were the U.S. contacts and interests in this case sufficiently strong for U.S. courts to take jurisdiction, compared, for example, to the courts of the United Kingdom or Liberia? What *harm* might be done if U.S. courts were to take jurisdiction in such cases? Would a decision taking jurisdiction have carried the risk that U.S. courts might become a world judiciary in actions grounded on international law violations of foreign governments? What remedies remained for Amerada Hess after this proceeding was concluded against it?

Note: *Gould Inc. v. Mitsui Min. & Smelting Co.,* 750 F.Supp. 838 (N.D.Ohio 1990), involved issues of trade secret misappropriation sufficient to amount to a "pattern of racketeering (per RICO)". The action was dismissed because the predicate acts of "mail and wire fraud" were insufficiently alleged. Gould alleged that some of its trade secrets were transferred to foreign companies and that a plant was built in France based at least partly upon the trade secrets. Defendants argued that, at the time of the alleged predicate acts, they were owned by France and that the FSIA, therefore, applied. They claimed that the FSIA was the only basis of jurisdiction and that a foreign sovereign is not subject to U.S. criminal jurisdiction, hence, the concomitant RICO claim falls. Plaintiff countered that the FSIA applies only to civil actions and that RICO was irrelevant. The Court held that the language of RICO suggests that the kind of fraud which may be a "predicate act" may only be criminal fraud. Hence, it may function only when the defendant is subject to being prosecuted. Sovereigns, not being subject to prosecution, are not jurisdiction. *See,* 18 U.S.C. § 1961(1)(B); 18 U.S.C. §§ 1341, 1343. As an interesting aside, the law firm which represented plaintiff also ended up representing defendant (in patent matters), due to the merger of law firms.

　　　　　　　　* * *

Question: Why do you think that the criminal nature of the RICO proceeding figured so prominently in this case?

2. APPLICATIONS OF RESTRICTIVE PRINCIPLE TO COMMERCIAL AND OTHER ACTIVITIES

REPUBLIC OF ARGENTINA AND BANCO CENTRAL DE LA REPUBLICA ARGENTINA, PETITIONERS v. WELTOVER, INC., ET AL.

United States Supreme Court, 1992.
112 S.Ct. 2160, 119 L.Ed.2d 394.

Justice SCALIA delivered the opinion of the Court.

This case requires us to decide whether the Republic of Argentina's default on certain bonds issued as part of a plan to stabilize its currency was an act taken "in connection with a commercial activity" that had a "direct effect in the United States" so as to subject Argentina to suit in an American court under the Foreign Sovereign Immunities Act of 1976, 28 U.S.C. §§ 1602 et seq.

I

* * * Argentina's currency is not one of the mediums of exchange accepted on the international market. Argentine businesses engaging in foreign transactions must pay in U.S. dollars or some other internationally accepted currency. [It has been] difficult for Argentine borrowers to obtain such funds, principally because of the instability of the Argentine currency. To address these problems, petitioners, the Republic of Argentina and its central bank, Banco Central (collectively Argentina), in 1981 instituted a foreign exchange insurance contract program (FEIC), under which Argentina effectively agreed to assume the risk of currency depreciation in cross-border transactions involving Argentine borrowers. This was accomplished by Argentina's agreeing to sell to domestic borrowers, in exchange for a contractually predetermined amount of local currency, the necessary U.S. dollars to repay their foreign debts when they matured, irrespective of intervening devaluations.

* * * Argentina did not possess sufficient reserves of U.S. dollars to cover the FEIC contracts as they became due in 1982. The Argentine government thereupon adopted certain emergency measures, including refinancing of the FEIC-backed debts by issuing to the creditors government bonds. These bonds, called "Bonods," provide for payment of interest and principal in U.S. dollars; payment may be made through transfer on the London, Frankfurt, Zurich, or New York market, at the election of the creditor. [T]he foreign creditor had the option of either

accepting the Bonods in satisfaction of the initial debt, thereby substituting the Argentine government for the private debtor, or maintaining the debtor/creditor relationship with the private borrower and accepting the Argentine government as guarantor.

When the Bonods began to mature in May 1986, Argentina concluded that it lacked sufficient foreign exchange to retire them. Pursuant to a Presidential Decree, Argentina unilaterally extended the time for payment, and offered bondholders substitute instruments as a means of rescheduling the debts. [Three creditors] refused to accept the rescheduling, and insisted on full payment, specifying New York as the place where payment should be made. Argentina did not pay, and respondents then brought this breach-of-contract action, * * * relying on the Foreign Sovereign Immunities Act of 1976 as the basis for jurisdiction. * * *

II

The Foreign Sovereign Immunities Act of 1976, 28 U.S.C. § 1602 et seq., establishes a comprehensive framework for determining whether a court in this country, state or federal, may exercise jurisdiction over a foreign state. Under the Act, a "foreign state *shall* be immune from the jurisdiction of the courts of the United States and of the States" unless one of several statutorily defined exceptions applies. § 1604 (emphasis added). The FSIA thus provides the "sole basis" for obtaining jurisdiction over a foreign sovereign in the United States. See Argentine Republic v. Amerada Hess [supra.] The most significant of the FSIA's exceptions—and the one at issue in this case—is the "commercial" exception of § 1605(a)(2). * * *

In the proceedings below, respondents relied only on the third clause of § 1605(a)(2) to establish jurisdiction and our analysis is therefore limited to considering whether this lawsuit is (1) "based * * * upon an act outside the territory of the United States"; (2) that was taken "in connection with a commercial activity" of Argentina outside this country; and (3) that "cause[d] a direct effect in the United States." The complaint in this case alleges only one cause of action on behalf of each of the respondents, viz., a breach-of-contract claim based on Argentina's attempt to refinance the Bonods rather than to pay them according to their terms. The fact that the cause of action is in compliance with the first of the three requirements—that it is "based upon an act outside the territory of the United States" (presumably Argentina's unilateral extension)—is uncontested. The dispute pertains to whether the unilateral refinancing of the Bonods was taken "in connection with a commercial activity" of Argentina, and whether it had a "direct effect in the United States." We address these issues in turn.

A

Respondents and their *amicus,* the United States, contend that Argentina's issuance of, and continued liability under, the Bonods constitute a "commercial activity" and that the extension of the payment schedules was taken "in connection with" that activity. The latter point is obvious enough, and Argentina does not contest it; the key question is whether the activity is "commercial" under the FSIA. The FSIA defines "commercial activity" to mean: "[E]ither a regular course of commercial conduct or a particular commercial transaction or act. The commercial character of an activity shall be determined by reference to the nature of the course of conduct or particular transaction or act, rather than by reference to its purpose." 28 U.S.C. § 1603(d).

This definition, however, leaves the critical term "commercial" largely undefined: The first sentence simply establishes that the commercial nature of an activity does *not* depend upon whether it is a single act or a regular course of conduct, and the second sentence merely specifies what element of the conduct determines commerciality (i.e., nature rather than purpose), but still without saying what "commercial" means. Fortunately, however, the FSIA was not written on a clean slate. As we have noted, see Verlinden B.V. v. Central Bank of Nigeria, 461 U.S. 480, 486–489 (1983), the Act (and the commercial exception in particular) largely codifies the so-called "restrictive" theory of foreign sovereign immunity first endorsed by the State Department in 1952. The meaning of "commercial" is the meaning generally attached to that term under the restrictive theory at the time the statute was enacted. See McDermott Int'l, Inc. v. Wilander, * * * ("[W]e assume that when a statute uses [a term of art], Congress intended it to have its established meaning").

This Court did not have occasion to discuss the scope or validity of the restrictive theory of sovereign immunity until our 1976 decision in Alfred Dunhill v. Cuba, 425 U.S. 682. Although the Court there was evenly divided on the question whether the "commercial" exception that applied in the foreign-sovereign-immunity context also limited the availability of an act-of-state defense, compare id., at 695–706 (plurality) with id., at 725–730 (Marshall, J., dissenting), there was little disagreement over the general scope of the exception. The plurality noted that, after the State Department endorsed the restrictive theory of foreign sovereign immunity in 1952, the lower courts consistently held that foreign sovereigns were not immune from the jurisdiction of American courts in cases "arising out of purely commercial transactions." [The plurality also noted that the "state sovereign" and "state commercial" acts were not entirely novel to U.S. law]. * * * The plurality stated that the restrictive theory of foreign sovereign immunity would not bar a suit based upon a foreign state's participation in the marketplace in the manner of a private citizen or corporation. 425 U.S., at 698–705. A foreign state engaging in "commercial" activities "do[es] not exercise powers peculiar to sovereigns"; rather, it "exercise[s] only those powers that can also be exercised by private citizens." The dissenters did not disagree with this general description. Given that the FSIA was enacted less than six months after our decision in *Alfred Dunhill* was announced, we think the plurality's contemporaneous description of the then-prevailing restrictive theory of sovereign immunity is of significant assistance in construing the scope of the Act.

In accord with that description, we conclude that when a foreign government acts, not as regulator of a market, but in the manner of a private player within it, the foreign sovereign's actions are "commercial" within the meaning of the FSIA. Moreover, because the Act provides that the commercial character of an act is to be determined by reference to its "nature" rather than its "purpose," 28 U.S.C. § 1603(d), the question is not whether the foreign government is acting with a profit motive or instead with the aim of fulfilling uniquely sovereign objectives. Rather, the issue is whether the particular actions that the foreign state performs (whatever the motive behind them) are the *type* of actions by which a private party engages in "trade and traffic or commerce," Black's Law Dictionary 270 (6th ed. 1990). See, e.g., Rush–Presbyterian–St. Luke's Medical Center v. Hellenic Republic, 877 F.2d 574, 578 (CA7), cert. denied. Thus, a foreign government's issuance of regulations limiting foreign currency exchange is a sovereign activity, because such authoritative control of commerce cannot be exercised by a private party; whereas a contract to buy army boots or even bullets is a "commercial" activity, because private companies can similarly use sales contracts to acquire goods, see, e.g., Stato di Rumania v. Trutta, [1926] Foro It. I 584, 585–586, 589 (Corte di Cass. del Regno, Italy), translated and reprinted in part in 26 Am.J.Int'l L. 626–629 (Supp.1932).

Argentina contends that, although the FSIA bars consideration of "purpose," a court must nonetheless fully consider the *context* of a transaction in order to determine whether it is "commercial." Accordingly, Argentina claims that the Court of Appeals erred by defining the relevant conduct in what Argentina considers an overly generalized, a contextual manner and by essentially adopting a *per se* rule that all "issuance of debt instruments" is "commercial."

Argentina points to the fact that the transactions in which the Bonods were issued did not have the ordinary commercial consequence of raising capital or financing acquisitions. Assuming for the sake of argument that this is not an example of judging the commerciality of a transaction by its purpose, the ready answer is that private parties regularly issue bonds, not just to raise capital or to finance purchases, but also to refinance debt. * * * Engaging in a commercial act does not require the receipt of fair value, or even compliance with the common-law requirements of consideration.

     * * *

However difficult it may be in some cases to separate "purpose" (i.e., the *reason* why the foreign state engages in the activity) from "nature" (i.e., the outward form of the conduct that the foreign state performs or agrees to perform), see De Sanchez, supra, at 1393, the statute unmistakably commands that to be done. 28 U.S.C. § 1603(d). We agree with the Court of Appeals, see 941 F.2d, at 151, that it is irrelevant *why* Argentina participated in the bond market in the manner of a private actor; it matters only that it did so. We conclude that Argentina's issuance of the Bonods was a "commercial activity" under the FSIA.

B

The remaining question is whether Argentina's unilateral rescheduling of the Bonods had a "direct effect" in the United States, 28 U.S.C. § 1605(a)(2).

We * * * have little difficulty concluding that Argentina's unilateral rescheduling of the maturity dates on the Bonods had a "direct effect" in the United States. Respondents had designated their accounts in New York as the place of payment, and Argentina made some interest payments into those accounts before announcing that it was rescheduling the payments. Because New York was thus the place of performance for Argentina's ultimate contractual obligations, the rescheduling of those obligations necessarily had a "direct effect" in the United States: Money that was supposed to have been delivered to a New York bank for deposit was not forthcoming. We reject Argentina's suggestion that the "direct effect" requirement cannot be satisfied where the plaintiffs are all foreign corporations with no other connections to the United States. We expressly stated in *Verlinden* that the FSIA permits "a foreign plaintiff to sue a foreign sovereign in the courts of the United States, provided the substantive requirements of the Act are satisfied." * * *

     * * *

We conclude that Argentina's issuance of the Bonods was a "commercial activity" under the FSIA; that its rescheduling of the maturity dates on those instruments was taken in connection with that commercial activity and had a "direct effect" in the United States; and that the District Court therefore properly asserted jurisdiction, under the FSIA, over the breach-of-contract claim based on that rescheduling. Accordingly, the judgment of the Court of Appeals is *Affirmed.*

Question: If the I.L.C's Draft Article 1(c) definition (see Documentary Supplement) were applicable, do you think that Mr. Justice Scalia would have reached the same result? If the "context" of the transaction indicated potentially extreme public importance to a respondent state, would this be taken into account under the FSIA? Should it? Comparing the French case NIGC above at p. 589, what are the differences in conceptual approach which led to different outcomes?

THE UNITED STATES OF AMERICA v. THE PUBLIC SERVICE ALLIANCE OF CANADA, THE ATTORNEY GENERAL OF CANADA AND THE CANADA LABOUR RELATIONS BOARD

Supreme Court of Canada, 1992.
32 I.L.M. 1 (1993).

[The Canadian Supreme Court addressed sovereign immunity in a case involving Canadian civilian employees of a U.S. naval base (leased by the U.S.) in Argentia, Newfoundland. The U.S. claimed immunity from proceedings before the Canadian Labor Relations Board. The issue was whether the Board's proceedings "relate to any U.S. commercial activity." The base was used by the U.S. in its anti-submarine warfare command. The Canadian employees did most of the base's maintenance and had only minimal exposure to the military operations. A dispute arose relating to unionization and a no-strike clause in the employment contracts].

La Forest, J.: Before delving into the specific questions posed by this case, it is useful to consider first the common law antecedents of the

State Immunity Act, and then to compare Canada's codification of the common law with the statutory model in the United States. As will become apparent, the law in this area reveals a consistent pattern of development that has arrived at a point where state activity can be characterized only after appreciating its entire context. Rigid dichotomies between the "nature" and "purpose" of state activity are not helpful in this analysis.   * * *

In determining the nature of the activity in question, it is useful to begin by acknowledging that employment at a military base is a multi-faceted relationship. It is simply not valid to isolate one aspect of this activity and label it as either "sovereign" or "commercial" in nature. A better approach is to determine which aspects of the activity are relevant to the proceedings in issue, and then to assess the impact of the proceedings on these attributes as a whole.

The United States argues that the work performed by the Canadian civilian personnel is an integral and indispensable part of its stated defence mission and that it takes place within the context of an international agreement—the Lease—which gives the United States the right of management and control over the base. The Board, on the other hand, argues that this Court should only consider the threshold nature of the activity, namely a contract of employment, and ignore its context or purpose. PSAC is prepared to go a little further and characterizes the relevant activity as employment to provide maintenance services to a military base in return for remuneration. The Canadian personnel involved are essentially tradesmen who "fix water pipes, run boilers, perform new construction, and generally maintain the physical buildings on the base". The nature of the contract of employment is similar to an employment contract in the private sector, because the employees are * * *.

It is impossible to ignore the sovereign purpose of this latter aspect of the employment relationship. Argentia is a military post, conceived in times of war as an air and naval base. In peacetime it has served as a highly sensitive communications and surveillance post. In another war the base could play a crucial role in American military activities in the North Atlantic. I can think of no activity of a foreign state that is more inherently sovereign than the operation of such a base. As such, the United States government must be granted the unfettered authority to manage and control employment activity at the base.

* * *

In the result, the "activity" at Argentia has a double aspect. It is at once sovereign and commercial. The question becomes, do the certification proceedings "relate" to the commercial aspect of this activity? To this issue I now turn.

* * *

I also agree with the Attorney General of Canada that the objective of the Board's proceedings is the imposition of collective bargaining by the Canadian state, and under the control of a Canadian court. The nexus between this objective and the management of the base constitutes an unacceptable interference with American sovereignty. This is more than just a theoretical concern, as becomes apparent upon consideration of the consequences of submission to the Board's * * * Collective bargaining carries with it the right of employees to strike to enforce their contract demands. A strike at the Argentia base would, at a minimum, disrupt its military mission. It is true that the employees' services are not directly required to achieve this mission. However, the indirect effect of the loss of 60 full-time employees cannot be lightly dismissed. I am not prepared to concede that a boiler plant operator or an engineer at the base does not contribute in some important way to the successful operation of the base. Simply put, the United States is entitled to absolute control of the base and so over the availability of its labour force, particularly in times of war. At all events, it can hardly be said not to interfere seriously with the control of the base, which is expressly conferred upon the United States by the Lease.

* * *

Finally, PSAC points out that the effect of granting immunity to the United States is to deprive Canadian employees of their right to the protection of labour relations legislation, a right enjoyed by all other Canadians. However, this regrettable result is a necessary consequence of Canada's commitment to policies of international comity and reciprocity. Any time sovereign immunity is asserted, the inevitable result is that certain domestic parties will be left without legal recourse. This is a policy choice implicit in the Act itself. A policy choice with a similar effect in the field of labour law is the exclusion from union membership of "a person who performs management functions or is employed in a confidential capacity in matters relating to industrial relations," under § 3 of the *Canada Labour Code*. That regrettable exclusion is necessitated by valid labour relations policy considerations. The exclusion in the present case is required by policy considerations of international comity and reciprocity. Indeed, more than mere comity comes into play here. As noted, it is required by Canada's obligation under the Lease— an international agreement. Article 1 of that document, we saw, accords the United States "all the rights, power and authority within the Leased Areas which are necessary for the establishment, use, operation and defence thereof, or appropriate for their control. * * * " I find it difficult to see how the United States can fully exercise these rights without having full control of its labour relations on the base.

Disposition

For these reasons I would allow the appeal, and answer the first referred question in the affirmative.

Notes and Questions:

How do you think Justice La Forest would have approached the Weltover case? The Canadian case being later in time than Weltover, do you think that the U.S. Supreme Court might look at "context" in a more flexible way the next time the issue is presented?

Plaintiff in *Saudi Arabia v. Nelson*, 113 S.Ct. 1471 (1993), alleged that he had been detained and tortured by Saudi Arabian authorities.

He had been hired in the United States to work as a monitoring systems engineer at a Saudi Arabian (government) hospital. Nelson alleged that agents of the Saudi Government arrested him after he made complaints about safety defects in the hospital. He claimed that he was shackled, beaten, kept for days without food, tortured and confined in a rat infested overcrowded cell. In addition, he claimed that his wife was told by a government official that her husband's release could be arranged, if she provided sexual favors.

Nelson was released after 39 days of confinement. Upon his return, he brought an action in the Federal District Court for the Southern District of Florida, claiming that the Saudi conduct was a violation of his human rights. He sought damages from the Saudi Government for, among other things, negligent failure to warn him of the dangers of working in a Saudi hospital, for various intentional torts, including "battery, unlawful detainment, wrongful arrest and imprisonment, false imprisonment, inhuman torture, disruption of normal family life, and infliction of mental anguish."

A majority of the Supreme Court held that the suit could not properly be maintained under the FSIA, because the conduct of which Nelson complained was not "based upon commercial activity," but "upon an abuse of sovereign power." It noted that the Act requires more than "mere connection with" or "relation to" commerce for conduct to be "based upon commercial activity." 28 U.S.C. § 1603(d). Justices White and Blackmun concurred, arguing that the conduct *was, indeed, based upon commercial activity,* "but went along with the decision, because they found that the activity was neither carried on in nor connected to the United States."

————

Query: What should be the test for "commercial activity" under the FSIA: the overall character of the operation or the particular actions complained of? Is there an element of subjectivity in determinations of this kind? With the uncertainty which remains, do you think that this subject is ready for codification or would codification simply continue the uncertainty? See the I.L.C.'s Draft Articles in the Documentary Supplement.

Note: In *Siderman de Blake v. Republic of Argentina,* 965 F.2d 699 (9th Cir.1992), the plaintiffs sued in the United States for damages from the Argentine Republic for torture and wrongful seizure of property. The opinion relating to torture and wrongful seizure of property by Argentine authorities is presented in Chapter 10. Their complaint alleged eighteen causes of action arising out of the torture of Jose Siderman and the expropriation of the Sidermans' property by Argentine military officials. The District Court dismissed the expropriation claims on the basis of the act of state doctrine, but granted a default judgment on the torture claims. The Court of Appeals ruled that Argentina had waived its sovereign immunity defense when it requested California State Courts by letter rogatory to assist it in proceedings it had undertaken in Argentina against the plaintiffs in this case and based upon the conduct in Argentina that prompted plaintiffs' action in the United States:

> "Here, we confront a situation where Argentina apparently not only envisioned United States court participation in its persecution of the Sidermans, but by its actions deliberately implicated our courts in that persecution. The Sidermans have presented evidence that a year after Jose, Lea and Carlos Siderman fled Argentina in fear for their lives, the Argentine military authorities altered the Tucuman provincial land records to show that they had held title only to 127, as opposed to 127,000 acres of land in the Province, and that in their last-minute efforts to raise cash they had thus sold property which did not belong to them. The Tucuman Public Prosecutor then initiated criminal proceedings against Jose Siderman for this 'fraudulent' sale, and had the Tucuman Supreme Court enlist the aid of our courts, via a letter rogatory, in serving him with process. 'The letter rogatory, dated May 11, 1980, informed the Presiding Judge of the Los Angeles Superior Court that criminal proceedings were pending against Jose Siderman in the Supreme Court of Tucuman. It requested the court's assistance in serving papers on Siderman, who was living in Los Angeles at the time. While the court complied with the request, the record is not clear as to the subsequent course of lawsuit. In their papers in support of jurisdiction, the Sidermans suggest that the Argentine military authorities sought to obtain Jose's return to Argentina in order to further torture and perhaps even to kill him.'

> Shortly after the Los Angeles Superior Court received Argentina's letter rogatory, indeed, Argentina requested that the Italian authorities arrest Siderman, who had travelled to Italy for a wedding, and extradite him to Argentina for having allegedly forged certain travel documents. Siderman was detained in Italy for seven months, twenty-seven days of which time was spent in prison, before an Italian court dismissed the charges against him as pretextual and denied Argentina's extradition request.

> We conclude that the Sidermans have presented evidence sufficient to support a finding that Argentina has implicitly waived its sovereign immunity with respect to their claims for torture. The evidence indicates that Argentina deliberately involved United States courts in its efforts to persecute Jose Siderman. If Argentina has engaged our courts in the very course of activity for which the Sidermans seek redress, it has waived its immunity as to that redress." [965 F.2d 699, 722].

The Sidermans argued that their claims fall within the international takings exception to the FSIA's rule of immunity. The Ninth Circuit held that advertising and receiving profits from the Sidermans' expropriated hotel in Argentina *constituted commercial activity. Id.,* at 708–09. It also held that the Sidermans could take advantage of the *"commercial activities exception "* to sovereignty, but could not benefit from the *"expropriation exception."* It held that even a claim based on a foreign government's violation of a *jus cogens principle* (a peremptory norm) could be heard in a U.S. court only if it falls within one of the exceptions to sovereignty. (For more on this, see Ch. 10).

———

Question: Do you find that any of the theories justifying sovereign immunity would be properly applied to cases of this kind? Is there a case to be made for universal jurisdiction in cases of alleged violations of international law? See Chapters 3 and 10.

———

Arbitration. Section 1605(a)(6) of the U.S. Foreign Sovereign Immunities Act of 1976 as amended (see text in the Documentary Supplement) establishes the rules governing an exception for actions brought to enforce an agreement made by the foreign state with or for the benefit of a private party to submit to arbitration or an action to confirm an award made pursuant to the agreement. Section 1610(a)(6) states the rules for a parallel exception from attachment or execution. In *Cargill International S.A. v. M/T Pavel Dybenko*, 991 F.2d 1012 (2d Cir.1993), the Court of Appeals affirmed jurisdiction to determine whether the plaintiff was a third party beneficiary of an arbitration agreement entered into by an instrumentality of the former Soviet Union and whether the arbitration exception was applicable in that case.

* * *

3. MEASURES OF CONSTRAINT

UNITED STATES, FOREIGN SOVEREIGN IMMUNITIES ACT OF 1976, EXCEPTIONS TO IMMUNITY FROM ATTACHMENT OR EXECUTION IN DOCUMENTARY SUPPLEMENT.

28 U.S.C. 1610.

LIBERIAN EASTERN TIMBER CORP. v. GOVERNMENT OF THE REPUBLIC OF LIBERIA

United States District Court, S.D.N.Y., 1986.
650 F.Supp. 73 (1986), aff'd without opinion, 854 F.2d 1314 (2d Cir.1987).

EDWARD WEINFELD, District Judge.

The Government of the Republic of Liberia ("Liberia" or "Republic") moves to vacate a judgment entered ex parte by Judge John F. Keenan enforcing an arbitration award issued under the rules of the International Centre for the Settlement of Investment Disputes ("ICSID"). The Republic also moves for a preliminary injunction enjoining the enforcement of, and execution upon, the aforesaid judgment pending determination of Liberia's motion: (1) to vacate the judgment, or, in the alternative, (2) to vacate the execution of that judgment on its property located in the United States. Liberia's contention is that the ex parte judgment violated its sovereign immunity which it did not waive.

In 1970 Liberia granted a concession to Liberian Eastern Timber Corporation ("LETCO") to harvest and exploit over 400,000 acres of Liberian timber. In 1972 LETCO began to exploit its concession and harvest, process and export the timber. In 1980, Liberia, based upon alleged shortcomings of LETCO and concerned over conservation and proper utilization of its timber resources, reduced LETCO's concession area by 279,000 acres. It later terminated the concession entirely, whereupon LETCO commenced arbitration under the Convention on the Settlement of Investment Disputes Between States and Nationals of Other States (the "Convention") pursuant to Article IX of the parties' Concession Agreement, which provides that if there:

> * * * shall be any question or dispute with respect to the Construction, meaning or effect of this Agreement or arising out of this Agreement or concerning the rights or obligations hereunder the parties shall have the right to require the dispute to be settled by conciliation and arbitration as hereinafter provided. Any of the parties to such dispute may commence conciliation or arbitration proceedings by giving notice to the other party and to the Secretary–General of the International Centre for Settlement of Investment Disputes * * *.
>
> (2) The Rules of Conciliation and Arbitration of the International Centre for Settlement of Investment Disputes shall govern the conciliation and arbitration * * *.
>
> (4) The decision of the arbitrator shall be final and binding upon the parties of this Agreement * * *.

After nominating an arbitrator on its behalf and designating a law firm to represent it, Liberia refused to participate in the arbitration and commenced an action against LETCO in the Liberian courts to resolve the dispute. Nonetheless, the arbitration panel proceeded with the arbitration and it awarded LETCO $8,793,280, plus interest.

Judge Keenan, sitting in the Motion Term, Part 1, signed an ex parte order directing entry of judgment for $9,076,857.25, including interest, based upon and as specified in the award issued by the ICSID arbitration panel. A Writ of Execution was issued to the United States Marshal for the Southern District of New York, pursuant to the Judgment, on September 25, 1986.

DISCUSSION

LETCO's opposition to Liberia's motion misapprehends Liberia's position. The Republic does not, in this litigation, seek to vacate the award as determined by the arbitration conducted pursuant to the ICSID Convention and Rules. What Liberia seeks to vacate is the judgment entered in this court based upon the arbitration award and to enjoin the issuance of executions to seize its property or assets in order to satisfy the judgment. It contends that this court was without jurisdiction to enter the judgment or to enforce the award by the issuance of executions against its property in the United States under the Foreign Sovereign Immunities Act ("FSIA"), and that it did not surrender or waive its sovereign immunity by entering into the Concession Agreement, by agreeing to arbitration, or by reducing the forestry area and then finally cancelling the contract.

In broad outline, the concession contract, which involved the Liberian forest, one of its most valuable resources, was intended to bolster Liberia's economy, create new jobs, protect the forest preserve, stimulate reforestation, and provide funds for the needs of the people of Liberia. LETCO and other entities engaged by Liberia for that purpose were regulated to ensure better utilization of the forest and to prevent waste. The granting of a concession to exploit that natural resource and the subsequent revocation of that concession were regulations of Liberia's natural resources and entailed an exercise of powers peculiar to a sovereign. Indeed, LETCO does not dispute that such activities were a governmental function. However, LETCO contends that Liberia waived its sovereign immunity in this case by entering into the concession contract whereby it agreed to submit any disputes arising under that contract to ICSID arbitration pursuant to the Convention, a treaty ratified by more than seventy-five countries, including the United States, the Liberian Republic and France.[4] In support of its position plaintiff emphasizes Article 54 of the Convention, which provides:

> Each Contracting State shall recognize an award rendered pursuant to this Convention as binding and enforce the pecuniary obligations imposed by that award within its territories as if it were a final judgment of a court in that State.

* * *

Liberia, as a signatory to the Convention, waived its sovereign immunity in the United States with respect to the enforcement of any arbitration award entered pursuant to the Convention. When it entered into the concession contract with LETCO, with its specific provision that any dispute thereunder be settled by arbitration under the rules of ICSID and its enforcement provision thereunder, it invoked the provision contained in Article 54 of the Convention which requires enforcement of such an award by Contracting States. That action, and reading the treaty as a whole, leaves little doubt that the signatories to the Convention intended that awards made pursuant to its provisions be given full faith and credit in their respective jurisdictions subject to such rights as are reserved by signatories thereunder. Therefore, Liberia clearly contemplated the involvement of the courts of any of the Contracting States, including the United States as a signatory to the Convention, in enforcing the pecuniary obligations of the award.

The fact that LETCO is a French entity and Liberia a foreign sovereign does not deprive the district court of subject matter jurisdiction. Thus, this Court had jurisdiction to direct the entry of judgment against Liberia to enforce the pecuniary obligations of the arbitration award in favor of LETCO. The motion to vacate the judgment is denied.

---

4. LETCO is owned and controlled by French nationals, and the parties agreed to treat it as a national of another Contracting State for purposes of the Convention, pursuant to Article 25(2)(b); hence the Convention was applicable to the contract.

We next consider the separate issue of Liberia's motion to vacate the executions issued against Liberia's property or assets to enforce and collect the judgment. Article 55 of the Convention provides that "Nothing in Article 54 shall be construed as derogating from the law in force in any Contracting State relating to immunity of that State or of any foreign state from *execution.*" (emphasis supplied). 28 U.S.C. § 1610(a) provides exceptions to the immunity of a foreign state from execution upon a judgment entered by a Court of the United States if the property is or was "used for a commercial activity in the United States."

The essence of Liberia's argument concerning its immunity from execution of the judgment, however variously stated, is that the executions upon the judgment entered in this court have been served on, among other entities, shipowners located in the United States and agents of Liberia appointed to collect from such shipowners tonnage fees, registration fees and other taxes due the government—that these fees are collected as taxes designed to raise revenues for the Republic of Liberia and, as such, are sovereign not commercial assets under the Liberian maritime law and regulations, and thus immune from execution since they are not "property * * * used for a commercial activity."

LETCO, with respect to the registry fees and tonnage taxes that have been levied upon within this district, does not dispute that they are tax revenues ultimately payable to Liberia, but asserts that of the gross amounts due and collected from companies under Liberian registry, 27% is retained for operating and administrative expenses and profits by United States corporations or citizens who render services in collecting the funds. In consequence, LETCO argues that those payments reflect commercial activities within the purview of section 1610(a). Upon the argument of this motion, LETCO conceded that if, instead of employing United States corporations or citizens to collect the registry fees and tonnage taxes, Liberia had engaged personnel of the Liberian Consulate stationed in the United States, that taxes so collected would be beyond the reach of execution. This rather fine distinction is without substance. It does not make sense to say that because Liberia engaged and gave employment to United States citizens, instead of utilizing the services of its consulate employees stationed in the United States, it thereby forfeited its sovereign immunity with respect to its right to the taxes so collected. The nature of the amounts due from ships flying the Liberian flag, the registration fees or taxes, is constant. They are tax revenues for the benefit of the Government of Liberia, and the method employed to effect their collection does not destroy the basic nature of that collection. The levy and collection of taxes intended to serve as revenues for the support and maintenance of governmental functions are an exercise of powers particular to a sovereign. Accordingly, Liberia's motion to vacate the executions upon such funds is granted and the United States Marshal is directed to release the funds so attached (less his lawful fees). Further, LETCO is enjoined from issuing executions against such registry fees and taxes; however, LETCO is not enjoined from issuing executions with respect to any properties which are used for commercial activities and that may fall within one of the exceptions delineated in section 1610.

So ordered.

Question: What is the practical difference between immunity from jurisdiction for the determination of claims and immunity from jurisdiction from execution of judgments on those claims? What policy considerations would support the denial of immunity in the first case but not in the second?

Note: LETCO later recorded the judgement in the U.S. District Court in the District of Columbia and writs of attachment were thereafter served on Riggs National Bank and First American Bank where Liberia held accounts. On Liberia's emergency motion for relief from orders attaching the accounts, treated as a motion to quash the writs of attachment, the Court stated:

> In conclusion, the bank accounts of the Liberian Embassy are immune from attachment both because they enjoy diplomatic immunity under the Vienna Convention and because no exception of the FSIA applies to deprive the bank accounts of their grant of sovereign immunity. Also, as noted above, the bank account used for the central bank of Liberia is immune under 28 U.S.C. § 1611(b)(1).

UNITED STATES, FOREIGN SOVEREIGN IMMUNITIES ACT OF 1976
(certain types of property immune from execution, 28 U.S.C. 1611 (Study this part of the *Act* in the Documentary Supplement.))

---

4. SOME HORIZONTAL QUESTIONS: STATES, WAIVERS, RELATION BETWEEN INTERNATIONAL LAW AND NATIONAL LAW IN THIS SECTOR

1. ***States.*** Sovereign immunity applies to states. Thus, the issue of what is a state arises. (See Chapter 2 above.) The international law rule for sovereign immunity reaches statehood in all of its manifestations. See for example, Krajina v. The Tass Agency, [1949] 2 All E.R. 274 (1949) where Cohen, L.J. stated in the Court of Appeal that the evidence "falls far short of that which would be necessary to establish that Tass is a legal entity and that the USSR, by procuring its incorporation, has deprived that particular department of the immunity which normally attaches to a department of a sovereign State in accordance with the principles of comity established by international law and recognized by this country. * * * I ought to say just a few words on what the position would be had we come to the opposite conclusion and been of opinion that the evidence did establish that Tass was given the status of a separate juridical entity. It does not seem necessary to follow that it would thereby have been deprived of its immunity." (Lord Justice Cohen then analyzed the parallel situation in the U.K. and concluded that "One must look at every case at the facts to reach a

conclusion whether the Crown had intended to give up its immunity generally or only for limited and defined purposes."

Courts should no longer find it troublesome, as did the Court in Krajina, to deal with the separate legal entity problem, for the statutory and treaty provisions now clearly recognize the state owned or controlled entity. For example Article 2.1(b) of the International Law Commission's Draft Articles (in the Documentary Supplement) define "State" for the purpose of those draft articles to mean:

(i) the State and its various organs of government;

(ii) constituent units of a federal state

(iii) political subdivisions of the State which are entitled to perform acts in the exercise of the sovereign authority of the State;

(iv) agencies or instrumentalities of the State and other entities, to the extent that they are entitled to perform acts in the exercise of the sovereign authority of the State;

(v) representatives of the State acting in that capacity;

In the 1991 General Assembly Sixth Committee discussion of this, one representative felt that "the definition should not include State enterprises and corporations, because as independent legal persons, such entities could both institute a proceeding and be sued and should not, therefore enjoy jurisdictional immunities." (U.N. Doc. A/CN.4/L. 456, February 6, 1991, p. 54).

The U.S. Foreign Sovereign Immunities Act of 1976 (in the Documentary Supplement) also contains a definition of "foreign state" which is more specific than the definition contained in the Draft Articles above. Section 1603 includes in the definition, "an agency or instrumentality of a foreign state as defined in subsection (b) which refers to any entity

(1) which is a separate legal person, corporate or otherwise and

(2) which is an organ of a foreign state or political subdivision thereof or a majority of whose shares or other ownership interest is owned by a foreign state or political subdivision thereof, and

(3) which is neither a citizen of a State of the United States as defined in section 1332(c) of this title, nor created under the laws of any third country."

For applications of the foregoing rules see Vermeulen v. Renault, U.S.A., Inc., 985 F.2d 1534 (11th Cir.1993) and Gould, Inc. v. Mitsui Mining and Smelting Co., Ltd. where the courts acted favorably upon claims that two French industrial corporations (Regie National des Usines Renault and Pechiney/Trefimetaux) were owned by France.

Can an individual qualify as a foreign sovereign under the U.S. Act? Although the language does not suggest individuals, States act through individuals who should be protected where a corporate entity would be protected under the circumstances. See Chuidian v. Philippine National Bank, 912 F.2d 1095 (9th Cir.1990) (upholding an individual's FSIA claim).

Any tendency to recognize claims for FSIA status for a state, has not been extended to an association which seeks that status but has failed to satisfy fully the established criteria for statehood. In Klinghoffer v. S.N.C. Achille Lauro, 937 F.2d 44 (2d Cir.1991), an action was brought against the PLO in connection with the 1985 seizure of the passenger liner "Achille Lauro". The PLO claimed the status of state entitled to immunity under the FSIA, but the court, finding the absence of a defined territory, permanent population and a government in control, held that the PLO does not qualify as a FSIA "state." This, despite the fact that the PLO had been recognized by other countries (but not the United States). What would the status of the PLO be today?

A final question, about the qualification of entities as "states" for immunity purposes when the entity is "in transition" from the public to the private sector. What happens when an entity qualifies as a "state" at the time the acts in question are performed but not at the time of suit or judgement? In General Electric Capital Corporation v. N. Bud Grossman, 991 F.2d 1376 (8th Cir.1993), the defendant Air Canada was a crown corporation owned by the Government of Canada at the time of the acts complained of, but was an investor owned corporation at the time of suit. In Cargill Intern. S.A. v. M/T Pavel Dybenko, 991 F.2d 1012 (2d Cir.1993), a Russian shipping company was in the "early stages" of denationalization when the conduct occurred. Russia had approved the company's plan to denationalize but no shares had been sold. No other steps toward privatization had been taken and even after the first shares were distributed, nearly half of the shares remained with the Russian State Property Fund for a period of three years. The Court in both cases held that the entity was sovereign under the FSIA. *Question:* Do you think the underlying policies supporting sovereign immunity should apply in the circumstances of the Air Canada and Russian shipping company cases?

---

2. *Waiver.* Waivers have at times been ignored when they are contained in commercial-type contracts by a state instrumentality but the state has not itself appeared in court to make an official and definitive waiver or when the State Department has recommended immunity. Isbrandtsen Tankers, Inc. v. President of India, 446 F.2d 1198 (2d Cir.1971). Moreover, waiver has not been given effect when the waiver is quite general and not specific as to the forum country or court. (See Argentine Republic v. Amerada Hess Shipping Corp., above, p. 591). In a continuing limitation, waiver of jurisdiction may not be expected to include waiver of execution under FSIA section 1610(a)(1). The forum's policy considerations perhaps underlie these cases of reluctance to apply waivers in circumstances where one would have thought that the waivers would have been permitted. (Cf. Siderman de Blake v. Republic of Argentina, above at p. 603).

In the FSIA section 1605(a)(1), waiver is the first mentioned exception to immunity. It applies in any case: "(1) in which the foreign state has waived its immunity either explicitly or by implication, notwithstanding any withdrawal of the waiver which the foreign state may purport to effect except in accordance with the terms of the waiver." For example, waivers were applied in Proyecfin de Venezuela v. Banco Industrial, 760 F.2d 390, 393 (2d Cir.1985) ("immunity [waived] to the full extent permitted by the laws of such jurisdiction and, in particular, to the intent [sic] that in any proceedings taken in New York the foregoing waiver of immunity shall have effect under and be construed in accordance with the * * *" [FSIA].) *See also* National Union Fire Insurance Co. of Pittsburgh v. Peoples Republic of the Congo, 729 F.Supp. 936 (D.C.S.D.N.Y.1989) ("hereby irrevocably agrees not to claim and hereby irrevocably waives such sovereign immunity in respect of suit [and] jurisdiction of any court"—waiver not disputed by the Congo).

Yet the trend is not uniform. In General Electric Capital Corporation v. N. Bud Grossman, 991 F.2d 1376, 1386 (8th Cir.1993), the Court rejected claims of waiver of sovereign immunity of Air Canada, a crown corporation. The claims of waiver were based upon: (1) the public sale by the Canadian government of its Air Canada stock before the case began; (2) the provision in the Air Canada Act that Air Canada "is not an agent of Her Majesty and its officers and employees are not part of the public service of Canada;" (3) Air Canada's agreeing in the Share Purchase Agreement "to submit to the 'non-exclusive' jurisdiction of the Ontario courts;" and (4) Air Canada's "engaging a private agent and acting in conjunction with co-conspirators."

Waiver of measures of execution has also arisen in the arbitration system developed by the World Bank. *See,* the International Centre for Settlement of Investment Disputes (ICSID, see Doc. Supp.) ICSID Model Clauses, Doc. ICSID/5/Rev. 2, at 15, February 1, 1993 states:

> Under Article 54 of the [ICSID] Convention, all Contracting States, whether or not parties to the dispute, must recognize awards rendered pursuant to the Convention as binding and enforce the pecuniary obligations imposed thereby. Article 55 of the Convention nevertheless makes it clear that a State does not by becoming a party to the Convention waive such immunity from execution of an award as the State might enjoy under national laws. Such a waiver may, however, be effected by an express stipulation of which the following is an example.

Clause 15

> The Host State hereby waives any right of sovereign immunity as to it and its property in respect of the enforcement and execution of any award rendered by an Arbitral Tribunal constituted pursuant to this agreement.

3. *Relation Between International Law and National Law in this Sector.* How does the international legal system deal with a conflict between the international system and a national one? Although some deny that an international system exists, the existence of the *international* law rules on sovereign immunity can not be seriously doubted. (See *Siderman de Blake* above at p. 603).

The European Convention treaties are improving the coherency of the international law on sovereign immunity (see above pp. 587) and the I.L.C. Draft Articles (see above pp. 587, et seq.). Those texts can be taken as a codification of existing customary law.

In the event of conflict between national and international law, national courts will apply their national law as required by their constitutions (see Chs. 1, 17 and 18). Whether there is a true conflict depends on whether the international rule is a mandatory or permissive one. If the rule in question is a mandatory rule of immunity, for example the rule affording immunity to warships, the application of an inconsistent national rule by national courts would necessarily constitute a violation of international law and give rise to the international responsibility of the state denying immunity. If, on the other hand, a state extends immunity on the basis of national law to a merchant ship, when international law permits but does not seem to require such immunity, there is no violation of international law.

Attention is naturally paid to the means of protecting claimants who are damaged when immunity is applied. *Are the alternative means of redress adequate?* In *Aldona*, above at p. 581, the Polish court referred to the possibilities of Aldona's seeking justice before English courts or making in effect an international claim through her Foreign Ministry to its British counterpart. *Are these alternatives realistic? Can you envisage other means?* Could the immune government be encouraged or required to waive immunity except in cases of demonstrable risk of disruption of government operations? Or should the immune government be required to accept arbitration? Should the immunity be relaxed except in cases where the court might make a specific finding of the disruption risk?

SECTION B. THE IMMUNITY OF INTERNATIONAL ORGANIZATIONS

International organizations are not treated as tantamount to states under international law. They are not entitled to the privileges and immunities of states. However, international organizations are legal entities created as "collections of states", and the protection of their public functions requires a legal status which is not identical to state privileges and immunities but resembles them in certain respects. The privileges and immunities of international organizations are designed mainly to protect the *independence* of organizations from undue outside influence and otherwise to ensure that they are able to carry out their missions.

Organizations expect to receive protection for the organization itself, its staff and representatives of member states. Organizations need legal capacity to act, competence to enter into treaties and contracts and to bring legal actions. They need power to make internal legal rules which may vary from those of the host state and in other countries in which they operate.

Their protection requires immunities from legal actions which might be brought in national courts against them, their staff or representatives of member states. These privileges and immunities are normally limited to the extent necessary for the fulfillment of the purposes of the organization and hence are charterized as "functional immunities". There are parallels between them and the privileges and immunities of consuls as seen in Chapter 12 below.

While there are common threads running through the privileges and immunities of most international organizations, usually set out generally in the treaty establishing the organization, the rules may vary from one organization to another. Often more detailed rules are developed in separate agreements, such as the Convention on the Privileges and Immunities of the United Nations and the Headquarters Agreement which appear in the Doc. Supp.

Read U.N. Charter Article 105 in the Doc. Supp. Do you find Article 105 to be sufficient? If not, what additional provisions are needed? Do you find them in the United Nations Convention and the Headquarters Agreement? Review Chapter 2, Section C. 1 above. How does the problem in the United States v. Palestine Liberation Organization Case, at pp. 66 et seq. below affect your view of Article 105?

1987 RESTATEMENT: IMMUNITIES OF INTERNATIONAL ORGANIZATIONS *

Introductory Note:

International organizations have achieved independent legal personality under international law largely since the Second World War. * * * Earlier, they were seen largely as "unincorporated" associations of individual states and sometimes claimed the immunities of one or all of their member states. When international organizations acquired legal personality by international agreement, they also acquired privileges and immunities in their own right.

The privileges and immunities of an international organization and its officials, and of member representatives, are generally established by the constitution of the organization, e.g., Article 105 of the United Nations Charter, and are often supplemented by special agreement. See, e.g., the Convention on Privileges and Immunities of the United Nations, 21 U.S.T., to which (as of 1986) 120 states (including the United States) were party, and the Convention on Privileges and Immunities of the Specialized Agencies, 33 U.N.T.S. 261, to which (as of 1986) 88 states were party (but not the United States). An international organization sometimes enjoys additional privileges and immunities by agreement with a particular state, for example, an agreement between the organization and the state that is the seat of its headquarters, such as the Headquarters Agreement between the United States and the United Nations. * * * Strictly, those agreements are binding only on

* Copyright 1987 by the American Law Institute. Reprinted with permission of the American Law Institute.

states' parties to them, but an organization may also enjoy basic privileges and immunities vis-à-vis non-member states under customary law. * * *

The privileges and immunities of international organizations are "functional," and, though modeled after those of states, differ from them in some measure, both in conception and content. Unlike states, international organizations are not "sovereign" and draw on no history of sovereignty and no tradition of sovereign immunity. State and diplomatic immunities apply equally and reciprocally between one state and another; the immunities of an international organization are claimed, without reciprocity, by an organization vis-à-vis a state, generally a member state. Most such claims, in fact, arise in the few particular states in whose territories the organizations have their headquarters or conduct their principal activities. Officials of an international organization represent no sending state but may be "sent" to all states; unlike diplomatic personnel they are not nationals of a sending state but bear various nationalities, in some instances the nationality of the state from whose laws they seek immunity. The absence of reciprocity is reflected also in the privileges and immunities enjoyed by representatives of member states to international organizations, as compared with the privileges and immunities of diplomatic agents. * * *

BROADBENT v. ORGANIZATION OF AMERICAN STATES

United States Court of Appeals, District of Columbia Circuit, 1980.
628 F.2d 27.

LEVENTHAL, Circuit Judge: This is an appeal from a District Court judgment dismissing an action by the appellants claiming they had been improperly discharged by the Organization of American States (OAS). The district court held the OAS was absolutely immune from suit. We affirm on the ground that, even assuming for discussion the applicability of the lesser, "restrictive" immunity doctrine, which permits a lawsuit based on "commercial" activity to be maintained against a sovereign without its consent, this case does not present such "commercial" activity.

I. BACKGROUND

The plaintiffs-appellants are seven former staff members of the General Secretariat of OAS. Before their termination, they had been employed at the permanent headquarters of the organization in Washington, D.C., for periods ranging from six to twenty-four years. They are all United States citizens or foreign nationals admitted to permanent residency in the United States.

The appellants were dismissed from the Secretariat on August 31, 1976, due to a reduction in force mandated by the OAS General Assembly. At various times between October 31 and November 8, 1976, they filed complaints with the Administrative Tribunal of the OAS, the internal court created to resolve personnel disputes. On June 1, 1977, the Tribunal held that the discharges had been improper and that the appellants should be reinstated at the grades they held when they were separated from service. In accordance with its governing statute, the Tribunal also fixed an indemnity to be paid to each appellant should the Secretary General choose to exercise the option of refusing to reinstate them. Subsequently, the Secretary General denied reinstatement, and each appellant received the indicated indemnity.[3]

* * * [A]ppellants brought this action in the district court, alleging breach of contract and seeking damages totalling three million dollars. The OAS moved to quash service and dismiss the complaint, asserting that the district court lacked subject matter jurisdiction and that the OAS is immune from service of process; but the district court denied the motion in an order dated January 25, 1978. On February 28, the OAS filed a request for certification under 28 U.S.C. § 1292(b) so as to take an interlocutory appeal of the January order to this court. In a final order dated March 28, 1978, the district court vacated its order of January 25 and dismissed the lawsuit. The March 28 order stated:

> On January 25, 1978, this Court held that the express language of 22 U.S.C. § 288a(b) and the statutory purposes underlying the International Organizations Immunities Act of 1945 bring international organizations within the terms of the Foreign Sovereign Immunities Act of 1976, and that pursuant to 28 U.S.C. § 1330 this Court had jurisdiction over the parties and controversy involved in the case. Upon careful review of that decision, the Court finds that it did not properly weigh the facts that international organizations, and particularly the Organization of American States, are creatures of treaty and by virtue of treaty stand in a different position with respect to the issue of immunity than sovereign nations. The Court is persuaded that international organizations are immune from every form of legal process except insofar as that immunity is expressly waived by treaty or expressly limited by statute. The Court is further persuaded that this Court has jurisdiction over lawsuits involving international organizations only insofar as such jurisdiction is expressly provided for by statute.

> The Foreign Sovereign Immunities Act of 1976 makes no mention of international organizations. The jurisdictional grant of 28 U.S.C. § 1330 refers only to foreign states. Nothing in the International Organizations Immunities Act of 1945 provides for jurisdiction in the district courts over civil actions against international organizations.

On April 19, 1978, appellants filed their notice of appeal from this ruling.

II. ANALYSIS

A. Jurisdiction

In its final order, the district court concluded that it lacked subject matter jurisdiction, and the OAS advances that position on appeal.

---

3. The amounts of the indemnities ranged from $9,000 to $12,000 plus attorney's fees.

Appellants—and the district court in its January 25 order—rely upon a conjunctive reading of the International Organizations Immunity Act (IOIA) of 1945, 22 U.S.C. § 288a(b) (1979), and the Foreign Sovereign Immunities Act (FSIA) of 1976, 28 U.S.C. § 1330 (1979), to establish jurisdiction. The OAS counters that § 288a(b) confers immunity, not jurisdiction, and that § 1330 establishes jurisdiction over suits against foreign *states,* not international organizations.

The United Nations (U.N.), appearing amicus curiae, offers a different approach to the question of jurisdiction. It contends that jurisdiction over suits involving international organizations exists under 28 U.S.C. § 1331(a). In support of this contention, amicus cited International Refugee Organization v. Republic Steamship Co., 189 F.2d 858, 861 (4th Cir.1951), which held that "an international organization created by treaties to which the United States is a party may invoke [federal question] jurisdiction because it is created by a treaty of the United States." That case also found an alternate basis for federal court jurisdiction over suits brought by international organizations in the provisions of 28 U.S.C. § 288a(a) that confer capacity to sue upon international organizations. Id. at 860. Counsel for the U.N. reasons from this alternative holding that, if international organizations may institute suits in a federal court, they should be permitted to defend them there; thus, he argues that § 1331 should be construed to confer federal jurisdiction over such suits.

Because clear and adequate non-judicial grounds for the disposal of this case exist, we need not and do not decide the difficult jurisdictional issues it presents.

B. The Immunity of International Organizations

The International Organizations Immunities Act of 1945, 22 U.S.C. § 288a(b) (1979), grants to international organizations which are designated by the President [10] "the same immunity from suit and every form of judicial process as is enjoyed by foreign governments, except to the extent that such organizations may expressly waive their immunity for the purpose of any proceedings or by the terms of any contract." As of 1945, the statute granted absolute immunity to international organizations, for that was the immunity then enjoyed by foreign governments.

The Foreign Sovereign Immunities Act of 1976, 28 U.S.C. § 1602 et seq. (1979), codified what, in the period between 1946 and 1976, had come to be the immunity enjoyed by sovereign states—restrictive immunity. The central feature of restrictive immunity is the distinction between the governmental or sovereign activities of a state (acts jure imperii) and its commercial activities (acts jure gestionis). Foreign states may not be found liable for their governmental activities by American courts; but they enjoy no immunity from liability for their commercial activities.

---

10. By Executive Order 10533 (June 3, 1954), 19 Fed.Reg. 3289 (1954), President Eisenhower designated the OAS an international organization entitled to the privileges and immunities conferred by the IOIA.

Contention for restrictive immunity

Appellants—and the United States as amicus curiae—submit the following syllogism: the IOIA conferred on international organizations the same immunity enjoyed by foreign governments; the FSIA indicates that foreign governments now enjoy only restrictive immunity; therefore, international organizations enjoy only restrictive immunity. They are supported by the general doctrine that ordinarily, "[a] statute which refers to the law of a subject generally adopts the law on the subject as of the time the law was invoked * * * includ[ing] all the amendments and modifications of the law subsequent to the time the reference statute was enacted."

Contention for absolute immunity

The OAS and several other international organizations as amici curiae counter that Congress granted international organizations absolute immunity in the IOIA, and it has never modified that grant. They rely on three implications of a legislative intent *not* to apply to international organizations the post World War II evolutions in the doctrine of sovereign immunity.

[T]he FSIA is generally silent about international organizations. No reference to such organizations is made in the elaborate definition of "state" in § 1603, and only § 1611 even alludes to their existence. True, § 1611, dealing as it does with the attachment of property belonging to international organizations, presupposes a successful action against an international organization. However, that could follow a waiver of immunity. Alternatively, § 1611 would have application in case of an attempt to execute a judgment against a foreign state by attaching funds of that foreign state held by an international organization.[16]

[B]y its own terms the IOIA provides for the modification, where appropriate, of the immunity enjoyed by one or more international organizations.

Under the statute, the President can withdraw or restrict the immunity and privileges thereby conferred. Specifically, it provides:

> The president (is) authorized, in the light of the functions performed by any such international organization, by appropriate executive order to withhold or withdraw from any such organization or its officers or employees any of the privileges, exemptions, and immunities provided for in this title * * * or to condition or limit the

---

16. According to the House Report: The purpose of this section is to permit international organizations designated by the President pursuant to the International Organization Immunities Act, 22 U.S.C. 288 et seq., to carry out their functions from their offices located in the United States without hindrance by private claimants seeking to attach the payment of funds to a foreign state; such attachments would also violate the immunities accorded to such international institutions. H.R.Rep. No. 94–1487, 94th Cong., 2d Sess. 30 (1976). The Report continues, even more pointedly

This reference to "international organizations" in this subsection is not intended to restrict any immunity accorded to such international organizations under any law or international agreement.

enjoyment by any such organization or its officers or employees of any such privilege, exemption, or immunity.[17]

The Senate Report on the IOIA stated: "This provision will permit the adjustment or limitation of the privileges in the event that any international organization should engage for example, in activities of a commercial nature." And, in floor debate on the legislation, its supporters pointed again to this provision as a limitation on commercial abuses by an international organization.[19] Hence this provision may reveal that Congress intended to grant absolute immunity to international organizations giving to the President the authority to relax that immunity, including removal or restriction of immunity in cases involving the commercial activities of international organizations.

Finally, Congress may have concluded that the policies and considerations that led to the development of the restrictive immunity concept for foreign nations do not apply to international organizations like the OAS.[20]

We need not decide this difficult question of statutory construction. On *either* theory of immunity—absolute or restrictive—an immunity exists sufficient to shield the organization from lawsuit on the basis of acts involved here.

C. The "Commercial" Activity Concept in the Restrictive Immunity Doctrine

Even under the restrictive immunity doctrine, there is immunity from lawsuits based on governmental or sovereign activities—the jure imperii—as distinct from commercial activities. We discuss the narrower standard of restrictive immunity not because it is necessarily the governing principle, but because we discern that an organization conducting the activities at issue in this case is shielded even under the restrictive immunity formula, and a fortiori on the absolute immunity theory.

Section 1605 of the FSIA provides that foreign states shall not be immune from the jurisdiction of American courts in any case based upon

---

17. 22 U.S.C. § 288a(a) (1979).

19. See 91 Cong.Rec. 12,432 (daily ed. Dec. 20, 1945) and 12,530 (daily ed. Dec. 21, 1945).

20. Prior to its modification, the absolute immunity of states was justified by "the desirability of avoiding adjudication which might affront a foreign nation and thus embarrass the executive branch in its conduct of foreign relations." See Hearings on H.R. 11315 before the Subcommittee on Administrative Law and Governmental Relations, House Committee on the Judiciary, 94th Cong., 2d Sess. 29 (1976). As sovereign nations become more and more involved in the market place, as merchants rather than sovereigns, claims arising out of commercial transactions do not affront the sovereignty of the nations involved. Id. Recognition of this growing involvement in

commercial activity was the basis of the movement to a restrictive concept. Moreover, most other commercial nations embrace restrictive immunity with regard to sovereigns. Thus, when our government and its instrumentalities are sued abroad in commercial litigation, the sovereign immunity defense is rarely available. H.R.Rep. [supra]. Congressional proponents of the restrictive immunity could thus indicate that use of the restrictive immunity concept would bring the United States into step with foreign nations. But neither rationale for adopting the restrictive notion of immunity would seem to apply to international organizations. Such organizations do not regularly engage in commercial activities, nor do other nations apply the concept of restrictive immunity to them. Cf. Alfred Dunhill of London, Inc. v. Cuba, 425 U.S. 682, 699–702 (1975).

their commercial activity in the United States, with the commercial character of an activity determined by reference to its "nature" rather than to its "purpose." The conceptual difficulties involved in differentiating jure gestionis from jure imperii have led some commentators to declare the distinction unworkable. The restrictive immunity doctrine is designed to accommodate the legal interests of citizens doing business with foreign governments on the one hand, with the interests of foreign states in avoiding the embarrassment of defending the propriety of political acts before a foreign court.

In our view, the employment by a foreign state or international organization of internal administrative personnel—civil servants—is not properly characterized as "doing business." That view is supported by the legislative history of the FSIA, and the definition of "commercial activity" in § 1603. The House Report commented:

(d) Commercial activity.—Paragraph (c) of section 1603 defines the term "commercial activity" as including a broad spectrum of endeavor, from an individual commercial transaction or act to a regular course of commercial conduct. A "regular course of commercial conduct" includes the carrying on of a commercial enterprise such as a mineral extraction company, an airline or a state trading corporation. Certainly, if an activity is customarily carried on for profit, its commercial nature could readily be assumed. At the other end of the spectrum, a single contract, if of the same character as a contract which might be made by a private person, could constitute a "particular transaction or act."

As the definition indicates, the fact that goods or services to be procured through a contract are to be used for a public purpose is irrelevant; it is the essentially commercial nature of an activity or transaction that is critical. Thus, a contract by a foreign government to buy provisions or equipment for its armed forces or to construct a government building constitutes a commercial activity. The same would be true of a contract to make repairs on an embassy building. Such contracts should be considered to be commercial contracts, even if their ultimate object is to further a public function.

By contrast, a foreign state's mere participation in a foreign assistance program administered by the Agency for International Development (AID) is an activity whose essential nature is public or governmental, and it would not itself constitute a commercial activity. By the same token, a foreign state's activities in and "contacts" with the United States resulting from or necessitated by participation in such a program would not in themselves constitute a sufficient commercial nexus with the United States so as to give rise to jurisdiction (see sec. 1330) or to assets which could be subjected to attachment or execution with respect to unrelated commercial transactions (see sec. 1610(b)). However, a transaction to obtain goods or services from private parties would not lose its otherwise commercial character because it was entered into in connection with an AID program. Also public or governmental and not commercial in nature, would be the employment of diplomatic, civil service, or military personnel, but not the employment of American citizens or third country nationals by the foreign state in the United States.[23]

This report clearly marks employment of civil servants as noncommercial for purposes of restrictive immunity. The Committee Reports establish an exception from the general rule in the case of employment of American citizens or third country nationals by foreign states. The exception leaves foreign states free to conduct "governmental" matters through their own citizens. A comparable exception is not applicable to international organizations, because their civil servants are inevitably drawn from either American citizens or "third" country nations. In the case of international organizations, such an exception would swallow up the rule of immunity for civil service employment disputes.

The United States has accepted without qualification the principles that international organizations must be free to perform their functions and that no member state may take action to hinder the organization.[24] The unique nature of the international civil service is relevant. International officials should be as free as possible, within the mandate granted by the member states, to perform their duties free from the peculiarities of national politics. The OAS charter, for example, imposes constraints on the organization's employment practices.[25] Such constraints may not coincide with the employment policies pursued by its various member states.[26] It would seem singularly inappropriate for the international organization to bind itself to the employment law of any particular member, and we have no reason to think that either the President or Congress intended this result. An attempt by the courts of one nation to adjudicate the personnel claims of international civil servants would entangle those courts in the internal administration of those organizations. Denial of immunity opens the door to divided decisions of the courts of different member states passing judgment on the rules, regulations, and decisions of the international bodies. Undercutting uniformity in the application of staff rules or regulations would undermine the ability of the organization to function effectively.

23. H.Rep. No. 94–1487, 94th Cong., 2d Sess. 16 (1976) (emphasis added).

24. See e.g., XIII Documents of the United Nations Conference on International Organizations 704–05 (1945), reprinted in 13 Whiteman, Digest of International Law 36 (1968).

25. See e.g., OAS Charter, Article 143 (forbidding discrimination on the basis of "race, creed or sex"), Article 126 (requiring staff recruitment on as wide a geographic basis as possible).

26. For example, the Age Discrimination in Employment Act of 1978, (ADEA) 29 U.S.C. § 621 et seq., forbids in most circumstances a requirement that a person retire at a particular age. Yet other countries consider early retirement an important social goal, the achievement of which facilitates advancement by younger people. Since there is no inconsistent provision in the OAS Charter (and since, even if there were, the ADEA was enacted after the latest amendment to the OAS Charter), the ADEA presumably would govern, and unless its provisions were construed not to cover international employment, see 29 U.S.C. §§ 630 and 633a, the OAS and other international organizations who are thought not immune from suit would be required to abide by the terms of the Act in their employment here.

Or for another example, the rigid quotas employed as an integral part of recruiting a "balanced" international civil service, see, e.g., General Assembly Resolution 33/143, December 18, 1978, might run afoul of the emerging law of "affirmative action" in the United States.

We hold that the relationship of an international organization with its internal administrative staff is noncommercial, and, absent waiver, activities defining or arising out of that relationship may not be the basis of an action against the organization—regardless of whether international organizations enjoy absolute or restrictive immunity.

D.   The Activities at Issue Here

The appellants were staff members of the General Secretariat of the OAS.   Their appointments, terms of employment, salaries and allowances, and the termination of employment were governed by detailed "Staff Rules of the General Secretariat" promulgated by the OAS.   The Staff Rules further establish an elaborate grievance procedure within the OAS, with ultimate appeal to the Administrative Tribunal of the OAS.

The Tribunal is competent to determine the lawfulness of an employee's termination of employment.   If an employee has been wrongfully discharged, the Tribunal may order reinstatement.   If reinstatement is ordered, the Tribunal may also establish an indemnity to be paid to the employee in the event the Secretary General exercises his authority to indemnify the employee rather than effect the reinstatement.

The employment disputes between the appellants and OAS were disputes concerning the internal administrative staff of the Organization.   The internal administration of the OAS is a non-commercial activity shielded by the doctrine of immunity.   There was no waiver, and accordingly the appellant's action had to be dismissed.

Affirmed.

––––––––

Note on Broadbent: The uncertainty about whether international organizations enjoy absolute immunity under the IOIA or restricted immunity as provided in the FSIA has remained unsettled.   See Tuck v. Pan American Health Organization, 668 F.2d 547 (D.C.Cir.1981); Mendaro v. World Bank, 717 F.2d 610 (D.C.Cir.1983); Morgan v. International Bank for Reconstruction and Development, 752 F.Supp. 492 (D.D.C.1990).

Convention on the Privileges and Immunities of the Specialized Agencies.   (The text of which is at 33 U.N.T.S. 261).   States, in acceding to this convention indicate to which of the specialized agencies they choose to apply it.   The United States is not a party, although, pursuant to the International Organization Immunities Act, 22 U.S.C. § 288, the President of the United States has designated virtually all U.N. agencies as entitled to the benefits of the act.

––––––––

Question: What is the argument for maintaining the immunity for international organizations?   Purely textual?   See a Food & Agriculture Org. v. INPDAI, 87 I.L.R. 1 (1992) (Italy Cour de Cass.).

Chapter 8

THE ACT OF STATE DOCTRINE

Perspective. The subject matter of this Chapter, together with some aspects of the preceding one, influenced us to call this book "The International Legal System," rather than one on international public law. What is analyzed here involves treatment in national legal systems of matters that are not as yet governed by widely-accepted rules of international public law, but which do, nonetheless, involve legal issues that connect with the interests and attitudes of other states. These issues are usually ignored in courses on domestic law, such as Conflicts of Law. Note that the resulting issue is not necessarily one of illegality under international public law. Sections 443 and 444 of the 1987 Restatement of the Foreign Relations Law, especially the Reporters' Notes, are helpful in understanding the setting tersely stated here.

The act of state doctrine presented here arises in a litigation context. It involves the question whether an otherwise governing foreign dispositive legal principle is to be invalidated by a "municipal" court. It does not arise in a purely foreign relations context, as where the foreign office of State A should reject official conduct of State B, either in a diplomatic protection case (refer to Chapters 9 and 15–B). A foreign ministry might assert that the foreign state's conduct violates international law, and it might even try to proceed in an international tribunal, where official conduct and major policy are concerned. But no state sues another in its own courts to invalidate official conduct of the latter, especially that taken in that state's territory. True, in the leading U.S. case, *Banco Nacional de Cuba v. Sabbatino,* the plaintiff was an agency of Cuba, but you will understand how it came to be the plaintiff shortly. In all other act of state cases in American courts the plaintiffs are private parties who have taken the initiative to bring cases, but whether the act of a foreign state is legitimate becomes the dispositive issue, this is usually at the defendant's initiative.

* * * The act of state doctrine is a judicially-created limitation on the exercise of federal adjudicatory jurisdiction. It is not a jurisdictional bar, but is a mechanism of judicial abstention to allow the judiciary prudentially to avoid litigating a foreign sovereign's public conduct committed within its own territory. The judiciary avoids being enmeshed in matters of foreign affairs which could risk embarrassment to the executive. Most of the Supreme Court decisions have related to expropriation of private property, or political crises in foreign countries. Questions of civil damages for loss of consortium or for *"Foreign Corrupt Practices"* relating to alleged bribery of foreign officials by a U.S. contractor have also recently been at issue.

The act of state doctrine is not part of the Foreign Sovereign Immunities Act and is governed by different variables as to application, *vel non*, although it will cause a plaintiff to lose in a similar fashion. Such a case could be dealt with as an ordinary, strictly judicial, conflicts of law case. The choice of law would be to apply that of the foreign state, unless the plaintiff could convince the court that the foreign law should be rejected as fundamentally and inherently contrary to the law and policy of the forum. But major act of state cases did not take this approach. Why? Simply put: it is because non-judicial issues arise, including issues of concern to the executive and the legislative branches.

The title of Section A is accurate: the Supreme Court has been the major actor in the fashioning of the American version of act of state. Why? Should it have been? Should it continue to take the lead in fashioning the Doctrine? If so, along what lines? Should Congress enact, on the model of the Foreign Sovereign Immunities Act, an "act of state" Act?

As to the use by courts in Britain of the principle of non-examination of the acts of a foreign state, *see* the United States Supreme Court's note 21 to its opinion in *Banco Nacional de Cuba v. Sabbatino, Receiver,* page 627 herein, citing the classic case of Luther v. Sagor & Co., [1921] 3 K.B. 532. For House of Lords decisions in 1981 and 1986 adopting the American view of act of state and declaring a change of title by nationalization of property in a foreign state non-reviewable, see Reporters' Note 12 to Section 443 of the 1987 Restatement. The United States Supreme Court also makes brief reference in its note 21 to the manner in which tribunals in civil law systems use the principle against examination of the legitimacy of an otherwise applicable foreign legal rule. The term act of state, however, is rarely used.

* * * Civil law systems will not apply an otherwise applicable foreign rule that is violative of the public order of the forum state. The notion of public order is not the same as that in a common law court. The civilian doctrine of *ordre public* concerns itself only with exceptional or highly significant manifestations of foreign sovereign will. The issue is whether in certain situations that will clash with an equally highly held principle of proper governance and national interest in the forum state.

Is it possible to argue today, on re-examination of state consent, that an abuse of jurisdiction [unreasonable exercise of jurisdiction] arises under customary international law where a court of one state reviews and invalidates the governmental act of another state as to non-immune persons, relationships, and assets localized in its territory?

————

SECTION A. THE BASIC COURT–MADE DOCTRINE IN THE UNITED STATES

————

The American act of state doctrine and political crises in foreign relations. The American act of state doctrine is closely linked to political crises abroad in the course of which officials of a foreign government take actions harmful or outrageous to a person who, later, seeks redress by bringing a suit in the United States.

In the agreement for the release of American hostages in Teheran in 1981, the United States undertook to bar the hostages from prosecuting claims against Iran for their seizure and detention. Suppose, however, the United States had not done so and some of hostages were able to find and serve in the United States former officials of the government in control in Iran at the time it violated the diplomatic immunity and human dignity of the plaintiffs. The defendants would plead that under the law of the United States governing its foreign relations, their conduct was an Iranian act of state. It would be beyond review by American courts.

The link to political crises abroad is apparent, startlingly so in retrospect, in the extensive history of the doctrine given in the majority opinion of the Supreme Court in the *Sabbatino* case, infra p. 627. The first case it cites, *Underhill v. Hernandez,* involved an insurgent general in Venezuela in the 1890s who mounted a successful coup, and was recognized as the head of government, but later fell from power. He came to the United States, only to find himself sued for mistreating the plaintiff in Venezuela during the insurgency. The chronology of the cases after *Underhill* takes the doctrine through the Mexican revolution of 1910–21, the outrages of Nazi Germany, the crisis between the United States and Castro's Cuba, a relatively recent dictatorship in Venezuela and the overthrow of the king of Libya by the military regime of Colonel Qadhafi.

A troublesome aspect of the doctrine is that it tends to keep the courts from serving justice. The point is dramatically made in two suits brought by a former German, Bernstein, a Jewish person whose ships, while he was still a German citizen, were seized by the Nazi government and sold for value to purchasers with notice. In the first, Judge Learned

Hand reluctantly applied the act of state doctrine and threw the case out of court. In the second, the Legal Adviser of the Department of State informed the court by letter that it would be contrary to the policy of the United States towards occupied Germany to recognize as valid the title to ships acquired by the purchaser under the notorious racial laws of Hitlerian Germany. The court gave effect to this view and did not apply the act of state doctrine.

As a result of the second case, the way was open for efforts, through legislation and executive action, to require that the act of state doctrine not apply unless the Department of State says it should. The justification for side-tracking the doctrine is that the courts should be allowed in less sensitive cases to do justice for plaintiffs in some cases who are victims of governmental acts of foreign states even though done in their own territories. But are we to assume that the courts, if left alone by Congress and the executive branch, would continue to apply the doctrine, no matter how brutal or uncivilized the conduct of the state involved? What happens to justice when the Executive or the Congress intervene in support of one outcome or the other as to the rejection or acceptance of the foreign act of state? The potential separation-of-powers problem is obvious. *Should the Supreme Court be the final arbiter? Cf. Baker v. Carr, 369 U.S. 186 (1962). Should the trial court solicit the foreign policy view of the Department of State on the matter? Should the court be required to follow the view of the Department of State position?* Should either the court or the Department of State (or any other executive department) make its choice on the basis of whether the foreign state is "liberal" (in the broad sense of a general political similarity to to the United States) or "nonliberal" (e.g., patently adverse to the American value system)? For analytical, inter-disciplinary speculation on this question and detailed analysis of American cases on Act of State, see *Burley, Law Among Liberal States: Liberal Internationalism and The Act of State Doctrine,* 92 Columbia L.Rev. 1907 (1992). Very generally, the writer's conclusion is that if the state whose act is in question is a "liberal" state, all three branches of the United States Government should accept that the case be decided by the courts on normal conflict of laws grounds, including, judicial authority to reject an otherwise applicable foreign law on the standard conflicts ground of fundamental incompatibility with the law of the forum. If the foreign state is "nonliberal," the issue becomes a "political question." The courts should defer to the political branches.

Where is the determination of "liberal" vs. "non-liberal" state to be made? By the federal judiciary? By the Department of State? * * * Of course, the Department of State and the Senate when it gives its "Advice & Consent" to our extradition treaties, currently make such a decision. They do the same when they eliminate the political offense exception, for relative political offenses. E.g., U.S.–U.K. Treaty; the *U.S.–German Extradition Treaty,* where former Department of State Legal Adviser, Judge Abraham Soafer, stated that we would only provide such a clause in treaties with our "liberal" democratic allies. It is said that we actually had negotiated a similar exception to the political offense exception in a proposed treaty with Marcos's Philippines. The latter treaty was never sent over for the advice and consent of the Senate.[1] Consider that possibility after you read Justice Scalia's opinion for a unanimous Supreme Court in the Kirkpatrick Case, p. 638 *infra.*

In the matter of American business investment abroad the customary tensions escalated into crises when Castro nationalized American private property in Cuba in retaliation for United States actions such as Congressional suspension of the Cuban sugar quota. Later, Allende in Chile nationalized what had already been reduced to minority American interests in Chilean copper mining companies. [He evaded paying compensation by inducing the enactment of a retroactive excess profits tax that exceeded the compensation claim.] In Peru, elements of the military overthrew an elected president who tried to settle a long-smouldering controversy about sub-surface oil and gas rights and had trumped up a claim for bad faith extraction that washed out compensation. Qadhafi cancelled some (but not all) oil concessions that had been made by the deposed king of Libya, without compensation.

Earlier, in 1951, Tories in Britain were narrowly prevented from gunboat diplomacy when Mosadegh, an austere traditional in Iranian politics, badly miscast by the West as a leftist, nationalized the Anglo-Iranian Oil Company, with an undertaking to compensate. Instead of force, Britain ultimately evolved the hot product doctrine, exemplified in the favorable (to dispossessed investors) decision of the Supreme Court of the then-British protectorate of Aden. This pioneering effort spawned a whole series of instances, including that in Sabbatino, where (ignored in the Aden decision, see p. 665 act of state loomed as an obstacle in limine to vindication of dispossessed investors in municipal judicial systems of other states.

Most recently courts have had to face the question whether an officially-directed act of torture or other outrage—historically and tragically a most classic act of state—is beyond scrutiny in non-international courts of states other than the acting state. (See, inter alia the *Filartiga* case infra, chapter 10 (Human Rights).

BANCO NACIONAL DE CUBA v. SABBATINO, RECEIVER

United States Supreme Court, 1964.
376 U.S. 398, 84 S.Ct. 923, 11 L.Ed.2d 804.[a]

Mr. Justice HARLAN delivered the opinion of the Court.

The question which brought this case here, and is now found to be the dispositive issue, is whether the so-called act of state doctrine serves to sustain petitioner's claims in this litigation. Such claims are ultimately founded on a decree of the Government of Cuba expropriating certain property, the right to the proceeds of which is here in controver-

---

1. Republic of the Philippines v. Marcos, 862 F.2d 1355, 1368–69 (9th Cir.1988).

a. See Chapter 12, Section A, for that part of the opinion which declares irrelevant the fact that the United States had severed diplomatic relations with Cuba.

sy. The act of state doctrine in its traditional formulation precludes the courts of this country from inquiring into the validity of the public acts a recognized foreign sovereign power committed within its own territory.

[In 1960, the U.S. Congress reduced the import quota for Cuban sugar. The Cuban government characterized the reduction as "aggression" and retaliated by nationalizing the sugar industry, expropriating many U.S. owned companies or companies in which Americans held significant interests. Farr Whitlock, an American commodities broker had entered into a contract to buy a shipload of C.A.V. (*Compañia Azucarera Vertientes,* one of the U.S. companies) sugar. Farr Whitlock entered into a new agreement to buy the shipload of sugar from the Cuban government, turned the proceeds over to *C.A.V.,* instead of Cuba. Farr Whitlock had arranged for indemnification, and assigned the bills of lading to the *Banco National de Cuba.* When Farr Whitlock negotiated the shipping documents to its clients, *Banco National* sued them for conversion. It also attempted to enjoin *Sabbatino,* the temporary receiver of C.A.V.'s assets, from taking any action in regard to the money that might result in its removal from New York. Farr Whitlock's defense was that title to the sugar never actually passed to Cuba, because the expropriation violated international law].

* * *

The classic American statement of the act of state doctrine, which appears to have taken root in England as early as 1674, and began to emerge in the jurisprudence of this country in the late eighteenth and early nineteenth centuries, see e.g., Ware v. Hylton, 3 Dall. 199, 230; The Santissima Trinidad, 7 Wheat. 283, 336, is found in Underhill v. Hernandez, where Chief Justice Fuller said for a unanimous Court: "Every sovereign State is bound to respect the independence of every other sovereign State, and the courts of one country will not sit in judgment on the acts of the government of another done within its own territory. Redress of grievances by reason of such acts must be obtained through the means open to be availed of by sovereign powers as between themselves." Following this precept the Court in that case refused to inquire into acts of Hernandez, a revolutionary Venezuelan military commander whose government had been later recognized by the United States, which were made the basis of a damage action in this country by Underhill, an American citizen, who claimed that he had been unlawfully assaulted, coerced, and detained in Venezuela by Hernandez.

None of this Court's subsequent cases in which the act of state doctrine was directly or peripherally involved manifest any retreat from Underhill. * * * On the contrary in two of these cases, Oetjen and Ricaud, the doctrine as announced in Underhill was reaffirmed in unequivocal terms.

* * *

The Court of Appeals relied in part upon an exception to the unqualified teachings of Underhill, Oetjen, and Ricaud which that court had earlier indicated. In Bernstein v. Van Heyghen Freres Société Anonyme, suit was brought to recover from an assignee property allegedly taken, in effect, by the Nazi Government because plaintiff was Jewish. Recognizing the odious nature of this act of state, the court, through Judge Learned Hand, nonetheless refused to consider it invalid on that ground. Rather, it looked to see if the Executive had acted in any manner that would indicate that United States Courts should refuse to give effect to such a foreign decree. Finding no such evidence, the court sustained dismissal of the complaint. In a later case involving similar facts the same court again assumed examination of the German acts improper, Bernstein v. N.V. Nederlandsche–Amerikaansche Stoomvaart–Maatschappij, 2 Cir., but, quite evidently following the implications of Judge Hand's opinion in the earlier case, amended its mandate to permit evidence of alleged invalidity, subsequent to receipt by plaintiff's attorney of a letter from the Acting Legal Adviser to the State Department written for the purpose of relieving the court from any constraint upon the exercise of its jurisdiction to pass on that question.

This Court has never had occasion to pass upon the so-called Bernstein exception, nor need it do so now. For whatever ambiguity may be thought to exist in the two letters from State Department officials on which the Court of Appeals relied, is now removed by the position which the Executive has taken in this Court on the act of state claim; respondents do not indeed contest the view that these letters were intended to reflect no more than the Department's then wish not to make any statement bearing on this litigation.

The outcome of this case, therefore, turns upon whether any of the contentions urged by respondents against the application of the act of state doctrine in the premises is acceptable: (1) that the doctrine does not apply to acts of state which violate international law, as is claimed to be the case here; (2) that the doctrine is inapplicable unless the Executive specifically interposes it in a particular case; and (3) that, in any event, the doctrine may not be invoked by a foreign government plaintiff in our courts.

Preliminarily, we discuss the foundations on which we deem the act of state doctrine to rest, and more particularly the question of whether state or federal law governs its application in a federal diversity case.

We do not believe that this doctrine is compelled either by the inherent nature of sovereign authority, as some of the earlier decisions seem to imply, see Underhill, supra; American Banana, supra; Oetjen, supra, or by some principle of international law. If a transaction takes place in one jurisdiction and the forum is in another, the forum does not by dismissing an action or by applying its own law purport to divest the first jurisdiction of its territorial sovereignty; it merely declines to adjudicate or makes applicable its own law to parties or property before it. The refusal of one country to enforce the penal laws of another * * * is a typical example of an instance when a court will not entertain a cause of action arising in another jurisdiction. While historic notions of sovereign authority do bear upon the wisdom of employing the act of state doctrine, they do not dictate its existence.

That international law does not require application of the doctrine is evidenced by the practice of nations. Most of the countries rendering decisions on the subject fail to follow the rule rigidly. No international arbitral or judicial decision discovered suggests that international law prescribes recognition of sovereign acts of foreign governments and apparently no claim has ever been raised before an international tribunal that failure to apply the act of state doctrine constitutes a breach of international obligation. If international law does not prescribe use of the doctrine, neither does it forbid application of the rule even if it is claimed that the act of state in question violated international law. The traditional view of international law is that it establishes substantive principles for determining whether one country has wronged another. Because of its peculiar nation-to-nation character the usual method for an individual to seek relief is to exhaust local remedies and then repair to the executive authorities of his own state to persuade them to champion his claim in diplomacy or before an international tribunal. Although it is, of course, true that United States courts apply international law as a part of our own in appropriate circumstances. The Paquete Habana, the public law of nations can hardly dictate to a country which is in theory wronged how to treat that wrong within its domestic borders.

Despite the broad statement in Oetjen that "The conduct of the foreign relations of our Government is committed by the Constitution to the Executive and Legislative * * * Departments," it cannot of course be thought that "every case or controversy which touches foreign relations lies beyond judicial cognizance." The text of the Constitution does not require the act of state doctrine; it does not irrevocably remove from the judiciary the capacity to review the validity of foreign acts of state.

The act of state doctrine does, however, have "constitutional" underpinnings. It arises out of the basic relationships between branches of government in a system of separation of powers. It concerns the competency of dissimilar institutions to make and implement particular kinds of decisions in the area of international relations. The doctrine as formulated in past decisions expresses the strong sense of the Judicial Branch that its engagement in the task of passing on the validity of foreign acts of state may hinder rather than further this country's pursuit of goals both for itself and for the community of nations as a whole in the international sphere. Many commentators disagree with this view; they have striven by means of distinguishing and limiting past decisions and by advancing various considerations of policy to stimulate a narrowing of the apparent scope of the rule. Whatever considerations are thought to predominate, it is plain that the problems involved are uniquely federal in nature. If federal authority, in this instance this Court, orders the field of judicial competence in this area for the federal courts, and the state courts are left free to formulate their own rules, the purposes behind the doctrine could be as effectively undermined as if there had been no federal pronouncement on the subject.

We could perhaps in this diversity action avoid the question of deciding whether federal or state law is applicable to this aspect of the litigation. New York has enunciated the act of state doctrine in terms that echo those of federal decisions decided during the reign of Swift v. Tyson, 16 Pet. 1. In Hatch v. Baez, 7 Hun. 596, 599 (N.Y.Sup.Ct.),

Underhill was foreshadowed by the words, "the courts of one country are bound to abstain from sitting in judgment on the acts of another government done within its own territory." More recently, the Court of Appeals in Salimoff & Co. v. Standard Oil Co., has declared, "The courts of one independent government will not sit in judgment upon the validity of the acts of another done within its own territory, even when such government seizes and sells the property of an American citizen within its boundaries." Thus our conclusions might well be the same whether we dealt with this problem as one of state law, see Erie R. Co. v. Tompkins, [supra].

However, we are constrained to make it clear that an issue concerned with a basic choice regarding the competence and function of the Judiciary and the National Executive in ordering our relationships with other members of the international community must be treated exclusively as an aspect of federal law. It seems fair to assume that the Court did not have rules like the act of state doctrine in mind when it decided Erie R. Co. v. Tompkins. Soon thereafter, Professor Philip C. Jessup, now a judge of the International Court of Justice, recognized the potential dangers were Erie extended to legal problems affecting international relations.[24] He cautioned that rules of international law should not be left to divergent and perhaps parochial state interpretations. His basic rationale is equally applicable to the act of state doctrine.

The Court in the pre-Erie act of state cases, although not burdened by the problem of the source of applicable law, used language sufficiently strong and broad-sweeping to suggest that state courts were not left free to develop their own doctrines (as they would have been had this Court merely been interpreting common law under Swift v. Tyson).

* * *

If the act of state doctrine is a principle of decision binding on federal and state courts alike but compelled by neither international law nor the Constitution, its continuing vitality depends on its capacity to reflect the proper distribution of functions between the judicial and political branches of the Government on matters bearing upon foreign affairs. It should be apparent that the greater the degree of codification or consensus concerning a particular area of international law, the more appropriate it is for the judiciary to render decisions regarding it, since the courts can then focus on the application of an agreed principle to circumstances of fact rather than on the sensitive task of establishing a principle not inconsistent with the national interest or with international justice. It is also evident that some aspects of international law touch much more sharply on national nerves than do others; the less important the implications of an issue are for our foreign relations, the weaker the justification for exclusivity in the political branches. The balance of relevant considerations may also be shifted if the government which perpetrated the challenged act of state is no longer in existence, as in the Bernstein case, for the political interest of this country may, as a result,

---

24. The Doctrine of Erie Railroad v. Tompkins Applied to International Law, 33 Am.J.Int'l L. 740 (1939).

be measurably altered. Therefore, rather than laying down or reaffirming an inflexible and all-encompassing rule in this case, we decide only that the Judicial Branch will not examine the validity of a taking of property within its own territory by a foreign sovereign government, extant and recognized by this country at the time of suit, in the absence of a treaty or other unambiguous agreement regarding controlling legal principles, even if the complaint alleges that the taking violates customary international law.

There are few if any issues in international law today on which opinion seems to be so divided as the limitations on a state's power to expropriate the property of aliens. There is, of course, authority, in international judicial and arbitral decisions, in the expressions of national governments, and among commentators for the view that a taking is improper under international law if it is not for a public purpose, is discriminatory, or is without provision for prompt, adequate, and effective compensation. However, Communist countries, although they have in fact provided a degree of compensation after diplomatic efforts, commonly recognize no obligation on the part of the taking country. Certain representatives of the newly independent and underdeveloped countries have questioned whether rules of state responsibility toward aliens can bind nations that have not consented to them and it is argued that the traditionally articulated standards governing expropriation of property reflect "imperialist" interests and are inappropriate to the circumstances of emergent states.

* * *

The possible adverse consequences of a conclusion to the contrary of that implicit in these cases is highlighted by contrasting the practices of the political branch with the limitations of the judicial process in matters of this kind. Following an expropriation of any significance, the Executive engages in diplomacy aimed to assure that United States citizens who are harmed are compensated fairly. Representing all claimants of this country, it will often be able, either by bilateral or multilateral talks, by submission to the United Nations, or by the employment of economic and political sanctions, to achieve some degree of general redress. Judicial determinations of invalidity of title can, on the other hand, have only an occasional impact, since they depend on the fortuitous circumstance of the property in question being brought into this country. Such decisions would, if the acts involved were declared invalid, often be likely to give offense to the expropriating country; since the concept of territorial sovereignty is so deep seated, any state may resent the refusal of the courts of another sovereign to accord validity to acts within its territorial borders. * * *

The dangers of such adjudication are present regardless of whether the State Department has, as it did in this case, asserted that the relevant act violated international law. If the Executive Branch has undertaken negotiations with an expropriating country, but has refrained from claims of violation of the law of nations, a determination to that effect by a court might be regarded as a serious insult, while a finding of compliance with international law, would greatly strengthen the bargaining hand of the other state with consequent detriment to American interests.

Even if the State Department has proclaimed the impropriety of the expropriation, the stamp of approval of its view by a judicial tribunal, however impartial, might increase any affront and the judicial decision might occur at a time, almost always well after the taking, when such an impact would be contrary to our national interest. Considerably more serious and far-reaching consequences would flow from a judicial finding that international law standards had been met if that determination flew in the face of a State Department proclamation to the contrary. When articulating principles of international law in its relations with other states, the Executive Branch speaks not only as an interpreter of generally accepted and traditional rules, as would the courts, but also as an advocate of standards it believes desirable for the community of nations and protective of national concerns. In short, whatever way the matter is cut, the possibility of conflict between the Judicial and Executive Branches could hardly be avoided.

* * *

Another serious consequence of the exception pressed by respondents would be to render uncertain titles in foreign commerce, with the possible consequence of altering the flow of international trade. If the attitude of the United States courts were unclear, one buying expropriated goods would not know if he could safely import them into this country. Even were takings known to be invalid, one would have difficulty determining after goods had changed hands several times whether the particular articles in question were the product of an ineffective state act.

Against the force of such considerations, we find respondents' countervailing arguments quite unpersuasive. Their basic contention is that United States courts could make a significant contribution to the growth of international law, a contribution whose importance, it is said, would be magnified by the relative paucity of decisional law by international bodies. But given the fluidity of present world conditions, the effectiveness of such a patchwork approach toward the formulation of an acceptable body of law concerning state responsibility for expropriations, is, to say the least, highly conjectural. Moreover, it rests upon the sanguine presupposition that the decisions of the courts of the world's major capital exporting country and principal exponent of the free enterprise system would be accepted as disinterested expressions of sound legal principle by those adhering to widely different ideologies.

* * *

Respondents claim that the economic pressure resulting from the proposed exception to the act of state doctrine will materially add to the protection of United States investors. We are not convinced, even assuming the relevance of this contention. * * *

It is suggested that if the act of state doctrine is applicable to violations of international law, it should only be so when the Executive Branch expressly stipulates that it does not wish the courts to pass on the question of validity. We should be slow to reject the representations of the Government that such a reversal of the Bernstein principle would work serious inroads on the maximum effectiveness of United States diplomacy. Often the State Department will wish to refrain from taking an official position particularly at a moment that would be dictated by the developing of private litigation but might be inopportune diplomatically. Adverse domestic consequences might flow from an official stand which could be assuaged, if at all, only by revealing matters best kept secret. Of course, a relevant consideration for the State Department would be the position contemplated in the court to hear the case. It is highly questionable whether the examination of validity by the judiciary should depend on an educated guess by the Executive as to probable result and, at any rate, should a prediction be wrong, the Executive might be embarrassed in its dealings with other countries. We do not now pass on the Bernstein exception, but even if it were deemed valid, its suggested extension is unwarranted.

However offensive to the public policy of this country and its constituent States an expropriation of this kind may be, we conclude that both the national interest and progress toward the goal of establishing the rule of law among nations are best served by maintaining intact the act of state doctrine in this realm of its application.

* * *

The judgment of the Court of Appeals is reversed and the case is remanded to the District Court for proceedings consistent with this opinion.

It is so ordered.

Mr. Justice WHITE dissenting.

I am dismayed that the Court has, with one broad stroke, declared the ascertainment and application of international law beyond the competence of the courts of the United States in a large and important category of cases. I am also disappointed in the Court's declaration that the acts of a sovereign state with regard to the property of aliens within its borders are beyond the reach of international law in the courts of this country. However clearly established that law may be, a sovereign may violate it with impunity, except insofar as the political branches of the government may provide a remedy. This backward-looking doctrine, never before declared in this Court, is carried a disconcerting step further: not only are the courts powerless to question acts of state proscribed by international law but they are likewise powerless to refuse to adjudicate the claim founded upon a foreign law; they must render judgment and thereby validate the lawless act. Since the Court expressly extends its ruling to all acts of state expropriating property, however clearly inconsistent with the international community, all discriminatory expropriations of the property of aliens, as for example the taking of properties of persons belonging to certain races, religions or nationalities, are entitled to automatic validation in the courts of the United States. No other civilized country has found such a rigid rule necessary for the survival of the executive branch of its government; the executive of no other government seems to require such insulation from international law adjudications in its courts; and no other judiciary is apparently so incompetent to ascertain and apply international law.

I do not believe that the act of state doctrine as judicially fashioned in this Court, and the reasons underlying it, require American courts to decide cases in disregard of international law and of the rights of litigants to a full determination on the merits.

[The remaining text of Mr. Justice WHITE's extensive dissenting opinion is omitted.]

———

Notes & Questions: How much of United States foreign affairs law is conclusively determinable only by the United States Supreme Court, despite the doctrine of Erie R.R. Co. v. Tompkins? Students of federal courts law, admiralty, and conflicts of law will recognize the possibilities inherent in the breadth of the *Sabbatino* court's statement covering its holding that the act of state doctrine falls, even in diversity of citizenship cases, within the penumbra of federal interest, i.e. where the federal courts find or make law: " * * * [W]e are constrained to make it clear that an issue concerned with a basic choice regarding the competence and function of the Judiciary and the National Executive in ordering our relationships with other members of the international community *must* be treated *exclusively* as an aspect of federal law." [Emphasis supplied.] This statement is certainly sufficient to cover all the concerns about the *Erie* decision that Jessup had in mind in his 1939 article, cited in the court's note 24. Additionally it could serve to expand the authority of the federal courts to declare the rules governing private rights and duties in a variety of international transactions. The trend has been for the Supreme Court to enlarge the sectors of federal interest in which, even in diversity cases, the federal courts make or find or create rules. This occurs even where there is no specific federal statutory norm. The same phenomenon is occurring in the continual development of the general maritime law which governs even in state court proceedings.

———

1. THE UNITED STATES SUPREME COURT POST–SABBATINO APPLICATION OF THE ACT OF STATE DOCTRINE

* * *

ALFRED DUNHILL OF LONDON, INC. v. REPUBLIC OF CUBA

United States Supreme Court, 1976.
425 U.S. 682, 695, 96 S.Ct. 1854, 1861, 48 L.Ed.2d 301, 312.

[In his plurality decision, the Castro regime in Cuba, [on a sad day for U.S. citizens] nationalized the cigar manufacturing industry, which had been run by Cuban corporations owned almost entirely by Cuban nationals. Dunhill and other cigar importers had done business with the Cuban industry and continued to do so with the Castro intervenors placed in charge of cigar production and sales. The dispossessed owners, by then in the United States made claims for pre- and post-nationalization cigar sales and for trademark infringements by Dunhill and other importers of the American-registered trademarks. Dunhill and other importers, however, paid all accounts due to the intervenors. The importers and the dispossessed owners eventually resolved their differences, encouraged by the district and circuit court decisions in Dunhill's suit against the Cuban intervenors for the restitution to Dunhill of sums paid to them on account of pre-intervention sales. The Cuban government, however, refused to make restitution to Dunhill and, when sued, justified its action on act of state grounds. The circuit court held that the Cuban Government's repudiation of the restitution obligation was an act of state. An opinion by Justice White, disagreeing with this conclusion, argued that the activity was commercial, not sovereign. Three other justices agreed with him. Justice Powell concurred in the result but strongly rejected the view that great weight should be given to the views of the executive branch as to whether an activity should fall on one side or another of the sovereignty line. Four justices dissented in toto, and Stevens, J. did not concur in Part III of the opinion given below.]

Mr. Justice WHITE:

III

If we assume with the Court of Appeals that the Cuban Government itself had purported to exercise sovereign power to confiscate the mistaken payments * * * and to repudiate intervenors' adjudicated obligation to return those funds, we are nevertheless persuaded by the arguments of petitioner and by those of the United States that the concept of an act of state should not be extended to include the repudiation of a purely commercial obligation owed by a foreign sovereign or by one of its commercial instrumentalities. Our cases have not yet gone so far, and we decline to expand their reach to the extent necessary to affirm the Court of Appeals. * * *

It is the position of the United States,[a] stated in an amicus brief * * * that * * * a line should be drawn in defining the outer limits of the act of state concept and that repudiations by a foreign sovereign of its commercial debts should not be considered to be acts of state beyond legal question in our courts. * * *

---

a. The Court appended to its opinion at Appendix 1 a letter from the Legal Adviser, Department of State, to the Court of Appeals and incorporated in the government brief amicus referred to in the above text.

Questions. 1. In view of the divisions of viewpoints expressed by the justices, what is the precedential effect of Dunhill? What is its *holding?* Note that Justice White characterizes the quasi-contractual obligation to repay fashioned by the American courts below as "a purely commercial obligation." Is this convincing? If not as to this case, what about a clearly commercial breach of contract by a foreign state agency? What is a *"quasi-contract"* in domestic U.S. law? In international law? In "continental law?"

2. As to clearly commercial transactions, should the test for act of state be the same as it is for foreign state immunity under the Foreign Sovereign Immunities Act? Should the test of commercial versus sovereign conduct be the same in both situations? If "yes", should the courts make this judgment or should Congress, considering that the executive branch gratefully ceded such decisions in immunity cases to the Congress and to the courts (through the required interpretation of the FSIA)? Are there any arguments of importance that in some situations what is commercial under the FSIA may not be commercial under the act of state doctrine?

FIRST NATIONAL CITY BANK v. BANCO NACIONAL DE CUBA

United States Supreme Court, 1972.
406 U.S. 759, 92 S.Ct. 1808, 32 L.Ed.2d 466.

[The Bank refused to return to the depositor a surplus of collateral following satisfaction of a loan, on the ground that it was entitled to set off and/or counterclaim for the nationalization by the Castro regime of its branch in Cuba. A five to four majority reached the result that the act of state doctrine did not bar the Bank's action, but there was no agreement on the basis for this result. Three members of the Court, Rehnquist, J., the opinion-writer, Burger, C.J., and White, J., concurred, based upon the Bernstein letter from the Department of State, which expressed the view of the executive that the act of state doctrine should not apply. These three were willing to follow the executive branch lead, citing *Belmont* and *Curtiss–Wright* as authority for "the exclusive competence of the Executive Branch in the field of foreign affairs." Justice Douglas decided for the Bank on the ground that it was entitled to assert a counterclaim under National City Bank v. Republic of China, 348 U.S. 356 (1955). Powell, J. decided for the Bank on the grounds stated below. Four dissenting justices characterized the remand order as "anomalous."]

Mr. Justice POWELL, concurring in the judgment.

* * * While Banco Nacional de Cuba v. Sabbatino * * * technically reserves the question of the validity of the Bernstein exception, as Mr. Justice BRENNAN notes in his dissenting opinion, the reasoning of Sabbatino implicitly rejects that exception. *Moreover, I would be uncomfortable with a doctrine which would require the judiciary to receive the executive's permission before invoking its jurisdiction.* [Emphasis sup-

plied.] Such a notion, in the name of the doctrine of separation of powers, seems to me to conflict with that very doctrine.

* * *

I nevertheless concur in the judgment of the Court because I believe that the broad holding of Sabbatino was not compelled by the principles, as expressed therein, which underlie the act of state doctrine. As Mr. Justice Harlan stated in Sabbatino, *the act of state doctrine is not dictated either by "international law [or] the Constitution," but is based on a judgment as to "the proper distribution of functions between the judicial and the political branches of the Government on matters bearing upon foreign affairs."* (emphasis added). Moreover, as noted in Sabbatino, there was no intention of "laying down or reaffirming an inflexible and all-encompassing rule. * * *."

* * * The balancing of interests, recognized as appropriate by Sabbatino, requires a careful examination of the facts in each case and of the position, if any, taken by the political branches of government. I do not agree, however, that balancing the functions of the judiciary and those of the political branches compels the judiciary to eschew acting in all cases in which the underlying issue is the validity of expropriation under customary international law. Such a result would be an abdication of the judiciary's responsibility to persons who seek to resolve their grievances by the judicial process.

Nor do I think the doctrine of separation of powers dictates such an abdication. To so argue is to assume that there is no such thing as international law but only international political disputes that can be resolved only by the exercise of power. * * *

* * *

Questions. 1. Is there evidence in the lower court precedents that a Bernstein letter exception exists? See discussion and cases in § 2, *infra.*

2. Justice Powell's rejection of executive domination of outcomes in act of state situations was repeated in the Dunhill decision, where he also concurred in the result in opposition to the application of the act of state doctrine. Where do you suppose Justice Powell would, under his judicial flexibility approach, be willing to apply the doctrine?

W.S. KIRKPATRICK & CO., INC. v. ENVIRONMENTAL TECTONICS CORPORATION, INTERNATIONAL

United States Supreme Court, 1990.
493 U.S. 400, 110 S.Ct. 701, 107 L.Ed.2d 816.

Justice SCALIA delivered the opinion of the Court.

In this case we must decide whether the act of state doctrine bars a court in the United States from entertaining a cause of action that does not rest upon the asserted invalidity of an official act of a foreign sovereign, but that does require imputing to foreign officials an unlawful motivation (the obtaining of bribes) in the performance of such an official act.

I

[Facts]: * * * In 1981, Harry Carpenter, who was then Chairman of the Board and Chief Executive Officer of petitioner W.S. Kirkpatrick & Co., Inc. (Kirkpatrick) learned that the Republic of Nigeria was interested in contracting for the construction and equipment of an aeromedical center at Kaduna Air Force Base in Nigeria. He made arrangements with Benson "Tunde" Akindele, a Nigerian citizen, whereby Akindele would endeavor to secure the contract for Kirkpatrick. It was agreed that, in the event the contract was awarded to Kirkpatrick, Kirkpatrick would pay to two Panamanian entities controlled by Akindele a "commission" equal to 20% of the contract price, which would in turn be given as a bribe to officials of the Nigerian Government. In accordance with this plan, the contract was awarded to petitioner W.S. Kirkpatrick & Co., International (Kirkpatrick International), a wholly owned subsidiary of Kirkpatrick; Kirkpatrick paid the promised "commission" to the appointed Panamanian entities; and those funds were disbursed as bribes. All parties agree that Nigerian law prohibits both the payment and the receipt of bribes in connection with the award of a government contract.

Respondent Environmental Tectonics, * * * an unsuccessful bidder for the Kaduna contract, learned of the 20% "commission" and brought the matter to the attention of the Nigerian Air Force and the United States Embassy in Lagos. Following an investigation by the Federal Bureau of Investigation, the United States Attorney for the District of New Jersey brought charges against both Kirkpatrick and Carpenter for violations of the Foreign Corrupt Practices Act of 1977, 15 U.S.C. § 78dd–1 et seq., and both pleaded guilty.

Respondent then brought this civil action against Carpenter, Akindele, petitioners, and others, seeking damages under the Racketeer Influenced and Corrupt Organizations Act [RICO], 18 U.S.C. § 1961 et seq., the Robinson–Patman Act, 15 U.S.C. § 13 et seq., and the New Jersey Anti–Racketeering Act. The defendants moved to dismiss the complaint under Rule 12(b)(6) of the Federal Rules of Civil Procedure on the ground that the action was barred by the act of state doctrine.

The District Court, having requested and received a letter expressing the views of the legal advisor to the United States Department of State as to the applicability of the act of state doctrine, treated the motion as one for summary judgment under Rule 56 of the Federal Rules of Civil Procedure, and granted the motion. Environmental Tectonics v. Kirkpatrick, 659 F.Supp. 1381 (1987). The District Court concluded that the act of state doctrine applies "if the inquiry presented for judicial determination includes the motivation of a sovereign act which would result in embarrassment to the sovereign or constitute interference in the conduct of foreign policy of the United States." Applying that principle to the facts at hand, the court held that respondent's suit had to be dismissed * * *

The Court of Appeals for the Third Circuit reversed. Although agreeing with the District Court that "the award of a military procurement contract can be, in certain circumstances, a sufficiently formal expression of a government's public interests to trigger application" of the act of state doctrine, it found application of the doctrine unwarranted on the facts of this case. The Court of Appeals found particularly persuasive the letter to the District Court from the legal advisor to the Department of State, which had stated that in the opinion of the Department judicial inquiry into the purpose behind the act of a foreign sovereign would not produce the "unique embarrassment, and the particular interference with the conduct of foreign affairs, that may result from the judicial determination that a foreign sovereign's acts are invalid." The Court * * * acknowledged that "the Department's legal conclusions as to the reach of the act of state doctrine are not controlling on the courts," but concluded that "the Department's factual assessment of whether fulfillment of its responsibilities will be prejudiced by the course of civil litigation is entitled to substantial respect." In light of the Department's view that the interests of the Executive Branch would not be harmed by prosecution of the action, the Court of Appeals held that Kirkpatrick had not met its burden of showing that the case should not go forward; accordingly, it reversed the judgment of the District Court and remanded the case for trial. We granted certiorari.

II

This Court's description of the jurisprudential foundation for the act of state doctrine has undergone some evolution over the years. We once viewed the doctrine as an expression of international law, resting upon "the highest considerations of international comity and expediency," Oetjen v. Central Leather Co. We have more recently described it, however, as a consequence of domestic separation of powers, reflecting "the strong sense of the Judicial Branch that its engagement in the task of passing on the validity of foreign acts of state may hinder" the conduct of foreign affairs, Banco Nacional de Cuba v. Sabbatino. Some Justices have suggested possible exceptions to application of the doctrine, where one or both of the foregoing policies would seemingly not be served: an exception, for example, for acts of state that consist of commercial transactions, since neither modern international comity nor the current position of our Executive Branch accorded sovereign immunity to such acts, see Alfred Dunhill of London, (opinion of WHITE, J.), or an exception for cases in which the Executive Branch has represented that it has no objection to denying validity to the foreign sovereign act, since then the courts would be impeding no foreign policy goals, see First National City Bank v. Banco Nacional de Cuba, (opinion of REHNQUIST, J.).

The parties have argued at length about the applicability of these possible exceptions, and, more generally, about whether the purpose of the act of state doctrine would be furthered by its application in this case. We find it unnecessary, however, to pursue those inquiries, since the factual predicate for application of the act of state doctrine does not exist. Nothing in the present suit requires the court to declare invalid, and thus ineffective as "a rule of decision for the courts of this country," the official act of a foreign sovereign.

In every case in which we have held the act of state doctrine applicable, the relief sought or the defense interposed would have required a court in the United States to declare invalid the official act of a foreign sovereign performed within its own territory. In Underhill v. Hernandez, [supra], holding the defendant's detention of the plaintiff to be tortious would have required denying legal effect to "acts of a military commander representing the authority of the revolutionary party as government, which afterwards succeeded and was recognized by the United States." In Oetjen, supra, and in Ricaud, supra, denying title to the party who claimed through purchase from Mexico would have required declaring that government's prior seizure of the property, within its own territory, legally ineffective. See Oetjen, supra, Ricaud, supra. In *Sabbatino*, upholding the defendant's claim to the funds would have required a holding that Cuba's expropriation of goods located in Havana was null and void. In the present case, by contrast, neither the claim nor any asserted defense requires a determination that Nigeria's contract with Kirkpatrick International was, or was not, effective.

Petitioners point out, however, that the facts necessary to establish respondent's claim will also establish that the contract was unlawful. Specifically, they note that in order to prevail respondent must prove that petitioner Kirkpatrick made, and Nigerian officials received, payments that violate Nigerian law, which would, they assert, support a finding that the contract is invalid under Nigerian law. Assuming that to be true, it still does not suffice. The act of state doctrine is not some vague doctrine of abstention but a "principle of decision binding on federal and state courts alike." *Sabbatino,* supra, (emphasis added). As we said in *Ricaud*, "the act within its own boundaries of one sovereign State * * * becomes * * * a rule of decision for the courts of this country." Act of state issues only arise when a court *must decide*—that is, when the outcome of the case turns upon—the effect of official action by a foreign sovereign. When that question is not in the case, neither is the act of state doctrine. That is the situation here. Regardless of what the court's factual findings may suggest as to the legality of the Nigerian contract, its legality is simply not a question to be decided in the present suit, and there is thus no occasion to apply the rule of decision that the act of state doctrine requires. Cf. Sharon v. Time, Inc., ("The issue in this litigation is not whether [the alleged] acts are valid, but whether they occurred").

In support of their position that the act of state doctrine bars any factual findings that may cast doubt upon the validity of foreign sovereign acts, petitioners cite Justice Holmes' opinion for the Court in American Banana Co. v. United Fruit Co., [supra]. That was a suit under the United States antitrust laws, alleging that Costa Rica's seizure of the plaintiff's property had been induced by an unlawful conspiracy. In the course of a lengthy opinion Justice Holmes observed, citing *Underhill,* that "a seizure by a state is not a thing that can be complained of elsewhere in the courts." *Id.* The statement is concededly puzzling. *Underhill* does indeed stand for the proposition that a seizure by a state cannot be complained of elsewhere—in the sense of being sought to be declared *ineffective* elsewhere. The plaintiff in American Banana, however, like the plaintiff here, was not trying to undo or disregard the governmental action, but only to obtain damages from private parties who had procured it. Arguably, then, the statement did imply that suit would not lie if a foreign state's actions would be, though not invalidated, impugned.

Whatever Justice Holmes may have had in mind, his statement lends inadequate support to petitioners' position here, for two reasons. First, it was a brief aside, entirely unnecessary to the decision. American Banana was squarely decided on the ground (later substantially overruled, see Continental Ore Co. v. Union Carbide & Carbon Corp., that the antitrust laws had no extraterritorial application, so that "what the defendant did in Panama or Costa Rica is not within the scope of the statute." Second, whatever support the dictum might provide for petitioners' position is more than overcome by our later holding in United States v. Sisal Sales Corp. There we held that, *American Banana* notwithstanding, the defendant's actions in obtaining Mexico's enactment of "discriminating legislation" could form part of the basis for suit under the United States antitrust laws. Simply put, *American Banana* was not an act of state case; and whatever it said by way of dictum that might be relevant to the present case has not survived *Sisal Sales.*

Petitioners insist, however, that the policies underlying our act of state cases—international comity, respect for the sovereignty of foreign nations on their own territory, and the avoidance of embarrassment to the Executive Branch in its conduct of foreign relations—are implicated in the present case because, as the District Court found, a determination that Nigerian officials demanded and accepted a bribe "would impugn or question the nobility of a foreign nation's motivations," and would "result in embarrassment to the sovereign or constitute interference in the conduct of foreign policy of the United States." The United States, as *amicus curiae*, favors the same approach to the act of state doctrine, though disagreeing with petitioners as to the outcome it produces in the present case. We should not, the United States urges, "attach dispositive significance to the fact that this suit involves only the 'motivation' for, rather than the 'validity' of, a foreign sovereign act," and should eschew "any rigid formula for the resolution of act of state cases generally." In some future case, perhaps, "litigation * * * based on alleged corruption in the award of contracts or other commercially oriented activities of foreign governments could sufficiently touch on 'national nerves' that the act of state doctrine or related principles of abstention would appropriately be found to bar the suit," (quoting *Sabbatino*) and we should therefore resolve this case on the narrowest possible ground, viz., that the letter from the legal advisor to the District Court gives sufficient indication that, "in the setting of this case," the act of state doctrine poses no bar to adjudication, ibid.**

** Even if we agreed with the Government's fundamental approach, we would question its characterization of the legal advisor's letter as reflecting the absence of

These urgings are deceptively similar to what we said in *Sabbatino,* where we observed that sometimes, even though the validity of the act of a foreign sovereign within its own territory is called into question, the policies underlying the act of state doctrine may not justify its application. We suggested that a sort of balancing approach could be applied— the balance shifting against application of the doctrine, for example, if the government that committed the "challenged act of state" is no longer in existence. But what is appropriate in order to avoid unquestioning judicial acceptance of the acts of foreign sovereigns is not similarly appropriate for the quite opposite purpose of expanding judicial incapacities where such acts are not directly (or even indirectly) involved. It is one thing to suggest, as we have, that the policies underlying the act of state doctrine should be considered in deciding whether, despite the doctrine's technical availability, it should nonetheless not be invoked; it is something quite different to suggest that those underlying policies are a doctrine unto themselves, justifying expansion of the act of state doctrine (or, as the United States puts it, unspecified "related principles of abstention") into new and uncharted fields.

The short of the matter is this: Courts in the United States have the power, and ordinarily the obligation, to decide cases and controversies properly presented to them. The act of state doctrine does not establish an exception for cases and controversies that may embarrass foreign governments, but merely requires that, in the process of deciding, the acts of foreign sovereigns taken within their own jurisdictions shall be deemed valid. That doctrine has no application to the present case because the validity of no foreign sovereign act is at issue.

The judgment of the Court of Appeals * * * is affirmed. *It is so ordered.*

Query: Some say that the act of state doctrine is in desuetude. It has long confounded international lawyers and the *Kirkpatrick case* has done nothing to provide guidance. Indeed, it has been argued that, since *Kirkpatrick,* the act of state doctrine cannot be understood in any coherent fashion. As you saw in Justice Scalia's terse opinion, the Court held that the act of state doctrine functions as a special "rule of decision" or special choice of law rule, which requires courts faced with challenges to apparently official acts of sovereign foreign governments, to apply the law of the latter state. *See,* Gregory H. Fox, *Reexamining the Act of State Doctrine: An Integrated Conflicts Analysis,* 33 Harv.Int'l L.J. 521 (1992). Did Justice Scalia oversimplify? If so, does that invite further use by counsel for foreign states and agencies, who would otherwise not be immune from suit under the restrictive theories of the FSIA? Sovereign immunity is an important shield where applicable. When it is removed, however, defense of the foreign state falls back to

any policy objection to the adjudication. The letter, which is reprinted as an appendix to the opinion of the Court of Appeals, see 847 F.2d 1052, 1067–1069 (CA3 1988), did not purport to say whether the State Department would like the suit to proceed, but rather responded (correctly, as we hold today) to the question whether the act of state doctrine was applicable.

the *act of state* doctrine. Does Justice Scalia's opinion create enough incoherence on these issues to breed additional such use? Ambiguity may be the medium of good lawyers.

BILLY LAMB AND CARMON WILLIS v. PHILLIP MORRIS, INC. AND B.A.T.

United States Court of Appeals, Sixth Circuit, 1990.
915 F.2d 1024.

[This is an early post-*Kirkpatrick* opinion. The plaintiffs, tobacco importers, sued Phillip Morris, Inc. under the antitrust laws and the Foreign Corrupt Practices Act of 1977, 15 U.S.C. §§ 78dd–1 & 2. The latter was held inapplicable to a private claim; and the trial court's application of the Act of State doctrine to bar the suit was reversed. The excerpts below show the influence of *Kirkpatrick* toward narrowing the application of the doctrine.]

Although the act of state doctrine typically involves an assessment of "the likely impact on international relations that would result from judicial consideration of the foreign sovereign's act," Allied Bank Int'l v. Banco Credito Agricola de Cartago, 757 F.2d 516, 520–21 (2d Cir.), we must initially determine whether the defendants in this case have established the factual predicate for application of the act of state doctrine. Act of state analysis is not generally guided by "an inflexible and all-encompassing rule," see *Sabbatino* [supra]. The Supreme Court recently indicated [however,] that, as a threshold matter, "[a]ct of state issues only arise when a court must decide—that is, when the outcome of the case turns upon—the effect of official action by a foreign sovereign." *Kirkpatrick* (emphasis omitted). Here, the defendants failed to make such a showing.

The defendants view Justice Holmes' discussion of the act of state doctrine in American Banana Co., *supra* (1909), as supportive of their position that the doctrine may be applied if a legal claim impugns the motivations of a foreign state. See also the *Clayco Petroleum Corp. case.* However, the Supreme Court's recent decision in *Kirkpatrick*—a case involving civil RICO and Robinson–Patman Act claims relating to a New Jersey corporation's bribery of Nigerian officials—undercuts their contention by explicitly eschewing the logic of *American Banana*. The Court explained in *Kirkpatrick*, the act of state doctrine in its present formulation "does not establish an exception for cases and controversies that may embarrass foreign governments, but merely requires that, in the process of deciding, the acts of foreign sovereigns taken within their own jurisdiction shall be deemed valid." In reaching this conclusion and permitting the plaintiffs' claims to go forward, Justice Scalia's opinion for the unanimous Court held that the act of state doctrine *does not* "bar a court in the United States from entertaining a cause of action that * * * require[s] imputing to foreign officials an unlawful motivation (the obtaining of bribes) in the performance of * * * an official act."

Notes and Questions. *What has the Kirkpatrick Case settled as to the American version of the act of state doctrine?*

In the last paragraph of the above opinion, Justice Scalia, for a unanimous Court, compresses the decision into a pithy rule: " * * * the acts of foreign sovereigns taken within their own jurisdictions shall be deemed valid * * * " Is this a rule absolute, or does it hide some uncertainties? Consider this issue from both the standpoints of a lawyer wanting to rely on the application in an American court of an Act of State, (a) as to a bar to a plaintiff's suit against a non-immune foreign state; (b) to avoid Justice Scalia's rule as a bar by limiting its scope. What questions come to mind?

Is there a commercial exception to the act of state? A commercial exception only if the act of state produces effects outside the acting state? Anywhere? In the United States? What is a "sovereign act?" "Deemed valid," for what purposes? What about the "balancing acts" in some Circuit Court decisions not reviewed by the Supreme Court? Is the Supreme Court in *Kirkpatrick* deliberately simplifying the Act of State doctrine as to applications? If so, why? What weight will now be given to a letter from the Department of State to the effect that in its opinion the foreign action was taken *ultra vires* by "down-the-line" (but honest) bureaucrats? What if congress should enact a law that acts taken by foreign sovereigns in their territory against Americans in violation of customary international law shall be deemed invalid in the United States?

Justice Scalia wrote the *Weltover* opinion also. (*See* Ch. 7, p. 596). Reread *Weltover*. Compare the following with both *Kirkpatrick* and *Weltover*. A Stanford graduate student fell in love while in the USSR and married Frilova, a Soviet citizen. She returned to the United States (the Chicago area) and found that the USSR would not give Frilova an exit visa. A human rights activist lawyer brought an action on her behalf against the USSR for loss of consortium. The USSR did not appear. Jurisdiction in Federal Court was posited on Foreign Sovereign Immunities Act § 1605(a)(5), the so-called "torts exception." The trial court's ruling on act of state follows:

FRILOVA v. UNION OF SOVIET SOCIALIST REPUBLICS

United States District Court, Northern District of Illinois, 1983.
558 F.Supp. 358.

The denial of immigration is a public act. Additionally, the tenor of the legislative history suggests that suits are to be allowed only for ordinary claims, such as contract or tort claims arising from the foreign states activities in the United States. This court believes that the consortium claim, which resulted from a public act, falls outside of this scope. The court need not, however, decide the FSIA issue as it finds that the act of state doctrine clearly requires dismissal.

THE ACT OF STATE DOCTRINE

The act of state doctrine was established in the 1897 case of Underhill v. Hernandez, [supra], in which the Supreme Court held that:

Every sovereign state is bound to respect the independence of every other sovereign state, and the courts of one country will not sit in judgment on the acts of the government of another done within its own territory. Redress of grievances by reason of such acts must be obtained through the means open to be availed of by sovereign powers as between themselves.

In *Sabbatino,* [supra], the Court articulated the act of state doctrine's modern rationale. Justice Harlan, writing for a majority of eight, described the doctrine as one arising "out of the basic relationships between branches of government in a system of separation of powers." The act of state doctrine therefore reflects general concern about the competency of the judiciary to decide questions in the area of foreign relations—an area the Constitution commits primarily to the Executive Branch. In short, the act of state doctrine operates to preclude United States courts from ruling on the validity of foreign governmental acts so as not to hinder or embarrass the Executive Branch in its foreign policy endeavors.

The act of state doctrine was not abolished in *Dunhill* [supra], as plaintiff would have this court believe. That portion of the *Dunhill* opinion which commanded a majority of the Court held the Cuban government liable merely because no act of state was present.

The issue before the Court in *Dunhill* was whether certain acts by the Cuban government constituted acts of state immune from suit in United States courts. The disputed act was Cuba's refusal to return funds U.S. purchasers advanced for cigar shipments which were never delivered. The majority in *Dunhill* expressed no doubt as to the continuing validity of the act of state doctrine. It simply held the Cuban government liable for a purely commercial transaction because "nothing in the record [revealed] an act of state * * *."

———

Note: The continuing validity of the act of state doctrine was also recognized by the dissenting opinion: [T]he act of state doctrine reflects the notion that the validity of an act of a foreign sovereign is, under some circumstances, a "political question" not cognizable in our courts.

The Court of Appeals affirmed on the non-applicability of the FSIA provision, and found that it did not have to deal with the act of state issue. The litigation was directed generally toward the vindication of a claimed human right against a foreign state before an American court, under the FSIA, because the plaintiff, a United States citizen, was not eligible to claim under the "alien torts" provision of the Judicial Code, 28 U.S.C. § 1350. (*See,* Chapter 10). What if there had been judicial jurisdiction, either under the FSIA provision or 28 U.S.C. § 1350? Would act of state bar such a human rights claim in an American court? Does the "Rule in *Kirkpatrick's Case*" apply inexorably to a "nonliberal" state's denial of an exit visa to its national?

2. EXPRESSIONS OF EXECUTIVE BRANCH VIEW-POINTS ON THE APPLICABILITY OF THE ACT OF STATE DOCTRINE: A RESUME

Several Legal Advisers to the Department of State have addressed the courts through the Department of Justice in pending cases where the act of state doctrine had been pleaded. In 1949, regarding the second *Bernstein* case, the Department of State took the initiative, informing the circuit court that American occupation policy in Germany invalidated Nazi racist legal action and thus the courts should feel relieved from any constraint linked to the act of state doctrine. 20 Dept. of State Bull. 592, 1949. Justice Harlan's majority opinion in *Sabbatino* notes that the Supreme Court had "never had occasion to pass on the so-called *Bernstein* exception." In *Sabbatino* itself, the Department of State expressed the view that it did not wish to make any statement bearing on the litigation, as Justice Harlan noted. This disinclination may have links to the pre-Tate Letter State Department discomfiture with involvement in sovereign immunity cases. In any event, it continued throughout the Kennedy–Johnson years but was replaced thereafter by various efforts of the executive branch to preclude or limit the application of the act of state doctrine in cases involving foreign nationalizations of Americans' foreign investments.

The communication that follows, from a Reagan-era Legal Adviser, focuses explicitly on the so-called *treaty exception* to the act of state doctrine. It also expresses a broader, general opposition to the application of the act of state doctrine in nationalization cases. A preference for national court decisions on the merits in nationalization cases, except for such as the executive might not wish to have brought, was consistently expressed by Legal Advisers in the Nixon–Ford period. The views of the various groupings of justices in the Supreme Court as to the weight to be given such executive branch initiatives may be appraised with benefit in the light of this summary.

ACT OF STATE DOCTRINE: FOREIGN EXPROPRIATIONS

Letter of the Legal Adviser
United States Department of State Bulletin, January 1983, p. 70.

November 19, 1982

The Honorable Rex E. Lee, Solicitor General of the United States, Department of Justice

Dear Mr. Solicitor General:

The Department of State has requested that the views of the United States be submitted to the United States Court of Appeals for the Sixth Circuit in a case styled Kalamazoo Spice Extraction Co. v. The Provisional Military Government of Socialist Ethiopia. This case involves an appeal from a decision by the United States District Court for the

Western District of Michigan in which the District Court abstained from ruling on the merits of the suit because of the act of state doctrine. Two aspects of the decision are of concern to the Department of State—the Court's characterization of the Treaty of Amity and Economic Relations between the United States and Ethiopia as being too "general * * * and susceptible of multiple interpretation" to constitute an agreed legal standard capable of judicial application, and the significance attached by the Court to the absence of a "Bernstein letter" from this Department stating that adjudication would not be harmful to the conduct of foreign relations.

We have worked closely with the Department of Justice in the preparation of a brief to convey to the Court of Appeals the views of the Executive Branch as amicus curiae on these two issues of special concern. The brief sets forth the reasons why the treaty provides a precise, administrable and, by agreement, governing rule of law. The brief also sets forth, partially in reliance upon this letter, why the courts should not infer from the silence of the Department of State that adjudication in this case would be harmful to the foreign policy of the United States. Since the latter issue involves the inferences to be drawn by the courts generally from actions of this Department, I wish to make clear the practice that we intend to follow in cases like this.

As expressed in *Sabbatino*, the presumption that the courts should abstain from considering the expropriatory acts of foreign states appears to have reflected two major concerns of the Supreme Court. The first was that articulation by United States courts of an applicable international law standard for compensation would pose special difficulties, including a perceived risk of conflict with the Executive Branch's assertion of a governing legal standard in the conduct of foreign relations. The second of the Court's principal concerns was that adjudication could complicate the conduct of bilateral relations with the expropriating state—for example, by frustrating ongoing claims settlement negotiations between the two governments. Where, as in the present case, there is an applicable treaty standard, the first of these concerns falls away. The second concern—potential interference with ongoing claims negotiations or other foreign relations interests—does not, in our view, warrant automatic abstention by the courts on act of state grounds. As Legal Adviser Monroe Leigh wrote to the Solicitor General concerning foreign expropriations in 1975: In general this Department's experience provides little support for a presumption that adjudication of acts of foreign states in accordance with relevant principles of international law would embarrass the conduct of foreign policy. [Letter of November 25, 1975, reprinted at Appendix I to Alfred Dunhill v. Cuba, [supra].]

The experience of the past seven years has reinforced this conclusion. Accordingly, we believe that a broad, inflexible rule of abstention in expropriation cases is not necessary to safeguard our foreign policy interests. When, as in this case, there is a controlling legal standard for compensation, we believe that the presumption should be that adjudication would not be inconsistent with foreign policy interests under the act of state doctrine.

If, however, the Department of State determines in a given case that judicial abstention is necessary for foreign policy reasons, it will request the Department of Justice to communicate that determination to the appropriate court. Such a communication could be either in response to an inquiry from a court concerned about the foreign policy implications of the case before it or on the initiative of the Executive Branch. (Private litigants and foreign governments frequently bring cases to the attention of the Department of State which they believe raise Act of State concerns.) If we indicate that adjudication would be consistent with foreign policy interests of the United States, we trust that the court will give appropriate weight to our views. As a general rule, however, where there is a controlling legal standard for compensation we would not plan to inform the courts of the absence of foreign policy objectives to adjudication of expropriation claims. Therefore, we would anticipate that silence on the part of the Executive in such cases would not be relied upon as a basis for judicial abstention under the act of state doctrine.

Sincerely, Davis R. Robinson

Questions. In the last two paragraphs, what is the meaning of the phrase, "a controlling legal standard for compensation"? Where does it come from? Does it exist only if established by a controlling international agreement, or does it include a customary international law standard?

------

3. PRE–KIRKPATRICK FEDERAL CIRCUIT COURT DECISIONS ON THE ACT OF STATE DOCTRINE NOT REVIEWED BY THE UNITED STATES SUPREME COURT

The act of state doctrine has figured more prominently in national court litigation than might be inferred from the number of cases reviewed by the United States Supreme Court. In fact, for over a decade the Supreme Court did not make a significant decision in this area. Thus, a full awareness of the doctrine's status and significance requires consideration of a selected number of intermediate-level federal court opinions read in the light of the *Kirkpatrick Case*.

INTERNATIONAL ASSOCIATION OF MACHINISTS v. OPEC

United States Court of Appeals, Ninth Circuit, 1981.
649 F.2d 1354.

CHOY, Circuit Judge:

I.   Introduction

The members of the International Association of Machinists and Aerospace Workers (IAM) were disturbed by the high price of oil and petroleum-derived products in the United States.   They believed the actions of the Organization of the Petroleum Exporting Countries, popularly known as OPEC, were the cause of this burden on the American public.   Accordingly, IAM sued OPEC and its member nations in December of 1978, alleging that their price-setting activities violated United States anti-trust laws.

* * *

OPEC achieves its goals by a system of production limits and royalties which its members unanimously adopt.   There is no enforcement arm of OPEC.   The force behind OPEC decrees is the collective self-interest of the 13 nations.

After formation of OPEC, it is alleged, the price of crude oil increased tenfold and more.   Whether or not a causal relation exists, there is no doubt that the price of oil has risen dramatically in recent years, and that this has become of international concern.

Supporters of OPEC argue that its actions result in fair world prices for oil, and allow OPEC members to achieve a measure of economic and political independence.   Without OPEC, they say, in the rush to the marketplace these nations would rapidly deplete their only valuable resource for ridiculously low prices.

Detractors accuse OPEC of price fixing and worse in its deliberate manipulation of the world market and withholding of a resource which many world citizens have not learned to do without.

In December 1978, IAM brought suit against OPEC and its member nations.   IAM's complaint alleged price fixing in violation of the Sherman Act, 15 U.S.C. § 1, and requested treble damages and injunctive relief under the Clayton Act, 15 U.S.C. §§ 15, 16.   IAM claimed a deliberate targeting and victimization of the United States market, directly resulting in higher prices for Americans.

The defendants refused to recognize the jurisdiction of the district court, and they did not appear in the proceedings below.   Their cause was argued by various amici, with additional information provided by court-appointed experts.   The district court ordered a full hearing, noting that the Foreign Sovereign Immunities Act (FSIA) prohibits the entry of a default judgment against a foreign sovereignty "unless the claimant establishes his claim or right to relief by evidence satisfactory to the court."   28 U.S.C. § 1608(e).

III.   Discussion

* * *

B.   The Act of State Doctrine

The act of state doctrine declares that a United States court will not adjudicate a politically sensitive dispute which would require the court to judge the legality of the sovereign act of a foreign state. This doctrine was expressed by the Supreme Court in Underhill v. Hernandez, [supra]. "Every sovereign State is bound to respect the independence of every other sovereign State, and the courts of one country will not sit in judgment on the acts of the government of another done within its own territory." The doctrine recognizes the institutional limitations of the courts and the peculiar requirements of successful foreign relations. To participate adeptly in the global community, the United States must speak with one voice and pursue a careful and deliberate foreign policy. * * *

The principle of separation of powers is central to our form of democratic government. Just as the courts have carefully guarded their primary role as interpreters of the Constitution and the laws of the United States, so have they recognized the primary role of the President and Congress in resolution of political conflict and the adoption of foreign policy. Compare Marbury v. Madison, 5 U.S. 137 (Cranch 1803); Baker v. Carr, 369 U.S. 186 (1962); Sabbatino, [supra].

The doctrine of sovereign immunity is similar to the act of state doctrine in that it also represents the need to respect the sovereignty of foreign states. The two doctrines differ, however, in significant respects. The law of sovereign immunity goes to the jurisdiction of the court. The act of state doctrine is not jurisdictional. Rather, it is a prudential doctrine designed to avoid judicial action in sensitive areas. Sovereign immunity is a principle of international law, recognized in the United States by statute. It is the states themselves, as defendants, who may claim sovereign immunity. The act of state doctrine is a domestic legal principle, arising from the peculiar role of American courts. It recognizes not only the sovereignty of foreign states, but also the spheres of power of the co-equal branches of our government. Thus a private litigant may raise the act of state doctrine, even when no sovereign state is a party to the action.

* * *

The act of state doctrine is not diluted by the commercial activity exception which limits the doctrine of sovereign immunity. While purely commercial activity may not rise to the level of an act of state, certain seemingly commercial activity will trigger act of state considerations. As the district court noted, OPEC's "price-fixing" activity has a significant sovereign component. While the FSIA ignores the underlying purpose of a state's action, the act of state doctrine does not. This court has stated that the motivations of the sovereign must be examined for a public interest basis. Timberlane, [supra]. When the state qua state acts in the public interest, its sovereignty is asserted. The courts must proceed cautiously to avoid an affront to that sovereignty. Because the act of state doctrine and the doctrine of sovereign immunity address different concerns and apply in different circumstances, we find that the act of state doctrine remains available when such caution is appropriate, regardless of any commercial component of the activity involved.

* * *

This court has stated: "we do not wish to challenge the sovereignty of another nation, the wisdom of its policy, or the integrity and motivation of its action. On the other hand, repeating the terms of Sabbatino, 'the less important the implications of an issue are for our foreign relations, the weaker the justification for exclusivity in the political branches.' Id. (citations omitted.)" There is no question that the availability of oil has become a significant factor in international relations. The growing world energy crisis has been judicially recognized in other cases. * * * The record in this case contains extensive documentation of the involvement of our executive and legislative branches with the oil question. IAM does not dispute that the United States has a grave interest in the petro-politics of the Middle East, or that the foreign policy arms of the executive and legislative branches are intimately involved in this sensitive area. It is clear that OPEC and its activities are carefully considered in the formulation of American foreign policy.

The remedy IAM seeks is an injunction against the OPEC nations. The possibility of insult to the OPEC states and of interference with the efforts of the political branches to seek favorable relations with them is apparent from the very nature of this action and the remedy sought. While the case is formulated as an anti-trust action, the granting of any relief would in effect amount to an order from a domestic court instructing a foreign sovereign to alter its chosen means of allocating and profiting from its own valuable natural resources. On the other hand, should the court hold that OPEC's actions are legal, this "would greatly strengthen the bargaining hand" of the OPEC nations in the event that Congress or the executive chooses to condemn OPEC's actions.

A further consideration is the availability of internationally-accepted legal principles which would render the issues appropriate for judicial disposition. As the Supreme Court stated in Sabbatino,

> It should be apparent that the greater the degree of codification or consensus concerning a particular area of international law, the more appropriate it is for the judiciary to render decisions regarding it, since the courts can then focus on the application of an agreed principle to circumstances of fact rather than on the sensitive task of establishing a principle not inconsistent with the national interest or with international justice. 376 U.S. at 428.

While conspiracies in restraint of trade are clearly illegal under domestic law, the record reveals no international consensus condemning cartels, royalties, and production agreements. The United States and other nations have supported the principle of supreme state sovereignty over natural resources. The OPEC nations themselves obviously will not agree that their actions are illegal. We are reluctant to allow judicial interference in an area so void of international consensus. An injunction against OPEC's alleged price-fixing activity would require condemnation of a cartel system which the community of nations has thus far been unwilling to denounce. The admonition in Sabbatino that the courts should consider the degree of codification and consensus in the area of law is another indication that judicial action is inappropriate here.

* * *

IV. Conclusion

The act of state doctrine is applicable in this case. The courts should not enter at the will of litigants into a delicate area of foreign policy which the executive and legislative branches have chosen to approach with restraint.

* * *

———

Questions. In the *Dunhill* case (supra, p. 636) White, J. (and those concurring in his opinion) attempted to develop a "purely commercial obligation" exception to the act of state doctrine, on the ground, inter alia, of desirable parallelism with the FSIA. Is the Ninth Circuit in the suit against OPEC disagreeing with the White approach or finding that whatever might have been the result under FSIA, activity of the OPEC states is not "purely commercial"? At what point do state buy-sell-trade-financial activities cease to be "purely commercial"?

———

4. THE CIRCUIT COURTS' BALANCING METHODOLOGY: WHAT IS BEING BALANCED? WHEN?

The *Sabbatino* majority opinion contains language against inflexibility in the application of the act of state doctrine. Some justices, notably White and Powell, limited themselves to an examination of each situation on its own facts. This approach and Justice Powell's insistence upon judicial independence in decisions as to the applicability of the act of state doctrine, seem to be the bases for any balancing process to determine whether to apply the act of state doctrine. The Supreme Court has not specifically reviewed any lower court approaches.

In 1987, the date of the previous edition of this book, litigation emphasis regarding act of state, however, had shifted away from the effort to remove the doctrine as a barrier to the enforcement of an American version of customary international law about nationalizations. This was accomplished either by ruling out act of state entirely in nationalization cases (as failed ultimately in Sabbatino) or by limiting its application through the development of various exceptions: the categories: "purely commercial" activity; the Bernstein Letter; and treaty exceptions. A case to case relativism now exists. This may be provisional. Many questions about this balancing approach are still open, if it survives *Kirkpatrick:* (i) Does the balancing approach eliminate the precedents as to this or that exception? (ii) What factors are being weighed? (iii) What weight does each factor have? (iv) In application, does balancing result in outcomes more or less favorable to the application of the act of state doctrine than earlier approaches? (v) What is the true American version of the act of state doctrine today? (vi) Is the act of state doctrine evolving toward a forum-controlled choice of law process where two or more states have some degree of public (regulatory) law interest?

There should not be any more decisions on the question whether the imposition of foreign exchange control by a state is an act of state that stops American proceedings, for the courts have made it clear that the doctrine applies. There continue to be cases in which plaintiffs claim against non-state parties that they conspired with a foreign state, which then acted in a state-like way to plaintiff's detriment, either in tort or under antitrust law.

SECTION B. CONGRESS AND THE ACT OF STATE DOCTRINE

----

1. *A few paragraphs of history.* Various interests concerned about nationalizations of direct foreign investment, and others hoping to reduce or prevent even legal nationalizations combined immediately after the decision by the Supreme Court in *Sabbatino* to add a second anti-nationalization provision to the Foreign Assistance [AID] Act. A key congressional figure in the drive was the late senator whose name is given to the Hickenlooper amendments.

The first Hickenlooper Amendment mandated that the President cut off development assistance to any country that did not (within a time frame for reassessment) conform as to Americans' investments to the international minimum standard for nationalizations asserted by the United States [refer to Chapter 15–B].

Shortly after the remand of the *Sabbatino case* for disposition in conformity with the Supreme Court decision, Congress enacted the second Hickenlooper Amendment.

FOREIGN ASSISTANCE ACT
22 U.S.C. § 2370.

* * *

(e)(2) Notwithstanding any other provision of law, no court in the United States shall decline on the ground of the federal act of state doctrine to make a determination on the merits giving effect to the principles of international law in a case in which a claim of title or other right to property is asserted by any party including a foreign state (or a party claiming through such state) based upon (or traced through) a confiscation or other taking after January 1, 1959, by an act of that state in violation of the principles of international law [according to the standards set by Congress]: Provided, That this subparagraph shall not be applicable (1) in any case in which an act of a foreign state is not contrary to international law or with respect to a claim of title or other right to property acquired pursuant to an irrevocable letter of credit of not more than 180 days duration issued in good faith prior to the time of the confiscation or other taking, or (2) in any case with respect to which the President determines that application of the act of state doctrine is required in that particular case by the foreign policy interests of the United States and a suggestion to this effect is filed on his behalf in that case with the court.

---

1. ***Retroactive application to include the nationalization in Sabbatino.*** January 1, 1959 was the date that Fidel Castro occupied Havana. His regime was almost immediately recognized by the United States as the Government of Cuba. Both the United States Government and the American people were happy that the dictator Batista had been toppled. But attitudes soon changed. Castro was prickly and anti-American. His midnight trials and firing squad executions seen on American TV shocked American viewers. An exasperated Congress suspended the Cuban sugar quota in the price-supported American sugar market. The sugar quota dollars were, and long had been, Cuba's principal source of hard currency foreign exchange. Castro's responses were (i) to issue the nationalization decree involved in *Sabbatino* and (ii) to turn to the Soviet Union. Later he declared that he had always been a Communist, a statement that as to its truth still divides experts on Cuba. By the time the second Hickenlooper Amendment was enacted, the Cuban–American cold war was in full swing. Probably this explains why the amendment was rolled back to the beginning of the Castro regime, i.e. January 1, 1959.

2. ***The second Hickenlooper Amendment, 22 U.S.C. § 2370(e)(2), held not to violate separation of powers or other constitutional requirements.*** The Supreme Court let stand the decision of the Second Circuit Court of Appeals to the above effect in *Banco Nacional de Cuba v. Farr, Whitlock [supra]*. In deciding the *Farr, Whitlock* case the Court of Appeals reiterated its earlier holding in *Sabbatino* that the taking by Cuba had violated customary international law, an issue that the Supreme Court did not reach in its *Sabbatino* decision, because of its holding that the act of state doctrine precluded decision on the merits. As a result, the denial of certiorari in *Farr, Whitlock* also let stand the consequence of the Court of Appeals decision in *Sabbatino*, that the violation of international law by the act of nationalization authorized the remedy of invalidation of title to the property (and its produce) sought to have been nationalized. Also, in

Farr, Whitlock the Court of Appeals found nothing constitutionally wrong with the application to the same real parties and the same cause of action of the intervening second Hickenlooper Amendment. This Amendment was enacted after the Supreme Court remanded the *Sabbatino case*; it was explained in a Senate report as being legislation designed "to reverse in part the recent *[Sabbatino]* decision of the Supreme Court". In fact, the Court of Appeals quoted this report in support of its decision in *Farr, Whitlock*.

In the United Kingdom an act of Parliament overrules a final judgment of the highest court in the land. *Is this possible also under the Constitution of the United States?* Normally it is not. Should the issue of valid or invalid retroactive application of the second Hickenlooper Amendment turn on the legal effect of the Supreme Court's remand order? Did the successful parties in the Sabbatino case have a vested right in the decision in their favor on the act of state doctrine? Or, did the remand leave the case open as if not previously decided, so as to be reachable legally by the later enacted second Hickenlooper Amendment?

SECTION C. THE SECOND HICKENLOOPER AMENDMENT IN THE COURTS

Approach. Re-read 22 U.S.C. § 2370(e)(2), supra. What resorts to the otherwise applicable act of state doctrine does Congress exclude from the jurisdiction of courts in the United States? What is a "claim of title"? Title to what? All economic interests? Property interests? What kinds of property interests? The first case that follows was chosen because it is unusual in that the final decision on the meaning of (e)(2) is left to a state supreme court. The majority of that court gave a narrow interpretation to the statutory provision. On what authority? Why?

HUNT v. COASTAL STATES GAS PRODUCING CO.

United States Supreme Court of Texas, 1979.
583 S.W.2d 322

BARROW, Justice.

This suit was instituted by Nelson Bunker Hunt, Herbert Hunt and Lamar Hunt (Hunt) seeking damages against Coastal States Gas Producing Company and Coastal States Marketing, Inc. (Coastal States) for the alleged conversion of oil to which Hunt was entitled by virtue of a concession agreement with Libya. Coastal States counterclaimed for damages for Hunt's allegedly tortious interference with the contract and business opportunities of Coastal States. Both parties moved for summary judgment on the issue of liability after extensive development of the case. The trial court denied relief on all claims and the court of civil appeals affirmed. We affirm the judgment of the court of civil appeals.

In 1957 the Government of Libya granted Hunt a concession which gave him the right, for fifty years, to explore, drill and extract oil in an area now identified as the Sarir field. Hunt assigned a one-half undivided interest in this concession to (British Petroleum) in 1960. Oil was discovered in the concession area in 1961 and, by 1967, it was produced in marketable quantities. In September 1969, Colonel Mu'ammar al-Qadhafi assumed power in Libya under a new government, the Revolutionary Command Council, and commenced making changes in the existing contractual relations with the various oil producers holding concession agreements with Libya. In 1971, the Libyan Government nationalized the operations and interest of British Petroleum in the Sarir field and transferred its rights to the Arabian Gulf Exploration Company (AGECO). AGECO is a corporation whose entire capital stock is owned by the Libyan Government.

On June 20, 1973, by Libyan Law No. 42 of 1973, the Libyan Government nationalized all the rights and assets of Hunt in the concession agreement and assigned these rights to AGECO. Although Libya agreed to pay compensation, the amount was to be determined by a committee designated by the State. In response to this action, Hunt published notices in newspapers throughout the world claiming that the Libyan nationalization violated international law and threatened suit against anyone who came into possession of Sarir oil. In May 1973, Coastal States entered into a contract with AGECO to purchase oil from the Sarir field and it continued to purchase oil under this contract despite Hunt's claims against Libya and threatened suits. This oil was transported by Coastal States to a refinery in Italy where it was processed and sold to third parties. It was stipulated that a portion of the products derived from this oil was subsequently taken to the United States, although it was not stipulated that Coastal States transported or caused any of such products to be brought here. Nevertheless, Coastal States is domiciled in the United States and, at least, the net proceeds derived from the Sarir oil were brought here and are the basis of Hunt's suit for conversion.

British Petroleum was a party to the controversy with Coastal States at one time, but it subsequently entered into a full settlement with the Libyan Government after arbitration of its claim and it does not now assert any claim against Coastal States.[1] In May 1975 Hunt entered into a settlement agreement with the Libyan Government whereby, for the sum of approximately $19,000,000, it released any and all claims against the Libyan Government arising out of the nationalization of the Sarir field. Coastal States was not a party to this agreement and Hunt now seeks to recover the proceeds realized by Coastal States from oil allegedly purchased from AGECO prior to the May 1975 settlement.

Both the trial court and the court of civil appeals concluded that the trial court was foreclosed from inquiring into the validity of the Libyan nationalization of Hunt's interest in the Sarir field by the Act of State Doctrine. These courts further concluded that as a matter of law,

---

1. The arbitrator held that Hunt did not acquire title to the oil in the strata.

Hunt's actions in giving notice of his claim to oil from the Sarir field did not violate either state or federal law and would not support Coastal States' claim for damages for tortious interference. Hunt and Coastal States both filed applications for writ of error and complain of the take-nothing judgment entered on the claim of each.

Appeal by Hunt

Hunt's claim against Coastal States is necessarily based upon the assertion that Libya's expropriation was invalid so that Coastal States acquired no title from AGECO. The critical question involved in Hunt's appeal is the applicability of the Act of State Doctrine and more precisely, whether Hunt's suit comes within the exception to the doctrine created by the Hickenlooper Amendment, 22 U.S.C. § 2370(e)(2). The lower courts have held that the doctrine bars inquiry by a Texas court into the validity of acts done by a foreign sovereign.

The Act of State Doctrine is a judicially created doctrine of restraint. The landmark case of *Sabbatino* (1964), reaffirmed the doctrine as originally articulated in *Underhill v. Hernandez,* in the following language:

> Every sovereign State is bound to respect the independence of every other sovereign State, and the courts of one country will not sit in judgment on the acts of the government of another, done within its own territory. Redress of grievances by reason of such acts must be obtained through the means open to be availed of by sovereign powers as between themselves.

In Sabbatino it was stated that the doctrine "arises out of the basic relationships between branches of government in a system of separation" and the court's prior recognition of the doctrine "expresses the strong sense of the Judicial Branch that its engagement in the task of passing on the validity of foreign acts of state may hinder rather than further this country's pursuit of goals both for itself and for the community of nations as a whole in the international sphere."

In Hunt v. Mobil Oil Corp., the Act of State Doctrine was held to bar Hunt's inquiry into the validity of Libya's nationalization of Hunt's concession. In holding that the trial court properly dismissed Hunt's claim against seven major oil producers in the Persian Gulf area for damages under the anti-trust statute, the circuit court said: "We conclude that the political act complained of here was clearly within the act of state doctrine and that since the disputed pleadings inevitably call for a judgment on the sovereign acts of Libya the claim is non-justiciable." This final judgment against Hunt in that case controls his present suit for conversion unless it comes within the exception to the Act of State Doctrine created by the Hickenlooper Amendment.

The Hickenlooper Amendment was enacted by Congress in 1964 shortly after the Sabbatino holding and in obvious reaction to it. It provides in part: "[N]o court in the United States shall decline on the ground of the federal act of state doctrine to make a determination on the merits giving effect to the principles of international law in a case in which a *claim of title or other right to property* is asserted by any party including a foreign state * * * based upon (or traced through) a confisca-tion or other taking * * * by an act of that state in violation of the principles of international law * * *." (Emphasis Added) It must be recognized at the outset that this exception which was adopted over the objections of the Executive Department of the United States has been narrowly construed by our courts.

The statute enumerates three requirements which must exist in order to avoid the act of state doctrine under the Hickenlooper Amend-ment. 1. Expropriated property must come within the territorial jurisdiction of the United States. 2. The act of the expropriating nation must be in violation of international law. 3. The asserted claim must be a claim of title or other right to property. 22 U.S.C. § 2370(e)(2). The court of civil appeals concluded, without consideration of the first two requirements, that the Hickenlooper Amendment is not applicable to this case because Hunt acquired only a contract right by the agreement with Libya. We agree with this conclusion and therefore limit our consideration to the third requirement stated above.

Since Libya is both the place of the contract's execution and perfor-mance as well as the location of the subject matter, Libyan substantive law governs the interpretation and construction of the rights conferred to Hunt by the Concession Agreement. The Concession Agreement expressly provides that the applicable law is the Libyan Petroleum Law No. 25 of 1955 and this law provides: (1) All petroleum in Libya in its natural state in strata is the property of the Libyan State. (2) No person shall explore or prospect for, mine or produce petroleum in any part of Libya, unless authorized by a permit or concession issued under this Law.

The expressed intent of the Concession Agreement was to grant Hunt the *right* to search for and to extract oil within the defined area for the stated term. It did not grant Hunt title to the oil in the strata. Under Libyan law title to the oil passed at the wellhead. In 1966 Hunt and Libya voluntarily amended the 1957 Concession Agreement. Clause 16 of the amended agreement states:

> (1) The Government of Libya will take all the steps necessary to ensure that the Company enjoys all the rights conferred by the Concession. The *contractual rights* expressly created by this conces-sion shall not be altered except by mutual consent of the parties.

> (2) This Concession shall throughout the period of its validity be construed in accordance with the Petroleum Law and the Regula-tions in force on the date of the execution of the agreement of amendment by which this paragraph (2) was incorporated into this concession agreement. Any amendment to or repeal of such Regula-tions shall not affect the *contractual rights* of the Company without its consent. (Emphasis added)

This language is significant in that it not only refers to Hunt's rights as "contractual," but it also recognizes Libya's ownership of the oil. We conclude that Hunt obtained only a contractual right under the Conces-sion Agreement.

The Hickenlooper Amendment by its express terms applies only to a claim of title or other right to property. This construction was made abundantly clear in 1965 when Congress added the words "to property" following the phrase "claim of title or other right." Thus this exception to the act of state doctrine has no application here where only a contractual right was expropriated from Hunt. We have been cited to no case, and have discovered no case, holding to the contrary. The trial court and the court of civil appeals did not err in concluding that the act of state doctrine bars judicial inquiry into the validity of Libya's actions.

Appeal by Coastal States

We agree with the holding of the court of civil appeals that Hunt's motion for summary judgment was properly granted on Coastal States' claim of tortious interference with business contracts and business relations. Hunt's contractual rights in the Sarir field were expropriated by Libya and Hunt was fully justified in apprising the international community of his intent to file suit if they dealt with oil from this field.

The judgment of the court of civil appeals is affirmed.

––––––

1. ***The Hunts' legal actions involving oil from Libya.*** The revolutionary regime that deposed the King of Libya cancelled the Hunt brothers' concessions from the latter. The efforts of the brothers to reach all parties possibly involved against their interests in oil from Libya have become litigation legend. Here you observe a post-nationalization hot oil suit against a purchaser of oil from the Hunts' concessions that were taken over by the revolutionary regime. In Chapter 15, you will consider two arbitral awards dealing with the Hunts' claims that the revolutionary regime must respect the concession rights granted them by the King. In other litigation the Hunt brothers have sued certain major American oil companies on theories of conspiracies with the revolutionary regime that, as to the majors, were claimed to violate the plaintiffs' rights under the antitrust laws of the United States.

2. ***Equivalent to property in nationalization situations.*** Suppose that under customary international law an oil concession cancellation does not give rise to a state obligation to compensate, but that under a national version of international law such cancellations are equivalent to a taking of property: how should a statute such as the second Hickenlooper Amendment be applied by an American court? Those who induced Congress to pass the amendment assumed that oil concessions were within the ambit of protection from application of the act of state doctrine. Inasmuch as Congress did so assume, why should the courts cut back on the statute? Which is the more dubious assumption: (i) that customary international law gives standing and remedies to private parties if they sue in national courts, even if they have no standing or direct remedies in international tribunals, or (ii) that a concession contract—or an arrangement to operate a foreign oil industry for a share of the profits (management-service contract)—is equivalent to property under the second Hickenlooper Amendment? If the first

assumption is the more dubious but is applied when act of state doctrine does not stop the proceeding, why not the less dubious?

———

WEST v. MULTIBANCO COMERMEX, S.A.
United States Court of Appeals, Ninth Circuit, 1987.
807 F.2d 820, 829–30.

[A group of American investors in dollar and Mexican peso certificates of deposit sue the issuing Mexican banks for payment at face value, even though thĕ banks have been turned over to governmental interventors (a type of nationalization) and the Mexican foreign exchange controls permit payments only under license and fix an unfavorable rate of exchange for permitted transfers. The act of state doctrine is one defense put forward; the plaintiffs respond with the second Hickenlooper Amendment. Thereupon the defendants argue that the second Hickenlooper Amendment does not apply to certificates of deposit.]

REINHARDT, Circuit Judge.

* * *

Defendants argue that Hickenlooper is inapplicable because rights arising out of ownership of certificates of deposit are contractual, and hence not "tangible property" which can be taken by expropriation within the meaning of the amendment. Although this proposition finds support in case law, e.g. French v. Banco Nacional de Cuba, 242 N.E.2d 704 (1968), it is based largely upon an overly formalistic attachment to private law categories and is contrary to the motivating policies of the Hickenlooper Amendment.

Defendants' construction would unnecessarily restrict the scope of Hickenlooper. As the District of Columbia Circuit has noted, the "broad, unqualified language of the carefully drafted amendment" should not be undermined by the importation of external constraints on interpretation. Ramirez de Arellano v. Weinberger, 745 F.2d 1500, 1542 n. 180 (D.C.Cir.1984) (en banc), vacated and remanded because of subsequent legislation. The legislative history to Hickenlooper supports the rejection of a constricted interpretation and makes it clear that the protection afforded U.S. investments was to be broad in scope:

> The sponsors of the amendment referred to it as the "Rule of Law" amendment; they viewed it as authorizing courts to apply established law [in] suits challenging expropriations. Congressional intent to overturn Sabbatino was never limited to a single narrow class of cases. The purposes of the amendment include the promotion and protection of United States investment in foreign countries (which characteristically has always principally been land, minerals, and large fixed immovables), and securing the right of a property holder to a court hearing on the merits.

Moreover, the tangible/intangible characterization of property interests, urged by the defendants, is a distinction without a difference. This distinction is not generally recognized in international, federal, or state law.

Although the certificates of deposit may be characterized as intangible property or contracts, they are "property interests" that are protected under international law from expropriation. For example, in its adjudication of disputes involving claims for compensation for alleged takings of property—bank deposits in Czechoslovakia—the Foreign Claims Settlement Commission observed that while "[t]he relationship between a depositor and bank arises only out of contract[,] * * * a contract right is property." The Commission ruled that the "right to payment of [a] deposit is regarded as 'property' and provides a basis for an expropriation claim. Here, we have citizens who purchased certificates of deposit." Such contracts are properly understood as investments and are therefore the type of "property" that Hickenlooper sought to protect.

In sum, the rights arising from a certificate of deposit are "rights to property" capable of being expropriated by foreign states under international law within the meaning of Hickenlooper. We reject the construction suggested by the defendants and hold that the "tangibleness" of property is not the dispositive factor. Accordingly, the amendment is applicable * * *.

Question. The plaintiffs lost anyway. The court held that foreign exchange control losses are not "takings." So, why did the court belabor the scope of the second Hickenlooper issue?

SECTION D. SIMILAR RESULTS IN OTHER LEGAL SYSTEMS

BUTTES GAS AND OIL COMPANY v. HAMMER

United Kingdom, House of Lords, 1981.
[1981] 3 All E.R. 616.*

[Two California oil companies quarreled about oil concession rights in the waters surrounding a small island in the Gulf of Arabia governed by the sovereign of a minor Arab emirate (Sharjah). Armand Hammer, holder of the commanding position in the Occidental Petroleum Company, at a press conference in London, accused the Buttes Gas and Oil Company of colluding with the then ruler of Sharjah to backdate a decree of that ruler extending the territorial waters of Sharjah around the island from 3 to 12 miles, to the detriment of Occidental. The Occidental–Buttes feud is as classic as that of the Hunt brothers against certain major oil companies in Libya.

---

* Reprinted with the permission of Butterworth's, London.

Buttes sued Occidental and Dr. Hammer personally in the United Kingdom, under a long-arm statute, for slander. The defendants pleaded truth as a defense, and Buttes responded that British courts could not examine the conduct of the ruler of Sharjah, as to his conduct regarding acts taken by him in his own territory, especially as to property interests therein. The Court of Appeal agreed that Occidental's defense should be considered on the merits. The Master of the Rolls (Lord Denning) rejected what he called a "second" American version of act of state, because it was "ill-defined in English law" and not as extensively applicable as in the United States. (A "first" version of the act of state doctrine, as explained in the introductory note to this chapter, would be in Britain the principle that a minister of the Crown cannot be held to answer within the realm for ministerial action outside the realm.) Roskill, L.J., reached the same result, but on the ground that the judicial power to strike a defense for collateral reasons should be used only sparingly, in very clear cases. In the House of Lords, Buttes continued its reliance on the second American version of the act of state doctrine. The House of Lords agreed with Buttes in the following terms.]

LORD WILBERFORCE.

* * *

So I think that the essential question is whether, apart from such particular rules as I have discussed, established by [cases cited], there exists in English law a more general principle that the courts will not adjudicate on the transactions of foreign sovereign states. Though I would prefer to avoid argument on terminology, it seems desirable to consider this principle, if existing, not as a variety of act of state but one for judicial restraint or abstention. The respondents' argument was that although there may have been traces of such a general principle, it has now been crystallised into particular rules (such as those I have mentioned) within one of which the appellants must bring the case, or fail. The Nile, once separated into a multi-channel delta, cannot be reconstituted.

In my opinion there is, and for long has been, such a general principle, starting in English law, adopted and generalised in the law of the USA, which is effective and compelling in English courts. This principle is not one of discretion, but is inherent in the very nature of the judicial process. The first trace of it is in the seventeenth century in Blad's Case.

* * *

More clearly as a recognition of a general principle is Duke of Brunswick v. King of Hanover (1844), a case in this House which is still authoritative and which has influenced the law both here and overseas. There are two elements in the case, not always clearly separated, that of sovereign immunity ratione personae, and that of immunity from jurisdiction ratione materiae; it is the second that is relevant. I find the principle clearly stated that the courts in England will not adjudicate on acts done abroad by virtue of sovereign authority. Thus Lord Cottenham LC states the question, quite apart from any personal immunity, as being whether the courts of this country can "sit in judgment" on the act of a sovereign, effected by virtue of his sovereign authority abroad. His decision is conveyed in the words: "It is true, the bill states that the instrument was contrary to the laws of Hanover and Brunswick, but, notwithstanding that it is so stated, still if it is a sovereign act, then, whether it be according to law or not according to law, we cannot inquire into it." And he continues by distinguishing cases of private rights (cf. Aksionairnove Obschestvo Luther v. Sagor & Co.): If it were a private transaction * * * then the law upon which the rights of individuals may depend, might have been a matter of fact to have been inquired into * * *. But * * * if it be a matter of sovereign authority, we cannot try the fact whether it be right or wrong.

Lord Campbell is still more definite. The question he says is "as to the validity of an act of sovereignty", and he expresses the view that even if the Duke of Cambridge (i.e., not the sovereign) had been sued, "it would equally have been a matter of state".

It is justly said of this case, and of their Lordships' observations, that they are directed to the question whether a sovereign can be brought to account in this country in respect of sovereign acts, and that such general phrases as "sitting in judgment on", "inquiring into", "entertaining questions" must be read in their context. I agree that these phrases are not to be used without circumspection; the nature of the judgment or inquiry or entertainment must be carefully analysed. It is also to be noted that the acts in question were performed within the territory of the sovereign concerned (reliance is placed on this in some passages); an argument on this I have already dealt with. These qualifications accepted, the case is nevertheless supported, no doubt by reference to the issue in dispute, for a principle of non-justiciability by the English courts of a certain class of sovereign acts.

* * *

The constitutional position and the relationship between the executive and the judiciary in the United States is neither identical with our own nor in itself constant. Moreover the passages which I have cited lay emphasis on the "foreign relations" aspect of the matter which appeared important to the United States at the time. These matters I have no wish to overlook or minimise. I appreciate also the argument of counsel for Occidental that no indication has been given that Her Majesty's government would be embarrassed by the court entering on these issues. But, the ultimate question what issues are capable, and what are incapable, of judicial determination must be answered in closely similar terms in whatever country they arise, depending, as they must, on an appreciation of the nature and limits of the judicial function. This has clearly received the consideration of the United States courts. When the judicial approach to an identical problem between the same parties has been spelt out with such articulation in a country, one not only so closely akin to ours in legal approach, the fabric of whose legal doctrine in this area is so closely interwoven with ours, but that to which all the parties before us belong, spelt out moreover in convincing language and reasoning, we should be unwise not to take the benefit of it.

* * *

And thus farewell to the Rose Mary! In 1953, the Supreme Court of the then British protectorate of Aden held that the Iranian nationalization of the Anglo–Iranian Oil Company did not divest title to oil subsequently produced in Iran, despite its sale to a purchaser for value in international commerce. Anglo–Iranian Oil Co. Ltd. v. Jaffrate (The Rose Mary), 20 International Law Reports 316 (1957). Although civil law courts in Italy and Japan refused to follow suit, The Rose Mary spawned numerous "pursuit of the product" litigations involving sugar, tobacco, copper ore, and of course, petroleum. In the Buttes decision, followed with a strong ruling against foreign review of title to property nationalized at its situs, *Rumasa, S.A. v. Multinvest (UK) Ltd.* [1986] 1 All ER 129, the Aden court's decision, ignoring act of state, has been rejected by Anglo-Commonwealth law.

ANGLO–IRANIAN OIL CO. LTD. v. S.U.P.O.R. CO.

Italy, Court of Venice, 1953.
22 Int'l L.Rep. 19 (1958).*

The Facts: The respondent Company had purchased in Persia certain oil which was shipped in the Miriella from Abadan and lay in store in Venice. The Anglo–Iranian Oil Company (A.I.O.C.) claimed the oil on the ground that the Persian Law of May 1, 1951, nationalizing the petroleum industry had not affected the ownership of A.I.O.C. in this particular cargo of oil and that in any event the Oil Nationalization Law could not properly be enforced by an Italian court as it violated the principles of Italian "public order". The A.I.O.C. applied for "judicial sequestration" [an order for interim custody] of the oil pending the hearing of their claim. S.U.P.O.R. objected on the ground that for the Court to grant such an order would amount to prejudging the substantive claim and so to "annulling" the law of a foreign sovereign State, namely, the Persian Oil Nationalization Law.

Held: that the application must fail. Although the respondents were in error in contending that the Court had no power to examine, and if necessary to refuse to apply, the law of a foreign State, on the merits of the substantive claim the Court found that the Persian Oil Nationalization Law was not contrary to Italian "public order"; the applicant Company therefore had no claim to the ownership of the oil in question.

If, however, the question is tested by examining the Nationalization Law in regard to public order, which has been referred to at some length in the contentions put forward on behalf of A.I.O.C., the claim of

---

* Reprinted with the permission of the Editor of the International Law Reports.

ownership appears unjustified, which supports the rejection of the request for sequestration.

* * *

It can be seen * * * that the Nationalization Law does not exclude the payment of compensation to A.I.O.C.; moreover, it unequivocally recognizes the right to claim such compensation. In fact, whilst Article 2 envisages a deposit to meet the claims of the Company, Article 3 contains the solemn undertaking on the part of the Persian Government to examine, in addition to its own claims, those of the Company; these claims, which are not specified in Article 2 but which are "likely" ("probable" in the English text produced by A.I.O.C.), are in Article 3 defined as being "rightful", and the argument maintained by A.I.O.C. that among these legitimate claims the Law does not include the claim for compensation—which is the most likely and most legitimate, though not the only one—must be regarded as being an entirely arbitrary view.

Little importance, from a legal point of view, can be attached to the argument of A.I.O.C. that the Law does not fix the measure of compensation nor require promptness in payment. Even considering the exceptional nature of the question, which—it must be recognized—as compared with the normal application of a foreign Law almost touches the limits contemplated by Article 31 of the Preliminary Rules, the Persian Law can be examined only with a view to establishing whether it fails to provide for the payment of any compensation, so as to be contrary to our Constitution, the provisions of which present the principle of public order and which admits expropriation "provided that compensation is paid". And other questions, such as the measure of compensation, its form, and promptness in payment, do not concern the public order: these are accessory elements which should be agreed upon the basis of present historical, political, social and economic conditions, which should be proportionate to the nature and importance of the property in question, and which do not enter the sphere of public order provided that they do not in practice annul the compensation and make it illusory.

* * *

———

The decisions of French courts. *Union des Républiques Socialistes Soviétiques v. Intendant Général Bourgeois és qual. et Soc. La Ropit, Court of Cassation,* 1928, [1927–1928] Ann.Dig. 67 (No. 43). The ships of the Russian company La Ropit were nationalized by decree while they were in Odessa. Odessa at the time was not yet under the control of the Soviet revolutionary government and a number of the ships escaped to Marseilles. After being recognized by France, the government of the USSR sued in the French courts claiming title to the ships. The supreme court rejected the claim because giving effect in France to foreign legislation expropriating property without compensation would conflict with French established order (i.e. *ordre public*).

Société Potasas Ibericas v. Bloch, Court of Cassation, [1939] Dalloz Rec.Heb. 257. The plaintiff was a corporation whose mines and other facilities in Spain had been nationalized. Bloch was the consignee of a shipment of chemical products from the Spanish state company which had taken over the facilities. The plaintiff claimed title to the shipment. A first decree of nationalization had been issued on August 8, 1936, against industries belonging to absent owners, but without specific mention of the plaintiff and without provision for compensation. The shipment arrived in France before the issuance of a second decree which specifically took the property of the plaintiff and provided for compensation. The court held that the second decree could not take effect retroactively in France with respect to a shipment already there and hence the consignee could not justify his possession of it.

Société Hardmuth, Court of Appeal of Paris, 1950, 44 R.Crit.Dr. Int'l Pr. 501 (1955). Hardmuth, a corporation in Czechoslovakia, was nationalized. Its new directors claimed the property of the corporation in France as against the former owners. The court rejected the claim relating to the tangible property in France, such as buildings, because measures of nationalization without compensation could not be given effect in France. But it recognized the claim concerning trademarks. Their nationalization was effective in Czechoslovakia and their protection in France was required by a convention on industrial property to which France and Czechoslovakia were parties.

Martin v. Bank of Spain, Court of Cassation, 1952, 42 R.Crit.Dr. Int'l Pr. 425 (1953). Spanish law required bills of Spanish currency, especially those coming in from France, to be embossed with a special seal in order to be legal tender. The plaintiff acquired in France bills of Spanish currency which were not so embossed and presented them for exchange against valid ones at the Spanish customs. They were given a receipt, but no money. Their invalid bills were turned over to the Bank of Spain. They sued the bank for payment in valid currency of the amount of their receipt. The court said that, even if the principle of immunity were disregarded, the refusal to pay the plaintiffs in valid currency "constituted acts of authority outside the control of the French courts."

De Keller v. Maison de la Pensée Française, Tribunal Civil de la Seine (référés) 1954, 44 R.Crit.Dr. Int'l Pr. 503 (1955). The plaintiff invoked an emergency and summary procedure by which the court was requested to take temporary custody of 37 out of 49 paintings by Pablo Picasso exhibited by the defendant, a nonprofit organization. The defendant had the 37 Picassos on loan from the Russian state art galleries in Leningrad and Moscow. The plaintiffs alleged that the paintings belonged to their deceased father, whose private art gallery the Russian state had confiscated in 1918, and contended they would establish their title to them in further proceedings. The court denied the request. It would have to determine whether the presence in France of paintings acquired by a foreign state in its own territory, and by a method legally valid there, violated French juridical order. Such a determination raised difficult questions which could not be resolved in the instant procedure without prejudging the merits as well as the jurisdiction of the French courts in the matter.

The nationalizations in Algeria led to substantial litigation in France, listed in Cour de Cassation Lachaume, Chronique de Jurisprudence Française Relative au Droit International Public 1969, Ann.Dr. Int'l Fr. 1970, at 874, 898 (1971).

SECTION E.   EXTRATERRITORIAL NATIONALIZATIONS DISTINGUISHED

REPUBLIC OF IRAQ v. FIRST NATIONAL CITY BANK

United States Court of Appeals, Second Circuit, 1965.
353 F.2d 47.

FRIENDLY, Circuit Judge.   King Faisal II of Iraq was killed on July 14, 1958, in the midst of a revolution in that country which led to the establishment of a republic, recognized by the United States in August. On July 19, 1958, the new government issued Ordinance No. 23 which decreed that "all property [of the dynasty] * * * whether moveable or immoveable * * * should be confiscated."   At the time of his death King Faisal had a balance of $55,925 and 4,008 shares of Canada General Fund, Ltd., a Canadian investment trust, in deposit and custody accounts with Irving Trust Company in New York.   In October 1958, the Surrogate's Court for New York County issued to the defendant letters of administration with respect to King Faisal's New York assets.   During that month the Consul General of the Republic of Iraq notified Irving Trust that the Republic claimed all assets of King Faisal by virtue of Ordinance No. 23.   Notwithstanding the notice, Irving Trust subsequently transferred to the administrator the balance in the account and certificates for the shares, which were later sold.

In March 1962, the Republic brought this action against the administrator in the District Court for the Southern District of New York to recover the bank balance and the proceeds of the shares.   From a judgment dismissing the complaint, the Republic appeals.   We affirm.

The District Court properly held that it had jurisdiction of the action.   Under 28 U.S.C. § 1332(a) the district courts are vested with original jurisdiction of all civil actions "where the matter in controversy exceeds the sum or value of $10,000, exclusive of interest and costs, and is between * * * (2) citizens of a State, and foreign states or citizens or subjects thereof."   Although this general language does not grant jurisdiction to probate a will or administer an estate, it has been established by a long series of decisions "that federal courts of equity have jurisdiction to entertain suits 'in favor of creditors, legatees and heirs' and other claimants against a decedent's estate 'to establish their claims' so long as the federal court does not interfere with the probate proceedings or assume general jurisdiction of the probate or control of the property in the custody of the state court."

The principal questions raised in this appeal are the proper definition of the act of state doctrine and its application to foreign confiscation decrees purporting to affect property within the United States. Although difficulty is sometimes encountered in drawing the line between an "act of state" and more conventional foreign decrees or statutes claimed to be entitled to respect by the forum, the Ordinance involved in this case is nowhere near the boundary. A confiscation decree, which is precisely what Ordinance No. 23 purported to be, is the very archetype of an act of state. *See* Restatement of Foreign Relations Law of the United States § 41c [hereinafter Restatement].

* * *

Under the traditional application of the act of state doctrine, the principle of judicial refusal of examination applies only to a taking by a foreign sovereign of property within its own territory. Cf. *Sabbatino, supra*; when property confiscated is within the United States at the time of the attempted confiscation, our courts will give effect to acts of state "only if they are consistent with the policy and law of the United States." Restatement § 46.

In this case, neither the bank account nor the shares in the Canadian investment trust can realistically be considered as being within Iraq simply because King Faisal resided and was physically present there at the time of his death; in the absence of any showing that Irving Trust had an office in Iraq or would be in any way answerable to its courts, we need not consider whether the conclusion would differ if it did. So far as appears on this record, only a court in the United States could compel the bank to pay the balance in the account or to deliver the certificates it held in custody. The property here at issue thus was within the United States. Although the nationality of King Faisal provided a jurisdictional basis for the Republic of Iraq to prescribe a rule relating to his property outside Iraq, Restatement § 30(1)(b), this simply gives the confiscation decree a claim to consideration by the forum which, in the absence of such jurisdiction, it would not possess—not a basis for insisting on the absolute respect which, subject to the qualifications of Sabbatino, [supra], the decree would enjoy as to property within Iraq at the time.

Extra-territorial enforcement of the Iraqi ordinance as to property within the United States at the date of its promulgation turns on whether the decree is consistent with our policy and laws. We perceive no basis for thinking it to be. Confiscation of the assets of a corporation has been said to be "contrary to our public policy and shocking to our sense of justice,". Confiscation of the assets of an individual is no less so, even if he wears a crown. Our Constitution sets itself against confiscations such as that decreed by Ordinance No. 23 not only by the general guarantees of due process in the Fifth and Fourteenth Amendments but by the specific prohibitions of bills of attainder in Article I. It is true that since these provisions are addressed to action by the United

States or a state, they might not prevent a court of the United States from giving effect to a confiscatory act of a foreign state with respect to property in the United States. But at least they show that, from its earliest days under the Constitution, this nation has had scant liking for legislative proscription of members of a defeated faction, although—or perhaps because—many states, in their dealings with property of the loyalists immediately after the Revolution, had practiced exactly that. Foreigners entrusting their property to custodians in this country are entitled to expect this historic policy to be followed save when the weightiest reasons call for a departure. In saying this we are not guilty of disrespect to the recitals in the preamble of Ordinance No. 23; subject to the narrow exception discussed below, the policy of the United States is that there is no such thing as a "good" confiscation by legislative or executive decree.

* * *

Affirmed.

———

1. *The problem of jurisdiction to nationalise.* A number of decisions in other countries also hold that a state's purported act of state in seeking to take into public ownership assets not within its territory will not be recognized. These decisions hold either that the act of state doctrine does not apply to such situations, that such takings are clearly against *ordre public,* or that the state has no jurisdiction to nationalize property that is within the jurisdiction to nationalize of the forum state or some third state. Problems of extraterritorial nationalization, then, should be distinguished from the act of state doctrine, and decisions denying recognition of extraterritorial nationalization should not be counted as decisions rejecting the act of state doctrine where the extraterritorial issue is not present. See Reeves, *The Sabbatino Case and the Sabbatino Amendment: Comedy—or Tragedy—of Errors,* 20 Vand.L.Rev. 429 (1966–1967), especially Appendix II.

As in conflict of laws, there is a problem as to the localization—or ascribed situs—of intangibles, in a range from unliquidated claims against a debtor to negotiable securities. Most nationalization cases, however, involve either land or movables that are capable of having an actual physical location. *Illustration*: when Egyptian President Nasser nationalized the assets of the Universal Suez Canal Corporation, he got the canal, but the big investment portfolio of the company kept in Paris remained beyond his grasp.

2. *The act of state doctrine and customary international law.* In a suit by one state against another in the International Court of Justice, or in an arbitration to be governed by customary international law, would act of state or a similar principle justify the court or arbitral panel to rule that the respondent state should have applied it? You have

noted that national legal systems do not claim international legal status for the principle. Nonetheless, can a case be made for the existence of such a principle? Cf. the Statute of the International Court of Justice, Article 38(1)(b) and (c), in the Doc. Supp. As between (b) and (c) which has the greater supportive potential for such a principle?

———

Chapter 9

NATIONALITY, PROTECTION
AND ALLEGIANCE

Section A.   Nationality: Loss of Its Benefits.
            Consequences of Statelessness.
Section B.   International Criteria for State Protection.
Section C.   Obligations of Nationality or Allegiance.
            1. The Crime of Treason.
            2. Taxation.
            3. Compulsory Military Service.
            4. Other?
Section D.   Situation of International Officials.

A basic feature of the system of nation states is the relative dependency of the individual. At birth a person becomes a member of some political institution (typically a state in the international system) which, more or less, affords protection from the violence of other individuals and groups of individuals. In the domestic legal system of that state, its police and courts may offer protection from harm inflicted within the state; its military may offer protection from harm caused by aggression from outside the state.

If the individual goes outside the home state, security diminishes. If injured by someone in another state, the individual must look for redress, if any, in the courts of that other state. Doctrines of sovereign immunity may be a bar to redress for injuries caused by that state. As a last resort the individual must appeal to the home state's government for assistance. If the home state chooses, it may come to the individual's aid by espousing a claim against the wrongdoing state through diplomatic channels (or possibly through arbitration or through judicial means such as the International Court of Justice).

For the protection it offers at home and the protection it may afford against foreign injuries, the home state demands obligations of the individual in return: to obey its laws, to pay its taxes, to help to defend it against aggression by other states.

The fact of an individual's presence within a state has been the major basis from which the state exerts its power to protect the individual and to demand allegiance. But the processes of history have developed legal relationships between the state and the individual that do not depend solely upon physical presence in the territory of the state. The state has a special relationship to those it designates as its nationals. In broad and inexact terms, the state's nationals are entitled to greater rights than non-nationals (e.g., in states with voting systems, the national is permitted to vote, the non-national is not); the state is more ready to demand that the national perform obligations (e.g., the national may be subject to laws prescribed by the state even though the national is not physically present in its territory).

The practices of states in creating the classes of people upon whom they confer nationality vary widely. Some states accord nationality to individuals born within the territory; this right of nationality is referred to as jus soli. Some states accord nationality at birth only to individuals born of parents who are already nationals: this right of nationality is referred to as jus sanguinis. An increasing number of states recognize both bases. In addition to according nationality based upon facts associated with birth, states afford naturalization processes by which individuals may apply for and be granted nationality. With such a variety of bases for nationality existing in the international system it is possible for an individual to be designated a national by more than one state and thus to have dual nationality or even multiple nationality. Also, there are circumstances under which a person may have no nationality at all and thus be stateless.

From the perspective of the international legal system, several important questions arise:

1. Is a state free to set its own standards for conferring its nationality upon an individual? Or does international law set some minimum standard?

2. What is the significance of nationality as a base for the state's requiring the performance of obligations by an individual? For example, can the state draft into its army someone who is not its national?

This chapter explores these two questions. In succeeding chapters the question will be asked whether the developments in the law of human rights and individual responsibility significantly modify the legal situation of the individual as sketched above.

––––––

The U.N. Staff Regulations, the Rules which govern that body, its subjects, and employees, are in the Documentary Supplement.

SECTION A. NATIONALITY:
LOSS OF ITS BENEFITS
––––––

RE IMMIGRATION ACT AND HANNA
Canada, Supreme Court of British Columbia, 1957.
21 Western Weekly Rep. 400.*

SULLIVAN, J. This is a "hard case" of the kind of which it is said that bad law is made. The applicant George Christian Hanna, whom I

* Reprinted by permission of Burroughs & Co., Ltd., Calgary, Alberta, Canada.

shall refer to as "Hanna" in these reasons for judgment, is a young man without a country—one of those unfortunate "stateless" persons of the world whose status is a matter of concern to humanitarians and has prompted men and women of good will of all countries to seek relief for such persons through the agency of the Economic and Social Council of the United Nations. A convention was adopted by that council in September 1954, to which, however, Canada is not a signatory.

The matter comes before me by way of habeas corpus with certiorari in aid. Hanna seeks a judicial declaration that his detention under a deportation order made by F. Wragg, an immigration officer (acting as a special inquiry officer) dated January 18, 1957, and confirmed on appeal to an immigration appeal board duly constituted under the provisions of the Immigration Act, RSC, 1952, ch. 325, is illegal, (1) Because the deportation order is defective, incomplete, impossible of interpretation or enforcement and beyond the statutory authority of Mr. Wragg to make; and (2) Because the immigration appeal board improperly denied Hanna the right to be heard, either in person or by counsel, at the appeal proceedings before such board.

The issues thus presented for my determination are strictly legal in nature and narrow in their scope. I have no right to reflect upon and must guard against the danger that the strictly legal opinion which I am required to express should be influenced in any degree by considerations of human sympathy for this unfortunate (23–year–old) young applicant in the frustrating dilemma with which fate seems to have confronted him throughout his lifetime prior to his last arrival in Canada as ship-bound prisoner aboard a tramp motor-ship in her ceaseless meanderings from port to port throughout the world. The deportation order in question is in the words and figures following:

DEPARTMENT OF CITIZENSHIP AND IMMIGRATION DEPORTATION ORDER
AGAINST CHRISTIAN GEORGE HANNA OF DJIBOUTI,
FRENCH SOMALILAND

under section 28 of the Immigration Act. On the basis of the evidence adduced at an inquiry held at the Immigration Building, Vancouver, B.C., on January 18, 1957 I have reached the decision that you may not come into or remain in Canada as of right and that you are a member of the prohibited class described in paragraph (t) of Section 5 of the Immigration Act, in that you do not fulfil or comply with the conditions or requirements of Subsection (1), Subsection (3) and Subsection (8) of Section 18 of the Immigration Regulations.

I hereby order you to be detained and to be deported to the place whence you came to Canada, or to the country of which you are a national or citizen, or to the country of your birth, or to such country as may be approved by the minister.

Date 18 January 1957, [Sgd.] F. WRAGG, Special Inquiry Officer [Sgd.] C.G. HANNA.

Subsecs. (1), (3) and (8) of sec. 18 of the regulations to which said deportation order refers require that an immigrant possess a passport and visa; and that his passport or other travel document bear a medical certificate in approved form.

It should be stated at the outset that no Canadian court has power to assist Hanna in his plea that he be given right of residence in Canada. That is a decision for immigration officials, and for them alone, to make. Similarly all right of exercise of discretionary power to exempt from strict compliance with the requirements of the Immigration Act or regulations made thereunder is vested in and is the prerogative of only the minister, deputy minister, director, or such other persons as may be authorized to act for the director.   * * *

* * *

It may be helpful to outline Hanna's history and background as it is disclosed by the scanty material before me. Most of such material consists of Hanna's sworn testimony, given in the English language, when he was before Mr. Wragg on January 18, 1957, at which time his knowledge and proficiency in the use of our language was not as great as it may be now. He says that he was born at sea and that no known record of his birth is extant. The name of the vessel aboard which he was born, and particulars of her nationality or port of registry are unknown. His father was named George Hanna and supposedly travelled to French Somaliland from Liberia, a small republic situate on the west coast of Africa. His mother's maiden name was Marian Marika and she was a native of Ethiopia (or Abyssinia)—a country whose status either as empire or vassal of Italy at any given time can be determined only by reference to historical data bearing upon Emperor Haile Selassie's struggles in warfare with the late Benito Mussolini. Hanna understands that his parents met and were married at Djibouti, the capital city of French Somaliland. The accuracy of his information in this respect should be easy to check. French Somaliland is a very small country. It has been a French colony for about 80 years. * * * Hanna was the only child born of his parents' marriage and both of his parents are dead. Continuing the narrative according to Hanna's understanding of events, his father left his mother to seek employment in Liberia. Subsequently his mother, being pregnant at the time, and seeking to rejoin her husband, took passage on a ship sailing out of Djibouti. She became ill and gave birth to Hanna when the ship was one day at sea, and because of her illness the ship was put about and returned to Djibouti where she and her newborn child were placed in a hospital or home for women. Thereafter Hanna was cared for by his mother who worked at various times at Addis Ababa and Dire Wawa (both in Ethiopia) and at Djibouti in French Somaliland, until Hanna was six years of age. She then died and thereafter Hanna more or less "raised himself" as he puts it, with some assistance from a kindly old Turkish gentleman at Djibouti and others, including a Japanese gentleman at Dire Wawa in Ethiopia.

During his years of infancy and adolescence Hanna seems to have crossed and recrossed the international boundaries of Ethiopia, French Somaliland, British Somaliland and Eritrea (formerly an Italian colony but now a province of Ethiopia by virtue of the recommendation of a United Nations' committee adopted by the General Assembly in 1952) without encountering difficulty with the immigration officials of those countries. I suppose that youth was in his favour at the outset, and I suppose, too, that the international boundaries referred to were not too well defined at that time. That still seems to be the case. I understand that the accurate fixation of the international borders convergent upon the small area of French Somaliland is a problem which presently engages the attention of the United Nations' General Assembly.

In this way Hanna lived and worked from time to time (inter alia) in the ports of Zeila and Berbera in British Somaliland where he picked up a smattering of English. He says that his mother spoke English and, although he never saw his father, it is his understanding that his parents conversed in English. This would be consistent with Hanna's theory that his father was a native of Liberia—a republic which most people look upon as a virtual protectorate of the United States of America, and where English is spoken.

As he grew older Hanna seems to have encountered and had difficulty with the immigration officers of these adjacent countries, in none of which he could claim right of residence. He thereby learned that possession of a birth certificate is an indispensable requirement of modern society. He learned "the hard way" that some of the fundamental human rights with which all men are endowed by their Creator at birth were not his to enjoy without the intervention and benevolent assistance of some temporal power—a power to be exercised in many cases according to the whim or opinion of immigration officers whose numbers are legion in most sovereign states. That is not to say, of course, that he or anyone else possesses an inherent right to enter or remain in Canada unless born here. The late Right Honorable W.L. Mackenzie King, Prime Minister of Canada, said in the House of Commons on May 1, 1947, that "It is not a 'fundamental human right' of an alien to enter Canada. It is a privilege. It is a matter of domestic policy."

The same thing might be said with respect to every sovereign state of the world, but one doubts that the Prime Minister intended his statement to be a repudiation of Canadian interest or sympathy in such a case of distress as this one, the like of which, I venture to say, has little chance of recurring. It is probable that the Prime Minister made use of the term "alien" in the popular sense of reference to a person who resides or seeks to reside in a country other than his own; and in that connotation it could be argued that a stateless person like Hanna is not an "alien" since he has no country of his own.

I [should remind] myself again that the issue before me is a strictly legal one which I am required to divorce from any considerations of equity or humanitarianism. Those things must be deemed to have been embodied in the statute at the time of its enactment.

Almost three years ago, when he was in the port of Massaua, Eritrea, Hanna stowed away in an Italian tramp steamer in the hope of being carried in her to some country which would grant him asylum and right of residence. His plan met with frustration because upon arrival of such ship at any port he was immediately locked up and denied permission to land. After a year or more of such aimless wandering and imprisonment, Hanna escaped from the Italian vessel when she called at Beirut in the republic of Lebanon, and concealed himself in the hold of the Norwegian motor-ship "Gudveig." As a stowaway in such latter vessel he fared no better than before. He was held prisoner aboard The "Gudveig" for more than 16 months and made three or more trips to Canada in her until his release under writ of habeas corpus in these proceedings. He first came before Clyne, J., upon return of a show cause summons on January 18, 1957, wherein he challenged the legality of his detention by the master of The "Gudveig." My learned brother there held (correctly, in my respectful opinion) that the master's detention of Hanna was not illegal since the master was subject to and bound by the regulations applicable to "stowaways" as passed pursuant to the provisions of the Immigration Act. Thereafter Hanna made application to enter Canada and his status was thereby changed from that of "stowaway" to that of "immigrant." An immigrant is defined by sec. 2(i) of the Immigration Act as follows: (i) "immigrant" means a person who seeks admission to Canada for permanent residence.

* * * And so, at a time when it had become a widely publicized matter of general public knowledge or repute that Hanna possessed no proof of birth nor documents of any kind, he was granted the privilege of appearing before three separate departmental tribunals for the purpose of proving—if he could—that he did in fact possess such documents. Of course, he was unable to discharge that onus, and the deportation order followed which is now under attack in these proceedings.

[Now to] that deportation order. Was it an order which the special inquiry officer had legal authority to make in all of the circumstances existing at the time of its making? It contains four separate directives which are stated in the alternative and, presumably, in the order of their importance.

The most important directive is, No. 1, that Hanna be deported to the place whence he came to Canada. The next directive is, No. 2, that he be deported to the country of which he is a national or citizen. The next is, No. 3, that he be deported to the country of his birth. The final alternative is, No. 4, that he be deported to such country as may be approved by the minister.

The No. 4 directive is meaningless in the absence of anything to show a possibility of the minister ever finding a country which would be willing to admit this young man in the face of Canada's refusal to admit him. It cannot be assumed that travel documents are of less significance in other countries than here. The thing goes further than that, however, because sec. 40(2) of our Act makes the minister's power of designation and approval of "such country" conditional upon the owners of the M.S. "Gudveig" first making request for such ministerial approval. Even then, as I interpret the statute, the approval of the minister could have no effect unless after finding "a country that is willing to receive him," Hanna were to indicate that such country is "acceptable" to him.

Directives No. 2 and No. 3 referring, respectively, to country of nationality or citizenship and country of birth, may be discussed together. Neither of these directives could possibly be complied with. In the absence of satisfactory evidence of nationality of a legitimate father and lack of any evidence as to the nationality or registry of the ship aboard which Hanna was born, these directives of the deportation order are meaningless.

The inescapable fact is that Hanna is a "stateless person," and the efforts of the department to prove otherwise have not been impressive. I was presented with evidence (consisting of affidavits by lawyers in Oslo, Norway, and a Canadian immigration officer) in support of the submission that Hanna is not "stateless" and that the words of the directive "country of your birth," therefore, are not meaningless. The trouble is that whilst the affidavit of the immigration officer fixes Hanna's birthplace as Djibouti in French Somaliland, the Norwegian lawyers suggest that he is an Egyptian who was born at Alexandria. None of this conflicting evidence is credible. It is all based on hearsay and, perhaps, the least said about it, the better.

[Now for] consideration of directive No. 1—that Hanna be deported to the place whence he came to Canada. What does it mean?

The department's position, as I understand it, is that it could mean a number of things which it leaves to other people to determine for themselves. The place whence Hanna came to Canada might be the port of Beirut in the republic of Lebanon since that is the place where he first stowed away in the M.S. "Gudveig." Perhaps that interpretation is favoured by the department since it has presented certain material tending to show that if Lebanese authorities can be satisfied that Hanna stowed away at Beirut, they might permit him to land in their country— a country, incidentally, which is quite as foreign to Hanna as it is to me. Then again the department seems to suggest that the place whence Hanna came to Canada could be the United Kingdom and an affidavit is presented for the purpose of showing that The "Gudveig" sailed non-stop from the United Kingdom to Vancouver on her last voyage with Hanna aboard. Perhaps the place whence Hanna came to Canada could be the port of Massaua in Eritrea, since that was the starting point of his aimless wanderings as a stowaway in search of a country which would give him right of residence. Other interpretations are possible, but it seems to me that the matter of correct interpretation is of comparative unimportance here. The thing of importance, is that the special inquiry officer delegated to the master or owners of The "Gudveig" the responsibility for saying what his deportation order means; and, apart from the circumstances that he himself does not seem to know what it means, I am of opinion that he has not that power of delegation under the Act. I have had reference to the authorities cited by counsel wherein it was held that deportation orders made (as this one was) in form approved by the minister were valid and enforceable notwithstanding their multiplicity of alternative directives, but in none of such cases were the facts comparable to the extraordinary facts of this amazing case. In each of such cases the meaning of the deportation order in the form used was clearly apparent to everyone concerned or affected by it. In no case did the deportation order require subsequent inquiry or investigation by anyone for determination of its meaning. In none was there a necessarily incidental delegation of his authority by the special inquiry officer who made the order for deportation. These are some of the things which distinguish Hanna's case from all others.

From whatever angle one views it, so far as Hanna is concerned, this deportation order amounted to a sentence of imprisonment aboard The "Gudveig" for an indefinite term, and in my opinion and finding, no immigration officer has the legal right to exercise such drastic power.

* * *

For the reasons previously expressed, there will be judgment for Hanna in these proceedings, with costs. That does not mean that he has established any legal right to enter or remain in Canada. As previously stated, it is for immigration officials and for them alone to grant or withhold that privilege. This judgment does not mean that Hanna may not be deported legally from Canada by further proceedings properly instituted and conducted in accordance with the provisions and intent of the Immigration Act. It means only that the present deportation order is illegal and that Hanna is entitled to be released from detention thereunder; and I so order.

* * *

CONSEQUENCES OF STATELESSNESS

1. **What happens to Hanna now?** In *Staniszewski v. Watkins,* 80 F.Supp. 132 (S.D.N.Y.1948), a stateless seaman was released after being detained at Ellis Island for about seven months. The court observed that the government was "willing that he go back to the ship, but if he were sent back aboard ship and sailed to the port * * * from which he last sailed to the United States, he would probably be denied permission to land." The court said, "There is no other country that would take him, without proper documents." The court sustained the seaman's writ of habeas corpus and ordered his release: "He will be required to inform the immigration officials at Ellis Island by mail on the 15th of each month, stating where he is employed and where he can be reached. If the government does succeed in arranging for petitioner's deportation to a country that will be ready to receive him as a resident, it may then advise the petitioner to that effect and arrange for his deportation in the manner provided by law."

Similarly, in Public Prosecutor v. Zinger, France, Tribunal of the Seine, 1936, [1935–37] Ann.Dig. 307 (No. 138), the court ordered the release of a stateless person who had been imprisoned for failure to obey expulsion orders. The court weighed the alternatives of releasing the man or imprisoning him "at the cost of the French taxpayer" for an offence which he could not help committing, since he was unable to leave French territory. The court concluded: "release is the best solution."

2. ***Discrimination between aliens and stateless persons.*** If a stateless person is allowed to remain in the United States, may that person be treated differently from an alien who has the nationality of some other state? Aliens have been held entitled to constitutional protections like the Fifth Amendment guarantee against expropriation of property without compensation. If the United States should discriminate between aliens with nationality and those without nationality, to the disadvantage of the latter, would there be any international consequence? A state whose national has been the subject of discrimination could call the United States to account under international law. Who would, or could, espouse the claim of the stateless alien?

3. ***Espousal of claims of stateless persons.*** Suppose a stateless person is allowed to remain in the United States and there reside for a number of years. If he then enters a foreign state and is injured severely at the hands of state officials (e.g. illegal imprisonment and subjection to torture and other inhumane treatment). Will the United States espouse a claim on the individual's behalf? 22 U.S.C. 732 provides:

> Whenever it is made known to the President that any citizen of the United States has been unjustly deprived of his liberty by or under the authority of any foreign government, it shall be the duty of the President forthwith to demand of that government the reasons of such imprisonment; and if it appears to be wrongful and in violation of the rights of American citizenship, the President shall forthwith demand the release of such citizen, and if the release so demanded is unreasonably delayed or refused, the President shall use such means, not amounting to acts of war, as he may think necessary and proper to obtain or effectuate the release; and all the facts and proceedings relative thereto shall as soon as practicable be communicated by the President to Congress.

The protection of the United States is not confined to native-born citizens. 22 U.S.C. 1731 provides: "All naturalized citizens of the United States while in foreign countries are entitled to and shall receive from this Government the same protection of persons and property which is accorded to native-born citizens." Suppose it is decided by the United States that it will espouse the stateless alien's claim. It is permitted by international law to do so? See the *Nottebohm case,* below.

4. ***Statelessness decreed against members of a class of persons.*** Statelessness has resulted from a state's decree that members of a whole class of persons are no longer citizens. During World War II, Germany withdrew German nationality from Jews permanently resident abroad. In France, this loss of nationality relieved an individual from the strictures applied by French law to enemy (German) subjects, even though the German denationalization law was repealed by the Allies at

the end of the war. Terhoch v. Daudin et Assistance Publique, France, Court of Appeal of Paris, [1947] Ann.Dig. 121 (No. 54).

5. Some states today withhold from women the right to acquire, change, retain their nationality or to pass on their nationality to their children. Article 9 of the Convention on the Elimination of All Forms of Discrimination Against Women [a] sought to remedy this inequality. A number of states that signed the Convention, nevertheless, claimed reservations to Article 9. See ch. 10.

RESERVATIONS TO THE CONVENTION ON THE ELIMINATION OF ALL FORMS OF DISCRIMINATION AGAINST WOMEN

REBECCA J. COOK, 30 Va.J.Int'l L. 643, 693–696 (1990).*

* * *

"C. *Nationality: Article 9*

Women's capacity to possess citizenship and nationality separate from their husbands' affects both their capacity to be represented by state subjects of international law and their ability legally to transmit such capacity to their children. The ability to invoke the protection of a country with which they retain a genuine and effective link [251] while they reside in another may be an important source of security for women who go to live in a country where they are disadvantaged as aliens.

Article 9 of the Women's Convention requires that:

1. States Parties shall grant women equal rights with men to acquire, change or retain their nationality. They shall ensure in particular that neither marriage to an alien nor change of nationality by the husband during marriage shall automatically change the nationality of the wife, render her stateless or force upon her the nationality of the husband.

2. States Parties shall grant women equal rights with men with respect to the nationality of their children.

Explanations on reservations to this article vary.[252] A traditional explanation is that family solidarity and cohesiveness is served by the family having the same nationality, which should be that of its leader, who traditionally has been an adult man. Another explanation is the

---

a. Convention on the Elimination of All Forms of Discrimination Against Women, 18 December 1979, 34 UN GAOR Supp. (No. 21) (A/34/46) at 193, UN Doc. A/RES/34/180 (entry into force 3 September 1981) [hereinafter Women's Convention].

* Reprinted by permission of Virginia Jnl. of Int'l Law.

251. The test for nationality was established in the *Nottebohm Case* (Liechtenstein v. Guatemala), 1955 I.C.J. 4, 22 (Judgment of April 6).

252. Countries which have not reserved this article are not necessarily in compliance. For example in Gabon, which ratified the Women's Convention without reservations, a Gabonese woman must renounce her nationality in order to marry a foreigner, and if she divorces she cannot have her nationality reinstated. Moreover, a foreign woman who marries a Gabonese man cannot retain her nationality. Implementation in Africa of the Convention on the Elimination of All Forms of Discrimination Against Women, Doc. E/ECA/CM.13/27 at para. 33 (1987).

prevention of statelessness that would arise when a woman's original national law attributes to her on marriage her husband's nationality, but her husband's national law recognizes her separate nationality and does not extend its nationality to her. The Republic of Korea, Iraq and Tunisia consider themselves not to be bound by this article.

Egypt's reservation to article 9(2) was made to afford a child born within marriage its father's nationality 'in order to prevent a child's acquisition of two nationalities, since this may be prejudicial to his future.' This goal would be served, of course, if the child had only its mother's nationality, but another explanation is offered: [I]t is clear that the child's acquisition of his father's nationality is the procedure most suitable for the child and that this does not infringe upon the principle of equality between men and women, since it is the custom for a woman to agree, on marrying an alien, that her children shall be of the father's nationality. Since Egypt claims that its existing law does not infringe upon equality of men and women, it is questionable why it reserved with respect to this article.

The proposition that the man's nationality should govern his wife and his child was rejected by the Inter–American Court on Human Rights and the Human Rights Committee. The Inter–American Court referred to article 9 in an Advisory Opinion sought by Costa Rica on a number of amendments proposed to the naturalization provisions of its Constitution. One of the proposed amendments would have distinguished the naturalization provisions governing foreign women and foreign men who marry Costa Ricans. The Court noted that the proposed amendment follows the formula

> adopted in the current Constitution, which gives women but not men who marry Costa Ricans a special status for * * * naturalization. This approach or system was based on the so-called principle of family unity and is traceable to two assumptions * * * [that] all members of a family should have the same nationality. The other derives from notions about paternal authority and the fact that authority over minor children was as a rule vested in the father and that it was the husband on whom the law conferred a privileged status of power, giving him authority, for example to fix the marital domicile and to administer the marital property. Viewed in this light, the right accorded to women to acquire the nationality of their husbands was an outgrowth of conjugal inequality.

The Court unanimously expressed the opinion that this proposed naturalization amendment 'which favors only one of the spouses, does constitute discrimination incompatible with article 17(4) [on equality of rights and responsibilities within marriage] and article 24 [on equal protection of the law] of the [American] Convention'. The Human Rights Committee in the *Aumeeruddy–Cziffra* decision considered that a Mauritian woman's inability (in contrast to a Mauritian man's ability) to transmit her nationality to her children constituted sex discrimination in the field of family life and cannot be justified on grounds of national security.

Discriminatory nationality laws between the sexes might have a marginal impact among static, perhaps isolated, populations but will be of major significance in countries where sizeable numbers of immigrants, such as workers, refugees and students, have intermarried. A reservation to the Women's Convention that upholds the imposition of a husband's alien nationality on a married woman, and the related withdrawal of the nationality of the country in which she and her family have lived and in which she intends to rear her children, will cause a comprehensive withdrawal of legal rights and capacities that the Women's Convention is designed to prevent. Such reservations, if permitted, would undermine the object and purpose of the Convention. The reservations themselves, founded on a stereotype of women's domestic roles, indicate an attitude or perception that states parties to the Women's Convention undertake to strive to change. It is inconsistent with adherence to the Women's Convention and its principle of progressive development for a country anchor women's enduring incapacity in such a stereotypical attitude.

---

6. ***Loss of nationality under the law of the United States.*** Congress has provided that a person who is a national of the United States by birth or by naturalization shall lose his nationality for a variety of reasons. 8 U.S.C. § 1481.[a] What is the meaning of the statutory phrase "lose his nationality"? In *Kennedy v. Mendoza–Martinez*, 372 U.S. 144, 160 (1963), the Court said:

> We recognize at the outset that we are confronted here with an issue of the utmost import. Deprivation of citizenship—particularly American citizenship, which is "one of the most valuable rights in the world today," Report of the President's Commission on Immigration and Naturalization (1953), 235—has grave practical consequences. An expatriate who, like Cort, had no other nationality becomes a stateless person—a person who not only has no rights as an American citizen, but no membership in any national entity whatsoever. "Such individuals as do not possess any nationality enjoy, in general, no protection whatever, and if they are aggrieved by a State they have no means of redress, since there is no State which is competent to take up their case. As far as the Law of Nations is concerned, there is, apart from restraints of morality or obligations expressly laid down by treaty * * * no restriction whatever to cause a State to abstain from maltreating to any extent such stateless individuals." The calamity is "[n]ot the loss of specific rights, then, but the loss of a community willing and able to guarantee any rights whatsoever * * *." Arendt, The Origins of Totalitarianism (1951), 294. * * *

In holding that denationalization as a punishment is barred by the Eighth Amendment, the court said in *Trop v. Dulles*:

> There may be involved no physical mistreatment, no primitive torture. There is instead the total destruction of the individual's

---

a. A thorough analysis of the legislative history of this statute is made in Mikva and Neuman, The Hostage Crisis and the "Hostage Act," 49 U. of Chi.L.Rev. 292 (1982).

status in organized society. It is a form of punishment more primitive than torture for it destroys for the individual the political existence that was centuries in the development. The punishment strips the citizen of his status in the national and international political community. His very existence is at the sufferance of the country in which he happens to find himself. While any one country may accord him some rights, and presumably as long as he remained in this country he would enjoy the limited rights of an alien, no country need do so because he is stateless. Furthermore, his enjoyment of even the limited rights of an alien might be subject to termination at any time by reason of deportation. In short, the expatriate has lost the right to have rights.

In Trop, the provision held unconstitutional involved conviction by court-martial and dishonorable discharge for desertion in wartime. Denationalization provisions have suffered at the hands of the Supreme Court. In the Kennedy case, the court held that the provision for loss of nationality by remaining outside the United States to avoid military service was punitive and lacked due process safeguards guaranteed by the Constitution of the United States. In *Schneider v. Rusk,* 377 U.S. 163 (1964), the court struck down the provisions for loss of nationality by a naturalized citizen who had continuously resided for three years in the country of his origin. Although in *Perez v. Brownell,* 356 U.S. 44 (1958), the court held that it was within Congress's foreign affairs power to provide for loss of citizenship by one who votes in a foreign election, this case was overruled in *Afroyim v. Rusk,* 387 U.S. 253 (1967). In Afroyim, the court held that the Fourteenth Amendment gives an individual "a constitutional right to remain a citizen in a free country unless he voluntarily relinquishes that citizenship." The relationship between the expatriating acts specified by Congress and the voluntary relinquishment required by the Afroyim ruling was elucidated in *Vance v. Terrazas,* 444 U.S. 252, reh. denied 445 U.S. 920 (1980):

> In sum, we hold that in proving expatriation, an expatriating act and an intent to relinquish citizenship must be proved by a preponderance of the evidence. We also hold that when one of the statutory expatriating acts is proved, it is constitutional to presume it to have been a voluntary act until and unless proved otherwise by the actor. If he succeeds, there can be no expatriation. If he fails, the question remains whether on all the evidence the Government has satisfied its burden of proof that the expatriating act was performed with the necessary intent to relinquish citizenship.

The requirements of Vance were found satisfied in *Richards v. Secretary of State,* 752 F.2d 1413 (9th Cir.1985). A United States citizen obtained Canadian citizenship and, in the process, took an oath of allegiance to Canada. These were both expatriating acts under United States legislation. He also expressly renounced his United States citizenship, as required for acquisition of Canadian citizenship. The court found that he had performed the expatriating acts voluntarily and that the oath of renunciation of United States citizenship had been taken with specific intent to renounce that citizenship. That the individual's motive in acquiring Canadian citizenship and taking the required oath had been only to advance his career in Canada did not negate his specific intent to renounce his United States citizenship.

One of the grounds for loss of nationality is "making a formal renunciation of nationality before a diplomatic or consular officer of the United States in a foreign state." 8 U.S.C. § 1481(a)(5). If a citizen of the United States makes such a renunciation and later seeks return to the United States, can he be excluded? If he is later found in the United States, can he be deported? To what state? See *Jolley v. Immigration and Naturalization Service*, 441 F.2d 1245 (5th Cir.), cert. denied.

7. ***Denaturalization and deportation.*** The United States has sought to deport individuals who committed war crimes during the Second World War. Although these individuals had become citizens of the United States by naturalization, their citizenship was revoked as a predicate to deportation. See chs. 10 and 16.

8. ***Other sources of utility:*** See the 1987 Restatement, § 212, especially Reporters' Note 4, on immigration law.

SECTION B. INTERNATIONAL CRITERIA FOR STATE PROTECTION

NOTTEBOHM CASE (LIECHTENSTEIN v. GUATEMALA)

International Court of Justice, 1955.
[1955] I.C.J.Rep. 4.

* * *

By the Application filed, the Government of Liechtenstein instituted proceedings before the Court in which it claimed restitution and compensation on the ground that the Government of Guatemala had "acted towards the person and property of Mr. Friedric Nottebohm, a citizen of Liechtenstein, in a manner contrary to international law". In its Counter–Memorial, the Government of Guatemala contended that this claim was inadmissible on a number of grounds, and one of its objections to the admissibility of the claim related to the nationality of the person for whose protection Liechtenstein had seised the Court.

It appears to the Court that this plea in bar is of fundamental importance and that it is therefore desirable to consider it at the outset.

Guatemala has referred to a well-established principle of international law, which it expressed in Counter–Memorial, where it is stated that "it is the bond of nationality between the State and the individual which alone confers upon the State the right of diplomatic protection".
* * *

Liechtenstein considers itself to be acting in conformity with this principle and contends that Nottebohm is its national by virtue of the naturalization conferred upon him. Nottebohm was born at Hamburg [in] 1881. He was German by birth, and still possessed German nationality when, in October 1939, he applied for naturalization in Liechtenstein.

In 1905 he went to Guatemala. He took up residence there and made that country the headquarters of his business activities, which increased and prospered; these activities developed in the field of commerce, banking and plantations. Having been an employee in the firm of Nottebohm Hermanos, which had been founded by his brothers Juan and Arturo, he became their partner in 1912 and later, in 1937, he was made head of the firm. After 1905 he sometimes went to Germany on business and to other countries for holidays. He continued to have business connections in Germany. He paid a few visits to a brother who had lived in Liechtenstein since 1931. Some of his other brothers, relatives and friends were in Germany, others in Guatemala. He himself continued to have his fixed abode in Guatemala until 1943, until the occurrence of the events which constitute the basis of the present dispute.

In 1939, after having provided for the safeguarding of his interests in Guatemala by a power of attorney given to the firm of Nottebohm Hermanos on March 22nd, he left that country at a date fixed by Counsel for Liechtenstein as at approximately the end of March or the beginning of April, when he seems to have gone to Hamburg, and later to have paid a few brief visits to Vaduz where he was at the beginning of October 1939. It was then, on October 9th, a little more than a month after the opening of the second World War marked by Germany's attack on Poland, that his attorney, Dr. Marxer, submitted an application for naturalization on behalf of Nottebohm.

The Liechtenstein Law of January 4th, 1934, lays down the conditions for the naturalization of foreigners, specifies the supporting documents to be submitted and the undertakings to be given and defines the competent organs for giving a decision and the procedure to be followed. The Law specifies certain mandatory requirements, namely, that the applicant for naturalization should prove: (1) "that the acceptance into the Home Corporation (Heimatverband) of a Liechtenstein commune has been promised to him in case of acquisition of the nationality of the State"; (2) that he will lose his former nationality as a result of naturalization, although this requirement may be waived under stated conditions. It further makes naturalization conditional upon compliance with the requirement of residence for at least three years in the territory of the Principality, although it is provided that "this requirement can be dispensed with in circumstances deserving special consideration and by way of exception". In addition, the applicant for naturalization is required to submit a number of documents, such as evidence of his residence in the territory of the Principality, a certificate of good conduct issued by the competent authority of the place of residence, documents relating to his property and income and, if he is not a resident in the Principality, proof that he has concluded an agreement with the Revenue authorities, "subsequent to the revenue commission of the presumptive home commune having been heard". The Law further provides for the payment by the applicant of a naturalization fee, which is fixed by the Princely Government and amounts to at least one half of the sum payable by the applicant for reception into the Home Corporation of a Liechtenstein commune, the promise of such reception constituting a condition under the Law for the grant of naturalization.

* * *

As to the consideration of the application by the competent organs and the procedure to be followed by them, the Law provides that the Government, after having examined the application and the documents pertaining thereto, and after having obtained satisfactory information concerning the applicant, shall submit the application to the Diet. If the latter approves the application, the Government shall submit the requisite request to the Prince, who alone is entitled to confer nationality of the Principality.

* * *

This was the legal position with regard to applications for naturalization at the time when Nottebohm's application was submitted.

On October 9th, 1939, Nottebohm, "resident in Guatemala since 1905 (at present residing as a visitor with his brother, Hermann Nottebohm, in Vaduz)", applied for admission as a national of Liechtenstein and, at the same time, for the previous conferment of citizenship in the Commune of Mauren. He sought dispensation from the condition of three years' residence as prescribed by law, without indicating the special circumstances warranting such waiver. He submitted a statement of the Crédit Suisse in Zurich concerning his assets, and undertook to pay 25,000 Swiss francs to the Commune of Mauren, 12,500 Swiss francs to the State, to which was to be added the payment of dues in connection with the proceedings. He further stated that he had made "arrangements with the Revenue Authorities of the Government of Liechtenstein for the conclusion of a formal agreement to the effect that he will pay an annual tax of naturalization amounting to Swiss francs 1,000, of which Swiss francs 600 are payable to the Commune of Mauren and Swiss francs 400 are payable to the Principality of Liechtenstein, subject to the proviso that the payments of these taxes will be set off against ordinary taxes which will fall due if the applicant takes up residence in one of the Communes of the Principality". He further undertook to deposit as security a sum of 30,000 Swiss francs. He also gave certain general information as to his financial position and indicated that he would never become a burden to the Commune whose citizenship he was seeking.

* * *

A document dated October 15th, 1939, certifies that on that date the Commune of Mauren conferred the privilege of its citizenship upon Mr. Nottebohm and requested the Government to transmit it to the Diet for approval. A certificate of October 17th, 1939, evidences the payment of the taxes required to be paid by Mr. Nottebohm. On October 20th, 1939, Mr. Nottebohm took the oath of allegiance and a final arrangement concerning liability to taxation was concluded on October 23rd. This was the procedure followed in the case of the naturalization of

Nottebohm. A certificate of nationality has also been produced, signed on behalf of the Government of the Principality and dated October 20th, 1939, to the effect that Nottebohm was naturalized by Supreme Resolution of the Reigning Prince dated October 13th, 1939.

Having obtained a Liechtenstein passport, Nottebohm had it visaed by the Consul General of Guatemala in Zurich on December 1st, 1939, and returned to Guatemala at the beginning of 1940, where he resumed his former business activities and in particular the management of the firm of Nottebohm Hermanos.

* * * Liechtenstein requests the Court to find and declare, first, "that the naturalization of Mr. Nottebohm in Liechtenstein on October 13th, 1939, was not contrary to international law", and, secondly, "that Liechtenstein's claim on behalf of Mr. Nottebohm as a national of Liechtenstein is admissible before the Court".

The Final Conclusions of Guatemala, on the other hand, request the Court "to declare that the claim of the Principality of Liechtenstein is inadmissible", and set forth a number of grounds relating to the nationality of Liechtenstein granted to Nottebohm by naturalization.

Thus, the real issue before the Court is the admissibility of the claim of Liechtenstein in respect of Nottebohm. Liechtenstein's first submission referred to above is a reason advanced for a decision by the Court in favour of Liechtenstein, while the several grounds given by Guatemala on the question of nationality are intended as reasons for the inadmissibility of Liechtenstein's claim. The present task of the Court is limited to adjudicating upon the admissibility of the claim of Liechtenstein in respect of Nottebohm on the basis of such reasons as it may itself consider relevant and proper.

To decide upon the admissibility of the Application, the Court must ascertain whether the nationality conferred on Nottebohm by Liechtenstein by means of a naturalization which took place in the circumstances which have been described, can be validly invoked as against Guatemala, whether it bestows upon Liechtenstein a sufficient title to the exercise of protection in respect of Nottebohm as against Guatemala and therefore entitles it to seise the Court of a claim relating to him. In this connection, Counsel for Liechtenstein said: "the essential question is whether Mr. Nottebohm, having acquired the nationality of Liechtenstein, that acquisition of nationality is one which must be recognized by other States". This formulation is accurate, subject to the twofold reservation that, in the first place, what is involved is not recognition for all purposes but merely for the purposes of the admissibility of the Application, and, secondly, that what is involved is not recognition by all States but only by Guatemala.

The Court does not propose to go beyond the limited scope of the question which it has to decide, namely whether the nationality conferred on Nottebohm can be relied upon as against Guatemala in justification of the proceedings instituted before the Court. It must decide this question on the basis of international law; to do so is consistent with the nature of the question and with the nature of the Court's own function.

* * *

Since no proof has been adduced that Guatemala has recognized the title to the exercise of protection relied upon by Liechtenstein as being derived from the naturalization which it granted to Nottebohm, the Court must consider whether such an act of granting nationality by Liechtenstein directly entails an obligation on the part of Guatemala to recognize its effect, namely, Liechtenstein's right to exercise its protection. In other words, it must be determined whether that unilateral act by Liechtenstein is one which can be relied upon against Guatemala in regard to the exercise of protection. The Court will deal with this question without considering that of the validity of Nottebohm's naturalization according to the law of Liechtenstein.

It is for Liechtenstein, as it is for every sovereign State, to settle by its own legislation the rules relating to the acquisition of its nationality, and to confer that nationality by naturalization granted by its own organs in accordance with that legislation. It is not necessary to determine whether international law imposes any limitations on its freedom of decision in this domain. Furthermore, nationality has its most immediate, its most far-reaching and, for most people, its only effects within the legal system of the State conferring it. Nationality serves above all to determine that the person upon whom it is conferred enjoys the rights and is bound by the obligations which the law of the State in question grants to or imposes on its nationals. This is implied in the wider concept that nationality is within the domestic jurisdiction of the State.

But the issue which the Court must decide is not one which pertains to the legal system of Liechtenstein. It does not depend on the law or on the decision of Liechtenstein whether that State is entitled to exercise its protection, in the case under consideration. To exercise protection, to apply to the Court, is to place oneself on the plane of international law. It is international law which determines whether a State is entitled to exercise protection and to seise the Court. The naturalization of Nottebohm was an act performed by Liechtenstein in the exercise of its domestic jurisdiction. The question to be decided is whether that act has the international effect here under consideration.

* * *

* * * International arbitrators, having before them allegations of nationality by the applicant State which were contested by the respondent State, have sought to ascertain whether nationality had been conferred by the applicant State in circumstances such as to give rise to an obligation on the part of the respondent State to recognize the effect of that nationality. To decide this question arbitrators have evolved certain principles for determining whether full international effect was to be attributed to the nationality invoked. The same issue is now before the Court: it must be resolved by applying the same principles.

The courts of third States, when confronted by a similar situation, have dealt with it in the same way. * * *

International arbitrators have decided in the same way numerous cases of dual nationality, where the question arose with regard to the exercise of protection. They have given their preference to the real and effective nationality, that which accorded with the facts, that based on stronger factual ties between the person concerned and one of the States whose nationality is involved. Different factors are taken into consideration, and their importance will vary from one case to the next: the habitual residence of the individual concerned is an important factor, but there are other factors such as the centre of his interests, his family ties, his participation in public life, attachment shown by him for a given country and inculcated in his children, etc.

Similarly, the courts of third States, when they have before them an individual whom two other States hold to be their national, seek to resolve the conflict by having recourse to international criteria and their prevailing tendency is to prefer the real and effective nationality.

The same tendency prevails in the writings of publicists and in practice. This notion is inherent in the provisions of Article 3, ¶ 2, of the court's Statute. National laws reflect this tendency. * * *

The practice of certain States which refrain from exercising protection in favour of a naturalized person when the latter has in fact, by his prolonged absence, severed his links with what is no longer for him anything but his nominal country, manifests the view of these States that, in order to be capable of being invoked against another State, nationality must correspond with the factual situation. * * *

The character thus recognized on the international level as pertaining to nationality is in no way inconsistent with the fact that international law leaves it to each State to lay down the rules governing the grant of its own nationality. The reason for this is that the diversity of demographic conditions has thus far made it impossible for any general agreement to be reached on the rules relating to nationality, although the latter by its very nature affects international relations. It has been considered that the best way of making such rules accord with the varying demographic conditions in different countries is to leave the fixing of such rules to the competence of each State. On the other hand, a State cannot claim that the rules it has thus laid down are entitled to recognition by another State unless it has acted in conformity with this general aim of making the legal bond of nationality accord with the individual's genuine connection with the State which assumes the defence of its citizens by means of protection as against other States.

* * *

According to the practice of States, to arbitral and judicial decisions and to the opinions of writers, nationality is a legal bond having as its basis a social fact of attachment, a genuine connection of existence, interests and sentiments, together with the existence of reciprocal rights and duties. It may be said to constitute the juridical expression of the fact that the individual upon whom it is conferred, either directly by the law or as the result of an act of the authorities, is in fact more closely connected with the population of the State conferring nationality than with that of any other State.   Conferred by a State, it only entitles that State to exercise protection vis-à-vis another State, if it constitutes a translation into juridical terms of the individual's connection with the State which has made him its national.

Diplomatic protection and protection by means of international judicial proceedings constitute measures for the defence of the rights of the State.   * * *

Since this is the character which nationality must present when it is invoked to furnish the State which has granted it with a title to the exercise of protection and to the institution of international judicial proceedings, the Court must ascertain whether the nationality granted to Nottebohm by means of naturalization is of this character or, in other words, whether the factual connection between Nottebohm and Liechtenstein in the period preceding, contemporaneous with and following his naturalization appears to be sufficiently close, so preponderant in relation to any connection which may have existed between him and any other State, that it is possible to regard the nationality conferred upon him as real and effective, as the exact juridical expression of a social fact of a connection which existed previously or came into existence thereafter.

Naturalization is not a matter to be taken lightly. * * *

To appraise its international effect, it is impossible to disregard the circumstances in which it was conferred, the serious character which attaches to it, the real and effective, and not merely the verbal preference of the individual seeking it for the country which grants it to him.

At the time of his naturalization does Nottebohm appear to have been more closely attached by his tradition, his establishment, his interests, his activities, his family ties, his intentions for the near future to Liechtenstein than to any other State?   * * *

                * * *

The essential facts are as follows: At the date when he applied for naturalization Nottebohm had been a German national from the time of his birth.   He had always retained his connections with members of his family who had remained in Germany and he had always had business connections with that country.   His country had been at war for more than a month, and there is nothing to indicate that the application for naturalization then made by Nottebohm was motivated by any desire to dissociate himself from the Government of his country.

He had been settled in Guatemala for 34 years.   He had carried on his activities there.   It was the main seat of his interests.   He returned there shortly after his naturalization, and it remained the centre of his interests and of his business activities.   He stayed there until his removal as a result of war measures in 1943.   He subsequently attempted to return there, and he now complains of Guatemala's refusal to admit him.   There, too, were several members of his family who sought to safeguard his interests.

In contrast, his actual connections with Liechtenstein were extremely tenuous. No settled abode, no prolonged residence in that country at the time of his application for naturalization: the application indicates that he was paying a visit there and confirms the transient character of this visit by its request that the naturalization proceedings should be initiated and concluded without delay. No intention of settling there was shown at that time or realized in the ensuing weeks, months or years—on the contrary, he returned to Guatemala very shortly after his naturalization and showed every intention of remaining there. If Nottebohm went to Liechtenstein in 1946, this was because of the refusal of Guatemala to admit him. No indication is given of the grounds warranting the waiver of the condition of residence, required by the 1934 Nationality Law, which waiver was implicitly granted to him. There is no allegation of any economic interests or of any activities exercised or to be exercised in Liechtenstein, and no manifestation of any intention whatsoever to transfer all or some of his interests and his business activities to Liechtenstein. It is unnecessary in this connection to attribute much importance to the promise to pay the taxes levied at the time of his naturalization. The only links to be discovered between the Principality and Nottebohm are the short sojourns already referred to and the presence in Vaduz of one of his brothers: but his brother's presence is referred to in his application for naturalization only as a reference to his good conduct. Furthermore, other members of his family have asserted Nottebohm's desire to spend his old age in Guatemala.

These facts establish, on the one hand, the absence of any bond of attachment between Nottebohm and Liechtenstein and, on the other hand, the existence of a long-standing and close connection between him and Guatemala, a link which his naturalization in no way weakened. That naturalization was not based on any real prior connection with Liechtenstein, nor did it in any way alter the manner of life of the person upon whom it was conferred in exceptional circumstances of speed and accommodation. In both respects, it was lacking in the genuineness requisite to an act of such importance, if it is to be entitled to be respected by a State in the position of Guatemala. It was granted without regard to the concept of nationality. * * *

Naturalization was asked for not so much for the purpose of obtaining a legal recognition of Nottebohm's membership in fact in the population of Liechtenstein, as it was to enable him to substitute for his status as a national of a belligerent State that of a national of a neutral State, with the sole aim of thus coming within the protection of Liechtenstein but not of becoming wedded to its traditions, its interests, its way of life or of assuming the obligations—other than fiscal obligations— and exercising the rights pertaining to the status thus acquired.

Guatemala is under no obligation to recognize a nationality granted in such circumstances. Liechtenstein consequently is not entitled to extend its protection to Nottebohm vis-à-vis Guatemala and its claim must, for this reason, be held to be inadmissible.

The Court is not therefore called upon to deal with the other pleas in bar put forward by Guatemala or the Conclusions of the Parties other than those on which it is adjudicating in accordance with the reasons indicated above. For these reasons, The COURT, by eleven votes to three, Holds that the claim submitted by the Government of the Principality of Liechtenstein is inadmissible. * * * [Dissenting opinions omitted.]

---

1. ***Earlier adjudication in the Permanent Court of International Justice.*** In its *Advisory Opinion on Nationality Decrees in Tunis and Morocco* (France and Great Britain), 1923, P.C.I.J., Ser. B, No. 4, the court was asked whether a dispute between France and Great Britain as to nationality decrees in Tunis and Morocco was or was not, by international law, solely a matter of domestic jurisdiction under Article 15, paragraph 8, of the Covenant of the League of Nations. Apparently on the ground that the relations between France and Great Britain and their protectorates were determined by international agreements and that "it will be necessary to resort to international law in order to decide what the value of an agreement of this kind may be as regards third States," the court expressed the opinion that the dispute was not, by international law, solely a matter of domestic jurisdiction. But for the existence of the agreements, however, the court presumably would not have taken jurisdiction: "The question whether a certain matter is or is not solely within the jurisdiction of a State is an essentially relative question; it depends upon the development of international relations. Thus, in the present state of international law, questions of nationality are, in the opinion of the Court, in principle within this reserved domain."

2. ***How far does Nottebohm reach?*** Liechtenstein's claim was asserted against a state, Guatemala, with which Nottebohm had, in the language of the court, "a long-standing and close connection," "a link which his naturalization in no way weakened."

a. Nottebohm had been sent by Guatemala to the United States for internment during World War II. Suppose that the United States had injured Nottebohm by seizing and retaining, without compensation, property he had removed to a bank in the United States. Liechtenstein now brings an action against the United States in the International Court of Justice; the United States asks the court to declare the claim inadmissible on the grounds that Liechtenstein has no standing. *How should the court rule? See Flegenheimer Case,* 14 Rep. of Int'l Arb. Awards 327 (Italian–United States Conciliation Commission, 1958).

b. Refer to the *Hanna case,* pp. 673. Suppose that Hanna has resided in Canada for a period of twenty years, is married there, raises a family and conducts a business. As a result of the international operation of his business, he accumulates large sums of money in a bank in State X. State X expropriates his bank account without compensation. Although he has not been declared a national by Canada, Canada espouses his claim against State X and eventually brings an action against State X in the International Court of Justice. State X asks the court to declare the claim inadmissible on the ground that Hanna is not Canada's national. How should the court rule?

If Canada has in fact accorded Hanna its protection domestically over the years, and if in fact he has established a close link or tie with Canada, with its acquiescence, is the formal grant of nationality by Canada necessary? See Leigh, Nationality and Diplomatic Protection, 20 Int'l. & Comp.L.Q. 453 (1971). What interest does State X have in Canada's according Hanna formal nationality?

c. If a stateless person is able to persuade *any* state to espouse his claim against a wrongdoing state with which he has previously had no link, why should that state not be permitted to claim on his behalf in the court?

3. *Continuity of nationality of individual claimant.*

a. Oppenheim: A State which puts forward a claim before a claims commission or other international tribunal must be in a position to show that it has locus standi for that purpose. The principal, and almost the exclusive, factor creating that locus standi is the nationality of the claimant, and it may be stated as a general principle that from the time of the occurrence of the injury until the making of the award the claim must continuously and without interruption have belonged to a person or to a series of persons (a) having the nationality of the State by whom it is put forward, and (b) not having the nationality of the State against whom it is put forward. International Law 347 (8th ed. 1955) (Vol. I).

b. Judge Van Eysinga: Those who maintain that this is a hard and fast rule rely mainly on the jurisprudence of the Claims Commissions (Mixed Commissions) * * *. The Mixed Commissions are set up by treaty when, especially after stormy events such as a revolution or civil war, a great number of the nationals of both parties to the treaty have suffered injury. A desire to liquidate all these claims leads the two parties to refer them by treaty to a commission set up especially to deal with them. Accordingly the commission is a special tribunal for certain groups of the nationals of both sides, and it is obvious that such treaties have in view only the nationals of the two parties who have suffered injury but not non-nationals, who may be in the same situation and who, in order to take advantage of the existence of the commission, get themselves naturalized, or nationals who may have brought the claims of non-nationals. In the domain of treaties setting up Mixed Commissions, the rule relied on by the Lithuanian Agent is perfectly comprehensible and perhaps in this sphere it is possible to speak of a rule of international law in the sense that, in the absence of a definite treaty provision, it must be observed by the Mixed Commissions. *Panevezys–Saldutiskis Railway Case* (Estonia v. Lithuania), 1939, P.C.I.J., Ser. A/B, No. 76, at 33.

c. Schwarzenberger and Brown: International judicial practice interprets this test so strictly as to demand the continuity of nationality from the time of the injury (dies a quo) until the date of judgment (dies ad quem). If the ratio legis behind the rule on the continuity of nationality were protection of the individual, the hardships resulting from this rule would lay it open to serious objections. For instance, if, before the award is delivered, the claimant dies and his heirs have a different nationality, the claim lapses. Actually, the rule serves a completely different purpose. It is to limit intervention in the domestic affairs of other States even if, in marginal cases, this object can be attained only at the price of considerable hardship to the individual. A Manual of International Law 143 (6th ed. 1976).

MERGÉ CASE

Italian–United States Conciliation Commission, 1955.
14 U.N.Rep.Int'l Arb.Awards 236.

The Facts: On October 26, 1948, the Embassy of the United States in Rome submitted to the Ministry of the Treasury of the Italian Republic on behalf of Mrs. Florence Mergé, a national of the United States, a claim based upon Article 78 of the Treaty of Peace with Italy for compensation for the loss as a result of the war of a grand piano and other personal property located at Frascati, Italy, and owned by Mrs. Mergé.

As the Italian Ministry of the Treasury had rejected the claim on the grounds that Mrs. Mergé is to be deemed, under Italian law, an Italian national by marriage, the U.N. submitted to this Commission the dispute which had arisen between the two Governments with respect to the claim. * * *

        * * *

The following facts relating to the two nationalities, Italian and United States, possessed by Mrs. Mergé are revealed by the record: Florence was born in New York City on April 7, 1909, thereby acquiring United States nationality according to the law of the United States. On December 21, 1933, at the age of 24, Florence Strunsky married Salvatore Mergé in Rome, Italy. As Mr. Mergé is an Italian national, Florence Strunsky acquired Italian nationality by operation of Italian law.

The United States Department of State issued a passport to Mrs. Mergé, then Miss Strunsky, on March 17, 1931. This passport was renewed on July 11, 1933, to be valid until March 16, 1935. Mrs. Mergé lived with her husband in Italy during the four years following her marriage until 1937. Her husband was an employee of the Italian Government, working as an interpreter and translator of the Japanese language in the Ministry of Communications. In 1937 he was sent to the Italian Embassy at Tokyo as a translator and interpreter.

Mrs. Mergé accompanied her husband to Tokyo, travelling on Italian passport No. 681688, issued on August 27, 1937 by the Ministry of Foreign Affairs in Rome. The passport was of the type issued by the Italian Government to employees and their families bound for foreign posts. After her arrival in Japan, Mrs. Mergé on February 21, 1940 was registered, at her request, as a national of the United States at the American Consulate General at Tokyo.

Mrs. Mergé states that, when hostilities ceased between Japan and the United States of America, she refused to be returned to the United States by the United States military authorities, having preferred to remain with her husband.

On December 10, 1946, the American Consulate at Yokohama issued an American passport to Mrs. Mergé, valid only for travel to the United States, with which she travelled to the United States. She remained in the United States for nine months, from December, 1946, until September, 1947. The American passport issued to her at Yokohama and valid originally only for travel to the United States, was validated for travel to Italy, and the Italian Consulate General at New York, on July 31, 1947, granted Mrs. Mergé a visa for Italy as a visitor, valid for three months.

On September 19, 1947, Mrs. Mergé arrived in Italy where she has since resided with her husband. Immediately after returning to Italy, on October 8, 1947, Mrs. Mergé registered as a United States national at the Consular Section of the American Embassy in Rome. On October 16, 1947, Mrs. Mergé executed an affidavit before an American consular officer at the American Embassy in Rome for the purpose of explaining her protracted residence outside of the United States. In that affidavit she lists her mother and father as her only ties with the United States, and states that she does not pay income taxes to the Government of the United States. On September 11, 1950, Mrs. Mergé requested and was granted by the Consular Section of the American Embassy at Rome a new American passport to replace the one which had been issued to her on December 10, 1946, by the American Consulate at Yokohama and which had expired. In her application for the new American passport, Mrs. Mergé states that her "legal residence" is at New York, and that she intends to return to the United States to reside permanently at some indefinite time in the future.

So far as the record indicates, Mrs. Mergé is still residing with her husband in Italy.

The Issue: It is not disputed between the Parties that the claimant possesses both nationalities. The issue is not one of choosing one of the two, but rather one of deciding whether in such case the Government of the United States may exercise before the Conciliation Commission the rights granted by the Treaty of Peace with reference to the property in Italy of United Nations nationals (Articles 78 and 83).

(1). Position of the Government of the United States of America:

(a) The Treaty of Peace between the United Nations and Italy provides the rules necessary to a solution of the case. The first subparagraph of paragraph 9(a) of Article 78 states:

> "United Nations nationals" means individuals who are nationals of any of the United Nations, or corporations or associations organized under the laws of any of the United Nations, at the coming into force of the present Treaty, provided that the said

individuals, corporations or associations also had this status on September 3, 1943, the date of the Armistice with Italy.

All United Nations nationals are therefore entitled to claim, and it is irrelevant for such purpose that they possess or have possessed Italian nationality as well.

* * *

(c) The principle, according to which one State cannot afford diplomatic protection to one of its nationals against a State whose nationality such person also possesses, cannot be applied to the Treaty of Peace with Italy because such principle is based on the equal sovereignty of States, whereas this Treaty of Peace was not negotiated between equal Powers but between the United Nations and Italy, a State defeated and obliged to accept the clauses imposed by the victors who at that time did not consider Italy a sovereign State.

(2).   Position of the Italian Government:

* * *

(b) A defeated State, even when it is obliged to undergo the imposition of the conqueror, continues to be a sovereign State.   From the juridical point of view, the Treaty of Peace is an international convention, not a unilateral act.   In cases of doubt, its interpretation must be that more favourable to the debtor.

(c) There exists a principle of international law, universally recognized and constantly applied, by virtue of which diplomatic protection cannot be exercised in cases of dual nationality when the claimant possesses also the nationality of the State against which the claim is being made.

* * *

Considerations of law: (1).   The rules of the Hague Convention of 1930 and the customary law manifested in international precedents and in the legal writings of the authors attest the existence and the practice of two principles in the problem of diplomatic protection in dual nationality cases.

The first of these, specifically referring to the scope of diplomatic protection, as a question of public international law, is based on the sovereign equality of the States in the matter of nationality and bars protection in behalf of those who are simultaneously also nationals of the defendant State.

The second of the principles had its origin in *private* international law, in those cases, that is, in which the courts of a third State had to resolve a conflict of nationality Laws.   Thus, the principle of effective nationality was created with relation to the individual.   But decisions and legal writings, because of its evident justice, quickly transported it to the sphere of *public* international law.

(2). It is not a question of adopting one nationality to the exclusion of the other. Even less when it is recognized by both Parties that the claimant possesses the two nationalities. The problem to be explained is, simply, that of determining whether diplomatic protection can be exercised in such cases.

(3). A prior question requires a solution: are the two principles which have just been set forth incompatible with each other, so that the acceptance of one of them necessarily implies the exclusion of the other? If the reply is in the affirmative, the problem presented is that of a choice; if it is in the negative, one must determine the sphere of application of each one of the two principles.

The Commission is of the opinion that no irreconcilable opposition between the two principles exists; in fact, to the contrary, it believes that they complement each other reciprocally. The principle according to which a State cannot protect one of its nationals against a State which also considers him its national and the principle of effective, in the sense of dominant, nationality, have both been accepted by the Hague Convention (Articles 4 and 5) and by the International Court of Justice (Advisory Opinion of April 11, 1949 and the Nottebohm Decision of April 6, 1955). If these two principles were irreconcilable, the acceptance of both by the Hague Convention and by the International Court of Justice would be incomprehensible.

(4). The International Court of Justice, in its recent decision in the Nottebohm Case, after having said that " * * * international law leaves to each State to lay down the rules governing the grant of its own nationality", adds: "On the other hand, a State cannot claim that the rules it has thus laid down are entitled to recognition by another State unless it has acted in conformity with this general aim of making the legal bond of nationality accord with the individual's genuine connexion with the State which assumes the defence of its citizens by means of protection as against other States. * * * Conferred by a State, it only entitles that State to exercise protection vis-à-vis another State, if it constitutes a translation into juridical terms of the individual's connexion with the State which has made him its national."

For even greater reason, this theory must be understood to be applicable to the problem of dual nationality which concerns the two contesting States, in view of the fact that in such case effective nationality does not mean only the existence of a real bond, but means also the prevalence of that nationality over the other, by virtue of facts which exist in the case.

(5). The principle, based on the sovereign equality of States, which excludes diplomatic protection in the case of dual nationality, must yield before the principle of effective nationality whenever such nationality is that of the claiming State. But it must not yield when such predominance is not proved because the first of these two principles is generally recognized and may constitute a criterion of practical application for the elimination of any possible uncertainty.

(6).   * * * In view of the principles accepted, it is considered that the Government of the United States of America shall be entitled to protect its nationals before this Commission in cases of dual nationality, United States and Italian, whenever the United States nationality is the effective nationality.   To establish the prevalence of the United States nationality in individual cases, habitual residence can be one of the criteria of evaluation, but not the only one.   The conduct of the individual in his economic, social, political, civic and family life, as well as the closer and more effective bond with one of the two States must also be considered.

(7).   It is considered that in this connexion the following principles may serve as guides:

(a) The United States nationality shall be prevalent in cases of children born in the United States of an Italian father and who have habitually lived there.

(b) The United States nationality shall also be prevalent in cases involving Italians who, after having acquired United States nationality by naturalization and having thus lost Italian nationality, have reacquired their nationality of origin as a matter of law as a result of having sojourned in Italy for more than two years, without the intention of retransferring their residence permanently to Italy.

(c) With respect to cases of dual nationality involving American women married to Italian nationals, the United States nationality shall be prevalent in cases in which the family has had habitual residence in the United States and the interests and the permanent professional life of the head of the family were established in the United States.

(d) In case of dissolution of marriage, if the family was established in Italy and the widow transfers her residence to the United States of America, whether or not the new residence is of an habitual nature must be evaluated, case by case, bearing in mind also the widow's conduct, especially with regard to the raising of her children, for the purpose of deciding which is the prevalent nationality.

(8).   United States nationals who did not possess Italian nationality but the nationality of a third State can be considered "United Nations nationals" under the Treaty, even if their prevalent nationality was the nationality of the third State.

(9).   In all other cases of dual nationality, Italian and United States, when, that is, the United States nationality is not prevalent in accordance with the above, the principle of international law, according to which a claim is not admissible against a State, Italy in our case, when this State also considers the claimant as its national and such bestowal of nationality is, as in the case of Italian law, in harmony (Article 1 of the Hague Convention of 1930) with international custom and generally recognized principles of law in the matter of nationality, will reacquire its force.

Decision: Examining the facts of the case in bar, in the light of the aforementioned criteria, especially paragraph 6, in relation to paragraph 7(c), the Commission holds that Mrs. Mergé can in no way be considered to be dominantly a United States national within the meaning of Article 78 of the Treaty of Peace, because the family did not have its habitual residence in the United States and the interests and the permanent professional life of the head of the family were not established there. In fact, Mrs. Mergé has not lived in the United States since her marriage, she used an Italian passport in travelling to Japan from Italy in 1937, she stayed in Japan from 1937 until 1946 with her husband, an official of the Italian Embassy in Tokyo, and it does not appear that she was ever interned as a national of a country enemy to Japan.

Inasmuch as Mrs. Mergé, for the foregoing reasons, cannot be considered to be dominantly a United States national within the meaning of Article 78 of the Treaty of Peace, the Commission is of the opinion that the Government of the United States of America is not entitled to present a claim against the Italian Government in her behalf.

* * *

———

1. *Limiting the applicability of the principle of effective nationality.* Number (8) of the commission's Considerations of Law was further amplified in its 1958 decision in the *Flegenheimer Case,* supra. Flegenheimer's claim (for cancellation of a sale of stock made under duress) depended upon his being a United States national. The commission found that he had lost his United States nationality upon acquiring German nationality in 1894 (and that this German nationality had been lost in 1940, so that he became stateless). Therefore, the claim was dismissed.

It had been argued by Italy, however, that because of close ties between Flegenheimer and Germany during the long period from 1894 until 1940 when he was a German national, "Italy therefore considers that no effective bond of nationality exists between the United States and Albert Flegenheimer, even if it were to be admitted that he was an American national on purely legal and nominal grounds." Thus, "the United States is not entitled to exercise, in his behalf, the right of diplomatic protection, nor can they resort to the Commission to plead his case." (at 375) The commission's opinion further stated:

"The Commission is of the opinion that it is doubtful that the International Court of Justice intended to establish a rule of general international law in requiring, in the Nottebohm Case, that there must exist an effective link between the person and the State in order that the latter may exercise its right of diplomatic protection in behalf of the former. * * *

* * *

The theory of effective or active nationality was established, in the Law of Nations, and above all in international private law, for the purpose of settling conflicts between two national States, or two national laws, regarding persons simultaneously vested with both nationalities, in order to decide which of them is to be dominant, whether that described as nominal, based on legal provisions of a given legal system, or that described as effective or active,[a] equally based on legal provisions of another legal system, but confirmed by elements of fact (domicile, participation in the political life, the center of family and business interests, etc.). It must allow one to make a distinction, between two bonds of nationality equally founded in law, which is the stronger and hence the effective one.

* * *

But when a person is vested with only one nationality, which is attributed to him or her either jure sanguinis or jure soli, or by a valid naturalization entailing the positive loss of the former nationality, the theory of effective nationality cannot be applied without the risk of causing confusion. It lacks a sufficiently positive basis to be applied to a nationality which finds support in a state law. There does not in fact exist any criterion of proven effectiveness for disclosing the effectiveness of a bond with a political collectivity, and the persons by the thousands who, because of the facility of travel in the modern world, possess the positive legal nationality of a State, but live in foreign States where they are domiciled and where their family and business center is located, would be exposed to nonrecognition, at the international level, of the nationality with which they are undeniably vested by virtue of the laws of their national State, if this doctrine were to be generalized. (at 376–377)."

PROTECTION AND ALLEGIANCE: INDIVIDUALS IN THE INTERNATIONAL LEGAL SYSTEM

1. *Nationality of corporations*. Chapter 15–B deals in some detail with the standing of states to assert diplomatic protection as to corporations. The decision of the International Court of Justice in the *Barcelona Traction Case* (1970) is excerpted there. Its basic holding is that a corporation may be protected diplomatically only by the state in which it is incorporated. Belgium lost the case, brought against Spain on behalf of the Belgian shareholders, because the corporation was chartered in Canada, and thus had the nationality of that country. This is the prevailing rule; *see* 1987 Restatement § 213, especially Reporters' Notes 1–9. Civil law countries have been said to ascribe nationality on the basis of the locus of corporate activity (*siège social*), but the Restatement takes the position that this is an additional, not a different,

---

a. See, e.g., Uzan and Sultan v. Minis-   is, 1967, 48 Int'l L.Rep. 162 (1975).
tère Public, France, Court of Appeal of Par-

requirement; see Reporters' Note 6. What does this mean? What if a corporation organized in Canada has its *siège social* in France? American corporation law tends to permit "piercing the veil" between a corporation and its shareholders when the court finds police-power public interest. Would this make a difference? Transnational and international decisions do not seem to have accepted this practice, except as to antitrust actions under European Community law. At a time when the United Kingdom was not a community member, *Imperial Chemicals Industries, Ltd.*, a British parent corporation, was held subject to (then) EEC (now EC) prosecution as a member of the dye-stuffs cartel, because it was "present" within the EEC through subsidiaries. See, *Imperial Chemical Industries Ltd. v. Commission,* Case, 11 Com.Mkt.L.R. 557 (1972). Would the then EEC countries have accepted a British claim to assert diplomatic protection as to ICI on the "present-through-subsidiary" principle, if the subsidiary, but not ICI, had a *siège social* in an EEC country? What if the subsidiary, organized in an EEC country were entirely managed from London? Britain is now in the E.V. so the hypothetical will have to be shifted to say, Norway?

2. ***Effective nationality in the Iran–United States Claims Tribunal.*** The tribunal adopted the principle of effective nationality in Case No. A/18 Concerning the Question of Jurisdiction Over Claims of Persons with Dual Nationality, 23 I.L.M. 489 (1984). The tribunal rested its decision principally on the *Nottebohm* and *Mergé* cases, declining to apply Article 4 of the 1930 Hague Convention Concerning Certain Questions Relating to the Conflict of Nationality Laws. Article 4 of the convention provides: "A State may not afford diplomatic protection to one of its nationals against a State whose nationality such person also possesses." The tribunal rejected the Hague Convention rule for two reasons: (1) the Iran–United States Claims Tribunal deals principally with claims by persons against states and not with diplomatic protection in the normal sense (i.e., claims by states against states), and (2) the tribunal doubted that the Hague Convention states a currently recognized rule (even of the international law of diplomatic protection), in view of its age, its limited number of states parties, and the changes and expansion in the concept of diplomatic protection since the conclusion of the convention. The Iranian members dissented from the tribunal's opinion.

4. ***Protection:*** The recent U.S. Supreme Court decision in *Alvarez–Machain,* makes it more difficult for the United States Government to fulfill its obligation to protect its own nationals. One of the dangers of that decision, in addition to the general erosion of the rule of law around the world and negative impact of mocking international law, as signalled by Justice Stevens in his dissent, U.S. nationals have probably become more vulnerable when they travel abroad. No doubt, neither Mexico, nor other nations are going to attack the United States for such violations of their sovereignty, but radical groups may feel more justified in committing terrorist acts against American interests both in the U.S. and abroad. What legal leg do U.S. officials have to stand on when an American is abducted to be "prosecuted?" The decision eroded the basis for diplomatic/legal protest. Moreover, the experience of our hostages in

Lebanon suggests that the U.S. Government will not attack another nation to free hostages. That option probably was never significant, and, certainly from the perspective of self defense in international law, ought not to be. Thus, the most serious basis of protecting nationals abroad, deterring abductions (which we call kidnapping or terroristic hostage taking when others do it), and promoting amelioration of their situation, once taken captive, has been eviscerated by our own Supreme Court. *See,* Christopher L. Blakesley, Terrorism, Drugs, International Law and the Protection of Human Liberty 276–79 (1992); Note, Hostages' Rights: The Unhappy Legal Predicament of an American Held in Foreign Captivity, 26 Colum.J.L. & Soc.Probs. 555 (1993).

The Iran–U.S. Claims Settlement Tribunal is said to be " * * * the most significant arbitral body in history * * * ". See, Caron, The Nature of the Iran–United States Claims Tribunal and the Evolving Structure of International Dispute Resolution, 84 Am.J. of Int'l Law 104 (1990). It was created in 1981 as an element of the release of the American hostages held by Iran at the United States Embassy in Teheran. The Tribunal sits at the Hague, applies Netherlands law and has disposed of about 4,000 cases involving claims arising out of commercial contracts, business investments, and other private sector economic activities. The provisions of the agreement to arbitrate make it clear that private claims are to be asserted by the claimant, on a nationality basis, not by the state of nationality as a diplomatic protection claim by it against the other state. Professor Caron reports, however, that in several instances Iran has asserted defenses (such as the requirement of exhaustion of other remedies prior to claiming before the Tribunal) that are pertinent only to classic diplomatic protection. The Tribunal has not agreed with the Iranian position in such instances. Successful American claimants are paid out of blocked Iranian assets through Algeria as "escrow agent," and the award earns the United States a service charge in some circumstances. This contrasts with state-to-state espousal of claims by the United States, where there are no such charges.

Is old fashioned diplomatic protection passé? Not quite or not yet. But other means are more and more available and used, including arbitration clauses between the foreign investor and the host state in contractual arrangements for entry to do business in the host state. See Chapter 15–B.

CHOSEN DUAL NATIONALITY AND U.S. CITIZENSHIP

It should be noted that the various provisions of the Immigration and Nationality Act governing loss of U.S. citizenship apply to all U.S. citizens equally, regardless of whether the individual acquired citizenship at birth or subsequently by virtue of naturalization. The Supreme Court has stated that there cannot be two classes of U.S. citizens based upon how that citizenship was attained. *Schneider v. Rusk,* 377 U.S. 163 (1964).

Section 349(a)(4) of the Immigration and Nationality Act pertains to potential loss of nationality as a consequence of acceptance of high political office in foreign governments. That subsection provides that a person who is a national of the United States risks loss of U.S. citizenship if he/she accepts employment with a foreign government *and* either (1) has the nationality of that foreign state or (2) the employment requires an oath or declaration of allegiance. However, even assuming that a person's actions are encompassed by Section 349(a)(4), his intent toward retaining U.S. citizenship is still relevant. Thus, in addition to committing one of the acts defined in INA 349(a)(4) as potentially expatriating, loss of U.S. citizenship cannot occur unless and until it is determined that the individual acted voluntarily and intended to relinquish his citizenship.

Intent to relinquish citizenship was the focus of *Kahane v. Shultz*, 653 F.Supp. 1486 (E.D.N.Y.1987). The *Kahane* court held that a declaration of intent to retain citizenship is sufficient to retain it, even when made simultaneously with the commission of an act made potentially expatriating by statute. Once acquired, citizenship can not be diluted or canceled at the will of the federal government. *Afroyim v. Rusk, supra.*

It has not been established that the act of serving as Prime Minister of a foreign country is necessarily inconsistent with and would automatically deprive the actor of U.S. citizenship. It is worth noting that every citizenship case is judged solely on its merits and decided on a case-by-case basis.

Dual nationals are required to use their U.S. passport when entering or leaving the United States by Section 215 INA. While dual nationals may be required to use their non-U.S. passport when entering or leaving the country of issuance, the Department of State recommends that dual nationals use their U.S. passport for travel to other countries. For purposes of consular protection, the Department generally does not distinguish between dual nationals and other U.S. citizens. The assistance which can be provided to persons while in the country of their other nationality, however, is necessarily limited.

SECTION C.   OBLIGATIONS OF NATIONALITY OR ALLEGIANCE

It is not uncommon for a state to apply its law to acts performed by its own nationals beyond its territorial limits. As stated by Chief Justice Hughes in *Blackmer v. United States* [*supra*],

> While it appears that the petitioner removed his residence to France in the year 1924, it is undisputed that he was, and continued to be, a citizen of the United States. He continued to owe allegiance to the United States. By virtue of the obligations of citizenship, the United States retained its authority over him, and he was bound by its laws made applicable to him in a foreign country. Thus although resident abroad, the petitioner remained subject to the taxing power of the United States. For disobedience to its laws through conduct abroad he was subject to punishment in the courts of the United

States * * *. With respect to such an exercise of authority, there is no question of international law, but solely of the purport of the municipal law which establishes the duties of the citizen in relation to his own government. * * *

The basis for the rule permitting this reach of a state's law was the subject of speculation by the Mexican Supreme Court in a case involving jurisdiction over an offense committed by a Mexican national in Texas:

> It is well known that it is the federal judge who has jurisdiction notwithstanding that it is the principle of territoriality which fundamentally regulates the special application of the penal law in accordance with Article 4 of the Federal Criminal Code, even though this precept, in its first hypothesis—a crime committed abroad by a Mexican national—admits the principle of personal law. This is so because of the respect due * * * to the ties of allegiance which should bind the subject to his State, or because it is not possible to conceive that a State should be transformed into a safe refuge for its own nationals who have committed crimes outside its frontiers, or because the rule of prosecution is merely a just corollary to the nonextradition of nationals, which is the practice of the majority of countries. *Re Gutierrez,* 24 Int'l L.Rep. 265, 266 (1961).

For discussion of nationality and crime, including extraditions, see Chapter 3. Should the reach of a state's laws based upon the relationship of the individual with the state be confined to those who have the state's nationality? The question is posed below in connection with laws relating to (a) the crime of treason, (b) taxation and (c) compulsory military service.

---

1.   THE CRIME OF TREASON

D'AQUINO v. UNITED STATES

United States Court of Appeals, Ninth Circuit, 1951.
192 F.2d 338.

POPE, Circuit Judge.

Appellant was convicted of treason against the United States. The indictment charged that she adhered to the enemies of the United States giving them aid and comfort by working as a radio speaker, announcer, script writer and broadcaster for the Imperial Japanese Government and the Broadcasting Corporation of Japan, between November 1, 1943, and August 13, 1945; that such activities were in connection with the broadcasting of programs specially beamed and directed to the American Armed Forces in the Pacific Ocean area; and, that appellant's activities were intended to destroy the confidence of the members of the Armed Forces of the United States and their allies in the war effort, to undermine and lower American and Allied military morale, to create nostalgia in their minds, to create war weariness among the members of such armed forces, to discourage them, and to impair the capacity of the United States to wage war against its enemies. The indictment alleged the commission of eight overt acts. Appellant (Tokyo Rose) was found guilty of the commission of overt act No. 6 only, which in the language of the indictment, was: "That on a day during October, 1944, the exact date being to the Grand Jurors unknown, said defendant, at Tokyo, Japan, in a broadcasting studio of the Broadcasting Corporation of Japan, did speak into a microphone concerning the loss of ships."

* * *

Appellant's contentions fall into two categories: the first, call for a judgment that the defendant-appellant must be discharged; the second relate to alleged errors which would require a new trial.

1. Whether the applicable clause of the Act relating to treason was unconstitutional as applied to appellant.

Appellant contends that those provisions of the treason statute, 18 U.S.C.A. § 1, 1946 under which she was convicted were void and wanting in due process under the Fifth Amendment by reason of the co-existence of those provisions of the Nationality Act of 1940, 8 U.S.C.A. § 501 et seq., which repealed the former expressed prohibition against expatriation in time of war. In consequence of this, says appellant, the law provided that a person in like position as appellant, might lawfully have been naturalized to an enemy belligerent, and that under the Government's naturalization policy the appellant could, as many other persons of Japanese ancestry did, have transferred allegiance to Japan.
* * *

We are unable to perceive any sound basis for such an argument. The reference to licensed and unlicensed adherence to the enemy is, we think, but a play on words. The classification here, of which appellant complains, is none other than the ancient distinction drawn between those who do and those who do not owe allegiance.[2]

Whether the provisions of the Nationality Act which appellant thinks work unfairly represent a wise or sound legislative policy is a problem for Congress, not for us. We are unable to observe anything unreasonable or arbitrary about preserving the ancient distinction between those who do and those who do not owe allegiance regardless of whether the transfer of allegiance could be made in wartime or not. Reasons both historical and logical exist for the distinction and we find no want of due process here. Since we find no prejudicial error in the record the judgment is affirmed.

---

2. TAXATION

NATIONALITY AS A BASIS OF JURISDICTION TO TAX

There are so many bases upon which taxes of various kinds may be levied that nationality, although one such base, does not loom large.

---

2. Title 18, § 1, Criminal Code, (1946 Ed.): "Whoever, owing allegiance to the United States, levies war against them or adheres to their enemies, giving them aid and comfort within the United States or elsewhere, is guilty of treason."

Technically, a state would not be impeded by international law to demand, on a fair treatment basis, all that its national might have, anywhere. But, fortunately, that is not a normal state practice. In the world as it is, domicile or residence probably gather more revenue than citizenship. And dual nationals could be double-taxed, but are not. See, generally, the 1987 Restatement, §§ 411 and 412.

* * *

DI PORTANOVA v. UNITED STATES

United States Court of Claims, 1982.
690 F.2d 169.

* * *

The government argues further that one of the principal purposes of the plaintiff's renunciation of his United States citizenship was the avoidance of taxes—a fact that under section 877(a) of the Code would bar him from obtaining the 30 percent tax rate and would subject his trust income to the regular graduated rates. The government seeks a trial on the tax avoidance issue. * * *

* * *

* * * The case is remanded to the Trial Division to determine whether a principal purpose of the plaintiff's renunciation of his United States citizenship was the avoidance of taxes * * *.

Basis of taxation of aliens. As noted international law has recognizes a number of bases for the imposition of taxes. Here as elsewhere it is essential to distinguish between a state's jurisdiction to prescribe a rule imposing a tax and its jurisdiction to enforce such a rule. The practical difficulties of enforcing taxes upon persons not physically within its territory and not owning property within its territory realistically limit the voraciousness of the tax collecting state. International controversy as to jurisdiction to tax has been relatively infrequent. Consequently the principal evidence of the international law on the subject is state practice.

The territorial base supports state taxation measured by property located and income produced within the state. States impose such taxes on the individuals owning such property, or producing or claiming such income, even though the individuals do not have a personal relationship with the taxing state such as that of nationality. At the other extreme, as in the Rexach case, states impose taxes upon their own nationals, even though the nationals are physically located outside the state and their property is located and income produced outside the state.

Will international law permit taxation measured by property located outside the state or income produced outside the state when the individual to be taxed is not its national? The United States imposes income tax upon aliens who are resident within the United States. The resident alien is taxed, in general, the same as a citizen, i.e., on worldwide income. 26 U.S.C. § 7701(b) includes in its definition of resident alien a substantial presence test, involving a strict calculation of numbers of days of presence in the United States. Consider the following general definition of residence:

> It appears that most governments consider that an alien who remains in its territory for a certain period of time, six months or more, is resident in such territory for purposes of income taxation. Asst. Sec. of State Macomber to U.S. Senator Carl Hayden, letter quoted in 8 Whiteman, Digest of International Law 536 (1967).

If, then, nationality is not a necessary prerequisite to taxability, is there some minimum personal connection that must exist before a state can lawfully prescribe a tax based on events that occur outside the state? What should that connection be? Could a state lawfully tax a mere transient or sojourner? What would be a lawful measure of such a tax? "On the one hand it is agreed that a State cannot tax a transient on the whole of his year's income as if he were a resident but on the other it is equally agreed that his presence may render him subject to poll tax, and sojourn tax, which, indeed, could be of an equivalent amount."

Taxation of corporations: the problem of the unitary tax. Corporations may also be accorded a nationality for a variety of purposes, including taxation. United States practice is to recognize the place of incorporation as the basis for determining nationality; civil law jurisdictions use the criterion of the seat of the corporation (location of the administration or principal place of business). Taxation of the worldwide income of a corporation having the nationality of the taxing state does not violate rules of international law, but the inevitable multiple taxation that results has encouraged states to negotiate tax treaties to avoid such overlapping jurisdiction.

Taxation of a wholly foreign corporation that has no connection with the taxing state would clearly violate international law (aside from the obvious legal and practical problems of enforcement of such a law). Taxation of a non-national or non-resident corporation with respect to income that has its source in the taxing state would not, however, be a violation of international legal principles. Calculation of the income that has its source in the taxing state poses problems with respect to multinational enterprises that typically consist of a parent company (or other controlling mechanism) with subsidiaries in a variety of countries.

A system of taxation employed by California and a number of other states in the United States has created international controversy. The unitary tax system used by those states has the potential for taxing some income of non-national and non-resident corporations that does not have its source in the taxing state. Under the unitary tax system, the worldwide income of a multinational enterprise doing business through one of its segments in the taxing state is first calculated. An arbitrary formula is then applied to determine the portion of that income that may be considered as having its source in the taxing state (e.g., the proportion that the sales prices, property values and wage rates of the enterprise in the taxing state bear to those items in the worldwide unit). Since, for example, wage rates in the taxing state may be substantially higher than in other states in which the multinational unit does business, the income attributable under the formula to the taxing state may be artificially higher than it is in fact. In essence, the taxing state would be taxing, in part, foreign income of a non-resident alien corporation.

Although the unitary tax system was held by the United States Supreme Court not to be unconstitutional, at least as regarded a multinational enterprise whose parent was a United States national (Container Corporation of America v. Franchise Tax Board, 463 U.S. 159 (1983), the question of its constitutionality (particularly with respect to foreign affairs) when applied to an enterprise whose parent is a foreign national remains in question. [See brief] that the unitary system conflicts with federal policy and with the international standard of separate accounting (the so-called arm's length adjustment method) employed by the United States in its bilateral tax treaties. Foreign states have protested the imposition of the unitary tax. In particular, the United Kingdom enacted defensive, retaliatory legislation. See Born, Recent British References to the Extraterritorial Application of United States Law: The Midland Bank Decision and Retaliatory Legislation Involving Unitary Taxation, 26 Virginia Journal of International Law 91 (1985). In addition to opposing the unitary tax in litigation, the federal administration proposed legislation to prohibit states from taxing on the basis of the unitary system.

Active opposition to the unitary system relaxed when California, a leading state in the use of that system, amended its law in 1986. The amendment allows a corporation to elect to include in its tax return only so-called "water's edge" affiliates (in effect, affiliates with substantial contacts within the United States). The administration is not pushing its proposed legislation. The British government has stated that, in view of developments in resolving the unitary tax problem, it will not apply its retaliatory legislation against United States companies. See 33 Tax Notes 1096 (1986).

Treaties Eliminating Double Taxation. There are numerous such treaties, usually between developed countries. The treaties deal with situations where two or more states have jurisdiction to prescribe (assess) taxes, in which the treaty parties agree to allocate exclusive jurisdiction, from situation to situation, to one or the other of them. Transnational tax law is an important aspect of a highly-developed speciality; see Chapter 15.

3. COMPULSORY MILITARY SERVICE
AND OTHER POSSIBLE DUTIES

UNITED STATES v. RUMSA

United States Court of Appeals, Seventh Circuit, 1954.
212 F.2d 927

SWAIM, Circuit Judge. This opinion disposes of two appeals by
Antanas Juratis Rumsa, the first being an appeal in a criminal case and
the second being an appeal from the order and judgment of the District
Court dismissing Rumsa's amended complaint in an action to enjoin the
defendants from inducting and causing him to be inducted and for a
declaratory judgment.

* * *

We consider the appeal of Rumsa from the judgment of the District
Court entered on a verdict of guilty on an indictment which charged him
with refusing to submit to induction into the armed forces of the United
States in violation of [50 U.S.C. 462], and the prescribed rules and
regulations thereunder.

The defendant was born in Lithuania on October 9, 1929, and
resided there until sometime in 1944 when the Russians invaded that
country and the defendant was forced to flee to Western Germany. In
Germany he was placed in a labor camp and kept there until he was
finally liberated by the American forces. On February 27, 1950, the
defendant executed a printed form of Application for Immigration Visa
and Alien Registration. This form stated that the defendant's purpose
in going to the United States was "to reside" and that he intended "to
remain permanently." This form also indicated that the defendant had
had five years in elementary school and eight years in secondary school
and that he was able to speak, read and write Lithuanian and a little
English and German. The American Vice Consul approved this application and granted the immigration visa to the defendant as a displaced
person pursuant to Public Law 774. Pursuant to the authority granted
by the United States on this application, the defendant was admitted to,
and did, enter the United States on April 6, 1950, coming to Chicago,
Illinois, to live. On August 12, 1950, he registered under the Selective
Service Act with Local Board No. 65, located at 63rd Street and Western
Avenue in Chicago. A little more than a month later, September 15,
1950, the defendant filled out a Selective Service Questionnaire and on
October 9, 1950, he was classified I–A (ready for service). On January
11, 1951, the defendant was ordered by the local board to report for
physical examination on January 29, 1951.

* * *

Defendant [contends] that, since he is an alien, he cannot be
required to submit to induction into the armed forces of the United
States; that requiring him to be inducted violates international law and
also violates the Fifth Amendment to our Constitution; that, further, as
a temporary resident alien, he had the right to be deferred from military

service by waiving the right ever to become an American citizen; that by his executing and filing Form 130, he did waive his right to ever become an American citizen; and that he thereby acquired the right to be permanently classified as IV–C, a right to exemption which could not thereafter be taken away even by a change in the law by Congress.

It is true that the Selective Training and Service Act which was in effect when Rumsa came to this country and when he first registered did provide that any citizen or subject of a neutral country should be relieved from liability for training and service if, prior to his induction, he had made application to be relieved of such liability. But in 1951 the Congress, alarmed by the international situation, determined that the safety of this nation required that more men be inducted for training and service. In the Conference Report, we find the recommendation that the law should be so changed that "All aliens admitted for permanent residence in the United States shall be immediately liable for induction into the Armed Forces or the National Security Training Corps under the same conditions applicable to citizens. * * *"

There can be no question but that the Universal Military Training and Service Act as amended authorized the selection and induction of aliens who had been admitted to the United States for permanent residence. * * *

* * *

It necessarily remained within the province and was the duty of Congress to be constantly alert to impending danger, to appraise such danger, and to raise and support armies of a sufficient number of men to be able to meet the danger successfully. Signs of increasing danger in 1951 were apparent to all. This naturally called for increased numbers in the armed services. The increased numbers could be secured only by enlarging the field from which to draw. This was accomplished by certain amendments which, among other things, reduced the age at which men were eligible, reduced the physical and mental standards required for induction *and made all aliens admitted for permanent residence in the United States immediately available for induction.* No classification of any individual could be considered permanent as against changes in the law, changes in the circumstances of the individual on which the classification was made or changes in valid regulations promulgated under the changed law. To hold that a classification, once made, was binding on the Government regardless of changing conditions and amended laws to meet such changing conditions might, in effect, destroy the power of Congress to raise and support armies.

The defendant had come to the United States from Germany in 1950 with his father and mother. On August 12, 1950, he registered for Selective Service, giving the family address in Chicago as his residence. At that time he had already secured work with the National Video Corporation, and a short time later he enrolled in the Chicago Navy Pier Branch of the University of Illinois. He was a national of Lithuania and, since the Russians had taken over that country and had set up a puppet government, it was uncertain when, if ever, he might be able to return to his native land.

* * *

The conscription law which the defendant violated by refusing to submit to induction does not say that aliens who have come here intending to stay permanently shall be subject to military service; instead it says that those who are qualified for and who are *admitted* for permanent residence are to be inducted. The emphasis is therefore on the intention of the officials who approve the Application for Immigration Visa and those who consent to the alien's admission into the United States, not necessarily on the intention of the alien. With an application for a visa such as we have here before the officials whose duty it was to decide as to his admission, there cannot be much doubt but that Rumsa was *admitted* to the United States for permanent residence regardless of what his secret intention may actually have been.

* * *

Counsel for the defendant have earnestly argued to us that the conscription of aliens is extremely bad policy on the part of the United States; that prior to the enactment of the Universal Military Training and Service Act the United States and most other nations had consistently refused to draft aliens; that the new policy which Congress adopted in 1951, if followed, will in effect invite other nations to force our nationals who may be residing in those countries to submit to service in their armies; and that, therefore, none of our nationals residing abroad will be safe from conscription by those countries or from the many dangers which service in foreign armies entail.

Even if all this be true there is nothing the courts can do about it. The question of whether or not aliens should be conscripted is a question of policy—a political question which is for the executive and legislative branches of the Government to solve. Such questions are entirely outside the realm of the judicial branch. * * *

The grant of power to Congress to raise and support armies is certainly sufficient to authorize the adoption of the present policy to conscript aliens. It is, of course, also within the power of Congress to change the conscription law to again excuse aliens from service in our armed forces at any time Congress determines that the services of aliens are either unnecessary or should not as a matter of policy be required. And as to this defendant and other aliens who have been convicted of violations of the present draft law, a pardon is always within the power of the President. Neither of these courses is open to the judiciary.

Finding no error, the judgment of the District Court is affirmed.

———

1. *United States legislation on drafting aliens.* During World War I, citizens and "male persons not alien enemies who have declared their intention to become citizens" were subject to the draft. Act of May 18, 1917, ch. 15, § 2. The Selective Training and Service Act of 1940,

ch. 720, § 3(a), contained similar provisions until amended in 1941, ch. 602, § 2. This World War II amendment made liable for training and service every male citizen and every other male person "residing in the United States," with the proviso that a citizen or subject of a neutral country could apply for and be granted relief, "but any person who makes such application shall thereafter be debarred from becoming a citizen of the United States." The phrase "residing in the United States" was held in *McGrath v. Kristensen,* 340 U.S. 162 (1950), not to include a Danish citizen who entered the United States on August 17, 1939 as a temporary visitor for sixty days (to attend the New York World's Fair and visit relatives) and was prevented from returning to Denmark by the outbreak of World War II in September of that year.

The Selective Service Act of 1948, ch. 625, § 4(a), broadened the category of resident aliens able to apply for relief to include "any citizen of a foreign country," retaining the provision for debarring such an applicant from citizenship. The dramatic change in policy in the 1951 Universal Military Training and Service Act, ch. 144, § 1(d), as pointed out in the Rumsa case, was to apply the draft even-handedly to United States citizens and aliens admitted for permanent residence, with no provisions for relief. Non-resident aliens were also subject to the draft, but only if they had remained in the United States for a period exceeding one year; the provisions for application for relief (and debarring from citizenship) were retained as to those non-resident aliens. For the text of the relevant statutes referred to above in this note, see 8 Whiteman, Digest of International Law 549 (1967).

By amendments in 1971, which changed the title of the draft statute to Military Selective Service Act, a wider exclusion of aliens from the draft was provided for. The draft applied to every male citizen and "every other male person residing in the United States" 50 U.S.C.App. §§ 453 and 455(a)(1), but not to any alien lawfully admitted as a "nonimmigrant" as defined in a long list of categories in the Immigration and Nationality Act. 8 U.S.C. § 1101(a)(15).[a] In addition, induction of an alien who is draftable is not to take place until "such alien shall have resided in the United States for one year." Thus the statute applies to aliens admitted for permanent residence, who can be drafted only after a year's residence. There is no authorization for drafting any other class of aliens and no provision for application for relief or debarring from citizenship.

Notwithstanding these changes in the draft statute, the Immigration and Nationality Act continues to provide in 8 U.S.C. § 1426(a): " * * * [A]ny alien who applies or has applied for exemption or discharge from training or service in the Armed Forces * * * on the ground that he is an alien, and is or was relieved or discharged from such training * * * on such ground, shall be permanently ineligible to become a citizen of the United States." Is this provision still viable? In *Gramaglia v. United States,* 766 F.2d 88 (2d Cir.1985), § 1426(a) was held to bar from citizenship an alien who had been honorably discharged from the United

---

a. Administratively, only the registration requirements of the act are operative at the present time.

States Army at his request. His release from military service had been based upon a treaty between the United States and Italy exempting nationals of one nation from compulsory service in the armed forces of the other nation. In *McGrath v. Kristensen,* above, the provision debarring aliens from citizenship was not held to apply to the alien who had been found not to be residing in the United States: "As there was no 'liability' for service, his act in applying for relief from a nonexistent duty could not create the bar against naturalization. By the terms of the statute, that bar only comes into existence when an alien resident liable for service asks to be relieved."

2. ***International law on drafting aliens.*** " * * * On the other hand, an alien does not fall under the personal supremacy of the local State; therefore he cannot, unless his own state consents, be made to serve in its army or navy, and cannot, like a citizen, be treated according to discretion." I. Oppenheim, International Law 681 (Lauterpacht, 8th ed. 1955). Is this the law today? If a state should require military service of all persons *present* in its territory, whether resident or not and without regard to the length of time that person was present, would that state be in violation of international law? Does the state lack *jurisdiction* to prescribe a rule of law requiring military service of such a person in fact physically present in the state? If there is no lack of jurisdiction, for what reason is the state precluded from exercising that jurisdiction? Is the alien who is only temporarily within the state entitled to something akin to immunity? Can such an immunity be grounded on the customary behavior of states; on the expectations of aliens who are temporarily sojourning in host states?

3. ***French point of view on drafting aliens.*** In Chronique des Faits Internationaux, 71 Rev. Générale de Dr. Int'l Public 143, 174 (1967), Rousseau comments on the Australian legislation, which subjected immigrant aliens to compulsory military service and hence some of them to duty in South Vietnam. Greece and Italy formally protested the legislation and Rousseau comments: "The most surprising aspect of the situation is that only two governments seem to have protested an act which constitutes a clear violation of the traditional status of aliens."

He qualifies the French practice of declining even voluntary military service by aliens in time of peace as "perhaps [showing] an excessive respect for foreign sovereignty." He then discusses an exception to the practice, i.e. voluntary service in the French Foreign Legion and the difficulties to which this voluntary service had given rise between France and other states, notably Belgium, Germany and Switzerland. He reviews in particular a serious diplomatic dispute with Switzerland in 1959, concerning the service in the Foreign Legion of Swiss citizens who falsified documents to make it appear they were 21 years of age at the time they enlisted, but were in fact still below that age. Once they enlisted, the Foreign Legion refused to release them.

In time of war, Rousseau points out, the French practice is to permit voluntary military service by aliens and to subject them to compulsory service in the labor force. He then states that Anglo–Saxon states have a different point of view in the matter of drafting aliens and reviews critically the dispute between France and the United States with respect to the drafting of French citizens in the American forces under the Service Act of 1951, the drafting of aliens by the United Kingdom during World War II, and an Australian decision of 1945 upholding the domestic validity of World War II legislation for the drafting of aliens while recognizing it was in violation of international law. The Australian decision to which Rousseau refers is Polites v. The Commonwealth, and Kandiliotes v. The Commonwealth, High Court of Australia, 1945, [1943–1945] Ann.Dig. 208 (No. 61).

4. ***Military service by the dual national.*** If mere presence of the individual in the territory of a state is not sufficient to support the draft, is the fact of nationality sufficient? The issue will not arise unless a state which claims that a person is its national complains to the drafting state and the latter defends its action on the ground that the individual was (also) its national.

IN RE M.M. AND X.M.

Greece, Conseil d'Etat, 1934 (No. 2).
[1933–1934] Ann.Dig. 295 (No. 117.) *

The Facts. The petitioners were born in England of a Greek father, in 1895 and 1898 respectively. By the Greek Law of Nationality (of October 9, 1856) children of a Greek father, wheresoever they may be born, are Greek. Greek nationality is lost (i) by naturalisation with the consent of the Greek Government, (ii) in certain circumstances, by entering foreign public service, and (iii) by leaving Greek territory with no intention of returning. The petitioners contended (I) that they were British subjects, having opted for British nationality by declarations made at the British Consulate at Patras and by entering themselves as British subjects on the British census of 1915; that they had voted at an election in England; and that they had travelled with British passports. They contended (II) that they had not registered as Greek nationals with the Greek Consulate in London, had no Greek domicile, and had not done their military service in Greece.

Held: that they were nevertheless Greek subjects. They had in fact two nationalities. The facts recited above were matters entirely for British law, which was irrelevant in this case. The facts recited were not sufficient to effect loss of Greek nationality. The provisions of Greek law for the loss of nationality were precise and were to be construed restrictively. Mere acquisition of a foreign nationality without the consent of the Greek Government did not entail loss of Greek nationality (although this was so before the passing of the Law of 1914).

---

* Reprinted with the permission of the Editor of the International Law Reports.

1. ***Problem***. Although the foregoing case of M.M. and X.M. did not involve the question of Greece's right to draft those individuals, consider in the light of the Greek law of nationality expressed in the opinion the problem which follows.

Client's son was born in the United States. Client is a wealthy Greek alien resident of the U.S. The son went AWOL from the United States Army in Germany and began hitchhiking through Europe. In Greece he was picked up while visiting relatives in a remote village and inducted into the Greek army.

Client wants you to do all you can, vis-à-vis the Department of State, the Greek Embassy, and if necessary vis-à-vis the authorities in Greece, to get the son released from Greek military service. The son is presently serving a military prison sentence for insubordination, at hard labor along the Corinth Canal. The client says he would rather take chances on the AWOL charge (U.S.) than to leave his boy in the Greek military prison. *Does the state with whom an individual has a more effective link have a claim on the merits against the drafting state?*

2. ***The law in treaties***. The United States is a party to a Protocol Relating to Military Obligations in Certain Cases of Double Nationality which was concluded at the Hague April 12, 1930. Only 25 states were parties to this international agreement as of January 1, 1980. Article 1 provided: "A person possessing two or more nationalities who habitually resides in one of the countries whose nationality he possesses, and who is in fact most closely connected with that country, shall be exempt from all military obligations in the other country or countries. This exemption may involve the loss of the nationality of the other country or countries." For bilateral agreements to which the United States is a party, dealing not only with the drafting of dual nationals but also with the drafting of aliens, see 8 Whitcman, Digest of International Law 561–573 (1967). The Convention on the Reduction of Cases of Plurality of Nationalities and on Military Obligations in Cases of Plurality of Nationalities of May 6, 1963, was prepared by the Council of Europe. The provisions in Chapter 11 of the convention are designed to insure that a person having two or more nationalities shall discharge his military obligations only once and be dispensed from serving them again in other states parties to the convention. Documents, 95 J. du Droit Int'l 760, 781 (1968).

---

4. OTHER?

ARE CITIZENS' (NATIONALS') POTENTIAL OBLIGATIONS OPEN–ENDED?

Persons are potentially at risk as to state demands for services beyond the payment of taxes and serving in the military. What about a compulsory Peace Corps or an Environmental Service? A Nuclear Waste Cleanup Squad? Only constitutions (fairness and equal treatment) and politics stand in the way of much heavier demands on nationals and resident aliens. Are there limits on what the state can demand? Will limits develop as a part of the now-emerging law of human rights? Compare at review-time the powers of states (Chapter 2) with Chapter 10 (Human Rights).

SECTION D. SITUATION OF INTERNATIONAL OFFICIALS

Note: "International officials" are persons appointed to positions of responsibility in the United Nations, the specialized agencies of the United Nations (e.g., WHO, FAO, UNESCO) and many other universal, regional and functional intergovernmental organizations. They are usually nationals of member countries of the organization. They do not relinquish their personal nationality as a consequence of accepting the status of international officials. Nor do they acquire anything like an internationally created special nationality. They do, however, enjoy certain privileges and immunities (see Chapter 12) and they undertake certain obligations of loyalty to their organization. Those obligations sometimes to the exercise of the officials' functions vis-a-vis their own governments. This raises the potential for sharp conflict between the two loyalties. International officials are not to take instructions from their governments and the governments are obligated not to seek to influence their nationals in the exercise of their international responsibilities. International officials are responsible solely to the executive heads and to the designated organs of the organizations and owe a duty of loyalty to those organizations and to their purposes and principles. This is essential to the objective and effective operations of the organizations which are created to serve the entire community of their member countries. In order to carry out their individual responsibilities effectively, international officials must give their professional loyalty to the organizations they serve, even in cases of conflict with their own governments. *If there is a conflict, can an international civil servant be prosecuted for "treason?"*

CHARTER OF THE UNITED NATIONS

Article 100

1. In the performance of their duties the Secretary–General and the staff shall not seek or receive instructions from any government or from any other authority external to the Organization. They shall refrain from any action which might reflect on their position as international officials responsible only to the Organization.

2. Each Member of the United Nations undertakes to respect the exclusively international character of the responsibilities of the Secre-

tary–General and the staff and not to seek to influence them in the discharge of their responsibilities.

––––––––

STATUTE OF THE INTERNATIONAL COURT OF JUSTICE

Article 20

Every member of the Court shall, before taking up his duties, make a solemn declaration in open court that he will exercise his powers impartially and conscientiously.

––––––––

Questions about loyalty. If the international official owes a duty of loyalty to the organization, does his government have any proper interest in his continuing national loyalty? Are international officials in a sense also representatives of their own governments? Could that be legally compatible with the provisions quoted above? How should executive heads of international organizations handle such questions when they arise in the form of a demand by a government that only its nationals holding a national loyalty clearance be appointed? In the event a United Nations official carries out instructions of the Secretary–General for certain actions which are considered by his national government to violate his duty of loyalty to his *own* country, would international law permit his prosecution in his own country? What if he acted beyond instructions and violated international law or the law of his own country? If the Secretary–General waived the official's immunity, would that affect your views?

––––––––

HINTON v. DEVINE

United States District Court, Eastern District of Pennsylvania, 1986.
633 F.Supp. 1023.

MEMORANDUM AND ORDER

TROUTMAN, Senior District Judge.

In 1953 the President of the United States issued Executive Order No. 10422, providing for an investigation of United States citizens employed or being considered for employment by the United Nations or other international organizations. The Order establishes an International Organizations Employees Loyalty Board, the function of which is to evaluate all such citizens and render an advisory opinion as to their loyalty to the United States. That opinion is transmitted to the Secretary of State for ultimate transmittal to the executive head of the involved international organization. The opinion is developed in accordance with procedures described in the Order, and rules and regulations promulgated by the Board.[1] The plaintiff, William Hinton, a resident of Fleetwood, Pennsylvania, and a graduate of the Cornell College of Agriculture and the author of several books on China, challenges the constitutionality of Executive Order No. 10422.

In 1980 Hinton was hired by the Food and Agriculture Organization (FAO), an agency of the United Nations, to serve for six months as a consultant to the Grasslands Development Project in the Inner Mongolia Region of the Peoples Republic of China (PRC). Pursuant to Executive Order No. 10422, he requested and received a loyalty clearance. In 1981 and 1982 he received similar FAO offers of employment and again sought and received loyalty clearances. In 1983, having once again been advised that he was being considered for an FAO consultancy, Hinton, for his fourth consecutive year, requested a loyalty clearance. This time his clearance was unaccountably delayed. Having failed to receive a clearance for 1983, Hinton was not offered FAO employment, but did return to the project, on which he had served for the preceding three years, as an employee of the PRC.

Early in 1984, with another FAO offer allegedly on the horizon, Hinton filed the instant suit, contending that because his 1983 loyalty clearance request had not been processed for over a year, he lost an employment opportunity in 1983. More importantly, he feared that the lack of a clearance would adversely affect his expected 1984 FAO appointment. Accordingly, plaintiff filed a motion for a preliminary injunction, requesting that the Court direct immediate action on his pending application for a loyalty clearance. On April 5, 1984, after a March 28 conference before the Court, Hinton received a loyalty clearance, obviating the need for an immediate ruling on his request for a preliminary injunction. Thereafter, on June 26, 1984, plaintiff filed a motion for summary judgment seeking a declaratory judgment that Executive Order No. 10422 is unconstitutional and a permanent injunction against its further and continued enforcement. * * *

II. *Lack of Presidential Authority*

We now consider the plaintiff's contention that the authority and power of the President over foreign affairs does not extend to regulating the employment of United States citizens by international organizations. The government contends that the breadth of authority over foreign affairs conferred by Article II of the Constitution, combined with Congress's acquiescence in the loyalty clearance program and its purported support by the United Nations, is sufficient to establish the legitimacy of Executive Order 10422. * * *

* * * It is unnecessary to test the outer bounds of the President's power over foreign affairs. The heart of the matter here is not whether, under any conceivable circumstances, the President lacks all authority to regulate or oversee in any manner the employment of United States citizens by international organizations. The true issue presented for our consideration is whether the loyalty clearance program, as presently operating, is a valid exercise of whatever power the President may have

---

1. Executive Order No. 10422, as amended, is found at 22 U.S.C. § 287.

in this area. This requires the Court to determine whether there is a sufficiently developed and articulated governmental interest to support investigations into the loyalty of United States citizens employed or being considered for employment by international organizations and whether the methods chosen to vindicate that interest, if it exists, show proper regard for safeguarding other constitutional interests.

III. *Overbreadth/Vagueness*

The analysis involved when a law is challenged as overbroad is somewhat different from that required when the same law is challenged as vague, but a statute that fails constitutional scrutiny on either ground suffers from the same basic infirmity, *i.e.*, the danger that in seeking to avoid the sanctions imposed by the law, an individual's legitimate exercise of First Amendment rights may be "chilled".

* * *

Part I of the Order deals with the nature and extent of the investigation to be conducted into the activities of any United States citizen employed by or seeking employment with an international organization. The investigation begins with a search of State Department files for "derogatory information". If any is found, the investigation proceeds to the Office of Personnel Management for a National Agency check, involving a search of more files for "derogatory information". For this second phase of the investigation, the files of certain agencies must be included but those of any other "appropriate" agency may also be included, thereby expanding the search to virtually all government investigative or intelligence agencies at the unfettered discretion of the person compiling the relevant information. If this phase reveals "derogatory information", the matter is referred to the FBI for a full field investigation. If that investigation reveals "derogatory information", the due process procedures of Part IV of the Order are triggered. Importantly, Part I 6 of the Order empowers the IOELB, through the Secretary of State, to inform the Secretary General of the United Nations or the director of any other international organization of whatever "derogatory information" may have been discovered at any stage of the proceeding *without* invoking the due process provisions.

If the investigation outlined above discloses no "derogatory information", the Secretary of State will so advise the Secretary General or international agency director. Otherwise, the IOELB renders an advisory opinion to the Secretary of State as to the loyalty of the person investigated on the basis of the information compiled as a result of the investigation. The Secretary of State then transmits the Board's recommendation to the head of the international organization.

Throughout Part I, wherever the term "derogatory information" appears it is accompanied by the phrase, "within the meaning of the standard set forth in Part II of this order". Nowhere in Part II does the term "derogatory information" appear, however. Instead, the "standard" is defined in Part II 1 as, "whether or not on all the evidence there is a reasonable doubt as to the loyalty of the person involved to the Government of the United States". The "derogatory information", which presumably will become part of that evidence, remains undefined, as does the term "loyalty". Part II 2 provides a list of "activities and associations * * * which may be considered" in determining whether or not there exists a reasonable doubt as to the person's loyalty. Engaging in any of the enumerated activities is presumably evidence of disloyalty or at least can raise a reasonable doubt as to loyalty. In any event, engaging in such activities would appear to be the sort of "derogatory information" that would be revealed in a check of the various files which may be perused in the search for such information.

It should be readily apparent from the Court's having to guess at the meaning of the terms in Part II that the purported standard fails to give fair notice to a person targeted for investigation of what conduct or activity may trigger a reasonable doubt as to his "loyalty" in the minds of those examining whatever files the investigators choose to select. * * *

Part II 2(a) and (f) concern associations both informal and formal, including, "knowingly associating with spies or saboteurs" and "[k]nowing membership with the specific intent of furthering the aims of, or adherence to and active participation in", virtually any "combination" of persons who advocate the use of violence to overthrow the Government of the United States or any state or political subdivision thereof.

* * *

Even the proscription against "sabotage, espionage or attempts or preparations therefor" found in Part II 2(a) are not sufficiently clear to survive constitutional scrutiny, as they are not limited to criminal convictions for such activities. Without that limitation, the terms are unconstitutionally vague. * * *

IV. *Nature of the Government's Interest*

We begin this phase of the analysis by examining the government's stated interest as set forth in § [6] of the Preamble to Executive Order No. 10422: " * * * it is in the interest of the United States that United States citizens who are employees of the Secretariat of the United Nations be of the highest integrity and not persons who have been, are, or are likely to be, engaged in espionage or subversive activities against the United States;". Conceding that this is an important interest, it would be ludicrous to conclude that the Order as it is written approaches the "precision of regulation" contemplated by the Supreme Court in situations where government regulation impinges upon First Amendment freedoms. Our exhaustive analysis of the means used to fulfill the government's stated purpose reveals that the procedures for obtaining a loyalty clearance are not narrowly drawn to reach only subversion, espionage or even lack of integrity. Instead, a wide range of activities and associations may be examined, and the resulting advisory opinion purports to pass upon the individual's "loyalty", a vague and sometimes illusory concept. Another inherent problem is the fact that the need for an advisory opinion as to loyalty extends to all employees or prospective employees of international organizations regardless of their duty stations or the nature of their duties.

* * *

The government made no effort to identify specific positions that might implicate significant foreign policy concerns of the United States. Instead, it seeks to justify the loyalty clearance program on the insubstantial and conclusory basis that all employees of international organizations are *"de facto"* representatives of the United States and have "affirmatively chosen to enmesh themselves in the delicate foreign affairs concerns of the United States". Just as the Supreme Court declined to allow "war powers" to "be invoked as a talismanic incantation" to support overbroad Congressional action because even that power "does not remove constitutional limitations safeguarding essential liberties", so this Court, for the same reason, may not allow the President's power over foreign affairs to be invoked in that manner.

A closer scrutiny of the government's rationale for the loyalty clearance program, particularly as it concerns the plaintiff in this case, reveals the true nature of what the government seeks to accomplish and clearly illustrates why it is legally and constitutionally impermissible. The *Ozonoff* court concluded, and we agree, that the government's interest in regulating the employment of United States citizens by international organizations is more attenuated than if the individuals subject to investigation were employees of this government. In doing so, the court observed that: "The appellee is a medical doctor. He does not want to represent the United States abroad, engage in diplomacy, or practice politics. His object—prolonging human life—is technical and scientific, not political. His employer is an international organization, not the American government."

Although we believe that only the last sentence of the foregoing observation is truly relevant to the issue, the government argues vigorously and at length that the issue of expertise was essential to the result reached in the *Ozonoff* case. Upon that premise, the government argues that Hinton does not fit the criteria set forth by the First Circuit and, hence, that it has a stronger interest in investigating his loyalty. To support that contention, defendant characterized the plaintiff as an "author of political propaganda who resides on a one-man farm" and who "has interacted with international political figures and practices politics". * * * Thus, it appears that the government is contending, at the least, that politically active citizens who seek to work for international organizations in whatever capacity ought to be subject to investigations into their loyalty to the United States.

* * *

From the government's more general defense of the loyalty clearance program, it appears that it seeks to use the Executive Order, if necessary, to discriminate against United States citizens on the basis of their political beliefs and activities. Defendant's most basic rationale for the Order can best be summarized by the following: In addition, * * * the international organization will not be misled into assuming that, for example, if it assigns such an individual to a 'balanced' team (one representing the conflicting interests of the constituent members of the international organization), that the organization is thereby fairly representing the interests of the United States on that team.   * * *"

As previously stated, an appropriate order will issue invalidating and enjoining the Order in question.

Chapter 10

HUMAN RIGHTS: THE GROWTH OF STATE RESPONSIBILITY TO INDIVIDUALS

The catalog of abuses to which human beings have subjected each other is one of unrelieved horror. Abuses range from murder and physical torture and rape of the individual to the slaughter and rape of religious, racial and ethnic masses. They also include slavery, mass rape, forced labor and deprivations of liberty of movement from one place or one state to another. Freedom to speak, to practice one's religion, to select one's own occupation, to marry whom one pleases have been repressed. Arbitrary arrest, imprisonment without trial, unfair trials and degrading punishments have been common ingredients of life. This has been true throughout history. And, what is worse, still is. In his stunning book, A Miracle, A Universe: Settling Accounts With

Torturers (1990), Lawrence Weschler chronicles the story of torture and its impact on Brazil and Uruguay mainly during the 1960's and 1970's: "They [the political prisoners] have all been tortured, kept in secret places of detention, questioned—all of them, without exception * * * In some units, prisoners are tortured with electrodes, in others they are suspended by their arms, which have been previously tied behind their backs, or kept with their heads under water until suffocation, not to mention similar refinements * * *." Weschler causes us to pause. He reminds us that we must be ever vigilant in minding ourselves, when he provides details on how the U.S. provided Uruguayan officers with up-to-date "anti-subversion techniques," and "more scientifically effective methods of interrogation."

All of these abuses to the human personality, recently called human dignity, are committed by people upon people. Some, such as murder, are often matters of private endeavor. Others are perpetrated by people acting in some capacity as a part of the organizations of state or its opponents. Protections against these abuses are frequently afforded by the internal laws of the state. Domestic laws are designed not only to deter private individuals from harming their fellows but also, as in the case of the United States Constitution, to protect the individual from abuses by the state. But suppose the machinery of domestic law fails to protect the individual. Does the international legal system offer any protection? Does it afford protection against abuses by the individual's own state? A generation ago, the rule was suggested in a chilling phrase that a state could treat its own citizens "according to discretion." I Oppenheim, International Law 682 (Lauterpacht, 8th ed. 1955). *This is not the law today.*

Questions such as the above and the following will be explored below. What substantive legal norms have been developed in the international system for the protection of the individual? What classes of individuals are protected by such norms—aliens alone or citizens of the acting state as well? By what processes are those norms applied and protections afforded?

As the nation-state became the organizing unit of the European peoples there was an early, if halting, recognition that, in some circumstances, a state might be circumscribed in the way it treated some of its own nationals. Doctrines of natural law furnished a major impetus. Pressure for such recognition came from groups to which those persons had formerly been attached. "The treaties by which States bound themselves to treat their own nationals in a certain way appear only as isolated phenomena inspired first by political interest and later by considerations of humanity. The series of particular agreements inaugurated in 1660 by the Treaty of Oliva after a century and a half of religious commotions bore this aspect. In these, states receiving cessions of territory guaranteed to the ceding states the continuance and protection of the religion existing in the ceded territories. This protection, granted first to individuals, was gradually extended to minority groups, to religious minorities first and afterwards ethnic or national minorities." DeVisscher, Theory and Reality in Public International Law 126 (Corbett trans., 1968).

SECTION A. RESPONSIBILITY OF STATES FOR INJURIES TO ALIENS

This process of looking after one's own kind is reflected in the practice of diplomatic protection in the 18th and 19th centuries. By this practice the state sought protection for its own nationals when they had left its territory to travel, reside or trade in a foreign state. If its nationals were injured by the foreign state, diplomatic protests were made, asserting that the foreign state had violated its treaty obligations or, in many cases, obligations imposed by international law generally. In theory, rights of the protecting state had been violated, not the rights of the injured individual. In the absence of an international judiciary in which the rights of the offended state could be litigated, states occasionally resorted to arbitration and authorized ad hoc tribunals to decide claims based upon alleged injuries to individuals. A substantial body of precedent, establishing a primitive law of human rights, was developed until the practice of arbitrating violations of personal rights began to slacken after World War II. The diplomatic protest remains a major vehicle for the assertion of human rights claims.

----

1. THE PRINCIPLE OF DIPLOMATIC PROTECTION

The traditional principle of diplomatic protection has been that an injury to an alien is actually an injury to the state of which the alien is a national. Thus, a claim for injury to an alien is the claim of the state of which the alien is a national. Does this artificial theory still underlie doctrine of diplomatic protection? Has it been modified? Do individuals have any standing to assert their own interests or "rights" against a foreign state? Keep these questions in mind as you read the following materials. Certainly, the reality of the claim, as being one by the state on behalf of the individual has been recognized.

ADMINISTRATIVE DECISION NO. V

Mixed Claims Commission (United States–Germany), 1924.
7 U.N.Rep.Int'l Arb. Awards 119, 152.

* * *

Ordinarily a nation will not espouse a claim on behalf of its national against another nation unless requested so to do by such national.

When on such request a claim is espoused, the nation's absolute right to control it is necessarily exclusive. In exercising such control it is governed not only by the interest of the particular claimant but by the larger interests of the whole people of the nation and must exercise an untrammeled discretion in determining when and how the claim will be presented and pressed, or withdrawn or compromised, and the private owner will be bound by the action taken. Even if payment is made to the espousing nation in pursuance of an award, it has complete control over the fund so paid to and held by it and may, to prevent fraud, correct a mistake, or protect the national honor, at its election return the fund to the nation paying it or otherwise dispose of it. * * *

---

2. THE INTERNATIONAL MINIMUM STANDARD

---

1. ***Equality versus international minimum standard.*** The General Claims Commission in *Roberts v. Mexico,* 4 U.N.Rpt. Int'l Arb. Awards 17 (1976) rejected, as the ultimate test, equality of treatment of aliens and nationals and adopted a test: whether aliens are treated in accordance with *ordinary standards of civilization.* When European nationals began to travel for colonization and trade, their governments became concerned for their personal safety. In diplomatic protests on behalf of their nationals, European states asserted that there existed a *minimum standard of justice* to which all states must adhere in their treatment of aliens. See Dawson and Head, International Law, National Tribunals and the Rights of Aliens, Chapter I (1971). Does such a minimum standard in fact exist as a matter of international law? Or must a state merely assure that aliens are not treated any worse than the state treats its own nationals? What standards are (or are supposed to be) comprehended by the minimum standard? Does an Islamic nation's prohibition of the consumption of alcohol or of women being in public unveiled violate the minimum standard? Is the "minimum standard" really only an imposition of Western values?

2. ***Standard for determining that there has been a denial of justice.*** By what standard would a court decide that there has been a denial of justice? Must the complaining party show that there has been a failure to meet the standards of local law? Or may the standards of local law be so high that a failure to meet those high standards is not, of itself, a denial of justice? Would the local court hold, on the other hand, that even though the standards of municipal law have been met there may be a denial of justice because those standards do not meet the higher standards of international law? Do aliens have more protection than nationals? *See, e.g.,* Cantero Herrera v. Canevaro, S.Ct., Peru (1927), [1927–1928] Ann.Dig. 219 (No. 149).

3. ***Traditional view.*** Traditionally, some jurists have denied that there is an international standard to which each state's jurisprudence must attain. It is frequently stated that the alien is entitled only

to equality of treatment with nationals. In analyzing this proposition it should be noted that the broad question of state responsibility for injury to aliens has been discussed somewhat indiscriminately in connection with two types of problems: injury to an alien individual in his personal rights (e.g., rights to physical security and personal freedom, rights to fair trial in cases involving personal liberty) on one hand and the alien individual's (or corporation's) rights to property, on the other. During much of the 20th Century, the latter rights have been the subject of considerable controversy, particularly with respect to the expropriation of property by states socializing and collectivizing the means of production. See Chapter 15. Would you expect a system of international law to be more protective of personal rights than of property rights?

4. *Influence of the creation of new states on the question of the international standard.* The Western World prior to World War II debated the question of an international minimum standard versus a standard of national treatment. This debate may be viewed as one within an established legal system in which the members of that system sought to delineate the contours of a body of customary law acceptable to them. With the influx of new states into the community of nations, mostly former colonies, the debate took on a different tone. Guha Roy notes:

> The international community in its inception was confined to only some Christian states of Europe. It expanded within very narrow limits to embrace, first, the other Christian states of Europe and next their own offshoots in other continents. It thus retained until recently its racial exclusiveness in full and its geographical and other limitations in part. The international law which the world-wide community of states today inherits is the law which owes its genesis and growth, first, to the attempts of these states to regulate their mutual intercourse in their own interests and, secondly, to the use made of it during the period of colonialism.

> The contacts of the members of the restricted international community of the past with other states and peoples of the much larger world outside its own charmed circle were not governed by any law or scruples beyond what expediency dictated. The history of the establishment and consolidation of empires overseas by some of the members of the old international community and of the acquisition therein of vast economic interests by their nationals teems with instances of a total disregard of all ethical considerations. A strange irony of fate now compels those very members of the community of nations on the ebb tide of their imperial power to hold up principles of morality as shields against the liquidation of interests acquired and held by an abuse of international intercourse. Rights and interests acquired and consolidated during periods of such abuse cannot for obvious reasons carry with them in the mind of the victims of that abuse anything like the sanctity the holders of those rights and interests may and do attach to them. To the extent to which the law of responsibility of states for injuries to aliens favors such rights and interests, it protects an unjustified

status quo or, to put it more bluntly, makes itself a handmaid of power in the preservation of its spoils.

* * *

The law of responsibility then, is not founded on any universal principles of law or morality. Its sole foundation is custom, which is binding only among states where it either grew up or came to be adopted. It is thus hardly possible to maintain that it is still part of universal international law. Whatever the basis of obligation in international law in the past, when the international community was restricted to only a few states, including those, fewer still, admitted into it from time to time, the birth of a new world community has brought about a radical change which makes the traditional basis of obligation outmoded.

Once it is found that the right of diplomatic protection of their nationals abroad, claimed by states as a customary right, is not universally binding, the structure of this law as part of universal international law crumbles, for this right is assumed to be the sole basis of a state's claim to stretch out its protecting hand to its nationals in the territory of another state independently of its consent. Its elimination from universal international law necessarily means that, even outside the limited zone of the applicability of this law, the responsibility of a state for injuries to aliens remains in every case in which it may be held to be responsible exactly in the same way as in the case of its own nationals, but it remains its responsibility not to the home state of the injured alien but to the injured alien himself. It ceases to be an international responsibility and becomes a responsibility only under the municipal law of the state concerned. Guha Roy, *Is the Law of Responsibility of States for Injuries to Aliens a Part of Universal International Law?* 55 AJIL 863, 866, 888 (1961).*

---

1. ***What variations in legal systems are comprehended by the international minimum standard?*** National legal systems differ considerably as to how they deal with an accused in a criminal proceeding pending trial on the merits. In some countries, the accusation of a criminal offense results in the accused being put into detention pending investigation by a magistrate on the question of whether there is a probable case against him. In most Civil Law countries, bail is not allowed for the period pending trial (they consider it scandalous that one with money can buy this liberty). Individuals who do not pose a threat of danger or pose a risk of disappearing are not detained. Often, the physical conditions of detention centers are rather grim. In many Civil Law countries, exclusionary and other rigorous rules of evidence are sparse and the defendant is not allowed in all cases directly to confront the witnesses against him. In view of these differences, can it be said

* Reprinted with the permission of the American Society of International Law.

that the international minimum standard of criminal procedural justice takes its contents from Anglo–American Systems? Moreover, as stated by the dissent in the *Chattin Case,* General Claims Commission, 1927, 4 U.N.Rpt. Int'l Awards 282, in ¶¶ 17–23, the majority did not understand the Mexican Legal System. The dissent noted:

> "All the criticism which has been made of these proceedings, I regret to say, appears to arise from lack of knowledge of the judicial system and practice of Mexico, and, what is more dangerous, from the application thereto of tests belonging to foreign systems of law. For example, in some of the latter the investigation of a crime is made only by the police magistrates and the trial proper is conducted by the Judge. Hence the reluctance in accepting that one same judge may have the two functions and that, therefore, he may have to receive in the preliminary investigation (instrucción) of the case all kinds of data, with the obligation, of course, of not taking them into account at the time of judgment, if they have no probative weight."

It is certain that the secret report, so much discussed in this case, would have been received by the police of the countries which place the investigation exclusively in the hands of such branch. This same police would have been free to follow all the clues or to abandon them at its discretion; but the Judge is criticized here because he did not follow up completely the clue given by Ramirez with respect to Chattin. The same domestic test—to call it such—is used to understand what is a trial or open trial imagining at the same time that it must have the sacred forms of common-law and without remembering that the same goal is reached by many roads. And the same can be said when speaking of the manner of taking testimony of witnesses, of cross-examination, of holding confrontations, etc. Trials in Mexico, like in other "Civil Law" systems are generally short and formal "confirmations of the written documents * * * ". The protections for the accused are supposed to be built into the investigative stage, where a judge, trained to protect the "liberty interests" of the accused, is supposed to oversee the process. Civil Law Systems do not allow cross-examination like in the U.S. (see last ½ of ¶ 22). Thus, the complaint about the process in Mexico may obtain for any "Civil Law" system. Does this mean that there is not international minimum standard? "Civil Law Systems" build in protections in a completely different way. Or does this suggest that the task of determining the content of such a standard does not consist of asking whether the foreign state has conformed to the requirements of the United States Constitution as interpreted by the Supreme Court from time to time?

The content of this minimum international standard is currently under discussion and, perhaps even being created, in relation to the *Ad Hoc* Tribunal for the territory of the former Yugoslavia and regarding the debate over creation of a permanent war crimes tribunal.

FROM CHRISTOPHER L. BLAKESLEY, OBSTACLES TO THE CREATION OF A PERMANENT WAR CRIMES TRIBUNAL

18, The Fletcher Forum of World Affairs 77 (1994) * (FOOTNOTES OMITTED).

Basic notions of fairness and human rights in relation to investigation, prosecution, and trial are paramount, and are part of the minimum standard. *But what are these basic notions of fairness?* If we are not scrupulous in protecting individuals accused from abuses and deprivation of civil liberties, we will ultimately condemn the viability of an international criminal tribunal. Justice Jackson summed up the importance of this point in his opening statement during the Nuremberg Trial: "Before I discuss the particulars of evidence, some general considerations which may affect the credit of this trial in the eyes of the world should be candidly faced. There is a dramatic disparity between the circumstances of the accusers and the accused that might discredit our work if we should falter, in even minor matters, in being fair and temperate. Unfortunately, the nature of these crimes is such that both prosecution and judgment must be by victor nations over vanquished foes [*a problem (or blessing?) not faced by the Ad Hoc Tribunal for the former Yugoslavia*] * * *. We must never forget that the record on which we judge these defendants is the record on which history will judge us tomorrow. To pass these defendants a poisoned chalice is to put it to our lips as well. We must summon such detachment and intellectual integrity to our task that this Trial will commend itself to posterity as fulfilling humanity's aspirations to do justice." [Justice Robert H. Jackson, Chief Counsel for the Prosecution in the Nuremberg Trials, *Opening Statement,* delivered, November 20, 1945, *quoted in* Telford Taylor, The Anatomy of the Nuremberg Trials: a Personal Memoir 167–169 (1992)].

International human rights law provides the minimum standard of protection for an accused person. Increasingly, United States requests for extradition and renditions under status of forces agreements have been overridden by international and foreign courts which have ruled that international human rights provisions take precedence. In two cases, concerns over capital punishment in the United States have resulted in litigation in which courts outside the United States have held that turning persons over to states with the death penalty (and the concomitant death row syndrome) would in certain circumstances violate provisions of international human rights conventions. See, e.g., Soering v. U.S. International human rights conventions contain analogues to many of the protections guaranteed by the U.S. Constitution, including the right to a fair trial, to "equality of arms" and access to court, to the presumption of innocence, to the right of confrontation, and to the right to counsel of choice. Though some of the international human rights protections meet, and even exceed, U.S. constitutional standards, some do not. Article 20(1) of the *Statute for the Ad Hoc Tribunal* for

* (Reprinted with the permission of the Fletcher Forum of World Affairs).

Yugoslavia provides that the "[t]rial chambers shall ensure that a trial is fair and expeditious and that proceedings are rendered in accordance with the rules of procedure and evidence, with full respect for the rights of the accused and due regard for the protection of victims and witnesses." The accused's Geneva Law and human right to consult a lawyer and to have adequate time to prepare a defense must be ensured. To be acceptable, this protection must be applicable to the entire process. Does this meet the minimum standard? Does it help create it? Is it sufficient to meet U.S. constitutional standards? Suppose that a U.S.–Serbian dual national had been fighting in the Bosnian war and that he has been charged with violations of humanitarian law. Suppose that he was sought for prosecution before the Ad Hoc Tribunal. If he were present in the U.S., could the U.S. Government constitutionally send him to the prosecution? If you were assigned as defense counsel, what would you argue? As prosecutor? If "minimum international standards" do not meet minimum U.S. Constitutional Standards, can our courts accept the U.S. participation in the creation of a court that does not apply the protections afforded U.S. citizens and send one there for prosecution? If so, upon what rationale? If not, why not? Do we do just that in extradition? Is there a difference? Is this extradition? See Ch. 3, supra.

Consider the following in this regard. To bring an individual accused of one or more of the atrocities covered by the *Ad Hoc Tribunal's* statute to trial, must sufficient evidence to establish "probable cause" be required? The notion of probable cause relates to the decision to arrest or to hold a person over for trial or to extradite to serve an already extant conviction and sentence). For conviction, it is necessary, if significant U.S., UK, Canadian, Australian, and other "common law countries" support is to be forthcoming, that the standard of proof be "beyond a reasonable doubt." This standard is the controlling standard for conviction in these nations, and has been for over two hundred years. John Locke and even on the continent, the famous German Lutheran jurist Samuel Pufendorf linked the concept of *"conscience"* (similar to the French notion of *"intîme conviction"*) to notions of moral certainty and of proof beyond a reasonable doubt. The perception and understanding of the "reasonable doubt" standard requires that the evidence be sufficient to establish that there is no reasonable hypothesis or explanation of the evidence other than that of the defendant's guilt. The equivalent standard was recently applied by the Israeli Supreme Court in the *Demjanjuk Case.* It is a difficult burden to meet, and it ought to be when a person's life or liberty is at stake.

The Right of Confrontation: *Similarly, should ex-parte affidavits or video-taped depositions, etc., be admissible in trial? Is their use inconsistent with the right [under article 21(4)(e) of the Statute for the Ad Hoc Tribunal or of some minimum standard] of an accused person to "examine, or have examined, the witnesses against him"?* This right is protected under Article 21(4)(e), of the Statute. *But see,* id., art. 21(4)(d): A person has a "[right] to be tried in his presence." Article 21(4)(e), was taken verbatim from article 14(3)(e) of the International Covenant on Civil and Political Rights. *Is this the same as the right of a* *defendant to confront the witnesses against him? Does that include a concomitant right to cross-examine those witnesses? It certainly does under U.S. law, but is that part of the minimum international standard? How many nations allow cross-examination?*

The Report of the A.B.A. Task Force concludes that the right is concomitant to cross-examination. This relationship is *not self-evident,* however, especially given the broad "civil law" practice of allowing the judge to do the questioning (not always so vigorously as the Anglo–American trial attorney). Moreover, during the Nuremberg Trials, where cross-examination was actually allowed, it was generally ineffective, because of defense counsels' general lack of experience.

However, there is *serious tension* between the primary responsibility of a tribunal to ensure a fair trial that comports with *due process* and the *obligation to protect victims and witnesses.* To provide protections for the accused without adequate safeguards for victims of war crimes, rape, and torture risks not only severe psychological harm to those victims, but even jeopardizes their very lives and those of their family members. The perpetrators of such crimes often have militia or other forces available to intimidate or harm the witnesses and victims. In the case of the former Yugoslavia, the ABA Task Force suggested that any derogation from the principle *against the use* of *ex-parte* affidavits should be limited to permitting their use as corroborative evidence in cases involving sexual assault against women, and that an *ex-parte* affidavit might be used at the investigatory stage, but not at trial.

Professor Cherif Bassiouni has strong reservations about the use of the U.S. model of confrontation and cross-examination without adequate safeguards for rape and torture victims. First, these procedural safeguards may be easily abused and cause distortion of the "truth-seeking" process. Second, the U.S. model disregards the legitimate rights and interests of the victim-witness. Third, the model assumes that other mechanisms in society will protect the victim-witness, which is unlikely in an international tribunal. Finally, the model lends itself to the further victimization of witnesses, including assassination and other forms of reprisals and harassment. Hence, while it is clear that human rights norms require some sort of "confrontation-type" examination (or the right to "have examined"), there is disagreement over what that means and should mean in the international tribunal context. Whatever approach one takes presents serious problems.

In a meeting held under the auspices of the International Scientific and Professional Advisory Council (ISPAC) in Spain on 3 May 1993, several recommendations were made with a view to protecting victims and witnesses while still providing for the accused's right to confrontation. Suggested protections included adding the following passage to Article 21 (*Rights of the Accused*) paragraph 4(e) of the Statute for the Ad Hoc Tribunal: "With regard to child witnesses this examination will be restricted to questions through the Tribunal only. In other cases where the International Tribunal considers it appropriate for the protection of the witness, it may similarly restrict the questioning." Article 18 (*Investigation and Preparation of Indictment*) paragraph 3 was to be amended to include: "The views and concerns of victims shall be presented and considered at appropriate stages of the proceedings where their personal interests are affected, without prejudice to the accused and consistent with the other rules of the International Tribunal." Further, it was recommended that the Tribunal "[take] into account the victims' needs for privacy and their special sensitivities. For example, screens or facilities for giving evidence from a separate room and separate waiting areas for defence and prosecution witnesses can be provided for protection. In this context, child victims should be offered special protection and interview procedures." These recommendations are to be taken into consideration in drafting the *Rules of Procedure and Evidence* and the general administrative structure of the Ad Hoc Tribunal, based on the notion that the United Nations ought to be prepared to incorporate the essence of its *Declaration on Victims* into this effort. These improvements should also be applicable to any permanent tribunal.

Even if done well, would these safeguards be sufficient for the victims, the witnesses, and the accused? Providing some of the traditional Anglo–American safeguards for the accused without establishing serious protective measures for victims will simply ensure that no victims will come forth, or if they do, that the risk of harm will be significant. Not including them will render the tribunal suspect. The international community would run the risk of facing another fiasco such as that at the Leipzig Trials. The result may be no serious or important convictions, but plenty of trauma for the victims and witnesses. Does this discussion suggest a minimum standard?

———

Other situations raising the question on "an international standard." In 1994, we have been treated to expansive converage of the *"Michael Fay"* incident in Singapore. Michael Fay had been charged with vandalism, among other offenses. Although there are claims that he was coerced into confessing, he did so. The result of his confession was sentencing to four months in prison and *caning (six "lashes"* with a ratan *"cane"*). The caning part of his sentence was eventually "commuted" to four lashes. The reader may also recall the incident in which Malaysia executed (hanged) a young Australian who had smuggled drugs into that country, apparently naively believing that if he travelled first class, he would not be searched at customs. Thus, one must wonder about the existence of "an international standard," or, if there is one, what it is. The U.S. State Department consistently warns U.S. travellers and has attempted to ameliorate the situation through *prisoner transfer treaties.*

———

Transfer of American prisoners by treaty arrangement. See Rosado v. Civiletti, 621 F.2d 1179 (2d Cir.), cert. denied 449 U.S. 856, reh. denied 449 U.S. 1027 (1980) for an excruciatingly graphic account of brutal treatment of several Americans arrested by Mexican authorities and ultimately convicted in Mexico for illegal importation of cocaine. Sentenced to eight years and nine months imprisonment, they were subsequently transferred to the United States to complete their sentences there, under the terms of a United States–Mexican treaty permitting such transfers reciprocally.   The Americans subsequently sought release from confinement in the United States on the ground that they had been coerced into giving their consents to transfer and that their continued detention in the United States was a deprivation of due process.   The court denied their release, holding that they had voluntarily and intelligently given their consents.   The court concluded:

> * * * [T]he congressional decision to require offenders transferring to American custody to agree to abide by the jurisdictional provision was neither needless nor arbitrary.   Moreover, we believe the conditional requirement that prisoners agree to challenge their convictions solely in the courts of the transferring nation legitimately serves two important interests that can be vindicated only by holding these prisoners to their agreements.
>
> In assessing the interacting interests of the United States and foreign nations, "we must move with the circumspection appropriate when [a court adjudicates] issues inevitably entangled in the conduct of our international relations."   Romero v. International Terminal, 358 U.S. 354, 383 (1959).   Since Mexico was unwilling to enter a treaty that provided for review of its criminal judgments by United States courts, American negotiators did not have a completely free hand in structuring the Treaty's terms.   Guided throughout by their humane concern to ameliorate the plight of hundreds of United States citizens imprisoned in Mexico, the negotiators obviously extracted a significant number of important concessions.   At the same time, however, our negotiators were anxious to improve relations with Mexico and hopefully eliminate what had become an important source of tension between the two nations.
>
> Of paramount importance, however, is the interest of those Americans currently incarcerated in Mexico.   Whatever hope the Treaty extends of escaping the harsh realities of confinement abroad will be dashed for hundreds of Americans if we permit these three petitioners to rescind their agreement to limit their attacks upon their convictions to Mexico's courts.   We refuse to scuttle the one certain opportunity open to Americans incarcerated abroad to return home, an opportunity, we note, the benefit of which Caban, Velez, and Rosado have already received.   In holding these petitioners to their bargain, we by no means condone the shockingly brutal treatment to which they fell prey.   Rather, we hold open the door for others similarly victimized to escape their torment.

On prisoner transfer treaties generally, see Michael Abbell and Bruno Ristau, 6 International Judicial Assistance (vol. 6, on Prisoner Transfers) (1990).   In a 1993 article in the International Enforcement Law Reporter, Mike Abbell writes:

PROPOSED POLICY FOR UNITED STATES
PRISONER TRANSFER TREATIES

by Michael Abbell* reprinted.

United States prisoner transfer treaties permit foreign nationals sentenced by all federal courts and most state courts to be transferred to their countries of nationality to serve the remainder of their United States sentences, and Americans sentenced in foreign countries to transfer to the United States to serve their foreign sentences. * * *

1. *Liberalization of Transfer Criteria for Foreign Nationals Convicted in United States*

During the Bush and Reagan Administrations, the Department increasingly refused to authorize the transfer of federal prisoners to their countries of nationality. For example, in 1992, the Department refused to authorize the transfer of 25 of the 39 Canadians who applied for transfer. The primary reason for this low approval rate is most likely the increasingly restrictive transfer criteria applied during those Administrations. However, it may also in part be due to the fact that the principal Department official responsible for approving transfers is the official in charge of the Witness Protection Program. Indeed, criticism has been levied by federal prisoners whose transfers were refused that unless [they cooperated] with the government or were very minor offenders * * *

2. *Removal of All Offense Related Restrictions on the Transfer to the United States of Americans Convicted Abroad*

* * * Former Senator Paula Hawkins attempted to have [U.S. nationals convicted abroad of heroin offenses] placed on transfer to the U.S. The Bush and Reagan Departments [of Justice] refused to approve the transfer of a significant number of Americans in Thai prisons—some of whom have since died in those prisons of hepatitis and * * * AIDS. This non-statutorily mandated restriction on the transfer of such Americans *must* be eliminated.

3. *Signature and Ratification of OAS Prisoner Transfer Convention*

[In] June the OAS opened for signature a new prisoner transfer Convention that potentially could permit prisoner transfers between all countries in this hemisphere. The Clinton Administration should not only sign this Convention and press for its rapid approval by the Senate, but also should actively lobby other Western Hemisphere countries to join it. This Convention could facilitate the transfer of numerous foreign nationals in United States prisons to prisons in their countries of nationality, thereby significantly reducing the cost of maintaining foreign prisoners in [the U.S.] and the capital costs of building new prisons.

4. *Increase of Personnel in Department's Prisoner Transfer Office*

The Criminal Division office responsible for processing prisoner transfer requests is understaffed in view of its ever-increasing workload.

---

* Reprinted with the permission, Int'l Enforcement Law Rptr.

* * * As a result, there is an increasing backlog of pending prisoner transfer requests with a concomitant increase in the length of time prisoners requesting transfer must spend in United States prisons prior to transfer. The cost of maintaining this increased backlog of potential transferees in United States prisons far exceeds the cost of the relatively small number of additional personnel that would be required to process their requests quickly and efficiently.

In 1991, the D.C. Circuit Court of Appeals held that *neither* the Transfer of Offenders to and from Foreign Countries Act, 18 U.S.C. § 1400 et seq. [the] Convention on the Transfer of Sentenced Persons, T.I.A.S. No. 10824, 22 I.L.M. 530 (1983), create a liberty interest in being transferred to one's home country, because the Conventions do not limit official discretion.

———

*3. **NATO Status of Forces Agreement [S.O.F.A.]**.* The United States has concluded agreements with states on whose territory American military forces are stationed. Among other matters, these agreements deal with the division of jurisdiction, over criminal offenses committed by members of the forces, between the United States and the state on whose territory the forces are stationed. In general, military or duty-related offenses are triable by the United States, other offenses by the receiving state. In the Agreement between the Parties to the North Atlantic Treaty Regarding the Status of their Forces, June 19, 1951, [1953] 4 U.S.T. 1792, 199 U.N.T.S. 67, express provision is made regarding the principles which must govern a criminal trial conducted by the receiving state when it exercises its jurisdiction. Paragraph 9 of Article VII provides: Whenever a member of a force or civilian component or a dependent is prosecuted under the jurisdiction of a receiving State he shall be entitled—

(a) to a prompt and speedy trial;

(b) to be informed, in advance of trial, of the specific charge or charges made against him;

(c) to be confronted with the witnesses against him;

(d) to have compulsory process for obtaining witnesses in his favor, if they are within the jurisdiction of the receiving State;

(e) to have legal representation of his own choice for his defence or to have free or assisted legal representation under the conditions prevailing for the time being in the receiving State;

(f) if he considers it necessary, to have the services of a competent interpreter; and

(g) to communicate with a representative of the Government of the sending State and, when the rules of the court permit, to have such a representative present at his trial.

Are these guarantees different from those which would be provided under the international minimum standard in accordance with ordinary standards of civilization? Would all the members of NATO provide these guarantees without reference to the agreement? Does paragraph 9 incorporate into status of forces jurisprudence the procedural guarantees of the United States Constitution?

* * *

Under U.S. law, the guarantees of the NATO Status of Forces Agreement are enforceable through diplomatic channels rather than directly available to the accused in the courts of the sending state. Members of the U.S. armed forces were tried in a German court under the terms of an agreement extending the terms of the Status of Forces Agreement. They were convicted of attempted rape but remained in United States custody. The United States was prepared to surrender them to the German authorities pursuant to the agreement. The servicemen, however, sought an injunction in a court, on the ground that procedures in the German trial had violated the guarantees of the Status of Forces Agreement. Their claim was held to be non-justiciable.

Evolution—Europe sometimes affords more protection than the U.S.: *Short v. Kingdom of the Netherlands*, 92 ILM 1388 (1990), noted in Steven J. Lepper, *Jurisdiction—NATO Status of Forces Agreement—U.S. Serviceman Charged with Criminal Offenses Overseas—European Convention on Human Rights*, 85 AJIL 698, 701 (1991) (footnotes omitted):*

* * *

The *Short* case represents perhaps the most serious example of this dilemma. On March 30, 1988, Staff Sergeant Charles D. Short, a member of the United States Air Force stationed at Soesterberg Air Base in the Netherlands, was arrested by the Dutch Royal Marechaussee (military police) as a suspect in the murder of his wife, a Turkish national. At some point during his interrogation, SSgt Short admitted killing his wife, dismembering her, and placing her remains in plastic bags by a dike somewhere near Amsterdam. Depending on such additional factors as his state of mind at the time of the murder, SSgt Short clearly might have been charged with capital murder under the Uniform Code of Military Justice. Knowing this, the Dutch authorities refused to turn him over to his superiors at the Soesterberg base. Although the NATO SOFA vested jurisdiction over this offense in the United States, the Dutch rationale for refusing to comply with that treaty was that to do so would subject SSgt Short to the risk of capital punishment.

The path this case traveled through the Dutch courts was just as interesting to the U.S. military as the High Court's ultimate refusal to surrender SSgt Short. Requests for the surrender of visiting force members to the state with primary jurisdiction are generally made and approved (or disapproved) at the lowest levels possible. Rarely will the host nation's courts get involved; the local police chief or prosecutor is usually the decisional authority. SSgt Short's case was destined to be different when his appointed Dutch attorney's first act was to secure a local court injunction preventing his surrender. After a full hearing, the civil trial court at The Hague acknowledged that the NATO SOFA gave

* Reprinted with the permission of the American Society of Int'l Law.

the United States primary jurisdiction over the alleged offense. Nevertheless, it refused to allow the Dutch Government to surrender SSgt Short because the Netherlands was bound by the Sixth Protocol to the European Convention not to subject anyone to the risk of capital punishment. The court added that it would order his surrender to U.S. authorities only if they could guarantee that the death penalty either would not be imposed or would not be carried out. For policy and legal reasons, the Commander in Chief, United States Air Forces in Europe (CinCUSAFE), refused to give such assurances.

While the Dutch Ministry of Justice appealed the civil trial court's decision, a Dutch criminal trial court convicted SSgt Short of manslaughter and sentenced him to six years' imprisonment. Very shortly thereafter, the civil appeals court in The Hague reversed the initial civil court decision on the ground that the NATO SOFA allocates primary jurisdiction to the United States. Instead of interpreting the Convention and Dutch law as superseding the SOFA, it construed them as consistent with it: since the SOFA exempted Short from Dutch criminal jurisdiction, it also removed him from its civil and convention-based jurisdiction. Thus, the latter laws and treaty did not apply. The appeals court accordingly ordered his surrender but agreed to stay execution of its judgment until the High Court had an opportunity to review it.

At this point, the decisions of the criminal trial court and the civil appeals court conflicted. Both were appealed. The criminal appeals court reversed the criminal trial court, holding that since the United States had jurisdiction, Dutch courts lacked authority to hear the criminal case. The Dutch High Court (Hoge Raad), however, reversed the civil appeals court, ruling that the state's obligations under the Convention must prevail over the conflicting SOFA allocation of jurisdiction. This double reversal led to an even more frightening paradox: unless either decision was somehow reversed, the ultimate result would be that SSgt Short—by his own admission, a brutal murderer—would be a free man in the Netherlands. Both judgments stood.

5. *Law applicable in international arbitrations.* In appraising the utility as precedent for international law of arbitral decisions, it is important to determine the legal context in which the opinion was rendered. As noted in Chapters 13, 17 and 1, arbitrations are customarily conducted in accordance with an agreement between the contending states (the *compromis*) which not only sets the terms under which the arbitration will be conducted but also may indicate the governing rules to be applied by the arbitrators. The convention often provided for the application of principles of international law, justice and equity. In *Perry (United States) v. Panama,* General Claims Commission, 1933, 6 U.N.Rep.Int'l Arb.Awards 315, the commission was authorized to decide in accordance with these principles. In awarding the United States the sum of $10,000 because of Panama's arrest and imprisonment of an American citizen "without a proper order," who "remained imprisoned through the failure of the authorities to give to his case proper attention," the majority of the commissioners stated: "There is no reason to scrutinize whether these terms [i.e. international law, justice, and equity] embody an indivisible rule or mean that international law, justice

and equity have to be considered in the order in which they are mentioned, because either of these constructions leads to the conclusion that the commission shall be guided rather by broad conceptions than by narrow interpretations." The dissenting Panamanian Commissioner stated that the majority opinion suggests "the Tribunal believes it proper to award Perry damages for simple reasons of equity." See extensive discussion of arbitration in Chapters 1 & 16.

———

6. ***Exhaustion of local remedies.*** "The rule that local remedies must be exhausted before international proceedings may be instituted is a well-established rule of customary international law. It has been generally observed in cases in which a state has adopted the cause of its national where rights are claimed to have been disregarded in another State in violation of international law. Before resort may be had to an international court in such a situation, it has been considered necessary that the State where the violation occurred should have an opportunity to redress it by its own means, within the framework of its own domestic legal system." *Interhandel Case* (Switzerland v. United States), [1959] I.C.J.Rep. 6, 27. As stated, the rule is applicable to claims based upon violations of personal human rights as well as to claims arising from violations of rights of property. Detailed examination of the rule is deferred to Chapter 15 dealing with economic interests.

The rule is subject to exceptions; for example, if it is clear that exhaustion of local remedies would not be effective, there is no need to pursue them. Should the rule apply to diplomatic protests, or only to claims in litigation, before the International Court of Justice or an arbitral tribunal?

In view of the exhaustion of local remedies rule, how can a claimant state assert that the acting state has violated its own law? If, for example, an individual has been imprisoned for a long time before trial and complains of this through appropriate court proceedings until a court of final appeal has ruled that the local law does not prohibit such imprisonment, can an international tribunal properly hold that there has been a violation of local law? In the famous *Roberts Case,* cited supra, the commission asserted that Roberts' imprisonment was a violation of the Mexican Constitution. *Does the answer to this question lie in the fact that the General Claims Convention governing the Roberts arbitration provided in Article V as follows?*

> The High Contracting Parties, being desirous of effecting an equitable settlement of the claims of their respective citizens thereby affording them just and adequate compensation for their losses or damages, agree that no claim shall be disallowed or rejected by the Commission by the application of the general principle of international law that the legal remedies must be exhausted as a condition precedent to the validity or allowance of any claim.

Does the exhaustion of remedies rule, created and applied in matters of diplomatic protection, also apply to human rights

cases? C.F. Amerasinghe, in his book Local Remedies in International Law (1990) argues that it does, but is refuted forcefully by A.A. Cançado Trindate, of the University of Brazilia, reviewing the book, in 86 AJIL 626, 631 (1992) (reprinted by permission AJIL):

> * * * to claim that the local remedies rule should be applied in human rights protection exactly as diplomatic protection, to claim that the content or scope of the rule is not affected by contextual differences, and, in particular, by considerations of superior common values or *ordre public* in respect of the protection of the rights of the human person and not of the state, is to close one's eyes to reality. Generally recognized rules of international law, besides undergoing an evolution of their own within the contexts in which they are applied, necessarily undergo, when enshrined in human rights treaties, some adjustment, dictated by the special character of the object and purpose of those treaties and by the generally recognized specificity of the international protection of human rights.

> This is the lesson drawn from the experience accumulated in this domain; progress in the international protection of human rights has been made possible in the last decades, as well as in relation to the operation of the local remedies rule, by an awareness of the specificity of this *droit de protection* (which calls for an interpretation of its own), by a proper understanding of the basic premises underlying the mechanisms of protection and by faithful pursuit of their object and purpose. It is fortunate that international supervisory organs in the domain of human rights protection have espoused an understanding of the local remedies rule and have proceeded on a basis wholly at variance with [its application in matters of diplomatic protection].

The *Optional Protocol to the International Covenant on Civil and Political Rights,* [U.N.Doc. A/6316 (1966), 999 UNTS 302] to which the United States, and most Western nations are not parties, allows, in its article 5, the Human Rights Committee to hear submissions by individuals without exhaustion of local remedies, "where the application of the [local] remedies is unreasonably prolonged." Is this law?

This *Optional Protocol* has created a body of law via the Human Rights Committee, providing that gross violations of human rights will have a remedy via the Committee, including the obligation to pay adequate compensation to the victims or their families. Gross violations have been deemed to include gross violations of human rights and fundamental freedoms, genocide, torture or other cruel, inhuman or degrading treatment or punishment, systematic racial discrimination, and a consistent pattern of gross violations of internationally recognized human rights. *See,* Theo van Boven, Special Rapporteur, for the *Study Concerning Right to Restitution, Compensation and Rehabilitation for Victims of Gross Violations of Human Rights and Fundamental Freedoms,* U.N.Doc. E/CN.4/Sub.2/10, at 8 (1990); reported in Luke T. Lee, *The Preventive Approach to the Refugee Problem,* 28 Willamette L.Rev. 821 (1992). The Inter–American Court of Human Rights granted jurisdiction on the ground that there were no meaningful local remedies to exhaust in Honduras, in *Valásquez Rodriguez Case,* Inter.Am.Ct.H.Rts., OAS/ser. L./V./III.19, doc. 13 (1988), 28 I.L.M. 291, 305–06 (1989).

7. *A new view of the older precedents.* The flow of third party decisions on questions of violation of personal human rights practically ceased with World War II. It has been observed that the desire of states for freedom to act unilaterally has been strong during the whole life of the United Nations and that states have been reluctant to take disputes to the International Court of Justice. "It may be noted in this context that, whereas the number of arbitral decisions since 1945 was not spectacular, it was not insignificant, although it is probably true that, as the Secretary General of the United Nations pointed out, 'most of them concerned minor questions, many of them of a commercial nature, which were not in the least likely to disturb peace and security.' " Leo Gross, *The International Court of Justice: Consideration of Requirements for Enhancing its Role in the International Legal Order,* 65 AJIL 253, 268 (1971).

Although the body of arbitral precedents with respect to personal human rights is static, the United Nations has made the development of new legal norms in that field a major matter of concern. *Query* : can an arbitral tribunal today ignore the Universal Declaration of Human Rights or the relevant draft covenants and United Nations regional conventions promulgated in recent decades?

SECTION B.   THE ARTICULATION OF HUMAN RIGHTS STANDARDS

1.   THEORIES OF HUMAN RIGHTS

a.   *Natural Law:*

de Vattel, The Law of Nations or Principles of the Law of Nature, Applied to the Conduct and Affairs of Nations and Sovereigns (1758), Book II ch. VI, p. 162 (Chitty, ed. 1849):

§ 71.   * * * [I]t remains for us to examine what share a state may have in the actions of her citizens, and what are the rights and obligations of sovereigns in this respect.

Whoever offends the state, injures its rights, disturbs its tranquility, or does it a prejudice in any manner whatsoever, declares himself its enemy, and exposes himself to be justly punished for it. Whoever uses a citizen ill, indirectly offends the state, which is bound to protect this citizen; and the sovereign of the latter should avenge his wrongs, punish the aggressor, and, if possible, oblige him to make full reparation; since otherwise the citizen would not obtain the great end of the civil association, which is, safety.

§ 72.   But, on the other hand, the nation or the sovereign, ought not to suffer the citizens to do an injury to the subjects of another state, much less to offend that state itself: and this, not only because no sovereign ought to permit those who are under his command to violate the precepts of the law of nature, which forbids all injuries,—but also because nations ought mutually to respect each other, to abstain from all offence from all injury, from all wrong,—in a word, from every thing that may be of prejudice to others. If a sovereign, who might keep his subject within the rules of justice and peace, suffers them to injure a foreign nation either in its body or its members, he does not less injury to that nation than if he injured it himself. In short, the safety of the state, and that of human society, requires this attention from every sovereign. If you let loose the reigns to your subjects against foreign nations, these will behave in the same manner to you; and, instead of that friendly intercourse which nature has established between all men, we shall see nothing but one vast and dreadful scene of plunder between nation and nation.

During the reign of *"Natural Law,"* it was a matter of principle that the law protected individuals from certain abuses. John Locke, therefore, provided the following thoughts:

JOHN LOCKE, SECOND TREATISE OF GOVERNMENT (1690) IN TWO TREATISES OF GOVERNMENT

§ 123, p. 368 (critical edition 1963).

Of the Ends of Political Society and Government.

If Man in the State of Nature be so free, as has been said; If he be absolute Lord of his own Person and Possessions, equal to the greatest, and subject to no Body, why will he part with his Freedom? Why will he give up this Empire, and subject himself to the Dominion and Controul of any other Power? To which 'tis obvious to Answer, that though in the state of Nature he hath such a right, yet the Enjoyment of it is very uncertain, and constantly exposed to the Invasion of others. For all being Kings as much as he, every Man his Equal, and the greater part no strict Observers of Equity and Justice, the enjoyment of the property he has in this state is very unsafe, very unsecure. This makes him willing to quit a Condition, which however free, is full of fears and continual dangers: And 'tis not without reason, that he seeks out, and is willing to joyn in Society with others who are already united, or have a mind to unite for the mutual *Preservation* of their Lives, Liberties and Estates, which I call by the general Name, *Property*.

2. POSITIVISM

BRITISH LAW OFFICERS OPINION IN THE SILESIAN LOAN CASE

1753, in 2 McNair, International Law Opinions, (Cambridge 1956) 303–304.

In the famous Report of the Law Officers of 18 January 1753 upon what is known as the Silesian Loan, the matter is touched upon incidentally. It was signed by Lee, Paul, Ryder and Murray (then

Solicitor–General, later Lord Chief Justice Mansfield). * * * If the Matter of Complaint be a Capture at Sea during War, and the Question relative to Prize, he ought to apply to the Judicatures established to try these Questions.

The Law of Nations, founded upon Justice, Equity, Convenience and the Reason of the Thing, and confirmed by long Usage, don't allow of Reprizals, except in Case of violent Injuries, directed or supported by the State, and Justice, absolutely denied, *in Re minime dubiâ,* by all the Tribunals, and afterwards by the Prince.

When the Judges are left free, and give Sentence according to their Conscience, though it should be erroneous, that would be no Ground for Reprizals. Upon doubtful Questions, different Men think and judge differently; and all a Friend can desire, is, that Justice should be as impartially administered to him, as it is to the Subjects of that Prince, in whose Courts the Matter is try'd.

On 6 November 1819, Robinson, in reporting upon certain depredations upon British trade by armed vessels acting under the orders of the captain-general of Valencia, which amounted "to an absolute denial of justice or failure of justice on appeal by reason of the acts of a principal officer of the Spanish Government", remarked:

The ancient remedy in such cases was by granting Special Letters of Reprizal to the injured party. But that practice has been disused, not on account of any intrinsic injustice in the principle, but on account of the inconveniences attending it. The remedy of Force however must always remain the last resort of the injured Government. But it is a question of extreme delicacy when and in what manner it may be expedient to use it.

———

Notes & Questions: Do philosophical positivists recognize the validity of Human Rights law? Can they, if given their position on the status of the individual in international law? If they can, how do they rationalize it? For more detail and writings of Austin and others, see Ch. 18, *infra.*

3. OTHER THEORIES

a. "Cross–Cultural Perspectives"

ABDULLAHI AHMED AN–NA'IM

Human Rights in Cross–Cultural Perspectives, pp. 1–6 (1992) *

* * * [A] cross-cultural approach may be helpful in deepening our understanding of the underlying causes of the continuing discrepancy between the theory and practice of human rights, and in addressing those causes more effectively. Clearly, the credibility and practical efficacy of national and international human rights standards would be enhanced by increasing their legitimacy in the widest possible range of cultural traditions. Current and foreseeable new human rights cannot

* Reprinted with the permission of University of Pennsylvania Press.

be seen as truly universal unless they are conceived and articulated within the widest possible range of cultural traditions.

The term *culture* is used here in its broadest sense as the "totality of values, institutions and forms of behavior transmitted within a society * * * this wide conception of culture covers *Weltanschauung* [world view], ideologies and cognitive behavior." In this sense, liberalism and Marxism, for example, are part of, or ideological manifestations of, the culture of some societies. As normative propositions, human rights are much more credible and thereby stand a better chance of implementation if they are perceived to be legitimate within the various cultural traditions of the world.

Some scholars and political leaders have argued that the current international standards of human rights, together with the machinery for promoting and implementing them, may not be sufficiently universal because they lack legitimacy in major cultural traditions. Others argue that these standards and machinery are universal because the vast majority of governments have either participated in the formulation process or subsequently ratified the relevant international instruments. They also warn against the dangers of claiming cultural relativity as a pretext for justifying human rights violations. While appreciating that the first position might be adopted cynically to justify human rights violations, and that the second position might reflect undue formalism or naive idealism, I suggest that a constructive approach can draw on the element of truth in each position in order to enhance the credibility and efficacy of international human rights standards.

* * * [It] is not realistic to deny the real or apparent insufficiency of cultural legitimacy of some human rights standards. Because there are obvious areas of conflict and tension between the current international standards of human rights and major cultural traditions, relativist arguments often seem plausible. Nevertheless, the dangers of extreme relativism should not be underestimated. My view, therefore, is that scholars and activists should neither underestimate the challenge of cultural relativism to the universality of human rights nor concede too much to its claims. Rather, it is preferable to adopt a constructive approach that recognizes the problems and addresses them in the context of each cultural tradition, as well as across cultural boundaries.

The proposed approach seeks to explore the possibilities of cultural reinterpretation and reconstruction through *internal cultural discourse and cross-cultural dialogue,* as a means to enhancing the universal legitimacy of human rights. * * *

Since cultural norms and attitudes influence individual and collective or institutional human behavior, one may reasonably expect cultural antagonism toward some human rights standards to diminish the efficacy of these standards in a particular society. Although such antagonism may reflect the prevailing or dominant view of the cultural position, it may not necessarily be the only available view. There may therefore be room for changing a cultural position from within, through *internal* *discourse* about the fundamental values of the culture and the rationale for these values.   * * *

---

b. A "Feminist" Approach to Human Rights Law:

Are women's human rights different from those of men? Does feminist legal scholarship provide different perspective from which to consider human rights law? See generally, Engle, Int'l Human Rights, *infra.* Goldberg & Kelly, *Recent Developments: International Human Rights and Violence Against Women,* 6 Harv.Hum.Rts.J. 195 (1993); Halberstam & Defeis, Women's Legal Rights (1987); Charlesworth, et al., *Feminist Approaches to International Law,* 85 AJIL 613 (1991); Bunch, *Women's Rights as Human Rights: Toward a Revision of Human Rights,* 12 Hum.Rts.Q. 486 (1990); Eisler, *Toward an Integrated Theory of Action,* 9 Hum.Rts.Q. 287 (1987).

Of the atrocities in Bosnia and Herzegovina, none was worse than the use of women as vessels of a strategic and genocidal rape. Women were singled out for mass rape which was used as a weapon of mass destruction. Women were not the only ones slaughtered, but they were the unique and purposeful victims of this tactic, even strategy, of terror and psychic genocide.[a] Perhaps women have a perspective on human rights violations in general that men do not have. Does the perspective extend beyond that particular crime? If so, is it based on anything other than being a particular type of victim? Feminists, of course, are not of one view on human rights. *See,* as an example, Goldberg and Kelly, *Violence Against Women,* supra, report:

* * *

   In recent years, scholars and advocates have criticized human rights law for its failure to accord protection to women facing gender-based violence. Although physical abuse of women is pervasive, cutting across cultural, class, and economic lines, traditional concepts of human rights have developed within a public, male-dominated framework which does not recognize the experiences of women as women. Violence against women, particularly that which occurs within the intimate sphere, is viewed as the result of private disputes and not as having an important, political context. Gender-based violence is not recognized as a violation of human rights, but rather as the product of particular cultural or religious practices or the isolated actions of individuals. Feminists have attributed this failure to a male-dominated conception of human rights which privileges public over private activity. They also fault a narrow western conception of human rights which focuses on state violations of civil and political rights, thereby subordinating economic, social, and cultural rights. Feminists have sought to address these shortcomings by calling for the following: (1) an expansion of the

---

a. Similarly, however, some men in concentration camps have reportedly been forced to bite off each others testicles. Editor's interview with investigators.

responsibility of states, at the local, national, and international levels, to protect women under existing legal mechanisms; (2) the creation of new mechanisms that address the human rights concerns of women as women; (3) increased awareness of abuses which occur because of gender and abuses imposed in a gender-specific manner; and (4) expansion of the conception and practice of human rights to incorporate the specific experiences of women.

The "voice" of women, of course, is not unified; there is an ongoing debate among feminists regarding the role of "culture" in human rights:

KAREN ENGLE, INTERNATIONAL HUMAN RIGHTS AND FEMINISM: WHEN DISCOURSES MEET
13 Mich.J.I.L. 517, 518–521 (1992) *

The literature on women's human rights is a particularly rich site for an analysis of rights discourse deployment, because in this literature two different, and sometimes competing, models of rights converge. Although it might seem that international human rights law would naturally incorporate women's rights, since women are human, women's rights advocates have suggested that such incorporation cannot be assumed. While some maintain that women's rights are already included in international human rights law, others argue that the international human rights régime will have to change before it can take women into account. In either case, women's rights discourse is generally positioned at the periphery of human rights discourse, both challenging and defending the dominant human rights model as it attempts to fit its causes into that model. * * *.

Although a critique of rights has not been launched at human rights law, it has not escaped challenge. Two attacks are generally aimed at the law. First, it is often seen as a Western-conceived and -dominated project that fails to address adequately the concerns of the East and the Third World. While some critics raise the possibility that a Western system of rights cannot accommodate non-Western needs, most believe that the system can rearrange its priorities to address those needs. Second, and more often, human rights law is attacked for not being expansive enough. It is encouraged, for example, to take more seriously economic or social rights, or the rights of women or cultural and ethnic minorities. These two critiques, of course, are not unrelated. For both sets of critics, whatever deficiencies the law might have, can be addressed through expansion, either through new sets of rights or through a reordering of the rights that exist. None of the critics believes that taking into account her or his concerns will radically disrupt the system.

The international law of human rights has been built largely by its own criticism. Since its inception, different groups and causes have situated themselves at its margins and challenged it to respond better to more and different types of oppression. In many ways, they have been successful. As different groups have suggested new rights and rein-

* Reprinted with the permission of the Michigan J. Int'l Law and Karen Engle.

terpretations of old rights, they have contributed to a proliferation of international human rights documents and conventions.

Feminists form one of the groups that has attempted to expand human rights, urging it to better encompass women's rights. Through their work, they have not only identified those international legal instruments that include provisions prohibiting sex discrimination, but they have also helped establish international legal instruments that pertain specifically to women's rights. Using the number of such instruments as a measure of progress, it would appear feminists' work has paid off: in 1986, Natalie Hevener identified twenty-two international documents relating to the status of women. Much of the work of women's rights advocates was realized during the United Nations Decade for Women, with the creation of the 1979 Convention on the Elimination of All Forms of Discrimination Against Women (Women's Convention). Although that Convention has only been open for signature since 1980, it already has been ratified by as many States as have ratified the International Covenant on Civil and Political Rights, and the International Covenant on Economic, Social and Cultural Rights.

As the number of legal instruments has increased, so has the scholarly literature on women's human rights. Before the Women's Convention, only a few works had been written about women's rights, but since then the number of works has skyrocketed. Some of those written since the Women's Convention focus specifically on that Convention, while others deal generally with women's human rights. The Women's Convention, then, has both generated and reflected a renewed interest in women's human rights, as much as it has been the actual subject of discourse * * *.

———

See also, Engle, Female Subjects of Public International Law: Human Rights and the Exotic Other Female, 26 New Eng.L.Rev. 1509 (1992).

———

4. HUMAN RIGHTS PROVISIONS OF THE CHARTER OF THE UNITED NATIONS

Articles 1, 2, 55, and 56 are most commonly cited in the UN Charter in relation to Human Rights. Read each of them carefully from the Documentary Supplement.

Highlights of the drafting history of Chapter IX, Article 56 of the Charter. Does Article 56 impose on states an international legal obligation to take immediate national action to correct internal deficiencies in the area of human rights? or does that article serve merely as a statement of political principle, i.e. that states intend to do something about human rights?

The United States was particularly concerned that nothing in Chapter IX of the charter "be construed as giving authority to the 'Organization' to intervene in the domestic affairs of member states." 10 U.N.Conf.Int'l Org. 83 (1945). The United States was, at one point, of the opinion that the reservation for domestic jurisdiction in Article 2(7) of the charter would not alone be sufficient to keep human rights from becoming matters of international concern if Article 56 were worded to include a pledge by members "to take such independent action as they deem appropriate to achieve these purposes within their own territories." *Id.,* at 140. Nevertheless, the United States ultimately supported the language of Article 56 as it appears in the charter, without insisting upon a special reservation to retain domestic jurisdiction over human rights matters. *Id.,* at 161.

As to the nature of the commitment, the following submission from a drafting sub-committee was rejected: "All members undertake to cooperate jointly and severally with the Organization for the achievement of these purposes." *Id.,* at 394 and 139.

The proposal noted above, for a pledge to take "independent action", was likewise not accepted. The ultimate language as found in the charter includes "*separate action* in cooperation with the Organization." [Emphasis supplied.]

THE MEANING OF ARTICLE 56

In the formative stages of the United Nations the members sought to give content to the commitments made in Article 56. An obvious place to begin was South Africa's practice of apartheid. The South African Government responded that the United Nations was, by the law of the Charter, forbidden to intervene in its domestic jurisdiction and that its laws on racial matters were within that jurisdiction. The South African position posed very sharply the issue whether the United Nations had broken decisively with the past; with the idea that how a nation treated its own citizens was its own business. The following is an extract from a debate in a General Assembly Committee. It illustrates the legal argumentation that was advanced at this early stage in the development of the relation between Article 56 of the Charter and Article 2(7)'s prohibition against intervention in domestic jurisdiction. An understanding of the organization's commitment in Article 56 is a predicate to appreciation of its later work in articulating human rights standards and pursuing their implementation. This is enlightening given the history-making events of 1994, including the end of apartheid and the election of Nelson Mandela in an election in which all races had a right to participate.

THE QUESTION OF RACE CONFLICT IN SOUTH AFRICA RESULTING FROM THE POLICIES OF APARTHEID

United Nations, Resolution 721 (VIII) Adopted by the General Assembly, Dec. 8, 1953.
U.N.G.A.Off.Rec., 8th Sess.1953 Supp. No. 17(A/2630).

The General Assembly,

Having considered the report of the United Nations Commission on the Racial Situation in * * * South Africa established by resolution 616A (VII) of 5 December 1952,

Noting with concern that the Commission, in its study of the racial policies of the Government of South Africa, has concluded that these policies and their consequences are contrary to the Charter and the Universal Declaration of Human Rights,

Noting that the Commission had also concluded that:

(a) "It is highly unlikely, and indeed improbable, that the policy of apartheid will ever be willingly accepted by the masses subjected to discrimination", and [that]

(b) the continuance of this policy [makes] peaceful solutions increasingly difficult and endanger friendly relations among nations,

Noting further that the Commission considers it desirable that the United Nations should request the Government of South Africa to reconsider the components of its policy towards various ethnic groups,

* * *

Considering the Commission's view that one of the difficulties encountered by it was the lack of cooperation from the Government of South Africa and, in particular, its refusal to permit the Commission to enter its territory,

1. Reaffirms its resolutions 103(I) of 19 November 1946, 377 A(V), section E, of 3 November 1950 and 616B (VII) of 5 December 1952, particularly the passages in those resolutions which state respectively that "it is in the higher interests of humanity to put an immediate end to religious and so-called racial persecution and discrimination"; that "enduring peace will not be secured solely by collective security arrangements against breaches of international peace and acts of aggression, but that a genuine and lasting peace depends also upon the observance of all the Principles and Purposes established in the Charter, of the United Nations, * * * and especially upon respect for an observance of human rights and fundamental freedoms for all and on the establishment and maintenance of conditions of economic and social well-being in all countries"; and that "in a multi-racial society harmony and respect for human rights and freedoms and the peaceful development of a unified community are best assured when patterns of legislation and practice are directed towards ensuring the equality before the law of all persons regardless of race, creed or colour, and when economic, social, cultural and political participation of all racial groups is on a basis of equality";

2. Expresses appreciation of the work of the United Nations Commission on the Racial Situation in * * * South Africa;

* * *

4. Requests the Commission:

(a) To continue its study of the development of the racial situation in * * * South Africa; * * *

(b) To suggest measures which would help to alleviate the situation and promote a peaceful settlement;

5. Invites the Government of South Africa to extend its full cooperation to the Commission;

* * *

ADVISORY OPINION ON THE CONTINUED PRESENCE OF SOUTH AFRICA IN NAMIBIA (SOUTH WEST AFRICA) [a]

International Court of Justice, 1971. [1971] I.C.J.Rep. 16.

[At the conclusion of World War I, South Africa accepted a Mandate with respect to German South West Africa pursuant to the Covenant of the League of Nations. Upon the demise of the League, South Africa refused to accept the principle urged upon it by the United Nations that the latter had the right to supervise its administration of South West Africa. After fruitless negotiations, and the rendering of advisory opinions on various aspects of the matter by the International Court of Justice, the General Assembly adopted a resolution terminating the Mandate for South West Africa, now called Namibia. South Africa having failed to alter its policies with respect to South West Africa, the Security Council adopted a resolution declaring the continued presence of South Africa in Namibia to be illegal and called on states to act accordingly. The Council thereafter requested the court to render an advisory opinion on the question: What are the legal consequences for States of the continued presence of South Africa in Namibia, notwithstanding Security Council resolution 276 (1970)? *Read* the comprehensive opinion answering this question:

* * * 128. In its oral statement and in written communications to the Court, the Government of South Africa expressed the desire to supply the Court with further factual information concerning the purposes and objectives of South Africa's policy of separate development or apartheid, contending that to establish a breach of South Africa's substantive international obligations under the Mandate it would be necessary to prove that a particular exercise of South Africa's legislative or administrative powers was not directed in good faith towards the purpose of promoting to the utmost the well-being and progress of the

---

a. The full name of the case is: Legal Consequences for States of the Continued Presence of South Africa in Namibia (South West Africa), notwithstanding Security Council Resolution 276 (1970), Advisory Opinion.

inhabitants. It is claimed by the Government of South Africa that no act or omission on its part would constitute a violation of its international obligations unless it is shown that such act or omission was actuated by a motive, or directed towards a purpose other than one to promote the interests of the inhabitants of the Territory.

129. The Government of South Africa having made this request, the Court finds that no factual evidence is needed for the purpose of determining whether the policy of apartheid as applied by South Africa in Namibia is in conformity with the international obligations assumed by South Africa under the Charter of the United Nations. To determine whether the laws and decrees applied by South Africa in Namibia, which are a matter of public record, constitute a violation of the purposes and principles of the Charter of the United Nations, the question of intent or governmental discretion is not relevant; nor is it necessary to investigate or determine the effects of those measures upon the welfare of the inhabitants.

130. It is undisputed, and is amply supported by documents annexed to South Africa's written statement in these proceedings, that the official governmental policy pursued by South Africa in Namibia is to achieve a complete physical separation of races and ethnic groups in separate areas within the Territory. The application of this policy has required, as has been conceded by South Africa, restrictive measures of control officially adopted and enforced in the Territory by the coercive power of the former Mandatary. These measures establish limitations, exclusions or restrictions for the members of the indigenous population groups in respect of their participation in certain types of activities, fields of study or of training, labour or employment and also submit them to restrictions or exclusions of residence and movement in large parts of the Territory.

131. Under the Charter of the United Nations, the former Mandatary had pledged itself to observe and respect, in a territory having an international status, human rights and fundamental freedoms for all without distinction as to race. To establish instead, and to enforce, distinctions, exclusions, restrictions and limitations exclusively based on grounds of race, colour, descent or national or ethnic origin which constitute a denial of fundamental human rights is a flagrant violation of the purposes and principles of the Charter.

* * *

ARTICLE 56 AND SELF–EXECUTION OF A TREATY UNDER UNITED STATES LAW

As will be developed further in Chapter 14, some treaties become domestic law in the United States immediately upon promulgation by the President, without implementing legislation. Such so-called self-executing treaties may also afford individual rights that are immediately enforceable in the courts. Is Article 56 of the United Nations Charter self-executing? Does it afford such enforceable rights? It was held not to be such a treaty in Sei Fujii v. State, 242 P.2d 617 (1952). Although holding that California's law that prohibited ownership of land by a Japanese citizen ineligible for American citizenship was unconstitutional under the Fourteenth Amendment, the court said, with respect to the Charter: "The provisions in the charter pledging cooperation in promoting observance of fundamental freedoms lack the mandatory quality and definitiveness which would indicate an intent to create justiciable rights in private persons immediately upon ratification." Is the California court correct in its appraisal of the provisions of Article 56? Would the result be different if mandatory quality were found? Can the self-executing theory lead to the conclusion, in a particular case, that the state is obligated internationally at some time after ratification not to discriminate on the basis of alien status but that, without promulgation of additional law, the alien, even after ratification, is not protected by national law? If this occurs, what is the status of the United States in relation to the treaty and international law? Was it inevitable in 1952 that a court would find the alien land law unconstitutional?

5. THE TORTURE CONVENTION

The United States Senate gave its Advice & Consent to the Torture Convention, *The Convention Against Torture and other Cruel, Inhuman, or Degrading Treatment or Punishment* [see Doc.Supp.] This Convention codifies, in a specific and comprehensive manner, an internationally recognized human right. The Convention, in article 1, *defines torture* as any act by which severe physical or mental pain or suffering is intentionally inflicted for purposes of punishment, intimidation, coercion, or discrimination, by or at the instigation of or with the consent or acquiescence of a public official or agent of an official, acting in an official capacity. The definition exempts lawful sanctions. The Convention includes *non-refoulement* or the protection that no state party shall expel, return (*refouler*) or extradite an individual where there exists substantial grounds to believe that he or she would be in danger of being tortured. *What does "substantial grounds" mean?* Would the standard in the U.S. for determining this be the same as under the Refugee Act of 1980, which provides that grounds for *non-refoulement* exist when the evidence indicates that it *"is more likely than not"* that the person will suffer or be threatened with persecution, etc. upon return? *See,* INS v. Stevic, 467 U.S. 407 (1984); *Sales v. Haitian Refugee Center,* infra p. 827.

Article 14 of the Torture Convention calls for each Party to accord the victim of torture both a legal right to redress and an enforceable right to fair and adequate compensation. The U.S. Congress promulgated the **Torture Victim Protection Act** of 1991, which provides: "An Act to carry out obligations of the United States under the United Nations Charter and other international agreements pertaining to the protection of human rights by establishing a civil action for recovery of damages from an individual who engages in torture or extrajudicial killing * * *."

Sec. 2. Establishment of Civil Action

(a) Liability.—An individual who, under actual or apparent authority, or color of law, of any foreign nation—

   (1) subjects an individual to torture shall, in a civil action, be liable for damages to that individual; or

   (2) subjects an individual to extrajudicial killing shall, in a civil action, be liable for damages to the individual's legal representative, or to any person who may be a claimant in an action for wrongful death.

(b) Exhaustion of Remedies.—A court shall decline to hear a claim under this section if the claimant has not exhausted adequate and available remedies in the place in which the conduct giving rise to the claim occurred.

(c) Statute of Limitations.—No action shall be maintained under this section unless it is commenced within 10 years after the cause of action arose.

Sec. 3. Definitions

(a) Extrajudicial Killing.—For the purposes of this Act, the term "extrajudicial killing" means a deliberated killing not authorized by a previous judgment pronounced by a regularly constituted court affording all the judicial guarantees which are recognized as indispensable by civilized peoples. Such term, however, does not include any such killing that, under international law, is lawfully carried out under the authority of a foreign nation.

(b) Torture.—For the purposes of this Act—

   (1) * * * means any act, directed against an individual in the offender's custody or physical control, by which severe pain or suffering (other than pain or suffering arising only from or inherent in, or incidental to, lawful sanctions), whether physical or mental, is intentionally inflicted on that individual for such purposes as obtaining from that individual or a third person information or a confession, punishing that individual for an act that individual or a third person has committed or is suspected of having committed, intimidating or coercing that individual or a third person, or for any reason based on discrimination of any kind; and

   (2) mental pain or suffering refers to prolonged mental harm caused by or resulting from—

      (A) the intentional infliction or threatened infliction of severe physical pain or suffering;

      (B) the administration or application, or threatened administration or application, of mind altering substances or other procedures calculated to disrupt profoundly the senses or the personality;

(C) the threat of imminent death; or

(D) the threat that another individual will imminently be subjected to death, severe physical pain or suffering, or the administration or application of mind altering substances or other procedures calculated to disrupt profoundly the senses or personality. Approved March 12, 1992.

In the manner of its approach to other human rights conventions, such as that on *Genocide*, the United States Senate adhered to the Convention, however, subject to significant reservations. For example, it provided that the Convention was *"non-self-executing."* This means that the Convention is non-effective under U.S. law, until enabling legislation has been promulgated. For discussion of this, see Chapter 1, Applications of International Law, and Chapter 14, U.S. Constitution and International Agreements. The U.S. also reserved a limitation on Convention Article 16's obligation to prevent "cruel, inhuman or degrading treatment or punishment," to what is meant by those terms under U.S. Constitutional Law, namely, pursuant to the Fifth, Eighth, and Fourteenth Amendments. U.S. ratification includes the "understanding" that this exemption for lawful sanctions includes judicially-imposed punishments and other enforcement measures authorized by U.S. law. Thus, the U.S. position is that the death penalty does not violate the Convention. The Senate included a "Federal–State" understanding, which provided that the federal government will implement the Convention, "to the extent that it exercises legislative and judicial jurisdiction over the matters covered by the Convention and otherwise by the state and local governments * * *." *What is the difference between a "reservation" and an "understanding?"* See Chapter 13, *infra.*

See Burgers & Danelius, The United Nations Convention Against Torture: A Handbook (1988); Stewart, The Torture Convention and the Reception of International Criminal Law Within the United States, 15 Nova L.Rev. 449 (1991) provides a thorough analysis of the Convention.

6. THE GENOCIDE CONVENTION

One day before the General Assembly adopted the Universal Declaration of Human Rights, it addressed the holocaust of World War II. On December 9, 1948, by a unanimous vote, it adopted the text of the Genocide Convention, which provides that genocide is a crime under international law which the contracting states undertake to prevent and punish. The text of the convention is set forth in full in the Documentary Supplement. Article II of the convention defines the crime:

In the present Convention, *genocide means* any of the following acts committed with intent to destroy, in whole or in part, a national, ethnical, racial or religious group, as such:

(a) Killing members of the group;

(b) Causing serious bodily or mental harm to members of the group;

(c) Deliberately inflicting on the group conditions of life calculated to bring about its physical destruction in whole or in part;

(d) Imposing measures intended to prevent births within the group;

(e) Forcibly transferring children of the group to another group.

Would the laws you would expect to find in a country's municipal criminal code cover the acts specified in Article II? In the United States, would the current state and federal laws on murder, assault and kidnapping satisfy the convention's obligation to prevent and punish genocide?

Is every instance of mass destruction of people genocide? What of a government's mass execution of its political opponents? Or of a government's administration of a policy of resettlement of its population for economic and political reasons that is so brutally or recklessly carried out that many people are killed, deliberately or otherwise? What about dropping a hydrogen bomb?

Does the convention impose any obligation upon the state aside from the obligation to enact legislation under Article V? Even if legislation is enacted, does the state (as distinct from the individuals under its jurisdiction) have any treaty obligation not to commit genocide? If a state has not become a party to the convention, does it violate international law if it commits genocide as a matter of state policy? If it condones genocide by individuals under its jurisdiction? Or if it fails to take action to prevent or punish genocide by individuals? If a state were obligated without a treaty, on what would the obligation be based?

HUMAN RIGHTS IN CAMBODIA

Extract from Hearing before the Subcommittee on International Organizations of the House Committee on International Relations, 95th Congress, First Session, May 3, 1977, p. 9.

Statement of John Barron, Senior Editor, Reader's Digest: Our accumulated data, I believe, conclusively demonstrate that the following has happened in Cambodia:

Within a few hours after occupying Phnom Penh on April 17, 1975, the Communists, known as the Khmer Rouge, ordered the capital evacuated. Within the next days, the entire population, estimated at the time [to be] approximately 3 million, was expelled at gunpoint.

Hospitals and convalescent homes were emptied and their patients, regardless of conditions, swept away with the masses. Numerous people who protested or were perceived to be resisting the evacuation order were summarily shot.

Soon other Cambodian cities, harboring all together approximately half a million people, were similarly evacuated. And later, probably another half a million were driven from the larger villages to the territories controlled by the Government prior to April 17. While draining the cities of all human life, the Khmer Rouge mounted a methodical assault on the physical symbols and sinews of preexisting Cambodian society and culture. Troops ransacked libraries, offices, and homes, burning books by the hundreds of thousands, along with written matter. They smashed hospital equipment, wrecked furniture, and hurled the contents of homes into the streets to ruin. Temples were despoiled and sacked, and automobiles by the thousands were overturned and vandalized. The purpose here, it seems to me, was to obliterate every vestige of Cambodian culture as it existed prior to April 1975.

Simultaneously, the Khmer Rouge commenced killing former military officers and civil servants of the Lon Nol government. Thousands were slaughtered in organized massacres conducted outside the cities according to the same basic pattern. Personnel who had been induced to surrender en masse were taken, usually by truck or bus, under various guises to outlying fields, where Communist troops waited in ambush. The actual extermination was accomplished by differing means, which included artillery fire, explosions of hand grenades and land mines, machinegun and automatic rifle fire, bayoneting, stabbing, and bludgeoning.

* * *

The very young and the very old were the first to die. Adults and children alike slaked their thirst in roadside ditches. Consequently, acute dysentery racked and sapped life from bodies already weakened by hunger and fatigue. A Cambodian physician, Dr. Vann Hay, who on April 17 was rousted from a Phnom Penh clinic along with all his patients, spent almost a month on various roads and trails before escaping to Vietnam. Dr. Hay told us:

> We must have passed the body of a child every 200 yards. Most of them died of gastrointestinal afflictions which cause complete dehydration. I had some medication with me, but most children brought to me required massive dosages and lengthy rest afterward. Neither was available.

> Thinking of all the bodies I saw, plus the sick who came to see me, between 20 and 30 every day, half of whom were not going to live, I figure that between 20,000 and 30,000 people must have died the first month, just in the area described (the route along which he walked to Vietnam).

* * *

The eventual destination of most [exiles] was a new settlement. Thousands of these new settlements were hewn out of the bush, scrubland, and jungle. Typically, upon arriving, a new villager family would be ordered to construct a hut out of bamboo leaves, whatever could be foraged from the jungle, and then were put into a work group normally comprised of 10 families.

* * *

There were in many areas a lack of agricultural implements, tools, and so much of the work had to be done by hand by people who were unaccustomed to arduous physical labor. Every phase of life soon strictly was regimented according to dictates from Angka Loeu, the High Organization or Organization on High, in whose name Cambodia has been ruled since the Communist conquest.

* * *

Generally, anyone violating the strictures of Angka or thought to be violating them received a warning known as a "kosang." A second transgression brought a second warning. A third transgression resulted in execution or "disappearance," which was widely believed—and, I believe, correctly—to be the same as execution. Anyone caught trying to escape usually was shot without warning. By late summer of 1975, food shortages reached famine level in large portions of the country. Epidemics of cholera, malaria, and dysentery incapacitated a sizable percentage of the new villagers. Given the demanding work regimen, the tropical squalor [sic] and the almost total lack of modern medicine, the death rate inevitably was high in the settlements.

In the autumn of 1975, Angka Loeu ordered field commanders to prepare for the extermination, after the forthcoming harvest, of all former government soldiers and civil servants, regardless of rank, and their families.

* * *

Soon word spread among Communist soldiers that former teachers, village chiefs, and students also were to be massacred. The second organized slaughter began early in 1976. Now the lowliest private, the most humble civil servant, and most innocent teachers, even foresters and public health officials, became prey. The testimony of one Cambodian physician indicates that some intellectuals after servitude in the fields or incarceration in prison were concentrated in special villages for reeducation. However, the physician's own experiences, as well as accounts of numerous other refugees, indicates that many teachers, students, and educated people were killed simply because of their class or education.

* * *

Possibly, some of the atrocities and barbarities committed against the populace in the first hours or even first days after the conquest were the result of uncontrolled excesses by individual soldiers, many of whom were very young and haggard, most of whom had been taught to hate and kill. However, the evacuation of the cities, the methodical assault upon symbols of the past, the carefully organized massacres in different parts of the country, the establishment of thousands of new villages, the imposition of more or less uniform work patterns, modes of behavior, and discipline, clearly reflect systematic central planning and direction.

As a consequence of this central rule by the Communist leaders who enshroud themselves under the title Angka Loeu, the people of Cambodia systematically are being denied virtually all human rights.

* * *

And, unless the rest of the world effectively brings pressure to bear in their behalf, they have no right or grounds to expect surcease from the ubiquitous fear and terror that now envelopes them.

———

* * * For discussion of U.N. reaction, see Chapter 16.

———

UN SUB–COMMISSION ON DISCRIMINATION AND MINORITIES

35 Review of the International Commission of Jurists 12 (1985).*

The Sub–Commission met in Geneva in August 1985.

Genocide

Under the Item Review of further developments in fields with which the Sub–Commission has been concerned, it discussed the revised and updated report on the question of the prevention and punishment of the crime of genocide, prepared by the Special Rapporteur, Mr. Whitaker.

Besides referring to the Nazi holocaust in Europe, he also cited as cases of genocide the German massacre of Hereros in 1904, the Ottoman massacre of Armenians in 1915–1916, the Ukranian pogrom of Jews in 1919, the Tutsi massacre of Hutu in Burundi in 1965 and 1972, [note the dialectic recurrence of terror in 1994], the Paraguayan massacre of Ache Indians prior to 1974, the Khmer Rouge massacre in Kampuchea between 1975–78 and the contemporary killings of Bahai'is in Iran. This passage in the report was criticised by many members of the Sub–Commission. After analysing the Convention on Genocide, he has made the following recommendations:

— the definition should be extended to include a sexual group, such as women, men or homosexuals;

— the inclusion of cultural genocide or ethnocide, meaning the physical destruction of indigenous communities, and also ecocide in terms of irreparable damage to the environment;

— an additional protocol to include the killings of political and other groups;

— addition to Article II of the Convention of words such as "in any of the above conduct, a conscious act or acts of advertent omission may be as culpable as an act of commission";

— to include specific wording in the Convention to the effect that in judging culpability a plea of obeying superior orders shall not be a defence;

— to include State responsibility for genocide, together with reparations;

* Reprinted with the permission of the International Commission of Jurists, Gene-   va, Switzerland.

— to make genocide a matter of universal jurisdiction and include in the Convention a provision similar to that of Article 8 of the Convention against torture;

— renewed efforts by the UN to persuade the remaining Member States to ratify the Convention;

— conducting interdisciplinary research into the psychological character and motivation of individuals and groups who commit genocide or acts of racism;

— developing an effective early warning system to monitor impending genocidal conflict and taking timely action on receiving such a warning; and

— establishment of a new impartial and respected international body to deal with genocide.

Speaking under this item, the Secretary–General of the International Commission of Jurists suggested that rather than seek to amend the Convention to include the "acts of omission", the International Law Commission might be asked to express an opinion on whether the words in Article II include acts of conscious and deliberate omission with that intent. He also suggested that the Commission on Human Rights could establish a working group to deal with alleged cases of genocide, as well as to consider the proposals for universal jurisdiction and/or for an international penal tribunal and other additions and amendments to the Convention recommended by the Special Rapporteur.

The Sub–Commission, in a resolution, took note of the revised and updated study and recommended that the UN renew its efforts to make ratification of the Convention * * * universal as soon as possible. *See* General Assembly Resolution and Declaration on the Rights of Persons Belonging to National or Ethnic, Religious and Linguistic Minorities, December 18, 1992, 32 I.L.M. 911 (1993), in Doc. Supp.

———

CASE CONCERNING APPLICATION OF THE CONVENTION ON THE PREVENTION AND PUNISHMENT OF THE CRIME OF GENOCIDE (BOSNIA AND HERZEGOVINA V. YUGOSLAVIA (SERBIA AND MONTENEGRO), REQUEST FOR THE INDICATION OF PROVISIONAL MEASURES, [1993] I.C.J.Reports 3, 32 I.L.M. 890 (1993) (wherein Bosnia and Herzegovina brought an action against Serbia and Montenegro "for violating the Genocide Convention" and other illegal conduct in violation of customary international law). On April 8, 1993, the International Court of Justice in response to the suit filed by Bosnia and Herzegovina, called upon Serbia and Montenegro to "immediately * * * take all measures within its power to prevent commission of the crime of genocide * * * whether directed against the Muslim population of Bosnia and Herzegovina or against any other national, ethnical, racial, or religious group." This was an interim decision. The Court noted that facts were still in dispute. It also noted that it was unable to render a decision in relation to disputed rights falling outside the ambit of the Genocide Convention.

———

The United States and the Genocide Convention. The United States signed the Convention two days after it was adopted by the General Assembly in 1948. President Truman submitted it to the Senate in 1949. The Senate did not give its advice and consent until February 1986, although each president from President Kennedy to President Reagan urged the Senate's approval. The Senate conditioned its action upon two reservations, five understandings and one declaration:

RESERVATIONS:

1. [Regarding] Article IX of the Convention, before any dispute to which the United States is a party may be submitted to the jurisdiction of the International Court of Justice under this article, the specific consent of the United States is required in each case.

2. That nothing in the Convention requires or authorizes legislation or other action by the United States prohibited by the Constitution of the United States as interpreted by the United States.

UNDERSTANDINGS:

1. That the term "intent to destroy, in whole or in part, a national, ethnical, racial, or religious group, as such" appearing in Article II means the specific intent to destroy, in whole or in substantial part, a national, ethnical, racial, or religious group as such by the acts specified in Article II.

2. That the term "mental harm" in Article II(b) means permanent impairment of mental faculties through drugs, torture or similar techniques.

3. That the pledge to grant extradition in accordance with a state's laws and treaties in force found in Article VII extends only to acts which are criminal under the laws of both the requesting and the requested state and nothing in Article VI affects the right of any state to bring to trial before its own tribunals any of its nationals for acts committed outside a state.

4. That acts in the course of armed conflicts committed without the specific intent required by Article II are not sufficient to constitute genocide as defined by this Convention.

5. That with regard to the reference to an international penal tribunal in Article VI of the Convention, the United States declares that it reserves the right to effect its participation in any such tribunal only by a treaty entered into specifically for that purpose with the advice and consent of the Senate.

DECLARATION:

>   That the President will not deposit the instrument of ratification until after the implementing legislation referred to in Article V has been enacted. 132 Congressional Record S–1377–8 (daily ed., Feb. 19, 1986).

Draft legislation to implement the convention was submitted to the Congress by the Attorney General in June 1986.

What do you think of these reservations, understandings, and declaration? For example, "[t]hat nothing in the [Genocide] Convention requires or authorizes legislation or other action by the United States of America prohibited by the Constitution of the United States as interpreted by the United States." This is the so-called "Sovereignty" reservation. Was it necessary? Is the Constitution primary U.S. law? Does it prevail over Treaties? *See* Chapter 14 on International Agreements and Domestic Constitutions. With regard to the Convention, what does such a reservation included with the U.S. instruments of ratification do to the perception that the other States Parties to the Convention have as to the U.S. commitment to the treaty, indeed, to whether the U.S. has even really become a party?

Due to the problems caused by the *"Sovereignty" reservation,* the U.S. Senate did not include one for the Torture Convention *supra.* Because of pressure by some Senators, it did include a "statement" in its Resolution of Advice and Consent, that "[t]he President of the United States shall not deposit the instrument of ratification until such time as he has notified all present and prospective ratifying party [sic] to this Convention that nothing in this Convention requires or authorizes legislation, or other action, by the United States prohibited by the Constitution of the United States as interpreted by the United States." This was not considered to be a "reservation" or an "understanding." David P. Stewart, The Torture Convention, supra.

Current developments relating to the Genocide Convention. Consider the following by Louis René Beres regarding crimes against humanity during and after the Gulf War.

LOUIS RENÉ BERES, AFTER THE GULF WAR: IRAQ, GENOCIDE AND INTERNATIONAL LAW

Det.Mercy L.Rev. 13 (1991) (footnotes omitted) *

>   "Truly, I live in dark times! The guileless word is folly. A smooth forehead suggests insensitivity. The man who laughs has simply not yet had the terrible news." (Bertolt Brecht)

---

* Reprinted with the permission of Detroit-Mercy Law Rev. and Louis René Beres.

The poet Brecht's "terrible news" has now been heard by all, but there is still considerable laughter. Tragically embedded in a world system that seemingly draws comfort from the outermost extremes of human torment, we residents of this defiled planet have not yet learned that politics is unheroic and that innocence counts for nothing. Aware, as legal scholars, that reason of state always preempts human rights, we know that Realpolitik has produced our Age of Atrocity, yet we steadfastly refuse to place enforceable limits around Realpolitik. As a result, the shadow of crimes against humanity darkens not only our discredited recent past but also our most probable immediate future.

* * *

Genocide, of course, is a crime under international law. This is the case whether one speaks of literal genocide, genocidal extermination without genocidal intent, or any other forms of "ethnocide" or "politicide." Yet, in all instances of genocide and genocide-like crimes, there is still significant divergence between the binding expectations of international law and actual compliance by states * * *

But first, what is genocide? Based upon a combination of the Greek genos (meaning race or tribe) with the Latin cide (meaning killing), it means the commission of certain specific acts with intent to destroy, wholly or in part, a national, ethnic, racial or religious group as such. Coined in 1944 by Raphael Lemkin, a Polish–Jewish lawyer who escaped the German occupation of his homeland, it describes what Winston Churchill once called "a crime without a name." In this connection, it describes a crime that is juristically distinct from other sorts of wartime killing (killing long since prohibited by the laws of war of international law) and from other sorts of non-wartime political repression * * *.

Although legal scholars may understand that genocide has always been prohibited by international law, the post World War II criminalization of genocide has been especially explicit and far-reaching. Building upon the norms established by international custom, the general principles of law recognized by civilized nations, the writings of highly qualified publicists, various treaties and conventions, and the overriding principles of natural law, this criminalization has flowed almost entirely from universal reaction to the Holocaust.

* * *

Today, there exists a well-established regime for the protection of all human rights. This regime is comprised of peremptory norms, rules that endow all human beings with a basic measure of dignity and that permit no derogation by States. These internationally protected human rights can be grouped into three broad categories:

— First, the right to be free from governmental violations of the integrity of the person—violations such as torture, cruel, inhuman or degrading treatment or punishment; arbitrary arrest or imprisonment; denial of fair public trial; and invasion of the home.

— Second, the right to the fulfillment of vital needs such as food, shelter, health care and education;

— Third, the right to enjoy civil and political liberties, including freedom of speech, press, religion and assembly; the right to participate in government; the right to travel freely within and outside one's own country; the right to be free from discrimination based on race or sex.

Taken together with other important covenants, treaties and declarations which comprise the human rights regime, the Genocide Convention represents the end of the idea of absolute sovereignty concerning non-intervention when human rights are in grievous jeopardy. The Charter * * * stipulates in its Preamble and several articles that human rights are protected by international law. In the Preamble, the peoples of the United Nations reaffirm their faith "in fundamental human rights, in the dignity and worth of the human person, in the equal rights of men and women and of nations large and small" and their determination "to promote social progress and better standards of life in larger freedom."

In light of these codified expressions of the international law of human rights, it is abundantly clear that individual states can no longer claim sovereign immunity from responsibility for gross mistreatment of their own citizens. Notwithstanding Article 2(7) of the U.N. Charter, which reaffirms certain areas of "domestic jurisdiction," each state is now clearly obligated to uphold basic human rights. Even the failure to ratify specific treaties or conventions does not confer immunity from responsibility, since all states are bound by the law of the Charter and by the customs and general principles of law from which such agreements derive * * *.

Looking over the current landscape of international relations, we recognize immediately that politics has become the primary ground of total misfortune. The myth of progress has run its course and calculated visions of a more perfect global society are no longer the reasonable product of creative imaginations. Against genocide and genocide-like crimes, collective legal sanctions and deterrents are indispensable, yet we are sobered by the timeless remark of the poet Yeats: "There is no longer a virtuous nation, and the best of us live by candle light."

* * *

---

7. THE UNIVERSAL DECLARATION OF HUMAN RIGHTS [a]

The declaration was adopted by the United Nations General Assembly, Resolution 217A(III), on December 10, 1948, by a vote of 48 to 0,

a. Other Human Rights Declarations. In addition to the Universal Declaration, a number of other declarations dealing with particular aspects of human rights have been adopted by the General Assembly. Among them are:

Gen.Ass.Off.Rec., 3rd Sess., Part 1, Resolutions, p. 71.   Although there were no dissenting votes, the following states abstained: Byelorussia SSR, Czechoslovakia, Poland, Saudi Arabia, Ukranian SSR, USSR, Union of South Africa and Yugoslavia.

CONTENTS OF THE DECLARATION

The full text of the Universal Declaration is in the Doc. Supp.   The General Assembly proclaims the listed rights as a "common standard of achievement."   These rights are applicable to "all human beings," to "everyone."   The rights include such personal rights as equal protection of the law, right to a fair hearing, to be presumed innocent, to freedom of movement and asylum, to marry and found a family.   Also included are economic and social rights such as to social security, to work, to form and join trade unions, to a standard of living adequate for health and well-being, to education.   For example:

Article 5

No one shall be subjected to torture or to cruel, inhuman or degrading treatment or punishment.

Article 9

No one shall be subjected to arbitrary arrest, detention or exile.

Declaration of the Rights of the Child, November 20, 1959, G.A.Res. 1386 (XIV), U.N.Gen.Ass.Off.Rec., 14th Sess., Supp. 16(A/4354), p. 19.

Declaration on the Granting of Independence to Colonial Countries and Peoples, December 14, 1960, G.A.Res. 1514(XV), U.N.Gen.Ass.Off.Rec., 15th Sess., Supp. 16(A/4684), p. 66.

United Nations Declaration on the Elimination of All Forms of Racial Discrimination, November 20, 1963, G.A.Res. 1904(XVIII), U.N.Gen.Ass.Off.Rec., 18th Sess., Supp. 15(A/5515), p. 35.

Declaration on the Elimination of Discrimination Against Women, November 7, 1967, G.A.Res. 2263(XXII), U.N.Gen.Ass.Off.Rec., 22nd Sess., Supp. 16(A/6716), p. 35.

Declaration on Territorial Asylum, December 14, 1967, G.A.Res. 2312(XXII), U.N.Gen.Ass.Off.Rec., 22nd Sess., Supp. 16(A/6716), p. 81.

Declaration on the Protection of all Persons from Being Subjected to Torture and Other

Cruel, Inhuman or Degrading Treatment or Punishment, December 9, 1975, G.A.Res. 3452(XXX), U.N.Gen.Ass.Off.Rec., 30th Sess., Supp. 34(A/10034), p. 91.

Declaration on the Rights of Mentally Retarded Persons, December 20, 1971, G.A.Res. 2856(26), U.N.Gen.Ass.Off.Rec., 26th Sess., Supp. 29(A/8429), p. 93.

Declaration on the Protection of Women and Children in Emergency and Armed Conflict, December 14, 1974, G.A.Res. 3318(29), U.N.Gen.Ass.Off.Rec., 29th Sess., Supp. 31(A/9631), p. 146.

Declaration on the Rights of Disabled Persons, December 9, 1975, G.A.Res. 3447(30), U.N.Gen.Ass.Off.Rec., 30th Sess., Supp. 34(A/10034), p. 88.

Declaration on the Elimination of All Forms of Intolerance and of Discrimination Based on Religion or Belief, November 25, 1981, G.A.Res. 36/55, U.N.Gen.Ass.Off.Rec., 36th Sess., Supp. 51(A/36/51), p. 171.

Article 10

Everyone is entitled in full equality to a fair and public hearing by an independent and impartial tribunal, in the determination of his rights and obligations and of any criminal charge against him.

THE QUESTION OF THE DECLARATION AS LAW
A DRAFTER'S VIEW

5 Whiteman, Digest of International Law 243 (1965).

As the General Assembly neared its final vote on the Declaration, Mrs. Franklin D. Roosevelt, as the Chairman of the Commission on Human Rights and a representative of the United States in the Assembly, stated:

> In giving our approval to the declaration today, it is of primary importance that we keep clearly in mind the basic character of the document. It is not a treaty; it is not an international agreement. It is not and does not purport to be a statement of law or of legal obligation. It is a declaration of basic principles of human rights and freedoms, to be stamped with the approval of the General Assembly by formal vote of its members, and to serve as a common standard of achievement for all peoples of all nations.

A DIPLOMATIC VIEW

2 Kiss, Répertoire de la Pratique Française en Matière de Droit International Public 651 (1966).[a]

Declaration of the French Government of August 1, 1951

The French Government has followed with the greatest attention the measures of deportation taken in Hungary against numerous components of the population [which have been] suddenly declared "undesirable." According to the information received [by the French Government] these measures appear to have been extraordinarily far reaching and harsh and to strike pitilessly a great diversity of persons within the population. Such acts constitute a flagrant violation of the principle of respect for human beings and the rights of man [which is] recognized by the international community and embodied in the Declaration of the United Nations of December 10, 1948.

The French Government notes with the greatest concern that the information has now been confirmed by official statements of the Hungarian authorities. Faithful to its traditions, the French Government regards it as its duty solemnly to denounce practices which openly violate the human rights that the Government of the People's Republic of Hungary has formally committed itself to observe in the Peace Treaty of February 10, 1947.

a. Translation by the editors. Reprinted by permission, Éditions du Centre National de la Recherche Scientifique, Paris.

A PUBLICIST'S VIEW

Humphrey, The UN Charter and the Universal Declaration of Human Rights,
The International Protection of Human Rights 39, 51 (Luard, ed. 1967).

Even more remarkable than the performance of the United Nations in adopting the Declaration has been its impact and the role which it almost immediately began to play both within and outside the United Nations—an impact and a role which probably exceed the most sanguine hopes of its authors.   No other act of the United Nations has had anything like the same impact on the thinking of our time, the best aspirations of which it incorporates and proclaims.   It may well be that it will live in history chiefly as a statement of great moral principles.   As such its influence is deeper and more lasting than any political document or legal instrument.   [Some] are more apt to be impressed by the political and legal authority which it has established for itself.   Its political authority is now second only to that of the charter itself. Indeed its reception at all levels has been such that, contrary to the expressed intention of its authors, it may have now become part of international law.

A JURIST'S VIEW

Separate Opinion of Vice–President Ammoun in Advisory Opinion
on the Continued Presence of South Africa in Namibia
(South West Africa) [1971] I.C.J. Reports 16, 76.

The Advisory Opinion takes judicial notice of the Universal Declaration of Human Rights.   In the case of certain of the Declaration's provisions, attracted by the conduct of South Africa, it would have been an improvement to have dealt in terms with their comminatory nature, which is implied in paragraphs 130 and 131 of the Opinion by the references to their violation.

In its written statement the French Government, alluding to the obligations which South Africa accepted under the Mandate and assumed on becoming a Member of the United Nations, and to the norms laid down in the Universal Declaration of Human Rights, stated that there was no doubt that the Government of South Africa had, in a very real sense, systematically infringed those rules and those obligations. Nevertheless, referring to the mention by resolution 2145(XXI) of the Universal Declaration of Human Rights, it objected that it was plainly impossible for non-compliance with the norms it enshrined to be sanctioned with the revocation of the Mandate, inasmuch as that Declaration was not in the nature of a treaty binding upon States.

Although the affirmations of the Declaration are not binding qua international convention within the meaning of Article 38, paragraph 1(a), of the Statute of the Court, they can bind States on the basis of custom within the meaning of paragraph 1(b) of the same Article, whether because they constituted a codification of customary law as was said in respect of Article 6 of the Vienna Convention on the Law of Treaties, or because they have acquired the force of custom through a general practice accepted as law, in the words of Article 38, paragraph 1(b), of the Statute. One right which must certainly be considered a preexisting binding customary norm which the Universal Declaration of Human Rights codified is the right to equality, which by common consent has ever since the remotest times been deemed inherent in human nature.

The equality demanded by the Namibians and by other peoples of every colour, the right to which is the outcome of prolonged struggles to make it a reality, is something of vital interest to us here, on the one hand because it is the foundation of other human rights which are no more than its corollaries and, on the other, because it naturally rules out racial discrimination and apartheid, which are the gravest of the facts with which South Africa, as also other States, stands charged. The attention I am devoting to it in these observations can therefore by no means be regarded as exaggerated or out of proportion.

It is not by mere chance that in Article 1 of the Universal Declaration of the Rights * * * there stands * * * this primordial principle or axiom: "All human beings are born free and equal in dignity and rights." From this first principle flow most rights and freedoms.

* * * The ground was thus prepared for the legislative and constitutional process which began with the first declarations or bills of rights in America and Europe, continued with the constitutions of the nineteenth century, and culminated in positive international law in the San Francisco, Bogota and Addis Ababa charters, and in the Universal Declaration of Human Rights which has been confirmed by numerous resolutions of the United Nations, in particular the above-mentioned declarations adopted by the General Assembly in resolutions 1514(15), 2625(25) and 2627(25). The Court in its turn has now confirmed it. *See,* The Filartiga and the *Siderman* cases, infra.

* * *

---

8. THE HUMAN RIGHTS COVENANTS

Under the aegis of the League of Nations and the United Nations, a number of conventions on particular human rights have been prepared by a variety of conferences, committees and commissions. Drafts of these conventions have progressed through a variety of stages. They are typically given final approval by some plenary international body before being submitted to states for ratification or other indication of intention to be bound. In some cases that approval has been given by resolution of the General Assembly. In others, the final text is prepared and approved by an ad hoc United Nations conference. In still other cases, the final text has come from a specialized agency, such as the International Labor Organization.

Among conventions in force are two that are the most general in scope of all of the human rights conventions. These are the International Covenant on Economic, Social and Cultural Rights and the International Covenant on Civil and Political Rights, set forth in full in the Doc. Supp.[a] These two covenants comprehensively carry into detailed treaty form most of the provisions of the Universal Declaration of Human Rights, although they do not parallel the declaration. A close comparison should be made between the declaration on one hand and the covenants on the other. For example, the declaration provides for the right to asylum; the matter is not treated in the covenants. The right to compensation for unlawful arrest or detention is provided for by the Covenant on Civil and Political Rights, but not by the declaration. Other disparities include the right to own property and the right of self-determination.

Queries: What other disparities exist? Is the fact of these disparities significant? Does the fact that certain rights were included in the declaration but not in the more detailed legislation weaken the general legal significance that has been accorded the declaration? Does the fact that certain rights appear in the covenants but not in the declaration (such as self-determination) suggest that they are less than universal, that they do not reflect general principles of international law? Or does the worldwide recognition of a particular right as international law depend upon factors more complex than whether the verbal recognition of that right was made in the declaration or one or the other of the covenants? If so, what are the factors?

The covenants were the product of many years' work, first in the Commission on Human Rights (from 1949 until 1954) and thereafter in the Third Committee of the General Assembly of the United Nations (from 1954 until 1966), and finally at the plenary session of the Assembly in 1966. Although the original conception in the commission had been to prepare a single draft covenant, the insistence by some states that the covenant include provisions for economic, social and cultural rights resulted in a decision by the General Assembly while the draft covenant was still under consideration by the commission that two covenants be drafted, one dealing with those rights and the other with civil and political rights. Contrast the language of the two covenants as ultimately adopted with respect to the sense of assurance by which the various rights are asserted in each of the documents. Contrast also the wide difference between the two covenants with respect to methods of implementation. *Where does the Convention on the Elimination of All Forms of Discrimination Against Women fit?* Also currently, there is a debate between those who argue for recognition of economic and social rights and those who argue that such rights do not exist. *See, e.g.,* Alston & Quinn, *The Nature and Scope of States Parties' Obligations Under the International Covenant on Economic, Social and Cultural Rights,* 9 Hum.Rts.Q. 156 (1987).

---

a. In 1978, the Office of Public Information of the United Nations published the texts of the Universal Declaration, these two covenants, and an official protocol relating to implementation of the latter covenant under the title: The International Bill of Human Rights.

Study the International Covenant on Civil and Political Rights, 993 U.N.T.S. 3 in the Documentary Supplement. Focus especially on article 14.

Comparison with the precedents on state responsibility. How do the rights provided for in such conventions as the Covenant on Civil and Political Rights compare with those recognized early decisions of commissions for the protection of refugees, minorities, or ethnic groups, or with the Ad Hoc Tribunal for the former Yugoslavia. Who is entitled to these rights? Are the substantive standards different? See discussion of International War Crimes tribunals, *supra* in this chapter and in chapter 11, *infra*.

9. U.S. RATIFICATION OF THE INTERNATIONAL COVENANT ON CIVIL AND POLITICAL RIGHTS:

In June 1992, the United States Senate gave its Advice and Consent to the *International Covenant on Civil and Political Rights*. [See Doc. Supp.] Reservations and understandings, similar to those discussed above were attached to the ratification.

EXCERPT FROM JOHN QUIGLEY, CRIMINAL LAW AND HUMAN RIGHTS: IMPLICATIONS OF THE UNITED STATES RATIFICATION OF THE INTERNATIONAL COVENANT ON CIVIL AND POLITICAL RIGHTS

6 Harv.Hum.Rts.J. 59, 59–63 (1993).*

The 1992 ratification by the United States of the International Covenant on Civil and Political Rights ("Covenant") opens U.S. practice on human rights issues to scrutiny under international standards. To be sure, human rights standards found in the customary law of nations already bound the United States, apart from this country's adherence to any human rights treaty. With every decision, domestic courts around the globe contribute to the customary law of nations; in a similar way, the opinions and practices of intergovernmental human rights committees and courts claim authority in the domestic courts of the United States. Customary law notwithstanding, accession to the Covenant may significantly enlarge our obligations under human rights standards. Ideally, the Covenant provides the human rights advocate with what customary law is wanting: an authoritative, textual exposition of protected rights and routinized mechanisms for their enforcement.

The Covenant requires governments to observe a broad spectrum of standards in their treatment of individuals and provide remedies for violations. It is no less than an international bill of rights, part of an effort to codify the Universal Declaration of Human Rights, the United Nations' post-war proclamation of the rights of man. As of February 1993, 116 member states of the United Nations had acceded to its terms.

---

* Reprinted with the permission of the Harvard Human Rights Journal.

The General Assembly approved the text and opened the Covenant for ratification in 1966; at the prospect of accession, the United States demurred. It was not until 1977 that President Carter made the United States a treaty signatory and asked the Senate to give its advice and consent to ratification. The Senate did not act during Carter's term, and President Reagan did not seek Senate action.

In 1991, President Bush requested the Senate's consent to ratification, but, seeking to limit U.S. obligations under the Covenant, submitted a package of formal reservations and qualifying statements. The Senate Foreign Relations Committee unanimously recommended the Covenant to the Senate, and the Senate voted in favor of ratification, subject to the Administration's proposed emendations. On June 8, 1992, the President deposited the signed instrument of ratification with the U.N. Secretary–General; three months later, on September 8, 1992, the treaty entered into force in the United States.

Criminal law is a principal area of concern in the Covenant. Rights guarantees in such areas as speech, assembly, and privacy limit the criminalization of conduct. The Covenant provides certain procedural protections to criminal suspects, the accused, and convicted prisoners,[15] and several provisions pertain to the conduct of criminal trials.[16] * * * I will next address the general question of the Covenant's enforceability.

II. LIMITATIONS ON U.S. OBLIGATIONS UNDER THE COVENANT

The U.S. government took steps, in ratifying the Covenant, to minimize international scrutiny into its domestic policies. The Bush Administration hedged U.S. acceptance of the Covenant with reservations, understandings, and declarations; the Administration sought to ensure that present practice would prevail where it conflicts with the Covenant. To the qualifications proposed by President Bush, the Senate added the so-called "Helms proviso": the Covenant should not be read to require or authorize legislation or other action by the United States that the U.S. Constitution would prohibit.

On the international level, the United States has protected itself from effective legal oversight on its compliance with Covenant provisions, particularly in refusing to sign the treaty's Optional Protocol. Pursuant to the Optional Protocol, individuals whose protected rights

---

15. The Covenant treats the following procedural topics: capital punishment, Covenant, supra note 1, art. 6; torture and lesser forms of brutality, id., art. 7; arbitrary arrest, id., art. 9(1); the right upon arrest to be informed of the charges, id., art. 9(2); prompt arraignment, id., art. 9(3); habeas corpus, id., art. 9(4); compensation for unlawful detention, id., art. 9(5); and prison conditions, id., art. 10; prosecution only for an act that was an offense at the time committed, id., art. 15(1).

16. A partial list: the right to a fair hearing, Covenant, supra note 1, art. 14(1); openness of court proceedings, id.; the presumption of innocence, id., art. 14(2); the right to be informed in detail of the

charges, id., art. 14(3)(a); an opportunity to prepare a defense, id., art. 14(3)(b); speedy trial, id., art. 14(3)(c); the right to defend oneself in person or through counsel of choice, including free counsel where required, id., art. 14(3)(d); the right to cross-examine prosecution witnesses and to compel the attendance of defense witnesses, id., art. 14(3)(e); assistance without charge of an interpreter, id., art. 14(3)(f); protection against self-incrimination, id., art. 14(3)(g); special proceedings for juveniles, id., art. 14(4); the right to appeal a conviction, id., art. 14(5); compensation for punishment under a false conviction, id., art. 14(6).

* * *

have "been violated by State action" have filed complaints with the Human Rights Committee, the body established by the treaty to monitor compliance with its provisions. As of February 1993, sixty-seven states were parties to the Optional Protocol.

The enforcement mechanisms to which the United States is subject have little bite. As a party to the Covenant, the United States must submit a periodic report to the Human Rights Committee; but the Committee has few investigatory powers and has been reluctant to take other affirmative steps toward more effective monitoring. Having acceded to an optional provision of the Covenant, the United States has opened itself to complaints by other states. Any state party that has acceded to the provision may lodge a complaint against the United States and have it heard before the Human Rights Committee. The Committee would then sit in closed, confidential session to entertain oral and written statements from the two states; pursuant to these hearings, it would issue a non-binding written report. To date, not one state party has filed a complaint against another under this procedure: states are loath to jeopardize relations, or to invite retaliatory filings. As it stands, this procedure will not provide effective international enforcement of U.S. obligations.

Article 2 mandates that states provide enforcement mechanisms through their domestic law. The United States government, however, entered a declaration in apparent opposition to this mandate. The declaration asserts that the prescriptive provisions of the Covenant (Articles 1 to 27) are not "self-executing": absent further action by the Congress to incorporate provisions into the domestic law, the courts may not enforce them. "The intent," explained the Foreign Relations Committee, was "to clarify that the Covenant will not create a private cause of action in U.S. courts * * *. [E]xisting U.S. law generally complies with the covenant; hence implementing legislation is not contemplated."

The Senate declaration has uncertain legal status. It is neither an Act of Congress, having the force of federal law, nor a reservation to the Covenant, having all the authority of treaty law under the Supremacy Clause. The declaration has effect only insofar as it bears upon a judicial appraisal of the Covenant's force. This appraisal is not a *fait accompli;* it is not clear how much weight the Senate's declaration will carry with the courts.

———

Notes: To determine whether treaty provisions are "self-executing," the U.S. Supreme Court examines the intent of the parties to the treaty: did the states parties intend to confer legal rights upon individuals? If it is true that the United States already provides, by constitution or statute, most of the rights granted by these conventions, what is to be gained by binding the United States *by treaty* to provide for those rights? What is to be lost? To the extent that some of the rights granted by the conventions are not already provided for by constitution or statute in the United States, should they be? Presumably the main purpose of these conventions is to require states who become parties to raise their human rights standards to the level required by the conventions. Is that purpose served by the United States when it makes reservations to provisions in the convention because they "go beyond United States law?"

The Department of State's position with respect to the four human rights conventions submitted in 1978 can fairly be described as cautious. Why has the United States been so hesitant?

Humanitarian law, which developed out of the law of war, is dealt with in Chapter 11.

The Helsinki Accord. In contrast to the legal commitments a state makes by becoming a party to the human rights conventions described above are the commitments that were made at the Helsinki conference. The Conference on Security and Cooperation in Europe, meeting from September 1973 to August 1975, concluded with a Final Act, signed by representatives of 35 states, including the countries of Western Europe, the "Soviet-bloc" countries of Europe, the United States and Canada. The legal status of this document was described by President Ford before he attended the closing days of the conference: "I would emphasize that the document I will sign is neither a treaty nor is it legally binding on any participating state. The Helsinki documents involve political and moral commitments aimed at lessening tensions and opening further the lines of communication between the peoples of East and West." 73 U.S. Dept. State Bull. 204, 205 (1975).

The delegate of Finland (the depository government) informed the Coordinating Committee at the Conference of his government's intention to send the Final Act to the Secretary General of the United Nations with a letter containing the following statement: "I have also been asked * * * to draw your attention to the fact that this Final Act is not eligible, in whole or in part, for registration with the Secretariat under Article 102 of the Charter, * * * as would be the case were it a matter of a treaty or international agreement. * * *

The Final Act is a comprehensive document covering the following matters: Questions Relating to Security in Europe (so-called Basket I); Cooperation in the Field of Economics, of Science and Technology, and of the Environment (Basket II); Questions Relating to Security and Cooperation in the Mediterranean, and Cooperation in Humanitarian and Other Fields (Basket III).

A major outcome of the conference was an assurance that existing European territorial arrangements (e.g. borders) would not be disturbed by force. Human rights matters were also included in the Final Act, as Principle VII in a Declaration of Principles Guiding Relations between Participating States. The declaration contained in the Final Act is in the Documentary Supplement. The complete text of the Final Act may be found at 73 U.S. Dept. State Bull. 323 (1975).

At a follow-up conference in Madrid in 1983, a Concluding Document amplified the Helsinki agreements with respect to cooperation in the humanitarian field. United States Department of State Bulletin, October 1983, p. 53.

Although the Helsinki Final Act does not constitute a legally binding international agreement, Principle VII of the Declaration of Principles seeks to tie the signatory states to international law with the following statement: "In the field of human rights and fundamental freedoms, the participating States will act in conformity with the purposes and principles of the Charter of the United Nations and with the Universal Declaration of Human Rights. They will also fulfill their obligations as set forth in the international declarations and agreements in this field, including inter alia the International Covenants on Human Rights, by which they may be bound." The United States has sought implementation of the Helsinki commitments by periodic reports on foreign states' compliance with the Final Act.

DEPARTMENT COMMENTS ON SUBJECT OF HUMAN RIGHTS IN CZECHOSLOVAKIA

76 United States Department of State Bulletin 154 (1977).

Following is a statement read to news correspondents on January 26 by Frederick Z. Brown, Director, Office of Press Relations: I would like to make a brief statement on the subject of human rights in Czechoslovakia. Some 300 individuals in that country have petitioned the government to guarantee the rights accorded them by the Czechoslovak Constitution, the International Covenants on Civil and Political and on Economic, Social, and Cultural Rights, and by the Helsinki Final Act. We have noted that the signers of Charter 77 explicitly state that it is not a document of political opposition. Some of the signers have reportedly been detained or harassed. As you know, the Helsinki Final Act provides that:

> In the field of human rights and fundamental freedoms, the participating States will act in conformity with the purposes and principles of the Charter of the United Nations and with the Universal Declaration of Human Rights. They will also fulfill their obligations as set forth in the international declarations and agreements in this field, including inter alia the International Covenants on Human Rights, by which they may be bound.

* * *

The "Soft–Law" of the Helsinki Final Act was used by the dissidents to accomplish the "Velvet Revolution."

Human Rights and the Environment. Do you think human rights law should encompass todays environmental concerns? Consider the following excerpt from the Keynote Address by Kerry Kennedy Cuomo.

KENNEDY CUOMO, HUMAN RIGHTS AND THE ENVIRONMENT: COMMON GROUND

18 Yale J.Int'l.L. 227 (1993) (footnotes omitted).*

* * *

As an international human rights attorney, I have focused my efforts on individuals who, in their pursuit of human rights, have stood up to government oppression at great personal risk. Many of these individuals have been imprisoned, tortured, or killed for their political beliefs. Untold numbers of journalists have been silenced, lawyers jailed, scientists stifled, and trade unionists crushed. What all of these brave individuals have in common is their commitment to justice, non-violence, and the rule of law.

Like civil rights lawyers in the United States who look to the Bill of Rights under the Constitution to guide their practice, international human rights lawyers look to a number of international instruments for the laws by which we expect governments to abide. Most human rights norms are based upon the Universal Declaration of Human Rights and the International Covenants on human rights. The Declaration was signed in 1948 in reaction to the Nazi atrocities during World War II, and set forth principles which members of the United Nations agreed to recognize. The Covenants were drafted and signed a few years later, and they set forth specific rights which states are bound to uphold. If states violate the terms of the Covenants, they can be brought before a tribunal and held accountable.

Our world has changed drastically since the Declaration and Covenants were written, and certainly the drafters did not anticipate all of today's problems. Clearly they did not foresee the enormity of our ecological degradation and the consequent necessity for human rights norms to encompass environmental considerations. Promoting the right to a healthy environment is the most obvious mechanism to fulfill this need. That right is just now being fleshed out. We are only beginning to explore the questions it raises: What entitlements does it anticipate? What constitutes a violation? Who will monitor nations? What form will relief take? And so many other queries. Meanwhile, people are being tortured and rainforests are disappearing. We can't afford to wait until all the answers are sorted out. The need for human rights activists and environmentalists to work together is urgent. And there are at least three circumstances under which, indisputably, we can work together right now, right here, today.

The first occurs when governments deliberately withhold life-saving information about environmental degradation from those affected; here we'll look at Chernobyl. The second occurs when governments target environmentalists for persecution; here we'll look at Wangari Maathai in Kenya. And the third occurs when exploitation of natural resources threatens the viability of indigenous cultures; here we'll look at the Tagbanwa people on the island of Palawan in the Philippines.

* * *

* (Reprinted with the permission of the Yale Journal of Int'l Law).

Governments that suppress information violate the right of their citizens to "seek, receive and impart information" and their right to "life, liberty and security of person." The Chernobyl incident is a dramatic example of the dangers of environmental censorship. Human rights activists and environmentalists can work together to hold governments responsible when withholding information directly causes death or other violations of human rights. After Chernobyl, those who had the information and the access to mass communications failed to speak out. Why? Perhaps they were afraid of the consequences, the consequences for their governments if the people found out, or the consequences to themselves personally if their governments found out who told the people.

The exercise of free speech about the dangers of pollution—speech which totalitarian governments view as a challenge to their survival—is all too often the catalyst for a series of human rights violations, including the rights to be free from arbitrary arrest, torture, or extra-judicial execution. Perhaps the clearest example of the inextricable link between human rights and the environment is a government that targets an environmental activist for persecution—someone who speaks out despite the consequences, someone like Wangari Maathai of Kenya. Today, she personifies the perfect marriage of human rights advocacy and environmental activism.

* * *

Question: Do you think there is a common ground between human rights and the environment? If so, how should this common ground be addressed within the international human rights arena? For more on the environment, see Ch. 6, *supra.*

SECTION C. HUMAN RIGHTS AS CUSTOMARY INTERNATIONAL LAW

———

The Declaration of Human Rights and the human rights conventions spell out in considerable detail a great number of rights. The conventions are legally binding documents detailing the correlative duties of state parties to give effect to human rights. Is the Universal Declaration a codification of international law? Does it create law? Are conventions more than contractual obligations; do they reflect international law that exists outside the treaty regime, law that is binding on parties and non-parties alike? The American Law Institute has taken the position that there are certain core human rights that have entered into the body of international law, rights that must be recognized by each state whether or not the state has become otherwise bound to do so by international agreement.

1987 RESTATEMENT, SECTION 702
CUSTOMARY INTERNATIONAL LAW OF HUMAN RIGHTS

A state violates international law if, as a matter of state policy, it practices, encourages or condones

(a) genocide,

(b) slavery or slave trade,

(c) the murder or causing the disappearance of individuals,

(d) torture or other cruel, inhuman or degrading treatment or punishment,

(e) prolonged arbitrary detention,

(f) systematic racial discrimination, or

(g) a consistent pattern of gross violations of internationally recognized human rights.

Comment:

k. Consistent pattern of gross violations of human rights. The acts enumerated in clauses (a) to (f) are violations of customary law even if the practice is not consistent, or not part of a "pattern," and those acts are inherently "gross" violations of human rights. Clause (g) includes other infringements of recognized human rights which, when committed singly or sporadically, are not violations of customary law (although they may be forbidden to states parties to the International Covenants or other particular agreements); they become violations of customary law if the state is guilty of a "consistent pattern of gross violations" as state policy. A violation is gross if it is particularly shocking because of the importance of the right or the gravity of the violation. While all the rights proclaimed in the Universal Declaration and protected by the principal International Covenants * * * are internationally recognized human rights, some rights are fundamental and intrinsic to human dignity, and a consistent pattern of violation of such rights as state policy may be deemed "gross" ipso facto. It includes, for example, systematic harassment, invasions of the privacy of the home, arbitrary arrest and detention (even if not prolonged); denial of fair trial in criminal cases; grossly disproportionate punishment; denial of freedom to leave a country when a country of haven is available; denial of the right to return to one's own country; mass uprooting of a country's population; denial of freedom of conscience and religion; denial of personality before the law; denial of basic privacy such as the right to marry and raise a family; invidious racial or religious discrimination. A party to the Covenant on Civil and Political Rights is responsible even for a single, isolated violation of one of these rights; any state is liable under customary law for a consistent pattern of violations of any such right as state policy. See also, the *Filartiga* and *Siderman* cases, *infra*.

SECTION D.   IMPLEMENTATION OF THE INTERNATIONAL LAW OF HUMAN RIGHTS

1.   IMPLEMENTATION AT THE UNITED NATIONS

STATEMENT ON HUMAN RIGHTS BY THE SECRETARY GENERAL OF THE INTERNATIONAL COMMISSION OF JURISTS, NOVEMBER 1978

Human Rights in United States and United Kingdom
Foreign Policy 23–26, 72 (Stewart ed. 1979).*

[Speaking at a colloquium on human rights in November 1978, Niall MacDermot, Secretary–General of the International Commission of Jurists, described the United Nations processes as follows.]

The UN bodies concerned with human rights are chiefly the Commission on Human Rights; its Sub–Commission on the Prevention of Discrimination and Protection of Minorities; and the Human Rights Committee set up under the International Covenant on Civil and Political Rights.   Many other UN bodies also cope with human rights issues.

Because of the four-tier UN structure, there is an unending cycle of human rights meetings, all with almost identical agendas, producing the same discussions, speeches, arguments and resolutions throughout the year:

- In August/September the Sub–Commission meets in Geneva.   Theoretically, it is a body of independent experts.

- In February/March the Human Rights Commission meets in Geneva for a six-week session.   More than 30 nations are represented.   The Commission reports to the Economic and Social Council (ECOSOC).

- In April/May ECOSOC meets in New York to deal with human rights.

- In September/December the General Assembly meets.   Human rights are dealt with by the Third Committee in December.

There are clearly too many tiers.   * * *

* * *

There is a frequent complaint about too much politics in the Human Rights Commission; but human rights are a very political subject.   One must accept that.   Paradoxically, it is very rare for politicians to attend the Human Rights Commission.

* Reprinted with the permission of the   Commission of Jurists.
American Association of the International

There is a need for people with continuing experience in human rights to head delegations. This is UK practice. The US changes its representatives on the Human Rights Commission frequently, to its disadvantage. It takes time to make influential contacts and understand the politicking that occurs.

A substantial delegation is needed by any government wanting to play a significant role. The UK's is often too small. * * *

The Human Rights Commission and the Sub–Commission's work is threefold: standard setting, studies, and implementation.

STANDARD SETTING is the formulation of principles in Conventions or Declarations of Principles such as the two International Covenants prepared by the Commission, and the Draft Convention on Torture. The Draft Body of Principles for the Protection of Persons in All Forms of Detention or Imprisonment was delegated to the Sub–Commission.

STUDIES cover many subjects, some very political. Most start in the Sub–Commission. One recently completed is sponsored by the UK on the Rights of Non–Citizens, arising from the expulsion of the Ugandan Asians. Two newer studies are worth mentioning: Human Rights under States of Exception or Emergency; and the Independence of the Judiciary, proposed by Sri Lanka.

Partly because the Sub–Commission is an independent body of experts, Western governments tend not to consider future studies. It should be part of government policy to think ahead and propose useful subjects. When asked for information, governments normally respond only about their own countries. NGOs must provide information that governments do not give. There is a feeling that the Human Rights Commission has done enough in the field of standard setting and should concentrate on implementation; but there is still a lot to do. Most of the Conventions state very general principles. Much detail needs to be worked out.

* * *

IMPLEMENTATION takes two forms:

Reports from States and Parties on legislative and administrative action to implement the various conventions and declarations. A number of them, such as on Freedom of Information and of the Press, go to the Commission. They do not form a large part of the Commission's activities and are not very effective. More impressive are the reporting procedures under the Convention on the Elimination of Racial Discrimination and under the Convention on Civil and Political Rights.

Alleged Violations Procedures can be public or private. They are public when a government raises an issue: the UK brought up Cambodia in the last session. Until recently, public investigations were confined to South Africa, Chile and Israel. An ad hoc committee is set up to study the subject and receive evidence, usually from NGOs and individuals. They tend to be one-sided in their views, often because the government under investigation has failed to cooperate. Governments do not regard them as fair tribunals.

The other system is the confidential so-called communications procedure directed to situations of a consistent pattern of gross violations of
human rights, rather than to individual complaints. The UN receives
30,000–40,000 complaints yearly, mostly from individuals and most of
which do not begin to provide evidence of a consistent pattern. * * *
The Commission acts on complaints from NGOs. The Human Rights
Commission can set up a Commission of Enquiry with the consent of the
concerned government; or it can order a thorough study. Neither has
ever been done. Occasionally a complaint has been referred to a
government for its comment. That is another delaying tactic. At that
stage the government usually takes the matter very seriously, as it wants
to avoid a condemnation by the Commission. Very, very slowly progress
is being made to strengthen and improve implementation.

* * *

To be effective, the UN fact-finding capacity must be increased. At
the moment the Human Rights Commission has neither the facilities nor
staff to be an effective fact-finding body. This provides one of the strong
arguments for a Human Rights Commissioner with his own staff to
fulfill the function. The Human Rights Committee under the International Covenant on Civil and Political Rights is in many ways the best
UN body on human rights. Its independent experts are all lawyers.
Their study of States–Parties' reports and cross-examination of States'
representatives on those reports has been done very well. * * *

Apart from the reports, they can investigate individual complaints
under the Optional Protocol * * *

———

1. ***Investigation of human rights violations.*** For the most
part, the work of the United Nations bodies in implementation of its
human rights policies consists of resolutions condemning massive violations of human rights standards, such as those claimed to have been
committed by South Africa in the administration of its apartheid system.
Ad hoc groups of experts or working groups are occasionally created by
the General Assembly or the Human Rights Commission, charged with
the responsibility of investigating and publicizing human rights violations. From time to time, a special rapporteur may be asked to address
a specific problem. The General Assembly may request the Secretary–
General * * * to investigate and publicize violations. For many years,
the Human Rights Commission has discussed the creation of a High
Commissioner for Human Rights, who could serve as an ombudsman,
dealing with specific situations as the need might arise. The Soviets,
among others, vigorously opposed the creation of this office. The High
Commissioner position was created in 1994.

2. ***The work of the Human Rights Commission,*** is illustrated
in the following report of one of its annual sessions.

HUMAN RIGHTS COMMITTEE CONCLUDES
FORTY–NINTH SESSION (1994)

Adopts Comments on Respect and Promotion Of Civil and Political Rights in Five Countries

GENEVA, 5 November (UN Information Service)—The Human Rights Committee concluded its forty-ninth session today after adopting comments on the promotion and protection of civil and political rights in Iceland, Norway, Japan, Malta and Romania.

In its report to the General Assembly, the 18–member Committee of experts notes the efforts undertaken in those countries concerning the implementation of the International Covenant on Civil and Political Rights. The Committee also cites areas of concern, such as the status of the Covenant in the legal orders of Norway and Iceland; the legacy of Romania's totalitarian past; and the treatment of minorities and women in Japan. The examination of a report from Libya was not completed at this session and would be resumed during the fifty-first session.

During its three-week meeting, the Committee also considered, in closed session, communications from individuals complaining that their rights under the Covenant had been violated by a State party to it.

In addition, the Committee, acting under its urgent action procedure, asked the Governments of Angola and Burundi to send reports on their application of rights protected under the Covenant in view of recent events in both countries. The reports, to be submitted by 31 January 1994, should relate, in particular, to the application of the articles of the Covenant concerning the imposition of a state of emergency, the right to life, torture, personal security, freedom of movement and the right to participate in public life.

Also at this session, the 18–member expert body began the adoption of a general comment to assist States parties to the Covenant implement the provisions of article 27 of the pact on the rights of ethnic, religious and linguistic minorities. At its next session, to take place at Headquarters from 21 March to 8 April 1994, the Committee will examine the reports from Mexico, Cameroon, El Salvador, Costa Rica and Cyprus.

Committee Comments on Reports

* * *

Japan: The Committee took note with satisfaction of the serious approach the Japanese Government had taken in dealing with issues relating to civil and political rights, and of its commitment to fulfil its obligations under the Covenant. The expert body was of the view that the human rights situation in Japan had improved since the consideration of its previous report in 1988.

The Committee expressed concern at continuing discriminatory practices against such groups as Korean permanent residents, members of the Buraku communities and persons belonging to the Ainu minority. It also expressed concern at discriminatory practices that appeared to persist against women with regard to renumeration in employment, and noted that de facto problems of discrimination more generally continued to exist. The Committee was disturbed by the number and nature of crimes punishable by death under the Japanese Penal Code.

Among the Committee's recommendations were that Japan become a party to both Optional Protocols to the Covenant and to the Convention against Torture and Other Cruel, Inhuman or Degrading Treatment or Punishment.

Malta: The Committee noted the efforts undertaken by the Government in order to guarantee effectively the protection of civil and political rights. The Committee was concerned at the fact that the Covenant, unlike the European Convention, had not yet been incorporated into the national legal order. It also expressed concern over the apparent preference accorded to the latter in Malta's domestic law, as well as in legal doctrines and jurisprudence. The Committee recommended, among other things, that Malta take appropriate measures to incorporate the substantive provisions of the Covenant into domestic law and ensure that the restrictions imposed under that law do not go beyond those permissible under the pact.

Romania: The Committee welcomed the many recent developments in Romania, which represented significant progress in the transition towards democracy and pluralism.

Considering the factors and difficulties affecting the implementation of the Covenant in Romania, the Committee noted with concern the legacy of that country's totalitarian past. It noted, in particular, that some prevailing and generally tolerated political and social attitudes in Romania were not conducive to the promotion and protection of human rights. The Committee expressed concern at the continuing problems in Romania regarding discrimination against persons belonging to minority groups and, in particular, offences committed as a result of incitement to ethnic or religious intolerance. That situation was especially threatening to vulnerable groups, such as the Roma (gypsies).

The Committee recommended that further measures be taken to protect persons belonging to minority groups and to enable them to exercise their rights under the Covenant, including participation at all levels in public institutions. It also emphasized the need for greater control over the police, particularly in view of the recent authoritarian past from which the Romanian society was emerging.

International Covenant on Civil and Political Rights

Adopted by the General Assembly in 1966, the Covenant entered into force 10 years later. It states in its first article that all peoples have the right to self-determination. It recognizes, among other things, the rights to life, liberty and security of person. It prohibits torture, cruel or degrading treatment or punishment, and the arbitrary deprivation of life. It states that anyone arrested is to be informed of the reasons for the arrest, and anyone arrested or detained on a criminal charge is to be brought promptly before a judge or other legally authorized person.

The Covenant also enshrines freedom of movement and places limitations on the expulsion of aliens present lawfully in the territory of a State party. In addition, it recognizes the rights to freedom of thought, conscience and religion, and to freedom of expression. It also prohibits any propaganda for war or any advocacy of national, racial or religious hatred.

States Parties to Covenant

As at 1 October, the following 124 States have ratified or acceded to the Covenant: Afghanistan, Albania, Algeria, Angola, Argentina, Armenia, Australia, Austria, Azerbaijan, Barbados, Belarus, Belgium, Benin, Bolivia, Bosnia and Herzegovina, Brazil, Bulgaria, Burundi, Cambodia, Cameroon, Canada, Cape Verde, Central African Republic, Chile, Colombia, Congo, Costa Rica, Cote d'Ivoire, Croatia, Cyprus, Czech Republic, Democratic People's Republic of Korea, Denmark, Dominica, Dominican Republic, Ecuador, Egypt, El Salvador, Equatorial Guinea, Estonia, Ethiopia, Finland, France, Gabon, Gambia, Germany, Grenada, Guatemala, Guinea, Guyana, Haiti, Hungary, Iceland, India and Iran.

Also, Iraq, Ireland, Israel, Italy, Jamaica, Japan, Jordan, Kenya, Latvia, Lebanon, Lesotho, Libya, Lithuania, Luxembourg, Madagascar, Mali, Malta, Mauritius, Mexico, Moldova, Mongolia, Morocco, Mozambique, Nepal, Netherlands, New Zealand, Nicaragua, Niger, Nigeria, Norway, Panama, Paraguay, Peru, Philippines, Poland, Portugal, Republic of Korea, Romania, Russian Federation, Rwanda, Saint Vincent and the Grenadines, San Marino, Senegal, Seychelles, Slovak Republic, Slovenia, Somalia, Spain, Sri Lanka, Sudan, Suriname, Sweden, Switzerland, Syria, Togo, Trinidad and Tobago, Tunisia, Ukraine, United Kingdom, United Republic of Tanzania, United States, Uruguay, Venezuela, Viet Nam, Yemen, Yugoslavia, Zaire, Zambia and Zimbabwe.

Optional Protocols to Covenant

The first Optional Protocol to the Covenant provides for the confidential consideration of communications from individuals who claim to be victims of a violation of any of the rights proclaimed in the Covenant. No communication can be received by the Committee if it concerns a State party to the Covenant that is not also a party to the Optional Protocol.

The following 74 States are parties to this Optional Protocol: Algeria, Angola, Argentina, Armenia, Australia, Austria, Barbados, Belarus, Benin, Bolivia, Bulgaria, Cameroon, Canada, Central African Republic, Chile, Colombia, Congo, Costa Rica, Cyprus, Czech Republic, Denmark, Dominican Republic, Ecuador, Equatorial Guinea, Estonia, Finland, France, Gambia, Germany, Guinea, Guyana, Hungary, Iceland, Ireland, Italy, Jamaica, Libya, Lithuania, Luxembourg, Madagascar, Malta, Mauritius, Mongolia, Nepal, Netherlands, New Zealand, Nicaragua, Niger, Norway, Panama, Peru, Philippines, Poland, Portugal, Republic of Korea, Romania, Russian Federation, Saint Vincent and the Grenadines, San Marino, Senegal, Seychelles, Slovak Republic, Slovenia, Somalia, Spain, Suriname, Sweden, Togo, Trinidad and Tobago, Ukraine, Uruguay, Venezuela, Zaire and Zambia.

The Second Optional Protocol to the Covenant, which aims at the abolition of the death penalty, was adopted by the General Assembly on 15 December 1989 and entered into force on 11 July 1991. It has been ratified or acceded to by 20 States: Australia, Austria, Ecuador, Finland, Germany, Iceland, Ireland, Luxembourg, Mozambique, Netherlands, New Zealand, Norway, Panama, Portugal, Romania, Slovenia, Spain, Sweden, Uruguay and Venezuela.

The Committee is also mandated, under article 41 of the Covenant, to consider communications from a State party alleging violation of the Covenant's provisions by another State party. This procedure can be applied when both States recognize this competence of the Committee by a relevant declaration. So far, the following 43 States have done so: Algeria, Argentina, Australia, Austria, Belarus, Belgium, Bosnia and Herzegovina, Bulgaria, Canada, Czech Republic, Chile, Congo, Denmark, Ecuador, Finland, Gambia, Germany, Guyana, Hungary, Iceland, Ireland, Italy, Luxembourg, Malta, Netherlands, New Zealand, Norway, Peru, Philippines, Poland, Republic of Korea, Russian Federation, Senegal, Slovenia, Spain, Sri Lanka, Sweden, Switzerland, Tunisia, Ukraine, United Kingdom, United States and Zimbabwe.

* * *

2. INTERNATIONAL ADJUDICATION

There is no universal court in which an individual can maintain an action to enforce the rights that international law has begun to recognize substantively. The only universal court is the International Court of Justice and only states may be parties in cases before the court. Are there nevertheless means by which an individual's rights can be vindicated in this court?

Problem. N is a national of State D, a party to the International Convention on the Elimination of All Forms of Racial Discrimination. (See the Documentary Supplement.) N claims that because of his race he has been denied equal opportunity by State D with respect to housing and employment, in violation of Article 5 of the convention. N persuades the foreign office of State P to become interested in his case by reason of the opportunity it affords State P to publicly embarrass State D over its racial policies. State P is unsuccessful in procuring any change in State D's policies or its treatment of N. All of the procedures provided for in the convention—see Articles 11, 12 and 13 in the Documentary Supplement—are exhausted without effect. Pursuant to Article 22 of the convention, State P refers its dispute with State D, over D's treatment of N, to the International Court of Justice. (Article 22 provides: "Any dispute between two or more States Parties with respect to the interpretation or application of this Convention, which is not settled by negotiation or by the procedures expressly provided for in this Convention, shall, at the request of any of the parties to the dispute, be referred to the International Court of Justice for decision, unless the disputants agree to another mode of settlement.") Will the court take jurisdiction of such a claim? Will it recognize the standing or interest of the complainant state?

NOTTEBOHM CASE (LIECHTENSTEIN v. GUATEMALA)

International Court of Justice, 1955.
[1955] I.C.J.Rep. 4.

The opinion of the court is set forth at p. 685. In the problem case the individual, N, whose rights were allegedly violated, is not a national of State P by any definition of nationality. Does the reasoning of Nottebohm suggest that P cannot maintain this proceeding?

––––––

INTER–AMERICAN COURT OF HUMAN RIGHTS: JUDGMENT IN *VELÁSQUEZ RODRÍGUEZ* CASE*

(Forced Disappearance and Death of Individual in Honduras)
[July 29, 1988], 28 I.L.M. 291 (1989).**

Introductory Note by Thomas Buergenthal

In 1986 the Inter–American Commission on Human Rights referred three cases to the Inter–American Court of Human Rights for adjudication in accordance with the provisions of the American Convention of Human Rights. [See 9 I.L.M. 673 (1970)]. In all three cases—*Velásquez Rodríguez, Godínez Cruz,* and *Fairen Garbi and Sollis Corrales*— the Republic of Honduras was charged with a series of violations of human rights that were allegedly committed in that country between 1981–1984 and resulted in the forced disappearance and death of four individuals.

The Government of Honduras, which had accepted the Court's jurisdiction in accordance with the provisions of Article 62 of the Convention, challenged the admissibility of the cases and the tribunal's jurisdiction to hear them on various grounds relating to the Commission's handling of the cases and for failure to exhaust domestic remedies. The Court dealt with these contentions in separate but almost identical judgments which were rendered on June 26, 1987. * * * In them, it rejected all but one of the preliminary objections of the Government. As to that objection, which alleged the failure to exhaust domestic remedies, the Court ordered it joined to the merits of the proceedings. This decision, the Court concluded, was compelled by the fact that it could not dispose of the objection without examining the question whether there existed in Honduras, between 1981 and 1984, a practice of disappearances, carried out or tolerated by the Government, which was the very issue the Court would have to address in dealing with the merits.

Although the Court was able to dispose of the preliminary objections in three separate judgments rendered on the same day, it has thus far adjudicated the merits of only two of the cases, *viz., Velásquez Rodríguez,*

* [Reproduced from the English text provided to *International Legal Materials* by the Inter–American Court of Human Rights. The Introductory Note was prepared for *International Legal Materials* by

Thomas Buergenthal, Professor of Law, George Washington University School of Law.]

** (Reprinted with the permission of the American Society of Int'l Law).

the instant case, and the *Godínez Cruz* case. The Court's reasoning in the latter case, which was decided on January 20, 1989, is for all practical purposes identical to that of *Velásquez.*

* * * In all three cases the Commission invited Messrs. Claudio Grossman, Juan Méndez and José Miguel Vivanco, the lawyers who represented the private parties in the proceedings before the Commission, to serve as advisers to its delegation in the proceedings. * * *

Notes: 1. The case concerning the Barcelona Traction, Light and Power Company, Limited (Belgium v. Spain). The case was decided in 1970, [1970] I.C.J.Rep. 3. A portion of the text of the decision appears in Chapter 15. The case concerned claimed injury to a corporation's property. In the course of an opinion dealing with the question of the proper state to maintain an action to redress this injury, the court stated:

> 33. When a State admits into its territory foreign investments or foreign nationals, * * * it is bound to extend to them the protection of the law and assumes obligations concerning the treatment to be afforded them. These obligations, however, are neither absolute nor unqualified. In particular, an essential distinction should be drawn between the obligations of a State towards the international community as a whole, and those arising vis-à-vis another State in the field of diplomatic protection. By their very nature the former are the concern of all States. In view of the importance of the rights involved, all States can be held to have a legal interest in their protection; they are obligations erga omnes.

> 34. Such obligations derive, for example, in contemporary international law, from the outlawing of acts of aggression, and of genocide, as also from the principles and rules concerning the basic rights of the human person, including protection from slavery and racial discrimination. Some of the corresponding rights of protection have entered into the body of general international law (Reservations to the Convention on the Prevention and Punishment of the Crime of Genocide, Advisory Opinion, I.C.J. Reports 1951, p. 23); others are conferred by international instruments of a universal or quasi-universal character.

> 35. Obligations the performance of which is the subject of diplomatic protection are not of the same category. It cannot be held, when one such obligation in particular is in question, in a specific case, that all States have a legal interest in its observance. In order to bring a claim in respect of the breach of such an obligation, a State must first establish its right to do so, for the rules on the subject rest on two suppositions:

>> The first is that the defendant State has broken an obligation towards the national State in respect of its nationals. The second is that only the party to whom an international obligation is due can bring a claim in respect of its breach.

(Reparation for Injuries Suffered in the Service of the United Nations, Advisory Opinion, I.C.J. Reports 1949, pp. 181–182.)

* * *

Despite the expansiveness of its language in paragraphs 33 and 34, the court made the following puzzling observation later in its opinion:

> 91. With regard more particularly to human rights, to which reference has already been made in paragraph 34 of this Judgment, it should be noted that these also include protection against denial of justice. However, on the universal level, the instruments which embody human rights do not confer on States the capacity to protect the victims of infringements of such rights irrespective of their nationality. It is therefore still on the regional level that a solution to this problem has had to be sought; thus, within the Council of Europe, of which Spain is not a member, the problem of admissibility encountered by the claim in the present case has been resolved by the European Convention on Human Rights, which entitles each State which is a party to the Convention to lodge a complaint against any other contracting State for violation of the Convention, irrespective of the nationality of the victim.

The Reporters of the 1987 Restatement addressed the court's statement:

> * * * Apparently, the Court meant that, as a matter of interpretation, general human rights agreements ordinarily do not contemplate diplomatic protection by one state party on behalf of an individual victim of a violation by another state party, at least where the victim was not a national of the protecting state. However, unless otherwise provided or clearly implied, there appears to be no reason why a party may not make an inter-state claim for a violation of such an agreement as for any other multilateral agreement. * * * Section 703, Reporters' Note 2.

2. **Remedies.** If a state refers to the court a dispute about a second state's treatment of the second state's own nationals, what relief should be requested or granted? Would monetary relief be administrable? Would a declaratory judgment be more workable? Would it be effective? See Judge Jessup's dissenting opinion in the South West Africa cases, [1966] I.C.J.Rep. at 329.

3. **Advisory Opinions.** How could an individual injured by his own state seek relief by way of an advisory opinion? The individual would need the support of some other state, to enlist the aid of the General Assembly or the Security Council (or some other body authorized under Article 65 of the Statute of the International Court of Justice) to ask for the opinion. It is obvious that the political difficulties that would be encountered by a single individual in pursuit of an advisory opinion through these channels would be virtually insurmountable. On the other hand, a group of individuals alleging a gross violation of a convention or general international legal obligation might possibly have more success, assuming a political context favorable to their cause. Beyond the political problems involved in procuring the request for an advisory opinion, there is the problem of inducing the

court to render the opinion. The question put to the court would have to be constructed in terms that would permit the court to find it had been asked for an opinion on a legal question under Article 65 of the statute. In addition, the court might have to be persuaded it was not in effect deciding a dispute involving a state without that state's consent to its jurisdiction.

ADVISORY OPINION ON THE WESTERN SAHARA

International Court of Justice, 1975.
[1975] I.C.J.Rep. 12, 22.

[The General Assembly, in 1975, focused on the decolonization of formerly Spanish Western Sahara and the claims to territorial sovereignty made by Morocco and Mauritania. The General Assembly finally requested the International Court of Justice to issue an *"advisory opinion"* addressing two problems: (1) When Spain colonized the Western Sahara, was the latter *terra nullius?* If no, (2) what is the legal nexus between the Western Sahara and Morocco or Mauritania?

27. Spain considers that the subject of the dispute which Morocco invited it to submit jointly to the Court for decision in contentious proceedings, and the subject of the questions on which the advisory opinion is requested are substantially identical; thus the advisory procedure is said to have been used as an alternative after the failure of an attempt to make use of the contentious jurisdiction with regard to the same question. Consequently, to give a reply would, according to Spain, be to allow the advisory procedure to be used as a means of bypassing the consent of a State, which constitutes the basis of the Court's jurisdiction. If the Court were to countenance such a use of its advisory jurisdiction, the outcome would be to obliterate the distinction between the two spheres of the Court's jurisdiction, and the fundamental principle of the independence of States would be affected, for States would find their disputes with other States being submitted to the Court, by this indirect means, without their consent; this might result in compulsory jurisdiction being achieved by majority vote in a political organ. [Thus, there are compelling reasons to deny the request].

Spain had not consented to the proceedings and had consistently and persistently objected. Spain invoked the fundamental rule that a state may not be compelled to submit its disputes to the Court's jurisdiction. *Citing, inter alia, the Status of Eastern Carilia Case, supra.*

30. In other respects, however, Spain's position in relation to the present proceedings finds no parallel in the circumstances of the advisory proceedings concerning the Status of Eastern Carelia in 1923. In that case, one of the States concerned was neither a party to the Statute of the Permanent Court nor, at the time, a Member of the League of Nations, and lack of competence of the League to deal with a dispute involving non-member States which refused its intervention was a decisive reason for the Court's declining to give an answer. In the present case, Spain is a Member of the United Nations and has accepted the

provisions of the Charter and Statute; it has thereby in general given its consent to the exercise by the Court of its advisory jurisdiction. It has not objected, and could not validly object, to the General Assembly's exercise of its powers to deal with the decolonization of a non-self-governing territory and to seek an opinion on questions relevant to the exercise of those powers. In the proceedings in the General Assembly, Spain did not oppose the reference of the Western Sahara question as such to the Court's advisory jurisdiction; it objected rather to the restriction of that reference to the historical aspects of that question.

31. In the proceedings concerning the Interpretation of Peace Treaties with Bulgaria, Hungary and Romania, First Phase, this Court had to consider how far the views expressed by the Permanent Court in the Status of Eastern Carelia case were still pertinent in relation to the applicable provisions of the Charter of the United Nations and the Statute of the Court. It stated, inter alia:

> "This objection reveals a confusion between the principles governing contentious procedure and those which are applicable to Advisory Opinions. The consent of States, parties to a dispute, is the basis of the Court's jurisdiction in contentious cases. The situation is different in regard to advisory proceedings even where the Request for an Opinion relates to a legal question actually pending between States. The Court's reply is only of an advisory character: as such, it has no binding force. It follows that no State, whether a Member of the United Nations or not, can prevent the giving of an Advisory Opinion which the United Nations considers to be desirable in order to obtain enlightenment as to the course of action it should take. The Court's Opinion is given not to the States, but to the organ which is entitled to request it; the reply of the Court, itself an 'organ of the United Nations', represents its participation in the activities of the organization, and, in principle, should not be refused." * * *

32. The Court affirmed in this pronouncement that its competence to give an opinion did not depend on the consent of the interested States, even when the case concerned a legal question actually pending between them. However, the Court proceeded not merely to stress its judicial character and the permissive nature of Article 65, paragraph 1, of the Statute but to examine, specifically in relation to the opposition of some of the interested States, the question of the judicial propriety of giving the opinion. Moreover, the Court emphasized the circumstances differentiating the case then under consideration from the Status of Eastern Carelia case and explained the particular grounds which led it to conclude that there was no reason requiring the Court to refuse to reply to the request. Thus the Court recognized that lack of consent might constitute a ground for declining to give the opinion requested if, in the circumstances of a given case, considerations of judicial propriety should oblige the Court to refuse an opinion. In short, the consent of an interested State continues to be relevant not for the Court's competence, but for the appreciation of the propriety of giving an opinion.

33. In certain circumstances, therefore, the lack of consent of an interested State may render the giving of an advisory opinion incompatible with the Court's judicial character. An instance of this would be when the circumstances disclose that to give a reply would have the effect of circumventing the principle that a State is not obliged to allow its disputes to be submitted to judicial settlement without its consent. If such a situation should arise, the powers of the Court under the discretion given to it by Article 65, paragraph 1, of the Statute, would afford sufficient legal means to ensure respect for the fundamental principle of consent to jurisdiction.

34. The situation existing in the present case is not, however, the one envisaged above. There is in this case a legal controversy, but one which arose during the proceedings of the General Assembly and in relation to matters with which it was dealing. It did not arise independently in bilateral relations. In a communication addressed on 10 November 1958 to the Secretary–General, * * * the Spanish Government stated: "Spain possesses no non-self-governing territories, since the territories subject to its sovereignty in Africa are, in accordance with the legislation now in force, considered to be and classified as provinces of Spain". This gave rise to the "most explicit reservations" of the Government of Morocco, which, in a communication to the Secretary–General of 20 November 1958, stated that it "claim[ed] certain African territories at present under Spanish control as an integral part of Moroccan national territory".

* * *

3. INDIVIDUAL PETITIONS

Gross and reliably attested violations. The Human Rights Commission and the Economic and Social Council decided in 1947 that the Commission "has no power to take any action in regard to any complaints concerning human rights." ECOSOC Off.Rec., 4th Sess., Supp. 3, Report of the Commission on Human Rights, First Sess., p. 6. Although attempts were made for two decades to reverse this position, the many communications from individuals that came to the United Nations informally each year were not acted upon, although a state named in a complaint was sent an anonymous copy.

This situation was changed by ECOSOC Resolution 1503 (XLVIII) of May 27, 1970, ECOSOC Off.Rec., Resumed 48th Sess., Resolutions, Supp. 1A, p. 8. It provides that the Sub–Commission on Prevention of Discrimination and Protection of Minorities may appoint a working group to consider communications from individuals and to bring to the sub-commission's attention those communications "which appear to reveal a consistent pattern of gross and reliably attested violations of human rights and fundamental freedoms within the terms of reference of the sub-commission." The resolution provides for consideration of the communications by the sub-commission, with reference thereafter to the Human Rights Commission and possibly a study and report by the commission or an investigation by an ad hoc committee appointed by the commission and recommendation to ECOSOC. Limitations of significance are that the ad hoc investigation can be made only with the consent of the state concerned and that the matter must remain confidential until the commission decides to make a recommendation to ECOSOC. The resolution is in the Documentary Supplement.

Procedures to carry out ECOSOC Resolution 1503 were adopted by the sub-commission in August 1971. Paragraph 2 of the procedures discloses that a broad range of persons and groups is empowered to originate communications. Paragraph 1 indicates that the procedures are useful for a single individual only if he is a victim of a "consistent pattern of gross and reliably attested violations of human rights and fundamental freedoms." It is significant, however, that the injured person can communicate directly with the United Nations without the necessity of enlisting the aid of a foreign state.

Although the 1503 procedure was hailed at the time of its creation as a major advance in human rights law, its accomplishments have largely been shrouded by the requirement of confidentiality, as illustrated by the following critique.

———

1. *Racial discrimination.* A procedure for hearing individual communications is contained in the International Convention on the Elimination of All Forms of Racial Discrimination and a Committee on the Elimination of Racial Discrimination exists under Article 8 of that Convention. Under Article 14, no communication from individuals is to be received by the committee if it concerns a state party that has not made a declaration recognizing the competence of the committee.

2. *Civil and political rights.* The right to make individual communications is also provided by the Optional Protocol to the International Covenant on Civil and Political Rights. The Human Rights Committee, established by Part IV of the covenant, is the mechanism for dealing with such communications.[a] Under Article 1 of the protocol, a state party to the protocol "recognizes the competence of the Committee to receive and consider communications from individuals subject to its jurisdiction who claim to be victims of a violation by that State Party of any of the rights set forth in the Covenant." It should be noted that this provision allows an individual to claim a single violation (i.e. it is not necessary to identify a pattern of violations as under the 1503 procedure). In addition, although Article 5(3) of the protocol calls for closed meetings, the committee is not held to the level of confidentiality that

a. The Human Rights Committee under the Optional Protocol is a different institution from the United Nations Commission on Human Rights and is not to be confused therewith.

surrounds the 1503 procedure. It has issued a number of reports with respect to communications that it has received, as shown below.

----

4. PUBLIC DENUNCIATION

The United States has taken a strong position with respect to violations of the human rights provisions of the Helsinki Final Act and the Madrid Concluding Document. It is the practice of the Department of State to issue periodic reports on the implementation of these provisions. In 1960's, '70's and 80's, the focus of these reports was often on the countries of Eastern Europe. Recently, they have focused on the nations in the territory of the former Yugoslavia, on the Peoples Republic of China, among others. A representative example follows:

----

* * *

CHINESE COMPLIANCE WITH MOU GOVERNING PRISON LABOR EXPORTS

Winston Lord, Assistant Secretary for East Asian and Pacific Affairs. Statement before the Subcommittee on International Economic Policy, the House Foreign Affairs Committee, Sept. 9, 1993

Mr. Chairman, members of the subcommittee: I appreciate the opportunity to provide an update on the problem of Chinese prison labor exports to the United States. With certain exceptions, U.S. law prohibits the importation of "all goods mined, produced, or manufactured wholly or in part in any foreign country by convict labor or/and forced labor or/and indentured labor under penal sanctions." The U.S. Government has devoted great efforts to prevent products produced by prison labor from being imported into this country. We at the State Department work closely with the U.S. Customs Service all over the world to support law enforcement both at our borders and overseas. Specifically regarding China, we have striven to identify and report on the export of prison labor products to the United States since the beginning of this decade. It is no mistake or quirk of bureaucratic policy-making that linked labor with our MFN process for China. Along with other areas of human rights, we are deeply concerned about this issue. This Administration has a commitment to human rights and enforcement of the prison labor MOU. China's MFN status is conditioned on it. It will not be extended if there is not satisfactory implementation of the MOU and overall progress on human rights.

There is reason for concern. Recent human rights problems have overtaken positive gestures by the Chinese Government. The overall implementation of the prison labor agreement has, generally, been characterized by poor communications, slow and cursory responses to investigation questions, and stonewalling or rejections of requests for visits.

Early U.S. Efforts:

Early efforts by the U.S. Government to learn about prison labor exports were not successful. Increasing information from sources like Harry Wu, Asia Watch, and others, coupled with interest on the part of the Congress, raised the level of public and governmental attention * * *.

In October 1991, partly in response, the Chinese issued a regulation prohibiting the export of products made with prison labor. However, there was still the need to ensure that these exports did not reach our shores. Concern in the previous Administration and the Congress prompted the U.S. to seek a Memorandum of Understanding on procedures for prompt investigation of allegations that specific imports from China were produced by prison labor.

We did not wait, however, for the prison labor MOU to be signed before we took action. U.S. law provides that Customs may issue detention orders when information reasonably, but not conclusively, indicates that merchandise produced by forced labor is being, or is likely to be, imported. Detention orders do not necessarily imply that goods have, in fact, been seized, but they prohibit the import of goods from subject facilities into the United States. The detention order cannot be lifted until Customs makes a clear determination that the facility in question does not utilize prison labor on the production line.

The detention order on Bliss Machine Tools, which resulted in effective prosecution and prohibition of imports of machine tools made by prison labor, is one example. I am sure Commissioner Weise has many more. We hoped that an MOU would assist Customs in making these determinations with regard to Chinese facilities.

Thus, after a long, laborious negotiation in which we were ably assisted by our colleagues in the Customs Service, the U.S. and China signed a Memorandum of Understanding on trade in prison labor products in August 1992. This was a significant step forward in strengthening compliance with both American and Chinese laws and regulations prohibiting trade in prison labor products. Effective implementation is an important U.S. priority in our bilateral relations with China.

The Memorandum of Understanding provides for:

— Prompt investigation of suspected violations of the laws and regulations of each side relating to trade in prison labor products:

— Exchanges of information; Meetings between officials and experts of the two sides; Furnishing of evidence that can be used in judicial or administrative proceedings against violators; and Prompt facilitation of visits to relevant facilities upon the request of either party.

Almost immediately after the signing, the U.S. Customs Service assigned a U.S.-based officer to the embassy to facilitate implementation of the MOU. Since then, Customs Officers have traveled frequently to

China on temporary assignment to conduct investigations. This month, the U.S. will assign two full-time officers to staff its new office in Beijing. One of these will be responsible primarily for prison labor issues. This will substantially boost our efforts to work with our Chinese counterparts to carry out the MOU.

Procedures for Investigations * * * have had problems at almost every stage of this process. First, we request the Chinese to investigate facilities which we have reason to believe use prison labor to produce goods for export. At this time, we present the Chinese with whatever hard evidence we have that a firm is engaging in prison labor trade. Depending on the results of the Chinese Ministry of Justice investigation, we may ask to make a verification visit to the site.

Since the signing of the MOU, we have presented 31 cases of suspected prison labor violations to the Chinese for investigation. Until yesterday, the Chinese had provided reports on 16 of these cases, and we were awaiting responses to another 15 which were presented to the Chinese in June. Mr. Chairman, I am pleased to report today that our embassy in Beijing has just received the results of the 15 outstanding cases. The results of these investigations could have a bearing on our ability to implement the MOU in the short term. Both State and Customs officials will be following up on these cases shortly in meetings with the Chinese in Beijing. That the Chinese have concluded these investigations despite their concerns about other outstanding cases may signal an increased willingness to work with us * * *

New Chinese Reports

The Chinese indicated that 11 of the 15 firms either do not export their products or do not export to the U.S. On August 25, 1992, we requested visits to five sites. We have visited only one of these facilities, the Jinma Diesel Factory, while our repeated requests to see the others have been rejected. For example, the Chinese responded that, since consulate officers had seen several of the other sites prior to the signing of the MOU, visits to these facilities were unnecessary. On the other hand, we have visited two sites which we did not ask to see but on which we had requested investigations.

In response to the first five cases submitted, the Chinese stated that they found no evidence that prison labor had been used to produce exports. The Chinese, subsequently, reported the results of 11 other cases. Of these 11, they claim that 6 facilities are prisons which do not produce goods for export, and that another one is a workers' collective which also does not export. The Chinese maintain that in many cases, factories employ family members of prison system employees but not prisoners themselves.

In the remaining four cases, the Chinese found that prison labor has been used for export production in the past. However, they maintain that these factories—the Sichuan Zigong Machine Tool Factory, the Sichuan Miaoxi Tea Plantation, the Shandong Dezhou Shengjian Machinery Factory, and the Hubei Xiangyang Machine Tool Factory—either have ceased exporting or have removed prisoners from the production line. Sichuan Zigong Machine Tool Factory was found to have exported prison labor-produced goods to Southeast Asia. Destinations of past exports from the other facilities were not reported.

* * * [I]nspection teams, comprising both State and Customs officials, have visited three suspected prison labor facilities, and we have long-standing requests to see five others. This includes one in Yunnan, the Jinma Diesel Engine Factory, where the first visit was inconclusive because local authorities denied the inspection team access to three areas of the factory compound. Up to now, requests for a revisit have been denied. Accordingly, the detention order on products from the Yunnan facility remains in effect, pending receipt of more definitive information * * *.

In two cases, the Qinghe Farm and Beijing Number One Prison (Qinghe Hosiery Factory), examination of prison records and facilities produced no evidence that these facilities were exporting any of their products. As a result, the joint Customs–State investigation team, in June, recommended the closure of these two cases. Customs is currently studying evidence obtained from visits to these two sites to make a final determination on them. * * *

Chinese Cooperation Following U.S. Trip

Implementation of the MOU has been slow from the start, but the Chinese exhibited greater willingness to work with us following the March visit here of a Chinese delegation of officials from the Ministry of Justice, the Ministry of Foreign Affairs, and the Ministry of Foreign Trade and Economic Cooperation. The trip, which both American and Chinese officials termed successful, allowed Chinese officials to hear first-hand the concerns of Congress and U.S. business on this important issue.

We have registered complaints many times with the Chinese. Perhaps predictably, the Chinese have some complaints of their own. They have recently expressed frustration at our failure, thus far, to close any of the outstanding cases. Chinese Ministry of Justice officials have suggested that we should reach final determinations on facilities already seen before requesting any more site visits. * * * They have recently indicated that they may withhold results of ongoing investigations until some outstanding cases, notably those involving the Qinghe Farm and the Beijing Number One Prison, are closed.

Chinese authorities have also repeatedly questioned the adequacy and timeliness of our evidence. Most information we have comes from Chinese publications, in some cases government ones which are 5 years old or more. Other evidence comes from company brochures, again many years old, which may include exaggerated or misleading claims about a company's activities. The lack of hard, recent evidence hampers our ability to work with Chinese justice officials and makes implementation of the MOU all the more difficult.

For our part, we have repeatedly encountered Chinese delays in providing responses to our requests for visits, and their investigation reports often lack detail. Prompt investigation of suspected facilities is in the interest of both the U.S. and China. Yet we have been granted access to only one facility for which we asked a visit.

As in many other issues in Sino–U.S. relations, the decentralization of authority within China, which accelerates the economic changes beneficial to a freer environment, also hampers prompt enforcement of our agreement. Conversely, the visits to Qinghe Farm and the Beijing Number One Prison—both in the Beijing area—were efficiently arranged and provided broad access both to facilities and, perhaps more importantly, to records. Chinese MOJ officials have repeatedly blamed the stonewalling of provincial and local officials at sites further from central control for the lack of more rapid progress on investigations and visits. However, this is no excuse for footdragging on a bilateral agreement * * *.

Perhaps even more than in prison labor, the MOU has encouraged Chinese cooperation in several other Customs-related areas. Customs sponsored a series of highly successful trade fairs which outlined for Chinese attendees how our Customs procedures and regulations apply to Chinese businesses. We have encouraged the Chinese to consider a similar program in the U.S. to acquaint U.S. businesses with Chinese laws. At the same time, Customs is currently negotiating a mutual assistance agreement with China.

Conclusion

There are encouraging signs, but much more remains to be done. I have already mentioned the increase in staff at the embassy. Although we have a number of Customs-related issues with the Chinese, the impetus behind setting up an office and a major part of its workload will be prison labor. Even with increased involvement on the ground, it is difficult to estimate whether, or how many, prison labor-made goods enter the U.S. through export to a third country and subsequent re-export here. Similarly, it can be hard to determine the origin of goods shipped to local trading companies and then exported to the U.S.

U.S. business can assist U.S. officials in these efforts. We should urge American businesspeople who travel frequently to China to consult with Chinese trading partners and encourage them to watch for possible violations of our regulations * * *. In addition, we welcome information from other organizations which might identify violations. * * *

The good faith of both parties, the United States and China, is critical to the successful implementation of the MOU. We have repeatedly underscored the importance we attach to this issue. This year China's progress in stemming exports of prison labor-produced goods through implementation of the MOU, together with freedom of emigration and other human rights concerns, will be scrutinized in determining our recommendations on most-favored-nation trade treatment for China.

5. PURSUIT OF HUMAN RIGHTS UNDER CUSTOMARY INTERNATIONAL LAW IN A NATIONAL COURT

FILARTIGA v. PENA–IRALA

United States Court of Appeals, Second Circuit, 1980.
630 F.2d 876.

KAUFMAN, Circuit Judge:

Upon ratification of the Constitution, the thirteen former colonies were fused into a single nation, one which, in its relations with foreign states, is bound both to observe and construe the accepted norms of international law, formerly known as the law of nations. Under the Articles of Confederation, the several states had interpreted and applied this body of doctrine as a part of their common law, but with the founding of the "more perfect Union" of 1789, the law of nations became preeminently a federal concern.

Implementing the constitutional mandate for national control over foreign relations, the First Congress established original district court jurisdiction over "all causes where an alien sues for a tort only [committed] in violation of the law of nations." Judiciary Act of 1789, ch. 20, § 9(b), (1789), codified at 28 U.S.C. § 1350. Construing this rarely-invoked provision, we hold that deliberate torture perpetrated under color of official authority violates universally accepted norms of the international law of human rights, regardless of the nationality of the parties. Thus, whenever an alleged torturer is found and served with process by an alien within our borders, § 1350 provides federal jurisdiction. Accordingly, we reverse the judgment of the district court dismissing the complaint for want of federal jurisdiction.

I

The appellants, plaintiffs below, are citizens of * * * Paraguay. Dr. Joel Filartiga, a physician, describes himself as a longstanding opponent of the government of President Alfredo Stroessner, which held power in Paraguay since 1954. His daughter, Dolly Filartiga, arrived in the U.S. in 1978 under a visitor's visa, and has since applied for permanent political asylum. The Filartigas brought this action in the Eastern District of New York against Pena–Irala (Pena), also a citizen of Paraguay, for wrongfully causing the death of Dr. Filartiga's seventeen-year old son, Joelito. Because the district court dismissed the action for want of subject matter jurisdiction, we must accept as true the allegations contained in the Filartigas' complaint and affidavits.

The appellants contend that on March 29, 1976, Joelito Filartiga was kidnapped and tortured to death by Pena, who was then Inspector General of Police in Asuncion, Paraguay. Later that day, the police brought Dolly Filartiga to Pena's home where she was confronted with the body of her brother, which evidenced marks of severe torture. As she fled, horrified, from the house, Pena followed after her shouting, "Here you have what you have been looking for for so long and what you deserve. Now shut up." The Filartigas claim that Joelito was tortured and killed in retaliation for his father's political activities and beliefs.

Shortly thereafter, Dr. Filartiga commenced a criminal action in the Paraguayan courts against Pena and the police for the murder of his son. * * *

During the course of the Paraguayan criminal proceeding, which is apparently still pending after four years, another man, Hugo Duarte, confessed to the murder. Duarte, who was a member of the Pena household,[1] claimed that he had discovered his wife and Joelito in flagrante delicto, and that the crime was one of passion. The Filartigas have submitted a photograph of Joelito's corpse showing injuries they believe refute this claim. Dolly Filartiga, moreover, has stated that she will offer evidence of three independent autopsies demonstrating that her brother's death "was the result of professional methods of torture." Despite his confession, Duarte, we are told, has never been convicted or sentenced in connection with the crime.

In July of 1978, Pena sold his house in Paraguay and entered the United States under a visitor's visa. He was accompanied by Juana Bautista Fernandez Villalba, who had lived with him in Paraguay. The couple remained in the United States beyond the term of their visas, and were living in Brooklyn, New York, when Dolly Filartiga, who was then living in Washington, D.C., learned of their presence. Acting on information provided by Dolly, the Immigration and Naturalization Service arrested Pena and his companion, both of whom were subsequently ordered deported on April 5, 1979 following a hearing. They had then resided in the United States for more than nine months.

Immediately, Dolly [had Pena served] with a summons and civil complaint at the Brooklyn Navy Yard, where he was being held pending deportation. The complaint alleged that Pena had wrongfully caused Joelito's death by torture and sought compensatory and punitive damages of $10,000,000. The Filartigas also sought to enjoin Pena's deportation to ensure his availability for testimony at trial. The cause of action is stated as arising under "wrongful death statutes; the U.N. Charter; the Universal Declaration on Human Rights; the U.N. Declaration Against Torture; the American Declaration of the Rights and Duties of Man; and other pertinent declarations, documents and practices constituting the customary international law of human rights and the law of nations," as well as 28 U.S.C. § 1350, Article II, sec. 2 and the Supremacy Clause of the U.S. Constitution. Jurisdiction is claimed under the general federal question provision, 28 U.S.C. § 1331 and, principally on this appeal, under the Alien Tort Statute, 28 U.S.C. § 1350.[3]

Judge Nickerson stayed the order of deportation, and Pena immediately moved to dismiss the complaint on the grounds that subject matter jurisdiction was absent and for forum non conveniens. * * * Pena, in

---

1. Duarte is the son of Pena's companion, Juana Bautista Fernandez Villalba, who later accompanied Pena to the United States.

3. Jurisdiction was also invoked pursuant to 28 U.S.C. §§ 1651, 2201 & 2202, presumably in connection with appellants' attempt to delay Pena's return to Paraguay.

support of his motion to dismiss on the ground of forum non conveniens, submitted the affidavit of his Paraguayan counsel, Jose Emilio Gorostiaga, who averred that Paraguayan law provides a full and adequate civil remedy for the wrong alleged. Dr. Filartiga has not commenced such an action, however, believing that further resort to the courts of his own country would be futile.

Judge Nickerson heard argument on the motion to dismiss on May 14, 1979, and on May 15 dismissed the complaint on jurisdictional grounds. The district judge recognized the strength of appellants' argument that official torture violates an emerging norm of customary international law. Nonetheless, he felt constrained by dicta contained in two recent opinions of this Court, Dreyfus v. von Finck, 534 F.2d 24 (2d Cir.), cert. denied (1976), to construe narrowly "the law of nations," as employed in § 1350, as excluding that law which governs a state's treatment of its own citizens.

The district court continued the stay of deportation for forty-eight hours while appellants applied for further stays. These applications were denied by a panel of this Court on May 22, 1979, and by the Supreme Court two days later. Shortly thereafter, Pena and his companion returned to Paraguay.

II

Appellants rest their principal argument in support of federal jurisdiction upon the Alien Tort Statute, 28 U.S.C. § 1350, which provides: "The district courts shall have original jurisdiction of any civil action by an alien for a tort only, committed in violation of the law of nations or a treaty of the United States." Since appellants do not contend that their action arises directly under a treaty of the United States, a threshold question on the jurisdictional issue is whether the conduct alleged violates the law of nations. In light of the universal condemnation of torture in numerous international agreements, and the renunciation of torture as an instrument of official policy by virtually all of the nations of the world (in principle if not in practice), we find that an act of torture committed by a state official against one held in detention violates established norms of the international law of human rights, and hence the law of nations.

The Supreme Court has enumerated the appropriate sources of international law. The law of nations "may be ascertained by consulting the works of jurists, writing professedly on public law; or by the general usage and practice of nations; or by judicial decisions recognizing and enforcing that law."

* * *

"[*The Paquete Habana*], ... is particularly instructive for present purposes, for it held that [a] traditional prohibition ..., [which] began as one of comity only, had ripened over the preceding century into 'a settled rule of international law' by 'general assent of civilized nationa.' Thus, it is clear that courts must interpret international law not as it was in 1789, but as it has evolved and exists among the nations of the world today."

The requirement that a rule command the "general assent of civilized nations" to become binding upon them all is a stringent one. Were this not so, the courts of one nation might feel free to impose idosyncratic legal rules upon others, in the name of applying international law. Thus, in Sabbatino, 376 U.S. 398 (1964), the Court declined to pass on the validity of the Cuban government's expropriation of a foreign-owned corporation's assets, noting the sharply conflicting views on the issue propounded by the capital-exporting, capital-importing, socialist and capitalist nations. Id.

The case at bar presents * * * situation diametrically opposed to the conflicted state of law that confronted the Sabbatino Court. Indeed, to paraphrase that Court's statement, there are few, if any, issues in international law today on which opinion seems to be so united as the limitations on a state's power to torture persons held in its custody.

The United Nations Charter (a treaty of the United States, (1945)) makes it clear that in this modern age a state's treatment of its own citizens is a matter of international concern. * * * [The court quotes United Nations Charter Articles 55 and 56, see, Doc. Supp.].

* * * [This broad mandate has been held not fully self-executing, but this does not end the inquiry]. [A]lthough there is no universal agreement as to the precise extent of the "human rights and fundamental freedoms" guaranteed to all by the Charter, there is at present no dissent from the view that the guaranties include, at a bare minimum, the right to be free from torture. This prohibition has become part of customary international law, as evidenced and defined by the Universal Declaration of Human Rights, General Assembly Resolution 217(III)(A) (Dec. 10, 1948) which states, in the plainest of terms, "no one shall be subjected to torture." [10] The General Assembly has declared that the Charter precepts embodied in this Universal Declaration "constitute basic principles of international law." G.A.Res. 2625(25) (Oct. 24, 1970).

Particularly relevant is the Declaration on the Protection of All Persons from Being Subjected to Torture, General Assembly Resolution 3452, 30 U.N. GAOR Supp., (n. 34) 91, U.S.Doc. A/1034 (1975) * * *.[a] The Declaration expressly prohibits any state from permitting the dastardly and totally inhuman act of torture. Torture, in turn, is defined as "any act by which severe pain and suffering, whether physical or mental, is intentionally inflicted by or at the instigation of a public official on a person for such purposes as * * * intimidating him or other persons." The Declaration goes on to provide that "[w]here it is proved that an act of torture or other cruel, inhuman or degrading treatment or punishment has been committed by or at the instigation of a public official, the victim shall be afforded redress and compensation, in accordance with national law." This Declaration, like the Declaration of Human Rights before it, was adopted without dissent by the General Assembly. * * *

10. Eighteen nations have incorporated the Universal Declaration into their own constitutions.

a. The General Assembly adopted a Convention Against Torture and Other Cruel, Inhuman or Degrading Treatment or Punishment on December 10, 1984. The definition of torture in the convention, although somewhat more detailed, is substantially the same as that set forth in the declaration. The text of the convention is set forth in the Documentary Supplement.

These U.N. declarations are significant because they specify with great precision the obligations of member nations under the Charter. Since their adoption, "[m]embers can no longer contend that they do not know what human rights they promised in the Charter to promote." * * * Moreover, a U.N. Declaration is, according to one authoritative definition, "a formal and solemn instrument, suitable for rare occasions when principles of great and lasting importance are being enunciated." * * * Accordingly, it has been observed that the Universal Declaration of Human Rights "no longer fits into the dichotomy of 'binding treaty' against 'non-binding pronouncement,' but is rather an authoritative statement of the international community." * * * Thus, a Declaration creates an expectation of adherence, and "insofar as the expectation is gradually justified by State practice, a declaration may by custom become recognized as laying down rules binding upon the States." Indeed, several commentators have concluded that the Universal Declaration has become, in toto, a part of binding, customary international law. * * *

Turning to the act of torture, we have little difficulty discerning its universal renunciation in the modern usage and practice of nations. The international consensus surrounding torture has found expression in numerous international treaties and accords. * * * The substance of these international agreements is reflected in modern municipal—i.e. national—law as well. Although torture was once a routine concomitant of criminal interrogations in many nations, during the modern and hopefully more enlightened era it has been universally renounced. According to one survey, torture is prohibited, expressly or implicitly, by the constitutions of over fifty-five nations, including both the United States and Paraguay.

* * *

Having examined the sources from which customary international law is derived—the usage of nations, judicial opinions and the works of jurists—we conclude that official torture is now prohibited by the law of nations. The prohibition is clear and unambiguous, and admits of no distinction between treatment of aliens and citizens. Accordingly, we must conclude that the dictum in Dreyfus v. von Finck, supra, to the effect that "violations of international law do not occur when the aggrieved parties are nationals of the acting state," is clearly out of tune with the current usage and practice of international law. The treaties and accords cited above, as well as the express foreign policy of our own government, all make it clear that international law confers fundamental rights upon all people vis-a-vis their own governments. While the ultimate scope of those rights will be a subject for continuing refinement and elaboration, we hold that the right to be free from torture is now among them. We therefore turn to the question whether the other requirements for jurisdiction are met.

III

Appellee submits that even if the tort alleged is a violation of modern international law, federal jurisdiction may not be exercised consistent with the dictates of Article III of the Constitution. The claim is without merit. Common law courts of general jurisdiction regularly adjudicate transitory tort claims between individuals over whom they exercise personal jurisdiction, wherever the tort occurred. Moreover, as part of an articulated scheme of federal control over external affairs, Congress provided, in the First Judiciary Act, Sec. 9(b), 1 Stat. 73, 77 (1789), for federal jurisdiction over suits by aliens where principles of international law are in issue. The constitutional basis for the Alien Tort Statute is the Law of Nations, which has always been part of the federal common law. [Article III of the U.S. Constitution provides that the "judicial power" applies to all cases which "arise under" "the Laws of the United States."]

* * *

Although the Alien Tort Statute has rarely been the basis for jurisdiction during its long history [28 USC 1350] in light of the foregoing discussion, there can be little doubt that this action is properly brought in federal court. This is undeniably an action by an alien, for a tort only, committed in violation of the law of nations. * * *

* * *

Since federal jurisdiction may properly be exercised over the Filartigas' claim, the action must be remanded for further proceedings. Appellee Pena, however, advances several additional points that lie beyond the scope of our holding on jurisdiction. Both to emphasize the boundaries of our holding, and to clarify some of the issues reserved for the district court on remand, we will address these contentions briefly.

IV

Pena argues that the customary law of nations, as reflected in treaties and declarations that are not self-executing, should not be applied as rules of decision in this case. In doing so, he confuses the question of federal jurisdiction under the Alien Tort Statute, which requires consideration of the law of nations, with the issue of the choice of law to be applied, which will be addressed at a later stage in the proceedings. The two issues are distinct. Our holding on subject matter jurisdiction decides only whether Congress intended to confer judicial power, and whether it is authorized to do so by Article III. The choice of law inquiry is a much broader one, primarily concerned with fairness. Should the district court decide that the Lauritzen analysis requires it to apply Paraguayan law, our courts will not have occasion to consider what law would govern a suit under the Alien Tort Statute where the challenged conduct is actionable under the law of the forum and the law of nations, but not the law of the jurisdiction in which the tort occurred.

Pena also argues that "[i]f the conduct complained of is alleged to be the act of the Paraguayan government, the suit is barred by the Act of State doctrine." This argument was not advanced below, and is therefore not before us on this appeal. We note in passing, however, that we doubt whether action by a state official in violation of the Constitution and laws of the Republic of Paraguay, and wholly unratified by that nation's government, could properly be characterized as an act of state. See *Sabbatino, supra*; Underhill v. Hernandez. Paraguay's renunciation of torture as a legitimate instrument of state policy, however, does not strip the tort of its character as an international law violation, if it in fact occurred under color of government authority. See Declaration on the Protection of All Persons from Being Subjected to Torture, supra; cf. Ex parte Young (state official subject to suit for constitutional violations despite immunity of state).

* * *

In the twentieth century the international community has come to recognize the common danger posed by the flagrant disregard of basic human rights and particularly the right to be free of torture. Spurred first by the Great War, and then the Second, civilized nations have banded together to prescribe acceptable norms of international behavior. From the ashes of the Second World War arose the United Nations Organization, amid hopes that an era of peace and cooperation had at last begun. Though many of these aspirations have remained elusive goals, that circumstance cannot diminish the true progress that has been made. In the modern age, humanitarian and practical considerations have combined to lead the nations of the world to recognize that respect for fundamental human rights is in their individual and collective interest. Among the rights universally proclaimed by all nations, as we have noted, is the right to be free of physical torture. Indeed, for purposes of civil liability, the torturer has become—like the pirate and slave trader before him—hostis humani generis, an enemy of all mankind. Our holding today, giving effect to a jurisdictional provision enacted by our First Congress, is a small but important step in the fulfillment of the ageless dream to free all people from brutal violence.

———

1. ***Further proceedings in the Filartiga case.*** On remand, the District Court granted a default judgment to plaintiffs and, in addition to actual damages recommended by a master, awarded punitive damages of $5,000,000 to each plaintiff. In looking for the applicable law, the court concluded that Section 1350 did not merely provide jurisdiction but also set the substantive principles to be applied, i.e., international law and not just the national law of the state where the tort was committed. The court devised the remedy of punitive damages after stating the following syllogism: "The international law prohibiting torture established the standard and referred to the national states the task of enforcing it. By enacting Section 1350 Congress entrusted that task to the federal courts and gave them power to choose and develop federal remedies to effectuate the purposes of the international law incorporated into United States common law." Filartiga v. Pena–Irala, 577 F.Supp. 860, 863 (E.D.N.Y.1984).

2. ***Release from indefinite detention.*** Making a search for legal principles in a manner similar to that employed by the court in the Filartiga case, the court in Rodriguez Fernandez v. Wilkinson, 505

F.Supp. 787 (D.Kan.1980) found that customary international law required release from indefinite detention of an excludable alien whose country (Cuba) would not take him back. The court of appeals, in Rodriguez–Fernandez v. Wilkinson, 654 F.2d 1382 (10th Cir.1981), affirmed, specifically on United States domestic law, although noting that its construction of the relevant statute was "consistent with accepted international law principles that individuals are entitled to be free of arbitrary imprisonment."

3. ***Tel–Oren v. Libyan Arab Republic,*** 726 F.2d 774 (D.C.Cir. 1984), cert. denied 470 U.S. 1003 (1985) addressed the Alien Tort Statute and came up with the opposite result.

Survivors of an armed attack in Israel by the PLO on two Israeli buses, a taxi, and a passing car and representatives of those who did not survive sued in the U.S. for compensatory and punitive damages. Their claim was that the damages arose from the above-indicated events, which violated international law. The case was dismissed at the trial level for want of subject matter jurisdiction. A three-judge panel of the Washington D.C. Court of Appeal affirmed the dismissal. Each judge wrote a separate opinion. ***Tel–Oren v. Libyan Arab Republic,*** 726 F.2d 774 (D.C.Cir.1984).

Judge Edwards: Judge Edwards "endorsed the legal principles [in] *Filartiga,* but found that 28 USC 1350 (the Alien Tort Statute) was inapplicable because the 'law of nations [fails to impose] the same responsibility or liability on non-state actors, such as the PLO, as it does in states and persons acting under color of state law.'" ***Judge Bork,*** on the other hand, argued that *Filartiga* was fundamentally wrong on the merits. Section 1350 simply did not apply—there was no jurisdiction and could be no cause of action, unless it were granted explicitly either by international law (general principles, custom, or treaty). Finding that the alleged conduct violated international law did not suffice; it was necessary to find an explicit grant of a cause of action. Finally, ***Judge Robb*** simply found that the case was non-justiciable; it came within the political question doctrine. *See also, Forti v. Suarez–Mason,* 672 F.Supp. 1531 (N.D.Cal.1987), *modified* in 694 F.Supp. 707 (N.D.Cal.1988); *Republic of Phillippines v. Marcos,* 818 F.2d 1473 (9th Cir.1987). ***Is it correct to hold that the Alien Tort Statute, which applies to offenses (wrongs) in violation of international law applies only to "state actors?"***

Notes & Questions:

1. ***In Jane Doe I, et al. v. Karadzic, 866 F.Supp. 734 (S.D.N.Y.1994),*** defendants' motion to dismiss was granted. Defendant, Radovan Karadzic, the self-proclaimed president of the Bosnian–Serb entity and leader of the Bosnian–Serb military faction, was sued for injunctive relief, compensatory, and punitive damages. The action was based upon the claim that plaintiffs were victims of a genocidal campaign ("ethnic cleansing"), designed, authorized, and directed by defendant. The alleged acts included rape and other human rights violations committed by forces under defendant's command. "Genocide, war crimes,

summary execution, wrongful death, torture, cruel, inhuman or degrading treatment, assault and battery, rape and intentional infliction of emotional harm" were the specifically alleged offenses. The action was brought pursuant to, inter alia: *the Alien Tort Act,* 28 U.S.C. § 1350; the *Torture Victim Protection Act,* 106 Stat. 73 (1992), also codified in 28 U.S.C. § 1350. Plaintiffs argued that the genocidal conduct was perpetrated in furtherance of "defendant's attempt to gain power and control of Bosnia–Herzegovina." The Court held that it did not have jurisdiction under the indicated laws, [*see discussion in Filartiga, supra*], because "only conduct which rises to the level of an international common law tort," which are committed by "state actors." *Citing, inter alia: Filartiga; Tel–Oren* (Edwards, J.'s opinion).

2. *Given the evolution of international law in the past 50 years, could it be possible that international law does not condemn and allow punishment of "not state actors?"* Is it necessary to prove agency of the state. Could it be true that just because an entity which is not recognized as a state performs terrorism and the like it is not a violation of the law of nations? Was this even true in the past? What about so-called pirates? What about hijackers? What about torture and terrorism committed by individuals involved in attempts to overthrow a state? Certainly, the requirement of a "state actor," if were ever true, has been abrogated.

2. *Even if one assumed that "state action" were required, is there any way to consider the defendants in this case to have acted under "apparent authority . . . of any foreign nation"?*

3. *Do you agree the Court's view of customary international law and its refusal to find an implied right of action?*

4. *Is it true, as the court claimed, that "[c]ourts have found causes of action to lie pursuant to § 1350," only when the perpetrators are state actors? See, contra, Abdul–Rahman Omar Adra v. Clift,* 195 F.Supp. 857 (D.Md.1961); *cf., Bolchos v. Darrell,* 3 Fed.Cas. 810 (D.S.C.1795) (No. 1607); 1 Op.Atty.Gen. 57, 58 (1795) (violations of neutrality by private U.S. perpetrators within the original Alien Tort Claims Act).

5. *Is there any series of treaties which impact on this analysis? Would such a series of treaties have any impact on the creation of a customary rule of international law? Would it be applicable to this case?*

4. *Subsequent judicial analysis of the Tel–Oren case.* 1. Von Dardel v. USSR, 623 F.Supp. 246 (D.D.C.1985) was an action for declaratory and injunctive relief and for damages against the Soviet Union on behalf of Raoul Wallenberg, a Swedish diplomat claimed to have been held, illegally under international law, by the Soviets for over thirty-five years following World War II. The Soviet Union did not participate in the litigation, claiming sovereign immunity. The court entered a default judgment for the plaintiffs. Section 1350 was held to provide federal jurisdiction as well as a substantive legal claim. The court found plaintiff's claim on behalf of a diplomat against a state to

satisfy all of the concerns expressed by the three judges in the Tel–Oren case. In particular Judge Bork's doubts about the existence of a cause of action under international law in the Tel–Oren case were found not applicable in a case involving well-settled principles of law regarding diplomats. Judge Bork, quoting Blackstone, had noted that "Infringement of the rights of embassadors" was one of the "kinds of offenses for which Congress wished to provide tort jurisdiction for suits by aliens." The court in the Von Dardel case held that the Wallenberg detention was one such offense.

5. ***U.S. Courts and Human Rights Law.*** Is it your impression that U.S. courts have been receptive to international human rights or humanitarian law? If not, why not? The U.S. generally includes many severely limiting reservations on its ratifying instruments. For example, it often includes a reservation that the convention is non-self-executing. What does this mean? If it is non-self-executing, what international effect does our "ratification" have? Domestic effect? Why do you think it has taken so long for the U.S. to ratify so many human rights conventions? As mentioned earlier, on April 2, 1992, the U.S. Senate gave its advice and consent to the *International Covenant on Civil and Political Rights*. It had been open for signature since 1966. Why did it take the U.S. Senate so long? When it filed its ratification papers, the U.S. Government included several reservations, including one that provided that the Convention is non-self-executing. For answers to these questions, see Chapter 14, infra.

6. ***Would the Torture Victim Protection Act of 1991, supra and the Victims of Crime Act of 1984,*** P.L. 102–572 § 1003, 106 Stat. 4521, et seq. (42 U.S.C. § 10601), which includes penalties for "international terrorism" change the outcome in cases like Tel–Oren?

SIDERMAN v. THE REPUBLIC OF ARGENTINA

United States Court of Appeals, Ninth Circuit, 1992.
Cert. denied 113 S.Ct. 1812 (1993) (most fns. omitted, other fn. numbers changed).

Before: FLETCHER, CANBY and BOOCHEVER, Circuit Judges.
FLETCHER, Circuit Judge:

* * *

FACTS

The factual record, which consists only of the Sidermans' complaint and numerous declarations they submitted in support of their claims, tells a horrifying tale of the violent and brutal excesses of an anti-Semitic military junta that ruled Argentina. On March 24, 1976, the Argentine military overthrew the government of President Maria Estela Peron and seized the reins of power for itself, installing military leaders of the central government and the provincial governments of Argentina. That night, ten masked men carrying machine guns forcibly entered the home of Jose and Lea Siderman, husband and wife, in Tucuman Province, Argentina. The men, who were acting under the direction of the military governor of Tucuman, ransacked the home and locked Lea in the bathroom. They then blindfolded and shackled 65–year old Jose, dragged him out of his home, tossed him into a waiting car, and drove off to an unknown building. For seven days the men beat and tortured Jose. Among their tools of torture was an electric cattle prod, which they used to shock Jose until he fainted. As they tortured him, the men repeatedly shouted anti-Semitic epithets, calling him a "Jew Bastard" and a "Shitty Jew." They inflicted all of these cruelties upon Jose Siderman because of his Jewish faith.

At the end of this nightmarish week, his body badly bruised and his ribs broken, Jose was taken out of the building and driven to an isolated area, where the masked men tossed him out of the car. The men told Jose that if he and his family did not leave Tucuman and Argentina immediately, they would be killed. On the day of Jose's release, he and Lea fled to Buenos Aires in fear for their lives. Their son Carlos followed shortly thereafter, and the night Carlos left Tucuman, military authorities ransacked his home. In June 1976, Jose, Lea, and Carlos left Argentina for the United States, where they joined Susana Siderman de Blake. She is the daughter of Jose and Lea and is a United States citizen.

Before the hasty flight from Tucuman to Buenos Aires, Jose was forced to raise cash by selling at a steep discount part of his interest in 127,000 acres of land. Prior to their departure for the United States, the Sidermans also made arrangements for someone to oversee their family business, Inmobiliaria del Nor–Oeste, S.A. ("INOSA"), an Argentine corporation. Susana Siderman de Blake, Carlos Siderman and Lea Siderman each owned 33% of INOSA and Jose owned the remaining one percent. Its assets comprised numerous real estate holdings including a large hotel in Tucuman, the Hotel Gran Corona. The Sidermans granted management powers over INOSA to a certified public accountant in Argentina.

After the Sidermans left Argentina for the United States, Argentine military officers renewed their persecution of Jose. They altered real property records in Tucuman to show that he had owned not 127,000, but 127, acres of land in the province. They then initiated a criminal action against him in Argentina, claiming that since he owned only 127 acres he had sold land that did not belong to him. Argentina sought the assistance of our courts in obtaining jurisdiction over his person, requesting via a letter rogatory that the Los Angeles Superior Court serve him with documents relating to the action. The court, unaware of Argentina's motives, complied with the request.

Soon thereafter, while he was travelling in Italy, Jose was arrested pursuant to an extradition request from Argentina to the Italian government. Argentina charged that Jose had fraudulently obtained the travel documents enabling him to leave Argentina in 1976. Jose was not permitted to leave Cremora, Italy, for seven months, and actually was imprisoned for 27 days, before an Italian Appeals Court finally held that Argentina's extradition request would not be honored, as it was politically motivated and founded on pretextual charges.

The Argentine military also pursued INOSA with vigor. In April 1977, INOSA was seized through a sham "judicial intervention," a proceeding in which property is put into receivership. The purported reasons for the intervention were that INOSA lacked a representative in Argentina and that INOSA had obtained excessive funds from a Tucuman provincial bank. Though these reasons were pretexts for persecuting the Sidermans because of their religion and profiting from their economic success, the Sidermans were unable to oppose the intervention because Argentine officials had imprisoned and killed the accountant to whom they had granted management powers over INOSA. In 1978, the Sidermans retained an attorney in Argentina and brought a derivative action in a Tucuman court in an effort to end the intervention. The court ordered that the intervention cease, and the order was upheld by the Supreme Court of Tucuman, but the order remains unenforced and the intervention has continued. Argentine military officials and INOSA's appointed receivers have extracted funds from INOSA, purchased various assets owned by INOSA at sharply discounted prices, and diverted INOSA's profits and revenues to themselves.

In 1982, Jose, Lea, and Carlos, who by then had become permanent residents of the United States, and Susana, a United States citizen since 1967, turned to federal court for relief. They filed a complaint asserting eighteen causes of action based on the torture and harassment of Jose by Argentine officials and the expropriation of their property in Argentina. Named defendants included the Republic of Argentina, the Province of Tucuman, INOSA, and numerous individual defendants who participated in the wrongdoing. In December 1982, the Sidermans properly served Argentina and Tucuman with the Summons and Complaint. The Argentine Embassy subsequently sought assistance from the U.S. State Department, which informed Argentina that it would have to appear and present any defenses it wished to assert to the district court, including the defense of sovereign immunity, or risk a default judgment. The State Department also provided a directory of lawyer referral services. Despite receiving this information, Argentina did not enter an appearance, and the Sidermans filed a motion for default judgment.

On March 12, 1984, the district court dismissed the Sidermans' expropriation claims sua sponte on the basis of the act of state doctrine and ordered a hearing for the Sidermans to prove up their damages on the torture claims. The Sidermans moved for reconsideration of the court's dismissal of the expropriation claims. On September 28, 1984, the court denied the motion for reconsideration and entered a default judgment on the torture claims, awarding Jose damages and expenses totalling $2.6 million for his torture claims and awarding Lea $100,000 for her loss of consortium claim.

The damages award finally elicited a response from Argentina, which filed a motion for relief from judgment on the ground that it was immune from suit under the FSIA and that the district court therefore lacked both subject matter and personal jurisdiction. The United States filed a suggestion of interest, asking the court to consider the issue of foreign sovereign immunity but indicating no view of the merits. On March 7, 1985, the district court vacated the default judgment and dismissed the Sidermans' action on the ground of Argentina's immunity under the FSIA.[1] The Sidermans filed a timely notice of appeal. We have jurisdiction over the appeal pursuant to 28 U.S.C. § 1291.

* * *

II. Torture Claims

The question of Argentina's immunity from the Sidermans' torture claims is squarely presented, without the procedural complications surrounding the district court's treatment of the expropriation claims. The district court dismissed the torture claims on the ground that they fell within no exception to immunity under the FSIA.[2] In defending the district court's decision on appeal, Argentina argues that the Sidermans' claims are foreclosed by the Supreme Court's opinion in Argentine Republic v. Amerada Hess. Since Amerada Hess represents the Court's most extensive treatment of the FSIA and its exceptions to immunity, we begin with a discussion of the case before turning to the Sidermans' arguments about why the case does not preclude their torture claims.

* * *

A. Jus Cogens

The Sidermans contend that Argentina does not enjoy sovereign immunity with respect to its violation of the jus cogens norm of international law condemning official torture. While we agree with the Sidermans that official acts of torture of the sort they allege Argentina to have committed constitute a jus cogens violation, we conclude that Amerada Hess forecloses their attempt to posit a basis for jurisdiction not expressly countenanced by the FSIA.

As defined in the Vienna Convention on the Law of Treaties, a jus cogens norm, also known as a "peremptory norm" of international law, "is a norm accepted and recognized by the international community of states as a whole as a norm from which no derogation is permitted and which can be modified only by a subsequent norm of general international law having the same character." Vienna Convention on the Law of Treaties, art. 53, May 23, 1969, 1155 U.N.T.S. 332, 8 I.L.M. 679

---

1. The court did not reach the question of personal jurisdiction, nor do the parties argue the issue on appeal. The FSIA provides that personal jurisdiction exists if subject matter jurisdiction exists and proper service has been made under the FSIA. See 28 U.S.C. § 1330(b). Nevertheless, the exercise of personal jurisdiction also must comport with the constitutional requirement of due process. [See discussion of Sovereign Immunity in Ch. 7, supra).

2. When the district court granted the initial default judgment in favor of Jose and Lea Siderman on the torture claims, it relied on the Alien Tort Statute, which provides the federal courts with jurisdiction over "any civil action by an alien for a tort only, committed in violation of the law of nations or a treaty of the United States." 28 U.S.C. § 1350. When the district court

later granted Argentina's motion for relief from the default judgment, it held that the Alien Tort Statute did not provide an exception to foreign sovereign immunity and that no exception in the FSIA encompassed the Sidermans' torture claims. The Supreme Court since has held that the Alien Tort Statute does not provide jurisdiction over suits against foreign states; the FSIA is the sole basis for jurisdiction over such actions. Argentine Republic v. Amerada Hess Shipping Corp. In light of Amerada Hess, and because the FSIA links immunity to subject matter jurisdiction, the district court's determination that no FSIA exception applied to the torture claims necessarily constituted a determination that the court lacked subject matter jurisdiction.

[hereinafter "Vienna Convention"]; see also Restatement § 102 Reporter's Note 6. Jus cogens is related to customary international law (the direct descendant of the law of nations), which the Restatement defines as the "general and consistent practice of states followed by them from a sense of legal obligation." Restatement § 102(2). Courts ascertain customary international law "by consulting the works of jurists, writing professedly on public law; or by the general usage and practice of nations; or by judicial decisions recognizing and enforcing that law." United States v. Smith, * * * (Story, J.); see also The Paquete Habana * * * (in ascertaining and administering customary international law, courts should resort "to the customs and usages of civilized nations, and, as evidence of these, to the works of jurists and commentators"); Filartiga v. Pena–Irala * * * Courts seeking to determine whether a norm of customary international law has attained the status of jus cogens look to the same sources, but must also determine whether the international community recognizes the norm as one "from which no derogation is permitted." Committee of U.S. Citizens Living in Nicaragua v. Reagan * * * [hereinafter "CUSCLIN"] (quoting Vienna Convention, art. 53). In CUSCLIN, the only reported federal decision to give extended treatment to jus cogens, the court described jus cogens as an elite subset of the norms recognized as customary international law. Id.

While jus cogens and customary international law are related, they differ in one important respect. Customary international law, like international law defined by treaties and other international agreements, rests on the consent of states. A state that persistently objects to a norm of customary international law that other states accept is not bound by that norm, see Restatement § 102 Comment d, just as a state that is not party to an international agreement is not bound by the terms of that agreement. International agreements and customary international law create norms known as jus dispositivum, the category of international law that "consists of norms derived from the consent of states" and that is founded "on the self-interest of the participating states * * *." Jus dispositivum binds only "those states consenting to be governed by it."

In contrast, jus cogens "embraces customary laws considered binding on all nations," * * * and "is derived from values taken to be fundamental by the international community, rather than from the fortuitous or self-interested choices of nations * * *." Whereas customary international law derives solely from the consent of states, the fundamental and universal norms constituting jus cogens transcend such consent, as exemplified by the theories underlying the judgments of the Nuremberg tribunals following World War II * * *. The legitimacy of the Nuremberg prosecutions rested not on the consent of the Axis Powers and individual defendants, but on the nature of the acts they committed: acts that the laws of all civilized nations define as criminal * * *. The universal and fundamental rights of human beings identified by Nuremberg—rights against genocide, enslavement, and other inhumane acts * * * are the direct ancestors of the universal and fundamental norms recognized as jus cogens. In the words of the International Court of Justice, these norms, which include "principles and rules concerning the basic rights of the human person," are the concern of all states; "they are obligations erga omnes." *The Barcelona Traction* (Belgium v. Spain), 1970 I.C.J. 3, 32.

Because jus cogens norms do not depend solely on the consent of states for their binding force, they "enjoy the highest status within international law." CUSCLIN, 859 F.2d at 940. For example, a treaty that contravenes jus cogens is considered under international law to be void ab initio. See Vienna Convention, art. 53; Restatement § 102 Comment k. Indeed, the supremacy of jus cogens extends over all rules of international law; norms that have attained the status of jus cogens "prevail over and invalidate international agreements and other rules of international law in conflict with them." Restatement § 102 Comment k. A jus cogens norm is subject to modification or derogation only by a subsequent jus cogens norm. Id.

The Sidermans claim that the prohibition against official torture has attained the status of a jus cogens norm. There is no doubt that the prohibition against official torture is a norm of customary international law, as the Second Circuit recognized more than ten years ago in the landmark case of Filartiga v. Pena–Irala * * *. Dr. Filartiga and his daughter, citizens of Paraguay, [sued] Paraguayan officials who had tortured Dr. Filartiga's son to death. They alleged jurisdiction under the Alien Tort Statute, which grants the district courts "original jurisdiction of any civil action by an alien for a tort only, committed in violation of the law of nations or a treaty of the United States." 28 U.S.C. § 1350. Dr. Filartiga claimed that the defendants' torture of his son, perpetrated under color of official authority, violated a norm of customary international law prohibiting official torture, and the court agreed. Judge Kaufman, writing for the court, explained that "there are few, if any, issues in international law today on which opinion seems to be so united as the limitations on a state's power to torture persons held in its custody." * * * Judge Kaufman catalogued the evidence in support of this view, citing several declarations of the United Nations General Assembly and human rights conventions prohibiting torture,[14] modern municipal law to the same effect, and the works of jurists, and finally concluded "that official torture is now prohibited by the law of nations."

Other authorities have also recognized that official torture is prohibited by customary international law. In Forti v. Suarez–Mason [*supra*], a suit predicated on atrocities committed by the same Argentine military government alleged to be responsible for the torture of Jose Siderman, the district court held that "official torture constitutes a cognizable violation of the law of nations," and described the prohibition against

---

14. Judge Kaufman cited the Universal Declaration of Human Rights, G.A.Res. 217A(III), 3 U.N.GAOR Supp. (No. 16), U.N.Doc. A/810 (1948); Declaration on the Protection of All Persons from Being Subjected to Torture, G.A.Res. 3452, 30 U.N.GAOR Supp. (No. 34) at 91, U.N.Doc. A/1034 (1975); American Convention on Human Rights, Nov. 22, 1969, 36 O.A.S.T.S. 1, O.A.S. Official Records OEA/Ser. 4 v/II 23, Doc. 21, rev. 2 (1975); International Covenant on Civil and Political Rights, Annex to G.A.Res. 2200(XXI)a, 21 U.N.GAOR Supp. (No. 16), U.N.Doc. A/6316 (1966); European Convention for the Protection of Human Rights and Fundamental Freedoms, Art. 3, Council of Europe, Europ.T.S. No. 5, 213 U.N.T.S. 211 (1968).

official torture as "universal, obligatory, and definable." Similarly, in Tel–Oren v. Libyan Arab Republic, [*supra*] (opinion of Edwards, J.) which involved an action against the Palestine Liberation Organization for its acts of terrorism, Judge Edwards identified torture as a violation of customary international law. Judge Bork, although raising considerable opposition to the application of customary international law in U.S. courts, see id. (opinion of Bork, J.), at the same time conceded that the international law prohibition against torture is not disputed. Id. The Restatement of Foreign Relations also holds to the view that customary international law prohibits official torture. Restatement § 702(d). Finally, the world now has an international agreement focused specifically on the prohibition against torture: The Convention Against Torture and Other Cruel, Inhuman or Degrading Treatment or Punishment, 39 U.N.GAOR Supp. (No. 51), 23 I.L.M. 1027 (1984) [hereinafter "Torture Convention"], which entered into force on June 26, 1987. The United States signed the Torture Convention in April 1988, the United States Senate gave its advice and consent in October 1988, see 136 Cong.Rec. S17486–92 (daily ed. October 27, 1990), and it now awaits the President's filing of the instrument of ratification with the Secretary–General of the United Nations.[15]

In light of the unanimous view of these authoritative voices, it would be unthinkable to conclude other than that acts of official torture violate customary international law. And while not all customary international law carries with it the force of a jus cogens norm, the prohibition against official torture has attained that status. In CUSCLIN, 859 F.2d at 941–42, the D.C. Circuit announced that torture is one of a handful of acts that constitute violations of jus cogens. In Filartiga, though the court was not explicitly considering jus cogens, Judge Kaufman's survey of the universal condemnation of torture provides much support for the view that torture violates jus cogens. In Judge Kaufman's words, "[a]mong the rights universally proclaimed by all nations, as we have noted, is the right to be free of physical torture." Supporting this case law is the Restatement, which recognizes the prohibition against official torture as one of only a few jus cogens norms. Restatement § 702 Comment n (also identifying jus cogens norms prohibiting genocide, slavery, murder or causing disappearance of individuals, prolonged arbitrary detention, and systematic racial discrimination). Finally, there is widespread

---

15. The Torture Convention defines torture as any act by which severe pain or suffering, whether physical or mental, is intentionally inflicted on a person for such purposes as obtaining from him or a third person information or a confession, punishing him for an act he or a third person has committed or is suspected of having committed, or intimidating or coercing him or a third person, or for any reason based on discrimination of any kind, when such pain or suffering is inflicted by or at the instigation of or with the consent or acquiescence of a public official or other person acting in an official capacity. Torture Convention, art. 1. The agreement also calls on each state party to take measures to prevent torture within its territory, id., art. 2, and to "ensure that all acts of torture are offenses under its criminal law," Id., art. 4. States parties must either prosecute or extradite persons charged with torture. Id., arts. 5–8. Each state party also must ensure that torture victims or their decedents "obtain[ ] redress and ha[ve] an enforceable right to fair and adequate compensation including the means for as full rehabilitation as possible." Id., art. 14(1). Finally, the Torture Convention creates a "Committee against Torture," which is responsible for receiving and reviewing states' compliance with the agreement. Id., arts. 17–24.

agreement among scholars that the prohibition against official torture has achieved the status of a jus cogens norm * * *.

Given this extraordinary consensus, we conclude that the right to be free from official torture is fundamental and universal, a right deserving of the highest status under international law, a norm of jus cogens. The crack of the whip, the clamp of the thumb screw, the crush of the iron maiden, and, in these more efficient modern times, the shock of the electric cattle prod are forms of torture that the international order will not tolerate. To subject a person to such horrors is to commit one of the most egregious violations of the personal security and dignity * * *. That states engage in official torture cannot be doubted, but all states believe it is wrong, all that engage in torture deny it, and no state claims a sovereign right to torture its own citizens. See Filartiga, * * * (noting that no contemporary state asserts "a right to torture its own or another nation's citizens"); at n. 15 ("The fact that the prohibition against torture is often honored in the breach does not diminish its binding effect as a norm of international law."). Under international law, any state that engages in official torture violates jus cogens.

The question in the present case is what flows from the allegation that Argentina tortured Jose Siderman and thereby violated a jus cogens norm. The Sidermans contend that when a foreign state's act violates jus cogens, the state is not entitled to sovereign immunity with respect to that act. This argument begins from the principle that jus cogens norms "enjoy the highest status within international law," CUSCLIN, [*supra*] and thus "prevail over and invalidate * * * other rules of international law in conflict with them," Restatement § 102 Comment k. The Sidermans argue that since sovereign immunity itself is a principle of international law, it is trumped by jus cogens. In short, they argue that when a state violates jus cogens, the cloak of immunity provided by international law falls away, leaving the state amenable to suit. [*For the sovereign immunity discussion in Siderman, see Chapter 7, supra*].

* * *

* * * [W]e conclude that if violations of jus cogens committed outside the United States are to be exceptions to immunity, Congress must make them so. The fact that there has been a violation of jus cogens does not confer jurisdiction under the FSIA.

* * *

The district court erred in dismissing the Sidermans' torture claims.

CONCLUSION

The Sidermans' complaint and the evidence they have presented in support of their allegations paint a horrifying portrait of anti-Semitic, government-sponsored tyranny. The record that so far has been developed in this case reveals no ground for shielding Argentina from the Sidermans' claims that their family business was stolen from them by the military junta that took over the Argentine government in 1976. It further suggests that Argentina has implicitly waived its sovereign immunity with respect to the Sidermans' claims for torture.

We REVERSE and REMAND for further proceedings consistent with this opinion.

————

Query: Are jus cogens normal pacts of customary international law or general principles?

————

SECTION E.   HUMAN RIGHTS AND REGIONAL ORGANIZATIONS

On regional human rights regimes, generally, see gen., Weston, Lukes, and Hnatt, Regional Human Rights Regimes: A Comparison and Appraisal, 20 Vand.J.Trans'l L. 585 (1987).   These include Western Europe, the Organisation of American States, Africa, and the Middle East.   The first three of these have enforcement mechanisms including Human Rights Commissions and Courts.   See also, Lillich, International Human Rights (2d ed. 1991).

1.   THE COUNCIL OF EUROPE

The Council of Europe was created in 1949 by European states with the aim, in the language of the statute, 87 U.N.T.S. 103, "to achieve a greater unity [among] its Members for the purpose of safeguarding and realising the ideals and principles which are their common heritage," this aim to be pursued "by discussion of questions of common concern * * * and in the maintenance and further realisation of human rights and fundamental freedoms."   Pursuant to that aim, and in the light of the Universal Declaration of Human Rights, the European Convention for the Protection of Human Rights and Fundamental Freedoms was brought into force in 1953, 213 U.N.T.S. 221.[a]   The Convention and protocols thereto are in the Documentary Supplement.

European Commission and European Court of Human Rights.   The Convention is notable because it is a working system for the international protection of human rights.   The international organs of enforcement are the European Commission on Human Rights and the European Court of Human Rights; these organs have established a substantial body of precedent under the convention.   The function of the Commission is to ascertain the facts as to alleged breaches of the convention and to secure a friendly settlement.   There are two ways in which the Commission can be activated.   One, any state party to the convention may refer an alleged breach by another party.   Second,

a. States that had ratified the Convention as of December 31, 1986, were Austria, Belgium, Cyprus, Denmark, Federal Republic of Germany, France, Greece, Iceland, Ireland, Italy, Liechtenstein, Luxembourg, Malta, Netherlands, Norway, Portugal, Spain, Sweden, Switzerland, Turkey and the United Kingdom. (The Council of Europe is a different institution from the European Community and is not to be confused therewith.)

individual victims [a] of a violation by a state party can petition the Commission; but this right of petition can be exercised against a state only if it has declared that it recognizes the competence of the Commission to receive petitions. In the event a friendly settlement is not reached through its conciliation processes, the Commission renders a report in which it states "its opinion as to whether the facts found disclose a breach by the State concerned of its obligations under the Convention." The convention provides for further decision and the requirement of measures by the Committee of Ministers, an organ of the Council of Europe.

The Court on the other hand, has a jurisdiction which is more remote from the individual. Its jurisdiction comprises cases referred to it by the Commission or by a state party to the convention; a state may refer the case to the Court if its national is alleged to be a victim, or if it had referred the case to the Commission or was the state against which the complaint had been lodged. As in the case of the International Court of Justice, jurisdiction depends upon the consent of the state concerned. A case cannot be brought to the Court until after the Commission's efforts for a friendly settlement have failed. From the individual victim's point of view, he is protected only derivatively in a case before the Court.

Nevertheless, a state other than that of the claimant's nationality can "represent" him. Also, if remedies are exhausted and the Commission deems it appropriate, it can trigger action in the Court. *Why are states, even in a regional organization of states with a common heritage, reluctant to permit individuals to have direct access to a court of human rights?* A textual exposition of the work of these two institutions is in Cassese, Human Rights and the European Community: Methods of Protection (1991); Cassese, Human Rights and the European Community: Substantive Law (1991); Janis, European Human Rights Law (1990).

CASE OF IRELAND v. THE UNITED KINGDOM

European Court of Human Rights.
Judgment of January 18, 1978, Series A, No. 25.

"[The judgment of the European Court of Human Rights begins with a long presentation of the history of the *'troubles'* in Northern Ireland. The case was 'referred to the Court' by the Government of Ireland against the United Kingdom (U.K.). This historical presentation ends with the U.K.'s introduction in 1971 of internment without trial of persons suspected of being *'suspected terrorists'* and *'key members of the I.R.A. (the Special Powers Act).'* It also includes the U.K.'s 1972 imposition of its own *direct rule* over Northern Ireland. The Court then focuses in some detail on two principal claims: (1) that suspects taken pursuant to the *Special Powers Act* after August 9, 1971 had been subjected to treatment which constituted torture and inhuman and

---

a. Article 25 of the convention: "Any person, non-governmental organisation or group of individuals claiming to be the victim of a violation * * *."

degrading treatment contrary to Article 3 of the European Convention on Human Rights; and (2) that whether or not (1) was established, internment without trial as implemented after August 9, 1971, constituted a violation of Article 5 of the European Convention, which guarantees security of the person and liberty.]''

* * *

[The "methods" applied] sometimes termed "disorientation" or "sensory deprivation" techniques, were not used in any cases other than the fourteen so indicated above. It emerges from the Commission's establishment of the facts that the techniques consisted of:

    (a) *wall-standing:* forcing the detainees to remain for periods of some hours in a "stress position", described by those who underwent it as being "spreadeagled against the wall, with their fingers put high above the head against the wall, the legs spread apart and the feet back, causing them to stand on their toes with the weight of the body mainly on the fingers";

    (b) *hooding:* putting a black or navy coloured bag over the detainees' heads and, at least initially, keeping it there all the time except during interrogation;

    (c) *subjection to noise:* pending their interrogations, holding the detainees in a room where there was a continuous loud and hissing noise;

    (d) *deprivation of sleep:* pending their interrogations, depriving the detainees of sleep;

    (e) *deprivation of food and drink:* subjecting detainees to a reduced diet pending interrogations.

* * *

97. From the start, it has been conceded by the respondent Government that the use of the five techniques was authorised at "high level". Although never committed to writing or authorised in any official document, the techniques had been orally taught to members of the RUC by the English Intelligence Centre at a [1971] seminar.

* * *

152. The U.K. Government contest neither the breaches of Article 3 as found by the Commission * * *, nor—a point moreover that is beyond doubt—the Court's jurisdiction to examine such breaches. However, relying inter alia on the case-law of the International Court of Justice (Northern Cameroons case, judgment of 2 December 1963, and Nuclear Tests cases, judgments of 20 December 1974), they argue that the European Court has power to decline to exercise its jurisdiction where the objective of an application has been accomplished or where adjudication on the merits would be devoid of purpose. Such, they claim, is the situation here. They maintain that the findings in question not only are not contested but also have been widely publicised and that they do not give rise to problems of interpretation or application of the Convention sufficiently important to require a decision by the Court.

Furthermore, for them the subject-matter of those findings now belongs to past history in view of the abandonment of the five techniques (1972), the solemn and unqualified undertaking not to reintroduce these techniques (8 February 1977) and the other measures taken by the United Kingdom to remedy, impose punishment for, and prevent the recurrence of, the various violations found by the Commission.

This argument is disputed by the applicant Government. Neither is it accepted in a general way by the delegates of the Commission; they stated, however, that they would express no conclusion as to whether or not the above-mentioned undertaking had deprived the claim concerning the five techniques of its object.

153. The Court takes formal note of the undertaking given before it, at the hearing on 8 February 1977, by the United Kingdom Attorney–General on behalf of the respondent Government. The terms of this undertaking were as follows:

> "The Government of the United Kingdom have considered the question of the use of the 'five techniques' with very great care and with particular regard to Article 3 of the Convention. They now give this unqualified undertaking, that the 'five techniques' will not in any circumstances be reintroduced as an aid to interrogation."

The Court also notes that the United Kingdom has taken various measures designed to prevent the recurrence of the events complained of and to afford reparation for their consequences. For example, it has issued to the police and the army instructions and directives on the arrest, interrogation and treatment of persons in custody, reinforced the procedures for investigating complaints, appointed commissions of enquiry and paid or offered compensation in many cases * * *.

154. Nevertheless, the Court considers that the responsibilities assigned to it within the framework of the system under the Convention extend to pronouncing on the non-contested allegations of violation of Article 3. The Court's judgments in fact serve not only to decide those cases brought before the Court but, more generally, to elucidate, safeguard and develop the rules instituted by the Convention, thereby contributing to the observance by the States of the engagements undertaken by them as Contracting Parties (Article 19).

* * *

155. Accordingly, that part of the present case which concerns the said allegations cannot be said to have become without object; the Court considers that it should rule thereon, notwithstanding the initiatives taken by the respondent State.

162. As was emphasized by the Commission, ill-treatment must attain a minimum level of severity if it is to fall within the scope of Article 3. The assessment of this minimum is, in the nature of things, relative; it depends on all the circumstances of the case, such as the duration of the treatment, its physical or mental effects and, in some cases, the sex, age and state of health of the victim, etc.

163. The Convention prohibits in absolute terms torture and inhuman or degrading treatment or punishment, irrespective of the victim's conduct. Unlike most of the substantive clauses of the Convention and of Protocols Nos. 1 and 4, Article 3 makes no provision for exceptions and, under Article 15 § 2, there can be no derogation therefrom even in the event of a public emergency threatening the life of the nation.

164. In the instant case, the only relevant concepts are "torture" and "inhuman or degrading treatment", to the exclusion of "inhuman or degrading punishment".

165. The facts concerning the five techniques are summarised * * * above. In the Commission's estimation, those facts constituted a practice not only of inhuman and degrading treatment but also of torture. The applicant Government ask for confirmation of this opinion which is not contested before the Court by the respondent Government.

166. The police used the five techniques on fourteen persons in 1971, that is on twelve, including T 6 and T 13, in August before the Compton Committee was set up, and on two in October whilst that Committee was carrying out its enquiry. Although never authorised in writing in any official document, the five techniques were taught orally by the English Intelligence Centre to members of the RUC at a seminar held in April 1971. There was accordingly a practice.

167. The five techniques were applied in combination, with premeditation and for hours at a stretch; they caused, if not actual bodily injury, at least intense physical and mental suffering to the persons subjected thereto and also led to acute psychiatric disturbances during interrogation. They accordingly fell into the category of inhuman treatment within the meaning of Article 3. The techniques were also degrading since they were such as to arouse in their victims feelings of fear, anguish and inferiority capable of humiliating and debasing them and possibly breaking their physical or moral resistance.

On these two points, the Court [agrees with] the Commission.

In order to determine whether the five techniques should also be qualified as torture, the Court must have regard to the distinction, embodied in Article 3, between this notion and that of inhuman or degrading treatment. In the Court's view, this distinction derives principally from a difference in the intensity of the suffering inflicted.

The Court considers in fact that, whilst there exists on the one hand violence which is to be condemned both on moral grounds and also in most cases under the domestic law of the Contracting States but which does not fall within Article 3 of the Convention, it appears on the other hand that it was the intention that the Convention, with its distinction between "torture" and "inhuman or degrading treatment", should by the first of these terms attach a special stigma to deliberate inhuman treatment causing very serious and cruel suffering. Moreover, this seems to be the thinking lying behind Article 1 *in fine* of Resolution 3452(30) adopted by the General Assembly of the United Nations on 9 December 1975, which declares:

"Torture constitutes an *aggravated* and deliberate form of cruel, inhuman or degrading treatment or punishment".

Although the five techniques, as applied in combination, undoubtedly amounted to inhuman and degrading treatment, although their object was the extraction of confessions, the naming of others and/or information and although they were used systematically, they did not occasion suffering of the particular intensity and cruelty implied by the word torture as so understood.

168.   The Court concludes that recourse to the five techniques amounted to a practice of inhuman and degrading treatment, which practice was in breach of Article 3.

186.   In a letter dated 5 January 1977, the applicant Government requested the Court to order that the respondent Government refrain from reintroducing the five techniques, as a method of interrogation or otherwise; proceed as appropriate, under the criminal law of the United Kingdom and the relevant disciplinary code, against those members of the security forces who have committed acts in breach of Article 3 referred to in the Commission's findings and conclusions, and against those who condoned or tolerated them.

At the hearings, the applicant Government withdrew the first request following the solemn undertaking given on behalf of the United Kingdom Government on 8 February 1977 (see paragraph 153 above); on the other hand, the second request was maintained.

187.   The Court does not have to consider in these proceedings whether its functions extend, in certain circumstances, to addressing consequential orders to Contracting States.   In the present case, the Court finds that the sanctions available to it do not include the power to direct one of those States to institute criminal or disciplinary proceedings in accordance with its domestic law.

* * *

FOR THESE REASONS, THE COURT

I.   *ON ARTICLE* 3, 1.   holds unanimously that, although certain violations of Article 3 were not contested, a ruling should nevertheless be given thereon; 2.   holds unanimously that it has jurisdiction to take cognisance of the cases of alleged violation of Article 3 to the extent that the applicant Government put them forward as establishing the existence of a practice; 3.   holds by sixteen votes to one that the use of the five techniques in August and October 1971 constituted a practice of inhuman and degrading treatment, which practice was in breach of Article 3; 4.   holds by thirteen votes to four that the said use of the five techniques did not constitute a practice of torture within the meaning of Article 3; * * * 10. holds unanimously that it cannot direct the respondent State to institute criminal or disciplinary proceedings against those members of the security forces who have committed the breaches of Article 3 found by the Court and against those who condoned or tolerated such breaches;

* * *

[Separate opinions omitted.]

—————

2. THE ORGANIZATION OF AMERICAN STATES

In the Charter of the Organization of American States, which entered into force on December 13, 1951, "proclaim(s) the fundamental rights of the individual without distinction as to race, nationality, creed or sex." 2 U.S.T. 2394, 119 U.N.T.S. 3. Amendments to the Charter entered into force February 27, 1970. At the 1948 Conference of the American States which gave birth to the Charter, there was also adopted the American Declaration of the Rights and Duties of Man. In 1959, by resolution of the Ministers of Foreign Affairs meeting as an organ of the Organization, the Inter–American Commission on Human Rights was created. In addition to its powers of study and advice, the commission was given the power to receive and examine individual communications charging the violation of fundamental human rights set forth in the American Declaration and to make recommendations to governments with respect thereto.

A conference in 1969 approved the American Convention on Human Rights, which contains provisions widening the American Declaration, re-establishing the Inter–American Commission and establishing the Inter–American Court of Human Rights. Individuals do not have access to the court, since the only states parties and the commission have the right to submit a case to the court; as usual, the court's jurisdiction depends upon the state's consenting thereto. For the statute of the court, see 19 ILM 634 (1980). President Carter submitted this convention to the Senate for its advice and consent in 1978. Ratification of the convention does not, of itself, constitute a state's consent to the court's jurisdiction. As in the case of the International Court of Justice, a further declaration of submission to the court's jurisdiction (or a special agreement) is necessary. See Article 62 of the Convention, in the Documentary Supplement. The President did not call upon the Senate to make such a declaration.

* * *

—————

BUERGENTHAL, THE ADVISORY PRACTICE OF THE INTER–AMERICAN HUMAN RIGHTS COURT

79 American Journal of International Law 1, 8 (1985).*

* * *

Disguised Contentious Cases. International tribunals exercising advisory and contentious jurisdiction have at times had to confront a problem that arises when they are asked to render an advisory opinion

—————

* Reprinted with the permission of the American Society of International Law.

on an issue that is, at one and the same time, the subject of a dispute between two or more states or between a state and an international organization. Here the argument frequently made is that the request for an advisory opinion is a disguised contentious case and that it should be heard only if all the parties have accepted the tribunal's contentious jurisdiction. The International Court of Justice, for example, has consistently rejected such arguments and complied with the requests. The inter-American human rights system adds a new dimension to this problem that is unique to the advisory functions of the Court. Under Article 64(1) of the Convention, the Court's advisory jurisdiction may be invoked not only by organs or organizations, as is the case in the UN system, for example, but also by states. The Court might therefore confront a petition by a state asking it to render an advisory opinion relating to a dispute between the petitioner and another state, which dispute could not be referred to the Court as a case because one of the states had not accepted its contentious jurisdiction. Moreover, the Inter–American Commission on Human Rights, which has the right to request advisory opinions, exercises powers under the Convention comparable to that of a tribunal of first instance in dealing with charges alleging violations of human rights by a state party and may also refer contentious cases to the Court. Since the Commission may only bring such cases to the Court if the states concerned have accepted the Court's jurisdiction, the question arises whether the Commission has the power, in the absence of a state's consent, to seek an advisory opinion under Article 64(1) regarding a legal issue in dispute in a case being considered by the Commission.

The Court has dealt with only one case bearing on these issues. The Inter–American Commission had embarked on a country study of the human rights situation in Guatemala, which was charged with numerous human rights violations. The authority of the Commission to prepare country reports derives from its status as an OAS Charter organ and is governed by different provisions of the Convention and its Statute from those which deal with the disposition of petitions filed by individuals and communications presented by states parties charging another state party with violations of the human rights guaranteed in the Convention. When the Commission prepares country studies and reports, it acts first and foremost as an OAS Charter organ; whereas, when it deals with petitions and communications filed under the Convention, it discharges the functions of a tribunal of first instance or Convention institution which, together with the Court, comprises the judicial and enforcement machinery provided for by the Convention.

These different functions need to be kept in mind when analyzing the Court's advisory opinion involving Guatemala. The Court was asked by the Commission to render an advisory opinion on a legal issue only. The issue was one of a number of disputed matters, both legal and factual, to arise between the Commission and the Government of Guatemala while the former was examining the human rights situation in that country. In rejecting Guatemala's claim that there was a dispute between it and the Commission and that, as a result, the Court lacked the power to hear the dispute because Guatemala had not accepted its jurisdiction, the Court emphasized that the Commission's request was designed to assist it in performing its functions under Article 112 of the OAS Charter:

> The powers conferred on the Commission require it to apply the Convention or other human rights treaties. In order to discharge fully its obligations, the Commission may find it necessary or appropriate to consult the Court regarding the meaning of certain provisions whether or not at the given moment in time there exists a difference between a government and the Commission concerning an interpretation, which might justify the request for an advisory opinion. If the Commission were to be barred from seeking an advisory opinion merely because one or more governments are involved in a controversy with the Commission over the interpreta- tion of a disputed provision, the Commission would seldom, if ever, be able to avail itself of the Court's advisory jurisdiction. Not only would this be true of the Commission, but the OAS General Assem- bly, for example, would be in a similar position were it to seek an advisory opinion from the Court in the course of the Assembly's consideration of a draft resolution calling on a Member State to comply with its international human rights obligations.

This language suggests that the Court treated the request for an advisory opinion * * * as it would have treated a similar request from any other OAS organ acting in the discharge of its OAS Charter functions. If the holding is limited to matters under consideration by the Commission in its role as OAS Charter organ, it permits the argument that the advisory route may not be used to circumvent the restrictions applicable to the contentious process, which is initiated by individual petition or interstate communication. There is a great deal of language in the Court's opinion, however, that suggests that the holding is much broader. Thus, for example, the Court noted that "[t]he mere fact that this provision [Article 4] may also have been invoked before the Commission in petitions and communications filed under Articles 44 and 45 of the Convention" did not affect the Court's conclusion about the legitimacy of the Commission's request. The Court indicated, moreover, that "the Convention, by permitting Member States and OAS organs to seek advisory opinions, creates a parallel system to that provided for under Article 62 [on the Court's contentious jurisdiction] and offers an alternate judicial method of a consultative nature, which is designed to assist states and organs to comply with and to apply human rights treaties without subjecting them to the formalism and the sanctions associated with the contentious judicial process." If the advisory route is in fact seen as in all respects a "parallel system" and "alternate judicial method" to the Court's contentious jurisdiction, the Commission or any interested state would be able to resort to it in the midst of a pending contentious proceeding. Here one might hypothesize a situa- tion in which an individual has lodged a petition with the Commission against state X, a party to the Convention, alleging that X has violated various rights guaranteed in the Convention. Let us assume further that in the course of the proceedings state X and the individual litigant disagree as to the meaning of one of the disputed provisions of the

Convention. May the Commission at that stage request an advisory opinion from the Court on the meaning of the disputed provision? May state X do so? Does it matter at all whether state X has accepted the jurisdiction of the Court? Is the consent of state X necessary before the Commission may request the advisory opinion?

The Court's advisory opinion relating to Guatemala does not provide any ready answers to these questions. However, one consideration mentioned in the opinion deserves to be noted. In dealing with the question whether to comply with the Commission's request, the Court made the following observation:

> The Court has already indicated that situations might arise when it would deem itself compelled to decline to comply with a request for an advisory opinion. In *Other Treaties* * * * the Court acknowledged that resort to the advisory opinion route might in certain situations interfere with the proper functioning of the system of protection spelled out in the Convention or that it might adversely affect the interests of the victim of human rights violations....
>
> . * * * The instant request of the Commission does not fall within the category of advisory opinion requests that need to be rejected on those grounds because nothing in it can be deemed to interfere with the proper functioning of the system or might be deemed to have an adverse effect on the interests of a victim.

It may well be, therefore, that the crucial question for the Court will not be whether the advisory opinion is or is not tied to proceedings pending in the Commission. Instead, the Court might seek to ascertain what impact in a particular case its decision to grant the request for an advisory opinion would have on the victim or on the Convention system.

* * *

---

3. THE ORGANIZATION OF AFRICAN UNITY
NOWAK, THE AFRICAN CHARTER ON HUMAN AND PEOPLES' RIGHTS
7 Human Rights Law Journal 399 (1986).*

On 21 October 1986 the African Charter on Human and Peoples' Rights, adopted by the 18th Ordinary Session of the Assembly of Heads of State and Government of the Organization of African Unity (OAU) held in June 1981, entered into force. This date marks an important day in the history of international promotion and protection of human rights. After the European and American Conventions on Human Rights the African Charter is the third regional human rights instrument of great political and legal significance. It provides for the establishment of an African Commission on Human and Peoples' Rights

* Reprinted with the permission of N.P. Engel, Publisher, Kehlam Rhein/Stras-bourg/Arlington, Va.

consisting of eleven African experts in the field of human rights. The members of the Commission will be elected at the 23rd Ordinary Session of the Assembly of Heads of State and Government which [was] in 1987.

The idea of establishing both an African Human Rights Convention and Commission dates back to 1961 when the first congress of African jurists was organized by the International Commission of Jurists at Lagos. It was further discussed at several regional human rights seminars organized by the United Nations. The decisive step forward was taken however only after the bitter experiences of serious human rights violations which had occurred in Africa during the seventies, above all in Uganda, the Central African Empire and Equatorial Guinea. In July 1979 the Assembly of Heads of State * * * at its 16th Ordinary Session held in Monrovia called on the Secretary–General of the OAU to "organize as soon as possible in an African capital a restricted meeting of highly qualified experts to prepare a preliminary draft of an African Charter on Human Rights providing, inter alia, for the establishment of bodies to promote and protect human rights". After less than two years of drafting negotiations the African Charter was adopted in Nairobi in June 1981.

The African Charter on Human and Peoples' Rights contains some major *conceptual innovations* in the field of international human rights law. By incorporating a number of collective rights of peoples it marks a major step forward in the development of a third generation of human rights. For the first time an international treaty undertakes to ensure to peoples not only the right to self-determination, but as well the rights of existence, equality, development, peace, security and a general satisfactory environment. Secondly, the African Charter provides for a number of fundamental duties of the individual towards his family and society, the State, other legally recognized communities and the international community. One of these duties is to preserve and strengthen positive African cultural values in the relation with other members of the society. The emphasis on the protection of morals and traditional values recognized by the community and on the family as the natural unit and basis of society underlines the specific *community-oriented approach* that distinguishes the African Charter from other international human rights instruments.

Eleven members of an African Commission on Human and Peoples' Rights will be elected by the Assembly of Heads of State and Government. The functions of the Commission will be primarily promotional: to collect documents, undertake studies, organize seminars or disseminate information. In addition the African Charter provides for more judicial functions as interpreting the Charter's provisions, conducting investigations and ensuring the protection of human and peoples' rights by deciding on communications from States parties, individuals or other bodies like non-governmental organizations. In the case of inter-State-communications, the Commission may publish a report stating the facts and its findings and make such recommendations as it deems useful. The Charter does not limit the right to submit "other communications" to the victims of an alleged violation or to individuals, but it provides, however, that those communications shall be considered by the Commission only if a simple majority of its members so decide. Furthermore the Commission shall draw the attention of the Assembly of Heads of State and Government exclusively to communications which apparently reveal the existence of a series of serious or massive violations of human and peoples' rights. In this case it may be authorized to undertake an in-depth study of these situations and publish a factual report including its findings and recommendations. Hence the communication procedure under the African Charter seems to be inspired both by the complaints procedures of other human rights conventions and the confidential investigation procedure established by ECOSOC–Res 1503 (XLVIII).

* * *

SECTION F.   SELF–HELP: ASYLUM AND REFUGEE LAW

So long as the level of human rights protections varies among the states of the world, the individual will continue the age-old human practice of leaving a state where he is oppressed to live in another state where, he believes, his rights will be protected. But it is said: "The reception of aliens is a matter of discretion, and every state is by reason of its territorial supremacy competent to exclude aliens from the whole, or any part, of its territory." I. Oppenheim, International Law 675 (Lauterpacht, 8th ed. 1955). The writer further asserts that the Universal Declaration of Human Rights does not give an alien a right to demand asylum. The declaration provides:

Article 13

1. Everyone has the right to freedom of movement and residence within the borders of each State. * * *

Article 14

1. Everyone has the right to seek and to enjoy in other countries asylum from persecution.

2. This right may not be invoked in the case of prosecutions genuinely arising from non-political crimes or from acts contrary to the purposes and principles of the United Nations.

If an alien cannot lawfully demand that a state grant him asylum, what is the content of the right to seek asylum?

The United Nations adopted a Declaration on Territorial Asylum, Resolution 2312(22) of December 14, 1967, U.N.Gen.Ass.Off.Rec., 22nd Sess., Supp. 16(A/6716), p. 81. It stated:

Article 1

1. Asylum granted by a State, in the exercise of its sovereignty, to persons entitled to invoke article 14 of the Universal Declaration

of Human Rights, including persons struggling against colonialism, shall be respected by all other States.

Article 3

1. No person referred to in article 1, paragraph 1, shall be subjected to measures such as rejection at the frontier or, if he has already entered the territory in which he seeks asylum, expulsion or compulsory return to any State where he may be subjected to persecution.

———

It is doubtful that the international community is prepared to accept an absolute obligation on the part of each state to grant asylum. In the preparation of a draft convention designed to give real effect to the apparent rights proclaimed in Article 14, what interests should be taken into account? Would a convention binding a state to "use its best endeavors to grant asylum in its territory" promote the humanitarian objectives of the Universal Declaration of Human Rights?

———

Note: David Carliner, *Book Review: Refugees—The Trauma of Exile: The Humanitarian Role of Red Cross and Red Crescent Edited by Diana Miseres. Dordrecht, Boston, London: Martinus Nijhoff Publishers, 1988.* 85 Am.J.Int'l L. 569 (1991) (footnotes omitted).

The International Red Cross movement has left its mark in the history of humanitarian law, beginning with the initiative taken in 1863 by its founder, Henri Dunant, for the relief of the wounded on the battlefield, and culminating in four successive Geneva Conventions governing the treatment of wounded soldiers in armed conflicts, whether international or not, prisoners of war and civilians in internal disturbances. These provisions, in the impersonal and cold language of legal drafters, prohibit taking any measure of such a character as to cause the physical suffering or extermination of protected persons in their hands * * * [and applies] * * * to murder, torture, corporal punishment, mutilation and medical or scientific experiments not necessitated by the medical treatment of a protected person, * * * [and] * * * any other measures of brutality whether applied by civilian or military agents.

Refugees—The Trauma of Exile puts a human face on the suffering of these victims. The book is a collection of papers presented at a workshop sponsored by the League of the Red Cross and Red Crescent Societies in 1987, dealing with the psychological and medical problems of persons uprooted by war, revolution, counterrevolution and naked terror. As narrated by the editor:

> We heard about some of the worst forms of evil man can perpetrate against man: physical and psychological torture, incarceration in inhuman conditions, forced separation of families, sud-

den deportation, violence on the high seas * * * [death or murder] * * * in prison * * *. Many of the victims of gross human rights abuses are children, some of whom have been forced to witness unspeakable horrors * * *. (Miseres, p. 6)

The persons who have been treated by the International Red Cross societies have come from diverse cultural, linguistic and religious backgrounds and from every continent, including the millions who fled Laos, Cambodia and Vietnam; the Tamils from Sri Lanka; the tens of thousands from Chile, El Salvador, Nicaragua and Cuba; the thousands who left Iran, Iraq and Afghanistan; countless people who have fled from the various African countries—Ethiopia, Sudan, Zaire and Ghana, among others—and refugees from Eastern European countries, including Jewish Holocaust survivors. [See further discussion in Chapter 2B, *supra*.]

SALE v. HAITIAN CENTERS COUNCIL, INC.

United States Supreme Court, 1993.
___ U.S. ___, 113 S.Ct. 2549, 125 L.Ed.2d 128.

[After the coup that ousted elected President Jean-Bertrand Aristide, unprecedented numbers of Haitians began to flee Haiti for the U.S.]

STEVENS, J., delivered the opinion of the Court, in which REHNQUIST, C.J., and WHITE, O'CONNOR, SCALIA, KENNEDY, SOUTER, and THOMAS, JJ., joined. BLACKMUN, J., filed a dissenting opinion.

Justice STEVENS delivered the opinion of the Court.

The President has directed the Coast Guard to intercept vessels illegally transporting passengers from Haiti to the United States and to return those passengers to Haiti without first determining whether they may qualify as refugees. The question presented in this case is whether such forced repatriation, "authorized to be undertaken only beyond the territorial sea of the United States," [1] violates § 243(h)(1) of the Immigration and Nationality Act of 1952 (INA or Act).[2] We hold that neither

---

1. This language appears in both Executive Order No. 12324, 3 CFR 181 (1981–1983 Comp.), issued by President Reagan, and Executive Order No. 12807, 57 Fed. Reg. 23133 (1992), issued by President Bush.

2. Title 8 U.S.C. § 1253(h) (1988 ed. and Supp. IV), as amended by § 203(e) of the Refugee Act of 1980, Pub.L. 96–212, 94 Stat. 107. Section 243(h)(1) provides:

"(h) Withholding of deportation or return. (1) The Attorney General shall not deport or return any alien (other than an alien described in section 1251(a)(4)(D) of this title) to a country if the Attorney General determines that such alien's life or freedom would be threatened in such country on account of race, religion, nationality, membership in a particular social group, or political opinion."

Section 243(h)(2), 8 U.S.C. § 1253(h)(2), provides, in part:

"(2) Paragraph (1) shall not apply to any alien if the Attorney General determines that—

* * *

"(D) there are reasonable grounds for regarding the alien as a danger to the security of the United States."

Before its amendment in 1965, § 243(h), 66 Stat. 214, read as follows: "The Attorney General is authorized to withhold deportation of any alien within the United States to any country in which in his opinion the alien would be subject to physical persecution on account of race, religion, or political opinion and for such period of time he deems to be

§ 243(h) nor Article 33 of the United Nations Protocol Relating to the Status of Refugees applies to action taken by the Coast Guard on the high seas. [Jan. 31, 1967, 19 U.S.T. 6223, T.I.A.S. No. 6577.]

* * *

III

Both parties argue that the plain language of § 243(h)(1) is dispositive. It reads as follows:

> "The Attorney General shall not deport or return any alien (other than an alien described in section 1251(a)(4)(D) of this title) to a country if the Attorney General determines that such alien's life or freedom would be threatened in such country on account of race, religion, nationality, membership in a particular social group, or political opinion." 8 U.S.C. § 1253(h)(1) (1988 ed., Supp. IV).

Respondents emphasize the words "any alien" and "return"; neither term is limited to aliens within the United States. Respondents also contend that the 1980 amendment deleting the words "within the United States" from the prior text of § 243(h), see n. 2, supra, obviously gave the statute an extraterritorial effect. This change, they further argue, was required in order to conform the statute to the text of Article 33.1 of the Convention, which they find as unambiguous as the present statutory text.

Petitioners' response is that a fair reading of the INA as a whole demonstrates that § 243(h) does not apply to actions taken by the President or Coast Guard outside the United States; that the legislative history of the 1980 amendment supports their reading; and that both the text and the negotiating history of Article 33 of the Convention indicate that it was not intended to have any extraterritorial effect.

We shall first review the text and structure of the statute and its 1980 amendment, and then consider the text and negotiating history of the Convention.

* * *

B.   The History of the Refugee Act of 1980

As enacted in 1952, § 243(h) authorized the Attorney General to withhold deportation of aliens "within the United States." Six years later we considered the question whether it applied to an alien who had been paroled into the country while her admissibility was being determined. We held that even though she was physically present within our borders, she was not "within the United States" as those words were used in § 243(h). Leng May Ma v. Barber, 357 U.S. 185, 186 (1958). We explained the important distinction between "deportation" or "expulsion," on the one hand, and "exclusion," on the other:

> "It is important to note at the outset that our immigration laws have long made a distinction between those aliens who have come to

necessary for such reason."   8 U.S.C.   Stevic, 467 U.S. 407, 414, n. 6 (1984).
§ 1253(h) (1976 ed.);   see also INS v.

our shores seeking admission, such as petitioner, and those who are within the United States after an entry, irrespective of its legality. In the latter instance the Court has recognized additional rights and privileges not extended to those in the former category who are merely 'on the threshold of initial entry.' * * * The distinction was carefully preserved in Title II of the Immigration and Nationality Act * * *."

Under the INA, both then and now, those seeking "admission" and trying to avoid "exclusion" were already within our territory (or at its border), but the law treated them as though they had never entered the United States at all; they were within United States territory but not "within the United States." Those who had been admitted (or found their way in) but sought to avoid "expulsion" had the added benefit of "deportation proceedings"; they were both within United States territory and "within the United States." Although the phrase "within the United States" presumed the alien's actual presence in the United States, it had more to do with an alien's legal status than with his location.

The 1980 amendment erased the long-maintained distinction between deportable and excludable aliens for purposes of § 243(h). By adding the word "return" and removing the words "within the United States" from § 243(h), Congress extended the statute's protection to both types of aliens, but it did nothing to change the presumption that both types of aliens would continue to be found only within United States territory. The removal of the phrase "within the United States" cured the most obvious drawback of § 243(h): as interpreted in Leng May Ma, its protection was available only to aliens subject to deportation proceedings.

Of course, in addition to this most obvious purpose, it is possible that the 1980 amendment *also* removed any territorial limitation of the statute, and Congress might have intended a double-barreled result. That possibility, however, is not a substitute for the affirmative evidence of intended extraterritorial application that our cases require. Moreover, in our review of the history of the amendment, we have found no support whatsoever for that latter, alternative, purpose.

The addition of the phrase "or return" and the deletion of the phrase "within the United States" are the only relevant changes made by the 1980 amendment to § 243(h)(1), and they are fully explained by the intent to apply § 243(h) to exclusion as well as to deportation proceedings. That intent is plainly identified in the legislative history of the amendment.[7] There is no change in the 1980 amendment, however, that could only be explained by an assumption that Congress also intended to provide for the statute's extraterritorial application. It would have been extraordinary for Congress to make such an important change in the law without any mention of that possible effect. Not a

---

7. See H.R.Rep. No. 96–608, p. 30 (1979) (the changes "require * * * the Attorney General to withhold deportation of aliens who qualify as refugees and who are in exclusion as well as deportation proceedings"); see also S.Rep. No. 96–256, p. 17 (1979), * * *.

scintilla of evidence of such an intent can be found in the legislative history.

In sum, all available evidence about the meaning of § 243(h)—the government official at whom it is directed, its location in the Act, its failure to suggest any extraterritorial application, the 1980 amendment that gave it a dual reference to "deport or return," and the relevance of that dual structure to immigration law in general—leads unerringly to the conclusion that it applies in only one context: the domestic procedures by which the Attorney General determines whether deportable and excludable aliens may remain in the United States.

IV

Although the protection afforded by § 243(h) did not apply in exclusion proceedings before 1980, other provisions of the Act did authorize relief for aliens at the border seeking protection as refugees in the United States. See INS v. Stevic, [*supra*]. When the United States acceded to the Protocol in 1968, therefore, the INA already offered *some* protection to both classes of refugees. It offered no such protection to any alien who was beyond the territorial waters of the United States, though, and we would not expect the Government to assume a burden as to those aliens without some acknowledgment of its dramatically broadened scope. Both Congress and the Executive Branch gave extensive consideration to the Protocol before ratifying it in 1968; in all of their published consideration of it there appears no mention of the possibility that the United States was assuming any extraterritorial obligations.[8] Nevertheless, because the history of the 1980 Act does disclose a general intent to conform our law to Article 33 of the Convention, it might be argued that the extraterritorial obligations imposed by Article 33 were so clear that Congress, in acceding to the Protocol, and then in amending the statute to harmonize the two, meant to give the latter a correspondingly extraterritorial effect. Or, just as the statute might have imposed an extraterritorial obligation that the Convention does not (the argument we have just rejected), the Convention might have established an extraterritorial obligation which the statute does not; under the Supremacy Clause, that broader treaty obligation might then provide the controlling rule of law.[9] With those possibilities in mind we shall consider both the text and negotiating history of the Convention itself.

Like the text and the history of § 243(h), the text and negotiating history of Article 33 of the United Nations Convention are both completely silent with respect to the Article's possible application to actions

8. "The President and the Senate believed that the Protocol was largely consistent with existing law. There are many statements to that effect in the legislative history of the accession to the Protocol. E.g., S.Exec.Rep. No. 14, 90th Cong., 2d Sess., 4 (1968) ('refugees in the United States have long enjoyed the protection and the rights which the Protocol calls for'); id., at 6, 7 ('the United States already meets the standards of the Protocol')."

9. U.S. Const., Art. VI, cl. 2 provides: "This Constitution, and the Laws of the United States which shall be made in Pursuance thereof; and all Treaties made, or which shall be made, under the Authority of the United States, shall be the supreme Law of the Land; * * *" In Murray v. The Charming Betsy, 2 Cranch 64, 117–118 (1804), Chief Justice Marshall wrote that "an act of congress ought never to be construed to violate the law of nations if any other possible construction remains * * *."

taken by a country outside its own borders. Respondents argue that the Protocol's broad remedial goals require that a nation be prevented from repatriating refugees to their potential oppressors whether or not the refugees are within that nation's borders. In spite of the moral weight of that argument, both the text and negotiating history of Article 33 affirmatively indicate that it was not intended to have extraterritorial effect.

A. The Text of the Convention

Two aspects of Article 33's text are persuasive. The first is the explicit reference in Article 33.2 to the country in which the alien is located; the second is the parallel use of the terms "expel or return," the latter term explained by the French word "refouler."

The full text of Article 33 reads as follows: *"Article 33.—Prohibition of expulsion or return ('refoulement')*

"1. No Contracting State shall expel or return ('refouler') a refugee in any manner whatsoever to the frontiers of territories where his life or freedom would be threatened on account of his race, religion, nationality, membership in a particular social group or political opinion.

"2. The benefit of the present provision may not, however, be claimed by a refugee whom there are reasonable grounds for regarding as a danger to the security *of the country in which he is,* or who, having been convicted by a final judgment of a particularly serious crime, constitutes a danger to the community of that country." Convention Relating to the Status of Refugees, July 28, 1951, 19 U.S.T. 6259, 6276 (emphasis added).

Under the second paragraph of Article 33 an alien may not claim the benefit of the first paragraph if he poses a danger to the country in which he is located. If the first paragraph did apply on the high seas, no nation could invoke the second paragraph's exception with respect to an alien there: an alien intercepted on the high seas is in no country at all. If Article 33.1 applied extraterritorially, therefore, Article 33.2 would create an absurd anomaly: dangerous aliens on the high seas would be entitled to the benefits of 33.1 while those residing in the country that sought to expel them would not. It is more reasonable to assume that the coverage of 33.2 was limited to those already in the country because it was understood that 33.1 obligated the signatory state only with respect to aliens within its territory.

Article 33.1 uses the words "expel or return ('refouler')" as an obvious parallel to the words "deport or return" in § 243(h)(1). There is no dispute that "expel" has the same meaning as "deport"; it refers to the deportation or expulsion of an alien who is already present in the host country. The dual reference identified and explained in our opinion in *Leng May Ma v. Barber,* suggests that the term "return ('refouler')" refers to the exclusion of aliens who are merely " 'on the threshold of initial entry.' "

This suggestion—that "return" has a legal meaning narrower than its common meaning—is reinforced by the parenthetical reference to "*refouler* ", a French word that is not an exact synonym for the English word "return." Neither of two respected English–French Dictionaries mentions "*refouler* " as one of many possible French translations of "return." Conversely, the English translations of "*refouler* " do not include the word "return." They do, however, include words like "repulse," "repel," "drive back," and even "expel." To the extent that they are relevant, these translations imply that "return" means a defensive act of resistance or exclusion at a border rather than an act of transporting someone to a particular destination. In the context of the Convention, to "return" means to "repulse" rather than to "reinstate."

The text of Article 33 thus fits with Judge Edwards' understanding "that 'expulsion' would refer to a 'refugee already admitted into a country' and that 'return' would refer to a 'refugee already within the territory but not yet resident there.' Thus, the Protocol was not intended to govern parties' conduct outside of their national borders." Haitian Refugee Center v. Gracey, 257 U.S.App.D.C., at 413, 809 F.2d, at 840 (footnotes omitted). From the time of the Convention, commentators have consistently agreed with this view.

The drafters of the Convention and the parties to the Protocol—like the drafters of § 243(h)—may not have contemplated that any nation would gather fleeing refugees and return them to the one country they had desperately sought to escape; such actions may even violate the spirit of Article 33; but a treaty cannot impose uncontemplated extraterritorial obligations on those who ratify it through no more than its general humanitarian intent. Because the text of Article 33 cannot reasonably be read to say anything at all about a nation's actions toward aliens outside its own territory, it does not prohibit such actions.[15]

* * *

V

Respondents contend that the dangers faced by Haitians who are unwillingly repatriated demonstrate that the judgment of the Court of Appeals fulfilled the central purpose of the Convention and the Refugee Act of 1980. While we must, of course, be guided by the high purpose of both the treaty and the statute, we are not persuaded that either one places any limit on the President's authority to repatriate aliens interdicted beyond the territorial seas of the United States.

It is perfectly clear that 8 U.S.C. § 1182(f), grants the President ample power to establish a naval blockade that would simply deny illegal Haitian migrants the ability to disembark on our shores. Whether the President's chosen method of preventing the "attempted mass migration" of thousands of Haitians—to use the Dutch delegate's phrase—poses a greater risk of harm to Haitians who might otherwise face a long and dangerous return voyage, is irrelevant to the scope of his authority to take action that neither the Convention nor the statute clearly prohibits. As we have already noted, Acts of Congress normally do not have extraterritorial application unless such an intent is clearly mani-

---

15. The Convention's failure to prevent the extraterritorial reconduction of aliens has been generally acknowledged (and regretted). * * *

fested. That presumption has special force when we are construing treaty and statutory provisions that may involve foreign and military affairs for which the President has unique responsibility. Cf. United States v. Curtiss–Wright Export Corp., 299 U.S. 304 (1936). We therefore find ourselves in agreement with the conclusion expressed in Judge Edwards' concurring opinion in Gracey: "This case presents a painfully common situation in which desperate people, convinced that they can no longer remain in their homeland, take desperate measures to escape. Although the human crisis is compelling, there is no solution to be found in a judicial remedy."

The judgment of the Court of Appeals is reversed.

It is so ordered.

Justice BLACKMUN, dissenting.

When, in 1968, the United States acceded to the United Nations Protocol Relating to the Status of Refugees, Jan. 31, 1967, [1968] 19 U.S.T. 6223, T.I.A.S. 6577, it pledged not to "return (*'refouler'*) a refugee in any manner whatsoever" to a place where he would face political persecution. In 1980, Congress amended our immigration law to reflect the Protocol's directives. Refugee Act of 1980, 94 Stat. 102. See INS v. Cardoza–Fonseca, [*supra;*] INS v. Stevic, [supra]. Today's majority nevertheless decides that the forced repatriation of the Haitian refugees is perfectly legal, because the word "return" does not mean return, because the opposite of "within the United States" is not outside the United States, and because the official charged with controlling immigration has no role in enforcing an order to control immigration.

I believe that the duty of nonreturn expressed in both the Protocol and the statute is clear. The majority finds it "extraordinary," that Congress would have intended the ban on returning "any alien" to apply to aliens at sea. That Congress would have meant what it said is not remarkable. What is extraordinary in this case is that the Executive, in disregard of the law, would take to the seas to intercept fleeing refugees and force them back to their persecutors—and that the Court would strain to sanction that conduct.

I

I begin with the Convention, for it is undisputed that the Refugee Act of 1980 was passed to conform our law to Article 33, and that "the nondiscretionary duty imposed by § 243(h) parallels the United States' mandatory *nonrefoulement* obligations under Article 33.1 * * *." INS v. Doherty, 112 S.Ct. 719, 729 (1992), (SCALIA, J., concurring in the judgment in part and dissenting in part). The Convention thus constitutes the backdrop against which the statute must be understood.

A

Article 33.1 of the Convention states categorically and without geographical limitation:

"No Contracting State shall expel or return (*'refouler'*) a refugee in any manner whatsoever to the frontiers of territories where his life or freedom would be threatened on account of his race, religion, nationality, membership in a particular social group or political opinion."

The terms are unambiguous. Vulnerable refugees shall not be returned. The language is clear, and the command is straightforward; that should be the end of the inquiry. Indeed, until litigation ensued, see Haitian Refugee Center v. Gracey, the Government consistently acknowledged that the Convention applied on the high seas.

The majority * * * has difficulty with the Treaty's use of the term "return (*'refouler'*)." "Return," it claims, does not mean return, but instead has a distinctive legal meaning. For this proposition the Court relies almost entirely on the fact that *American* law makes a general distinction between *deportation* and *exclusion*. Without explanation, the majority asserts that in light of this distinction the word "return" as used in the Treaty somehow must refer only to "the exclusion of aliens who are * * * 'on the threshold of initial entry' " * * *

* * * The text of the Convention does not ban the "exclusion" of aliens who have reached some indeterminate "threshold"; it bans their "return." It is well settled that a treaty must first be construed according to its "ordinary meaning." Article 31.1 of the Vienna Convention on the Law of Treaties, 1155 U.N.T.S. 331 (1980). The ordinary meaning of "return" is "to bring, send, or put (a person or thing) back to or in a former position." Webster's Third New International Dictionary 1941 (1986). That describes precisely what petitioners are doing to the Haitians. By dispensing with ordinary meaning at the outset, and by taking instead as its starting point the assumption that "return," as used in the Treaty, "has a legal meaning narrower than its common meaning," the majority leads itself astray.

The straightforward interpretation of the duty of nonreturn is strongly reinforced by the Convention's use of the French term "*refouler*." The ordinary meaning of "*refouler*," as the majority concedes, is "[t]o repulse, * * *; to drive back, to repel." *Dictionnaire Larousse* 631 (1981).[19] Thus construed, Article 33.1 of the Convention reads: "No contracting state shall expel or [repulse, drive back, or repel] a refugee in any manner whatsoever to the frontiers of territories where his life or freedom would be threatened * * *." That, of course, is exactly what the Government is doing. It thus is no surprise that when the French press has described the very policy challenged here, the term it has used is "*refouler*." See, e.g., Le bourbier haitian, Le Monde, May 31–June 1, 1992 ("[L]es Etats–Unis ont decide de *refouler* directement les refugies recueillis par la garde cotire." (The United States has decided [de refouler] directly the refugees picked up by the Coast Guard)).

And yet the majority insists that what has occurred is not, in fact, "*refoulement*." It reaches this conclusion in a peculiar fashion. After acknowledging that the ordinary meaning of "*refouler*" is "repulse," "repel," and "drive back," the majority without elaboration declares:

---

19. The Court seems no more convinced than I am by the Government's argument that "refouler" is best translated as "expel." That interpretation, as the Second Circuit observed, would leave the Treaty redundantly forbidding a nation to "expel" a refugee. Haitian Centers Council, Inc. v. McNary, 969 F.2d 1350, 1363 (1992).

"To the extent that they are relevant, these translations imply that 'return' means a defensive act of resistance or exclusion at a border * * *." I am at a loss to find the narrow notion of "exclusion at a border" in broad terms like "repulse," "repel," and "drive back." * * *

Article 33.1 is clear not only in what it says, but also in what it does not say: it does not include any geographical limitation. It limits only where a refugee may be sent "to", not where he may be sent from. This is not surprising, given that the aim of the provision is to protect refugees against persecution.

Article 33.2, by contrast, *does* contain a geographical reference, and the majority seizes upon this as evidence that the section as a whole applies only within a signatory's borders. That inference is flawed. Article 33.2 states that the benefit of Article 33.1

"may not * * * be claimed by a refugee whom there are reasonable grounds for regarding as a danger to the security of the country in which he is, or who, having been convicted by a final judgment of a particularly serious crime, constitutes a danger to the community of that country."

The signatories' understandable decision to allow nations to deport criminal aliens who have entered their territory hardly suggests an intent to permit the apprehension and return of noncriminal aliens who have not entered their territory, and who may have no desire ever to enter it. One wonders what the majority would make of an exception that removed from the Article's protection all refugees who "constitute a danger to their families." By the majority's logic, the inclusion of such an exception presumably would render Article 33.1 applicable only to refugees with families.

Far from constituting "an absurd anomaly," the fact that a state is permitted to "expel or return" a small class of refugees found within its territory but may not seize and return refugees who remain outside its frontiers expresses precisely the objectives and concerns of the Convention. Non-return is the rule; the sole exception (neither applicable nor invoked here) is that a nation endangered by a refugee's very presence may "expel or return" him to an unsafe country if it chooses. The tautological observation that only a refugee already in a country can pose a danger to the country "in which he is" proves nothing.

* * *

II

* * *

C

That the clarity of the text and the implausibility of its theories do not give the majority more pause is due, I think, to the majority's heavy reliance on the presumption against extraterritoriality. The presumption runs throughout the majority's opinion, and it stacks the deck by requiring the Haitians to produce "affirmative evidence" that when Congress prohibited the return of "any" alien, it indeed meant to prohibit the interception and return of aliens at sea.

The judicially created canon of statutory construction against extra-territorial application of United States law has no role here, however. It applies only where congressional intent is "unexpressed." Here there is no room for doubt: a territorial restriction has been deliberately deleted from the statute.

Even where congressional intent is unexpressed, however, a statute must be assessed according to its intended scope. The primary basis for the application of the presumption (besides the desire—not relevant here—to avoid conflict with the laws of other nations) is "the common-sense notion that Congress generally legislates with domestic concerns in mind." Where that notion seems unjustified or unenlightening, however, generally-worded laws covering varying subject matters are routinely applied extraterritorially * * *.

In this case we deal with a statute that regulates a distinctively international subject matter: immigration, nationalities, and refugees. Whatever force the presumption may have with regard to a primarily domestic statute evaporates in this context. There is no danger that the Congress that enacted the Refugee Act was blind to the fact that the laws it was crafting had implications beyond this Nation's borders. The "common-sense notion" that Congress was looking inwards—perfectly valid in a case involving the Federal Tort Claims Act, such as Smith,—cannot be reasonably applied to the Refugee Act of 1980.

In this regard, the majority's dictum that the presumption has "special force" when we construe "statutory provisions that may involve foreign and military affairs for which the President has unique responsibility," is completely wrong. The presumption that Congress did not intend to legislate extraterritorially has less force—perhaps, indeed, no force at all—when a statute on its face relates to foreign affairs. What the majority appears to be getting at, as its citation to United States v. Curtiss–Wright Export Corp., suggests, is that in some areas, the President, and not Congress, has sole constitutional authority. Immigration is decidedly not one of those areas. " '[O]ver no conceivable subject is the legislative power of Congress more complete * * *.' " And the suggestion that the President somehow is acting in his capacity as Commander-in-Chief is thwarted by the fact that nowhere among Executive Order No. 12,807's numerous references to the immigration laws is that authority even once invoked.[20]

If any canon of construction should be applied in this case, it is the well-settled rule that "an act of congress ought never to be construed to violate the law of nations if any other possible construction remains." Murray v. The Charming Betsy. The majority's improbable construction of § 243(h), which flies in the face of the international obligations imposed by Article 33 of the Convention, violates that established principle.

---

20. Indeed, petitioners are hard-pressed to argue that restraints on the Coast Guard infringe upon the Commander-in-Chief power when the President himself has placed that agency under the direct control of the Department of Transportation. * * *

III

The Convention that the Refugee Act embodies was enacted largely in response to the experience of Jewish refugees in Europe during the period of World War II. The tragic consequences of the world's indifference at that time are well known. The resulting ban on *refoulement,* as broad as the humanitarian purpose that inspired it, is easily applicable here, the Court's protestations of impotence and regret notwithstanding.

The refugees attempting to escape from Haiti do not claim a right of admission to this country. They do not even argue that the Government has no right to intercept their boats. They demand only that the United States, land of refugees and guardian of freedom, cease forcibly driving them back to detention, abuse, and death. That is a modest plea, vindicated by the Treaty and the statute. We should not close our ears to it.

I dissent.

Note: *See Haitian Centers Council v. Sale,* 823 F.Supp. 1028, 1042 (E.D.N.Y.1993); Koh, Reflections on Refoulement and Haitian Centers Council, 34 Harv.Int'l L.J. 1 (1994).

Additional problems. Several additional problems concerning asylum and the reception of refugees require consideration. (1) Is a state that grants asylum to the national of another state violating the rights of that state? See the language of Article 1 of the Declaration on Territorial Asylum. (2) If a state admits individuals seeking asylum or refuge, how must they be treated? On a basis of equality with other aliens; with nationals of the asylum state? See the Convention Relating to the Status of Refugees, 1951, 189 U.N.T.S. 137. At what locations may a state receive persons seeking asylum so as not to violate the rights of the state of which he is a national or from which he is fleeing? Compare the following two cases.

DEFECTION FROM THE "UKRAINA"

8 Whiteman, Digest of International Law 669 (1967).

In connection with the circumstances in which a refugee escaping from a Soviet fishing fleet off Shetland was pursued by Soviets across British soil in June 1958, the Secretary of State for the Home Department and Lord Privy Seal, R.A. Butler, furnished the House of Commons with the following information:

> A man named Erich Teayn, stated to be an Estonian, came ashore in the Shetland Islands early this morning from the Russian fishing vessel "Ukraina", one of three Russian trawlers anchored in a bay at Walls. He made his way to a crofter's house and indicated that he did not want to go back to the Russian vessel. He was

followed by a party of Russians, said to number about 30, who landed from two small boats in pursuit of him. He was taken into custody for interrogation under the Aliens Order. Three Russians subsequently called at Lerwick police station and sought access to him. This was refused.

In response to a question whether immediate protest would be made to the Russians if the facts as stated were confirmed, and the person involved were a genuine political refugee, Mr. Butler replied: "First, we have to examine the case. If this man asks for political asylum, it will certainly be considered." * * *

ASYLUM ON A VESSEL

II Hackworth, Digest of International Law 641 (1941).

The American Minister in Guatemala reported to the Department of State, in October 1922, that in reply to an inquiry of the Mexican Minister as to whether a certain Guatemalan to whom the Mexican Legation had given asylum would be safe from arrest if placed aboard an American vessel in a Guatemalan harbor, he had informed the Minister that the Guatemalan authorities would have the right to effect the arrest of a person in such circumstances so long as the vessel was within Guatemalan waters. In an instruction of November 3, 1922 the Department approved the attitude assumed by the Minister.

Would the result be different if the Guatemalan were placed aboard a United States naval vessel in Guatemalan waters? That is, could Guatemala lawfully arrest the man; would Guatemala have a basis for diplomatic protest in such a case? For the United States Department of State statement of general policy for dealing with requests for asylum by foreign nationals, see 66 U.S.Dept. of State Bull. 124 (1972).

SECTION G.   HUMAN RIGHTS AND
THE NEW WORLD ORDER

With all the cataclysmic changes that have occurred world-wide during the past few years, many feel that it is necessary to re-examine and re-think the concept of human rights within the context of international law. What do you think? Refer back to the works by feminists and cross-cultural writers *supra*. Following are excerpts from more articles dealing with this issue.

B. COSSMAN REFORM, REVOLUTION, OR RETRENCHMENT? INTERNATIONAL HUMAN RIGHTS IN THE POST–COLD WAR ERA

32 Harv.J.Int'l L. 339 (1991) (Footnotes omitted).*

————

As Europe East and West struggles to come in from the cold, international human rights must confront the implications of profound social, economic, and political change. It is a moment of both opportunity and challenge. The end of the Cold War may signal a renewed possibility for the cooperation so essential for the realization of the normative vision of international human rights. Notwithstanding such hopes, I would argue that fundamental changes in the relationship between East and West may undermine important dimensions of the discourse of international human rights. Moreover, the focus of attention on the changes in the East may have devastating effects on the relationship between North and South, and on the conception of human rights law emerging from developing countries. As the Wall is dismantled in Europe, new walls may only be going up elsewhere.

I. Rights Discourse and Democratic Possibilities

The end of the Cold War may bring renewed international commitment to human rights. From its beginnings, international human rights law has been limited by problems of enforcement. As one commentator [wrote], "[i]nternational remedial paths remain fragile, often illusory." It has relied primarily on international cooperation, moral suasion and condemnation to ensure compliance. Moreover, this cooperation was often elusive in the Cold War world, where deep political and ideological divides constrained the sanctioning of human rights abuses by the international community. In a polarized world, the discourse on human rights was often no more than a rhetorical device in a political game of legitimation and delegitimation which coexisted with superpowers turning a blind eye to the human rights abuses in their own sphere of influence. Yet, despite the weakness * * * there remains a strong commitment to the discourse of human rights principles. As Philip Alston wrote in 1988, "It is now widely accepted that the characterization of a specific goal as a human right elevates it above the rank and file of competing social goals, gives it a degree of immunity from challenge and generally endows it with an aura of timelessness, absoluteness and universal validity."

Human rights is a powerful political discourse—indeed, it is often the only discourse in which disadvantaged groups may claim a voice and legitimately make universal claims. International, national and grassroots organizations continue to make human rights the discourse of choice in their struggles. Despite its institutional limitations, the discourse provides an important source of political inspiration and energy through which people can be educated and mobilized.

* (Reprinted with the permission of the Harv.J.Int'l L.

In a world no longer divided along the East/West axis, this political discourse may have heightened possibilities. A world no longer divided may better lend itself to the international cooperation so essential to the realization of the vision of international human rights. On the international level, we are witnessing the emergence of a renewed commitment to the United Nations as a forum for the resolution of international conflict. Such international cooperation could assume many forms in the area of human rights. The mechanisms for enforcing and monitoring compliance with international human rights norms could be improved within both Charter- and Convention-based procedures. States which have not already done so could ratify article 41 of the International Covenant on Civil and Political Rights (ICCPR), which provides for interstate complaints to the Human Rights Committee, as well as the Optional Protocol of the Covenant, which allows the Committee to hear complaints from individuals. Much room exists for strengthening the procedures and remedies in the International Convention on the Elimination of All Forms of Racial Discrimination (CERD), and the Convention for the Elimination of All Forms of Discrimination Against Women (CEDAW). * * * Many more states could ratify the Declaration regarding article 14 of CERD, allowing the Committee on the Elimination of All Forms of Racial Discrimination to receive communications from individuals. A provision similar to article 14 could be added to CEDAW.

Even short of precipitating formal changes in the enforcement machinery of international instruments, the end of the Cold War may open other and perhaps more significant opportunities for human rights. Improved international cooperation may facilitate the work of the various agencies, committees, and working groups engaged in monitoring compliance with human rights obligations. Until now, the operations of these groups and institutions have been severely limited by the deep and often hostile political and ideological differences of their members.

* * *

The changing international climate may also enlarge the role regional organizations play in human rights enforcement. Non-binding regional standards such as those contained in the Helsinki Final Act of the Conference on Security and Cooperation in Europe may acquire new importance in the wake of the CSCE's emergence as a key vehicle for shaping the post-Cold War Europe. Despite their focus on security issues, recent meetings of the CSCE have directed considerable attention to human rights. Indeed, the Concluding Document of the Follow–Up of the CSCE in January 1989 has been described as signifying "great progress as regards human rights." Under the new conditions of cooperation, non-binding human rights standards such as those promulgated by the CSCE might be as effective as, if not more so than, binding instruments lacking cooperative context.

II. HUMAN RIGHTS IN TRANSITION

The transcendence of oppositions in the post-Cold War era may open possibilities for international human rights in democratic struggles. Yet, the failure to transcend the oppositions of political philosophy may limit these possibilities. The collapse of the Communist bloc has been accompanied by a radical shift to the right in the political orientation of the countries of Eastern Europe, and the post-Cold War political climate may be less one of transcendence than it is of retrenchment.

Most current international human rights norms emerged in the aftermath of World War II, a product of the competing political ideologies of that period. The three generations of human rights correspond to three different political visions: civil and political rights associated with Western liberal democracies; social and economic rights associated with Eastern socialist states; and development rights associated with post-colonial, developing countries. The very division of the International Bill of Rights into two Covenants—one dealing with civil and political rights, the other dealing with social, economic, and cultural rights—was in large part due to the political and ideological divisions of the post-war world. It took almost two decades from the adoption of the Universal Declaration to the adoption of the Covenants to accommodate fundamental differences between liberal and socialist conceptions of individual rights, and of the individual's relation to society. While the international community has recognized the indivisibility of all human rights on several occasions, contemporary international human rights discourse remains the product of a precarious balance of ideological differences.

As the East embraces laissez-faire economics, what will become of the social and economic rights the East has historically advocated? A trend away from social and economic rights towards civil and political rights is becoming increasingly visible throughout Eastern Europe. Although it is important to recognize the progress that has been made within the United Nations system in advancing social and economic rights, we must consider the real possibility of a backslide on recent commitments. The countries of East and West may now agree on the priority of civil and political rights over social and economic rights. Indeed, they may even agree that the latter are not appropriately understood as rights, but only as aspirations. Paradoxically, the possibility for heightened cooperation in the promotion of human rights may be a product of the narrowing of the discourse itself.

Even within the realm of civil and political rights, we must further ask whether some rights will be more equal than others. Will all civil and political rights be given equal significance, or will the shifting ideological balance privilege individualistic, libertarian rights of freedom from state intervention over collective, egalitarian rights, such as the freedom from discrimination? Two examples, although far from conclusive, are illustrative of the political mood of Eastern Europe, and suggest reason to be concerned about the future of human rights.

The first example is the attack on ethnic minorities throughout Eastern Europe. Nationalist movements * * * have engaged in widespread ethnic violence. In Romania, extremist groups are fueling hatred against ethnic Hungarians, Germans, Gypsies, and Jews. In the [former] Soviet Union, violence erupted between Armenians and Azeris, Uzbeks and Meskhetian Turks, Georgians and Abkhazians. In Bulgaria, nationalism has been directed against the Turkish minority. In Yugoslavia, tensions between the six national republics, as well as the eighteen other nationalities, [have torn] the country apart. Throughout Eastern Europe and the [former] Soviet Union, anti-Semitism is experiencing a tragic revival.

The second example is the assault on women's rights. Women are experiencing a disproportionate impact of the inflation and unemployment that accompany the transition to free-market economies in Eastern Europe. Most East European women are in the workforce. However, they are at high risk of losing their job security and their maternity [and other] benefits. With rising unemployment, women are the first to be laid off and thereby forced to return to the sphere of domestic labor. Moreover, social pressure is mounting on women to return to the home voluntarily. Further, divorce and abortion rights are under attack in many Eastern European countries. In Poland, where the anti-abortion movement has been the strongest, a woman now must visit three doctors and a psychologist before she can have an abortion at a publicly funded hospital. Last November, a bill which proposed banning abortion passed the Polish Senate.

Such discrimination, harassment, and violence directed against women and minorities constitute a clear violation of international human rights standards. The attack on the rights of ethnic minorities has been identified as a serious problem at both the international and regional level. For example, in 1988, the U.N. Sub–Commission on Prevention of Discrimination and Protection of Minorities, after many years of sidestepping this divisive issue, decided to consider the protection of racial, ethnic, religious, and linguistic minorities. Similarly, increased attention has been directed toward the rights of minorities within the CSCE, which has been called upon to meet the challenges of the anti-Semitism and ethnic hatred that is sweeping across Eastern Europe. At its recent meetings, the CSCE has directed increased attention to develop protections for the rights of ethnic minorities. While some observers still argue that international instruments are inadequate for the protection of ethnic minorities, some official efforts are being made to offset the rising intolerance toward ethnic minorities. There is at least some evidence that the states of Eastern Europe are resisting the assault on the rights of ethnic minorities by adopting official measures to protect them. The same, however, cannot be said of women's rights. On the contrary, official state discourse often encourages discrimination against women. It may be that women's rights, tied as they are to social and economic rights, will be first among the victims of retrenchment in human rights discourse.

> * * *

IV. Conclusion

The post-Cold War international order opens windows of opportunity for stronger enforcement mechanisms, more non-binding standards, and increased international and regional cooperation for the promotion of international human rights. However, it is essential that the discourse of international human rights is not itself compromised in the efforts to achieve these ends. The real challenge facing international human rights in this era lies in resisting the homogenization of human rights as civil and political rights. While regional organizations, such as the CSCE, are well-positioned to assume a prominent role in fostering new international cooperation, they cannot be expected to take the lead in promoting social and economic rights. The reorientation of human rights promotion and economic development along the East–West axis may only serve to deepen the divide between North and South. A renewed commitment to the existing discourse and fora for international human rights is required to ensure that the political changes in Eastern Europe bring about a real increase in democratic space within which rights claims can be made, rather than simply a rise in conservative ideologies within which rights claims will go largely unheard. But there may also be possibility in paradox. Perhaps the depoliticized East–West dialogue offers a possibility of political space for more substantive and less rhetorical debate on the essential meaning of human dignity.

M. KOSKENNIEMI THE FUTURE OF STATEHOOD

32 Harv.J.Int'l L. 397 (1991) (Footnotes omitted).*

* * *

I. Human Rights and Statehood

An international law of sovereign equality has always contained the unfortunate implication of providing legitimacy for the national repression of citizens, or at least impunity for tyrants. The emergence of a body of human rights law may seem to be "competing—if not at loggerheads—with the traditional principles of respect for sovereign equality of States and of non-interference * * *." The 1966 U.N. Covenants on Economic, Social and Cultural Rights and on Civil and Political Rights have affirmed that states have international obligations to their citizens. Along with the more recent instruments on the prevention of racial and sexual discrimination and torture, and on the establishment of rights for children and migrant workers, these covenants have also instituted a universally applicable system of international inspection and supervision. The practical effects of such international standards may still be rather small, but their existence means that a state may not claim that mere statehood justifies any internal activities.

During the 1970's and 1980's, many U.N. policies, such as developmental and peace programs, were characterized as a right of the policies' beneficiaries. This practice may have somewhat obscured the meaning of human rights as legally cognizable claims by an individual or a community against the state. Developments in Eastern Europe, however, have again focused global attention on the right to be free from state interference. In essence, "[l]iberation in these countries means curtailing the power of the state and its bureaucracy." Similarly, the "Charter of Paris for a New Europe," adopted at the Summit Meeting of Heads of State or Government of States participating in the Conference on Securi-

* (Reprinted with the permission of the Harv.J.Int'l L.).

ty and Cooperation in Europe (CSCE), begins with a section entitled "Human Rights, Democracy and the Rule of Law": "Human rights and fundamental freedoms are the birthright of all human beings, are inalienable and are guaranteed by law. Their protection and promotion is the first responsibility of government. Respect for them is an essential safeguard against an over-mighty State." Forums like the CSCE, the Council of Europe, and the U.N. Human Rights Commission are developing and strengthening mechanisms to curtail state power. Such developments may even have supported claims regarding the customary character of certain core restraints on the power of states.

The protection of human rights, however, cannot form a meaningful basis for social order. If we are to define our polity in terms of human rights, we must ascertain the number and content of such rights. If our polity is to be orderly, these rights must form a harmonious whole. Rights discourse, insofar as it is carried to the level of political theory, consequently rests on two naturalistic assumptions: knowability and harmony. Sad experience reveals that neither assumption can be sustained in a manner sufficiently compelling for the conduct of politics.

Much of rights discourse is no more than the transformation of substantive political goals into human rights language, perhaps most evident in the perennial argument about whether economic and social rights and, *a fortiori,* the so-called third generation or solidarity rights are "real" human rights. But even in the core area of personal freedom and inviolability, agreement reigns only on the general formulation of some rights, such as the right to life, the prevention of torture, and the right to a fair trial. The appearance of consensus is soon dispelled by interpretative controversy: Does the right to life preclude capital punishment? Is solitary confinement "torture"? Is trial by politically elected bureaucrats "fair"? The indeterminacy of human rights language may not be any greater than the indeterminacy of legal rules and principles in general. But the omnipresent debate over rights highlights the fact that such rights cannot *replace* the institutions that are needed to enumerate and interpret them. Rights discourse cannot form a polity because it relies on (conceptually independent) political institutions to define rights. We do not know our rights; we create them through our political processes.

Rights—legally cognizable powers— are scarce resources and are more often than not mutually exclusive. For example, political rights may be achieved only at the cost of economic sustainability, just as free speech overlaps with the right of privacy. Regardless of how we enumerate and construe human rights, we cannot avoid these conflicts. The assumption that human rights exist in some pre-established harmony may only be held with a prior commitment to the kind of naturalism that not only defines rights as coterminous with each other, but in doing so, also provides an inherently authoritarian standpoint towards existing conflict.

Insofar as we do not understand political controversy between the substance and the delimitation of a human right as requiring the determination of the right's essence, that is, insofar as naturalism is not an option for the resolution of political conflict, we can only conclude that as a set of social norms, human rights owe their existence and meaning to decision-making processes. There is no reason to construe those processes in such a way that one political position would be permanently privileged. Thus, something very much like the (ideal) liberal state, which aims to maintain the integrity of the decision-making process, may be a precondition for the proper administration of human rights.

* * *

IV. Theorizing the Challenges

The values of the international system as expressed in public international law are those of liberal individualism transposed to the inter-state level. The system denies the existence of an external standard of judgment that is valid regardless of whether it is held by states themselves. Its law, Louis Henkin observed recently, "is designed to further each state's realization of its own notion of the Good." The "system" exists only in the formal sense of a shared vocabulary and a set of institutional practices that states use for cooperation or conflict. It is an artificial creation, a contrived synthesis of power and ideas. In short, it is not an organism that embodies some autonomous ideal of authentic communal life.

This is the understanding of the present state system shared and challenged by each of the discourses discussed above: human rights, nationalism, and world order. Each posits an ideal of *authenticity* outside the system that contrasts with the formal and artificial character of statehood. These ideals, however, cannot be sustained within liberal political rhetoric. To the contrary, their enforcement might appear as precisely the kind of authoritarianism against which the state system was created.

Human rights discourse builds on the psychological assumption of an authentic self and a normative rejoinder regarding the character of communal life as an instrument for the realization of the self's authentic potential. As we have seen, the difficulty with this assumption is the absence of agreement about the content of that authenticity, that is, what should actually be held to be inalienable "human" rights. Perhaps our lack of consensus is more than ignorance about our true natures. Perhaps no authentic self exists. Instead of a socially circumscribed instantiation of human nature, personhood itself is likely to be a social construct. But if the self is more like a bottomless pit than a set of determinate potentials, any rigorous effort to ground society on personal self-realization would do away with normativity altogether. Under these circumstances, a demand for self-fulfillment and its corollary, a general presumption against restricting liberty, accompanied by an absence of faith in a natural law—a set of natural constraints on liberty—argues for Leviathan. A generalized call for unmitigated, compulsive egoism is bound to make social life impossible, and thereby justify an authoritarian reaction for the purpose of restoring order and protecting everyone's "real interests."

* * *

We also have little reason to be confident that some subject-matters—such as peace, economy, and the environment—are authentically global and must be dealt with by globally uniform solutions. The types of social life constituting or advancing "true peace," "a stable economy," or "a healthy environment" are determined with reference to political values. The increasing recourse to justice, equity, and general principles by international lawyers resembles the turn in national societies away from the *Rechtstaat* into a more contextually responsive social order. Thus, the paradox emerges in that universalizing, although still indeterminate, rhetoric in fact contextualizes the law. As flexible standards tend to increase the power of the institutions which intend to apply them, the *dédoublement fonctionnelle* guarantees that states remain in control.

* * *

By establishing and consenting to human rights limitations on their own sovereignty, states actually define, delimit, and contain those rights, thereby domesticating their use and affirming the authority of the state as the source from which such rights spring. * * * If the revolution in Eastern Europe is now followed by frustration, this may reflect a mass realization that the revolution failed to provide a compelling sense of authenticity to society. Thus, one set of state apparatuses was replaced by another, sturdier ideology in 1989.

* * *

VI. FORM OR SUBSTANCE?

The preoccupation of international lawyers with change in the international system may be connected with the more general turn in contemporary thought and experience from bureaucratic formalism to substantive ideals of communal life. Just as the responsiveness of the strictly formal *Rechtstaat* to these ideals appears inadequate, the extreme rationalism of the Westphalian system may also seem responsible for such unacceptable consequences as economic disparity and the permanent threat of nuclear war.

Despite the dismantling of both intermediate-range nuclear weapons and the Berlin Wall, the romantic ideal of a "new world order" based on substantive values that transcend statehood may not have come much closer to realization. People still disagree about the political good. In normal circumstances, states still provide the means to direct substantive disagreement into institutionalized debate. When such disagreement extends beyond the state, it is soon formalized into regular diplomatic intercourse.

At the time that I wrote this, war had begun in the Gulf, and the Soviet Union had increased military pressure on the Baltic republics. Both crises involved statehood: the former involved an attempt to restore it, the latter an effort to preserve the boundaries claimed by one state and to prevent the creation of a new state. In these cases, statehood no longer performs its formalizing function of channeling political debate into institutions. As the Marxist critique once claimed, form has become a camouflage for substance. Statehood has become a pretense for enforcing politics. Attempts to discuss these situations as if they only manifested a formal-legal difficulty about "right to statehood" sound increasingly hollow. Inasmuch as statehood, too, has its substantive reasons, it is difficult to see how international lawyers could discuss these two cases without invoking *those* substances. This, of course, creates difficulties for an agnostic legal rhetoric, denying its reliance on any particular substance. Nonetheless, it challenges international lawyers to formulate and agree upon some very basic ideals of communal life, however tentative. Without this, it is hard to see how we might feel justified in looking beyond today's crises with any confidence in a shared future.

Chapter 11

INDIVIDUAL RESPONSIBILITY

———

———

SECTION A.   TRADITIONAL WAR CRIMES

"When we neither punish nor reproach evildoers, we are not simply protecting their trivial old age, we are thereby ripping the foundations of justice from beneath new generations." Alexander Solzhenitsyn, The Gulag Archipelago 178 (T. Whitney trans. 1974).

———

JUDGMENT IN CASE OF LIEUTENANTS DITHMAR AND BOLDT HOSPITAL SHIP "LLANDOVERY CASTLE"

Germany, Supreme Court of Leipzig, 1921.
16 American Journal of International Law 708 (1922).*

* * *

Up to 1916 the steamer Llandovery Castle, had, according to the statements of the witnesses Chapman and Heather, been used for the transport of troops. In that year she was commissioned by the British Government to carry wounded and sick Canadian soldiers home to Canada from the European theatre of war. The vessel was suitably fitted out for the purpose and was provided with the distinguishing marks, which the Tenth Hague Convention of the 18th October, 1907 (relating to the application to naval warfare of the principles of the Geneva Convention) requires in the case of naval hospital ships. The name of the vessel was communicated to the enemy powers. From that time on she was exclusively employed in the transport of sick and wounded. She never again carried troops, and never had taken munitions. * * *

* * *

[In] 1918, the Llandovery Castle was on her way back to England from Halifax, after having carried sick and wounded there. She had on board the crew consisting of 164 men, 80 officers and men of the Canadian Medical Corps, and 14 nurses, a total of 258 persons. There were no combatants on board, and, in particular, no American airmen. The vessel had not taken on board any munitions or other war material. * * *

In the evening of 27th June, 1918, at about 9:30 the Llandovery Castle was sunk in the Atlantic Ocean, about 116 miles south-west of Fastnet (Ireland), by a torpedo from the German U-boat 86. Of those on board only 24 persons were saved, 234 having been drowned. The commander * * * was First–Lieutenant Patzig, who was subsequently promoted captain. His present whereabouts are unknown. The accused Dithmar was the first officer and the accused Boldt the second. Patzig recognized the character of the ship, which he had been pursuing for a long time, at the latest when she exhibited at dusk the lights prescribed for hospital ships by the Tenth Hague Convention. In accordance with international law, the German U-boats were forbidden to torpedo hospital ships. According both to the German and the British Governments' interpretation of the said Hague Convention, ships, which were used for the transport of military persons wounded and fallen ill in war on land, belonged to this category. * * * Patzig knew this and was aware that by torpedoing the Llandovery Castle he was acting against orders. But he was of the opinion, founded on various information (including some from official sources, the accuracy of which cannot be verified, and does not require to be verified in these proceedings), that on the enemy side, hospital ships were being used for transporting troops and combatants,

* Reprinted with the permission of the American Society of International Law.

as well as munitions. He, therefore, presumed that, contrary to international law, a similar use was being made of the Llandovery Castle. In particular, he seems to have expected (what grounds he had for this has not been made clear) that she had American airmen on board. Acting on this suspicion, he decided to torpedo the ship, in spite of his having been advised not to do so by the accused Dithmar and the witness Popitz. Both were with him in the conning tower, the accused Boldt being at the depth rudder.

The torpedo struck the Llandovery Castle amidship on the port side and damaged the ship to such an extent that she sank in about 10 minutes. There were 19 lifeboats on board. Each could take a maximum of 52 persons. Only two of them were smaller, and these could not take more than 23 persons. Some of the boats on the port side were destroyed by the explosion of the torpedo. A good number of undamaged boats were, however, successfully lowered. The favorable weather assisted life-saving operations.

* * *

After the sinking of the Llandovery Castle, there were still left three of her boats with people on board. Some time after the torpedoing, the U-boat came to the surface and approached the lifeboats, in order to ascertain by examination whether the Llandovery Castle had airmen and munitions on board. * * *

* * *

After passing by the second time, the U-boat once more went away. The lifeboat, which had hoisted a sail in the meantime, endeavored to get away. But after a brief period, the occupants of the boat noticed firing from the U-boat. The first two shells passed over the lifeboat. Then firing took place in another direction; about 12 to 14 shots fell all told. The flash at the mouth of the gun and the flash of the exploding shells were noticed almost at the same time, so that, as the expert also assumes, the firing was at a very near target. After firing had ceased, the occupants of the lifeboat saw nothing more of the U-boat.

The captain's boat cruised about for some 36 hours altogether. On the 29th June, in the morning, it was found by the English destroyer Lysander. The crew were taken on board and the boat left to its fate. During the 29th June, the commander of the English Fleet caused a search to be made for the other lifeboats of the Llandovery Castle.

* * *

The prosecution assumes that the firing of the U-boat was directed against the lifeboats of the Llandovery Castle. The court has arrived at the same conclusion as the result of the evidence given at this time.

* * *

In this connection we must refer to the opinion of the actual witnesses, both English and German. * * *

If finally the question is asked—what can have induced Patzig to sink the lifeboats, the answer is to be found in the previous torpedoing of the Llandovery Castle. Patzig wished to keep this quiet and to prevent any news of it reaching England. * * * He may have argued to himself that, if the sinking of the ship became known (the legality of which he, in view of the fruitlessness of his endeavors to prove the misuse of the ship, was not able to establish) great difficulties would be caused to the German Government in their relations with other powers. Irregular torpedoings had already brought the German Government several times into complications with other states and there was the possibility that this fresh case might still further prejudice the international position of Germany. This might bring powers, that were still neutral, into the field against her. Patzig may have wished to prevent this, by wiping out all traces of his action. The false entries in the log-book and the chart, which have already been mentioned, were intended, having regard to his position in the service, to achieve this object. This illusion could be, however, of but short duration, if the passengers in the lifeboats, some of whom had been on board the U-boat, and who, therefore could fully describe it, were allowed to get home. It was, therefore, necessary to get rid of them, if Patzig did not wish the sinking of the Llandovery Castle to be known. [There] the explanation of the unholy decision. * * *

* * * The court has decided that the lifeboats of the Llandovery Castle were fired on in order to sink them. This is the only conclusion possible, [given statements] by the witnesses. It is only on this basis that the behavior of Patzig and of the accused men can be explained.

The court finds that it is beyond all doubt that, even though no witness had direct observation of the effect of the fire, Patzig attained his object so far as two of the boats were concerned. * * *

For the firing on the lifeboats only those persons can be held responsible, who at the time were on the deck of the U-boat; namely Patzig, the two accused and the chief boatswain's mate Meissner. Patzig gave the decisive order, which was carried out without demur in virtue of his position as commander. It is possible that he asked the opinion of the two accused beforehand, though of this there is no evidence. As Meissner was the gunlayer and remained on deck by special orders, it may be assumed with certainty that he manned the after gun which was fired. In the opinion of the naval expert, he was able to act without assistance. According to this view, owing to the nearness of the objects under fire, there was no need for the fire to be directed by an artillery officer, such as the accused Dithmar. The only technical explanation, which both the accused have given and which fits in with the facts, is that they themselves did not fire. Under the circumstances this is quite credible. They confined themselves to making observations while the firing was going on. The naval expert also assumes that they kept a look-out. Such a look-out must have brought the lifeboats, which were being fired on, within their view. By reporting their position and the varying distances of the lifeboats and such like, the accused assisted in the firing on the lifeboats, and this, quite apart from the fact that their observations saved the U-boat from danger from any other quarter, and that they thereby enabled Patzig to do what he intended as regards the lifeboats. The statement of the accused Boldt that "so far as he took part in what happened, he acted in accordance with his orders" has reference to the question whether the accused took part in the firing on the lifeboats. He does not appear to admit any participation. But the two accused must be held guilty for the destruction of the lifeboats.

With regard to the question of the guilt of the accused, no importance is to be attached to the statements put forward by the defence, that the enemies of Germany were making improper use of hospital ships for military purposes, and that they had repeatedly fired on German lifeboats and shipwrecked people. * * * [T]hroughout the German fleet it was a matter of general belief that improper use of hospital ships was made by the enemy. It must, therefore, be assumed for the benefit of the accused, that they also held this belief. Whether this belief was founded on fact or not, is of less importance as affecting the case before the court, than the established fact that the Llandovery Castle at the time was not carrying any cargo or troops prohibited under clause 10 of the Hague Convention.

The act of Patzig is homicide, according to Penal Code ¶ 212. By sinking the lifeboats he purposely killed the people who were in them. * * *

　　　* * *

The firing on the boats was an offence against the law of nations. In war on land the killing of unarmed enemies is not allowed (compare the Hague regulations as to war on land, para. 23(c)), similarly in war at sea, the killing of shipwrecked people, who have taken refuge in lifeboats, is forbidden. It is certainly possible to imagine exceptions to this rule, as, for example, if the inmates of the lifeboats take part in the fight. But there was no such state of affairs in the present case, as Patzig and the accused persons were well aware, when they cruised around and examined the boats.

Any violation of the law of nations in warfare is, as the Senate has already pointed out, a punishable offence, so far as in general, a penalty is attached to the deed. The killing of enemies in war is in accordance with the will of the State that makes war, (whose laws as to the legality or illegality on the question of killing are decisive), only in so far as such killing is in accordance with the conditions and limitations imposed by the law of nations. The fact that his deed is a violation of international law must be well-known to the doer, apart from acts of carelessness, in which careless ignorance is a sufficient excuse. In examining the question of the existence of this knowledge, the ambiguity of many of the rules of international law, as well as the actual circumstances of the case, must be borne in mind, because in war time decisions of great importance have frequently to be made on very insufficient material. This consideration, however, cannot be applied to the case at present before the court. The rule of international law, which is here involved, is simple and is universally known. No possible doubt can exist with regard to the question of its applicability. The court must in this instance affirm Patzig's guilt of killing contrary to international law.

The two accused knowingly assisted Patzig in this killing, by the very fact of their having accorded him their support in the manner, which has already been set out. It is not proved that they were in agreement with his intentions. The decision rested with Patzig as the commander. The others who took part in this deed carried out his orders. It must be accepted that the deed was carried out on his responsibility, the accused only wishing to support him. * * * They are, therefore, only liable to punishment as accessories.

Patzig's order does not free the accused from guilt. It is true that according to para. 47 of the Military Penal Code, if the execution of an order in the ordinary course of duty involves such a violation of the law as is punishable, the superior officer issuing such an order is alone responsible. According to No. 2, however, the subordinate obeying such an order is liable to punishment, if it was known to him that the order of the superior involved the infringement of civil or military law. This applies in the case of the accused. It is certainly to be urged in favor of the military subordinates, that they are under no obligation to question the order of their superior officer, and they can count upon its legality. But no such confidence can be held to exist, if such an order is universally known to everybody, including also the accused, to be without any doubt whatever against the law. This happens only in rare and exceptional cases. But this case was precisely one of them, for * * * it was perfectly clear to the accused that killing defenceless people in the lifeboats could be nothing else but a breach of the law. As naval officers by profession they were well aware, as the naval expert Saalwächter has strikingly stated, that one is not legally authorized to kill defenceless people. They well knew that this was the case here. They quickly found out the facts by questioning the occupants in the boats when these were stopped. They could only have gathered, from the order given by Patzig, that he wished to make use of his subordinates to carryout a breach of the law. They should, therefore, have refused to obey. As they did not do so, they must be punished.

* * *

The defence finally points out that the accused must have considered that Patzig would have enforced his orders, weapon in hand, if they had not obeyed them. This possibility is rejected. If Patzig had been faced by refusal on the part of his subordinates, he would have been obliged to desist from his purpose, as then it would have been impossible for him to attain his object, namely, the concealment of the torpedoing of the Llandovery Castle. This was also quite well-known to the accused, who had witnessed the affair. From the point of view of necessity (para. 52 of the Penal Code), they can thus not claim to be acquitted.

In estimating the punishment, it has, in the first place, to be borne in mind that the principal guilt rests with Commander Patzig, under whose orders the accused acted. They should certainly have refused to obey the order. This would have required a specially high degree of resolution. A refusal to obey the commander on a submarine would have been something so unusual, that it is humanly possible to understand that the accused could not bring themselves to disobey. That certainly does not make them innocent, as has been stated above. They had acquired the habit of obedience to military authority and could not rid themselves of it. This justifies the recognition of mitigating circumstances. In determining the punishment, a severe sentence must, however, be passed. * * *

* * *

CHRISTOPHER L. BLAKESLEY, TERRORISM, DRUGS, INTERNATIONAL LAW AND THE PROTECTION OF LIBERTY

18–22; 177–179 (1992).

There have been "crimes against humanity" since antiquity. See, the Code of Hammurabi (1728–1686 B.C.), the Laws of Eshnunna (2000 B.C.), and even in the earlier Code of Ur–Nammu (© 2100, B.C.). The Lex Talionis, or law of exact retaliation, is found in the Jewish Torah or Biblical Pentateuch. In virtually all ancient cultures, metaphysics and law were merged; the social cell felt obliged to purge itself of the threat of destruction by the wrath of God or gods. There was a sense that when the group was tainted by crime committed by one of its own or by another against the group, the taint had to be removed to make the group whole again. Punishment of the wrongdoer, combined with religious ceremony, was the cleansing or expiating mechanism. The Code of Manu, [Bk. VII, 18, 23–24; Bk. VIII, 17] provided that rest and happiness for the wrongdoer and society is obtained only by soul-purging punishment of the perpetrator. Blood atonement was required by the Israelites for heinous offenses. [See I Kings 2:28–34]. The Cheyenne banished the one who tainted the food or water supply. The ritual of the "breaking of the arrows," followed to cleanse the group.

In the very early "modern era," Jean Bodin, Hugo Grotius, and Emerich de Vattel all called for the rule that punishment was necessary for those who commit serious offenses, in their requirement that there be no sanctuary for the criminal. Each nation has an obligation to "prosecute or extradite." The ascendancy of "positivism" in the nineteenth century created the perception that international law was binding only on states and could not impose obligations or impose punishment directly on individuals; that was solely for states to do.

> "For centuries military commanders—from Henry V of England, under his famous ordinances of war in 1419, to the American military prosecutions of soldiers involved in the My Lai massacre under the U.S. Code of Military Justice—have enforced such laws against violators. In other cases, states have brought to trial captured prisoners of war for offenses committed against the customary laws of war. Thus, both the accused's own state and the captor state have standing to prosecute. Neither system, however, has functioned with any degree of efficiency."

Note: Theodor Meron, The Case for War Crimes Trials in Yugoslavia, 72 For.Aff. 122, 123 (1993); C. Blakesley, Obstacles to the Creation of a Permament War Crimes Tribunal, 18 Fleth.Forum Wld. Affr's 77 (1994). See Schwarzenberger, The Problem of an International Criminal Law, in International Criminal Law 3, 10, 16 (Mueller & Wise eds. 1965); Kelsen, Collective and Individual Responsibility in International Law with Particular Regard to the Punishment of War Criminals, 31 Calif.L.Rev. 530, 553–56 (1943) (noting that international law provides for some offenses as criminal, though enforcement is to be undertaken by domestic courts); Orentlicher, Settling Accounts: The Duty to Prosecute Human Rights Violations of a Prior Regime, 100 Yale L.J. 2537 (1991); Bassiouni, International Criminal Law and Human Rights, 9 Yale J.Wld.Pub.Order 193 (1982); Q. Wright, The Outlawry of War and the Law of War, 47 A.J.I.L. 365 (1953).

Nuremberg Principle I (1946): "[a]ny person who commits an act which constitutes a crime under international law is responsible therefore and liable to punishment." While you are considering the issues in this chapter, think about chapter 10, on Human Rights. One question considered herein is whether the growth of individual human rights law has caused a concomitant development of individual duties under international law? Other questions to keep in mind include the following. Does such individual criminal responsibility exist? If so, did it pre-exist the Nuremberg Trials or did those trials create a rule that individuals may be recognized as objective actors in international law who may be held accountable for their conduct? If this is a rule, is it part of customary international law or does it require a treaty? What do you think the future holds for the Nuremberg principles?

The Nuremberg Tribunal concluded the following:

"It was submitted that international law is concerned with the actions of sovereign States, and provides no punishment for individuals; and further, that where the act in question is an act of State, those who carry it out are not personally responsible but are protected by the doctrine of the sovereignty of the State. In the opinion of the Tribunal, both these submissions must be rejected. That international law imposes duties and liabilities upon individuals as upon States has long been recognized * * * citing Ex parte Quierin, 317 U.S. 1 (1942) * * * Crimes against international law are committed by men, not by abstract entities, and only by punishing individuals who commit such crimes can the provisions of international law be enforced * * * [T]he very essence of the Charter is that individuals have international duties which transcend the national obligations of obedience imposed by the individual State. He who violates the laws of war cannot obtain immunity while acting in pursuance of the authority of the State, if the State in authorizing action moves outside its competence under international law * * * " International Military Tribunal, Judgment, 6 F.R.D. 69, 110 (1946), reprinted in 41 A.J.I.L. 172, 220–21 (1947).

"Offenses against the peace and security of mankind * * * are crimes under international law, for which the responsible individuals shall be punished." See, Draft Code of Offenses Against the Peace and Security of Mankind. This rule of punishment for "crimes against humanity" or crimes against some "higher law" has existed from antiquity.

The monist/dualist debate (presented in Chapter 18, *infra*) is exemplified in the arena of international criminal law. Reference is often made to offenses against the "Law of Nations" (see U.S. Constitution, article 1, § 8). Does this mean that international law proscribes the conduct and provides for punishment? Or does it mean simply that international law provides nations with jurisdiction to apply their own law for conduct which otherwise would not be within their competence? Judge Harry T. Edwards, concurring in *Tel–Oren, supra,* Ch. 10, presented a bit of the historical evolution of the individual's role in international law. Through the 18th century and into the 19th, writers and jurists believed that rules of international law bound individuals as well as states. See, e.g., United States v. Smith, 18 U.S. (5 Wheat.) 153, 5 L.Ed. 57 (1820) (piracy violates law of nations; individual liable); Respublica v. De Longchamps, 1 U.S. (1 Dall.) 111, 1 L.Ed. 59 (1784) (assault on French consul-general violates law of nations; individual liable); 4 Blackstone's Commentaries 66–73 (Welsby ed. 1854) (recounting various offenses against law of nations, committed by private persons, punishable under English statutory law). In the 19th century, the view emerged that states alone were subjects of international law, and they alone were able to assert rights and be held to duties devolved from the law of nations. See, also, Dickenson, The Law of Nations as Part of the National Law of the United States (pt. 1), 101 U.Pa.L.Rev. 26, 29–30 (1952); (pt. 2) 101 U.Pa.L.Rev. 792, 792–95 (1953); 2 Moore, International Law 951, et seq. (1906); Harvard Research in International Law, Piracy, 26 A.J.I.L. 739, 754, 759–60 (1932); Korowitz, The Problem of the International Personality of Individuals, 50 A.J.I.L. 533, 534 (1956); Alfred P. Rubin, The Law of Piracy 305, et seq. (1988). Consider the following history by Telford Taylor, one of the prosecutors at the Nuremberg Trials.

T. TAYLOR, NUREMBERG AND VIETNAM
20 (1970).*

What, then, are the "laws of war"? They are of ancient origin, and followed two main streams of development. The first flowed from medieval notions of knightly chivalry. Over the course of the centuries the stream has thinned to a trickle; it had a brief spurt during the days of single-handed aerial combat, and survives today in rules (often violated) prohibiting various deceptions such as the use of the enemy's uniforms or battle insignia, or the launching of a war without fair warning by formal declaration.

The second and far more important concept is that the ravages of war should be mitigated as far as possible by prohibiting needless cruelties, and other acts that spread death and destruction and are not reasonably related to the conduct of hostilities. The seeds of such a

* Reprinted with permission of Quadrangle Books, Inc., New York.

principle must be nearly as old as human society, and ancient literature abounds with condemnation of pillage and massacre. In more recent times, both religious humanitarianism and the opposition of merchants to unnecessary disruptions of commerce have furnished the motivation for restricting customs and understandings. In the 17th century these ideas began to find expression in learned writings, especially those of the Dutch jurist-philosopher Hugo Grotius.

The formalization of military organization in the 18th–century brought the establishment of military courts, empowered to try violations of the laws of war as well as other offenses by soldiers. During the American Revolution, both Captain Nathan Hale and the British Major John André were convicted as spies and ordered to be hanged, the former by a British military court and the latter by a "Board of General Officers" appointed by George Washington. During the Mexican War, General Winfield Scott created "military commissions," with jurisdiction over violations of the laws of war committed either by American troops against Mexican civilians, or vice versa.

Up to that time the laws of war had remained largely a matter of unwritten tradition, and it was the United States, during the Civil War, that took the lead in reducing them to systematic, written form. In 1863 President Lincoln approved the promulgation by the War Department of "Instructions for the Government of Armies of the United States in the Field," prepared by Francis Lieber, a German veteran of the Napoleonic wars, who emigrated to the United States and became professor of law and political science at Columbia University. These comprised 159 articles, covering such subjects as "military necessity," "punishment of crimes against the inhabitants of hostile countries," "prisoners of war," and "spies." It was by a military commission appointed in accordance with these instructions that Mary Surratt and the others accused of conspiring to assassinate Lincoln were tried.

In the wake of the Crimean War, the Civil War and the Franco–Prussian War of 1870 there arose, in Europe and America, a tide of sentiment for codification of the laws of war and their embodiment in international agreements. The principal fruits of that movement were the series of treaties known today as the Hague and Geneva Conventions. For present purposes, the most important of these are the Fourth Hague Convention of 1907, and the Geneva Prisoner of War, Red Cross, and Protection of Civilians Conventions of 1929 and 1949.

"The right of belligerents to adopt means of injuring the enemy is not unlimited," declared Article 22 of the Fourth Hague Convention, and ensuing articles specify a number of limitations: Enemy soldiers who surrender must not be killed, and are to be taken prisoner; captured cities and towns must not be pillaged, nor "undefended" places bombarded; poisoned weapons and other arms "calculated to cause unnecessary suffering" are forbidden. Other provisions make it clear that war is not a free-for-all between the populations of the countries at war; only members of the armed forces can claim protection of the laws of war, and if a noncombatant civilian takes hostile action against the enemy he is guilty of a war crime. When an army occupies enemy territory, it must endeavor to restore public order, and respect "family honor and rights, the lives of persons, and private property, as well as religious convictions and practices."

Rules requiring humane treatment of prisoners, and for protection of the sick and wounded, are prescribed in the Geneva Conventions. While there is no general treaty on naval warfare, the Ninth Hague Convention prohibited the bombardment of undefended "ports," and the London Naval Treaty of 1930 condemned submarine sinkings of merchant vessels, unless passengers and crews were first placed in "safety."

In all of these treaties, the laws of war are stated as general principles of conduct, and neither the means of enforcement nor the penalties for violations are specified. The substance of their provisions, however, has been taken into the military law of many countries, and is often set forth in general orders, manuals of instruction, or other official documents. In the United States, for example, the Lieber rules of 1863 were replaced in 1914 by an army field manual which, up-dated, is still in force under the title "The Law of Land Warfare." It is set forth therein that the laws of war are part of the law of the United States, and that they may be enforced against both soldiers and civilians, including enemy personnel, by general courts-martial, military commissions, or other military or international tribunals.

Comparable though not identical publications have been issued by the military authorities of Britain, France, Germany and many other countries. These documents, and the treaties on which they are largely based, are regarded as a comprehensive but not necessarily complete exposition of what is really a body of international common law—the laws of war.

Since the mid–19th century, with increasing frequency, the major powers have utilized military courts for the trial of persons accused of war crimes. An early and now famous trial, depicted in a successful Broadway play, was the post-Civil War proceeding against the Confederate Major Henry Wirz on charges of responsibility for the death of thousands of Union prisoners in the Andersonville prison camp, of which he had been commandant. War crimes tribunals were convened by the United States after the Spanish–American War, and by the British after the Boer War.

Following the defeat of Germany in the First World War, the Allies demanded that nearly 900 Germans accused of war crimes, including military and political leaders, be handed over for trial on war crimes charges. The Germans resisted the demand, and in the upshot they were allowed to try their own "war criminals." The trials in 1921 and 1922 were not conducted by military courts, but by the Supreme Court of Germany, sitting in Leipzig. From the Allied standpoint they were a fiasco, as only a handful of accused were tried, and of these nearly all were acquitted or allowed to escape their very short prison sentences. The German court did, however, affirm that violations of the laws of war are punishable offenses, and in the Llandovery Castle case sentenced two German U-boat officers to four-year prison terms (from which both soon escaped) for complicity in the torpedoing of a British hospital ship and the shelling and sinking of her lifeboats. * * * *See also,* Telford Taylor, The Anatomy of the Nuremberg Trials: A Personal Memoir (1992).

Notes & Questions: Does international law, itself, condemn certain conduct and call for the punishment of individuals who breach it? If so, what legal philosophy backs it up? Consider the following thoughts on Natural Law and Positivism:

DAVID LUBAN, ALAN STRUDLER, AND DAVID WASSERMAN, MORAL RESPONSIBILITY IN THE AGE OF BUREAUCRACY
90 Mich.L.Rev. 2348, 2350–53 (1993).*

The doctrine of individual responsibility on the part of rulers and ruled alike has played a prominent role in the development of twentieth-century international law. Positivism, including legal realism, was the ascendant view among legal theorists outside the Catholic Church for the country between the 1830's and the 1930's. World War II changed that. If there is a single historical event that accounts for the survival of serious macular interest in natural law, it is surely the Nuremberg trials. The Nuremberg Tribunal held individual Nazi officials responsible for acts that positive law did not forbid at the time they were committed— so-called "crimes against peace" and "crimes against humanity." Antic-ipating the defendants' protest that they were merely following official orders that carried the force of positive law, Article 8 of the Nuremberg Charter specifically provided that "[t]he fact that the defendant acted pursuant to an order of his government or of a superior shall not free him from responsibility."

That Article 8 represents a flat-out rejection of what might be called the *positivist excuse* for atrocious official acts—the excuse that the acts were licensed by positive law—is intuitively clear. As Stanley Panlson has shown, the defense at Nuremberg relied extensively upon the posi-tivist excuse, which the Tribunal had little difficulty rejecting. The natural law argument that unjust laws lose their obligatory character provides a straightforward philosophical justification for Article 8. Simi-larly, appeals to natural law * * * form the most obvious justification for criminalizing "murder, extermination, enslavement, deportation, and other inhumane acts * * * whether or not in violation of domestic law * * * where perpetrated." Such crimes against humanity are radically inconsistent with the common good, and any domestic legal system that permits them must violate natural law. In addition, Article 7 of the Charter eliminated the act-of-state defense on the part of those in command positions, thereby recognizing that those who legislate bear moral responsibilities just as surely as do those who follow orders.

* Reprinted with the permission of the Michigan Law Review.

Indeed, the view that the Nazi era exposes the moral deficiency of positivism compared with natural law is a commonplace. As early as the mid–1940's, Gustav Radbruch, an eminent pre-War German positivist, repudiated positivism and embraced natural law, arguing in several influential essays that positivism had disarmed German jurists in the face of Nazism. Thus, international revulsion at the official criminality of Hitler's regime, as manifested legally in the Nuremberg trials, represents a triumph for natural law thinking. At the very least, this worldwide condemnation provisionally lays to rest the positivist excuse in international law. But the excuse that "I was only following orders," or "I was only doing my job," was not the only one offered by those implicated in Nazi crimes. In the aftermath of World War II, the world heard with equal frequency the cry, "I didn't know!" This is the *epistemological excuse,* whose elements present the problem that will occupy our attention in this article. Though it is often insincere, and seldom entirely persuasive, the epistemological excuse seems to come naturally to those who commit wrongs in a bureaucratic setting. We shall argue (1) that bureaucracies function (often by design) to permit their functionaries to truthfully plead the excuse "I didn't know"; (2) that traditional accounts of moral responsibility typically recognize this epistemological excuse, and (3) that it is therefore very difficult to find a workable account of moral responsibility within bureaucratic institutions. The strength and prevalence of the epistemological excuse may render the historic rejection of the positivist excuse an empty or very partial victory.

Perhaps the single most salient characteristic of the Nazi crimes was their bureaucratic nature. They were committed, not by a lawless gang of criminals, but by a regularly functioning state bureaucracy executing official policies. Not only Nazi crimes have this bureaucratic character—it exists as well in the misdeeds of the recently departed regimes of the Soviet empire. Emerging democracies of Eastern Europe—if democracies are what they prove to be—are beginning to come to grips with the bureaucratic crimes committed for generations by officials of their former regimes, many of whom will surely enter the epistemological excuse. Czech novelist Milan Kundera [focuses] directly in *The Unbearable Lightness of Being:*

> Let us concede that a Czech public prosecutor in the early fifties who called for the death of an innocent man was deceived by the Russian secret police and the government of his own country. But now that we all know the accusations to have been absurd and the executed to have been innocent, how can that selfsame public prosecutor defend his purity of heart by beating himself on the chest and proclaiming, "My conscience is clear I didn't know."

One might respond with an equally rhetorical question: how can the prosecutor be blamed if he truly did not know? Kundera's rage clearly stems from the ready availability of the epistemological excuse within the secretive Communist bureaucracies, but the fact that an excuse is a bit too handy does not in itself undercut its viability. Thus, the problem of bureaucratic irresponsibility faces post-Communist societies much as it faced post-Nazi Germany.

* * *

1. ***Protocols I and II to the Geneva Conventions of 1949.*** On June 8, 1977, the Geneva Diplomatic Conference on the Reaffirmation and Development of International Humanitarian Law Applicable in Armed Conflicts adopted two protocols supplementing these conventions: the Protocol Additional to the Geneva Conventions of 12 August 1949, and relating to the Protection of Victims of International Armed Conflicts (Protocol I), with annexes, and the Protocol Additional to the Geneva Conventions of August 12, 1949, and relating to the Protection of Victims of Non–International Armed Conflicts (Protocol II). The protocols entered into force December 7, 1978; they were not in force for the United States as of January 1, 1980. The text of the protocols appears at 72 AJIL 457 (1978) and at 16 ILM 1391 (1977) (Protocol I) and 16 ILM 1442 (1977) (Protocol II).

In January 1987, President Reagan transmitted Protocol II to the Senate for its advice and consent, stating that the protocol,

> is essentially an expansion of the fundamental humanitarian provisions contained in the 1949 Geneva Conventions with respect to non-international armed conflicts, including humane treatment and basic due process for detained persons, protection of the wounded, sick and medical units, and protection of noncombatants from attack and deliberate starvation. If these fundamental rules were observed, many of the worst human tragedies of current internal armed conflicts could be avoided. In particular, among other things, the mass murder of civilians is made illegal, even if such killings would not amount to genocide because they lacked racial or religious motives. Several Senators asked me to keep this objective in mind when adopting the Genocide Convention. I remember my commitment to them. This Protocol makes clear that any deliberate killing of a noncombatant in the course of a non-international armed conflict is a violation of the laws of war and a crime against humanity, and is therefore also punishable as murder.

> While I recommend that the Senate grant advice and consent to this agreement, I have at the same time concluded that the United States cannot ratify a second agreement on the law of armed conflict negotiated during the same period. I am referring to Protocol I additional to the 1949 Geneva Conventions, which would revise the rules applicable to international armed conflicts. Like all other efforts associated with the International Committee of the Red Cross, this agreement has certain meritorious elements. But Protocol I is fundamentally and irreconcilably flawed. It contains provisions that would undermine humanitarian law and endanger civilians in war. One of its provisions, for example, would automatically treat as an international conflict any so-called 'war of national liberation.' Whether such wars are international or non-international should turn exclusively on objective reality, not on one's view of the moral qualities of each conflict. To rest on such subjective

distinctions based on a war's alleged purposes would politicize humanitarian law and eliminate the distinction between international and non-international conflicts. It would give special status to 'wars of national liberation,' an ill-defined concept expressed in vague, subjective, politicized terminology. Another provision would grant combatant status to irregular forces even if they do not satisfy the traditional requirements to distinguish themselves from the civilian population and otherwise comply with the laws of war. This would endanger civilians among whom terrorists and other irregulars attempt to conceal themselves. These problems are so fundamental in character that they cannot be remedied through reservations, and I therefore have decided not to submit the Protocol to the Senate in any form, and I would invite an expression of the sense of the Senate that it shares this view. Finally, the Joint Chiefs of Staff have also concluded that a number of the provisions of the Protocol are militarily unacceptable.

[81 AJIL 910 (1987)].

———

Queries: Do you agree or disagree with President Reagan's reasons for not becoming party to Protocol I? Even if you agree with them, do they retain their validity after the demise of the Soviet Empire and the end of the Cold War? Protocol I, article 51(2) prohibits "[a]cts or threats of violence the primary purpose of which is to spread terror among the civilian population." Is it appropriate to refuse ratification of this and other salutary rules in Protocol I, because it would provide "national liberation movements" a "rhetorical and political victory"? There may be other reasons for opposing Protocol I. Did it go far enough? Protocol I is not beyond criticism. Professor Michael Reisman suggests that it presents a shift away from the status quo in international affairs. He notes that an existing state that has suffered low intensity incursions or aggression is not allowed by Protocol I to attack another state in which the original low-intensity attackers have found haven, which is an innovation contrary to self-defense in customary international law. This is a valid criticism. One can criticize Protocol I for a basic confusion between humanitarian rules for protecting victims during armed conflict (jus in bello) and rules aimed at determining the status of parties to conflict (jus ad bellum). To the extent that Protocol I makes jus in bello dependent on jus ad bellum it is unfortunate. Jus in bello originally were undertaken as a matter of self-interest, but had the effect of protecting victims within the embattled state, no matter what "morality" was seen to reside with their "side." Jus in bello in Protocol I is viewed as applying only in certain "acceptable" wars. Protocols I and II made the humanitarian rules applicable to more conflicts, but, unfortunately Protocol I limits their applicability on the basis of an ideological litmus test. Do you agree? What are the arguments favoring Protocol I? See, M. Reisman, Old Wine in New Bottles: The Reagan & Brezhnov

Doctrines, 13 Yale Int'l J. 171, 193–97 (1988); A. Rubin, Int'l Law and the Use of Force by National Liberation Movements, 13 Fletch.For.Wld.Affairs 410, 414 (1989).

President Reagan's position with respect to Protocol I is vigorously rebutted by the Legal Adviser to the Directorate of the International Committee of the Red Cross in An Appeal for Ratification by the United States, 81 AJIL 912 (1987).

2. *The law of war, humanitarian law and human rights law.* Conventional and customary legal developments in the law of war during this century have led scholars to refer to this body of law as humanitarian law. The relationship between humanitarian law and the law of human rights is discussed in the following excerpt.

MERON, ON THE INADEQUATE REACH OF HUMANITARIAN AND HUMAN RIGHTS LAW AND THE NEED FOR A NEW INSTRUMENT
77 American Journal of International Law 589 (1983).*

* * *

Certain initial general observations may be useful. * * * [H]umanitarian law has been more systematically codified than ordinary peacetime human rights, a fact that should not be surprising in view of the comparative age of these two systems of law. While humanitarian law has undergone more than a century of fairly intensive codification, human rights instruments are a product of the post-UN Charter era.

Humanitarian law instruments have been accepted far more than human rights instruments as the positive law of the international community. Baxter has observed that "[t]he Hague Regulations of 1907, which have passed into customary international law, and the Geneva Conventions of 1949 have achieved almost universal acceptance and are probably binding on a larger number of states than any other treaties save only the constitutional instruments of international organizations." It is remarkable indeed that as of December 31, 1982, there were 159 state parties to each of the four Geneva Conventions. The most parties to any human rights instrument, as of 1993, were 115 to the International Convention on the Elimination of All Forms of Racial Discrimination. The number of state parties to other instruments was significantly lower: 73 to the International Covenant on Economic, Social and Cultural Rights (Economic Covenant); 70 to the International Covenant on Civil and Political Rights (Political Covenant); 27 to the Optional Protocol to the International Covenant on Civil and Political Rights; 89 to the Convention on Prevention and Punishment of the Crime of Genocide; and 39 to the Convention on the Elimination of All Forms of Discrimination Against Women. In comparing the extent of ratifications of human rights and humanitarian instruments, however, account should be taken of the fact that the former instruments apply to day-to-day life, while the latter govern exceptional situations only.

* Reprinted with the permission of the American Society of International Law.

There is a considerable difference between the customary law status of many of the norms contained in the humanitarian law instruments and those in the human rights instruments. It is generally accepted that the Regulations Respecting the Laws and Customs of War on Land annexed to Hague Convention No. IV are now part of the corpus of customary international law. The acceptance of the Hague Regulations as customary law resolves the difficulties posed by Article 2 of the fourth Hague Convention, which states that the provisions contained in the Convention and in the Regulations annexed to it "do not apply except between Contracting Powers, and then only if all the belligerents are parties to the Convention." This *si omnes* or general participation clause can now be regarded as irrelevant.

While the binding nature of the Geneva Conventions of 1949 is generally based on their status as treaties, some of their provisions can be traced to earlier Geneva Conventions and to the Hague Regulations of 1907. Thus, certain provisions of the Conventions of 1949 reflect customary law. This can only be determined *in concreto* with regard to each particular provision. However, the extent to which provisions of the Conventions are declaratory of customary law is of limited significance because of the universal acceptance of these Conventions qua binding treaties. Nevertheless, when a government contests the applicability of one of the Conventions, it may be useful for the International Committee of the Red Cross (ICRC) to invoke a certain rule as customary, rather than as a treaty provision.

The status of the 1977 Protocols Additional to the Geneva Conventions of August 12, 1949 is altogether different. By the end of 1982, Protocol I had been ratified by only 27 states and Protocol II by only 23 states. The Protocols have introduced many changes and innovations, some of which are controversial in nature, into humanitarian law. Some scholars view such provisions as not codifying customary law.

* * *

Human rights law and humanitarian law have different historical sources and, originally, different jurisprudential underpinnings. * * * [O]ne of the fundamental sources and guiding principles of human rights is the principle of humanity. The ideas that lie behind the law of war and humanitarian law are different in origin. The law of war originates in the tension between military necessity and restraints (whether motivated by humanitarian or other considerations such as economic advantage) on the conduct of belligerents. The weight of these two conflicting factors has changed greatly in the course of history. Originally, military necessity was dominant. The principle of humanitarian restraints, originally in a weak position, is of growing importance, particularly in the elaboration of new instruments, but not necessarily in actual practice. A central concept of the law of war is that of reciprocity, regarded both as a reason behind the norms and as an important factor in their efficacy. Not surprisingly, humanitarian law has focused, historically, on the reciprocal protection of a few strictly limited categories of persons, especially persons "belonging to the enemy."

It goes without saying that the post-UN Charter international human rights instruments have the humanitarian object of recognizing human rights and extending international protection to them. But it should be pointed out that humanitarian law, while protecting the rights of states and governing their duties, also contains a prominent human rights component, dating back to the 19th century when the law of war had "come to be seen as a law of humanitarian restraints upon the conduct of the belligerents." This humanitarian and humanizing aspect of the law of war finds a significant reflection in the preambular (Martens) clause to Hague Convention No. IV.[24] The post-UN Charter human rights, as reflected in the Universal Declaration of Human Rights (Universal Declaration), had an influence on the humanitarian character of the Geneva Conventions of 1949. The 1977 Additional Protocols also reflect the influence of international human rights, in some instances by taking those rights into consideration, and in others by making explicit reference to them. In matters such as the prohibition of torture and cruel, inhuman, or degrading treatment or punishment, arbitrary arrest and detention, discrimination on grounds of race, sex, language, or religion, and the norm of due process, there exists a very large measure of convergence and parallelism between norms originating in human rights instruments and those originating in instruments on international humanitarian law. * * *

The dominance of the humanitarian principle in the most recent elaboration of the laws of armed conflict is apparent, inter alia, in Articles 50–56 of Protocol I, which concern the protection of the civilian population in the case of an international armed conflict, and in the provisions of Protocol II, which confer significant human rights on persons living in a country involved in an internal armed conflict. If the former example can be seen as reflecting also the principle of reciprocity, the latter can and should be explained primarily on the basis of the principle of humanity. Indeed, the protection afforded in certain circumstances by humanitarian law to citizens of a particular state vis-à-vis their own government * * * did not originate in the principle of reciprocity, but in that of humanity. The idea of humanity has become the common denominator of human rights law and of humanitarian law. The fact that these two systems of law have different historical and doctrinal origins must not deter us from realizing that a tremendous rapprochement has already taken place between them and that the trends point to an ever greater reliance on the shared idea of humanity.

---

24. This clause reads as follows:

Until a more complete code of the laws of war has been issued, the High Contracting Parties deem it expedient to declare that, in cases not included in the Regulations adopted by them, the inhabitants and the belligerents remain under the protection and the rule of the principles of the law of nations, as they result from the usages established among civilized peoples, from the laws of humanity, and the dictates of the public conscience.

* * *

1. *Some background to the My Lai Massacre.*

M. LIPPMAN, WAR CRIMES: THE MY LAI MASSACRE AND THE VIETNAM WAR

1 S.D.Just.J. 295, 299–319 (1993).

* * *

After C Company was alerted in mid–1967 that they would be sent to Vietnam, they underwent an accelerated training program, much of which was compressed * * * Although the company received routine training in the handling of prisoners, little emphasis was placed on the appropriate treatment of civilians or refugees or on the obligation to report war crimes and atrocities * * * [t]he soldiers had received only "marginal training in several key areas: (1) provisions of the General Conventions, (2) handling and safeguarding of non-combatants, and (3) rules of engagement."

Upon arriving in Vietnam, C Company received a month long indoctrination before being assigned in January 1968 to Task Force Barker, a specially constituted force * * * Task Force Barker was assigned to the northeast portion of Quang Ngai Province which was designated on the military maps as "Pinkville," adjacent to the North Vietnamese border. The five hundred man task force was faced with a daunting challenge—this was " 'indian country,' " meaning it was firmly under the control of the Viet Cong. Between January 22 and March 15, 1968, Task Force Barker suffered over one hundred friendly casualties, roughly forty percent of which occurred in the month of February. During the same period, the task force killed and wounded an estimated three hundred enemy soldiers, captured fifty combatants and seized roughly twenty weapons. * * *

Calley reported to Officer Candidate School (OCS) in March 1967, a year before the My Lai massacre, and graduated 120th out of a class of 156. He recounted that the overriding lesson taught at OCS was how to kill, with a jungle vine, knife and rifle. It was stressed that the important thing in Vietnam was to get a big kill ratio or body count. Calley learned that in " 'combat you haven't friends! You have enemies! * * * I told myself, I'll act as if I'm never secure. As if everyone in Vietnam would do me in. As if everyone's bad.' " * * *—all Vietnamese were the enemy. "Everyone there was VC. The old men, the women, the children—the babies were all VC or would be VC in about three years. And inside of VC women, I guess there were a thousand little VC now." Calley did not recognize complexity—he assumed that all orders were legal * * *

* * *

* * * The daily grind of search and destroy missions and life in the jungle took its toll. C Company encountered land mines and snipers and felt frustrated over their failure to directly engage the enemy. The men began to lash out, beating and abusing civilians and prisoners. Various soldiers were assigned by Medina to kill and torture prisoners. In one instance, Calley shot an elderly Vietnamese who had been dropped into a well by his men. Calley reported to Medina that the victim was a

Vietnamese sniper who had jumped into the well in order to avoid captivity. Eventually, even those who had initially objected to this brutality began to tolerate the violence. * * *

On February 25, six were killed and twelve were seriously wounded when C Company wandered into a minefield north of Pinkville. Many of the Americans blamed the villagers for having failed to alert them to the mines. The violence escalated—in one case, two platoon members raped a young woman and killed her baby. Calley was on leave at the time of the ambush and coincidentally found himself in a helicopter loaded with gear which had been retrieved from the ambush.

> The chopper was filled with gear, rifles, rucksacks * * *. There must have been six boots there with the feet still in them, brains all over the place and everything was just saturated with blood. I believe there was one arm on it and a piece of a man's face, half of man's face on the chopper with the gear.

By March 1968, murder, rape and arson had become commonplace. Many units ignored established policy and established "zippo squads," groups whose mission was to follow combat troops through the hamlets and to set them on fire. Few questions were raised over the fact that weapons were seldom recorded as having been seized from dead enemy soldiers. The suspicion was that these were civilian casualties. During a three-day operation in February, Task Force Barker reported having killed eighty Viet Cong and having recovered no weapons. In another February operation, seventy-five Viet Cong were reportedly killed and six weapons were captured. Ronald Grezesik, a member of Calley's platoon, later reflected that the platoon was caught in a vicious cycle which would later culminate in slaughter.

> It was like going from one step to another * * * [f]irst, you'd stop the people, question them, and let them go. Second, you'd stop the people, beat up an old man, and let them go. Third, you'd stop the people, beat up an old man, and then shoot him. Fourth, you go in and wipe out a village.

On March 14, two days before the My Lai mission, a small squad from the third platoon, C Company, wandered into a booby trap. George Cox, a popular sergeant, was killed and another GI lost his eyes, an arm and a leg. In retribution, the remaining squad members entered a nearby hamlet, stole a radio and killed a fifteen year old girl and stole her ring. Medina later justified their actions, explaining that the young girl had detonated the booby trap with a remote control device. Gregory Olsen, a devout Mormon, described the incident in a letter to his father: "It was murder, and I'm ashamed of myself for not trying to do anything about it. This isn't the first time * * *. My faith in my fellow men is shot to hell. I just want the time to pass and I just want to come home."

Journalist Richard Hammer writes that the men of C Company had been reduced to killers and thugs:

> In dehumanizing and depersonalizing the Vietnamese, the Americans had themselves become depersonalized and dehumanized, had become vultures on the land, scavengers, * * * leaving in their wake

nothing but death and destruction, and the hatred of those they had wronged. * * * like some horrible never-ending chain, they sensed hatred and fear of the Vietnamese toward Americans was translated into even deeper hatred and fear of Americans toward Vietnamese. So the mask of the killer was donned.

Despite this brutality, not a single member of Task Force Barker was court-martialed for an offense against Vietnamese civilians. By mid-March, Task Force Barker had been in the field for almost ten weeks without a respite. Fifteen GI's in the three company task force had been killed and eighty-five wounded. C Company of Task Force Barker soon would be presented with the opportunity [for] revenge.

B. THE MY LAI MASSACRE

Quang Ngai had been a center of nationalist sentiment. During the struggle against the French, it was a stronghold of Viet Minh strength. * * *

In March 1968, the United States' objective was to engage and to destroy the 48th Battalion of the North Vietnam Army (NVA) which reportedly was headquartered in Son My Village * * * Frustrated at their inability to attract support among the local population, the Americans determined that they would decimate the province. The United States military declared the area to be a "free fire zone," which meant that all targets and suspected targets could be freely attacked without obtaining prior approval. Tens of thousands of tons of bombs, rockets, napalm and artillery ordinance were poured into northeastern Quang Ngai between 1965–1967. Planes with excess ordinance frequently unloaded their bombs on any convenient target, and artillery fire was randomly fired into the area. By 1967, 138,000 civilians had been rendered homeless and about seventy percent of the dwellings in the province had been destroyed.

* * *

Medina also reportedly ordered his men to burn and destroy My Lai (4) and to kill the livestock and to destroy the foodstuffs. No instructions were issued as to the treatment of civilians. According to the Peers inquiry, a significant number of the men reported that Medina had "left little or no doubt" that all persons remaining in the vicinity of My Lai (4) "were enemy, and that C Company's mission was to destroy the enemy." Various witnesses also agreed that Medina made reference to the casualties which had been inflicted by enemy mines, booby traps and sniper fire and that he characterized the forthcoming operation as an opportunity to take revenge against the VC. The Peers inquiry concluded that "[i]n a very real sense ... it appears that the operation took the added aspect of a grudge match between C Company and an enemy force in My Lai." Medina also conceded that he had endeavored to work his men into a determined frenzy. He explained that he was attempting to build their morale and to give them the " 'psychological bread to go in and do battle with the 48th VC Battalion.' " Some sense of the mood of C Company is indicated by the question posed to Medina as to whether they should kill women and children. * * *

The platoons split into separate squads. All the participants could hear the continuous stream of weapons firing, and grenade rocket launchers exploding.

* * *

* * * English journalists Michael Bilton and Kevin Sim describe the impressions of Dennis Conti, who operated a mine sweeper:

> To Conti the men appeared all psyched up when they landed. The shooting, once it began, created almost a chain reaction * * *. Inside the village his comrades appeared out of control. Families had huddled together for safety in houses, in the yards and in bunkers only to be mown down with automatic weapon fire or blown apart by fragmentation grenades. Women and children were pushed into bunkers and grenades thrown in after them * * *. At one point, wandering off on his own, Conti found a woman aged about 20 with a 4–year–old child. He forced her to perform oral sex on him while he held a gun at the child's head, threatening to kill it. Just at that moment Calley happened along and angrily told him to pull on his pants and get over to where he was supposed to be.

C Company still had not yet received any enemy fire or had encountered any VC. At approximately 0830 hours, Captain Medina reported that the body count now had risen to eighty-four enemy dead. Only a few refused to participate in the brutalities or offered assistance to the Vietnamese. The only American injury in Calley's platoon was an American soldier who shot himself in the foot.

The atrocities escalated. Many GI's became " 'double veterans,' " slang for raping and murdering a Vietnamese woman. Many females reportedly were raped, sodomized, mutilated, and then had their vaginas torn open with knives or bayonets or blasted apart by rifle fire. Victims were stabbed, had their limbs cut off, or were beheaded. Others were scalped, had their tongues cut out or throats slit. Vietnamese were beaten, clubbed, bayoneted and were shot at point blank range. The signature " 'C Company' " or the shape of an Ace of Spades, a Vietnamese sign of bad luck, was carved into the chests of the dead.

The events which made My Lai infamous were now to unfold. Paul Meadlo was standing guard over a group of elderly people, young women and children. *[see decision, infra]* * * *

Dennis Conti corroborated Meadlo's testimony.

> Lieutenant Calley came out and said take care of these people. So we said, okay, so we stood there and watched them. He went away, then he came back and said, "I thought I told you to take care of these people." We said, "We are." He said, "I mean, kill them."
>
> So they—Calley and Meadlo—got on line and fired directly into the people. There were bursts and single shots for two minutes. It was automatic. The people screamed and yelled and fell * * *. The people were pretty well messed up. Lots of heads was shot off, pieces of heads and pieces of flesh flew off the sides and arms. Meadlo fired a little bit and broke down * * *. He gave his weapon

into my hands. I said I wouldn't. "If they're going to be killed, I'm not going to do it. Let Lieutenant Calley do it," I told him.

Conti reportedly wandered away and later saw Calley and Sergeant David Mitchell firing into a ditch.

I moved to the left to see what they were shooting at. It was a ditch and there were people there, and Calley and Mitchell were firing down into them. The fire * * * was both automatic and semi-automatic, single shots. A lot of them, the people, were trying to get up and mostly they was just screaming and pretty bad shot up.

The people were lying in the ditch right beneath Calley and Mitchell * * * and both men were holding their weapons at their shoulders and I could see muzzle flashes. I seen a woman tried to get up. I seen Lieutenant Calley fire. He hit the side of her head and blew it off.

Calley was not finished; Radio operator, Charles Sledge, testified.

We went up the ditch * * * we came upon a priest almost at the end of the ditch. At least I think he was a priest; he was dressed in white robes. Lieutenant Calley started to ask him some questions and the priest, he would fold his hands and bow his head and say, "No Viet, no Viet." Calley asked him a few more questions and he kept saying, "No Viet." Then Lieutenant Calley hit him with the butt of his rifle.

* * * His mouth was bleeding and then he fell back a little and folded his hands and, sort of like pleading. Lieutenant Calley took his rifle and point-blank pulled the trigger right in his face and blew half his head off. The priest fell. Half his head was blown away.

Sledge then testified that someone shouted that a child was running back toward the village. "* * * Calley ran back and grabbed the baby by one arm. I don't know whether it was a boy or a girl. He picked it up by one arm and threw it into the ditch, and shot it. He flung it into the ditch, the deep end of it. The child was maybe one or two. Calley fired one shot."

Calley, in an interview with journalist John Sack, explained his motivation. "As for me, killing those men in My Lai didn't haunt me. I didn't—I couldn't kill for the pleasure of it. We weren't in My Lai to kill human beings, really. We were there to kill ideology. That is carried by—I don't know. Pawns. Blobs. Pieces of flesh, and I wasn't in My Lai to destroy intelligent men. I was there to destroy an intangible idea [communism]. Those people are monsters, [they] have no qualms, no hang-ups, no holding-backs to the extremes they'll go to. I mean butcherings: that is what communism does, and we were there in My Lai to destroy it. Personally, I didn't kill any Vietnamese that day: I mean personally. I represented the United States of America. My country."

The Peers inquiry concluded that C Company killed between 175 and 200 Vietnamese. The Army Criminal Investigation Division (CID) estimated that the number of dead Vietnamese totaled 347. The company suffered only one self-inflicted injury. Only three or four of the dead Vietnamese were confirmed VC. Three enemy weapons and several sets of web gear and grenades were also captured. The inquiry concluded that there was no evidence that the company had received any enemy fire or had encountered any other form of resistance prior to or after entering My Lai (4).

————

Notes: 1. Standard applied in the Calley case. Should a soldier be convicted of murder (as opposed to, say, manslaughter) only if he *subjectively knew* that an order to kill was illegal? Or can he be convicted of murder even if he did not in his own mind know of its illegality but other soldiers knew it was illegal? Was Calley convicted because of what he knew or because of what other people knew? The debate in the opinions in the Calley case centers around what some other person would know: i.e. a person of ordinary sense and understanding, or a person of commonest understanding. Are all the judges saying that Calley can be found guilty, even though he didn't know subjectively, if the person meeting that standard would have known? Or is the standard some rule of evidence, e.g., since an individual of ordinary sense and understanding would know the order was illegal and since Calley is a man of ordinary sense and understanding, therefore Calley *"must have known"* the order was illegal?

In *Public Prosecutor v. Leopold,* Austria Supreme Court 1967, 47 Int'l L.Rep. 464 (1974), defendant was convicted of the murder of Poles and Jews, inmates of a labor camp in Poland during the Second World War. Defendant was a German S.S. deputy troop leader, a member of the guard at the labor camp, who claimed to be acting pursuant to orders. The defendant's appeal asserted, inter alia, that he was "unable, owing to his limited intelligence, to realize the criminal nature of the execution of an illegal order." In denying the appeal, the court stated:

> * * * [I]t must be said that orders to kill, given without previous proceedings, in respect of individual or groups of inmates of this labour camp could not even as a matter of form have any legal justification. They were therefore *straightaway recognizable as illegal.* Furthermore, the fact must be considered that orders to kill inmates of the labour camp, irrespective of their form and extent, which were *clearly recognizable by anybody as illegal,* could never have justified the person executing such orders but could only, in certain circumstances, have excused him from the point of view of absolute coercion (§ 2(g) Penal Code), that is, only if non-execution of such orders would have meant immediate danger to life for the person disregarding them. The reference in the appeal to the power of a commander under martial law to reinforce his orders, in face of the enemy, if necessary immediately by the use of his weapon (which incidentally—as is generally known—was only applied in the last phase of the Second World War), is out of place in this context, since

the defendant was not involved in belligerent action by a fighting unit but performed only a guarding function. [Emphasis supplied.]

UNITED STATES v. CALLEY

United States Court of Military Appeals, 1973.
48 C.–M.Rep. 19.

QUINN, Judge:

First Lieutenant Calley stands convicted of the premeditated murder of 22 infants, children, women, and old men, and of assault with intent to murder a child of about 2 years of age. All the killings and the assault took place on March 16, 1968 in the area of the village of My Lai in the Republic of South Vietnam. The Army Court of Military Review affirmed the findings of guilty and the sentence, which, as reduced by the convening authority, includes dismissal and confinement at hard labor for 20 years. The accused petitioned this Court for further review * * *

* * *

[Defendant's second assignment of error is that the evidence is insufficient to meet the reasonable doubt standard. Summary of pertinent evidence follows].

Lieutenant Calley was a platoon leader in C Company, a unit that was part of an organization known as Task Force Barker, whose mission was to subdue and drive out the enemy in an area in the Republic of Vietnam known popularly as Pinkville. Before March 16, 1968, this area, which included the village of My Lai 4, was a Viet Cong stronghold. C Company had operated in the area several times. Each time the unit had entered the area it suffered casualties by sniper fire, machine gun fire, mines, and other forms of attack. Lieutenant Calley had accompanied his platoon on some of the incursions.

On March 15, 1968, a memorial service for members of the company killed in the area during the preceding weeks was held. After the service Captain Ernest L. Medina, the commanding officer of C Company, briefed the company on a mission in the Pinkville area set for the next day. C Company was to serve as the main attack formation for Task Force Barker. In that role it would assault and neutralize My Lai 4, 5, and 6 and then mass for an assault on My Lai 1. Intelligence reports indicated that the unit would be opposed by a veteran enemy battalion, and that all civilians would be absent from the area. The objective was to destroy the enemy. Disagreement exists as to the instructions on the specifics of destruction.

Captain Medina testified that he instructed his troops that they were to destroy My Lai 4 by "burning the hootches, to kill the livestock, to close the wells and to destroy the food crops." Asked if women and children were to be killed, Medina said he replied in the negative, adding that, "You must use common sense. If they have a weapon and are trying to engage you, then you can shoot back, but you must use common sense." However, Lieutenant Calley testified that Captain Medina informed the troops they were to kill every living thing—men, women, children, and animals—and under no circumstances were they to leave any Vietnamese behind them as they passed through the villages enroute to their final objective. Other witnesses gave more or less support to both versions of the briefing.

On March 16, 1968, the operation began with interdicting fire. C Company was then brought to the area by helicopters. Lieutenant Calley's platoon was on the first lift. This platoon formed a defense perimeter until the remainder of the force was landed. The unit received no hostile fire from the village.

Calley's platoon passed the approaches to the village with his men firing heavily. Entering the village, the platoon encountered only unarmed, unresisting men, women, and children. The villagers, including infants held in their mothers' arms, were assembled and moved in separate groups to collection points. Calley testified that during this time he was radioed twice by Captain Medina, who demanded to know what was delaying the platoon. On being told that a large number of villagers had been detained, Calley said Medina ordered him to "waste them." Calley further testified that he obeyed the orders because he had been taught the doctrine of obedience throughout his military career. Medina denied that he gave any such order.

One of the collection points for the villagers was in the southern part of the village. There, Private First Class Paul D. Meadlo guarded a group of between 30 to 40 old men, women, and children. Lieutenant Calley approached Meadlo and told him, "You know what to do," and left. He returned shortly and asked Meadlo why the people were not yet dead. Meadlo replied he did not know that Calley had meant that they should be killed. Calley declared that he wanted them dead. He and Meadlo then opened fire on the group, until all but a few children fell. Calley then personally shot these children. He expended 4 or 5 magazines from his M–16 rifle in the incident.

Lieutenant Calley and Meadlo moved from this point to an irrigation ditch on the east side of My Lai 4. There, they encountered another group of civilians being held by several soldiers. Meadlo estimated that this group contained from 75 to 100 persons. Calley stated, "We got another job to do, Meadlo," and he ordered the group into the ditch. When all were in the ditch, Calley and Meadlo opened fire on them. Although ordered by Calley to shoot, Private First Class James J. Dursi refused to join in the killings, and Specialist Four Robert E. Maples refused to give his machine gun to Calley for use in the killings. Lieutenant Calley admitted that he fired into the ditch, with the muzzle of his weapon within 5 feet of people in it. He expended between 10 to 15 magazines of ammunition on this occasion.

With his radio operator, Private Charles Sledge, Calley moved to the north end of the ditch. There, he found an elderly Vietnamese monk, whom he interrogated. Calley struck the man with his rifle butt and then shot him in the head. Other testimony indicates that immediately afterwards a young child was observed running toward the village. Calley seized him by the arm, threw him into the ditch, and fired at him. Calley admitted interrogating and striking the monk, but denied shooting him. He also denied the incident involving the child.

Appellate defense counsel contend that the evidence is insufficient to establish the accused's guilt. They do not dispute Calley's participation in the homicides, but they argue that he did not act with the malice or mens rea essential to a conviction of murder; that the orders he received to kill everyone in the village were not palpably illegal; that he was acting in ignorance of the laws of war; that since he was told that only "the enemy" would be in the village, his honest belief that there were no innocent civilians in the village exonerates him of criminal responsibility for their deaths; and, finally, that his actions were in the heat of passion caused by reasonable provocation.

* * *

The testimony of Meadlo and others provided the court members with ample evidence from which to find that Lieutenant Calley directed and personally participated in the intentional killing of men, women, and children, who were unarmed and in the custody of armed soldiers of C Company. If the prosecution's witnesses are believed, there is also ample evidence to support a finding that the accused deliberately shot the Vietnamese monk whom he interrogated, and that he seized, threw into a ditch, and fired on a child with the intent to kill.

Enemy prisoners are not subject to summary execution * * *. Military law has long held that the killing of an unresisting prisoner is murder. * * * "While it is lawful to kill an enemy 'in the heat and exercise of war,' yet 'to kill such an enemy after he has laid down his arms * * * is murder.' "

Conceding for the purposes of this assignment of error that Calley believed the villagers were part of "the enemy," the uncontradicted evidence is that they were under the control of armed soldiers and were offering no resistance. In his testimony, Calley admitted he was aware of the requirement that prisoners be treated with respect. He also admitted he knew that the normal practice was to interrogate villagers, release those who could satisfactorily account for themselves, and evacuate the suspect among them for further examination. Instead of proceeding in the usual way, Calley executed all, without regard to age, condition, or possibility of suspicion. On the evidence, the court-martial could reasonably find Calley guilty of the offenses before us.

At trial, Calley's principal defense was that he acted in execution of Captain Medina's order to kill everyone in My Lai 4. Appellate defense counsel urge this defense as the most important factor in assessment of the legal sufficiency of the evidence. The argument, however, is inapplicable to whether the evidence is *legally* sufficient. Captain Medina denied that he issued any such order, either during the previous day's briefing or on the date the killings were carried out. Resolution of the conflict between his testimony and that of the accused was for the triers of the facts. The general finding of guilty, with exceptions as to the number of persons killed, does not indicate whether the court members found that Captain Medina did not issue the alleged order to kill, or whether, if he did, the court members believed that the accused knew the order was illegal. For the purpose of the legal sufficiency of the evidence, the record supports the findings of guilty.

In the third assignment of error, appellate defense counsel assert gross deficiencies in the military judge's instructions to the court members. Only two assertions merit discussion. One contention is that the judge should have, but did not, advise the court members of the necessity to find the existence of "malice aforethought" in connection with the murder charges; the second allegation is that the defense of compliance with superior orders was not properly submitted to the court members.

The existence vel non of malice, say appellate defense counsel, is the factor that distinguishes murder from manslaughter. * * *

* * * In enactment of the Uniform Code of Military Justice, Congress eliminated malice as an element of murder by codifying the common circumstances under which that state of mind was deemed to be present. * * * One of the stated purposes of the Code was the "listing and definition of offenses, redrafted and rephrased in modern legislative language." That purpose was accomplished by defining murder as the unlawful killing of a human being, without justification or excuse. * * *

The trial judge delineated the elements of premeditated murder for the court members in accordance with the statutory language. He instructed them that to convict Lieutenant Calley, they must be convinced beyond a reasonable doubt that the victims were dead; that their respective deaths resulted from specified acts of the accused; that the killings were unlawful; and that Calley acted with a premeditated design to kill. The judge defined accurately the meaning of an unlawful killing and the meaning of a "premeditated design to kill." These instructions comported fully with requirements of existing law for the offense of premeditated murder, and neither statute nor judicial precedent requires that reference also be made to the pre-Code concept of malice.

We turn to the contention that the judge erred in his submission of the defense of superior orders to the court. After fairly summarizing the evidence, the judge gave the following instructions pertinent to the issue:

> The killing of resisting or fleeing enemy forces is generally recognized as a justifiable act of war, and you may consider any such killings justifiable in this case. The law attempts to protect those persons not actually engaged in warfare, however; and limits the circumstances under which their lives may be taken.
>
> Both combatants captured by and noncombatants detained by the opposing force, regardless of their loyalties, political views, or prior acts, have the right to be treated as prisoners until released, confined, or executed, in accordance with law and established procedures, by competent authority sitting in judgment of such detained or captured individuals. Summary execution of detainees or prisoners is forbidden by law. Further, it's clear under the evidence presented in this case, that hostile acts or support of the enemy

North Vietnamese or Viet Cong forces by inhabitants of My Lai (4) at some time prior to 16 March 1968, would not justify the summary execution of all or a part of the occupants of My Lai (4) on 16 March, nor would hostile acts committed that day, if, following the hostility, the belligerents surrendered or were captured by our forces. I therefore instruct you, as a matter of law, that if unresisting human beings were killed at My Lai (4) while within the effective custody and control of our military forces, their deaths cannot be considered justified, and any order to kill such people would be, as a matter of law, an illegal order. Thus, if you find that Lieutenant Calley received an order directing him to kill unresisting Vietnamese within his control or within the control of his troops, *that order would be an illegal order.*

A determination that an order is illegal does not, of itself, assign criminal responsibility to the person following the order for acts done in compliance with it. Soldiers are taught to follow orders, and special attention is given to obedience of orders on the battlefield. Military effectiveness depends upon obedience to orders. On the other hand, the obedience of a soldier is not the obedience of an automaton. A soldier is a reasoning agent, obliged to respond, not as a machine, but as a person. The law takes these factors into account in assessing criminal responsibility for acts done in compliance with illegal orders.

The acts of a subordinate done in compliance with an unlawful order given him by his superior are excused and impose no criminal liability upon him unless the superior's order is one which a man of *ordinary sense and understanding* would, under the circumstances, know to be unlawful, or if the order in question is actually known to the accused to be unlawful.

* * *

* * * In determining what orders, if any, Lieutenant Calley acted under, if you find him to have acted, you should consider all of the matters which he has testified reached him and which you can infer from other evidence that he saw and heard. Then, unless you find beyond a reasonable doubt that he was not acting under orders directing him in substance and effect to kill unresisting occupants of My Lai (4), you must determine whether Lieutenant Calley actually knew those orders to be unlawful.

* * * In determining whether or not Lieutenant Calley had knowledge of the unlawfulness of any order found by you to have been given, you may consider all relevant facts and circumstances, including Lieutenant Calley's rank; educational background; OCS schooling; other training while in the Army, including basic training, and his training in Hawaii and Vietnam; his experience on prior operations involving contact with hostile and friendly Vietnamese; his age; and any other evidence tending to prove or disprove that on 16 March 1968, Lieutenant Calley knew the order was unlawful. If you find beyond a reasonable doubt, on the basis of all the evidence, that *Lieutenant Calley actually knew* the order under which he asserts he operated was unlawful, the fact that the order was given operates as no defense.

Unless you find beyond reasonable doubt that the accused acted with actual knowledge that the order was unlawful, you must proceed to determine whether, under the circumstances, *a man of ordinary sense and understanding would have known the order was unlawful. Your deliberations on this question do not focus on Lieutenant Calley and the manner in which he perceived the legality of the order found to have been given him. The standard is that of a man of ordinary sense and understanding under the circumstances.*

Think back to the events of 15 and 16 March 1968. * * * Then determine, in light of all the surrounding circumstances, whether the order, which to reach this point you will have found him to be operating in accordance with, is one which a man of ordinary sense and understanding would know to be unlawful. Apply this to each charged act which you have found Lieutenant Calley to have committed. Unless you are satisfied from the evidence, beyond a reasonable doubt, that a man of ordinary sense and understanding would have known the order to be unlawful, you must acquit Lieutenant Calley for committing acts done in accordance with the order. (Emphasis added.)

Appellate defense counsel contend that these instructions are prejudicially erroneous in that they require the court members to determine that Lieutenant Calley knew that an order to kill human beings in the circumstances under which he killed was illegal by the standard of whether "a man of ordinary sense and understanding" would know the order was illegal. They urge us to adopt as the governing test whether the order is so palpably or manifestly illegal that a person of "the commonest understanding" would be aware of its illegality. They maintain the standard stated by the judge is too strict and unjust; that it confronts members of the armed forces who are not persons of ordinary sense and understanding with the dilemma of choosing between the penalty of death for disobedience of an order in time of war on the one hand and the equally serious punishment for obedience on the other. Some thoughtful commentators on military law have presented much the same argument.

The "ordinary sense and understanding" standard is set forth in the present Manual for Courts–Martial, United States, 1969 (Rev.) and was the standard accepted by this Court in United States v. Schultz; and United States v. Keenan. It appeared as early as 1917. Manual for Courts–Martial, U.S. Army, 1917, paragraph 442. Apparently, it originated in a quotation from F. Wharton, Homicide § 485 (3d ed. 1907). Wharton's authority is Riggs v. State (Tenn.1866), in which the court approved a charge to the jury as follows: "[I]n its substance being clearly illegal, so that a man of ordinary sense and understanding would know as soon as he heard the order read or given that such order was illegal, would afford a private no protection for a crime committed under such order."

* * *

In the stress of combat, a member of the armed forces cannot reasonably be expected to make a refined legal judgment and be held criminally responsible if he guesses wrong on a question as to which there may be considerable disagreement. But there is no disagreement as to the illegality of the order to kill in this case. For 100 years, it has been a settled rule of American law that even in war the summary killing of an enemy, who has submitted to, and is under, effective physical control, is murder. Appellate defense counsel acknowledge that rule of law and its continued viability, but they say that Lieutenant Calley should not be held accountable for the men, women and children he killed because the court-martial could have found that he was a person of "commonest understanding" and such a person might not know what our law provides; that his captain had ordered him to kill these unarmed and submissive people and he only carried out that order as a good disciplined soldier should.

Whether Lieutenant Calley was the most ignorant person in the United States Army in Vietnam, or the most intelligent, he must be presumed to know that he could not kill the people involved here. The U.S. Supreme Court has pointed out that "[t]he rule that 'ignorance of the law will not excuse' [a positive act that constitutes a crime] * * * is deep in our law." Lambert v. California. An order to kill infants and unarmed civilians who were so demonstrably incapable of resistance to the armed might of a military force as were those killed by Lieutenant Calley is, in my opinion, so palpably illegal that whatever conceptional difference there may be between a person of "commonest understanding" and a person of "common understanding," that difference could not have had any "impact on a court of lay members receiving the respective wordings in instructions," as appellate defense counsel contend. In my judgment, there is no possibility of prejudice to Lieutenant Calley in the trial judge's reliance upon the established standard of excuse of criminal conduct, rather than the standard of "commonest understanding" presented by the defense, or by the new variable test postulated in the dissent, which, with the inclusion of such factors for consideration as grade and experience, would appear to exact a higher standard of understanding from Lieutenant Calley than that of the person of ordinary understanding.

In summary, as reflected in the record, the judge was capable and fair, and dedicated to assuring the accused a trial on the merits as provided by law; his instructions on all issues were comprehensive and correct. * * *

The decision of the Court of Military Review is affirmed.

DUNCAN, Judge (concurring in the result):

My difference of opinion from Judge Quinn's view of the defense of obedience to orders is narrow. The issue of obedience to orders was raised in defense by the evidence. Contrary to Judge Quinn, I do not consider that a presumption arose that the appellant knew he could not kill the people involved. The Government, as I see it, is not entitled to a presumption of what the appellant knew of the illegality of an order. It is a matter for the factfinders under proper instructions.

Paragraph 216, Manual for Courts–Martial, United States, 1969 (Rev.), provides for special defenses: excuse because of accident or misadventure; self-defense; entrapment; coercion or duress; physical or financial inability; and obedience to apparently lawful orders. Subparagraph *d* of paragraph 216 [reads]:

> An order requiring the performance of a military duty may be inferred to be legal. An act performed manifestly beyond the scope of authority, or pursuant to an order that a man of ordinary sense and understanding would know to be illegal, or in a wanton manner in the discharge of a lawful duty, is not excusable.

The military judge clearly instructed the members pursuant to this provision of the Manual. The heart of the issue is whether, under the circumstances of this case, he should have abandoned the Manual standard and fashioned another. The defense urges a purely subjective standard; the dissent herein yet another. * * *

* * *

Perhaps a new standard, such as the dissent suggests, has merit; however, I would leave that for the legislative authority or for the cause where the record demonstrates harm from the instructions given. I perceive none in this case. The general verdict in this case implies that the jury believed a man of ordinary sense and understanding would have known the order in question to be illegal.[4] Even conceding arguendo that this issue should have been resolved under instructions requiring a finding that almost every member of the armed forces would have immediately recognized that the order was unlawful, as well as a finding that as a consequence of his age, grade, intelligence, experience, and training, Lieutenant Calley should have recognized the order's illegality, I do not believe the result in this case would have been different.

* * *

DARDEN, Chief Judge (dissenting):

Although the charge the military judge gave on the defense of superior orders was not inconsistent with the Manual treatment of this subject, I believe the Manual provision is too strict in a combat environment. Among other things, this standard permits serious punishment of persons whose training and attitude incline them either to be enthusiastic about compliance with orders or not to challenge the authority of their superiors. The standard also permits conviction of members who are not persons of ordinary sense and understanding.

* * *

The test of palpable illegality to the commonest understanding properly balances punishment for the obedience of an obviously illegal order against protection to an accused for following his elementary duty of obeying his superiors. Such a test reinforces the need for obedience as an essential element of military discipline by broadly protecting the

---

4. This assumes that the jury found that the order the appellant contends he obeyed was given.

soldier who has been effectively trained to look to his superiors for direction. It also promotes fairness by permitting the military jury to consider the particular accused's intelligence, grade, training, and other elements directly related to the issue of whether he should have known an order was illegal. Finally, that test imputes such knowledge to an accused not as a result of simple negligence but on the much stronger circumstantial concept that almost anyone in the armed forces would have immediately recognized that the order was palpably illegal.

I would adopt this standard as the correct instruction for the jury when the defense of superior orders is in issue. Because the original case language is archaic and somewhat ungrammatical, I would rephrase it to require that the military jury be instructed that, despite his asserted defense of superior orders, an accused may be held criminally accountable for his acts, allegedly committed pursuant to such orders, if the court members are convinced beyond a reasonable doubt (1) that almost every member of the armed forces would have immediately recognized that the order was unlawful, and (2) that the accused should have recognized the order's illegality as a consequence of his age, grade, intelligence, experience, and training.

* * *

In the instant case, Lieutenant Calley's testimony placed the defense of superior orders in issue even though he conceded that he knew prisoners were normally to be treated with respect and that the unit's normal practice was to interrogate Vietnamese villagers, release those who could account for themselves, and evacuate those suspected of being a part of the enemy forces. Although crucial parts of his testimony were sharply contested, according to Lieutenant Calley, (1) he had received a briefing before the assault in which he was instructed that every living thing in the village was to be killed, including women and children; (2) he was informed that speed was important in securing the village and moving forward; (3) he was ordered that under no circumstances were any Vietnamese to be allowed to stay behind the lines of his forces; (4) the residents of the village who were taken into custody were hindering the progress of his platoon in taking up the position it was to occupy; and (5) when he informed Captain Medina of this hindrance, he was ordered to kill the villagers and to move his platoon to a proper position.

In addition to the briefing, Lieutenant Calley's experience in the Pinkville area caused him to know that, in the past, when villagers had been left behind his unit, the unit had immediately received sniper fire from the rear as it pressed forward. Faulty intelligence apparently led him also to believe that those persons in the village were not innocent civilians but were either enemies or enemy sympathizers. For a participant in the My Lai operation, the circumstances that could have obtained there may have caused the illegality of alleged orders to kill civilians to be much less clear than they are in a hindsight review.

Since the defense of superior orders was not submitted to the military jury under what I consider to be the proper standard, I would grant Lieutenant Calley a rehearing.

———

Notes: 1. ***Further proceedings in the Calley case.*** In Calley v. Callaway, 382 F.Supp. 650 (M.D.Ga.1974), Calley was ordered released on habeas corpus because of pretrial publicity. This was reversed, 519 F.2d 184 (5th Cir.1975), cert. denied sub. nom. Calley v. Hoffman, 425 U.S. 911 (1976). While these cases were in process, Calley was first paroled by the United States Army and then released on bail by the District Court in November 1974, pending appeal. After the Supreme Court denied certiorari, the United States Army announced in April 1976 that it would not seek to return Calley to custody for the remaining ten days of his sentence (previously reduced). *See* The New York Times, Nov. 9, 1974, p. 1; Nov. 10, 1974, p. 1; Sept. 11, 1975, p. 26; Apr. 6, 1976, p. 1.

2. In Calley's appeal, he argued that the deaths of the villagers at My Lai were not "legally requitable in that the villagers had no right to continued life cognizable in our law." His argument was founded on the claim that the villagers' support and sympathy for the Viet–Cong was so complete and extensive that they were not entitled to "civilian status." He simultaneously argued that they were not entitled to irregular belligerent status, which would allow them protection of the Geneva POW Convention. *See,* Geneva Convention Relative to the Treatment of Prisoners of War, 12 Aug. 1949, 6 UST 3316 (1956). The Court of Military Appeals rejected Calley's arguments: "[Even if it were true that some of the villagers may have sympathized with and assisted the Viet–Cong, this does not justify killing] 'infants in arms or children of toddler age * * *.' [Moreover, summary executions of 'irregular combatants' may not be condoned], whether an armed conflict be a local uprising or a global war, summary executions as in My Lai (4) are not justifiable * * *." Discussed in Matthew Lippman, War Crimes, *supra* at 320.

INDIVIDUAL CRIMINAL RESPONSIBILITY IN THE STATUTE FOR THE AD HOC TRIBUNAL FOR THE PROSECUTION OF PERSONS RESPONSIBLE FOR SERIOUS VIOLATIONS OF INTERNATIONAL HUMANITARIAN LAW IN THE TERRITORY OF THE FORMER YUGOSLAVIA

Article 7 of the Secretary General's Statute provides for individual criminal responsibility. It reads:

    1. A person who planned, instigated, ordered, committed or otherwise aided and abetted in the planning, preparation or execution of a crime referred to in articles 2 to 5 of the present Statute, shall be individually responsible for the crime.

    2. The official position of any accused person, whether as Head of State or Government or as a responsible Government official, shall not relieve such person of criminal responsibility nor mitigate punishment.

    3. The fact that any of the acts referred to in articles 2 to 5 of the present Statute was committed by a subordinate does not relieve

his superior of criminal responsibility if he knew or had reason to know that the subordinate was about to commit such acts or had done so and the superior failed to take the necessary and reasonable measures to prevent such acts or to punish the perpetrators thereof.

4. The fact that an accused person acted pursuant to an order of a Government or of a superior shall not relieve him of criminal responsibility, but may be considered in mitigation of punishment if the International Tribunal determines that justice so requires.

C. BLAKESLEY, OBSTACLES TO THE CREATION OF A PERMANENT WAR CRIMES TRIBUNAL

18 The Fletch. Forum of World Affairs 77, 93–96 (1994).

Defenses:[1] [Head of State immunity or immunity for acts of government officials or for acts done in an official capacity will not constitute a defense to criminality or even a mitigating factor. Political leaders or other officials, therefore, may be held responsible for giving orders to commit an offense. Liability for criminal negligence is also imposed on a person in a position of superior authority who knew or had reason to know that his or her subordinates were about to commit an offense under the statute and who failed to take whatever action was necessary and reasonable to prevent, deter, or to repress the commission of such crimes by subordinates. On this standard, see, e.g., Jordan J. Paust, My Lai and Vietnam: Norms, Myths and Leader Responsibility, 57 Mil.L.Rev. 99, 147–83 (1972), and the numerous cases cited therein. The Report talks of "imputed responsibility or criminal negligence." The same would be true in case of failure to punish those who had committed such an offense. Moreover, Superior Orders is not a defense, but may be considered a mitigating factor, "should the Tribunal determine that justice so requires." The superior *orders defense* acknowledges that soldiers must obey their superiors.[2] Obviously, if superior officers have the power to inflict punishment, pain or death on a soldier who refuses to obey, duress may be involved, although *duress* is actually a separate defense. In addition, the ABA Task Force on the Ad Hoc Tribunal for the former Yugoslavia recommended that superior orders should be a legitimate defense if "a defendant acting under military authority in armed conflict did not know the orders to be unlawful and a person of ordinary sense and understanding would not have known the orders to be unlawful." It is hard to conceive, however, of a situation in which the grave breaches covered by the statute of a war crimes tribunal would not be understood to be illegal.]

Duress is traditionally a separate defense from superior orders. It would likely be considered only a mitigating factor when combined with the superior orders defense, where superior orders are conjoined with

1. These defenses are detailed and analyzed in A. D'Amato, "National Prosecution for International Crimes," in M. Cherif Bassiouni, ed., 3 International Criminal Law (1987), 169, 172–78.

2. On the superior orders defense, see gen., Dinstein, The Defense of Superior Orders.

circumstances of coercion or lack of moral choice. Other standard criminal law defenses, such as minimum age or mental incapacity, for example, would be determined by the Tribunal itself. Certainly, criminal liability would obtain for complicity in such crimes.

In the case of the former Yugoslavia, the ABA Task Force has recommended that mitigation due to duress should be the *only* type of mitigation allowed under superior orders. This recommendation is sound, but as duress is a distinct defense, it should be separated from the superior orders defense. The mistake-of-law type of superior orders defense should be eliminated and duress retained. It is true that the aspect of the superior orders defense that gives rise to the lack of "moral choice" is a duress-like defense. This relationship was recognized at the Nuremberg Trial, although literally excluded in the London Charter. A second aspect or type of superior orders defense is that based on "ignorance of the illegality." The U.S. Military Field Manual formulates its mistake-based superior orders defense on that basis. Should both types of defense be allowed if a war crimes tribunal were created, or should only duress be allowed as the ABA suggests?

COMMENT, PUNISHMENT FOR WAR CRIMES: DUTY OR DISCRETION?

69 Michigan Law Review 1312 (1971).*

* * * Immediately prior to the adoption of the 1949 Conventions, it was remarked in reference to one of these earlier conventions that "[i]t is one of the greatest weaknesses of the existing rules on prisoners of war that they do not contain definite and written provisions on sanctions." In view of such criticisms and the ad hoc measures taken to deal with the war crimes of World War II, negotiators in 1949 agreed that specific provisions for punishment of breaches of the new Conventions were essential. Accordingly, each of the Four Conventions adopted in 1949 contained an article requiring each Party to "enact any legislation necessary to provide effective penal sanctions for persons committing * * * grave breaches" of the Conventions. * * *

Although granted a writ of immunity from military prosecution by the Commanding General of Fort Benning, Georgia, where the trial by court-martial of Lieutenant Calley was conducted, Meadlo consistently refused to testify until the Government issued a federal immunity order protecting him from civilian prosecution. Finally, under threat of arrest for further refusal to testify after having been granted federal *immunity,* Meadlo took the witness stand on January 11, 1971. Ten days later, Assistant United States Attorney General *William H. Rehnquist* struck a disquieting note that has been overlooked in the wake of the Calley conviction: Has the United States violated its treaty obligation under the 1949 Geneva Conventions to prosecute those persons accused of

* Reprinted by permission of the Michigan Law Review.

"grave breaches" of the Conventions by granting immunity to a confessed participant in the My Lai slayings?

* * *

Notes & Questions: Did the U.S. not have legislation sufficient to allow effectual penal sanctions? Can compliance with a treaty require elimination of constitutional protection? Could the U.S. enter into a treaty which allows infringement of constitutional rights of U.S. citizens? Could the U.S. enter into a treaty creating an International Criminal Court, wherein defendants (including U.S. nationals) would be tried under circumstances which do not comport with the U.S. Constitution? *See* Blakesley, *Obstacles to the Creation of a Permanent War Crimes Tribunal, supra.*

BISHOP, JUSTICE UNDER FIRE 290 (1974) *

* * * All of the Geneva Conventions obligate each signatory power to search for persons alleged to have committed "grave breaches" of those Conventions and to "bring such persons, regardless of their nationality, before its own courts." There is still too little precedent for such enforcement of the law of war. I know of no instance in which * * * any * * * totalitarian government has ever accused a member of its own forces of a violation of the Geneva Conventions or any other war crime. But the most recent available figures show that, as of April, 1971, American courts-martial had tried 117 servicemen and convicted 60 on charges of murdering civilians in Vietnam; an unknown, but probably larger, number had been tried for lesser offenses, such as rape and robbery, against civilians. Murder and other violence against the persons of noncombatants or captured enemies violate the Geneva Conventions, but they are also, of course, violations of the Uniform Code of Military Justice and have been charged as such. The main practical difference is that trial by court-martial for a violation of the Code guarantees the accused procedural protections and appellate review to which he might not be entitled if he were tried by a military commission for a war crime.

Some of the acquittals were probably unjustified, and in at least one case, that of Captain Ernest Medina, the acquittal may have been based on the military judge's erroneous instruction that Medina had no responsibility for the My Lai massacre unless he had "actual knowledge" of it: as laid down by the Supreme Court in General Yamashita's case, the law is that a commander is responsible for war crimes committed by his subordinates if he knew, *or should have known,* that they were going on and failed to do what he could to prevent or punish them. It is also safe to assume that many war crimes committed by Americans have never been investigated, tried, or punished. The Pentagon has not shown much enthusiasm for investigating the possible failures of commanders

---

* Reprinted by permission of Joseph W. Bishop, Jr.

884   INDIVIDUAL RESPONSIBILITY   Ch. 11

at divisional and higher levels to take adequate measures to prevent and punish war crimes. Moreover, the Department of Justice seems to [have taken] the position that an honorably discharged serviceman cannot be tried for a war crime committed prior to his discharge. The Supreme Court did hold some years ago that such a discharged soldier could not be tried for an ordinary offense—i.e., one that was not a war crime—committed prior to his discharge. But it had earlier held, in World War II, that a Nazi saboteur who was an American civilian could constitutionally be tried by a military commission for a war crime, and it did not overrule that decision. I am myself of the opinion (though I seem to be in the minority) that a discharged serviceman *can* be tried by a military court on a charge of violating the law of war. In any case, Congress could and should give the federal courts jurisdiction to try such cases: under the Geneva Conventions, in fact, the United States is obligated to "enact any legislation necessary to provide effective penal sanctions" for * * * "grave breaches."

The record is thus very far from perfect. All that can be said is that it is a better record than that of any other nation in the world and that it lends a degree of credibility to the Pentagon's numerous orders and regulations that aim to prevent and punish war crimes by requiring a report and an investigation of such incidents, and the training and indoctrination of the troops on the subject.

* * *

Query: If the obligation is "to prosecute" will it suffice to allow a U.S. prosecutor simply to decide whether or not to go forward with a case? Could the U.S. require more?

Notes: Study the law of land warfare, United States Department of the Army Field Manual. [FM 27–10] at 4 (1956) (as amended by Change No. 1, 1976), in the Doc.Supp.

* * *

1. *Atomic weapons.* Paragraph 35 of the Army Field Manual in the Doc.Supp. asserts that the use of explosive atomic weapons cannot as such be regarded as violative of international law in the absence of any customary rule of international law or international convention restricting their employment. Compare this bald statement with the specific prohibitions that are recognized in the manual: against so-called dum-dum bullets (paragraph 34), poison (paragraph 37), and chemical and bacteriological weapons (paragraph 38). Why are atomic weapons not included among these groups? Paragraph 34 states that the prohibition against the use of arms calculated to cause unnecessary suffering does not extend to the use of explosives contained in artillery projectiles, mines, rockets, or hand grenades. Are atomic weapons to be considered as only a new form of explosive device comparable to such devices?

State practice for over fifty years has been *not* to use atomic weapons in battle. If state practice is some test of a customary rule of international law, it should be noted that the only *use* of atomic weapons was the two explosions in Japan ending World War II, before the destructive capacity of the atomic bomb and its collateral consequences were fully appreciated. Further, the policy of the atomic superpowers has been based, not upon a claimed lawful first use of atomic weapons, but upon the development of a second strike capacity in response to a first use. The Russians recently indicated that they might consider a first use under certain circumstances.

Richard Falk argues that any use of nuclear weapons is illegal. *Is this argument naive, utopian and irrelevant to the real world? Or is it quintessentially practical?* Trimble counters that Falk argues that "[t]he effects of nuclear weapons are the 'functional equivalent' of the effects of chemical and biological weapons, therefore nuclear weapons are illegal by virtue of various, prenuclear agreements prohibiting the use of chemical and biological weapons. *The use of international law for this argument is neither normative nor persuasive.*" (emphasis ours). *Is this criticism well taken?* Do the development of nuclear weapons and the subsequent international agreements relating to possession and testing indicate that the states-parties sanction the possession and certain uses? *What impact do nonproliferation treaties have on this? Does the existence of nonproliferation treaties suggest that the nations holding the weapons consider them to be unacceptable?*

Nuclear nations have claimed that earlier treaties on chemical, biological, and other prohibited weapons were not intended to cover *all* new forms of warfare and weaponry. Nonproliferation treaties have been used to prevent nations from obtaining nuclear weapons. Many nations have not wanted anything to do with nuclear weapons. Some who have the weapons wish to get rid of them. What should be the U.S. position today, now that access to developing or purchasing nuclear weapons is more readily available to other nations or groups? What is the international law? What should it be?

2. *Reprisals.* The description of the law of reprisals in Paragraph 497 of the Army Field Manual should be considered in the light of the material in Chapters 16 and 17 on the law governing the use of force. That the manual's use of the term refers only to the conduct of war rather than to the instigation of war itself is suggested by the following.

———

REPRISALS

Starke, Introduction to International Law 499 (9th ed. 1984).*

Reprisals are methods adopted by states for securing redress from another state by taking retaliatory measures. Formerly, the term was restricted to the seizure of property or persons, but [today it] connotes coercive measures adopted by one state against another for the purpose of settling some dispute brought about by the latter's illegal or unjustified conduct. The distinction between reprisals and retorsion is that reprisals consist of acts which would generally otherwise be quite illegal whereas retorsion consists of retaliatory conduct to which no legal objection can be taken. Reprisals may assume various forms—boycott of

* Reprinted with the permission of Butterworth's, London.

the goods of a particular state, an embargo, a naval demonstration, or bombardment. Few topics of international practice are more controversial than that of reprisals, and this was well illustrated in 1973–1974 when the Arab oil producing states introduced an oil export embargo as to certain states of destination; the views expressed on the legality or illegality of this embargo were irreconcilable, and are indicative of the extent to which the law in this respect is unsettled.

It is now generally established by international practice that a reprisal is only justified, if at all, where the state against which it is directed has been guilty of conduct in the nature of an international delinquency. Moreover, a reprisal would not be justified if the delinquent state had not been previously requested to give satisfaction for the wrong done, or if the measures of reprisals were "excessive" proportionately in relation to the injury suffered. There have been several vivid illustrations of purported reprisal action by states, for example the expulsion of Hungarians from Yugoslavia in 1935, in alleged retaliation for Hungarian responsibility for the murder of King Alexander of Yugoslavia at Marseilles, and the shelling of the Spanish port of Almeria by German warships in 1937, as reprisal for an alleged bombardment of the battleship Deutschland by a Spanish aircraft belonging to the Spanish Republican forces.

Some authorities hold that reprisals are only justified if their purpose is to bring about a satisfactory settlement of a dispute. Hence the principle referred to above that reprisals should not be resorted to unless and until negotiations for the purpose of securing redress from the delinquent state fail.

Strictly speaking, retaliatory acts between belligerent states in the course of a war are a different matter altogether from reprisals, although they also are termed "reprisals". The object of such acts is generally to force an opponent state to stop breaking the laws of war; as, for example, in 1939–1940, when Great Britain commenced the seizure of German exports on neutral vessels in retaliation for the unlawful sinking of merchant ships by German-sown naval magnetic mines. No less than peace-time reprisals, the topic of reprisals as between belligerents is the subject of deep controversy, as reflected in the acute division of views on the matter at the Sessions in 1974–1977 of the Diplomatic Conference at Geneva on the Reaffirmation and Development of International Humanitarian Law Applicable in Armed Conflicts * * *.

As in the case of retorsion, the use of reprisals by member states of the United Nations has been affected by the Charter. Not only is there paragraph 3 of article 2 mentioned above in connection with retorsion, but there is also the provision in paragraph 4 of the same article that member states are to refrain from the threat or use of force against the territorial integrity or political independence of any state, or in any other manner inconsistent with the Purposes of the United Nations. Also, the Declaration on Principles of International Law Concerning Friendly Relations and Co-operation Among States in Accordance with the United Nations Charter, adopted by the General Assembly on 24 October 1970, expressly declares: "States have a duty to refrain from acts of reprisal involving the use of force". The United Nations Security Council had earlier, in 1964, by a majority, condemned reprisals as being "incompatible with the Purposes and Principles of the United Nations". A reprisal, therefore, being an act otherwise than for the purpose of lawful defence, under article 51 of the United Nations Charter, against armed attack, and which consisted in the threat or the exercise of military force against another state in such a way as to prejudice its territorial integrity, or political independence would presumably be illegal. Moreover under article 33 the states parties to a dispute, the continuance of which is likely to endanger peace and security are "first of all" to seek a solution by negotiation, and other peaceful means. Thus a resort to force by way of retaliation would seemingly be excluded as illegal.

JURISDICTION & WAR CRIMES
MATTER OF DEMJANJUK

United States District Court, N.D.Ohio, 1985.
603 F.Supp. 1468.

[Israel requested the extradition of Demjanjuk, a Ukranian who had become a naturalized American citizen in 1958, *charging him with having murdered tens of thousands of Jews and non-Jews while operating the gas chambers to exterminate prisoners at the Treblinka concentration camp in Poland in 1942.* The history of Demjanjuk's denaturalization and deportation proceedings and the disposition of Israel's extradition request are in *Demjanjuk v. Petrovsky,* 776 F.2d 571 (6th Cir.1985). The disposition of the extradition request required consideration of the question of the subject matter jurisdiction with respect to *war crimes.*]

BATTISTI, Chief Judge.

ON JURISDICTION

* * * [*Issue:*] "Whether a United States civilian court has subject-matter jurisdiction in an extradition proceeding where the crimes alleged occurred during wartime or whether only a properly constituted military tribunal has jurisdiction over alleged war crimes?" * * *

On February 21, 1985, * * * this Court found that it had subject matter jurisdiction to hear and decide the instant extradition proceeding. This opinion more fully presents the reasons for that decision.

I.

Throughout the briefing and argument of this case, respondent has referred to the question of military tribunals as a "jurisdictional issue". At times, this term has caused confusion because 18 U.S.C. § 3184 explicitly grants jurisdiction to federal courts in extradition proceedings.[1]

---

1. 18 U.S.C. § 3184 reads in pertinent part: Whenever there is a treaty or convention for extradition between the United States and any foreign government, any justice or judge of the United States, or any magistrate authorized so to do by a court of the United States, or any judge of a court of record of general jurisdiction of any State,

The statute, therefore, has resolved the only jurisdictional issue this Court is required to answer. Counsel for respondent, however, has insisted that the extradition action cannot proceed because of the special nature of the charges against the respondent.

Although respondent has nowhere set out his views in a clear and logical progression, this Court interprets the argument he makes to be as follows. Respondent acknowledges that § 3184 enables a United States judicial officer to hear extradition matters. * * * Respondent argues, however, that while there is an extradition treaty in force between Israel and the United States, this treaty does not give a United States district court § 3184 jurisdiction in this matter because of the "subject matter" of the extradition. * * * He contends that in determining jurisdiction, the judicial officer must examine the charge, specifically the type of conduct for which extradition is sought. If the conduct charged is "war crimes or genocide," respondent contends a civilian court lacks jurisdiction. He argues that Article 1 of the United States Constitution gives Congress the exclusive power to regulate the land and naval forces and that Congress has authorized military tribunals to try "war criminals" exclusively. * * * Respondent claims that "a determination has been made historically in this country based on international law and comity, that the rules of land warfare and the punishment of men in uniform will always take place in front of a military tribunal." * * * Respondent asserts that "a man in uniform" has never been tried by a civilian tribunal in the history of the United States. * * * Thus, * * * this Court lacks subject matter jurisdiction in this proceeding. For the reasons * * * below, respondent's arguments and conclusion are erroneous.

II.

Respondent's interpretation of domestic law, both cases and statutes, is misplaced on at least two grounds. First, this is an extradition proceeding and not a civil or criminal trial on the merits. Second, neither the United States Constitution nor statutes vest exclusive jurisdiction in military tribunals for so-called "war crimes". Each of these conclusions will be examined below.

A.

No American cases have been * * * or found in which a civilian court * * * lacked jurisdiction to preside over an extradition proceeding because the "subject matter" of the extradition charge was alleged "war crimes". In the few reported United States judicial decisions addressing requests to extradite persons for so-called war crimes, courts have not found that they lack jurisdiction to determine extraditability.

In In re Ryan, [supra], the Federal Republic of Germany requested the extradition of a naturalized American citizen, Hermine Braunsteiner

may, upon complaint made under oath, charging any person found within his jurisdiction, with having committed within the jurisdiction of any such foreign government any of the crimes provided for by such treaty or convention, issue his warrant for the apprehension of the person so charged, that he may be brought before such justice, judge, or magistrate, to the end that the evidence of criminality may be heard and considered.

Ryan, pursuant to a 1931 treaty. 360 F.Supp. at 272 (United States–Germany Treaty of Extradition). Petitioner alleged that Ryan had been a warden at the Lublin concentration camp in Poland during World War II. She was charged with multiple counts of murder in Germany. A United States district court judge exercised jurisdiction pursuant to 18 U.S.C. § 3184 and certified to the Secretary of State that the evidence * * * [sustained] the charges under the Extradition Treaty. Ryan was * * * surrendered to the government of West Germany, where she stood trial and was found guilty of war crimes and sentenced to life imprisonment in June of 1981. * * *

* * * The extradition of Artukovic [was sought] for "murder." On March 5, 1985, a United States magistrate exercised jurisdiction pursuant to 18 U.S.C. § 3184 and certified that Artukovic is extraditable to Yugoslavia for a murder committed during World War II. * * * Extradition proceedings against Artukovic were originally initiated in 1951. Artukovic was accused of ordering the killings of thousands of persons while a high ranking official in a puppet government installed by the Nazi regime which controlled much of prewar Yugoslavia during World War II. Artukovic was found nonextraditable in 1959 because of insufficient evidence and the "political character" of the alleged offenses. Pursuant to Yugoslavia's second extradition request, petitioner United States of America filed a second extradition complaint on November 14, 1984. In the course of these proceedings, none of the federal courts which examined Artukovic's extraditability even questioned whether they could assert jurisdiction in an extradition proceeding because the crimes alleged were war-related.

B.

Neither the United States Constitution nor United States legislation provides that crimes committed by military personnel, crimes which violate the laws of war, or crimes related to the conduct of war must be tried before military authorities. The Supreme Court has characterized as "well-established" the power of military tribunals to exercise jurisdiction over enemy belligerents, prisoners of war and others charged with violating the laws of war. Johnson v. Eisentrager, 339 U.S. 763, 786 (1950). The Supreme Court, however, has never stated or implied that such jurisdiction is exclusive ("the Military Commission is a lawful tribunal to adjudge enemy offenses against the laws of war.")

Article I, Section 8, clause 14 of the Constitution grants Congress the power to "make Rules for the Government and Regulation of the land and naval Forces." Article I, section 8, clause 10 gives Congress the power to "define and punish * * * Offenses against the Law of Nations," of which the law of war is a part. Pursuant to these constitutional provisions, Congress may have the power to vest exclusive jurisdiction over crimes relating to war in military tribunals. This issue, however, need not be reached in the instant case. Congress has not enacted legislation intended to give military authorities exclusive jurisdiction over war-related crimes, let alone over persons accused of murder, manslaughter and causing grievous bodily harm during wartime while at a Nazi concentration camp.

Congress historically has granted military authorities the power to establish military tribunals to try enemy nationals accused of war crimes. Articles of War, 10 U.S.C. §§ 1471–1593 repealed in part, incorporated in part, 10 U.S.C. §§ 801–835 (1948, 1950). Nonetheless, this jurisdictional grant was not intended to be exclusive. The Articles of War provided that courts martial would have concurrent jurisdiction with other military tribunals in certain instances. Accord In re Yamashita 327 U.S. 1, 7–8 (1946). See also 10 U.S.C. § 821 (1950). Indeed, during the time the Articles of War were in effect, Congress had authorized federal district courts to try certain war-related offenses. Espionage Act of 1917 (repealed 1948). Cf. Ex parte Quirin. [Prisoners of war are subject to prosecution for offenses malum in se; although they may be tried by courts martial, they may also be tried by courts of general jurisdiction in the country in which the crime is committed].

No United States cases have been found which specifically address civilian court jurisdiction over "war crimes". Nonetheless, courts have examined the related issue of civilian court jurisdiction over American military personnel whom Congress has subjected to the jurisdiction of courts martial. During the Civil War, World War I, and World War II periods, courts have found that civil courts have jurisdiction concurrent with military tribunals. They have held that civilian courts may try a member of the armed forces for an offense which is punishable by a military court, if the civilian court has taken jurisdiction first or if the military consents. See Kennedy v. Sanford, 166 F.2d 568 (5th Cir.1948) (Articles of War provide for concurrent jurisdiction over an American soldier, even during war time; commanding officer has discretion regarding the surrender of a soldier for crimes against federal or state laws); Scott v. State, 22 So.2d 529 (Ala.1945) (state court properly asserted jurisdiction over defendant member of the armed forces during time of war for crime of robbery, when military authorities did not request surrender of the accused); People v. Denman, 177 P. 461 (Cal.1918) (felony murder charge brought against American soldier who committed crime during time of war properly brought in state court).

The cases cited above clearly illustrate that Congress has not provided nor have courts found that military tribunals or courts martial have exclusive jurisdiction over military matters or crimes related to the conduct of war. The United States government has never surrendered control of civilian affairs to the army, in peace time. Americans have historically been very cautious about giving the military powers beyond those that it needs to maintain the security of the United States. Coleman v. Tennessee, 7 Otto 509, 97 U.S. 509 (1878).

Israel has charged John Demjanjuk of murdering "tens of thousands" of persons while operating the gas chambers of the Treblinka death camp. There is no reason why jurisdiction to try John Demjanjuk should be vested exclusively in an American military tribunal. Indeed, no American military tribunal presently exists to try persons accused of "war crimes". Congress * * * did not intend for persons physically present in the United States * * * accused of "war crimes" to be able to avoid trial and punishment because no American court had jurisdiction to hear an extradition request. If respondent is found extraditable under 18 U.S.C. § 3184, it would not be consistent with American policy, as reflected in this nation's participation in the Nuremberg trials, to shield him from extradition. Matter of Doherty, 599 F.Supp. at 274.

C.

Respondent, contending that "military law is regarded as entirely separate" from civilian law, cites several Supreme Court decisions which are inapposite to the instant case. * * * In re Yamashita, and Ex parte Quirin, both involve habeas corpus proceedings initiated by petitioners tried by military commissions for alleged crimes growing out of their actions during World War Two.[4] In neither case did the Supreme Court address whether a civilian tribunal could have asserted original jurisdiction in these cases. In both cases, the Supreme Court found that its scope of review was limited to the authority and jurisdiction of the military commissions. The Court said in Yamashita:

> We also emphasized in Ex parte Quirin, as we do here, that on application for habeas corpus we are not concerned with the guilt or innocence of the petitioners. *We consider here only the lawful power of the commission to try the petitioner for the offense charged.* In the present cases it must be recognized throughout that the military tribunals which Congress has sanctioned by the Articles of War are not courts whose rulings and judgments are made subject to review by this Court. See Ex parte Vallandigham.

The Court held that the detention of General Yamashita and the Quirin petitioners for trial and upon conviction, subject to the prescribed review by the military authorities, was lawful. Contrary to respondent's assertions, * * * these Supreme Court decisions addressing the appealability of military tribunal decisions do not limit the jurisdiction of this Court to proceed with the instant extradition proceeding.

III.

Respondent's argument that international law provides that trials of military personnel for war crimes will always take place before a military tribunal also lacks merit. International law[5] is a part of the law of the United States. The Paquete Habana. Respondent has not met his burden of proving his contention that if a civilian court tries him for alleged war crimes, a violation of international law would occur.

First, the United Nations Convention on the Prevention and Punishment of the Crime of Genocide, 78 U.N.T.S. 277 (opened for signature December 9, 1948) was adopted by the United Nations General Assembly in 1948, G.A.Res. 260(A), U.N.Doc. A/810 at 174 (1948) and has been ratified by 93 nations. The Convention defines genocide to include various acts, including killing, committed "with intent to destroy * * * a

4. In re Yamashita involved the trial of the Commanding General of the Fourteenth Army Group of the Imperial Japanese Army in the Philippine Islands. 327 U.S. at 5. Ex parte Quirin involved the trial of German spies and saboteurs arrested in the United States for actions during World War II. 327 U.S. at 4.

5. "International law" develops from a number of sources, including treaties and conventions, international declarations and charters, and the customs and usages of civilized nations. Cf. Statute of the International Court of Justice Art. 38(1). * * *

national, ethnical, racial or religious group" and "confirms" that genocide is a punishable crime under international law. Article 6 provides
that both national courts and a supranational tribunal, as yet uncreated,
have the power to try persons charged with genocide. See also G.A.Res.
3074, 28 U.N.GAOR Supp. (No. 30) at 78, U.N.Doc. A/9030 (1973) (sets
forth principles regarding international cooperation in the extradition
and punishment of war criminals, including the right of each state to try
its own war criminals). While this Convention may not have a binding
effect on nations, such as the United States, which have not ratified it, it
does not support respondent's contentions.

Second, at the end of World War II, the wartime Allies agreed to
prosecute accused "war criminals" for "atrocities, massacres and executions" which occurred during the war. The "major war criminals" were
tried by an International Military Tribunal. The Nurnberg Trial, 6
F.R.D. 69 (1946). The agreements reached between the Allies, however,
explicitly provided that "national courts" had jurisdiction to try "war
criminals." Moscow Declaration of German Atrocities, 9 Dep't State
Bull. 310 (November 1, 1943) (signed by Roosevelt, Churchill, Stalin);
Agreement by the Government of the United States of America, the
Provisional Government of the French Republic, the Government of the
United Kingdom of Great Britain and North Ireland and the Govern-
ment of the Union of Soviet Socialist Republics for the Prosecution and
Punishment of the Major War Criminals of the European Axis (London
Agreement) arts. 4, 6 (August 8, 1945).[6] Whether the agreements reflect
international law at the time of agreement or begin to create a new
standard, they indicate that international law does not prohibit the trial
of alleged war criminals before national civil tribunals.

Third, the practice of several European nations in the years following World War II also shows that the trial of war criminals by non-
military courts is widely accepted in international practice. Since World
War Two, a number of European countries have tried alleged perpetrators of various "war crimes" or "crimes against humanity" in their
civilian courts. Civilian courts in Norway and Sweden asserted jurisdiction over Nazi war criminals in instances where their own municipal law
was violated. See Appleman, Military Tribunals and International
Crimes (1954) at 307. Poland's civilian tribunals also asserted jurisdiction over war criminals. * * * Indeed, during the period from 1944 to
1948, the United States extradited over 1,200 alleged Nazi war criminals
from the American zones of occupied Germany and Austria to European
nations, including Norway, Denmark and Poland. * * *

French law currently provides for trying and punishing the perpetrators of both "war crimes" and "crimes against humanity" in civilian
courts. A French civilian court, for example, is presiding over the
pending prosecution of Klaus Barbie, allegedly a former Gestapo chief.
Bolivia expelled Barbie to France in 1983. French prosecutors * * *
charged Barbie with "crimes against humanity" for the part he played in
the torture, deportation and murder of several thousand Jews and non-

---

6. Art. 6 provides: Nothing in this
Agreement shall prejudice the jurisdiction
or the powers of any national or occupation
court established or to be established in any
allied territory or in Germany for the trial
of war criminals.

Jews during World War II. See Goldberg, "Klaus Barbie and the United States Government", 19 Harv.C.R.–C.L.L.Rev. 1 (1984). * * *

In addition to trials in the civilian courts of the Allied powers, civil courts in occupied Germany and later in the Federal Republic of Germany have tried thousands of people accused of "war crimes" and crimes against humanity committed during the Nazi era. * * * See also *In re Ryan,* [*supra*]; Re Federal Republic of Germany and Rauca, 141 D.L.R.3d 412, 30 C.R.3d 97, 38 O.R.2d 705 (1982) (extradition by Canada to West Germany of Rauca, to stand trial for war crimes committed during World War II). No evidence has been presented that the "customs and usages of civilized nations" prohibit civilian courts from exercising jurisdiction over war-related crimes.

IV.

Respondent's arguments have not shown that this Court lacks subject matter jurisdiction to proceed with an extradition hearing in the above captioned case. Clearly, the accused cannot choose the tribunal in which he is to be tried.

The State of Israel has requested respondent Ivan Demjanjuk's extradition, pursuant to the 1963 Convention on Extradition between the Government of the United States of America and [Israel.] T.I.A.S. 5476, 14 U.S.T. 717. This Court has personal jurisdiction over Respondent. Title 18 U.S.C. § 3184, therefore, imposes a responsibility on this Court to proceed with an extradition hearing forthwith.

———

* * *

Notes & Questions: In 1993, the Supreme Court of Israel found that the evidence was insufficient to prove beyond a reasonable doubt that Demjanjuk was "Ivan the Terrible" from Treblinka. The 6th Circuit Court of Appeals, sua sponte ordered the U.S. Government to respond to allegations that the prosecution had not disclosed information to the Court in the original extradition hearing that suggested Demjanjuk was not the person named in the extradition request as having been "Ivan the Terrible" of the Treblinka death camp. After Demjanjuk had been returned to the United States, a three-judge federal appeals court panel revoked the 1986 extradition order, which had sent Demjanjuk to Israel. The panel found that Justice Department lawyers committed "fraud on the court," and displayed a "win at any cost" attitude, in failing to disclose key evidence that might have caused the extradition request to be turned down. OSI failed turn-over statements by two Treblinka guards (made to officials of the former Soviet Union) identifying another man (Ivan Marchenko) as "Ivan the Terrible." The OSI also failed to provide a list of Ukranian guards that it had received from the Polish Government, which included Marchenko and not Demjanjuk. They also did not disclose conflicting statements about whether Demjanjuk was "Ivan the Terrible", obtained from a German guard interviewed by the Justice Department. A "Special Master" had found that the Department of Justice had erred in "good faith", but the three-judge panel disregarded the special master's finding. The Panel noted that the OSI had acted in "bad faith," and in "reckless disregard of the truth." The Justice Department's Office of Special Investigations (OSI) has declared its intent to seek to expel Demjanjuk for being a guard in another Nazi concentration camp (Sobibor) and for lying about his past in his visa application (for which he was stripped of his citizenship in 1981). *See, gen.,* Isikoff, *Appellate Panel Rebukes Justice Dept. on Demjanjuk,* The Wash. Post, Nov. 18, 1993 section A, p. A–01.

SECTION B.   THE INNOVATIONS OF NUREMBERG: CRIMES AGAINST PEACE AND CRIMES AGAINST HUMANITY

CHARTER OF THE INTERNATIONAL MILITARY TRIBUNAL [a]

59 Stat. 1544, 1546.

Article 1.   In pursuance of the Agreement signed on the 8th day of August 1945 by the Government of the United States, * * * the Provisional Government of the French Republic, the Government of the United Kingdom * * * and the Government of the Union of Soviet Socialist Republics, there shall be established an International Military Tribunal (hereinafter called "the Tribunal") for the just and prompt trial and punishment of the major war criminals of the European Axis.

Article 2.   The Tribunal shall consist of four members, each with an alternate. One member and one alternate shall be appointed by each of the Signatories.   * * *

Article 6.   The Tribunal established by the Agreement referred to in Article 1 hereof for the trial and punishment of the major war criminals of the European Axis countries shall have the power to try and punish persons who, acting in the interests of the European Axis countries, whether as individuals or as members of organizations, committed any of the following crimes. The following acts, or any of them, are crimes coming within the jurisdiction of the Tribunal for which there shall be individual responsibility:

   (a) CRIMES AGAINST PEACE: namely, planning, preparation, initiation or waging of a war of aggression, or a war in violation of international treaties, agreements or assurances, or participation in a common plan or conspiracy for the accomplishment of any of the foregoing;

a. The Charter was annexed to an Agreement for the Prosecution and Punishment of the Major War Criminals of the European Axis, which came into force on signature, August 8, 1945, by France, the U.S.S.R., U.K. and the U.S.   11 Whiteman, Digest 881–82 (1968). In the United States it was treated as an executive agreement and was not submitted to the United States Senate as a treaty for its advice and consent. For the distinction between executive agreements and treaties, see Chapters 13 & 14.

(b) WAR CRIMES: namely, violations of the laws or customs of war. Such violations shall include, but not be limited to, murder, ill-treatment or deportation to slave labor or for any other purpose of civilian population of or in occupied territory, murder or ill-treatment of prisoners of war or persons on the seas, killing of hostages, plunder of public or private property, wanton destruction of cities, towns or villages, or devastation not justified by military necessity;

(c) CRIMES AGAINST HUMANITY: namely, murder, extermination, enslavement, deportation, and other inhumane acts committed against any civilian population, before or during the war; [1] or persecutions on political, racial or religious grounds in execution of or in connection with any crime within the jurisdiction of the Tribunal, whether or not in violation of the domestic law of the country where perpetrated.

Leaders, organizers, instigators and accomplices participating in the formulation or execution of a common plan or conspiracy to commit any of the foregoing crimes are responsible for all acts performed by any persons in execution of such plan.

Article 7.   The official position of defendants, whether as Heads of State or responsible officials in Government Departments, shall not be considered as freeing them from responsibility or mitigating punishment.

Article 8.   The fact that the Defendant acted pursuant to order of his Government or of a superior shall not free him from responsibility, but may be considered in mitigation of punishment if the Tribunal determines that justice so requires.

Article 9.   At the trial of any individual member of any group or organization the Tribunal may declare (in connection with any act of which the individual may be convicted) that the group or organization of which the individual was a member was a criminal organization.

After receipt of the Indictment the Tribunal shall give such notice as it thinks fit that the prosecution intends to ask the Tribunal to make such declaration and any member of the organization will be entitled to apply to the Tribunal for leave to be heard by the Tribunal upon the question of the criminal character of the organization. The Tribunal shall have power to allow or reject the application. If the application is allowed, the Tribunal may direct in what manner the applicants shall be represented and heard.

Article 10.   In cases where a group or organization is declared criminal by the Tribunal, the competent national authority of any Signatory shall have the right to bring individuals to trial for membership therein before national, military or occupation courts. In any such case the criminal nature of the group or organization is considered proved and shall not be questioned.

---

1. [The contracting governments signed a protocol at Berlin on Oct. 6, 1945 * * * which provides that this semi-colon in the English text should be changed to a comma.]

Article 11.   Any person convicted by the Tribunal may be charged before a national, military or occupation court, referred to in Article 10 of this Charter, with a crime other than of membership in a criminal group or organization and such court may, after convicting him, impose upon him punishment independent of and additional to the punishment imposed by the Tribunal for participation in the criminal activities of such group or organization.

Article 12.   The Tribunal shall have the right to take proceedings against a person charged with crimes set out in Article 6 of this Charter in his absence, if he has not been found or if the Tribunal, for any reason, finds it necessary, in the interests of justice, to conduct the hearing in his absence.

Article 26.   The judgment of the Tribunal as to the guilt or the innocence of any Defendant shall give the reasons on which it is based, and shall be final and not subject to review.

Article 27.   The Tribunal shall have the right to impose upon a Defendant, on conviction, death or such other punishment as shall be determined by it to be just.

* * *

JUDGMENT OF THE INTERNATIONAL MILITARY TRIBUNAL, NUREMBERG, GERMANY, 1946

22 I.M.T., Trial of the Major War Criminals 411, 427 (1948).

* * *

III.   The Common Plan of Conspiracy and Aggressive War

The Tribunal now turns to the consideration of the crimes against peace charged in the indictment.   Count one of the indictment charges the defendants with conspiring or having a common plan to commit crimes against peace.   Count two of the indictment charges the defendants with committing specific crimes against peace by planning, preparing, initiating, and waging wars of aggression against a number of other States.   It will be convenient to consider the question of the existence of a common plan and the question of aggressive war together, and to deal later in this judgment with the question of aggressive war together, and to deal later in this judgment with the question of the individual responsibility of the defendants.

The charges in the indictment that the defendants planned and waged aggressive wars are charges of the utmost gravity.   War is essentially an evil thing.   Its consequences are not confined to the belligerent states alone, but affect the whole world.

To initiate a war of aggression, therefore, is * * * an international crime [it is] the supreme international crime differing only from other war crimes in that it contains within itself the accumulated evil of the whole.   The first acts of aggression referred to in the indictment are the seizure of Austria and Czechoslovakia; and the first war of aggression charged in the indictment is the war against Poland begun on the 1st September 1939.

Before examining that charge it is necessary to look more closely at some of the events which preceded these acts of aggression. The war against Poland did not come suddenly out of an otherwise clear sky; the evidence has made it plain that this war of aggression, as well as the seizure of Austria and Czechoslovakia, was premeditated and carefully prepared, and was not undertaken until the moment was thought opportune for it to be carried through as a definite part of the preordained scheme and plan. For the aggressive designs of the Nazi Government were not accidents arising out of the immediate political situation in Europe and the world; they were a deliberate and essential part of Nazi foreign policy. From the beginning, the National Socialist movement claimed that its object was to unite the German people in the consciousness of their mission and destiny, based on inherent qualities of race, and under the guidance of the Fuehrer.

For its achievement, two things were deemed to be essential: The disruption of the European order as it had existed since the Treaty of Versailles, and the creation of a Greater Germany beyond the frontiers of 1914. This necessarily involved the seizure of foreign territories.

War was seen to be inevitable, or at the very least, highly probable, if these purposes were to be accomplished. The German people, therefore, with all their resources, were to be organized as a great political-military army, schooled to obey without question any policy decreed by the State.

* * *

IV. Violations of International Treaties

The Charter defines as a crime the planning or waging of war that is a war of aggression or a war in violation of international treaties. The Tribunal has decided that certain of the defendants planned and waged aggressive wars against 10 nations, and were therefore guilty of this series of crimes. This makes it unnecessary to discuss the subject in further detail, or even to consider at any length the extent to which these aggressive wars were also "wars in violation of international treaties, agreements, or assurances."

These treaties are set out in appendix C of the indictment. Those of principal importance are the following:

(A) Hague Conventions

In the 1899 Convention the signatory powers agreed: "before an appeal to arms * * * to have recourse, as far as circumstances allow, to the good offices or mediation of one or more friendly powers." A similar clause was inserted in the Convention for Pacific Settlement of International Disputes of 1907. In the accompanying Convention Relative to Opening of Hostilities, article I contains this far more specific language:

The Contracting Powers recognize that hostilities between them must not commence without a previous and explicit warning, in the form of either a declaration of war, giving reasons, or an ultimatum with a conditional declaration of war.

Germany was a party to these conventions.

(B) Versailles Treaty

Breaches of certain provisions of the Versailles Treaty are also relied on by the prosecution—not to fortify the left bank of the Rhine (art. 42–44); to "respect strictly the independence of Austria" (art. 80); renunciation of any rights in Memel (art. 99) and the Free City of Danzig (art. 100); the recognition of the independence of the Czecho–Slovak State; and the Military, Naval, and Air Clauses against German rearmament found in part V. There is no doubt that action was taken by the German Government contrary to all these provisions, the details of which are set out in appendix C. With regard to the Treaty of Versailles, the matters relied on are:

1.   The violation of articles 42 to 44 in respect of the demilitarized zone of the Rhineland.

2.   The annexation of Austria on the 13th March 1938, in violation of article 80.

3.   The incorporation of the district of Memel on the 22d March 1939, in violation of article 99.

4.   The incorporation of the Free City of Danzig on the 1st September 1939, in violation of article 100.

5.   The incorporation of the provinces of Bohemia and Moravia on the 16th March 1939, in violation of article 81.

6.   The repudiation of the military, naval and air clauses of the treaty in or about March of 1935.

On the 21st May 1935, Germany announced that, whilst renouncing the disarmament clauses of the treaty, she would still respect the territorial limitations, and would comply with the Locarno Pact. (With regard to the first five breaches alleged, therefore, the Tribunal finds the allegation proved.)

* * *

(E) The Law of the Charter

The jurisdiction of the Tribunal is defined in the Agreement and Charter, and the crimes coming within the jurisdiction of the Tribunal, for which there shall be individual responsibility, are set out in Article 6. The law of the Charter is decisive, and binding upon the Tribunal.

The making of the Charter was the exercise of the sovereign legislative power by the countries to which the German Reich unconditionally surrendered; and the undoubted right to these countries to legislate for the occupied territories has been recognized by the civilized world. The Charter is not an arbitrary exercise of power on the part of the victorious nations, but in the view of the Tribunal, as will be shown, it is the expression of international law existing at the time of its creation; and to that extent is itself a contribution to international law.

* * *

* * * [T]he very essence of the Charter is that individuals have international duties which transcend the national obligations of obedience imposed by the individual State. He who violates the laws of war cannot obtain immunity while acting in pursuance of the authority of the State if the State is authorizing action moves outside its competence under international law.

It was also submitted on behalf of most of these defendants that in doing what they did they were acting under the orders of Hitler, and therefore cannot be held responsible for the acts committed by them in carrying out these orders. The Charter specifically provides in Article 8:

> The fact that the defendant acted pursuant to order of his Government or of a superior shall not free him from responsibility, but may be considered in mitigation of punishment.

The provisions of this Article are in conformity with the law of all nations. That a soldier was ordered to kill or torture in violation of the international law of war has never been recognized as a defense to such acts of brutality, though, as the Charter here provides, the order may be urged in mitigation of the punishment. The true test, which is found in varying degrees in the criminal law of most nations, is not the existence of the order, but whether moral choice was in fact possible.

V. The Law as to the Common Plan or Conspiracy

In the previous recital of the facts relating to aggressive war, it is clear that planning and preparation had been carried out in the most systematic way at every stage of the history.

* * *

In the opinion of the Tribunal, the evidence establishes the common planning to prepare and wage war by certain of the defendants. It is immaterial to consider whether a single conspiracy to the extent and over the time set out in the indictment has been conclusively proved. Continued planning, with aggressive war as the objective, has been established beyond doubt. The truth of the situation was well stated by [the] official interpreter of the German Foreign Office:

> The general objectives of the Nazi leadership were apparent from the start, namely the domination of the European Continent, to be achieved first by the incorporation of all German-speaking groups in the Reich, and, secondly, by territorial expansion under the slogan "Lebensraum." The execution of these basic objectives, however, seemed to be characterized by improvisation. Each succeeding step was apparently carried out as each new situation arose, but all consistent with the ultimate objectives mentioned above.

The argument that such common planning cannot exist where there is complete dictatorship is unsound. A plan in the execution of which a number of persons participate is still a plan, even though conceived by only one of them; and those who execute the plan do not avoid responsibility by showing that they acted under the direction of the man who conceived it. Hitler could not make aggressive war by himself. He had to have the cooperation of statesmen, military leaders, diplomats, and businessmen. When they, with knowledge of his aims, gave him their cooperation, they made themselves parties to the plan he had initiated. They are not to be deemed innocent because Hitler made use of them, if they knew what they were doing. That they were assigned to their tasks by a dictator does not absolve them from responsibility for their acts. The relation of leader and follower does not preclude responsibility here any more than it does in the comparable tyranny of organized domestic crime.

* * *

VI. War Crimes and Crimes Against Humanity

The evidence relating to war crimes has been overwhelming, in its volume and its detail. It is impossible for this judgment adequately to review it, or to record the mass of documentary and oral evidence that has been presented. The truth remains that war crimes were committed on a vast scale, never before seen in the history of war. They were perpetrated in all the countries occupied by Germany, and on the high seas, and were attended by every conceivable circumstance of cruelty and horror. There can be no doubt that the majority of them arose from the Nazi conception of "total war," with which the aggressive wars were waged. For in this conception of "total war" the moral ideas underlying the conventions which seek to make war more humane are no longer regarded as having force or validity. Everything is made subordinate to the overmastering dictates of war. Rules, regulations, assurances, and treaties, all alike, are of no moment; and so, freed from the restraining influence of international law, the aggressive war is conducted by the Nazi leaders in the most barbaric way. Accordingly, war crimes were committed when and wherever the Fuehrer and his close associates thought them to be advantageous. They were for the most part the result of cold and criminal calculation.

On some occasions war crimes were deliberately planned long in advance. In the case of the Soviet Union, the plunder of the territories to be occupied, and the ill-treatment of the civilian population, were settled in minute detail before the attack was begun. As early as the autumn of 1940, the invasion of the territories of the Soviet Union was being considered. From that date onwards, the methods to be employed in destroying all possible opposition were continuously under discussion.

Similarly, when planning to exploit the inhabitants of the occupied countries for slave labor on the very greatest scale, the German Government conceived it as an integral part of the war economy, and planned and organized this particular war crime down to the last elaborate detail.

Other war crimes, such as the murder of prisoners of war who had escaped and been recaptured, or the murder of commandos or captured airmen, or the destruction of the Soviet commissars, were the result of direct orders circulated through the highest official channels.

The Tribunal proposes, therefore, to deal quite generally with the question of war crimes, and to refer to them later when examining the responsibility of the individual defendants in relation to them. Prisoners of war were ill-treated and tortured and murdered, not only in defiance of the well-established rules of international law, but in complete disregard of the elementary dictates of humanity. Civilian populations in occupied territories suffered the same fate. Whole populations were deported to Germany for the purposes of slave labor upon defense works, armament production and similar tasks connected with the war effort. Hostages were taken in very large numbers from the civilian populations in all the occupied countries, and were shot as suited the German purposes. Public and private property was systematically plundered and pillaged in order to enlarge the resources of Germany at the expense of the rest of Europe. Cities and towns and villages were wantonly destroyed without military justification or necessity.

(A) Murder and Ill–Treatment of Prisoners of War

Article 6(b) of the Charter defines war crimes in these words:

War Crimes: namely, violations of the laws or customs of war. Such violations shall include, but not be limited to, murder, ill-treatment or deportation to slave labor or for any other purpose of civilian population of or in occupied territory, murder or ill-treatment of prisoners of war or persons on the seas, killing of hostages, plunder of public or private property, wanton destruction of cities, towns, or villages, or devastation not justified by military necessity.

Many Allied soldiers who had surrendered to the Germans were shot immediately, often as a matter of deliberate, calculated policy. * * *

* * *

When Allied airmen were forced to land in Germany they were sometimes killed at once by the civilian population. The police were instructed not to interfere with these killings, and the Ministry of Justice was informed that no one should be prosecuted for taking part in them. The treatment of Soviet prisoners of war was characterized by particular inhumanity. The death of so many of them was not due merely to the action of individual guards, or to the exigencies of life in the camps. It was the result of systematic plans to murder. * * *

* * *

(B) Murder and Ill–Treatment of Civilian Population

Article 6(b) of the Charter provides that "ill-treatment * * * of civilian population of or in occupied territory * * * killing of hostages * * * wanton destruction of cities, towns, or villages" shall be a war crime. In the main, these provisions are merely declaratory of the existing laws of war as expressed by the Hague Convention, Article 46, which stated: "Family honor and rights, the lives of persons and private property, as well as religious convictions and practice, must be respected." The territories occupied by Germany were administered in violation of the laws of war. The evidence is quite overwhelming of a systematic rule of violence, brutality, and terror. On the 7th December

1941, Hitler issued the directive since known as the "Nacht und Nebel Erlass" (night and fog decree), under which persons who committed offenses against the Reich or the German forces in occupied territories, except where the death sentence was certain, were to be taken secretly to Germany and handed over to the SIPO and SD for trial or punishment in Germany. * * *

Even persons who were only suspected of opposing any of the policies of the German occupation authorities were arrested, and on arrest were interrogated by the Gestapo and the SD in the most shameful manner. * * *

* * *

The practice of keeping hostages to prevent and to punish any form of civil disorder was resorted to by the Germans; an order issued by the defendant Keitel on the 16th September 1941, spoke in terms of fifty or a hundred lives from the occupied areas of the Soviet Union for one German life taken. The order stated that "it should be remembered that a human life in unsettled countries frequently counts for nothing, and a deterrent effect can be obtained only by unusual severity." The exact number of persons killed as a result of this policy is not known, but large numbers were killed in France and the other occupied territories; in the east the slaughter was on [a massive] scale. * * *

* * *

(D) Slave Labor Policy

Article 6(b) of the Charter provides that the "ill-treatment or deportation to slave labor or for any other purpose, of civilian population of or in occupied territory" shall be a war crime. The laws relating to forced labor by the inhabitants of occupied territories are found in Article 52 of the Hague Convention, which provides: "Requisition in kind and services shall not be demanded from municipalities or inhabitants except for the needs of the army of occupation. They shall be in proportion to the resources of the country, and of such a nature as not to involve the inhabitants in the obligation of taking part in military operations against their own country." The policy of the German occupation authorities was in flagrant violation of the terms of this convention. Some idea of this policy may be gathered from the statement made by Hitler in a speech on November 9, 1941:

> The territory which now works for us contains more than 250,000,000 men, but the territory which works indirectly for us includes now more than 350,000,000. In the measure in which it concerns German territory, the domain which we have taken under our administration, it is not doubtful that we shall succeed in harnessing the very last man to this work.

The actual results achieved were not so complete as this, but the German occupation authorities did succeed in forcing many of the inhabitants of the occupied territories to work for the German war effort, and in deporting at least 5,000,000 persons to Germany to serve German industry and agriculture.

* * *

(E) Persecution of the Jews

The persecution of the Jews at the hands of the Nazi Government has been proved in the greatest detail before the Tribunal. It is a record of consistent and systematic inhumanity on the greatest scale.   * * *

* * *

* * * Adolf Eichmann, who had been put in charge of this program by Hitler, has estimated that the policy pursued resulted in the killing of 6,000,000 Jews, of which 4,000,000 were killed in the extermination institutions.

(F) The Law Relating to War Crimes and Crimes Against Humanity

* * *

The Tribunal is of course bound by the Charter, in the definition which it gives both of war crimes and crimes against humanity. With respect to war crimes, however, as has already been pointed out, the crimes defined by Article 6, section (b), of the Charter were already recognized as war crimes under international law. They were covered by Articles 46, 50, 52, and 56 of the Hague Convention of 1907, and Articles 2, 3, 4, 46, and 51 of the Geneva Convention of 1929. That violation of these provisions constituted crimes for which the guilty individuals were punishable is too well settled to admit of argument.

But it is argued that the Hague Convention does not apply in this case, because of the "general participation" clause in Article 2 of the Hague Convention of 1907. That clause provided: "The provisions contained in the regulations (rules of land warfare) referred to in Article I as well as in the present convention do not apply except between contracting powers, and then only if all the belligerents are parties to the convention." Several of the belligerents in the recent war were not parties to this convention.

In the opinion of the Tribunal it is not necessary to decide this question. The rules of land warfare expressed in the convention undoubtedly represented an advance over existing international law at the time of their adoption. But the convention expressly stated that it was an attempt "to revise the general laws and customs of war," which it thus recognized to be then existing, but by 1939 these rules laid down in the convention were recognized by all civilized nations, and were regarded as being declaratory of the laws and customs of war which are referred to in Article 6(b) of the Charter.

A further submission was made that Germany was no longer bound by the rules of land warfare in many of the territories occupied during the war, because Germany had completely subjugated those countries and incorporated them into the German Reich, a fact which gave Germany authority to deal with the occupied countries as though they were part of Germany. In the view of the Tribunal it is unnecessary in this case to decide whether this doctrine of subjugation, dependent as it is upon military conquest, has any application where the subjugation is the result of the crime of aggressive war. * * *

With regard to crimes against humanity, there is no doubt whatsoever that political opponents were murdered in Germany before the war, and that many of them were kept in concentration camps in circumstances of great horror and cruelty. The policy of terror was certainly carried out on a vast scale, and in many cases was organized and systematic. The policy of persecution, repression, and murder of civilians in Germany before the war of 1939, who were likely to be hostile to the Government, was most ruthlessly carried out. The persecution of Jews during the same period is established beyond all doubt. To constitute crimes against humanity, the acts relied on before the outbreak of war must have been in execution of, or in connection with, any crime within the jurisdiction of the Tribunal. The Tribunal is of the opinion that revolting and horrible as many of these crimes were, it has not been satisfactorily proved that they were done in execution of, or in connection with, any such crime. The Tribunal therefore cannot make a general declaration that the acts before 1939 were crimes against humanity within the meaning of the Charter, but from the beginning of the war in 1939 war crimes were committed on a vast scale, which were also crimes against humanity; and insofar as the inhumane acts charged in the indictment, and committed after the beginning of the war, did not constitute war crimes, they were all committed in execution of, or in connection with, the aggressive war, and therefore constituted crimes against humanity.

* * *

VERDICTS AND SENTENCES OF THE INTERNATIONAL MILITARY TRIBUNAL

Calvocaressi, Nuremberg 141 (1947).

	Table of								
	Charges Counts				Verdicts Counts				Sentences
	1	2	3	4	1	2	3	4	
Goering...................	X	X	X	X	X	X	X	X	Death.
Ribbentrop................	X	X	X	X	X	X	X	X	
Keitel....................	X	X	X	X	X	X	X	X	
Jodl	X	X	X	X	X	X	X	X	
Rosenberg.................	X	X	X	X	X	X	X	X	
Frick	X	X	X	X		X	X	X	
Seyss–Inquart	X	X	X	X		X	X	X	
Sauckel	X	X	X	X			X	X	
Bormann..................	X		X	X			X	X	
Kaltenbrunner	X		X	X			X	X	
Frank	X		X	X			X	X	
Streicher.................	X			X				X	
Raeder...................	X	X	X	X	X	X	X		Life.
Funk	X	X	X	X		X	X	X	

	Table of								
	Charges Counts				Verdicts Counts				Sentences
	1	2	3	4	1	2	3	4	
Hess	X	X	X	X	X	X			Life.
Speer	X	X	X	X			X	X	20 years.
Schirach	X			X				X	20 years.
Neurath	X	X	X	X	X	X	X	X	15 years.
Doenitz	X	X	X			X	X		10 years.
Fritzsche	X		X	X					Acquitted.
von Papen	X	X							Acquitted.
Schacht	X			X					Acquitted.

Notes: Other trials in Germany.

LIPPERT, THE EICHMANN CASE AND THE NUREMBERG TRIALS

48 A.B.A.J. 738 (1962).

As a follow-up to the International Military Tribunal (IMT) case, the United States had planned to prosecute high-ranking officials of the security and police services, but after investigation it was realized that few were available for trial. Justice Jackson's successor as United States Prosecutor, Brigadier General Telford Taylor, reported that "Many of them were known to be dead and others missing could not be located." It cannot be doubted that the missing Eichmann, the very man named by the IMT, was one of those whose trial had been contemplated, such to be held before one of the United States courts that were established in Nuremberg in 1946 after the IMT finished its work.

These courts which were known as United States Military Tribunals, were staffed by judges who were drawn from the Bench and Bar of the United States. Before one or the other of them, there appeared 177 members of the SS and police, doctors, judges, lawyers, industrialists, government ministers and military leaders. Of this total 142 were found guilty, in greater or less degree, of the war crimes, crimes against peace, and crimes against humanity, of which they were charged, and twelve were executed pursuant to the death penalty imposed. The trial of the jurists has become well known by reason of the fictional version of it portrayed in the film "Judgment at Nuremberg."

Moreover, there were still other United States courts in Germany which could have taken jurisdiction of Eichmann's case at the time. Concurrently with the trials in Nuremberg an equally monumental judicial undertaking was in progress in Dachau, a suburb of Munich, and previously the site of one of the infamous extermination camps, complete with gas chamber and ovens. Here the United States Army in a staggering total of 489 trials prosecuted those charged with crimes committed against United States soldiers and those having complicity in the operation of the concentration camps liberated by United States troops. Of the 1,672 persons accused, 1,347 were found guilty and 258 suffered the death penalty. * * * *See, e.g., U.S. v. von Leeb (The High Command Case)*, U.S. Military Trib. (V) (1948), 11 Trials of War Criminals 462 (1950).

---

1. ***Trial of Japanese leaders.*** An International Military Tribunal for the Far East conducted a trial of Japanese leaders in Tokyo and rendered a judgment in November, 1948. Parts of judgment and other opinions are reported in Sohn, Cases on United Nations Law (1956).

2. ***The Nuremberg principles in the United Nations.*** In December, 1946, the General Assembly adopted a resolution affirming "the principles of international law recognized by the Charter of the Nuremberg Tribunal and the judgment of the Tribunal." Resolution 95(1). The International Law Commission, an organ of the United Nations established by the General Assembly to carry out Article 13 of the Charter, was requested by the General Assembly to formulate the Nuremberg principles. In 1950, the Commission submitted a draft of seven principles which were discussed by the General Assembly but never formally affirmed by the assembly. Extensive efforts in the United Nations to prepare and agree upon a Draft Code of Offenses against the Peace and Security of Mankind and to establish an international criminal court have not succeeded.

3. ***The Draft Code of Crimes Against the Peace and Security of Mankind*** was completed in 1991 in 30 I.L.M. 1584 (1991). The International Law Commission had been struggling with the Code since 1950, 2 Yb.I.L.C. 253; [1951] 2 Yb.I.L.C. 43. The early Draft Code was never approved by the General Assembly, mainly due to problems relating to defining *"aggression."* The current Draft Code focuses on articles for which individuals are responsible. *Article 1*, provides: "[t]he crimes [under international law] defined in this Code constitute crimes against the peace and security of mankind." *Article 3*: "[a]n individual who commits a crime against the peace and security of mankind is responsible therefor and is liable to punishment." *Article 5*: "prosecution of an individual [for such crimes] does not relieve a State of any responsibility under international law * * *." *Article 6*: "[a] State in whose territory an individual alleged to have committed a crime against the peace and security of mankind is present shall either try or extradite him * * *." Crimes listed include: aggression, threat of aggression, intervention, colonial domination, genocide, apartheid, systematic or mass violations of human rights, exceptionally serious war crimes, recruitment, use, financing and training mercenaries, international terrorism, illicit drug trafficking, and wilful and severe damage to the environment. What do you think of the breadth of some of these offenses? What are "exceptionally serious war crimes?" What is "colonial domination?" What is included in these offenses and in the notion of "intervention?"

4. ***Does the notion of "crimes against humanity" include rape when committed on a mass or systematic scale?*** See, Y.

Khusalani, *Dignity and Honour of Women as Basic and Fundamental Rights* (1982), *and* Nuremberg Charter and Control Council Law No. 10. Certain acts, such as torture and wilfully causing great suffering or serious injury to body or health, are strictly prohibited. *In addition to being a "crime against humanity" could rape on such a systematic and massive scale be considered a type of genocide?* See, Meron, *Rape as a Crime under International Criminal Law*, 87 A.J.I.L. 424, 425 (1993).

5. There have been suggestions made that Saddam Hussein be brought to trial in an international tribunal for his conduct during the Persian Gulf War. See, Beres, Prosecuting Iraqui Gulf War Crimes: Allied and Israeli Rights Under International Law, 16 Hastings Int'l & Comp.L.Rev. 41 (1992); O'Brien, The Nuremberg Precedent and the Gulf War, 31 Va.J.I.L. 391 (1991); Moore, War Crimes and the Rule of Law in the Gulf Crisis, 31 Va.J.I.L. 403 (1991).

6. ***Nuremberg's aftermath: an appraisal.*** In Justice Under Fire (1974), Professor Bishop asked at 284:

> What, then, has the Magna Carta of international law done for the welfare of humanity since its promulgation? The answer is clear and simple: nothing. Since Nuremberg, there have been at least eighty or ninety wars (some calculators exclude armed invasions of neighbors too weak to attempt resistance), some of them on a very large scale. The list includes the Korean war, the Suez invasion of 1956, the Algerian rebellion, the four Arab–Israeli wars, the Vietnam wars (including the accompanying fighting in Laos and Cambodia), and the invasion of Czechoslovakia by the Soviet Union and its myrmidons. In none of these cases, nor in any other, was an aggressor arrested and brought to the bar of international justice, and none is likely to be. For all the good it has done, the doctrine that aggressive war is a crime might as well be relegated to the divinity schools.

Is Professor Bishop correct? Could there be an influence not discernable by looking at the numbers of wars? As to some of the wars referred to by Bishop, the relevance of the provisions of the United Nations Charter is examined in Chapters 16 and 17.

7. ***Ad Hoc Tribunal for the Prosecution of Persons Responsible for Serious Violations of International Humanitarian Law in the territory of the former Yugoslavia:*** Nuremberg Principle I is applicable to the depredations which have taken place in the former Yugoslavia. On May 25, 1993, the Security Council, in Resolution 827, established a tribunal *to try serious violations* of international humanitarian law, committed in the territory of the former Yugoslavia, including: murders of men, women and children, mass executions, torture, and forced deportations or expulsion pursuant to "ethnic cleansing." Resolution 827 was based on the Report of the Secretary–General made pursuant to paragraph 2 of Security Council Resolution 808 (1993) (May 3, 1993). [Security Council Doc. S/25704, 3 May 1993]. On November 18, 1993, Professor Antonio Cassese of Italy was elected President of the International Tribunal. The other judges are: Georges Michel Abi–Saab (Egypt), Antonio Cassese (Italy), Jules Deschenes (Canada), Adolphus

Godwin Karibi–Whyte (Nigeria), Germain Le Foyer de Costil (France), Li Haopei (China), Gabrielle Kirk McDonald (United States), Elizabeth Odio Benito (Costa Rica), Rustam S. Sidhwa (Pakistan), Sir Ninian Stephen (Australia) and Lal CHand Vohra (Malaysia). The Prosecutor is _____. The inaugural meeting of the Tribunal was held on Wednesday, November 17, 1993.

The Tribunal has three Chambers which are, an Appeals Chamber consisting of five members and two Trial Chambers with three members each. The President of the Tribunal also presides over the Appeals Chamber. The President, in consultation with the members, will determine who is assigned to each Chamber. Each Trial Chamber elects its own President. At another meeting, the members decided that assignments to the Chambers would be for a period of one year, and thereafter by rotation. * * *

The Appeals Chamber, under the presidency of Antonio Cassese, has as its members Judges Georges Abi–Saab, Jules Deschenes, Li Haopei and Sir Ninian Stephen. Judge Elizabeth Odio Benito (Costa Rica) was unanimously elected as Vice–President of the Tribunal. Having established its organizational structure and elected its officials, the Tribunal decided that its title should be abbreviated as "The International Tribunal for Crimes in former Yugoslavia."

BLAKESLEY, REPORT ON THE OBSTACLES TO THE CREATION OF A PERMANENT WAR CRIMES TRIBUNAL

18 The Fletcher Forum of World Affairs 77, 78, 81–86, 97–98 (1994) (most fns. omitted).*

Individual criminal responsibility is the cornerstone of any international war crimes tribunal. Nuremberg Principle I provides that "[a]ny person who commits an act which constitutes a crime under international law is responsible therefor and liable to punishment." [2] Acts by heads of state or other government officials, even if committed in an official capacity, may not provide an immunity defense or mitigate criminality.[3]

---

* (Reprinted with the permission of The Fletcher Forum of World Affairs and l'Association Int'l de Droit Pénal).

2. The Charter and Judgment of Nuremberg recognize five principles: I.) as indicated in the text; II.) "The fact that domestic law does not punish an act which is an international crime does not free the perpetrator of such crimes from responsibility under international law"; III.) "The fact that a person who committed an international crime acted as Head of State or public official does not free him from responsibility under international law or mitigate punishment"; IV.) "The fact that a person acted pursuant to order of his Government or of a superior does not free him

from responsibility under international law. It may, however, be considered in mitigation of punishment, if justice so requires"; V.) "Any person charged with a crime under international law has the right to a fair trial on the facts and law." "Nazi Conspiracy and Aggression Opinion and Judgment, Nuremberg, 30 September 1945," reprinted in 41 A.J.I.L. 186–218 (1946); see also J. Spiropoulos, "Special Rapporteur, Formulation of Nuremberg Principles," 2 1950 Yrbk. Int'l L.Comm. 181, 191–193.

3. See, e.g., Secretary–General's Report on the Tribunal for the former Yugoslavia, Pursuant to para. 2 of S.C.Res. 808 (1993) (hereafter "Secretary–General's Report"), at para. 55. * * *

These officials, therefore, could also be held responsible for offenses committed pursuant to their orders.   Additionally, liability for criminal negligence may be imposed on a person in a position of authority who knew, or had reason to know, that his or her subordinates were about to commit a war crime, and who failed to take whatever action was necessary and reasonable to prevent, to deter, or to repress its commission.   The same liability obtains for failure to prosecute those who commit such offenses.

When it comes to enforcement or effecting jurisdiction, will nations unilaterally agree to such liability? Is agreement required? If not, are they liable pursuant to customary international law or general principles? Who or what institution will be able to enforce this liability?

Historical and Conceptual Background

Efforts to establish an international criminal tribunal are not new, although they have intensified recently.   One wonders whether this history of so many attempts and so few successes suggests that the time is ripe for a permanent tribunal, or that a complete change in the international system is required before one will succeed.   Professor Cherif Bassiouni notes that "the first prosecution for initiating an unjust war is reported to have been in Naples, in 1268, when Conradin von Hohenstaufen was executed for that offense."   The "modern" idea of establishing an international criminal court could be said to have been launched in 1899 with the Hague Convention for the Pacific Settlement of International Disputes [discussed *supra* this chapter and in chapters 16 & 17, *infra*].

The 1919 Versailles Treaty was another early step toward establishing a war crimes court.   The face of the treaty provided for the prosecution of Kaiser Wilhelm II for a supreme offense against the "international morality and the sanctity of treaties" and for war crimes charged against German officers and soldiers.   Also in 1919, the Allies established a special commission to investigate the responsibility *"for acts of war"* and crimes against *"the laws of humanity."*   The Report of the Commission contained the following conclusion: "All persons * * * who have been guilty of offenses against the laws and customs of war or the laws of humanity, are liable to criminal prosecution."   This provision was developed in response to the killing of an estimated one million Armenians by Turkish authorities and the Turkish people, supported or abetted by the state's public policy.   There can be no doubt that those who committed such atrocities knew they were committing * * * "crimes against humanity." [22]   United States [opposition], however, *prevented* the Commission's report from including this type of conduct among the offenses that an international criminal court would prosecute. Subsequently, the Treaty of Sèvres, which was the 1920 Treaty of Peace between the Allies and the Ottoman Empire, provided for the surrender

---

22. See, e.g., B. Wright, History of the United Nations War Crimes Commission (London: H.M. Stationery Office, 1948), 35 (the governments of Great Britain, France, and Russia had condemned the massacres of Armenians by Turks in 1915 as "crimes against humanity and civilization"); see also, Robert Lansing, "Notes on World Sovereignty," 15 A.J.I.L.: 13, 25 (1921) (former U.S. Secretary of State writing that the slave trade had become a "crime against humanity") * * *.

by Turkey of such persons as might be accused of crimes against "the laws of humanity," but unfortunately, in 1923, the Treaty of Lausanne gave them amnesty.

Between the two world wars, a wave of terror swept Europe, mostly in connection with nationalist claims in the Balkans. In 1936, Adolf Hitler [exploited] the international community's inability to prosecute or sanction crimes against humanity stating, "And who now remembers the Armenians?" Indeed, it is particularly revealing that he would preface his policy of exterminating Jews, Gypsies, and Slavs by revealing the absence of interest by the world community [to prosecute] such conduct. [That failure and the inability to create efficient] international structures to enforce this proscription, gave Hitler the comfort of knowing that he might succeed in genocide, as others had in the past. In 1937, the League of Nations adopted a Convention Against Terrorism; an annexed Protocol provided for the establishment of a special international criminal court to prosecute such crimes. India was the only country to ratify the Convention. It never entered into force.

After World War II, it became obvious that crimes against peace, war crimes, and what became known, with the London Charter, as "crimes against humanity" had been committed. The London Charter established the International Military Tribunal (IMT) at Nuremberg, which was designed to prosecute major war criminals in the European theater. In 1946, a similar international military tribunal was established in Tokyo to prosecute major Japanese war criminals.

Since World War II, there have been many examples of conduct that violate the Nuremberg principles and which could have been tried in a war crimes tribunal. During the Vietnam War, atrocities were committed by both sides. The depredations of the Khmer Rouge in Cambodia are infamous. The Iraqi Air Force appears to have bombed villages in Kurdistan with both mustard gas and nerve gas. The former Soviet Union is alleged to have booby-trapped dolls belonging to Afghan Mujahideen children. Bosnia, Rwanda and Haiti provide more recent examples. The macabre list could go on.

In 1989, the General Assembly urged consideration of the establishment of an international criminal court. This recommendation was predicated on growing international concern for drug trafficking * * * and international terrorism. The International Law Commission (ILC) was requested to prepare a report and, in 1990, proposed the creation of an international criminal court. The G.A. Sixth Committee addressed the issue in 1991, and proposed that it be studied further.

On 8 April 1993 the International Court of Justice (ICJ), in response to the suit filed by Bosnia and Herzegovina, called upon Serbia and Montenegro "immediately * * * [to] take all measures within their power to prevent commission of the crime of genocide * * * whether directed against the Muslim population of Bosnia and Herzegovina or against any other national, ethnical, racial, or religious group." [35] This

---

35. "Case Concerning Application of the Convention on the Prevention and Punishment of the Crime of Genocide (Bosnia and Herzegovina v. Yugoslavia [Serbia and

was an interim decision. The Court noted that facts were still in dispute. It was also unable to render a decision on disputed rights falling outside the ambit of the Genocide Convention.

The creation of the Ad Hoc Tribunal for crimes against humanitarian law was the culmination of several earlier Security Council resolutions. * * * In early 1992, Resolution 771 called for preliminary investigations. Resolution 780 of 6 October 1992 created a "War Crimes Commission," which analyzed the information garnered by the earlier investigations, conducted its own investigations, and reported its findings to the Secretary–General. Subsequently, the Secretary–General recommended that the Security Council create the Ad Hoc Tribunal. On 11 February 1993, the Council adopted this recommendation and called for the creation of the Ad Hoc Tribunal in its Resolution 808.

Security Council Resolution 808, paragraph 1, provides: "an international tribunal shall be established for the prosecution of persons responsible for serious violations of international humanitarian law committed in the territory of the former Yugoslavia since 1991."

The Legal Basis and Authority to Establish a Permanent Tribunal

The usual and most appropriate method for establishing an international criminal tribunal would be a convention. All member states, however, are likely under a binding obligation to take whatever action is required to enforce the statute under U.N. Charter, Chapter VII. The Secretary–General suggested that the treaty approach would be too long and arduous; drafting an instrument and obtaining the required ratifications for entry into force would not be reconcilable with the urgency expressed by the Security Council in Resolution 808 (Secretary–General's Report, at paras. 20–21). Thus, it was recommended that the authority or legal basis for the tribunal be predicated on Chapter VII of the U.N. Charter, which covers Action with respect to Threats to the Peace, Breaches of the Peace, and Acts of Aggression. The creation of the tribunal would be a "*measure* to maintain or restore international peace and security, following the requisite determination of the existence of a threat to the peace, breach of the peace or act of aggression."

Article 41 of the U.N. Charter provides: "The Security Council may decide what measures not involving the use of armed force are to be employed to give effect to its decisions, and it may call upon the members of the United Nations to apply such measures." *Article 42* adds: "Should the Security Council consider that measures provided for in Article 41 would be inadequate or have proved to be inadequate, it may take such action by air, sea, or land forces as may be necessary to maintain or restore international peace and security. Such action may include demonstrations, blockade, and other operations by air, sea, or land forces of Members of the [U.N.]" The argument is that if the use of force is allowed as a "*measure*" under Article 42, *a fortiori,* the

Montenegro]), request for the indication of provisional measures, (1993) I.C.J. Reports 3, 32 I.L.M. 890 (1993) (wherein Bosnia and Herzegovina filed suit against Serbia and Montenegro "for violating the Genocide Convention" and other illegal conduct in violation of customary international law).

creation of an ad hoc international criminal court should also be allowed. In "the particular case of the former Yugoslavia, the Secretary–General believes that the establishment of the International Tribunal by means of a Chapter VII decision would be legally justified, both in terms of the object and purpose of the decision [as indicated in the purpose statement in his report] and of past Security Council practice." [Sec.Gen.Report ¶¶ 24, 27].

The Secretary–General's Report relating to the atrocities there noted that the creation of the Tribunal for the prosecution of the alleged breaches of international humanitarian law will apply existing law, including the Geneva Conventions of 1949, and that the Security Council would not be creating law or purporting to legislate. Is this assertion accurate? Where, besides in the Geneva and Hague Conventions, would these crimes be found? Would they be found with sufficient clarity to satisfy due process concerns? Would the Secretary–General's assertions hold for a permanent war crimes tribunal?

Specific Tribunal Characteristics

Propriety

A tribunal will only be acceptable if it proceeds in a manner that is beyond reproach. Basic notions of fairness and human rights in relation to investigation, prosecution, and trial are paramount. Any tribunal unscrupulous in protecting the accused from abuses and deprivation of civil liberties would be a dangerous institution. Justice Jackson summed up the importance of this point in his opening statement during the Nuremberg Trial.

> Before I discuss the particulars of evidence, some general considerations which may affect the credit of this trial in the eyes of the world should be candidly faced. There is a dramatic disparity between the circumstances of the accusers and the accused that might discredit our work if we should falter, in even minor matters, in being fair and temperate. Unfortunately, the nature of these crimes is such that both prosecution and judgment must be by victor nations over vanquished foes [*a problem not faced by the Ad Hoc Tribunal for the former Yugoslavia*].

> . . . We must never forget that the record on which we judge these defendants is the record on which history will judge us tomorrow. To pass these defendants a poisoned chalice is to put it to our lips as well. We must summon such detachment and intellectual integrity to our task that this Trial will commend itself to posterity as fulfilling humanity's aspirations to do justice.

International Human Rights Law provides the minimum standards for protection of an accused person. Increasingly, U.S. requests for extradition and hand-overs under Status of Forces agreements have been overridden by international and foreign courts, which have ruled that international human rights provisions take precedence. In two recent cases, concerns over capital punishment have resulted in litigation in which courts outside the United States have held that extradition to states where the death penalty applied would, in certain circumstances, violate provisions of international human rights conventions.

International human rights conventions contain analogues to many of the protections guaranteed by the U.S. Constitution, including the right to fair trial, to "equality of arms" and access to court, to the presumption of innocence, to the right to confrontation, and to the right to counsel of choice. Though some of the international human rights protections meet, and even exceed, U.S. constitutional standards, some do not. Article 20(1) of the Statute for the Ad Hoc Tribunal provides that the "[t]rial chambers shall ensure that a trial is fair and expeditious and that proceedings are rendered in accordance with the rules of procedure and evidence, with full respect for the rights of the accused and due regard for the protection of victims and witnesses." The accused's Geneva Law and human right to consult a lawyer and to have adequate time to prepare a defense must be ensured. To be acceptable, this protection must be applicable to the entire trial process.

* * *

SECTION C. USE OF NUREMBERG PRINCIPLES UNDER UNITED STATES LAW

1. ARE THE NUREMBERG PRINCIPLES A SOURCE OF CIVIL LIABILITY?

HANDEL v. ARTUKOVIC

United States District Court, C.D. California, 1985.
601 F.Supp. 1421.

RYMER, District Judge.

Plaintiffs in this class action seek compensatory and punitive damages against defendant for his alleged involvement in the deprivations of life and property suffered by the Jews in Yugoslavia during World War II. The complaint, which must be taken as true for purposes of this motion, alleges that defendant was the Commissioner of Public Security and Internal Administration and later the Minister of the Interior for the Independent State of Croatia, a puppet state of the German Reich established after its invasion of the Kingdom of Yugoslavia. In his official capacity, defendant oversaw and implemented Croatia's solution to "the Jewish question." The result of defendant's implementation of this policy was the passage of anti-Jewish legislation; the seizure of property owned by Croatian Jews; and the imprisonment and eventual execution of tens of thousands of Jewish men, women, and children.

The complaint avers that defendant fled Croatia in 1945, and that he entered this country illegally in 1949. In May 1951, defendant was the subject of deportation proceedings. These proceedings eventually culminated in the grant to defendant in 1959 of a temporary stay of deportation, and defendant has remained in the United States until the present. Plaintiffs [all now U.S. citizens] state that they were Jewish citizens of Yugoslavia in 1941, and each had close relatives who were murdered under the auspices of Croatian authority.

In their complaint, plaintiffs state four causes of action: (1) violation of the Hague Convention of 1907 and the Geneva Convention of 1929; (2) war crimes in violation of international law; (3) crimes against humanity in violation of international law; and (4) violation of Articles 100, 125, 141, and 145 of the Yugoslavian Criminal Code. Jurisdiction for the first three causes of action is based on 28 U.S.C. § 1331; jurisdiction over the fourth claim is predicated upon diversity jurisdiction pursuant to 28 U.S.C. § 1332(a)(2). Defendant has moved to dismiss under Fed.R.Civ.P. 12(b)(1) and (6).

* * * [T]he Court concludes that the international law claims should be dismissed under Fed.R.Civ.P. 12(b)(1) for lack of subject matter jurisdiction. The war crime and crime against humanity claims are * * * barred by the statute of limitations, and therefore fail to state a claim for relief. Fed.R.Civ.P. 12(b)(6). The * * * Yugoslavian * * * claim is barred by the applicable statute of limitations; and that to apply Yugoslavian substantive law as requested would in any event be unconstitutional under United States law as well as unenforceable under Yugoslavian and international law.[a] The Yugoslavian law count therefore also fails to state a claim upon which relief can be granted.[1]

I. Violation of the Hague and Geneva Conventions.

Pursuant to 28 U.S.C. § 1331, the Court has jurisdiction over actions "arising under" the "Constitution, laws, or treaties" of the United States. In plaintiffs' third count, they assert a cause of action under two United States treaties: the Convention Respecting the Laws and Customs of War on Land, 1907, T.S. No. 539 ("Hague Convention"); and the Convention Between the United States of America and other Powers Relating to Prisoners of War, 1929 (1932), revised in Geneva Convention Relative to the Treatment of Prisoners of War, 1949, 6 U.S.T. 3316, T.I.A.S. 3364, 75 U.N.T.S. 135 ("Geneva Convention"). [The court held that the two treaties were not self-executing and thus did not provide judicially enforceable obligations. For analysis of the question of self-executing treaties, see Chapter 14, *infra*. Thus, neither of the treaties relied upon by plaintiffs gives them a private right of action "arising under" the treaties within the meaning of section 1331. The first count therefore must be dismissed for want of jurisdiction under Rule 12(b)(1).

II. Violation of Customary International Law.

Plaintiffs' second and third claims for relief are based on alleged

---

a. The court concluded that the Yugoslavian criminal statutes on which plaintiffs' claim was based ran afoul of prohibitions against ex post facto laws.

1. Since the time that the Court took this matter under submission, extradition proceedings have been initiated against the defendant. Because this is a civil action and involves altogether different considerations, nothing said or held in this matter should be taken in any way as bearing on the issues or the proper result in that proceeding.

violations of the laws of war [2] and the laws of humanity. Two issues are presented by these claims: first, whether the Court has jurisdiction over such claims under section 1331; and second, if the Court does have jurisdiction, whether plaintiffs have stated a cognizable claim for relief under international law. The Court concludes that it does not have jurisdiction under section 1331, and, even if it did, plaintiffs fail to state a claim upon which relief may be granted.

A. Jurisdiction under Section 1331: Plaintiffs' international law claims, like their treaty claims, must "arise under" the "laws of the United States" for jurisdiction to lie. It is clear that the law of nations "is part of our law, and must be ascertained and administered by the courts of justice of appropriate jurisdiction, as often as questions of right depending upon it are duly presented for their determination." The Paquete Habana. As Judge Kaufman stated in Filartiga v. Pena–Irala [supra]: "The law of nations forms an integral part of the common law, and a review of the history surrounding the adoption of the Constitution demonstrates that it became a part of the common law of the United States upon the adoption of the Constitution."

* * *

The more difficult issue is whether plaintiffs have a claim "arising under" the law of nations. Plaintiffs contend that because international law is part of federal common law, the Court should find an explicit or implicit right of action for its enforcement. There are three possible sources for such a private right of action: an explicit grant of authority under 28 U.S.C. § 1331; an implicit right derived from the law of nations; or an implicit right derived from federal common law.

Section 1331 does not provide plaintiffs with a right of action. Although two recent circuit court opinions, Filartiga and Judge Edwards' concurrence in Tel–Oren, have found that 28 U.S.C. § 1350 creates a private right to sue for violations of the law of nations, it is clear that the result would be different if section 1331 rather than section 1350 were the applicable jurisdictional statute:

Unlike section 1331, which requires that an action "arise under" the laws of the United States, section 1350 does not require that the action "arise under" the law of nations, but only mandates

---

2. Although the Court does not need to reach the issue for purposes of this motion, plaintiffs do not appear to have stated a cognizable claim under the laws of war. "War crimes" refers to criminal actions taken against the soldiers or civilians of *another* country rather than against the defendant's fellow citizens. This limitation on the meaning of "war crimes" is reflected in the Charter of the International Military Tribunal annexed to the Agreement for the Establishment of an International Military Tribunal, U.S. Department of State, Trial of War Criminals 13, Department of State Pub. No. 2420 (1945), 39 AJIL Supp. 257 (1945). The Charter defines war crimes in relevant part as "murder, ill-treatment or deportation to slave labor or for any other purpose of civilian population *of or in occupied territory*." By contrast, crimes against humanity include "murder, extermination, enslavement, deportation, and other inhumane *acts* committed against *any* civilian population." Plaintiffs lived within the boundaries of the Croatian state, and therefore defendant's conduct violated the laws of humanity but not the laws of war.

> a "violation of the law of nations" in order to create a cause of action. The language of the statute is explicit on this issue: by its express terms, nothing more than a *violation* of the law of nations is required to invoke section 1350. Judge Bork nevertheless would propose to write into section 1350 an additional restriction that is not even suggested by the statutory language. Congress, of course, knew full well that it could draft section 1350 with "arising under" language, or the equivalent, to require a "cause of action" or "right to sue," but it chose not to do so.

Tel–Oren, supra (Edwards, J., concurring). Thus, while the "violation" language of section 1350 may be interpreted as explicitly granting a cause of action, the "arising under" language of section 1331 cannot be so interpreted. Section 1331, standing alone, does not give the Court jurisdiction over plaintiffs' claims.

Nor may plaintiffs urge that a right of action can be inferred from the law of nations. While international law may provide the substantive rule of law in a given situation, the enforcement of international law is left to individual states. * * * As Judge Edwards stated in Tel–Oren: "[T]he law of nations never has been perceived to create or define the civil actions to be made available by each member of the community of nations; by consensus, the states leave that determination to their respective municipal laws."

It is important that this distinction be maintained for two reasons. First, as a matter of policy, the distinction is a fundamental aspect of international law's accommodation to principles of national sovereignty. The Nuremberg tribunal articulated this interest in United States v. Altstoetter (The "Justice Case"), (Trials of War Criminals, Vol. III:

> This universality and superiority of international law does not necessarily imply universality of its enforcement * * * The law is universal, but such a state reserves unto itself the exclusive power within its boundaries to apply or withhold sanctions. Thus, notwithstanding the paramount authority of the substantive rules of common international law, the doctrine of national sovereignty has been preserved through the control of enforcement machinery.

Second, the distinction reflects the practical limits on enforcement of international law by municipal courts. The absence of a consensus on international law, particularly with respect to technical issues created by the wide array of legal systems in the world, makes it "hard even to imagine that harmony ever would characterize this issue." Tel–Oren, * * * (Edwards, J., concurring).

Thus, although plaintiffs cite a number of jurists and commentators who describe customary international law *substantively*, they have not pointed to any source, and the Court has found none, for the proposition that one looks to the law of nations to determine the *actionability* of conduct condemned by that body of law. The Court declines to rewrite a long-established rule based on sound policy concerns. The law of nations therefore does not provide plaintiffs with a private right of action in this municipal court.

The third possible source of a right of action, urged particularly by amicus ACLU, is federal common law. They argue that the present case is analogous to Bivens v. Six Unknown Federal Narcotics Agents, in that "where federally protected rights have been invaded, it has been the rule from the beginning that courts will be alert to adjust their remedies so as to grant the necessary relief." Bivens, quoting from Bell v. Hood. As amicus puts the argument, "the legal prohibition of such conduct entitles the plaintiffs to sue for damages, just as the rights guaranteed by treaties, statutes, and the Constitution may by their very nature justify private enforcement."

However, the step encouraged by amicus fails to recognize the fundamental difference between municipal enforcement of municipal law and municipal enforcement of international law. The Supreme Court has noted that, under Bivens, there may be "special factors counseling hesitation in the absence of affirmative action by Congress." In the present case, the "special factor" is the absence of any affirmative legislative action at all. Unlike violations of federal statutes or the Constitution, no American legislative body has acted in any way with respect to customary international law. To imply a cause of action from the law of nations would completely defeat the critical right of the sovereign to determine whether and how international rights should be enforced in that municipality. The Restatement (Second) Foreign Relations § 3 (1965) [states] a violation of international law gives to individual litigants such remedies or defenses in a forum of a state *"as are provided by its domestic law."* Until Congress evinces an intent to give effect to international law, either by passing a jurisdictional statute or by incorporating international rights into the statutes of the United States, the Court declines to infer such an intent solely from the United States' membership in the community of nations.

B.   Stating a Claim under International Law.

Even assuming that the Court has jurisdiction over plaintiffs' customary international law claims, plaintiffs have not stated an actionable claim pursuant to Fed.R.Civ.P. 12(b)(6). Two issues are raised by plaintiffs' claims: first, whether the alleged acts constituted a violation of international law at the time they were committed; and second, whether the claims would be time barred.

It appears clear that the acts of genocide, torture, enslavement, and religious discrimination alleged in plaintiffs' complaint constituted violations of the laws of humanity at the time they were committed. In the late nineteenth century, occasional treaties began to reflect a growing consciousness of fundamental human rights. For example, in 1878, under the Treaty of Berlin, the people of Serbia, Montenegro, and Rumania were guaranteed freedom of religious practice. * * * Finally, at the Hague Conferences of 1899 and 1907, the signatory countries established detailed rules for land and naval warfare as well as for the treatment of prisoners of war.

Despite this increasing awareness of international human rights, at the end of World War I there was not a generalized recognition of the "laws of humanity." For example, the American delegates to the 1919

Paris Convention expressed considerable reservations regarding the condemnation of violations of "the laws of humanity" contained in the report of the Paris Commission on Responsibility of Authors of the War.

Nevertheless, international law continued to develop in the decades between the two world wars. Protection for minority groups received particular attention as multi-national kingdoms were replaced with nation states:

> On the one hand, with the disappearance of multi-national, non-racial states, such as the old Austro–Hungarian and Turkish Empires, almost every European nation came to be dominated by a single nationality which, without special measures of protection, might abuse its position at the expense of the minorities. On the other [hand], the ideal of self-determination itself presupposed a special concern to protect all national groups even if, for reasons of their geographical distribution, they were not able to enjoy that right in a direct form.

* * * This concern for minority groups led to a League of Nations requirement that all new or substantially enlarged states, including Yugoslavia, assume obligations for the protection of their minorities as a condition of recognition of their independence or new frontiers. The minority treaty signed by Yugoslavia as well as many other European countries placed members of racial, religious, or linguistic minorities "under the guarantee of the League of Nations," and "guaranteed such rights as freedom from discrimination in civil and political affairs, and the free exercise of speech and religion." * * *

The work of the League of Nations suggests that there was a general recognition of the rights of religious and ethnic minorities by the time of the outbreak of World War II. The existence of this consensus was confirmed by the Nuremberg court sitting immediately after World War II. That court, when faced with the issue of whether "crimes against humanity" were part of the law of nations prior to World War II, quoted with approval from Sir David Maxwell–Fyfe: With regard to "crimes against humanity," this at any rate is clear. The Nazis, when they persecuted and murdered countless Jews and political opponents in Germany, knew that what they were doing was wrong and that their actions were crimes which had been condemned by the criminal law of every civilized state. When these crimes were mixed with the preparation for aggressive war and later with the commission of war crimes in occupied territories, it cannot be a matter of complaint that a procedure is established for their punishment.

Although the law of nations was not codified until after the war, the court concluded that the notion of the "laws of humanity," put forward initially in the 1919 Paris Commission on Responsibility of Authors of the War, had clearly become an international consensus by the time of World War II. It therefore seems clear that defendant's alleged actions constituted a violation of international law when they were committed. Turning to the second question raised by plaintiffs' claim, namely, what is the applicable statute of limitations for this violation, plaintiffs urge the Court to look to international law, noting that "the incorporation of the law of nations into federal common law permits a federal court to determine an appropriate period of limitations without regard to the parochial interests of the forum state." * * * [Further], in applying this federal common law, the universal consensus condemning defendant's behavior "requires this court to look to international standards before applying any limitations for actions of this nature." * * *

Assuming, arguendo, plaintiff's initial premise that federal rather than state law should provide the applicable rule of decision regarding the limitation of actions, there is no basis in the cases or commentaries for the conclusion that international law should govern the procedural aspects of plaintiffs' claim. Even plaintiffs' expert, Professor Almond, states that "the practice of states does not show that statutes of limitation have been established, as such, applicable as part of the international law shared among nations." * * *

It is therefore municipal, rather than international, law that must provide the rule of decision for plaintiffs' international law claims.

In ascertaining the federal law that should govern plaintiffs' claims, considerable energy has been expended by the parties on the issue of whether or not the United States has endorsed the statute of no limitation set forth in the Convention on the Non–Applicability of Statutes of Limitation to War Crimes and Crimes Against Humanity, adopted and opened for signature (entered into force November 11, 1970). From the proceedings in the United Nations General Assembly, it appears that the United States did support the principle of a statute of no limitations. In Press Release, November 26, 1968, the United States delegation stated that: the original purposes of this convention were— (1) to make clear that under international law there are no periods of limitation applicable to war crimes and crimes against humanity, and (2) to establish a new rule of international law by treaty that states which become parties to the convention should adopt necessary measures to abolish domestic statutes of limitation insofar as they might apply to war crimes and crimes against humanity. The reasons enumerated by the delegation for opposing the draft convention do not suggest that the United States had any reservations about this initial purpose. Indeed, in a prior press release, the delegation had "urge[d] the Committee to reconsider whether it would not be better to return to the original purpose of this item—namely, to produce a convention limited simply to non-application of statutes of limitations to war crimes and crimes against humanity." Thus, while the United States did not sign the resulting convention, it appears to recognize the principle that a statute of no limitation should be applied to the criminal prosecution of war crimes and crimes against humanity.

Regardless of what was the position of the United States, however, the period of limitations appropriate for criminal prosecution does not suggest that a similar rule should be adopted for civil actions. In American jurisprudence, criminal and civil statutes of limitations have different conceptual underpinnings. For criminal violations, the common law rule was that there was no limitation as to the time within which offenses might be prosecuted. Criminal statutes of limitations were therefore adopted at the will of the legislature, and were, in effect, an act of grace by which the sovereign surrendered its right to prosecute. Because these statutes are equivalent to acts of amnesty, the length of the statute of limitations bears a necessary relation to the heinousness of the crime.

Civil statutes of limitation, by contrast, are viewed as a procedural requirement designed to protect against stale claims, and are unrelated to the underlying merits of the action.

Considering these factors, plaintiffs' international law claims should have a shorter rather than a longer limitations period. First, like instances of wrongful death, crimes against humanity are immediately known to the victims and their families. Second, a claim of a crime against humanity is one that is particularly susceptible to the loss of evidence through the death or disappearance of witnesses and the loss of documents; it is unlike a claim for breach of a written contract, where the most critical evidence does not change with time. Finally, the gravity of international law violations mandates a reasonably short period to protect individuals from fraudulent claims.

In light of these considerations, the Court does not need to determine the precise limit applicable to plaintiff's cause of action, * * * to hold that thirty five years is beyond the time within which plaintiffs should have brought their claims. The parties have not brought to the Court's attention any civil statute of limitations, either in domestic law or in an international forum, that comes close to the length of time involved here. While defendant's alleged activities shock the conscience, the gravity of this conduct does not play the role in civil limitation statutes that it fulfills in criminal statutes. Criminal prosecutions of crimes against humanity should be and are subject to a statute of no limitations; but civil actions cannot be subjected to this rule under American law. [Discussion of plaintiff's claim based on violation of the Yugoslavian criminal code omitted.] IT IS THEREFORE ORDERED that plaintiffs' complaint be dismissed with prejudice.

---

2. CAN THE NUREMBERG PRINCIPLES BE USED DEFENSIVELY IN CRIMINAL PROSECUTIONS?

MITCHELL v. UNITED STATES

United States Supreme Court, 1967.
386 U.S. 972, 87 S.Ct. 1162, 18 L.Ed.2d 132.[a]

Certiorari denied.

Mr. Justice DOUGLAS, dissenting.

a. Reh. denied 386 U.S. 1042 (1967).

Petitioner did not report for induction as ordered, was indicted, convicted, and sentenced to five years' imprisonment and his conviction was affirmed. His defense was that the "war" in Vietnam was being conducted in violation of various treaties to which we were a signatory, especially the Treaty of London of August 8, 1945, * * * which in Article 6(a) declares that "waging of a war of aggression" is a "crime against peace" imposing "individual responsibility." Article 8 provides: "The fact that the Defendant acted pursuant to order of his Government or of a superior shall not free him from responsibility, but may be considered in mitigation of punishment if the Tribunal determines that justice so requires." Petitioner claimed that the "war" in Vietnam was a "war of aggression" within the meaning of the Treaty of London and that Article 8 makes him responsible for participating in it even though he is ordered to do so.[1]

Mr. Justice Jackson, the U.S. prosecutor at Nuremberg, stated: "If certain acts in violation of treaties are crimes, they are crimes whether the United States does them or whether Germany does them, and we are not prepared to lay down a rule of criminal conduct against others which we would not be willing to have invoked against us."

Article VI, cl. 2, of the Constitution states that "Treaties" are a part of the "supreme Law of the Land; and the Judges in every State shall be bound thereby." There is a considerable body of opinion that our actions in Vietnam constitute the waging of an aggressive "war."

This case presents the questions:

(1) whether the Treaty of London is a treaty within the meaning of Art. VI, cl. 2;

(2) whether the question as to the waging of an aggressive "war" is in the context of this criminal prosecution a justiciable question;

(3) whether the Vietnam episode is a "war" in the sense of the Treaty;

(4) whether petitioner has standing to raise the question;

(5) whether, if he has, the Treaty may be tendered as a defense in this criminal case or in amelioration of the punishment.

These are extremely sensitive and delicate questions. But they should, I think, be answered. Even those who think that the Nuremberg judgments were unconstitutional by our guarantee relating to ex post facto laws would have to take a different view of the Treaty of London that purports to lay down a standard of future conduct for all the signatories.

I intimate no opinion on the merits. But I think the petition for certiorari should be granted. We have here a recurring question in

1. The trial court charged the jury that the Treaty of London did not interfere "in any manner in respect to this defendant fulfilling his duty under this order."

present-day Selective Service cases.[a]

RANDALL v. COMMISSIONER OF INTERNAL REVENUE SERVICE

United States Court of Appeals, Eleventh Circuit, 1984.
733 F.2d 1565.

PER CURIAM:

This case presents a new twist in two respects to the attempt to claim a credit against income taxes because of the religious beliefs of the taxpayer. First, rather than claiming a credit for just the percentage of his tax that reflects the percentage of the Government's budget utilized for military spending, roughly 61% according to taxpayer, the claim here is for 100% of the taxes he would owe based on the assertion that the payment of any money to the United States Treasury would be the commission of a mortal sin. Second, rather than basing his claim on the First Amendment of the Constitution, taxpayer contends that 26 U.S.C.A. § 7852(d) protects him from payment of taxes. Section 7852(d) states that no provision of the Internal Revenue Code shall apply where it "would be contrary to any treaty obligation of the United States." Taxpayer contends that the requirement that he pay taxes violates treaties of the United States in two ways. First, United States military spending is in violation of international treaty obligations. Second, the United States is obligated by treaty to observe the religious freedom of its citizens, and it is contrary to this treaty obligation to fail to honor taxpayers' free practice of religion by requiring him to pay taxes to the general treasury of the United States, from which military expenditures are made.

* * *

In sustaining the Commissioner's refusal to allow the tax credit claimed on this basis, the tax court recognized that the sole purpose of section 7852(d) was to insure that the application of the Internal Revenue Code would in no way abrogate any existing tax treaties in the collection of taxes. Plainly, that section is not concerned with the ways in which Government funds, generated by tax revenues, are ultimately spent. * * *

Contrary to taxpayer's argument as to the thrust of the Nuremberg Principles and other principles of international law, the act of paying taxes does not amount to complicity in any war crime committed by the Government. * * * With respect to any violation of international law committed by the Government, the taxpayer as a taxpayer is exempted from complicity by his remoteness and utter lack of direct involvement.

---

a. Problems posed by this case are more fully analyzed in Forman, The Nuremberg Trials and Conscientious Objection to War: Justiciability Under United States Munici-pal Law, in 1969 Proceedings of the American Society of International Law 157 and comments by Telford Taylor and others in 1969 Proceedings 165 ff.

* * * It has been consistently held that the Nuremberg Principles furnish no excuse for the non-payment of taxes.   * * *

AFFIRMED.

———

Nuremberg's apparent adoption of transcendant principles of individual responsibility would seem to provide the individual conscientious objector or disobedient a promising basis for legal defense for refusal to participate. The U.S. judiciary, however, has chosen to interpret the Nuremberg rules strictly, not in favor of the policies they enunciate, but in favor of the state. In Nuremberg itself, were there any other than high ranking officials charged with committing or having a legal duty to prevent war crimes from occurring? If war crimes trials are limited to high ranking officials, does that establish a rule that only high ranking officials have the legal duty? If the average conscript, citizen or member of the armed forces was not charged at Nuremberg, does it mean that those individuals do not have a legal duty and, hence, no defense for refusing to participate? Is this logical or appropriate? If it is the "law" after Nuremberg, has that Judgment been eviscerated? What do the decisions you just read suggest? See Lippman, *Civil Resistance: Revitalizing International Law in the Nuclear Age,* 13 Whitt.L.Rev. 17 (1992).

3. INDIRECT USE OF NUREMBERG PRINCIPLES: DENATURALIZATION AND DEPORTATION OR DISGUISED EXTRADITION?

Courts have applied the Nuremberg principles to Nazi war criminals by expelling, deporting, or other slight-of-hand extraditions.

ETHAN NADELMAN, THE EVOLUTION OF U.S. INVOLVEMENT IN THE INTERNATIONAL RENDITION OF FUGITIVE CRIMINALS

25 N.Y.U.J.Int'l L. & Pol. 313, 324 (1993) (most fns. omitted) *

The courts have similarly refrained from according any sanctuary to Nazi war criminals who thought they had found a safe refuge in the United States. The one exception occurred in 1959, when a California federal court rejected a request from the government of Yogoslavia for the extradition of Andrija Artukovic, Minister of the Interior of the Independent State of Croatia during World War II. (*Karadzole v. Artukovic,* 170 F.Supp. 838 (S.D.Cal.1959). His alleged crimes, which included control over concentration camps and the murders of thousands of civilians, were viewed by the court as political offenses for which extradition could not be granted. Moreover, until well into the 1970s, the Immigration and Naturalization Service devoted little effort to identifying and deporting Nazi war criminals. During the late 1970s, however, Elizabeth Holtzman, chairperson of the House Judiciary Com-

* Reprinted with the permission of N.Y.U.J.Int'l L. & Pol.

mittee's Subcommittee on Immigration, pushed through legislation requiring the Justice Department to assume responsibility for Nazi war crime cases. Attorney General Griffin Bell responded in 1979 by creating an Office of Special Investigations (OSI), dedicated to finding Nazi war criminals and arranging their extradition or deportation to face charges in foreign courts. The OSI's efforts were aided by the widespread repudiation of the 1959 Artukovic decision by most commentators and all federal courts. By 1991, seventy-five extraditions and deportations had resulted from OSI's investigations, including: the 1986 extradition of Artukovic to Yogoslavia, where he died before his sentenced execution; the 1973 extradition of Hermine Brausteiner–Ryan, a former SS member and Maidanek concentration camp guard, to West Germany, where she was sentenced to life imprisonment for multiple murders; the 1984 deportation of Deodor Fedorenko, a Ukrainian guard in the Treblinka concentration camp, to the Soviet Union, where he was executed for his crimes; the 1987 deportation of Karl Linnas, an Estonian who supervised the killing of Jews in the concentration camps at Tartu, to the Soviet Union, where he died while awaiting action on an appeal for a pardon (*see, U.S. v. Linnas*, 527 F.Supp. 426 (EDNY 1981); *Linnas v. I.N.S.*, 790 F.2d 1024 (2d Cir.1986)); and the 1986 extradition of John Demjanjuk, a Ukrainian initially identified as a notorious SS guard at the Treblinka and Sobibor death camps known as "Ivan the Terrible," to Israel, where he was tried and sentenced to death.

SECTION D.   UNIVERSAL JURISDICTION AND NUREMBERG PRINCIPLES

ATTORNEY GENERAL OF ISRAEL v. EICHMANN
Israel, Supreme Court 1962.
36 Int'l L.Rep. 277 (1968).*

1.   The appellant, Adolf Eichmann, was found guilty by the District Court of Jerusalem of offenses of the most extreme gravity against the Nazi and Nazi Collaborators (Punishment) Law, 1950 (hereinafter referred to as "the Law") and was sentenced to death. These offences may be divided into four groups:

   (a) Crimes against the Jewish people, contrary to Section I(a)(1) of the Law;

   (b) Crimes against humanity, contrary to Section I(a)(2);

   (c) War crimes, contrary to Section I(a)(3);

   (d) Membership of hostile organizations, contrary to Section 3.

2.   The acts constituting these offences, which the Court attributed to the appellant, have been specified in paragraph 244 of the judgment of the District Court * * *. The acts comprised in Group (a) are:

---

* Reprinted with the permission of the
Editor of the International Law Reports.

(1) that during the period from August 1941 to May 1945, in Germany, in the Axis States and in the areas which were subject to the authority of Germany and the Axis States, he, together with others, caused the killing of millions of Jews for the purpose of carrying out the plan known as "the Final Solution of the Jewish Problem" with the intent to exterminate the Jewish people;

(2) that during that period and in the same places he, together with others, placed millions of Jews in living conditions which were calculated to bring about their physical destruction, for the purpose of carrying out the plan above mentioned with the intent to exterminate the Jewish people;

(3) that during that period and in the same places he, together with others, caused serious physical and mental harm to millions of Jews with the intent to exterminate the Jewish people;

(4) that during the years 1943 and 1944 he, together with others, "devised measures the purpose of which was to prevent births among Jews by his instructions forbidding child bearing and ordering the interruption of pregnancies of Jewish women in the Theresin Ghetto with the intent to exterminate the Jewish people".

The acts constituting the crimes in Group (b) are as follows:

(5) that during the period from August 1941 to May 1945 he, together with others, caused in the territories and areas mentioned in clause (1) the murder, extermination, enslavement, starvation and deportation of the civilian Jewish population;

(6) that during the period from December 1939 to March 1941 he, together with others, caused the deportation of Jews to Nisco, and the deportation of Jews from the areas in the East annexed to the Reich, and from the Reich area proper, to the German Occupied Territories in the East, and to France;

(7) that in carrying out the above-mentioned activities he persecuted Jews on national, racial, religious and political grounds;

(8) that during the period from March 1938 to May 1945 in the places mentioned above he, together with others, caused the spoliation of the property of millions of Jews by means of mass terror linked with the murder, extermination, starvation and deportation of these Jews;

(9) that during the years 1940–1942 he, together with others, caused the expulsion of hundreds of thousands of Poles from their places of residence;

(10) that during 1941 he, together with others, caused the expulsion of more than 14,000 Slovenes from their places of residence;

(11) that during the Second World War he, together with others, caused the expulsion of scores of thousands of Gypsies from Germany and German-occupied areas and their transportation to the German-occupied areas in the East;

(12) that in 1942 he, together with others, caused the expulsion of 93 children of the Czech village of Lidice.

The acts comprised in Group (c) are:

that he committed the acts of persecution, expulsion and murder mentioned in Counts 1 to 7, in so far as these were done during the Second World War against Jews from among the populations of the States occupied by the Germans and by the other Axis States.

The acts comprised in Group (d) are:

that as from May 1940 he was a member of three Nazi Police organizations which were declared criminal organizations by the International Military Tribunal which tried the Major War Criminals, and as a member of such organizations he took part in acts which were declared criminal in Article 6 of the London Charter of August 8, 1945.

3.   The appellant has appealed to this Court against both conviction and sentence.

4.   The oral and written submissions of learned counsel who supported the appeal, Dr. Servatius, may, in so far as they are directed against conviction, be classified under two heads:

(1) Purely legal contentions, the principal object of which was to undermine the jurisdiction of a court in Israel to try the appellant for the crimes in question;

(2) Factual contentions the object of which was in essence to upset the finding of the District Court that there was no foundation for the defence of the appellant that he played the part of a "small cog" in the machine of Nazi destruction, that in all the above-mentioned chapters of events he functioned as a minor official without any independent initiative, and that nothing but the compulsion of orders and blind obedience to commands from above guided him in carrying out his work at all stages.

> * * *

5.   The District Court has in its judgment dealt with both categories of contentions in an exhaustive, profound and most convincing manner. We should say at once that we fully concur, without hesitation or reserve, in all its conclusions and reasons.   * * *

[The Jurisdiction of the Court]

6.   Most of the legal contentions of counsel for the appellant revolve around the argument that in assuming jurisdiction to try the appellant the District Court acted contrary to the principles of international law. These contentions are as follows:

(1) The Law of 1950, which is the only source of the jurisdiction of the Court in this case, constitutes ex post facto penal legislation which prescribes as offences acts that were committed before the State of Israel came into existence; therefore the validity of this Law is confined to its citizens alone.

(2) The offences for which the appellant was tried are "extra-territorial offences", that is to say, offences that were committed outside the territory of Israel by a citizen of a foreign State, and even though the Law confers jurisdiction in respect of such offences, it conflicts in so doing with the principle of territorial sovereignty, which postulates that only the country within whose territory the offence was committed or to which the offender belongs—in this case, Germany—has the right to punish therefor.

(3) The acts constituting the offence of which the appellant was convicted were at the time of their commission Acts of State.

(4) The appellant was brought to Israeli territory, to be tried for the offences in question, unwillingly and without the consent of the country in which he resided, and this was done through agents of the State of Israel, who acted on the orders of their Government.

(5) The judges of the District Court, being Jews and feeling affinity with the victims of the plan of extermination and Nazi persecution, were psychologically incapable of giving the appellant an objective trial.

* * *

7. We reject all these contentions.

* * *

[Portions of the court's opinion dealing with the second contention—the "extraterritoriality" of the offences—are set forth as follows.]

[Universal Jurisdiction]

12. * * * [I]t is the universal character of the crimes in question which vests in every State the authority to try and punish those who participated in their commission. This proposition is closely linked with the one advanced in the preceding paragraph, from which indeed it follows as a logical outcome. The grounds upon which it rests are as follows:

(a) One of the principles whereby States assume in one degree or another the power to try and punish a person for an offence is the principle of universality. Its meaning is substantially that such power is vested in every State regardless of the fact that the offence was committed outside its territory by a person who did not belong to it, provided he is in its custody when brought to trial. This principle has wide currency and is universally acknowledged with respect to the offence of piracy jure gentium. But while general agreement exists as to this offence, the question of the scope of its application is in dispute * * *.

* * *

(b) The brief survey of views set out above shows that, notwithstanding the differences between them, there is full justification for applying here the principle of universal jurisdiction since the international character of "crimes against humanity" (in the wide meaning of the term) dealt with in this case is no longer in doubt, while the unprecedented extent of their injurious and murderous effects is not to be disputed at the present time. In other words, the basic reason for which international law recognizes the right of each State to exercise such jurisdiction in piracy offences—notwithstanding the fact that its own sovereignty does not extend to the scene of the commission of the offence (the high seas) and the offender is a national of another State or is stateless—applies with even greater force to the above-mentioned crimes. That reason is, it will be recalled, that the interest to prevent bodily and material harm to those who sail the seas and to persons engaged in trade between nations, is a vital interest common to all civilized States and of universal scope * * *.

It follows that the State which prosecutes and punishes a person for piracy acts merely as the organ and agent of the international community and metes out punishment to the offender for his breach of the prohibition imposed by the law of nations * * *.

The above explanation of the substantive basis upon which the exercise of the principle of universal jurisdiction in respect of the crime of piracy rests, justifies its exercise in regard also to the crimes which are the subject of the present case.

(c) The truth is—and this further supports our conclusion—that the application of this principle has for some time been moving beyond the international crime of piracy. We have in mind its application to conventional war crimes as well. As we observed in paragraph 11(c) of this judgment, whenever a "belligerent" country tries and punishes a member of the armed forces of the enemy for an act contrary to "the laws and customs of war", it does so because the matter involves an international crime in the prevention of which the countries of the whole world have an interest. * * *

* * *

(f) We sum up our views on this subject as follows. Not only do all the crimes attributed to the appellant bear an international character, but their harmful and murderous effects were so embracing and widespread as to shake the international community to its very foundations. The State of Israel therefore was entitled, pursuant to the principle of universal jurisdiction and in the capacity of a guardian of international law and an agent for its enforcement, to try the appellant. That being the case, no importance attaches to the fact that the State of Israel did not exist when the offences were committed. Here therefore is an additional reason—and one based on a positive approach—for rejecting the second, "jurisdictional", submission of counsel for the appellant.

* * *

DEMJANJUK v. PETROVSKY

United States Court of Appeals, Sixth Circuit, 1985.
776 F.2d 571.[a]

LIVELY, Chief Judge.

This international extradition case is before the court on appeal from the denial of a petition for a writ of habeas corpus.

I.

The petitioner, John Demjanjuk, is a native of the Ukraine, one of the republics of the Soviet Union. Demjanjuk was admitted to the United States in 1952 under the Displaced Persons Act of 1948 and became a naturalized United States citizen in 1958. He has resided in the Cleveland, Ohio area since his arrival in this country.

In 1981 the United States District Court for the Northern District of Ohio revoked Demjanjuk's certificate of naturalization and vacated the order admitting him to United States citizenship. * * * Chief Judge Battisti of the district court entered extensive findings of fact from which he concluded that the certificate and order "were illegally procured and were procured by willful misrepresentation of material facts under 8 U.S.C. § 1451(a)."

The district court found that Demjanjuk was conscripted into the Soviet Army in 1940 and was captured by the Germans in 1942. After short stays in several German POW camps and a probable tour at the Trawniki SS training camp in Poland, Demjanjuk became a guard at the Treblinka concentration camp, also in Poland, late in 1942. In his various applications for immigration to the United States the petitioner misstated his place of residence during the period 1937–1948 and did not reveal that he had worked for the SS at Treblinka or served in a German military unit later in the war. In the denaturalization proceedings Demjanjuk admitted that his statements concerning residence were false. * * * He steadfastly denied that he had been at Trawniki or Treblinka, though documentary evidence placed him at Trawniki and five Treblinka survivors and one former German guard at the camp identified Demjanjuk as a Ukrainian guard who was known as "Ivan or Iwan Grozny," that is, "Ivan the Terrible."

Following the denaturalization order the government began deportation proceedings against Demjanjuk. While these proceedings were underway Israel filed with the United States Department of State a request for the extradition of Demjanjuk. The United States Attorney, acting on behalf of the State of Israel, filed a complaint in the district court seeking the arrest of Demjanjuk and a hearing on the extradition request. Following a hearing the district court entered an order certifying to the Secretary of State that Demjanjuk was subject to extradition at the request of the State of Israel pursuant to a treaty on extradition between the United States and Israel. * * *

---

a. Cert. denied 475 U.S. 1016 (1986).

II.

* * *

B.

Before reaching the more technical arguments related to jurisdiction [and] whether the crimes charged were within the treaty provisions, we deal with the sufficiency of the evidence. There was sworn testimony by affidavits from six witnesses who were at Treblinka in 1942 and 1943 who identified Demjanjuk. These witnesses stated that Demjanjuk was a guard who herded prisoners into the gas chambers and then actually operated the mechanism which filled the chambers with gas. In addition, several of the witnesses testified that they saw Demjanjuk beat and maim prisoners, some of whom died. * * *

* * * The only evidentiary function of the extradition court is to determine whether there is sufficient evidence to justify holding a person for trial in another place. We are satisfied that the district court relied upon admissible evidence in making its determination in this case.

* * *

III.

A.

The pertinent portions of the treaty (Convention on Extradition) between the United States and Israel (hereafter the Treaty) found in the first three articles and the thirteenth article, are set forth:

Article I

Each Contracting Party agrees, under the conditions and circumstances established by the present Convention, reciprocally to deliver up persons found in its territory who have been charged with or convicted of any of the offenses mentioned in Article II of the present Convention committed within the territorial jurisdiction of the other, or outside thereof under the conditions specified in Article III of the present Convention.

Article II

Persons shall be delivered up according to the provisions of the present Convention for prosecution when they have been charged with, or to undergo sentence when they have been convicted of, any of the following offenses:

1.   Murder.

2.   Manslaughter.

3.   Malicious wounding; inflicting grievous bodily harm.

* * *

Article III

When the offense has been committed outside the territorial jurisdiction of the requesting Party, extradition need not be granted unless the laws of the requested Party provide for the punishment of such an offense committed in similar circumstances.

The words "territorial jurisdiction" as used in this Article and in Article I of the present Convention mean: territory, including territorial waters, and the airspace thereover belonging to or under the control of one of the Contracting Parties, and vessels and aircraft belonging to one of the Contracting Parties or to a citizen or corporation thereof when such vessel is on the high seas or such aircraft is over the high seas.

* * *

Article XIII

A person extradited under the present Convention shall not be detained, tried or punished in the territory of the requesting Party for any offense other than that for which extradition has been granted nor be extradited by that Party to a third State unless:

(Exceptions not applicable).

The Israeli warrant on which the extradition request was based was issued pursuant to a request which charged Demjanjuk with having "murdered tens of thousands of Jews and non-Jews" while operating the gas chambers to exterminate prisoners at Treblinka. It further asserts that the acts charged were committed "with the intention of destroying the Jewish people and to commit crimes against humanity." The complaint in the district court equated this charge with the crimes of "murder and malicious wounding [and] inflicting grievous bodily harm," listed in the Treaty. The warrant was issued pursuant to a 1950 Israeli statute, the Nazis and Nazi Collaborators (Punishment) Law. This statute made certain acts, including "crimes against the Jewish people," "crimes against humanity" and "war crimes committed during the Nazi period" punishable under Israeli law. The statute defines these crimes: "crime against the Jewish people" means any of the following acts, committed with intent to destroy the Jewish people in whole or in part:

1. killing Jews;

2. causing serious bodily or mental harm to Jews;

3. placing Jews in living conditions calculated to bring about their physical destruction;

4. imposing measures intended to prevent births among Jews;

5. forcibly transferring Jewish children to another national or religious group;

6. destroying or desecrating Jewish religious or cultural assets or values;

7. inciting to hatred of Jews;

"crime against humanity" means any of the following acts: murder, extermination, enslavement, starvation or deportation and other inhumane acts committed against any civilian population, and persecution on national, racial, religious or political grounds;

"war crime" means any of the following acts:

> murder, ill-treatment or deportation to forced labour or for any other purpose, of civilian population of or in occupied territory; murder or ill-treatment of prisoners of war or persons on the seas; killing of hostages; plunder of public or private property; wanton destruction of cities, towns or villages; and devastation not justified by military necessity.

B.

Demjanjuk contends that the district court had no jurisdiction to consider the request for extradition. He advances several discrete arguments in support of this position. As he did in the district court, Demjanjuk maintains that the crime he is charged with is not included in the listing of offenses in the treaty. It is his position that "murdering thousands of Jews and non-Jews" is not covered by the treaty designation of "murder." It is a fundamental requirement for international extradition that the crime for which extradition is sought be one provided for by the treaty between the requesting and the requested nation. 18 U.S.C. § 3184; Fernandez v. Phillips, 268 U.S. at 213. We have no difficulty concluding that "murder" includes the mass murder of Jews. This is a logical reading of the treaty language and is the interpretation given the treaty by the Department of State. That interpretation is entitled to considerable deference, as this court noted in Argento v. Horn, 241 F.2d 258, 263 (6th Cir.1957):

> A construction of a treaty by the political department of the government, while not conclusive upon a court called upon to construe such a treaty in a matter involving personal rights, is nevertheless of much weight. [Quoting Charlton v. Kelly.]

Demjanjuk also argues that the district court had no jurisdiction because there is a requirement of "double criminality" in international extradition cases. The Restatement of the Foreign Relations Law of the U.S. (1984) (hereafter "Restatement"), provides in § 487: (1) No person may be extradited pursuant to § 486 [The Basic Rule]

> * * *

> (c) If the offense with which he is charged or of which he has been convicted is not punishable as a serious crime both in the requesting and in the requested state.

The Supreme Court stated in Collins v. Loisel, "It is true that an offense is extraditable only if the acts charged are criminal by the laws of both countries." See also Brauch v. Raiche ("The requirement that the acts alleged be criminal in both jurisdictions is central to extradition law * * *").

We believe the double criminality requirement was met in this case. As the Court stated in Collins v. Loisel: "The law does not require that the name by which the crime is described in the two countries shall be the same; nor that the scope of the liability shall be coextensive, or, in other respects, the same in the two countries. It is enough if the particular act charged is criminal in both jurisdictions." If the acts upon which the charges of the requesting country are based are also proscribed by a law of the requested nation, the requirement of double criminality is satisfied. Murder is a crime in every state of the United States. The fact that there is no separate offense of mass murder or murder of tens of thousands of Jews in this country is beside the point. The act of unlawfully killing one or more persons with the requisite malice is punishable as murder. That is the test. The acts charged are criminal both in Israel and throughout the United States, including Ohio. Demjanjuk's argument that to interpret murder to include murder of Jews would amount to judicial amendment of the Treaty is absurd and offensive.

IV.

A.

A separate jurisdictional argument concerns the territorial reach of the statutory law of Israel. Demjanjuk relies on two facts to question the power of the State of Israel to proceed against him. He is not a citizen or resident of Israel and the crimes with which he is charged allegedly were committed in Poland. He also points out that the acts which are the basis of the Israeli arrest warrant allegedly took place in 1942 or 1943, before the State of Israel came into existence. Thus, Demjanjuk maintains that the district court had no jurisdiction because Israel did not charge him with extraditable offenses.

The scope of this nation's international extradition power and the function of the federal courts in the extradition process are set forth in 18 U.S.C. § 3184: * * * Section 3184 clearly provides that the extradition complaint must charge the person sought to be extradited with having committed crimes "within the jurisdiction of any such foreign government," that is, the requesting state. This same condition is reflected in § 486(a) of the Restatement, which requires the requested state to comply with the request to arrest and deliver a person sought "on charges of having committed a serious crime within the jurisdiction of the requesting state." The question is whether the murder of Jews in a Nazi extermination camp in Poland during the 1939–1945 war can be considered, for purposes of extradition, crimes within the jurisdiction of the State of Israel.

B.

We look first at the Treaty. Article III provides that when an offense has been committed outside the territorial jurisdiction of the requesting party, "extradition need not be granted unless the laws of the requested party provide for the punishment of such an offense committed in similar circumstances." Demjanjuk maintains that the "need not" language of Article III prohibits extradition in this case because the laws of the United States do not provide punishment for war crimes or crimes against humanity. * * *

* * *

* * * In our view the treaty language makes two things clear: (1) the parties recognize the right to request extradition for extra-territorial

crimes, and (2) the requested party has the discretion to deny extradition if its laws do not provide for punishment of offenses committed under similar circumstances. This provision does not affect the authority of a court to certify extraditability; it merely distinguishes between cases where the requested party is required to honor a request and those where it has discretion to deny a request. That the specific offense charged is not a crime in the United States does not necessarily rule out extradition.

The Israeli statute under which Demjanjuk was charged deals with "crimes against the Jewish people," "crimes against humanity" and "war crimes" committed during the Nazi years. It is clear from the language defining the crimes, and other references to acts directed at persecuted persons and committed in places of confinement, that Israel intended to punish under this law those involved in carrying out Hitler's "final solution." This was made explicit in the prosecution of Adolph Eichmann in 1961. Attorney General v. Eichmann [*supra*]. Such a claim of extraterritorial jurisdiction over criminal offenses is not unique to Israel. For example, statutes of the United States provide for punishment in domestic district courts for murder or manslaughter committed within the maritime jurisdiction (18 U.S.C. § 1111) and murder or manslaughter of internationally protected persons wherever they are killed (18 U.S.C. § 1116(c)). We conclude that the reference in 18 U.S.C. § 3184 to crimes committed within the jurisdiction of the requesting government does not refer solely to territorial jurisdiction. Rather, it refers to the authority of a nation to apply its laws to particular conduct. In international law this is referred to as "jurisdiction to prescribe." Restatement § 401(1).

C.

The law of the United States includes international law. The Paquete Habana, 175 U.S. 667, 712 (1900). International law recognizes a "universal jurisdiction" over certain offenses. Section 404 of the Restatement defines universal jurisdiction: § 404: Universal Jurisdiction to Define and Punish Selected Offenses

> A state may exercise jurisdiction to define and punish certain offenses recognized by the community of nations as of universal concern, such as piracy, slave trade, attacks on or hijacking of aircraft, genocide, war crimes, and perhaps terrorism, even where none of the bases of jurisdiction indicated in § 402 is present.

This "universality principle" is based on the assumption that some crimes are so universally condemned that the perpetrators are the enemies of all people. Therefore, any nation which has custody of the perpetrators may punish them according to its law applicable to such offenses. This principle is a departure from the general rule that "the character of an act as lawful or unlawful must be determined wholly by the law of the country where the act is done."

The wartime allies created the International Military Tribunal which tried major Nazi officials at Nuremberg and courts within the four occupation zones of post-war Germany which tried lesser Nazis. All were tried for committing war crimes, and it is generally agreed that the establishment of these tribunals and their proceedings were based on universal jurisdiction. * * *

Demjanjuk argues that the post-war trials were all based on the military defeat of Germany and that with the disestablishment of the special tribunals there are no courts with jurisdiction over alleged war crimes. This argument overlooks the fact that the post-war tribunals were not military courts, though their presence in Germany was made possible by the military defeat of that country. These tribunals did not operate within the limits of traditional military courts. They claimed and exercised a much broader jurisdiction which necessarily derived from the universality principle. Whatever doubts existed prior to 1945 have been erased by the general recognition since that time that there is a jurisdiction over some types of crimes which extends beyond the territorial limits of any nation.

Turning again to the Restatement, § 443 appears to apply to the present case: "§ 443. Jurisdiction to Adjudicate in Aid of Universal and Other Non–Territorial Crimes. A state's courts may exercise jurisdiction to enforce the state's criminal laws which punish universal crimes (§ 404) or other nonterritorial offenses within the state's jurisdiction to prescribe (§§ 402–403)." Israel is seeking to enforce its criminal law for the punishment of Nazis and Nazi collaborators for crimes universally recognized and condemned by the community of nations. The fact that Demjanjuk is charged with committing these acts in Poland does not deprive Israel of authority to bring him to trial.

Further, the fact that the State of Israel was not in existence when Demjanjuk allegedly committed the offenses is no bar to Israel's exercising jurisdiction under the universality principle. When proceeding on that jurisdictional premise, neither the nationality of the accused or the victim(s), nor the location of the crime is significant. The underlying assumption is that the crimes are offenses against the law of nations or against humanity and that the prosecuting nation is acting for all nations. This being so, Israel or any other nation, regardless of its status in 1942 or 1943, may undertake to vindicate the interest of all nations by seeking to punish the perpetrators of such crimes.

D.

We conclude that the jurisdictional challenges to the district court's order must fail. The crime of murder is clearly included in the offenses for which extradition is to be granted under the treaty. Murder is a crime both in Israel and in the United States and is included in the specifications of the Nazis and Nazi Collaborators (Punishment) Law; the requirement of "double criminality" is met; and, the State of Israel has jurisdiction to punish for war crimes and crimes against humanity committed outside of its geographic boundaries.

Though it was not explicitly argued, we have considered whether recognition of the power of Israeli courts to punish for war crimes committed outside of its national territory violates any right of Demjanjuk under the Constitution of the United States. Demjanjuk had notice before he applied for residence or citizenship in the United States that this country, by participating in post-war trials of German and Japanese war criminals, recognized the universality principle. Israel has chosen to proceed under that principle, and we do not supervise the conduct of another judicial system. To do so "would directly conflict with the principle of comity upon which extradition is based." Jhirad v. Ferrandina. In the absence of any showing that Demjanjuk will be subjected to procedures "antipathetic to a federal court's sense of decency," Gallina v. Fraser, this court will not inquire into the procedures which will apply after he is surrendered to Israel. There is absolutely no showing in this record that Israel will follow procedures which would shock this court's "sense of decency." United States ex rel. Bloomfield v. Gengler. * * *

    * * *

The judgment of the district court is affirmed.

———

Questions. Is there any theory upon which Demjanjuk could have been prosecuted in the U.S. for the killings in Poland? Would a state murder statute reach those events? A federal statute? The federal statutes for common crimes listed in Title 18 of the United States Code cover events that take place only within precisely defined jurisdictions (e.g., special maritime and territorial jurisdiction, 18 U.S.C. § 7, supra, special aircraft jurisdiction, 49 U.S.C. §§ 1301(38) and 1472(k)). Federal criminal law has expanded only incrementally to reach specific problems that demand extraterritorial prescription, as we have seen with respect to, hostage taking, hijacking and terrorism. Although the court in Demjanjuk identified murder within maritime jurisdiction and murder of internationally protected persons as offenses involving extraterritorial jurisdiction, the killings in that case did not fall within either of those categories.

Lieutenant Calley was convicted of murder under the Uniform Code of Military Justice, 10 U.S.C. § 801ff., a code applicable to a limited body of persons (e.g., members of the U.S. armed forces and prisoners of war in custody of the armed forces, 10 U.S.C. § 802). There is no statute, state or federal, that in precise terms makes the commission of war crimes punishable. Articles 18 and 21 of the Uniform Code of Military Justice (10 U.S.C. §§ 818 and 821) do so inferentially by conferring jurisdiction on courts-martial, and sanctioning the jurisdiction of military commissions, with respect to the law of war. In Ex parte Quirin, 317 U.S. 1 (1942), the Supreme Court stated that Congress, by its recognition of such jurisdiction, "had the choice of crystallizing in permanent form and in minute detail every offense against the law of war, or of adopting the system of common law applied by military tribunals so far as it should be recognized and deemed applicable by the courts. It chose the latter course." But the Quirin case involved enemy saboteurs taken in time of war. And the Yamashita case, 327 U.S. 1 (1946), involved an enemy general in custody immediately following the cessation of hostilities. But see the argument in Paust, After My Lai:

The Case for War Crime Jurisdiction Over Civilians in Federal District Courts, 50 Tex.L.Rev. 6 (1971).

Would you favor legislation making war crimes punishable in the United States, beyond the extent to which they may presently be punished under the Uniform Code of Military Justice? Would you provide for universal prescriptive jurisdiction, i.e., would the statute apply to any war crime, in any war, anywhere in the world, whether or not the United States is a party to the conflict, or whether or not a United States citizen is the actor or the victim? Would such a statute make punishable war crimes in general terms, or would it list specific offenses? What offenses? See Komarow, Individual Responsibility Under International Law: The Nuremberg Principles in Domestic Legal Systems, 29 Int'l & Comp.L.Q. 21 (1980).

Would you favor legislation making violations of the other Nuremberg principles (crimes against humanity and crimes against peace) punishable in the United States? Who would be subject to the statute? Foreign citizens, including foreign officials? United States citizens, including United States officials? Again, would the statute apply to any event, anywhere in the world, irrespective of whether United States citizens were the actors or victims, or whether the United States was otherwise involved?

———

Chapter 12

DIPLOMATIC AND CONSULAR IMMUNITIES AND IMMUNITIES OF PERSONS CONNECTED WITH INTERNATIONAL ORGANIZATIONS

SECTION A. CRIMES AGAINST DIPLOMATIC AGENTS AND OTHER PERSONS ENTITLED TO IMMUNITIES

1. *The Vienna Convention on Diplomatic Relations (1961)* in the Documentary Supplement, provides in Article 3:

1. The functions of a diplomatic mission consist inter alia in:

(a) representing the sending State in the receiving State;

(b) protecting in the receiving State the interests of the sending State and of its nationals, within the limits permitted by international law;

(c) negotiating with the Government of the receiving State;

(d) ascertaining by all lawful means conditions and developments in the receiving State, and reporting thereon to the Government of the sending State;

(e) promoting friendly relations between the sending State and the receiving State, and developing their economic, cultural and scientific relations.

2. Nothing in the present Convention shall be construed as preventing the performance of consular functions by a diplomatic mission.

2. **Risks of diplomatic life.** Diplomatic representation is essential to the operation of the international legal system. For diplomatic representation to function effectively, diplomatic representatives must be protected from receiving state interference with the discharge of diplomatic duties. Lord Mansfield in *Triquet v. Bath* noted the verity of this in the incident which led to the enactment in England of the Diplomatic Privileges Act of 1708:

> This privilege of foreign ministers and their domestic servants depends upon the law of nations. The Act of Parliament of 7 Ann. c. 12, is declaratory of it. All that is new in this Act, is the clause which gives a summary jurisdiction for the punishment of the infractors of this law.

> The Act of Parliament was made upon occasion of the Czar's Ambassador being arrested. If proper application had been immediately made for his discharge from the arrest, the matter might and doubtless would have been set right. Instead of that, bail was put in, before any complaint was made. An information was filed by the then Attorney General against the persons who were thus concerned, as infractors of the law of nations: and they were found guilty; but never brought up to judgment.

> The Czar took the matter up, highly. No punishment would have been thought, by him, an adequate reparation. Such a sentence as the Court could have given, he might have thought a fresh insult.

> Another expedient was fallen upon and agreed to: this Act of Parliament passed, as an apology and humiliation from the whole nation. It was sent to the Czar, finely illuminated by an ambassador extraordinary, who made excuses in a solemn oration. 3 Burr. 1478, 1480 (K.B.1764).

Protection from the authorities in the receiving state has not always been sufficient, however, to insure the inviolability of diplomatic representatives. Private individuals have at times felt compelled physically to vent frustrations of one kind or another upon the persons of foreign ambassadors. On the whole, though, interference with the function of diplomatic representation, either by the authorities of the receiving states or by individuals resorting to violence, seems, until recently, to have been minimal.

3. **The Revue Générale de Droit International Public publishes in each of its quarterly issues a Chronique des Faits Internationaux.** This chronicle of diplomatic and legal happenings is prepared by Professor Charles Rousseau: "It is based upon official and unofficial sources, including newspaper reports. It discloses a rather constant stream of violence concerning diplomatic personnel, premises and property in violation of international law. Professor Rousseau's reports on two recent cases, Panama and Kuwait, are noteworthy:

Rousseau, Chronique des Faits Internationaux, 95 Rev. Gén. de Droit Int'l Pub. 495 and 1096 (1991).[a]

On Panama: Infringements of Diplomatic Privileges. General Noriega surrendered voluntarily on January 3, 1990 to American armed forces without any bargaining or negotiation and was immediately transferred by a C–130 aircraft from Howard military base to Holmstead in Florida. The fact that he had taken refuge at the Papal Nonciature in Panama as early as December 24 (a building enjoying diplomatic immunity) posed "unsolvable" problems for the American "occupation forces." The position of the United States consisted in not recognizing in this instance diplomatic asylum which in its opinion could benefit only political refugees and not common criminals such as General Noriega. President Endara terminated Noriega's command, thereby ending his special status and of personnel immunity.

The encirclement of the Cuban and Peruvian Embassies in Panama, the search of the Nicaraguan Embassy [3], the searches of the Noncio's car on each of his departures from the Nonciature were [serious] infringements of immunities traditionally recognized to diplomatic personnel and buildings. This resulted in the expulsion by the government of Nicaragua of 20 out of the 28 American diplomats accredited to Managua and the reduction from 120 to 100 non-diplomatic members of the American Embassy.

On Iraq: Measures against Diplomatic Missions and Agents. From the moment the annexation of Kuwait was proclaimed, the government of Iraq announced the expulsion of the foreign diplomatic missions established in Kuwait. Iraq indicated that it would no longer recognize the diplomatic status of agents accredited to a State "which no longer existed." But 28 out of 60 embassies, as of September 1, 1990—refused to bow to the orders of Iraq and continued to function, declaring that they would give way only in the face of force.

The Iraqi government responded by blocking the embassies. They were encircled by the army and police and deprived of any communication with the outside, the Iraqi authorities cut off water, electricity and telephone.

Two incidents constituting a particularly serious infringement of the inviolability of embassies and their members occurred: (1) The arrest by the Iraqi army—announced on August 27 but carried out several days earlier—of the Ambassador of Lebanon and twelve members of his staff, followed by their transfer to the Lebanese Embassy in Baghdad which they were forbidden to leave; (2) the invasion by the Iraqi army on September 14 of several foreign embassies in Kuwait (France, Belgium, Netherlands and Canada) and the arrest of the French military attaché, the consuls of the United States, Canada, Ireland and Austria, as well as three French refugees. All were taken to an unknown destination, but

a. Translation by the editors.

3. [The search was on Jan. 3]. on January 8 the OAS protested this measure which was characterized by President Bush as a "screw-up". It nevertheless permitted the discovery of machine guns, rifles, bayonets and a rocket launcher, materials not habitually seen in the private residence of a foreign ambassador.

the French military attaché and the consuls were released in the evening. The residence of the French Ambassador was pillaged and ransacked.

This conduct infringed international law; it was a scandalous violation of the principle of the inviolability of embassies and diplomatic agents. Articles 22.1, 9 and 30 of the Vienna Convention of April 18, 1961 on Diplomatic Relations condemn it. * * * Iraq would also expel on September 20 and October 4 the military attachés of several Member States of the E.U. (France, Great Britain, FRG, Spain and Italy), the military attaché of the United States, seven French diplomats (but not the Chargé d'affaires), Egyptian diplomats.[a]

4. ***United States legislation to protect foreign representatives.*** Threats of violence and violent acts against foreign representatives have also been on the rise in the United States. The situation in New York, with repeated hostile demonstrations and attacks on diplomatic representatives to the United Nations, led the General Assembly to pass a resolution urging the United States to take measures for ensuring the protection and security of the United Nations Headquarters, the missions accredited to it and their personnel. See the statements of the Deputy Under Secretary of State for Management and of the United States Representative to the United Nations, 67 U.S. Dept. St.Bull. 609 (1972). At the request of the Department of State, legislation was enacted on October 24, 1972 making it a federal offense to commit certain crimes, e.g., murder, kidnapping, assault, harassment, property damage, against foreign embassy personnel and their families and representatives to international organizations and their families. See 18 U.S. Code §§ 112, 970, 1116, 1117 and 1201.

5. ***Convention on the Prevention and Punishment of Crimes against Internationally Protected Persons, Including Diplomatic Agents.*** The Convention, signed December 14, 1973, entered into force for the United States on February 20, 1977. 28 U.S.T. 1975, 1035 U.N.T.S. 167. More than 80 countries are parties. Article 1 of the convention provides that "internationally protected person" means:

> * * * (a) a Head of State, including any member of a collegial body performing the functions of a Head of State under the constitution of the State concerned, a Head of Government or a Minister for Foreign Affairs, whenever any such person is in a foreign State, as well as members of his family who accompany him;
>
> (b) any representative of a State or any agent of an international organization of an intergovernmental character who, at the time when and in the place where a crime against him, his official premises, his private accommodation or his means of transport is committed, is entitled pursuant to international law to special protection from any attack on his person, freedom or dignity, as well as members of his family forming part of his household;
>
> * * *

a. Translation by the editors.

The convention is designed to deny safe haven to those who attack, kidnap or inflict grievous bodily harm upon diplomatic agents or other internationally protected persons. A main feature of the convention is the requirement that a party in whose territory the offender is found must either prosecute or extradite him.

YENER AND EREZ DECEASED

France, Conseil d'Etat (1987).
89 Int'l L.Rptr. 1 (1992).

The following is the text of the judgment of the *Conseil d'Etat* :

1. The application of the dependants of Mr. Yener seeks:

a) the annulment of the judgment of 7 July 1982 of the *Tribunal administratif* of Paris which rejected their claim against the State for the award of damages as compensation for the loss suffered by them as a result of the assassination of Mr. Yener, the chauffeur of the Turkish Ambassador in France, which occurred on 24 October 1975 in Paris; and

b) the award of various sums as compensation for this loss.

2. The application of the dependants of Mr. Erez seeks:

a) the annulment of the judgment of 7 July 1982 of the *Tribunal administratif* of Paris which rejected their claim for damages against the State as compensation for the loss suffered by them as a result of the assassination of Mr. Erez, Turkish Ambassador in France, which occurred on 24 October 1975 in Paris; and

b) the award of various sums as compensation for this loss.

The *Conseil d'Etat* has considered the Decree of 29 March 1971 whereby the Vienna Convention on Diplomatic Relations was published * * *.

[The *Conseil d'Etat* decided to join the two applications and continued:] Mr. Erez, Turkish Ambassador in France, and Mr. Yener, his chauffeur, were the victims of a terrorist attack in Paris on 24 October 1975 at approximately 1.30 p.m., when they were travelling in a car on the bridge of Bir–Hakeim in the direction of the embassy premises, which were a few hundred metres away. In the circumstances of the case, proceedings to establish State responsibility for the alleged inadequacy of measures taken to ensure the protection of the victims of the attack in question, having regard to their membership of a diplomatic mission, do not bring into question the conduct of international relations by France. Their outcome merely depends upon an assessment which can be separated from questions of international relations.

It does not appear from the available information that the police ought to have provided tighter security surveillance than they actually gave. In particular it is not established from the documents in the file that the Turkish Ambassador made any request for special protection (*protection rapprochée*) in the days leading up to the attack. In failing to take additional measures the French police did not therefore commit any serious fault capable of engaging the responsibility of the State.

In the absence of any express legislative provision, the responsibility of the State cannot be engaged merely on the basis of the actual risk of acts of terrorism on French territory. It follows * * * that the dependents of Erez and Yener are not entitled to claim that, in the judgments being challenged, the *Tribunal administratif* of Paris wrongly rejected their claims that the State should be declared responsible for the consequences of the attack in question and ordered to pay damages. * * * [The applications were rejected.]

SECTION B.   DIPLOMATIC IMMUNITY

---

1.   INVIOLABILITY OF DIPLOMATIC PREMISES

RADWAN v. RADWAN

England, Family Division, 1972.
[1972] 3 W.L.R. 735.*

CUMMING–BRUCE J.   Mrs. Mary Isobel Radwan filed a petition for dissolution of marriage on November 27, 1970, seeking dissolution on the ground of her husband's cruelty.   * * *

* * *

The facts are as follows. The husband was born in Cairo. He is and at all material times was a Mohammedan. He was and remains a subject of the United Arab Republic. By the date of the institution of these proceedings, and by the date of the pronouncement of divorce by talaq in April 1970, he had acquired a domicile of choice in England. On April 1, 1970, he entered the Egyptian Consulate in London; the procedure stated in the affidavit of the deputy consul of the Consulate General was followed. The husband three times declared the prescribed form of divorce in the presence of two witnesses. All the steps were carried out in accordance with Egyptian law. After the prescribed 90 days the divorce was finalised in accordance with Egyptian law, and in accordance with that law it was no impediment to the efficacy of the proceedings that the wife knew nothing about it at all. The deputy consul states * * * that the Egyptian Consulate in London is regarded as being Egyptian territory on Egyptian soil. I take it that he means so regarded by the sending sovereign state * * *.

The question for my decision is whether by English law the Egyptian Consulate General is part of a country outside the British Isles within the meaning of section 2(a) of the Divorce Act. By that Act the relevant sections providing for recognition will have effect in respect of overseas divorces if they have been obtained by means of judicial or

* Reprinted by permission of The Incorporated Council of Law Reporting for England and Wales, London.

other proceedings in any country outside the British Isles, and it is necessary for the efficacy of the talaq divorce that it should have been obtained outside the British Isles by reason of the fact that at the material time the husband had acquired English domicile. Curiously, the question has not arisen for decision in England before—the question whether the premises of an embassy or consulate are part of the territory of the sending state as compared to the territory of the receiving state. * * *

        * * *

The term "extraterritorial" has been used to describe in a compendious phrase that bundle of immunities and privileges which are accorded by receiving civilized states to the envoys sent by foreign states. One such immunity included in the term is the inviolable character of the premises of a mission, which the agents of the receiving state may not enter without the consent of the head of the mission. The phrase was used by Grotius * * *. The word "extra-territorialitas" was used by Wolff in 1749 and has been in use in English, French and German for some 250 years. Three theories have been invoked to explain the admitted principles that diplomatic premises and property are inviolable by the agents of the receiving state:

> (a) The strict extraterritorial fiction. The premises are regarded by a legal fiction as outside the territory of the receiving state and as part of the territory of the sending state. (b) The representative theory. The premises are immune from entry without consent of the head of the mission, as the mission represents or personifies the sovereignty of the sending state. (c) The theory of functional necessity. The immunity is granted by the receiving state because it is necessary to enable the mission to carry out its functions.

Mr. Ewbank submits, and I agree, that (a) should be discarded as obsolete in the sense that international lawyers have long regarded it as unsound, and it is inconsistent with modern foreign decisions and international convention. He asks me to prefer (c) to (b), though both avoid the practical dangers which (a) is liable to produce.

This view is rested on the foundation of the consensus of authors learned in international law, the approach of courts of law abroad in such cases in modern times as have involved consideration of the immunity of diplomatic land and buildings, and inferences from the international conventions by which civilized states in modern times have sought to define the immunities which they will accord to diplomatic missions. I develop these three heads separately.

1. The opinion of authors. [There follows a list of the 11 works examined by the judge.] In all of them I find a consensus of opinion that there is no valid foundation for the proposition, or alleged rule, that diplomatic premises are to be regarded as outside the territory of the receiving state. The history of the confusion is given concisely by Professor Lauterpacht:

The exterritoriality which must be granted to diplomatic envoys by the municipal laws of all the members of the international community is not, as in case of sovereign Heads of States, based on the principle par in parem non habet imperium, but on the necessity that envoys must, for the purpose of fulfilling their duties, be independent of the jurisdiction, control, and the like, of the receiving states. Exterritoriality, in this as in every other case, is a fiction only, for diplomatic envoys are in reality not without, but within, the territories of the receiving states. The term "exterritoriality" is nevertheless valuable because it demonstrates clearly the fact that envoys must, in most respects, be treated as though they were not within the territory of the receiving states. * * *

* * * Nowadays the official residences of envoys are, *in a sense and in some respects only,* considered as though they were outside the territory of the receiving states.

And he continues: "But such immunity of domicile is granted only so far as it is necessary for the independence and inviolability of envoys, and the inviolability of their official documents and archives." A little further down: "If a crime is committed inside the house of an envoy by an individual who does not enjoy personally the privilege of exterritoriality, the criminal must be surrendered to the local government." I quote and adopt the observations of Mr. J.E.S. Fawcett.

But there are two popular myths about diplomats and their immunities which we must clear away; one is that an embassy is foreign territory * * * The premises of a mission are inviolable, and the local authorities may enter them only with the consent of the head of the mission. But this does not make the premises foreign territory or take them out of the reach of the local law for many purposes: for example, a commercial transaction in an embassy may be governed by the local law, particularly tax law; marriages may be celebrated there only if conditions laid down by the local law are met; and a child born in it will, unless his father has diplomatic status, acquire the local nationality.

This so exactly represents the conclusion to which I have come, after looking at the textbooks, that I think it unnecessary in this judgment to quote other passages of eminent authorities. * * *

[Discusses cases in Australia, France, Germany and Italy in which] the court rejected the argument that diplomatic premises were not part of the territory of the receiving state * * *

* * *

3. International conventions.

Though international conventions do not have the force of law unless embodied in municipal legislation, they may in the field of international law be valuable as a guide to the rules of international law which this country as a signatory respects. The Vienna Convention on Consular Relations in 1963, by article 31 sets out the agreed immunities adherent to consular premises under the heading: "Inviolability of the consular premises": "1. Consular premises shall be inviolable to the extent provided in this article," and the article then sets out that extent in its several different ways. There is no suggestion that it was in the mind of any of the signatories that the premises themselves were part of the territory of the sending state. So, too, the Vienna Convention on Diplomatic Relations 1961, by article 22: [had been incorporated].

> 1. The premises of the mission shall be inviolable. The agents of the receiving state may not enter them, except with the consent of the head of the mission.

The next paragraph deals with protection, and the third:

> 3. The premises of the mission, their furnishings and other property thereon and the means of transport of the mission shall be immune from search, requisition, attachment or execution.

What is significant about those articles is not so much what they say as what they do not say. If it was the view of the high contracting parties that the premises of missions were part of the territory of the sending state, that would undoubtedly be formulated and it would have been quite unnecessary to set out the immunities in the way in which it has been done.

* * *

For those reasons the husband, being at the material time a gentlemen of English domicile, did not go through a proceeding for divorce in a country outside the British Isles when he pronounced the talaq three times in the Consulate General in 1970.

* * *

————

1. *Jurisdiction of sending state over crimes committed within diplomatic premises.* In United States v. Erdos, 474 F.2d 157 (4th Cir.1973), the chargé d'affairs at the American embassy in Equitorial Guinea was convicted of killing another embassy employee within the embassy compound. The Court construed 18 U.S.C. § 7(3), which deals with the special maritime and territorial jurisdiction of the United States, as embracing an embassy in a foreign country.

In 1978, the former ambassador of Austria to Yugoslavia was sentenced by an Austrian court to a heavy fine for accidentally killing the French ambassador to Yugoslavia upon their return from a hunting trip. The court relied on Article 31(4) of the Vienna Convention which specifies that immunity from the jurisdiction of the receiving state does not exempt the diplomat from the jurisdiction of the sending state. 82 Revue Générale de Droit International Public 1086 (1978).

2. *Diplomatic asylum.* Latin American states assert that a right to grant asylum in the diplomatic premises exists by virtue of a regional custom peculiar to them. The existence of such a right was tested and denied in the *Asylum Case* (Colombia v. Peru) [1950] I.C.J.Rep. 266. The holding of the court that the Colombian government had failed to prove the existence of a regional custom of asylum may have induced the adoption of a new convention on asylum by the Tenth Inter–American Conference at Caracas in 1954. 6 Whiteman Digest *supra* at 436.

The United States Department of State has consistently maintained that a state does not have a right to grant asylum under international law. The granting of asylum to Cardinal Mindszenty by the American embassy in Budapest in 1956 was explained as "exceptional." 6 Whiteman Digest supra at 463–464. It lasted for 15 years.

GOLDBERG,[a] THE SHOOT–OUT AT THE LIBYAN SELF–STYLED PEOPLE'S BUREAU: A CASE OF STATE–SUPPORTED TERRORISM

30 South Dakota Law Review 1 (1984).[*]

* * *

The facts of the shoot-out at the Libyan People's Bureau in London have been extensively reported. Two gunmen in the Libyan self-styled "People's Bureau" in London opened fire on a crowd of peaceful anti-Qaddafi demonstrators. These demonstrators were conducting their peaceful protest on a sidewalk adjacent to the Libyan People's Bureau, yet the gunmen inside chose to shoot at them, killing Constable Fletcher and wounding eleven demonstrators and bystanders. Ten days after this barbaric incident, the British Government provided the killers and their murder weapons with safe passage out of the country.

On the same day that British police escorted the murderers to Heathrow Airport, Constable Fletcher was buried. At the time of her funeral, the Home Secretary, Mr. Leon Brittan, stated that the British police were prevented under the terms of the Vienna Convention on Diplomatic Relations from storming the so-called People's Bureau to apprehend the killers and bring them to justice. Mr. Brittan asserted Her Majesty's government could not act because the murderers, the premises of the People's Bureau, and the bags within which the lethal weapons were concealed were all immune according to the Convention. Prime Minister Thatcher and the Foreign Secretary Howe, supported the Home Secretary's view in the debate in the House of Commons. With all respect, I disagree. The Vienna Convention, like all treaties, must be sensibly interpreted. In this unruly age of state-sponsored terrorism, the Vienna Convention must not be construed so as to be a suicide pact for civilized countries. Treaties must be read in their entirety, with some provisions necessarily modified by others. Nothing could be more foolish than to accept a simple-minded, literal reading of each of the Convention's articles. The privileges and immunities granted by the Convention are rights declared in words, but rights declared in words are not to be lost in reality.

* * *

a. The author, Arthur G. Goldberg, was formerly Associate Justice of the Supreme Court of the United States and Ambassador to the United Nations.

* Reprinted with the permission of the South Dakota Law Review.

[T]he Home Secretary * * * claimed the British police under the Vienna Convention could not storm the so-called Libyan People's Bureau to capture the killers and confiscate their weapons as material evidence. * * * I disagree. Colonel Qaddafi's People's Bureau in London scarcely qualifies as a *bona fide* embassy whose premises are inviolable under the Vienna Convention. * * * [T]he London People's Bureau, according to reliable evidence, has harbored assassination teams directed by Qaddafi against Libyan dissidents. Murder factories are not embassies, and therefore do not come within the scope of the Vienna Convention. That treaty is designed to grant immunity to a proper embassy devoted to diplomatic relations. Article 41, section 3 of the Convention states that the "premises of the mission must not be used in any manner incompatible with the functions of the mission as laid down in the * * * Convention or by other rules of general international law * * *." Harboring hit squads clearly does not come within the protection of that provision.

The People's Bureau in London therefore is not a *bona fide* embassy. It was, in my opinion, subject under established rules of international law to search and seizure by the British police after the brutal murder of Constable Fletcher and the wounding of others.

       * * *

       ———

Question concerning the seizure of the United States Embassy in Teheran. If, as maintained above, the premises of the Libyan People's Bureau in London were not inviolable because their use was not in conformity with article 41 of the Vienna Convention, what of the assertion by the government of Iran that the United States Embassy in Teheran was used for criminal activities and, hence, the seizure and taking hostage of its personnel were justified? Case Concerning United States Diplomatic and Consular Staff in Teheran (United States v. Iran). What might Saddam Hussein have done in 1990–1991 with such a doctrine? Who is to decide the current meaning of art. 41?

       ———

LETTER DATED 2 APRIL 1992 FROM THE PERMANENT REPRESENTATIVE OF VENEZUELA TO THE UNITED NATIONS ADDRESSED TO THE PRESIDENT OF THE SECURITY COUNCIL

31 I.L.M. 753 (1992) (reprinted by permission of the American Society of Int'l Law).

I have the honour to transmit to Your Excellency the text in Spanish of the Declaration of the Government of Venezuela, in regard to the violation to the diplomatic mission of Venezuela in Tripoli, on 2 April 1992. I would greatly appreciate if Your Excellency distributed the text of the present letter and its annex as a document of the Security Council.

(*Signed*) Diego ARRIA Ambassador of Venezuela
Permanent Representative to the United Nations
Annex [Original: Spanish]

The Ministry of Foreign Affairs hereby informs public opinion that today, at 10:30 a.m. Libyan time, the administrative headquarters of the Venezuelan Embassy in Tripoli was attacked.   A mob consisting of students who had arrived in two buses and people from the street broke into the Embassy shouting slogans against Venezuela because of the latter's vote in the Security Council in favour of the anti-terrorist resolution on 31 March 1992.   The mob then began to ransack and destroy the premises of our diplomatic representation.   Neither the four Libyan guards assigned to protect the Embassy nor anyone from the police force of the city of Tripoli intervened to stop the looting and arson of the diplomatic premises, which were carried out with total impunity. The members of the Venezuelan diplomatic staff, with whom this Ministry remains in contact through various channels, suffered no physical injury to speak of.

On the same date, the Ministry of Foreign Affairs delivered an official note to the representative of the Libyan Government in Venezuela to protest about the violation of the standards of protection for diplomatic premises which are laid down in the relevant international agreements, and to demand assurances guaranteeing the physical integrity of the Venezuelan diplomats accredited to Libya and the inviolability of the Venezuelan Embassy residence, together with an adequate official explanation of the incident in question within 48 hours.

Caracas, 2 April 1992

LETTER DATED 8 APRIL 1992 FROM THE PERMANENT REPRESENTATIVE OF VENEZUELA TO THE UNITED NATIONS ADDRESSED TO THE PRESIDENT OF THE SECURITY COUNCIL

31 I.L.M. 754 (1992) (reprinted by permission of the American Society of Int'l Law).

With regard to the letter dated 2 April 1992 from the Permanent Representative of Venezuela to the United Nations addressed to the President of the Security Council, concerning the attack on the Venezuelan diplomatic mission at Tripoli, Libya, I have the honour to transmit herewith the communiqué issued on 5 April 1992 by the Ministry of Foreign Affairs of Venezuela concerning the official reply by the People's Bureau for Foreign Liaison and International Cooperation of the Libyan Arab Jamahiriya to the Venezuelan protest note.   I should be grateful if you would have this text issued as a document of the Security Council.

(*Signed*) Diego Arria Permanent Representative of Venezuela to the United Nations

Annex

The Ministry of Foreign Affairs reports that on 5 April Venezuela received from the People's Bureau for Foreign Liaison and International Cooperation of Libya (Ministry of Foreign Affairs) the official reply to the Venezuelan protest note concerning the attack on the Venezuelan Embassy in Tripoli conveying " * * * the deepest regret and apologies of the Socialist People's Libyan Arab Jamahiriya for the damage sustained by the Venezuelan Embassy at Tripoli". The note of apology adds:

> "The Jamahiriya, in condemning this act, feels that it was directed in the first place against the Jamahiriya, rather than against Venezuela, a friendly country. The Jamahiriya takes responsibility for the consequences of this incident and will provide compensation in the fairest manner so as to satisfy the Government of Venezuela since this is a legitimate right of the Government of Venezuela. The Jamahiriya reiterates that what occurred will not be repeated in respect of the Venezuelan Embassy or of the other Embassies accredited to the Jamahiriya. The Jamahiriya hopes that this passing incident will not have any adverse effect on the good relations between our two countries."

The Ministry of Foreign Affairs accepts the apologies of the Government of Libya on the understanding that there will be no repetition of such acts of violence, that there will be full compensation for the material damage and that the diplomatic relations between the two countries will be conducted, both in matters on which they agree and in matters on which they disagree, in accordance with the norms of international law and of civilized coexistence among nations. At all events, national public opinion will be informed that Venezuela's diplomatic representatives in Libya have been called back to Caracas for consultations with the Ministry.

---

2. IMMUNITY AND INVIOLABILITY OF DIPLOMATIC AGENTS

The Vienna Convention on Diplomatic Relations was signed by 81 states on April 18, 1961. It entered into force on April 24, 1964. As of Jan. 1, 1992, 156 states were parties to the Convention. The Convention entered into force for the United States on December 13, 1972. The legislation prior to ratification dated from the eighteenth century (Act of 30 April 1790, ch. 9, § 25, 22 U.S.C. § 252). It conferred broad immunity from both criminal and civil jurisdiction upon ambassadors, their domestic servants, and upon other diplomatic personnel. The Convention on the other hand granted a narrower measure of immunity to all diplomatic personnel. The Department of Justice took the position that the Convention did not repeal or supersede the greater measure of immunity provided by existing legislation. Rovine, Digest of United States Practice in International Law 1973, at 143 (1974). The Diplomatic Relations Act, repealing the previous legislation and giving effect to the Convention as controlling domestic law, was enacted on September 30, 1978. 22 U.S.C. §§ 254a–254e, 28 U.S.C. § 1364. The text of the Act and the Convention are in the Doc. Supp.

Rationale: immunity of diplomatic agents. Diplomatic immunity rests on two grounds: (1) it ensures the effective performance by the diplomatic agent; and (2) it protects the diplomatic agent's person and dignity. Before the Vienna Convention, however, a number of states rejected the *representational* considerations, i.e., those pertaining to the personal dignity of diplomatic agents. They took the position that *functional* necessity was the sole basis of diplomatic immunity.

In the states adopting the rationale of functional necessity, the courts distinguished between the official acts and the private acts of a diplomatic representative, immunity being granted for the former, but not for the latter. The distinction had an obvious parallel in the distinction made by many courts in civil law states between the public acts of a foreign state (for which immunity is granted) and its private acts (for which no immunity is given). See Chapter 7.

MARIAN NASH LEICH, CONTEMPORARY PRACTICE OF THE UNITED STATES RELATING TO INTERNATIONAL LAW

83 A.J.I.L. 905, 910 (1989).*

DIPLOMATIC MISSIONS AND EMBASSY PROPERTY (U.S. *Digest,* Ch. 4, § 1)

Appointment, Accreditation and Notification: The Department of State has observed that it is necessary and useful periodically to reiterate and clarify the standards for the accreditation of foreign diplomatic personnel assigned to the United States. By a circular note to the Chiefs of Mission at Washington, dated May 23, 1989, Secretary of State James A. Baker III reiterated the Department's requirement that, to be recognized as a diplomatic agent, a person must possess a recognized diplomatic title and must, as well, perform duties of a diplomatic nature. Secretary Baker reminded the Chiefs of Mission that the accreditation of diplomats was solely within the discretion of the Department of State and that requests for accreditation in diplomatic status of personnel performing duties of an administrative and technical nature were incompatible with both Department policy and the Vienna Convention on Diplomatic Relations (1961). The Secretary informed them, further, that any promotion from the administrative and technical staff to diplomatic agent status must be accompanied by a formal position description for each person * * *.

Enclosed with the note of May 23, 1989, was an earlier circular note in greater detail on the same subject, dated May 1, 1985, and reading, in part, as follows:

> Requests for exceptions to the general guidelines will be considered infrequently and only in extenuating circumstances. Such requests must be forwarded in the form of a diplomatic note to the Department and must set forth in detail the exact nature of the exception requested, justification for such exception, the duration thereof, and possible alternative courses of action.

* Reprinted with the permission of the American Society of Int'l Law.

So that the accreditation policy of the United States Government may be uniformly a matter of record for all missions, the criteria governing accreditation are set forth as follows:

"DIPLOMATIC AGENTS"

To be recognized as a "diplomatic agent", and in order to retain such status, a person must: (1) possess a valid diplomatic passport if diplomatic passports are issued by his government or, if diplomatic passports are not issued, present a diplomatic note from the mission formally representing the intention of the sending government to assign to him diplomatic duties; (2) possess a recognized diplomatic title; (3) be a holder of an A–1 nonimmigrant visa; (4) be over 21 years of age; (5) with the exception of certain designated senior financial, economic, and commercial positions in New York City or certain other positions expressly agreed to by the Department, reside in the Washington, D.C. area * * *; and (6) devote official activities to diplomatic functions on an essentially full-time basis. * * *

For "diplomatic agents", the only exception to the requirement to reside in the Washington, D.C. area, is residence in the New York City area, which is permissible only upon the express agreement of the Department that such persons may be assigned to perform specific functions [there]. No such exception exists for "members of the administrative and technical staff". Accordingly, persons employed by the sending State in support of "diplomatic agents" residing outside the Washington, D.C., area have no claim to the privileges and immunities provided in the Vienna Convention on Diplomatic Relations. They have only such privileges and immunities as expressly agreed upon by the United States and the sending State of the "diplomatic agent".

The Department reiterates the emphasis placed on the performance of traditional and accepted diplomatic functions by recognized foreign diplomatic personnel assigned to the United States. Accordingly, the Department will not consider for accreditation any person who, during assignment in the United States, is, or will be, a student or trainee at any college, university, vocational school, military institution, or private or governmental foundation, or who is engaged in any pursuit inconsistent with regular and accepted diplomatic functions. In the past some governments have selected officials for assignment to the United States who, following arrival and subsequent recognition as diplomats by the Department of State, have entered upon intergovernmental military training courses or have been assigned for training at private research institutions. This practice also is unacceptable. Each mission is required to notify the Department promptly whenever any of its personnel terminate diplomatic duties to engage in nondiplomatic pursuits and should return immediately all diplomatic credentials issued to such persons.

Occasionally the Department learns of persons who, although accredited as diplomatic agents, are performing duties principally, if not solely, under contract at or by appointment with international organizations headquartered in Washington. Although the Vienna Convention on Diplomatic Relations (Article 5, paragraph 3) states that members of the diplomatic staffs of missions also may act as representatives to international organizations, the Convention provides no basis for them to serve on the staffs of international organizations. The Department of State views such service as incompatible with the functions of a diplomat, whose principal concern must be to assist in the conduct of bilateral relations between the sending State and the United States. Accordingly, the Department will require the return of all diplomatic credentials issued to any such individual and will delete his name from the Diplomatic List. A person who is duly accredited to the staff of an international organization will have only such privileges and immunities as are provided by U.S. law or by international agreement to the staff of the international organization concerned.

———

Questions: How much leeway should the receiving state have in imposing conditions, going beyond the terms of Vienna Convention Articles 4, 7 and 10, for recognizing "diplomatic agent" status? Should there be any at all? In your opinion, is the author citing *legal* views of Secretary Baker or a probable pragmatic outcome?

———

Abuse of Immunities. In the aftermath of the "shoot-out" at the Libyan Peoples' Bureau in London and other developments, there were a number of reviews and second thoughts about the scope of diplomatic immunity, particularly in relation to criminal prosecution where the immunity could be abused. The U.S. Congress ordered a State Department study and report. Hearings were held in the spring of 1988. The State Department reported that there were in the U.S. 26,282 persons with criminal immunity, 29,689 with official acts immunity, for a total of 55,971, but that the number of crimes committed by those persons is "very small" and there was not a "diplomatic crime wave." Draft legislation before the Congress to tighten procedures was not adopted. *See The Diplomatic Privileges and Immunities Act, Hearing before the Subcommittee on International Operations of the Committee on Foreign Affairs*, 100th Cong. 2nd Sess. 7, March 30 and April 13, 1988; and Miscellaneous International Affaires Authorizations Act of 1988, Report to accompany S. 2757, submitted by Mr. Pell, from the Committee on Foreign Relations 100th Cong. 2nd Sess. Report 100–500, September 7, 1988. In the United Kingdom, the review process and report are described in Higgins, U.K. Foreign Affaires Committee Report on the Abuse of Diplomatic Immunities and Privileges: Government Response and Report, 80 A.J.I.L. 135 (1986).

Questions: Had there been evidence of more rampant and serious abuse—or should there be rampant and serious abuse in the future—what remedies might be employed by the receiving state without impairing the diplomatic immunity? What might be the risk to the receiving state in limiting the scope of the immunity?

SANCTIONS AGAINST DIPLOMATS

Statement of the Minister for Foreign Affairs of the Netherlands.
2 Netherlands Yearbook of International Law 170 (1971).*

During a * * * debate in the Parliamentary Standing Committee for Foreign Affairs, the Minister for Foreign Affairs made, inter alia, the following remarks: * * * a foreign diplomat cannot be prosecuted, unless his Government or he himself waives his right to immunity * * *

Yet, there are some sanctions. First, expulsion from the host country, which goes further than recall. * * * Secondly, the person in question can be called to account through his ambassador * * * and one can ensure that civil liability, at least, be assumed. Thirdly, the foreign government does sometimes take this liability on itself. There have been cases of ordinary offences such as nonpayment of large amounts for the purchase of cars, food, etc. being committed; in these cases the nomination of a new ambassador was made conditional on previous settlement of those questions. * * * [I]t is a principle of public international law that the host country should put nothing in the way of a diplomat which would hinder him from complete freedom to exercise his functions and should remove any existing hindrances. [But there] are of course limits; for instance, when a diplomat obviously abuses his position. I am thinking of cases in which espionage activities lead to expulsion. Then there are local customs: one should behave according to local standards. One also oversteps the limit, therefore, by violating unwritten morals of a host country, by behaving in a provocative manner, by being drunk in a public place or, in countries where ladies go veiled, by insisting on seeing what is going on behind the veil. I just give a few examples that do not require the exercise of much imagination on the part of this illustrious assembly. In these cases of what I would call overstepping the limit, the diplomat concerned may be declared *persona non grata* * * *

CASE CONCERNING UNITED STATES DIPLOMATIC AND CONSULAR STAFF IN TEHERAN (UNITED STATES v. IRAN)

International Court of Justice, 1980.
[1980] I.C.J.Rep. 3.

[On November 27, 1979, the United States instituted proceedings in the International Court of Justice against Iran with respect to the seizure and holding as hostages in Teheran on November 4, 1979, of

---

* Reprinted by permission of T.M.C. Asser Instituut, The Hague.

American diplomatic and consular personnel. Iran did not file any pleading and did not appoint an agent to appear on its behalf. It sent to the court, however, two letters in which it defined its position and contended that the taking of the hostages might be justified by the existence of special circumstances. The court examined that contention]:

* * *

81. In his letters of 9 December 1979 and 16 March 1980, as previously recalled, Iran's Minister for Foreign Affairs referred to the present case as only "a marginal and secondary aspect of an overall problem". This problem, he maintained, "involves, inter alia, more than 25 years of continual interference by the United States in the internal affairs of Iran, the shameless exploitation of our country, and numerous crimes perpetrated against the Iranian people, contrary to and in conflict with all international and humanitarian norms". In the first of the two letters he indeed singled out amongst the "crimes" which he attributed to the United States an alleged complicity on the part of the [CIA] in the coup d'état of 1953 and in the restoration of the Shah to the throne of Iran. Invoking these alleged crimes, the Iranian Foreign Minister took the position that the United States' Application could not be examined by the Court divorced from its proper context, which he insisted was "the whole political dossier of the relations between Iran and the United States over the last 25 years".

82. [Other information before the court suggested that the criminal activities asserted in the letter consisted of espionage and U.S. interference in Iran centered upon its embassy in Teheran.]

* * *

85. * * * It is for the very purpose of providing a remedy for such possible abuses of diplomatic functions that Article 9 of the 1961 Convention on Diplomatic Relations stipulates:

> 1. The receiving State may at any time and without having to explain its decision, notify the sending State that the head of the mission or any member of the diplomatic staff of the mission is persona non grata or that any other member of the staff of the mission is not acceptable. In any such case, the sending State shall, as appropriate, either recall the person concerned or terminate his functions with the mission. A person may be declared non grata or not acceptable before arriving in the territory of the receiving State.

> 2. If the sending State refuses or fails within a reasonable period to carry out its obligations under paragraph 1 of this Article, the receiving State may refuse to recognize the person concerned as a member of the mission.

The 1963 Convention contains, in Article 23, paragraphs 1 and 4, analogous provisions in respect of consular officers and consular staff. Paragraph 1 of Article 9 of the 1961 Convention, and paragraph 4 of Article 23 of the 1963 Convention, take account of the difficulty that may be experienced in practice of proving such abuses in every case or, indeed, of determining exactly when exercise of the diplomatic function, expressly recognized in Article 3(1)(d) of the 1961 Convention, of "ascertaining by all lawful means conditions and developments in the receiving State" may be considered as involving such acts as "espionage" or "interference in internal affairs". The way in which Article 9, paragraph 1, takes account of any such difficulty is by providing expressly in its opening sentence that the receiving State may "at any time and without having to explain its decision" notify the sending State that any particular member of its diplomatic mission is "persona non grata" or "not acceptable" (and similarly Article 23, paragraph 4, of the 1963 Convention provides that "the receiving State is not obliged to give to the sending State reasons for its decision"). Beyond that remedy for dealing with abuses of the diplomatic function by individual members of a mission, a receiving State has in its hands a more radical remedy if abuses of their functions by members of a mission reach serious proportions. This is the power which every receiving State has, at its own discretion, to break off diplomatic relations with a sending State and to call for the immediate closure of the offending mission.

86. The rules of diplomatic law, in short, constitute a self-contained regime which, on the one hand, lays down the receiving State's obligations regarding the facilities, privileges and immunities to be accorded to diplomatic missions and, on the other, foresees their possible abuse by members of the mission and specifies the means at the disposal of the receiving State to counter any such abuse. These means are, by their nature, entirely efficacious, for unless the sending State recalls the member of the mission objected to forthwith, the prospect of the almost immediate loss of his privileges and immunities, because of the withdrawal by the receiving State of his recognition as a member of the mission, will in practice compel that person, in his own interest, to depart at once. But the principle of the inviolability of the persons of diplomatic agents and the premises of diplomatic missions is one of the very foundations of this long-established regime, to the evolution of which the traditions of Islam made a substantial contribution. The fundamental character of the principle of inviolability is, moreover, strongly underlined by the provisions of Articles 44 and 45 of the Convention of 1961 (cf. also Articles 26 and 27 of the Convention of 1963). Even in the case of armed conflict or in the case of a breach in diplomatic relations those provisions require that both the inviolability of the members of a diplomatic mission and of the premises, property and archives of the mission must be respected by the receiving State. Naturally, the observance of this principle does not mean—and this the Applicant Government expressly acknowledges—that a diplomatic agent caught in the act of committing an assault or other offence may not, on occasion, be briefly arrested by the police of the receiving State in order to prevent the commission of the particular crime. But such eventualities bear no relation at all to what occurred in the present case.

* * *

[By 13 votes to 2, the court decided, inter alia, that the conduct of Iran was in violation of the rules of international law on diplomatic immunity and by 12 votes to 3 decided that Iran was under an obligation to make reparation to the United States for the injury.]

STATUS OF THE DIPLOMATIC BAG
McCAFFREY, THE FORTY–FIRST SESSION OF THE INTERNATIONAL LAW COMMISSION
83 A.J.I.L. 937 (1989).*

* * *

The Diplomatic Courier and Bag

The Commission initially took up this topic in 1977 pursuant to General Assembly Resolution 31/76 of December 13, 1976. Work began in earnest in 1980 with the consideration of the first report of the special rapporteur, Professor Alexander Yankov. In 1986 the Commission adopted a set of 33 draft articles on first reading and transmitted them through the Secretary–General to governments for their comments. Beginning in 1988, the Commission undertook a second reading of the draft articles on the basis of observations that had been received from approximately 30 governments. At its 1989 session, the Commission completed the second reading, making several significant changes in the 1986 draft. The full set of draft articles, together with the Commission's commentaries thereto, are set out in the Commission's report to the General Assembly.   * * *

One of the principal objects of the draft is to establish a comprehensive and essentially uniform regime for all kinds of couriers and bags employed by states for official communications. Its provisions apply to diplomatic and consular couriers and bags, within the meaning of the Vienna Conventions on Diplomatic and Consular Relations, as well as those of permanent missions, permanent observer missions and observer delegations, within the meaning of the Vienna Convention on the Representation of States in Their Relations with International Organizations of a Universal Character. Couriers and bags of international organizations of a universal character, as well as those of special missions, are dealt with in separate optional protocols to the draft. This is a change from the version adopted on first reading, which included the two latter categories of couriers and bags in the draft articles themselves. Since the Conventions on Special Missions and on the Representation of States are not nearly so widely ratified as the Conventions on Diplomatic and Consular Relations, the Commission believed that states would be more likely to find the draft acceptable if they were given the option of extending its application to couriers and bags of special missions and of international organizations of a universal character.

The centerpiece of the draft is Article 28, Protection of the diplomatic bag. This article deals with the fundamental issue of whether any sort of inspection or challenge procedure is to be allowed as to diplomat-

* Reprinted with the permission of the American Society of Int'l Law.

ic [7] bags. Some * * * had argued that a regime of complete inviolability was unrealistic in today's world, as the pouch is used for the transport of everything from drugs to weapons and even human beings. They believed that some means of inspection that would not violate the confidentiality of official communications was essential to stem the widespread abuses of the diplomatic bag. Other[s] had maintained that absolute inviolability of the bag was essential to the free communication between sending states and their missions, consular posts and delegations that is the cornerstone of diplomatic relations. * * *

The version of the article adopted on first reading reflected the deep division in the Commission between these schools of thought. It contained, in brackets, various alternative regimes. One alternative simply reproduced Article 27, paragraph 3 of the 1961 Vienna Convention on Diplomatic Relations; [9] another added that the bag "shall be exempt from examination directly or through electronic or other technical devices"; a third would have preserved the separate "challenge procedure" for consular bags currently provided for under Article 35, paragraph 3 of the 1963 Vienna Convention on Consular Relations; a fourth would have subjected all kinds of bags to the challenge procedure currently applicable only to consular bags; and the final alternative would have created new challenge procedures, applicable to all kinds of bags. As finally adopted by the Commission on second reading, Article 28 reads as follows:

Protection of the diplomatic bag

1. The diplomatic bag shall be inviolable wherever it may be; it shall not be opened or detained and shall be exempt from examination directly or through electronic or other technical devices.

2. Nevertheless, if the competent authorities of the receiving State or the transit State have serious reason to believe that the consular bag contains something other than the correspondence, documents or articles referred to in paragraph 1 of article 25, they may request that the bag be opened in their presence by an authorized representative of the sending State. If this request is refused by the authorities of the sending State, the bag shall be returned to its place of origin.

Paragraph 1 reproduces language found in the four Conventions on diplomatic and consular law ("The diplomatic bag shall * * * not be opened or detained") and adds the concept of "inviolability" as well as a specific exemption from direct or remote examination. In the view of the Commission's special rapporteur, these additions only clarify the conventional rule and are already observed in state practice but are necessary to protect the confidentiality of official communications, encoding equipment and the like. Paragraph 2 reproduces Article 35,

---

7. Article 2 of the draft defines "diplomatic bag" to include diplomatic and consular bags, as well as bags of a permanent mission, a permanent observer mission, a delegation and an observer delegation.

9. Article 27(3) of the Convention, supra note 3, provides simply: "The diplomatic bag shall not be opened or detained."

paragraph 3 of the Vienna Convention on Consular Relations, and preserves the separate "challenge" procedure for consular bags provided for in that article. There was a considerable and strongly held opinion in the Commission that this sort of procedure should be applicable [even to diplomatic bags] to address the problem of abuse. This view is reflected in one of the alternative versions of paragraph 2 adopted on first reading, described above. In the end, however, the Commission decided simply to preserve existing law. The Commission's failure to make proposals for the "progressive development" of the law in this area seems unfortunate, since states look to the Commission for guidance and leadership, particularly with regard to problems as notorious as abuse of the diplomatic bag.

The Commission recommended to the General Assembly that it convoke a diplomatic conference to elaborate a convention on the diplomatic courier and bag on the basis of the ILC's draft. While it seems doubtful that there is a pressing need for a new convention on the subject, the draft should be relatively uncontroversial. The Commission has accomplished its basic purposes of establishing a uniform regime for all kinds of couriers and bags, and filling in gaps in existing law. If the draft does engender controversy, it may well be because the articles resolve most, if not all, doubts in favor of increased protection of the courier and bag. This may not sit particularly well with those receiving and transit states for which even the current regime of the bag has caused difficulties.

* * *

WAIVER OF IMMUNITY

DAME NZIE v. VESSAH

France, Court of Appeal of Paris, 1978.
105 Journal du Droit International 605 (1978).[a]

[The wife of Vessah, Julienne Nzie, from the Republic of Cameroon, filed for divorce under both French law and the law of Cameroon. The court held that it had no jurisdiction because Vessah, as First Secretary of the Embassy of Cameroon in Paris (thus, registered on the diplomatic list) was entitled to immunity. He had not waived it.

The plaintiff appealed on two grounds. First, the court should not have declared itself without jurisdiction on its own initiative. Second, her husband had written to her family, in accordance with the customary law in force in Cameroon, that he agreed to divorce her according to her wishes. Hence, she contended, he had waived his diplomatic immunity. She finally argued only French courts could assure her physical safety by giving her permission to live separately from her husband.

---

a. Translation by the editors. Reprint-   S.A., Paris.
ed by permission of Editions Techniques,

* * * The Vienna Convention on diplomatic relations, made effective in France by the decree * * * and ratified by the [Republic of] Cameroon provides in Article 31 that a diplomatic agent enjoys immunity from jurisdiction save in exceptional cases, which are limited to those enumerated, and do not include a divorce proceeding. According to the terms of Article 32 of the Convention, the accrediting state may waive the immunity of jurisdiction of its diplomatic agents, but the waiver must always be express, [and] if a diplomatic agent brings suit, he may not invoke his immunity with regard to any counterclaim directly connected with the principal claim. It follows that the waiver by a diplomatic agent who is summoned to appear before a court must always be expressly authorized by his government.

* * * In the case at bar, the Republic of Cameroon has not indicated any waiver of immunity.

* * * In the absence of a waiver of immunity, the judge for matrimonial matters did not have the power to proceed with attempts at reconciliation, nor could he continue in force his preliminary ruling of December 17, 1976, by which * * * he authorized Julienne Nzie to live apart from her husband. The appeal is thus without foundation.

––––––

ABDULAZIZ v. METROPOLITAN DADE COUNTY

United States Court of Appeals, Eleventh Circuit, 1984.
741 F.2d 1328.

RONEY, Circuit Judge:

* * *

H.R.H. Prince Turki Bin Abdulaziz, a member of the ruling family of the Kingdom of Saudi Arabia, Princess Hend Al–Fassi, his wife, and Sheikha Faiza Ali Helmi, his mother-in-law, were residents of the Cricket Club condominium in Dade County, Florida. On February 26, 1982, representatives from a Florida State Attorney's office obtained a search warrant after inquiry with the United States Department of State revealed that Prince Turki and his family did not have diplomatic status. The warrant was based on the affidavit of Abdelmejid Daifi, a former employee of Prince Turki, who alleged that Prince Turki was holding an Egyptian named Nadia Lutefi against her will. Miami Dade Police officers attempted to execute the warrant. A "scuffle" ensued at the apartment between Prince Turki, his family and bodyguards, and the officers that were attempting to execute the warrant. On March 2, 1982, Prince Turki and his family brought this § 1983 action for violation of their civil rights against Metropolitan Dade County and the officers and the agents involved.

On March 11, 1982, the defendants counterclaimed alleging injuries from the encounter. Subsequently the State Department certified that on April 1, 1982, papers were filed which qualified Prince Turki and his family for diplomatic status. The plaintiffs moved to dismiss their complaint, and to dismiss the counterclaims on the ground that they had diplomatic immunity from suit. The district court dismissed the action November 30, 1982.

* * *

Defendants argue that plaintiff's classification as "special envoy" is not protected by the Diplomatic Relations Act. Under the Vienna Convention, the State Department has the broad discretion to classify diplomats. The broadness in the language of the Vienna Convention is necessary, since it is the foreign country that actually ranks its envoys, not the State Department. Article 14 of the Vienna Convention classifies "envoys" as Heads of Missions. Heads of Missions are defined in § 254a of the Diplomatic Relations Act, and are protected by the Act.

The State Department was notified by the Embassy of Saudi Arabia of Turki's status as "special envoy" for matters concerning the Government of Saudi Arabia. The designation of "special envoy" reflects the designation provided by the sending state. As special envoy Turki was afforded full protection pursuant to the Diplomatic Relations Act. This protection extended to his family, members of his service staff, and servants. See 22 U.S.C.A. §§ 254a(1)(C) and 254a(2).

* * *

Diplomatic immunity can be waived by continuing to assert a claim while at the same time seeking immunity from a counterclaim. Cf. National City Banks v. Republic of China. Here, however, immediately after receiving the certificate from the State Department that his papers from Saudi Arabia were properly on file and that he was entitled to immunity, Prince Turki moved to dismiss his action and the counterclaims. Turki's immediate seeking of a dismissal of his own suit forecloses any argument that defendants may have as to waiver. Defendants' argument that plaintiffs' initiation of the suit waived immunity is without merit because at the time the suit was brought his entitlement to immunity was not clear. He could not knowingly waive the benefit of a status to which he was not clearly entitled.

* * *

———

1. ***Question.*** Is it consistent to require the express authorization of waiver by the sending state when the diplomatic agent is sued and not require any authorization of waiver when he brings the proceeding himself?

2. ***Waiver of inviolability of diplomatic agent's private residence.*** The Office for Public International Law of the Swiss Federal Political Department gave an opinion regarding whether a diplomatic agent—or a member of the administrative and technical staff of a mission—could waive the inviolability of his private residence. It stated that the Vienna Convention did not provide a clear answer as to who could give the authorities of the receiving state consent to enter the diplomatic agent's private residence. It declined to assimilate the inviol-

ability of the personal residence to the inviolability of the premises of the mission. It refused, therefore, to conclude that, since the consent of the head of the mission was required for entry into the premises of the mission, it was required as well for entry into the agent's personal residence. The Office concluded the inviolability of the premises of the mission availed the sending state while the inviolability of the private residence of the agent attached to his person, thus providing him with it even in a temporary residence. Accordingly, the agent could validly waive the inviolability of his residence. 31 Annuaire Suisse de Dr. Int'l 147 (1976).

3. *Private acts of diplomatic agent not covered by immunity.* The Division of Juridical Affairs of the Swiss Federal Political Department issued an opinion as to whether a lien could be secured on a building owned by a high official of an international organization. Workers who provide services and materials for the construction of a building are protected for their payment under the Swiss Code by a lien against the property, even if the owner is not the one owing the debt. The lien must be recorded and this can be done only if the debtor acknowledges the debt or if a court orders the recordation following a summary proceeding. Where a cantonal court ordered provisional recordation of a lien upon the property of a high official of the United Nations, the lien is effective. Under Article 31(1) of the Vienna Convention, a diplomatic agent shall enjoy immunity from civil and administrative jurisdiction of the receiving state, but not with respect to private immovable property in the territory of the receiving state. Since the property was private in this case, the opinion concluded there was no need to seek a waiver of diplomatic immunity. 32 Ann. Suisse de Dr. Int'l 143 (1976).

For the other two types of private acts not covered by diplomatic immunity, see Article 31(1) in the Doc. Supp.

4. *Termination of diplomatic function: effect upon diplomatic immunity.* Under Article 39(2) of the Vienna Convention, the effect differs as between the diplomat's official and private acts. Thus with respect to a car accident, the following statement appears in 11 Japanese Ann.Int'l L. 94 (1967):

> On February 17, 1964, a secretary of the Malaysian Embassy in Tokyo, while driving home from a reception, ran over a Japanese student causing his death. The police made the necessary inquest and found that the accident was caused by his reckless driving, but, in view of the diplomatic status of the driver, no further action was taken by way of criminal proceedings against him. In August 1964, the secretary was recalled back home after completion of his term in Tokyo, and he left Japan without coming to a settlement with the family of the victim on the question of the damages. When this case was taken up for debate in the House of Councillors, the Director of the Treaties Bureau of the Ministry of Foreign Affairs stated that although the Civil Code of Japan was applicable to such a case of car accident, which might constitute a tort in civil law, the man had been immune from the jurisdiction of the court to entertain an

action against him at the time of the accident because of his status as a [member of the] diplomatic staff of the Embassy. Further to a question whether he continued to enjoy the immunity from jurisdiction after returning to his own country, the Director of the Treaties Bureau stated that in accordance with the provisions of the Vienna Convention on Diplomatic Relations, the jurisdictional immunity of a diplomat will cease to exist when the sending State gives notice of the termination of his mission to the receiving State, and that in law the secretary was now not immune from the civil jurisdiction of the court in Japan.

The U.S. Department of State took the same position in 1987. The ambassador of Papua New Guinea struck with the car he was driving several parked cars on a main thoroughfare in Washington D.C. Two people were injured, one seriously. The ambassador immediately returned to his country, but his embassy requested assurances that any criminal indictment against him be quashed. The Department refused to give such assurances and stated "the immunities of former diplomats do not subsist in respect of acts that, during the period of performance of diplomatic functions, were not performed in the exercise of functions as a member of the mission." 81 AJIL 937 (1987).

Suppose that a diplomatic agent performs an official act such as the preparation of a report on a highly sensitive political matter in the receiving state, at the request of his chief of mission. The report is made public in the sending state and is eventually reprinted in a newspaper in the receiving state. The diplomatic agent retires from the diplomatic service and remains in the state where he formerly exercised his function. Thereupon he is sued for libel in the report he prepared. Does Section 39(2) of the Vienna Convention entitle him to immunity?

OTHER PERSONS ENTITLED TO DIPLOMATIC IMMUNITY

1. *Organization of a diplomatic mission.* The Vienna Convention divides the personnel of a diplomatic mission into four categories and assigns different privileges and immunities to each. In assessing the difference in treatment of each of these categories, it is useful to know who are the persons in each and what they do. The information below is a simplified organization of a diplomatic mission.

The first category is the diplomatic staff. Its members have diplomatic rank. They are the ones who are engaged in the performance of the diplomatic function in the strict sense of the term. These diplomatic agents, as they are called in the Vienna Convention, include the chief of mission (ambassador, or minister or chargé d'affaires), counsellor or deputy chief of mission, the first, second and third secretaries (of embassy), the military attachés (air, army, navy) and such other attachés (for commerce, labor, treasury and other matters) as the receiving state may agree to recognize as diplomatic agents.

The next two categories—which may be looked upon as part of the official family of the diplomatic agent—are the administrative and technical staff on the one hand and the service staff on the other. The administrative staff includes administrative officers, persons in charge of communications (code and mail), secretary-typists and file clerks. The service staff includes drivers of the mission cars, butlers, cooks, maids and gardeners. The last category—which may be seen as part of the personal family of the diplomatic agent—consists of private servants.

2. *Variant state interests as to the reach of immunity.* Many diplomatic missions, including those of the United States, make heavy use of nationals of the host state. It is in the general interest of states housing missions to have a fairly wide reach of immunity for all members of the embassy community, including the local employees. On the other hand, objections are often publicly raised if diplomatic immunity were widely accorded to fellow nationals and resident aliens because of their employment by a foreign mission.

3. *Effect of nationality upon diplomatic immunity.* Under Article 38 of the Vienna Convention, a diplomatic agent who is a national of, or a permanent resident in, the receiving state is entitled to immunity only in respect of acts performed in the exercise of his functions. Thus in *Querouil v. Breton,* Court of Appeal of Paris, 1976, 57 Rev.Crit. de Dr. Int'l Priv. 478 (1968), plaintiffs were owners of an apartment rented to a Frenchman who was counsellor of the embassy of Chad in Paris. They brought a proceeding for his eviction. He pleaded diplomatic immunity. The court held that, even though the Vienna Convention was not yet ratified by France, it was a codification of current practice. Thus, defendant, being French, could not claim diplomatic immunity for a suit arising from his private act. No personnel are entitled to any immunity if they are nationals of the receiving state, unless and except to the extent such state accords it to them.

STATUS OF HUSBAND-IN-FACT OF DIPLOMAT
Opinion of the Office for Public International Law
of the Swiss Federal Political Department.
33 Annuaire Suisse De Droit International 224 (1977).[a]

[In a note dated July 13, 1976, the Office for Public International Law of the Federal Political Department handed down a ruling on the question whether the de facto husband of a woman diplomat accredited to Switzerland could avail himself of the privileges and immunities accorded by Article 37, paragraph 1, of the Vienna Convention on Diplomatic Relations of April 18, 1961, " * * * to members of the family of a diplomatic agent who are part of his household and not nationals of the accrediting state."]

Doctrine is silent on this question. Jurisprudence [case law] appears to be nonexistent. Albeit, we can cite a decision of the Tribunal

a. Translation by the editors. Reprint-　phischer Verlag AG, Zurich.
ed by permission of Schulthess Polygra-

Civil of the Seine in 1907 holding that the wife of a diplomat, who had been authorized to establish a separate domicile as a result of a suit for separation, continued to enjoy diplomatic privileges and immunities.

The working papers of the International Law Commission (ILC) do not address themselves to the precise question of a spouse-in-fact. But they do furnish useful guidelines as to the circle of members of the family entitled to diplomatic privileges. The ILC has noted in particular that the chief, or member, of a mission may be elderly or a bachelor and be assisted by a sister, an adult daughter or even a sister-in-law, who acts as lady of the house * * *. In its comments on Article 36 (practically identical to the future Article 37 of the Convention) of the draft articles (concerning diplomatic relations and immunities), the ILC comments:

> So far as concerns diplomatic agents * * * who enjoy the full range of privileges and immunities, the Commission, in conformity with existing practice, proposed that these prerogatives be equally accorded to members of their families, on the condition they be members of their households and they not be nationals of the accrediting state. The Commission did not want to go so far as precisely to define the meaning of the term "members of the family" or to set a maximum age for children. The spouse and the minor children, at least, are universally acknowledged to be members of the family, but there can be cases where other relatives also qualify if they are part of the household. In stipulating that in order to claim privileges and immunities, a member of the family must be part of the household, the Commission means to indicate that close relationships or special circumstances must be involved. These special circumstances may exist when a relative keeps house for the ambassador though they may not be closely related or when a distant relative has lived in the bosom of the family for so long he ends up being a part of it.

Strictly speaking the term *family* means a group of persons linked to each other by marriage (relationship by affinity), by descent (relationship by consanguinity) or by adoption. But the commentary clearly leads one to think that the ILC preferred to put the emphasis on the common household rather than on the links of marriage. Therefore it seems to be in conformity with the spirit of the Convention to include a spouse-in-fact among the members of the family. The Convention never made it its goal to regulate the private lives of diplomatic agents, but [rather made it its goal] to regulate the granting of diplomatic privileges.

In conformity with the preamble to the Vienna Convention, the purpose of the Convention's privileges is not to create advantages for individuals but to insure the effective performance of the functions of diplomatic missions insofar as they represent states. They are extended to the family that is part of the household of the diplomatic agent because the family is supposed to represent that which is dearest to him and because, by threats to it, one would be able to compromise the free exercise of the mission of the agent. Besides, the family in the sense of the Convention includes a limited number of persons. Giving a privileged status to its members would not in itself involve major risks of abuse. The family does not vary every day in its composition. It is relatively stable. It exists within the orbit of the diplomatic agent who can exert upon it a certain control.

All of these elements are present in the case at bar. The theoretical foundation of the law of diplomatic privileges and immunities rests on the idea that certain persons—first of all the members of his family— may be considered as an extension of the personality of the diplomatic agent * * *. As it were, there are sometimes circumstances under which one must hold them to be special and assimilate a person, even though a stranger to the agent (diplomat) by blood or by marriage, to a member of the family within the meaning of Article 37, paragraph 1, of the Convention. Such is the case with a long-time liaison, officially recognized as such by the accrediting state, between two spouses-in-fact who travel together, each with an official passport. The closeness of the bond seems to us further strengthened when the husband-in-fact, far from wanting to create his own center of interests and exercise a gainful activity in the accrediting state, manifests an intention to live under the same roof and in the financial orbit of the diplomatic agent. * * *

---

3. SPECIAL MISSIONS AND HEADS OF STATE OR PERSONS OF HIGH RANK

1. ***Special missions.*** On December 8, 1969, the General Assembly of the United Nations adopted and opened for signature on December 16, 1969, a Convention on Special Missions. For its text, see U.N. Document A/Res/2530(24) of December 8, 1969 and A/Res/2530(24)/Corr. 1 of January 2, 1970. The convention entered into force on June 21, 1985. As of December 31, 1990, 24 states were parties to the convention. In Article I, a special mission is defined as a "temporary mission, representing the State, which is sent by one State to another State with the consent of the latter for the purpose of dealing with it on specific questions or of performing in relation to it a specific task."

Like the Vienna Convention on Diplomatic Relations, the Convention on Special Missions breaks down their personnel into four categories—diplomatic staff, administrative and technical staff, service staff and private staff—and grants to the members in each the same immunities, subject to one qualification, as are granted to personnel in the corresponding categories by the Vienna Convention on Diplomatic Relations. The qualification is that in addition to the three types of private acts for which a diplomatic agent is not entitled to immunity from civil and administrative jurisdiction under the Vienna Convention on Diplomatic Relations, a member of the diplomatic staff of a special mission has no immunity from civil and administrative jurisdiction in the case of "an action for damages arising out of an accident caused by a vehicle used outside the official functions of the person concerned." Article 31, 2, (d). By Article 25, the premises of a special mission are made inviolable, and the members of its diplomatic staff enjoy personal inviolability under Article 29.

2. ***Heads of state and persons of high rank.*** Article 21 of the Convention on Special Missions provides:

1. The Head of the sending State, when he leads a special mission, shall enjoy in the receiving State or in a third State the facilities, privileges and immunities accorded by international law to Heads of State on an official visit.

2. The Head of the Government, the Minister for Foreign Affairs and other persons of high rank, when they take part in a special mission of the sending State, shall enjoy in the receiving State or in a third State, in addition to what is granted by the present Convention, the facilities, privileges and immunities accorded by international law.

The federal department of foreign affairs in Switzerland sent to an embassy in Berne in 1983 a note setting forth its views on the immunities, under customary international law, of foreign chiefs of state and their families. The note stated that a head of state is entitled in a foreign state to absolute immunity from criminal jurisdiction, as are the members of his close family. As to immunity from jurisdiction in civil matters, the practice of states varies. Some states distinguish between the official acts of the head of state and his private acts, the immunity extending only to the official ones. If the department were asked to take a position regarding the private acts of a foreign head of state in Switzerland, it would recognize the immunity, except for litigation involving an interest in immovable property, an interest in an estate locally administered, or an illegal act committed in his private capacity. 40 Ann. Suisse Dr. Int'l 182 (1984).

UNITED STATES v. NORIEGA
746 F.Supp. 1506 (U.S.D.C., S.D.Fla.1990.)

OMNIBUS ORDER

HOEVELER, District Judge. [The facts and non-immunity aspects of the case are presented in Ch. 17].

* * *

Subsequent to the indictment, the Court granted General Noriega's motion to allow special appearance of counsel, despite the fact that Noriega was a fugitive and not before the Court at that time. Noriega's counsel then moved to dismiss the indictment on the ground that United States laws could not be applied to a foreign leader whose alleged illegal activities all occurred outside the territorial bounds of the United States. Counsel further argued that Noriega was immune from prosecution as a head of state and diplomat, and that his alleged narcotics offenses constituted acts of state not properly reviewable by this Court.

* * *

This case, the Court is presented with several issues of first impression. This is the first time that a leader or de facto leader of a sovereign nation has been forcibly brought to the United States to face criminal charges. The fact that General Noriega's apprehension occurred in the course of a military action only further underscores the complexity of the issues involved. * * *

* * *

A. Head of State Immunity

Grounded in customary international law, the doctrine of head of state immunity provides that a head of state is not subject to the jurisdiction of foreign courts, at least as to official acts taken during the ruler's term of office. The rationale behind the doctrine is to promote international comity and respect among sovereign nations by ensuring that leaders are free to perform their governmental duties without being subject to detention, arrest, or embarrassment in a foreign country's legal system.[11] * * *

To assert head of state immunity, a government official must be recognized as a head of state. Noriega has never been recognized as Panama's Head of State either under the Panamanian Constitution or by the United States. Title VI, Article 170 of the Panamanian Constitution provides for an executive branch composed of the President and Ministers of State, neither of which applies to Noriega. Officially, Noriega is the *Commandante* of the Panamanian Defense Forces, but he was never elected to head Panama's government and in fact abrogated the Panamanian presidential elections of May 7, 1989. More importantly, the United States government has never accorded Noriega head of state status, but rather continued to recognize President Delvalle as the legitimate leader of Panama while Noriega was in power. As this Court held in a previous case involving the Republic of Panama, the Executive's decision to recognize President Delvalle and not the Defendant as Panama's head of state is binding on the Court. The ruling in that case—which I find no reason to depart from here—was based on a line of case law holding that recognition of foreign governments and their leaders is a discretionary foreign policy decision committed to the Executive branch and thus conclusive upon the courts.

* * *

Aside from the fact that neither Panama nor the United States recognizes Noriega as a head of state, the defendant concedes that he does not fit within traditional notions of a head of state as defined by customary international law.[13] He nonetheless argues that he is entitled

---

11. Given this rationale, there is ample doubt whether head of state immunity extends to private or criminal acts in violation of U.S. law. See In re Doe, 860 F.2d at 45; In re Grand Jury Proceedings, Doe # 700, 817 F.2d at 1111; Philippines v. Marcos (Marcos I), 806 F.2d 344, 360 (2d Cir.1986). Criminal activities such as the narcotics trafficking with which Defendant is charged can hardly be considered official acts or governmental duties which promote a sovereign state's interests, especially where, as here, the activity was allegedly undertaken for the sole personal benefit of the foreign leader.

13. The provision of customary international law cited by Defendant as an acceptable definition of a head of state would not

to head of state immunity as the *de facto* ruler of Panama, "regardless of the source of his power or the nature of his rule." The defendant cites numerous newspaper reports and excerpts of congressional testimony to the effect that Noriega effectively controlled Panama. In fact, this Court has previously acknowledged that, despite the official recognition of Delvalle, Noriega was the *de facto* head of Panama's government. United States v. Noriega, 683 F.Supp. at 1374, n. 3. But simply because Noriega may have in fact run the country of Panama does not mean he is entitled to head of state immunity, since the grant of immunity is a privilege which the United States may withhold from any claimant. The Schooner Exchange v. M'Faddon * * * Indeed, deference to the Executive branch in matters concerning relations with foreign nations is the primary rationale supporting immunity for heads of state. Since the only reason Noriega would be entitled to immunity as a head of state is because of such judicial deference to the Executive, his claim to a "right" of immunity against the express wishes of the Government is wholly without merit.

The "head of state" argument comes to the Court unencumbered by evidence; the arguments were made largely on the basis of general information made available by the media. However, accepting as true statements of counsel regarding Defendant's position of power, to hold that immunity from prosecution must be granted "regardless of his source of power or nature of rule" would allow illegitimate dictators the benefit of their unscrupulous and possibly brutal seizures of power. No authority exists for such a novel extension of head of state immunity, and the Court declines to create one here. Since the United States has never recognized General Noriega as Panama's head of state, he has no claim to head of state immunity.

* * *

SECTION C.   CONSULAR IMMUNITY

CONSULAR FUNCTION

Vienna Convention on Consular Relations was signed on April 24, 1963. The Convention entered into force on March 19, 1967; as of January 1, 1992, 38 states were parties. It entered into force for the United States on December 24, 1969. 21 U.S.T. 77, 596 U.N.T.S. 261. It is reproduced in the Doc. Supp.

---

include Noriega. The Convention on the Prevention and Punishment of Crimes Against Internationally Protected Persons, Including Diplomatic Agents (T.I.A.S. No. 8532; 28 U.S.T.1975) defines "internationally protected person" as "(a) a Head of State, including any member of a collegial body performing the functions of a Head of State under the constitution of the State concerned, a Head of Government or a Minister of Foreign Affairs * * *" Noriega has not shown that he was either the ceremonial or official head of government, and he does not otherwise fulfill the definition.

RE RISSMANN

Italy, Court of Genoa, 1970.
1 Italian Yearbook of International Law 254 (1975).*

Facts.—By complaint lodged with the Prosecutor of Genoa dated 13 July 1966, Mrs. Mancuso Santa in Cucco declared: * * * by decision dated 21 July 1964 the Genoa Minors Court had given her custody of her minor daughter Maria Luisa, born in Genoa [in] 1947 from her first marriage with the German citizen Muller Werner; which marriage was dissolved by the Hannover Court with a sentence of divorce on 2 October 1956, recognized and made effective in Italy by the Court of Appeal of Genoa by judgment dated 31 March 1961; that following such judgment the minor had acquired Italian citizenship, in accordance with a note dated 5 July 1965 from the Prefettura of Genoa; that by letter dated 8 March 1966 addressed to the Consul General for Germany in Genoa and, with a copy to the Head of the Police, she, as legitimate guardian of the said minor child, had given notice of her disapproval to the issuing of a passport or of any other equivalent document to the said minor, even if requested by a third party; * * * that in March 1966, she, following a serious act of indiscipline by the minor * * * had agreed for her to stay in the boarding house Istituto Madri Pie, Genoa * * *; that, however, on the morning of 11 July 1966 a nun of the Institute had informed her that her daughter had gone out * * * and had not come back * * *.

* * *

Therefore the complainant formally called for punishment of whoever was responsible for the disappearance of her daughter, a minor, of the removal of her from her mother's guardianship and of any other criminal action arising from the facts reported by her or subsequently arising therefrom * * *. Following the summons the Prosecutor proceeded to verify the facts reported therein and the further circumstances arising therefrom * * *. On the basis of such results and after acquiring copies of the statements made during the guardianship proceedings by the minor to the President of the Genoa Court for Minors, * * * the Prosecutor made the charge referred to in the heading against Dr. Rissmann, sending a copy thereof to the Consulate of the German Federal Republic in Genoa under cover of a note dated 8 August 1966.

However, the German Embassy in Rome, by memorandum dated 25 August 1966 addressed to the Ministry of Foreign Affairs and through it transmitted to the Ministry of Justice who also sent a copy to the Prosecutor in Genoa, stated that Dr. Rissmann had "in the exercise of his functions and following written request by the father of the German national Maria Luisa Muller, born 7 June 1947, whom he had the right to legally represent, issued her with a German passport", and invoked for the Consul Rissmann the consular immunity provided for in the first paragraph of art. 43 of the Vienna Convention on Consular Relations ratified by both Italy and Germany, stating that in view of this the Consul Rissmann had been ordered not to appear in Court.

* * *

* Reprinted with the permission of Editoriale Scientifica, s.r.l., Naples.

Law.—The question as to whether or not consular immunity exists is clearly a preliminary question to be decided since it is relevant to whether or not Dr. Rissmann is exempt from the jurisdiction of this criminal Court. First and foremost, it calls for consideration as to the nationality of the minor Maria Luisa Muller. There is no doubt that she, German iure sanguinis having been born of parents who were both German at that time, never lost German nationality according to the German law on citizenship.

* * *

It is * * * established that in the same way as Italy, maintaining that Muller had acquired Italian nationality iure communicationis, could legitimately consider her purely as an Italian citizen ignoring her dual nationality, so also could the German Federal Republic, and consequently also the Consul, Rissmann, who was one of the representatives operating abroad, legitimately consider her a German citizen.

Clearly, in view of the fact that, inter alia, the minor had been legally entrusted by the Italian judge to her mother, the Consul in issuing her with a passport as a German citizen and facilitating her return to Germany was certainly acting in conflict with the Italian legal system and behaving in a manner liable to give rise to the criminal charge contained in the indictment in this case.

But it is necessary to clarify the question as to whether there exists in the present case the necessary conditions and circumstances for the application of consular immunity. According to agreed doctrine (developed from jurisprudence of the principal States) and to general international law, even prior to the last Convention on Consular Relations concluded in Vienna [in] 1963 in conformity with the principles of the Charter of the United Nations, there existed functional immunity for Consuls: namely, exemption from local jurisdiction in civil and criminal matters in respect of acts performed in the exercise of their office. Following the same doctrine, a demonstration of the common feeling of states on this matter was afforded by Article II of the Convention of Montreux dated 8 May 1937. This provided that "foreign consuls are subject to the jurisdiction of mixed Courts subject always to the exceptions recognised by international law. In particular, they are not subject to indictment in respect of actions carried out in the exercise of their office".

It should be added that functional immunity, already then generally recognised even in the absence of specific provisions in consular conventions, finds its justification in the general principle according to which the Consul's acts, even though they may be valid within the legal system of territorial State and thus produce legal consequences therein, constitute an activity of the State to which the Consul belongs, and not of the Consul personally, since, in the exercise of his office, he must answer to his government. Such an immunity is not, therefore, confined to judicial proceedings. It is based on a principle of substantive law, and continues even after his tour of office as Consul has terminated.

* * *

We now come to the Convention on Consular Relations signed in Vienna [in] 1963 by 92 States members of the United Nations, including Italy and the German Federal Republic, and implemented by law. The Court observes that the functional immunity of consuls is explicitly covered by Art. 43 of the Convention, under the title "Immunity from Jurisdiction", the first paragraph of which provides as follows: "Consular officers and consular employees shall not be amenable to the jurisdiction of the judicial or administrative authorities of the receiving State in respect of acts performed in the exercise of consular functions". * * *

We must now examine whether or not the action of the Consul Rissmann which gives rise to this case fell within the scope of his consular functions. As far as concerns the present judgment, suffice to observe that Art. 5 of the Convention includes among consular functions at letters *d*) and *e*) respectively, the issuing of passports and travel documents to citizens of the State concerned and the giving of assistance to the same: textually "Consular functions consist in: * * * *d*) issuing passports and travel documents to nationals of the sending State, * * * *e*) helping and assisting nationals of the sending State." It is certain that Muller was a German citizen, [so] there can be no doubt that Rissmann, in issuing her with a German passport, was carrying out a true and proper official act as Consul, and this is because, in view of the fact that a minor was in question, he had not only the consent but even the express request on the part of the father, a German citizen, entitled to guardianship of her which entitlement had never lapsed * * *.

It should not be forgotten that Consuls, being State agents operating abroad, do not exceed the scope of their functions when they act in accordance with the laws of their country which they must comply with in so far as these laws are to be applied abroad.

As far as concerns the cooperation of Rissmann in furthering the return of the minor to Germany by means of booking and acquiring the air ticket and the assistance given to her for this purpose, it must be stressed that this undoubtedly pertains to the consular office. First and foremost, such an assistance was given to a minor German citizen, upon the request of the father, a German national, exercising guardianship rights over her. From the knowledge that the Consul had of the history of Muller, as it had been referred to him by her and her father, he had valid reason—even independently from actual truth of the case that, as proved by evidence before the Court, had been explained to him only by the afore-mentioned as a situation of dramatic tension and intolerability—to respond to the appeal for assistance directed to him by a fellow country woman who, among other things, was by then 19 years of age.

* * * [W]e must * * * hold that proceedings cannot be brought against Rissmann in respect of the charges made against him, since, as a person who enjoys consular immunity, he is exempted from criminal action * * *.

SECTION D. IMMUNITIES OF PERSONS CONNECTED WITH INTERNATIONAL ORGANIZATIONS

1. OFFICIALS OF INTERNATIONAL ORGANIZATIONS
PEOPLE v. LEO

United States, Criminal Court of the City of New York, 1978.
95 Misc.2d 408, 407 N.Y.S.2d 941.

BETTY WEINBERG ELLERIN, Judge:

Defendant moves for dismissal of the complaint charging him with assault in the third degree (Penal Law § 120.00) and resisting arrest (Penal Law § 205.30) on the ground that he "is a person who has international diplomatic immunity and as such the court lacks jurisdiction". The relevant facts underlying the charges arose on July 29, 1977, when defendant, who was then working at his office in the United Nations Building at about 10 P.M., received a telephone call from his wife advising him of the uninvited presence of complainant in their apartment and her refusal to leave despite requests that she do so. Defendant then left his office and returned home, where a scuffle with complainant ensued resulting in the arrival of the police to place defendant under arrest for assault and his resistance to such arrest.

Defendant contends that a dismissal is mandated in this case because he is insulated from prosecution by the cloak of diplomatic immunity and, further, because this court lacks jurisdiction over the subject matter which, according to defendant, constitutes the commission of a federal crime by the complainant. It may be noted that defendant has pressed a cross-complaint against complainant in this court and has also made a formal complaint to the U.S. Attorney's office against her apparently under 18 U.S.C. § 112.

It is essential to establish the precise status occupied by defendant in this country. It is uncontradicted that he is a Tanzanian national who is employed by the United Nations at its headquarters in New York in the capacity of Economic Affairs Officer, Economic Affairs Section, Centre for Natural Resources, Energy, and Transportation. While defendant is concededly sponsored for this position by the government of Tanzania, he holds no other diplomatic position on behalf of the government of Tanzania, has never been issued a diplomatic passport and he resides in the United States under a G4 visa which is issued to international civil servants. Thus, it is clear that defendant's status is solely that of an employee of the United Nations with whatever rights and immunities may inure to him by virtue of that position.

The controlling authorities are in Article 105 of the United Nations Charter, of which the United States is a signatory, and in the International Organizations Immunities Act (22 U.S.C. § 288d[b]) which was enacted in 1945 to implement the immunities provisions embodied in the

United Nations Charter and was made applicable to that organization by Executive Order No. 9698 of February 19, 1946.

Article 105 of the United Nations Charter, provides that:

1. The Organization shall enjoy in the territory of each of its Members such privileges and immunities as are necessary for the fulfillment of its purposes.

2. Representatives of Members of the United Nations and officials of the Organization shall similarly enjoy such privileges and immunities as are necessary for the independent exercise of their functions in connection with the Organization.

Section 288d, sub-paragraph (b) of Title 22 of the United States Code states that:

Representatives of foreign governments in or to international organizations and officers and employees of such organization shall be immune from suit and legal process relating to acts performed by them in their official capacity and falling within their function as such representatives, officers, or employees except insofar as such immunity may be waived by the foreign government or international organization concerned. (underscoring added.)

The underscored language clearly delineates the perimeters of the immunity applicable to defendant, as an employee of the United Nations. It is limited in scope and purpose to protection for acts committed by United Nations officials in the course of accomplishing their functions as United Nations' employees in distinction to the unlimited form of immunity traditionally accorded to diplomats.

While defendant asserts that the statutory immunity under Section 288d(b) applies in this instance because complainant did in fact obstruct him "in the performance of his duties", an analysis of the facts in this case, in the most liberal perspective possible, fails to demonstrate any basis whatsoever upon which to conclude that defendant was acting in his official capacity or that there was some reasonable relationship between the alleged altercation and defendant's United Nations employment. On the contrary, the acts underlying the charges took place away from defendant's office when he returned home in response to his wife's call concerning an unwanted visitor whose presence at defendant's residence has not been shown to have been in any way connected with defendant's employment. The defendant's acts took place wholly within the context of a personal, domestic matter and as such are outside the scope of the limited immunity to which he is entitled as a United Nations' employee. The tenuous circumstance that he was at his office when he received his wife's call affords no rational basis for holding that his subsequent acts of violence in ejecting complainant and in resisting arrest were in some way related to the purposes of the United Nations or to the performance or fulfillment of defendant's duties and functions as an Economic Affairs Officer of that organization.

Nor is there merit to defendant's argument that this court lacks jurisdiction over the subject matter herein because such jurisdiction is vested solely in the Federal Courts. In support of this contention defendant points to the fact that, under his version of the incident, complainant is chargeable with a violation of the federal law (i.e. 18 U.S.C. § 112[a] and [b]) which provides for the imposition of criminal penalties for injury to the person or property of a foreign official, including trespass upon the residence of such official. It is apparently defendant's position that if he initiates charges against complainant under such statute, he is thereby rendered immune from criminal prosecution for any acts committed against complainant, however egregious. Aside from the fact that defendant does not fall within the category of "foreign official" covered by the statute, he seriously misapprehends its scope and purpose. The statute is designed to provide foreign officials with a protective shield against harm by imposing severe criminal penalties upon those who would interfere with such foreign officials in the performance of their functions and duties. There is no language whatsoever in Section 112(a) and (b) of Title 18 which deals with the granting of immunity or which can give rise to a construction of the statute permitting it to be converted into a sword authorizing the perpetration of criminal acts with impunity by those whom the statute seeks to protect. The purpose of this legislation is simply to deal with the protection of diplomatic officials by preventing and discouraging crimes against such persons. Any immunities from prosecution which they or other persons may enjoy derive from other statutory provisions. Insofar as defendant is concerned the controlling statute is 22 U.S.C. § 288d(b) which, as has already been discussed, affords him only the limited diplomatic immunity applicable to a United Nations employee, an immunity which in no way proscribes the instant prosecution. It is undoubtedly in recognition of the limited scope of 22 U.S.C. § 288 that defendant seeks to create a more expansive immunity by a strained and distorted interpretation of 18 U.S.C. § 112. Significantly, defendant has submitted no authority whatsoever in support of such untenable construction of that statute.

* * *

Accordingly, defendant's motion to dismiss on the ground of diplomatic immunity is in all respects denied.

———

1. *Is immunity derivative?* In Westchester County v. Ranollo, 187 Misc. 777, 67 N.Y.S.2d 31 (1946), defendant was prosecuted for speeding. Defendant automobile operator claimed immunity as an employee of the United Nations; he asserted that, in fact, he was accompanied at the time by the Secretary–General of the United Nations, Trygve Lie. The court noted that the International Organizations Immunities Act accorded immunity to "officers and employees of such organizations * * * from suit and legal process relating to acts performed by them in their official capacity and falling within their functions * * *." It held that "the defendant is not entitled to immunity as a matter of law without a trial of the issue of fact * * *." What issue of fact remains to be tried? Suppose that defendant proves that he was chauffeuring the

Secretary–General to an official United Nations meeting (cocktail party?) and was speeding because the Secretary was late for the appointment.

2. ***The Vienna Convention on the Representation of States in Their Relations with International Organizations of a Universal Character.*** This Convention was adopted by a United Nations conference in March 1975 and was not in force as of December 31, 1990. The United States abstained on the vote adopting the text of the convention and did not become a signatory. The head of the United States delegation to the conference explained that the United States viewed the convention as needlessly expanding the obligations of host states. "Article 66, for example, is an expansion of current privileges and immunities for which no justification has been given. Administrative and technical staff, who have no representational functions, are accorded virtually the same privileges and immunities as would be accorded the ambassador to the host state." McDowell, Digest of United States Practice in International Law 1975, at 40 (1976).

3. ***When the state of nationality of a United Nations employee confers diplomatic rank upon him.*** U.S. v. Melekh, 190 F.Supp. 67 (S.D.N.Y.1960), involved an indictment of a Russian citizen for a conspiracy to obtain United States defense information. Melekh was employed in the Secretariat of the United Nations as chief of the Russian language section in the office of Conference Services. Melekh's defense of immunity was based upon the assertion that the Soviet Union has conferred on him the diplomatic rank of Second Secretary of the Ministry of Foreign Affairs of the USSR. The court rejected Melekh's claim of immunity. The defendant had not been designated as a representative of the USSR to the United Nations, was not a member of the staff of the Soviet delegation, was not assigned by the USSR to diplomatic duties with the United States or any other government and had not been received by the United States as a diplomat. Diplomatic immunity was therefore unavailable under 22 U.S.C. § 252 and the Headquarters Agreement. Functional immunity was unavailable under the International Organizations Immunities Act: " * * * the defendant does not argue that the alleged criminal acts * * * grew out of or were incidental to his official activities as a United Nations officer or employee." The court also found no basis for immunity in Article 105 of the charter or international law. In response to the argument that diplomatic status arose out of the relationship between the defendant's government and the United Nations, the court stated: "It is neither the defendant's position with his own government, as such, nor the relationship of the defendant's government, as such, with the United Nations that is decisive. What counts is the actual position occupied by the defendant in the United Nations and his actual duties and functions in the United Nations."

In support of an identical holding in U.S. v. Enger, 472 F.Supp. 490 (D.N.J.1978), the court remarked, drily: "[e]spionage, the crime with which the defendants are charged, is, of course, not one of the functions performed in the defendants' official capacities with the United Nations." The defendants' titles within the United Nations secretariat were, in one case, "Political Affairs Officer attached to the Unit for

Coordination and Political Information, Office of the Undersecretary General for Political Information" and, in the other, "Administrative Officer, * * * a member of the Training and Examination Service, Office of Personnel Service." In explaining why diplomatic status is not accorded to all employees of the United Nations the court stated:

> There is a practical justification based on the legitimate self-interest of the United States. The fact that the United Nations has its headquarters in the United States requires a large number of foreign government representatives and foreign national employees to reside in the New York City area for substantial periods of time. From the standpoint of providing diplomatic immunity, it would be impractical for all concerned if each of those individuals had to be "approved" by the United States in advance. The accommodation reached is not to afford all such foreign nationals full immunity status. Rather, it is to permit the foreign government or international organization to undertake the selection of representatives and employees but, as a means of protecting this country's interests, to limit the availability and scope of immunity. Accordingly, under the Headquarters Agreement and 22 U.S.C. § 288d(b), only a limited number of persons may receive full immunity and then only after prior government approval; all others are cloaked with immunity only when acting within the scope of their employment.

4. *Immunity of official of the International Atomic Energy Agency.* A high official of the agency, of Lebanese nationality, was divorced from his wife, an Austrian national, and sought custody of their child in an action before the Austrian courts. She opposed his claim and sought an order awarding her custody of the child. Thereupon he withdrew his action and pleaded immunity to hers. The supreme court held that, under the international agreement between the agency and Austria, he was entitled to the immunity of a diplomatic agent and had not waived it by bringing the action. 106 J. de Dr. Int'l. 165 (1979).

---

2. REPRESENTATIVES OF MEMBER STATES AND OFFICIAL INVITEES

UNITED STATES EX REL. CASANOVA v. FITZPATRICK

United States District Court, S.D. New York, 1963.
214 F.Supp. 425.

WEINFELD, District Judge. The petitioner, Roberto Santiesteban Casanova, seeks his release from custody on a writ of habeas corpus on the ground of lack of the Court's jurisdiction over his person. He is under arrest and detention by virtue of a two-count indictment wherein he, two codefendants and two others not named as defendants are charged with conspiracy to commit sabotage and to violate the Foreign Agents Registration Act. He was originally arrested on a warrant issued by the United States Commissioner, based upon a complaint, and held in $250,000 bail fixed by the Commissioner. Thereafter, following his indictment by a grand jury, this Court set bail in the sum of $75,000, which it later reduced to $50,000. Petitioner has been confined since his arrest in default of bail.

Petitioner contends he is entitled to diplomatic immunity and is not subject to Federal arrest, detention or prosecution. The basic facts upon which his claim to immunity rests are not in dispute. He is a Cuban national, appointed by his government as an attache and Resident Member of the Staff of the Permanent Mission of Cuba to the United Nations (hereafter "Cuban Mission.") He entered the United States on October 3, 1962 with a diplomatic passport issued by his own government, a nonimmigrant visa issued by our Department of State, and a landing card issued by the Immigration and Naturalization Service. From the time of his admission to the United States to the date of his arrest he was employed as a Resident Member of the staff of the Cuban Mission.

Petitioner contends that he enjoys diplomatic immunity from arrest and prosecution under (1) Article 105 of the United Nations Charter, (2) Section 15(2) of the Headquarters Agreement, and (3) the Law of Nations. He further contends that even if his claim to immunity is overruled, nonetheless the writ must be sustained, since the Supreme Court of the United States has exclusive and original jurisdiction to try him under Article III of the Constitution of the United States and 28 U.S.C. § 1251. Before considering his contentions, it is desirable to localize the issue with which we deal. The petitioner is not a member of a diplomatic staff accredited to, and recognized by, the United States Government. He is not a representative to, or an employee of, the United Nations. His claim to diplomatic immunity derives solely from his status as a Resident Member of the Cuban Permanent Mission to the United Nations. Whatever right to immunity exists must be considered within the context of that status.

A.   THE CLAIM OF DIPLOMATIC IMMUNITY UNDER THE UNITED NATIONS CHARTER

* * *

The thrust of the relator's contention is that the declaration in section 2 is self-executing and requires absolute diplomatic immunity be accorded to representatives of members and their staffs. The argument rests upon the postulate, universally recognized in international law, that diplomatic agents are accorded immunity from judicial process so that their governments may not be hampered in their foreign relations by the arrest or harassment of, or interference with, their diplomatic representatives. Petitioner urges that this rationale applies with equal force to the members of a mission to the United Nations and its staff; that unless they enjoy diplomatic immunity they can be prevented from fulfilling their diplomatic functions vis-a-vis the United Nations, if the host country, in this instance the United States, were able to arrest and detain them—in short, that diplomatic immunity is required to assure the independence of the Organization and its members in the discharge of their duties and functions. Accordingly, he contends that Article 105 intended, and in fact confers, full diplomatic immunity. The language of

Article 105, its history, as well as subsequent acts by the United States and the United Nations, require rejection of petitioner's claim that by its own force full diplomatic immunity was either intended or granted.

* * *

The Court concludes that Article 105 of the Charter does not purport to nor does it confer diplomatic immunity. The broadest claim that can be made is that it is self-operative with respect to functional activities. And even if it were so construed, it avails not the petitioner, since by its very language the immunity is confined to acts necessary for the independent exercise of functions in connection with the United Nations. Conspiracy to commit sabotage against the Government of the United States is not a function of any mission or member of a mission to the United Nations. Accordingly, the Court holds that the petitioner does not enjoy diplomatic immunity against prosecution on the indictment by virtue of Article 105 of the United Nations Charter.

B. THE CLAIM OF DIPLOMATIC IMMUNITY UNDER THE HEADQUARTERS AGREEMENT

(1) Is the Court concluded by the certificate of the State Department?

The development and growth of international organizations over the past two decades, particularly the United Nations as a world force, have brought into being new problems and concepts relating to the immunities and privileges to be accorded the organization, its officials and representatives of member states and their staffs. From the start it was evident that unless adequate immunity was provided to protect them in the exercise of their respective functions, the independence of the organization would be undermined and its effectiveness greatly hampered, if not destroyed. The location of the headquarters presents special problems to the host country and the organization. Access to the headquarters to all persons having legitimate business with the organization is required and, on the other hand, the host country is entitled to protection against the admission of persons likely to engage in activities subversive of its national interests and internal security. These matters are usually provided for by the basic charter or constitution, special agreements or national legislation. With the United States as the site of the United Nations headquarters, our Government was particularly sensitive to the problem of assuring the independence and proper functioning of the United Nations, and also to the protection of its own security. The Headquarters Agreement was one of the means adopted to protect the respective interests.

* * *

Under the above provisions, those who come within its embrace are entitled to the broad diplomatic privileges and immunities enjoyed by diplomatic envoys accredited to the United States. And there would appear to be no question that if the petitioner is entitled to the benefits of Article 15, he is immune from prosecution upon the charges contained in the indictment. Petitioner relies upon section 15(2) as conferring diplomatic immunity upon him by reason of his position as an attache and a Resident Member of the Cuban Mission. The Government challenges his claim, pointing out that the subsection expressly provides that immunity thereunder is accorded only to "such resident members * * * as may be agreed upon between the Secretary–General, the Government of the United States and the Government of the Member concerned." It denies that any such agreement was ever manifested, although it admits that an application therefor was made by the Secretary–General of the United Nations pursuant to the request of the Cuban Mission.

The prosecution has filed an authenticated affidavit of the Chief Protocol Officer of the Department of State certifying that the Government of the United States has not agreed to grant diplomatic immunity to petitioner under section 15(2) of the Headquarters Agreement, "and that he does not enjoy any diplomatic privileges and immunities under the aforesaid Article 15 of the Agreement." Accordingly, it presses that the Court is concluded by this certification. Thus, a threshold question is presented. The precise issue before the Court is whether, in the light of section 15(2) of the Headquarters Agreement, certification by the Department of State that an individual acknowledged to be a resident attache of the Permanent Cuban Mission to the United Nations has not been "agreed upon" by the Government as entitled to diplomatic privileges and immunities thereunder, concludes the question. A number of leading authorities do hold that the State Department certification is conclusive where the issue pertains to a diplomatic envoy accredited to the United States. This Court is of the view that such authorities do not control the question here presented. There is a sharp distinction between a diplomatic envoy accredited to the Government of the United States and a representative of a member state to the United Nations, an international organization. The status of each is different and immunity rests upon and is derived from entirely different desiderata.

Acceptance of a diplomatic envoy from a foreign government to the United States rests upon the exercise by our Executive of its power to conduct foreign affairs. It either accepts or rejects the diplomat in its sole and absolute discretion and, if he is received, he thereby is entitled, without more, under the Law of Nations, to full diplomatic immunity. These are political judgments by the Executive Branch of the Government and the Court is concluded thereby. In contrast, a representative of a member state to an international organization, such as the United Nations, is designated by his Government entirely independent of the views of other member states and indeed of the Organization. The United States has no say or veto power with respect to such representative of any member state. These representatives acquire immunity only to the extent that it is granted by legislation, or by agreement, whether under the basic charter, a general convention, or a separate agreement, as in the instant case by the Headquarters Agreement. Accordingly, whether or not a particular individual is entitled to immunity is to be decided within the framework of the applicable document. The Headquarters Agreement simply provides that the three designated parties are to agree upon those entitled to immunity. * * *

Whether, upon the facts presented by both the Government and the individual involved or his government, immunity exists by reason of the agreement, is not a political question, but a justiciable controversy involving the interpretation of the agreement and its application to the particular facts. In this instance the decision is for the Court and it is not concluded by the unilateral statement of the Government, a party to that agreement and to this controversy, that the individual is not entitled to immunity thereunder.   * * *

The scope of the inquiry is narrowly confined. Did the United States of America, as one of the parties to the Headquarters Agreement, make its decision under section 15(2) either that it agreed or did not agree that petitioner was entitled to diplomatic immunity? The Government's statement that it did not so agree is evidential but not conclusive. Petitioner asserts that by various acts the necessary agreement was manifested; the Government denies it.   * * *   Thus we proceed to consider the petitioner's contention upon the merits.

(2) The claim that section 15(2) of the Headquarters Agreement contemplates agreement only as to categories and not as to individuals.

The petitioner's contention is that the clause "such resident members as may be agreed upon" contemplates an agreement with respect to categories of persons and does not require agreement upon persons within the category. The petitioner's main props in support of his contention are comments and reports of committees of the United Nations with respect to immunity proposals. While the unilateral views of any United Nations committee or member cannot serve to defeat the express language of the final agreement (the Headquarters Agreement), nonetheless, analysis of such comments and reports negates rather than supports the plaintiff's position.

* * *

The argument that unless petitioner's construction of class agreement is adopted the United States would obtain "a discriminatory, unilateral and effective control of and sanctions against nations of equal sovereignty in the United Nations" is unpersuasive. As already demonstrated, full diplomatic immunity is accorded under subdivision 1 of section 15 to top echelon representatives of member nations identical to that accorded to accredited diplomats to the United States. As to their staff members, pending agreement by the United States under section 15(2), which would entitle them to diplomatic immunity, there is available under the International Organizations Immunities Act the immunity necessary for the independent exercise of their functions, apart from Article 105 of the Charter, if in fact it is self-executing. No member state is prevented from appointing whomever it will to serve on the resident staff of its mission to the United Nations, but the United States, under section 15(2), is not required, simply by reason of one's employment in a particular category, to grant diplomatic immunity. It retains the rights thereunder to agree or not to agree that diplomatic immunity shall extend to individuals who qualify under the broad category "Resident Members of their Staffs." While it has exercised this right sparingly, it has refused, in the instance of at least five individuals, to agree to the request for immunity, without objection by either the Secretary–General or the member state who submitted the request.

The construction advanced would mean that a member state of the United Nations which may be hostile to our interests is free to send to the United States individuals designated as resident members of their staffs, to engage in conduct destructive of our national interest and security and yet have them protected from criminal prosecution on the theory that their designated status cloaked them with diplomatic immunity. It would open the flood gates for the entry of saboteurs, agents provocateur and others under a built-in guarantee that no matter what the criminal conduct, the Government could not prosecute them.

The language of the section controls. There is nothing in its history or in the practice under it to support petitioner's claim. To accept his contention would in effect amend section 15(2) by inserting therein the words "classes of" to read "such classes of resident members * * *."

The Court holds that the status of petitioner as an attache and resident member of the Cuban Mission does not by itself entitle him to diplomatic immunity under section 15(2) and that unless there was the agreement of the United States, as provided therein, the prosecution is not barred. The petitioner claims there was such agreement.

    (3) The claim that the United States did agree that petitioner was entitled to diplomatic immunity.

The essence of petitioner's claim is that the issuance of the visa and the landing permit constituted, under the facts and law, the agreement of the Government of the United States that he was entitled to diplomatic privileges and immunities under section 15(2) of the Headquarters Agreement. * * *

    * * *

I am of the view that petitioner's contention cannot be upheld. To do so is to transmute the G–1 visa issued by the State Department into the agreement of the United States required under section 15(2) before diplomatic immunity extends to staff members of missions to the United Nations. The fact that the G–1 visa recognized that petitioner had the status encompassed within section 15(2) does not mean that by reason thereof the United States gave the required agreement thereunder. The visa was issued at the request of the Cuban Mission upon presentation of a diplomatic passport issued by the Cuban government and its representation of petitioner's appointment as "diplomatic attache." Since the designation rested with the Cuban government, the United States was obligated under sections 11 and 13 of the Headquarters Agreement not to impose any impediment in his transit to and from the Headquarters District and to provide him with the necessary visa. The visa was the basic document of entry into the United States enroute to his post with his mission.

Petitioner argues that the State Department did not have to issue a G–1 visa in order to fulfill its obligations under the Headquarters Agreement; that so long as petitioner was accorded free access to the

Headquarters District, the obligations of the United States Government were met. But as the prosecution contends, once the State Department determined that petitioner, upon the documents and representations contained therein, qualified for a G–1 visa, its issuance to the petitioner was pursuant to rules promulgated under the Immigration and Naturalization Act. The question of the agreement of the United States Government to diplomatic immunity was entirely separate from facilitating petitioner's entry to assume his duties with his mission.

I conclude that the Government of the United States did not, by the issuance of the visa and the landing permit, give its agreement that petitioner, on his entry into the United States to assume his duties as a member of the Cuban Mission, was thereby entitled to diplomatic immunity under section 15(2) of the Headquarters Agreement.

C. The Claim of Diplomatic Immunity Under the Law of Nations

Here the petitioner's position is that under the Law of Nations he had diplomatic immunity from the time of his entry until the Government of the United States took definitive action upon the request of the Cuban Mission that he be "agreed upon" for diplomatic immunity under the Headquarters Agreement. Again, the claim centers in part about the G–1 visa and landing permit. He urges in substance that by this issuance the United States acknowledged his status for the purpose of entry into the United States to assume his duties with his mission, aware that he was eligible for diplomatic immunity. Accordingly, he contends that he was entitled to diplomatic immunity from the time of his entry on the same principle as that applicable under the Law of Nations to diplomats awaiting acknowledgment by governments to which they are accredited and which attaches even before they have been received by it—in fine, that until he was either agreed upon or rejected in response to his government's request, he was protected.   * * *

　　* * *

Petitioner's path is blocked by the same reasoning upon which the Court rejected the Government's position that its unilateral determination that he was not entitled to diplomatic immunity under the Headquarters Agreement was conclusive. As the Government's suggestion of an analogy to diplomats accredited to the United States was refused above, so is petitioner's in this instance. It is the Headquarters Agreement, the Charter and the applicable statutes of the United States that govern the determination of his rights, not the Law of Nations. The Law of Nations comes into play and has applicability in defining the nature and scope of diplomatic immunity only once it is found a person is entitled thereto under an applicable agreement or statute.

The Court concludes that petitioner is not entitled to diplomatic immunity by virtue of the Law of Nations.

　　* * *

The petition for a writ of habeas corpus is dismissed upon the merits.

———

UNITED STATES v. PALESTINE LIBERATION ORGANIZATION

United States District Court, S.D.N.Y.1988.
695 F.Supp. 1456, 27 I.L.M. 1055.

PALMIERI, J.:

The Anti-terrorism Act of 1987 (the "ATA"), is the focal point of this lawsuit. At the center of controversy is the right of the Palestine Liberation Organization (the "PLO") to maintain its office in conjunction with its work as a Permanent Observer to the United Nations. The case comes before the court on the government's motion for an injunction closing this office and on the defendants' motions to dismiss.

I

Background

The United Nations' Headquarters in New York were established as an international enclave by the Agreement Between the United States and the United Nations Regarding the Headquarters of the United Nations[2] (the "Headquarters Agreement"). This agreement followed an invitation extended to the United Nations by the United States, one of its principal founders, to establish its seat within the United States.

As a meeting place and forum for all nations, the United Nations, according to its charter, was formed to:

> maintain international peace and security * * *; to develop friendly relations among nations, based on the principle of equal rights and self-determination of peoples * * *; to achieve international cooperation in solving international problems of an economic, social, cultural or humanitarian character * * *; and be a centre for harmonizing the actions of nations in the attainment of these common ends.

U.N. Charter art. 1. Today, 159 of the United Nations' members maintain missions to the U.N. in New York. U.N. Protocol and Liaison Service, *Permanent Missions to the United Nations No. 262* 3–4 (1988) (hereinafter *"Permanent Missions No. 262 "*). In addition, the United Nations has, from its incipiency, welcomed various non-member observers to participate in its proceedings. *See Permanent Missions to the United Nations: Report of the Secretary–General,* (hereinafter *Permanent Missions: Report of the Secretary–General*). Of these, several non-member nations, intergovernmental organizations, and other organizations currently maintain "Permanent Observer Missions" in New York.

The PLO falls into the last of these categories and is present at the United Nations as its invitee. See Headquarters Agreement, § 11 (22 U.S.C. § 287 note). The PLO has none of the usual attributes of sovereignty. It is not accredited to the United States and does not have the benefits of diplomatic immunity. There is no recognized state it

---

2. G.A.Res. 169(II), 11 U.N.T.S. 11, No. 147 (1947). T.I.A.S. No. 1676, *authorized by* S.J.Res. 144, 80th Cong., 1st Sess., *set out in* 22 U.S.C. § 287 note (1982). We refer to the Headquarters Agreement as a treaty, since we are not concerned here with making a distinction among different forms of international agreement. The applicable law implicates all forms, including the Headquarters Agreement. Weinberger v. Rossi, 456 U.S. 25, 29–30 (1982).

claims to govern. It purports to serve as the sole political representative of the Palestinian people. The PLO nevertheless considers itself to be the representative of a state, entitled to recognition in its relations with other governments, and is said to have diplomatic relations with approximately one hundred countries throughout the world.

In 1974, the United Nations invited the PLO to become an observer at the U.N., to "participate in the sessions and the work of the General Assembly in the capacity of observer." The right of its representatives to admission to the United States as well as access to the U.N. was immediately challenged under American law. Judge Costantino rejected that challenge in Anti–Defamation League of B'nai B'rith v. Kissinger. The court upheld the presence of a PLO representative in New York with access to the United Nations, albeit under certain entrance visa restrictions which limited PLO personnel movements to a radius of 25 miles from Columbus Circle in Manhattan. It stated from the bench:

> This problem must be viewed in the context of the special responsibility which the United States has to provide access to the United Nations under the Headquarters Agreement. It is important to note that a primary goal of the United Nations is to provide a forum where peaceful discussions may displace violence as a means of resolving disputed issues. At times our responsibility to the United Nations may require us to issue visas to persons who are objectionable to certain segments of our society.

* * *

Since 1974, the PLO has continued to function without interruption as a permanent observer and has maintained its Mission to the United Nations without trammel, largely because of the Headquarters Agreement, which we discuss below.

II

The Anti–Terrorism Act

In October 1986, members of Congress requested the United States Department of State to close the PLO offices located in the United States. That request proved unsuccessful, and proponents of the request introduced legislation with the explicit purpose of doing so. The result was the ATA, 22 U.S.C. §§ 5201–5203. It is of a unique nature. We have been unable to find any comparable statute in the long history of Congressional enactments. The PLO is stated to be "a terrorist organization and a threat to the interests of the United States, its allies, and to international law and should not benefit from operating in the United States." 22 U.S.C. § 5201(b). The ATA was added, without committee hearings, as a rider to the Foreign Relations Authorization Act for Fiscal Years 1988–89, which provided funds for the operation of the State Department, including the operation of the United States Mission to the United Nations. The bill also authorized payments to the United Nations for maintenance and operation. Id., § 102(a)(1); see also id. § 143.

The ATA, which became effective on March 21, 1988, forbids the establishment or maintenance of "an office, headquarters, premises, or other facilities or establishments within the jurisdiction of the United States at the behest or direction of, or with funds provided by" the PLO, if the purpose is to further the PLO's interests. 22 U.S.C. § 5202(3). The ATA also forbids spending the PLO's funds or receiving anything of value except informational material from the PLO, with the same mens rea requirement.

* * *

The United States commenced this lawsuit the day the ATA took effect, seeking injunctive relief to accomplish the closure of the Mission. The United States Attorney for this District has personally represented that no action would be taken to enforce the ATA pending resolution of the litigation in this court.

* * *

V

The Anti–Terrorism Act and the Headquarters Agreement

If the ATA were construed as the government suggests, it would be tantamount to a direction to the PLO Observer Mission at the United Nations that it close its doors and cease its operations *instanter*. Such an interpretation would fly in the face of the Headquarters Agreement, a prior treaty between the United Nations and the United States, and would abruptly terminate the functions the Mission has performed for many years. This conflict requires the court to seek out a reconciliation between the two.

* * *

We believe the ATA and the Headquarters Agreement cannot be reconciled except by finding the ATA inapplicable to the PLO Observer Mission.

A. The Obligations of the United States under the Headquarters Agreement.

The obligation of the United States to allow transit, entry and access stems not only from the language of the Headquarters Agreement but also from forty years of practice under it. Section 11 of the Headquarters Agreement reads, in part: "The federal, state or local authorities of the United States shall not impose any impediments to transit to or from the headquarters district of: (1) representatives of Members * * *, (5) other persons invited to the headquarters district by the United Nations * * * on official business." (22 U.S.C. § 287 note).[23] These rights could not be effectively exercised without the use of offices. The ability to effectively organize and carry out one's work, especially as a liaison to an international organization, would not be possible otherwise. It is particularly significant that Section 13 limits the application of United

---

23. Section 12 requires that the provisions of Section 11 be applicable "irrespective of the relations existing between the Governments of the persons referred to in that Section and the Government of the United States." (22 U.S.C. § 287 note).

Section 13 limits the applicability of the United States laws and regulations regarding the entry and residence of aliens, when applied to those affiliated with the United Nations by virtue of Section 11. (22 U.S.C. § 287 note).

States law not only with respect to the entry of aliens, but also their residence. The Headquarters Agreement thus contemplates a continuity limited to official United Nations functions and is entirely consistent with the maintenance of missions to the United Nations. The exemptions of Section 13 are not limited to members, but extend to invitees as well.

There can be no dispute that over the forty years since the United States entered into the Headquarters Agreement it has taken a number of actions consistent with its recognition of a duty to refrain from impeding the functions of observer missions to the U.N. It has, since the early days of the U.N.'s presence in New York, acquiesced in the presence of observer missions to the U.N. in New York. See Permanent Missions: Report of the Secretary–General.

After the United Nations invited the PLO to participate as a permanent observer, the Department of State took the position that it was required to provide access to the U.N. for the PLO. The State Department at no time disputed the notion that the rights of entry, access and residence guaranteed to invitees include the right to maintain offices.

* * *

In sum, the language of the Headquarters Agreement, the long-standing practice under it, and the interpretation given it by the parties to it leave no doubt that it places an obligation upon the United States to refrain from impairing the function of the PLO Observer Mission to the United Nations. The ATA and its legislative history do not manifest Congress' intent to abrogate this obligation. We are therefore constrained to interpret the ATA as failing to supersede the Headquarters Agreement and inapplicable to the Mission.

* * *

VI

Conclusions

The Anti–Terrorism Act does not require the closure of the PLO Permanent Observer Mission to the United Nations nor do the act's provisions impair the continued exercise of its appropriate functions as a Permanent Observer at the United Nations. The PLO Mission to the United Nations is an invitee of the United Nations under the Headquarters Agreement and its status is protected by that agreement. The Headquarters Agreement remains a valid and outstanding treaty obligation of the United States. It has not been superceded by the Anti–Terrorism Act, which is a valid enactment of general application.

* * *

The motion of the United States for summary judgment is denied, and summary judgment is entered for the defendants, dismissing this action with prejudice.

Note: On August 29, 1988, the U.S. Dept. of Justice announced that the Administration would not appeal this decision in the P.L.O. case. "The Administration based its decision on foreign policy considerations. Specifically, the State Department expressed concern that the closure of the mission would violate the U.S. obligations as the host country under the United Nations Headquarters Agreement." 27 I.L.M. 1704 (1988).

SECTION E.   UNITED STATES ADMINISTRATIVE PRACTICE

Note: *Study the United States: Department of State Guidance for Law Enforcement Officers With Regard to Personal Rights and Immunities of Foreign Diplomatic and Consular Personnel (1988). 27 I.L.M. 1617 (1988) found in the Doc.Supp. and following chart.*

* * *

Diplomatic and Consular Privileges and Immunities
Summary of Law Enforcement Aspects

	Category	May be Arrested or Detained	Residence May be Entered Subject to Ordinary Procedures	May be Issued Traffic Citation	May be Subpoenaed as Witness	May be Prosecuted	Recognized Family Member
Diplomatic	Diplomatic Agent	No [2]	No	Yes	No	No	Same as sponsor (full immunity & inviolability).
Diplomatic	Member of Admin. and Tech. Staff	No [2]	No	Yes	No	No	Same as sponsor (full immunity & inviolability).
Diplomatic	Service Staff	Yes [1]	Yes	Yes	Yes	No—for official acts. Otherwise, Yes [1]	No immunity or inviolability. [1]
Consular	Career Consular Officers	Yes, if for a felony & pursuant to a warrant [1]	Yes [4]	Yes	No—for official acts. Testimony may not be compelled in any case.	No—for official acts. Otherwise, Yes [1]	No immunity or inviolability. [1]
Consular	Honorable Consular Officers	Yes	Yes	Yes	No—for official acts. Yes, in all other cases.	No—for official acts. Otherwise, Yes	No immunity or inviolability.
Consular	Consular Employees	Yes [1]	Yes	Yes	No—for official acts. Yes, in all other cases.	No—for official acts. Otherwise, Yes [1]	No immunity or inviolability. [1]
International Organizations	International Organization Staff [3]	Yes [3]	Yes [3]	Yes	Yes [3]	No—for official acts. Otherwise, Yes [3]	No immunity or inviolability.
International Organizations	Diplomatic-Level Staff of Missions to Int'l Orgs.	No [2]	No	Yes	No	No	Same as sponsor (full immunity & inviolability).
International Organizations	Support Staff of Missions to International Organizations	Yes	Yes	Yes	Yes	No—for official acts. Otherwise, Yes	No immunity or inviolability.

[1] This table presents general rules. Particularly in the cases indicated, the employees of certain foreign countries may enjoy higher levels of privileges and immunities on the basis of special bilateral agreements.

[2] Reasonable constraints, however, may be applied in emergency circumstances involving self-defense, public safety, or the prevention of serious criminal acts.

[3] A small number of senior officers are entitled to be treated identically to "diplomatic agents."

[4] Note that consular residences are sometimes located within the official consular premises. In such cases, only the official office space is protected from police entry.

Chapter 13

THE INTERNATIONAL LAW ABOUT INTERNATIONAL AGREEMENTS

Introduction: 1. *The Law of Treaties* is a segment of international law governing treaties. The Vienna Convention article 2.1(a), defines treaty, for purposes of the convention as "an international agreement concluded between States in written form and governed by international law, whether embodied in a single instrument or in two or more related instruments and whatever its particular designation." Ask yourself the following questions as you study this and the next chapter. Is there a difference between general international law on treaties and the Vienna Convention on Treaties? Is this definition broader or narrower than a treaty in general international law? Is it possible to have a treaty between a state and an international organization or between a state and a multinational corporation, or between a state and an organization not [yet] a state? In this regard, note the recent ground-breaking *agreement* between Israel and the Palestinian Liberation Organization. Note also that the only *"treaty"* in U.S. constitutional law is an international agreement that is entered into by the President and receives the Advice & Consent of ⅔ of the Senators present, Art. II, § 2[2]. Its relationship with international law is explored in the next chapter. We saw in Chapter 1, supra, that article 38 of the Statute of the International Court of Justice sets out the *sources* of international law. "[I]nternational conventions, whether general or particular, establishing rules expressly recognized by the contesting

990

states * * * " is the first in the hierarchy. Not only are treaties a basic source of international law, they are *the* key vehicle by which the international system changes most rapidly. They are the modii vivendi of states; they provide the mechanism for the various subjects of international law to arrange their relations, indeed, to make their own law. This aspect of treaties is really not much different from citizens of states in their contractual relationships. They are called treaties, conventions, modii vivendi, concordats, charters, articles of agreement, pacts, protocols, and accords, agreements, memoranda of understanding, among other designations. These labels are not significant. It is important to note differences such as multilateral versus bilateral or agreements in which special rules are allowed to govern (e.g. reservations).

Studying the law on treaties helps one understand law in general. *What makes treaties binding?* By the same token, why are contracts in a domestic system binding? The *Code Civil* in France provides that the conventional obligation (i.e., the contract) is the means by which the parties make their own law as between themselves (as long as what they do does not violate important public policy). Is there a parallel in international treaty law? If the Code makes the treaty binding, what makes the Code binding? The Constitution? What makes the Constitution binding? The social contract? Public policy? General principles? In antiquity, religious solemnity provided the obligatory force for both contracts and treaties. The general principle, *pacta sunt servunda,* is often said to be *The Law* of international relations and apparently makes them binding. *Why?*

2. *The Treaty on Treaties: present status and significance as evidence of customary law.* We had you read the Vienna Convention on the Law of Treaties (in Doc.Supp.) at the outset of this course. The Convention entered into force January 27, 1980. Although not yet acted upon in the Senate of the United States, to which the President referred it on November 21, 1971, the Vienna Convention is good evidence of what customary international law about treaties and other international agreements is, at least with respect to most of its provisions. We will consider some problematic provisions. The Department of State has stated since 1973 that it considers the convention as a codification of customary international law. Is it correct to say that the Vienna Convention is a codification of customary international law on treaties? A "common-law lawyer" may say yes, but a "civilian" would cringe. *What is a code?* Is the Vienna Convention comprehensive, complete and exclusive? Is it coherent and systematic? A true Code preempts the field. Thus, given the definition of treaty in article 2.1(a), quoted above, does a treaty really have to be written? Do you believe that agreements are found to be binding whether they are written or not? If not written, are they treaties? What body of law controls? If some other body of law controls, is the Convention a code? Does this mean that those who designated it a codification understood the term not in the continental or civil law sense (from which the term arises and retains its meaning), but in the "common law" sense, wherein it has no meaning other than a compilation of rules or a digest of some sort. The

Convention's preamble, states: "rules of customary international law will continue to govern questions not regulated by the * * * Convention." Does this mean that if an issue is "regulated by the Convention," no new custom may develop? Will custom modify the Convention? Is Custom a source of law relating to agreements along with the Convention? Does pre-existing custom control interpretation? Can inconsistent custom, still followed even by member states, overrule the Convention?

The Vienna Convention on Treaties has been considered authoritative with respect to the executive's treatment of issues related to international agreements arising after May 22, 1969. See, Rovine, Digest of U.S. Practice in International Law 1973, at 307, 482–83 (1974). Several judicial decisions in the U.S. have also followed the Convention. These executive and judicial acceptances may raise problems of separation of powers and of "supreme law" under Article VI of the Constitution (cf. Chapter 14), especially if the Senate buries the Convention or rejects it as a result of the opposition of one-third of the Senate plus one. Nevertheless, study of the law about treaties during the usable life of this edition ought to be undertaken with knowledge of the Convention's treatment of the various international legal issues that follow. Ask yourselves when you finish this chapter: Is the Vienna Convention either silent or a poor guide on any of the issues raised in this chapter? What issues does it clarify well or seem to settle? Where does it fall? Where, if anywhere, does the convention expand doctrine?

The Convention was developed from draft articles prepared by the International Law Commission (ILC). The work of the last rapporteur (Sir Humphrey Waldock, later a judge of the International Court of Justice) was overwhelmingly the most influential on the commission as it prepared the draft that went to the Convention at Vienna. The ILC's Draft Articles, with commentary, can be found in 61 AJIL 263 (1967). The Convention itself is authoritatively commented upon by two of the American negotiators, Kearney and Dalton, in The Treaty on Treaties, 64 AJIL 495 (1970):

> The Convention on the Law of Treaties sets forth the code of rules that will govern the indispensable element in the conduct of foreign affairs, the mechanism without which international intercourse could not exist, much less function. It is possible to imagine a future in which the treaty will no longer be the standard device for dealing with any and all international problems—a future in which for example, the use of regulations promulgated by international organizations in special fields of activity, such as the World Health Organization's sanitary regulations, will become the accepted substitute for the lawmaking activity now effected through international agreement. But, in the present state of international development, this is crystal-gazing. For the foreseeable future, the treaty will remain the cement that holds the world community together.

3. *The wide range of utilization of international agreements.* Undertakings between states are major tools of operations in the international legal system. Rules of customary law, derived from

the usual modes of conduct of international relations, right reason, judicial decisions, general principles of law common to the world's major legal systems and the like, usually lag behind developing needs within the international community. Moreover, for technologically complicated and politically sophisticated situations they lack specificity. International agreements, on the other hand, are often made because the parties have realized a need to reach specific accord upon some issue, matter, or common concern. Like contracts or trusts in private law, international agreements are cut to the cloth of the interests of the parties.

Functionally, international agreements cover a wide range of interests, extending from certain types of agreements that are in effect conveyances of real estate (treaties of lease, cession and admeasurement of boundaries) through mutual promises to pursue common lines of action (military alliances, mutual defense, safety at sea) to organic arrangements that function much as constitutions (the U.N. Charter). Some international agreements are regarded as executed internationally as between the parties when made (boundary treaties). Others are executory, such as the mutual promises of the members of the NATO to consider an attack on one an attack on all and to respond effectively.

In Chapter 15 we shall see that international agreements have given the international legal system almost all the rules that exist as to international economic law. In the more traditional political areas, international agreements alter or expand customary international law. Also, they may restate it. Finally, given the lack so far of an effective international parallel to national legislatures, international agreements of the multipartite sort are used to make new law such as with respect to pollution of the high seas, uses of the moon, Antarctica, aerial hijacking, human rights. These latter have legislative characteristics, (are sometimes called *traité-lois,* or law-making treaties) establish a series of legislation-like rules among nations, (e.g., the Hague and the Geneva Conventions, or UNCLOS, the U.N. Treaty on Drug Trafficking or a multilateral, or series of bi-lateral consular relations treaty(s)). It is with respect to them that the analytical issue whether the rules therein stated are themselves international law arises. Treaties and other international agreements have *constitutional* characteristics (i.e., they are creative of institutions and organizations, e.g., the U.N. Charter, the Treaty of Rome Maastricht—in force since Nov. 1, 1993, and the constituent treaties of most international organizations). Some treaties have "common-law" like customary law-creating, characteristics (a series of treaties or even one adopted by all nations may create customary international law). Treaties also may "codify" rules of customary international law. Finally, they have simple contract-like characteristics (*un traité contrat*) (e.g., the Louisiana Purchase). Some treaties may be seen as being "*merely*" aspirational, such as the Helsinki Final Act, although it is worth wondering whether such aspirational treaties do not sometimes in the long-run create law. Ask the Czechoslovak underground if Helsinki helped them and whether it is now incorporated in their domestic law. See, Chapters 10 (Human Rights), 11 (Individual Responsibility), 16 (International Resolution of Disputes), and 17 (States and the Use of Force).

Suffice it to note that the modern international practitioner must of necessity have a lot to do with international agreements and that the International Court of Justice has subject-matter jurisdiction as to issues concerning international agreements. Treaties are a most vital part of international law; they promote trade and commerce, allow cooperation in other economic and even criminal law matters, provide for common defense, they promote friendship, cooperation in all areas of international intercourse, such as providing for the post, protect the environment, protect the rights and interests of individuals.

Treaties & the E.U. One of the most significant modern uses of treaties is to create structures such as the multipartite international agreements that underlie the European Union (EU). This establishes new institutions, binds the member states to uniform courses of action, makes EU law (and that deriving therefrom as declared by EU agencies) superior to member state national law in enumerated situations, and provides for centralized budgeting and financing of important activities, such as the Community Agricultural Policy (CAP), under the community treaty on economic matters (the European Economic Community treaty). The EU system is neither a conventional international organization nor (so far) a federation that eliminates the international statehood of its members. If community authority to make superior law that is directly applicable in some, but not all, situations of governance should expand appreciably into general governmental affairs, the EU might one day become a new federated state. If the authority of the EU should decline to the extent of becoming non-binding directly within member states, it would become indistinguishable from ordinary international organizations.

SECTION A. INTERNATIONAL AGREEMENTS AS BASES OF LEGAL RIGHTS AND DUTIES

Pacta sunt servanda, the standard of performance. Even before the Vienna Convention, the prevailing rule was that a treaty undertaking should be performed in good faith, but some authorities contended that the proper standard, if not for all, then for some types of treaties, was utmost fidelity (*uberrima fides*). The concept is similar to that of fiduciary obligation in anglo-american law. Article 26 of the Vienna Convention adopts the first (pacta sunt servanda) standard, although some delegates at the Vienna treaty conference wanted it stated that only valid treaties in force should be so entitled. Some others wished to confine the performance standard to treaties in force which conformed to the convention, which would have raised a serious retroactivity problem. What is the difference between the two standards? Judge Lauterpacht's separate opinion in the *Norwegian Loans Case* (1957), noted that "[u]nquestionably, the obligation to act in accordance with good faith, being a general principle of law, is also part of international law." Did Judge Lauterpacht see *pacta sunt servanda* as a rule of customary international law? As a general principle of international law? As both?

YALTA CONFERENCE, AGREEMENT REGARDING ENTRY OF THE SOVIET UNION INTO THE WAR AGAINST JAPAN, FEB. 11, 1945

59 Stat. 1823.

The leaders of the three Great Powers—the Soviet Union, the United States of America and Great Britain—have agreed that in two or three months after Germany has surrendered and the war in Europe has terminated the Soviet Union shall enter into the war against Japan on the side of the Allies on condition that:

1. The status quo in Outer–Mongolia (The Mongolian People's Republic) shall be preserved;

2. The former rights of Russia violated by the treacherous attack of Japan in 1904 shall be restored, viz:

(a) the southern part of Sakhalin as well as all the islands adjacent to it shall be returned to the Soviet Union,

(b) the commercial port of Dairen shall be internationalized, the preeminent interests of the Soviet Union in this port being safeguarded and the lease of Port Arthur as a naval base of the USSR restored,

(c) the Chinese–Eastern Railroad and the South–Manchurian Railroad which provides an outlet to Dairen shall be jointly operated by the establishment of a joint Soviet–Chinese Company it being understood that the preeminent interests of the Soviet Union shall be safeguarded and that China shall retain full sovereignty in Manchuria;

3. The Kuril islands shall be handed over to the Soviet Union.

It is understood, that the agreement concerning Outer–Mongolia and the ports and railroads referred to above will require concurrence of Generalissimo Chiang Kai–Shek. The President will take measures in order to obtain this concurrence on advice from Marshal Stalin. The Heads of the three Great Powers have agreed that these claims of the Soviet Union shall be unquestionably fulfilled after Japan has been defeated. For its part the Soviet Union expresses its readiness to conclude with the National Government of China a pact of friendship and alliance between the USSR and China in order to render assistance to China with its armed forces for the purpose of liberating China from the Japanese yoke.

> И. Сталин (J. Stalin)
> Franklin D. Roosevelt
> Winston S. Churchill

UNITED STATES POSITION ON SOVIET–JAPANESE PEACE TREATY NEGOTIATIONS

35 United States Department of State Bulletin 484 (1956).

Following is the text of an *aide memoire* which was given to the Japanese Ambassador at Washington on September 7 and to the Japanese Foreign Minister at Tokyo on September 8. Pursuant to the request made by the Japanese Foreign Minister, Mr. Shigemitsu, in the course of recent conversations in London with the Secretary of State, Mr. Dulles, the Department of State has reviewed the problems presented in the course of the current negotiations for a treaty of peace between the Union of Soviet Socialist Republics and Japan, with particular reference to the interest of the United States as a signatory of the San Francisco Peace Treaty, and on the basis of such review makes the following observations.

The Government of the United States believes that the state of war between Japan and the Soviet Union should be formally terminated. Such action has been overdue since 1951, when the Soviet Union declined to sign the San Francisco Peace Treaty. Japan should also long since have been admitted to the United Nations, for which it is fully qualified; and Japanese prisoners of war in Soviet hands should long since have been returned in accordance with the surrender terms.

With respect to the territorial question, as the Japanese Government has been previously informed, the United States regards the so-called Yalta agreement as simply a statement of common purposes by the then heads of the participating powers, and not as a final determination by those powers or of any legal effect in transferring territories. The San Francisco Peace Treaty (which conferred no rights upon the Soviet Union because it refused to sign) did not determine the sovereignty of the territories renounced by Japan, leaving that question, as was stated by the Delegate of the United States at San Francisco, to "international solvents other than this treaty".

* * *

DEPARTMENT OF STATE, Washington, September 7, 1956.

———

LEGAL STATUS OF EASTERN GREENLAND (DENMARK v. NORWAY)

Permanent Court of International Justice, 1933.
P.C.I.J., ser. A/B, No. 53.

* * *

By an Application instituting proceedings, filed with the Registry of the Court on July 12th, 1931, in accordance with Article 40 of the Statute and Article 35 of the Rules of Court, the Danish Government, relying on the optional clause of Article 36, paragraph 2, of the Statute, brought before the Permanent Court of International Justice a suit against the Norwegian Government on the ground that the latter had, on July 10th, 1931, published a proclamation declaring that it had proceeded to occupy certain territories in Eastern Greenland, which, in the contention of the Danish Government, were subject to the sovereignty of the Crown of Denmark. The Application, after thus indicating the subject of the dispute, proceeds to formulate the claim by asking the Court for judgment to the effect that "the promulgation of the above-mentioned declaration of occupation and any steps taken in this respect by the Norwegian Government constitute a violation of the existing legal situation and are accordingly unlawful and invalid."

* * *

The Danish submission in the written pleading, that the Norwegian occupation of July 10th, 1931, is invalid, is founded upon the contention that the area occupied was at the time of the occupation subject to Danish sovereignty; that the area is part of Greenland, and at the time of the occupation Danish sovereignty existed over all Greenland; consequently it could not be occupied by another Power. In support of this contention, the Danish Government advances two propositions. First, that the sovereignty which Denmark now enjoys over Greenland has existed for a long time, has been continuously and peacefully exercised and, until the present dispute, has not been contested by any Power. This proposition Denmark sets out to establish as a fact. Second, that Norway has by treaty or otherwise herself recognized Danish sovereignty over Greenland as a whole and therefore cannot now dispute it.

* * *

The Court will now consider the second Danish proposition that Norway had given certain undertakings which recognized Danish sovereignty over all Greenland. These undertakings have been fully discussed by the two Parties, and in three cases the Court considers that undertakings were given.

* * *

In addition to the [above] engagements, the Ihlen declaration, viz. the reply given by M. Ihlen, the Norwegian Minister for Foreign Affairs, to the Danish Minister on July 22nd, 1919, must also be considered.

* * *

* * * [T]he point is whether the Ihlen declaration—even if not constituting a definitive recognition of Danish sovereignty—did not constitute an engagement obliging Norway to refrain from occupying any part of Greenland. The Danish request and M. Ihlen's reply were recorded by him in a minute, worded as follows:

> I. The Danish Minister informed me to-day that his Government has heard from Paris that the question of Spitzbergen will be examined by a Commission of four members (American, British, French, Italian). If the Danish Government is questioned by this Commission, it is prepared to reply that Denmark has no interests

in Spitzbergen, and that it has no reason to oppose the wishes of Norway in regard to the settlement of this question.

Furthermore, the Danish Minister [stated]:

> The Danish Government has for some years been anxious to obtain the recognition of all the interested Powers of Denmark's sovereignty over the whole of Greenland, and it proposes to place this question before the above-mentioned Committee * * *. During the negotiations with the U.S.A. over the cession of the Danish West Indies, the Danish Government raised this question in so far as concerns recognition by the Government of the U.S.A., and it succeeded in inducing the latter to agree that, concurrently with the conclusion of a convention regarding the cession of the said islands, it would make a declaration to the effect that the Government of the U.S.A. would not object to the Danish Government extending their political and economic interests to the whole of Greenland.

> * * *

> I replied that the question would be examined.

> 14/7—19 Ih.

II. Today I informed the Danish Minister that the Norwegian Government would not make any difficulties in the settlement of this question. 22/7—19Ih.

The incident has reference, first to the attitude to be observed by Denmark before the Committee of the Peace Conference at Paris in regard to Spitzbergen, this attitude being that Denmark would not "oppose the wishes of Norway in regard to the settlement of this question"; as is known, these wishes related to the sovereignty over Spitzbergen. Secondly, the request showed that "the Danish Government was confident that the Norwegian Government would not make any difficulty" in the settlement of the Greenland question; the aims that Denmark had in view in regard to the last-named island were to secure the "recognition by all the Powers concerned of Danish sovereignty over the whole of Greenland," and that there should be no opposition "to the Danish Government extending their political and economic interests to the whole of Greenland." It is clear from the relevant Danish documents which preceded the Danish Minister's démarche at Christiania on July 14th, 1919, that the Danish attitude in the Spitzbergen question and the Norwegian attitude in the Greenland question were regarded in Denmark as interdependent, and this interdependence appears to be reflected also in M. Ihlen's minutes of the interview. Even if this interdependence—which, in view of the affirmative reply of the Norwegian Government, in whose name the Minister for Foreign Affairs was speaking, would have created a bilateral engagement—is not held to have been established, it can hardly be denied that what Denmark was asking of Norway ("not to make any difficulties in the settlement of the [Greenland] question") was equivalent to * * * indicating her readiness to concede in the Spitzbergen question (to refrain from opposing "the wishes of Norway in regard to the settlement of this question"). What Denmark desired to obtain from Norway was that the latter should do nothing to obstruct the Danish plans [for] Greenland. The declaration which the Minister * * * gave on July 22nd, 1919, on behalf of the Norwegian Government, was definitely affirmative: "I told the Danish Minister to-day that the Norwegian Government would not make any difficulty in the settlement of this question."

The Court considers it beyond all dispute that a reply of this nature given by the Minister for Foreign Affairs on behalf of his Government in response to a request by the diplomatic representative of a foreign Power, in regard to a question falling within his province, *is binding upon the country to which the Minister belongs.* (emphasis added).

* * *

It follows that, as a result of the undertaking involved in the Ihlen declaration of July 22nd, 1919, Norway is under an obligation to refrain from contesting Danish sovereignty over Greenland as a whole, and a fortiori to refrain from occupying a part of Greenland.

* * *

For these reasons, the court, by twelve votes to two, (1) decides that the declaration of occupation promulgated by the Norwegian Government on July 10th, 1931, and any steps taken in this respect by that Government, constitute a violation of the existing legal situation and are accordingly unlawful and invalid;

* * *

Dissenting Opinion of Mr. ANZILOTTI:

* * *

The question whether the so-called Ihlen declaration was merely a provisional indication (Norwegian contention) or a definitive undertaking (Danish contention) has been debated at length. * * *

* * *

The outcome of all this is therefore an agreement, concluded between the Danish Minister, on behalf of the Danish Government, and the Norwegian Minister for Foreign Affairs, on behalf of the Norwegian Government, by means of purely verbal declarations. The validity of this agreement has been questioned, having regard, in the first place, to its verbal form, and to the competence of the Minister for Foreign Affairs. As regards the form, it should be noted that as both Parties are agreed as to the existence and tenor of these declarations, the question of proof does not arise. Moreover, there does not seem to be any rule of international law requiring that agreements of this kind must necessarily be in writing, in order to be valid. The question of the competence of the Minister for Foreign Affairs is closely connected with the contents of the agreement in question; and these have already been determined.

No arbitral or judicial decision relating to the international competence of a Minister for Foreign Affairs has been brought to the knowledge of the Court; nor has this question been exhaustively treated by legal authorities. In my opinion, it must be recognized that the constant and general practice of States has been to invest the Minister for Foreign Affairs—the direct agent of the chief of the State—with authority to make statements on current affairs to foreign diplomatic representatives, and in particular to inform them as to the attitude which the government, in whose name he speaks, will adopt in a given question. Declarations of this kind are binding upon the State.

As regards the question whether Norwegian constitutional law authorized the Minister for Foreign Affairs to make the declaration, that is a point which, in my opinion, does not concern the Danish Government: it was M. Ihlen's duty to refrain from giving his reply until he had obtained any assent that might be requisite under the Norwegian laws. * * *

[Observations and another dissenting opinion omitted.]

———

Comment on the Anzilotti dissent. This luminary of the Permanent Court of International Justice agreed with the majority on the issues of oral treaties and the binding effect internationally of a foreign minister's commitment in excess of his constitutional authority. (Cf. Articles 27, 46, and 47 of the Vienna Convention.) His dissent was on a broader ground: he was not prepared to rule that the Norwegian occupation was invalid, even though unlawful. For further explanation see Hudson, The Twelfth Year of the Permanent Court of International Justice, 28 AJIL 1, 8 (1934). Did the majority opinion, and especially the dissent, accept agency principles as part of international law? If so, by what authority? What are the boundaries of this "agency" that the Court and international law recognize? See, *Vienna Convention Article 7(1)(b):* "[if it] appears from the practice of the states concerned or from other circumstances that their intention was to consider that person as representing the state for such purposes and to dispense with full powers * * *." See also article 47. Was this pure application of agency law or were there aspects of contract involved; was there any sort of quid pro quo? Was any sort of agreement made? Did Denmark give anything to Norway? Denmark conceded that Norway had sovereignty over Spitzbergen. Is that sufficient for a contract?

———

RIGHTS AND OBLIGATIONS OF STATES NOT PARTIES TO AN INTERNATIONAL AGREEMENT

Read Articles 34 through 37 of the Vienna Convention in the Documentary Supplement.

———

FREE ZONES OF UPPER SAVOY AND THE DISTRICT OF GEX (FRANCE v. SWITZERLAND)

Permanent Court of International Justice, 1932.
P.C.I.J., ser. A/B, No. 46.

[France contended that the Treaty of Versailles (1919) abrogated certain tariff-free areas within France, on the border with Switzerland in the region of Geneva. Switzerland claimed that her rights in these areas had been provided in the post-Napoleonic settlement of Europe, by various treaties stemming from the Congress of Vienna, in the years 1814–15. The court found that Switzerland had sufficiently participated in the earlier arrangements as to have acquired rights as to the free zones. It also decided that the Treaty of Versailles was not intended to abrogate these rights. Nevertheless, the court expressed a viewpoint on the question whether rights that Switzerland might have acquired as a non-party to the 1814–15 treaties could have been taken away by France and other parties to the Versailles treaty, to which Switzerland was not a party. On third party rights the court made a statement which a common law lawyer would call obiter dictum. It appears below.]

It cannot be lightly presumed that stipulations favourable to a third State have been adopted with the object of creating an actual right in its favour. There is however nothing to prevent the will of sovereign States from having this object and this effect. The question of the existence of a right acquired under an instrument drawn between other States is therefore one to be decided in each particular case: it must be ascertained whether the States which have stipulated in favour of a third State meant to create for that State an actual right *which the latter has accepted as such.* [Emphasis supplied.]

Question. Before the Vienna Convention the statement above was the main authority on the point. Does the Convention follow the dictum squarely? See Article 36.

JUS COGENS

Question. Are there overriding restrictions on what states may do by international agreement? The Latin term jus cogens (compelling law) may supply an answer. Read article 53 of the Vienna Convention on Treaties in the Doc.Supp. What is a peremptory norm?

SCHWELB, SOME ASPECTS OF INTERNATIONAL JUS COGENS AS FORMULATED BY THE INTERNATIONAL LAW COMMISSION

61 American Journal of International Law 946, 949 (1967).*

Jurisprudence on International Jus Cogens

* * * [There have been very few instances involving authoritative invocation of jus cogens. Many of its invocations have been in dissenting opinions or in domestic judicial decisions.]

* * *

In the case of the S.S. Wimbledon the question was whether Germany, as a neutral in the Polish–Russian war, was in 1921 under the obligation to permit contraband destined for Poland to pass through the Kiel Canal. The Court decided that Article 380 of the Peace Treaty of Versailles applied, under which the Canal was to be maintained open to the vessels of all nations at peace with Germany. Mr. Schücking, the German national judge, dissented. One of his arguments was the consideration that, by permitting the passage of the ship carrying contraband, Germany would have violated the duties of a neutral. It cannot have been the intention of the victorious states, he said, to bind Germany to commit offenses against third states. It would have been impossible to give effect to such an intention because it is impossible to undertake by treaty a valid obligation to perform acts which would violate the rights of third parties. Judges Anzilotti and Huber, who also dissented from the decision of the Court, did not adduce an argument based on the partial invalidity of the Peace Treaty article.

* * *

THE NEGOTIATING HISTORY OF JUS COGENS AT VIENNA

Kearney and Dalton, The Treaty on Treaties, 64 American Journal of International Law 495, 535 (1970).

* * * The committee of the whole moved immediately to one of the most controversial articles produced by the Commission—Article 53 on treaties conflicting with a peremptory norm of international law or, as it is customarily described, the Jus Cogens Doctrine. The Commission [proposed]: "A treaty is void if it conflicts with a peremptory norm of general international law from which no derogation is permitted and which can be modified only by a subsequent norm of general international law having the same character." Although the principle that there are fundamental requirements of international behavior that cannot be set aside by treaty is considered a fairly recent development, it has been incorporated into Section 116 of the Restatement in the following terms: "An international agreement may be made with respect to any matter

* Reprinted with the permission of the American Society of International Law.

except to the extent that the agreement conflicts with, a) the rules of international law incorporating basic standards of international conduct. * * * " Both the Commission's article and the Restatement, however, present the same difficulty: they leave open the question what is a peremptory norm or what is a basic standard of international conduct.

* * *

In his second report Waldock had proposed three categories of jus cogens: (a) the use or threat of force in contravention of the principles of the United Nations Charter; (b) international crimes so characterized by international law; (c) acts or omissions whose suppression is required by international law. The discussion in the Commission indicated such varying viewpoints on what constituted jus cogens that the categories were dropped. A comment regarding the resulting draft is pertinent: "Mr. Bartoš explained that the drafting committee had been compelled to refrain from giving any definition of jus cogens whatever, because two-thirds of the Commission had been opposed to each formula proposed." The position in the conference reflected the position in the Commission. There was no substantial attack made upon the concept of jus cogens. Indeed, it would be very difficult to make a sustainable case that two states are free to make a treaty in which they agree to attack and carve up a third state or to sell some of their residents to each other as slaves. But as Minagawa points out, "examples such as the treaty permitting piracy or re-establishing slavery appear to concern merely *'une pure hypothèse d'école'.*" The real problem was how to define the test for recognizing a rule of jus cogens.

* * *

The Austrian jurist, Hanspeter Neuhold, gives in his analysis of the 1968 session a lively account of the conclusion of debate:

After five meetings had been devoted to discussing the various problems of jus cogens, the scene was set for the final showdown at a night meeting which lasted almost till midnight. It was fought with all the weapons which the arsenal of the rules of procedure offered the delegates. Thus, the representative of the USA introduced a motion to defer the vote on article [53] and to refer all amendments to the Drafting Committee with a view to working out a more acceptable text. This proposal was endorsed by the United Kingdom and France. Conversely, the Ghanaian delegate, who was supported by the representatives of India and the USSR, moved to take a vote immediately, since the various delegations had made their positions sufficiently clear. Motions to adjourn the debate and to close the discussion were defeated. Other motions requesting a division of the original United States proposal caused considerable confusion. At last, a roll call was taken on the motion submitted by the USA to defer voting on article [53] and the amendments thereto, which failed to obtain the necessary majority by the narrowest margin possible: 42 votes were cast in favour, the same number against, with 7 abstentions! Ironically enough, if a request by Ghana for priority of her motion to vote at once had been adopted and the votes cast in the same way, the United States motion would have prevailed indirectly * * *. [r]eference to recognition of jus cogens by the national and regional legal systems of the world was rejected. * * *

A dispute then arose as to the meaning of that vote and whether the principle of jus cogens had been adopted. The chairman settled the matter by ruling that the jus cogens principle had been adopted and that the drafting committee was to see if the text could be made clearer. A peremptory norm was defined as "a norm accepted and recognized by the international community of States as a whole * * *."

----

1. ***Ruminations on jus cogens?*** Where does it fit in the schema of sources of international law presented in article 38 of the Permanent Court of International Justice hierarchy of sources? Is it customary international law? A super custom? A general principle? What is the difference? Could you say that it is a form of fundamental or constitutional Law? The basic notion seems simple enough; certain norms are so compelling that they have reached the level of being *peremptory*. They cannot be violated at all. They are nonderogable in treaties. Nations may not agree to brutalize or destroy whole peoples. Does this suggest that there is a *world order* that is not controlled by nation-states? Can *jus cogens* principles be modified? If so, how? Can custom overcome them or does it take a subsequent formulation of a new peremptory norm—a new "super-custom?" Is there some analogy between the notion of *jus cogens* and principles of public policy in both civilian jurisdictions and common law states, which will not countenance derogation by contract? Can a treaty derogate from a regular (*non-jus cogens*) rule of customary international law?

Does *jus cogens supersede domestic law? From the point of view of international law? From the point of view of domestic law?* See, Committee of U.S. Citizens Living in Nicaragua v. Reagan, 859 F.2d 929, 940 (D.C.Cir.1988) ("*Jus cogens* describes peremptory norms of law, which are nonderogable and form the highest level of international law"); Siderman v. Argentina, *supra* (the prohibition against official torture "carries with it the force of *jus cogens*.") ("*[Jus cogens] is an elite subset of norms recognized as customary international law.*") We present the pertinent part of Siderman in chapter 10. Read the *jus cogens* portion again.

2. ***Note that article 53 defines a peremptory norm as one "accepted and recognized by the international community of States as a whole * * *." What is the "international community of states?"*** What norms reach the level of being peremptory? Who decides? What does it mean?—Every nation? A majority? A two-thirds majority? The most influential? The ones with the most population? If there is a community, does it ever accept anything "as a whole?" If it can be argued that the "community" has accepted the prohibition of the slave trade, genocide, etc., could it be argued that it has also accepted a principle prohibiting environmental pollution? See Chapter 6.

3. *How may the substantive content of jus cogens be established?* What state conduct beyond Waldock's three categories may come to be included in *jus cogens*? What institutions, by what modalities, will, or may, add to the basic list of peremptory norms? Category (a) in Waldock's enumeration is generally assumed to be established by opinio juris and the United Nations Charter, although in Ch. 17 the argument is raised that the anti-force provisions of the Charter are not as firm as the language and negotiating history of the United Nations Charter might otherwise indicate. Analytically, *jus cogens* is a rule about valid and invalid treaties, classified as to purpose; it is not a rule about legal and illegal use of force by states, which would come into issue even if no agreement were involved. However, look at ¶ 190 of the Nicaragua Case, supra p. 53, where the International Court states that the principle against the use of force, is "a conspicuous example of a rule of international law having the character of *jus cogens*." Also, look at Article 103 of the Charter. Does this make the Charter a general *jus cogens* principle invalidating any treaty inconsistent with the Charter?

4. *Treatment of jus cogens in the 1987 Restatement.* See Section 331(2), especially Comment *e* and Reporters' Note 4. In general, the treatment of the content of *jus cogens* is cursory and the importance of who is to determine such content is stressed.

SECTION B.   RESERVATIONS TO INTERNATIONAL AGREEMENTS

1. *What is a reservation and why are they made?* Sometimes a nation will wish to have the advantages of a treaty and to be a party to it, except for certain aspects which it either does not wish to follow or cannot follow for domestic constitutional reasons. In such cases, a state will become a party to the convention, but except itself out of or modify offending provisions. A *reservation* is "a unilateral statement, however phrased or named, made by a State, when signing, ratifying, accepting, approving or acceding to a treaty, whereby it purports to exclude or to modify the legal effect of certain provisions of the treaty in their application to that state." Vienna Convention, art. 1(d). Would this make a unilateral interpretation of an ambiguous clause in a treaty a reservation? Can there be a reservation to a bi-lateral treaty?

A state interested in entering into a treaty relationship will attempt during the negotiations to shape the agreement to its wishes. If it succeeds, there is no further problem. But if it cannot convince its negotiating partners but wishes to protect itself against becoming obligated in a manner or to a degree that it unsuccessfully tried to avoid in the negotiations, it may want to attempt to enter into the treaty relationship under the safeguard of a reservation.

Sometimes parties to or drafters of conventions allow reservations to increase world-wide participation. The price to be paid for this, however, may be to compromise the value or integrity of the convention. *See, e.g.,* Rebecca J. Cook, Reservations to the Convention on the Elimination of All Forms of Discrimination Against Women, 30 Va.J.Int'l L. 643 (1990). Some recent treaties have not allowed reservations. For example, *see* "fast track" (up or down vote—no amendments) procedures in the Law of the Sea, and NAFTA treaties.

Where the negotiations are between two, or a few states, reservations have little utility. They may be a rejection of the treaty. In the context of bilateral negotiations it is sometimes said that a reservation is a counter-offer, which if not accepted by the offeree, means no treaty.

2. *When are reservations put?* In the case of some multinational agreements, such as the Vienna Convention on the Law of Treaties, particular issues are intensely disputed in the negotiating conference. A reservation will be put forward by a state that has made the decision to try to keep its point and to enter the treaty community, simultaneously with its manifestation of intent to become bound. In times past, when most chiefs of state were autocrats, this occurred at the time their representatives purported to sign for them. Today, the signature of the final act of the negotiating conference is almost always ad referendum to an internal authorization process, leading to ratification. Signature indicates that the language of the text has been agreed upon. Even so, reservations are sometimes made at signature, so as to give a clear showing of viewpoint to the other states involved or to protect the negotiators from criticism at home. An international agreement may provide that it is open for acceptance or accession by states that did not participate in the negotiation. In such cases, obviously, an acceding state wishing to make a reservation would do so at the time of attempted accession.

In many states the internal authorization to become bound involves the consent of the legislative branch. In the United States, the Senate, by a two-thirds majority of the senators present, gives the legislative authorization. The legislative authorization may itself be conditioned upon the making of a reservation. Under most constitutional systems when this happens the executive has no alternative, if it wishes to go forward with the treaty association, but to put the reservation forward internationally. Such a second stage reservation often reflects imperfect foresight on the part of the executive at the time of the negotiations as to the views of the legislature on the particular point. The classic and tragic case is that of President Woodrow Wilson and a minority (more than one-third) of the Senate as to the Covenant of the League of Nations. In negotiating the Covenant at Paris in 1919, the President did not take into account that a group of dissident senators would block approval, unless their reservations were accepted. When he discovered that they did have such power, it was too late. The Covenant was an annex to the Versailles peace treaty with Germany, and a re-convention of the peace conference was politically impossible because Germany was in internal turmoil, with the Weimar Republic weak, hyperinflation raging, and the revanchist elements that Hitler later mobilized already active against the treaty. Eventually the Nazis denounced the treaty. The relationships between the President and the Senate with respect to the conclusion of treaties makes for both domestic and international complications. See Chap. 14.

3. **_Effect of reservation on other states in multilateral treaties._** When a reservation is put forward, it presents other states with this problem: shall State X come into the treaty community on its altered version of the treaty or shall we try to exclude State X from the agreement? This issue has a substantive and a procedural aspect. The pre-WWII rule was blunt. State X could not come in, unless its reservation was unanimously accepted. In modern times, as reflected in the Vienna Convention, there has been a shift in viewpoint with the result that the rules provide greater flexibility. See Restatement § 313(2)(c). The materials that follow deal with this shift.

4. **_Stipulations against reservations._** There is a growing use of prohibitions on reservations, especially in complicated, multisubject, multiparty conventions, such as the United Nations Convention on the Law of the Sea. Such prohibitions, obviously, hinder universality in acceptance but preserve uniformity of treatment. On final review of this course, you might ask yourselves: if the convention were to have permitted reservations, how many of those the United States might have proposed would meet the test of the Advisory Opinion of the International Court of Justice in the following case?

RESERVATIONS TO THE CONVENTION ON GENOCIDE (ADVISORY OPINION)

International Court of Justice, 1951.
[1951] I.C.J.Rep. 15.

[On November 16th, 1950, the General Assembly requested the Court to respond to the following questions concerning the Genocide Convention:] I. Can the reserving State be regarded as being a party to the Convention while still maintaining its reservation if the reservation is objected to by one or more of the parties to the Convention but not by others? II. If the answer to Question I is in the affirmative, what is the effect of the reservation as between the reserving State and: (a) The parties which object to the reservation? (b) Those which accept it? III. What would be the legal effect as regards the answer to Question I if an objection to a reservation is made: (a) By a signatory which has not yet ratified? (b) By a State entitled to sign or accede but which has not yet done so?

* * *

The Court observes that the three questions referred to it for an Opinion have certain common characteristics. All three questions are expressly limited by the terms of the Resolution of the General Assembly to the Convention on the Prevention and Punishment of the Crime of Genocide, * * * [t]he replies which the Court is called upon to give to them are necessarily and strictly limited to that Convention. The Court will seek these replies in the rules of law relating to the effect to be given to the intention of the parties to multilateral conventions. The * * * questions are purely abstract in character. They refer neither to the reservations which have, in fact, been made to the Convention by certain States, nor to the objections which have been made to such reservations by other States. They do not even refer to the reservations which may in future be made in respect of any particular article; nor do they refer to the objections to which these reservations might give rise. * * *

The Court observes that this question [I] refers, not to the possibility of making reservations to the Genocide Convention, but solely to the question whether a contracting State which has made a reservation can, while still maintaining it, be regarded as being a party to the Convention, when there is a divergence of views between the contracting parties concerning this reservation, some accepting the reservation, others refusing to accept it.

* * *

The Court recognizes that an understanding was reached within the General Assembly on the faculty to make reservations to the Genocide Convention and that it is permitted to conclude therefrom that States becoming parties to the Convention gave their assent thereto. It must now determine what kind of reservations may be made and what kind of objections may be taken to them.

The solution of these problems must be found in the special characteristics of the Genocide Convention. * * * The origins of the Convention show that it was the intention of the United Nations to condemn and punish genocide as "a crime under international law" involving a denial of the right of existence of entire human groups, a denial which shocks the conscience of mankind and results in great losses to humanity, and which is contrary to moral law and to the spirit and aims of the United Nations (Resolution 96(I) of the General Assembly, December 11th 1946). The first consequence arising from this conception is that the principles underlying the Convention are principles which are recognized by civilized nations as binding on States, even without any conventional obligation. A second consequence is the universal character both of the condemnation of genocide and of the co-operation required "in order to liberate mankind from such an odious scourge" (Preamble to the Convention). The Genocide Convention was therefore intended by the General Assembly and by the contracting parties to be definitely universal in scope. It was in fact approved on December 9th, 1948, by a resolution which was unanimously adopted by fifty-six States.

The objects of such a convention must also be considered. The Convention was manifestly adopted for a purely humanitarian and civilizing purpose. It is indeed difficult to imagine a convention that might have this dual character to a greater degree, since its object on the one hand is to safeguard the very existence of certain human groups and on the other to confirm and endorse the most elementary principles of morality. In such a convention the contracting States do not have any interests of their own; they merely have, one and all, a common interest, namely, the accomplishment of those high purposes which are the raison d'être of the convention. Consequently, in a convention of this type one cannot speak of individual advantages or disadvantages to States, or of the maintenance of a perfect contractual balance between rights and duties. The high ideals which inspired the Convention provide, by virtue of the common will of the parties, the foundation and measure of all its provisions.

* * *

The object and purpose of the Genocide Convention imply that it was the intention of the General Assembly and of the States which adopted it that as many States as possible should participate. The complete exclusion from the Convention of one or more States would not only restrict the scope of its application, but would detract from the authority of the moral and humanitarian principles which are its basis. It is inconceivable that the contracting parties readily contemplated that an objection to a minor reservation should produce such a result. But even less could the contracting parties have intended to sacrifice the very object of the Convention in favour of a vain desire to secure as many participants as possible. The object and purpose of the Convention thus limit both the freedom of making reservations and that of objecting to them. It follows that it is the compatibility of a reservation with the object and purpose of the Convention that must furnish the criterion for the attitude of a State in making the reservation on accession as well as for the appraisal by a State in objecting to the reservation. Such is the rule of conduct which must guide every State in the appraisal which it must make, individually and from its own standpoint, of the admissibility of any reservation.

Any other view would lead either to the acceptance of reservations which frustrate the purposes which the General Assembly and the contracting parties had in mind, or to recognition that the parties to the Convention have the power of excluding from it the author of a reservation, even a minor one, which may be quite compatible with those purposes. It has nevertheless been argued that any State entitled to become a party to the Genocide Convention may do so while making any reservation it chooses by virtue of its sovereignty. The Court cannot share this view. It is obvious that so extreme an application of the idea of State sovereignty could lead to a complete disregard of the object and purpose of the Convention.

On the other hand, it has been argued that there exists a rule of international law subjecting the effect of a reservation to the express or tacit assent of all the contracting parties. This theory rests essentially on a contractual conception of the absolute integrity of the convention as adopted. This view, however, cannot prevail if, having regard to the character of the convention, its purpose and its mode of adoption, it can be established that the parties intended to derogate from that rule by admitting the faculty to make reservations thereto.

It does not appear, moreover, that the conception of the absolute integrity of a convention has been transformed into a rule of international law. The considerable part which tacit assent has always played in estimating the effect which is to be given to reservations scarcely permits one to state that such a rule exists, determining with sufficient precision the effect of objections made to reservations. In fact, the examples of objections made to reservations appear to be too rare in international practice to have given rise to such a rule. It cannot be recognized that the report which was adopted on the subject by the Council of the League of Nations on June 17th, 1927, has had this effect. At best, the recommendation made on that date by the council constitutes the point of departure of an administrative practice which, after being observed by the Secretariat of the League of Nations, imposed itself, so to speak, in the ordinary course of things on the Secretary-General of the United Nations in his capacity of depositary of conventions concluded under the auspices of the League. But it cannot be concluded that the legal problem of the effect of objections to reservations has in this way been solved.   * * *

It may, however, be asked whether the General Assembly of the United Nations, in approving the Genocide Convention, had in mind the practice according to which the Secretary–General, in exercising his functions as a depositary, did not regard a reservation as definitively accepted until it had been established that none of the other contracting States objected to it. If this were the case, it might be argued that the implied intention of the contracting parties was to make the effectiveness of any reservation to the Genocide Convention conditional on the assent of all the parties. The Court does not consider that this view corresponds to reality. It must be pointed out, first of all, that the existence of an administrative practice does not in itself constitute a decisive factor in ascertaining what views the contracting States to the Genocide Convention may have had concerning the rights and duties resulting therefrom. It must also be pointed out that there existed among the American States members both of the United Nations and of the Organization of American States, a different practice which goes so far as to permit a reserving State to become a party irrespective of the nature of the reservations or of the objections raised by other contracting States. The preparatory work of the Convention contains nothing to justify the statement that the contracting States implicitly had any definite practice in mind. Nor is there any such indication in the subsequent attitude of the contracting States: neither the reservations made by certain States nor the position adopted by other States towards those reservations permit the conclusion that assent to one or the other of these practices had been given. Finally, * * * the debate on reservations to multilateral treaties which took place in the Sixth Committee at the fifth session of the General Assembly reveals a profound divergence of views, some delegations being attached to the idea of the absolute integrity of the Convention, others favouring a more flexible practice which would bring about the participation of as many States as possible. It results from the foregoing considerations that Question I, on account of its abstract character, cannot be given an absolute answer. The appraisal of a reservation and the effect of objections that might be made to it depend upon the particular circumstances of each individual case.

[Portions of the opinion setting forth the Court's reasoning as to Questions II and III omitted.]

The COURT is of opinion,

In so far as concerns the Convention on the Prevention and Punishment of the Crime of Genocide, in the event of a State ratifying or acceding to the Convention subject to a reservation made either on ratification or on accession, or on signature followed by ratification,

On Question I: by seven votes to five, that a State which has made and maintained a reservation which has been objected to by one or more of the parties to the Convention but not by others, can be regarded as being a party to the Convention if the reservation is compatible with the object and purpose of the Convention; otherwise, that State cannot be regarded as being a party to the Convention.

On Question II: by seven votes to five, (a) that if a party to the Convention objects to a reservation which it considers to be incompatible with the object and purpose of the Convention, it can in fact consider that the reserving State is not a party to the Convention; (b) that if, on the other hand, a party accepts the reservation as being compatible with the object and purpose of the Convention, it can in fact consider that the reserving State is a party to the Convention. * * * That an objection to a reservation made by a State which is entitled to sign or accede but which has not yet done so, is without legal effect. * * * [Dissenting opinions omitted.]

———

Notes & Questions. On November 4, 1988, President Reagan signed the *Genocide Convention Implementation Act,* which the Senate had given its Advice and Consent, enabling the U.S. to become the 88th party to the Genocide Convention. The U.S. adhered to the Genocide Convention, subject to significant reservations, understandings and a declaration. These were intended to modify the legal effects of certain provisions of the Convention. For example, the Senate stipulated that the U.S. must consent specifically before being required to appear before the International Court of Justice. In addition, the Senate provided that the Convention was "non-self-executing." This means that the Convention is not effective under U.S. law, until enabling or implementing legislation has been promulgated. *See, e.g.,* Asakura, Sei Fijii, and others in Chapter 14, *infra.*

The Senate further provided "[t]hat nothing in the [Genocide] Convention requires or authorizes legislation or other action by the United States of America prohibited by the Constitution of the United States as interpreted by the United States." This is the so-called "Sovereignty" reservation. Was this reservation necessary? There was also a "World Court" reservation, requiring specific consent to jurisdiction in each case.

Does it make the Genocide Convention meaningless vis-a-vis the United States? Does it give other nations the argument that the U.S. may claim the right of non-compliance with any obligation under the Convention? Is this reservation *"compatible with the object and purpose of the Convention?"* as required by the *Vienna Convention on Treaties, arts.* 18 and 19? On Genocide and Human Rights, see Chapter 10. For more on the U.S. Constitution and Treaties, see Chapter 14. Does such a reservation included with the U.S. instruments of ratification invite the perception by the other parties to the Convention that the United States does not take the Convention seriously? Or that the United States may not really be a party?

Due to the problems caused by the "sovereignty" reservation, the U.S. Senate did not include one for the Torture Convention, discussed in Ch. 10, *supra*. It did include a *"declaration"* in its Resolution of Advice and Consent, that "[t]he President of the United States shall not deposit the instrument of ratification until such time as he has notified all present and prospective ratifying party [sic] to this Convention that nothing in this Convention requires or authorizes legislation, or other action, by the United States prohibited by the Constitution of the United States as interpreted by the United States." This was not considered to be a *"reservation"* or an *"understanding." See, gen.*, D. Stewart, The Torture Convention and the Reception of International Criminal Law Within the United States, 15 Nova L.Rev. 449 (1991), an excellent article presenting a thorough analysis of the Convention by a member of the U.S. Department of State Office of the Legal Adviser.

The Senate also stipulated five *understandings,* designed to clarify interpretation of the Convention and the obligations that arise thereunder. They included the claim that the type of "intent [to destroy a group]" used in article II of the Convention means "specific intent." Other *understandings* relate to: defining "mental harm;" to the obligation to extradite (the Convention is not necessarily an extradition treaty); to protecting members of the U.S. armed forces from prosecution for genocide in combat situations; to limiting the jurisdiction of any future international criminal court. Are the terms *"understanding"* and *"declarations"* used in the Vienna Convention? *Is an understanding any different from a reservation? What impact do they have on the Convention?*

In the **International Covenant on Civil and Political Rights,** the U.S. Senate gave its advice and consent, but included the so-called *"states rights"* understanding, which provides that the United States Government will only "take appropriate measures to the end" of meeting the requirement of Covenant article 50. Article 50 provides that "the Covenant shall extend to all parts of federal States without any limitations or exceptions" and to fulfill "this Covenant." What do you think the effect of this *understanding* will be? See Ch. 10, *supra*.

VIENNA CONVENTION ON THE LAW OF TREATIES

[The text of the convention is in the Documentary Supplement. Read Articles 20 through 23 in conjunction with Article 19, below.]

Article 19
Formulation of reservations

A State may, when signing, ratifying, accepting, approving or acceding to a treaty, formulate a reservation unless:

(a) the reservation is prohibited by the treaty;

(b) the treaty provides that only specified reservations, which do not include the reservation in question, may be made; or

(c) in cases not falling under sub-paragraphs (a) and (b), the reservation is incompatible with the object and purpose of the treaty.

----

1. *Vienna Convention provisions on reservations: illustrations of treaties providing for the codification and progressive development of international law.* Articles 19–23 of the Convention are the end product of the General Assembly's request to the International Law Commission, referred to in the Genocide case, to deal with the matter of reservations. The formulation of a law-making international agreement (see the second introductory note to this chapter, p. 991) may call for an orderly formulation in concise text of widely accepted norms of customary international law [*codification*] or the formulation of proposed new rules where there were none before [*progressive development*], or both of these, in the same international agreement. The Treaty on Treaties, as the Convention is colloquially named, is, on the whole, more digest than code or progressive development, but some aspects of the articles on reservations may go beyond what is clearly accepted as customary international law. *Can you identify these?*

2. *Problems.*

a. State X, with nuclear capability, has not yet acceded to the Nuclear Test Ban Treaty. What would be the legal consequences (a) under the Genocide case and (b) under the Vienna Convention if State X were to deposit the following instrument with the three depositary governments? "State X accedes to the Treaty Banning Nuclear Weapons Tests in the Atmosphere, in Outer Space and under Water done at Moscow, August 5, 1963, subject to the reservation that the treaty shall not be deemed to inhibit the use of nuclear weapons in armed conflict."

b. State Y, a new state that has just come into existence, proposes to accede to a number of multipartite international agreements open for accession including the Geneva Convention Relative to the Treatment of Prisoners of War, 75 U.N.T.S. 135. It offers for deposit this reservation: "Provided, however, that persons guilty of war crimes shall not be entitled in State Y to treatment as prisoners of war under this Convention." At the time this proposal is made, military personnel of State A, which is engaged in armed conflict with State Y, have been captured in large numbers by State Y. State A is a party to the Geneva Convention. Assume the Vienna Convention is in force. What position would you as an official of State A take as to this reservation under the Vienna Convention?

c. The United States and Canada negotiated a Treaty Concerning the Uses of the Waters of the Niagara River, 1 U.S.T. 694 (1950). The major purpose of the treaty was to allocate as between the two countries the amount of hydro-static potential each could use for the generation of electrical power. The Senate resolution of advice and consent included a reservation that the United States for its part reserves the right to provide by legislation for the use of the United States' share of the waters of the Niagara and that no project for the use of the United States' share should be undertaken until specifically authorized by Congress. This reservation was officially called to the attention of the government of Canada. What, if any, response do you think Canada should make? *See* Reporters' Note 7 to Section 133 of the 1965 Restatement. Internal legal aspects of this situation, in relationship to the Federal Power Act of 1920 and the jurisdiction of the Federal Power Commission in the absence of any new legislation, were involved in Power Authority of New York v. Federal Power Commission, 247 F.2d 538 (D.C.App.1957).

SECTION C. INTERPRETATION OF INTERNATIONAL AGREEMENTS

General aspects of the problem. The basic principles for interpreting treaties are: ordinary meaning in context, good faith, and object and purpose. *See* art. 31 of the Vienna Convention. The determination of the meaning of language in relationship to rights and duties of parties to an international agreement is a process that parallels interpretation of contracts, wills, trusts and other consensual arrangements in private law. It also presents problems particularly linked to operations in the international legal system. Here we assume the parallels and focus on the special problems.

Are there formalized guidelines for interpretation of international agreements? Older systemic scholarship sometimes presented canons for interpretation. These have fallen into disuetude. Do words and phrases in international agreements always, sometimes, or never, have clear, mutually understood, and constant meanings? The influences of relatively modern developments of thought about semiotics, semantics, social psychology, linguistics, and mental processes are manifest. A restraining influence on the movement away from lexicographical emphasis is the continued validity of an international relations assumption that states, being free to make agreements, always intend to make the least detrimental of several otherwise plausible interpretative alternatives.

To what extent is the type or nature of the international agreement involved to be taken into account, as say, between a land boundary agreement, an international agreement codifying private carriage of goods at sea, and the Charter of the United Nations? How is the authority of the authorized interpreter to interpret the agreement to be determined? Is an arbitral panel chosen by the states concerned more or less free to interpret than the legal adviser of one of the foreign offices involved? The International Court of Justice, if its jurisdiction is invoked? A national court, where the issue is one of asserted private party rights under an international agreement?

How and when, if at all, is the negotiating history of the agreement legally acceptable as relevant to the interpretative process? Would acceptable negotiating history include actions taken and statements made during the internal ratification of the agreement by a party?

INTERNATIONAL LAW COMMISSION, DRAFT ARTICLES ON THE LAW OF TREATIES

61 American Journal of International Law 255, 349 (1967).*

Commentary on Rules of Interpretation [a]

(1) The utility and even the existence of rules of international law governing the interpretation of treaties are sometimes questioned. The first two of the Commission's Special Rapporteurs on the law of treaties in their private writings also expressed doubts as to the existence in international law of any general rules for the interpretation of treaties. Other jurists, although they express reservations as to the obligatory character of certain of the so-called canons of interpretation, show less hesitation in recognizing the existence of some general rules for the interpretation of treaties. * * *

(2) Jurists also differ to some extent in their basic approach to the interpretation of treaties according to the relative weight which they give to: (a) The text of the treaty as the authentic expression of the intentions of the parties; (b) The intentions of the parties as a subjective element distinct from the text; and (c) The declared or apparent objects and purposes of the treaty.

* * *

(3) Most cases submitted to international adjudication involve the interpretation of treaties, and the jurisprudence of international tribunals is rich in reference to principles and maxims of interpretation. In fact, statements can be found in the decisions of international tribunals to support the use of almost every principle or maxim of which use is made in national systems of law in the interpretation of statutes and contracts. Treaty interpretation is, of course, equally part of the everyday work of Foreign Ministries.

* * *

(11) The article as already indicated is based on the view that the text must be presumed to be the authentic expression of the intentions of the parties; and, that, in consequence, the starting point of interpretation is the elucidation of the meaning of the text, not an investigation

---

* Reprinted with the permission of the American Society of International Law.

a. Draft Articles 27 and 28, which correspond to Articles 31 (as supplemented) and 32 in the Convention.

ab initio into the intentions of the parties. The Institute of International Law adopted this—the textual—approach to treaty interpretation. The objections to giving too large a place to the intentions of the parties as an independent basis of interpretation find expression in the proceedings of the Institute. The textual approach on the other hand, commends itself by the fact that, as one authority has put it, "le texte signé est, sauf de rares exceptions, la seule et la plus récente expression de la volonté commune des parties." Moreover, the jurisprudence of the International Court contains many pronouncements from which it is permissible to conclude that the textual approach to treaty interpretation is regarded by it as established law. In particular, the Court has more than once stressed that it is not the function of interpretation to revise treaties or to read into them what they do not, expressly or by implication, contain.

KEARNEY AND DALTON, THE TREATY ON TREATIES

64 American Journal of International Law 495, 518 (1970).*

* * *

The articles on interpretation demonstrate that a quite conservative (even old-fashioned) series of rules would be accepted by the conference if endorsed by the Commission. Articles 31 and 32 deal, respectively, with the general rule and supplementary means of interpretation. The Commission's formulation established a hierarchy of sources in which primacy was accorded to the text.

Paragraph 1 of Article 31 requires that a treaty be "interpreted in good faith in accordance with the ordinary meaning to be given to the terms of the treaty in their context and the light of its object and purpose." Context is narrowly defined as comprising, "in addition to the text, including its preamble and annexes," related agreements made by all the parties and instruments made by less than all the parties but accepted by all as related to the treaty. Paragraph 3 of Article 31, listing elements "extrinsic to the text" which shall be "taken into account" in interpretation, is limited to subsequent agreements between the parties, subsequent practice establishing agreement and relevant rules of international law.

Article 32 allows "supplementary means of interpretation" to be resorted to, "including preparatory work on the treaty and the circumstances of its conclusion, in order to confirm the meaning resulting from the application of article 31, or to determine the meaning when the interpretation according to article 31: (a) leaves the meaning ambiguous or obscure; or (b) leads to a result which is manifestly absurd or unreasonable."

A member of the Commission has observed that the method of presentation in both Articles 31 and 32 "is designed to stress the dominant position of the text itself in the interpretative process."

* Reprinted with the permission of the American Society of International Law.

In the Commission Messrs. Briggs, El Erian, Rosenne and Tsuruoka supported a proposal to combine the substance of Articles 31 and 32 into a single article. In addition, Mr. Bartoš stated that he was inclined to favor the proposal, and Mr. Amado that he had no strong feelings either way. Among the governments which in their comments on the Commission's articles criticized treating the travaux préparatoires as a secondary means of interpretation were Hungary and the United States.

In light of the division in the Commission on the subject, the expressions of concern in governmental comments, and the traditional United States position in favor of according equal weight to travaux, the United States formally proposed an amendment, the principal objective of which was to eliminate the hierarchy between the sources of evidence for interpretation of treaties by combining the articles containing the general rule and the supplementary means of interpretation: "A treaty shall be interpreted in good faith in order to determine the meaning to be given to its terms in the light of all relevant factors, including in particular:

(a) the context of the treaty;

(b) its objects and purposes;

(c) any agreement between the parties regarding the interpretation of the treaty;

(d) any instrument made by one or more parties in connexion with the conclusion of the treaty and accepted by the other parties as an instrument related to the treaty;

(e) any subsequent practice in the application of the treaty which establishes the common understanding of the meaning of the terms as between the parties generally;

(f) the preparatory work of the treaty;

(g) the circumstances of its conclusion;

(h) any relevant rules of international law applicable in the relations between the parties;

(i) the special meaning to be given to a term if the parties intended such term to have a special meaning.

In introducing the amendment Professor McDougal adverted to the practice of Ministries of Foreign Affairs in looking at the travaux when considering a problem of treaty interpretation and to the practice of international tribunals, as illustrated by the Lotus case, of looking at the preparatory work before reaching a decision on the interpretation of a treaty described as "sufficiently clear in itself."

In the ensuing debate in the committee of the whole, the U.S. amendment received scant support. A principal source of arguments against it was the 1950 debates in the Institute of International Law which had adopted the textual approach. Fear was expressed that "too ready admission of the preparatory work" would afford an opportunity to a state which had "found a clear provision of a treaty inconvenient" to allege a different interpretation "because there was generally something in the preparatory work that could be found to support almost any intention." Other arguments advanced included the assertion that recourse to travaux would favor wealthy states with large and well-indexed archives, fear that non-negotiating states would hesitate to accede to multilateral conventions, since they could hardly be aware of or wish to have their rights based on recourse to the travaux, and the characterization of the International Law Commission text as a "neutral and fair formulation of the generally recognized canons of treaty interpretation." Given the tenor of the debate, the rejection of the amendment was a foregone conclusion.

The adoption by the conference of two articles which the United States viewed as somewhat archaic and unduly rigid does not seriously weaken the value of the convention. It seems unlikely that Foreign Offices will cease to take into consideration the preparatory work and the circumstances of the conclusion of treaties when faced with problems of treaty interpretation, or that international tribunals will be less disposed to consult Article 32 sources in determining questions of treaty interpretation.

The reaction of the conference to a United States amendment to Article 33, which deals with interpretation of plurilingual treaties, was more favorable. The amendment was referred to the drafting committee, which incorporated it in paragraph 4. The new rule provides that when a treaty has been authenticated in two or more languages, neither of which has been accorded priority, and a difference in meaning persists after recourse to the other articles on interpretation, "the meaning which best reconciles the texts, having regard to the object and purpose of the treaty, shall be adopted."

———

See McDougal, Lasswell, & Miller, The Interpretation of Agreements and World Public Order: Principles of Content and Procedure (1967), where these authors of the "Yale School" argue that the rules of interpretation ought to permit consideration of *any* relevant evidence to achieve the goal of determining the *"shared expectations of the parties."* They argue that this should be done even when to do so would require contravention of the clear meaning of the text. *What approach does the Vienna Convention on Treaties take? See, articles 31 and 32.*

FITZMAURICE, VAE VICTIS OR WOE TO THE NEGOTIATORS! YOUR TREATY OR OUR "INTERPRETATION" OF IT?

65 American Journal of International Law 358, 370 (1971).*

[Taken from an article-length book review of McDougal, Lasswell and Miller, The Interpretation of Agreements, *supra.*] The most striking feature of the authors' system is, however, that it subordinates the interpretation of a treaty—or rather (for the matter has little to do with interpretation stricto sensu) its application—to the attainment of certain objectives,—a process which is summed up * * * under the head of the "policing * * * goal." This is defined in general terms * * * as "requir-

* Reprinted with the permission of the American Society of International Law.

ing the rejection of the parties' explicit expectations which [sc. if and insofar as they] contradict community policies." In other words the intentions of the parties, even if clear and ascertained and—what is even more important—common to them both, or all (in short the intentions of the *treaty*—* * *), are not to be given effect to if, in the opinion of the "decision-maker," such intentions are inconsistent with * * * "the goals of public order." Since it is thus left to the adjudicator to decide not only whether there is such inconsistency but also what *are* the goals of public order (and of which public order) to be taken into account, it is evident that on this wideranging, indeed almost illimitable basis, the parties could never be sure how their treaty would be applied or whether it would be applied at all. The process would, in fact, confer on the "decision-maker" a discretion of a kind altogether exceeding the normal limits of the judicial function, amounting rather to the exercise of an administrative rôle. This is well illustrated by the character of the only "community goal" which, so far as this reviewer can see, the authors themselves actually specify, namely, that of the preservation of "human dignity" * * *.

* * *

The *second* goal contemplates the case where the search for * * * the "genuine shared expectations" of the parties "must falter or fail because of gaps, contradictions or ambiguities" in their "communication"—(an unclear term which might mean in the course of the negotiations leading up to the agreement, or in the agreement itself). In such event (ibid.) "a decision-maker should supplement or *augment* (our italics) the relatively more explicit expressions of the parties [sc. what they actually wrote into the agreement] by making reference to the basic constitutive policies of the larger community * * *." Here again, therefore, community policies come in as a criterion, and also, once more, human dignity,—for (ibid.) "no conceivable alternative goal" could be "in accord with the aspiration to defend and expand a social system compatible with the overriding objectives of human dignity."

This, however excellent, is not law but sociology; and although the aim is said to be "in support of search for the genuine shared expectations of the parties," it would in many cases have—and is perhaps subconsciously designed to have—quite a different effect, namely, in the guise of interpretation, to substitute the will of the adjudicator for that of the parties, since the intentions of the latter are, by definition (in the given circumstances) unascertainable because not sufficiently clearly or fully expressed,—and therefore presumed intentions, based on what the adjudicator thinks would be good for the community, or in accordance with "overriding objectives of human dignity" etc., must be attributed to them.

* * *

TEXTUALITY OR CONTEXTUALITY

CASE ON INTERPRETATION OF THE AUSTRIAN STATE TREATY

Seidl–Hohenveldern, Notes on Austrian Judicial Decisions.
86 J. du Droit International 835, 837 (1959).[a]

The German text of Article 16, Austrian State Treaty (BGBl., Nr. 152/1955; J.O. 2nd Sept. 1955; 49 AJIL, 1955, Off.Doc., p. 162), is worded as follows: "Prohibition relating to Civil Aircraft of German and Japanese Design". "Austria shall not acquire or manufacture civil aircraft which are of German or Japanese design or which embody major assemblies of German or Japanese manufacture or design". Pursuant to this regulation, the Federal Ministry of communications and electric power—Air Navigation Division—denied the request filed by an Austrian glider club for licensing a glider of German construction type; and the glider club, in protest, brought an action before the Verwaltungsgerichtshof. It pointed out, to start with, that in the German language version of the Treaty there was an inherent contradiction, since the Title of Article 16 read "Zivilflugzeuge" (airplanes), whereas in the Article proper one referred to "Luftfahrtzeugen" (aircraft). In Austrian terminology, the plaintiff asserted, "Zivilflugzeuge" indicates in principle that the plane is engine-driven, while "Luftfahrtzeuge" covers gliders as well. Pursuant to Article 38, State Treaty, the Russian, English, French and German texts are authentic. The French version makes use, for both title and text of Article 16, of the word "Avion", which corresponds to the "Zivilflugzeug" concept, instead of using "aéronef", which would render "Luftfahrtzeug"; and so does the Russian text. The English version, on the contrary, reads—for both title and text of Article 16—"aircraft", which corresponds to "Luftfahrtzeug", whereas "Zivilflugzeug", in English, would be "airplane".

The glider club considered that, account being taken of the aforementioned discrepancies between texts, one was faced here, essentially, with an error in the translation into German. Article 16 * * * brings about a limitation of Austrian sovereignty, but even according to the basic principles of international law the existence of diverging authentic texts of a State Treaty results in considering that version which infringes least on sovereignty, as the only one which may be regarded as consonant with the will of the contracting parties and the principles of International Law. Moreover, it claimed, the French text is most authoritative, because in the Convention on International Civil Aviation French terminology is clearly defined—French being the official language of ICAO. * * * French wording does not provide any reason for further limiting Austria's sovereignty.

The Verwaltungsgerichtshof decided that, for the purpose of implementing the State Treaty—which in the domestic sphere is to be

---

a. English text in the Journal. Reprinted by permission of Editions Techniques, S.A., Paris.

regarded as directly applicable law—one must infer from its Article 39, paragraph 1, that its German version became domestic law. Pursuant to Austrian practice, headings are to be called upon for construing a legal text only in the event that the text proper is not clear or does not make sense—which is not the case here. In the light of the purpose which, among others, underlies Part II of the State Treaty—namely, to prevent coordination of the Austrian Air Force and civilian aviation with those of Germany and Japan—, the importance of civil aviation as a whole in war time, together with the widespread use of all types of aircraft, including gliders and balloons, for war aims, make a prohibition against any aircraft (even one which is not engine-propelled) appear perfectly logical, however harsh such a rule may seem to glider pilots.

Nor is anything to be gained in favour of thus construing this legal text by underlining the existing contradictions between the German version and those in other languages, since the latter turn out to be just as diverging. Therefore, as long as the differences are not settled by an authentic interpretation of Article 16, made in accordance with the procedure provided for in Article 35 of the Treaty—a procedure which can only be initiated at the international public law level—, the Austrian authorities must continue to abide by the German text, application of which as positive law is mandatory for them and in which the wording does not admit—as already pointed out—of the kind of interpretation proposed by the plaintiff. A legal text may be interpreted in the manner most favourable to the sovereignty of the country concerned only when there exists a doubt as to how that regulation ought to be interpreted; since the provisions of Article 16, in its German version, are unambiguous, this does not apply here.

* * *

TEXTUALITY OR CONTEXTUALITY IN THE LIGHT OF SPECIAL CIRCUMSTANCES

In the Anglo–Iranian Oil Co. Case, United Kingdom v. Iran, [1952] I.C.J.Rep. 4, the optional clause jurisdiction of the World Court turned on the interpretation of the Iranian declaration under Article 36(2) of the Statute of the Court. The issue was whether the limitation of acceptance of jurisdiction was as to (i) treaties or (ii) events coming after the ratification of the Iranian declaration. On linguistic grounds, stressing the French text of the declaration, the court held for Iran, but in doing so it went into the background of why, at the time of making its declaration, Iran sought to be as restrictive as possible as to old treaties. Iran wished to exclude "capitulations treaties," and other impositions on middle eastern countries, made in the Age of Imperialism.

In dissent, Judge Alvarez strongly rejected any notion that a declaration under Article 36(2) should be interpreted on linguistic grounds and then listed and rejected a set of old-fashioned canons of interpretation: The traditional methods of interpretation may be summarized by the following points:

(1) It is considered that the texts have an everlasting and fixed character as long as they have not been expressly abrogated.

(2) Strict respect for the letter of the legal or conventional texts.

(3) Examination of these texts, considered by themselves without regard to their relations with the institution or convention as a whole.

(4) Recourse to travaux préparatoires in case of doubt as to the scope of these texts.

(5) Use, in reasoning, of out-and-out logic, almost as in the case of problems of mathematics or philosophy.

(6) Application of legal concepts or doctrines of the law of nations as traditionally conceived.

(7) Application of the decisions of the present International Court, or of the earlier Court, in similar cases which arise, without regard to the question whether the law so laid down must be modified by reason of the new conditions of international life.

(8) Disregard for the social or international consequences which may result from the construction applied.

Some form of reaction is necessary against these postulates because they have had their day. In the first place the legal or conventional texts must be modified and even regarded as abrogated if the new conditions of international life or of States which participated in the establishment of those texts, have undergone profound change. Then it is necessary to avoid slavish adherence to the literal meaning of legal or conventional texts; those who drafted them did not do so with a grammar and a dictionary in front of them; very often, they used vague or inadequate expressions. The important point is to have regard above all to the spirit of such documents, to the intention of the parties in the case of a treaty, as they emerge from the institution or convention as a whole, and indeed from the new requirements of international life.

Recourse should only be had to travaux préparatoires when it is necessary to discover the will of the parties with regard to matters which affect their interests alone. A legal institution, a convention, once established, acquires a life of its own and evolves not in accordance with the ideas or the will of those who drafted its provisions, but in accordance with the changing conditions of the life of peoples.

A single example will suffice to show the correctness of this assertion. Let us assume that in a commercial convention there is a stipulation that all questions relating to maritime trade are to be governed by the principles of international law in force. These principles may have been followed by the parties for a century, perhaps, without any disputes arising between them; but one of the parties may, at the present time, by reason of the changes which have recently taken place in such matters, come to Court to claim that the century-old practice hitherto followed should be changed on the ground that it must be held that the will of the parties is no longer the same as it was at the time when the convention was signed. This is in many ways similar to the rebus sic stantibus clause which is so well known in the law of nations.

It is to be observed that out-and-out reliance upon the rules of logic is not the best method of interpretation of legal or conventional texts, for international life is not based on logic; States follow, above all, their own interests and feelings in their relations with one another. Reason, pushed to extremes, may easily result in absurdity. It is also necessary to bear in mind the fact that certain fundamental legal conceptions have changed and that certain institutions and certain problems are not everywhere understood in the same way. * * *

SECTION D. PERFORMANCE OF INTERNATIONAL AGREEMENTS

1. NOVATION, AMENDMENT AND MODIFICATION OF INTERNATIONAL AGREEMENTS

As in the private law of contracts, the parties to an international agreement may, if third party rights protected by international law are not involved, agree to end the agreement, substitute another agreement for it, or otherwise change particulars in it. Consult Articles 37, 39, 40, and 41 of the Vienna Convention. Cf. The 1987 Restatement, §§ 334 and 339 (semble, as to modification).

2. INVALIDATION

As in the private law of contracts, an international agreement may be or become unenforcible for strong public policy reasons. Jus cogens, to the extent it has developed or will develop, is one such reason; see p. 1001, et seq. The niceties of common law distinctions between void and voidable contracts do not carry over into customary international law, but under certain circumstances an obligated party under a treaty may prevail against performance by succeeding in establishing a legal basis for invalidation. Such bases have been expanded by the Vienna Convention beyond what they were in pre-convention customary international law, thus providing an instance in which the Vienna Convention progressively develops, rather than merely codifies, customary international law. A significant example involves force and duress. In pre-Charter times, force and duress (military, political, or economic) were two of the legitimate means by which a state was required to become legally obligated to another state or states, contrary to the obligated states' wishes. Many grabs of territory were thus established over many centuries. Likewise, error, even fraud in the inducement, were not defenses. Study now Articles 46 through 53 of the Vienna Convention.

Only Article 51 (coercion of the representative of a state) was an assuredly recognized legal basis for later invalidation prior to the Vienna Convention. Does the Vienna Convention go too far the other way, say as to fraud (Article 49)? In diplomacy, as in war, ruses and deceptions have a long history of usage, and it cannot assuredly be affirmed that their actual use has ended in post-Charter, post-Vienna Convention days. Treaty capitulations imposed upon a state by use or threat of force impermissible under the United Nations Charter, however, seem clear targets for subsequent successful invalidation. On what ground, other than Article 52 of the Vienna Convention? See also the 1987 Restatement, § 331, especially Comment *d* and Reporters' Note 3.

---

3. DURATION, SUCCESSION, SUSPENSION, TERMINATION

1. ***Duration, (general).*** International agreements may be for fixed time periods, ending automatically at the expiration of the time set. Some provide for automatic renewal if nothing is done at the end of the period. If no time period is fixed, international agreements continue until legally terminated. International agreements may declare that they continue in perpetuity, but some, such as the 1903 canal treaty between the United States and Panama have not so continued.

See, Vienna Convention article 4, which allows for termination * * * when and in the manner indicated in the agreement. It also allows termination of an agreement when all of the parties agree. Does this apply to multilateral treaties? What would be the result if a sufficient number of parties withdrew from a multilateral agreement to put the number of parties remaining below that required for *"entry into force?" Do articles 54 or 55 help?*

A few international agreements that fix no time period are considered to be of perpetual duration, such as those creating the European Community (EC). Many treaties that create international organizations (often called constitutive treaties) provide procedures for amendment (see the United Nations Charter, Articles 108 and 109.) Typically such treaties do not provide for withdrawal but withdrawals have taken place nevertheless.

2. ***Relative durability of various types of international agreements.*** While international agreements are in strict legal analysis all equally durable, in the actual practices of states some agreements are more durable than others. Bilateral treaties that are or become out of balance as to mutuality of interests between the parties are susceptible to unilateral denunciation that politically the advantaged party may be unable to complain of. In international relations practice treaties, bipartite and multipartite, that create territorial rights (said to be executed treaties) are usually stable. So are treaties that deal with a common problem or need shared by the parties. Where, in the past, war has either terminated or suspended international agreements, peace

treaties may clarify the situation by stipulating the pre-war bilateral treaties that the parties deem still to be in force and by stating for the negotiating history of the peace treaty that multipartite treaties, unless specifically stipulated against, continue in force. The peace treaties negotiated with Italy, Finland, Hungary, Rumania and Bulgaria at Paris in 1946 followed the method just described.

When the issue is whether an international agreement has an internal legal effect, as in cases in national courts where a party claims under a treaty, the court looks to the element of the national government that is in charge of international relations for guidance as to whether the agreement is still in effect. In some states subsequent inconsistent national law may affect the internal legal standing of the international agreement, although internationally it has not been legally ended. Various cases in the next chapter illustrate aspects of this problem in United States law.

3. *Two significant instances of treaty instability.*

The Treaty of Versailles, 1919. This treaty was negotiated to end World War I with Germany. The Covenant of the League of Nations was an annex to it. President Woodrow Wilson went to Paris to negotiate it. The stroke that led to his death happened while he was trying to convince the American people to support the treaty after far less than half the Senate balked at approving it without reservations that politically could not have been re-negotiated with Germany and the other Allies. A young John Maynard Keynes became famous for his attack on its reparations provisions and his study of the disintegration of Wilson's principles under the pounding of vengeful European leaders, especially Georges Clémenceau, premier of France. Keynes, The Economic Consequences of the Peace (1919). In addition to reparations that Germany claimed it could not pay without an expansion of its export trade unacceptable to the Allies, Germany from the beginning evaded the arms limitations provisions of the treaty. Hitler, after he was elected chancellor in 1933, denounced the treaty, armed openly and stated as an objective of his 1,000 year Reich the elimination of the injustices done to Germany under Versailles, including the Allies' imposition on Germany of onerous terms that would not have been acceptable in the first instance but for disintegration of the German economy following the Armistice of November 11, 1918. Many asked themselves, as World War II approached and during that war, whether a more benign Versailles Treaty would have avoided a second terrible war in Europe, or whether a more severe and effectively policed 1919 treaty would have prevented World War II. Unconditional surrender and Allied military occupation were imposed upon Germany following World War II. No peace treaty has yet been made with Germany, including either the former Federal German Republic or the German Democratic Republic. The western Allies successfully resisted Soviet demands for heavy reparations charges (20 billion dollars in current production), so far as the occupation zones administered by France, the United Kingdom and the United States were concerned; and this resistance is historically directly linked to the division of Germany into two states.

The Panama Canal Treaty of 1903. A zone eleven miles wide through the fledgling state of Panama was granted to the United States in perpetuity, along with authority to act there " * * * as if sovereign." In 1964 internal objection in Panama erupted into riot at a high school within the zone when the Panamanian flag was hauled down by U.S. students. To avoid further unrest negotiations to replace the treaty of 1903 began in 1965 but did not result in mutually agreed terms until after a military coup in Panama in 1968 and the subsequent mobilization by Panama of world opinion in its favor, including a special session of the Security Council held in Panama. Under two treaties still in force Panama and the United States are jointly responsible for the security of the Panama Canal, United States law has been replaced in the zone by Panamanian law and courts, various public installations in the zone are in the process of being transferred to Panama, and by the year 2000 the canal itself is to pass to Panamanian ownership and control.

See, generally and as to other instances, Malawer, Imposed Treaties and International Law, 7 Cal.W.I.L.J. 1 (1977); Stone, De Victoribus Victis: The International Law Commission and Imposed Treaties of Peace, 8 Va.J. of Int'l L. 356 (1968); David, The Strategy of Treaty Termination—Lawful Breaches and Retaliations (1975). Cf., the meta-legal literature of conflict resolution and negotiating science, such as Deutsch, Cooperation and Trust, Some Theoretical Notes, Nebraska Symposium on Motivation (1962); R. Bilder, Managing the Risks in International Agreements (1981). M. Halberstam, *A Treaty is a Treaty is a Treaty*, 33 Va.J.Int'l L. 51 (1992); I. Johnstone, *Treaty Interpretation: The Authority of Interpretive Communities*, 12 Mich.J.Int'l L. 371 (1991).

4. *Duration and the territorial applicability of international agreements as affected by the life of states and the growth and division of states.* International agreements lose states as parties if such states cease to exist. But short of complete subjugation by different ethnic groups, states have always had a high survival rate. As to international agreements not otherwise terminated, the treaties to which the former German Reich was a party were carried on through the former two divided Germanies to today's Germany, despite the unconditional surrender of the Reich and the exercise of supreme authority in the territory of the former Reich by the occupying powers for from seven to ten years and technically much longer for Berlin. However, it was decided that the statehood of Austria should be re-established by treaty after the 1938 incorporation of Austria into the Reich by Hitler. Technically the Republic of Italy is the Kingdom of Savoy territorially expanded and governmentally altered insofar as treaties are concerned.

The USSR was the Tsarist Russian Empire with a different ideology, even though propagandistically the Marxist–Leninist structure was depicted as a new arrangement for a new species of humanity. Shortly after the 1917 Revolution, Lenin cancelled unilaterally some treaties giving Russia imperialistic territorial and other rights in Iran. This attitude has long since been cast upon the ash heap of history by Lenin's successors, clung tenaciously to all Russian rights under Tsarist treaties.

The post World War I Treaty of St. Germain split up the Austro–Hungarian Empire into a vestigial Austria and a somewhat altered Hungary, restored Serbia as a part of a new Yugoslav state (which has now dissolved or re-created itself in such tragic fashion) and made Bohemia, after centuries of non-treatment as a state, into a new Czechoslovak state, which has now divided itself in two. Many of the "nations" created in this era are now becoming independent; all of them have retained the treaties of their predecessors.

In the decades since World War II, many former colonies have spun off as new states, and in the arrangements for their independence it has been usual to deal with the determination of what treaties of the metropole shall continue in force for the new entity. Then, if third states are concerned, the mother country carries out the negotiations for the continuation or cessation of such treaties as to the people or territory of the new state. Usually newly-created states opt for the continuation of boundary and other territorial interests, including servitudes, transit rights, and similar arrangement. Sometimes the retiring sovereignty is able to negotiate for the new state the continuation for it of advantages it formerly enjoyed as a colony under multilateral treaties, such as (GATT); see § B of Chapter 15. The new state usually elects to decide for itself what multipartite treaties open for accession it will become a party to. As to the United Nations, the new state must apply to be admitted as a member under Article 4(2) of the Charter.

Historically, the appearance of entirely new states out of revolution is comparatively rare, except for the states of the Western Hemisphere, beginning with the United States of America. The former French Indochina, Israel, Bangladesh, and, possibly the Republic of Indonesia, are the major post World War II instances.

Treaty provisions on termination and related matters. Treaties contained in the Documentary Supplement display a variety of approaches to the question of termination. These include:

    a.   No express provision appears in the following:

        (i) International Covenant on Economic, Social and Cultural Rights.

        (ii) International Covenant on Civil and Political Rights.

        (iii) Vienna Convention on the Law of Treaties.

        (iv) Vienna Convention on Diplomatic Relations.

        (v) 1958 Conventions on the Law of the Sea.

    b.   Denunciation at any time by notice to Secretary–General of United Nations (to take effect one year after receipt of notice): International Convention on the Elimination of all forms of Racial Discrimination, Article 21.

    c.   After ten years the convention remains in force for successive periods of five years, for parties that have not denounced (by notice to Secretary–General) six months before end of current period: Convention on the Prevention and Punishment of the Crime of Genocide, Article XIV.

d.   Notice of withdrawal may be given to Depository Governments after one year after treaty in force (to take effect one year after receipt of notice): Space Treaty, Article XVI.

Some conventions provide an amendment process (e.g., Nuclear Test Ban, Space Treaty, United Nations Charter, and the 1982 Law of the Sea Convention). Some conventions provide that parties may request revision by notifying the Secretary–General of the United Nations, in which event the General Assembly shall decide what steps to take (e.g., conventions on Racial Discrimination, the Territorial Sea, the High Seas, the Continental Shelf). The 1958 Law of the Sea Conventions provide that such requests can be made only after five years from the date the relevant convention has come into force.

Article 56 of the Vienna Convention on the Law of Treaties provides that if there is no provision for termination, denunciation or withdrawal, a treaty is not subject to denunciation unless "it is established that the parties intended to admit the possibility of denunciation or withdrawal" or "a right of denunciation or withdrawal may be implied by the *nature* of the treaty." [Emphasis supplied.]

Query: *Who has the authority to withdraw from or to terminate a treaty? Do Agency Law principles apply, as discussed supra? We discuss the issue relating to U.S. law in the next chapter.*

––––––––

1. ***Outbreak of hostilities.*** In *Clark v. Allen,* 331 U.S. 503, 508 (1947), the court said: "We start from the premise that the outbreak of war does not necessarily suspend or abrogate treaty provisions. *Society for the Propagation of the Gospel v. New Haven,* 8 Wheat. 464, 494–495. There may be such an incompatibility between a particular treaty provision and the maintenance of a state of war as to make clear that it should not be enforced. *Karnuth v. United States,* 279 U.S. 231. Or the Chief Executive or the Congress may have formulated a national policy quite inconsistent with the enforcement of a treaty in whole or in part. This was the view stated in *Techt v. Hughes* * * * and we believe it to be the correct one. That case concerned the right of a resident alien enemy to inherit real property in New York. Under New York law, as it then stood, an alien enemy had no such right. The question was whether the right was granted by a reciprocal inheritance provision in a treaty with Austria which was couched in terms practically identical with those we have here. The court found nothing incompatible with national policy in permitting the resident alien enemy to have the right of inheritance granted by the treaty. * * *

Article 73, Vienna Convention on the Law of Treaties provides: "The provisions of the present Convention shall not prejudge any question that may arise in regard to a treaty * * * from the outbreak of hostilities between States."

2. ***Suspension and revival of treaties.*** The Supreme Court view in *Clark v. Allen, supra,* that hostilities do not necessarily suspend or abrogate treaty provisions is elaborated by some text-writers. Focusing on types of treaties, rather than provisions in treaties, they say that hostilities abrogate political treaties, such as those for mutual security or alliance, but only suspend less sensitive ones, such as consular, navigation, and commercial arrangements. Suspension is sometimes used as an alternative to cancellation for failure of performance by the other party either in the same treaty or under general international law. Suspension of treaty concessions is common in international trade law under the General Agreement on Tariffs and Trade (GATT). Suspension is also used in some instances to manifest political disapproval of another treaty party's policies. See also, Resolution, The Effects of Armed Conflicts on Treaties, 61 Ann.Inst.Dr.Int'l de l'Institut de Droit Int'l (1986); *Sedco Inc. v. National Iranian Oil Co.* and the Islamic Republic of Iran, 84 ILR 521 (Iran—US Claims Trib. 1986).

---

4. CHANGE OF CIRCUMSTANCES (REBUS SIC STANTIBUS)

BREMEN (FREE HANSA CITY OF) v. PRUSSIA

Germany, Staatsgerichtshof, 1925.
[1925–1926] Ann.Dig. 352 (No. 266).*

Facts. A treaty entered into on 21 May, 1904, between Bremen and Prussia provided for an exchange of portions of territory belonging to each of the two States mainly with the view of enabling Bremen to extend the facilities for transport by sea. Article 13 of the Treaty laid down that a specified portion of the territory received by Bremen in exchange should be used by Bremen only for the purpose of constructing ports and other works connected with navigation, and Article 22 provided that no works connected with the fishing industry should be constructed or allowed by Bremen. The area of the territories exchanged was 595 and 597 hectares, but it appears from the judgment that the territory received by Prussia was only useful for agricultural purposes and, therefore, less valuable. Prussia, therefore, asked for further consideration, and received it in the form of the above restrictive clauses calculated to safeguard the interests of her adjoining provinces menaced by the competition of the neighbouring Bremen fishing industry. Before the Staatsgerichtshof Bremen asked for a rescission of the restrictive clauses, subject, if necessary, to adequate compensation to be paid by her. She claimed that, as a result of the outcome of the War of 1914–1918, there had taken place a *total change in the circumstances* (emphasis added) which underlay the conclusion of the Treaty. It was expected in 1904 that not only would the commercial fleet of Bremen, especially

---

* Reprinted with the permission of E. Lauterpacht and Grotius Publications, Ltd., Cambridge, England.

the North German Lloyd, continue to exist, but also that a rapid development of that fleet would take place. It was in view of this expectation that Bremen agreed to the restrictions contemplated in Articles 13 and 22. Bremen pointed out before the court that the Treaty of Versailles effected a complete change in the situation in that the German commercial fleet was handed over to the Allied Powers; that the position of Bremen as a centre of shipping and navigation was irretrievably lost; and that the operation of the restrictive clauses had become most oppressive as the prohibited activities had now become the only sphere open to Bremen as a maritime State. *Held:* That the application of Bremen must be refused;

1. International Law recognizes to a large extent the possibility of termination of treaties on account of changed circumstances in accordance with the principle rebus sic stantibus.

2. This principle applies also to treaties concluded between State members of the German Reich. Although rules of International Law do not eo ipso form part of German constitutional law, they may be resorted to in order to supplement the latter. The regard for the interests of the other contracting party which International Law expects from a State, cannot be regarded as inequitable and devoid of a legal foundation within the German Federation.

3. However, as the two restrictive clauses formed an integral part of the treaties in question and as Prussia would not, in the opinion of the Court, have agreed to the treaties but for the restrictive clauses they could not be abrogated without her consent.

4. Neither could the clauses in question be abrogated subject to compensation to be paid to Prussia by Bremen. No such alteration of individual provisions of the treaty is admissible as would compel one contracting party to remain subject to the obligation while surrendering what it intended to achieve as the principal object of the treaty, at the time of the conclusion of the treaty.

5. The above decision [is not] a rejection of the doctrine rebus sic stantibus. The doctrine could still be applied in regard to certain payments or time limits contemplated in several provisions. * * *

The clause rebus sic stantibus. The Vienna Convention on the Law of Treaties provides in Article 62 (in somewhat negative language) for terminating, withdrawing from or suspending a treaty because of a ***fundamental change of circumstances.*** Read article 62 carefully (in Doc. Supp.) This provision should be read in conjunction with the procedures established in Articles 65–68, which also refer to invalidity, termination, withdrawal from or suspension of a treaty. Why is article 62 couched in negative terms? Does article 62 appear to limit the application of rebus sic stantibus? When is a change of a "fundamental character" an "essential basis" of the consent? What is meant by the term to "radically transform" the party's obligations? What happens if one of the parties to a treaty has a change in government? What if the change occurs as a result of the acts of the party raising the issue of rebus sic stantibus? These questions raise serious difficulties with rebus sic stantibus. Can a private party raise rebus sic stantibus—say, for example, that a person's extradition has been requested and the regime of the requesting state is now much more hostile to him than the prior one? The U.S. answer seems to be no. *See, T.W.A. v. Franklin Mint Corp.,* 466 U.S. 243, 253 (1984). Many scholars have raised doubts about the viability and wisdom of rebus sic stantibus. See, e.g., Schwarzenberger, Clausula Rebus Sic Stantibus, 7 Ency.Pub.Int'l L. 22 (1984). Others have signalled some value to the rule, such as being a mechanism for enhancing stability and peace, through providing an outlet for intolerably burdensome treaties or for those in which the community no longer has a strong interest. This latter point was made by O. Lissitzyn, *Stability and Change: Unilateral Denunciation or Suspension of Treaties by Reason of Changed Circumstances,* 61 ASIL Proceedings 186 (1967); *see also,* the creative article by D. Bederman, *The 1871 London Declaration, Rebus Sic Stantibus and a Primitivist View of the Law of Nations,* 82 A.J.I.L. 1 (1988).

Suppose a state simply ceases to comply with a treaty and is subsequently called to account by the other party. Is rebus sic stantibus a defense? Can be invoked unilaterally by a state after it breaches? Does the Vienna Convention allow an unlimited right to terminate a treaty unilaterally on the basis of rebus sic stantibus? This is exactly what was suggested by the Attorney General in his opinion to the President in 1941. Is this a wise policy to promote or was it an expedient? Do you think that unilateral denunciation of a treaty based on rebus sic stantibus is often tested in the courts or in arbitration?

To avoid the doctrinal implication of the term rebus sic stantibus, the International Law Commission decided not to use it either in the text or the title of the Vienna Convention article on fundamental change. See the Commentary of the International Law Commission in its draft Article 59 (now Treaty Article 62), 61 AJIL 428 (1967). It is clear, however, that the Commission was carefully and narrowly stating its preferred version of the rule of rebus sic stantibus. The commission noted that the International Court of Justice had avoided taking a position on the existence of the rule by finding, in the one case which posed the question, that the facts of that case did not warrant application of the rule. Free Zones of Savoy and Gex, P.C.I.J., 1932, Series A/B, No. 46. The commission further noted that, although municipal courts "have not infrequently recognized the relevance of the principle in international law," they have "always ended by rejecting the application of it in the particular circumstances of the case before them." (*See, Bremen v. Prussia, supra.*) However, the commission found in state practice "a wide acceptance of the view that a fundamental change of circumstances may justify * * * termination or revision of a treaty."

The doctrine of rebus sic stantibus, either in those terms or in other words, is to be found in the domestic law of states in cases not involving treaties but, rather, commercial contracts between private persons. Article 610 of the German Civil Code provides that one who promises to make a loan can revoke the promise in case of misgivings if a material deterioration develops in the pecuniary circumstances of the other party, through which the claim for repayment is jeopardized. See also Article 321 of that Code on bilateral contracts. Article 2–615 of the United States Uniform Commercial Code provides: " * * * (a) Delay in delivery or non-delivery in whole or in part by a seller * * * is not a breach of his duty under a contract for sale if performance as agreed has been made impracticable by the occurrence of a contingency the nonoccurrence of which was a basic assumption on which the contract was made * * *." *Are there differences?* Is there reticence by domestic courts to use it? If rebus sic stantibus is common to municipal systems of law, why, then, should there be such hesitancy to recognize that the rule is a rule of international law? Are there any peculiar risks to its application in international law that do not exist, or exist to a lesser extent, in municipal law? Is the weakness of international adjudication one such risk?

Impossibility of performance. Article 61 of the Vienna Convention sharply differentiates supervening impossibility of performance from fundamental change of circumstances (Article 62). But, like the latter, Article 61 is tightly drafted against excuse from performance. Is impossibility related to rebus sic stantibus? Does it have a legal foundation at least as solid as that of rebus sic stantibus? It would seem so. It has been utilized less than has rebus sic stantibus, however.

---

5. DENUNCIATION: PRIOR BREACH BY THE OTHER PARTY

Similarities to the private law of contracts. Neither parties to private contracts nor states parties to treaties are disposed to carry out their obligations if the other side has not lived up to its undertaking to do something first, or has made it clear it does not intend to perform. There are public international public law parallels to failure of consideration (in the common law world, or failure of cause in the civilian world (one type of which is failure of consideration)), prior breach of condition precedent, material breach, anticipatory breach, or frustration of expectations, and the like, but they are not sharply etched in the conduct of states as legal principles.

Most jurists agree that a violation of a treaty by one party provides a right in the other party to abrogate the treaty or to suspend its own performance. Reprisals, otherwise unlawful may be available. There is a split of opinion on the scope of the right to abrogate. Some jurists see it as the only viable sanction for some countries, while others see it as being too risky for wide use. Generally the right is limited to breaches of *material, fundamental,* or other *primary* aspects of a treaty. Of course, these "limitations" give rise to uncertainty and potential dispute.

See gen., International Law Commission Draft Articles on the Law of Treaties, Commentary on "Breach." 61 AJIL 263, 422 (1967).

Vienna Convention on the Law of Treaties, on Breach—see Article 60 in the Documentary Supplement. What is a *material breach*? Take for example the case of the attempted extradition of hijacker Willie Holder, where failure to understand a foreign criminal justice system or the desire to ensure adoption of a treaty by avoiding a negotiation snag that would be impossible to overcome, ultimately caused a heated exchange of diplomatic notes; claiming breach of treaty:

BLAKESLEY, COMPARATIVE LAW: ITS PURPOSES & POSSIBILITIES, 27 TEX.I.L.J. 315, 320–22 (1992)*.

* * * [L]anguage and perception of etymology tell us a great deal of each other's legal culture. This enables us to understand how each other thinks about legal issues. We take our own world-view for granted as the product of our natural common sense, but in reality it is provided by our mother tongue. Vox populi, vox dei. This feeling is a weakness [and] a strength. Paradoxically, it is a weakness that many international lawyers and scholars suffer. To be a good international lawyer, one needs to be a good comparativist.

An example of this comes to mind. The word "to represent" in English is the same in French: *"représenter."* Yet the conceptual meaning and mental picture created by the word in the mind of a United States attorney and his or her French counterpart is startlingly different. In a case in which the United States sought the extradition of Willie Holder, who had been charged with the hijacking of an American airliner, the French *Avocat Général,* who *"represents"* the United States Government before the French courts in extradition matters, presented the evidence against Holder and then proceeded to *recommend* to the French court that Holder not be extradited. As the *Avocat Général* saw it, the crime was excepted from extradition because it was a political offense. The United States Government was outraged that the *Avocat Général,* the person ostensibly *"representing"* the United States in France, would simply present the evidence and then argue against the United States' position.

The problem arose because of the differing meanings given to the term "represent." The American vision of "represent" conjured up the aggressive adversarial paradigm. The French *Avocat Général* was functioning, however, under the French concept of the term "représenter," which requires him to present all the papers, but to speak to the court as his perception of justice would require (*la parole est libre*). Thus, he must present exculpatory evidence and arguments, if he feels that they are appropriate. Both sides in this controversy were right, based on their own notion of "representation." Notwithstanding the use of the same term, misunderstanding arose because of the different visions of criminal justice triggered

* Reprinted with the permission of the Tex. Int'l L.J.

by the term. *See, In re Holder,* 1975 Digest of U.S. Foreign Relations Law 168.

———

CHARLTON v. KELLY

United States Supreme Court, 1913.
229 U.S. 447, 33 S.Ct. 945, 57 L.Ed. 1274.

Mr. Justice LURTON delivered the opinion of the court.

[This is an appeal from a judgment dismissing a petition for a writ of habeas corpus and remanding the petitioner to custody under a warrant for his extradition as a fugitive from Italy.]

* * *

The objections relied upon for the purpose of defeating extradition may be conveniently summarized and considered under four heads:

* * *

3. That appellant is a citizen of the United States, and that the treaty in providing for the extradition of "persons" accused of crime does not include persons who are citizens or subjects of the nation upon whom the demand is made.

4. That if the word "person" as used in the treaty includes citizens of the asylum country, the treaty, in so far as it covers that subject, has been abrogated by the conduct of Italy in refusing to deliver up its own citizens upon the demand of the United States, and by the enactment of a municipal law, since the treaty, forbidding the extradition of citizens.

We will consider these objections in their order:

* * *

3. By Article I of the extradition treaty with Italy the two governments mutually agree to deliver up all persons, who, having been convicted of or charged with any of the crimes specified in the following article, committed within the jurisdiction of one of the contracting parties, shall seek an asylum in the other, etc. It is claimed by counsel for the appellant that the word "persons" as used in this article does not include persons who are citizens of the asylum country. That the word "persons" etymologically includes citizens as well as those who are not, can hardly be debatable. The treaty contains no reservation of citizens of the country of asylum. The contention is that an express exclusion of citizens or subjects is not necessary, as by implication, from accepted principles of public law, persons who are citizens of the asylum country are excluded from extradition conventions unless expressly included.
* * *

     * * *

* * * This interpretation has been consistently upheld by the United States, and enforced under the several treaties which do not exempt citizens. That Italy has not conformed to this view, and the effect of this attitude will be considered later. But that the United States has always construed its obligation as embracing its citizens is illustrated by the action of the executive branch of the Government in this very instance. A construction of a treaty by the political department of the Government, while not conclusive in a matter involving personal rights, is nevertheless of much weight.

* * *

4. We come now to the contention that by the refusal of Italy to deliver up fugitives of Italian nationality, the treaty has thereby ceased to be of obligation on the United States. The attitude of Italy is indicated by its Penal Code of 1900 which forbids the extradition of citizens, and by the denial in two or more instances to recognize this obligation of the treaty as extending to its citizens.

* * *

This adherence to a view of the obligation of the treaty as not requiring one country to surrender its nationals while it did the other, presented a situation in which the United States might do either of two things, namely: abandon its own interpretation of the word "persons" as including citizens, or adhere to its own interpretation and surrender the appellant, although the obligation had, as to nationals, ceased to be reciprocal. The United States could not yield its own interpretation of the treaty, since that would have had the most serious consequence on five other treaties in which the word "persons" had been used in its ordinary meaning, as including, all persons, and, therefore, not exempting citizens. If the attitude of Italy was, as contended, a violation of the obligation of the treaty, which, in international law, would have justified the United States in denouncing the treaty as no longer obligatory, it did not automatically have that effect. If the United States elected not to declare its abrogation, or come to a rupture, the treaty would remain in force. It was only voidable, not void; and if the United States should prefer, it might waive any breach which in its judgment had occurred and conform to its own obligation as if there had been no such breach.
* * *

* * *

That the political branch of the Government recognizes the treaty obligation as still existing is evidenced by its action in this case. In the memorandum giving the reasons of the Department of State for determining to surrender the appellant, after stating the difference between the two governments as to the interpretation of this clause of the treaty, Mr. Secretary Knox said:

> The question is now for the first time presented as to whether or not the United States is under obligation under treaty to surrender to Italy for trial and punishment citizens of the United States fugitive from the justice of Italy, notwithstanding the interpretation placed upon the treaty by Italy with reference to Italian subjects. In this connection it should be observed that the United States, although, as stated above, consistently contending that the Italian

interpretation was not the proper one, has not treated the Italian practice as a breach of the treaty obligation necessarily requiring abrogation, has not abrogated the treaty or taken any step looking thereto, and has, on the contrary, constantly regarded the treaty as in full force and effect and has answered the obligations imposed thereby and has invoked the rights therein granted. It should, moreover, be observed that even though the action of the Italian Government be regarded as a breach of the treaty, the treaty is binding until abrogated, and therefore the treaty not having been abrogated, its provisions are operative against us.

The question would, therefore, appear to reduce itself to one of interpretation of the meaning of the treaty, the Government of the United States being now for the first time called upon to declare whether it regards the treaty as obliging it to surrender its citizens to Italy, notwithstanding Italy has not and insists it can not surrender its citizens to us. It should be observed, in the first place, that we have always insisted not only with reference to the Italian extradition treaty, but with reference to the other extradition treaties similarly phrased that the word "persons" includes citizens. We are, therefore, committed to that interpretation. The fact that we have for reasons already given ceased generally to make requisition upon the Government of Italy for the surrender of Italian subjects under the treaty, would not require of necessity that we should, as a matter of logic or law, regard ourselves as free from the obligation of surrendering our citizens, we laboring under no such legal inhibition regarding surrender as operates against the government of Italy. Therefore, since extradition treaties need not be reciprocal, even in the matter of the surrendering of citizens, it would seem entirely sound to consider ourselves as bound to surrender our citizens to Italy even though Italy should not, by reason of the provisions of her municipal law be able to surrender its citizens to us.

The executive department having thus elected to waive any right to free itself from the obligation to deliver up its own citizens, it is the plain duty of this court to recognize the obligation to surrender the appellant as one imposed by the treaty as the supreme law of the land and as affording authority for the warrant of extradition.

Judgment affirmed.

———

Chapter 14

TREATIES AND OTHER INTERNATIONAL AGREEMENTS IN THE CONSTITUTION-AL AND STATUTORY LAW OF THE UNITED STATES

The Vienna Convention on the Law of Treaties has contributed significantly to the modernization of the law about treaties; but when the result is compared with any modern, developed legal system's treatment of the law of conventional obligations (contract), it is apparent that the international legal system lags. On review, ask yourselves, where does it lag? Absent compulsory judicial process against an alleged treaty breacher or non-performer, how much more improvement is reasonably foreseeable?

Confining inquiry to the policing and enforcement of treaties as contracts between states, the contrast between the array of remedies in the Anglo–American national legal systems and their scarcity in the international legal system is marked. As at common law, before the rise of equity, damages are still the basic remedy in the international system. Justice Holmes and other jurists have played contrapuntally with the notion that the common law of contract gives a "bad man" an option to breach his undertaking and pay damages. But equity will put him in jail until he does carry out his undertaking in a number of situations that matter. The civil law system, however, never developed injunction and specific performance, although it resorts to criminal law in promise-enforcement more widely than the Anglo–American system does. We have seen, though, that a promisee state can use the pressure of withholding its performance pending compliance with undertaking on the other side. This toleration is, functionally, a kind of invalidation, and as such is a sanction beyond damages. Some added inducement to performance also comes from the law *in* treaties, when it is also internal law to be applied by national courts. Can you think of situations where a state wishing to rid itself of a treaty obligation might provoke or induce non-performance on the other side, or charge that side with a bad record of treaty performance?

Study the Constitution of the United States: Article I, Section 10; Article II, § 2; Article II, § 3; Article VI; and Amendment X, in the Doc. Supp.

Focus. This chapter presents the American way of dealing with international agreements. It is unique, in the unmodifiable, true sense of the word. Largely this is caused by U.S. institutions of federalism and separation of powers. Problems result beyond those dealt with in Chapter 13. We consider them here because they are not usually analyzed in any depth in courses on constitutional law. Moreover, as an American practitioner of international law, you cannot function without it. Non–U.S. lawyers must understand this to deal with Americans. Against the background of Chapter 13, we begin with the Constitution of 1789, as amended. Problems involving the difficulty of the federal government under the American Constitution in requiring the states to respect the obligations of the nation under international agreements were significant among the reasons for convening at Philadelphia in 1787 the convention that drafted the Constitution. Federal-state issues as to foreign affairs operations under treaties and other international agreements still exist, but by far the most difficult and numerous problems are those involving the federal legislative chambers, between themselves and between Congress and the President. Another vital issue is the role and authority of the Supreme Court to decide contentions as to the respective foreign affairs powers of the Congress and the President.

A point as to word usage: in Chapter 13 we saw that what one called an international agreement was not very important. But in United States foreign affairs law, *"treaty"* has a very specific and significant meaning; and all other international agreements are usually called "executive agreements," even though not always made by the President's branch alone.

SECTION A. THE CONSTITUTION, THE FOREIGN AFFAIRS POWER, AND TREATIES AS FEDERAL LAW

WORMUTH & FIRMAGE, TO CHAIN THE DOG OF WAR

Excerpts from 1–15, 192–93 (2d ed. 1989) (most footnotes omitted).*

It is usually said that the United States has contributed two inventions to political science: federalism and judicial review. And this is more or less true. But two other ideas which have played a great part in our constitutional history were not American in origin: checks and balances and the separation of powers.

Herodotus, writing in the fifth century B.C., established the familiar classification of governments—the government of the one, of the few, and of the many. In the next century Aristotle reported that "some, indeed, say that the best constitution is a combination of all existing forms, and they praise the Lacedaemonian because it is made up of oligarchy, monarchy, and democracy. * * * Thereafter the idea of the mixed state, as it has come to be called, became common. Polybius gave final expression to the classical conception in the second century B.C. Accepting Plato's theory of an inevitable cycle of revolutions throughout the three simple forms, he said that Lycurgus had contrived a mixed government for Sparta.

> The royal power was prevented from growing insolent by fear of the people, which had also assigned to it an adequate share in the constitution. The people in their turn were restrained from a bold contempt of the kings by fear of the Gerousia: the members of which, being selected on grounds of merit, were certain to throw their influence on the side of justice in every question that arose; and thus the party placed at a disadvantage by its conservative tendency was always strengthened and supported by the weight and influence of the Gerousia. The result of this combination has been that the Lacedaemonians retained their freedom for the longest period of any people with which we are acquainted. * * *

The constitution that Lycurgus had invented by "the light of reason," the Romans had achieved "through many struggles and difficulties, and by continually adopting reforms from knowledge gained in disaster."

> As for the Roman constitution, it had three elements, each of them possessing sovereign powers and their respective share of power in the whole state had been regulated with such a scrupulous regard to equality and equilibrium, that no one could say for certain, not even a native, whether the constitution as a whole were an aristocracy or democracy or despotism * * *. When any one of the

* Reprinted with the permission of the University of Illinois press.

three classes becomes puffed up, and manifests an inclination to be contentious and unduly encroaching, the mutual interdependency of all the three, and the possibility of the pretensions of any one being checked and thwarted by the others, must plainly check this tendency: and so the proper equilibrium is maintained by the impulsiveness of the one part being checked by the fear of the other * * *.

Julius Caesar destroyed the Roman mixed state, and Caesar Augustus erected * * * an absolute monarchy on the ruins. Thereafter, for more than sixteen centuries, the mixed state lived a purely literary life, and a very attenuated one; it was mentioned—rarely—as a possible form of government or—very rarely—as a characterization of an actual institutional system. It was restored to the field of active political discussion by Charles I in 1642, at the outbreak of the English Civil Wars, in his reply to the Nineteen Propositions of Parliament: "There being three kinds of government amongst men, absolute monarchy, aristocracy, and democracy, and all these having their particular conveniences and inconveniences * * *.

The ill of absolute monarchy is tyranny, the ill of aristocracy is faction and division, the ills of democracy are tumults, violence, and licentiousness. The good of monarchy is the uniting of a nation under one head to resist invasion from abroad, and insurrection at home: the good of aristocracy is the conjunction of counsel in the ablest persons of a state for the public benefit: the good of democracy is liberty, and the courage and industry which liberty begets."

The King was, of course, the monarchical element, the House of Lords the aristocratic, the House of Commons the democratic. The King was charged with the conduct of foreign relations, the power of appointment, the pardoning power, and other functions; the Lords had power of judicature; the Commons possessed the sole right to propose taxes and to impeach. All three participated in legislation.

The theory of the mixed state immediately became the usual characterization of the English constitutional system. Oliver Cromwell's second written constitution, the Humble Petition and Advice, was a copy of the Stuart constitution. This plan governed England from May 1657 to May 1659 with Oliver Cromwell—and, after his death, his son Richard— as Lord Protector, an elective House of Commons, and an "other House" of appointed members as a surrogate for the Lords. Nathaniel Fiennes, one of Cromwell's Commissioners of the Great Seal, addressed the Parliament of the new government in 1658. He praised the plan because the power of legislation was divided among the three branches. "If anything inconvenient should chance to slip out at one door, must it not pass two more, before it come abroad, to the detriment of the people?" * * * An eminent lawyer, Sir John Maynard, [from the] House of Commons, echoed Fiennes: "I would give my negative, if it were put, that we should have a free legislature within these walls * * *. There is nothing can be well done by man. A check is necessary upon us."

The Humble Petition and Advice was scuttled by the army in 1659; yet after a series of republican expedients failed, Charles Stuart was recalled from exile as King. For two hundred years thereafter England was a mixed monarchy. Sir William Blackstone, for example, wrote in his *Commentaries on the Laws of England:*

> And herein indeed consists the true excellence of the English government, that all parts of it form a mutual check upon each other. In the legislature, the people are a check upon the nobility, and the nobility a check upon the people, by the mutual privilege of rejecting what the other has resolved: while the king is a check upon both, which preserves the executive power from encroachments. And this very executive power is again checked and kept within bounds by the two houses, through the privilege they have of inquiring into, impeaching and punishing the conduct (not indeed of the king, which would destroy his constitutional independence; but, which is more beneficial to the public) of his evil and pernicious counsellors * * *. Like three distinct powers in mechanics, they jointly impel the machine of government in a direction different from what either, acting by itself, would have done, but at the same time in a direction partaking of each, and formed out of all, a direction which constitutes the true line of the liberty and happiness of the community.

But in the latter part of the eighteenth century it came to be recognized by the more acute observers that the King was dependent on the Commons and must appoint ministers acceptable to that body. And the King, under pressure from the Commons, could bring the Lords to terms by threatening to create more peers. Finally, in 1869 Walter Bagehot reported the extinction of the mixed state. * * *

Matters went quite otherwise in the United States. During the colonial period the virtues of the mixed state and of checks and balances were learned from the mother country. In 1784 John Adams published his *Defense of the Constitutions of the United States.* Adams lauded the partition of power established by all the state constitutions of the revolutionary period, Luther Martin, in his report to the Maryland legislature on the Constitutional Convention, said that the reviewers had justly observed that Adams "appears to be as fond of *checks* and *balances* as Lord Chesterfield of the Graces." * * * But Martin himself thought checks and balances appropriate to a state government; he merely protested that bicameralism was unnecessary to a simple confederation of states, which the United States had been under the Articles of Confederation and which he hoped they would continue to be.

In England, checks and balances reflected social divisions: monarchy, the aristocracy, and the commonalty. But in the United States there was neither a monarchy nor an aristocracy. In No. 14 of the *Federalist* James Madison asserted that America had shown that representation might be made the basis of "unmixed and extensive republics." He might have added that America had also shown that checks and balances might exist in an unmixed republic, balancing institutions rather than social classes against each other. The institutions that the framers of the Constitution counter-poised were determined by the theory of the separation of powers.

Frank J. Goodnow observed in 1914 that there were only two functions of government—the formulation of policy and the execution of policy. This analysis had first been stated during the English Civil Wars: the formulation of policy was assigned to the legislative power, and the execution of policy was attributed to what was called either the executive or the judicial power. At its first appearance the separation of powers was therefore a twofold separation.

The proposition that the two powers should be in separate hands was first stated by John Lilburne, the leader of the Levellers, a democratic political faction during the Civil Wars. In 1645 he was arrested and interrogated by a committee of the House of Commons; he insisted that he should be dealt with according to known rules of law. This could be insured only if those who made the law had no power to execute it. In 1649 he was interrogated by the Council of State, which was in effect a committee of the Rump House of Commons, and he offered a further argument for distinct personnel in the executive branch: Parliament should correct errors of the executive, but the benefit would be lost if the members of the executive sat in Parliament and judged the appeals.

Thereafter the propriety of separating the legislative power from the executive or judicial function became universally accepted. * * * The distinction of "the legislative from the ministerial authority" was "the most vital part of freedom."

John Locke, in his *Two Treatises of Government,* offers us a view of the Stuart constitution as modified by the radical political theory that had developed during the Civil Wars: the doctrines of social contract, of individualism and equality, and of the separation of powers. The principal omission is the theory of the mixed state. Locke wrote the major part of the book between 1679 and 1683 to express the philosophy of the Whig party in its contest with Charles II * * *. That publication was extremely influential; it not only justified the Glorious Revolution but also helped shape constitutional discussion in England and America in the eighteenth century. Locke wrote:

> In all Cases, whilst the Government subsists, *the Legislative is the Supreme Power.* For what can give Laws to another, must needs be superior to him: and since the Legislative is no otherwise Legislative of the Society, but by the right it has to make Laws for all the parts and for every Member of the Society, prescribing Rules to their actions, and giving power of Execution, where they are transgressed, the *Legislative* must needs be the *Supreme,* and all other Powers in any Members or parts of the Society, derived from and subordinate to it. [Locke, Two Treatises of Government 385–86 (Lasswell ed. 1907)]

There are two other powers of government. "But because the Laws, that are at once, and in a short time made, have a constant and lasting force, and need a *perpetual Execution,* or an attendance thereunto: Therefore 'tis necessary there should be a *Power always in being,* which should see to the *Execution* of the Laws that are made, and remain in force. And thus the *Legislative* and *Executive* Power come often to be separated." * * *

This therefore contains the Power of War and Peace, Leagues and Alliances, and all the Transactions, with all Persons and Communities without the Commonwealth, and may be called *Federative,* if any one pleases.

The executive power may be placed in the hands of several persons or of one, who may also have a share in the legislative power. But he is merely the *"Supreme Executor* of the Law," and if he violates law "and acts by his own private Will, he degrades himself, and is but a single private person without power, and without Will, that has any right to *Obedience;* the Members owing no Obedience but to the publick Will of the Society."

Locke, although he, like Lilburne, believed that "the Ruling Power ought to govern by *declared* and *received Laws,* and not by extemporary Dictates and undetermined Resolutions", trusted the legislative supremacy to accomplish this result. There was one feature of the Stuart constitution that Locke felt unable to disavow. The King had long claimed a "prerogative" to act outside—that is, contrary to—the law in cases of necessity. Locke wrote that: "there is a latitude left to the Executive power, to do many things of choice, which the Laws do not prescribe * * *.

The old Question will be asked, in this matter of who shall be Judge when this Power is made a right use of? I answer: Between an Executive Power in being, and a Legislative that depends upon his will for their convening, there can be no *Judge on Earth:* As there can be none, between the Legislative, and the People, should either the Executive, or the Legislative, when they have got the Power in their hands, design, or go about to enslave, or destroy them. The People have no other remedy in this, as in all other cases where they have no Judge on Earth, but to *appeal to Heaven.*

It may strike the reader that Locke made a bad choice in granting a prerogative to violate the law for the public good and leaving no remedy for abuse of this power other than revolution. The inconveniences of the absence of prerogative are surely outweighed by the inconveniences of revolution. But the alternatives were those suggested by seventeenth-century English history. As we shall see, American law has made a better choice than either.

The federative power survived as a distinct power only until Montesquieu. The judicial power as a third power of government appears to owe its origin to the course of events in the struggle between King and Lords, and also to the King. But the King could control the advice of Lords, and its decisions in lawsuits, by appointing pliant judges and removing those who proved obdurate, for the judges' commissions appointed them only * * * to hold office at the King's pleasure, rather than * * * while they conducted themselves well. This of course allowed the King to decide constitutional disputes in his own favor. The independence of the judiciary was not insured until the passage of the Act of Settlement in 1701. This act provided that "judges' commissions be made *quam diu se bene gesserini,* and their salaries ascertained and established, but upon the addresses of both houses of parliament it may be lawful to remove them * * *." The act did not deny that the judges were executive officers but passed on the assumption that special considerations should guarantee them security of tenure.

Montesquieu spent eighteen months in England between 1729 and 1731. There he became acquainted with English political doctrine—the political value of liberty, the separation of powers, the mixed state. These he worked into *l'Esprit des Lois,* which was published in 1748. He rather muddled the subject. He begins with Locke's threefold division of powers: legislative, executive, and federative; but the federative power—the executive power in matters governed by the law of nations—disappears from Montesquieu's discussion almost immediately, and the executive power proper is subdivided. This gives us our present threefold analysis of powers. The political value of liberty requires that these three be separated. When the legislative and executive powers are united in the same person, or in the same body of magistracy, there can be no liberty; because apprehensions may arise, lest the same monarch or senate should enact tyrannical laws, to execute them in a tyrannical manner.

> Again, there is no liberty, if the power of judging be not separated from the legislative and executive powers. Were it joined with the legislative, the life and liberty of the subject would be exposed to arbitrary control; for the judge would then be the legislator. Were it joined to the executive power, the judge might behave with all the violence of an oppressor.

Lilburne's primary motive for the separation of powers was to insure impartiality: the legislature should be confined to the making of general rules, and the executive to the enforcement of these rules. Locke shared this view, but his principal purpose in separating the executive from the legislature was to make the King subject to the representative body, the Parliament. The first paragraph quoted from Montesquieu suggests Lilburne's view, but not clearly. Montesquieu may be repeating an English political axiom without thoroughly understanding it. Nor is he clear on the judicial power. He begins by putting it in the hands of the prince or magistrate but then separates it, lest the judge "behave with all the violence of an oppressor." Then he goes on to place the judicial power not in the hands of the magistrate, but in the control of a jury. And he concludes the whole discussion by saying: "Of the three powers above-mentioned the judiciary is *en quelque façon nulle* [in a way nothing]. There remain therefore only two; and as they have need of a regulating power to temper them, the part of the legislative body composed of the nobility, is extremely proper for this very purpose." Montesquieu then expatiates on the virtues of British mixed monarchy, where the executive power is in the King, and the legislative power in the King and a bicameral Parliament.

In his Commentaries on the Laws of England, Sir William Blackstone used the idea of checks and balances and the seventeenth-century twofold separation of powers, joined with the rule that counseled the independence of the judiciary. In his famous argument in the *Case of Writs of Assistance* in 1761, James Otis employed the same analysis and said that the "executive courts" must pass into disuse acts of Parliament that violated the British constitution. * * * The first New Hampshire constitution, of 1776, spoke of the "executive courts." As late as 1827 Chief Justice John Marshall spoke of "the judicial power as part of the executive."

But Montesquieu's was the dominant analysis in America. The first constitutions of Virginia, Maryland, North Carolina, Georgia, and Massachusetts, and the second constitution of New Hampshire, decreed that the legislative, executive, and judicial powers were and should remain distinct. This was more easily decreed than accomplished. In his *Notes on the State of Virginia,* first published in 1785, Thomas Jefferson, a former governor of the state, complained of "very capital defects" in the constitution. The principal defect was the fact that the constitution had been adopted by the legislature, and its provisions might be altered by any subsequent act of the legislature.

> The judiciary and the executive were left dependent on the legislative, for their subsistence in office, and some of them for their continuance in it. If therefore the legislature assumes executive and judiciary powers, no opposition is likely to be made; nor, if made, can it be effectual, because in that case they may put their proceedings into the form of an act of assembly, which will render them obligatory on the other branches. They have, accordingly, in many instances, decided rights which should have been left to judicial controversy: and the direction of the executive, during the whole time of their session, is becoming habitual and familiar. T. Jefferson, Notes on the State of Virginia 120 (Paden., ed. 1955).

To remedy this defect, Jefferson proposed that "the powers of government should be so divided and balanced among several bodies of magistracy, so that no one could transcend their legal limits, without being effectually checked and restrained by the others." So Jefferson called in checks and balances—not, as previously, of social classes, but of governmental institutions—to safeguard the separation of powers. Madison adopted the same argument in No. 48 of the *Federalist,* describing the arrangements he thought would perhaps accomplish the desired result. * * * The executive, legislative, and judicial officers should draw their authority from the people through channels having no communication with one another; the method of choosing the judiciary, however, offered difficulties. The legislature should consist of two branches chosen by different methods of election; perhaps the weaker branch of the legislature, the Senate, should have "some qualified connection" with the executive to assist it in defending its rights against the more popular branch of the legislature. In addition, the executive should have a "qualified veto" over acts of legislation. To these internal checks of the national government he added the states as further checks, and he revived the argument of No. 10 of the *Federalist:* in an extensive republic, interests would be so numerous that a tyrannical majority would not come into existence.

In No. 78 of the *Federalist* Alexander Hamilton completed the argument on checks and balances. In a discussion of the judiciary he quoted Montesquieu, "There is no liberty, if the power of judging be not separated from the legislative and executive powers." In a constitution that limits legislative power, the judiciary must pronounce legislative acts contrary to the constitution as void, for the constitution is a fundamental law, and the courts must prefer it to a statute inconsistent with it. Jefferson had expressed the same opinion two years earlier in his answer to the inquiries of Jean Nicolas Démeunier, who was compiling an article on the United States for the *Encyclopedia Methodique*. Repeating his complaint that people considered the constitution of Virginia an ordinary statute because it had been created by the legislature, and therefore many laws inconsistent with the constitution had been passed, Jefferson said, "I have not heard that in the other states they have ever infringed their constitutions; and I suppose they have not done it; as the judges would consider any law void, which was contrary to the constitution." [Thomas Jefferson, The Papers of Thomas Jefferson at X, ____ & XIV, ____ (Boyd ed. 1954).]

Like Madison, Jefferson believed that "the tyranny of the legislature is the most formidable dread at present." (Id.) * * * But at the Constitutional Convention of 1787 the liveliest apprehension centered on the executive. The Convention began its task with a consideration of the Virginia plan presented by Governor Edmund Randolph of Virginia. This called for a National Executive chosen by the National Legislature, but it did not specify as to whether the executive should consist of one or several persons. Randolph, however, "opposed a unity" in the executive. He regarded it as "the foetus of monarchy." James Wilson, the most vigorous champion of placing the executive power in a single person, argued, "Unity in the Executive instead of being the foetus of Monarchy would be the best safeguard against tyranny." The New Jersey plan provided for a collegial executive, but the plan offered by Charles Pinckney of South Carolina called for a President. At various times during the Convention, Randolph and George Mason spoke for a collegial executive but lost on two votes. * * * However, some of the most influential members of the Convention favored associating a council with the President. The Virginia plan had proposed a Council of Revision to exercise a qualified veto over legislation. This was not adopted, but James Madison, Benjamin Franklin, Gouverneur Morris, Elbridge Gerry, Roger Sherman, and John F. Mercer spoke for an executive council or Privy Council or Council of State. There was no agreement on the composition of the body or its powers. Most of the members seem to have thought of it as advisory, but Madison would have given the President "liberty to depart from their Opinion at his peril." * * * Morris would have created a Council of State composed of the chief justice and the secretaries of named departments. * * * His proposal shrank into the passage in Article II, Section 2 of the Constitution. "He [the President] may require the Opinion, in writing, of the principal Officer in each of the executive Departments, upon any Subject relating to the duties of their respective Offices * * *."

* * *

* * * *[The] treaty-making power* is allocated between the executive and legislative branches, reflecting the intent of the framers for a partnership in the conduct of foreign relations. But while the Constitution provides that the President "shall have Power, by and with the Advice and Consent of the Senate, to make treaties, provided two-thirds of the senators present concur," the Constitution does not indicate how the President is to "make" treaties or how the Senate is to give its advice and consent to presidential action. This lack of specificity on how the treaty power was to be exercised is probably the result of the fact that the framers simply assumed that the international customs and practices of their time would be the model for treaty making under the Constitution. * * * This assumption is supported by the fact that the treaty-making process received but little consideration in the Constitutional Convention.

[Authority to Negotiate Treaties] As a consequence of the lack of constitutional guidelines on how the treaty power is to be exercised, the treaty-making process has evolved as a matter of custom. For the most part, the President exclusively has exercised the power to negotiate treaties," and it is now commonly accepted that neither the Senate nor the Congress as a whole has the authority to enter into the negotiating process. In addition to the President's power to "make treaties," the President's constitutional power to "receive Ambassadors and other public Ministers" is customarily cited as a basis for this exclusive executive power of negotiation.

[The Senate's Advice & Consent] Once a treaty has been negotiated, it is submitted by the President to the Senate. The Senate does not formally advise the President on the treaty but rather exercises its "advice and consent" power by either accepting or rejecting the treaty as submitted or by amending it in some form. * * * Once the Senate has approved a treaty, the President may then "make" the treaty by formally concluding it with the nation(s) with which it was negotiated. The President, however, is free not to conclude a treaty that the Senate has approved, as when the Senate approves a treaty in amended form.

There is no *definition of a treaty* in the Constitution, apparently because the framers saw no need to define what was well known to them in international law. * * * The status of treaties in national law, however, was specified in the supremacy clause: "All Treaties made, or which shall be made, under the authority of the United States, shall be the supreme Law of the Land * * *." Thus the Supreme Court has regarded treaties as being legally equivalent to the laws of Congress. The traditional rule is that an act of Congress will therefore supersede a prior treaty obligation, while a treaty will likewise supersede a previously enacted statute.

———

Preliminary questions, based on the Constitution. Does Congress have a role in the conduct of foreign affairs? What is it? May Congress negotiate with other states? Directly? Indirectly? May Congress impose limitations or prior restraints on the President's power to negotiate? How, if at all? Are any such limitations on restraints unconstitutional? Will/should the federal court system attempt to decide such an issue?

In the first constitution, the Articles of Confederation, Congress and judiciary were the entire federal government. Working through its committees, Congress appointed and received envoys, negotiated international agreements, made and carried out foreign policy. Thus Congress was once master as to all the foreign affairs of the United States. What has Congress lost in this sector from the decision of the convention to separate the executive and legislative powers of government and assign the former to a President? How clean-cut is the separation as to foreign affairs (a) policy, (b) operations? Did the framers of the present Constitution answer the question: *"Who is master as to foreign affairs"*? If not, why not? *If so, how*? If not, how are the two branches to work together in the foreign affairs field?

The Constitution gives Congress the power to declare war and raise and support armed forces. It makes the President the commander-in-chief of such forces. If the President wants to deploy American forces in State X but Congress does not want to, what happens?

In Britain, Parliament tamed the monarchy through the money power. The Constitution gives the Congress the money power (taxing and appropriating federal funds). *Is it legitimate for Congress to use the money power to control American foreign policy*?

WARE v. HYLTON

Supreme Court of the United States, 1796.
3 U.S. (3 Dall.) 199, 220, 1 L.Ed. 568.

CHASE, Justice.—The Defendants in error, on the 7th day of July, 1774, passed their penal bond to Farrell and Jones, for the payment of £.2,976 11 6, of good British money; but the condition of the bond, or the time of payment, does not appear on the record.

On the 20th of October, 1777, the legislature of the commonwealth of Virginia, passed a law to sequester British property. In the 3d section of the law, it was enacted, "that it should be lawful for any citizen of Virginia, owing money to a subject of Great Britain, to pay the same, or any part thereof, from time to time, as he should think fit, into the loan office, taking thereout a certificate for the same, in the name of the creditor, with an indorsement, under the hand of the commissioner of the said office, expressing the name of the payer; and shall deliver such certificate to the governor and the council, whose receipt shall discharge him from so much of the debt. And the governor and the council shall, in like manner, lay before the General Assembly, once in every year, an account of these certificates, specifying the names of the persons by, and for whom they were paid; and shall see to the safe keeping of the same; subject to the future directions of the legislature: provided, that the governor and the council may make such allowance, as they shall think reasonable, out of the interest of the money so paid into the loan office, to the wives and children, residing in the state, of such creditor."

On the 26th of April, 1780, the Defendants in error, paid into the loan office of Virginia, part of their debt, to wit, 3,111 1–9 dollars, equal to £.933 14 0 Virginia currency; and obtained a certificate from the commissioners of the loan office, and a receipt from the governor and the council of Virginia, agreeably to the above, in part recited law.

The Defendants in error being sued, on the above bond, in the Circuit Court of Virginia, pleaded the above law, and the payment above stated, in bar of so much of the Plaintiff's debt. The plaintiff, to avoid this bar, replied the fourth article of the Definitive Treaty of Peace, between Great Britain and the United States, of the 3d of September, 1783. To this replication there was a general demurrer and joinder. The Circuit Court allowed the demurrer, and the plaintiff brought the present writ of error.

The case is of great importance, not only from the property that depends on the decision, but because the effect and operation of the treaty are necessarily involved. I wished to decline sitting in the cause, as I had been council, some years ago, in a suit in Maryland, in favour of American debtors; and I consulted with my brethren, who unanimously advised me not to withdraw from the bench. I have endeavored to divest myself of all former prejudices, and to form an opinion with impartiality. I have diligently attended to the arguments of the learned council. * * * I have given the subject, since the argument, my deliberate investigation, and shall, (as briefly as the case will permit,) deliver the result of it with great diffidence, and the highest respect for those, who entertain a different opinion. I solicit, and I hope I shall meet with, a candid allowance for the many imperfections, which may be discovered in observations hastily drawn up, in the intervals of attendance in court, and the consideration of other very important cases.

The first point raised by the council for the Plaintiff in error was, that the legislature of Virginia had no right to make the law, of the 20th October, 1777 * * *. If this objection is established, the judgment of the Circuit Court must be reversed; because it destroys the Defendant's plea in bar, and leaves him without defence to the Plaintiff's action.

This objection was maintained on different grounds by the Plaintiff's council. One of them contended, that the legislature of Virginia had no right to confiscate any British property, because Virginia was part of the dismembered empire of Great Britain, and the Plaintiff and Defendants were, all of them, members of the British nation, when the debt was contracted, and therefore, that the laws of independent nations do not apply to the case; and, if applicable, that the legislature of Virginia was not justified by the modern law and practice of European nations, in confiscating private debts. In support of this opinion, he cited Vattel who expresses himself thus: "The sovereign has naturally the same right over what his subjects may be indebted to enemies. Therefore, he may confiscate debts of this nature, if the term of payment happen in the time of war. But at present, in regard to the advantage and safety of Commerce, all the sovereigns of Europe have departed from this rigour * * * "

* * *

I am of opinion that the exclusive right of confiscating, during the war, all and every species of British property, within the territorial limits of Virginia, resided only in the Legislature of that commonwealth. * * *

* * *

The 4th article of the treaty is in these words: "It is agreed that creditor, on either side, shall meet with no lawful impediment to the recovery of the full value, in sterling money, of all bona fide debts, heretofore contracted."

* * * I will adopt the following remarks, which I think applicable, and which may be found in Dr. Rutherforth and Vattel. * * * The intention of the framers of the treaty, must be collected from a view of the whole instrument, and from the words made use of by them to express their intention, or from probable or rational conjectures. If the words express the meaning of the parties plainly, distinctly, and perfectly, there ought to be no other means of interpretation; but if the words are obscure, or ambiguous, or imperfect, recourse must be had to other means of interpretation, and in these three cases, we must collect the meaning from the words, or from probable or rational conjectures, or from both. When we collect the intention from the words only, as they lie in the writing before us, it is a literal interpretation; and indeed if the words, and, the construction of a writing, are clear and precise, we can scarce call it interpretation to collect the intention of the writer from thence. The principal rule to be observed in literal interpretation, is to follow that sense, in respect both of the words, and the construction, which is agreeable to common use.

* * *

WILSON, Justice.

* * *

* * * Even if Virginia had the power to confiscate, the treaty annuls the confiscation. The fourth article is well expressed to meet the very case: it is not confined to debts existing at the time of making the treaty; but is extended to debts heretofore contracted. It is impossible by any glossary, or argument, to make the words more perspicuous, more conclusive, than by a bare recital. Independent, therefore, of the Constitution of the United States, (which authoritatively inculcates the obligation of contracts) the treaty is sufficient to remove every impediment founded on the law of Virginia. The State made the law; the State was a party to the making of the treaty: a law does nothing more than express the will of a nation; and a treaty does the same. Under this general view of the subject, I think the judgment of the Circuit Court ought to be reversed.

[The court agreed, although some justices found the plight of the debtor who had paid his debt under the law of Virginia, very troublesome. The opinion of Justice Tredell is particularly anguished.]

———

MISSOURI v. HOLLAND

United States, Supreme Court, 1920.
252 U.S. 416, 40 S.Ct. 382, 64 L.Ed. 641.

Mr. Justice HOLMES delivered the opinion of the court.

This is a bill in equity brought by the State of Missouri to prevent a game warden of the United States from attempting to enforce the Migratory Bird Treaty Act of July 3, 1918, and the regulations made by the Secretary of Agriculture in pursuance of the same. The ground of the bill is that the statute is an unconstitutional interference with the rights reserved to the States by the Tenth Amendment, and that the acts of the defendant done and threatened under that authority invade the sovereign right of the State and contravene its will manifested in statutes. The State also alleges a pecuniary interest, as owner of the wild birds within its borders and otherwise, admitted by the Government to be sufficient, but it is enough that the bill is a reasonable and proper means to assert the alleged quasi sovereign rights of a State. A motion to dismiss was sustained by the District Court on the ground that the act of Congress is constitutional. The State appeals.

On December 8, 1916, a treaty between the United States and Great Britain was proclaimed by the President. It recited that many species of birds in their annual migrations traversed certain parts of the United States and of Canada, that they were of great value as a source of food and in destroying insects injurious to vegetation, but were in danger of extermination through lack of adequate protection. It therefore provided for specified close[d] seasons and protection in other forms, and agreed that the two powers would take or propose to their law-making bodies the necessary measures for carrying the treaty out. The above mentioned Act of July 3, 1918, entitled an act to give effect to the convention, prohibited the killing, capturing or selling any of the migratory birds included in the terms of the treaty except as permitted by regulations compatible with those terms, to be made by the Secretary of Agriculture. Regulations were proclaimed [in] 1918. It is unnecessary to go into any details, because, the question raised is the general one whether the treaty and statute are void as an interference with the rights reserved to the States.

To answer this question it is not enough to refer to the Tenth Amendment, reserving the powers not delegated to the United States, because by Article II, § 2, the power to make treaties is delegated expressly, and by Article VI treaties made under the authority of the United States, along with the Constitution and laws of the United States made in pursuance thereof, are declared the supreme law of the land. If the treaty is valid there can be no dispute about the validity of the statute under Article I, § 8, as a necessary and proper means to execute the powers of the Government. The language of the Constitution as to the supremacy of treaties being general, the question before us is narrowed to an inquiry into the ground upon which the present supposed exception is placed.

It is said that a treaty cannot be valid if it infringes the Constitution, that there are limits, therefore, to the treatymaking power, and that one such limit is that what an act of Congress could not do unaided, in derogation of the powers reserved to the States, a treaty cannot do. An earlier act of Congress that attempted by itself and not in pursuance of a treaty to regulate the killing of migratory birds within the States had been held bad in the District Court. Those decisions were supported by arguments that migratory birds were owned by the States in their sovereign capacity for the benefit of their people, and that under cases like Geer v. Connecticut, this control was one that Congress had no power to displace. The same argument is supposed to apply now with equal force.

Whether the two cases cited were decided rightly or not they cannot be accepted as a test of the treaty power. Acts of Congress are the supreme law of the land only when made in pursuance of the Constitution, while treaties are declared to be so when made under the authority of the United States. It is open to question whether the authority of the United States means more than the formal acts prescribed to make the convention. We do not mean to imply that there are no qualifications to the treaty-making power; but they must be ascertained in a different way. It is obvious that there may be matters of the sharpest exigency for the national well being that an act of Congress could not deal with but that a treaty followed by such an act could, and it is not lightly to be assumed that, in matters requiring national action, "a power which must belong to and somewhere reside in every civilized government" is not to be found. What was said in that case with regard to the powers of the States applies with equal force to the powers of the nation in cases where the States individually are incompetent to act. We are not yet discussing the particular case before us but only are considering the validity of the test proposed. With regard to that we may add that when we are dealing with words that also are a constituent act, like the Constitution of the United States, we must realize that they have called into life a being the development of which could not have been foreseen completely by the most gifted of its begetters. It was enough for them to realize or to hope that they had created an organism; it has taken a century and has cost their successors much sweat and blood to prove that they created a nation. The case before us must be considered in the light of our whole experience and not merely in that of what was said a hundred years ago. The treaty in question does not contravene any prohibitory words to be found in the Constitution. The only question is whether it is forbidden by some invisible radiation from the general terms of the Tenth Amendment. We must consider what this country has become in deciding what that Amendment has reserved.

The State as we have intimated founds its claim of exclusive authority upon an assertion of title to migratory birds, an assertion that is embodied in statute. No doubt it is true that as between a State and its inhabitants the State may regulate the killing and sale of such birds, but it does not follow that its authority is exclusive of paramount powers. To put the claim of the State upon title is to lean upon a slender reed. Wild birds are not in the possession of anyone; and possession is the beginning of ownership. The whole foundation of the State's rights is the presence within their jurisdiction of birds that yesterday had not arrived, tomorrow may be in another State and in a week a thousand miles away. If we are to be accurate we cannot put the case of the State upon higher ground than that the treaty deals with creatures that for the moment are within the state borders, that it must be carried out by officers of the United States within the same territory, and that but for the treaty the State would be free to regulate this subject itself.

As most of the laws of the United States are carried out within the States and as many of them deal with matters which in the silence of such laws the State might regulate, such general grounds are not enough to support Missouri's claim. Valid treaties of course "are as binding within the territorial limits of the States as they are elsewhere throughout the dominion of the United States." No doubt the great body of private relations usually fall within the control of the State, but a treaty may override its power. We do not have to invoke the later developments of constitutional law for this proposition; it was recognized early with regard to statutes of limitation, and even earlier, as to confiscation, in Ware v. Hylton. It was assumed by Chief Justice Marshall with regard to the escheat of land to the State in Chirac v. Chirac. So as to a limited jurisdiction of foreign consuls within a State. Wildenhus's Case. It only remains to consider the application of established rules to the present case.

Here a national interest of very nearly the first magnitude is involved. It can be protected only by national action in concert with that of another power. The subject-matter is only transitorily within the State and has no permanent habitat therein. But for the treaty and the statute there soon might be no birds for any powers to deal with. We see nothing in the Constitution that compels the Government to sit by while a food supply is cut off and the protectors of our forests and our crops are destroyed. It is not sufficient to rely upon the States. The reliance is vain, and were it otherwise, the question is whether the United States is forbidden to act. We are of opinion that the treaty and statute must be upheld.

Decree affirmed. Mr. Justice VAN DEVANTER and Mr. Justice PITNEY dissent.

REID v. COVERT

United States Supreme Court, 1957.
354 U.S. 1, 77 S.Ct. 1222, 1 L.Ed.2d 1148.

Mr. Justice BLACK announced the judgment of the Court and delivered an opinion, in which The Chief Justice, Mr. Justice DOUGLAS, and Mr. Justice BRENNAN join.

These cases raise basic constitutional issues of the utmost concern. They call into question the role of the military under our system of government. They involve the power of Congress to expose civilians to trial by military tribunals, under military regulations and procedures, for offenses against the United States thereby depriving them of trial in civilian courts, under civilian laws and procedures and with all the safeguards of the Bill of Rights. These cases are particularly significant because for the first time since the adoption of the Constitution wives of soldiers have been denied trial by jury in a court of law and forced to trial before courts-martial.

* * * Mrs. Clarice Covert killed her husband, a sergeant in the United States Air Force, at an airbase in England. Mrs. Covert, who was not a member of the armed services, was residing on the base with her husband at the time. She was tried by a court-martial for murder under Article 118 of the Uniform Code of Military Justice (UCMJ). The trial was on charges preferred by Air Force personnel and the court-martial was composed of Air Force officers. The court-martial asserted jurisdiction over Mrs. Covert under Article 2(11) of the UCMJ, which provides: "The following persons are subject to this code: * * * (11) Subject to the provisions of any treaty or agreement to which the United States is or may be a party or to any accepted rule of international law, all persons serving with, employed by, or accompanying the armed forces without the continental limits of the United States * * *."

Counsel for Mrs. Covert contended that she was insane at the time she killed her husband, but the military tribunal found her guilty of murder and sentenced her to life imprisonment. The judgment was affirmed by the Air Force Board of Review, but was reversed by the Court of Military Appeals, because of prejudicial errors concerning the defense of insanity. While Mrs. Covert was being held in this country pending a proposed retrial by court-martial in the District of Columbia, her counsel petitioned the District Court for a writ of habeas corpus to set her free on the ground that the Constitution forbade her trial by military authorities. Construing this Court's decision in *U.S. ex rel. Toth v. Quarles,* as holding that "a civilian is entitled to a civilian trial" the District Court held that Mrs. Covert could not be tried by court-martial and ordered her released from custody. The Government appealed directly to this Court under 28 U.S.C.A. § 1252.

* * * Mrs. Dorothy Smith killed her husband, an Army officer, at a post in Japan where she was living with him. She was tried for murder by a court-martial and despite considerable evidence that she was insane was found guilty and sentenced to life imprisonment. The judgment was approved by the Army Board of Review, and the Court of Military Appeals. Mrs. Smith was then confined in a federal penitentiary in West Virginia. Her father, respondent here, filed a petition for habeas corpus in a District Court for West Virginia. The petition charged that the court-martial was without jurisdiction because Article 2(11) of the UCMJ was unconstitutional insofar as it authorized the trial of civilian dependents accompanying servicemen overseas. The District Court refused to issue the writ, and while an appeal was pending in the Court of Appeals

for the Fourth Circuit we granted certiorari at the request of the Government.

The cases were consolidated and argued last Term and a majority of the Court, with three Justices dissenting and one reserving opinion, held that military trial of Mrs. Smith and Mrs. Covert for their alleged offenses was constitutional. The majority held that Article III and the Fifth and Sixth Amendments which require that crimes be tried by a jury after indictment by a grand jury did not protect an American citizen when he was tried by the American Government in foreign lands for offenses committed there and that Congress could provide for the trial of such offenses in any manner it saw fit so long as the procedures established were reasonable and consonant with due process. The opinion then [expressed] the view that military trials, as now practiced, were not unreasonable or arbitrary when applied to dependents accompanying members of the armed forces overseas. In reaching their conclusion the majority found it unnecessary to consider the power of Congress "To make Rules for the Government and Regulation of the land and navel Forces" under Article I of the Constitution.

* * * The Court granted a petition for rehearing. Now, after further argument and consideration, we conclude that the previous decisions cannot be permitted to stand. We hold that Mrs. Smith and Mrs. Covert could not constitutionally be tried by military authorities.

* * *

At the time of Mrs. Covert's alleged offense, an executive agreement was in effect between the United States and Great Britain which permitted United States' military courts to exercise exclusive jurisdiction over offenses committed in Great Britain by American servicemen or their dependents.[29] For its part, the United States agreed that these military courts would be willing and able to try and to punish all offenses against the laws of Great Britain by such persons. In all material respects, the same situation existed in Japan when Mrs. Smith killed her husband. Even though a court-martial does not give an accused trial by jury and other Bill of Rights protections, the Government contends that Art. 2(11) of the UCMJ, insofar as it provides for the military trial of dependents accompanying the armed forces in Great Britain and Japan, can be sustained as legislation which is necessary and proper to carry out the United States' obligations under the internation-

---

29. Executive Agreement of July 27, 1942. The arrangement now in effect in Great Britain and the other NATO nations, as well as in Japan, is the NATO Status of Forces Agreement, T.I.A.S. 2846, which by its terms gives the foreign nation primary jurisdiction to try dependents accompanying American servicemen for offenses which are violations of the law of both the foreign nation and the United States. Art. VII, §§ 1(b), 3(a). The foreign nation has exclusive criminal jurisdiction over dependents for offenses which only violate its laws. Art. VII, § 2(b). However, the Agreement contains provisions which require that the foreign nations provide procedural safeguards for our nationals tried under the terms of the Agreement in their courts. Art. VII, § 9.

Apart from those persons subject to the Status of Forces and comparable agreements and certain other restricted classes of Americans, a foreign nation has plenary criminal jurisdiction, of course, over all Americans—tourists, residents, businessmen, government employees and so forth—who commit offenses against its law within its territory.

al agreements made with those countries. The obvious and decisive answer to this, of course, is that no agreement with a foreign nation can confer power on the Congress, or on any other branch of Government, which is free from the restraints of the Constitution. Article VI, the Supremacy Clause of the Constitution, declares: "This Constitution, and the Laws of the United States which shall be made in Pursuance thereof; and all Treaties made, or which shall be made, under the Authority of the United States, shall be the supreme Law of the Land * * *."

There is nothing in this language which intimates the treaties and laws enacted pursuant to them do not have to comply with the provisions of the Constitution. Nor is there anything in the debates which accompanied the drafting and ratification of the Constitution which even suggests such a result. These debates as well as the history that surrounds the adoption of the treaty provision in Article VI make it clear that the reason treaties were not limited to those made in "pursuance" of the Constitution was so that agreements made by the United States under the Articles of Confederation, including the important peace treaties which concluded the Revolutionary War, would remain in effect. It would be manifestly contrary to the objectives of those who created the Constitution, as well as those who were responsible for the Bill of Rights—let alone alien to our entire constitutional history and tradition—to construe Article VI as permitting the United States to exercise power under an international agreement without observing constitutional prohibitions. In effect, such construction would permit amendment of that document in a manner not sanctioned by Article V. The prohibitions of the Constitution were designed to apply to all branches of the National Government and they cannot be nullified by the Executive or by the Executive and the Senate combined.

There is nothing new or unique about what we say here. This Court has regularly and uniformly recognized the supremacy of the Constitution over a treaty. For example, in Geofroy v. Riggs * * * it declared:

> The treaty power, as expressed in the Constitution, is in terms unlimited except by those restraints which are found in that instrument against the action of the government or of its departments, and those arising from the nature of the government itself and of that of the States. [It cannot extend] so far as to authorize what the Constitution forbids, or a change in the character of the government or in that of one of the States, or a cession of any portion of the territory of the latter, without its consent.

This Court has also repeatedly taken the position that an Act of Congress, which must comply with the Constitution, is on a full parity with a treaty, and that when a statute which is subsequent in time is inconsistent with a treaty, the statute to the extent of conflict renders the treaty null.[34] It would be completely anomalous to say that a treaty

---

34. In Whitney v. Robertson, the Court stated: "By the Constitution a treaty is placed on the same footing, and made of like obligation, with an act of legislation. Both are declared by that instrument to be the supreme law of the land, and no superior efficacy is given to either over the other * * *. [I]f the two are inconsistent, the

need not comply with the Constitution when such an agreement can be overridden by a statute that must conform to that instrument.

There is nothing in Missouri v. Holland, [*supra*], which is contrary to the position taken here. There the Court carefully noted that the treaty involved was not inconsistent with any specific provision of the Constitution. The Court was concerned with the Tenth Amendment which reserves to the States or the people all power not delegated to the National Government. To the extent that the United States can validly make treaties, the people and the States have delegated their power to the National Government and the Tenth Amendment is no barrier.

In summary, we conclude that the Constitution in its entirety applied to the trials of Mrs. Smith and Mrs. Covert. Since their court-martial did not meet the requirements of Art. III, § 2 or the Fifth and Sixth Amendments we are compelled to determine if there is anything within the Constitution which authorizes the military trial of dependents accompanying the armed forces overseas.

* * *

* * * The judgment of the District Court directing that Mrs. Covert be released from custody is affirmed. The judgment of the District Court is reversed and the case is remanded with instructions to order Mrs. Smith released from custody. Reversed and remanded. Mr. Justice WHITTAKER took no part in the consideration or decision of these cases. Mr. Justice FRANKFURTER, concurring in the result.

* * *

A further argument is made that a decision adverse to the Government would mean that only a foreign trial could be had. Even assuming that the NATO Status of Forces Agreement, covering countries where a large part of our armed forces are stationed, gives jurisdiction to the United States only through its military authorities, this Court cannot speculate that any given nation would be unwilling to grant or continue such extraterritorial jurisdiction over civilian dependents in capital cases if they were to be tried by some other manner than court-martial. And, even if such were the case, these civilian dependents would then merely be in the same position as are so many federal employees and their dependents and other United States citizens who are subject to the laws of foreign nations when residing there.

* * *

[Opinion of Mr. Justice HARLAN, concurring in the result, omitted.] Mr. Justice CLARK, with whom Mr. Justice BURTON joins, dissenting.

* * *

Before discussing the power of the Congress under Art. I, § 8, cl. 14, of the Constitution it is well to take our bearings. * * * [No question of] U.S. jurisdiction of a military court-martial sitting within U.S. territorial limits [is involved]. * * * The power of the Government to make treaties or the legal relationship between treaties and the Consti-

one last in date will control the other
* * *." [*See also*], Head Money Cases.

tution [is not at issue]. Nor are they concerned with the power of Congress to provide for the trial of Americans sojourning, touring, or temporarily residing in foreign nations. * * * We are to determine only whether the civilian dependents of American servicemen may constitutionally be tried by an American military court-martial in a foreign country for an offense committed in that country.

* * *

The only alternative remaining—probably the alternative that the Congress will now be forced to choose—is that Americans committing offenses on foreign soil be tried by the courts of the country in which the offense is committed. Foreign courts have exclusive jurisdiction under the principles of international law and many nations enjoy concurrent jurisdiction with the American military authorities pursuant to Article VII of the [SOFA] of Parties to NATO. Where the American military authorities do have jurisdiction, it is only by mutual agreement with the foreign sovereign concerned and pursuant to carefully drawn agreements conditioned on trial by the American military authorities. Typical of these agreements was the one concluded between the United States and Japan [in] 1952, and in force at the time one of these cases arose. Under this and like agreements, the jurisdiction so ceded to the United States military courts will surely be withdrawn if the services are impotent to exercise it. It is clear that trial before an American court-martial in which the fundamentals of due process are observed is preferable to leaving American servicemen and their dependents to the widely varying standards of justice in foreign courts throughout the world. Under these circumstances it is untenable to say that Congress could have exercised a lesser power adequate to the end proposed.

* * *

———

1. *"In Reid v. Covert, Justice Black held:* 'The United States is entirely a creature of the Constitution. Its power and authority have no other source. It can only act in accordance with all the limitations imposed by the Constitution.' Although Justice Black wrote for only four justices, the opinions of the two concurring justices and the two dissenting justices implied agreement with this general proposition. Three years later, in *Kinsella v. U.S.,* Justice Whittaker and Justice Stewart announced their adhesion to the proposition stated by Black in Reid v. Covert." *See* H. Koh, *Why the President (Almost) Always Wins in Foreign Affairs: Lessons of the Iran–Contra Affair,* 97 Yale L.J. 1255, 1261–63 (1988); Randall, *The Treaty Power,* 51 Ohio St.L.J. 1089 (1990).

2. *Questions on the constitutionality of the human rights conventions.* a. *Are there constitutional impediments to the United States becoming a party to the human rights conventions sponsored by the United Nations at least without reservations?* Refer in particular to the following conventions in the Doc. Supp. Economic, Social and Cultural Rights; Civil and Political Rights; Elimination of All Forms of Racial Discrimination. Consider for example,

Article 4 of the Convention on Racial Discrimination and Article 19 of the Convention on Civil and Political Rights. Is Article 5 of the Convention on Civil and Political Rights relevant to the question of the constitutionality of that convention as a whole? The U.S. Senate recently gave its Advice & Consent to the Genocide Convention and the International Covenant on Civil & Political Rights, but with expansive reservations, relating to the Senate's impression of their unconstitutionality. See Chapter 10, on Human Rights, and Chapter 13, on Treaties.

b. ***Do the human rights treaties embody a bargain with foreign states? Must they, to be within the treaty power?*** If a treaty does not involve a bargaining of concessions between the negotiating states, some have argued that it cannot involve a matter of international concern. If a putative treaty does not involve such a matter, the argument continues, the arrangement is not really a treaty within the meaning of the Constitution. Hence the overriding power given to the federal government in Article VI, clause 2, is not activated. This argument assumes that a decision maker, presumably a court, would pass on the question, whether the supposedly necessary international concern, exists in the particular case. Is this evaluation a proper function for courts in the United States? How would the Supreme Court go about making a determination as to whether a treaty was or was not a matter of international concern? The concern about international content as a constitutional requirement has greatly diminished. It is rejected in the 1987 Restatement, Section 302, Comment c.

Even if the courts will not review a treaty at the constitutional level on the basis of whether there is an international concern, senators in giving their advice and consent to the treaty are also obligated, by their oath of office, to consider the question. Even if the senators should find that the treaty is satisfactory in this respect, it lies within their responsibility and prerogative, to determine whether the treaty is, nonetheless, undesirable from a policy point of view.

c. ***Between roughly 1948 and 1953, a determined effort was made by a group of senators, elements of the American Bar Association, and others to amend the Constitution to limit the internal legal effect of treaties on the federal legislative power.*** The political history of the period shows that the proponents of the *Bricker Amendment* (named for the Ohio senator who led the fight) were neo-isolationists in general alignment. Many also had a serious concern lest the conventions on human rights then being negotiated in the United Nations be given internal effect within the United States in such matters as segregated education and travel facilities. The amendment effort failed, not too long before the Supreme Court, in 1954, interpreted the due process and equal protection clauses of the 5th and 14th Amendments to prohibit different treatment based on race in public education, thus setting the stage for the general dismantling of all forms of racial discrimination involving state action. In other areas of socio-political discrimination, such as to gender, disability, disease, and age, the potential of the treaty power as an alternative path to legalizing anti-discrimination at the federal level (thus imposing the legal change on the states) still exists. Should the treaty power be used in this way, if neither formal amendment nor judicial interpretation occurs? Objection might possibly go beyond the political to a revival of constitutional arguments against such use to change the allocation of federal-state powers. Is there a residual or ultimate inherent limitation on the use of the treaty power to achieve internal socio-political change? What might it be?

———

EDWARDS v. CARTER

United States Court of Appeals, District of Columbia Circuit, 1978.
580 F.2d 1055, cert. denied, 436 U.S. 907.

PER CURIAM: This is an appeal from the District Court's dismissal of a challenge to appellee's use of the treaty power to convey to the Republic of Panama United States properties, including the Panama Canal, located in the Panama Canal Zone.[1] Appellants, sixty members of the House of Representatives, sought a declaratory judgment that the exclusive means provided in the Constitution for disposal of United States property requires approval of both Houses of Congress, see Art. IV, § 3, cl. 2, and that therefore the Panama Canal Zone may not be returned to Panama through the Treaty process, which invests the treaty-making power in the President by and with the advice and consent of two-thirds of the Senators present, see Art. II, § 2, cl. 2. Appellee contends that the Constitution permits United States territory

---

1. *Property Transfer and Economic Participation by the Republic of Panama*

1. Upon termination of this Treaty, the Republic of Panama shall assume total responsibility for the management, operation, and maintenance of the Panama Canal, which shall be turned over in operating condition and free of liens and debts, except as the two Parties may otherwise agree.

2. The United States transfers, without charge, to Panama all right, title and interest the United States may have with respect to all real property, including non-removable improvements thereon, as set forth below:

(a) Upon the entry into force of this Treaty, the Panama Railroad and such property that was located in the former Canal Zone but that is not within the land and water areas the use of which is made available to the United States pursuant to this Treaty. However, it is agreed that the transfer on such date shall not include buildings and other facilities, except housing, the use of which is retained by the United States pursuant to this Treaty and related agreements, outside such areas;

(b) Such property located in an area or a portion thereof at such time as the use by the United States of such area or portion thereof ceases pursuant to agreement between the two Parties.

(c) Housing units made available for occupancy by members of the Armed Forces of Panama paragraph 5(b) of Annex B to the Agreement in Implementation of Article IV of this Treaty at such time as such units are made available to Panama.

(d) Upon termination of this Treaty, all real property and non-removable improvements that were used by the United States for the purposes of this Treaty and related agreements and equipment related to the management, operation and maintenance of the Canal remaining in Panama.

3. Panama agrees to hold the United States harmless with respect to any claims which may be made by third parties relating to rights, title and interest in such property.

4. Panama shall receive, in addition, from the Panama Canal Commission a just and equitable return on the national resources which it has dedicated to the efficient management, operation, maintenance, protection and defense of the Panama Canal * * *.

to be disposed of either through congressional legislation or through the treaty process, and that therefore the President's decision to proceed under the treaty power is constitutionally permissible. * * *

* * * For the reasons appearing below, we affirm the dismissal of the complaint, not on the jurisdictional ground relied on by the District Court but for failure to state a claim on which relief may be granted.

I

* * *

* * * [T]he precise question we address is whether the constitutional delegation found in Art. IV, § 3, cl. 2 is exclusive so as to prohibit the disposition of United States property by self-executing treaty—i.e., a treaty enacted in accordance with Art. II, § 2, cl. 2, which becomes effective without implementing legislation.

II

Article IV, § 3, cl. 2, in its entirety: "The Congress shall have Power to dispose of and make all needful Rules and Regulations respecting the Territory or other Property belonging to the United States; and nothing in this Constitution shall be so construed as to Prejudice any Claims of the United States, or of any particular State."

Appellants contend that this clause gives Congress exclusive power to convey to foreign nations any property, such as the Panama Canal, owned by the United States. We find such a construction to be at odds with the wording of this and similar grants of power to the Congress, and, most significantly, with the history of the constitutional debates.[4]

The grant of authority to Congress under the property clause states that "The Congress shall have Power * * *," not that only the Congress shall have power, or that the Congress shall have exclusive power. In this respect the property clause is parallel to Article I, § 8, which also states that "The Congress shall have Power * * *." Many of the powers thereafter enumerated in § 8 involve matters that were at the time the Constitution was adopted, and that are at the present time, also commonly the subject of treaties. The most prominent example of this is the regulation of commerce with foreign nations, Art. I, § 8, cl. 3, and appellants do not go so far as to contend that the treaty process is not a constitutionally allowable means for regulating foreign commerce. It thus seems to us that, on its face, the property clause is intended not to restrict the scope of the treaty clause, but, rather, is intended to permit

---

4. The Senate Foreign Relations Committee has thoroughly considered and rejected appellants' argument. That Committee reported the treaties with Panama to the full Senate by a 14 to 1 vote, and the one dissenting Senator did not dispute the power of the President, by and with the advice and consent of two-thirds of the Senate present, to transfer United States property. In addition to the American Law Institute's Restatement of Foreign Relations Law, see infra, other authorities in agreement with this conclusion include Professor Louis Henkin, see L. Henkin, Foreign Affairs and the Constitution 159–60 (1965); Professor Covey Oliver, Hearings Before the Committee on Foreign Relations, Part IV, at 95, 103, 112–13 (Jan. 19, 1978).

Congress to accomplish through legislation what may concurrently be accomplished through other means provided in the Constitution.

* * *

There are certain grants of authority to Congress which are, by their very terms, exclusive. In these areas, the treaty-making power and the power of Congress are not concurrent; rather, the only department of the federal government authorized to take action is the Congress. For instance, the Constitution expressly provides only one method—congressional enactment—for the appropriation of money: "No Money shall be drawn from the Treasury, but in Consequence of Appropriations made by Law." Art. I, § 9, cl. 7. Thus, the expenditure of funds by the United States cannot be accomplished by self-executing [a] treaty; implementing legislation appropriating such funds is indispensable. Similarly, the constitutional mandate that "all Bills for raising Revenue shall originate in the House of Representatives," Art. I, § 7, cl. 1, appears, by reason of the restrictive language used, to prohibit the use of the treaty power to impose taxes.

These particular grants of power to Congress operate to limit the treaty power because the language of these provisions clearly precludes any method of appropriating money or raising taxes other than through the enactment of laws by the full Congress. This is to be contrasted with the power-granting language in Art. I, § 8, and in Art. IV, § 3, cl. 2. Rather than stating the particular matter of concern and providing that the enactment of a law is the only way for the federal government to take action regarding that matter, these provisions state simply that Congress shall have power to take action on the matters enumerated.

Thus it appears from the very language used in the property clause that this provision was not intended to preclude the availability of self-executing treaties as a means for disposing of United States property. The history of the drafting and ratification of that clause confirms this conclusion. The other clause in Art. IV, § 3 concerns the procedures for admission of new states into the Union, and the debates at the Constitutional Convention clearly demonstrate that the property clause was intended to delineate the role to be played by the central government in the disposition of Western lands which were potential new states. Several individual states had made territorial claims to portions of these lands; and as finally enacted the property clause, introduced in the midst of the Convention's consideration of the admission of new states, sought to preserve both federal claims and conflicting state claims to certain portions of the Western lands.

The proceedings of the Virginia state ratifying convention provide further evidence of the limited scope of the property clause. During a debate in which the meaning of the clause was questioned, Mr. Grayson noted that the sole purpose for including this provision was to preserve

a. The self-executing treaty problem in United States law is mainly one of determining *when* a treaty is or is not self-executing. In this case the court is really dealing with the constitutional-level question: When can the President and two-thirds of the Senate, by treaty alone, deprive the House of Representatives of participation in a decision?

the property rights of the states and the federal government to the Western territory as these rights existed during the Confederation.

This history demonstrates the limited concerns giving rise to the inclusion of Article IV, § 3, cl. 2 in the Constitution. Whether or not this historical perspective might serve as a basis for restricting the scope of congressional power under the property clause, we view it as persuasive evidence for rejecting the claim that Article IV is an express limitation on the treaty power, foreclosing the availability of that process as a constitutionally permissible means of disposing of American interests in the Panama Canal Zone.

* * *

IV

In view of the lack of ambiguity as to the intended effects of the treaty and property clauses, it may be surprising that judicial pronouncements over the past two centuries relating to these constitutional provisions are somewhat vague and conflicting. However, none of the actual holdings in these cases addressed the precise issue before us—whether the property clause prohibits the transfer of United States property to foreign nations through self-executing treaties. While, therefore, neither the holdings nor the dicta of these previous cases are dispositive of the case before us, we believe that in the main they support the conclusions we have stated heretofore.

* * *

As is true of most of the cases in which the Supreme Court has addressed the scope of the treaty power * * * involved the federal government's interaction with Indian tribes. Because of the sui generis nature of the relationship between the Indian tribes and the federal government, it might be argued that these decisions are not dispositive. We think, however, that they are persuasively supportive of the authority of the President and the Senate under the treaty clause.

V

While certain earlier judicial interpretations of the interplay between the property clause and the treaty clause may be somewhat confused and less than dispositive of the precise issue before us, past treaty practice is thoroughly consistent with the revealed intention of the Framers of these clauses. In addition to the treaties with Indian tribes upheld in the cases discussed above, there are many other instances of self-executing treaties with foreign nations, including Panama, which cede land or other property assertedly owned by the United States. That some transfers have been effected through a congressional enactment instead of, or in addition to, a treaty signed by the President and ratified by two-thirds of the Senate present lends no support to appellants' position in this case, because, self-executing treaties and congressional enactments are alternative, concurrent means provided in the Constitution for disposal of United States property.

For instance, the Treaty with Panama of 1955, transferred certain property (a strip of water and other sites within the Canal Zone) to

Panama without concurring legislation by the Congress, while transfer of other property (owned by the United States but within the jurisdiction of Panama) was, under the terms of the treaty itself, dependent upon concurring legislation by the Congress. The decision to cast some but not all of the articles of conveyance in non-self-executing form was a policy choice; it was not required by the Constitution.

The transfer of property contemplated in the current instance is part of a broader effort in the conduct of our foreign affairs to strengthen relations with another country, and indeed with the whole of Latin America. The Framers in their wisdom have made the treaty power available to the President, the chief executant of foreign relations under our constitutional scheme, by and with the advice and consent of two-thirds of the members of the Senate present, as a means of accomplishing these public purposes. We do not think it is relevant that many previous treaties couched in self-executing terms have been different in scope, dealing with boundary issues or otherwise ceding land which was claimed both by the United States and by a foreign nation.   * * *

    * * *

[Thus], the judgment of the District Court dismissing the complaint is Affirmed.

[Dissenting opinion of MacKINNON, Circuit Judge, omitted.]

SECTION B. EXECUTIVE AGREEMENTS AND THE CONSTITUTION

---

1. PRESIDENTIAL POWER

The President, the Senate and the House of Representatives. What institutions of the federal government should participate in the formulation of foreign policy and in the making of internal law by international agreement? Despite the experience of President Washington, detailed below, Senate leaders in recent years have contended that the power as to advice and consent to treaties gives the Senate a special role of collaboration with the executive in the formulation of United States foreign policy, even where no specific international agreement is involved. Leaders of the House of Representatives have not shown enthusiasm for this concept of senatorial special responsibility.

Sometimes, as in the case of tax treaties, the special responsibility of the House as to revenue measures is respected by the practice of making such treaties subject to the enactment of tax legislation by Congress. Further, in a revenue measure, Congress delegates to the executive, before the fact, the power to make certain types of international agreements, such as those for the reduction of tariffs or the elimination of non-tariff trade barriers. These delegations fix time limits, state maximum cuts and require periodic reports to Congress. More recently, they specify procedural steps. See Ch. 15, Section A.

Concern as to the possibility that executive agreements not authorized bicamerally by Congress might force it to go along with the President, both as to foreign policy choices and as to internal legal effects, has from time to time been voiced in both chambers. The Senate has been more active institutionally in this regard than the House. In 1971, the Senate Committee on Foreign Relations held hearings [a] that are still significant because they covered many aspects of a basic problem of legislative participation in foreign affairs, from taxing and appropriating, through oversight of past executive actions, to the use of international agreements and the formulation of congressional foreign policy preferences. Other legislation, requiring seasonable reports from the President, is now in place, and in 1986–87 lay at the heart of the Reagan Administration's "Iran–Contragate" crisis.

---

2 SCHWARTZ, A COMMENTARY ON THE CONSTITUTION OF THE UNITED STATES: THE POWERS OF GOVERNMENT 101, 150 (1963) *

The conception of the Senate as a Presidential council in the diplomatic field broke down as soon as it was tried in practice. In August, 1789, Washington came personally to the Senate to seek its advice on a proposed treaty. As might have been expected, an independent legislative chamber (even one composed of only twenty-six members) was scarcely suited to perform the role of Council of State. Instead of giving the President the speedy advice he sought, the Senators made lengthy speeches on the procedure to be followed. "This defeats every purpose of my coming here!" Washington exclaimed. As he left the Senate Chamber, he is reported to have declared "That he would be damned if he ever went there again." The account is probably apocryphal, but the fact remains that, after Washington's experience in this respect, neither he nor any other President ever again sought the formal advice of the Senate on a proposed negotiation. The concept of the Senate as an executive council in the field of foreign affairs was thus all but still-born at the outset of the Republic.

* * *

That an executive agreement can, in fact, be employed to accomplish the identical purpose as a treaty covering the same subject-matter is dramatically demonstrated by Theodore Roosevelt's action in connection with a proposed treaty with the Dominican Republic. Plenipotentiaries of the two countries had signed an agreement in 1905 in treaty form providing for the collection and disbursement of Dominican customs revenues. The treaty was submitted to the Senate, but that body failed to give its constitutional consent. President Roosevelt then proceeded to put the proposed treaty provisions into effect as an executive agreement.

---

a. Hearings Before the Senate Committee on Foreign Relations on S. 596, 92nd Cong., First Sess., Oct. 20–21, 1971.

* © Bernard Schwartz 1962; reprinted by permission of the publisher, The Macmillan Company, New York.

As T.R. put it in his Autobiography: "Somebody had to do that duty, and accordingly I did it. I went ahead and administered the proposed treaty anyhow, considering it as a simple agreement on the part of the Executive." Does the fact that he "did it" make it Constitutional?

How easy would the President Theodore Roosevelt gambit be now? A few presidential exercises of the executive agreement alternative in earlier times fed a viewpoint much emphasized by the proponents of the Bricker amendment, that important international matters are dealt with by executive agreements, not Article II treaties, and that, in any event, the two modalities are interchangeable at the option of the President. It is doubtful that the first belief was ever true, and as to the second, consider the classification of executive agreements that follows, as well as the legislation that has been enacted since the first Roosevelt president acted so independently. Could any president whom you personally remember have gotten away with the gambit?

Examine the connection between the rise of legislation requiring the President to keep the Congress informed on foreign affairs operations, including executive agreements, and the carrot-stick inducement used by Congress in the Trade Act of 1974, i.e., the fast-track procedure of Section 151 of that Act.

WORMUTH & FIRMAGE, TO CHAIN THE DOG OF WAR
at 181–191, 198–200 (footnotes omitted).*

Articles I and II of the Constitution reveal the intent of the framers to give Congress the dominant hand in the establishment of basic policy regarding foreign relations. It has been observed that a stranger reading the Constitution would obtain little idea of the vast authority actually exercised by the President today. The constitutional text and the accounts of the Philadelphia Convention also make it clear that the framers envisioned a foreign affairs partnership between the two political branches. The treaty power, viewed (inaccurately as it turned out) as the major means by which our foreign relations were to be conducted * * * rests with the Senate and the President. Moreover, the ambiguities and potential overlaps of authority in the constitutional grants of power * * * as well as the theory of mixed powers articulated by some of the framers * * * provide additional evidence of the framers' anticipation: a foreign policy system emerging out of cooperation and conflict would be slow to take major steps, would lack consensus between the political branches. Finally, the constitutional text does not address all the issues that can be raised about authority in foreign affairs, indicating—or perhaps simply dictating—that custom would also play a role in the development of the allocation of power in foreign relations.

Thus, while some powers to act in foreign affairs are expressly granted, some may be implied from textual grants of power, and still

* (Reprinted with the permission of the University of Illinois press).

others, seemingly without any basis in the Constitution, have been "created" as a result of decades of custom and practice in the political branches. The outcome of this process is that the President almost certainly exercises greater authority over the conduct of foreign affairs than was contemplated by the framers of the Constitution. This acquisition of power by the executive proceeded at a rapid pace from the earliest days of the Republic and was aided and abetted by a Congress that recognized the natural advantages held by the executive branch. Nevertheless, in those areas where Congress has been granted clear authority, it has been given the final and authoritative word. Moreover, to recognize that presidents have on occasion robbed Congress and overstepped constitutional bounds in the process of check, balance, and accommodation previously described, is not to say that the precedents necessarily legitimate such acts. The secrecy with which some executive acts have been accomplished indicates that even the actors recognized the disparity between their acts and their legal authority.

Power in foreign relations is divided between the branches of the national government and is possessed largely by the political branches; however, the war power, meaning the power to decide on war and to authorize its initiation, resides in Congress. The executive, under the commander-in-chief powers, performs vital functions. But the decision for or against war resides with Congress. * * * In the Constitution, the powers of Congress to "provide for the common defense," to "raise and support armies," to "provide and maintain a navy," to "regulate commerce with foreign nations," to "define and punish piracies and felonies committed on the high seas, and offenses against the law of nations," to "grant letters of marque and reprisal," to "make rules concerning captures on land and water," to "make rules for the government and regulation of land and naval forces," to "provide for organizing, arming, and disciplining the militia, and for governing such part of them as may be employed in the service of the United States," to "provide for calling forth the militia to execute the laws of the union," to "suppress insurrections and repeal invasions," to "make all laws which shall be necessary and proper for carrying into execution the foregoing powers," and, most important, to "declare war"—all leave the executive war powers to be exercised largely within parameters determined by Congress. The textual grant of power to Congress to "declare war" provides, with only one qualification (the right of self-defensive response to sudden attack upon the U.S. and its armed forces), the exclusive power to initiate war. * * *

Some authors have attempted to bolster the claim for presidential war power by relying on the contention that the President is the "sole organ" of American foreign policy. According to this argument, the President's broad responsibility for America's foreign policy justified acting in the nation's interest by intervening in Vietnam. * * * A brief review of the history of the sole organ doctrine is therefore warranted.

John Marshall, speaking in the House of Representatives in defense of controversial action taken by President Adams, first described the President as "the sole organ of the nation in its external relations, and its sole representative with foreign nations." President Adams had given written instructions to a federal judge that a British deserter held in custody by a United States circuit court should be turned over to British authorities in accordance with extradition provisions of the Jay Treaty." In response to inaccurate charges that the President had actually delivered up an American citizen who had been impressed into British service, Marshall gave a speech outlining the facts of the case and the various legal arguments in support of the President's acts." At no time during Marshall's speech did he assert that the President's exclusive power to communicate with other nations on behalf of the United States involved power to make foreign policy.

It was Justice Sutherland who first attempted to read substantive power into the phrase. In *Curtiss–Wright*, Sutherland used Marshall's "sole organ" language to bolster his argument that the traditional prohibition against the delegation of legislative power to the President does not apply in the area of foreign affairs. In a relatively brief discussion, Sutherland moved from the accepted proposition that "the President alone has the power to speak or listen as a representative of the nation" to finding justification for the challenged delegation of authority in part in "the very delicate, plenary and exclusive power of the President as the sole organ of the federal government in the field of international relations." * * *

Just as Sutherland's theory of extra-constitutional power has been repudiated by the Supreme Court, his statements concerning the delegation doctrine and the President's authority as sole organ have been severely qualified. Two judicial statements bear repetition here. First, Justice Jackson, concurring in the *Steel Seizure Case*, reduced *Curtiss–Wright* to the holding that it would be unwise to require Congress "to lay down narrowly definite standards by which the President is to be governed." Chief Justice Warren later observed that *Curtiss–Wright* does not mean that Congress "can grant the Executive totally unrestricted freedom of choice." It is clear then that the sole organ language has been limited in its effect to a statement that the nature of the conduct of foreign relations, and the President's power over communications with foreign nations, ought to be taken into account in determining whether Congress, in granting the President contingent power, has provided sufficient statutory guidelines for presidential action. In short, *Curtiss–Wright* has been read as dealing with constitutional limits on the power of Congress, and its dictum on "sole organ" has been abandoned.

Viewed in this light, the sole organ doctrine is not novel constitutional theory. Other early officers of state had agreed with Marshall that the President held exclusive power to communicate officially with other nations * * * and this power has been continually recognized. It is also true that the President's control of the foreign affairs bureaucracy, recognized power to negotiate treaties and otherwise communicate officially with other nations, and authority to grant or withhold diplomatic recognition of other states, necessarily undermine the traditional claim that the President merely conducts foreign relations while Congress alone formulates foreign policy. Indeed, it has been correctly observed that "a President could not conduct foreign relations without thereby making foreign policy." More important, presidents do in fact formulate American foreign policy. * * *

But to acknowledge that the President makes foreign policy is a far cry from the assertion that he or she is the sole foreign policymaker. Set against the "sole organ" doctrine is what has been described as the "foreign affairs power" of Congress. It has been observed that "[n]o one knows the reaches" of this power—a power that, when combined with the generous grants of power to Congress specified in Article I, has enabled Congress to enact legislation covering a wide variety of subjects relating to the nation's foreign affairs.

Beginning with the debate between "Helvidius" (Madison) and "Pacificus" (Hamilton), recurring discussions have disputed whether Congress or the President should be dominant in determining "the condition of the nation" or in formulating American foreign policy. As part of this dialogue, Congress has frequently asserted its right to declare national policy in foreign affairs—whether by proclaiming American neutrality in times of war, repudiating treaties or directing Presidents to terminate treaties, recognizing the independence of nations formerly dominated by external powers, or directing Presidents to send delegates to international conferences and outlining the objectives to be sought and the limits of the delegates' authority. In 1864, the House of Representatives resolved:

> Congress has a constitutional right to an authoritative voice in declaring and prescribing the foreign policy of the United States, as well in the recognition of new Powers as in other matters; and it is the constitutional duty of the executive department to respect that policy, not less in diplomatic negotiations than in the use of national forces when authorized by law; and the propriety of any declaration of foreign policy by Congress is sufficiently proved by the vote which pronounces it. * * *

The "Helvidius" position has received other strong endorsements historically. In a famous 1906 debate with Senator John Spooner, Senator Augustus Bacon contended that "Congress and not the President is supreme under the Constitution in the control of foreign affairs." More recently, Senator Fulbright has maintained that, while we must acknowledge the inevitable overlap between shaping foreign policy and conducting foreign relations, Congress must no longer default on its duty "to participate actively in determining policy objectives and in the making of significant decisions."

Most significant, the Supreme Court has lent strength to the contention that Congress is the sovereign voice in determining the law and policy of the nation in its external relations. In 1889, in the *Chinese Exclusion Case*, the Supreme Court upheld the power of Congress to exclude aliens, despite the lack of any express constitutional grant of such power, on the ground that Congress could employ the "powers which belong to independent nations." Since then, the Court has frequently referred to these inherent powers of sovereignty sustaining congressional enactments and has suggested that these powers are held by the legislative branch. In *Perez v. Brownell*, the Court upheld a statute imposing loss of nationality to an American citizen for voting in a political election of a foreign state, using this reasoning: "Although there is in the Constitution no specific grant to Congress of power to enact legislation for the effective regulation of foreign affairs, there can be no doubt of the existence of this power in the law-making order of the Nation." Other judicial statements lend strength to the concept of sovereign power over foreign relations and provide additional support for the view that such sovereignty resides in Congress. On the other hand, the President has no power to change the law or even the applicability of comity in foreign affairs. [*See Sabbatino*].

1 O'CONNELL, INTERNATIONAL LAW

206 (2d ed. 1970).*

* * * If, in [U.S.] constitutional law, a mere agreement is not a treaty, and thereby does not require Senate endorsement, the President may, by resort to informal methods of contracting, oblige the nation without the democratic control that the legislative process aims at. Actually the President is rarely so isolated in the matter of executive agreements from Congressional action of some sort as to be independent of legislative control or approval. The term "executive agreement" is a wide one, designed to mark off the boundary between treaties which require the advice and consent of the Senate and those documents, widely but loosely described in international practices as "treaties," which do not. Three main categories of instruments are comprehended: (a) agreements or understandings entered into pursuant to or in accordance with specific directives or authorisation of Congress given antecedently; (b) those not given effect to without such direction or authorisation given subsequently; and (c) those made by the Executive solely in virtue of its constitutional power. Actually, those in the third category are relatively few. The critics of the executive agreements, therefore, must be taken to be attacking, not principally the dangers of Presidential commitment without legislative check, so much as the constitutional rule concerning the effect internally on the States of informal international agreements; implied in the argument is that State sovereignty is insufficiently protected by Joint Resolution of both Houses, and that the more obstructive process of a two-thirds Senate majority is necessary. The principal example of an executive agreement in the third category was the Litvinov Agreement between President Roosevelt and the Soviet Ambassador which affected suits between private claimants and the Soviet. * * *

        * * *

The question is whether an international commitment of the United States is required by the Constitution to be in treaty as distinct from agreement form. The question is usually resolved on an ad hoc basis by consultation between the Executive and Congress, taking into account

* Reprinted with the permission of Stevens & Sons, Ltd., London.

the extent to which the agreement can be carried out by the former without encroaching on the domain of the latter. * * *

———————

Comments upon O'Connell's classification. Recognition that not all American executive agreements are based upon presidential claims to inherent power did not begin with Professor O'Connell. Their tripartite classification had been noted by writers and courts prior to its use in 1965 Restatement. Even so, the O'Connell analysis was influential in two respects: (i) it differentiated clearly the issue of interchangeability of executive agreements with Senate-approved treaties and the issue of executive agreements as sources, or not, of internal law; (ii) it analyzed the uses made of executive agreements of the various classes in foreign affairs operations. O'Connell's research showed that presidents have not widely interchanged treaties and wholly-presidential executive agreements (*à la* Theodore Roosevelt). It disproved Bricker amendment-era assertions that treaties were used by presidents for relatively secondary matters and executive agreements for highly significant ones. It also supports the view that even presidents know when they cannot act internally on the basis of international agreement. Finally, it shows how often, in important matters, the President and the whole Congress, through presidential negotiation and congressional delegation or ratification, have combined forces in categories 1 and 2.

Unfortunately, Professor O'Connell's research in this area has not been updated. Nevertheless, the validity of his analysis can be checked as to particular instances by examination of a very useful research tool for American law in treaties, the Department of State yearly publication, Treaties in Force—A List of Treaties and Other International Agreements of the United States in Force. The late Professor O'Connell's analysis and classification of United States executive agreements has been useful in clarifying the situation. It has been particularly admired, because Professor O'Connell worked normally in the [British] Commonwealth environment as to domestic effects of international agreements. At the time of his last writing on the subject, Professor O'Connell expressed the belief that Congress and the President had worked out a protocol of general applicability as to their roles in the making of various types of executive agreements. Has time proved him right in this? Does the fast track procedure for international trade agreements support his hypothesis? Is it perhaps true that the choice between modalities of cooperation (or co-existence) between the legislative and executive branches in the United States has narrowed to either a bicameral, simple majorities legislative approval of an executively negotiated international agreement of the non-treaty type, or to presidential-senate cooperation on a non-self-executing treaty followed by bicameral implementation by bill or joint resolution?

———————

WORMUTH & FIRMAGE, TO CHAIN THE DOG OF WAR
196–200 (2d ed. 1989).*

Because the "sole organ" rationale is properly disregarded as a justification for the practice of entering into international agreements without Senate approval, scholars have sought to justify the practice on other grounds. One theory posits that the authority to enter into such agreements falls within a "zone of twilight" between presidential and congressional powers. This "zone of twilight," according to the theory, "may be occupied by Congress at will." The failure of Congress to fill this gray area, however, leaves a void which the President may fill. Presidential authority to enter into executive agreements has also been justified as a concomitant of the powers as commander in chief and chief executive. A recurring issue in this area is whether a given international agreement should be embodied in treaty form or in the form of an executive agreement. *United States v. Belmont* has been interpreted by some as intimating that the permissible scope of executive agreements is virtually coextensive with that of treaties. Since so much attention has centered on the case, it requires extended discussion.

It has long been the task of the chief executive of a nation, under the rules of international law, to seek the satisfaction of the claims of its nationals against a foreign state by diplomatic negotiation. In 1918 the Soviet Union confiscated the property of Russian corporations abroad and also nationalized without compensation the property of American nationals within the USSR. A Russian corporation had a sum of money on deposit in the Belmont Bank in New York in 1918. In 1933 President Roosevelt made an agreement by which he recognized the Soviet government. The Soviet government transferred its claims of property in the United States, including the deposit in the Belmont Bank, to the United States, and the Soviet government recognized the claims of American citizens affected by the confiscation. It was agreed that after the rival claims had been computed, whichever government had gained an advantage would pay the surplus to the other. Thus the American creditors would at last gain satisfaction. The Belmont Bank refused to pay the deposit to the United States, alleging that it was founded on confiscation and that the public policy of New York did not recognize claims resulting from confiscation. In United States v. Belmont in 1937, the Supreme Court, in an opinion by Justice Sutherland, held that the recognition validated the Soviet confiscation under the act of state doctrine, and the executive agreement transferred the Soviet claim to the United States. Sutherland said: "But an international compact, as this was, is not always a treaty which requires the consent of the Senate. There are many such compacts, of which a protocol, a modus vivendi, a postal convention, and agreements like that now under consideration are illustrations."

Moore uses the term protocol to signify the adjustment of inconsiderable claims of citizens and also to describe agreements as to the

---

* Reprinted with the permission of University of Illinois, press.

purpose and scope of future negotiations. A modus vivendi is a provisional agreement pending formal legal action. Moore speaks of postal conventions as agreements made by the postmaster general with the advice and consent of the President under the authority of an act of Congress of 1872. By "agreements like that now under consideration" Sutherland must have referred to numerous agreements detailed by Moore to obtain the satisfaction of the claims or guarantee of the rights of American citizens. In short, the Belmont case introduced no new principle. Since the recognition and the assignment of the Soviet claim were valid at national law, the public policy of no state could stand against them.

UNITED STATES DEPARTMENT OF STATE
CIRCULAR NUMBER 175

50 American Journal of International Law 784 (1956).*

1. Purpose of Circular: 1.1 The purpose of this circular is to insure (a) that the function of making treaties and other international agreements is carried out within traditional and constitutional limits; (b) that the objectives to be sought in the negotiation of particular treaties and other international agreements are approved by the Secretary or Under Secretary; (c) that firm positions resulting from negotiations are not undertaken without the approval of the interested Assistant Secretaries or their Deputies; (d) that the final texts developed are approved by the interested Assistant Secretaries or their Deputies and brought to the attention of the Secretary or Under Secretary a reasonable time before signature; and (e) that authorization to sign the final text is secured and appropriate arrangements for signature are made.

* * *

2. Scope of the Treaty–Making Power: Treaties should be designed to promote United States interests by securing action by foreign governments in a way deemed advantageous to the United States. Treaties are not to be used as a device for the purpose of effecting internal social changes or to try to circumvent the constitutional procedures established in relation to what are essentially matters of domestic concern.

3. Scope of the Executive Agreement–Making Power: Executive agreements shall not be used when the subject matter should be covered by a treaty. The executive agreement form shall be used only for agreements which fall into one or more of the following categories:

    a. Agreements which are made pursuant to or in accordance with existing legislation or a treaty;

    b. Agreements which are made subject to Congressional approval or implementation; or

* Reprinted with the permission of the American Society of International Law.

    c.   Agreements which are made under and in accordance with the President's Constitutional power.

* * *

TRANSMITTAL OF UNITED STATES INTERNATIONAL AGREEMENTS TO CONGRESS
1 U.S.C. 112b.

§ 112b.   United States international agreements; transmission to Congress: (a) The Secretary of State shall transmit to the Congress the text of any international agreement (including the text of any oral international agreement, which agreement shall be reduced to writing), other than a treaty, to which the United States is a party, as soon as practicable after such agreement has entered into force with respect to the United States but in no event later than sixty days thereafter. However, any such agreement the immediate public disclosure of which would, in the opinion of the President, be prejudicial to the national security of the United States shall not be so transmitted to the Congress but shall be transmitted to the Committee on Foreign Relations of the Senate and the Committee on International Relations of the House of Representatives under an appropriate injunction of secrecy to be removed only upon due notice from the President. Any department or agency of the United States Government which enters into any international agreement on behalf of the United States shall transmit to the Department of State the text of such agreement not later than twenty days after such agreement has been signed.

(b) Not later than March 1, 1979, and at yearly intervals thereafter, the President shall, under his own signature, transmit to the Speaker of the House of Representatives and the chairman of the Committee on Foreign Relations of the Senate a report with respect to each international agreement which, during the preceding year, was transmitted to the Congress after the expiration of the 60–day period referred to in the first sentence of subsection (a), describing fully and completely the reasons for the late transmittal.

(c) Notwithstanding any other provision of law, an international agreement may not be signed or otherwise concluded on behalf of the United States without prior consultation with the Secretary of State. Such consultation may encompass a class of agreements rather than a particular agreement.

(d) The Secretary of State shall determine for and within the executive branch whether an arrangement constitutes an international agreement within the meaning of this section.

(e) The President shall, through the Secretary of State, promulgate such rules and regulations as may be necessary to carry out this section.

The evolution of Circular 175 (1955). Circular 175 superseded an earlier Circular 25 of 1953. Both were mollifying executive responses to the Bricker amendment controversy, as the text of paragraphs 2 and 3 of Circular 175 show. To this end also, it established a procedure for keeping track of international commitments made in the Department of State. Circular 175 was, however, insufficient to head off the congressional requirement supra, that all executive agreements be reported to the House and Senate; and after the legislation was in effect, the Circular 175 procedure reinforced the reporting requirement. The Foreign Affairs Manual (excerpted below) goes into more procedural detail than Circular 175, pulling together various internal operational instructions and procedures not within the original Circular 175. The manual's opening paragraph (720.1) refers to it as "a codification of the substance" of Circular 175. The admonition against use of any type of international agreements power "as a device for the purpose of effecting internal social changes or to try to circumvent the constitutional procedures" is no longer explicit. However, the linkage to Circular 175 at the outset, and the general tone of the manual, probably make the admonition implicit, should need for reassurance arise. For specifics, see Coordination and Reporting of International Agreements, 22 CFR § 181.2–181.7 (4/1/93), in the Documentary Supplement.

NOTE: Study the Excerpt From Treaties and Other International Agreements, 11 Foreign Affairs Manual 720, United States Department of State, Publication, 1985, in the Documentary Supplement.

* * *

---

2. AGREEMENTS UNDER PRESIDENTIAL POWER: INTERNAL LAW OR PREEMPTION ON FOREIGN POLICY GROUNDS?

UNITED STATES v. PINK

United States Supreme Court, 1942.
315 U.S. 203, 62 S.Ct. 552, 86 L.Ed. 796.

[The Litvinov Agreement referred to in the quotation from O'Connell above was the subject of litigation in United States v. Belmont, 301 U.S. 324, and United States v. Pink. In the *Pink* case, the relevant document is referred to as the Litvinov Assignment. As an incident to the United States recognition of the USSR on November 16, 1933, the Soviet foreign minister, Litvinov, delivered a letter to the President of the United States by which the Soviet Union assigned to the United States amounts due to the Soviet Union from United States nationals. This assignment was stated to be preparatory to a final settlement mainly of United States claims for nationalization of property of citizens of the United States situated in the USSR. In Pink the United States, assignee of the Soviet Union, sued the New York Superintendent of Insurance, who had succeeded by a court order to the assets of the New York branch of a Russian insurance company (previously nationalized by Soviet law). One defense was that the Russian nationalization decrees were extraterritorial, confiscatory and contrary to the public policy of New York. The New York courts had dismissed the United States complaint, but the Supreme Court reversed. For the Court Mr. Justice DOUGLAS stated, in part:]

* * * The powers of the President in the conduct of foreign relations included the power, without consent of the Senate, to determine the public policy of the United States with respect to the Russian nationalization decrees. "What government is to be regarded here as representative of a foreign sovereign state is a political rather than a judicial question, and is to be determined by the political department of the government." That authority is not limited to a determination of the government to be recognized. It includes the power to determine the policy which is to govern the question of recognition. Objections to the underlying policy as well as objections to recognition are to be addressed to the political department and not to the courts. As we have noted, this Court in the Belmont case recognized that the Litvinov Assignment was an international compact which did not require the participation of the Senate. It stated: "There are many such compacts, of which a protocol, a modus vivendi, a postal convention, and agreements like that now under consideration are illustrations." Recognition is not always absolute; it is sometimes conditional. Power to remove such obstacles to full recognition as settlement of claims of our nationals certainly is a modest implied power of the President who is the "sole organ of the federal government in the field of international relations." Effectiveness in handling the delicate problems of foreign relations requires no less. Unless such a power exists, the power of recognition might be thwarted or seriously diluted. No such obstacle can be placed in the way of rehabilitation of relations between this country and another nation, unless the historic conception of the powers and responsibilities of the President in the conduct of foreign affairs * * * is to be drastically revised. It was the judgment of the political department that full recognition of the Soviet Government required the settlement of all outstanding problems including the claims of our nationals. Recognition and the Litvinov Assignment were interdependent. We would usurp the executive function if we held that that decision was not final and conclusive in the courts.

"All constitutional acts of power, whether in the executive or in the judicial department, have as much legal validity and obligation as if they proceeded from the legislature, * * *." The Federalist, No. 64. A treaty is a "Law of the Land" under the supremacy clause (Art. VI, Cl. 2) of the Constitution. Such international compacts and agreements as the Litvinov Assignment have a similar dignity. * * *

It is, of course, true that even treaties with foreign nations will be carefully construed so as not to derogate from the authority and jurisdiction of the States of this nation unless clearly necessary to effectuate the national policy. For example, in Todok v. Union State Bank, this Court took pains in its construction of a treaty, relating to the power of an alien to dispose of property in this country, not to invalidate the provisions of state law governing such dispositions. Frequently the obligation of a treaty will be dependent on state law. But state law must yield when it is inconsistent with, or impairs the policy or provisions of, a treaty or of an international compact or agreement. Then, the power of a State to refuse enforcement of rights based on foreign law which runs counter to the public policy of the forum must give way before the superior Federal policy evidenced by a treaty or international compact or agreement.

Enforcement of New York's policy as formulated by the Moscow case would collide with and subtract from the Federal policy, whether it was premised on the absence of extraterritorial effect of the Russian decrees, the conception of the New York branch as a distinct juristic personality, or disapproval by New York of the Russian program of nationalization.
* * *

---

1. ***Problem. The Nuclear Test Ban Treaty*** entered into force on October 10, 1963, following its ratification by the United States, the United Kingdom and the Soviet Union. For the text, see the Doc. Supp. In its operative Article I, the treaty provides "[e]ach of the Parties to this Treaty undertakes to prohibit, to prevent, and not to carry out any nuclear weapon test explosion, or any other nuclear explosion, at any place under its jurisdiction or control: (a) in the atmosphere; beyond its limits, including outer space; or underwater, including territorial waters or high seas; or (b) in any other environment if such explosion causes radioactive debris to be present outside the territorial limits of the State under whose jurisdiction or control such explosion is conducted. * * * " Article II of the treaty provides for amendment as follows: "1. Any Party may propose amendments to this Treaty. The text of any proposed amendment shall be submitted to the Depositary Governments which shall circulate it to all Parties to this Treaty. Thereafter, if requested to do so by one-third or more of the Parties, the Depositary Governments shall convene a conference, to which they shall invite all the Parties, to consider such amendment. 2. Any amendment to this Treaty must be approved by a majority of the votes of all the Parties to this Treaty, including the votes of all of the Original Parties. The amendment shall enter into force for all Parties upon the deposit of instruments of ratification by a majority of all the Parties, including the instruments of ratification of all of the Original Parties."

The resolution of the United States Senate giving its advice and consent to the ratification of the treaty provides as follows: "Whereas the President has submitted a limited nuclear test ban treaty, providing a method of amendment, to the Senate for its advice and consent in accordance with article II, section 2 of the Constitution; and Whereas the Constitution in article II, section 2, provides 'He shall have Power, by and with the Advice and Consent of the Senate, to make Treaties, provided two-thirds of the Senators present concur'; and Whereas amendments to treaties are subject to this constitutional provision: Now, therefore, be it Resolved (two-thirds of the Senators present concurring therein), That the Senate advise and consent to the ratification of the treaty banning nuclear weapon tests in the atmosphere, in outer space, and underwater, signed at Moscow on August 5, 1963, on behalf of the United States of America, the United Kingdom of Great Britain and Northern Ireland, and the Union of Soviet Socialist Republics."

Suppose that in conjunction with the negotiation of an arms limitation treaty the United States and the USSR agree to ban underground testing and that the President, because of expected delays in the Senate as to the approval of the entire treaty, undertakes to enforce the underground testing prohibition as an executive agreement pending Senate consent to the entire treaty: (i) Is the United States bound internationally not to test nuclear weapons underground? (ii) Does this executive agreement legally justify no further underground testing in the United States as against prior legislation directing a certain number of such tests and appropriating money for them?

2. ***Pink and separation of powers.*** After *Pink* was decided, the Supreme Court held in *Youngstown Sheet & Tube* [*supra*], that the President has neither explicit nor inherent power to set aside an act of Congress for the benefit of United States foreign affairs interests as seen by the President. The decision was based upon the separation of powers, a principle underlying the structure of the Constitution, though not stated explicitly therein. And under its self-asserted power to say what the law is that governs the outcome of litigation, the Supreme Court has invalidated presidential and congressional acts that, if justiciable, violate the judicial version of the separation of powers principle. The basic rationale of *Youngstown* is that a president has no inherent power to repeal or suspend an act of Congress. *Buckley v. Valeo,* 424 U.S. 1 (1976) holds invalid an act of Congress providing for congressional appointment of two representative members of the Federal Elections Commission, because such a commission exercises the executive power of management, denied to Congress under separation of powers. What, then, of the President's exercise of power in the next case?

DAMES & MOORE v. REGAN

United States Supreme Court, 1981.
453 U.S. 654, 101 S.Ct. 2972, 69 L.Ed.2d 918.

Justice REHNQUIST * * *.

The questions presented by this case touch fundamentally upon the manner in which our Republic is to be governed. Throughout the nearly two centuries of our Nation's existence under the Constitution, this subject has generated considerable debate. We have had the benefit of commentators such as John Jay, Alexander Hamilton, and James Madison writing in The Federalist Papers at the Nation's very inception, the benefit of astute foreign observers of our system such as Alexis de Tocqueville and James Bryce writing during the first century of the Nation's existence, and the benefit of many other treatises as well as more than 400 volumes of reports of decisions of this Court. * * *

The tensions present in any exercise of executive power under the tripartite system of Federal Government established by the Constitution have been reflected in opinions by Members of this Court more than once.   The Court stated in United States v. Curtiss–Wright Export Corp., [supra].

> "[W]e are here dealing not alone with an authority vested in the President by an exertion of legislative power, but with such an authority plus the very delicate, plenary and exclusive power of the President as the sole organ of the federal government in the field of international relations—a power which does not require as a basis for its exercise an act of Congress, but which, of course, like every other governmental power, must be exercised in subordination to the applicable provisions of the Constitution."

And yet 16 years later, Justice Jackson in his concurring opinion in *Youngstown, supra,* which both parties agree brings together as much combination of analysis and common sense as there is in this area, focused not on the "plenary and exclusive power of the President" but rather responded to a claim of virtually unlimited powers for the Executive by noting: "The example of such unlimited executive power that must have most impressed the forefathers was the prerogative exercised by George III, and the description of its evils in the Declaration of Independence leads me to doubt that they were creating their new Executive in his image."

As we now turn to the factual and legal issues in this case, we freely confess that we are obviously deciding only one more episode in the never-ending tension between the President exercising the executive authority in a world that presents each day some new challenge with which he must deal and the Constitution under which we all live and which no one disputes embodies some sort of system of checks and balances.

I

On November 4, 1979, the American Embassy in Tehran was seized and our diplomatic personnel were captured and held hostage.   In response to that crisis, President Carter, acting pursuant to the International Emergency Economic Powers Act, 50 U.S.C. §§ 1701–1706 (hereinafter IEEPA), declared a national emergency on November 14, 1979, and blocked the removal or transfer of "all property and interests in property of the Government of Iran, its instrumentalities and controlled entities and the Central Bank of Iran which are or become subject to the jurisdiction of the United States * * *."   President Carter authorized the Secretary of the Treasury to promulgate regulations carrying out the blocking order.   On November 15, 1979, the Treasury Department's Office of Foreign Assets Control issued a regulation providing that "[u]nless licensed or authorized * * * any attachment, judgment, decree, lien, execution, garnishment, or other judicial process is null and void with respect to any property in which on or since [November 14, 1979,] there existed an interest of Iran." The regulations also made clear that any licenses or authorizations granted could be "amended, modified, or revoked at any time."

On November 26, 1979, the President granted a general license authorizing certain judicial proceedings against Iran but which did not allow the "entry of any judgment or of any decree or order of similar or analogous effect * * *." On December 19, 1979, a clarifying regulation was issued stating that "the general authorization for judicial proceedings contained in § 535.504(a) includes pre-judgment attachment."

On December 19, 1979, * * * Dames & Moore filed suit in the United States District Court for the Central District of California against the Government of Iran, the Atomic Energy Organization of Iran, and a number of Iranian banks. In its complaint, petitioner alleged that its wholly owned subsidiary, Dames & Moore International, S.R.L., was a party to a written contract with the Atomic Energy Organization, and that the subsidiary's entire interest in the contract had been assigned to petitioner. Under the contract, the subsidiary was to conduct site studies for a proposed nuclear power plant in Iran. As provided in the terms of the contract, the Atomic Energy Organization terminated the agreement for its own convenience on June 30, 1979. Petitioner contended, however, that it was owed $3,436,694.30 plus interest for services performed under the contract prior to the date of termination.[4] The District Court issued orders of attachment directed against property of the defendants, and the property of certain Iranian banks was then attached to secure any judgment that might be entered against them.

On January 20, 1981, the Americans held hostage were released by Iran pursuant to an Agreement entered into the day before and embodied in two Declarations of the Democratic and Popular Republic of Algeria * * *. The Agreement stated that "[i]t is the purpose of [the United States and Iran] * * * to terminate all litigation as between the Government of each party and the nationals of the other, and to bring about the settlement and termination of all such claims through binding arbitration." In furtherance of this goal, the Agreement called for the establishment of an Iran–United States Claims Tribunal which would arbitrate any claims not settled within six months. Awards of the Claims Tribunal are to be "final and binding" and "enforceable * * * in the courts of any nation in accordance with its laws." Under the Agreement, the United States is obligated: "to terminate all legal proceedings in United States courts involving claims of United States persons and institutions against Iran and its state enterprises, to nullify all attachments and judgments obtained therein, to prohibit all further litigation based on such claims, and to bring about the termination of such claims through binding arbitration." In addition, the United

---

4. The contract stated that any dispute incapable of resolution by agreement of the parties would be submitted to conciliation and that, if either party was unwilling to accept the results of conciliation, "the matter shall be decided finally by resort to the courts of Iran." * * *

States must "act to bring about the transfer" by July 19, 1981, of all Iranian assets held in this country by American banks. One billion dollars of these assets will be deposited in a security account in the Bank of England, to the account of the Algerian Central Bank, and used to satisfy awards rendered against Iran by the Claims Tribunal. * * *

On January 19, 1981, President Carter issued a series of Executive Orders implementing the terms of the agreement. These Orders revoked all licenses permitting the exercise of "any right, power, or privilege" with regard to Iranian funds, securities, or deposits; "nullified" all non-Iranian interests in such assets acquired subsequent to the blocking order of November 14, 1979; and required those banks holding Iranian assets to transfer them "to the Federal Reserve Bank of New York, to be held or transferred as directed by the Secretary of the Treasury."

On February 24, 1981, President Reagan issued an Executive Order in which he "ratified" the January 19th Executive Orders. Moreover, he "suspended" all "claims which may be presented to the * * * Tribunal" and provided that such claims "shall have no legal effect in any action now pending in any court of the United States." The suspension of any particular claim terminates if the Claims Tribunal determines that it has no jurisdiction over that claim; claims are discharged for all purposes when the Claims Tribunal either awards some recovery and that amount is paid, or determines that no recovery is due.

Meanwhile, on January 27, 1981, petitioner moved for summary judgment in the District Court against the Government of Iran and the Atomic Energy Organization, but not against the Iranian banks. The District Court granted petitioner's motion and awarded petitioner the amount claimed under the contract plus interest. Thereafter, petitioner attempted to execute the judgment by obtaining writs of garnishment and execution in state court in the State of Washington, and a sheriff's sale of Iranian property in Washington was noticed to satisfy the judgment. However, by order of May 28, 1981, as amended by order of June 8, the District Court stayed execution of its judgment pending appeal by the Government of Iran and the Atomic Energy Organization. The District Court also ordered that all prejudgment attachments obtained against the Iranian defendants be vacated and that further proceedings against the bank defendants be stayed in light of the Executive Orders discussed above. * * *

On April 28, 1981, petitioner filed this action in the District Court for declaratory and injunctive relief against the United States and the Secretary of the Treasury, seeking to prevent enforcement of the Executive Orders and Treasury Department regulations implementing the Agreement with Iran. In its complaint, petitioner alleged that the actions of the President and the Secretary of the Treasury implementing the Agreement with Iran were beyond their statutory and constitutional powers and, in any event, were unconstitutional to the extent they adversely affect petitioner's final judgment against the Government of Iran and the Atomic Energy Organization, its execution of that judgment in the State of Washington, its prejudgment attachments, and its ability to continue to litigate against the Iranian banks.   * * *

 * * *

II

The parties and the lower courts, confronted with the instant questions, have all agreed that much relevant analysis is contained in *Youngstown* [*supra*]. Justice Black's opinion for the Court in that case, involving the validity of President Truman's effort to seize the country's steel mills in the wake of a nationwide strike, recognized that "[t]he President's power, if any, to issue the order must stem either from an act of Congress or from the Constitution itself." Justice Jackson's concurring opinion elaborated in a general way the consequences of different types of interaction between the two democratic branches in assessing Presidential authority to act in any given case. When the President acts pursuant to an express or implied authorization from Congress, he exercises not only his powers but also those delegated by Congress. In such a case the executive action "would be supported by the strongest of presumptions and the widest latitude of judicial inter-pretation, and the burden of persuasion would rest heavily upon any who might attack it." When the President acts in the absence of congres-sional authorization he may enter *"a zone of twilight* in which he and Congress may have concurrent authority, or in which its distribution is uncertain." In such a case the analysis becomes more complicated, and the validity of the President's action, at least so far as separation-of-powers principles are concerned, hinges on a consideration of all the circumstances which might shed light on the views of the Legislative Branch toward such action, including "congressional inertia, indifference or quiescence." Finally, when the President acts in contravention of the will of Congress, "his power is at its lowest ebb," and the Court can sustain his actions "only by disabling the Congress from acting upon the subject."

Although we have in the past found and do today find Justice Jackson's classification of executive actions into three general categories analytically useful, we should be mindful of Justice Holmes' admonition, quoted by Justice Frankfurter in *Youngstown,* supra, at 597 (concurring opinion), that "[t]he great ordinances of the Constitution do not estab-lish and divide fields of black and white." Justice Jackson himself recognized that his three categories represented "a somewhat over-simplified grouping," 343 U.S., at 635, and it is doubtless the case that executive action in any particular instance falls, not neatly in one of three pigeonholes, but rather at some point along a spectrum running from explicit congressional authorization to explicit congressional prohi-bition. This is particularly true as respects cases such as the one before us, involving responses to international crises the nature of which Congress can hardly have been expected to anticipate in any detail.

III

In nullifying post-November 14, 1979, attachments and directing those persons holding blocked Iranian funds and securities to transfer them to the Federal Reserve Bank of New York for ultimate transfer to Iran, President Carter cited five sources of express or inherent power. The Government, however, has principally relied on § 203 of the IEEPA, 50 U.S.C. § 1702(a)(1), as authorization for these actions. Section 1702(a)(1) provides in part:

> "At the times and to the extent specified in section 1701 of this title, the President may, under such regulations as he may prescribe, by means of instructions, licenses, or otherwise—

> "(A) investigate, regulate, or prohibit—

> "(i) any transactions in foreign exchange,

> "(ii) transfers of credit or payments between, by, through, or to any banking institution, to the extent that such transfers or payments involve any interest of any foreign country or a national thereof,

> "(iii) the importing or exporting of currency or securities, and

> "(B) investigate, regulate, direct and compel, nullify, void, prevent or prohibit, any acquisition, holding, withholding, use, transfer, withdrawal, transportation, importation or exportation of, or dealing in, or exercising any right, power, or privilege with respect to, or transactions involving, any property in which any foreign country or a national thereof has any interest;

> "by any person, or with respect to any property, subject to the jurisdiction of the United States."

The Government contends that the acts of "nullifying" the attachments and ordering the "transfer" of the frozen assets are specifically authorized by the plain language of the above statute. The two Courts of Appeals that have considered the issue agreed with this contention. * * *

　　* * *

IV

Although we have concluded that the IEEPA constitutes specific congressional authorization to the President to nullify the attachments and order the transfer of Iranian assets, there remains the question of the President's authority to suspend claims pending in American courts. Such claims have, of course, an existence apart from the attachments which accompanied them. * * *

We conclude that although the IEEPA authorized the nullification of the attachments, it cannot be read to authorize the suspension of the claims. The claims of American citizens against Iran are not in themselves transactions involving Iranian property or efforts to exercise any rights with respect to such property. An *in personam* lawsuit, although it might eventually be reduced to judgment and that judgment might be executed upon, is an effort to establish liability and fix damages and does not focus on any particular property within the jurisdiction. The terms of the IEEPA therefore do not authorize the President to suspend claims in American courts. * * *

Concluding that neither the IEEPA nor the Hostage Act constitutes specific authorization of the President's action suspending claims, however, is not to say that these statutory provisions are entirely irrelevant to the question of the validity of the President's action. We think both statutes highly relevant in the looser sense of indicating congressional acceptance of a broad scope for executive action in circumstances such as those presented in this case. * * *

Not infrequently in affairs between nations, outstanding claims by nationals of one country against the government of another country are "sources of friction" between the two sovereigns. *United States v. Pink* [*supra*]. To resolve these difficulties, nations have often entered into agreements settling the claims of their respective nationals. As one treatise writer puts it, international agreements settling claims by nationals of one state against the government of another "are established international practice reflecting traditional international theory." L. Henkin, Foreign Affairs and the Constitution 262 (1972). Consistent with that principle, the United States has repeatedly exercised its sovereign authority to settle the claims of its nationals against foreign countries. Though those settlements have sometimes been made by treaty, there has also been a longstanding practice of settling such claims by executive agreement without the advice and consent of the Senate. Under such agreements, the President has agreed to renounce or extinguish claims of United States nationals against foreign governments in return for lump-sum payments or the establishment of arbitration procedures. To be sure, many of these settlements were encouraged by the United States claimants themselves, since a claimant's only hope of obtaining any payment at all might lie in having his Government negotiate a diplomatic settlement on his behalf. But it is also undisputed that the "United States has sometimes disposed of the claims of its citizens without their consent, or even without consultation with them, usually without exclusive regard for their interests, as distinguished from those of the nation as a whole." It is clear that the practice of settling claims continues today. Since 1952, the President has entered into at least 10 binding settlements with foreign nations, including an $80 million settlement with the People's Republic of China.

Crucial to our decision today is the conclusion that Congress has implicitly approved the practice of claim settlement by executive agreement. This is best demonstrated by Congress' enactment of the International Claims Settlement Act of 1949, as amended, 22 U.S.C. § 1621 et seq. The Act had two purposes: (1) to allocate to United States nationals funds received in the course of an executive claims settlement with Yugoslavia, and (2) to provide a procedure whereby funds resulting from future settlements could be distributed. To achieve these ends Congress created the International Claims Commission, now the Foreign Claims Settlement Commission, and gave jurisdiction to make final and binding decisions with respect to claims by United States nationals against settlement funds. 22 U.S.C. § 1623(a). By creating a procedure to implement future settlement agreements, Congress placed its stamp of approval on such agreements. * * *

Over the years Congress has frequently amended the International Claims Settlement Act to provide for particular problems arising out of settlement agreements, thus demonstrating Congress' continuing acceptance of the President's claim settlement authority. With respect to the Executive Agreement with the People's Republic of China, for example, Congress established an allocation formula for distribution of the funds received pursuant to the Agreement. 22 U.S.C. § 1627(f). As with legislation involving other executive agreements, Congress did not question the fact of the settlement or the power of the President to have concluded it. * * * Finally, the legislative history of the IEEPA further reveals that Congress has accepted the authority of the Executive to enter into settlement agreements. Though the IEEPA was enacted to provide for some limitation on the President's emergency powers, Congress stressed that "[n]othing in this act is intended * * * to interfere with the authority of the President to [block assets], or to impede the settlement of claims of U.S. citizens against foreign countries." 50 U.S.C. § 1706(a)(1).

* * *

The judgment of the District Court is accordingly affirmed.   * * *

* * *

[Justices Steven's and Powell concurred] except re U.S. duty to compensate for "taking."]

———

Pink, Youngstown, Dames & Moore and federalism. Is the basis of the Pink decision presidential action as law under the supremacy clause [Constitution Article VI(2)] or federal preemption of a foreign affairs matter (recognition)? The Douglas opinion straddles this. The Youngstown decision cuts against presidential power to make law contrary to legislative enactment in the federal sphere. But does separation of powers in the federal system always prevent presidential law-making in the federal-state sphere? Dames & Moore put Youngstown into softer focus as to presidential power regarding foreign claims settlement matters, clearly a federal, not state, function. Does that focus extend to other matters, including the over-riding of state law?

In *Zschernig v. Miller*, 389 U.S. 429 (1968), the Supreme Court, in the absence of any federal legislation or claim of preemption, held that a state could not validly require reciprocity in the treatment of legatees as between the state and Iron Curtain countries. (An Iron Curtain legatee could not inherit in the state if an iron curtain bequest to a resident of the state would not be permitted.) In retrospect, is Pink a similar situation? Would the Supreme Court under Zschernig have ruled against the New York banking superintendent (Pink) even if President Roosevelt and Ambassador Litvinov had not made the agreement as to Russian bank assets a part of the act of recognition?

———

3.   WHERE LIES THE POWER TO END TREATIES?

The U.S. Constitution does not reveal explicitly which entity has the power to suspend or terminate treaties. *See,* Restatement (3rd), at § 339.   In 1979, the Supreme Court dismissed an action brought by Senator Goldwater and others, which complained that President Carter had failed to consult Congress properly in terminating the *Mutual Defense Treaty of 1954 (with Taiwan).*   Goldwater v. Carter, 444 U.S. 996, 998, et seq. (1979).   This Treaty in the constitutional sense, having received the two-thirds vote of the Senators present.   Thus, it was argued below that "proper consultation" with Congress was required before termination.   The suit was dismissed, four justices arguing that the issue was a "political question," beyond the Court's competence. Another concurring justice argued that the case was not ripe.

WORMUTH AND FIRMAGE, TO CHAIN THE DOG OF WAR

at 193–94.*

The Constitution makes no mention of treaty termination.   This omission leaves open questions as to the circumstances under which treaties may be terminated and, more important, whether the power to terminate treaty obligations is vested in the Senate or in the executive. Constitutional silence on the matter notwithstanding, there are several means whereby the United States may terminate its treaty obligations. Under international law, a nation has the right to terminate a treaty in response to another nation's breach of an important term of the treaty or in response to a fundamental change in the circumstances.   Also, a treaty's own terms, provide for termination, notice is given to the other nation(s) affected.   Finally, as a sovereign state the United States has the *power*—but not the right—to abrogate a treaty "and abide the international consequences" of that act.

Assuming that the United States has the right to terminate or abrogate treaties, the Constitution does not specify whether the President may act alone or must obtain the consent of the Senate in making the decision.   There is logic in the argument that if the President must obtain the Senate's consent to conclude a treaty, the President should also obtain its consent to terminate the treaty.   But it has also been argued that perhaps "the framers were concerned only to check the President in 'entangling' the United States" and that since " 'disentangling' is less risky and may have to be done quickly, and is often done piecemeal, or ad hoc, by various means or acts," senatorial approval of the President's decision to terminate a treaty should not be required. Apart from these theoretical arguments, the President has demonstrated an effective power to terminate treaties, and the Senate has not success-

* Reprinted with the permission of the
University of Illinois press.

fully challenged that right to do so. The first historical example of unilateral abrogation by a President came in 1864 under President Lincoln. Lincoln's notice to Great Britain of withdrawal from the Rush–Bagot Agreement of 1817 was subsequently ratified by Congress. It has been in the twentieth century, however, that the President has consistently and effectively asserted the right to terminate treaties. Presidents Taft, Wilson, Roosevelt, Truman, and Eisenhower invoked the power unilaterally to terminate or abrogate American treaties; more recent Presidents have followed their precedents. The larger number of modern scholars agree that the President has the effective power unilaterally to terminate treaties and that Congress is unlikely to be successful in any attempt to reassert its claim to a share in that power.

SECTION C.   SELF–EXECUTING TREATIES IN THE UNITED STATES

1. *A comparative perspective.* In absolute monarchies, dictatorships de jure and de facto, and in some continental democracies, there is normally no discontinuity as to the time that an international agreement comes into effect as an international obligation and when it becomes, should that be necessary to the international undertaking, the internal law of the land. Absolute monarchs and dictators could, if they wished, provide such discontinuities but normally they do not. Under some constitutions in democracies, in Germany for instance, the legislative act that ratifies the treaty as an international obligation simultaneously makes it law within the country.

In the United Kingdom and members of the Commonwealth that still recognize the Crown, making international agreements binding internationally is a part of the prerogative of the Crown, while, as a result of historical evolution, making internal law can only be done by Parliament. Thus, theoretically, discontinuity between international obligation and internal legal effect is possible. Yet there is no possibility of discontinuity in practice, because the government (the cabinet) controls both the will of the Crown to make a treaty internationally and the will of Parliament to make a treaty-conforming law. And it is also the practice in British-type democracies to lay the treaty on the table at Parliament as a template for any necessary legislation that might be required by the international obligation. Such laying on the table is not ratification, however; the ministers of the Crown have already committed the country internationally.

In the United States, and in the few countries with American-type governmental structures, discontinuities do occur. This is rare outside the United States, but in the United States the choice of either a self-executing or a non-self-executing international agreement is very often difficult; all too frequently the model selected by the treaty-makers is not pre-determined.

2. *Guidelines for the American system as to self-execution.* Some international agreements, usually treaties, require no changes or effects in internal law whatsoever. Sometimes Congress and the Presi-

dent work together and by their joint efforts bring into effect international agreements that in the same creative act make internal federal law. The President and two-thirds of the Senate have the power both to bind the United States internationally by treaty and to make necessary internal implementing law; i.e., the President and the Senate may make many types of self-executing treaties that require internal conformation to the international agreement. In important instances the President and the Senate either lack the power to legislate by treaty or wisely choose not to do so, e.g., where the House of Representatives must participate, as in revenue-raising, appropriations, and trade law (linked to revenue-raising). It is accepted also that the President and the Senate will not attempt to make federal criminal law by treaty. Why not? Does the Constitution speak to this? A serious operational problem arises because the President and the Senate almost never specify whether they consider a treaty self-executing. This means that when the treaty is brought into litigation as the asserted governing law, the courts must decide whether the treaty is or is not self-executing.

----

1. THE ROLE OF THE JUDICIARY
UNITED STATES v. PERCHEMAN

United States Supreme Court, 1833.
32 U.S. (7 Pet.) 51, 8 L.Ed. 604.

[Percheman claimed title to land in Florida under a grant to his predecessor in title made by the Spanish governor of Florida in 1815, when Spain still was sovereign there, even though American military penetration had commenced. In 1819, Spain ceded Florida to the United States by a peace treaty which contained standard provisions about ceded territory, including one that private rights previously granted would be respected. As noted in detail in omitted portions of the opinion that follows, the federal government made various arrangements by acts of Congress to deal with issues of title and ownership involving some 30 million acres of newly acquired territory, pursuant to Article IV, Section 3, Paragraph 2 of the Constitution. Under an 1828 federal act, a commission was created to pass on title claims. Apparently it fell considerably short of the due process and related provision of our modern Administrative Procedures Act, and the commission ruled against Percheman's claim. Congress, despite all its other activity as to land in Florida, had never got around to implementing the provision in the 1819 treaty safeguarding prior grants. Claiming directly under the treaty, Percheman sued the United States on some waiver of sovereign immunity not disclosed in the opinion and not common to the era. Perhaps it was taken for granted that the Fifth Amendment "takings" clause overrode immunity.]

MARSHALL, Chief Justice.

        * * *

This state of things [the status of private property in cases of cession of territory according to the modern usage of nations] ought to be kept in view when we construe the eighth article of the treaty, and the acts which have been passed by congress for the ascertainment and adjustment of titles acquired under the Spanish government. That article in the English part of it is in these words. "All the grants of land made before the 24th of January 1818 by his catholic majesty, or by his lawful authorities, in the said territories ceded by his majesty to the United States, shall be ratified and confirmed to the persons in possession of the lands, to the same extent that the same grants would be valid if the territories had remained under the dominion of his catholic majesty."

This article is apparently introduced on the part of Spain, and must be intended to stipulate expressly for that security to private property which the laws and usages of nations would, without express stipulation, have conferred. No construction which would impair that security further than its positive words require, would seem to be admissible. Without it, the titles of individuals would remain as valid under the new government as they were under the old; and those titles, so far at least as they were consummate, might be asserted in the courts of the United States, independently of this article.

The treaty was drawn up in the Spanish as well as in the English language. Both are originals, and were unquestionably intended by the parties to be identical. The Spanish has been translated, and we now understand that the article, as expressed in that language, is, that the grants "shall remain ratified and confirmed to the persons in possession of them, to the same extent, * * * "—thus conforming exactly to the universally received doctrine of the law of nations. If the English and the Spanish parts can, without violence, be made to agree, that construction which establishes this conformity ought to prevail. If, as we think must be admitted, the security of private property was intended by the parties; if this security would have been complete without the article, the United States could have no motive for insisting on the interposition of government in order to give validity to titles which, according to the usages of the civilized world, were already valid. No violence is done to the language of the treaty by a construction which conforms the English and Spanish to each other. Although the words "shall be ratified and confirmed," are properly the words of contract, stipulating for some future legislative act; they are not necessarily so. They may import that they "shall be ratified and confirmed" by force of the instrument itself. When we observe that in the counterpart of the same treaty, executed at the same time by the same parties, they are used in this sense, we think the construction proper, if not unavoidable.

In the case of Foster v. Elam, 2 Peters, 253, this court considered these words as importing contract. The Spanish part of the treaty was not then brought to our view, and we then supposed that there was no variance between them. We did not suppose that there was even a formal difference of expression in the same instrument, drawn up in the language of each party. Had this circumstance been known, we believe it would have produced the construction which we now give to the article.

* * *

___

ASAKURA v. CITY OF SEATTLE

United States Supreme Court, 1924.
265 U.S. 332, 44 S.Ct. 515, 68 L.Ed. 1041.

Mr. Justice BUTLER delivered the opinion of the Court.

Plaintiff in error is a subject of the Emperor of Japan, and, since 1904, has resided in Seattle, Washington. Since July, 1915, he has been engaged in business there as a pawnbroker. The city passed an ordinance, which took effect July 2, 1921, regulating the business of pawnbroker and repealing former ordinances on the same subject. It makes it unlawful for any person to engage in the business unless he shall have a license, and the ordinance provides "that no such license shall be granted unless the applicant be a citizen of the United States." Violations of the ordinance are punishable by fine or imprisonment or both. Plaintiff in error brought this suit in the Superior Court of King County, Washington, against the city, its Comptroller and its Chief of Police to restrain them from enforcing the ordinance against him. He attacked the ordinance on the ground that it violates the treaty between the United States and the Empire of Japan, proclaimed April 5, 1911 * * *. He had about $5,000 invested in his business, which would be broken up and destroyed by the enforcement of the ordinance. The Superior Court granted the relief. On appeal, the [State] Supreme Court held the ordinance valid and reversed the decree. * * *

Does the ordinance violate the treaty? Plaintiff in error invokes and relies upon the following provisions: "The citizens or subjects of each of the High Contracting Parties shall have liberty to enter, travel and reside in the territories of the other to carry on trade, wholesale and retail, to own or lease and occupy houses, manufactories, warehouses and shops, to employ agents of their choice, to lease land for residential and commercial purposes, and generally to do anything incident to or necessary for trade upon the same terms as native citizens or subjects, submitting themselves to the laws and regulations there established. * * * The citizens or subjects of each * * * shall receive, in the territories of the other, the most constant protection, and security for their persons and property * * *."

A treaty made under the authority of the United States "shall be the supreme law of the land; and the judges in every State shall be bound thereby, any thing in the constitution or laws of any State to the contrary notwithstanding." Constitution, Art. VI, § 2.

* * * The treaty was made to strengthen friendly relations between the two nations. The provision quoted establishes the rule of equality between Japanese subjects while in this country and native citizens. Treaties for the protection of citizens of one country residing in the territory of another are numerous, and make for good understanding between nations. The treaty is binding within the State of Washington. * * * The rule of equality established by it cannot be rendered nugatory in any part of the United States by municipal ordinances or state laws. It stands on the same footing of supremacy as do the provisions of the Constitution and laws of the United States. It operates of itself without the aid of any legislation, state or national; and it will be applied and given authoritative effect by the courts. * * *

The purpose of the ordinance complained of is to regulate, not to prohibit, the business of pawnbroker. But it makes it impossible for aliens to carry on the business. It need not be considered whether the State, if it sees fit, may forbid and destroy the business generally. Such a law would apply equally to aliens and citizens, and no question of conflict with the treaty would arise. The grievance here alleged is that plaintiff in error, in violation of the treaty, is denied equal opportunity.

* * *

Decree reversed.

Questions about the judicial characterization of treaties as self-executing. Are the characterizations made by American courts in the foregoing cases assuredly based upon the principles of interpretation of treaties? If so, are the interpretations textual or contextual in the terminology? Are some of the characterizations as self-executing linked to the court's response to plaintiff's claim of right based on the treaty alone? Can you formulate any reasonably reliable way of predicting outcomes on the issue, self-executing or not? If so, what is it?

When the Carter administration submitted three United Nations (and one Inter–American) human rights conventions to the Senate (where they were still awaiting action at the end of 1987), the executive branch reported that the treaties had been examined for any conflicts with the Constitution and existing legislation and that any potential conflicts had been dealt with by reservations prepared by the executive and recommended to the Senate as conditions to its advice and consent. This, the President's messages claimed, would reduce the necessity for the Senate to have to weigh consent to the treaties in terms of what legislative changes might be required to put the treaties into effect as law. Why should the Senate be concerned about possible legislative changes? Would it be apt to be more concerned about possible legislative changes in the Federal Criminal Code than in some other titles of the United States Code? As to an executive branch preference for non-self executing treaties on human rights, see Chapter 10. We have already noted the reservations made to the U.S. adherence to the Genocide Convention and the International Covenant on Civil and Political Rights. One of these is a declaration that they are not self-executing. Is this a wise thing to do? Would you think that there are more advantages to having a treaty self-executing or non-self-executing? See Ch. 10, supra.

In Cannon v. U.S. Dep't of Justice (Parole Commission), 973 F.2d 1190, 1197 (5th Cir.1992), relating to the U.S.—Mexico Treaty on Execution of Penal Sentences, the Fifth Circuit Court of Appeals held that the Parole Commission may not authorize a "release date which results in the total period of incarceration * * * [which is] less than or greater than the total foreign-court-imposed sentence * * *" The Court noted: "Aside from the ministerial task of appointing an 'Authority' to receive transferred prisoners, the Treaty *required* [emphasis the courts] no legislative action other than ratification. Procedural legislation which makes operation of a Treaty more convenient cannot amend or abrogate a self-executing Treaty [citing Cook v. U.S., Chew Heong v. U.S.]. Accordingly, a foreign-court-imposed sentence is in fact one imposed by the equivalent of an Act of Congress." See also, discussion on self-executing treaties in *United States v. Alvarez–Machain,* supra Chapters 1 and 3.

Is there a strong presumption that a treaty is self-executing?

PAUST, SELF–EXECUTING TREATIES
82 AJIL 760 (1988) *

" * * * it seems clear that the text of the Constitution, the predominant views of the Founders, and early and more modern trends in judicial decision all demand that certain notions of several text writers with respect to the inherently non-self-executing nature of certain types of treaties be abandoned. The constitutionally preferable view is that no treaty is inherently non-self-executing except those which would seek to declare war on behalf of the United States. * * * With the exception of the sui generis power of Congress to declare war, the mere existence of a congressional power does not mean that it is exclusive and would obviate any potentially self-executing effect of a treaty.

It also seems clear that all treaties are self-executing except those (or the portions of them) which, by their terms considered in context, require domestic implementing legislation or seek to declare war on behalf of the United States. All treaties are supreme federal law, but some treaties, by their terms, are not directly operative. Finally, even non-self-executing treaties can produce and have produced domestic legal effects through indirect incorporation, by which a treaty norm is utilized as an aid in interpreting the Constitution, a statute, common law or some other legal provision."

Notes and Questions. The word "self-executing" may or may not be felicitous, but awareness of the actual text of the Constitution, the predominant views of the Founders, early and more modern judicial opinions, and a proper separation of powers should prove a useful counter to ambiguity and the contrary assumptions. It is appropriate to reaffirm the text of the Constitution and expectations of the Founders

* Reprinted with the permission of the American Society of International Law.

that all treaties will be the supreme law of the land. Do you agree? Why or why not?

2. OTHER PROBLEMS ABOUT INTERNATIONAL AGREEMENTS AS INTERNAL LAW

a. ***A British problem: The European Community Treaties and British law.*** As we have seen, in British-type systems the treaties made by the Crown do not have internal legal effect. Only Parliament can provide such effect. The European Community treaties have no fixed duration and do not provide for withdrawal. Yet the treaties themselves contain legal rules that under the terms of the treaties have direct internal effects, over-riding conflicting internal law in member states. It was necessary for the United Kingdom Parliament to enact the [1974] European Communities Act before the United Kingdom could perform its obligations under the European Community system. But, technically, the superior law of the Community is applicable in Britain by act of Parliament. This raises problems concerning the authorized interpretation of Community law regarding internal effect and the continued "omnipotence of Parliament" as to the Community treaties. Some British jurists and scholars have wondered whether in fact Parliament any longer has the power to repeal the Communities Act. If it does not, it would be the only legislation that Parliament cannot change, including the Bill of Rights (1689).

A parallel problem is discussed regarding the power or lack of power of Parliament to reduce the legal effect in Britain of the European Convention on Human Rights, a problem further complicated by the fact that the Government did not ask Parliament to enact a European rights convention act. Some British suitors before the European Human Rights Commission and Court claim rights under the Convention that they do not have under British internal law, such as just compensation for property taken by eminent domain.

b. ***What are the operational limitations on the power of the President and the Senate to legislate by treaty?*** We previously noted operating limitations on the President–Senate power of making self-executing treaties regarding revenue measures, appropriations, and federal criminal law. How much farther does practice carry the treaty-as-legislation power of the President and the Senate so far as concerns other enumerated powers of Congress in Article I, Section 8 of the Constitution? Is the *Asakura case* the final answer as to all aspects of the foreign commerce power under Section 8(3)? An even more difficult question is whether the President and the Senate could make a self-executing treaty fixing the exchange rate for the dollar. Look also at Section 8(4, 11, 12 and 13). We have no answers based on what has been decided, and research has not been able to draw conclusions from the non-use of the power to make law by self-executing treaties.

The problem is not entirely or even principally a legal one. Institutional attitudes in the House and Senate—attitudes beyond political alignments—are also important. Among enduring House institutional attitudes are: (i) resentment of the Senate's constitution–given role in foreign relations (a role superseded by the history of American federalism and the amendment providing for the popular election of senators); (ii) suspicion of cozy fraternization between the foreign affairs executive branches and the Senate Committee on Foreign Relations; (iii) belief that the more popular branch of the Congress is closer to grass roots than the Senate and that senators are more susceptible to foreigners' blandishments, because they are fewer, more elitist, and often more prominent; (iv) fear and dislike as to appropriations, revenue, and national security matters, of finding themselves boxed-in by national interest needs to carry out international commitments which they had no part in making; (v) concern about the erosion of House rights to participate, as in the case of the disposition of United States property in the Panama Canal Zone.

Treaties, Congress, and Judicial Interpretation. Can Congress pass a law that violates an extant treaty? How does the judiciary interpret legislation that appears to do this? If legislation is found to violate a treaty, what is the result domestically? What is the result internationally? Read the excerpts from the following case relating to possible legislative violation of GATT.

MISSISSIPPI POULTRY ASS'N, INC. v. MADIGAN

United States Court of Appeals, Fifth Circuit, 1993.
992 F.2d 1359, 1369–67.

* * *

In another variation on the absurdity theme, the Agency insists that the interpretation urged by the Associations is absurd because it would place the PPIA in violation of the 1) General Agreement on Tariffs and Trade (GATT), 2) the ongoing trade negotiations under the auspices of GATT (the Uruguay Round) and 3) the United States–Canada Free–Trade Agreement (FTA). The Agency adamantly insists that Congress cannot violate an international obligation without making a clear statement that it intends to do so. The Agency maintains further that a clear statement is especially appropriate in the instant case because the Executive Branch has exclusive responsibility for conducting international affairs. We discern fatal flaws in the Agency's position.

* * * The Agency has obfuscatorily intertwined its arguments, but when they are untangled there appear three separate but related maxims governing the construction of statutes which implicate international obligations. First, Congress may abrogate a treaty or international obligation entered into by the United States only by a clear statement of its intent to do so. Second, the extraterritorial application of domestic laws requires a clear statement of congressional intent so as "to protect against unintended clashes between our laws and those of other nations which could result in international discord." And finally, "[i]t has been a maxim of statutory construction since the decision in *Murray v. The*

Charming Betsy, [*supra*] that 'an act of Congress ought never to be construed to violate the law of nations, if any other possible construction remains.' " Even when we grant arguendo that these truisms of statutory construction exist, we find them inapplicable and therefore not controlling in the instant case.

Despite the Agency's claim that Congress must clearly express its intention to violate the GATT, it fails to cite us to any authority for that specific proposition and we are aware of none. In fact, we are aware of strongly instructive authority to the contrary. The Federal Circuit recently rejected out of hand the argument that a statutory provision should be read consistently with the obligations of the United States as a signatory of GATT—the very position argued here by the Agency. The court reasoned that

> even if * * * [the] Commerce[ ] [Department's] interpretation conflicts with the GATT, * * * the GATT is not controlling. While we acknowledge Congress's interest in complying with U.S. responsibilities under the GATT, we are bound not by what we think Congress should or perhaps wanted to do, but by what Congress in fact did. The GATT does not trump domestic legislation; if the statutory provisions at issue here are inconsistent with GATT, it is a matter for Congress and not this court to decide and remedy.

We conclude that this same, flawless reasoning applies to the instant case and mandates that we give effect to Congress' intent, even if implementation of that intent is virtually certain to create a violation of the GATT.

Our adoption of this reasoning is unaffected by the maxims of statutory construction cited above. The first maxim—that a clear statement of Congress is required to abrogate a treaty—does not require a different result here because Congress is not abrogating a treaty or an international obligation. Abrogation or repeal involves nullifying an obligation. In the instant case, Congress has at most evinced an intent to place the PPIA *in violation of the GATT.* Certainly, United States has passed laws that, in a subsequent proceeding before a GATT panel, have been declared in violation of the GATT. Yet these violations have not signified the end of American involvement in the GATT.

Second, there is no need here for an Arabian American Oil Co. "clear statement" as required when Congress intends for its legislation to violate the GATT. The instant case is distinguishable from the situation in Arabian American Oil Co., which only requires such a clear statement when the intent of Congress is to apply domestic legislation extraterritorially, so as "to protect against unintended clashes between our laws and those of other nations which would result in international discord."

The factual circumstances in both of these cases are distinguishable from those in the instant case. In *Arabian American Oil Co.,* the question was whether Title VII applied to American corporations located in Saudi Arabia. Courts must be hesitant to apply American law when it would displace the law of the foreign forum. Similarly, in *Aerospatiale,* the defendants were corporations owned by France, so for all practical purposes a foreign sovereign was a party in the lawsuit. In both cases the key issue is clear: application of American law would directly *affect the sovereignty of a foreign nation*. That cannot be said of the case now before us. There is absolutely no issue of sovereignty in the instant case; in the absence of such an issue the concerns voiced in *Arabian American Oil Co.* and *Aerospatiale* are not implicated.

Like the first two maxims, the third—that an act of Congress should not be construed to violate the law of nations if there is an alternative construction available—cannot apply here. The Agency directs our attention to no supporting authority for its contention that the GATT— or for that matter any multi-lateral trade agreement—falls under the rubric of "the law of nations"; and again we have been unable to find any. Neither have we found a single case in which this canon was applied to international commercial law. Rather, all cases relying on the law-of-nations canon of construction either involve traditional rules of public international law or implicate the sovereignty of a foreign nation. We are loath, therefore, to extend this maxim to multi-lateral trade agreements. To do so in the absence of controlling authority would be to exercise raw judicial fiat.

The additional Agency argument—that a clear congressional statement is especially appropriate in this instance because the Executive Branch has exclusive authority over foreign affairs—borders on frivolity. The Agency overlooks or conveniently ignores the well recognized distinction between foreign *affairs* and *foreign commerce*. Even though the Executive Branch does have exclusive jurisdiction over foreign affairs, the Constitution grants Congress power to regulate commerce with foreign nations. To the extent that a dispute exists over possible foreign policy implications to the GATT, we decline to enter the fray.   * * *

* * *

RIESENFELD, THE DOCTRINE OF SELF-EXECUTING TREATIES AND U.S. v. POSTAL: WIN AT ANY PRICE?

Editorial Comment, 74 American Journal of International Law 892, 896 (1980).*

From a survey of the copious literature it emerges that the concept of self-executing treaties is in need of clarification. It has separate international and domestic constitutional aspects. The international aspect focuses on the issue of whether the treaty aims at the immediate creation of rights and duties of private individuals which are enforceable and to be enforced by domestic tribunals. The domestic constitutional aspect deals with the question whether and under what circumstances such enforceability and enforcement needs separate legislative action to accomplish this aim. The international aspect deals with the content or nature of the treaty obligation: what is to be accomplished and what is the time frame for such accomplishment. The domestic means for such accomplishment will usually not be of international concern.   * * *

* * *

---

* Reprinted with the permission of American Society of International Law.

A survey of the constitutions, cases, and scholarly writings in other countries leads to the conclusion that even in countries in which legislative approval is needed for the conclusion of international treaties, the creation of rights, privileges, duties, and immunities cognizable in domestic courts is primarily a function of the particular treaty provision. The power of parties to invoke it in domestic courts depends upon its import, as determined from its language, context, purpose, negotiating history, and general background. The internal applicability is created *by virtue of* and—save where publication requirements dictate otherwise— *upon* the international entry into effect of the treaty provision with respect to the nation involved. The legislative approval is a condition for the valid conclusion of the treaty. Normally it does not determine the domestic applicability of the treaty provisions. Of course, this does not exclude the possibility that the legislature, in giving approval to the international engagement of the nation, may prescribe its domestic cognizability irrespective of the treaty's mandate. Conversely, where the treaty expressly or by implication provides for domestic protection of the rights and privileges created thereby, the parliamentary approval of its conclusion may not deny such cognizability, unless the legislature is empowered to prescribe internationally valid reservations or is constitutionally authorized to postpone domestic applicability until the passage of further legislation.

This analysis compels a further semantic consequence: Strictly speaking, the term "self-executing" is not a notion whose meaning is determined by international law. The self-executing nature of a treaty provision is a product of international and domestic constitutional rules. Internationally relevant is merely the determination whether the treaty provision in question mandates the cognizability in and protection by domestic tribunals of the rights, duties, privileges, and immunities created thereby. Reservations or interpretative declarations, to the extent that they are internationally permissible and effective, may only relate to that aspect.

* * *

From what is said * * *, it follows that the panel of the United States Court of Appeals for the Fifth Circuit erred egregiously in the choice of the criteria for the determination of whether or not Article 6 of the High Seas Convention is self-executing. A treaty provision which by its terms and purpose is *meant* to stipulate the immediate and not merely progressive creation of rights, privileges, duties, and immunities cognizable in domestic courts and is *capable* of being applied by the courts without further concretization *is* self-executing by virtue of the constitutional mandate of Article VI of the U.S. Constitution. The intent or understanding of the Executive is at best an element in the interpretative task of the court. * * *

* * *

Questions. Does Professor Riesenfeld's test provide a workable basis for differentiating the questions, (a) whether a treaty is self-executing and (b) whether it creates private rights, duties, privileges or immunities? The 1965 Restatement asserts in Comment *h* to Section 131: "Whether a treaty is self-executing is not to be confused with whether the treaty creates rights and remedies." Is this merely a delphic utterance or a concurrence with Riesenfeld? Suppose that the President and two-thirds of the Senate specifically provide that the treaty they bring into effect internationally is to be deemed self-executing, but the right claimed by a private litigant is that he is entitled by the treaty to a tax break not sanctioned under the Internal Revenue Code. Would the Riesenfeld and Restatement statements lead to the same conclusion or to opposite ones? How would the Restatement utterance solve, as an original issue, Mr. Asakura's claim of right to engage in pawnbrokerage in Seattle? How does Riesenfeld know when a treaty, by its terms and purpose, is meant to be self-executing? He covers himself, does he not, if the treaty is meant to be self-executing (by whatever means of determination) but is incapable of being applied by the courts without further concretization?

United States v. Postal, 589 F.2d 862 (5th Cir.1979) involved a criminal case against persons arrested on the high seas, offshore the United States, for attempted narcotics smuggling from an unmarked, no-flag craft. The issue was whether the defendants had assertible private rights under the 1958 High Seas Convention not to be arrested by American authorities. The Court of Appeals for the Fifth Circuit held against the defense on the ground that the treaty was not executed as an international agreement, relying on the view of the executive branch that it was not such a treaty. How fundamental is Riesenfeld's critique under these circumstances? How useful the Restatement's cautionary statement? *But see, United States v. Juda*, [*supra* ch. 3] where the 9th Circuit required a nexus sufficient to meet due process, even for stateless vessels.

———

SECTION D. UNITED STATES LAW AND PRACTICE AS TO RESERVATIONS, AMENDMENTS AND UNDERSTANDINGS: THE PRESIDENT AND THE SENATE

1. *The Senate of the United States.* As a part of the solution to the large-small states issue at the Constitutional Convention (1787), the executive power article (II) conditions the President's treaty-making authority by requiring that treaties be made "by and with the Advice and Consent of the Senate * * * provided two-thirds of the Senators present concur." This enforced sharing of foreign affairs power and the two-thirds vote requirement for bringing a treaty into effect are at the root of many of the aspects of uniqueness that characterize the international agreements law of the United States. In broad effect, the Senate

expects (and the executive acquiesces) that any condition it attaches to its consent be respected. If the Senate does not have its way, there is no treaty, so far as United States law is concerned. The clearest form of Senate condition to consent is a reservation, i.e. a Senate imposed alterations of the legal undertaking. One notes that this type of condition is parallel to the concept of reservation in customary international law, as codified in this respect by the Vienna Convention. Sometimes, but not often, the Senate purports to amend a treaty, and this is regarded as tantamount to a reservation.

All too often (some say) the Senate approves a treaty with Senate interpretation, i.e., understandings of what it means. The rub is that while understandings are easier to get support for in the Senate (because deemed not alterations), executive practice is to communicate them to the other treaty party or parties for acceptance or rejection, exactly on the same basis as reservations. To complicate matters further, in recent times the senators have developed even less conditional caveats, such as declarations. If made by a senator or two, but not two-thirds of them, declarations would be no more than legislative history. But declarations by the approving two-thirds would seem to fall within the executive practice of transmitting all caveats by the Senate to other treaty parties. Finally, the executive may have made reservations at signature and more recently has formulated reservations recommended to the Senate. All executive reservations will be in the President's message to the Senate, and everything in that message will be sent to the other party or parties; and, eventually, if the Senate approves the treaty and the President ratifies it, the whole history of the treaty, including recitation of communication of reservations to the other side, is repeated in the presidential promulgation of the treaty. See discussion in ch. 10 of the U.S. Reservations and understandings relating to the Genocide Convention and the Covenant on Civil & Political Rights.

2. *Caveats made subsequent to a treaty entering into effect.* There are several open or only partially resolved questions here. *Reservations made by other states:* If these were made prior to approval by the Senate, they would be put before the Senate by the President. But if made and acquiesced in by the executive after the treaty has come into effect for the United States, we have no rule as yet. The other state's reservations to a bilateral treaty would virtually ensure it would not be sent to the Senate. Why?

Senate action after the treaty is in effect for the United States. In the only known case, *The Diamond Rings*, 183 U.S. 176, 180 (1901), the Supreme Court refused to take into account a Senate resolution seeking what in effect was a post-approval understanding, saying "the meaning of the treaty cannot be controlled by subsequent explanations of some of those who may have voted to ratify it". Experts on federal legislation could fashion a tighter case: the Senate is a continuing body and that body now votes by two-thirds to attach a post-promulgation reservation. Would the court ignore it?

Executive branch actions after the treaty is in effect for the United States. The treaty is in effect, and another party to it (by diplomatic note) asks whether the United States agrees with this or that interpretation of an article in the treaty. The Secretary of State says that the United States does agree. It is beyond dispute that the executive branch is the authorized interpreter of treaties vis-à-vis other states and that executive interpretations are entitled to great weight in courts in the United States. See Section 326 of the 1987 Restatement. However, the Senate, by two-thirds vote interposes a reservation to the above interpretation. What result?

This once largely hypothetical question became an acute issue of uncertain future dimensions in the spring of 1987. Responding to the President's activism in espousing a re-interpretation of the Anti–Ballistic Missile Treaty to accommodate the administration's wish to develop and (eventually) deploy the Strategic Defense Initiative, Senator Sam Nunn, a recognized Senate leader on national security and related issues, declared, for himself and some other senators, that such reinterpretation was contrary to the Senate's understanding of the ABM treaty when it was approved, and if not referred to the Senate again, would create a grave constitutional issue. Because of the unknowable possible significance of the ABM issue on United States law about treaties, we provide the following material. What issues remain the same and what new issues arise since the disintegration of the former Soviet Union?

Study the Treaty Between the United States of America and the Union of Soviet Socialist Republics on the Limitation of Anti-Ballistic Missiles Systems of May 26, 1972, 23 U.S.T. 3435, T.I.A.S. 7503, in Doc. Supp.

THE REAGAN RE-INTERPRETATION, 1985–1987

Prepared statement of Abraham D. Sofaer, Legal Adviser, U.S. Department of State, ABM Treaty Interpretation Dispute, Hearing Before the Sub–Committee on Arms Control, International Security and Science of the Committee on Foreign Affairs, House of Representatives, 99th Cong., 1st Sess., 9 (1986).

* * *

The ABM Treaty is an important element of our strategic arms control structure. When the President first announced the SDI program in March 1983, he made clear that it would be conducted "consistent with our obligations [under] the ABM treaty." This commitment has been maintained. The United States has scrupulously complied with the Treaty, notwithstanding such clear Soviet violations of it as the Krasnoyarsk radar station.

Soviet violations of the ABM Treaty, the implementation of our SDI program, and the ongoing arms negotiations at Geneva recently caused various agencies to consider more thoroughly than ever before the appropriate interpretation of the ABM Treaty as it relates to future or "exotic" systems. By that, I mean defensive systems that serve the same functions as ABM systems and components, but that use devices based on technology not understood in 1972 when the Treaty was negotiated and that are capable of substituting for ABM interceptor missiles, launchers, and radars. This examination has led to the conclusion that a reading of the ABM Treaty that would allow the development and testing of such systems based on physical principles other than those understood in 1972 is wholly justified.

* * *

I was well aware when I began my work on this issue that several officials associated with the SALT I negotiations, and others still in the Government, had advanced the view that the ABM Treaty is unambiguous in its treatment of such future systems. They argued that Article V of the Treaty forbids development, testing, or deployment of any future ABM systems and components other than those that are fixed land-based. They read Agreed Statement D as relevant only to fixed land-based systems and components, arguing that it permits "creation" of such systems and components when they are based on "other physical principles," but conditions their deployment on agreement between the parties on specific limitations. Other persons were contending, however, that this "restrictive" view of the ABM Treaty is based on unilateral assertions by U.S. negotiators; that the Treaty is ambiguous; and that the negotiating record supports a broader view of our freedom to develop, test, and deploy future systems.

My study of the Treaty led me to conclude that its language is ambiguous and can more reasonably be read to support a broader interpretation. An examination of the three provisions primarily at issue will demonstrate why this is so. * * *

The restrictive interpretation rests on the premise that Article V(1) is clear on its face: it says no development, testing, or deployment of "ABM systems or components" other than those that are fixed land-based. But this language does not settle the issue of the article's applicability to future systems or components. That issue depends on the meaning of the term "ABM systems or components": is that phrase limited to systems and components based on then-current technology, or does it also include those based on future technology?

In attempting to answer this question, one must turn to the definition of "ABM system" in Article II(1). Proponents of the restrictive view contend that this definition is functional: anything ever conceived that could serve the function of countering strategic missiles in flight falls within the definition. These persons argue that the three components identified in that paragraph—missiles, launchers, and radars—are merely listed as the elements of what an ABM system is "currently consisting of," and that all future components of a system that satisfies the functional definition are also covered by Article II(1). Only when armed with these meanings can proponents rely on Article V(1) as a ban on development, testing, and deployment of all non-fixed land-based systems or components, whether current or future.

* * *

Under international law, as under U.S. domestic law, once an agreement has been found ambiguous, one must seek guidance in the circumstances surrounding the drafting of the agreement. Thus, in the present situation, once we concluded that the Treaty is ambiguous, we turned to the negotiating record to see which of the possible constructions most accurately reflects the parties' intentions.

Examining the negotiating record for the ABM Treaty presented some real, albeit mundane, difficulties. No single agency has systematically collected and preserved the entire record in a readily usable form. My staff and I therefore obtained from various sources everything that we could find that might be relevant to the issue of future systems and components. Because we are still in the process of collecting material, I cannot tell you with certainty that I know every single step in the negotiating process. But we are far enough along that I can say with confidence that a much stronger case exists in the record for the broader interpretation of the Treaty than for the restrictive interpretation.

If, after this public session, the Committee chooses to go into executive session, I will be free to explain much more. I can tell you in general, however, that I personally reviewed all the significant statements and drafts in the available negotiating history regarding future systems. I reached the firm conclusion that, although the U.S. delegates initially sought to ban development and testing of non-land based systems or components based on future technology, the Soviets refused to go along, and no such agreement was reached. The Soviets stubbornly resisted U.S. attempts to adopt in the body of the Treaty any limits on such systems or components based on future technology; their arguments rested on a professed unwillingness to deal with unknown devices or technology. The farthest the Soviets were willing to go with respect to such future systems or components was to adopt a side agreement prohibiting only the deployment of such systems and components, once created, until the parties agreed on specific limitations. The parties did not agree to ban development and testing of such systems or components, whether on land or in space.

The negotiating record also contains strong support for a reading of Article II(1) that restricts the definitions of "ABM system" and "components" to those based on current physical principles. The Soviets specifically sought to prevent broad definitions of these terms, and our negotiators acceded to their wishes. Moreover, our negotiators ultimately convinced the Soviets to adopt Agreed Statement D by arguing that, without it, the Treaty would leave the parties free to deploy systems or components based on other physical principles, such as lasers.

* * *

SMITH,[a] FOREWORD TO SHERR, A LEGAL ANALYSIS OF THE "NEW INTERPRETATION" OF THE ANTI–BALLISTIC MISSILE TREATY (1986) *

The Anti–Ballistic Missile Treaty of 1972 is the only U.S.–Soviet strategic nuclear arms control agreement that has been ratified and remains in force today. It has effectively prevented the parties from expanding their strategic defensive arsenals as they have done so vigorously on the offensive side. It has permitted both governments to pursue—albeit with insufficient results to date—limits and reductions on strategic missiles, submarines, and bombers.

In October, 1985, the Reagan Administration suddenly revealed a new interpretation of the Treaty that would permit the development and testing of lasers and other exotic weapons that are space-, air-, sea-, or mobile land-based. This unilateral reinterpretation reversed the established understanding of the Treaty. It is inconsistent with the historic understanding accepted by the Treaty's negotiators, including myself; the U.S. Senate, which ratified it; and every Administration since President Nixon's, including the Reagan Administration itself before October, 1985.

When the supreme law of our land as set forth in this Treaty of unlimited duration is thus radically revised by an overreaching policy, it is the responsibility of the legal profession to examine the issue and support adherence to the law. In this instance, the pertinent provisions of the Treaty are clear, their meaning is readily apparent, and the public historical record is unambiguous. One does not have to be a technical expert or international lawyer to read the Treaty and the Administration's recent arguments and then draw an informed conclusion about the merits of the established and the "new" interpretations of the Treaty.

SECTION E. DOES UNITED STATES PUBLIC LAW ABOUT INTERNATIONAL AGREEMENTS NEED CHANGING AND IF SO WHAT IS FEASIBLE?

Focus for the questions posed in the title. Those using this book as students will, in their professional lifetimes, probably have occasions to discharge public affairs responsibilities involving the issue whether the system of public law about treaties and other international agreements currently in place should or should not be altered. The material you have studied shows that there is an American way as to international agreements (treaties and executive agreements) that is unique in the world community. The present public law of international agreements is, of course, an important part of the foreign affairs apparatus and the operations of a super-power, and there is need for the foreign affairs ways of the United States to be better understood worldwide. On the whole they are not well understood now by the world community and remain as enigmatic as the inner mysteries of the former Soviet Union, although for different reasons.

a. Ambassador Gerard C. Smith was Chief U.S. Delegate to SALT I and Director of the U.S. Arms Control and Disarmament Agency from 1969 to 1973.

* Reprinted with the permission of Lawyers Alliance for Nuclear Arms Control.

The present public law and practice of the United States as to international agreements, internally viewed, fits reasonably well, if not perfectly, into the foreign affairs system of the country. Some argue: why bother to consider changing the former, unless the foreign affairs system can be changed, which is not likely. Others, taking into account the unlikelihood of a third United States constitution, such as a shift to a cabinet form of government would require, and the political risks of a general constitutional convention to reconsider the present Constitution across the board, support only changes in the American way with international agreements which would not alter the version of separation of powers combined with checks and balances that is the bedrock of the Constitution of 1789.

Consider, individually, whether you would change anything, support major structural change, or consider adjustments within the present system that would reduce whatever operational deficiencies exist in current American public law and practice about international agreements. If you opt for the third, the modest goal, consider the feasibility of means for change in a range from the development of non-legislated practices between the political branches, through legislation, to constitutional amendment.

EXECUTIVE–CONGRESSIONAL INTERNATIONAL AGREEMENTS

1. ***Current extent of use.*** As Professor O'Connell's classification of executive agreements shows (p. 1070) international agreements resulting from congressional authorizations by way of delegation or ratification and presidential conclusion internationally are not unusual, but the executive-legislative agreement has not, as a modality, yet become the paramount way of committing the United States to other entities and simultaneously correlating such commitment with internal law. The use of the Executive–Congressional alternative is controlled by the President's choice; and political and other variables, such as tradition that certain types of international agreements be sent to the Senate (see paragraph 721.4 of the Foreign Affairs Manual), are often determinative. So far there is little indication that the convenience and practicality of the executive-congressional agreement for foreign affairs operations is the key factor in this choice. What are the advantages of choosing the executive-congressional agreement alternative? Its disadvantages?

2. ***The fast track provision in the Trade Act of 1974.*** This interesting development is considered more extensively in Chapter 16–A, but its essence is an offer along the following line. Congress, in effect, says: "Mr. President, only the executive can negotiate trade agreements, but only Congress can make trade law for the United States. When you go your way without consulting Congress in detail at every step, Congress always delays and sometimes frustrates your negotiation. But we in Congress know that Congress cannot, despite its power, actually make a national tariff schedule or set quotas or deal with non-tariff barriers on its own, because there are too many conflicting constituency issues.

"So, Mr. President, let us work together, but not in any way that would violate separation of powers. Separation of powers will not preclude this arrangement: (i) Congress sets the broad parameters of national trade law and authorizes you to negotiate trade agreements within them; (ii) if you, in such negotiations, beginning with the consultations and hearings in the United States with industry, labor, and other interest groups and continuing through the negotiations with other countries, keep the relevant committee and other elements in the Congress fully informed and show good faith in taking congressional viewpoints into account, Congress for its part will enact *now,* general legislation with respect to the procedural rules of both houses that will guarantee speedy enactment of the legislation necessary to put your international negotiation into effect."

In January, 1975, President Ford signed into law the Trade Reform Act of 1974. Section 151 of the act—19 M.S.C. § 2191—provides the above fast track. There was urgent need for the legislation, as the United States had had no trade legislation in place since the automatic demise of the Kennedy-era Trade Expansion Act of 1962. The 1974 act also contained several legislative veto provisions but President Ford could not risk using his veto.

Question: Is the result under the fast track properly classifiable as an executive-congressional agreement, or does it belong in a new, fourth classification?

3. *Executive-congressional international agreements at the initiative of the President: always constitutionally effective?* In a pioneering article, McDougal and Lans, *Treaties and Congressional–Executive or Presidential Agreements: Interchangeable Instruments of National Policy*, 54 Yale L.J. 181, 534 (1945), the viewpoint was that such types of executive agreements are absolutely (or almost always) interchangeable, with referral to the Senate for advice and consent and to both houses for implementation, if required. Cf., Oliver, *Getting the Senators to Accept the Reference of Treaties to Both Houses for Approval by Simple Majorities; Does the Sense Resolution in the 1979 Foreign Relations Authorization Act Point a Way?*, 74 AJIL 142 (1980), which focuses more on the political practicability of wide replacement of the orthodox system than on assured constitutionality in all or most situations. It is now generally assumed that the alternative of the executive-congressional international agreement has wider potential than presidents have chosen to utilize. Such agreements have not been specifically tested for constitutionality by the courts. Would members of the Senate, not the Senate as a body, have standing to contend that executive-congressional agreements cannot be used to deprive them of their individual rights as senators to use the two-thirds requirement for advice and consent to prevent treaties from coming into effect?

A perhaps more difficult issue might be whether an executive-congressional international agreement can have status as a "treaty" under the supremacy clause, Article VI of the Constitution. Suppose such agreements, rather than Senate-consented treaties, had been the basis of federal supremacy in *Ware v. Hylton* and *Missouri v. Holland?*

Would the marked expansion of the federal legislative power afforded by the Supreme Court suggest that de facto interchangeability exists under Article VI? Might the court decline to decide the controversy under the political question doctrine?

It is readily apparent that the American executive-congressional international agreement comes close to the simultaneous ratification and internal implementation-by-law models in continental constitutions. It has been mildly mooted in the literature whether a direct replacement of the Article II arrangement in the Constitution by a bicameral, simple majority, legislative act of approval would be acceptable constitutionally, even if the Supreme Court might not hear the issue. Would the political branches be violating their own oaths to "preserve, protect, and defend the Constitution" Could it be argued effectively that such a development would merely be another case of the evolution of the Constitution, as, say, in regard to the right of privacy? How far would you be willing to go? Why?

Chapter 15

INTERNATIONAL ECONOMIC LAW

The Why of This Chapter

We believe every person who is interested in or concerned about legal order in the world community needs to understand the basics covered in this Chapter, e.g. the emerging, growing, shifting and changing economic law sector of the international legal system. The materials chosen are broadly representative but are only a minimal introduction to specializations that are covered in advanced or graduate courses such as International Economic Law, Foreign Trade Law, Transnational Finance Law, Multinational Business Enterprise Law, Legal Controls of Planetary Resources, International Business Taxation and the like. This field engages more private practitioners and big law firms than any other sector. The monied levels of legal activity are so vast probably because the planet is fast-becoming one world economically—but not legally.

Overview

Economic equality does not prevail in our world of "legally equal states" and various types of international entities themselves linked to legally equal states. There are rich states, modestly endowed states, poor states and seemingly hopeless states. The economic condition of a state is a tremendous factor in its real-world state of development, including politics, potential for aggression, and human rights sensitivity.

While an equilibrium of assured economic equality cannot be fashioned, it is obvious that as much as possible should be done to provide a planetary maximization of asset-uses. The means are free and fair exchange of goods and services among states (Trade); permitted and reasonably-assured movements of investment capital from state to state (Foreign Investment); effective regulations to minimize theft and fraud as to capital movements across frontiers (Transnational Cooperation in Regulatory Activities); and fair and assured utilization of energy resources (Transnational Cooperation in Resource Management). The legal situation as to each of these headings will be taken up in this Chapter. But, first, consider these illustrative situations:

———

Problems. The problems sketched below are an introduction to the subject matter in this chapter.—*Problem A.* Denial of entry of foreign goods. For a long time private enterprise in State X has exported large quantities of electric home appliances to consumers in State Y, paying normal import duties. Suddenly, authorities in State Y decree a very low quota on foreign-made electric home appliances, stating that this is done to save the domestic home appliance industry from extinction. Business failures and serious unemployment result in the home appliance industry of State X.

Problem B. Denial of entry of foreign business capital. Home appliance manufacturers in State X decide to set up production in State Y for the State Y market, using Y labor. State Y refuses to permit the transfer of the requisite business capital from State X to it.

Problem C. Deprivation of rights flowing from ownership. A corporation organized in State Z owns 100% a corporation chartered in State Y that under State Y law owns subsurface rights to mine certain minerals. These rights are now worth $50,000,000. State Y expropriates these rights and pays no compensation, charging that the alien group from State Z paid only $500,000 for the rights to begin with and has since profited $100,000,000 from their exploitation.

Problem D. Deprivation of developmental opportunity. State M has a population growth rate of three percent a year and a Gross National Product per capita of $62 a year—a very poor state indeed. It has been receiving from State N and from International Organization O foreign assistance grants to help with its population problem and development loans on concessional terms (below the market cost of the money to the lenders) to support a National Development Plan designed to boost GNP per capita to $200 over ten years. In the fifth year of the assistance program State N objects to the denial of basic human rights in State M. N cuts off its bilateral development assistance to M and successfully prevents O from providing multilateral assistance.

Problem E. Security of Supply of an essential natural resource. The industrialized countries have become increasingly dependent upon foreign oil for heating, electricity generation, transport fuel and industrial uses. Some of the leading oil producers are concentrated in the unstable Middle East where they pursue foreign policies at times sharply at variance with those of some of the main oil consumer countries. The producers impose an oil embargo as an economic weapon against the consumer countries in order to induce policy changes; and by cartel actions the producers force a dramatic increase in the price of oil. The consumers in turn abruptly face the prospect of long-term foreign policy vulnerability to adversarial action of the producers as well as exposure to disruption of essential supplies by reason of natural disasters, military action in the producing regions, transport difficulties and other causes beyond their control, together with the prospect of economic loss through production controls and other cartel pricing practices.

* * *

Notwithstanding these major activities and needs, there is no customary international law imposing duties and creating correlative rights in the above cases, except possibly Case C, where capital-exporting states (or most of them) would argue that there is a rule of customary law requiring fair compensation and some capital-receiving (usually also poor and developing) nations would disagree. Except for the increasingly disputed nationalization area of Case C and some rules about the trading rights of neutrals in pre-UN wars—rules that in World War I and II were not followed because the enemy continued to breach closely related rules—the rules of the economic activity of international legal systems are found in international agreements. These rules are incomplete. The lawyer's role in the transnational economic field is currently active and highly important, although international lawyering takes one more often than not into national centers of law and policy and to the law in treaties, rather than to decisions of international tribunals or the doctrines of international law publicists. Students and law firms, as well as corporations and other businesses need to know that the market for good international lawyers is burgeoning. They often do not.

GENERALITIES ABOUT FOREIGN
TRADE AND INVESTMENT

Historically the movement of goods (but not services or capital) has been public and at least taxed for revenue purposes. In ancient times walled cities had a kiosk at the city gate for the tax-gatherers. (Whether the charges levied there were purely for revenue or to some degree "protection" we cannot say; but trade in goods was only very rarely entirely "free".) Capital, on the other hand, moved quietly or secretly, usually unmolested by minor authorities for obvious reasons. Trade in services is a modern concept. (As we shall see, it became a matter of debate in GATT, at the United States' initiative, only in the past few years). In earlier times personal services usually involved chattel slavery or indentures or simply the movement of medical or other skilled providers from one place to another, as from Athens to Rome. Services were not thought of as things, and even today, in GATT and elsewhere, "trade" in services is slightly exotic.

Capital movements, in contrast to Trade, do not raise "tariff-like" problems. We know of no direct taxes on capital movements. But there are sometimes prohibitions or hindrances. Conversion of capital from one money system to another involves the costs of the foreign exchange transaction; and under circumstances usually not entirely in the hands of any single government, foreign exchange controls may be imposed in certain circumstances on the conversion of local currency profits. The "charge" on a capital movement, thus, remains free of direct control by most state authorities, but it can be discouraged or encouraged by monetary management and other activities of host state agencies. In international law the major problems arising in regard to capital investment in foreign countries have been those of freedom to enter, protection from host state action or inaction in violation of international law, and freedom from discriminatory, larcenous, or patently unfair regulation by the state into which it moves.

Lawyers need to know about relevant trade law, foreign investment law and the different sets of international economic law rules with differences as to where to seek redress. *For instance:* do not take a trade hassle to the State Department or an expropriation of your client's Ruritanian factory to the International Trade Commission! (Not at first, anyway.)

SECTION A.   FOREIGN TRADE LAW

A SKETCH OF THE IMPORT–PROCESS AS TO TRADE IN GOODS AND THINGS

The shipment arrives at the frontier, usually pre-cleared, or delivered directly to a customs broker. The bill of lading describes the contents, using, if possible, the customs nomenclature of the receiving state. The goods or things are inspected for the accuracy and the veracity of the importer's classification. The customs inspector may change the classification and hence also the rate of duty, classifications being numerous, narrow, and sometimes surprisingly (or shockingly) variant as between items that seem not to be very different. (These differences may reflect hidden protectionism, sometimes ancient, with reasons forgotten.) If the importer does not accept a re-classification, a lawyer specializing in trade law has to be engaged to take the dispute through administrative review, and eventually, if necessary, judicial review. There is a whole body of specialist law about customs classification (and levy) issues. Note that the foregoing refers to trade in goods and things, not services. Services do not ordinarily receive customs classification for the levy of duties. Entry of them, vel non, is a matter of host state control not unlike those on direct foreign businesses, treated in Section B.

There are other import controls than custom duties: quotas, sanitary and safety regulations, and importing state sanctions or other inducements to the exporting state to conform to some value or standard of interest to the import state. Quotas as to quantity or value have been often of more concern to foreign suppliers than customs duties, particularly when rates of duty have been reduced to low percentages of value. You will see later that trade liberation arrangements, such as GATT, approach the rate of duty and quota problems along somewhat different lines. As to health, sanitary and safety regulations, contemporary news reports of American exporters' complaints about Japanese "testing" delays and alleged "Mickey–Mouse" standards have probably come to your attention. Ironically, at this writing, the American meat-consuming public is having a problem with the Great American Hamburger, "protected" from foreign beef by the Wholesome Meat Act, which inter-alia, requires American official inspection of slaughter houses abroad that would export to the United States.

Prohibition of imports from a particular source for foreign policy reasons or national moral values (such as human rights) involves the legal pros and cons of "economic sanctions" (also, known under more stressful conditions as "economic warfare"). So do controls (including absolute prohibitions) on the export of materials and devices deemed of national security concern. Until the dissolution of the Soviet Union and the warming of the Cold War, administrative practice before the Export Control Administration of the United States Department of Commerce and judicial review of the actions thereof, and lobbying, supported a number of specialist attorneys, both for the Government and for the contesting would-be exporters. We do not vouchsafe here present levels of activity in this field.

Finally, as to the customs process: beyond what happens at the customs frontier, there are in the United States and elsewhere, rather vast and complicated administrative law procedures, and in the United States, federal court judicial review.

A BRIEF HISTORY OF TARIFFS AND OF TRADE LIBERALIZATION

The era of European colonization of the Americas saw *mercantilism* practiced with varying degrees of exclusivity by the Spanish, Portuguese, French, and British colonizers. The metropoles, to varying degrees over time, sought to have their colonies trade with the world through them; and the same attitudes characterized later European colonizations in other parts of the world. A vestige of this era, (British) *Empire Preference* (as to terms of trade) lasted well into this century.

According to popular history, the British–Northamericans who revolted and created the United States of America, a revolution triggered by a trade-taxation issue, found themselves after Independence divided on a trade issue that persisted in national politics roughly until the Truman Administration. You may remember the issue from school history as: *Tariffs for Revenue Only* versus *Tariffs to Protect Infant Industry* (and later, *Tariffs to Protect the American Laborer*). The deep division on this issue reflected the conflicting aspirations of industrial states of the Union and agricultural states and areas. Why, then? What now? What is South Carolina today? Illinois? California?

In 1930 Congress enacted the highest levels of duty in American history. (The Smoot–Hawley Tariff Act). Why was this done in the first year of the Great Depression? What happened to these very high (often over 30%) ad valorem rates of duty? They still remain in the United States tariff schedules! But they are in Schedule 2 of the TSUS (Tariff Schedule of the United States), which means that they apply only when Schedule 1 of TSUS does not apply; Schedule 1 represents the rate of duty on imports from Most–Favored–Nations. Schedule 1 rates reflect many years of bilateral and multipartite tariff-lowering activities of the United States. President Franklin D. Roosevelt's choice for Secretary of State, "Judge" Cordell Hull, Senator from Tennessee, was a classic "Free Trade Democrat". (The Term "Free Trade" in the American lexicon did not mean, necessarily, zero duty, but lower duty.) The American initiative was nearly a solo one for years. Secretary Hull and his successors first used bilateral negotiations, then multipartite negotiations mainly through the General Agreement on Tariffs and Trade (GATT), to bring down rates of duty from Smoot–Hawley levels (Schedule 2) to a range which currently regards a 10 percent-of-value duty as quite high. How was this done? By the use of Unconditional Most–Favored–Nation procedures, which we shall consider now.

Even before the Roosevelt–Hull era, the United States occasionally experimented swapping tariff concessions with other countries; i.e., with Hawaii exchanging lower U.S. duties on Hawaiian pineapples for lower Hawaiian duties on iron plowshares. The United States would then inform another pineapple-producing state that it could have the same deal. This kind of relationship was known as Conditional–Most–Favored–Nation–Treatment (Conditional MFN). Sometimes the items in the swap varied a bit; but the basic principle remained that of a concession for a concession. Obviously, Conditional MFN could not be utilized to spread trade liberalization widely and quickly. In 1927 (before Roosevelt–Hull), the United States first moved to Unconditional MFN, when Brazil and the U.S. promised to give each other any break as to customs duty given to any third state. In the Roosevelt–Hull era, Unconditional MFN treaties were increasingly negotiated on a bi-lateral basis, with the MFN agreement usually part of rather standardized "treaties of friendship, commerce, and navigation", (FCN treaties). In theory, such bilateral treaties would be negotiated with a "principal supplier" of the commodity to be imported, in order to ensure mutual interest in making generous concessions as to rates of duty, or sometimes, quotas. The effect of such treaties was an across-the-board reduction in tariffs, because states with an MFN treaty right were automatically entitled to concessions given any other state that was the "nation-most-favored" as to that commodity.

In 1947–48 a multipartite version of Unconditional MFN became possible through tariff negotiation between any two members of the General Agreement on Tariffs and Trade (GATT), via Article I of the Gatt agreement (pp. 1116–1117). The optimistic assumption was that in GATT Negotiating Rounds (see infra), a pair of principal suppliers would negotiate to the bone, and both concessions could be claimed throughout the GATT membership. Hence, in Country C problem contained in the introduction to this Chapter, page 1114, Unconditional MFN is called "the heart of GATT". However, this does not mean that the United States can claim the zero rate of duty on, say, French wine, that prevails between France and the United Kingdom. In other words, states that are grouped together in common markets do not have to favor nonmembers of that market. What about free trade areas? You will come to them. Meanwhile, bilateral unconditional MFN still exists between a GATT member and a state not in GATT; see MFN for China.

1. MOST FAVORED NATION TREATMENT

Problem. At a time when its own tariffs were highly protectionist, State A analyzed world trade conditions and came to the conclusion that tariff barriers were undesirably high worldwide including the tariffs of States B, C and D. Up to that time, State A had given another state only such tariff cuts for its exports to State A as were compensated for by some corresponding cut in that state's duty on State A's exports to it. This requirement of compensation applied even where the other state had been promised most favored nation treatment in a treaty with State A, and State A had given a cut to a third state, which, in turn, had conceded a trade benefit to State A.

When State A decided to launch a worldwide effort to lower tariff barriers, it announced that it was changing its concept of most favored nation treaties to an unconditional form. Thereafter, States A, B, C and D each entered into unconditional most favored nation agreements (MFNs) with the other three. States A, B and C are highly-developed, producing wide ranges of manufactured goods. State D is a less well-developed country, largely an agricultural producer and non-competitive as to costs with A, B and C insofar as manufactured goods are concerned. If D did not have high tariffs or low quotas on goods (say automobiles) manufactured in A, B and C, its high cost domestic market would yield to the foreign imports of manufactured goods and D would lose scarce foreign exchange to pay for the imports.

States A and B enter into wide-ranging and hard-bargained bilateral trade treaties that result in average tariff cuts of 50% from schedules on both sides. C and D, under their MFN treaties with A and B, claim the benefits of these cuts but offer none in return, with the result that their tariff walls loom higher than ever as clogs on international trade. Considering the materials on pp. 1119 et seq. answer these *questions*: 1. Why did A move to unconditional MFN? 2. Why did A and B make their arrangement, assuming they knew that C and D might not offer cuts? 3. Could A and B legally withdraw their promises to C and D, if they had been led to believe by C or D that they, too, would offer cuts, which they did not in fact offer?

Questions to come back to: (after more on GATT, or on review):

Assume that states A, B, and C are members of GATT and:

1. A and B entered into a bilateral MFN arrangement: Are C and D entitled to claim MFN?

2. C is a member of the EU, which has no tariffs among EU countries, but a common external tariff applicable to all non-members of the EU. What are the recourses within GATT of A and B?

3. D is a member of a free trade area, wherein members have zero tariffs among themselves but keep their national tariffs as against non-members. What are A & B's recourses within GATT?

PATTERSON, DISCRIMINATION IN INTERNATIONAL TRADE, THE POLICY ISSUES 1945–1965

at 6 (1966) *

Discriminatory policies were sometimes defended on the much wider grounds that they fostered freer trade. In a world in which there are problems of unemployment and in which tariff barriers exist and are reduced by a process of negotiation and exchange of "concessions," in such a world a policy of nondiscrimination (unconditional-most-favored-nation treatment) by A and B reduces their future bargaining power in the quest for larger markets in C and D. The consequence, many held, could easily be a slowing down in tariff reductions all around the world. This case for discrimination was more difficult to deal with by those who favored more liberal trade policies and it was commonly accepted as a potent case for discrimination. Ways were found to partially meet the problem—notably, the development of the "principal supplier" rule and specialized tariff classification [6]—but at the cost of impairing the most-

---

* Copyright © 1966 by Princeton University Press. Reprinted by permission.

6. The principal supplier—or chief source—rule requires that a nation negotiate reductions in import barriers on a given product only with the country which had been supplying the greatest portion of the former's import of that product. It is thus intended that each concession will be negotiated with the country having the greatest interest in it. This practice preserves bargaining power when the unconditional-most-favored-nation practice is followed, because there is a tendency under it for some products of prime interest to other countries (those goods for which each is a major supplier) not to be the subject of negotiation between other pairs of countries. Specialized tariff classification facilitates the application of the principal supplier rule by so defining products for trade barrier cutting purposes that fewer, rather than more, of the exports important to those not participating in a given bilateral negotiation qualify for the bilaterally agreed cuts.

favored-nation principle.[7]

* * *

Trade liberalization and the rise of most favored national treatment in the unconditional form. Broadly, both the conditional and unconditional forms of most favored nation treatment reduce the discrimination that exists in international trade when two states restrict exclusively to themselves the trade advantages they give to each other. Bilateral and strictly exclusive trade bargains were the norm over much of the historical period of the modern state, often being linked to treaties of military and political alliance. To a considerable extent for some countries such arrangements existed until sometime after World War II in the Western world, usually those with foreign exchange difficulties. Bilateral trade arrangements of the exclusive sort still characterize the trading practices of the Eastern European socialist bloc.

However, there is evidence that, in past centuries, states sometimes found it in their respective national interests to make trade liberalization arrangements in the knowledge that there were outstanding most favored nation promises to third states, and in some instances these promises were of the unconditional type.

Between the two World Wars and after the second down to date, subject to questions that arise in relationship to material to follow in this section, the United States has been the prime mover toward trade liberalization (lower tariffs and the reduction of quotas on imports, i.e. quantitative restrictions). Exclusive trade agreements were not favored by the United States even when political parties favoring highly protective tariffs were in power. Until shortly before an exchange of notes with Brazil in 1923, the United States adhered to the practice of entering into conditional most favored nation treaty relationships. See *Whitney v. Robertson*, 124 U.S. 190, 8 S.Ct. 456 (1888), where an importer of goods from San Domingo (today the Dominican Republic) failed to get the lower than tariff schedule rate the United States had given the King of Hawaii on the same product, because the United States treaty with the country of the import's origin was of the conditional most favored nation variety and that country did not give American imports concessions comparable to those that the King of Hawaii had given. It was so held even though the treaty had not specifically stated that the United States treaty promise to that country was conditioned upon the giving of such compensation.

Nonetheless, the general level of United States and other tariffs remained high. What is said to be the highest general level of tariffs in United States history was reached in the Tariff Act of 1930, coinciding with the Great Depression and European defaults on war debts to the United States, because of the debtors' inability to sell enough for dollars and gold to pay without seriously impairing the credibility of their own monies and their capacity to pay for necessary imports. Franklin D.

---

7. The argument lost some more of its potency when, immediately after World War II, arrangements were made for simultaneous bilateral negotiations, a procedure which Germany had followed before World War I, and which became the hallmark of the General Agreement on Tariffs and Trade.

Roosevelt came to power in 1933 committed to trade liberalization through the negotiation of bilateral tariff reductions that by unconditional most favored nation treatment would spread throughout the world trading system. It was assumed that the maximum use of the principal supplier technique (see the excerpt from Patterson above) would ensure the requisite network of tariff-cutting agreements.

Congress responded with the Reciprocal Trade Agreements Act of 1933, which as codified and from time to time extended and amplified as to the scope of the President's delegated power to cut tariffs, is still the basis of United States trade liberalization treaties and for United States participation in the General Agreement on Tariffs and Trade (GATT).

TREATY OF FRIENDSHIP, COMMERCE AND NAVIGATION BETWEEN THE UNITED STATES AND JAPAN OF APRIL 2, 1953

4 U.S.T. 2063, 206 U.N.T.S. 143.

Article XIV

1. Each Party shall accord most-favored-nation treatment to products of the other Party, from whatever place and by whatever type of carrier arriving, and to products destined for exportation to the territories of such other Party, by whatever route and by whatever type of carrier, with respect to customs duties and charges of any kind imposed on or in connection with importation or exportation or imposed on the international transfer of payments for imports or exports, and with respect to the method of levying such duties and charges, and with respect to all rules and formalities [re] importation and exportation.

* * *

Article XXII

* * *

2. The term "most-favored-nation treatment" means treatment accorded within the territories of a Party upon terms no less favorable than the treatment accorded therein, in like situations, to nationals, companies, products, vessels or other objects, * * *, of any third country.

GENERAL AGREEMENT ON TARIFFS AND TRADE OF OCTOBER 30, 1947

61 Stat. Part 5, A12, 55 U.N.T.S. 187.

Article I

1. With respect to customs duties and charges of any kind imposed on or in connection with importation or exportation or imposed on the international transfer of payments for imports or exports, and with

respect to the method of levying such duties and charges, and with respect to all rules and formalities in connection with importation and exportation, and with respect to all matters referred to in paragraphs 1 and 2 of Article III, any advantage, favour, privilege or immunity granted by any contracting party to any product originating in or destined for any other country shall be accorded immediately and unconditionally to the like product originating in or destined for the territories of all other contracting parties.

2. The provisions of paragraph 1 of this Article shall not require the elimination of any preferences in respect of import duties or charges which do not exceed the levels provided for in paragraph 3 of this Article and which fall within the following descriptions:

[There follow specified excepted trade preferences, i.e. tariff advantages that are to remain exclusive. Generally, these were those between the United Kingdom and other Commonwealth entities; France and Territories of the French Union; the Customs Union of Belgium, Luxembourg and the Netherlands and the overseas territories of Belgium and the Netherlands; the United States and the Republics of Cuba and the Philippines and dependent territories of the United States; preferences between a few neighboring countries, the United States and Canada—Mexico not being included.]

---

1. *The institutional history of GATT.* The GATT, as a set of multipartite treaty rules about international trade and as a slightly developed international organization, is all that survives of an ambitious post-World War II effort to establish an International Trade Organization (ITO). The Charter of the International Trade Organization died aborning, in part because it attempted to regulate internationally restrictive trade practices and cartels and monopolies, as well as tariffs and quotas. GATT was put into effect pending sufficient state approvals to permit the ITO to come into being, which it never did. As the prospects for the ITO dimmed, GATT institutionalized itself, although it still is not, strictly speaking, a full-fledged international organization.

As to the expectations for the ITO, see Rubin, The Judicial Review Problem in the International Trade Organization, 63 Harv.L.Rev. 78 (1949). For the early period of GATT, consult Gorter, GATT after Six Years: An Appraisal, VIII Int'l Orgs. 1 (1954). The failure of the ITO also cost the less-developed countries (LDCs) their effort to write into MFN treatment an explicit exception for their development-related exports; the developed countries agreed to such a principle (Art. XV of the ITO) for the ITO, but successfully resisted its inclusion in the GATT part of that arrangement. As things turned out GATT was the only part of the total effort to regulate all major aspects of international trade that went into effect. As to the work of GATT, consult Hudec, The GATT Legal System and World Trade Diplomacy (1975), and Jackson, World Trade and the Law of GATT (1970), and Jackson & Davey, Legal Problems of International Economic Relations (2d ed. 1986).

2. ***GATT as a legal curiosity.*** It is often said that unconditional most favored treatment is the heart of GATT. It is also about the only part that requires GATT member states to alter pre-existing national legislation contrary to GATT. Technically, no state is a party to GATT as such. GATT is in force only through a Protocol of Provisional Application, and that Protocol allows states at signature to indicate that (or what) then-existing national legislation contrary to Part II of GATT will remain in effect. Part I of GATT, including Article I, above, is not affected by the "existing legislation" provision in the Protocol of Provisional Application.

3. ***Membership in GATT.*** A GATT publication, *Activities,* periodically updates GATT membership and is a useful source of general information about the organization, headquartered at Geneva, Switzerland. In July, 1992, 104 states were members; 28 states where GATT formerly applied during colonial periods were awaiting decisions on admission. Several members have divided or otherwise split-up since the above date, notably the former Czechoslovakia and the former Yugoslavia. The former U.S.S.R., which became an observer in 1990, has been succeeded by the Russian Federation as observer at GATT. Most states-members of the Commonwealth of Independent States, also derived from the former U.S.S.R., are reported by GATT to be adopting GATT–based guidelines for their evolving trade regimes and thus looking toward association. The three Baltic States, Estonia, Latvia and Lithuania, are reported to have expressed interest in observer status. Also, as of the above date, GATT working parties were considering the membership applications of Bulgaria, Paraguay, Mongolia; and Panama, Ecuador, Syria, Taiwan and Viet Nam had made formal or informal soundings about accession. Cuba is a long-standing member. (Does this surprise you?) Mexico became a member several years ago, thus making all states in the proposed North American Free Trade Agreement (NAFTA) members of GATT as well.

4. ***Other international economic structures.*** Dealing with international economic policy more broadly cast than trade alone are UNCTAD (United Nations Commission on Trade and Development); OECD (Organization for Economic Cooperation and Development), based at Paris and not a specialized agency of the United Nations or a commission thereof; and UNCITRAL (United Nations Commission on International Trade Law) which works in the field of research, negotiation and proposal of private law rules of international trade, including standardized rules for arbitration of trade disputes.

UNCTAD has very wide membership, including all major developed countries and the developing countries except Albania and North Korea. So far it has reflected the viewpoints of the developing world, but as we'll see later, the developing countries bloc in the Assembly is currently not very active. OECD is open to all countries, but its developing country membership, though appreciable, is short of UNCTAD's. OECD does very professional economic and social research, often leading to policy-linked proposals, but these, unlike those of the two United Nations Commissions (UNCTAD and UNCITRAL) do not have a track through the Economic and Social Council to the United Nations General

Assembly. OECD proposals, instead, go directly to member states' governments for further individual or collective consideration. The World Bank Group (formerly the International Bank for Reconstruction and Development and affiliates) and the International Monetary Fund (IMF) are strongly capitalized, specialized agencies of the United Nations, with weighted voting. Both have very important links to foreign trade, but most of these links are beyond the scope of this introductory presentation. Common markets and free trade areas are also, in a sense, types of "international" economic structures, and they are very significant in GATT and otherwise in world trade. However, they do not provide universal membership by states, and hence they are not ordinarily thought of as being "international", but either as "transnational" or *sui generis*.

---

2. DEPARTURES FROM MOST FAVORED NATION TREATMENT

Types of departures. The most favored nation principle is used in modern commercial treaties for more than just trade (tariffs and quotas). Custom dictates certain exclusions from the coverage of most favored nation provisions, civil aviation for example. Certain other activities are also excluded, sometimes explicitly or by the general understanding of the mutually promising states: defense industries and administration of aliens' estates. As to trade in the strict sense, there is a customary exclusion of preferences given to frontier traffic.

The more important departures are those arising where common markets (a more precise term than the older "customs unions") and free trade areas provide trade advantages for the participating states in their trade with each other that, if extended to nonparticipating states having most favored nation treaties with member states individually, would destroy a major incentive toward the customs union or the trade area. Article XXIV of GATT states the contours of the exception under reference, but in practice few of the arrangements that have been made have fitted GATT like a glove, with the result that waivers have been sought and usually granted. The U.S. quickly approved such a waiver as to the present European Union (EU), when, prior to the Treaty of Rome (1956), the then European Economic Community (EEC) was being created, on the basis of free trade among the member states and a common external tariff as to non-member states. By hindsight, should it have? Why did the U.S. not only tolerate, but welcome, the EEC concept as early as 1948? All EU states are GATT members; so the EU itself is also subject to the GATT system, and the sole tariff of its members is the common external tariff, which means that only it is the basis of the EU's MFN obligation.

The same general principle of MFN exception applies to the European Free Trade Association (EFTA), as to the tariff and quota preferences the member states give each other. But as there is no common external tariff in EFTA, each EFTA state, through GATT, is responsible for dealing properly with third states in the administration of its national tariff. The currently inoperative Central American Common Market (CACM) has the same MFN structure as the EC; and the Latin American Free Trade Association (LAFTA) (currently dormant) is like EFTA, as to unconditional most favored nation treatment. Other groupings in developing Africa, Southeast Asia, the Caribbean Basin, and Latin America (the Andean Group within LAFTA) are similarly classifiable as either common markets or customs unions.

The European Union (formerly ECC, then EC) is the world's largest trading unit, although this will change, if NAFTA works. It negotiates for all twelve member states at GATT, through the EU Commission based at Brussels. The member states also have presence at GATT, technically through observers, but there have been instances of de facto direct member state activity at GATT through negotiation.

The European Free Trade Area (EFTA) once included the United Kingdom, Ireland, and Denmark, but these shifted to the (then) EEC (now EC). EFTA still includes Austria and Sweden, both of which have applied to join the EU. Switzerland and Leichtenstein (whose foreign affairs are managed by Switzerland) may have some lingering problems about shifting from EFTA to the EU, due mainly to Switzerland's "neutralization" at the Congress of Vienna (1815). Norway left the EEC and joined EFTA because of EEC regulation and limitations on North Sea herring fisheries. Nevertheless, and despite internal opposition, Norway is a candidate. Finland, which before the collapse of the Soviet Union had made some bilateral free trade arrangements with members of the Eastern Bloc (but not the USSR), was freed from concern about USSR objection to Finland's joining either Western trade area, and is a definite candidate to follow Sweden into the EU.

Multi-member free trade areas and a few multi-member "almost" common markets have been attempted by less-well developed African and Western Hemisphere states, within significant success so far. A major obstacle is that there is usually very little trade among the countries attempting broader-based trading relationships. The Asian side of the Pacific Rim has made some moves toward multi-member arrangements, and the remarkable economic growth of some of these countries gives rise to expectations of success for such arrangements. There are two political problems, however: (i) memories of Japanese aggression and occupation, and, (ii) the Chinese economic and ideological monolith. Both problems impede the association of these two states with each other and with developing states.

The other major departures from MFN in GATT are those authorizing member states to offer generalized systems of import trade preferences (GSP) to developing countries; emergency foreign exchange situations in the importing country, under which disincentives to imports are permitted; and authorization for the imposition of over-schedule duties to rectify dumping (goods offered as exports below home country cost of production), governmental subsidization of exports, unfair trade practices as to exports, and temporary escape clause situations. These other departures from MFN tend to concentrate disputes in the importing country and hence in administrative agencies and courts there, while challenges to alleged Art. XXIV departure from MFN usually arise in negotiating arguments at a GATT "Round" of trade negotiations or by a specific referral of a dispute to a GATT dispute-settlement panel at Geneva. These matters are dealt with in much greater detail in specialty courses on international trade law.

Departures from MFN for developing countries. The United States, the European Economic Community, and various developed countries individually are authorized by a 1971 waiver to Article I of GATT (and by the later development of a new part added to the GATT agreement) to give developing countries tariff and quota trading advantages which are denied to developed countries.

The term GSP (generalized system of preferences) is in general usage to refer to this type of departure from unconditional most favored nation treatment. By 1987, it was seen that the developing countries had not been lifted out of their difficulties by GSP to the degree theoretically viewed as possible in 1961 and 1971. Apologists for developing countries blame ungenerous § 7 GSP concessions and sporadic tergiversations in policy by developed countries for their disappointment. Many observers in developed countries admit that GSP classifications are often narrow and even arbitrary, but they also claim they can identify other deficiencies in developing country economics which prevent full effectiveness for existing GSP. See in the Documentary Supplement excerpts from the United States GSP system, as provided in Title V of the Trade and Tariff Act of 1984.

---

3. DEPARTURES FROM IMPORT BINDINGS FOR REASONS OTHER THAN NON-ENTITLEMENT TO MFN TREATMENT

1. *Focus.* Under this sub-heading, there are presented, very briefly, the general types of situations in which the rate of duty, or other term of trade with respect to import, binding a state (by bilateral international agreement or by the bindings resulting from trade liberalization negotiations in the GATT tent under Article II) may be altered by special circumstances. In some circumstances, these alterations may have an incidental or an asserted or actual intended discriminatory effect on the most favored nation principle as well. A good deal of the work of American specialists in international trade law falls into this area.

2. *Foreign exchange and other stringencies.* What happens legally when a GATT member finds that its trade liberalization policy has brought it a flood of imports priced in a scarce foreign currency at a time when its own exports are lagging, with the result that its adverse balance of trade (trade deficit) affects or threatens to affect its balance of payments or even its reserves to back its own currency? See the incident that follows:

GENERAL AGREEMENT ON TARIFFS AND TRADE OF OCTOBER 30, 1947

61 Stat. Part 5, A12, 55 U.N.T.S. 187.

Article XII

1. Notwithstanding the provisions of paragraph 1 of Article XI [eliminating quotas], any contracting party, in order to safeguard its external financial position and its balance of payments, may restrict the quantity or value of merchandise permitted to be imported, subject to the provisions of the following paragraphs of this Article.

2. (a) Import restrictions instituted, maintained or intensified by a contracting party under this Article shall not exceed those necessary:

    (i) to forestall the imminent threat of, or to stop, a serious decline in its monetary reserves, or (ii) in the case of a contracting party with very low monetary reserves, to achieve a reasonable rate of increase in its reserves

    * * *

(b) Contracting parties applying restrictions under subparagraph (a) of this paragraph shall progressively relax them as such conditions improve * * *.

    * * *

---

1. ***The 1971 tariff surcharge and GATT.*** GATT Article XII provides that " * * * any contracting party, to safeguard its external financial position and its balance of payments, may restrict the quantity or value of merchandise * * * [imports.]" The language means quotas, not upward revision unilaterally of tariff bindings under GATT Article II. The distinction is based on an earlier focus on high tariffs, which only since 1974 is shifting to non-tariff barriers, as general levels of duties fall. So the 1971 Nixon surcharge violated GATT.

For a short time in the early 1970s the Soviet Union and the United States were reciprocally entitled to MFN treatment under a bilateral trade agreement; but the USSR withdrew from the agreement, because of objection to an emigration rider that Congress in the Trade Act of 1974 made applicable to Soviet exports to the United States. *What happens if the Russian Federation joins GATT? If the United States and the Russian Federation make a bilateral trade treaty?*

2. ***Tariff Schedules of the United States.*** They are made up of very narrow categories of products, with the result that the customs classification problem is often litigated. Are pregnant Holstein heifers weighing over 700 pounds "cows imported specially for dairy purposes" and thus entitled to a lower rate of duty per pound than "cattle generally"?

CURRENT STATUS OF CERTAIN OTHER COMMON MARKETS AND FREE TRADE AREAS

The Central American Common Market (CACM) has not revived from the political debacle of the eighties in that region. The Latin American Free Trade Association (LAFTA), while not moribund, has accomplished little. Other groupings in less-well-developed areas (LDC's) of Africa, Southeast Asia, and the Caribbean Basin also have shown little progress. Proposals for new attempts in developing or hope-to-be developing countries continue to be made, but structures remain unstarted or incomplete. Why so little forward movement? Could it be that common markets and free trade areas require for vigor substantial amounts of existent or feasibly-developable, normal commerce by members with each other? How much commerce is there, say, between Costa Rica and El Salvador, or Brazil and Chile? Why is a free trade area between Canada and the United States functioning? An elaborate North American Free Trade Agreement (NAFTA), linking Canada, the United States and Mexico, has been negotiated and obtained the advice and consent of the Senate. Implementing legislation is in process. In July, 1993, the Canadian Parliament completed approval of NAFTA. The President of Mexico and the long-governing political party that he heads, strongly support it. Will two developed and one developing country be able to make it work? In the time when the EU was a group of six advanced European countries with substantially equal foreign exchange reserves, it was thought by experts that substantial parity in levels of economic development was essential to success of a common market or free trade area. But now the twelve states in the EU are at three levels of economic capacity. Is it working? Will it hold? If so, can Mexico hold its own, as to foreign exchange resources, under NAFTA? Does the answer depend, inter alia, on what advantages NAFTA itself may throw Mexico's way as to employment, levels of industry, foreign capital investment, and less stringent environmental regulation? Will it be deemed in the long run interests of Canada and the United States to provide such advantages to Mexico? In the case of the United States, would the concession of advantages to Mexico be acceptable should such concessions help relieve the illegal alien problem? Mexican President Salinas believes so, and is reported to have committed thirty million dollars to lobbying NAFTA's approval by Congress!

CUSTOMS LAW IN ACTION: A SKETCH

Classifications (under categories of substances and manufactures) in the TSUS (Tariff Schedules of the United States) tend, as do those of other states, to be very narrow, with differences in the customs duties that often seem unjustified by the degree of difference in the items themselves. Why is this so? Does it reflect accumulations of special interests and political pressures on the tariff-makers? The answer is "Yes", to a considerable degree. (In the United States the ultimate tariff-makers are the Congress, with revenue bills initiating in the House of Representatives.) Transnational efforts to rationalize and standard-ize customs categories and classifications have been under way for some time and progress is being made toward greater uniformity. But, to illustrate a simple situation: "Cows imported specially for dairy pur-poses" enjoy a lower rate of duty than "cattle generally". *Issue:* Do pregnant Holstein heifers weighing over 700 pounds qualify? See E. Dillingham, Inc. v. United States, 490 F.2d 967 (C.R.PA.1974). *Make a bet:* Yes or No, then look it up. (*Note:* the Court of Customs and Patent Appeals (CCPA) has been abolished and its federal appellate jurisdiction transferred to the United States Court of Appeals for the Federal Circuit, an Article III (constitutional) court, which like the Circuit Court for the District of Columbia, sits exclusively in Washington.)

---

4. THE FAST TRACK: ANOTHER WAY FOR THE UNITED STATES TO MAKE TRADE AGREEMENTS

Coping with an Old Separation of Powers Problem. The Constitution gives the revenue power to Congress, with initiation in the House of Representatives. Because American trade law began with and still involves tariffs, which are revenues, and also, because trade is *commerce* under Article I, Congress has until recently (until it commit-ted to "fast-track") held onto detailed control of and micro-managed tariff and trade acts. Congress tended to "take care" of its constituen-cies, creating a hodge-podge of tariff classifications, rates of duty, quotas, and subsidies. Further, the House of Representatives would never tolerate the making of international trade law by the President and the Senate via self-executing treaties. As a result, tariff acts were both complicated and delayed by diverse special interest pressures presented to Congress; for instance, a proposal for a higher duty on sheep wool than goat wool (or even Toggenberg goat versus mohair-producing goat). The TSUS reveals ample examples of such gerrymandering of rates of duty and customs classifications.

The problem is even more difficult when a broad-ranging trade agreement is involved. Such an agreement requires negotiation; negoti-ation with other states is an Executive or Executive–Senate function. However, the agreement also involves tariffs and revenues; hence the entire Congress is entitled to approve or disapprove of its terms. In the process, amendments to the negotiated text would surely be made.

In another of several efforts to bridge the separation-of-powers gulf between the White House and the Hill, without turning the American Federal Government into a Parliamentary system, a procedure inevitably called "Fast Track" was devised and enacted into legislation in 1974, and has now been codified as 19 U.S.C. § 2501, et seq. (see the Doc. Supp.). In effect, Congress and the President agree that if (i) the President notifies Congress at least 90 days in advance that he is entering a trade negotiation and (ii) undertakes (presumably to the satisfaction of Congress) to keep the relevant Committees in both Houses fully informed as to all significant aspects of the negotiation, then each House shall adjust its rules to permit voting yea or nay without amendments on the trade agreement, provided that the President submits with it a proposed act of implementing legislation. So far, the Fast Track has functioned well and has brought efficiently into force a considerable number of technical agreements on specific international trade matters. The Fast Track has also enabled wider-ranging trade agreements of the EFTA sort to be implemented, including ones with Israel and Canada, with NAFTA negotiated but not yet submitted to Congress.

EXCERPT FROM THE TRADE AGREEMENTS ACT OF 1979

19 United States Code § 2501 et seq.

Sec. 2. Approval of Trade Agreements. [The fast track procedure in section 151 of the Trade Act of 1974—19 U.S.C. § 2191. The text of the Section is in the Doc. Supp.]

---

5. NON–TARIFF BARRIERS, TRADE IN SERVICES, EXPORT CONTROLS

Tour d'horizon. Rates of duty and quotas are no longer significant entry barriers in developed country market areas, except as to agricultural products. Japan, in fact, has the lowest tariff levels on manufactured goods as compared to the EC and the United States, and all three are on the average below 10%. A number of developing countries still use, or are compelled by the International Monetary Fund to use, import-reducing devices, including tariffs, to conserve foreign exchange resources by reducing the consumption of foreign goods. Today the major entry barriers in major markets, agriculture excluded, are: complicated import procedures; overly meticulous safety and other inspections of imports; governmental, private, or governmental-private informal arrangements providing biases against imports and ultimately favoring consumer preferences for domestic products, preferences obviously nearly non-existent in the United States. Non-tariff barriers are more difficult to negotiate than mere tariff cuts or quota increases. Hence, Congress has sought to keep its hand in non-tariff barriers, while as to tariffs it merely sets the range within which the President may negotiate cuts. One result is the fast-track, Section 151 procedure.

A problem for the United States is that it has low entry barriers (subject to the debatable charge previously mentioned that the whole United States customs system is a non-tariff barrier), whereas both the EC and Japan have some formidable ones. In the case of EC the great barrier is an automatic variable levy on imports of all agricultural products that, if produced in the EU are subsidized. This is a tariff barrier technically, but it works in an unconventional way for a tariff. It can be argued that it is essentially a non-tariff barrier.

The Japanese barriers are to a high degree difficult to understand, as seen by non-Japanese. With low duties, why should European Community alcoholic beverages be so costly in Japan? [The EC has raised this in GATT.] What arrangements [some westerns wonder] go on between Japanese industrialists and MITI, the powerful Japanese Ministry of International Trade and Industry?

On the whole, the array of legal proceedings brought against Japanese exporters to the United States have failed to give domestic American producers effective protection in steel, automobiles, color television receivers, barber chairs, shirt-pocket radios, etc. The result is that through executive action the United States has warned Japan of possible congressional intervention and negotiated voluntary restraint or orderly marketing arrangements [OMAs] through the Japanese government, although an early, controverted arrangement was purported to be a direct initiative by a Japanese steel manufacturer's association.

Parallel—some say—to the decline of its heavy manufacturers, the United States now wishes to see an international legal mechanism for trade in services: banking, insurance, legal, consultative, managerial, technology-transferring. In the next GATT round, the Uruguay Round, the issue of expanding GATT from goods to include services was on the agenda. And because services sometimes involve property rights under foreign law (patents and trademarks), or business establishments abroad, or special machinery located there, the services issue sometimes comes close to the direct foreign investment problems considered in Section B, to follow herein.

In some instances assured and non-discriminatory access to exports is the international trade problem involved. Most issues as to the export controls of the United States have related to national security or foreign policy goals, although access problems as to certain metals, industrial diamonds, and eventually, petroleum (again) might arise.

THE "ROUNDS" IN THE BIG GATT TENT

For roughly its first twenty years (1948–68) GATT operations were mainly directed to lowering tariffs. The general plan for this was that periodically the member states' representatives would gather at a particular place to open membership-wide tariff-cutting and terms-of-trade-easing negotiations. The concessions that any "negotiating pair" made to each other would spread automatically via Article I of GATT (by MFN). In theory the concessional negotiations would be between pairs or groups of principal suppliers, each of which would have some import goodie to trade for a concession to that suppliers' export. By the end of the Sixth ("Kennedy") Round (Geneva, 1964–67) tariffs within GATT were reduced substantially, to their present low levels. Also, in the Kennedy Round attention began to shift to "non-trade" barriers, but little was accomplished as to lowering or eliminating them at that Round. The Seventh (so-called "Tokyo") Round (1973–79) focused on "Codes" of trade conduct, which are not instantly spreadable through the GATT tent but depend on accession by members for binding effect. The agreement finally made through the Uruguay Round was put into effect in a signing ceremony at Marrakesh, Morocco, April 15, 1994. A major effect of this arrangement is that it provides for the transmutation of the GATT, in 1995, into a full-fledged specialized agency under Articles 57 and 63 of the U.N. Charter, to be called the INTERNATIONAL TRADE ORGANIZATION. Thus, a major, but failed objective of the 1948 Havana Conference is finally achieved, a half-a-century later. One general expectation is that the new International Trade Organization will provide greater effectiveness in the resolution of internal disputes between member states. Also, there are expectations that its existence will reduce or end the need for "GATT Rounds," described immediately above.

ENVOI ON TRADE: THE DEVIL IN THE DETAILS

The California press for May 23, 1993, reported that California congresspersons were urging the United States Trade Representative to take this matter up with Mexico, in the context of the North American Free Trade Agreement (NAFTA). Mexico has recently removed its prior import license requirement for foreign table wines and lowered its tariff on such wines to 20 percent of value (a high going-rate of duty today). At the same time, Mexico has given Chilean wines a four-year phase-out of the duty, whereas under NAFTA the duty on American wine is to be phased-out in ten years. One might enquire: What about MFN in NAFTA? Would Article I of GATT apply to the arrangement between Mexico and Chile, if (a) the agreement is bilateral, (b) there is a Mexican–Chilean free trade agreement, or (c) there is a wider free trade area of Latin–American countries? The California wine industry currently exports wine worth over 4 million dollars to Mexico, despite the import license requirement and duty barriers, but anticipates a larger Mexican market as that country becomes more prosperous under NAFTA. Of course, California wants a level playing field with competing wine-producing countries. One wonders: what is the EU rate of duty on wines from (a) Algeria, (b) Chile, (c) Australia, (d) the United States? Are there reasons why they might not be uniform?

---

1. ***Reasons for use of controls on export trade.*** Export controls have been used over time to gain advantages for states enjoying certain types of natural or technological monopolies; to reduce the force potential of other states; to evince extreme political dissatisfaction with the domestic or foreign policies of another state or states; and in time of war as an instrument of economic warfare.

2. ***Extraterritorial use of export controls historically by the United States.*** It is reasonably accurate to suggest that the United

States became familiar with export controls in the course of learning economic warfare from the British in two World Wars. In wartime, it sought to deny all sorts of economic advantages to the enemy using any possible shred of power which might exist, including sanctions against persons not nationals acting in any place designated as "enemy territory" for economic warfare purposes by the President.

In the Cold War period, beginning as early as 1946, the United States undertook an effort, that is still being made, to induce its allies to use denials policies ranging from keeping technology from the USSR (and for a long time the Peoples' Republic of China) to pressuring the communist leaders of Poland not to bear down on anti-socialist movements, such as Solidarity. The Export Administration Act, at the section numbers given above, shows what the potential range of objectives of denials policies is.

American presidents and congresses have all, since 1946, followed denials policies from time to time. And they have included in the ambit of their efforts the foreign subsidiaries and technology licensees of American parent corporations. These efforts have generated much opposition, even passion, in allied countries, and they have not been very successful. See the 1987 Restatement, Section 414, Comment b and Reporters' Notes 3, 4 and 8, and Section 431, Reporters' Note 3.

SECTION B. THE LEGAL SITUATION OF FOREIGN–OWNED ENTERPRISES

1. DIPLOMATIC PROTECTION AND CUSTOMARY INTERNATIONAL LAW: A BIT OF SOCIO–HISTORY

Until contemporary times, a dispute between a state asserting the right to espouse a claim against another state for its treatment of a foreign enterprise in the latter, if not settled by diplomacy in some pragmatic way, became an issue about the content of customary international law, whether the dispute was an unresolved public issue, before a court or, possibly, an arbitral body. Disputes of this sort almost always involved a foreign investment in an economic enterprise. The world has had few disputes about capital movements and other investment activities that did not involve host state treatment of a foreign-owned business establishment. In the absence of treaty coverage of the legal aspects of foreign business enterprise controversies, states asserting claims on a legal basis turned to customary international law; and, as might be expected, defending states sometimes disputed either the existence of any governing customary international law or its applicability in the particular situation.

Disputes between states as to the applicability or content of customary international law seldom arose between wealthier and more powerful states, where cross-investments in each others' economies were commonplace. But such disputes arose, and sometimes generated considerable heat, between developed (and usually older) states and less-well-developed ones (usually former colonies of some European power). International judicial settlement of the relevant issues of customary international law was slight, even after the first world court was created by the League of Nations in 1919. (When you studied the Permanent Court of International Justice and its successor, the International Court of Justice, you saw why: *the "optional clause".*) Arbitration ad hoc of such disputes could involve the application and content of customary law only if chosen as the basis of decisions by the arbitral agreement (the *compromise*).

Despite all these difficulties there is a large jurisprudence (in the sense of a body of law) as to customary international law about investment disputes, and its coverage is wide, from standing-to-claim through details of compensation. Earlier editions of this casebook covered the ins-and-outs of the classic terrain more completely than we think we should present it to you here, chiefly because the resolution of investment disputes is moving into new ways of settlement that we want to acquaint you with. We have, therefore, eliminated some of the less-significant aspects of the customary international law route to claims settlements. If these should become important again, during the life of this edition, or of yours in practice, you will not lack sources for dealing with them, beginning with the 1987 Restatement of the Foreign Relations Law of the United States, especially sections 711–713, et seq., and including any one of the first three editions of this casebook, other casebooks, and textbooks galore.

What were the causes of the old dispute about the content and reach of customary international law, a dispute that pitted the developed, capital-exporting world against certain portions of the developing world? *Socialism versus capitalism? No.* The socialist-communist states (except Castro–Cuba) never rejected the legal validity of existing foreign interests' nationalization claims as an element of the abolishment of private property, although admittedly some took time to settle; and the spur of American non-recognition of the Soviet Union from 1917 to early Franklin Roosevelt, is seen by some as based on Communist rejection of customary international law, but by others as an earlier version of President Reagan's "Evil Empire" syndrome (i.e., American non-recognition on politico-moral grounds).

Touchiness about sovereignty in new states arising out of former colonies? Definitely. The widely-popular *Calvo* and *Drago Doctrines,* to be explained shortly, were based on assertions of absolute sovereignty by states in Latin America that feared they would compromise their new independence, unless they resisted assertions of a higher authority for customary international law. Further, when such assertions came not from old masters of onetime colonies, but from another former colony, now a vigorous, powerful state given to sending its Marines to protect the foreign investments of its nationals, a complex emotional element was added. This element was intensified by the gross insensitivities of many of the early foreign entrepreneurs in Latin America, beginning with and especially in, the extractive industries, involving the processing and export of irreplaceable raw materials (inter alia, tin, copper, guano, iron ore, coal, silver, gold, precious stones, and petroleum). Attitudinal and political tensions were further accentuated by the following factors: low in-country profit sharing; internal misuses of whatever the national share was; low wages and poor working conditions; exclusion of national investors, either by their lack of money or choice of the foreigners, usually the latter; and a cultural inheritance going back to Roman law: the principle that sub-surface wealth is *Res Publica*.[a] This doctrine could be squared with grants of concessions, but foreign operators' attitudes too often left impressions that they acted as owners, which impressions were exploited as political gambits supporting the "return" of state property via uncompensated nationalizations. Further, hostility to foreign control of mining and the like became part of national "folklores" [b] against all types of foreign-dominated economic presence. Notwithstanding this, foreign ownership of manufacturing, mercantile, banking, and shipping establishments only rarely had troubles. Large scale agricultural enterprises, however, had some problems, e.g. bananas in Central America, sugarcane production and refining in Cuba (even before Castro), and marine-life food processing in several places. Railroads eventually came into national public ownership, as did telephone [c] companies in various countries.

2. THE CLASSIC INTERNATIONAL STATE-TO-STATE INTERNATIONAL CLAIMS PROCESS

Pre–View. The specifics of the now-aging classical claims process, along with the fundamental concept of an international minimum standard, are the ingredients of a mixture that is the customary international law of diplomatic protection and claims. Elements of this body of customary law survive in the newer modalities for settlement previously discussed and thus must be understood. To illustrate: regardless of the forum or institution selected for dealing with an international claim, the remedy would be some variant of a "make whole" principle, whether phrased as "full", "fair" or, in the American formula, "prompt, adequate and effective" compensation. And the claim, if asserted as a legal one, would be dealt with as an assertion of obligation under customary international law, not a voluntary act of generosity (*ex gratia* payment) with no admission of legal liability. Keep in mind that, although in this Chapter we are dealing with economic claims involving foreign business establishments, other types of claims arise that are governed by the same fundamental bases, such as claims for personal mis-treatment or worse by the respondent state of a plaintiff state's national.

STATEMENT OF POLICY BY THE PRESIDENT OF THE UNITED STATES [NIXON] CONCERNING THE INTERNATIONAL MINIMUM STANDARD
8 Weekly Compilation of Presidential Documents 64 (1972).

* * *

I * * * wish to make clear the approach of this administration to the role of private investment in developing countries, and in particular

---

a. Especially in the oil industry, except in Peru, where the Liberator from Spain (Simon Bolivar) either knew no Roman law, overlooked or chose to ignore it.

b. With charmed recollection of Thurman W. Arnold's Folklore of Capitalism.

c. A president of Chile, Dr. Salvador Allende, may have been killed because of induced military opposition to "socialistic" nationalization of a foreign-owned telephone system.

to one of the major problems affecting such private investment: upholding accepted principles of international law in the face of expropriations without adequate compensation.

A principal objective of foreign economic assistance programs is to assist developing countries in attracting private investment. A nation's ability to compete for this scarce and vital development ingredient is improved by programs which develop economic infrastructure, increase literacy, and raise health standards. Private investment, as a carrier of technology, of trade opportunities, and of capital itself, in turn becomes a major factor in promoting industrial and agricultural development. Further, a significant flow of private foreign capital stimulates the mobilization and formation of domestic capital within the recipient country.

       * * *

The wisdom of any expropriation is questionable, even when adequate compensation is paid. The resources diverted to compensate investments that are already producing employment and taxes often could be used more productively to finance new investment in the domestic economy, particularly in areas of high social priority to which foreign capital does not always flow. Consequently, countries that expropriate often postpone the attainment of their own development goals. Still more unfairly, expropriations in one developing country can and do impair the investment climate in other developing countries.

In light of all this, it seems to me imperative to state—to our citizens and to other nations—the policy of this Government in future situations involving expropriatory acts.

1. Under international law, the United States has a right to expect:

— That any taking of American private property will be nondiscriminatory;

— That it will be for a public purpose; and

— That its citizens will receive prompt, adequate, and effective compensation from the expropriating country.

Thus, when a country expropriates a significant U.S. interest without making reasonable provision for such compensation to U.S. citizens, we will presume that the U.S. will not extend new bilateral economic benefits to the expropriating country unless and until it is determined that the country is taking reasonable steps to provide adequate compensation or that there are major factors affecting U.S. interests which require continuance of all or part of these benefits. 2. In the face of the expropriatory circumstances just described, we will presume that the United States Government will withhold its support from loans under consideration in multilateral development banks. 3. Humanitarian assistance will, of course, continue to receive special consideration under such circumstances.

* * *

BARCELONA TRACTION, LIGHT AND POWER CO., LTD. (BELGIUM V. SPAIN)

International Court of Justice, 1970.
[1970] I.C.J.Rep. 3.

[The decision was on a narrow issue, the question whether Belgium had standing to espouse claims of its nationals who owned the majority of the shares of a corporation organized in Canada. In the course of 303 pages of separate opinions by members of a court, who except for one judge ad hoc, agreed on the disposition of the case, almost every aspect of the nationalization problem as it concerns investments in the corporate form is discussed by one or more of the judges. The selections that follow deal with the international minimum standard. It is perhaps revealing that the dispositive opinion and some of the separate opinions assume it exists. Other views, pro and con, are more explicitly stated.]

Separate Opinion of Judge TANAKA, at pp. 115, 116.

* * *

Here, it is not necessary to emphasize the spirit of a universally recognized rule of customary international law concerning every State's right of diplomatic protection over its nationals abroad, that is, a right to require that another State observe a certain standard of decent treatment to aliens in its territory. * * *

* * *

Briefly, the idea of diplomatic protection does not seem to be a blind extension of the sovereign power of a State to the territory of other countries; the spirit of this institution signifies the collaboration of the protecting State for the cause of the rule of law and justice.

* * *

Separate Opinion of Judge JESSUP at p. 162, 164–167.

* * *

10. In adjudicating upon [this] case the Court must apply rules from one of the most controversial branches of international law. The subject of the responsibility of States for injuries to aliens (otherwise referred to as the diplomatic protection of nationals), evokes in many current writings recollections of political abuses in past eras. The Court is not involved here in any conflict between great capital-exporting States and States in course of development. Belgium and Spain are States which, in those terms, belong in the same grouping. I do not agree with the Spanish contention on 20 May 1969 that Belgium was merely trying to get the Court to internationalize a private litigation, but

it is true that basically the conflict was between a powerful Spanish financial group and a comparable non-Spanish group. This case cannot be said to evoke problems of "neo-colonialism".

Moreover, the Court is not here in the least concerned with such provocative problems as State sovereignty over natural resources or the rules applicable to compensation in case of nationalizations or expropriations. Professor F.V. Garcia Amador, in his sixth report as Special Rapporteur of the International Law Commission on State responsibility set forth an admirable attitude:

> * * * his purpose was to take into account the profound changes which are occurring in international law, in so far as they are capable of affecting the traditional ideas and principles relating to responsibility. The only reason why, in this endeavour, he rejected notions or opinions for which acceptance is being sought in our time, is that he firmly believes that any notion or opinion which postulates extreme positions—whatever may be the underlying purpose or motive—is incompatible and irreconcilable with the idea of securing the recognition and adequate legal protection of all the legitimate interests involved. That has been the policy followed by the Commission hitherto and no doubt will continue to be its policy * * *.

11. The institution "of the right to give diplomatic protection to nationals abroad was recognized in * * * the Vienna Convention on Diplomatic Relations, 1961", as Mr. Gros (as he then was) reminded the sub-committee of the International Law Commission. The institution of the right to give diplomatic protection is surely not obsolete although new procedures are emerging. With reference to diplomatic protection of corporate interests, the customary international law began to change in the latter half of the nineteenth century. As Jennings writes, in somewhat picturesque and Kiplingesque language: "It is small wonder that difficulties arise when 19th century precedents about outrageous behaviour towards aliens residing in outlandish parts are sought to be pressed into service to yield principles apposite to sophisticated programmes of international investment." Since the critical date in this case is 1948, developments in the law and procedures during the ensuing last two decades are not controlling.

* * *

14. In States having different types of economic and financial problems, international law has become increasingly permissive of actions involving nationalizations. In place of what used to be denounced as illegal expropriation, the issues now turn largely on the measure of compensation, since even the famous General Assembly Resolution on Permanent Sovereignty Over Natural Resources, provides that compensation is due.

* * *

Separate Opinion of Judge PADILLA NERVO

* * *

The history of the responsibility of States in respect to the treatment of foreign nationals is the history of abuses, illegal interference in the domestic jurisdiction of weaker States, unjust claims, threats and even military aggression under the flag of exercising rights of protection, and the imposing of sanctions in order to oblige a government to make the reparations demanded. Special agreements to establish arbitral tribunals were on many occasions concluded under pressure, by political, economic or military threats.

The protecting States, in many instances, are more concerned with obtaining financial settlements than with preserving principles. Against the pressure of diplomatic protection, weaker States could do no more than to preserve and defend a principle of international law, while giving way under the guise of accepting friendly settlements, either giving the compensation demanded or by establishing claims commissions which had as a point of departure the acceptance of responsibility for acts or omissions, where the government was, neither in fact nor in law, really responsible. In the written and in the oral pleadings the Applicant has made reference, in support of his thesis, to arbitral decisions of claims commissions—among others those between Mexico and the United States, 1923. "These decisions do not necessarily give expression to rules of customary international law, as * * * the Commissions were authorized to decide these claims 'in accordance with principles of international law, justice and equity' and, therefore, may have been influenced by other than strictly legal considerations." * * *

In considering the needs and the good of the international community in our changing world, one must realize that there are more important aspects than those concerned with economic interests and profit making; other legitimate interests of a political and moral nature are at stake and should be considered in judging the behaviour and operation of the complex international scope of modern commercial enterprises.

* * *

Separate Opinion of Judge AMMOUN

* * *

5. In this connection, it is essential to stress the trends of Latin–American law and that of Asia and Africa, and their undeniable influence on the development of traditional international law. It seems indeed that among the principles and norms which have sprung from the regional law peculiar to Latin America are the norms and principles whose aim is to protect countries in that part of the world against the more powerful industrialized States of North America and Europe. An Afro–Asian law also seems to be developing as a result of the same preoccupations, springing from the same causes. In the field of the responsibility of States and of diplomatic protection, the same points of view have been adopted in the countries of the three continents, thus initiating a form of co-operation which will not be of slight effect on the renewal of law.

The first reaction to the rules of traditional law came however from the countries of Latin America; witness the vehement speech made by

Mr. Seijas, a former Venezuelan minister, at the 1891 Session of the Institut de droit international at Hamburg, which was no mere display of bad temper. Evidence of this too is the appearance of the Calvo Clause, excluding recourse to international adjudication in favour of internal remedies, on which the jurists of Latin America have never compromised, because of their lack of confidence in diplomatic protection as conceived by traditional law and the practices of western nations. This reaction on the part of the Latin American States would, moreover, explain their opposition from 1948 onwards to the draft insurance guarantee agreement proposed by the United States, providing for the exercise of diplomatic protection by that power without local remedies having been exhausted.

This attitude on the part of the Hispanic States, which is shared by the Afro–Asian States, is the more readily understandable if the extra-legal forms and means to which diplomatic protection formerly had recourse are borne in mind. It will be recalled that the claims of great States and their nationals abroad often led, during the period preceding the renewal of the law consequent upon two world wars and the creation of a means of international adjudication, to acute conflicts and to acts of deliberate violence going so far as armed intervention and permanent occupation, or to demonstrations of force, against which the Drago doctrine, which was endorsed by the Pan–American Conference of 1906 and has since become one of the basic principles of Latin American international law, has, since 1926, reacted not without success. Recourse to force, subject to an offer of arbitration, was nevertheless tolerated by The Hague Peace Conference of 1907, which admitted intervention sub modo by virtue of the Porter Convention, against which Convention Drago and his Latin American colleagues vainly protested at the Conference. This was not the least of the contradictions which attended it, contradictions which bespeak the still predominant influence of the colonialist era. Accordingly, one is entitled to suspect certain arbitral decisions of having been agreed to or accepted under duress, those decisions having been preceded by ultimata or menaces or by a deployment of force more or less in the spirit of the said Conference, which was struggling to free itself from a tyrannical tradition.

* * *

The development of Latin American thought concerning diplomatic protection and its limits must be particularly stressed in the present discussion, on account of the influence which it can have on the development of that institution. This thought is at present centered on the following aspects of the problem: A. The 20 States of South and Central America all reject the rule laid down by Vatel and endorsed by the Permanent Court of International Justice, according to which the right of diplomatic protection is "to ensure, in the person of its subjects, respect for the rules of international law". They hold it to be a fiction, which one of their most eminent jurists, Garcia Robles, has described as "a product of Hegelian influence, resulting from the expansionism of the nineteenth century". And all these States, at inter-American conferences, in the writings of publicists, in the positions adopted by governments, are united in their efforts for its elimination, on the understanding that the individual's status as a subject of the law is to be recognized thus enabling him to seek legal redress himself, and not under the cloak of his national State. But before what tribunal? Before an American regional tribunal. The resolution submitted to the Inter–American Conference at Buenos Aires and adopted almost unanimously reads: "American legal controversies should be decided by American judges * * * and a correct understanding of acts pertaining to the Americas is more readily to be obtained by Americans themselves".

* * *

B. The States of Latin America remain firmly attached to the Calvo Clause, which they habitually insert in contracts entered into with foreign undertakings. Their constitutions and laws generally make it compulsory. Their doctrine with regard thereto, founded upon the two principles of equality between States and non-intervention, was forcefully expressed by Judge Guerrero, a former President of the Court, in the report which he submitted on behalf of the Sub-committee set up by the Committee of Experts of the League of Nations to study the responsibility of States. Several non-American countries were not hostile to this point of view. China, Holland and Finland were frankly favourable to it. Finally, the United States, which had found in Borchard a vigorous defender of the thesis that the individual cannot dispose of a right which, according to Vatelian doctrine, is that of the State and not his own, allowed itself to be won over, with the inauguration of the "good neighbour" policy of F.D. Roosevelt, to the doctrine of its southern neighbours.

C. The Calvo Clause, which on the other side of the Atlantic is regarded merely as a compromise, was destined to prepare the way for the adoption of the Calvo doctrine, which is aimed at nothing less than the abolition of unilateral diplomatic protection in order to substitute for it a protection exercised by the collectivity on the basis of human rights.

The path towards this unconcealed objective is certainly a long and arduous one; its success seems bound up with the progress of mankind towards an inter-American or international organization less removed than the United Nations from the concept of the Super–State.

* * *

It was the more necessary to recall these features of American law in that other States are treading the same path towards the limitation of diplomatic protection. The States of Africa and of Asia, since they too have come to participate in international life, share the same concerns,— as witness the proceedings of the International Law Commission. At its Ninth Session in 1957, Mr. Padilla Nervo stated that: "* * * the history of the institution of State responsibility was the history of the obstacles placed in the way of the new Latin American countries—obstacles to the defense of their * * * independence, to the ownership and development of their resources, and to their social integration." And he added:

> "With State responsibility * * * international rules were established, not merely without reference to small States but against

them." And Mr. El–Erian, of the United Arab Republic, stressed the twofold consequence of the privileged condition accorded to nationals of Western countries in their relations with the countries of Africa or Asia, which on the one hand had led to the system of capitulations and on the other afforded a pretext for intervention in the domestic affairs of States.

The similarity of the essential views and objectives of the States of the three continents of America, Africa and Asia, and the action they are able to take to develop a positive international law of world-wide ambit, will tend to direct them toward a universalist concept of law and bring them back to a system of international adjudication which will no longer be of an exclusive nature but will, through its effective composition, meet the wishes expressed in the United Nations Charter, which would have it represent the main legal systems and principal forms of civilization of the world. It is in the light of these preliminary considerations that the connected problem of diplomatic protection and the jus standi of the applicant State should have been approached.

* * *

TYPES OF ECONOMIC INTERESTS TREATED AS ENTITLED TO DIPLOMATIC PROTECTION

Perspective. Here the focus is on what types of economic interests the state of nationality or other state entitled to make the claim will recognize and the host state will accept as constituting a taking of property. In many situations there is no problem in this regard. There is common agreement that land, physical things (artifacts), patents, copyrights, bank balances and other book assets are property for nationalization claims purposes. At the other extreme, the mere prospect of having made a gain is not property. When a business enterprise is taken from an alien the manner in which he holds his ownership interests therein may become important in the context of the present inquiry. In the field of direct foreign investment in minerals extraction and disposal for profit, the civil and the common law tend to have different viewpoints as to whether authorizations to explore, mine or drill, and remove create interests in property. In the common law world they do. The recipient of the authorization either has an estate in determinable fee simple in the subsurface, an incorporeal hereditament (profit à prendre), or a lessee's rights under a mining lease. But in most of Latin America, all subsurface minerals property pertains to the state, and the state is not authorized to alienate such property. A concession contract in such a country is not a grant of a real property interest; it is a contract with the state under which the private party is licensed to explore, extract and market.

* * *

In nationalization cases valuation is often a serious problem. However, in several nationalizations in Latin America the regime in control of the state has not contested its general responsibility to pay compensation, or even the amount, but has sought to offset the claim with charges for alleged back taxes, improper exploitation or illegality ab initio of removals, despite the good faith nature of the alien's operation. Whether such situations will fall into the category of denial of justice or be dealt with as defenses to taking cannot now be foretold.

GENERAL CREDITORS' CLAIMS: POLICY OF UNITED STATES DEPARTMENT OF STATE

6 Moore, Digest of International Law 707 (1906).

* * *

How far it may be justifiable or expedient formally to press all the claims upon the French Government for immediate payment is a consideration to be distinguished from the clear opinion which is entertained of their intrinsic justice. Wherever they originated in compulsory measures practiced upon the claimants, they are entitled to a full and immediate interposition of their Government; but where the bills have been received by virtue of voluntary contracts, whether with the agents of the French Government or individuals, the receivers, having regard, as they must have had, to the degree of credit and punctuality ascribed to that Government * * * any calculation and consequent disappointment ought not to be permitted to embarrass their own Government by binding it to pursue very pointed measures for their relief.

* * *

You appear not fully to have understood your powers and duties under the law of nations in regard to claims of American citizens on foreign governments. I can not explain these more clearly than by extracting a few sentences from a letter dated on the 11th November, 1847, and addressed by this Department to Vice–President Dallas, in answer to an application made by him in behalf of an American citizen: * * * "It has been the practice of this Department to confine its official action in the recovery of indemnity from foreign governments to tortious acts committed under their authority against the persons and property of our citizens. In the case of violation of contract, the rule has been not to interfere, unless under very peculiar circumstances, and then only to instruct our diplomatic agents abroad to use their good offices in behalf of American citizens with the Governments to which they are accredited. The distinction between claims arising from torts and from contracts is, I believe, recognized by all nations, and the reasons for this distinction will readily occur to your own mind." This letter was carefully considered and adopted by the President and the entire Cabinet. I might add, that if this were not the rule, governments, and especially our Government, would be involved in endless difficulties. Our citizens go abroad over the whole world and enter into contracts with all foreign governments. In doing this they must estimate the character of those with whom they contract and assume the risk of their ability and will to execute their contracts. Upon a different principle, it would become the duty of the Government of our country to enforce the payment of loans made by its citizens and subjects to the government of another country. This might prove exceedingly inconvenient to some of the States of this Union as well as to other sovereign States.

* * *

BOND HOLDERS' CLAIMS

8 Whiteman, Digest of International Law 933 (1967).

In response to a letter requesting information on steps which the United States Government could take to protect the interests of United States bondholders affected by the default of the Government of Cuba on payments of principal and interest on bonds, the policy of the Department of State with regard thereto was explained as follows:

A default in the payment of principal or interest on bonds of foreign governments is considered by the Department primarily a matter for direct negotiation and settlement by the American bondholders or their representatives and the foreign government concerned. The Department is, however, always ready to facilitate such negotiations and settlements when possible, but it has been its consistent policy, repeatedly stated by various Secretaries of State, generally to decline to intervene in the enforcement of such obligations, except under very unusual circumstances, as, for example, where American nationals are discriminated against in connection with payments made by a foreign government on its obligations.

It was because of this policy that the Government in the fall of 1933 encouraged the creation of the Foreign Bondholders Protective Council, a private nonprofit organization, with the view that it would assist the numerous and scattered American holders of defaulted foreign government securities in the protection of their interests. The Council has offices at 90 Broad Street, New York, New York. As it functions entirely independently of the Government, this reference to it is, of course, made without responsibility on the part of the Department.

The Department will consider the bonds to which you have referred in the event that a general settlement of claims against Cuba becomes feasible or in the event that unusual circumstances arise with respect to the bonds, such as those mentioned above.

* * *

* * * [Foreign Bondholders Protective Council, Inc.] was formed in 1933 by its original directors upon request of Mr. Cordell Hull, Secretary of State, Mr. W.H. Woodin, Secretary of the Treasury, and Mr. Charles H. March, Chairman of the Federal Trade Commission, who expressed the need for "an adequate and disinterested organization for the protection of American holders of foreign securities," this problem being of such "great and urgent importance to American investors, and of such public significance as to make its proper handling a public service."

The White House announcement to the press on October 20, 1933 stated that the making of satisfactory arrangements and protecting American interests was "a task primarily for private initiative and interests. The traditional policy of the American Government has been that such loan and investment transactions were primarily private actions, to be handled by the parties directly concerned. The Government realizes a duty, within the proper limits of international law and international amity, to defend American interests abroad. However, it would not be wise for the Government to undertake directly the settlement of private debt situations."

As a consequence, the Council was incorporated December 13, 1933 under the laws of the State of Maryland as a non-stock, non-profit organization. Among the purposes for which the corporation was formed is that of protecting the rights and interests of American holders of publicly offered dollar bonds issued or guaranteed by foreign governments and their political subdivisions.

* * *

SAUDI ARABIA v. ARABIAN AMERICAN OIL CO. (ARAMCO)

Arbitration Tribunal, 1958.
27 Int'l L.Rep. 117, 168, 170, 171 (1963).*

[This was an arbitration by an ad hoc panel pursuant to an agreement between the Arabian American Oil Co. (Aramco), a Delaware corporation, and the State of Saudi Arabia. A 1933 concession arrangement grants the company's predecessor in title (a company with a slightly different name and organized in California) " * * * the exclusive right * * * to explore, prospect, drill for, extract, treat, manufacture, transport, deal with, carry away and export petroleum * * * " within an "Exclusive Area" which included islands, territorial waters and all offshore areas as to which the Saudi State has or may claim dominion. In 1954 Aristotle Socrates Onassis made an agreement with Saudi Arabia under which Onassis' Saudi Arabian Tankers Company (Satco) was granted " * * * the right of priority to ship and transport oil and its products exported from Saudi Arabia to foreign countries by way of the sea * * *." This priority was conditioned upon a first priority for shipment by concessionaries up to the extent they actually engaged in the regular transportation of Saudi Arabian oil before December 31, 1953. Aramco asked the tribunal to declare the contracts in conflict and the second a nullity as to Aramco, i.e. that Aramco have an unlimited right to ship oil from Saudi Arabia. A majority of the panel did so declare. The appointee of Saudi Arabia dissented.

* * *

* Reprinted with the permission of the Editor of the International Law Reports.

The law in force in Saudi Arabia did not contain any definite rule relating to the exploitation of oil deposits, because no such exploitation existed in that State before 1933. This lacuna was filled by the 1933 Concession Agreement, whose validity and legality under Saudi Arabian law are not disputed by either side. The present dispute only concerns the effects of the provisions contained in the Agreement. The Concession Agreement is thus the fundamental law of the Parties, and the Arbitration Tribunal is bound to recognize its particular importance owing to the fact that it fills a gap in the legal system of Saudi Arabia with regard to the oil industry. The Tribunal holds that the Concession has the nature of a constitution which has the effect of conferring acquired rights on the contracting Parties. * * *

In so far as doubts may remain on the content or on the meaning of the agreements of the Parties, it is necessary to resort to the general principles of law and to apply them in order to interpret, and even to supplement, the respective rights and obligations of the Parties.

* * *

Aramco's right of ownership in the oil it extracts and the oil derivatives it produces is not expressly mentioned in the 1933 Concession Agreement and it has been questioned by the Government, although the latter admits that the Company does possess private rights of a sacred character. In the course of the oral hearings, the Government claimed that this omission was intentional and that neither one nor the other Party had any absolute right of ownership in the oil. Aramco has no such right, it was argued, because it is not entitled to enjoy and dispose freely of the object of the Concession. Under Moslem law, it cannot base its alleged right of ownership on the fact of prior discovery and extraction of the oil because the right of the first discoverer in Hanbali law is not an exclusive right and is only attributed to Moslems and to non-Moslems who are among the residents of the Moslem State (Ahl al Dar); Aramco, it was further argued, cannot claim to be the first discoverer of the oil by virtue of its exclusive right to explore the vast area reserved to it in the Concession [because]: as no one else had the right to explore and prospect, Aramco's privilege would destroy the rules of Hanbali law according to which the first discoverer cannot prevent others from taking their needs of the mineral resources he has discovered.

But these rules, evolved some centuries ago in respect of mineral deposits other than oil, have precisely been supplemented by the 1933 Concession Agreement, ratified by Royal Decree No. 1135 in the proper exercise of the powers vested, under Hanbali law, in the Ruler of the State. The right to sell the products of the conceded oil deposits is not disputed by the Government, for it is explicitly mentioned in Article I of the 1933 Concession, as follows: "It is understood, however that such right does not include the exclusive right to sell crude or refined products within the area described below or within Saudi Arabia." It follows, by an inescapable argument a contrario, that the concessionaire has the exclusive right to sell outside Saudi Arabia. This right of sale, which entails a transfer of title, implies a recognition of Aramco's right of ownership in the oil and oil products.

* * *

In conclusion, this analysis shows that, in Saudi Arabian law as in the laws of Western Countries, the oil concession is an institution which implies an authorization by the State, on the basis of a statute or of a contract, and necessarily entails the grant to the concessionaire of property rights in the oil. As a result of this, the Concession, even in the absence of an express clause to that effect, confers upon Aramco the right to dispose of the oil. Because of this fundamental similarity, the Tribunal will be led, in the case of gaps in the law of Saudi Arabia, of which the Concession Agreement is a part, to ascertain the applicable principles by resorting to the world-wide custom and practice in the oil business and industry; failing such custom and practice, the Tribunal will be influenced by the solutions recognized by world case-law and doctrine and by pure jurisprudence.

As regards the international effects of the Concession, such as the effects of the sale and transport of the oil and oil products to foreign countries, and in particular the f.o.b. sales, the Tribunal holds that these effects are governed by the custom and practice prevailing in maritime law and in the international oil business. Because of the American nationality of the concessionaire, a particular importance must be ascribed, in this connection, to the custom and practice followed by producers in the United States and their buyers all over the world. This does not mean that American law, as the law of the nationality and of the domicile of one of the Parties, should be given any priority in relation to the law of Saudi Arabia, as the national law of the grantor and the law of the place of exploration. What the Tribunal intends to take into account is only the world-wide practice adopted in the oil industry and business. The Tribunal holds that public international law should be applied to the effects of the Concession, when objective reasons lead it to conclude that certain matters cannot be governed by any rule of the municipal law of any State, as is the case in all matters relating to transport by sea, to the sovereignty of the State on its territorial waters and to the responsibility of States for the violation of its international obligations.

* * * [Dissenting opinion omitted.]

TEXACO OVERSEAS PETROLEUM CO. AND CALIFORNIA ASIATIC OIL CO. v. THE GOVERNMENT OF THE LIBYAN ARAB REPUBLIC

Dupuy, Sole Arbitrator, 1977.
Award on the Merits, 1977.
53 Int'l L.Rep. 389, 431 (1979).*

[An excerpt from the arbitral award on a different point is at p. ____. The question here is whether, under the choice of law provision in the concession contracts, these contracts are to be governed by Libyan law or international law. The applicable provision read: This concession shall be governed by and interpreted in accordance with the principles of law of Libya common to the principles of international law and, in the absence of such common principles, then by and in accordance with the general principles of law, including such of those principles as may have been applied by international tribunals.]

* * *

B.   The Law Governing the Arbitration

11.   The Arbitral Tribunal must now state precisely what law or what system of law is applicable to this arbitration, it being understood that the parties themselves are entitled freely to choose the law of procedure applicable to the arbitration and it is only, as is the case here, in the absence of any express agreement between them that the Arbitral Tribunal must determine the law or system of law applicable to the arbitration. Two solutions are theoretically possible:

12.   (a) The first solution, which was adopted with respect to the arbitration between Sapphire International Petroleum Limited and the National Iranian Oil Company (NIOC), consists in submitting the arbitration to a given municipal law which will generally, but not necessarily, be that of the place of arbitration * * *. [The Sole Arbitrator rejected this alternative.]

13.   (b) All the elements of this case support, on the contrary, the adoption of a second solution which is to consider this arbitration as being directly governed by international law.

* * *

[Reasoning and arbitral precedents omitted. The Sole Arbitrator then developed the following thesis.]

32.   For the time being, it will suffice to note that the evolution which has occurred in the old case law of the Permanent Court of International Justice is due to the fact that, while the old case law viewed the contract as something which could not come under international law because it could not be regarded as a treaty between States, under the new concept treaties are not the only type of agreements governed by such law. And, although they are not to be confused with treaties, contracts between States and private persons can, under certain

* Reprinted with the permission of the Editor of the International Law Reports.

conditions, come within the ambit of a particular and new branch of international law: the international law of contracts.

33. As Dr. F.A. Mann wrote: "* * * [I]n regard to treaties between international persons, the nature and subject matter of which frequently are not substantially different from contracts between international and private persons, those legal rules have been, or are capable of being, and, in any event, must be developed. The law which is available for application to the one type of contractual arrangement can, without difficulty, be applied to the other group of contracts."

* * *

————

1. *Question.* What is the holding? That concessions contracts are economic interests of aliens protected by international law? Or that the parties may choose international law to govern?

2. *Management-service contracts with the state.* As an alternative to foreign direct investment in enterprises within the territory, some developing countries are paying for foreign skills, technology and, to some extent, capital, by making contracts with foreign enterprise for the conduct of a particular type of economic operation on a fee basis. For example, Mexico, despite its state-owned oil industry and the full rigor of a constitutional prohibition on any kind of foreign-owned capital interest in oil and gas in place, has made many contracts with foreign oil companies for exploration and production of oil and gas. The foreign companies are usually paid an agreed percentage of the net returns from the operation, but they have only contract rights with the host state.

As to espousal of claims based on management-service contracts, so far there has been too little experience with unilateral cancellation, outside of contract stipulations, for any clear trend to have developed as to whether such cancellations would fall into the category of interests of aliens for which espousal is accepted or into that for which espousal is not generally recognized. It is likely that the foreign investment history of such arrangements (that of having developed as alternatives to foreign private sector entrepreneurial activity based on ownership of the means of production) will incline both capital-exporting and capital-importing states to regard management-service contracts as eligible for espousal— if, of course, the receiving country does not under Calvo clause doctrines or otherwise deny the validity of diplomatic protection in any case.

3. *Question.* Your client has been offered a management-service contract in a state where the constitution requires a Calvo clause undertaking from a foreign investor. Would you advise your client to reject the offer out of hand? Why or why not?

————

THE REQUIREMENT OF TAKING
FOR A PUBLIC PURPOSE

BANCO NACIONAL DE CUBA v. SABBATINO [a]

United States Court of Appeals, Second Circuit, 1962.
307 F.2d 845, 865–68.

WATERMAN, Circuit Judge. [Rejecting the Act of State defense *in limine,* the Court of Appeals decided that the Cuban nationalization violated international law and hence that the purchasers for value of sugar subsequently produced in the nationalized mills would have to pay the ousted owners for it.]

* * *

Several authorities have announced that confiscation of the property of the nationals of a particular country without the payment of compensation when done as an act of retaliation is contrary to international law. The American Branch of the International Law Association's Committee on Nationalization of Property has stated: "[U]nder International law, a State may not take foreign interests as a measure of political reprisal." Lord McNair declared in regard to Indonesian seizures of Dutch property during the dispute between the Netherlands and Indonesia over control of Dutch New Guinea:

> "In my opinion the absence of a *bona fide,* social or economic purpose involving the property nationalized is vital and alone suffices to render unlawful the [Indonesian] Nationalization Act of 1958 * * * ".

And in Anglo–Iranian Oil Co. v. S.U.P.O.R. Co., Italian Civil Court of Rome, 1954, [1955], the court stated: "Italian courts must refuse to apply in Italy any foreign law which decrees an expropriation, not for reasons of public interest, but for purely political persecutory, discriminatory, racial and confiscatory motives."

Unlike the situation presented by a failure to pay adequate compensation for expropriated property when the expropriation is part of a scheme of general social improvement, confiscation without compensation when the expropriation is an act of reprisal does not have significant support among disinterested international law commentators from any country. And despite our best efforts to deal fairly with political and social doctrines vastly different from our own, we also cannot find any reasonable justification for such procedure. Peacetime seizure of the property of nationals of a particular country, as an act of reprisal against that country, appears to this court to be contrary to generally accepted principles of morality throughout the world.

The appellant seeks to justify retaliatory confiscation by the Cuban government by asserting that the United States was the first offender against international law by an attempt to coerce Cuba through the

---

a. The Supreme Court reversal of this decision is at 376 U.S. 398 (1964) and in ch. 8, *supra* at 627.

reduction of American purchases of Cuban sugar. If the United States had seized Cuban assets in this country without compensating the owners, we might find some merit in this contention, for then Cuba would be treating American nationals exactly as the United States was treating Cuban nationals. But, whether she was wise or unwise, fair or unfair, in what she did, the United States did not breach a rule of international law in deciding, for whatever reason she deemed sufficient, the sources from which she would buy her sugar. We cannot find any established principle of international jurisprudence that requires a nation to continue buying commodities from an unfriendly source. Accordingly it follows that the amendment to the Sugar Act of 1948 did not excuse Cuba's prima facie breach of international law. * * *

BARCELONA TRACTION, LIGHT AND POWER CO., LTD. (BELGIUM v. SPAIN)

International Court of Justice, 1970.
[1970] I.C.J. Rep. 3, 168.

Separate Opinion of Judge JESSUP.

* * *

16. In connection with the instant case, the question arises from the argument that there can be no international right to damages for shareholders indirectly injured by damage to the company in which they hold shares, since no such right is generally established in municipal law. Much reliance is placed upon the proposition that under most systems of municipal law, shareholders have no rights in or to the assets of the corporation until after it is dissolved or wound up. Shareholders' suits are indeed provided by law in the United States and somewhat less extensively in Great Britain. In the United States "The derivative stockholder-plaintiff is not only a nominal plaintiff, but at the same time a real party in interest. He sues not solely upon a corporate cause of action but also upon his own cause of action". The provisions for shareholder suits in the European countries seem to be somewhat less favourable to the shareholder. But the trend in France is toward more protection of shareholders, as Judge Gros points out.

17. Although the concept of corporate personality is a creature of municipal law, none of the theories evolved in that frame of reference can be relied on universally to explain the legal relations surrounding that "technical legal device". * * * I would paraphrase and adapt a dictum from a recent decision of the Supreme Court of the United States in an anti-trust case: the International Court of Justice in the instant case is "not bound by formal conceptions of" corporation law. "We must look at the economic reality of the relevant transactions" and identify "the overwhelmingly dominant feature". The overwhelmingly dominant feature in the affairs of Barcelona Traction was not the fact of incorporation in Canada, but the controlling influence of far-flung international financial interests manifested in the Sofina grouping.

It may well be that the new structures of international enterprise will be increasingly important, but any glance at the world-wide picture today shows that non-governmental corporations still have a major role to play. That is why so many new States, and the United Nations itself, encourage the investment of private capital.

The Right to Extend Diplomatic Protection to Corporate Enterprises

18. The decision of the Court, in this case, is based on the legal conclusion that only Canada had a right to present a diplomatic claim on behalf of Barcelona Traction which was a company of Canadian nationality. My own conclusion is that, for reasons which I shall explain, Canada did not have, in this case, a right to claim on behalf of Barcelona Traction. As a matter of general international law, it is also my conclusion that a State, under certain circumstances, has a right to present a diplomatic claim on behalf of shareholders who are its nationals. As a matter of proof of fact, I find that Belgium did not succeed in proving the Belgian nationality, between the critical dates, of those natural and juristic persons on whose behalf it sought to claim. The Belgian claim must therefore be rejected.

* * *

———

1. *Creeping nationalization.* It is sometimes difficult to find a positive act of nationalization such as a statute or decree. Major political changes in the host country may alter the whole investment climate in reliance on which the investment was made. Or the tax laws of the host country may become much more severe. The zeal with which the police power is used may increase. At some point, in some situations, a design of harassment and discrimination against all, or a particular, foreign investment may become sufficiently clear as to be the basis of formal or informal diplomatic remonstrance by a state entitled to espouse the interests of the investor affected. But it is extremely difficult for such diplomatic actions to go to the point of claiming a constructive taking of the alien's economic interests thus making the objection one under international law.

In a few instances, such as in that of a deliberate course of police intimidation of foreign enterprise, some states of nationality have declared that the conduct of the host state was a constructive taking. Other states have been disinclined to make claims based on constructive nationalization. Why ever not?

2. *Questions.* From the standpoint of a host state, if a foreign investment has become internally unpopular or undesirable, why should the state nationalize instead of squeezing the foreign interest out? Would the host state not have an easier time internationally if it followed the latter course? Would the Hickenlooper amendments [see 22 U.S.C. § 2370(e)(1) and (2)] be activated by a program of tightening the noose to the point of practical strangulation of the foreign enterprise, but without taking title? Mexico has developed some refined ways of

inducing foreign enterprises, such as the American sulphur industry in Mexico, to scale down the foreign stock ownership through sale at fair prices. The inducement in the sulphur case was to cut down almost to zero on export licenses for sulphur, most of which was sold in the world market, not in Mexico. After the American interests sold down to a minority position, export licensing on a large scale was resumed. Eventually the American interest sold out entirely.

The fundamentals in a nutshell. The basic rules for international claims settlements are set out in a number of useful sources. Whatever the instrumentality or means of settlement, the major rules usually followed are: a. Local (nationalizing state) remedies must have been exhausted, if any exist in law and are not clearly unavailable in fact. b. The private claimant must have had the nationality, through a genuine link, of the espousing state at the time of the taking. This rule creates obvious problems where dual or corporate nationality is involved. In the settlements of the nationalizations that occurred in socialist states in Eastern Europe after World War II, sensitive issues arose as to persecuted persons who had had the nationality of the taking state at the time of the taking but had been naturalized in other states before the claims settlement.

c. The claimant must have continued to be a national of the espousing state down to the time of espousal, and possibly to the time of settlement. This rule has also created certain stresses of a politico-moral nature.

d. The most widely recognized remedy is compensation. Restitution or invalidation of title to the nationalized property has not been granted by international adjudication as a clear alternative to compensation possibly because international cases are not presented in the form of suits against private parties purchasing from the nationalizing states. However, some national courts have given these remedies in cases involving such parties, but others have not.

e. The doctrine of sovereign immunity bars suits against the taking state in the courts of another state.

f. Internationally the state authorized to espouse the claim has the power to bar it in whole or in part by arrangement with the taking state, even though no—or no adequate—compensation has been obtained.

g. Use of force by the espousing state to redress the injury suffered by the owner whose economic interests are taken in violation of international law is illicit under the United Nations Charter and the Charter of the Organization of American States. Also, for political reasons, it is extremely unlikely today that intervention in pursuit of such redress would be undertaken. The aborted British–French action at Suez, 1956, in redress of the nationalization of the Suez Canal by the United Arab Republic, is likely not to be often imitated.

WAIVER BY PRIVATE PARTY
OWNERS OF THE TATTLER (UNITED STATES) v. GREAT BRITAIN

Arbitral Tribunal, Great Britain–United States, 1920.
6 U.N. Rep. Int'l Arb. Awards 48 (1955).

[The Canadian authorities in Nova Scotia arrested and detained a fishing vessel of United States nationality on charges of having engaged in fishing in violation of an 1818 treaty between the United States and Great Britain, which in 1886 became internal law in Canada, then and at the time of this suit still a British dominion. The Tattler was released upon the payment of a fine and the signing by the private party of a waiver of further claim.]

* * *

The record shows that by an agreement made at Liverpool, Nova Scotia, April 15, 1905, the owners entered into the following undertaking: "In consideration of the release of the American schooner Tattler of Gloucester, Mass., now under detention at the port of Liverpool, Nova Scotia (on payment of the fine of five hundred dollars, demanded by the Honourable, Minister of Marine and Fisheries of Canada, or by the Collector of Customs at said port), we hereby guarantee His Majesty King Edward the Seventh, his successors and assigns, represented in this behalf by the said Minister, and all whom it doth or may concern, against any and all claims made or to be made on account of or in respect to such detention or for deterioration or otherwise in respect to said vessel or her tackle or apparel, outfits, supplies or voyage, hereby waiving all such claims and right of libel or otherwise before any courts or Tribunal in respect to said detention or to such or any of such claims or for loss or damage in the premises." It has been observed by the United States Government that on the same day the owners notified the Canadian authorities that the payment of the said sum of $500 was made under protest.

But neither this protest nor the receipt given by the Canadian authorities for the $500 contains any reservation to, or protest against, the guarantee given against "any and all claims made or to be made on account of or in respect to such detention". It does not appear, therefore, that the waiver in the undertaking of any claim or right "before any court or tribunal" was subject to any condition available before this tribunal. It is proved by the documents that the consent of the British Government to the release of the vessel was given on two conditions, first, on payment of $500, and, second, on the owners undertaking to waive any right or claim before any court, and the protest against the payment does not extend and can not in any way be held by implication to extend to this waiver. This protest appears to have been a precautionary measure in case the Canadian authorities should have been disposed to reduce the sum. Any protest or reserve as to the waiver of the right to damages would have been plainly inconsistent with the undertaking itself and would have rendered it nugatory if it had been accepted by the other party.

On the other hand, it has been objected that the renunciation of and guarantee against any claims are not binding upon the Government of the United States, which presents the claim. But in this case the only right the United States Government is supporting is that of its national, and consequently in presenting this claim before this Tribunal, it can rely on no legal ground other than those which would have been open to its national.

For these reasons

This Tribunal decides that the claim relating to the seizure and detention of the American schooner Tattler * * * must be dismissed.

* * *

1. ***Settlement acceptable to the private claimant.*** States usually espouse the claims of their nationals only because the claims have not otherwise been settled. If after causing or threatening to cause diplomatic problems, a claim is settled by the respondent state and the private claimant, the settlement is instinctively accepted as final. The potential plaintiff state's officials breathe a sign of relief and go on to other business. This is clearly so if there is no related but independent plaintiff-state claim and if the settlement is reached before formal espousal has been made. Technically this would not be so for a settlement made after espousal, but the resistance to a second settlement that the respondent state would surely interpose makes the technicality rather illusory. The state of nationality, however, will tend to be sensitive to the interests of its national as against undue pressure or duress in the settlement itself.

2. ***Waiver as a condition precedent to entry as a foreign contractor or investor; the Calvo clause problem.*** Some Latin American states in their constitutions, by statute, or by executive action make it a condition precedent to the entry of a foreign contractor or direct investor that the alien undertake at the time of entry and in consideration therefor not to invoke the diplomatic protection of the state of his nationality and to accept non-discriminatory national treatment as his sole basis of right. Contractually, this is an anticipatory waiver of claims. The foreign minister of Argentina who gave his name in the latter part of the last century to the Calvo doctrine, which the clauses seek to implement, grounded the doctrine firmly on a negation of any right of diplomatic protection inhering in states of nationality and on a denial of the existence of an international minimum standard.

Calvo clauses raise these questions: (i) may the private party bind or bar the state of his nationality (ii) if the promisor, again the private party, breaches his promise and goes tattling to the state of his nationality, what happens as to: (a) the investor vis-á-vis the state to which he gave his promise, (b) any independent right of action that the state of nationality otherwise might have had?

The questions posed do not have clear and satisfactory answers in either doctrinal writings or in international arbitrations or adjudications. Analytically, these questions raise the issue whether the notion that a nationalization claim is an injury to the state of espousal is an expression of a fundamental rule of customary international law, or whether it is really merely a doctrine of logical convenience, to get around underdevelopment of individuals' rights in customary international law.

Capital exporting states other than the United States seem to have been only rarely troubled by Calvo clauses. So far this device for subjecting the foreign investor to greater host state control has not spread throughout the developing half of the world. But recall the separate opinion of Judge Ammoun in Barcelona Traction p. 1134.

In diplomatic correspondence and in the position of at least one of its appointees to arbitral tribunals, the United States has rejected the notion that the international cause of action of the United States could be compromised by an agreement between a foreign state and a United States citizen. United States Commissioner F.K. Neilsen dissented vigorously in the International Fisheries Case, U.S.–Mexican General Claims Commission 1926 * * *. There a majority of the arbitral body followed the general line of a previous case in the same arbitral series (U.S.–Mexico General Claims) to the effect that a Calvo clause undertaking must be given a reasonable and circumspect interpretation. Such an interpretation includes these elements: (i) the undertaking covers only the economic and technical aspects of the contract or investment venture, not the general rights of alien private persons; (ii) a Calvo clause does not mean that the private party must abstain from pursuing international legal remedies for denial of procedural justice or outrageous conduct by the host state; (iii) a state's rights under international law cannot be taken away by a contract to which it is not a party; (iv) where, in an arbitration involving a Calvo clause-affected claim, the plaintiff state acts strictly on behalf of its national and the national does not resort to (or exhaust) his local remedies but instead complains to his government and seeks espousal, provisions in the arbitration agreement that exhaustion of remedies will be waived do not apply. That is, a waiver of exhaustion between the states parties to the agreement to arbitrate does not cover non-exhaustion in Calvo clause cases.

Consult the 1987 Restatement 713, Comment *g*, and Reporters' Note 5. Both the arbitral decisions referred to above and state practice seem to negate the view that Calvo clauses are nullities in international claims law and practice. And there is some evidence that in United States diplomatic practice the presence of a Calvo clause is a factor in determining either willingness to espouse or the degree and intensity with which the diplomatic protection function of the Department of State is discharged. This is where the legal trail ends.

3. ***Problem.*** An American investor makes a Calvo clause investment in State X. Later the investment is nationalized without compensation satisfactory to the investor. The investor complains to the

Department of State but does not pursue his remedies in X, which is under a military dictatorship that has made a big national issue out of this particular nationalization. Strictly on the bases of the two Hickenlooper amendments, one requiring the President to cut off foreign assistance to a country that does not give reasonable assurance of settling a nationalization claim in accordance with international law within six months of the taking and the other ordering the elimination of the act of state doctrine in Sabbatino-type nationalization cases, insofar as alleged violations of international law are concerned, what should be the effects, if any, of the disregard by the investor of his Calvo clause promises?

4. **Question.** Would it be reasonably accurate to say that the Hickenlooper amendments are hard-nosed, developed state responses to a too-clever developing state doctrinal device for making international law irrelevant in nationalization cases?

Espousal by a state of a claim on behalf of a person (also called the extension of diplomatic protection) requires the existence between the claimant and the state of a genuine link between the claimant and the state of a genuine link (see the *Nottebohm Case,* Ch. 9, p. 685). Usually it is the link of nationality. And the link must exist at the time of the taking or other injurious act by the defendant state. Claims of dual nationals of the states involved are also dealt with in Chapter 9.

Standing to Claim involves two often-litigated preconditions: first the existence of the required link between the injured party and the espousing state at the time of the taking. It is also assumed but not often provable from decisions, that loss of the link by a change of nationality before diplomatic settlement is sought (but after the taking) cancels espousal. What about a change of nationality after the taking and after the espousal but before the settlement? The second element of Standing to Claim is requirement of the exhaustion of other remedies before resorting to the assertion of an international claim. This will be considered briefly later in this Chapter, in addition to the question whether there has been a taking, as distinguished from strict regulation. This is sometimes referred to as the "problem of creeping nationalization".

ESPOUSAL OF CORPORATE CLAIMS

General requirement of effective nationality. Judge Jessup discusses this requirement in the Barcelona Traction Case, [1970] I.C.J.Rep. 3, at 182. [A portion of his opinion follows.]

38. There is no question that, under international law, a State has in general a right to extend its diplomatic protection to a corporation which has its nationality, or national character as it is more properly called. The proposition raises two questions:

(1) What are the tests to determine the national character of a corporation?

(2) Assuming the appropriate tests are met, must that national character be "real and effective" as shown by the "link" between

the corporation and the State, just as, in the Nottebohm case, this Court decided that a certain claim to nationality is not enough in all situations to justify a State in extending its diplomatic protection to a natural person?

39.   There are two standard tests of the "nationality" of a corporation.   The place of incorporation is the test generally favoured in the legal systems of the common law, while the siège social is more generally accepted in the civil law systems.   There is respectable authority for requiring that both tests be met.

It is not possible to speak of a single rule for all purposes.   The tests used in private international law have their own character.

Commercial treaties and claims conventions often contain their own definitions of which companies shall be considered to have the nationality of a State for purposes of the treaty.   The tests used for such purposes may be quite different—even in the practice of the same State—from the tests used for other purposes.   For example, the "control" test was widely used to determine the enemy character of property during war, but it is not established in international law as a general test of the nationality of a corporation.   On the other hand, control may constitute the essential link which, when joined to nationality, gives the State the right to extend diplomatic protection to the corporation.   It is a familiar fact that the laws of certain States provide favourable conditions for companies incorporating therein, especially in relation to taxation.   Canada is one such State, Lichtenstein is another.   In the United States, many companies find it advantageous, for various reasons, to incorporate in Delaware or New Jersey.   Charters secured for such reasons may be called "charters of convenience".

40.   The Judgment of the Court of Nottebohm, Second Phase, in 1955, has been widely discussed in the subsequent literature of international law particularly with reference to the so-called "link theory" by which the effectiveness of nationality may be tested.   It has been argued that the doctrine is equally applicable in the case of ships flying "flags of convenience" and in relation to the diplomatic protection of corporations.   I have maintained the view that it should apply in both those situations.

43.   It has also been argued that the Court should not pass judgment on the question whether there existed the necessary link between Canada and Barcelona Traction without hearing argument on behalf of Canada.   Canada might have sought to intervene in the instant case under Article 62 of the Statute, but it did not do so.   It is said that after judgment is pronounced in this case of Belgium v. Spain, Canada might find some jurisdictional ground to found an application to institute a case of Canada v. Spain.   It is known that no such jurisdictional ground now exists.   It seems quite unreal to suppose that Spain would now agree with Canada upon a compromise submitting to the Court a Canadian claim on behalf of Barcelona Traction, thus exposing Spain to the new hazard of being required to pay some two hundred millions of dollars of damages.

But if the Court were properly seised of an application by Canada, it would have to take cognizance of the fact that following Article 59 of the Statute, "The decision of the Court has no binding force except between the parties and in respect of that particular case". Had the Court endorsed the application of the link principle to juristic persons, in its present decision in Belgium v. Spain, Canada could have argued against that conclusion in the hypothetical case of Canada v. Spain, or might have relied on Spanish admissions that Canada was entitled to protect the company.

44. It seems to be widely thought that the "link" concept in connection with the nationality of claims, originated in the International Court of Justice's Judgment in Nottebohm. I do not agree that in that instance the Court created a new rule of law. Indeed the underlying principle was already well established in connection with diplomatic claims on behalf of corporations. To look for the link between a corporation and a State is merely another example of what is now the familiar practice of "lifting the veil". The practice of such States as the United States and Switzerland had already given weight to the proposition that a corporation would not be protected solely because it was incorporated in the State, i.e., had the State's nationality; some other link was required and that link usually was related to the ownership of shares. Such abstention, being as it were "against interest", has special probative value.

Three years after the decision in Nottebohm, the Italian–United States Conciliation Commission, under the presidency of the late Professor Sauser Hall, in the Flegenheimer case stated:

> The right of challenge of the international court, authorizing it to determine whether, behind the nationality certificate or the acts of naturalisation produced, the right to citizenship was regularly acquired, is in *conformity with the very broad rule* of *effectivity* which dominates the law of nationals entirely and allows the court to fulfill its legal function and remove the inconveniences specified. (Emphasis supplied.)

* * *

BARCELONA TRACTION, LIGHT AND POWER CO., LTD. (BELGIUM v. SPAIN)

International Court of Justice, 1970.
[1970] I.C.J.Rep. 3.

[In this case, the parent company in the corporate complex involved was incorporated in 1911 in Canada; but after the First World War approximately 85% of its shares came to be held by Belgian nationals, largely through complicated arrangements involving some very large Belgian holding companies. Belgium wished to be allowed to show that its nationals as shareholders had been seriously harmed by actions of the Spanish state after the Spanish Civil War. These included, according to the Belgian memorials in an earlier ICJ case dropped in 1961 in expectation of a diplomatic settlement: denial from 1940 on of foreign exchange licenses to the Traction Company and some of its Spanish subsidiaries to permit service on bonds payable in pounds sterling; a 1948 bankruptcy proceeding in Spain brought by Spanish purchasers of "defaulted" sterling bonds of which the Traction Company itself had not received fair notice; an unfair time limit on appeal in the bankruptcy case; and the eventual passage of very substantial influence over the corporate structures in Spain to one Juan March.

Although the memorials do not mention the matter in just this way, March, known widely as the "Match King" of Spain, was often reported to have been a significant financial supporter of Franco's insurgency against the Spanish Republic and known as a highly skilled and secretive financial operator. The essence of the Belgian claim on the merits in the case that follows would have been that Belgians had been the victims of foreign exchange, bankruptcy and related official actions that squeezed out the Belgian equity investment in the Barcelona Traction corporate complex. A portion of the opinion of the court appears below.]

31. The Court has to deal with a series of problems arising out of a triangular relationship involving the State whose nationals are shareholders in a company incorporated under the laws of another State, in whose territory it has its registered office; the State whose organs are alleged to have committed against the company unlawful acts prejudicial to both it and its shareholders; and the State under whose laws the company is incorporated, and in whose territory it has its registered office.

32. In these circumstances it is logical that the Court should first address itself to what was originally presented as the subject-matter of the third preliminary objection: namely the question of the right of Belgium to exercise diplomatic protection of Belgian shareholders in a company which is a juristic entity incorporated in Canada, the measures complained of having been taken in relation not to any Belgian national but to the company itself.

36. * * * [I]t is the existence or absence of a right, belonging to Belgium and recognized as such by international law, which is decisive for the problem of Belgium's capacity.

> This right is necessarily limited to intervention [by a State] on behalf of its own nationals because, in the absence of a special agreement, it is the bond of nationality between the State and the individual which alone confers upon the State the right of diplomatic protection, and it is as a part of the function of diplomatic protection that the right to take up a claim and to ensure respect for the rules of international law must be envisaged.

It follows that the same question is determinant in respect of Spain's responsibility towards Belgium. Responsibility is the necessary corollary of a right. In the absence of any treaty on the subject between the Parties, this essential issue has to be decided in the light of the general rules of diplomatic protection.

46. It has also been contended that the measures complained of, although taken with respect to Barcelona Traction and causing it direct damage, constituted an unlawful act vis-à-vis Belgium, because they also, though indirectly, caused damage to the Belgian shareholders in Barcelona Traction. This again is merely a different way of presenting the distinction between injury in respect of a right and injury to a simple interest. But, as the Court has indicated, evidence that damage was suffered does not ipso facto justify a diplomatic claim. Persons suffer damage or harm in most varied circumstances. This in itself does not involve the obligation to make reparation. Not a mere interest affected, but solely a right infringed involves responsibility, so that an act directed against and infringing only the company's rights does not involve responsibility towards the shareholders, even if their interests are affected.

50. Turning to the international legal aspects of the case, the Court must, as already indicated, start from the fact that the present case essentially involves factors derived from municipal law—the distinction and the community between the company and the shareholder—which the Parties, however widely their interpretations may differ, each take as the point of departure of their reasoning. If the Court were to decide the case in disregard of the relevant institutions of municipal law it would, without justification, invite serious legal difficulties. It would lose touch with reality, for there are no corresponding institutions of international law to which the Court could resort. Thus the Court has not only to take cognizance of municipal law but also to refer to it. It is to rules generally accepted by municipal legal systems which recognize the limited company whose capital is represented by shares, and not to the municipal law of a particular State, that international law refers. In referring to such rules, the Court cannot modify, still less deform them.

51. On the international plane, the Belgian Government has advanced the proposition that it is inadmissible to deny the shareholders' national State a right of diplomatic protection merely on the ground that another State possesses a corresponding right in respect of the company itself. In strict logic and law this formulation of the Belgian claim to jus standi assumes the existence of the very right that requires demonstration. In fact the Belgian Government has repeatedly stressed that there exists no rule of international law which would deny the national State of the shareholders the right of diplomatic protection for the purpose of seeking redress pursuant to unlawful acts committed by another State against the company in which they hold shares. This, by emphasizing the absence of any express denial of the right, conversely implies the admission that there is no rule of international law which expressly confers such a right on the shareholders' national State.

58. * * * [T]he process of lifting the veil, being an exceptional one admitted by municipal law in respect of an institution of its own making, is equally admissible to play a similar role in international law. It follows that on the international plane also there may in principle be special circumstances which justify the lifting of the veil in the interest of shareholders.

85.   The Court will now examine the Belgian claim from a different point of view, disregarding municipal law and relying on the rule that in inter-State relations, whether claims are made on behalf of a State's national or on behalf of the State itself, they are always the claims of the State.   As the Permanent Court said, "The question whether the * * * dispute originates in an injury to a private interest, which in point of fact is the case in many international disputes, is irrelevant from this standpoint." (Mavrommatis Palestine Concessions, Judgment; Nottebohm, Second Phase).

* * *

89.   Considering the important developments of the last half-century, the growth of foreign investments and the expansion of the international activities of corporations, in particular of holding companies, which are often multinational, and considering the way in which the economic interests of States have proliferated, it may at first sight appear surprising that the evolution of law has not gone further and that no generally accepted rules in the matter have crystallized on the international plane.   Nevertheless, a more thorough examination of the facts shows that the law on the subject has been formed in a period characterized by an intense conflict of systems and interests.   It is essentially bilateral relations which have been concerned, relations in which the rights of both the State exercising diplomatic protection and the State in respect of which protection is sought have had to be safeguarded.   Here as elsewhere, a body of rules could only have developed with the consent of those concerned.   The difficulties encountered have been reflected in the evolution of the law on the subject.

90.   Thus, in the present state of the law, the protection of shareholders requires that recourse be had to treaty stipulations or special agreements directly concluded between the private investor and the State in which the investment is placed.   States ever more frequently provide for such protection, in both bilateral and multilateral relations, either by means of special instruments or within the framework of wider economic arrangements.   Indeed, whether in the form of multilateral or bilateral treaties between States, or in that of agreements between States and companies, there has since the Second World War been considerable development in the protection of foreign investments.   The instruments in question contain provisions as to jurisdiction and procedure in case of disputes concerning the treatment of investing companies by the States in which they invest capital.   Sometimes companies are themselves vested with a direct right to defend their interests against States through prescribed procedures.   No such instrument is in force between the Parties to the present case.

92.   Since the general rule on the subject does not entitle the Belgian Government to put forward a claim in this case, the question remains to be considered whether nonetheless, as the Belgian Government has contended during the proceedings, considerations of equity do not require that it be held to possess a right of protection.   It is quite true that it has been maintained that, for reasons of equity, a State should be able, in certain cases, to take up the protection of its nationals,

shareholders in a company which has been the victim of a violation of international law. Thus a theory has been developed to the effect that the State of the shareholders has a right of diplomatic protection when the State whose responsibility is invoked is the national State of the company. Whatever the validity of this theory may be, it is certainly not applicable to the present case, since Spain is not the national State of Barcelona Traction.

93. On the other hand, the Court considers that, in the field of diplomatic protection as in all other fields of international law, it is necessary that the law be applied reasonably. It has been suggested that if in a given case it is not possible to apply the general rule that the right of diplomatic protection of a company belongs to its national State, considerations of equity might call for the possibility of protection of the shareholders in question by their own national State. This hypothesis does not correspond to the circumstances of the present case.

94. In view, however, of the discretionary nature of diplomatic protection, considerations of equity cannot require more than the possibility for some protector State to intervene, whether it be the national State of the company, by virtue of the general rule mentioned above, or, in a secondary capacity, the national State of the shareholders who claim protection. Account should also be taken of the practical effects of deducing from considerations of equity any broader right of protection for the national State of the shareholders. It must be observed that it would be difficult on an equitable basis to make distinctions according to any quantitative test: it would seem that the owner of 1 per cent. and the owner of 90 per cent. of the share-capital should have the same possibility of enjoying the benefit of diplomatic protection. The protector State may, of course, be disinclined to take up the case of the single small shareholder, but it could scarcely be denied the right to do so in the name of equitable considerations. In that field, protection by the national State of the shareholders can hardly be graduated according to the absolute or relative size of the shareholding involved.

95. The Belgian Government, it is true, has also contended that as high a proportion as 88 per cent. of the shares in Barcelona Traction belonged to natural or juristic persons of Belgian nationality, and it has used this as an argument for the purpose not only of determining the amount of the damages which it claims, but also of establishing its right of action on behalf of the Belgian shareholders. Nevertheless, this does not alter the Belgian Government's position, as expounded in the course of the proceedings, which implies, in the last analysis, that it might be sufficient for one single share to belong to a national of a given State for the latter to be entitled to exercise its diplomatic protection.

96. The Court considers that the adoption of the theory of diplomatic protection of shareholders as such, by opening the door to competing diplomatic claims, could create an atmosphere of confusion and insecurity in international economic relations. The danger would be all the greater inasmuch as the shares of companies whose activity is international are widely scattered and frequently change hands. It might be claimed that, if the right of protection belonging to the national

States of the shareholders were considered as only secondary to that of the national State of the company, there would be less danger of difficulties of the kind contemplated. However, the Court must state that the essence of a secondary right is that it only comes into existence at the time when the original right ceases to exist. As the right of protection vested in the national State of the company cannot be regarded as extinguished because it is not exercised, it is not possible to accept the proposition that in case of its non-exercise the national States of the shareholders have a right of protection secondary to that of the national State of the company. Study of factual situations in which this theory might possibly be applied gives rise to the following observations.

* * *

100. It is clear from what has been said above that Barcelona Traction was never reduced to a position of impotence such that it could not have approached its national State, Canada, to ask for its diplomatic protection, and that there was nothing to prevent Canada from continuing to grant its diplomatic protection to Barcelona Traction if it had considered that it should do so.

101. For the above reasons, the Court is not of the opinion that, in the particular circumstances of the present case, jus standi is conferred on the Belgian Government by considerations of equity.

* * *

103. Accordingly, The Court rejects the Belgian Government's claim by fifteen votes to one, twelve votes of the majority being based on the reasons set out in the present Judgment.

* * * [Declarations, separate opinions and dissenting opinion omitted.]

————

Characterization of the theory of action against the taking state. Some writers characterize a state that has violated international law (either in the taking itself or by failing to pay compensation) as having been guilty of tortious conduct. Others say that the theory of action is analogous to unjust enrichment, inasmuch as the taking state acquired property without paying for it. The first theory covers both injuries to aliens in their persons and their economic interests while the second does not. Historically, both types of injuries have given rise to international responsibilities, in some instances in the same case. The tort theory, therefore, has the utility of providing a conceptual basis for both situations. The unjust enrichment theory as to takings of economic interests, if followed in strict analogy to Anglo–American quasi-contract, also precludes an ab initio (at taking) concept that the wrong is the taking, not the withholding of compensation.

It should be borne in mind that both these characterizations draw heavily upon analogies to municipal legal systems, and that the analogies cannot be pushed very far beyond the fundamental concepts involved. As is well known, what is tort, with a whole array of sub-rules as to duty, proximate cause, damages, and the like, to a common law lawyer is not quite the same thing as civil responsibility to a civil law lawyer. And while legal systems agree that unjust enrichment should be redressed in some ways in some situations, the doctrines of quasi-contract and quantum meruit at common law are not of universal acceptance. Thus, it would seem inadmissible to derive conclusions about the remedies that international law provides for the taking of an alien's economic interest in violation of international law by logical deduction of explicit rules from these characterizations. If there is an international tort or an international cause of action for unjust enrichment it should be regarded as sui generis, rather than as a detailed transformation of national law into international law.

The remedy of compensation. There is common agreement that compensation ought to be sufficient in value to make the forcibly disinvested alien whole. The basic problem is *what value* of *what*. Valuation is an extremely difficult problem in domestic legal systems, and in such systems, too, there are questions as to what types of interests, expectations and prospects should be included. A fairly common problem in the international claims arena is as to the valuation of the interests of an oil company lost by the cancellation of its concession. Its physical installations raise only the problems of technique and criteria for fixing the value in money of what has been taken, not that these are simple. (Replacement value? Original cost depreciated? What kind of depreciation? etc.) But what of known but not extracted reserves of oil and gas in place? What of speculative value as to reserves not yet known? There is a natural tendency for claimants to put high valuations on what they have lost by nationalization and an equally natural tendency of the respondent state in any type of claims settlement proceeding to minimize the damage suffered.

Eventually some money value is going to have to be arrived at. On an individual case basis this may be done by party or diplomatic bargaining, a finding of the damages by an arbitral tribunal or a court (perhaps assisted by a fact-finding aide), or agreement of the parties to engage a professional and disinterested valuation expert to determine true value. In instances where a state has engaged in wholesale nationalization, as when Yugoslavia became socialist, a very great many claimants with many different types of losses exist. In such situations the settlement may take the form of the acceptance by the espousing state of a global or lump sum in complete satisfaction and waiver of all the claims included within the scope of the negotiation. The espousing state would, of course, find it necessary to analyze all the claims it had received as to amounts claimed, types of property involved, etc. and come to an overall negotiating figure that it would then use in bargaining with the other state concerned. (In a sense such an approach is not unlike the settlement out of court of a class action in the United States.)

In the Yugoslavian claims settlement negotiations of 1948–49, the United States Department of State received (as a result of published notice) the claims of United States citizens against Yugoslavia for the nationalization program carried on in that country. These submissions were then examined to determine espousibility by the United States and to estimate the degree of inflation or over-statement that might exist in particular claims. During the course of this operation, also, there were consultations with claimants and groups of claimants to explain the process and to seek general concurrence that a lump sum figure of such and such amount (to be divided ratably among the claimants in the proportion of total lump sum recovery to total eligible claims) would be acceptable. Eventually the United States decided that it could accept $17 million in gold in complete settlement and waiver of a total of espousible claims that, before analysis for overstatement of value, totaled $42 million. After the negotiation of an executive agreement with Yugoslavia for settlement along these lines, the Congress authorized the use of the value of the gold received for the benefit of the private claimants and set up an administrative body, now the Foreign Claims Settlement Commission, to pass upon the individual claims as to eligibility under the terms of the agreement and to award money recoveries.

The remedy of compensation is adjectivally stated in the classic United States formulation as "prompt, adequate and effective." The three adjectives are the subject of somewhat wishful further descriptions in standard sources for expression of United States viewpoints on what international law requires.

One of the American trilogy of adjectives, "effective," expresses a clear preference for compensation in freely convertible foreign exchange instead of compensation in inconvertible local currency. In the real world of today, the effect of this requirement, if strictly adhered to, would be to prevent a state short of foreign exchange from nationalizing aliens' interests even under programs of social reform. But, of course, it is not adhered to in such cases, beyond a kind of discounted foreign exchange receipt in quittance under lump sum agreements to pay in convertible monetary assets. Payment over time, as by the issuance of government or government-guaranteed bonds, is in state practice prompt enough and effective enough to be acceptable.

Finally, it should be noted that the nationalization of a going enterprise is a business disaster, and compensation under any criteria that the taking state would consider accepting is almost always below the real value of the economic loss. This reality properly justifies the classification of claims settlement as a species of salvage. It is important for lawyers to get salvage for their clients, but the law of salvage is hardly the best body of law to provide a secure and lasting basis for foreign investment that wants to stay in business.

Restitution, invalidation of title and other specific recovery of property as remedies; cross-reference to Chapter 6. The question whether customary international law has developed remedies for violations of an international minimum standard in addition to the remedy of fair compensation in state to state proceedings becomes pertinent at this point in consideration of what the injured private party's attorney can do. The cases bearing on the remedies of specific restitution, invalidation of the title derived from the nationalizing state, and other possible types of specific recovery of property have been dealt with in Chapter 6 as a necessary aspect of the act of state doctrine. Is it reasonable to conclude, from the leading cases bearing on this issue in Chapter 6, from the Supreme Court of the United States, the House of Lords, and the Supreme Court of Texas, that the normal principle that a state may control title to property having situs in its territory has prevailed? If so, have we seen the end of the pursuit into world commerce by the dispossessed former owners of hot oil, sugar, copper, tobacco, and whatever? Did the lawyers who sought so vigorously to equate a state with a thief at common law, act in the name of customary international law in innocent expectation that national courts would discover international law their way?

Investment insurance. The Marshall Plan (1948) was not only the world's first major foreign assistance program; it also broke new ground in providing that qualified private sector investors (mainly United States companies) could, for fees of approximately ¾ to 1% of the principal per type of risk, receive the promise of the United States to reimburse them for certain types of non-business losses, such as from nationalization without adequate compensation, non-convertibility of earnings in soft currencies into dollars and damages resulting from hostilities. The investment guaranty, as it was then called, was designed to encourage the outflow of capital from the United States' private sector to help rehabilitate the private sectors of the countries in Europe that were to benefit from the Marshall Plan. (The Soviet Union was included in the Marshall Plan's general invitation to participate, but it declined for itself and its dominated satellites.)

When, approximately a decade later, the United States began to engage for the first time in significant bilateral assistance to the world's poorer and developing countries, the investment guaranty program was extended to them, first for the above three risks, slightly expanded in the third instance (that of physical damage from hostilities, to include losses due to civil insurrection). By that time the writing of investment guaranties for developed countries had stopped. There had been no losses in Europe, but the amounts for which guaranties nonetheless were being sought were becoming too large to be prudently managed on the resource base Congress was willing to commit. In 1969 Congress took the investment guaranty program out of the United States Foreign Assistance Administration (USAID) and turned it over to a wholly-owned government corporation, the Overseas Private Investment Corporation (OPIC); see 22 U.S.C.A. §§ 2191–2200a.

The investment insurance program simplifies the problem of the foreign investor as to getting compensation for new investment, provided the coverage is available. However, there is considerable hostility in Latin America to United States (and probably other foreign country) investment insurance. In part this resistance arose from the insistence of Congress in earlier years on a precondition that an investment-receiving country have entered into a bilateral agreement with the

United States accepting the scheme and recognizing the right of the United States government to be subrogated to any covered claims it might discharge. Legislatures balked in a number of Latin countries as to contract subrogation and its implicit assertion of the international minimum standard. The Andean Investment Code binds the states members of the Andean Common Market (ANCOM) not to give foreign investors better than national treatment (Art. 50), and its Article 51 provides: "In no instrument relating to investments or the transfer of technology shall there be clauses that remove possible conflicts from the national jurisdiction and competence of the recipient country or allow the subrogation by States to the rights and actions of their national investors." 16 ILM 138 (1977).

These limitations do not apply literally to investment guaranties or insurance by multipartite assistance agencies, such as the International Finance Corporation of the World Bank Group. For some time the staff of the latter worked on a multipartite investment insurance plan which is in effect. We have heard reports that the former restrictions are being lifted in various Latin–American countries. In the North–American Free Trade Agreement (NAFTA), approved in December 1993 by the United States Congress, Mexico has accepted terms for the entry and treatment of direct foreign investment that are in startling contrast to her past. Foreign ownership of interests in the petroleum industry, however, are excluded.

––––––

1. *The possibility of new foreign investment arrangements.* The preceding material in Section B of this chapter deals with the jural pathology of direct foreign investment in the present international legal system. Better treatment of investment diseases, as by better opportunity for authoritative and neutral settlement of investment disputes under existing international law, would help. Also, clarifications and substantive modifications in the rules themselves might reduce fears, suspicions and tensions in both capital exporting and capital importing states. It is rather striking to note in this regard how little trouble creditor investments seem to give. Why? Is it because they are not very much protected by the international legal system, or is there some other reason? Would it help if for international purposes foreign equity investment should come to be regarded as limited rather than perpetual ownership, that is, to arrange the rules so that the foreign ownership investor is entitled to x times his total investment and then must get out?

Another factor that is coming more and more to planning attention in regard to direct foreign ownership investment, is that of the effect of development itself upon the stability of investment relationships. In general, investment disputes between the world's industrialized, rich countries are very few, except for the administration of prior restraints on entry in France and Japan and for some antitrust problems, especially with the United Kingdom and possibly other Commonwealth countries. It is between the private sector ownership investors of rich countries and the governments, politicians and publics of the less well-developed countries that most of the problems arise. To a considerable extent they seem to be related to differences in the levels of managerial skills of the foreign companies and the host country public administrators. But technological advances as host countries develop may tend toward the eventual tranquilization of the present general investment situation between the rich and poor halves of the planet and the evolution of more effective legal rules for the governance of relationships between capital exporting and capital receiving countries.

Codification efforts toward new rules for foreign investment have been made. Several proposed codes for foreign investment, to come into effect as law-making international agreements, have been made by groups within developed countries. In general these proposals have found little favor in developing countries. Why? Some developing countries individually have provided rules through legislation and administrative practice. These range from prior restraints and foreign ownership maxima to provisions designed actually to attract foreign investment, either generally or into lagging sectors of the national economies. The countries in the Andean Group within the Latin American Free Trade Association (LAFTA) apply a complete system of regulation designed to put into effect nationally in each of them a uniform basic law on foreign investment. All of these efforts are parts of a quest for rules for foreign investment of greater precision and sophistication than provided by the vague principles of customary international law, which as we have seen sound more in salvage than in prevention.

2. ***Bilateral treaties involving direct foreign investment.*** Some general aspects of the legal status of foreign investment have long been dealt with in general commercial treaties, usually referred to in United States practice as FCN (friendship, commerce and navigation) treaties. In Asakura v. City of Seattle, a Japanese pawnbroker was protected under an FCN bilateral against a municipal ordinance forbidding aliens from engaging in that business. More detailed investors' rights provisions exist in later FCN treaties with other developed countries, where, generally speaking, such enumerations are not often needed. More recently, particularly vis-à-vis developing countries, the United States has vigorously pursued detailed agreements limited to foreign business investment issues. Some other capital exporting countries attempt the same types of arrangements. Such treaties provide for national and most favored nation treatment for foreign investors of the nationality of the parties, on a basis of reciprocity. The term "investment" is broadly defined and includes intellectual and industrial property rights, expectations under contracts, and re-invested earnings. Compulsory arbitration is often sought. The international minimum standard, capital-exporting country version, is explicit; and the United States tries to get the compensation formula stated as "prompt, adequate, and effective." Israel and a few other developing countries where historically foreign investment has not been controversial or prominent have entered into such treaties. But it is still slow going with the classic opposition, particularly in Latin America. Several treaties of the new

sort negotiated by the United States and developing countries still await coming into effect some years later.

A particularly useful survey of the later type bilateral investment treaties, is Gudgeon, Valuation of Nationalized Property under United States and Other Bilateral Investment Treaties, Ch. III, Lillich (ed.), The Valuation of Nationalized Property in International Law, Volume 4 (1987), pp. 101 et seq.

————

Read and Discuss the Treaty of Friendship, Establishment and Navigation Between the United States and Belgium of February 21, 1961, 14 U.S.T. 1284, 480 U.N.T.S. 149, in the Doc. Supp.

Multipartite efforts. Over the past forty years many proposals for multipartite investment codes have been put forward: the German bankers' plan, OECD formulations, even the failed Havana Charter for an international trade organization. The arrangement that follows is the only success, so far as it goes. In the Uruguay GATT Round, the trade-in-services agenda item included some proposals for service-related establishments abroad. The Uruguay Round was completed and signed on December 15, 1993.

3. WHAT IS HAPPENING AS TO THE INVESTMENT DISPUTE SETTLEMENT PROCESS?

The classic procedure of invoking espousal of the claim by the claimant's state of nationality, and thus elevating the matter to one between states and possibly triggering a doctrinal dispute on issues of customary international law, is giving way to a new procedure. The new process involves claimant party versus defendant state proceedings where disputes about the content of customary law are avoided by the nature of the arrangement used, even though principles derived from customary law are accepted by the parties, as, for example, the nature of the taking, levels of compensation, standing, and the like.

Instead of involving his foreign office, a claimant today is apt to propose or accept arbitration, either ad hoc, governed by a prior agreement at the time of the entry of the business investment, or provided at the option of the parties by either an international organization, or one of a number of non-governmental arbitral groups, such as the American Arbitration Association.

Within this range of options, the trend in investment disputes that involve developing countries as defendants is to use the facilities of the International Centre for the Settlement of Investment Disputes (ICSID), an organ of the World Bank which within the Bank is linked to the legal affairs office of the institution. Where the dispute is more "commercial" than "developmental", the resort might be to the arbitral rules and procedures of the United Nations Commission for International Trade Law (UNCITRAL).

ICSID publishes numerous useful materials related to foreign investment matters of a legal nature and is generous in their distribution. Of particular utility is a two-volume publication, Legal Framework for the Treatment of Foreign Investment (1992). Volume I of this publication includes a useful survey of sources about direct foreign investment, including lists of multilateral and bilateral investment treaties, tables on expropriations and compensation therefor, and an argument (Part III, at 147 ff) for the application to party-foreign state contracts of the customary law principle applicable between states, *Pacta Sund Servanda*, considered in Chapter 13.

EXCERPT FROM SHIHATA*, TOWARDS A GREATER DEPOLITICIZATION OF INVESTMENT DISPUTES: THE ROLES OF ICSID AND MIGA **

* * * Like the World Bank, with which it is closely associated, or the Multilateral Investment Guarantee Agency (MIGA or the Agency), which I will describe later, ICSID must be regarded as an instrument of international policy for the promotion of investments and of economic development. The main features of the system ICSID's founders devised for this instrument include its voluntary character, its flexibility and its effectiveness.

1. ICSID's *Voluntary Character*. ICSID's facilities are available on a voluntary basis. States eligible to join ICSID (members of the World Bank and states invited to sign the ICSID Convention under its Article 67) are obviously free to decline to do so. Their decision has no bearing on their relations with the World Bank itself. Moreover, ratification of the ICSID Convention does not constitute an obligation to use the ICSID machinery. That obligation can arise only after the Contracting State concerned has specifically agreed to submit to ICSID arbitration a particular dispute or class of disputes. In other words, the decision of a state to consent to ICSID arbitration is a matter within the sole discretion of each Contracting State. Under Article 25(4) of the ICSID Convention, any Contracting State may in addition notify ICSID, either at the time of ratification or at any time thereafter, of the class or classes of disputes that it would or would not consider arbitrable under ICSID's auspices. However, only a few Contracting States have made such a notification. Saudi Arabia has indicated that it intends to exclude investment disputes relating to "oil and pertaining to acts of sovereignty" and Jamaica has excluded disputes relating to "minerals or other natural resources." Papua New Guinea has specified that "it will only consider submitting those disputes to the Centre which are fundamental to the investment itself" and Turkey has indicated that it will only consider submitting to ICSID disputes arising out of investments that have been approved in Turkey and do not relate to rights in land.

Within this framework, parties have considerably more freedom to determine whether their transaction is suitable for ICSID arbitration

---

* Vice President and General Counsel, World Bank; Secretary–General, ICSID.   ** World Bank Publication in monograph; footnotes deleted; pp. 6–7, 13.

than might be assumed from the limitation of the Centre's jurisdiction to investment disputes of a legal character. The ICSID Convention does not define the term "investment," and this deliberate lack of definition has enabled the ICSID Convention to accommodate not only traditional types of investment in the form of capital contributions, but also new types of investment—including service contracts and transfers of technology.

Disputes submitted to the Centre concerning traditional types of investment have included disputes relating to the exploitation of natural resources, such as bauxite, timber and petroleum; industrial investments, such as the manufacture of fibers and of bottles, natural gas liquefaction, and aluminum production; a shrimp-farming joint venture; and the construction of hotels, tourist centers, and urban housing. Disputes relating to new types of "investment" have included disputes arising out of agreements for the construction of a chemical plant on a turnkey basis, coupled with a management contract, a management contract for a cotton mill, a contract for equipping of vessels for fishing and training their crews, technical and licensing agreements for the manufacture of weapons, and a branch operation of a bank. Most of these cases are related to genuine contractual disputes concerning the interpretation of investment agreements or matters of performance. Only a few concern unilateral termination of investment agreements, e.g. in the form of outright nationalization or the revocation of investment licenses.

4. EXHAUSTION OF LOCAL REMEDIES

The ICSID Convention gives investors direct access to an international forum and assures them that the refusal or abstention of the state party to a dispute to participate in the proceedings after it has given its consent cannot frustrate the arbitral process. But the ICSID Convention (Article 26) also provides that a Contracting State may, as a condition of its consent to ICSID arbitration, require prior exhaustion of local remedies. This condition may be specified in various ways. It could, for instance, be stipulated in the investment of agreement, as has been done in agreements concluded by Latin American countries.

5. DIPLOMATIC PROTECTION

As to diplomatic protection, the ICSID Convention takes a radical position. It was recognized at the time the ICSID Convention was finalized that: When a host state consents to the submission of a dispute with an investor to the Centre, thereby giving the investor direct access to an international jurisdiction, the investor should not be in a position to ask his state to espouse his case and that state should not be permitted to do so.

This fundamental consideration, which is another aspect of the exclusivity of the ICSID system, finds its expression in Article 27 of the ICSID Convention. That provision expressly prohibits a contracting state from giving diplomatic protection, or bringing an international claim, with respect to a dispute which one of its nationals and another contracting state have consented to submit to ICSID arbitration.

FRIEDMANN AND BEGUIN, JOINT INTERNATIONAL BUSINESS VENTURES IN DEVELOPING COUNTRIES 23 (1971) *

* * * [The joint venture] cannot be regarded as a panacea. It is a device to be adopted, rejected, or modified after a sober consideration of the many legal, psychological, and technical factors prevailing in a given situation. Confidence between the partners will overcome the most difficult obstacles; lack of confidence will destroy the most perfect devices. As a major negative factor, we mentioned disparity of outlook between the foreign and local partners:

> * * * In joint ventures between industrially developed countries, such as the United States, Britain, West Germany, the Netherlands, Italy, or Sweden, there is a certain community not only of tradition and of scientific, technical, and legal standards, but there has also been more experience with responsible investment practices and legal supervision, although such standards have often evolved only after disastrous experiences with unscrupulous speculators. In many of the less developed countries, this stage has not yet been reached in the business environment. * * *

* * *

---

1. *Joint ventures between the private sector in market economy countries and socialist states.* The joint venture is being used increasingly as an alternative to licensing, exporting, and management-service contracts where the private sectors in market economy states and socialist states seek to do business with each other. In the normal (private sector to private sector) joint venture the foreigners and the locals jointly own a corporation. How do you suppose the joint venture is structured where in the host state private ownership of the means of production is forbidden? The People's Republic of China has relaxed Marxist doctrine pragmatically. Direct foreign investment, with or without joint-venture linkages, is now commonplace in the Russian Federation, Ukraine, and a number of the newly-independent states once part of the Soviet empire.

2. *Multinational enterprises (MNEs).* In the last 30 years there has been great growth in the size and number of corporate families (parents and foreign subsidiaries) that carry on economic activity on multi-country, regional, or even global, bases. Aside from the influence of fashions in thought about business structure, why have the joint

* Reprinted with the permission of the Columbia University Press.

venture, earlier, and the MNE now, raised so many expectations as to preferred forms of direct foreign investment?

Experienced observers know well that the classic American parent-wholly owned foreign subsidiary structure is tagged as very foreign in most host countries; and in socially volatile ones, such as the developing and highly nationalistic states of Latin America, the label can lead to uncomfortable results. Thus, from the perspective of reducing or preventing transnational investment conflicts, the issue as to the MNE is one of credibility. Is the MNE really something new that does not deserve to be feared, controlled or discriminated against as both foreign and especially dangerous? Or is the MNE just a new name for an old and basically unchanged and increasingly controversial foreign investment structure?

One difficulty the MNE image is apt to have, in developing countries at least, but possibly in others as well, is that some self-styled MNEs—and they fit the definition quoted above also—have been take-over conglomerates. Foreign take-over of the best indigenous enterprise is always politically unpopular in the host state. When to this there is added the controversies that swirl around the basic assumption in justification that undefined and largely still personalized asserted management skills make conglomerates economically and socially desirable, the damage that the asserted linkage can do to the general idea of MNEs is substantial. Another relationship that comes into play at this point is whether the worlds of today and tomorrow (short range) have put aside as no longer relevant the "Curse of Bigness" of late nineteenth century populism (and the late Louis D. Brandeis). MNEs are big; a little business MNE is almost unimaginable. Has business learned how to be big, yet agile, adaptive and efficient at the same time? Here new doctrines of management technology and earlier folk-doubts may face a moment of truth before long. Or, if not intellectual confrontations, then antitrust ones.

In the United States MNE parent corporations are not without domestic problems. Organized labor complains that MNEs are largely responsible for runaway plants that take jobs away from American workers and bring in foreign made goods under freer trade auspices. Others complain that certain self-styled MNEs conspire against, and seek to involve the United States government in pressuring certain foreign governments. Congress may have still to face what it will do about proposed legislation against imports here of goods made abroad by American-owned foreign companies. Some observers have seen in some patterns of European Economic Community antitrust enforcement action a bias against large American companies with numerous subsidiaries (some of them by take-over) within the EEC. On the other hand, others say that the industrialized Europeans and the Japanese have enthusiastic ideas of their own about the further use of MNEs. It is sometimes added that more true MNEs are based in Europe—and have been for some time—than in the United States, because Europeans, more than the Americans, have found it expedient in past to share participations in capital at the top—and sometimes at lower—levels within the structure of a corporate family.

Student users of these materials—and some of their teachers—will in their professional lifetimes probably see how the foregoing issues and problems work themselves out. Will one straight line projection or its opposite occur? Or will evolution take a now unforeseen twist? Meanwhile, the profession of international lawyering is already considerably involved with the MNE as a concept, a rhetoric, or a reality. More and more the term TNE (Transnational Enterprise) is used. Why?

---

6. REDUCTION OF TRANSNATIONAL INVESTMENT CONFLICT

Prior Restraints on Entry

It was noted earlier in this chapter that historically there have been more hindrances and prohibitions on the movement of merchandise across frontiers (trade) than as to the movement of business capital. However, some states control entry of foreign businesses by the requirement of licenses to enter. France for some time has required large direct foreign investments to apply for entry permits. The Latin–American States of the Andean Common Market developed and put into effect an elaborate prior restraint system. * * *

Reports at the April, 1993 annual meeting of the American Society of International Law, not yet published, indicated marked relaxation of business-entry controls. The earlier restraints are now seen as the waning of hostility toward foreign investment in Latin–America that was generated by situations that have either improved or become irrelevant. See, supra, § B–1. Generally, as to its background, outlook, and terms see Oliver, The Andean Foreign Investment Code: A New Phase in the Quest for Normative Order as to Direct Foreign Investment, American Journal of International Law 763 (1972).

Profile lowering devices. In the United States and in a number of other countries the legal profession, through practitioners specializing in international business transactions, is influential in the structuring of foreign investments. That clients prefer to be told how they can come somewhere near achieving their objectives, rather than to be told what they cannot do, is a reality here as in other sectors of practice involving prospective operations. Knowledge of the existing rules of the international legal system and of the lines along which these rules may evolve is highly important. It is also important that the lawyer be innovative, sensitive to the psycho-political setting in the potential host country and free of ideological prejudice. In particular, it is useful for him to consider ways in which the business venture itself can be organized and operated so as to avoid to the extent possible shifts for the worse in the investment climate after the client has become irrevocably committed to the venture, as by making a foreign investment in fixed assets. The fundamental principle of economics that such an investment is assuredly retrievable only for its scrap or salvage value should not be overlooked.

Among the possibilities that modern foreign investors ought to be induced to consider, in particular circumstances, are:

  a. Management-service contracts as an alternative to ownership interests. Some countries have already limited the foreign investor to the former in the extractive industries and public utilities.

  b. Joint ventures.

  c. Wider offerings of stock in the host-country operating company to investors of that country, i.e. a departure from the pattern so often found in the past of complete foreign stock ownership, except for qualifying shares, usually three percent or less of the total stock in that company. Such preponderance is not necessary for control.

  d. Due regard to national and regional preferences that foreign investors not dominate particular sectors of the economy, such as defense-related industries, telecommunications, etc.

  e. For the extractive industries, the possibility of negotiating the country-company sharing of the proceeds of the business at different ratios during the life of the concession, particularly if the term is a fairly long one. In many instances minerals concessions now giving the preponderant return to the country were originally contracted for on the basis of a far lower participation by the host, and as time went on pressures built up for changing the sharing that sometimes caused crises in the relationship, and even nationalizations under emotionally heated circumstances. It has been suggested that with the utilization of improved techniques of economic forecasting new concessions might be originally negotiated to provide for increasing the host share of the proceeds at successive stages in the life of the concession.

  f. Acceptance of partial disinvestment down to substantial minority stock ownership. See Hirschman, How to Divest in Latin America, and Why, Princeton Essays in International Finance (No. 76, 1969). However, experience shows that foreign business capital will not flow if the foreign element does not have control through the period of 100% payout.

  g. The multinationalization of the foreign ownership, thus reducing the association of the venture with any single foreign nationality. Oliver, Speculations on Developing Country Reception of Multinational Enterprise, 11 Va.J. of Int'l Law 192 (1971).

  h. Disassociation from particular nationalities by removing the parents' corporation control centers to relatively innocuous offshore places, usually in new, small, rule-of-law states. Does this tactic have a downside?

  Other possibilities involving legal structuring exist and still others will doubtless develop in the future. Outside the lawyer's sphere of specialization, but related, are managerial practices as to the use of nationals of the host country in executive suites as well as in the labor force, corporate good citizenship in the host country, maximum use of products of that country in the conduct of a manufacturing or sales business and the like.

———

Chapter 16

PEACEFUL RESOLUTION OF DISPUTES AND THE USE OF FORCE IN THE INTERNATIONAL SYSTEM

SECTION A. THE PEACEFUL RESOLUTION OF DISPUTES IN THE INTERNATIONAL SYSTEM

At its 44th Session, in 1989, the General Assembly declared 1990–1999 to be the U.N. Decade of International Law. Objectives were to further the acceptance of the principles of international law and to promote methods for the peaceful settlement of international disputes. In the modern era of nation-states since the treaties of Utrecht and Westphalia, international law has attempted to resolve disputes by means short of war in several ways. Inspired in part by legal and theological precepts of *"Just War,"* aggressive war was proscribed, means of peaceful resolution of disputes were developed, and rules mitigating the violent effects of war were promulgated.

Modalities and techniques for the peaceful resolution of disputes were instituted through the Hague Peace Conferences of 1899 and 1907, the Bryan Treaties, the Kellogg–Briand Pact, and the League of Nations. This early history is examined in this section, culminating in a review of attempts peacefully to resolve disputes under the provisions of Chapter VI of the U.N. Charter, including fact-finding and conciliation, good offices, mediation and arbitration. Finally, this chapter describes the international community's attempts to maintain conditions of peace and justice through the use of force short of war: economic boycott and United Nations "peace-keeping" under Chapter VII of the Charter. Chapter Seventeen, infra, completes the circle, exploring the traditional and residual rights of states to go to war.

For the most part, international disputes are resolved by negotiation between the disputants. In this way, on a day-to-day basis, international law works. If negotiation fails, the parties may seek to resolve their differences by mediation or conciliation.

Negotiation: Nations, like individuals, will attempt to resolve their problems in a non-violent way if it may give them an advantage. National leaders have negotiated with their foreign counterparts as the means to enter into relations, to prevent problems before they arise, and to resolve problems when they do arise. Thus, nations have expert negotiators in the *Legal Adviser's Office* of their Department of Foreign Affairs, who conduct "negotiations", and "consultations" (e.g., the various offices in the Department of State maintain ongoing consultation on the subject of their oversight or expertise). This is the ongoing, daily business of foreign affairs, which takes place through "diplomatic channels." These negotiators negotiate treaties, but also continue ongoing "consultation" and "negotiation" on issues in their expertise.

Mediation: When consultation fails to prevent a problem and negotiation fails to resolve it, a third party may be able to intervene to resolve the impasse, helping the parties create a solution acceptable to each of them. This is offering "good offices." The third party has no power or authority to force a settlement, such as in binding arbitration. He attempts to help the parties see solutions which will be mutually advantageous or at least an acceptable alternative to continuing the dispute. The mediator may also be charged with investigation and development of proposals for consideration. This is called "concilia-tion."

Conciliation: A commission is set-up by disputing parties. The commission may be permanent, to resolve ongoing disputes on a given subject, or, may be ad hoc. The commission is charged to investigate the dispute or incident and to establish the facts as a neutral observer. We will examine the minimally successful attempt to utilize conciliation in disputes in the early part of the 20th century. More recently, the General Assembly has adopted a plan, *U.N. Draft Rules for the Concilia-tion of Disputes Between States,* Nov. 28, 1990, 30 ILM 229 (1991), which we have included in the Doc. Supp.

Adjudication: If the above methods fail, nations may resort to international adjudication either in the International Court of Justice, discussed in Chapters 1, 10, and 11, or in domestic courts, examined in Chapters 1, 10, 11, and in 14. Other aspects of peaceful resolution are related to fact-finding and the success of the peaceful means attempted often depends on them. These include: jurisdiction, applicable law, effect or nature of outcomes (e.g., binding or non-binding), acceptability of the various procedures (waxing or waning, for example), and workabil-ity.

1. FACT FINDING AND DISPUTE RESOLUTION UNDER THE HAGUE CONVENTIONS AND LEAGUE OF NATIONS

For detailed historical analysis, see Firmage, Fact–Finding in the Resolution of International Disputes—From the Hague Peace Confer-ence to the United Nations, [1971] Utah L.Rev. 421; and, Firmage, The 1993 Kellogg Lectures, War, Peace & Faith, delivered at the Episcopal Divinity School in Cambridge, Mass. (1993) from which the following material was drawn.

The history of peaceful resolution of disputes through the Hague Conventions and the League of Nations is often seen as being negative, because the League and its member states failed to prevent the Second World War. While the League and its members failed adequately to confront aggressor states in the 1930's, the League was successful to some degree in resolving some disputes in Europe following the disinte-gration of imperial systems of government after the First World War. Then as now, contending ethnic and national groups threatened the peace. The League and its member states had somehow to redraw the map of Europe. Techniques and instruments of peaceful resolution were developed which may once again be useful in allowing contending parties in disputes to have available the means for peaceful resolution.

The enduring quest of the peacemaker has been to substitute peaceful means of dispute resolution for violent self help. The horizontal and uncentralized nature of the international system has lessened the capacity of international law to punish illegal violence and provide adequate means of peaceful resolution of disputes. There are few hierarchical, vertical, or centralizing factors in the international system to enforce its norms upon aberrant states.

Within this context of relative immaturity and weakness, the international system, nevertheless, has developed some institutional procedures to accomplish the peaceful resolution of disputes. For the most part, these procedures—good offices, conciliation, inquiry or fact-finding, negotiation, mediation, arbitration and judicial settlement—have counterparts within municipal systems. While this listing of techniques ranges from political or diplomatic to judicial, one process—inquiry or fact-finding—is instrumental to both.

Fact-finding has a common relationship to resultant conclusions of law, policy, or accommodation in dispute settlement whether the process of resolution is of a juridical or a diplomatic nature. Modern techniques of fact-finding in the process of the peaceful resolution of international disputes have an evolutionary history dating from the latter part of the last century. International commissions of inquiry have existed from before the Hague Conventions through the period of the Bryan treaties and the League of Nations to the less formal fact-finding bodies frequently created by the United Nations.

The Hague Conventions Through the League of Nations. The Hague Conventions of 1899 and 1907: Significant institutional development of international commissions of inquiry as a technique in the peaceful resolution of disputes began with the Hague Conventions of 1899 and 1907, although informal international commissions of inquiry had been employed before. Seven commissions of inquiry were established under the two Hague Conventions. The commissions all possessed the following characteristics: (1) resort to the commissions was voluntary; (2) only minor disputes were referred to the commissions; (3) each commission was *ad hoc;* (4) each commission was constituted so as to insure neutral dominance; (5) the report was recommendatory only; (6) commissions could investigate only factual differences. The Hague Convention of 1899 was invoked in only one dispute—the "Hull," or "*Dogger Bank,*" case, where the commission's report, though not binding, was implemented by the Parties. Russia accordingly paid damages.

The Bryan Treaties: Between 1913 and 1915 the United States signed over 30 bilateral treaties, all entitled "Treaty for the Advancement of Peace," with other American states and with several European states. The force behind the negotiation of the treaties was William Jennings Bryan, who made his acceptance of the office of Secretary of State dependent upon the integration of his concept of commissions of inquiry into the foreign policy of the Wilson administration. While there are obvious similarities between the Hague and Bryan Commissions, the differences are more significant. Where the Hague Conventions provided for ad hoc commissions to be established by agreement between the parties, the Bryan treaties established permanent commissions within guidelines provided by the Conventions. Under the Hague Conventions, the jurisdiction of the commissions was severely limited to disputes of an incidental nature, involving neither national honor "nor vital interests." In addition, the commissions' terms of reference under the Conventions were usually, though not always, limited to findings of fact rather than conclusions of law.

The League of Nations: Thirty disputes were handled by the League of Nations from 1920 to 1940. Most of these were border and territorial disputes stemming from the disintegration of the Austro-Hungarian, Turkish, and Russian empires. Franco–British solidarity accounted for the League's success in resolving most of the disputes which arose in the 1920's. This solidarity, however, proved insufficient to deal with the aggressive acts of other great powers in the 1930's.

Conclusions: Fact-finding worked best when simple, non-strategic issues were involved between parties who, in good faith, were disputing relatively simple questions of fact. All disputes handled under the Hague Conventions involved maritime incidents that did not affect the vital interests of the parties. The majority of the cases considered by the League of Nations concerned border disputes stemming them the disintegration of colonial empires.

The experience of the Hague Conventions and the League of Nations suggests that there are two essential elements of successful fact-finding efforts to aid in the peaceful settlement of international disputes: first, the parties must, to a certain degree, accept peaceful settlement as a customary means of dispute resolution; and second, the parties must believe that there is a credible threat of community sanction to enforce those means. There is a direct correlation between these two factors. As the first increases in the depth of its tradition, the necessity of the second decreases proportionally. The prerequisites are discernible in international relations, but since they are still weak, it is predictable and understandable that states will resolve the most complex and important disputes by more traditional means of diplomacy and by threatened or actual military action.

The functioning and composition of fact-finding through the League period reflects the tentative steps which the international community was willing to take along the road to increased community resolution of disputes through means of pacific settlement. The composition of most commissions was based upon individual expertise rather than national representation. Almost all commission members operated individually, without instructions from their governments. This, of course, was an operational reflection of the simplicity and relative unimportance of the disputes entrusted to their resolution. The terms of reference of the commissions became broader as the international community gained gradual confidence in this technique of dispute resolution.

The lines drawn and the nation building of the period resonate today. The disintegration of the Soviet Union and Yugoslavia and the end of Soviet hegemony throughout Eastern Europe again confront the world with ethnic, religious and nationalist civil strife. Older imperial or multi-ethnic and multi-national forms of government have crumbled and ethnic disputes have risen to the level of civil wars, for example, in Rwanda & Burundi, in the former Yugoslavia, in Georgia, and between Azerbaijan and Armenia within the former Soviet Union. The similarities to the disintegration of imperial systems and consequent ethnic strife following World War I are apparent. Sadly, many of the parties and issues from the earlier disputes have risen once again.

2. THE UNITED NATIONS CHARTER

At this point, consider Chapter VI of the U.N. Charter, especially Articles 33, 34, 35, 36, 37 and 38, available in the Doc. Supp. As you study, keep in mind the following: What are the means of peacemaking, peacekeeping and preventive diplomacy?

3. EARLY ATTEMPTS PEACEFULLY TO RESOLVE DISPUTES UNDER THE CHARTER

a. *General*

(1) The Greek Crisis. The Greek crisis was the first dispute to confront the United Nations. Following World War II, Greece suffered internal dissent and insurrection. The Acting Chair of the Greek delegation sent a letter to the Secretary–General, asking him to bring the problem to the attention of the U.N. pursuant to Articles 34 and 35 of the Charter. The Greek Government claimed that a condition of insurgency existed only in its northern provinces and that the insurgents were being trained and supplied by its northern neighbors, Yugoslavia, Albania, and Bulgaria.

The Security Council invited the representatives of the states involved to present their cases before the Council on December 10, 1946. After hearing the arguments the United States Representative to the U.N. proposed that the Security Council establish a Fact–Finding Commission to investigate the alleged border violations and to report its conclusions to the Council. The Security Council unanimously adopted the resolution on December 19, 1946. (See Doc. Supp.).

Despite being denied access to three of the four states for most of its tenure, the Commission's investigation was thorough and relatively successful. The Commission concluded that Yugoslavia and, to a lesser degree, Albania and Bulgaria, supported the guerrilla warfare in Greece. The Commission found that most of the violence had taken place in the three most northern Greek provinces, but that the level of violence did not constitute a civil war. The majority of the members of the Security Council approved the Commission's Report, but the USSR and Poland did not. The USSR vetoed the execution of the measures called for in the Commission's Report, concluding that the evidence in the report demonstrated that a state of civil war did exist throughout Greece and was the result of internal causes. See, 1946–47 Y.B.U.N. 369.

Following the Security Council's refusal to execute the Report, the General Assembly created the United Nations Special Committee on the Balkans (UNSCOB). The Assembly ordered UNSCOB to observe compliance with its collateral call for the four involved states to "establish good neighborly relations, establish frontier agreements, settle the refugee problems and study the possibility of transferring minority groups along the border." UNSCOB had authority to investigate within each of the four states, although only Greece ultimately allowed the observer force into their country. Nevertheless, UNSCOB was successful in collecting information and ultimately provided unambiguous evidence that the three northern, neighbor states were essential accomplices in the Greek insurgency. Armed with these reports, the General Assembly condemned the actions of Yugoslavia, Albania, and Bulgaria. *See*, Firmage, *Fact–Finding, supra* at 443–44.

(2) The India–Pakistan Conflict. Following independence, India and Pakistan went to war over Kashmir. The combatants reached a cease-fire agreement in July, 1949. United Nations Military Observer Group (UNMOGIP), was established to investigate complaints of violations of the agreement, to observe troop build-up and deployment, and to control civilian movement in and around the cease-fire line. Although initially UNMOGIP was successful, the violence began to increase after 1955. By 1965 it had reached crisis proportions. Based on UNMOGIP reports, the Secretary General reported the escalation of violence to the Security Council in a letter. *See, gen.,* Report by the Secretary–General On the Current Situation in Kashmir with Particular Reference to the Cease–Fire Agreement, the Cease–Fire Line and the Functioning of UNMOGIP. U.N. Doc. S/6650. Consider also U.N. S.C. Resolution 211 in Doc. Supp.

Despite Resolution 211 and others which followed, the combatants in Kashmir continued to violate the cease-fire agreement. The Secretary–General and UNMOGIP continued to report violations and to attempt to mediate the dispute. Finally, on February 17, 1966, the leaders of Pakistan and India agreed to withdraw their forces and to restore the cease-fire.

b. *Dispute Resolution Conducted By the General Assembly*

The Korean Conflict. Following World War II, Korea remained divided into two nations and was occupied by the major powers. The harmony that the drafters of the U.N. Charter believed would develop and continue after World War II evaporated long before the North Korean invasion of the South in 1950. The major powers after the War found themselves involved on either side in the Korea Conflict. The Security Council already reflected institutionally the bi-polarity of the Cold War in the veto power of the permanent members and consequent paralysis of the Council. The General Assembly, however, did not find itself so constrained. Article 18(2) of the Charter, which does not include a veto, allowed the Assembly to pass Resolution 112 (II) to establish a temporary commission to inquire into whether a lawful government had been established in the Republic of Korea. Pertinent resolutions include: G.A. Res. 112; G.A. Res. 195 (III), 12 Dec. 1948; G.A. Res. 293 (IV), 21 Oct. 1949. War came to Korea, despite the efforts of the United Nations Commission on Korea (UNCOK). After delays in placing reporters in country, observers were immediately dispatched to the 38th Parallel. The observers were not allowed into North Korea and were called back to Seoul just one day before the North attacked. The Commission's report was instrumental, however, in disproving the North Korean claims of self-defense to justify their attack. Moreover, the Commission's report established that an observer group could monitor developments in a tense situation and could provide useful information, even when confined to only one side of a border.

(d) *Report of the United Nations Commission on Korea to the Fifth Regular Session of the General Assembly.* UNCOK *concluded that:* The hostilities that had broken-out on June 25, 1950 were not caused by "a provocative attack by the troops of the Republic of Korea, [or] the launching of an invasion force across the [38th] parallel by the Republic of Korea, as has been alleged * * *." The Commission reported that it had observers with free access to all areas in South Korea, which were at all times aware of the military situation there. The Commission observers completed their report on June 24, 1950, the eve of the invasion from the North. Their report indicated that the forces in the South were not prepared to attack the North, and, therefore, "that no offensive could possibly have been launched across the parallel by the Republic of Korea on 25 June 1950 * * *. The invasion launched by North Korean forces on 25 June cannot have been the result of a decision taken suddenly to repel a mere border attack or in retaliation for such an attack. Such an invasion * * * presupposes a long-premeditated, well-prepared and well-timed act of aggression. The subsequent steady advance of the North Korean forces supplies further evidence * * * of the extensive nature of the planning and preparation for the aggression. * * * It is the considered opinion of the Commission that this planning and preparation were deliberate, and an essential part of the policy of the North Korean authorities. The objective of this policy was to secure by force what could not be gained by any other means. In furtherance of this policy the North Korean authorities, on 25 June 1950, initiated a war of aggression, without provocation and without warning * * *."

c. *Dispute Resolution Conducted By the Secretary–General*

The Secretary–General has initiated a dispute resolution without General Assembly or Security Council authority. This action has usually been met with one of two responses from either or both of the two bodies: (1) one or both issued a resolution providing post hoc authorization; (2) a member of the Security Council has attempted to thwart the action as an abuse of authority.

(1) The Cambodia—Thailand Border Dispute. Cambodia and Thailand have engaged in a border dispute for centuries. External pressures from Cold War conflicts in Southeast Asia led to "good offices" missions in 1959, 1963–64, and in 1966. In 1966, the Secretary–General initiated the good-offices mission on his own authority. The USSR objected that the crisis implicated international peace and security, thus, falling within Security Council, rather than the Secretary–General's jurisdiction. *See also* Section B of this Chapter.

(a) Letter from the Secretary–General to the President of the Security Council. 16 Aug. 1966:

I have the honour to inform you that, in consultation with the Governments of Cambodia and Thailand, I have designated Ambassador Herbert de Ribbing as my Special Representative in the two countries. Ambassador de Ribbing will examine with the Governments of Cambodia and Thailand the situation prevailing between them, endeavour to find ways and means of reducing tension in the area and explore the possibilities of resolving whatever problems may exist between them. The duration of the assignment of my Special Representative will be initially for six months. He will be expected to move from one country to the other as necessary.

Both Governments have signified to me their willingness to share on an equal basis all costs involved in the mission of the Special Representative—who will be assisted by a small staff as appropriate—so that no budgetary provisions on the part of the United Nations will be required. In view of the nature of the action envisaged, I thought it appropriate to inform the members of the Security Council.

(Signed) Accept, Sir, etc. U. Thant

(b) Letter from N. Fedorenko, Permanent Representative to the President of the Security Council. 27 Aug. 1966:

With reference to the Secretary–General's letter dated 26 August 1966 addressed to the President of the Security Council (S/7402), stating his intention to appoint a Special Representative to help to eliminate tension between Cambodia and Thailand, I consider it necessary to emphasize that under the United Nations Charter decisions on matters connected with action by the United Nations relating to the maintenance of international peace and security are taken by the Security Council. When the Security Council takes a decision on the particular candidate put forward for the post after consultation with the parties concerned, the Soviet Union will have no objection to make.

I should be grateful if you would arrange for this letter to be circulated as an official Security Council document. Accept, Sir, etc.

(Signed) N. FEDORENKO
Representative of the USSR
in the Security Council

(c) Letter from Raul Quijano, Deputy Permanent Representative of the Argentine Republic Addressed to the President of the Security Council. 30 Sept. 1966:

I have the honour to refer to the letter dated 27 August 1966 from the Permanent Representative of the Union of Soviet Socialist Republics to the United Nations addressed to the President of the Security Council (S/7478). The Argentine Government wishes to state that it cannot share the views expressed by the Permanent Representative of the USSR concerning the decision taken by the Secretary-General, in consultation with the Governments of Cambodia and Thailand, to appoint Ambassador Herbert de Ribbing as his Special Representative in these two countries. My Government considers that the action taken by the Secretary-General is fully justified and falls within the competence conferred upon him by the Charter of the United Nations.

In the light of the provisions of Article 99 of the Charter and the directives addressed by the General Assembly to the Secretary–General concerning his functions and responsibilities, my Government has no doubt whatever that the Secretary–General has the authority, and even the duty, to keep himself informed on all matters which may threaten the maintenance of international peace and security and to exert the utmost effort to relieve situations which may become threats to international peace and security. Most particularly, when a dispute arises between two or more countries, it lies within the authority of the Secretary–General to offer his good offices to the parties concerned, either directly or through a representative, to reduce tension and resolve the disagreement between them. The Secretary–General's appointment of a representative for this purpose is, in my Government's view, subject to only two requirements: that he should consult the parties concerned and obtain their consent to his appointment of a representative and that he should inform the Security Council of his decision.

> (*Signed*) Raul QUIJANO
> Deputy Permanent Representative
> of the Argentine
> Republic to the United Nations
> Chargé d'affaires a.1.

Query: Who do you think is correct?

(2) The Crisis in Lebanon (1958). On May 22, 1958, Lebanon's Representative to the United Nations sent a letter to the President of the Security Council complaining that the United Arab Republic was violating Lebanon's borders and was aiding insurgents within Lebanon.

(a) Letter from the Representative of Lebanon (S/4007).

Upon instructions from my Government, I have the honour to request you, in your capacity as President of the Security Council, to call an urgent meeting of the Council to consider the following question: "Complaint by Lebanon in respect of a situation arising from the intervention of the United Arab Republic in the internal affairs of Lebanon, the continuance of which is likely to endanger the maintenance of international peace and security."

The said intervention consists *inter alia* of the following acts: the infiltration of armed bands from Syria into Lebanon, the de-

struction of Lebanese life and property by such bands, the participation of United Arab Republic nationals in acts of terrorism and
rebellion against the established authorities in Lebanon, the supply
of arms from Syria to individuals and bands in Lebanon rebelling
against the established authorities, and the waging of a violent radio
and press campaign in the United Arab Republic calling for strikes,
demonstrations and the overthrow of the established authorities in
Lebanon, and through other provocative acts. * * *

This letter prompted the Security Council to invite Representatives
of Lebanon of those of the United Arab Republic to present their case
before it. Thereafter, the Security Council authorized the formation of
an observer mission to Lebanon (UNOGIL).

Security Council Resolution 128 (S/4023)

The Security Council, having heard the charges of the representative of Lebanon concerning interference by the United Arab Republic in
the internal affairs of Lebanon and the reply of the representative of the
United Arab Republic,

1. *Decides* to dispatch urgently an observation group to proceed to
Lebanon so as to ensure that there is no illegal infiltration of personnel
or supply of arms or other *material* across the Lebanese borders;

2. *Authorizes* the Secretary–General to take the necessary steps to
that end;

3. *Requests* the observation group to keep the Security Council
currently informed through the Secretary–General.

> *Adopted at the 825th meeting by 10
> votes to none, with 1 abstention
> (Union of Soviet Socialist
> Republics).*

The broad language of Resolution 128 could have been interpreted
to authorize interdiction of border violations, but the Secretary–General
chose to interpret it narrowly, to include only fact-finding. On November 25, 1958, the Security Council, manifesting structural paralysis, took
the approach that became its hallmark during this period. It decided
"to delete the Lebanese complaint from the list of matters of which it
was seized," thus leaving the parties to resolve (or to continue) their
own dispute. *See* Firmage, *Fact–Finding, supra* at 435.

Assassinations in Iraq of the King, the Crown Prince, and other
government leaders in a coup precipitated the landings of U.S. troops in
Lebanon and U.K. forces in Jordan, at the request of those governments.
The Secretary–General rejected U.S. and Lebanese requests that UNO-
GIL be transformed into a peace-keeping force, on the ground that such
an action had to be based on Security Council directives pursuant to
chapter VII of the Charter. In retrospect, it appears that fact-finding
produced better information for the Secretary–General than that obtained by U.S. intelligence. The Secretary–General's view seems to have

been correct, that the strife was internally caused and was not due to external forces, as the United States had argued.

4.   THE CONTADORA GROUP: U.N., REGIONAL ORGA-NIZATION, & THIRD PARTIES COORDINATION IN REGIONAL DISPUTE RESOLUTION.

On July 19, 1979, the Sandanistas seized power in Nicaragua, overthrowing the U.S.-backed former Nicaraguan dictator, General Anastazio Somoza. The Reagan Administration, feeling that another "Marxist-led" nation in the Western Hemisphere was intolerable and presented a threat to the security of the entire region, began a campaign to undermine and contain the Sandanista Government in Nicaragua. The assistance was actually initiated by a "request" from El Salvador and, eventually from other countries. Massive financial assistance and military training programs were begun by the United States to maintain what it considered "friendly" regimes in Honduras, El Salvador, and Costa Rica. The U.S. Government created, financed, and trained the *Contra* (anti-Sandanista) rebels fighting in Nicaragua. The *Contras,* were composed largely of former members of the deposed dictator Somoza's National Guard and *Sandanistas,* who had helped overthrow Somoza, but who had become disaffected. The CIA also took direct military action against Nicaragua by reconnaissance overflights of Nicaraguan airspace by military aircraft, and mining Nicaraguan harbors.

Colombia, Mexico, Panama and Venezuela organized the Contadora Group that sought peaceful resolution by promoting dialogue among Nicaragua, Honduras, El Salvador, Costa Rica and, the two principal third-party sponsors of the violence in Nicaragua, Cuba and the United States. The methodology was mediation with good-offices aimed at ending the long-standing warfare and violence. The Contadora movement sought to prevent military intervention and conflict through a broad range of political and economic cooperative measures and in limiting the introduction of arms and military bases. *See, The Contadora Act on Peace and Co-operation in Central America,* June 7, 1986, reprinted in 25 ILM 1302 (1986), and in Contadora and the Central American Peace Process: Selected Documents, 8 SAIS Papers in International Affairs 194–217 (Bagley, et al. eds. 1985). Unfortunately, the Draft Contadora Act was never ratified. *See also,* Caminos & Lavalle, *New Departures in the Exercise of Inherent Powers by the UN and OAS Secretaries–General: The Central American Situation,* 83 A.J.I.L. 395 (1989).

5.   ADJUSTING THE PEACE SYSTEM: RECENT AT-TEMPTS TO MODERNIZE THE PROCESS—NEGOTI-ATION, MEDIATION & CONCILIATION

a.   *The United Nations Handbook on the Peaceful Settlement of Disputes Between States.*

INTRODUCTION

By its resolutions 39/79 and 39/88 of 13 December 1984, the General Assembly requested the Secretary–General to prepare * * * in the light of the views expressed in the course of the discussions in the Sixth Committee and in the Special Committee, a draft handbook on the peaceful settlement of disputes between States.

In accordance with the conclusions reached by the Special Committee at its 1984 session with respect to the preparation of the draft handbook, the Secretary–General was instructed to consult periodically a representative group of competent individuals from among the members of the Permanent Missions of the States Members of the United Nations in order to obtain assistance in the performance of his task. At the 1985 session, it was agreed that the "representative group of competent individuals from among the members of the Permanent Missions of the States Members of the United Nations" would be open to all members of the Special Committee and that the group would have purely consultative functions.

The purpose of the handbook is to contribute to the peaceful settlement of disputes between States and to help to increase compliance with international law by providing States parties to a dispute, particularly those States which do not have the benefit of long-established and experienced legal departments, with the information they might need to select and apply procedures best suited to the settlement of particular disputes.

The handbook has been prepared in strict conformity with the Charter of the United Nations. It is descriptive in nature and is not a legal instrument. Although drawn up on consultation with Member States, it does not represent the views of Member States.

In conformity with the above-mentioned resolutions, the scope of the handbook was to be limited to disputes between States, excluding those disputes which although involving States fell under municipal law or were within the competence of domestic courts. However, at the request of the Consultative Group to the Secretary–General, the draft handbook now includes disputes to which subjects of law other than States may be parties. *United Nations Handbook on the Peaceful Settlement of Disputes Between States.* *(Handbook is in Doc. Supp.)*

* * *

b. See also, Guatamala Draft Resolution calling for U.N. rules for the conciliation of disputes between states: in the Doc. Supp.

c. The General Assembly Plan: U.N. Draft Rules for the Conciliation of Disputes Between States, Nov. 28, 1990, 30 ILM 229 (1991). (See, the Doc. Supp.)

d. The Secretary–General's Plan: Boutros Boutros–Ghali, Report On an Agenda for Peace—Preventive Diplomacy, Peacemaking and Peacekeeping (June 17, 1992, 31 ILM 953 (1992).

INTRODUCTION

1. In its statement of 31 January 1992, adopted at the conclusion of the first meeting held by the Security Council at the level of Heads of State and Government, I was invited to prepare, for circulation to the * * * United Nations * * *, an "analysis and recommendations on ways of strengthening and making more efficient within the framework and provisions of the Charter the capacity of the United Nations for preventive diplomacy, for peacemaking and for peace-keeping."

2. The United Nations is a gathering of sovereign States and what it can do depends on the common ground that they create between them. The adversarial decades of the cold war made the original promise of the Organization impossible to fulfil. The January 1992 Summit therefore represented an unprecedented recommitment, at the highest political level, to the Purposes and Principles of the Charter.

3. In these past months a conviction has grown, among nations large and small, that an opportunity has been regained to achieve the great objectives of the Charter—a United Nations capable of maintaining international peace and security, of securing justice and human rights and of promoting, in the words of the Charter, "social progress and better standards of life in larger freedom". This opportunity must not be squandered. The Organization must never again be crippled as it was in the era that has now passed.

4. I welcome the invitation of the Security Council, early in my tenure as Secretary–General, to prepare this report. It draws upon ideas and proposals transmitted to me by Governments, regional agencies, non-governmental organizations, and institutions and individuals from many countries. I am grateful for these, even as I emphasize that the responsibility for this report is my own.

5. The sources of conflict and war are pervasive and deep. To reach them will require our utmost effort to enhance respect for human rights and fundamental freedoms, to promote sustainable economic and social development for wider prosperity, to alleviate distress and to curtail the existence and use of massively destructive weapons. The U.N. Conference on Environment and Development, the largest summit ever held, has just met at Rio de Janeiro. The second World Conference on Human Rights [follows.] In 1994 Population and Development will be addressed. In 1995 the World Conference on Women will take place, and a World Summit for Social Development has been proposed. * * * I shall be addressing all these great issues. I bear them all in mind as, in the present report, I turn to the problems that the Council has specifically requested I consider: preventive diplomacy, peacemaking and peace-keeping—to which I have added a closely related concept, post-conflict peace-building.

6. The manifest desire of the membership to work together is a new source of strength in our common endeavour. Success is far from certain, however. While my report deals with ways to improve the Organization's capacity to pursue and preserve peace, it is crucial for all Member States to bear in mind that the search for improved mechanisms and techniques will be of little significance unless this new spirit of commonality is propelled by the will to make the hard decisions demanded by this time of opportunity.

* * *

14. Since the creation of the United Nations in 1945, over 100 major conflicts around the world have left some 20 million dead. The United Nations was rendered powerless to deal with many of these crises because of the vetoes—279 of them—cast in the Security Council, which were a vivid expression of the divisions of that period.

15. With the end of the cold war there have been no such vetoes since 31 May 1990, and demands on the United Nations have surged. Its security arm, once disabled by circumstances it was not created or equipped to control, has emerged as a central instrument for the prevention and resolution of conflicts and for the preservation of peace. Our aims must be:

- To seek to identify at the earliest possible stage situations that could produce conflict, and to try through diplomacy to remove the sources of danger before violence results;

- Where conflict erupts, to engage in peacemaking aimed at resolving the issues that have led to conflict;

- Through peace-keeping, to work to preserve peace, however fragile, where fighting has been halted and to assist in implementing agreements achieved by the peacemakers;

- To stand ready to assist in peace-building in its differing contexts: rebuilding the institutions and infrastructures of nations torn by civil war and strife; and building bonds of peaceful mutual benefit among nations formerly at war;

- And in the largest sense, to address the deepest causes of conflict: economic despair, social injustice and political oppression. It is possible to discern an increasingly common moral perception that spans the world's nations and peoples, and which is finding expression in international laws, many owing their genesis to the work of this Organization.

U.N.Doc. A/47/227 and S/2411 (17 June 1992), reprinted in, 31 I.L.M. 953 (1992).

Query: Do the recent plans improve on the old? Why? Why not?

SECTION B. THE USE OF FORCE BY THE UNITED NATIONS

1. EVOLUTION OF LAW AGAINST USE OF FORCE BY STATES:

a. Conceptual and Philosophical Introduction. Portions of this introduction were adapted from Firmage, Summary and Interpretation, concluding Chapter in International Law of Civil War 405–428 (Richard Falk, ed. 1971); Firmage, Kellogg Lectures, 1993 supra at 7–8.

Section A, On Peaceful Resolution of Disputes, precedes this section on the use of force by the United Nations, because we see it as being primary. Chapter VI of the U.N. Charter provides for a system of non-violent dispute resolution through fact-finding, good offices, negotiations, and mediation. There is a provision for binding third-party decisions through arbitration and judicial resolution through the International Court of Justice. The United Nations also has powers that go beyond techniques of peaceful resolution of disputes. Where the League of Nations was limited merely to recommending action, Chapter VII of the U.N. Charter allows the latter, with Security Council approval, to use force ranging from economic boycott and sanction to initiating war against an aggressive state. This section focuses on Chapter VII and provides opportunity to analyze the use of force and its limitations under the United Nations Charter.

At the end of the Cold War we face a fractionalized world of rival ethnic groups, racial, tribal, religious and national factions in conflict similar to conditions before and after the First World War. In the aftermath of that epochal confrontation, we saw the disintegration of major imperial and multi-national ethnic and linguistic systems leading to ethnic and national conflict. The aftershocks also gave birth to the Bolshevik Revolution, with profound consequences for Asia and Europe. In post-war Germany, hyper-inflation and political reaction to defeat in war brought the rise of Adolph Hitler and National Socialism. After World War II, the United Nations was created with the hope that peaceful resolution of disputes would be more feasible. The U.N. was to provide a mechanism to control violence. Soon, however, the world became divided into two, perhaps three, blocks. The Cold War dominated international law, including that relating to the use of force. The violence unleashed in World War II was only transmuted at its end as Cold War followed—overt, covert, and by proxy.

The disintegration of the former Soviet Union and the end of the Cold War provides an opportunity for the international system to function more efficiently. We now have an opportunity for peaceful resolution of disputes and an amelioration of violence to a degree not enjoyed by the leaders of nations at least since World War I. Now, however, with the disintegration of multi-ethnic states in Yugoslavia and the Soviet Union, the forms of violence which preceded and followed World War I confront us again. We now face violence among Hindu and

Muslim in India and Pakistan; Serbs, Croats and Muslims in Bosnia; Armenians and Azeris in the Caucuses; Tamils and Sinhalese in Sri Lanka; and Israelis and Palestinians in the West Bank, the Hutus and the Tutsis in Rwanda, to mention but a few.

A paradox of the nuclear era is that the existence of nuclear weapons has suppressed in some circumstances massive violence with conventional weaponry of the magnitude, at least, of World War II. The nature of war in our time has tended to be internecine: wars of national liberation, civil wars, ethnic and religious conflict. Now, with the breakdown of the last imperial system to survive both world wars, and the disintegration of multi-ethnic states associated with the former Soviet Union and Communism, ethnic or tribal war, internal war and civil strife are increasingly the sorts of conflict which will challenge the peace.

Solutions are not readily available. International law, when faced with the issue of third-party involvement in civil strife, has two competing lines of authority. One line of precedent allows third-party intervention in civil strife upon the invitation and in aid of the incumbent government, at least until a status of belligerency is achieved by the insurgent forces. When belligerency is reached, international law requires neutrality by third party states. The other line of cases simply requires neutrality on the part of third parties throughout the course of civil strife. There is a bias favoring incumbent governments in the former line of authority. One of the reasons for this bias is that incumbent governments perform certain invaluable services for the international community. Such an approach places value in a modicum of order provided by the incumbent government that allows for the provision of services and minimal amenities for citizens and non citizens. For a decentralized and horizontal system of law such as international law, the municipal government provides an essential role. Unlike a mature municipal system of law, with a vertical hierarchy of lawmakers, judges and police, the international system depends upon sovereign, independent incumbent governments to assure even minimal order. Do Protocols I & II change this?

But in periods of radical transformation and disintegration of old systems, this conceptually clean analysis becomes messy. When incumbent governments collapse, choosing an "incumbent" from among the various contenders may be impossible. And even if an incumbent can be identified, conditions can become so chaotic that the services normally performed by the incumbent government to earn the bias in its favor by the international community cannot be accomplished. In this situation, there is little reason to favor an incumbent.

Exceptions to the non-intervention principle exist, although colonial abuses have tarnished, if not destroyed the integrity of such exceptions. It is contended that third parties may intervene for humanitarian reasons, for example, when an incumbent government abuses its own citizens or the citizens of other states. The legality of humanitarian intervention is hotly debated and we will present the various arguments for your consideration. Protocols I and II to the 1949 Geneva Convention provide means to control internal warfare and international warfare in circumstances not covered by the Geneva Convention proper.

The neutrality principle also embodies the recognition that violence, including violent intervention in civil strife in another state, is rarely as successful, as determinative or as easily contained and terminated as it may have seemed initially. The world community has struggled with this issue in modern history for nearly a century—from the Hague Peace Conferences of 1899 and 1907, through the League of Nations, to the activities of the United Nations today. The United Nations has taken action in Suez, the Congo, Korea, Cyprus, in the Greek Civil War, in the war between India and Pakistan, in the creation of the State of Israel, and, most recently in Cambodia, the Persian Gulf War, Somalia, Rwanda, the territory of the former Yugoslavia, and Haiti.

The ending of the Cold War offers the first chance since the inception of the United Nations for a system of international dispute resolution truly to work. If the international system is to move beyond the present level of almost total reliance upon nation states either to keep the peace or to break it, as they wish, then international institutions of law must be strengthened. The accomplishments of this century provide a foundation for peace. The machinery of the Hague Conventions of 1899 and 1906 was used in the successful resolution of maritime disputes. The League of Nations and later United Nations fact-finding groups and other institutions for peaceful resolution of disputes enjoyed considerable success in resolving conflicts, including border disputes, disputes among racial, ethnic, and national groups recently freed from imperial governmental joinder and disputes involving the protection of human rights of ethnic and religious minorities in newly created states following the disintegration of imperial and colonial systems after World War I. These newly created states following through 1930 successfully redrew the map of Europe and quite possibly arrested war among rival ethnic and religious groups, particularly in the Balkans. These successes, presented in Section A of this chapter, unfortunately and unfairly, have been eclipsed in our minds by the spectacular failure of the League and the major states of the world, in or out of the League, to deal with the aggressor states of the 1930s: Japan in Manchuria; Germany; Italy and Portugal in the Spanish Civil War; and later in those directs acts of aggression in Poland and Czechoslovakia that led to World War II. This section moves from Chapter VI actions to Chapter VII actions, presenting the law relating to the use of force by the United Nations.

b. *Early Historical Development and Legal Authority*

International Organizations:

The League of Nations. The Covenant of the League did not outlaw war as such. Instead, it sought to obligate states to resort to methods of peaceful settlement; in turn, members of the League agreed under certain circumstances not to resort to war. See in particular the following articles of the Covenant: *Article 12* (" * * * they agree in no case to resort to war until three months after the award by the arbitrators or the report by the Council."); *Article 13* ("The Members of the League agree that they will carry out in full good faith any award that may be rendered, and that they will not resort to war against a Member of the League which complies therewith."); *Article 15* ("If a report by the Council is unanimously agreed to by the Members thereof other than the representatives of one or more of the parties to the dispute, the Members of the League agree that they will not go to war with any party to the dispute which complies ...")

These qualified commitments against waging war should be contrasted to the language of the Peace Pact of Paris and *Article 2(4)* of the United Nations Charter. Also to be contrasted with *Article 2(4)* of the Charter is *Article 10* of the Covenant, in which members of the League undertook to "respect and preserve as against external aggression the territorial integrity and existing political independence of all members of the League." The mechanisms for enforcing the ambiguous and qualified obligations not to wage war were contained in *Article 10* of the Covenant (" * * * the Council shall advise upon the means by which this obligation shall be fulfilled") and in *Article 16* (the provisions for collective measures by the members of the League in the event a member of the League should "resort to war in disregard of its Covenants under Article 12, 13 or 15").

The United States did not become a member of the League of Nations. The Covenant of the League was an integral part of the Treaty of Versailles. When it was submitted to the Senate for its advice and consent, Senator Henry Cabot Lodge led the Senate to the adoption of a number of reservations, notably one to Article 10, to the effect that the United States would not assume an obligation to preserve the territorial integrity or political independence of any country unless "in any particular case the Congress, which, under the Constitution, has the sole power to declare war or authorize the employment of the military or naval forces of the United States, shall by act or joint resolution so provide." Stone (ed.), Wilson and the League of Nations 98 (1967). President Wilson refused to accept the Lodge reservations. As a result, the treaty (with the Covenant) was rejected by the Senate.

As for the effect of the Covenant on the unilateral use of force by states and the efforts of the League to restrain that force, it can only be stated that the results were dismal.

MORGENTHAU, POLITICS AMONG NATIONS 290
(4th ed., 1967).*

* * * Collective measures of enforcement under Article 16 were applied in only one of the five cases in which undoubtedly a member of the League resorted to war in violation of the Covenant. With regard to the Sino–Japanese conflict that started in 1931, the Assembly of the League found unanimously that "without any declaration of war, part of the Chinese territory has been forcibly seized and occupied by the Japanese troops," and that far-flung hostilities, initiated by Japan, had

* © Reprinted with the permission of Alfred A. Knopf, Inc., New York.

taken place between troops of the Chinese and Japanese governments. Yet the Assembly found also that Japan had not resorted to war in violation of the Covenant and that, therefore, Article 16 did not apply.

During the Chaco War of 1932–35, when Paraguay continued hostilities against Bolivia in violation of the Covenant, many members of the League limited the arms embargo, originally imposed upon both belligerents, to Paraguay. This was a discriminatory measure falling far short of the spirit and the letter of the first paragraph of Article 16. When Japan, which by then had resigned from the League, invaded China in 1937, the Assembly found that Japan had violated the Nine Power Treaty of 1922 and the Briand–Kellogg Pact, that Article 16 was applicable, and that the members of the League had the right to take enforcement measures individually under that provision. No such measures were ever taken. When the USSR went to war with Finland in 1939, it was expelled from the League by virtue of Article 16, paragraph 4, but no collective action of enforcement was taken against it.

In contrast to these cases, the Assembly found in 1935 that the invasion of Ethiopia by Italy constituted resort to war within the meaning and in violation of the Covenant and that, therefore, Article 16, paragraph 1, was to apply. In consequence, collective economic sanctions against Italy were decided upon and applied. Yet the two measures, provided for by Article 16, paragraph 1, that offered the best chance of making international law prevail under the circumstances and that in all probability would have compelled Italy to desist from its attack upon Ethiopia—namely, an embargo on oil shipments to Italy and the closure of the Suez Canal—were not taken. "However," as Sir H. Lauterpacht puts it, "although the sanctions of Article 16, paragraph 1, were formally put into operation and although an elaborate machinery was set up with a view to their successive and gradual enforcement, the nature of the action taken was such as to suggest that the repressive measures were being adopted as a manifestation of moral reprobation rather than as an effective means of coercion."

[To sum up]: the attempts at establishing a centralized system of law enforcement under Article 16 of the Covenant by saying that in most cases that would have justified the application of sanctions, sanctions were not applied at all. In the sole case in which they were applied, they were applied in such an ineffective fashion as virtually to assure both their failure and the success of the recalcitrant state.

——————

It should also be noted that the League system had a measure of success in the 1925 crisis between Greece and Bulgaria, noted supra, and failures in Japanese invasion of Manchuria, the Spanish Civil War, and the German Reich's invasions of the Rhineland (1936), Austria (1938), Czechoslovakia (1939), and Poland (1939).

COVENANT OF THE LEAGUE OF NATIONS, JUNE 28, 1919
1 Hudson International Legislation 1 (1931).

* * *

ARTICLE XVI

Should any Member of the League resort to war in disregard of its covenants under Article 12, 13 or 15, it shall ipso facto be deemed to have committed an act of war against all other Members of the League, which hereby undertake immediately to subject it to the severance of all trade or financial relations, the prohibition of all intercourse between their nationals and the nationals of the covenant-breaking State, and the prevention of all financial, commercial or personal intercourse between the nationals of the covenant-breaking State and the nationals of any other State, whether a Member of the League or not.

It shall be the duty of the Council in such case to recommend to the several Governments concerned what effective military, naval or air force the Members of the League shall severally contribute to the armed forces to be used to protect the covenants of the League. The Members of the League agree, further, that they will mutually support one another in the financial and economic measures which are taken under this Article, to minimize the loss and inconvenience resulting from the above measures, and that they will mutually support one another in resisting any special measures aimed at one of their number by the covenant-breaking State, and that they will take the necessary steps to afford passage through their territory to the forces of any of the Members which are co-operating to protect the covenants of the League.

* * *

Questions: How does Article 16 of the League Covenant compare with the enforcement mechanisms in the U.N. Charter? As you read the material in this section (focusing on a series of crises, which eventuated in the use of force), ask yourself whether the result in each situation would have been different under the League Covenant or the U.N. Charter. Is "balance of power" the immutable "iron law of politics," which still [if it ever actually did] fits our "anarchic world of incorrigible power seekers," as the realists maintain? Are there viable alternative views?

TRAVAUX—PREPARATOIRES FOR THE PEACE PACT OF PARIS (THE KELLOGG–BRIAND PACT)
[1928] 1 Foreign Relations of the United States 32 (1942).

French Draft of Treaty for the Condemnation and Renunciation of War as an Instrument of National Policy

The President of the German Empire, the President of the United States of America, the President of the French Republic, His Majesty the King of England, Ireland and the British Dominions, Emperor of India, His Majesty the King of Italy, His Majesty the Emperor of Japan:

Equally desirous not only of perpetuating the happy relations of peace and friendship now existing among their peoples, but also of avoiding the danger of war between all other nations in the world.

Having agreed to consecrate in a solemn act their most formal and most definite resolution to condemn war as an instrument of national policy and to renounce it in favor of a peaceful settlement of international conflicts, expressing, finally, the hope that all the other nations of the world will be willing to join in this humane effort to bring about the association of the civilized peoples in a common renunciation of war as an instrument of national policy, have decided to conclude a treaty and to that end have designated as their respective plenipotentiaries:

* * *

The President of the German Empire:

The President of the United States of America:

The President of the French Republic:

His Majesty the King of Great Britain, Ireland and the British Dominions, Emperor of India:

His Majesty the King of Italy:

His Majesty the Emperor of Japan:

who, after exchanging their full powers found to be in good and due form have agreed on the following provisions:

Article One

The High Contracting Parties without any intention to infringe upon the exercise of their rights of legitimate self-defense within the framework of existing treaties, particularly when the violation of certain of the provisions of such treaties constitutes a hostile act, solemnly declare that they condemn recourse to war and renounce it as an instrument of national policy; that is to say, as an instrument of individual, spontaneous and independent political action taken on their own initiative and not action in respect of which they might become involved through the obligation of a treaty such as the covenant of the League of Nations or any other treaty registered with the League of Nations. They undertake on these conditions not to attack or invade one another.

Article Two

The settlement or solution of all disputes or conflicts of whatever nature or origin which might arise among the High Contracting Parties or between any two of them shall never be sought on either side except by pacific methods.

Article Three

In case one of the High Contracting Parties should contravene this treaty, the other Contracting Powers would ipso facto be released with respect to that Party from their obligations under this treaty.

Article Four

The provisions of this treaty in no wise affect the rights and obligations of the Contracting Parties resulting from prior international agreements to which they are parties.

Article Five

The present treaty will be offered for the accession of all Powers and will have no binding force until it has been generally accepted unless the signatory Powers in accord with those that may accede hereto shall agree to decide that it shall come into effect regardless of certain abstentions.

* * *

[Reply by Kellogg], Washington, April 23, 1928.

* * * In its present form the French draft treaty is wholly unacceptable to the United States since it cannot in any respect be regarded as an effective instrument for the promotion of world peace. It emphasizes war, not peace, and seems in effect to be a justification rather than a renunciation of the use of armed force. The United States will sign no treaty of the nature now under discussion which cannot reasonably be expected to lessen the danger of an outbreak of war and thus promote the cause of world peace.

* * *

There seem to be six major considerations which the French Government has emphasized in its correspondence and in its draft treaty, namely, that the treaty must not (1) impair the right of legitimate self-defense; (2) violate the Covenant of the League of Nations; (3) violate the treaties of Locarno; (4) violate certain unspecified treaties guaranteeing neutrality; (5) bind the parties in respect of a state breaking the treaty; (6) come into effect until accepted by all or substantially all of the Powers of the world. The views of the United States on these points are as follows: (1) Self-defense. There is nothing in the American draft of an anti-war treaty which restricts or impairs in any way the right of self-defense. That right is inherent in every sovereign state and is implicit in every treaty. Every nation is free at all times and regardless of treaty provisions to defend its territory from attack or invasion and it alone is competent to decide whether circumstances require recourse to war in self-defense. If it has a good case, the world will applaud and not condemn its action. Express recognition by treaty of this inalienable right, however, gives rise to the same difficulty encountered in any effort to define aggression. It is the identical question approached from the other side. Inasmuch as no treaty provision can add to the natural right of self-defense, it is not in the interest of peace that a treaty should stipulate a juristic conception of self-defense since it is far too easy for the unscrupulous to mold events to accord with an agreed definition.

* * *

KELLOGG

GENERAL TREATY FOR RENUNCIATION OF WAR
AS AN INSTRUMENT OF NATIONAL POLICY
OF AUGUST 27, 1928

46 Stat. 2343, 94 L.N.T.S. 59 (1929).

Article I

The High Contracting Parties solemnly declare in the names of their respective peoples that they condemn recourse to war for the solution of international controversies, and renounce it as an instrument of national policy in their relations with one another.

Article II

The High Contracting Parties agree that the settlement or solution of all disputes or conflicts of whatever nature or of whatever origin they may be, which may arise among them, shall never be sought except by pacific means.

———

1. ***Parties during World War II and Current Status.*** The Pact of Paris, TS 796; 2 Bevans 732; 94 LNTS 57, signed at Paris, August 27, 1928, entered into force for the United States on July 24, 1929. It is still in effect and, in 1993, has 66 adherents. Treaties in Force lists the parties and includes a disclaimer that the Department has not passed upon the effect of war on any of the treaties in the compilation.

2. ***Why was the Pact of Paris a futile bar to war?*** Even before the outbreak of World War II, armed conflict had been carried on by Japan in China, by Germany, Italy and the USSR in Spain, and by Italy in Ethiopia. Was it ever vindicated?

3. ***Was the Pact of Paris vindicated in any way in World War II?*** How was it to be enforced? Did it have an "enforcement clause"? Would it have been appropriate to include one? Was it vindicated at Nuremberg? For war crimes trials and related material, see Chapter 11.

BROWN, UNDECLARED WARS

33 American Journal of International Law 538, 540 (1939).*

* * *

We see, therefore, in the light of theory and practice, that the problem of the undeclared war remains largely an academic one which involves considerations more ethical than legal. And this is true also of the self-denying declaration embodied in the General Treaty of 1928 for the Renunciation of War, generally entitled the Kellogg Pact. This agreement, while purporting to renounce the use of war, really consecrated the vague and dangerous right of self-defence. The various signatories explicitly reserved the right to resort to war and to judge for

* Reprinted with the permission of the American Society of International Law.

themselves "whether circumstances require recourse to war in self-defence." Within four years of the signing of this Pact occurred three breaches of the Pact, namely, the aggression by Russia against China in 1929, the occupation of Manchuria by Japan in 1931, and the invasion of Colombia by Peru in 1932. The more recent instances of warlike acts by Japan, Germany, and Italy are too vividly in mind to require comment. It is necessary, however, to stress the lamentable and unforeseen consequence of the Kellogg Pact in encouraging aggressor nations hypocritically to avoid any formal declaration of war in order to elude the constraints of this pious declaration.

Still another most unexpected inducement to avoid a formal declaration of war, as revealed in the case of the conflict now going on between Japan and China, has been the natural desire to escape the disabilities of recent neutrality legislation of the United States, whereby the shipment of arms and munitions of war to belligerents is automatically forbidden. The question presents itself whether, in the absence of a formal declaration of war by either side, it should not be incumbent on neutral nations to brush all legal niceties aside and openly acknowledge a state of war where the laws of war and neutrality should apply. Nations intent on peace and determined to uphold the reign of law have a solemn duty to avoid any implied connivance in the evasion of international obligations. Neutrality is not merely to conserve national interests, but also to preserve an impartial rôle which may enable a nation to affirm with vigor the responsibilities and rights of peoples under international law.

The situation is certainly a most unhappy one. It is stultifying to discover that an idealistic agreement such as the Kellogg Pact, and neutrality legislation conceived for a generous purpose, should actually conduce to the fiction of the undeclared war. * * *

Questions: What are the reasons behind a requirement that war be declared? Did it serve as a caution to a nation of the awesome act contemplated? Did the Nuremberg Charter, Trials and Judgments have any effect on the Law relating to the Use of Force among states or the role of international alliances or organizations in relation to illegal use of force by states? Were these occurrences more important than the old rule requiring declaration of war? Less? The same? The Nuremberg Trials are discussed in Chapter 11, *on Individual Responsibility,* supra, and the role of the above-mentioned items considered in Chapter 17, Use of Force by States, infra.

CHARTER OF THE UNITED NATIONS

Turn to your Documentary Supplement and analyze articles 2(1) & (4), 7, 25, 39, 41, 42, 43, and 51.

JOST DELBRÜCK, A FRESH LOOK AT HUMANITARIAN INTERVENTION UNDER THE AUTHORITY OF THE UNITED NATIONS

67 Ind.L.J. 887, 889–91 (1992) (footnotes omitted) *

I. The Principle of Nonintervention Under General International Law and Under the UN Charter in Cases of Grave Human Rights Violations

* * *

The principle of nonintervention is deeply enshrined in general international law. It has its legal basis and legal policy foundations in the principles of the sovereignty and equality of states, the constitutive elements of the international legal order. Recognition of sovereignty—the independence and freedom of states from any external dominance in the determination of their domestic and foreign policies and the equality of states under law—excludes, in principle, the permissibility of interventions by third parties.

The scope, however, of the prohibition against intervention in the internal or domestic affairs of states is still controversial. On the one hand, there are those who support a broad construction of the concept of nonintervention that is based on a corresponding expansive interpretation of the concept of sovereignty. If sovereignty not only is to denote the legal independence and self-determination of states, but also is supposed to have a substantive meaning in the real world of international relations, it is argued, it must be protected from violations as a matter of law. Hence, a principle of nonintervention commensurate in scope to that of the principle of sovereignty must be recognized under international law. * * * [Some] advocate a restrictive interpretation of the principle of nonintervention. They argue that a broadly construed concept of sovereignty and a corresponding broad interpretation of the principle of nonintervention no longer meet the demands of the growing internationalization of states' responsibilities for the maintenance of international peace and security as well as for the protection of human rights. If such growing international responsibilities are recognized as a matter of law, sovereignty must be viewed as legally more limited than in the past. This, in turn, must result in a restrictive interpretation of the scope of the principle of nonintervention, leaving room for international interventions in the domestic affairs of states—if not generally, then at least under certain well-defined circumstances.

Qualifying the permissibility of international interventions in this way, however, indicates that within this second school of thought there is * * * no consensus as to the criteria or the circumstances allowing for interventions. Nor is there general agreement as to what kind of actions taken in the course of interventions could be considered legal; that is, whether such interventions could be carried out by the use of (military) force or whether they must be restricted to measures short of the use of force. According to widespread opinion, the general prohibi-

* Reprinted by permission of the University of Indiana Law Journal and Fred Rothman & Co.)

tion against the use of force under international law does not allow for unilateral forcible interventions by individual states even for the purpose of rescuing citizens of third states, or their own, from threats to their lives and physical safety. That is to say, so-called humanitarian interventions, once accepted as legal, are widely viewed as illegal today. Countermeasures even against grave and massive human rights violations are, for good reason, considered to be restricted to economic and diplomatic sanctions below the threshold of the use of force: Allowing military enforcement measures based on the "isolated" decisions of individual states would lead to an erosion of the general prohibition against the use of force and against "dictatorial interference[s]." Since the assessment of the factual situation, the determination of the appropriate means to be applied, and the execution of the intervention would all be administered by the intervening state, the door to purely arbitrary intervention, that is, acts of aggression in disguise, would be wide open.

In a world community heeding diverse values and pursuing different, often antagonistic, interests, it is easy to conceive of states invoking all kinds of justae causae as a justification for intervention. This objection to a more liberal regime governing the law of intervention need not necessarily hold true if interventions in the internal affairs of a state that commits grave human rights violations are decided on the basis of an orderly and lawful procedure and are executed by an international organization such as the UN as the representative of the international community of states. The question is, therefore, what the authority of the UN is in this regard. * * *

What do you think of Delbrück's proposition?

LETTER FROM EDWARD R. STETTINIUS, SECRETARY OF STATE OF THE UNITED STATES, TO PRESIDENT HARRY TRUMAN

13 United States Department of State Bulletin 77, 80 (1945).

Summary of Report on Results of San Francisco Conference

* * *

It will be the duty of the Security Council, supported by the pledged participation, and backed by military contingents to be made available by the member states, to use its great prestige to bring about by peaceful means the adjustment or the settlement of international disputes. Should these means fail, it is its duty, as it has the power, to take whatever measures are necessary, including measures of force, to suppress acts of aggression or other breaches of the peace. It will be the duty of the Security Council, in other words, to make good the commitment of the United Nations to maintain international peace and security, turning that lofty purpose into practice. To that end the Council will be given the use and the support of diplomatic, economic and military tools and weapons in the control of the United Nations.

* * *

———

1. ***The Grand Design.*** The Charter of the United Nations forbade the use of force by states (Article 2(4)), save in the limited area of self-defense (Article 51). A near monopoly of force was reposed in the Security Council, under Chapter VII, in which the Council was empowered to respond to the dramatic conditions of Article 39 ("any threat to the peace, breach of the peace, or act of aggression") by resort to the powerful measures of Articles 41 and 42, including armed forces at its disposal under the terms of Article 43, especially "immediately available national air-force contingents" (Article 45). It was a vision of many in 1945 that the military forces of the United Nations Security Council would restrain any nation that disturbed the peace following World War II.

The language of Charter article 2(4) comprehensively prohibits the use of force, replacing and surpassing the Kellogg–Briand Pact, which prohibited the use of war as a political tool. The language, however, has traditionally been read more narrowly, to prohibit the use or threat to use force only to the international arena. Thus, in Article 39, read in pari materia, the terms "breach of the peace," "aggression," and "threat to the peace" were interpreted to have only international application and implication. As you read the following material, ask whether the situations created by apartheid in South Africa and the racism in Southern Rhodesia were treated by the Security Council consistently with this traditional view? *See,* Oscar Schachter, International Law in Theory & Practice 110 (1991). Are these terms of articles 2(4) and 39, still used the same way today? Has there been a change since the end of the Cold War? Also, consider this issue when reading the material in this chapter on the Gulf War, Somalia, and the former Yugoslavia. Can the U.N. intervene militarily without a finding that there is a threat to international peace and security? Does the Secretary–General have authority to call for military action of any kind? Can the Ad Hoc Tribunal for the former Yugoslavia call for the Security Council to sanction a nation that does not deliver a fugitive for Prosecution? Its rules call for this. See ch. 11, *supra.*

The international legal system is decentralized; the primary international law enforcement vehicle remains the state. The notion of statehood includes the characteristic of autonomy, which includes integrity of territory and freedom from intervention or coercion. It also includes notions of reciprocity, legal equality, and general adherence to international law by sister states. Failure to respect these values and interests may allow retorsion, reprisal, and self-defense. Traditionally, the state had a right under international law to use force, even to go to war, for purposes of law enforcement (liberum ius ad bellum). Does this right still exist, or has international law eliminated it and replaced it with the U.N. Security Council's authority in Chapter VII of the Charter and the residual right of individual and collective self-defense under article 51? This state-based use of force is considered in Chapter 17, *infra,* but it is important to remember that states are the engine even for United Nations efforts to "keep the peace" or to "make peace" by use of force. Keep these issues in mind as you read the following material and note the interrelationship of the "system" envisaged under the U.N. Charter and the role of individual states or other international organizations such as NATO.

2. ***What went wrong?*** The Charter was grounded in a belief and a hope: the belief that only with the cooperation of the great powers could the United Nations succeed, and the hope that because they had cooperated in war they would continue to do so during the peace (hence, the veto). That cooperation was not forthcoming. An immediate effect of the fragmentation of great power policy was the failure of the powers to make the agreements called for in Article 43; the council thus did not have at its disposal the forces projected at the United Nation's founding. See Sohn, Basic Documents of the United Nations 89 (2nd ed. rev'd, 1968), especially Note at 98, detailing U.S.–Soviet disagreements over size and the relationships of the various force contributions to be made by the permanent members of the force.

A further factor of significance in the appraisal of the Charter provisions for dealing with threats to the peace is the fact that world tensions have taken new shapes since the days of World War II. The disintegration of old empires and the rise of the self-consciousness of formerly subject peoples have brought new demands on U.N. organs.

3. ***Scope of § B of this chapter.*** Section B is concerned with several principal themes that have become significant because of the foregoing political factors: first, the ways in which the United Nations has accommodated to the fact that the Security Council's monopoly of force has not worked as it was designed; and second, the development of the power of the United Nations to use its authority to assist the drive of subject peoples toward self-determination. After the Gulf–War, the events in Somalia and the former Yugoslavia, do you think that the Secretary–General's vision of having U.N. military forces ready to prevent or stop breaches of the peace is realistic? What are the alternatives? Has the Security Council begun to exercise its power? Is a more broadly constituted NATO an alternative, after the Cold War? How does the Ad Hoc Tribunal for the former Yugoslavia fit into this discussion?

2.   COLLECTIVE MEASURES IN THE USE OF FORCE

a. *Korea*

(1) ***Background.*** Korea was one of the pre-World War II states that found itself divided at the end of the war. As recounted above, the United Nations was unsuccessful in its effort to unite the country and its divisions hardened into a Republic of Korea in the south (whose government was established by elections supervised by the United Nations) and

a People's Republic in the north claiming jurisdiction over all of Korea. The North Korean invasion of the south precipitated a United Nations response. For discussion of attempts at Peaceful Resolution, *see* Section A of this Chapter. The resolutions adopted by the Council immediately following the North Korean attack on June 25, 1950, provided the authority for collective military action. They would doubtless have been vetoed by the USSR, but the Soviets were absent from the Council, having voluntarily left their seat vacant in protest over the Council's refusal to seat the Chinese communists instead of the Chinese nationalists. First, in an emergency meeting of the Council, S.C. Resolution 82 was adopted on June 25th, expressing grave concern over the "armed attack on the Republic of Korea by forces from North Korea" and "determin[ed] that this action constitutes a breach of the peace * * *." It also called for "the immediate cessation of hostilities * * * " and for the "authorities in North Korea to withdraw forthwith their armed forces to the 38th parallel." Resolution 82 also requested the previously created Commission on Korea: "to communicate its fully considered recommendations on the situation with the least possible delay," "to observe the withdrawal of North Korean forces to the 38th parallel," and "to keep the Security Council informed on the execution of this resolution." Finally, it called upon member states to "render every assistance to the U.N. in the execution of the Resolution and to refrain from giving assistance to the North Korean Authorities."

On June 27th, the Security Council met again and issued Resolution 83, which reiterated that it had determined that the "armed attack upon the Republic of Korea by the forces from North Korea constitutes a breach of the peace" and called "for an immediate cessation of hostilities" and for "the authorities in North Korea to withdraw forthwith" to the 38th parallel. It noted that the North Korean forces had not withdrawn and that *"urgent military measures are required to restore international peace and security "* and recommended *"that the Members of the United Nations furnish such assistance to the Republic of Korea as may be necessary to repel the armed attack and to restore international peace and security in the area."*

On July 7th, 1950, the Security Council welcomed the prompt and vigorous support it had received. It recommended that all members providing military forces and other assistance, *"make such forces and other assistance available to a unified command under the United States of America,"* requested that the United States "designate the commander of such forces," authorized the use of the U.N. flag along with the various flags of the participating states, and requested the United States to provide the Security Council with periodic reports. Consider the S.C. Resolutions, which are in the Documentary Supplement.

Notes/Questions:

1. ***How was this similar or different from the situation in Bosnia–Herzegovina? What was the legal basis for the Security Council's action?*** Resolution 82 (1950) determined that the armed attack by North Korea constituted a "breach of the peace," using the language of Article 39 of the Charter, although neither Article 39 nor

Chapter VII were actually cited. The Security Council's findings of
"threats to the [international] peace" *"breaches of the [international]*
peace" or *"acts of aggression"* have accelerated over the past fifteen
years. The first was in relation to Korea in 1950, when the North
invaded the South. Similar findings under Article 39 were made in the
Rhodesian and South African cases, but the Council did not authorize
the use of military force. On the other hand, the situation in Suez
(1956) and the Congo (1960), armed force was authorized by the United
Nations, without any Article 39 findings having been made. Article 39
findings were made concerning the 1980 attack by Argentina on the
Falkland Islands. A burst of activity began with Iraq's attack on Iran in
1987, followed by Iraq's invasion of Kuwait in 1990, and later the
warfare in the territory of the former Yugoslavia, beginning in 1991 and
the 1992 clan warfare in Somalia. By the end of 1993, the Security
Council has applied Chapter VII to authorize the collective use of force
in Korea, in the Gulf War, and has authorized actions very close to that
in Somalia and has considered similar action in Haiti. Can the Security
Council authorize the collective use of force without first finding a
"threat to international peace and security" under Article 39? Does the
Security Council have authority to take actions to preserve or maintain
international peace and security in a general way or is it limited to the
specific measures called for in Chapter VII? Professor Yoram Dinstein
discusses this issue in his book, War, Aggression and Self Defence 102–
121 (1956); *see also Certain Expenses Case, infra.* One argument about
the legality of the United Nations action in Korea was whether the
conflict was a civil war. A portion of the debate on that question
appears in chapter 2 with the concept of statehood. What is the
relevance of that argument? Does Article 2(7) exclude United Nations
action in a civil war? Note that Article 2(7) expressly preserves United
Nations application of enforcement measures under Chapter VII. (Article 39 is in Chapter VII.) Does the term "peace" in Article 39 mean
only international peace? What is "international peace?" Would that
interpretation exclude United Nations involvement in a civil war?
Would it have excluded United Nations involvement in the Korean case?

2. ***Nature of the forces.*** Article 43 of the Charter was an
agreement to agree on the composition of forces to be made available to
the Security Council. As noted above, the effort to create a standing
force failed for lack of agreement among the major powers. Despite
that, the Council authorized member states to provide military forces to
repel the North Koreans (specifically, it *recommended* that member
states furnish assistance to the Republic of Korea and, in fact, sixteen
member states fought in Korea under the United Nations' auspices).
Was the Council acting within its powers in creating a United Nations
force in this manner? Does the Charter confine the Security Council to
using only a standing force?

3. ***Nature of the command.*** The Security Council authorized a
unified command under the United States and requested the United
States to designate the commander (who was, initially, General Douglas
MacArthur). Was the Council acting within its powers by delegating
command, and the selection of the commander? Compare, with this

mode of dealing with the command question, the assumption of command responsibility directly by the U.N. in the Suez, Congo, Persian Gulf, Somalia, and former Yugoslavia cases, considered below.

---

b. *Uniting for Peace*

The Security Council's resolutions authorizing the creation of the United Nations forces in Korea were adopted in June and July of 1950. The representative of the USSR returned to the meetings of the Security Council in August, but it was too late for the Soviets to cast a veto to undo the prior action of the Council. The forces under the aegis of the U.N. continued to fight despite the vocal opposition of the USSR. However, it was plain that no further Security Council action would be possible in the Korean case in view of the Soviet's undoubted use of the veto. Indeed, the potential of the Security Council to act in future cases involving clashes of East–West interests was recognized as weak if not non-existent. The General Assembly was urged by a group of states acting under the leadership of the United States to assert its own authority in cases in which the Security Council failed to act because of the use of the veto. That assertion of authority was cast in the form of the Uniting for Peace Resolution. (*See,* Doc. Supp.)

Authority under the United Nations Charter. Article 11(2) of the Charter provides the basis for an argument that the General Assembly does not have the authority under the Charter to exercise the power it has asserted in operative paragraph 1 of the Uniting for Peace Resolution: "Any such question on which *action* is necessary shall be referred to the Security Council by the General Assembly either before or after discussion." [Emphasis supplied.] How do you appraise this argument? Would you make it today?

---

c. *The Persian Gulf War: Post–Cold War Enforcement of the Charter Scheme*

(1) Background: On August 2, 1990, Iraq invaded Kuwait; the Emir sought refuge in Saudi Arabia. By that time, the Cold War had eroded and on the very day of the invasion, the Security Council unanimously condemned the invasion and *demanded* that the Iraqi troops "withdraw immediately and unconditionally all its armed forces * * *" deeming the invasion a *"breach of international peace and security."* [*S.C.Res. 660 (1990)*]. The S.C. Resolutions are in the Doc. Supp.

On August 3rd, the United States dispatched naval forces to the Persian Gulf. On August 6th, the Security Council imposed a trade embargo on Iraq, except for medicine and food for humanitarian purposes. On August 7th, the U.S. deployed combat troops and planes to Saudi Arabia. On August 8th, Iraq formally annexed Kuwait. Twelve Arab leaders agreed on August 10th to send military forces to protect Saudi Arabia and on the 11th, Egyptian and British forces began to arrive in Saudi Arabia. On August 12th, Iraq ordered 4,000 Britains and 2,500 Americans in Kuwait to report to certain hotels or be rounded-up. On August 28th, Iraq declared Kuwait to be its 19th province and freed all western women and children who had been held hostage. For the ensuing three months, the United Nations attempted without success to resolve the crisis peacefully. During this period, the U.S. imposed significant and comprehensive economic sanctions on Iraq; the USSR, Japan, the European Union, and others followed suit.

On November 29th, the Security Council issued an ultimatum to Iraq, approving resolution 665 and authorizing the creation of a multinational force that would be allowed to apply military force to oust Iraqi troops from Kuwait, if they did not withdraw by January 15, 1991. On January 10, 1991, the U.S. Congress debated whether to give President Bush the authority to use force in Iraq and Kuwait. The January 15th deadline passed and on January 16th Operation *Desert Shield* was transformed into *Desert Storm*. The Senate and the House of Representatives passed a resolution supporting the engagement. For the next several weeks, the U.S. population was transfixed by the events of the War shown virtually non-stop on cable television. Ultimately several Security Council Resolutions (660–678) were issued (in Doc. Supp.). It has been reported that between 100,000 and 200,000 Iraqi troops and civilians were killed and 300,000 were injured, while fewer than 400 allied deaths occurred, most by "friendly fire." *See*, Prochaska, *Disappearing Iraqis,* 4 Public Culture 91 (1992); Krishna, *Review Essay: The Importance of Being Ironic: A Postcolonial View on Critical International Relations Theory,* 18 Alternatives 385, 397 (1993)]. On February 13th, U.S. bombs hit an underground facility in Baghdad. The U.S. claimed that the bunker was a military command center, but 500 civilians holed up in it died. By February 25th, Saddam Hussein ordered his troops to leave Kuwait; by the 26th Iraqi troops appeared to be in full retreat. On February 27th President Bush ordered suspension of all offensive operations. On March 3rd, Iraqi military leaders accepted the U.N. Security Council's terms for formal cease-fire. On March 12th the Iraqis crushed a Shiite Muslim rebellion in Southern Iraq. Iraq later did the same to the Kurdish rebellion in Northern Iraq, touching off a mass exodus of Kurds into Turkey. On April 5th, the President ordered emergency aid to be flown to the 450,000 Kurdish refugees along the Turkish/Iraqi border. On April 6th, Iraq accepted the U.N. conditions for a formal termination of the war, and on April 11th, the Security Council announced the formal end to the War and accepted Iraq's pledge to pay war damages and to destroy its weapons of mass destruction. The operation succeeded in restoring the independence of Kuwait, with far-reaching political and economic consequences. Since the end of the war, Iraq has continued intermittently to defy U.N. resolutions. It appears that the Shiite Muslim Marsh Arabs of Southern Iraq are still being decimated by starvation, poisoning and draining of their water. In

April, U.N. peacekeepers in a helicopter were destroyed by U.S. friendly fire. *See gen., Persian Gulf Chronology, Gannett News Service, June 26, 1993;* 7 Saudi Arabia 16–23, 6–11 (No. 4, Winter 1991); *Entre Les Lignes: La Guerre Du Golfe et Le Droit International* (Brussels 1991); Law & Force in the New International Order (Damrosch & Scheffer eds. 1991); Moore, Crisis in the Gulf: Enforcing the Rule of Law (1992).

Notes & Questions: *Should President Bush have reported to Congress prior to sending troops? Does the War Power of Congress require congressional authorization?* For discussion of the legality *and* constitutionality of the Gulf War and the process leading to it, *see,* chapters 14 and 17 of this coursebook; Firmage, *Book Review–Essay, War Power,* 59 G.W.L.Rev. 1684, 1704–1711 (1991); and Firmage, *The War Power of Congress and Revision of the War Powers Resolution,* 1 J.Contemp.L. 237 (1991). The Security Council Resolutions relating to the Gulf War are in the Doc. Supp. Study them and consider the following questions.

Notes & Questions for Resolutions. *Res. 661:* Was the embargo binding? What articles of the U.N. Charter make it so? Did this Resolution provide a basis for U.S. domestic action? See, 22 U.S.C. § 287c (1982) (U.N. Participation Act). Did Res. 661 provide the U.S. or other member nations with authority to use military force to stop Iraqi ships from going to third nations? See R.S. 665, in Doc. Supp.

Is Resolution 662 (1990) essentially security council *legislation declaring* the annexation of Kuwait null and void? Is it more like legislation, a judicial decision, or an executive ordinance?

Resolution 665 was an adoption of the U.S. position on Res. 661, that military force was authorized to enforce sanctions. What authority was to be in control of military forces? *In Resolution 666, Note* the coordination with and use of the International Committee of the Red Cross (ICRC) discussed in Chapter 1.

Note that Resolution 667 is a Security Council decision *enforcing* the Vienna Convention on Treaties, considered in Chapters 1 and 13.

In Resolution 670, the Security Council essentially sets aside the bilateral civil aviation treaties. This has not been done before. Is it an example of U.N. Charter Article 103 action?

In Res. 670, were nations authorized to order planes on their way to Iraq to land for inspection? If such a plane refused to land, was the "ordering" nation authorized to shoot it down? See, reference to the Chicago Convention (in Doc. Supp.). Did R.S. 670, issue any warning to third countries? If so, what was it and how would it enforce that warning?

Does R.S. 674 explicitly mention the use of force to expel Iraq from Kuwait? Virtually at the same time, leaders of nations which became allies during the Gulf War were sending threatening signals and were engaged in a significant military buildup in the region. The United States dispatched naval ships, combat aircraft, and troops to the Persian Gulf and to Saudi Arabia. France, Italy, Spain, Britain, Canada, and Argentina did similarly.

Did Res. 686 allow the Security Council play a judicial role in demanding that Iraq "accept in principle its liability under international law for any loss, damage, or injury arising in regard to Kuwait and third states...." or was this executive in nature?

S.C.Res. 687 is probably the most important resolution from the standpoint of continuing enforcement. Moreover, it may be the most far-reaching "legislative" act ever adopted by the Security Council. Is this an example of international government?

IRAQ'S ACCEPTANCE OF THE UNITED NATIONS "CEASE-FIRE" RESOLUTION 687 (1991)

Identical letters dated 6 April 1991 from the permanent representative of Iraq to the United Nations addressed respectively to the Secretary-General and the President of the Security Council

On instructions from my Government, I have the honour to enclose the text of a letter dated 6 April 1991 addressed to you by the Minister for Foreign Affairs of the Republic of Iraq. I should be grateful if you would have the text of this letter and its annex circulated as a document of the Security Council.

(*Signed*) Abdul Amir A. AL–ANBARI, Ambassador, Permanent Representative

Annex

Identical letters dated 6 April 1991 from the Minister for Foreign Affairs of the Republic of Iraq addressed respectively to the Secretary-General and the President of the Security Council

I have the honour to inform you that the Iraqi Government has taken note of the text of Security Council resolution 687 (1991), the authors of which are the first to recognize that it is unprecedented in the annals of the Organization, and wishes, before stating its official position, to make a number of fundamental comments regarding certain concepts and provisions contained therein:

I.   While in its preamble the resolution reaffirms that Iraq is an independent sovereign State, the fact remains that a good number of its iniquitous provisions impair that sovereignty. In fact, the resolution constitutes an unprecedented assault on the sovereignty, and the rights that stem therefrom, embodied in the Charter and in international law and practice. For example, where the question of boundaries is concerned, the Security Council has determined in advance the boundary between Iraq and Kuwait. And yet it is well known, from the juridical and practical standpoint, that in international relations boundary issues must be the subject of an agreement between States, since this is the only basis capable of guaranteeing the stability of frontiers.

The resolution fails to take into account Iraq's view, which is well known to the Council, that the provisions relating to the boundary between Iraq and Kuwait contained in the "Agreed Minutes Between the State of Kuwait and the Republic of Iraq Regarding the Restoration of

Friendly Relations, Recognition and Related Matters" dated 4 October 1963 have not yet been subjected to the constitutional procedures required for ratification of the Agreed Minutes by the legislative branch and the President of Iraq, thus leaving the question of the boundary pending and unresolved. The Council has nevertheless imposed on Iraq the line of its boundary with Kuwait. By acting in this strange manner, the Council itself has also violated one of the provisions of resolution 660, which served as the basis for its subsequent resolutions. In its paragraph 3, resolution 660 calls upon Iraq and Kuwait to resolve their differences through negotiation, and the question of the boundary is well known to be one of the main differences. Iraq officially informed the Council that it accepted resolution 660 and was prepared to apply it, but the Council has gone beyond this legal position, contradicting its previous resolution, and adopted an iniquitous resolution which imposes on Iraq, an independent and sovereign State and a Member of the United Nations, new conditions and a boundary line which deprive it of its right to establish its territorial rights in accordance with the principles of international law. Thus the Council is also depriving Iraq of its right to exercise its free choice and to affirm that it accepts that boundary without reservation. [Regarding the boundary], the Council resolution is an iniquitous resolution which constitutes a dangerous precedent, a first in the annals of the international Organization and—as some impartial members of the Council indicated in their statements when the resolution was voted on—an assault on the sovereignty of States.

It is also to be noted that the United States of America, the author of the draft resolution on which resolution 687, which imposes a solution to the boundary-related and other differences between Iraq and Kuwait, was based, refuses to impose any solution whatsoever on its ally, Israel, in accordance with conventions, United Nations resolutions and international law. Furthermore, the United States of America is preventing the Security Council from assuming the responsibilities incumbent upon it with respect to the Arab–Zionist conflict, the Israeli policy of annexation of the occupied Arab territories, the establishment of settlements, the displacement of populations and the disregard for the rights of the Palestinian people and the neighboring Arab countries, by vetoing any draft resolution approved by the remaining members of the Council, for the simple reason that Israel does not want a resolution which favours a just settlement of the conflict.

II. Iraq's position with regard to the prohibition of chemical and bacteriological weapons is clear. It is indeed a party to the Protocol for the Prohibition of the Use in War of Asphyxiating, Poisonous or Other Gases, and of Bacteriological Methods of Warfare, signed at Geneva in 1925. In a statement issued in September 1988, Iraq reiterated its attachment and adherence to the provisions of that Protocol. It also participated in the Conference of States Parties to the 1925 Geneva Protocol and Other Interested States, held at Paris from 7 to 11 January 1989, and signed the Declaration issued by the participating States. On that occasion, Iraq took a position which was unanimously shared by all the Arab countries, namely that all weapons of mass destruction, including nuclear weapons, must be eliminated from the Middle East region.

Iraq is also a party to the Treaty on the Non–Proliferation of Nuclear Weapons, of 1 July 1968. As the many reports of the International Atomic Energy Agency confirm, it is applying all the provisions of the Treaty. The Security Council resolution obliges only Iraq, and it alone, to undertake the destruction of the non-conventional weapons left to it after the heavy destruction inflicted both on these weapons and on the related installations by the military operations launched against Iraq by the 30 countries of the coalition. It does not deprive the other countries of the region, particularly Israel, of the right to possess weapons of this type, including nuclear weapons. Moreover, the Council has ignored its resolution 487 (1981), which calls on Israel to place all its nuclear facilities under international safeguards, and has not sought to ensure the implementation of that resolution in the same way as it is now seeking to impose the position it has taken against Iraq. It is thus clear that a double standard is being applied with respect to the elimination of weapons of mass destruction in the region, and an attempt being made to disrupt the military balance there. This is all the more apparent in that Iraq has not had recourse to weapons of this type. The application of this provision of the resolution cannot but seriously endanger the regional balance, as indeed was confirmed by certain impartial members of the Security Council in their statements when the resolution was voted upon. There can be no doubt that Israel, an expansionist aggressor country which is occupying the territory of neighbouring countries, usurping the right of the Palestinian Arab people against which it daily commits the most horrible atrocities, and refusing to comply with the resolutions of the Security Council, which it holds in contempt, as well as all the resolutions of the international Organization, will be the first to benefit from this imbalance.

Whereas, the resolution emphasizes the importance of all States adhering to the Convention on the Prohibition of the Development, Production and Stockpiling of Bacteriological (Biological) and Toxin Weapons, of a Convention on the Universal Prohibition of Chemical Weapons being drafted and of universal adherence thereto, it makes no mention whatsoever of the importance of universal adherence to the convention banning nuclear weapons or of the drafting of a convention on the universal prohibition of such weapons in the region. Instead, it emphasizes the importance of instituting a dialogue among the States of the region with a view to achieving a so-called balanced and comprehensive control of armaments in the region.

Proof of the resolution's biased and iniquitous nature is afforded by the Council's use of what it terms unprovoked attacks using ballistic missiles as grounds for calling for the destruction of all ballistic missiles with a range greater than 150 kilometers and of all repair and production facilities. The term unprovoked attacks is used of attacks against Israel, a country which itself launched an unprovoked attack in 1981, destroying Iraqi nuclear installations which were used for peaceful purposes and were under international safeguards. In this connection, the Security Council considered in its resolution 487 (1981), adopted unanimously, that that attack constituted a serious threat to the entire safeguards regime of the International Atomic Energy Agency, which is the foundation of the Treaty on the Non–Proliferation * * *. It should be pointed out as well that the Council had also considered in the same resolution that Iraq was entitled to appropriate redress for the destruction it had suffered. The Council has to date taken no steps for the implementation of that resolution, whereas it imposes particularly severe and iniquitous terms and mechanisms when it comes to the redress referred to in resolution 687 (1991), without taking into account even the basic humanitarian needs of the Iraqi people.

III. Furthermore, Iraq's internal and external security has been and remains seriously threatened, in that continuing efforts are being made to interfere, by force of arms, in the country's internal affairs. Thus the measures taken by the Council against Iraq to deprive it of its lawful right to acquire weapons and military matériel for defence directly contribute to the intensification of these threats and to the destabilization of Iraq, thus endangering the country's internal and external security and hence peace, security and stability throughout the region.

IV. * * * [T]he Council resolution provides mechanisms for obtaining redress from Iraq, [but] makes no reference to Iraq's rights to claim redress for the considerable losses it sustained and the massive destruction inflicted on civilian installations and infrastructures as a result of the abusive implementation of resolution 678 (1990), which were testified to by the delegation sent by the Secretary–General which visited Iraq recently, and have been referred to by the President of a permanent member of the Security Council (Soviet President Mikhail Gorbachev) and by all impartial observers who have seen with their own eyes the consequences of the military operations launched against Iraq. The Council has not explained to world public opinion and the conscience of mankind what the relationship is between its resolution 678 and the deliberate destruction of Iraq's infrastructure—generating stations, water distribution networks, irrigation dams, civilian bridges, telephone exchanges, factories producing powdered milk for infants and medicines, shelters, mosques, churches, commercial centres, residential neighbourhoods, etc. Moreover, the resolution authorizes third parties to claim compensation from Iraq for damage that may have been caused to them, even when such damage resulted from unfulfilment of their commitments to Iraq immediately following the adoption of resolution 661.

Further evidence of the resolution's biased and iniquitous nature is that it holds Iraq liable for environmental damage and the depletion of natural resources, although this liability has not been established; on the other hand, it makes no mention of Iraq's own right to obtain compensation for the established facts of damage to its environment and depletion of its natural resources as a result of more than 88,000 tons of explosives, or for the destruction of water distribution networks, generating stations and the road network, which has spread disease and epidemics and caused serious harm to the environment. These provisions partake of a desire to exact vengeance and cause harm, not to give effect to the relevant provisions of international law. The direct concrete consequences of their implementation will affect the potential and resources of millions of Iraqis, and deprive them of the right to live in dignity.

V.   After imposing compulsory and universal sanctions against Iraq by adopting resolution 661 (1990) in consequence, according to it, of Iraq's refusal to comply with the provisions of resolution 660 (1990), the Council has maintained most of them in force despite Iraq's acceptance of all the Council's resolutions and the implementation of a good number of their provisions.   The Council resolution provides for the progressive lifting of sanctions over an unspecified period, thus leaving broad discretionary authority to certain influential members of the Council which have drawn up the Council's resolutions in an arbitrary manner in order to impose them for political purposes which bear no relation to the Charter or to international law.

In essence, this procedure means that the Council has contradicted the initial resolution under which it imposed sanctions against Iraq, and moreover has not taken account of the offensive launched against Iraq, whereas the interests of the other parties have been taken into account, despite their wealth and their considerable resources.

VI.   The Council does not deal clearly and directly with the question of withdrawal of the foreign forces occupying part of Iraqi territory, although the resolution declares a formal cease-fire.

The very conditions invoked in support of the declaration of a formal cease-fire also necessitate the withdrawal.   The fact that the withdrawal is not explicitly mentioned is tantamount to authorizing the occupation of Iraqi territory for a period whose duration is at the discretion of the occupying countries, which make no secret of their intention to exploit the occupation for political purposes and to make use of it as a trump card in their hand.   This position on the part of the Council constitutes a flagrant violation of Iraq's sovereignty, independence and territorial integrity, and cannot be justified by any provision of resolution 678 (1990).   Under this same selective, premeditated and totally unjustifiable approach, the resolution stipulates that the observer forces will be deployed in Iraq to a distance of 10 kilometres from the boundary, and only [5] kilometres into the territory of the other party, despite the fact that the terrain in the region is flat everywhere, with no relief features that would justify this difference of treatment.

VII.   Numerous mechanisms are envisaged which will necessitate consultation in the context of the implementation of the resolution's provisions, but the resolution is not at all clear about Iraq's participation in these consultations.   The fact that Iraq is concerned to the highest degree in the application of the resolution makes its effective participation in all consultations bearing on the implementation of these provisions essential.   However, the Council has once again opted for an arbitrary and inequitable method.

The questions raised in the resolution and discussed in the foregoing preliminary comments constitute, in substance, an injustice, a severe assault on the Iraqi people's right to life and a flagrant denial of its inalienable rights to sovereignty and independence and its right to exercise its free choice.   *   *   *   [T]he provisions of the resolution embodying the criteria of duality in international relations and the application of a double standard to questions of the same kind hold Iraq and its population hostage to the designs harboured by certain Powers to take control of their resources, set quotas for their food and clothing needs, and deprive them of their right to live in dignity in the modern society to which they aspire.

Such injustices and such assaults on the rights of a member country of the United Nations and its people cannot under any circumstances be in conformity with the purposes and objectives of the Charter. The Council had a duty to discuss the issues before it with objectivity and in accordance with the provisions of international law and the principles of justice and equity. By adopting this unjust resolution and by this selective treatment of the Iraqi people, the Council has merely confirmed the fact that we have never ceased to emphasize, namely that the Council has become a puppet which the United States of America is manipulating in order to achieve its political designs in the region, the prime objective being to perpetuate Israel's policy of aggression and expansion, despite the empty words about peace and justice in the Middle East uttered by one or another of the Council members which voted for this resolution.

It could not be more clear to all men of honour and justice that these iniquitous and vengeful measures against Iraq are not a consequence of the events of 2 August 1990 and the subsequent period, for the essential motive underlying these measures stems from Iraq's rejection of the unjust situation imposed on the Arab nation and the countries of the region for decades, a situation which has enabled Israel, a belligerent Power heavily armed with the most modern and fearsome conventional weapons and with weapons of mass destruction, including nuclear weapons, to exercise hegemony in the region. This reality confirms what Iraq had stated before the events of 2 August 1990, namely that it was the target of a plot aimed at destroying the potential it had deployed with a view to arriving at a just balance in the region which would pave the way for the institution of justice and of a lasting peace.

It is unfortunate that States whose intention was not in any way to help the United States of America and Israel attain their objectives should involuntarily have contributed to their attainment by voting for this iniquitous resolution. As Iraq makes its preliminary comments on the juridical and legal aspects of this resolution, so as to encourage men of conscience in the countries members of the international community and world public opinion to make an effort to understand the truth as it is and the need to ensure the triumph of justice, it has no choice but to accept this resolution.

I should be grateful if you would have this letter circulated as a document of the Security Council.

(*Signed*) Ahmed HUSSEIN, Minister for Foreign Affairs of Iraq

BOB WOODWARD, THE COMMANDERS
319–321 (1991).*

* * *

[On] November 29, the * * * Security Council met to vote on an authorization to use force to expel Iraqi forces from Kuwait. If it passed, the resolution would be the broadest authority for war it had granted since Korea in 1950.

Baker had touched down in various world capitals to bring key heads of state on board and iron out the language of the resolution. He had spent ten weeks traveling 100,000 miles and had held more than 200 meetings with foreign ministers and heads of state.

His strategy had been to obtain ironclad assurances of support from the key U.N. countries before publicly acknowledging that the administration was even seeking a resolution on the use of force. He had hedged, saying repeatedly that he was taking soundings and that such a resolution was merely under consideration.

Any one of the five permanent members of the Security Council— the United States, China, Great Britain, France or the Soviet Union— could veto the resolution. The Chinese turned out not to be much of a problem; early on, they agreed not to veto. Britain's Prime Minister Thatcher was ready and willing to use force. The French were a problem and required a major effort, but Bush and Baker had succeeded in bringing them on board.

The Soviets were the big question mark. From the beginning of the crisis, Gorbachev had opposed the possibility of military force, but he had finally come around. Bush administration lawyers had said it would be best for the resolution language to be a model of clarity, spelling out directly the authority for use of force.

In a series of conversations and meetings in the weeks and days leading up to the U.N. vote, Baker and Soviet Foreign Minister Shevardnadze had hashed it out.

Baker presented Shevardnadze with a draft that included the phrase "use of force."

"Can you live with this?" Baker asked.

"After our Afghanistan experience, that won't fly with the Soviet people," Shevardnadze said. There had to be some other way, an indirect way of saying it, a euphemism. The Soviets could support the idea of force but the resolution itself had to be vague.

Baker said that would be hard. Force was force, after all, and they could not run the risk of not saying exactly what they meant. Scribbling on a piece of paper, Baker tried out some ideas—lawyerly phrases to substitute for "use of force." He tried five different formulations.

In one of their conversations, Shevardnadze said he wanted some language that would allow force but also encompass all other possible

* Reprinted with the permission of Pocket Star Books and Bob Woodward.

measures—diplomacy, negotiations, anything that might work. The broader the better.

How about "all necessary means," Baker proposed. In Russian, the same word could be used for "means" and "measures."

They went back and forth. Soon Shevardnadze was favoring "all necessary means." It was the broadest phrase they had found.

Now Baker backed off his own phrase. It was too indefinite.

"The United States knows what 'all necessary means' is," Shevardnadze said. "Don't embarrass us. Don't push us. Don't be extreme." Shevardnadze said for the Soviets it wasn't a moral problem, it was a practical problem. The Soviet Union could not go to the United Nations and be seen voting for war. At home, war still meant Afghanistan.

Baker said the United States wanted to avoid ambiguity. The Gulf policy was too volatile at home, and the Bush administration did not want a domestic debate on the meaning of a U.N. resolution.

Shevardnadze was immovable. Finally Baker gave in and they settled on "all necessary means." The coalition would be authorized to use "all necessary means" to eject Saddam's forces from Kuwait if he had not pulled them out by the resolution's deadline, January 15, 1991.

Baker said that since he would be the temporary president of the Security Council during the vote, he would speak afterwards and characterize the resolution as an unambiguous authority to use "force." That would be a permanent part of the record, and if no one objected, it would stand as the interpretation of "all necessary means." * * *

Fine, Shevardnadze said.

S/PV.2963, 29 November 1990

The Council had before it document S/21969 containing the text of a draft resolution tabled by Canada, the Union of Soviet Socialist Republics, the United Kingdom of Great Britain and Northern Ireland and the United States of America [statements of Secretary Baker and Minister Shevardnadze]:

The President: [Mr. BAKER, United States of America]:

I have been informed by the Secretary–General that at this meeting of the Security Council the following members of the Council are represented by their Foreign Ministers: Canada, China, Colombia, Cuba, Ethiopia, Finland, France, Malaysia, Romania, the Union of Soviet Socialist Republics, the United Kingdom of Great Britain and Northern Ireland, the United States of America and Zaire. Côte d'Ivoire and Yemen are represented by their Permanent Representatives to the United Nations. The participation of so many Foreign Ministers of the States members of the Council is testimony, I think, to the significance of this meeting. On behalf of the Council, I would like to express to them deep appreciation for their presence.

Colleagues, your very presence here, for only the fourth time in the Security Council's history that Foreign Ministers have assembled, symbolizes, I think, the seriousness of the present situation. I would like to begin today's discussion with a quotation that I believe aptly sets the context for our discussions today. The quotation is as follows:

> There is no precedent for a people being the victim of such injustice and of being at present threatened by abandonment to an aggressor. Also, there has never before been an example of any government proceeding with the systematic extermination of a nation by barbarous means in violation of the most solemn promises made to all the nations of the Earth that there should be no resort to a war of conquest and that there should not be used against innocent human beings terrible poison and harmful gases.

Those words, I think, could well have come from the Emir of Kuwait, but they do not. They were spoken in 1936, not in 1990. They come from Haile Selassie, the leader of Ethiopia, a man who saw his country conquered and occupied, much like Kuwait has been brutalized since 2 August. Sadly, that appeal to the League of Nations fell ultimately upon deaf ears. The League's efforts to redress aggression failed and international disorder and war ensued.

History has now given us another chance. With the cold war behind us, we now have the chance to build the world which was envisioned by the founders of this Organization—by the founders of the United Nations. We have the chance to make this Security Council and this United Nations true instruments for peace and for justice across the globe. We must not let the United Nations go the way of the League * * *. We must fulfil our common vision of a peaceful and just post-cold-war world.

But if we are to do so, we must meet the threat to international peace created by Saddam Hussein's aggression. And that is why the debate that we are about to begin will, I think, rank as one of the most important in the history of the United Nations. It will surely do much to determine the future of this body.

Our aim today must be to convince Saddam Hussein that the just and humane demands of this Council and of the international community cannot be ignored. If Iraq does not reverse its course peacefully, then other necessary measures, including the use of force, should be authorized. We must put the choice to Saddam Hussein in unmistakable terms. * * *

[88] Mr. Shevardnadze (U.S.S.R.) (interpretation from Russian): * * *

There is logic in the actions of our Council, which, from the outset of the crisis, has acted with cohesion and consistency and, at the same time, in a responsible, calm and prudent manner, in strict conformity with the letter and spirit of the U.N. Charter in its modern interpretation, which restores its original rights and authority. We have been faced with the first extremely grave test of the post-cold-war period, and we are coping with it, placing mankind's common interests at the centre of our policy and being guided by the principles of the new thinking in international affairs.

There is justice and a large measure of generosity in the resolution we have just adopted. As the end of the fourth month of the crisis approaches, the international community is showing genuine magnanimity and giving the side that has breached the peace time to think again. At the same time we are giving the victim in this crisis a firm pledge that it will not have to wait much longer, that help is on the way and that its rights will be fully restored.

Today we have started the count-down of the "pause of goodwill". We are confident that before the time is up events will take a turn towards peace and that the pause will usher in a transition to a political settlement. Had we thought otherwise, this resolution would have been unnecessary. It is one last sincere attempt to give common sense a chance to prevail; or, let us say, to give the instinct of self-preservation a chance to work; to give Iraq time to think about the consequences of any other than peaceful outcome of the crisis.

So we want to begin the pause of goodwill by calling upon Iraq and * * * Saddam Hussein to rise above considerations of prestige, to display wisdom and foresight and to place above all else the interests of the country and the fate of its people and of peace and stability on our planet. No member of the Council wants or seeks a tragic outcome; but nor should there be any mistake about the collective will of the international community as expressed here, or about its resolve and its readiness to act. The Council's action is based on the clear awareness and belief that shirking its duty now by failing to reverse the aggression would mean even greater hardship and suffering for the world and for all nations. Those who have breached the peace should know that "all necessary means" will indeed inexorably be used against them. All of us would be happy if only there were no need to resort to such means.

* * *

I say quite bluntly that what has happened in the Persian Gulf region strikes a blow at the emerging world of civilized behaviour. That is why it is so important to parry that blow and make sure that it does not do irreparable damage to the institutions of peace and democracy, thereby plunging the world into chaos. The world will not enter a more lucid, calm and stable phase unless it can meet the residual challenges of the past and rise to the new challenges of the present and the future.

It is of overriding importance that today we are no longer responding to these challenges in the same way as we did yesterday. We are giving preference to the law, to action under the authority of the Charter and of the Security Council, and to collective efforts. We have acted * * * collectively and in concert, throughout the long and difficult weeks of the Persian Gulf crisis, and we continue to do so. We are right to act in this way. I see it as a sign that we are truly entering a time of political maturity and have recognized that freedom and democracy are inseparable from an awareness by each one of us of our responsibility for order, for the state of our common home and for saving world civilization.

I have to say that, while it in no way minimizes our sympathy for Kuwait or our pain at its suffering, there is more at stake than the fate of that one State. Our common future is threatened. Hence the certainty that Kuwait will be reborn as an independent and sovereign State, as demanded by the resolutions adopted by the Security Council.

As some of my colleagues have rightly noted, we do not favour linkages in politics, least of all such absurd ones as those that seem to require the creation of a new problem in order to solve an old one, or the enslavement of one nation in order to promote the freedom of another. That would be truly absurd. But nor do we see any logic in artificially holding back efforts to solve a long-standing problem just because of the emergence of a new one that has to be addressed first.

　　　* * *

The purpose of the resolution we have just adopted is to put an end to the aggression and make it clear * * * that aggression cannot be rewarded. We hope the Iraqi leaders will find the strength to recognize the responsibility they bear to their own people and to history and comply with the will of the international community. We are serving them with a special warning about their personal responsibility for the fate of foreign nationals in Iraq. Endangering their lives will be regarded as a crime against humanity, with all the consequences that entails.

On behalf of the Soviet Union, I would like to state that in accordance with the support given by my Government to the concept of the "pause of goodwill" referred to in the resolution adopted today and for its duration, we will be guided by the following precepts, to which some of my colleagues have already referred.

First, assuming that there have been no adverse changes in the circumstances, my Government does not intend to introduce or to support any Security Council action to extend the scope or nature of the sanctions under Security Council resolution 661 (1990), 665 (1990) or 670 (1990), or any new measures of the Security Council regarding Iraq during the period between now and the date indicated in operative paragraph 2 of Security Council resolution 678 (1990).

Secondly, that undertaking is without prejudice to any and all rights of my Government under the Charter, including its rights should the Government of Iraq allow any harm to come to foreign nationals held against their will by the Government of Iraq.

Thirdly, my Government recalls the terms of operative paragraph 13 of Security Council resolution 670 (1990) under which individuals are held personally responsible for grave breaches of the Fourth Geneva Convention, and states that all those involved in violations of the laws of armed conflict, including the prohibition against initiating the use of chemical or biological weapons contrary to the Geneva Protocol of 1925, to which Iraq is a signatory, will similarly be held personally responsible.

In conclusion, I express the confidence that we will be able to overcome this crisis peacefully—I repeat, peacefully, and in a political way—and to end it on a note of hope for a better future for all of us.
* * *

* * *

The President [Mr. Baker, United States of America]: I thank the Minister for Foreign Affairs of Romania for the kind words he addressed to me. I should now like to make a statement in my capacity as Secretary of State of the United States of America. I think that today's vote marks a watershed in the history of the United Nations.

Earlier this week * * * the Security Council heard testimony of crimes committed against the citizens of Kuwait. There can be no doubt that these are crimes incompatible with any civilized order. They are part of the same pattern that includes—and many speakers have referred to this today—the taking of innocent hostages from many nations.

The entire international community has been affronted by a series of brutal acts. Iraqi forces have invaded and seized a small Arab neighbour. A once-prosperous country has been pillaged and looted. A once-peaceful country has been turned into an armed camp. A once-secure country has been terrorized. The nations of the world have not stood idly by. We have taken political, economic and military measures to quarantine Iraq and contain its aggression. We have worked out a coordinated international effort involving over 50 States to provide assistance to those nations most in need as a consequence of the economic embargo of Iraq. And military forces from over 27 nations have been deployed to defend Iraq's neighbours from further aggression and to implement the resolutions of this Council. The 12 resolutions adopted by the Council have clearly established that there is a peaceful way out of this conflict—and that is the complete, immediate and unconditional Iraqi withdrawal from Kuwait, the restoration of Kuwait's legitimate Government and the release of all hostages.

I do not think all this could have taken place unless most nations shared our vision of what is at stake. A dangerous man committed a blatant act of aggression in a vital region at a very critical moment in history. Saddam Hussein's actions, the vast arms he possesses and the weapons of mass destruction he seeks indicate clearly that Kuwait was not only not the first but probably not the last target on his list. If he should win this struggle, there will be no peace in the Middle East; only the prospect of more conflict and a far wider war. If he should come to dominate the resources of the Gulf, his ambitions will threaten all of us here and the economic well-being of all nations. Finally, if Iraq should emerge from this conflict with territory or with treasure or with political advantage, then the lesson will be very, very clear: aggression pays.

As I said earlier today, we must remember the lesson of the 1930s and aggression must not be rewarded. Since 2 August many nations have worked together to prove just that. Many unprecedented actions have been taken. The result is a new fact: a newly effective United Nations Security Council, free of the constraints of the cold war. Yet the sad truth is that the new fact has not yet erased the old fact of Iraqi aggression, and that—and that alone—is the ultimate test of success.

We must ask ourselves why Saddam has not recoiled from his aggression. We must wonder why he does not understand how great the forces are against him and how profound is the revulsion against his behaviour. The answer must be that he does not believe we really mean what we say. He does not believe we will stand united until he withdraws. He thinks that his fact of aggression is going to outlast our fact: that is, an international community opposed to aggression.

We are meeting here today, therefore, first and foremost—as many speakers here have already pointed out—to dispel Saddam Hussein's illusions. He must know from us that a refusal to comply peacefully with the Security Council resolutions risks disaster for him.

Fellow members of the Security Council, we are at a crossroads. Today we show Saddam Hussein that the sign marked "peace" is the direction he should take.

Today's resolution is very clear. The words authorize the use of force. But the purpose, I believe—and, again, many here have already said this—is to bring about a peaceful resolution of this problem. No one here has sought this conflict. Many nations here have had very good relations with the people of Iraq. But the Security Council of the United Nations cannot tolerate this aggression and still be faithful to the principles of the Charter of the United Nations.

With the adoption of today's resolution we concur with other Council members that this should lead to a pause in the Council's efforts— assuming, of course, no adverse change in circumstances. We do so while retaining our rights, as other nations have, to protect our foreign nationals in Iraq, and very mindful of the terms of the Fourth Geneva Convention and the Geneva Protocol of 1925, should Saddam Hussein use chemical or biological weapons.

By adopting today's resolution, which we think is a pause for peace, we say to Saddam Hussein: "We continue to seek a diplomatic solution. Peace is your only sensible option. You can choose peace by respecting the will of the international community. But if you fail to do so, you will risk all. The choice is yours."

If we fail to redress this aggression, more will be lost than just peace in the Persian Gulf. Only recently, in Europe, the nations party to the cold war assembled to bury that conflict. All the peoples of Europe and North America who had nothing to look forward to except an unending twilight struggle now have a fresh start, indeed a new opportunity. Conflict and war are no longer the watchwords of European politics.

We meet at the hinge of history. We can use the end of the cold war to get beyond the whole pattern of settling conflicts by force, or we can slip back into ever more savage regional conflicts in which might alone makes right. We can take the high road towards peace and the rule of law, or we can take Saddam Hussein's path of brutal aggression and the law of the jungle. Simply put, it is a choice between right and wrong. I think we have the courage and the fortitude to choose what is right. . . .

The Secretary–General:

The Security Council has taken a decision of immense portent. I should like to stress that, even on the most stringent reading, the resolution just adopted envisages at least 45 days of earnest effort to achieve a peaceful solution of the crisis. Mindful of the responsibility inherent in my office, I must express the hope that this time will be used to the most constructive purpose.

In my statement at the Council's ministerial meeting on 25 September I sought to point out the position of principle deriving from the Charter that is involved in this question. In requiring compliance with the resolutions of the Security Council, the United Nations seeks not surrender but the most honourable way of resolving a crisis in a manner that respects all legitimate interests and is conducive to the wider peace and the rule of law.

This * * * is not a matter simply of rhetoric. It is not a question of clothing a bellicose intent in persuasive language. To my mind, the situation requires that diplomatic efforts be made with renewed determination to put the present crisis on the road to a peaceful outcome.

A collective engagement, as I have observed before, requires a discipline all its own. Moreover, the actions of the United Nations to correct this international wrong must be perceived as part of the larger endeavour to establish peace through justice, wherever the one is imperilled and the other denied.

Questions and Discussion: Compare the role played by the Security Council in the Gulf War with that in the Korean Conflict. The Security Council in the Korean Conflict *"recommended"* that the member states defend South Korea. What did the Security Council do in relation to Iraq and Kuwait? Do the terms: *"recommend," "authorize,"* and *"determine"* have legal significance? While the use of the veto by the Soviet Union did not occur at the beginning of the Korean War, because the Soviet Representative was absent, later the allies had to resort to the General Assembly through the *Uniting for Peace Resolution*. Was the situation during the Gulf War significantly better? If so why? What were the legal differences? The institutional differences? The allies in the Gulf War faced the possibility of a veto, both from China and Russia at various points. Difficult negotiations ultimately settled the differences, but do you think it was likely that some of the primary U.S. objectives were ultimately not taken as a consequence of the give and take of negotiation? Is it possible that the decision ultimately not to press on to Baghdad or to overthrow Saddam Hussein was one of these? Was it wise? What were the positive impacts that the Gulf War had on international law in practice and theory? Can you think of any dangers to the way the Security Council was able to function during that War? Was it a fact, as some have supported, that the Council determined the aggressor without much discussion or dissent?

Note that the Security Council never did determine that *"aggression"* had occurred or that there was an *"aggressor,"* in exactly those words. The Security Council's acts were all based on *"breach of the peace,"* until S.C. Resolution 688, which was based on *"threat to the peace."* Is the action taken in the Gulf War best characterized as collective self-defense authorized by the Security Council or as Article 42 action? If the action is considered to be taken in self-defense authorized by the Security Council, do the usual requirements of proportionality and necessity obtain?

Questions of Domestic Constitutional Authority and the Gulf War Precedent: Did S.C. Resolution 678 provide the President of the United States with authority to deploy U.S. troops and armament into the Persian Gulf War? See discussion in Chapter 17, infra.

The Gulf War and notions of sovereignty. Did the Gulf War have an impact on the Austinian positivist notion that international law is not really law, because there is no "sovereign" to enforce it? If it could have been claimed before, can it be claimed any longer that there is no "enforcement mechanism" in international law? Could one say there *was* a sovereign? If so, what was it? The basic philosophies of international law are in Chapter 18, *infra.* Was the Gulf War an example of international government at work? Was the Security Council the "sovereign"? Did the Gulf War develop the notion of "collective sovereignty," not unlike that of popular sovereignty that developed in relation to the citizens of nation-states in the eighteenth and nineteenth centuries? Has the war in Bosnia dashed any notion of UN or other supra-national sovereignty?

The Gulf War and the Laws of War: Do the laws of war obtain for actions of the Security Council? What would be the appropriate and legal action to be taken if forces under the U.N. Command committed violations of the laws of war? Chapter 11 considers individual responsibility. For example, will the Ad Hoc Tribunal for the violations of humanitarian law in the territory of the former Yugoslavia hear cases of violations by U.N. forces, if there are any? See, Blakesley, *Obstacles to the Creation of a Permanent War Crimes Tribunal,* 18 The Fletcher Forum 77 (1994).

KAHN, ESSAY: LESSONS FOR INTERNATIONAL LAW FROM THE GULF WAR

45 Stan.L.Rev. 425 (1993) (footnotes omitted).*

Politically and militarily, the War in the Gulf remains an unsettled event. Although nearly two years have passed since the War, its political consequences are still evolving. Militarily, the recent reintroduction of allied forces into Iraqi air space suggests that the War continues, though at a much reduced level. In the long run, the War will probably be seen as a footnote to the larger political upheavals that marked the start of this decade—noteworthy because it made visible the realignment of the international order that had already occurred.

---

* Reprinted by permission of the Stanford Law Review.

[The war] is a major event from the perspective of international law. It marked one of the few occasions on which there was a deliberate invocation of international law to justify military force. An examination of the War can teach us much about the reality of, and possibilities for, international law. Given the continuing tumultuous politics of Eastern Europe and the former Soviet Union, this legal reconsideration is important. Already, the international-legal machinery deployed in the War has served as a precedent for Security Council action authorizing military intervention in Bosnia and Herzegovina.

We are moving rapidly toward a new world order of some sort. While it may be too early to predict the political shape of that order, it is not too early to consider the role that international law may play in it. Before we raise our hopes for a vital future for international law, we need to fully understand the character and power of existing international law. To that end, it is useful to examine international law as it operated, and failed to operate, in the Gulf War.

The international law at work during the Gulf War is the captive of an ideal of state sovereignty that assumes a harmonious relationship between a people and its government. All too often, however, the reality is not harmony but opposition. In its present form, international law cannot deal with this reality. Its focus on the ideal of state sovereignty leads international law to pursue morally unsupportable goals and to choose irrational means. When the international legal system acts to protect state sovereignty, too often the only real beneficiary is the political leadership, not the people. In those rare cases when modern international law responds to legal violations, it ends up punishing the people for the acts of their leaders, when the people too are victims.

While at some deep level international law has grasped that it will remain a tool of powerful interests of the status quo until it rests on a foundation of human rights, justice, and equality, these ideals are not yet operative aspects of the legal system. Until the international legal system embraces those ideals, the new world order must seek a foundation somewhere outside of international law.

These may seem overly pessimistic conclusions to draw from the defeat of Saddam Hussein's effort at international aggrandisement. Admittedly, the enterprise of drawing general lessons for international law from a single event is inherently controversial. Moreover, analysis of the Gulf War is particularly difficult because the events have a complicated sequential character. The lessons drawn depend not only upon the particular events one emphasizes, but equally upon where one ends the story. For example, although the immediate aftermath of the war was a human rights disaster for Iraqi Kurds and Shiites, that disaster elicited an international response that is itself an ongoing story.

Despite such problems, international legal analysis must look to single events. This is true because particular incidents of state behavior are an important source of innovation in international law. More important, only by looking to the operation of law in particular events are we able to discuss realistically the force and effect of the formal system of international law.

* * *

From the perspective of creating an effective international legal regime, the United States' action with respect to Iraq is particularly praiseworthy because a strong argument could have been made in support of unilateral action under Article 31 of the Charter. That Article recognizes a right of self-defense and, more importantly, of collective self-defense "until the Security Council has taken measures necessary to maintain international peace and security." Arguably, the United States could have defended Kuwait and Saudi Arabia merely upon a request from their governments. This exception for a unilateral recourse to force in "self-defense" has provided a large loophole through which much of the hope for the prohibition on the use of force in Article 2(4) has fallen over the last few decades. Yet another unilateral use of force, justified by reference to Article 31, would have done little to advance international law from a self-serving rhetorical system to an actual restraint on the behavior of states.

Discussions of international law tend to fade into discussions of the domestic law of foreign policy. This is inevitable for two reasons. First, we are interested not just in the formal system of international law but in how international law interacts with domestic legal institutions. Second, international law and constitutional law both address the problem of arresting institutional constraints on the unilateral use of force in international affairs. International law and domestic separation of powers doctrine share that goal of restraining the use of force through the dispersion of authority and the requirement of collective decision-making. Not surprisingly, therefore, the Gulf War triggered renewed debate over the constitutional division of responsibility for decisions to use force: Does Congress' war-making power require it to review military actions taken by the President as commander in chief?

* * *

Questions: Was Iraq's invasion of Kuwait a "failure" of international law, rather than a violation of it? Is a robbery or murder a "failure" of domestic law?

3. PEACEKEEPING FORCES [U.N. USE OF FORCE TO KEEP THE PEACE]:

In 1992, President Clinton presented new criteria for U.S. forces to become involved in "peacekeeping" efforts. In the beginning, the U.S. took the position that U.S. forces would not be allowed to participate unless they were able "to make a unique military contribution." President Clinton revised this to allow U.S. forces to participate in planning, training, and engagement in peacekeeping efforts, if and when U.S. national interests justified the participation, in addition to being able to make the "unique military contribution." Factors to be considered in making the decision to participate included: public support or the lack thereof, the risk of open-ended engagement, and the relative weight of U.S. national interests. See, e.g., Friedman, Clinton at UN, Lists Stiff Terms for Sending U.S. Force to Bosnia, The New York Times, Section A, p. 1, col. 5; Curtius, President Calls for a Cautious UN: U.S. Commitment Affirmed, but Limits Urged on Troop Use, The Boston Globe p. 1, Sept. 28, 1993. In addition, at the same time that the number and complexity of missions seemed to be multiplying, members of the U.N., including the U.S. continue to withhold funds. See, Preston, Members of U.N. Failing to Pay Up for Peace Keeping, As Global Missions Multiply * * *, Wash.Post, p. A–25, June 27, 1993. Several African states are collapsing and large areas of the Continent are not governed by any state: grave problems exist in [Rwanda & Burundi] Zaire, Gabon, Mozambique, Angola, Cameroon, Togo, Liberia, Ethiopia, Sudan and Sierra Leone. Gannett News Service, Dec. 10, 1992, citing Pauline Baker, an African expert at the Aspen Institute. Some world leaders have suggested that the triple crises of Somalia, Bosnia, and Cambodia indicate that the concept of absolute territorial sovereignty can no longer be considered the sole factor in maintaining order and ensuring the protection of humanity. See, Boutros–Ghali, Agenda for Peace, *supra*, June 1992, stating: "[t]he time for absolute and exclusive sovereignty * * * has passed * * *. Its theory was never matched by reality." We will briefly present the development of "peacekeeping" (or peace-making?) forces and suggest that you consider the past, present and future role of U.S. involvement in these operations.

a. Suez

The First Peacekeeping Force: A British–French Challenge to the prohibition of the Use of Force. In Suez, after President Nasser of Egypt nationalized the Suez Canal Company, the English and French met secretly to plan and proceed with an Anglo–French "police action following an Israeli attack upon Egypt." See, Higgins, United Nations Peacekeeping, 1946–1967, I., The Middle East 225 (1969). Thus, the French and British challenged the prohibition of the use of force, claiming, through Sir Pierson Dixon: that their armed military action was necessary to safeguard "the Suez Canal and the restoration of peaceful conditions in the Middle East * * *. [N]either we [the British] nor the French Government have any desire whatever that the military action which we have taken should be more than temporary in its duration. It will be terminated as soon as the emergency is over. It is our intention that our action to protect the Canal, to terminate hostilities and to separate the combatants should be as short as possible * * *. The action taken by my Government and by the Government of France has been called an act of aggression against Egypt. This is a charge which we emphatically deny * * *. The action of France and the United Kingdom is not aggression. We do not seek the domination of Egypt or of any part of Egyptian territory. Our purpose is peaceful, not warlike. Our aim is to re-establish the rule of law, not to violate it; to protect and not to destroy. What we have undertaken is a temporary police action necessitated by the turn of events in the Middle East and occasioned by the imperative need not only to protect the vital interests of my own and many other countries, but also to take immediate measures for the restoration of order * * *. Our action is in no way aimed at the sovereignty of Egypt, and still less at its territorial integrity." (G.A.Off. Rec., 1st Emergency Special Sess., 1956 Plenary, p. 5).

France and the United Kingdom thwarted any Security Council action with their negative votes. A special emergency session of the General Assembly was called pursuant to the Uniting for Peace Resolution. The Assembly adopted Resolution 997 (ES–I), on November 2, 1956, urging a cease-fire and withdrawal of troops and that steps be taken to re-open the Canal. The next day, France and the United Kingdom declared that they were willing to cease their military action, if the Egyptian and Israeli Governments would agree to accept a U.N. Force to keep the peace. The General Assembly then established an emergency international U.N. Force (United Nations Command for an emergency international Force to secure and supervise the cessation of hostilities," G.A. Res. 1000, later called the United Nations Emergency Force, UNEF, see, U.N.Doc.A/3317). *See gen.*, Seyersted, United Nations Forces in the Law of Peace and War 46 (1966); G.A. Resolutions (997, 998, 1000, and 1002) Establishing the Emergency Force (UNEF).

––––––––

1. *Legal basis for the United Nations Emergency Force.* In establishing the Emergency Force, did the General Assembly avail itself of all of the power it had asserted in the Uniting for Peace Resolution? The force was not physically located on Israeli territory. Could it have lawfully entered Israeli territory to perform its function without the consent of the government of Israel?

2. *Withdrawal of the Emergency Force.* At the request of the government of the United Arab Republic (Egypt), the Secretary–General of the United Nations (U Thant) withdrew the Emergency Force from the territory of the Republic in May and June 1967. The action of the Secretary–General in acceding to this request at that particular time was highly controversial. He explained his action in detail in a report to the United Nations. G.A.Off.Rec., 5th Emergency Spec.Sess. (1967), Annexes (A/6730/Add. 3), p. 9.

––––––––

b. *The Congo: Preventing Dismemberment of a New State*

The former Belgian Congo became independent in June 1960. Shortly after independence, the Katanga Province attempted to secede, with concomitant civilian riots, including attacks on Belgians and other Europeans, and mutiny by the Congolese military. Moise Tshombe, the leader in the Katanga Province, requested the intervention of Belgian troops to restore order. Belgian troops did intervene on July 10, 1960, causing panic and bitterness in the Katangan population. Tshombe sought recognition but never received it. The Security Council, at the request of President Kasavubu and Prime Minister Lumumba of the Congo, adopted a resolution on July 14, 1960, which called for the immediate withdrawal of Belgian troops and authorized the Secretary–General to provide the Congolese Government with sufficient military assistance to bring about order. Thus, the U.N. Peacekeeping Force for the Congo was created (ONUC) (S.C.Res. 143; U.N.Doc.S/4387 1960), which did intervene, engaging in heavy fighting in Katanga Province. During 1960, several S.C. resolutions were vetoed by the USSR and a rift developed between Prime Minister Lumumba and President Kasavubu. In the beginning of the crisis, the U.N. appeared to take a neutral position on the Katangan secession, but by July 22, 1960, it requested "all states to refrain from any action which might impede the restoration of law and order and the exercise by the Government of the Congo of its authority and also to refrain from any action which might undermine the territorial integrity and the political independence of the Republic of the Congo." (S.C.Res. 145 (1960). In 1961, this was reiterated as the purpose of the U.N. involvement. [S.C.Res.U.N.SCOR, 16th Sess., U.N.Doc.S/5002 (1961)]. *See,* Note, *Secession: State Practice and International Law After the Dissolution of the Soviet Union and Yugoslavia,* 3 Duke J.Comp. & Int'l L. 299, 304–307 (1993); Franck & Carey, Working Paper, The Role of the United Nations in the Congo—A Retrospective Perspective, in The Role of the United Nations in the Congo 1, 11–12 (Tondel ed. 1963); Hoskyns, The Congo: A Chronology of Events, January 1960–December 1961 (1962); Seyersted, United Nations Forces in the Law of Peace and War 60 (1966).

---

1. ***Legal basis for the United Nations operations in the Congo.*** The Congolese action was authorized by the Security Council. Was its legality firmly based on the Charter than the Emergency Force in the Middle East (which, as seen above, was authorized by the General Assembly)? Did the Council act pursuant to Article 39? If so, what was the requisite threat to the peace, breach of the peace, or act of aggression? Was it the sending of troops by Belgium to maintain and restore order? The Council never made a finding to that effect. Can the Council's action be grounded on the request of the Congolese government for aid? What is the Charter basis for the Council's response to such a request?

2. ***Analysis of the legal basis for peacekeeping forces by the International Court of Justice.*** The legal basis for both the Emergency Force and the Congolese operations was the subject of analysis by the International Court in the *Certain Expenses Case,* which follows. The Court was asked for an advisory opinion because certain members of the U.N. refused to pay amounts assessed against them as "expenses of the Organization" (Article 17). The members refusing claimed that the Middle East and Congolese operations did not qualify as such expenses. The case was significant because of its financial implications, since Article 19 of the Charter prescribes a loss of the right to vote in the General Assembly in the case of certain financial delinquencies on the part of a member. But the advisory opinion of the court is also

significant because of its analysis of the constitutional powers of the United Nations and its organs to employ or authorize military force.

———

CERTAIN EXPENSES OF THE UNITED NATIONS (ADVISORY OPINION)

International Court of Justice, 1962.
[1962] I.C.J.Rep. 151, 156, 162.

[The General Assembly requested an advisory opinion by Resolution 1731 (XVI), adopted on December 20, 1961. The request has been edited by omitting designations, by number and date, of specific resolutions adopted by the Security Council and the General Assembly.]

* * *

The question on which the Court is asked to give its opinion is whether certain expenditures which were authorized by the General Assembly to cover the costs of the United Nations operations in the Congo (hereinafter referred to as ONUC) and of the operations of the United Nations Emergency Force in the Middle East (hereinafter referred to as UNEF), "constitute 'expenses of the Organization' within the meaning of Article 17, paragraph 2, of the Charter * * *".

* * *

The text of Article 17 is in part as follows: 1. The General Assembly shall consider and approve the budget of the Organization. 2. The expenses of the Organization shall be borne by the Members as apportioned by the General Assembly.

* * *

Article 17 is the only article in the Charter which refers to budgetary authority or to the power to apportion expenses, or otherwise to raise revenue, except for Articles 33 and 35, paragraph 3, of the Statute of the Court which have no bearing on the point here under discussion. Nevertheless, it has been argued before the Court that one type of expenses, namely those resulting from operations for the maintenance of international peace and security, are not "expenses of the Organization" within the meaning of Article 17, paragraph 2, of the Charter, inasmuch as they fall to be dealt with exclusively by the Security Council, and more especially through agreements negotiated in accordance with Article 43 of the Charter.

The argument rests in part upon the view that when the maintenance of international peace and security is involved, it is only the Security Council which is authorized to decide on any action relative thereto. It is argued further that since the General Assembly's power is limited to discussing, considering, studying and recommending, it cannot impose an obligation to pay the expenses which result from the implementation of its recommendations. This argument leads to an examination of the respective functions of the General Assembly and of the

Security Council under the Charter, particularly with respect to the maintenance of international peace and security.

Article 24 of the Charter provides: "In order to ensure prompt and effective action by the United Nations, its Members confer on the Security Council primary responsibility for the maintenance of international peace and security. * * *"

The responsibility conferred is "primary", not exclusive. This primary responsibility is conferred upon the Security Council, as stated in Article 24, "in order to ensure prompt and effective action". To this end, it is the Security Council which is given a power to impose an explicit obligation of compliance if for example it issues an order or command to an aggressor under Chapter VII. It is only the Security Council which can require enforcement by coercive action against an aggressor.

The Charter makes it abundantly clear, however, that the General Assembly is also to be concerned with international peace and security. Article 14 authorizes the General Assembly to "recommend measures for the peaceful adjustment of any situation, regardless of origin, which it deems likely to impair the general welfare or friendly relations among nations, including situations resulting from a violation of the provisions of the present Charter setting forth the purposes and principles of the United Nations". The word "measures" implies some kind of action, and the only limitation which Article 14 imposes on the General Assembly is the restriction found in Article 12, namely, that the Assembly should not recommend measures while the Security Council is dealing with the same matter unless the Council requests it to do so. Thus, while it is the Security Council which, exclusively, may order coercive action, the functions and powers conferred by the Charter on the General Assembly are not confined to discussion, consideration, the initiation of studies and the making of recommendations; they are not merely hortatory. * * *

* * *

The Court has considered the general problem of the interpretation of Article 17, paragraph 2 * * *. In determining whether the actual expenditures authorized constitute "expenses of the Organization within the meaning of Article 17, paragraph 2, of the Charter", the Court agrees that such expenditures must be tested by their relationship to the purposes of the United Nations in the sense that if an expenditure were made for a purpose which is not one of the purposes of the United Nations, it could not be considered an "expense of the Organization."

The purposes of the United Nations are set forth in Article 1 of the Charter. The first two purposes as stated in paragraphs 1 and 2, may be summarily described as pointing to the goal of international peace and security and friendly relations. The third purpose is the achievement of economic, social, cultural and humanitarian goals and respect for human rights. The fourth and last purpose is: "To be a center for harmonizing the actions of nations in the attainment of these common ends".

The primary place ascribed to international peace and security is natural, since the fulfilment of the other purposes will be dependent upon the attainment of that basic condition. These purposes are broad indeed, but neither they nor the powers conferred to effectuate them are unlimited. Save as they have entrusted the Organization with the attainment of these common ends, the Member States retain their freedom of action. But when the Organization takes action which warrants the assertion that it was appropriate for the fulfilment of one of the stated purposes of the United Nations, the presumption is that such action is not ultra vires the Organization.

* * *

The expenditures enumerated in the request for an advisory opinion may conveniently be examined first with reference to UNEF and then to ONUC. In each case, attention will be paid first to the operations and then to the financing of the operations.

In considering the operations in the Middle East, the Court must analyze the functions of UNEF as set forth in resolutions of the General Assembly. Resolution 998 (ES–I) of 4 November 1956 requested the Secretary–General to submit a plan "for the setting up, with the consent of the nations concerned, of an emergency international United Nations Force to secure and supervise the cessation of hostilities in accordance with all the terms of" the General Assembly's previous resolution 997 (ES–I) of 2 November 1956. The verb "secure" as applied to such matters as halting the movement of military forces and arms into the area and the conclusion of a cease-fire, might suggest measures of enforcement, were it not that the Force was to be set up "with the consent of the nations concerned."

In his first report on the plan for an emergency international Force the Secretary–General used the language of resolution 998 (ES–I) in submitting his proposals. The same terms are used in [G.A.] resolution 1000 (ES–I) of 5 November in which operative paragraph 1 reads: "Establishes a United Nations Command for an emergency international Force to secure and supervise the cessation of hostilities in accordance with all the terms of General Assembly resolution 997 (ES–I) of 2 November 1956." This resolution was adopted without a dissenting vote. In his second and final report on the plan for an emergency international Force of 6 November, the Secretary–General, in paragraphs 9 and 10 stated:

> While the General Assembly is enabled to establish the Force with the consent of those parties which contribute units to the Force, it could not request the Force to be stationed or operate on the territory of a given country without the consent of the Government of that country. This does not exclude the possibility that the Security Council could use such a Force within the wider margins provided under Chapter VII of the Charter. I would not for the present consider it necessary to elaborate this point further, since no use of the Force under Chapter VII, with the rights in relation to Member States that this would entail, has been envisaged.

10. The point just made permits the conclusion that the setting up of the Force should not be guided by the needs which would have existed had the measure been considered as part of an enforcement action directed against a Member country.   There is an obvious difference between establishing the Force in order to secure the cessation of hostilities, with a withdrawal of forces, and establishing such a Force with a view to enforcing a withdrawal of forces.

Paragraph 12 of the Report is particularly important because in resolution 1001 (ES–I) the General Assembly, again without a dissenting vote, "Concurs in the definition of the functions of the Force as stated in paragraph 12 of the Secretary–General's report".   Paragraph 12 reads:

the functions of the United Nations Force would be, when a cease-fire is being established, to enter Egyptian territory with the consent of the Egyptian Government, in order to help maintain quiet during and after the withdrawal of non-Egyptian troops, and to secure compliance with the other terms established in the resolution of 2 November 1956.   The Force obviously should have no rights other than those necessary for the execution of its functions, in co-operation with local authorities.   It would be more than an observers' corps, but in no way a military force temporarily controlling the territory in which it is stationed; nor, moreover, should the Force have military functions exceeding those necessary to secure peaceful conditions on the assumption that the parties to the conflict take all necessary steps for compliance with the recommendations of the General Assembly.

It is not possible to find in this description of the functions of UNEF, as outlined by the Secretary–General and concurred in by the General Assembly without a dissenting vote, any evidence that the Force was to be used for purposes of enforcement.   Nor can such evidence be found in the subsequent operations of the Force, operations which did not exceed the scope of the functions ascribed to it.

It could not therefore have been patent on the face of the resolution that the establishment of UNEF was in effect "enforcement action" under Chapter VII which, in accordance with the Charter, could be authorized only by the Security Council.

On the other hand, it is apparent that the operations were undertaken to fulfil a prime purpose of the United Nations, that is, to promote and to maintain a peaceful settlement of the situation.   This being true, the Secretary–General properly exercised the authority given him to incur financial obligations of the Organization and expenses resulting from such obligations must be considered "expenses of the Organization within the meaning of Article 17, paragraph 2."

* * *

The operations in the Congo were initially authorized by the Security Council in the resolution of 14 July 1960 which was adopted without a dissenting vote.   The resolution, in the light of the appeal from the Government of the Congo, the report of the Secretary–General and the debate in the Security Council, was clearly adopted with a view to maintaining international peace and security.   However, it is argued that that resolution has been implemented, in violation of provisions of the Charter inasmuch as under the Charter it is the Security Council that determines which States are to participate in carrying out decisions involving the maintenance of international peace and security, whereas in the case of the Congo the Secretary–General himself determined which States were to participate with their armed forces or otherwise.

* * *

The Security Council resolutions of 14 July, 22 July and 9 August 1960 were noted by the General Assembly in its resolution 1474 (ES–IV) of 20 September, adopted without a dissenting vote, in which it "fully supports" these resolutions. Again without a dissenting vote, on 21 Feb. 1961 the Security Council reaffirmed its three previous resolutions "and the General Assembly resolution 1474 (ES–IV) of 20 September 1960" and reminded "all States of their obligations under these resolutions".

Again without a dissenting vote on 24 November 1961 the Security Council, once more recalling the previous resolutions, reaffirmed "the policies and purposes of the United Nations with respect to the Congo (Leopoldville) as set out" in those resolutions. Operative paragraphs 4 and 5 of this resolution renew the authority to the Secretary–General to continue the activities in the Congo.

In the light of such a record of reiterated consideration, confirmation, approval and ratification by the Security Council and by the General Assembly of the actions of the Secretary–General in implementing the resolution of 14 July 1960, it is impossible to reach the conclusion that the operations in question usurped or impinged upon the prerogatives conferred by the Charter on the Security Council. The Charter does not forbid the Security Council to act through instruments of its own choice: under Article 29 it "may establish such subsidiary organs as it deems necessary for the performance of its functions"; under Article 98 it may entrust "other functions" to the Secretary–General.

It is not necessary for the Court to express an opinion as to which article or articles of the Charter were the basis for the resolutions of the Security Council, but it can be said that the operations of ONUC did not include a use of armed force against a State which the Security Council, under Article 39, determined to have committed an act of aggression or to have breached the peace. The armed forces which were utilized in the Congo were not authorized to take military action against any State. The operation did not involve "preventive or enforcement measures" against any State under Chapter VII and therefore did not constitute "action" as that term is used in Article 11.

[Thus,] financial obligations which, in accordance with the clear and reiterated authority of both the Security Council and the General Assembly, the Secretary–General incurred on behalf of the United Nations, constitute obligations of the Organization for which the General Assembly was entitled to make provision under the authority of Article 17.

* * *

The COURT is of opinion, by nine votes to five, that the expenditures authorized in General Assembly resolutions * * * relating to the U.N. operations in the Congo * * * and the expenditures authorized in General Assembly resolutions * * * relating to the operations of the U.N. Emergency Force constitute "expenses of the Organization" within the meaning of Article 17, paragraph 2, of the Charter.

[A declaration, separate opinions and dissenting opinions omitted.]

Aftermath of Certain Expenses Case. Although the General Assembly subsequently adopted a resolution in which it accepted the advisory opinion of the International Court of Justice, members that had refused to recognize peacekeeping expenses as expenses of the organization (principally France and the USSR) continued to refuse to accept the Court's interpretation of the Charter and became in arrears in their payments. The United States at first intended to force the application of Article 19, entailing the loss of vote by non-paying members. The Nineteenth Session of the General Assembly did business without formal voting to avoid the question. The issue was subsequently dropped. The members reserved their positions and a constitutional crisis was avoided.

---

c. The Middle East: The Role of Peacekeeping Forces

(1) UNITED NATIONS DISENGAGEMENT OBSERVER FORCE *(UNDOF)*

Genesis of the force. UNDOF was created in 1974. It had its roots in the continuous flow of hostilities in the Middle East. You have considered material on the Suez Crisis, which was the impetus for the creation of the first U.N. peace-keeping force (UNEF). Tension decreased after the UNEF force withdrew and was replaced by UAR (Egyptian) forces. Immediately after the withdrawal, at the request of Egypt of the U.N. Emergency Force in 1967, Israel launched a broad-scale offensive against Egypt and Syria which resulted in territorial gains. Following the termination of hostilities, the Security Council adopted Resolution 242 (1967) detailing the principles deemed requisite to peace in that area. But hostilities were begun again in 1973, this time on the initiative of Egypt and Syria. The Security Council adopted Resolution 338 (1973), calling for a cease fire and for the implementation of the principles in Resolution 242 (1967). After Israel and Syria entered into an agreement of disengagement, pursuant to Security Council Resolution 338 (1973), the Council authorized the establishment of the *U.N. Disengagement Observer Force.* As has been its custom in the establishment of such forces, the Council put a short time limit on its authorization, subject to renewal. Three relevant resolutions were issued by the Security Council. The meaning of the resolution on principles has been the subject of debate: Resolution 242 affirms the principle of Israeli withdrawal from "territories occupied in the recent conflict;" it does not call for withdrawal from "all territories" or "the territories."   See Rostow, *The Illegality of the Arab Attack on Israel of October 6, 1973,* 69 AJIL 272 (1975)).

After the 1967 War, the Security Council's Resolution 242 enunciated two "principles:" that the Israeli forces withdraw "from the territories occupied in the recent conflict" (*French version: "[r]etrait des forces armées israéliennes des territoires occupés lor du récent conflit"*); and "[t]ermination of all claims or states of belligerency and respect for and acknowledgment of the sovereignty, territorial integrity and political independence of every State in the area and their right to live in peace within secure and recognized boundaries free from threats or acts of force."   Resolution 242 failed to produce peaceful settlement and Israel retained the territories occupied in the '67 War.   This caused Egypt, Syria and Iraq to launch, in 1973, an attack on Israel, which was repelled after some initial success.   The Security Council issued Resolution 338 (1973), which called upon the parties to "cease all firing and terminate all military activity immediately, no later than 12 hours after the moment of the adoption of this decision * * *; [T]o start immediately after the cease-fire the implementation of res. 242 (1967)," *supra;* and "that negotiations shall start between the parties * * * aimed at establishing a just and durable peace in the Middle East."   Security Council Resolution 340 (1973), established the U.N. Emergency Force (UNEF). Security Council Resolution 350 (1974) established the U.N. Disengagement Observer Force (UNDOF), with the strength of 1,250 individuals. UNDOF was charged with monitoring the disengagement that Israel had finally accepted in agreements with Egypt and Syria and to occupy the buffer zone between Israel and Syria (the Golan Heights).

The provisions of the agreements, which were stated not to be "peace agreements," included the cease-fire, the separation of the forces and an agreement not to have military forces in this buffer zone. Monitoring and inspection were to be done by UNDOF.   UNDOF was to have freedom of movement and communication required for its mission, was to be supplied with defensive weapons, but was required to comply with pertinent Syrian law and regulations and was not to hamper local civil administration.   UNDOF was under the command of the United Nations, executed by the Secretary–General under the authority of the Security Council.   The initial authorization was for six-months, renewable by the Security Council.   See, *Establishment of the U.N. Disengagement Observer Force* (UNDOF), 1974 Yb.U.N. 198, 199.   The mandate of UNDOF has been extended so that it continues to monitor the Golan Heights.

(2) *United Nations Interim Force in Lebanon (UNIFIL)*

In March of 1978, another U.N. peacekeeping force was established in the Middle East.   The United Nations Interim Force in Lebanon (UNIFIL), was created to oversee and confirm the withdrawal of Israeli "forces from all Lebanese territory, to restore international peace and security," and to assist "the Government of Lebanon in ensuring the return of its effective authority in the area * * *."   [S.C.Res. 425 (1978)].   UNIFIL remains today, having had its mandate extended. Some background follows.

THE SITUATION IN THE ISRAEL—LEBANON SECTOR

32 Yearbook of the United Nations 295, 296 (1978).

In a letter * * * to the Secretary–General, the representative of Israel charged that * * * a terrorist murder squad dispatched by the Palestine Liberation Organization (PLO) had infiltrated the Israeli coastline and carried out an indiscriminate attack against Israeli civilians along the Haifa–Tel Aviv highway, resulting in 37 dead and 76 wounded. The letter also contained excerpts from a statement by the Prime Minister of Israel in his press conference. * * * The Chief of Staff of UNTSO reported heavy Israeli ground, naval and air activity * * *. There were bombing attacks by Israeli forces to Beirut and against a Palestinian refugee camp south of Beirut, shelling in the vicinity of Tyre from Israeli naval vessels, and air attacks; mortar, artillery and tank fire were impacting in and around several other targets along the Lebanese frontier. All UNTSO personnel were reported to be safe.

In letters * * * to the President of the Security Council and the Secretary–General, the representative of Lebanon charged that * * *, Israel had committed an aggression against Lebanese territory, during which massive numbers of Israeli troops crossed into Lebanon from several axes, patrol vessels penetrated Lebanese territorial waters along the coastline from Tyre to Sidon, and Israeli warplanes bombarded several areas in Lebanese territory. An undetermined number of citizens were killed, notably in Tyre, and enormous damage was caused to property. He also stressed that Lebanon had no connection with the commando operation on the Haifa–Tel Aviv highway, that it was not responsible for the presence of Palestinian bases in southern Lebanon, and that the only solution to the problem lay in putting an end to Israeli aggression and in Israel's withdrawing its forces from Lebanon.

* * *

In a statement to the Council, the representative of Lebanon accused Israel of having committed a savage act of aggression against his country and urged the Council to demand the immediate cessation of hostilities and the withdrawal of the invaders. The United Nations should be enabled to uphold its Charter, he added, and prevent Israel from taking international law into its own hands and acting as judge, jury and executioner while the community of nations idly watched Lebanon's agony. He stressed the need for restoring the peace, restoring Lebanese sovereignty over its territory and re-establishing an acceptable international order in the Middle East.

The representative of Israel said he was convinced that the debate was unnecessary, since both parties involved in the issue wanted the same thing—the complete restoration of Lebanese sovereignty in the area in question. He charged the United Nations with blatant partiality vis-a-vis his country and regretted that neither the General Assembly nor the Security Council had issued a statement encouraging the peace talks between Israel and Egypt or urging their extension to Israel's other neighbours. Israel Defence Forces had crossed into Lebanon as a measure to deal with terror and terrorists, he continued, in carrying out Israel's inherent duty to exercise its right to self-defence in the protection of the inviolability of its territory and its people. He deplored the aid given by some Arab States and the USSR to PLO and maintained that the aim of the Israeli operation was not retaliation or to seize territory but to clear PLO from the area of southern Lebanon, bordering on Israel, where an absence of law and order reigned and over which the Lebanon Government had lost control, and to create conditions in which the Government of Lebanon could restore control and re-establish its sovereign right in the area.

* * *

REPORT OF THE SECRETARY–GENERAL

36 Yearbook of the United Nations 6 (1982).

* * *

Peace-keeping operations have generally been considered to be one of the most successful innovations of the United Nations, and certainly their record over the years is one of which to be proud. They have proved to be a most useful instrument of de-escalation and conflict control and have extended the influence of the Security Council into the field in a unique way. I may add that U.N. peace-keeping operations have traditionally shown an admirable degree of courage, objectivity and impartiality. This record, which is a great credit to the Organization, is sometimes overlooked in the heat of partisanship. The limitations of peace-keeping operations are less well understood. Thus when a peace-keeping operation is overrun or brushed aside, the credibility both of the United Nations and of peace-keeping operations as such is severely shaken.

It is not always realized that peace-keeping operations are the visible part of a complex framework of political and diplomatic efforts and of countervailing pressures designed to keep the peace-keeping efforts and related peace-making efforts effective. It is assumed that the Security Council itself and those Member States in a position to bring influence to bear will be able to act decisively to ensure respect for decisions of the Council. If this framework breaks down, as it did for example in Lebanon last June, there is little that a United Nations peace-keeping force can by itself do to rectify the situation. Indeed, in such circumstances it tends to become the scapegoat.

Peace-keeping operations can function properly only with the co-operation of the parties and on a clearly defined mandate from the Security Council. They are based on the assumption that the parties, in accepting a United Nations peace-keeping operation, commit themselves to co-operating with it. This commitment is also required by the Charter, under which all concerned have a clear obligation to abide by the decisions of the Council. United Nations peace-keeping operations are not equipped, authorized, or indeed made available, to take part in military activities other than peace-keeping. Their main strength is the will of the international community which they symbolize. Their weakness comes to light when the political assumptions on which they are based are ignored or overridden.

I recommend that Member States, especially the members of the Security Council, should again study urgently the means by which our peace-keeping operations could be strengthened. An increase in their military capacity or authority is only one possibility—a possibility which may well give rise in some circumstances to serious political and other objections. Another possibility is to underpin the authority of peace-keeping operations by guarantees, including explicit guarantees for collective or individual supportive action. In recent months, two multinational forces were set up outside the framework of the United Nations to perform peace-keeping tasks, because of opposition to United Nations involvement either within or outside the Security Council. While understanding the circumstances which led to the establishment of these forces, I find such a trend disturbing because it demonstrates the difficulties the Security Council encounters in fulfilling its responsibilities as the primary organ for the maintenance of international peace and security in the prevailing political conditions.

* * *

Multinational forces outside the framework of the United Nations.

1. *The Sinai Multinational Force and Observers.* This force was established to implement provisions of the 1979 Treaty of Peace between Egypt and Israel. The United States contributed personnel to the force. As explained to Congress by President Reagan:

> As you know, the 1979 Treaty of Peace between Egypt and Israel terminated the existing state of war between those countries, provided for the complete withdrawal from the Sinai of Israeli armed forces and civilians within three years after the date of the Treaty's entry into force (that is, by April 25, 1982), and provided for the establishment of normal friendly relations. To assist in assuring compliance with the terms of Annex I to the Treaty, so as to enhance the mutual confidence of the parties in the security of the Sinai border area, the Treaty calls for the establishment of a peacekeeping force and observers to be deployed prior to the final Israeli withdrawal. Although the Treaty called on the parties to request the United Nations to provide the peacekeeping force and observers, it was also recognized during the negotiations that it might not be possible to reach agreement in the United Nations for this purpose. For this reason, President Carter assured Israel and Egypt in separate letters that "if the Security Council fails to establish and maintain the arrangements called for in the Treaty, the President will be prepared to take those steps necessary to

ensure the establishment and maintenance of an acceptable alternative multinational force."

In fact, it proved impossible to secure U.N. action. As a result,
Egypt and Israel, with the participation of the United States, entered into negotiations for the creation of an alternative multinational force and observers. These negotiations resulted in the
signing on August 3, 1981 by Egypt and Israel of a Protocol for that
purpose. The Protocol established the MFO and provided in effect
that the MFO would have the same functions and responsibilities as
those provided in the 1979 Treaty for the planned U.N. force.
Included are: the operation of checkpoints, reconnaissance patrols,
and observation posts; verification of the implementation of Annex I
of the Peace Treaty; and ensuring freedom of navigation through
the Strait of Tiran in accordance with Article V of the Peace Treaty.
By means of an exchange of letters with Egypt and Israel, the
United States agreed, subject to Congressional authorization and
appropriations, to contribute an infantry battalion, a logistics support unit and civilian observers to the MFO, as well as a specified
portion of the annual costs of the MFO. The U.S. military personnel to be contributed comprise less than half of the anticipated total
MFO military complement of approximately 2,500 personnel. 76
AJIL 613 (1982).

2. ***The Multinational Force in Lebanon.*** The United States
entered into agreements in 1982 with the government of Lebanon for the
establishment of this force and contributed contingents along with
France, Italy and the United Kingdom. 78 AJIL 209 (1984).

----

d. *Cyprus*

The United Kingdom granted Cyprus its independence in 1960.
The circumstances of independence were difficult, because of vitriolic
conflict between Turkish and Greek Cypriot communities. *See,* Treaty
Concerning the Establishment of the Republic of Cyprus, August 16,
1960, 382 U.N.T.S. 8. Fighting erupted between the Greek and Turkish
Cypriot forces in December 1963. Greece supported the Greek Cypriot
forces, while Turkey supported those of the Turkish "Cypriot" community. This situation was extremely volatile. The Security Council, after
monitoring the situation for several weeks in early 1964, approved
Resolution 186, establishing a peacekeeping force (UNFICYP), which
was mandated "to prevent the recurrence of fighting, help maintain law
and order, and promote a return to normal conditions * * * "
[U.N.S.C.Res. 186, March 4, 1964]. Serious fighting, including air
strikes by Turkish air forces and ground attacks by the Greek Cypriots
continued until September 1964. Widespread fighting finally ceased, but
tensions have remained. UNFICYP resources have never been sufficient
to resolve the problem.

e. *Cambodia*

The Cambodians have suffered more than twenty years of civil war among at least four factions, preceded by saturation bombing by the U.S. during the Vietnam War. Cambodians have suffered interventions, genocide, and a series of gross violations of their human rights. Norodom Sihanouk, Cambodia's hereditary king, was overthrown. Later, the Kampuchean Communist Party (the Khmer Rouge) gained control of Cambodia in 1975 and renamed it Democratic Kampuchea, ruling from April 1975 until January 1979, when it was ousted by Vietnamese troops. During this four year period, the regime attempted total restructuring of the Khmer society, rejected all foreign influences, tried to create an agrarian economy, committed atrocities of a nature to constitute one of the worst examples of state-sponsored slaughter and other violations of human rights known to have occurred in this century. This ultimately resulted in the execution, starvation or death by disease or exhaustion of a significant portion of the Cambodian people. The 1979 Vietnamese invasion established the People's Republic of Kampuchea. The ousted Khmer Rouge occupied small rural enclaves principally close to the Thai–Cambodian border, while hundreds of thousands of Cambodians fled to Thailand and the West. The Vietnamese forces retained control throughout the 1980's, despite protestations and a call by the U.N. General Assembly to withdraw all "foreign forces." GA Res. 34/22, UN GAOR, 34th Sess., Supp. No. 46, at 16, UN Doc. A/34/46 (1979).

In 1980, the General Assembly convened an international conference to find "a comprehensive political settlement of the Kampuchean problem," [G.A.Res. 35/6, UN GAOR, 35th Sess., Supp. No. 48, at 13, 14, UN Doc. A/35/48 (1980)]. The Conference met in New York during July of 1981. It was attended by 79 states, including Democratic Kampuchea, but was boycotted by Vietnam and states aligned with the USSR. The General Assembly subsequently passed annual resolutions and Indonesia convened the Jakarta Informal Meeting (JIM I and II), initiating a process of reconciliation.

Vietnam announced troop withdrawal in April 1989 to be completed by the end of September. The French and Indonesian Governments agreed in 1989 to convene another international conference aimed at reaching a comprehensive settlement. This Paris Conference on Cambodia included the four Cambodian factions and the ASEAN States, the five permanent members of the UN Security Council, Vietnam, Laos, Japan, Australia, India and Canada. Zimbabwe was invited to represent the non-aligned States. This Conference finally led to several agreements. [See, Paris Peace Conference on Cambodian Agreements Elaborating the Framework for a Comprehensive Political Settlement of the Cambodian Conflict, UN Doc. A/46/608 and S/233177, reprinted in 31 I.L.M. 174 (1992)].

One of these agreements was to establish a Supreme National Council (SNC) made-up of the four formerly warring factions, to be the "unique * * * source of authority" in Cambodia, embodying Cambodian sovereignty. The SNC agreed to allow the U.N. to establish UNTAC, the U.N. Transitional Authority in Cambodia (ultimately composed of 15,000 individuals) to oversee the disarmament of the factions, to supervise free elections, and to provide some civil administrative services, including the functioning of at least five ministries. It has access to all governmental documents, to issue binding directives, and has control of all personnel. SNC and UNTAC are intertwined and present an unprecedented feature for international law. SNC virtually ran Cambodia.

Questions: Did Cambodia become a trusteeship? If so, was that legal? See U.N. Charter Articles 77 and 78. The Security Council did not authorize any Chapter VII action to "restore international peace" in the region. Did the "nation" of Cambodia delegate power to the U.N.? Was there a single government in Cambodia accepted by all factions and able to delegate power? Was such an "entity" ingeniously created by the Comprehensive Settlement Agreement in the Supreme National Council (SNC)? The latter was defined by the agreement as the, "unique legitimate body and source of authority in which, throughout the transitional period, the sovereignty, independence and unity of Cambodia are enshrined ..." and provides that the SNC would represent Cambodia externally during this transitional period. [Comprehensive Settlement Agreement, arts. 3 and 5]. What institution would have jurisdiction if [when] SNC forces committed crimes (including crimes against humanity?) There is evidence that such conduct has occurred without appropriate resolution.

SNC is sui generis in international law. To pose the questions raised earlier, some world leaders have suggested that the triple crises of Somalia, Bosnia, and Cambodia indicate that sovereignty and national self-determination are insufficient by themselves as guiding principles for international conduct. See, Boutros–Ghali, *Agenda for Peace,* stating: "[t]he time for absolute and exclusive sovereignty * * * has passed, * * * Its theory was never matched by reality." Does the Cambodian situation give credence to this proposition?

On November 14, 1993, the last official U.N. peacekeeping troops left Cambodia [CNN News, 11/14/93], pursuant to Security Council Resolution of August 1993, which called for a November 15th deadline for a safe and orderly withdrawal from Cambodia. King Norodom Sihanouk, once and future King of Cambodia, returned on September 23rd, 1993, to sign his nations's Constitution that will make him monarch once again. This completed the prerequisites for the withdrawal of the U.N. Peacekeeping force. *See,* Reuters, Limited, September 23, 1993, Sihanouk Returns to Cambodia to Become King Again; Xinhua General News Service, August 27, 1993, Item No. 0827014, Westlaw. Thus, ended the most expensive United Nations peace-keeping effort to date. *See,* Ratner, *The Cambodia Settlement Agreements,* 87 A.J.I.L. 1, 3–14 (1993) (from which most of this summary was developed); Quinn, The Pattern and Scope of Violence, in Cambodia 1975–1978 Rendezvous With Death (Karl D. Jackson ed. 1989); Chanda, Brother Enemy: The War After the War (1986); Kampuchea: Decade of the Genocide (R. Kiljunen ed. 1984). Consider the following in relation to peace-keeping forces in Cambodia and other places. Parker, *Cultural Autonomy: A Prime Directive for the Blue Helmets,* 55 U.Pitt.L.Rev. 207, 208 (1993) (footnotes omitted).*

---

* Reprinted with the permission of the U.Pitt.L.Rev.

United Nations forces increasingly are being used and promoted as tools for humanitarian intervention. The demise of the Cold War provided the catalyst for this development, resulting concurrently in a shift in international attention to the political and humanitarian concerns of individual nations, and the development of a cooperative ability within the U.N. Security Council to address those concerns using United Nations forces. As this method of intervention gains favor, important questions regarding the human rights of a subject nation's citizens, both individual and collective, must be answered.

Certain stories emerging from nations currently occupied by U.N. forces raise a subset of these questions—those relating to cultural rights. The effect of the 22,000 person United Nations Transitional Authority in Cambodia ("UNTAC") goes far beyond its official mission of preparing for elections and securing the peace. Newspaper reports describe upheavals in the economic, social, and legal life of Cambodians incidentally caused by UNTAC's authorized actions. UNTAC employees have created an unsustainable, artificial economy, luring farmers and others to Phnom Penh from their traditional vocations. Prostitution, previously almost unknown, is rampant in the larger cities. UNTAC's presence also is forcing changes in Cambodian educational practices, particularly in the language of instruction. The media, a key conduit of culture, is controlled by UNTAC monitors.

Queries: Are these concerns justified? Do similar concerns arise in other areas, such as Somalia? The Security Council Resolutions for Somalia are presented in the Doc. Supp. Analyze them. Relating the material on international peacekeeping forces and United States law, would the timing provisions of the War Powers Resolution be triggered if U.S. forces were participating in such an operation and hostilities commenced between belligerents. See Chapter 17. On Peacekeeping generally, see: Durch & Blechman, Keeping the Peace: The United Nations in the Emerging World Order (1992).

4. USE OF UNITED NATIONS AUTHORITY NOT INVOLVING MILITARY FORCE

a. *Southern Rhodesia*

Although Southern Rhodesia (now Zimbabwe) was largely a self-governing territory rather than strictly a colony in the British system, it was not fully independent until the 1960s. Because it was governed by a white majority, the United Kingdom was unwilling to grant it independence until satisfactory constitutional arrangements were arrived at in Rhodesia to provide improvements in the political powers of the black minority. Negotiations between the British and the governing regime in Southern Rhodesia having failed, Southern Rhodesia declared its independence on November 11, 1965 (an act referred to as Unilateral Declaration of Independence or UDI). The General Assembly immediately requested the Security Council to take-up the Rhodesian question as a "matter of urgency." (G.A.Res. 2024, 1965).

A series of resolutions in the Security Council condemned UDI, called on the United Kingdom to quell the rebellion and specifically called on the United Kingdom to prevent, by force if necessary, the delivery of oil by tankers destined for Rhodesia. Security Council Resolutions 216 and 217 [a] (1965) of November 12, 1965 and 221 [b] (1966) of April 9, 1966. Selective sanctions were voted by the Council in Resolution 232,[c] December 16, 1966. Stating that it was acting in accordance with Articles 39 and 41 of the Charter, the Council determined "that the present situation in Southern Rhodesia constitutes *a threat to international peace and security*." [Emphasis supplied.] The Council thereupon decided that all States Members of the United Nations shall prevent:

(a) the import into their territories of asbestos, iron ore, chrome, pig-iron, sugar, tobacco, copper, meat and meat products and hides, skins and leather originating in Southern Rhodesia and exported therefrom after the date of this resolution;

(b) any activities by their nationals or in their territories which promote or are calculated to promote the export of their commodities from Southern Rhodesia and any dealings by their nationals or in their territories in any of these commodities originating in Southern Rhodesia and exported therefrom after the date of this resolution, including in particular any transfer of funds to Southern Rhodesia for the purposes of such activities or dealings.

* * *

These measures having failed, the Council adopted more comprehensive sanctions two years later.

———

* * *

The Security Council called for selective sanctions in 1966. Two years later, the Security Council, in Resolution 253, noted the failure of these sanctions to bring the "rebellion in Southern Rhodesia to an end," called for the following sanctions, pursuant to article 25 of the Charter: a total economic blockade (inter alia, no importation of Rhodesian goods and no exportation to Rhodesia or even any activity tending to promote economic or commercial exchange or trade); cultural and political isolation, including preventing airline registration or operation to or from Rhodesia. The sanctions were finally lifted in December 1979. The dispute finally ended with an agreement reached at the Lancaster House Conference in London. The Security Council, on December 21, 1979,

a. Resolutions and Decisions of the Security Council 1965. U.N.Sec.Council Off. Rec., 20th Year, p. 8.

b. Resolutions and Decisions of the Security Council 1966. U.N.Sec.Council Off. Rec., 21st Year, p. 5.

c. Resolutions and Decisions of the Security Council 1966. U.N.Sec.Council Off. Rec., 21st Year, p. 7.

called upon Member States of the United Nations "to terminate the measures taken against Southern Rhodesia under Chapter VII of the Charter pursuant to resolutions 232 (1966), 253 (1968) and subsequent related resolutions * * *." Ultimately Zimbabwe became indpendent and a multi-racial nation.

* * *

b.   South Africa: Apartheid

The racial situation in South Africa concerned the United Nations since its founding. For years numerous resolutions directed toward the abolition of the system of racial separation (apartheid) in that country produced no discernible effect. *See,* for example, the General Assembly resolution and debate in Chapter 10 on human rights. In 1963, the members of the Security Council apparently decided that persuasion and exhortation were insufficient to correct at least one aspect of that country's policies. Resolution 181 (1963), the text of which is in the Documentary Supplement was adopted calling upon states to impose an arms embargo. Note the concern of the United States representative with the question of the legal basis under the Charter for the Council's action. The Council imposed a mandatory embargo by its 1977 resolution, the text of which is also in the Documentary Supplement. Read the resolutions carefully and answer the following questions. What was the legal basis for that action? Had the United States changed its position on the law, or on the facts? Note the legal position taken by South Africa with respect to the council's action.

The Security Council reiterated its condemnation of Apartheid in Resolution 282 (1970), as "evil and abhorrent policies * * * and the measures being taken by the Government of South Africa to enforce and extend those policies beyond its borders * * *." It noted that "the situation resulting from the continued application of the policies of apartheid and the constant build-up of the South African military and police forces * * * constitut[ed] a potential threat to international peace and security; and recogniz[ed] that the extensive arms build-up of the military force of South Africa poses a real threat to the security and sovereignty of independent African States opposed to the racial policies of the Government of South Africa * * *." Finally, the Security Council reiterated its call for the 1963 voluntary arms embargo. The Security Council adopted Resolution 418, in 1977, portions of which are in the Doc. Supp.

STRICT IMPLEMENTATION OF 1977 ARMS EMBARGO
AGAINST SOUTH AFRICA ASKED BY COUNCIL

24 UN Chronicle No. 1 (1987), p. 46.

The Security Council on 28 November asked States to implement strictly its 1977 mandatory arms embargo against South Africa and urged them to ensure that components of items included in that embargo did not reach the South African military establishment and police through third countries. States were also asked to refrain from any co-operation in the nuclear field with South Africa which would contribute to the manufacture and development by that country of nuclear weapons or nuclear explosive devices. The Council acted by adopting by consensus resolution 591 (1986), the text of which had been recommended by its Committee on sanctions against South Africa, formally known as the "Security Council Committee established by resolution 421 (1977) concerning the question of South Africa".

* * *

In resolution 591, States were called on to prohibit the export of spare parts for embargoed aircraft and other military equipment belonging to South Africa and any official involvement in the maintenance and service of such equipment. States were urged to ban export to South Africa of items which they had reason to believe were destined for its military and/or police forces, which had a military capacity and which were intended for military purposes—aircraft, aircraft engines, aircraft parts, electronic and telecommunication equipment, computers and four-wheel drive vehicles. The Council asked States to ensure that their national legislation or comparable policy directives guaranteed that specific provisions to implement resolution 418 included penalties to deter violations. States were also asked to adopt measures to investigate violations, prevent future circumventions and strengthen their machinery for the implementation of resolution 418 with a view to the effective monitoring and verification of transfers of arms and other equipment in violation of the arms embargo.

The embargo should, the Council stated, include—in addition to all nuclear, strategic and conventional weapons—all military, paramilitary police vehicles and equipment, "as well as weapons and ammunitions, spare parts and supplies for the aforementioned and the sale or transfer thereof". It renewed its request to States to refrain from importing arms, ammunition of all types and military vehicles produced in South Africa. States were called upon to prohibit the import or entry of all South African armaments for display in international fairs and exhibitions under their jurisdiction; to end exchanges as well as visits and exchanges of visits by government personnel, when such visits and exchanges maintained or increased South Africa's military or police capabilities; and to refrain from participating in any activities in South Africa which they had reason to believe might contribute to Pretoria's military capability. States, including those not United Nations members, were asked to act in accordance with the provisions of the resolution. * * *

* * *

Mr. Alleyne (Trinidad and Tobago) said that, while some countries had observed the letter and the spirit of Council resolutions providing for the prevention of arms shipments to South Africa, the embargo had itself been "something of a leaky barrier through which arms and military technology for bolstering a domestic arms industry in South Africa have flowed freely". The resolution sought to secure full implementation of the embargo by recommending measures to close loopholes in it, to reinforce it and to make it more effective.

* * *

Resistance to mandatory sanctions. In Resolution 569 of 1985, the Security Council voted for a series of voluntary sanctions against South Africa. The resolution: * * *

6. Urges States Members of the Organization to adopt measures against South Africa, such as the following:

(a) Suspension of all new investment in South Africa;

(b) Prohibition of the sale of krugerrands and all other coins minted in South Africa;

(c) Restrictions in the field of sports and cultural relations;

(d) Suspension of guaranteed export loans;

(e) Prohibition of all new contracts in the nuclear field;

(f) Prohibition of all sales of computer equipment that may be used by the South African army and police;

* * *

The resolution was adopted by a vote of thirteen to none, but with the United Kingdom and the United States abstaining.

In May, 1986, a resolution was proposed, declaring that South Africa's acts and policies were "a threat to international peace and security." Under this resolution, the sanctions listed in Resolution 569 would now become mandatory. The resolution failed by reason of the votes against it by the United Kingdom and the United States (with France abstaining). These three states explained their positions as follows (23 UN Chronicle, No. 4 (1986), p. 29):

* * * The United States said it could not support a call for imposition of mandatory sanctions. All States should be able to decide for themselves what measures were most appropriate "as we pursue our common goal of destroying apartheid".

The destruction of the South African economy served no one's interests, least of all those who suffered under apartheid. A severance of economic ties would lead ineluctably to severance of political ones, depriving the United States of any leverage over Pretoria, and depriving the international community of any ability to work for the timely and complete dismantling of apartheid. The United States would not turn its back on the millions of blacks in South Africa and on a growing number of whites there who looked to the West to lead the South African Government out of its "crude and inhuman" political system into one where the voice of the majority participated directly in the formulation of national and international policy.

The United Kingdom said the draft contained "unacceptable" passages. It would have voted for all its provisions except that calling for sanctions. It regretted that the draft's sponsors would not accept a paragraph-by-paragraph vote. Nothing must be done to undermine the chances of a successful outcome, however hard to achieve, to the Commonwealth initiative to peacefully abolish apartheid. The United Kingdom would not take short-term steps which might endanger that long-term and fundamental goal. France said there were no grounds for replacing national measures with mandatory sanctions.

* * *

Questions: The sanctions apparently helped cause at least a temporary financial crisis in South Africa in 1985 and brought pressure to bear upon the Government. The legislation establishing and promoting apartheid was slowly repealed throughout the latter part of the 1980's; sanctions were concomitantly eliminated. Finally, in mid–1993, Nelson Mandela has called for the elimination of the economic sanctions, and in April 1993, was elected President of South Africa, in the first elections in which all were able to participate.

c. Libya

LIBYA AND THE AERIAL INCIDENT AT LOCKERBIE: WHAT LESSONS FOR INTERNATIONAL EXTRADITION LAW

14 Mich.J.Int'l L. 222 (1993) by Christopher C. Joyner & Wayne P. Rothbaum.*

On December 21, 1988, Pan American Flight 103 took off from London's Heathrow Airport on its transatlantic flight to John F. Kennedy Airport in New York. At 6:56 P.M. EST, at an altitude of 31,000 feet, the Maid of the Seas made its last contact with ground control. Seven minutes later, the green cross-hair at air traffic control split into five bright blips as Pan Am Flight 103 exploded in midair. Her fiery skeleton, laden with the bodies of passengers and crew, rained down on the people of Lockerbie, Scotland. Within the hour, 243 passengers, 16 crew members, and 11 townspeople were dead.

* Reprinted by Permission, Michigan J. Int'l Law.

Nearly three years later, following extensive international investigations, the United States indicted two Libyan intelligence officers in November 1991 for the bombing of Pan Am Flight 103. The Libyan response to informal extradition claims was not unexpected: the government refused to surrender the officers on the grounds that such an act constituted direct interference in Libya's internal affairs.

In January 1992, and again in March 1992, the United Nations Security Council responded to the Libyan position with two resolutions: the first urged the government of Colonel Muammar el-Qadhafi to cooperate with the international investigation of the bombing; the second imposed sanctions on Libya for its failure to comply with the Security Council's requests. Taken together as legal prescriptions, the Security Council's actions marked the first time that the United Nations had ever demanded extradition of nationals of one State to face trial in a second State, despite the existence of international legal principles supporting Libya's position to refuse extradition of its nationals.

The U.N. Security Council resolutions in the Lockerbie case represent a salient, albeit as yet unconsummated, step toward strengthening the international extradition process for dealing with alleged terrorist acts. In the past, international fugitives who committed unlawful acts abroad often found sanctuary behind the political veils of customary and codified law, evading extradition with the shield of State sovereignty. The lack of a universally accepted rule of law has left extradition to bilateral treaties and acts of reciprocity and comity, which provide only malleable standards that States can interpret and reinterpret to suit their needs. The subjective nature of "relative" political acts, coupled with differing State penal laws and judicial systems, has further hampered the process of transnational extradition.

The Security Council's concerted action to compel legal cooperation from Libya provokes inquiry into whether supreme authority over extradition in the international community may be shifting slowly away from State sovereignty and toward the collective will of the United Nations. Although the full impact of the council resolutions is not yet known, such collective action is appropriate for particularly notorious cases, such as the Lockerbie bombing, fraught with myriad political complications.

The Lockerbie incident provides a means both for highlighting customary norms within the international extradition process and analyzing the legal implications of Security Council resolutions—for Libya in particular, but also for international law in general. Does concerted action taken by the U.N. Security Council against Libya bolster the international extradition process? Or do these resolutions represent little more than a new coat of legal paint on the same old political problems?

* * *

Libya, the Security Council & the World Court: *Does the International Court of Justice have the power of judicial review to* *challenge the validity of Security Council actions?*   While the issue was averted for the moment, the aftermath of the Lockerbie incident and the Libyan claim before the International Court of Justice revealed that possibility.   Geoffrey Watson notes that Libya recently challenged the view that the International Court of Justice has no power of judicial review by initiating an action "to enjoin the United States from pressing its claim for the extradition of the two Libyan nationals accused in the 1988 bombing of Pan Am flight 103 over Lockerbie, Scotland [Libya v. [U.S.] & U.K., 1992 I.C.J. 3 (Provisional Measures Order of April 14, 1992)].   Libya contended that the Security Council resolutions ordering extradition were ultra vires (and therefore invalid) because they disregarded a fundamental principle of international law—that a state cannot be forced to extradite its own nationals.   While a majority of the Court rejected Libya's request for provisional relief, a number of concurring and dissenting judges expressed a willingness to examine the validity of Security Council actions.   The majority opinion thus averted a potential constitutional confrontation between two organs of the United Nations, but the concurring and dissenting opinions suggest that such a confrontation is possible in the future."   Watson, *Constitutionalism, Judicial Review, The World Court,* 34 Harv.Int'l L.J. 1, 3 (1993).

THOMAS M. FRANCK, EDITORIAL COMMENT, THE "POWERS OF APPRECIATION": WHO IS THE ULTIMATE GUARDIAN OF UN LEGALITY?

86 AJIL 519, 520–23 (1992) (footnotes omitted).*

The Libyan case was based on the asserted illegality of U.S. (and UK) actions in demanding the extradition of Libyan citizens to stand trial in the United States or the United Kingdom.   The Council had first decided that the Libyan Government must surrender its two nationals accused of the Lockerbie bombing; then, after the Court's oral argument but before its decision, it imposed universal mandatory commercial and diplomatic sanctions to secure compliance.   In effect, Libya's request for interim relief invited the Court to decide that these Security Council resolutions might be *ultra vires* and thus sanctions would impose irreparable injuries.   In particular, Libya argued that, by its resolutions, "the Security Council infringes, or threatens to infringe, the enjoyment and the exercise of the rights conferred on Libya by the Montreal Convention and its economic, commercial and diplomatic rights."

Article 5(2) of the Montreal Convention for the Suppression of Unlawful Acts against the Safety of Civil Aviation of 1971, to which over 140 nations including Libya and the United States are parties, requires each state party either to take jurisdiction over persons present in its territory who are alleged to have committed acts of terrorism against a civil aircraft, or to extradite them to a state which has, and is willing to exercise, such jurisdiction.   Libya asserted that it had already taken the steps necessary for "complying in full with that Convention," having "submitted the case to its competent authorities for the purpose of prosecution."   Relying on those assertions, Libya asked the Court to

---

* Reprinted with the permission of the American Society of Int'l Law.

conclude that the Security Council's resolutions are "contrary to international law" and that "the Council has employed its power to characterize the situation for purposes of Chapter VII simply as a pretext to avoid applying the Montreal Convention."

The Libyan Application essentially left the Court with three jurisprudential choices. It could have held that the sanctions ordered by Resolution 748 should be suspended until such time as the Court ascertained, at the merits stage, that Libya's claim was groundless. Or it could have decided that, since no sufficient case of *mala fides* or *ultra vires* had been established by Libya at this preliminary stage, there were no grounds upon which the Court could order such interim relief. Or, third, the Court could have held that no relief would be forthcoming at any stage of the proceedings if granting that relief would require the Court to make a finding that a chapter VII decision of the Security Council exceeded its lawful authority. It will be evident that the first two of these three options assume an implicit right of judicial review, albeit leading to opposite results, while the third assumes judicial restraint or abdication.

What did the Court's majority choose to do? It appears to have elected, if rather softly, the *second* option. The very brief majority opinion appears to turn on a finding that "both Libya and the United States, as Members of the United Nations, are obliged to accept and carry out the decisions of the Security Council in accordance with Article 25 of the Charter," including the obligations imposed by Security Council Resolution 748. It concludes, further, that "the obligations of the Parties in that respect prevail over their obligations under any other international agreement, including the Montreal Convention." This conclusion the majority reaches by an interpretation of the effect of Charter Article 103.

Most significant, however, as also in Marbury v. Madison, is what the Court left unsaid. As in *Marbury,* the Court superficially appears to accede to the broad discretionary power of the system's political "branch." But, as in Marbury, it accedes not by refusing to decide, but by exercising its power of decision. The Security Council's action in imposing sanctions is adjudged *intra vires* precisely because the majority of judges seems to agree that, for purposes of interim measures, Article 103 of the Charter "trumps" any rights Libya might have under the Montreal Convention, and thus frees the Security Council to apply sanctions as a suitable remedy in exercise of its powers under chapter VII. On the other hand, had Libya been able to allege a more general ground of *ultra vires* —that a coercive demand for extradition of a state's own national "could be deemed contrary * * * to protection of sovereign rights under general international law"—then, in the words of Acting President Oda, that "would have instituted a totally different litigation, and whether or not the Court has jurisdiction to deal with that issue is certainly a different matter." It is interesting to speculate what might have happened had Libya been a party to the Court's mandatory jurisdiction under Article 36(2) of its Statute and had it brought its action "under general international law" against Britain, as another party to 36(2), rather than under the Montreal Convention.

As it is, the interim measures decision represents a delicate balancing. As Judge Lachs noted in his separate opinion confirming the majority's result: "While the Court has the vocation of applying international law as a universal law, operating both within and outside the United Nations, it is bound to respect, as part of that law, the binding decisions of the Security Council." The operative verb is "respect"—not "defer to." The Court's decision, Lachs emphasized, "should not * * * be seen as an abdication of the Court's powers."

This carefully crafted nonabdication is succinctly put by the separate opinion, concurring in the majority's result, by Judge Shahabuddeen:

> The question now raised by Libya's challenge to the validity of resolution 748 (1992) is whether a decision of the Security Council may override the legal rights of States, and, if so, whether there are any limitations on the power of the Council to characterize a situation as one justifying the making of a decision entailing such consequences. Are there any limits to the Council's *powers of appreciation?* In the equilibrium of forces underpinning the structure of the United Nations within the evolving international order, is there any conceivable point beyond which a legal issue may properly arise as to the competence of the Security Council to produce such overriding results? If there are any limits, what are those limits and what body, if other than the Security Council, is competent to say what those limits are?

That is the nub of the matter, although the case exhibits many other interesting aspects. For example, one of those joining in the decision, as well as one dissenting judge, expressed the view that the United States was obliged by its recourse to the Security Council to renounce any right to take unilateral measures against Libya. Central, however, is the issue highlighted in the dissent of Judge Weeramantry: "does * * * the Security Council discharge[ ] its variegated functions free of all limitations, or is there a circumscribing boundary of norms or principles within which its responsibilities are to be discharged?" The majority and dissenting opinions seem to be in agreement that there are such limits and that they cannot be left exclusively to the Security Council to interpret. The legality of actions by any UN organ must be judged by reference to the Charter as a "constitution" of *delegated* powers. In extreme cases, the Court may have to be the last-resort defender of the system's legitimacy if the United Nations is to continue to enjoy the adherence of its members. This seems to be tacitly acknowledged judicial common ground. * * *

5. HUMANITARIAN INTERVENTION

a. *Recent Collective Use of Military Force—A Hybrid? Iraq, the Former Yugoslavia & Somalia*

Is the U.N. action in the territory of the former Yugoslavia the use of military force in the nature of that applied in the Korean Conflict? Is the use of force short of military force? Have the Security Council and the Secretary–General created a hybrid in Iraq, the former Yugoslavia and in Somalia? If so, is it legal or, if you will, constitutional under the U.N. scheme? Are there differences among these cases?

The General Assembly created, in 1991, a new position of *Undersecretary–General for Humanitarian Affairs.* Security Council Resolution 688 (1991), was issued in the wake of Iraq's suppression of its civilian population, particularly the Kurds and the Shiites. The Kurds had taken refuge in Turkey and Iran. Resolution 688 (found in the Documentary Supplement) requested the Secretary–General to pursue humanitarian efforts and to use all resources at his disposal, including those of the relevant U.N. agencies, to address urgently the critical needs of the refugees and displaced Iraqi population. Resolution 688 could be read broadly to support writers such as Professors Lillich, McDougal, Reisman, and Téson to support humanitarian intervention. Others, such as Brownlie, Henkin, and Schachter oppose the legality of humanitarian intervention. Does U.N. Charter article 2(4) allow it? If so, on what theory? Does international law permit intervention to promote democracy? See, Schachter, The Legality of Pro–Democratic Invasion, 78 A.J.I.L. 645 (1984); Reisman Coercion and Self–Determination: Construing Charter article 2(4), 78 A.J.I.L. 642 (1984); Halberstam, The Copenhagen Document: Intervention in Support of Democracy, 34 Harv. Int'l L.J. 163 (1993). The Security Council, in Resolution 770, August 13, 1992, authorized forcible humanitarian intervention in Bosnia–Herzegovina. Resolution 770 stated: "humanitarian assistance in Bosnia–Herzegovina is an important element in the Council's effort to restore international peace and security in the area * * *." It also called for states to facilitate relief by "all necessary measures," a euphemistic term of art, understood to include military action. While peace-keeping forces have been present and frequently have operated under great difficulty and with courage, U.N. presence has been ineffectual due to defiance by the various parties. Actual military intervention in the traditional sense has not occurred. *See* Arnison, International Law and non-Intervention: When do Humanitarian Concerns Supersede Sovereignty, 17 Fletcher For.Wld.Aff. 199, 204–05 (1993).

The Security Council specifically authorized military intervention in Somalia to establish "a secure environment for humanitarian relief efforts." This was also a hybrid situation, as the nature or status of Somalia as a state had dissipated or ceased to exist due to the non-existence of a viable government. *See,* The Retreat (U.S. Intervention in Somalia Wanes), The Economist 45(2) (Oct. 16, 1993), WL Mag–ASAP, MI file 47; International Law and non-Intervention, supra; and Jöst Delbruck, A Fresh Look at Humanitarian Intervention Under the Authority of the United Nations, 67 Ind.L.J. 887 (1993).

b. *Somalia*

Read the pertinent Security Council Resolutions in the Doc. Supp. Somalia was created from an ad hoc grouping of six major clans into one state created from the 1960 merger of two former European colonies. Siad Barré seized power in a 1969 coup d' état and ruled brutally for twenty-one years, until he was overthrown in 1991 by coalition forces made up of the various clans and sub-clans. Civil war ensued wherein no one clan or coalition was able to seize control. Various clans and sub-clans maintained power over various areas by controlling resources, such as food, medicine, ammunition and weapons. The general population suffered terribly from the "civil war" and by October 1992, some 4.5 million people were near starvation.

In August 1992, the Security Council called for 3,500 troops to be sent to Somalia to protect food and other relief supplies from the warring factions. [S.C.Res. 775, Aug. 1992]. The U.N. Operation in Somalia [UNOSOM] was created to implement S.C. Resolution 733 (January 1992), which had called for the "general and complete embargo on all deliveries of weapons and military equipment to Somalia." At least 300,000 individuals had already died by that time. UNOSOM was largely prevented from performing and conditions deteriorated. The Secretary–General expressed his concern in letters to the President of the Security Council in November 1992. [See, UN Docs. S/24859 and S/24868 and S/24868, which recalled earlier S.C. Resolutions 733, 746, 571, 676 and 755 (1992)]. The Secretary–General called for military action pursuant to Article 39 of the U.N. Charter. He stated that military force was required to disarm the warring factions and to ensure the success of UNOSOM. The United States offered to commit a force of 20,000 troops to safeguard relief supplies, maintaining that its role was to be limited to opening supply lines and, then, to turn the operation over to other U.N. peacekeeping forces. Finally, on December 3, 1992, the Security Council unanimously authorized the U.S.-led military, humanitarian intervention, to ensure the success of UNOSOM. [U.N. Security Council Resolution 794, S/Res/794, Dec. 3, 1992)]. The Resolution noted the hybrid and "unique character" of the circumstances in Somalia (essentially that there was no viable government, hence, no state) and emphasized the "magnitude of the human tragedy * * * " which constituted *a threat to international peace and security.* Id.

c. The Former Yugoslavia

See, *Chronology: Developments Related to the Crisis in Bosnia,* March 10—September 22, 1992, 3 Dep't St. Dispatch, Supp. No. 7, Sept. 1992, at 15. The United States has refused to extend recognition to the recently self-proclaimed nation-state, the Federal Republic of Yugoslavia, formed out of former Serbia and Montenegro on April 27, 1992, and following the dissolution of the former Yugoslavia. The "Yugoslav People's Army (JNA) attacked the Slovenian capital of Ljubljana, but the Secretary–General did not call for U.N. involvement, because this was "an internal affair." On the other hand, Bosnia–Herzegovina, Croatia, and Slovenia became members of the U.N. on May 22, 1992. *See, Note, Secession: State Practice and International Law After the Dissolution of the Soviet Union and Yugoslavia,* 3 Duke J.Comp. & Int'l L. 299, 325–26 (1993).

WELLER, THE INTERNATIONAL RESPONSE TO THE DISSOLUTION OF THE SOCIALIST FEDERAL REPUBLIC OF YUGOSLAVIA

86 A.J.I.L. 569 (1992).*

CURRENT DEVELOPMENTS

THE INTERNATIONAL RESPONSE TO THE DISSOLUTION OF
THE SOCIALIST FEDERAL REPUBLIC OF YUGOSLAVIA

The [former] Yugoslavia consisted of six republics (Slovenia, Croatia, Serbia, Bosnia–Hercegovina, Montenegro and Macedonia) and two autonomous regions (Kosovo and Vojvodina).[1] Its overall population was recently estimated as 23.69 million. There were 8.14 million Serbs, 4.43 million Croats, 1.75 million Slovenes, 1.73 million Albanians, 1.34 million Macedonians and 1.22 million "Yugoslavs," as well as a variety of other minorities.

Slovenia has a population of 1.94 million, 90 percent of whom are ethnic Slovenes. There are small minorities of ethnic Serbs, Croats and Hungarians.

Croatia, with a population of 4.68 million, 85 percent of whom are ethnic Croats, contains a minority of 11.5 percent ethnic Serbs who, in 14 of 102 internal administrative districts, constitute a local majority. Among the areas predominantly inhabited by ethnic Serbs are Krajina and Petrinja.

Serbia's population totals 9.8 million, two-thirds of whom are ethnic Serbs. It includes Vojvodina and Kosovo, two formerly autonomous territories that were incorporated into Serbia in September 1990. Vojvodina contains a Hungarian minority of some 21 percent and Kosovo is home to a local Albanian majority of 91 percent.

Montenegro has a population of 650,000; two-thirds are ethnic Montenegrins. There are minority Muslims and Albanians.

Bosnia–Hercegovina has a population of 4.1 million, of whom some 40 percent are Muslims, 32 percent Serbs and 18 percent Croats. The various elements of the population are intermingled and pocketed throughout the territory.*

Macedonia's population of 2.1 million is composed of 67 percent Macedonians, 20 percent Albanians and various other minorities.

The Federal Government was directed by a Presidential Council, or collective presidency, whose chairmanship rotated among the heads of the republics and autonomous territories. On September

---

* Reprinted with the permission of the American Society of Int'l Law.

1. The following account is based on Whitacker's Almanac 1992, at 877–78 (1991); Fischer Almanac 1992, at 90–92 (1991); and 1990–92 Keesing's Contemporary Archive.

* *Editor's Note:* Interestingly many of the Bosnian Muslims are actually ethnic Serbs whose ancestors were converted to Islam centuries ago. Croats, of course are mostly Catholic, while the "Serbs" are Orthodox. Thus, this is in many ways a *religious*, not ethnic war.

27, 1990, the Slovenian parliament declared that legislation promulgated by the federal institutions would no longer be applied within the republic. In a referendum, held on December 23 of that year, 88.5 percent of the Slovenian voters opted for independence. The day before, the Croatian parliament had proclaimed the supremacy of its legislation over federal law.

Negotiations among the republics to achieve a loose federation of fully or semisovereign states, carried on in the spring of 1991, failed, apparently owing to the intransigence of the Serbian leadership, which had hitherto dominated the political structure of the federation. According to the London *Times,* "The Croats and Slovenes wanted a loose federation that would dilute Serbian influence. The Serbians wanted a tighter federation to preserve its centralized control of the economy and its dominant role in Yugoslav life." When agreement "on the basic functions of the future Yugoslavia" was reached among the other republics, the Serbian member of the Presidential Council walked out.

The support for maintaining the territorial integrity of the federation voiced by representatives of influential states and organizations, including the United States, the European Community (EC) and its members, and the Conference on Security and Co-operation in Europe (CSCE), undoubtedly strengthened Slobodan Milosevic, the Serbian leader, in his perception that flexibility was not required in negotiations, since independence for Slovenia and Croatia was not supported internationally. Instead of offering to accept a looser confederation, the Serbian leadership had the central army declare martial law, a move that had been explicitly ruled out by the federal presidency, which acted, or should have acted, as commander in chief.

In May, the federal council failed to elect Stipe Mesic, a Croat who, under the constitutional arrangements of the federation, was supposed to have assumed the federal presidency. Serbia, Montenegro and the representatives of the two autonomous republics effectively blocked the vote, despite Croatia's threat to secede if Mesic was not elected. On May 19, 93.24 percent of the voters in Croatia opted for independence. That month, the United States suspended all economic assistance to Yugoslavia, including support in international financial institutions for loans and credits, yet still voiced staunch support for the maintenance of national unity. On June 21, U.S. Secretary of State James A. Baker III, while visiting Belgrade, strongly endorsed a declaration adopted two days earlier at the Berlin meeting of the CSCE, which expressed support for "democratic development and [the] territorial integrity of Yugoslavia."

By June 24, 1991, after further abortive attempts at negotiations regarding secession or a loose federation of sovereign states, the Yugoslav Prime Minister warned the authorities in Zagreb and Ljubljana that "the Federal Government will use all means available to stop the republics' unilateral steps towards independence." Nevertheless, Slovenia and Croatia declared independence a day later.

On June 27, the armed forces of the central authorities (JNA) left their barracks in Slovenia and, supported by a column of heavy armor brought in through Croatia, attacked the provisional Slovenian militia. The authorities in Slovenia proclaimed that a "state of war" existed and appealed for international assistance, including action by the EC, the CSCE and the United Nations.

As the EU and the CSCE (*The Conference on Security and Cooperation in Europe*) were preparing for what they hoped would be the final phase of the *Maastricht Summit* negotiations, neither was expecting, let alone prepared for, the crisis about to arise in the territory of the former Yugoslavia. Within 72 hours of the outbreak of war, the foreign ministers of Italy, Luxembourg and the Netherlands went to the former Yugoslavia in an attempt to obtain a cease-fire. Serbia soon (in July 1991) attacked Croatia, claiming that the ethnic serbian minority in Croatia had a right to self-determination and to secede. The fighting intensified and spread in 1992–93 to Bosnia–Herzegovina, where reports of Serbian atrocities, including "ethnic cleansing" and rape as a military and political strategy, starvation, and attacks on non-combatants were widely reported.

Despite the atrocities, the Security Council remained inactive for three months. When it finally met, the Council did not invoke article 2(4), and registered no conclusion that an "act of aggression" had occurred. The Security Council first adopted Resolution 713 (September 25, 1991), which called upon the EU and CSCE to work collectively for peace in the territory of the former Yugoslavia, pursuant to Chapter VII of the United Nations Charter. Resolution 713 provided that no territorial gains or advantages within the former Yugoslavia brought about by violence were acceptable and proclaimed that "the continuation of this situation constitutes a threat to international peace and security * * *." Further, it called for a general and complete embargo on all deliveries of weapons and military equipment to Yugoslavia until the Security Council decides otherwise * * *."

Former U.S. Secretary of State Cyrus Vance undertook to obtain an agreement for a "peace-keeping" operation in the territory of the former Yugoslavia. He called for the deployment of troops and police monitors in certain areas of Croatia, designated and deemed to be demilitarized "United Nations Protected Areas" (UNPAs). [See, Report of the Secretary–General Pursuant to S.C. Res. *721 (1991)*]. In S.C.Res. *724, Dec. 15, 1991*, an advance team, of 12 military personnel, some police, plus supporting staff, was sent to Belgrade. *S.C. Resolution 727, Jan. 8, 1992*, provided for the dispatch of 50 military liaison officers to promote the continuation of cease-fires, but still determined that sending a larger force was not opportune.

Resolution 743 (Feb. 21, 1992) endorsed a proposal for a peacekeeping force of 13,870 personnel, and, pursuant to Charter Article 25, the Council established a U.N. Protection Force (UNPROFOR) for immediate deployment. *Security Council Resolution 757 (May 30, 1992)* ordered that air links with Serbia and Montenegro be eliminated and that export and import of goods to or from these "nations" be largely prohibited.

On October 6, 1992, Resolution 779 authorized the Peacekeeping Force, UNPROFOR, to monitor the withdrawal of the Serbian Army from Croatia. On the same date, *Resolution 780* called for international relief institutions to investigate and to compile statistics on the widely reported "ethnic cleansing." Also in October 1992, military flights were prohibited over Bosnia & Herzegovina (*S.C.Res. 781 (1992)* [this was later extended in *S.C. Resolution 816, March 31, 1993*] and in November 1992, a naval blockade of the Danube River and the Adriatic Sea was imposed [*S.C.Res. 787 (1992)*].

   In December 1992, the Security Council called for 700 peacekeeping troops (including U.S. forces) to be deployed to Macedonia as a preventive measure. Bell–Fialkoff, *A Brief History of Ethnic Cleansing,* 72 For.Aff. 110 (1993); William Pfaff, *Invitation to War,* 72 For.Aff. 97 (1993); Meron, *The Case for War Crimes Trials in Yugoslavia,* 72 For.Aff. 122 (1993).

Chapter 17

THE USE OF FORCE BY STATES

INTRODUCTION

1. *What is the law today governing the use of force by states?* This question will be explored in the context of a number of instances in which states have used force unilaterally or, even though collectively, outside the aegis of the United Nations. This raises another question: to what extent did the creation of the United Nations and promulgation of the U.N. Charter change the law relating to the use of force?

a. Law Designed to Discourage or Control the Use of Force Prior to the United Nations: Since the emergence of the nation-state and the international law that developed around the system of states, notions of autonomy, territorial integrity, sovereignty, and equality have been paramount. The use of force to violate those state interests violated international law as well.

When we speak of actual armed conflict, we need to distinguish two notions: the law governing resort to armed conflict, *jus ad bellum,* and that governing the conduct of armed conflict, *jus in bello.* Also, since Hugo Grotius wrote his classic, *De Jure Belli Ac Pacis* (1646), international law has been divided into the law relating to peace and that relating to war. Keep these distinctions in mind as you read the material in this chapter. Antiquity saw its own control of the use of force, generally ordained by holy law and powerful leaders. Force and war were "legal" when and if consistent with the will of deity. The Code of Manu (Law of the ancient Hindus), Law 91, provided that a king who fights his foes in battle should not "strike one who has climbed on an eminence, or a eunuch, nor one who joins the palms of his hands (in supplication), nor one who (flees) with flying hair, nor one who sits down, nor one who says 'I am thine;'" 92: "Nor one who sleeps, nor one who has lost his coat of mail, nor one who is naked, nor one who is disarmed, nor one who looks on without taking part in the fight, nor one who is fighting with another (foe);" 93: "Nor one whose weapons are broken, nor one afflicted (with sorrow), nor one who has been grievously wounded, nor one who is in fear, nor one who has turned to flight; (but in all these cases let him) remember the duty (of honorable warriors) * * *." Sun Tzu said: "[T]reat your captives well, and care for them. *Chang Yü*: all the soldiers taken must be cared for with magnanimity and sincerity so that they may be used by us * * *. Generally in war the best policy is to take a state intact; to ruin it is inferior to this * * *." In 634 A.D., Calif Abu Bakr charged the Moslem Arab Army invading Christian Syria: "Do not commit treachery, nor depart from the right path. You must not mutilate, neither kill a child or aged man or woman * * *."

Pascal thought, "unable to strengthen justice they have justified might; so that the just and the strong should unite, and there should be peace, which is the sovereign good * * *." St. Augustine (354–430), who contributed to the creation of the Christian doctrine of "just war," argued that *"just war"* could be fought to avenge the injuries caused by an enemy who has refused to make amends, to punish those wrongs, and to restore the status quo. Thomas Acquinas argued that *just war* was appropriate when entered for a *just cause,* such as when the wrongdoer (enemy) was *subjectively guilty;* no objective manifestation of that guilt was necessary. When the nation-state arose, it was jealous of the religious authority making such decisions, so *just war* was linked to the *divine right* of kings and *sovereignty.* Wars between Christian nations were difficult to justify. The attempt at justification became the impetus for the development of the gradation of causes for using military force. *Just War* doctrine was *jus ad bellum* at its bottom, but it contained (and still contains) threads of *jus in bello.* For example, innocents were not to be subject to the violence of even a *just war.* In addition, proportionality formed a primary component of both *jus ad bellum* and *jus in bello.*

In the seventeenth and eighteenth centuries, Hugo Grotius and Emerich de Vattel attempted to secularize just war notions and to apply evidence of state practice. They actually merged religious and secular notions, distinguishing moral and legal principles (the first based on religion and the latter on nature). Grotius argued for a balancing approach by which the legality of the use of military force depended on self-defense, the defense of property and the protection of citizens. He argued against a rash use of war even for a just cause.

Professor Shaw argued that the Peace of Westphalia killed the *just war* in international law. [*See*, Shaw, International Law 539–541 (1986)]. Is Shaw's claim too strong? At most, does it apply to jus ad bellum? Just war includes, among other things, the distinction between combatant and non-combatant, care of wounded and sick prisoners, proportionality, necessity, and the requirement to attempt peaceful resolution.

Current law on the use of force is significantly more restrictive than that of the "classical period of international law," which lasted from antiquity through Vitoria, Suarez, Grotius, de Vattel, Jean Bodin and others up to World War I and the Kellogg–Briand Pact. Prior to that, war was the prerogative of the sovereign, then the right of the state. It was a legal means to promote the state's vital interests. The late nineteenth and early twentieth centuries saw an attempt to define war, first to control its conduct, later to outlaw it. Chapter 11 (on individual responsibility) presents the Hague Convention and associated regulations, which attempted to provide the (*jus in bello*) rules of warfare.

The first timorous step toward outlawing war was in the Hague Convention II (1907), which provided in article I that, "[t]he contracting Powers agree not to have recourse to armed force for the recovery of contract debts claimed from the Government of one country by the Government of another country as being due to its nationals. This undertaking, however, was not applicable when the debtor State refused or neglected to reply to an offer of arbitration, or, after accepting the offer, prevented any *compromis* from being agreed on, or, after the arbitration, failed to submit to the award * * *." The League of Nations gave impetus to the attempt to outlaw war. The League was aimed at "promot[ing] international co-operation and to achiev[ing] international peace and security." Indeed, the League Covenant provided that the "resort to war in disregard of [a Member's] covenants * * * [shall cause it] *ipso facto* [to] be deemed to have committed an act of war against all other Members of the League, which hereby undertake immediately to subject it to the severance of all trade or financial relations * * *." Bowett notes that the League's approach to achieving this was based on disarmament (art. 8), a collective guarantee of each member's independence (art. 10), pacific settlement of disputes and the outlawry of war (arts. 11–15), and sanctions for violation of these principles (arts. 16 & 17).　Bowett, The Law of International Institutions 17–18 (4th ed. 1982).　*See,* Chapter 16, *supra,* on *Peaceful Resolution of Disputes and the Use of Force in the International System.* Finally, the Pact of Paris (Kellogg–Briand Pact) (July 24, 1929) in articles I and II, renounced war "as an instrument of national policy in [the Parties] relations with one another * * * [and that] the settlement or solution of all disputes or conflicts of whatever nature or whatever origin they may be, which may arise among them, shall never be sought except by pacific means."

b.　*The Law Today:* Today, the law of the U.N. Charter along with earlier treaties such as the *Kellogg–Briand Pact* and customary rules live on.　Since the end of World War II and the advent of the United Nations, reprisals have been rigorously limited to non-military countermeasures, and the former right of a sovereign state to use military force as a law enforcement measure has been abrogated.　Most authorities consider the use of force now to be legal only pursuant to self-defense under article 51, or as a measure of collective security under Chapter VII of the Charter.　***Two issues are central to the search for an answer to the question of what the law is today:*** (1) did the failure of the Security Council of the United Nations to use its theoretical near monopoly of force (during the Cold War after the Korean Conflict) affect not merely the practice of states but also the substance of the law governing the use of force by states?　(2) Has the resurgence of the Security Council had an impact on the lawful use of force by states? Chapter 16 presents the law and history of the use of force by the United Nations and provides background for the development of these questions in this chapter.

c.　*Limited Bibliography:* Christopher L. Blakesley, Terrorism, Drugs, International Law and the Protection of Human Liberty (1992); Wormuth & Firmage, To Chain the Dog of War (2d ed. 1989);　Henkin, How Nations Behave (2d ed. 1979);　Schachter, International Law in Theory and Practice (1991);　Dinstein, War, Aggression and Self–Defense (1988);　L.C. Green, Essays on the Modern Law of War (1985);　Gardam, Proportionality and Force in International Law, 87 A.J.I.L. 391 (1993); Grew, History of the Law of Nations: World War I to World War II, in 7 Encyclopedia of Public International Law 252 (Rudolf Bernhardt ed. 1984);　Henkin, et al. Right v. Might: International Law and the Use of Force (1991);　Shaw, International Law 539–541 (1986);　M. Khadduri, War and Peace in the Law of Islam (1955);　Sun Tzu, The Art of War 75–77 (S. Griffith trans. 1963);　The Laws of Manu (*Translated* by G. Butler, with extracts from seven commentaries, Sacred Books of the East Series, Delhi 1962).　Wilson, International Law and the Use of Force by National Liberation Movements (1988);　Law and Force in the New International Order (Damrosch & Scheffer, eds. 1991);　Cassese, Violence and Law in the Modern Age (Greenleaves trans. 1988).

Debate. *Boyle*: In the modern world of international relations, the only legitimate justifications and procedures for the perpetration of violence and coercion by one state against another are those set forth in the U.N. Charter. The Charter alone contains those rules which have been consented to by the virtual unanimity of the international community that has voluntarily joined the United Nations. These include and are limited to the right of individual and collective self-defense in the event of an "armed attack" as prescribed by article 51; chapter 7 "enforcement action" by the U.N. Security Council; chapter 8 "enforcement action" by the appropriate regional organizations acting with the authorization of the Security Council, as required by article 53; and the so-called "peacekeeping operations" organized under the jurisdiction of the Security Council pursuant to chapter 6, or under the auspices of the General Assembly in accordance with the Uniting for Peace Resolution (1950), or by the relevant regional organizations acting in conformity with their proper constitutional procedures and subject to the overall supervision of the Security Council, as specified in chapter 8 and articles 24 and 25. *"Remarks on Problems of the Law of Armed Conflict in Lebanon,"* Proceedings of the 77th Annual Meeting, AJIL 223 (1983).

Reisman: There is no need to recite yet again the desuetude of the collective security arrangements envisioned in the Charter. Intractable conflicts between contending public order systems with planetary aspirations paralyzed the Security Council. The UN Charter's mechanisms often proved ineffective. * * *

* * *

A sine qua non for any action—coercive or otherwise—I submit, is the maintenance of minimum order in a precarious international system. Will a particular use of force enhance or undermine world order? When this requirement is met, attention may be directed to the fundamental principle of political legitimacy in contemporary international politics: the enhancement of the ongoing right of peoples to determine their own political destinies. That obvious point bears renewed emphasis for it is the main purpose of contemporary international law: Article 2(4) is the means. The basic policy of contemporary international law has been to maintain the political independence of territorial communities so that they can continue to express their desire for political community in a form appropriate to them.

Article 2(4), like so much in the Charter and in contemporary international politics, rests on and must be interpreted in terms of this key postulate of political legitimacy in the 20th century. * * * *"Coercion and Self–Determination: Construing Charter Article 2(4),"* 78 AJIL 642, 643 (1984).

Schacter: "The difficulty with Reisman's argument is not merely that it lacks support in the text of the Charter or in the interpretations that states have given Article 2(4) in the past decades. It would

introduce a new normative basis for recourse to war that would give
powerful states an almost unlimited right to overthrow governments
alleged to be unresponsive to the popular will or to the goal of self-
determination.   The implications of this for interstate violence in a
period of superpower confrontation and obscurantist rhetoric are ominous.   That invasions may at times serve democratic values must be
weighed against the dangerous consequences of legitimizing armed attacks against peaceful governments.   * * * It is no answer to say that
invasions should be allowed where there is no abuse and only for the
higher good of self-determination.   In the absence of an effective international mechanism to restrain force, individual governments would
have wide latitude to decide on the 'reality' of democracy and self-
determination in various countries.   The test one side would favor would
not be acceptable to others.   Ideological confrontations would sooner or
later become clashes of power.   These considerations are so evident that
we can be quite sure that governments will not adopt the suggested
reinterpretation of Article 2(4) as law.   Not even its espousal by a
powerful state would make it law.   In short, it is not, will not and should
not be law.   * * * *"The Legality of Pro–Democratic Invasion,"* 78 AJIL
645, 649 (1984).

2.   ***Sources of the law governing the use of force by states.***
Discourse about the law governing the use of force has, until recently,
almost exclusively referred to the United Nations Charter, in particular
to Articles 2(4) and 51.   In the case of *Nicaragua v. United States,*[a] the
International Court of Justice decided that, in spite of the United States'
reservation to the compulsory jurisdiction of the Court excluding in
certain circumstances disputes arising under a multilateral treaty (i.e.,
the Charter), the Court could decide the claim of Nicaragua under
customary international law governing the use of force:

176.   As regards the suggestion that the areas covered by the
two sources of law are identical, the Court observes that the United
Nations Charter, the convention to which most of the United States
argument is directed, by no means covers the whole area of the
regulation of the use of force in international relations.   On one
essential point, this treaty itself refers to pre-existing customary
international law; this reference to customary law is contained in
the actual text of Article 51, which mentions the "inherent right"
(in the French text the "droit naturel") of individual or collective
self-defence, which "nothing in the present Charter shall impair"
and which applies in the event of an armed attack.   The Court
therefore finds that Article 51 of the Charter is only meaningful on
the basis that there is a "natural" or "inherent" right of self-
defence, and it is hard to see how this can be other than of a
customary nature, even if its present content has been confirmed
and influenced by the Charter.   Moreover the Charter, having itself
recognized the existence of this right, does not go on to regulate

a. The full name of the case is Case
Concerning Military and Paramilitary Activities In and Against Nicaragua (Nicaragua v. United States of America), [1986]
I.C.J. Reports 14.   The case is more fully
set forth at 1323.   As to the case before the
International Court of Justice on jurisdiction, see Chapter 1, p. 53.

directly all aspects of its content. For example, it does not contain any specific rule whereby self-defence would warrant only measures which are proportional to the armed attack and necessary to respond to it, a rule well established in customary international law. Moreover, a definition of the "armed attack" which, if found to exist, authorizes the exercise of the "inherent right" of self-defence, is not provided in the Charter, and is not part of treaty law. It cannot therefore be held that Article 51 is a provision which "subsumes and supervenes" customary international law. It rather demonstrates that in the field in question, the importance of which for the present dispute need hardly be stressed, customary international law continues to exist alongside treaty law. The areas governed by the two sources of law thus do not overlap exactly, and the rules do not have the same content. This could also be demonstrated for other subjects, in particular for the principle of non-intervention.

177.   * * * [E]ven if the customary norm and the treaty norm were to have exactly the same content, this would not be a reason for the Court to hold that the incorporation of the customary norm into treaty law must deprive the customary norm of its applicability as distinct from that of the treaty norm. The existence of identical rules in international treaty law and customary law has been clearly recognized by the Court in the North Sea Continental Shelf cases. To a large extent, those cases turned on the question whether a rule enshrined in a treaty also existed as a customary rule, either because the treaty had merely codified the custom, or caused it to "crystallize", or because it had influenced its subsequent adoption. The Court found that this identity of content in treaty law and in customary international law did not exist in the case of the rule invoked, which appeared in one article of the treaty, but did not suggest that such identity was debarred as a matter of principle: on the contrary, it considered it to be clear that certain other articles of the treaty in question "were * * * regarded as reflecting, or as crystallizing, received or at least emergent rules of customary international law" (I.C.J. Reports 1969, p. 39, para. 63). More generally, there are no grounds for holding that when customary international law is comprised of rules identical to those of treaty law, the latter "supervenes" the former, so that the customary international law has no further existence of its own.

179.   It will therefore be clear that customary international law continues to exist and to apply, separately from international treaty law, even where the two categories of law have an identical content.
   * * *

3. *The principle of non-intervention as customary international law.* The term "intervention" has factual, political and legal connotations. Common to all three meanings, in the context of international affairs, is the series of overriding or dominant influences of one state upon the will or capabilities of another state, particularly as to events and conditions in the latter. In the history of Latin American relations prior to the coming into being of the United Nations and the

Organization of American States, the opposition by Latin America to the penchant of the United States to land the Marines to protect American lives and property, and for other purposes viewed as good by the United States, coalesced into a principle of non-intervention. While some writers of that period contended that this principle was one of general international law, others viewed it as a political principle without legal content that ought eventually to be stated as a rule of international law. Since the creation of the United Nations, legal discourse has, with increased frequency, engaged the term. Does it now have legal meaning; if so, what is its scope?

The Charter of the United Nations does not apply the term in describing the rights and duties of states with respect to the employment of physical force. As seen, Article 2(4) forbids the use of force directed "against the territorial integrity or political independence of any state, or in any manner inconsistent with the Purposes of the United Nations." The existence of an act of aggression (not intervention), if found by the Security Council, triggers certain permissible United Nations responses, but even aggression is not in terms forbidden to states. It is from Article 2(7) of the Charter of the United Nations that emanations have emerged forbidding intervention by states although, in its terms, that provision is directed toward the organization rather than its members: "Nothing contained in the present Charter shall authorize the United Nations to intervene in matters which are essentially within the domestic jurisdiction of any state * * *." This provision is buttressed in the Charter by broadly stated principles: self-determination of peoples, Article 1(2); sovereign equality of states, Article 2(1).

In elucidation of this principle, the Assembly declared: "No State or group of States has the right to intervene directly or indirectly, for any reason whatever in the internal or external affairs of any other State." And further: "Every State has an inalienable right to choose its political, economic, social and cultural systems, without interference in any form by another State." In the Nicaragua case, the Court stated its recognition of this principle as a matter of international law and defined its content to some extent:

> 202. The principle of non-intervention involves the right of every sovereign State to conduct its affairs without outside interference; though examples of trespass against this principle are not infrequent, the Court considers that it is part and parcel of customary international law. As the Court has observed: "Between independent States, respect for territorial sovereignty is an essential foundation of international relations" (I.C.J. Reports 1949, p. 35), and international law requires political integrity also to be respected. Expressions of an opinio juris regarding the existence of the principle of non-intervention in customary international law are numerous and not difficult to find. Of course, statements whereby States avow their recognition of the principles of international law set forth in the United Nations Charter cannot strictly be interpreted as applying to the principle of non-intervention by States in the internal and external affairs of other States, since this principle is not, as such, spelt out in the Charter. But it was never intended

that the Charter should embody written confirmation of every essential principle of international law in force. The existence in the opinio juris of States of the principle of non-intervention is backed by established and substantial practice. It has moreover been presented as a corollary of the principle of the sovereign equality of States. A particular instance of this is General Assembly resolution 2625 (XXV), the Declaration on the Principles of International Law concerning Friendly Relations and Co-operation among States. In the Corfu Channel case, when a State claimed a right of intervention in order to secure evidence in the territory of another State for submission to an international tribunal (I.C.J. Reports 1949, p. 34), the Court observed that:

> "the alleged right of intervention as the manifestation of a policy of force, such as has, in the past, given rise to most serious abuses and such as cannot, whatever be the present defects in international organization, find a place in international law. Intervention is perhaps still less admissible in the particular form it would take here; for, from the nature of things, it would be reserved for the most powerful States, and might easily lead to perverting the administration of international justice itself." (I.C.J. Reports 1949, p. 35.)

203. The principle has since been reflected in numerous declarations adopted by international organizations and conferences in which the United States and Nicaragua have participated, e.g., General Assembly resolution 2131 (XX), the Declaration on the Inadmissibility of Intervention in the Domestic Affairs of States and the Protection of their Independence and Sovereignty. It is true that the United States, while it voted in favour of General Assembly resolution 2131 (XX), also declared at the time of its adoption in the First Committee that it considered the declaration in that resolution to be "only a statement of political intention and not a formulation of law." However, the essentials of resolution 2131 (XX) are repeated in the Declaration approved by resolution 2625 (XXV), which set out principles which the General Assembly declared to be "basic principles" of international law, and on the adoption of which no analogous statement was made by the United States representative.

205. Notwithstanding the multiplicity of declarations by States accepting the principle of non-intervention, there remain two questions: first, what is the exact content of the principle so accepted, and secondly, is the practice sufficiently in conformity with it for this to be a rule of customary international law? As regards the first problem—that of the content of the principle of non-intervention—the Court will define only those aspects of the principle which appear to be relevant to the resolution of the dispute. In this respect it notes that, in view of the generally accepted formulations, the principle forbids all States or groups of States to intervene directly or indirectly in internal or external affairs of other States. A prohibited intervention must accordingly be one bearing on matters in which each State is permitted, by the principle of State sovereignty, to decide freely. One of these is the choice of a political, economic, social and cultural system, and the formulation of

foreign policy. Intervention is wrongful when it uses methods of coercion in regard to such choices, which must remain free ones. The element of coercion, which defines, and indeed forms the very essence of, prohibited intervention, is particularly obvious in the case of an intervention which uses force, either in the direct form of military action, or in the indirect form of support for subversive or terrorist armed activities within another State. As noted above (paragraph 191), General Assembly resolution 2625 (XXV) equates assistance of this kind with the use of force by the assisting State when the acts committed in another State "involve a threat or use of force". These forms of action are therefore wrongful in the light of both the principle of non-use of force, and that of non-intervention. In view of the nature of Nicaragua's complaints against the United States, and those expressed by the United States in regard to Nicaragua's conduct towards El Salvador, it is primarily acts of intervention of this kind with which the Court is concerned in the present case.

———

[The Tribunal ultimately decided that the conduct of the United States constituted intervention and violated international law, including the customary rule against the use of force. It was not justified by any conduct by Nicaragua, and that the United States "should immediately cease and refrain from any action restricting, blocking, or endangering access to or from Nicaraguan ports, and, in particular, the laying of mines." Article 51 was held not to justify U.S. conduct. Did the Tribunal hold that the United States violated article 2(4)? For more discussion of the *Nicaragua Case,* including its text, see p. 1323, *infra.*

———

SECTION A. THE USE OF FORCE UNDER THE UNITED STATES CONSTITUTION AND OTHER LAWS

A state operates within the strictures of both international law and its own domestic law, as we saw in Chapter 14 (the law of international agreements and the Constitution). You will recall that a *monist* will argue that these are one and the same and that international law controls. On the other hand, a *dualist* argues that they are two separate systems, each of which functions within its own domain, albeit with mutual impact. The drafters of the United States Constitution, not without vitriolic debate, developed a sophisticated system of powers both shared and separate. The brilliant mix was aimed at protecting against any one branch of government developing too much power. A major arena of focus of this admixture was that of foreign affairs and especially the use of force. The U.S. Constitution went beyond Montesquieu or any other European Separation of Powers luminary. It provided an intricate balancing, refined by the clear understanding that if any one branch gained a monopoly on the use of force (even that applied abroad), that branch could endanger the Republic. The framers understood that what is allowed to be done abroad, especially by our agents, eventually affects the national community, as well. The Constitution grants to the Congress the decision for war or peace. The President, as Commander in Chief, may respond in self-defense to sudden attack. Scrutinize the following Constitutional provisions and the writings to see whether you agree.

Read the United States Constitution article I, sections 8 & 9; article II, sections 1, 2; Article III, sections 1, 2, 3; Article IV, section 4; and Article VI, found in Documentary Supplement.

4. *The War Powers.*

WORMUTH & FIRMAGE, TO CHAIN THE DOG OF WAR
298–300 (2d ed. 1989) (footnotes omitted).*

[W]e are not told under what conditions a virtuous state might resort to force and war in order to preserve or extend itself. No doctrine of just war appears, though it is possible to argue that the Constitution's references to the law of nations incorporated some such notions. Rather, the framers realized that the reasons [for deciding] to go to war must be left for every generation to work through within the political branches of government. Whether we should go to war and under what conditions were political questions. But the way we go to war was not. The procedural means were carefully stipulated. If these procedural means were wisely chosen in the first place, and if modern technology does not render them anachronistic, then we ignore this, under the ideologically fueled heat of the moment, at our peril. At various times in our history, our self-righteous assurance of our own virtue and our own infallibility has led us to ignore these procedures in favor of a total commitment to our perceived ends, however self-destructive.

Precisely because of their fear of one person's fallibility, the framers of our Constitution separated the power to decide for war from the power to conduct it. The power to initiate war, except for sudden attack upon our country, was lodged exclusively in the Congress. The President was confined to conducting war once Congress had decided upon such a course.

The assumptions behind this separation of war power are as vital to us two hundred years later as they were when these ideas were penned in Philadelphia. The executive or monarchical inclination to make war impulsively, without deliberate debate among a sizeable and varied body of people, was thought by many to have contributed to decades of war that ravaged Europe. War came almost to be the natural condition, interrupted rarely by periods of peace.

The framers thought that by denying to the President the monarchical power of raising armies and deciding for war, and placing such powers in the Congress, the sensitivities of the people who had to fight such wars and pay for them would be reflected through their representa-

* Reprinted with the permission of the University of Illinois Press.

tives. In other words, the condition of peace, not war, would be considered to be normal. The biases and presumptions of law and government, the inertia factor, were placed on the side of peace. Those who advocate war have a burden of persuasion not easily borne. Only after open debate in a deliberative body, a process intentionally meant to prevent precipitous, cavalier action, will the state move from peace to war.

A number of factors have eroded these constitutional checks against war. Two world wars and a depression in this century have moved much power in government from the deliberative body—Congress—to the executive. Certain advantages of administration and dispatch are obvious. But the costs of executive abuse—Watergate, Iran and Nicaragua, and executive war in Korea and Vietnam—have been devastating. Apparently, government based upon an assumption of perpetual crisis fulfills its own presumption.

More than half of the United States population now living have not known peace in a very real sense. We have been subject to a Cold War since World War II ended. Previous generations have enjoyed peace at least between wars. Now almost every problem, domestic and foreign, is considered within a matrix of Cold War. Hatreds that in times past were intentionally set loose in time of war were mercifully confined within the period of war—1914–18, 1941–45. Now endemic fear is maintained through generations.

Administrations preach hatred and suspicion of foreign foes for domestic political advantage as much as for preparedness actually to be able to meet an enemy. A military-industrial complex has become a permanent part of an economic structure addicted to massive military spending. With governmental officers who all too often join the companies with whom they dealt with in government, these industries perpetuate themselves without regard for the national interest. In decades past a peacetime economy for a discrete time would change temporarily to build instruments of war and then quickly revert to the productivity of peace. Now our scientists and engineers are increasingly drawn into producing the technology of war while the infrastructure of our economy, from our factories to our transportation systems, erode and our spending for social needs is squeezed below the minimal requirements of social justice.

The war power of Congress is an institutional means of controlling the inclination to make war [precipitately,] presumptuously. For us today, this provision is a structural, horizontal check on war—while arms control measures and the laws of war hit at vertical, singular issues. Even in 1789, Thomas Jefferson noted insightfully: "We have already given * * * some effectual check to the dog of war by transferring the power of letting him loose, from the executive to the legislative body, from those who are to spend to those who are to pay." Congress exclusively possesses the constitutional power to initiate war, whether declared or undeclared, public or private, perfect or imperfect, de jure or de facto. The only exception is the power in the President to respond self-defensively to sudden attack upon the United States. Three points also follow from constitutional text, our history, and pragmatic necessity. First, power over foreign relations was meant by the Framers to be jointly held by the Congress and the President. Today much congressional direction and control have been allowed to wither by congressional default and presidential usurpation.

Second, the existence of nuclear weapons and missile delivery systems reinforces this original understanding, not the reverse. The argument by presidents and presidential counselors that the President must have the power to wage nuclear war instantaneously because of nuclear missile delivery time of a few minutes simply does not hold when weighed against the cosmic implications of nuclear war. These implications favor more rather than less institutional restraint, collegial decision rather than the potential frailty and impetuosity of one human being who decides for or against the continuation of human society and, possibly, the human species.

Third, Congress possesses the power, through control over expenditure, appointment, the direction of foreign policy, the government of the armed forces, censure of the President and, if necessary, impeachment, to reassert its substantial power in foreign relations and its singular power to decide for peace or war. This position—that Congress possesses the sole power to decide for war or peace—is supported with absolute clarity of intent of the founding fathers. And our history, while checkered with congressional ratification of presidential acts and by presidential abuse and congressional malfeasance on occasion, clearly reveals the norm of congressional control and presidential dependence in the decision for war and peace. This was so through the Indian wars, the Whiskey Rebellion, the Barbary pirates, and the Civil War, and from our endemic preoccupation with intervention in the Caribbean to our border crossings into Mexico and Canada. Our pattern continued through two world wars until Korea and Vietnam.

James Madison noted that "the executive is the department of power most distinguished by its propensity to war: hence it is the practice of all states, in proportion as they are free, to disarm this propensity of its influence." Even Alexander Hamilton, the advocate of presidential power in the Philadelphia Convention, nevertheless recognized that the President's power "would amount to nothing more than the supreme command and direction of the military forces," since the President lacked the British Crown's authority to declare war and raise armies. The power given Congress rests upon the constitutional text that Congress be empowered to "declare war and grant letters of marque and reprisal." This entails the power to decide for war declared or undeclared, whether fought with regular public forces or by privateers under governmental mandate. While letters of marque and reprisal originally covered specific acts, by the eighteenth century letters of marque and reprisal referred to sovereign use of private and sometimes public forces to injure another state. It was within this context that the constitutional framers vested Congress with the power to issue letters of marque and reprisal. Clearly, only Congress has the constitutional power to wage overt or covert war by private parties as well as by the armed forces * * *. *See also,* Firmage, Rogue Presidents and the War

Power of Congress, 11 Geo.Mason L.Rev. 79, 80–82 (1988); Firmage, Book Review Essay: The War Power, 59 G.W.L.Rev. 1684, 1690–91 (1991). Were/are there any limits on *how* the president conducts war? If so, what are they?

Franck and Weisband note that especially after World War II, up until the Vietnam War and Watergate, the President gained predominance in the foreign policy arena, especially where there was a risk of or actual war. This had been achieved, "by a zealous patriotic rallying behind the Presidential colors * * *" Franck & Weisband, FOREIGN POLICY BY CONGRESS 3 (1979).

H. KOH, THE NATIONAL SECURITY CONSTITUTION
117–18 (1990).*

[The reasons may] be grouped under three headings, which not coincidentally mirror general institutional characteristics of the executive, legislative, and judicial branches. First, and most obviously, the president has won because the executive branch has taken the initiative in foreign affairs and has often done so by construing laws designed to constrain his actions as authorizations. Second, the president has won because, for all of its institutional activity, Congress has usually complied with or acquiesced in what the president has done, through legislative myopia, inadequate drafting, ineffective legislative tools, or sheer lack of political will. Third, the president has won because the federal courts have usually tolerated his acts, either by refusing to hear challenges to those acts or by hearing the challenges and then affirming presidential authority on the merits.

This simple, three-part combination of executive initiative, congressional acquiescence, and judicial tolerance explains why the president almost invariably wins in foreign affairs. Indeed, this three-part reasoning enters directly into the calculus of an executive branch lawyer asked to draft a legal opinion justifying a proposed foreign affairs initiative. If asked, for example, whether the president can impose economic sanctions on Libya or can bomb Colonel Qaddafi's headquarters, the president's lawyer must answer three questions: (1) Do we have the legal authority to act? (2) Can Congress stop us? and (3) Can anyone challenge our action in court? Or, to use the framework outlined above: (1) Do the Constitution and laws of the United States authorize the president to take this executive initiative? (2) If the executive branch takes the initiative, will Congress acquiesce? and (3) If Congress does not acquiesce and challenges the president's action (or if a private citizen sues), will the courts nevertheless tolerate the act, either by refusing to hear the challenge or by hearing it and ruling in the president's favor?

* * *

Negative reaction to the Vietnam War and to Watergate caused Congress ultimately to react, by way of the Joint War Powers Resolution.

---

* Reprinted with the permission of the Yale University Press.

Does the Resolution practically further its stated objective of reasserting congressional power to decide for war or peace? Consider the following:

WORMUTH AND FIRMAGE, TO CHAIN THE DOG OF WAR
12–16 (1989) (footnotes omitted).*

The President has become more than the executor of the laws; she or he is now the leader of a party and of the nation. There have been similar developments in other countries—de Riencourt has written of an evolution toward executive aggrandisement of power in *The Coming Caesars*. But our system of checks and balances has thus far proved to be an insuperable obstacle to the permanence of American Caesarism. Attempts have been made to revive the Stuart conception of an emergency power of the King, which John Locke recognized under the name of prerogative. In his dissenting opinion in the *Steel Seizure Case,* Chief Justice Fred Vinson spoke vaguely of "the leadership contemplated by the Framers" and claimed a limited emergency power for the President. "With or without statutory authorization, Presidents have at such times dealt with national emergencies by acting promptly and resolutely to enforce legislative programs, at least to save those programs until Congress could act." In 1971 Secretary of State Rogers asserted that "in emergency situations, the President has the power and responsibility to use the armed forces to protect the nation's security." The only evidence he cites is the framers' agreement that under the Constitution the President might use the armed forces to repel a sudden attack on the United States, since such an attack would initiate a state of war without a congressional joint resolution.

Of course the existence of an emergency does not redistribute the powers of government allocated by the Constitution. In 1869, Justice Miller held that the action of the secretary of war (imputed to the President)—accepting without statutory authority bills of exchange in order to buy necessary supplies for the army—was illegal. Miller remarked, "We have no officers in this government from the President down to the most subordinate agent, who does not hold office under the law, with prescribed duties and limited authority." The two dissenting justices argued that the statute authorizing the secretary to make contracts implicitly authorized him to accept the bills. Miller also wrote the unanimous opinion in United States v. Lee, decided in 1882, an ejection action against two army officers in possession of the Lee estate in Virginia. Miller said:

> Shall it be said, in the face of all this, * * * that the courts cannot give remedy when the citizen has been deprived of his property by force, his estate seized and converted to the use of the government without any lawful authority, because the president has ordered it and his officers are in possession? If such be the law, it sanctions a tyranny which has no existence in the monarchies of Europe, nor in any other government which has a just claim to well-regulated liberty and the protection of personal rights.

* Reprinted with the permission of the University of Illinois Press.

And in 1935, in Schechter Poultry Corp. v. U.S., Chief Justice Charles Evans Hughes said for eight justices (the ninth wrote a separate, concurring opinion), "Extraordinary conditions do not create or enlarge governmental power."

Of course it is true that a government of limited and divided powers does not grant an instant decision for every question that anyone, or even a large number of people, may believe requires instant decision. The price we pay for renouncing autocracy is the absence of autocracy.

Locke's prerogative, the "power to act according to discretion, for the publick good, without the prescription of the Law, and sometimes even against it," if it had endured, would have overthrown his whole system. Albert v. Dicey described the solution to problems of emergency that eventually emerged in English law: "There are times of tumult and invasion when for the sake of legality itself the rules must be broken. The course which the government must then take is clear. The ministry must break the law and trust for protection to an act of immunity."

American law followed the same course. [First] *Appollon,* [sic] decided unanimously in 1824 by the Supreme Court in an opinion by Justice Joseph Story. In 1820 Congress had levied a tonnage duty on French vessels. The *Appollon* was a French ship bound for Charleston, but on arrival off the port of Charleston the master learned that Congress had imposed the duty. He therefore sailed for Amelia Island, in Spanish territory, intending "to transship his cargo into the United States, and to receive from thence a cargo of cotton, without subjecting himself to the payment of the French tonnage duty." The collector of the port of St. Mary's caused the *Appollon* [sic] to be seized while in Spanish waters and brought to St. Mary's. The master of the vessel sued the collector for damages and recovered. Justice Story wrote:

> It cannot, however, escape observation, that this court has a plain path of duty marked out for it, and that is, to administer the law as it finds it. * * * Whatever may be the rights of the government, upon principles of the law of nations, to redress wrongs of this nature, and whatever the power of Congress to pass suitable laws to cure any defects in the present system, our duty lies in a more narrow compass; and we must administer the laws as they exist, without straining them to reach public mischiefs which they were never designed to remedy. It may be fit and proper for the government, in the exercise of the high discretion confided to the Executive, for great public purposes, to act on a sudden emergency, or to prevent an irreparable mischief, by summary measures which are not found in the text of laws. Such measures are properly matters of state, and if the responsibility is taken, under justifiable circumstances, the legislature will doubtless apply a proper indemnity. *Discuss this decision.*

The Prize Cases, decided in 1863, upheld the blockade of southern ports proclaimed by President Lincoln in 1861. Having held that the "sudden attack" of the seceding states instituted a state of war in which the President's action was constitutionally justified, Justice Grier said:

If it were necessary to the technical existence of a war, that it should have a legislative sanction, we find it in almost every Act passed at the extraordinary session of the Legislature of 1861 * * *. And finally, in 1861 we find Congress *"ex majore cautela,"* and in anticipation of such astute objections, passing an Act "approving, legalizing and making valid all the acts, proclamations, and orders of the President, &c., as if they had been done under the previous express authority and direction of the Congress * * *."

Without admitting that such an Act was necessary under the circumstances, it is plain that if the President had in any manner assumed powers which it was necessary should have the authority or sanction of Congress, that on the well known principle of law, *"omnis ratihabitio et mandata equiparatur,"* this ratification has operated to perfectly cure the defect.

Limited retroactive acts of immunity were passed for the protection of Union soldiers during and after the Civil War and were upheld. In 1913 the Supreme Court upheld the governor general of the Philippines in a damage suit by an alien whom he had unlawfully ordered deported because the territorial legislature had subsequently passed an act saying that his action was "approved and ratified and confirmed, and in all respects declared legal, and not subject to question or review." Justice Oliver Wendell Holmes said for a unanimous Court that "it generally is recognized that in cases like the present, where the act originally purports to be done in the name and by the authority of the state, a defect in that authority may be cured by the subsequent adoption of the act."

There is, then, a solution to the problem of emergency. If the President believes that the necessity is sufficiently great, he or she should act illegally and look to Congress for ratification of his actions. The President should not claim an emergency power to act against the law for the good of the nation, nor claim the exclusive right to determine what is good for the nation. In 1973 Congress administered a tardy rebuke for the actions of two Presidents in the War Powers Resolution, which reads in part:

The constitutional powers of the President as Commander-in-Chief to introduce United States Armed Forces into hostilities, or into situations where imminent involvement in hostilities is clearly indicated by the circumstances, are exercised only pursuant to (1) a declaration of war, (2) specific statutory authorization, or (3) a national emergency created by attack upon the United States, its territory or possessions, or its armed forces.

The War Clause of the Constitution reads, "The Congress shall have power * * *. To declare war, grant letters of marque and reprisal, and make rules concerning captures on land and water * * *." The corresponding provision of the Articles of Confederation, under which the United States was governed from March 2, 1781, to 1789, said, "The United States in Congress assembled shall have the sole and exclusive power of determining on peace and war, except in the cases mentioned in the sixth article * * *." The sixth article authorized the states to engage in war only if invaded or menaced with invasion by an Indian tribe. * * *

On May 29, 1787, Governor Randolph of Virginia presented to the Constitutional Convention a plan for a constitution * * * The seventh paragraph proposed "that a National Executive be instituted" and that the Executive "ought to enjoy the Executive rights vested in Congress by the Confederation." The Convention resolved itself into a committee of the whole to consider the Randolph plan. When the proposal to give the National Executive the executive powers possessed by the Continental Congress came before the Convention as a resolution on June 1, Charles Pinckney objected that "the Executive powers of [the existing] Congress might extend to peace & war which would render the Executive a Monarchy, of the worst kind, towit an elective one." James Wilson reassured him, "Making peace and war are generally determined by writers on the Laws of Nations to be legislative powers." James Madison conceded that the war power was legislative, but he nevertheless thought the resolution too broad. Rufus King noted: "Mad: agrees wth. Wilson in his definition of executive powers—executive powers ex vi termini, do not include the Rights of war & peace &c. but the powers should be confined and defined—if large we shall have the Evils of elective Monarchies * * *." Randolph did not defend his resolution but directed his advocacy to a plural executive. "A unity of the Executive he observed would savor too much of a monarchy." The resolution was not brought to a vote. Nevertheless the interchange seems to show a consensus that "determining on war"—which can only mean a decision to initiate war—was a legislative power.

Accordingly, the Committee of Detail distributed a printed draft constitution on August 6 providing, "The legislature of the United States shall have the power * * * To make war * * *." When this clause came up for debate on August 17, Pinckney opposed vesting the power in Congress; proceedings would be too slow. "The Senate would be the best depositary, being more acquainted with foreign affairs, and most capable of proper resolutions." Pierce Butler said that "he was for vesting the power in the President, who will have all the requisite qualities, and will not make war but when the Nation will support it." This drew from Elbridge Gerry the rejoinder that he "never expected to hear in a republic a motion to empower the Executive alone to declare war." Butler's motion received no second.

Butler was the only member of the Convention ever to suggest that the President should be given the power to initiate war. But Madison and Gerry were not quite satisfied with the proposal of the Committee of Detail that the legislature be given the power to make war. They moved to substitute *declare* for *make,* "leaving to the Executive the power to repel sudden attacks." The meaning of the motion was clear. The power to initiate war was left to Congress, with the reservation that the President need not await authorization from Congress to repel a sudden attack on the United States. The reservation on sudden attacks met with general approbation, but there was a difference of opinion as to whether the change of language effected the desired result. Roger Sherman of Connecticut opined: "The Executive shd. be able to repel and not to commence war. 'Make' much better than 'declare' the latter narrowing the power [of the Legislature] too much." The records of the Convention noted that George Mason of Virginia "was agst giving the power of war to the Executive, because not [safely] to be trusted with it; or to the Senate, because not so constructed as to be entitled to it. He was for clogging rather than facilitating war; but he was for facilitating peace. He preferred '*declare*' to '*make.*'" Madison's motion was carried by a vote of seven states to two. Then King observed that the verb *make* might be interpreted as authorizing Congress not only to initiate but also to conduct war, and Connecticut changed its vote, so that the verb *declare* was adopted by a vote of eight to one.

This is all the information we have on the debate. On the same day Congress was given the power to "make rules concerning captures on land and water," and on September 5, it was given the power to "grant letters of marque and reprisal." This completed the war clause.

The declaration of war in 1812 said, "That war be and the same is declared to exist between the United Kingdom of Great Britain and Ireland and the dependencies thereof, and the United States of America and their territories * * *." The same form was followed in all subsequent declarations of general war.

Emerich de Vattel, the most influential writer on the law of nations * * * at the time of the adoption of the Constitution, called such a declaration a "declaration of war pure and simple." It was desirable because it gave notice to the adversary, to neutral nations, and to the subjects of the sovereign initiating the war. It ought properly to be preceded by a "conditional declaration of war"—an ultimatum demanding the satisfaction of grievances—which would first offer an alternative to war. But it was possible to enter into the state of war without making either a conditional declaration or a declaration pure and simple. The state under attack was automatically at war. And by omitting the declaration, the attacking state gained the advantage of surprise.

The Dutch jurist Bynkershoek, writing in 1737, said: "Writers on the law of nations have laid down various elements that are essential in a lawful war, and among these is the requirement that a war should be openly declared either by a special proclamation or by sending a herald; and this opinion accords with the practices of the modern nations of Europe." But compliance with this practice, he said, was "not demanded by any exigency of reason." "War may begin by a declaration, but it may also begin by mutual hostilities." In 1779, in the case of the *Maria Magdalena*, the British High Court of Admiralty held that the fact of hostilities made war.

> Where is the difference, whether a war is proclaimed by a Herald at the Royal Exchange, with his trumpets, and on the Pont Neuf at Paris, and by reading and affixing a printed paper on public buildings; or whether war is announced by royal ships, and whole fleets, at the mouths of cannon? * * * If learned authorities are to be quoted, Bynkershoek has a whole chapter to prove, from the history of Europe, that a lawful and perfect state of war may exist without proclamation.

It has always been possible at British and American law to enter into war without a formal proclamation or the services of a herald. In the [U.S.], however, war cannot lawfully be initiated by the military or its commander but only by Congress. Consequently, although a formal declaration is unnecessary, there must be some legislative act directing the cannons to speak. One of the most respected jurists of the early days of the nation, Chancellor James Kent of New York, said:

> But, though a solemn declaration, or previous notice to the enemy, be now laid aside, it is essential that some formal public act, proceeding directly from the competent source, should announce to the people at home their new relations and duties growing out of a state of war, and which should equally apprise neutral nations of the fact * * *. As war cannot lawfully be commenced on the part of the United States without an act of Congress, such an act is, of course, a formal official notice to all the world, and equivalent to the most solemn declaration.

Chancellor Kent was following established usage when he interpreted *declare* to mean *commence*. The verb *declare* had much earlier acquired this secondary meaning. It did not cease to describe a formal public proclamation of hostilities, but it was used also to mean simply the initiation of hostilities, whether or not a formal proclamation was made. In 1552 Huloet's dictionary gave the definition: "Declare warres. *Arma canere, Bellum indicere.*" There are two meanings here: to summon to arms; to announce war.

In almost every monarchical state, the power to initiate war resided in the sovereign. In discussions of constitutional arrangements at municipal law, the terms *to declare war* and *to make war* came to be used interchangeably. And while a formal declaration should be made—on the basis of obligation, according to Vattel's interpretation of the law of nations, or on the premise of generosity and justice, according to Bynkershoek's—whether or not such a formal proclamation was made had no significance for the question of the residence of power to make war at municipal law.

Comyns' Digest, an authoritative work on English law first publish-ed in 1744, said, "To the king alone it belongs to make peace and war," and also, "the king has the sole authority to declare war and peace." In 1799 in the High Court of Admiralty, Sir William Scott said, "By the law and constitution of this country, the sovereign alone has the power of declaring war and peace." It will be recalled that in the debate in the Constitutional Convention quoted above, Gerry rephrased Butler's pro-posal that the President be given the power to "make war" as a motion "to empower the Executive alone to declare war." Hamilton spoke of Congress as "that department which is to declare *or make war.*" Henry Clay said that "the power of declaring war" did not reside with the executive but with the legislature, which was therefore "the war-making branch."

The question of the presidential power to initiate war can be approached in another way. Retorsion is the practice of peaceful retalia-tion on a foreign state. Congress has often passed acts of retorsion; in

1817, 1818, and 1820, Congress closed our ports to British shipping because the British navigation acts had restricted trade, allowing only British vessels to carry to British colonies in the Western Hemisphere. During this same historical period, decisions by Justice Story on circuit and by the Supreme Court both held that the executive has no inherent power to interrupt foreign commerce; this power belongs to Congress. If the President's authority over foreign affairs does not include the peaceful practice of retorsion, it can hardly justify the initiation of war.

It remains true that the President has dominated even the decision to initiate war in recent decades. But this course of events represents a departure from the balance actually struck by the framers; it is not a simple maneuver within the gray areas or spheres of apparently overlapping authority. For these reasons, congressional action during the last decade takes on particular significance. Congress not only repented of the blank check it handed the executive in the Tonkin Gulf Resolution by repealing the Resolution in 1971, but also took a series of steps to end the Vietnam War as well as to reassert congressional authority over war. Beginning in 1970, Congress enacted the Fulbright proviso, prohibiting the use of funds for military support of Cambodia, attached a similar prohibition to every subsequent military appropriation act, prohibited the construing of any American assistance to Cambodia as an American commitment to Cambodian defense, and prohibited the use of any appropriated funds for military operations in Cambodia. Finally, and most important, Congress passed through joint resolution (over presidential veto) the *War Powers Resolution of 1973*.

The Constitution also fails to address directly the question of whether Congress or the President has the power to end war, or "to make peace." While it is undisputed that a formal treaty of peace may only be concluded by the President after approval by the Senate, it is not clear from the Constitution whether either the President or Congress may unilaterally terminate hostilities. While the President, as commander in chief, has the effective power to end the deployment of troops engaged in conflict, it is also arguable that the power of Congress to declare war "is the power to decide for *war or peace*, and should imply the power to *unmake war* as well as to make it." * * * This potential conflict between the President and Congress is addressed to a limited extent by the War Powers Resolution. Under its terms, the President must remove American forces from hostilities, in the absence of statutory authorization or a declaration of war, if "Congress so directs by concurrent resolution." This provision reflects congressional commitment to its own power over war and its belief that the President has no independent war power that would allow legal retention of forces in conflict against the will of Congress. The provision leaves unanswered, however, the more difficult question on the scope of the President's power as commander in chief once war has been authorized by Congress. In theory, it seems that Congress should have the final decision as to whether American forces should be withdrawn from conflict, but it also seems likely that the decision will in practice be a cooperative one, requiring good faith and respect for coordinate branches by both sides.

The War Powers Resolution, 50 U.S.C. §§ 1541–1548.

WORMUTH & FIRMAGE, TO CHAIN THE DOG OF WAR

at 190–192; 194–95; 219–223 (1989).*

THE WAR POWERS RESOLUTION: The Resolution interprets presidential power to introduce American forces into hostilities as being limited to the power to respond to attack or to act pursuant to authorization by congressional statute or declaration of war. Presidential consultation with Congress is required "in every possible instance" before the introduction of American forces into hostilities or situations in which imminent involvement in hostilities is likely. The Senate report on its version of the War Powers Resolution makes clear the type of involvement that would be considered imminent.

> The purpose of this provision is to prevent secret, unauthorized military activities and to prevent a repetition of many of the most controversial and regrettable activities in Indochina. The ever deepening ground combat involvement of the United States in South Vietnam began with the assignment of U.S. "advisors" to accompany South Vietnamese units on combat patrols; and in Laos, secretly and without congressional authorization, U.S. "advisors" were deeply engaged in the war * * *.

The President must report to Congress the "circumstances necessitating the introduction" and the "constitutional and legislative authority" for the introduction. Within sixty days of the submission of such a report, the President must terminate the use of American armed forces, unless Congress "has declared war or has enacted a specific authorization for such use," has extended the sixty-day period, or has been unable to meet because of armed attack upon the country. The requirement that congressional authorization be specific was recently upheld in the case of Crockett v. Reagan, an action brought by twenty-nine members of Congress to curb presidential action in El Salvador. In Crockett, the President argued that the passage of the International Security and Development Cooperation Act of 1981 impliedly authorized presidential military action in El Salvador. Although the district court dismissed the suit without reaching the merits, it correctly held that under Section 8(a) of the War Powers Resolution, congressional authorization cannot be inferred. Furthermore, far from being an unwarranted infringement on inherent presidential power, as some have claimed, * * * the sixty-day provision is arguably an unconstitutional delegation of congressional war power to the President. * * * The provision is the result of political compromises which were essential to assure the votes required to pass the Resolution. * * * Notwithstanding the sixty-day provision, the President must remove American forces from hostilities outside the "United States, its possessions and territories" if there has been no declaration of war or statutory authorization for the use of the armed

* Reprinted with the permission of the
University of Illinois Press.

forces in hostilities and if "Congress so directs by concurrent resolution
* * * "

Of significance for judicial interpretation of the exercise of the war
power, the Resolution stipulates that congressional authorization for the
introduction of American armed forces into "hostilities or into situations
where the involvement in hostilities" may not be "inferred from any
provision of law," including "any appropriation Act, unless such provision specifically authorizes" such introduction. Nor shall such an inference be drawn from "any treaty" unless it is "implemented by legislation specifically authorizing the introduction" of military forces into
hostilities or into situations likely to result in hostilities. These provisions were drafted to prevent a recurrence of judicial rulings like those
near the end of the Vietnam conflict, which sustained the constitutionality of the war on the ground that Congress had ratified executive war
making by means of military appropriations, extensions of the draft, and
other supportive legislative acts.

In the future, it may be that Congress will remedy what it considers
to be gross presidential abuse of power in the conduct of foreign
relations by necessarily using the impeachment power weapon. The
framers clearly held the view that misuse of power, including power
exercised in the conduct of foreign relations, was itself a ground for
removal of the President.

* * * Indeed, serious encroachment by the executive upon the
constitutional prerogatives of another branch of government was one of
the major evils to be protected against by the impeachment clause. The
impeachment provision was seen by the framers as the therapeutic
corrective by which the proper balance and check between the branches
could be reestablished following abuse by one branch at the expense of
the other.

* * *

Congress appears not to have learned the lesson of the Indochina
War. After giving the President a blank check to embark on war and
spending years in a struggle to extricate the country from the consequent war, Congress then enacted the War Powers Resolution of 1973,
the recited purpose of which was to fulfill "the intent of the framers of
the Constitution * * * and to insure that the collective judgment of both
the Congress and the President will apply to the introduction of United
States Armed Forces into hostilities" but which actually endorsed future
delegations of power. According to Section 8, entitled "Interpretation of
Joint Resolution," the President may engage in hostilities if an act of
Congress has authorized this, or if a treaty should be ratified and should
be implemented by legislation authorizing the use of the armed forces.
This section contemplates that Congress shall make advance authorizations in general terms and that the President shall have the power,
although not the duty, of engaging in hostilities under such statutes.
Section 8 also holds that the President and the Senate may make
treaties promising to engage in hostilities in the future and that Congress may contemporaneously authorize the President to invoke the
treaty and plunge the country into war at any time during the life of the

treaty. This hardly fulfills the intent of the framers. The War Powers Resolution considers it proper for the President to engage in war if at an earlier date, perhaps at a very much earlier date, Congress—necessarily acting in total ignorance of the future problem, of the future circumstances, and even of the future antagonist—has issued a blank check.

Other sections of the War Powers Resolution raise similar constitutional issues. For example, Section 3 is full of ambiguities that permit the President to usurp the power of Congress. This section, entitled "Consultation," requires the President to "consult" with Congress "in every possible instance" before involving United States troops in "hostilities," actual or imminent. To "consult" supposedly means more than to inform; it is said to require advice, opinion, and, when appropriate, approval. "Every possible instance" is intended to exclude only such dire circumstances as a hostile missile attack. And "hostilities" are meant to encompass any state of confrontation, whether or not shots have been fired, including the provision of non-combat advisors. But those vague guidelines do not pass the constitutional tests of specificity required for any delegation of Congress. As a result, Presidents have largely ignored the consultation requirement. [The "Consultation" on Grenada is enlightening].

According to testimony by a senior State Department official, the President signed the directive ordering the invasion at 6:00 P.M. on October 24. At 8:00 P.M. the President met with the bipartisan congressional leadership to inform them of his decision. The invasion began at 5:30 A.M. the next day. Although the administration contended that the evening meeting satisfied the consultation requirement, one ranking member of the Senate Foreign Relations committee who was not even invited to the meeting commented, "There is a world of difference between being consulted and being asked do we think this is wise or not, or being informed, saying we are doing this at 5 A.M. tomorrow."

One justification for the failure to consult may be lack of time. In justifying the secrecy surrounding the invasion of Grenada, President Reagan stated, "We knew that we had little time and that complete secrecy was vital to insure both the safety of the young men who would undertake this mission and the Americans they were about to rescue." While it may be that sometimes circumstances will require an expediency that provides little opportunity for discussion, even then the President could consult secretly with members of Congress, as is done with the staff and executive branch officers, so that the decision-making process can more closely follow constitutional procedure.

Related constitutional issues are raised by the reporting requirements of the War Powers Resolution. Section 4(a)(1) allows the President to use military force without congressional authorization so long as she or he "reports" to Congress within forty-eight hours of deployment. This reporting requirement in turn triggers the running of a limited sixty-day time period. Under Section 5(b) the unauthorized deployment may continue for a period of sixty days unless Congress acts to either extend the time period for an additional thirty days or terminate the deployment altogether.

In practice, presidential reporting under Section 4(a)(1) has been less than ideal. For example, following the invasion of Grenada and the deployment of the marines in Lebanon, President Reagan reported to Congress: * * * "In accordance with my desire that the Congress be informed on this matter, and consistent with the War Powers Resolution, I am providing this report on the deployment of the United States Armed Forces * * *. This deployment * * * is being undertaken pursuant to my constitutional authority with respect to the conduct of foreign relations and as Commander-in-Chief * * *."

In neither situation did the President refer to Section 4(a)(1). By failing to mention Section 4(a)(1) in either report to Congress, the President indicated that he did not recognize any duty to withdraw the troops within the sixty day period if Congress had not acted. In the case of Lebanon, the marines were stationed in Beirut for over a year without congressional authorization. According to the Reagan administration, the resolution's "clock" did not start ticking when the marines were deployed because they were merely defensive and were not engaged in hostilities or imminent hostilities.

In refusing to acknowledge the constitutionality of the War Powers Resolution, presidents have often relied upon their power to conduct foreign policy and their position as commander-in-chief of the armed forces. However, the President's authority with respect to the conduct of foreign relations is a collegial authority to be exercised in concert with, not contrary to, congressional foreign policy authority. Moreover, the President's constitutional authority as commander-in-chief is limited to direction and conduct of hostilities following a congressional declaration of war or other congressional authorization. In fact, at the time the War Powers Resolution became law, opponents of the resolution argued that Sections 4(a)(1) and 5(b) granted "a legal basis for the President's broad claims of inherent power to initiate war" that was not present previously under the Constitution. These opponents preferred a Senate proposal that sought to reaffirm the proper role of Congress, limiting the circumstances under which the President could deploy the armed forces to those recognized by constitutional law. Instead, these limitations appear in the precatory "Purpose and Policy" section of the resolution and have no legal effect on the President's power to commence war.

Thus, perhaps not surprisingly, the most strident critics of the War Powers Resolution do not attack it as an unconstitutional delegation of the war power of Congress, but as an unconstitutional infringement on the President's war power—a reflection of how heavily the "constitutional 'balance' of authority over warmaking has swung * * * to the President in modern times." [See Harold Koh's work]. Since the passage of the resolution, almost all of the presidents have argued that it is an unconstitutional restriction upon the inherent presidential powers. President Nixon vetoed the resolution with indignation; President Ford challenged its constitutionality; and President Reagan refused to concede that congressional authorization was required for his various military excursions, though he purported to comply with the resolution.

For example, on October 12, 1983, when President Reagan signed into law the Multinational Force in Lebanon Resolution, which authorized the continued participation of the marines in the Multinational Force for a period of eighteen months, he expressed grave doubts as to the constitutionality of certain of its provisions. His statement, highly representative of the general Executive sentiment towards the War Powers Resolution, is worth quoting at length: "I would note that the initiation of isolated or infrequent acts of violence against United States Armed Forces does not necessarily constitute actual or imminent involvement in hostilities, even if casualties to those forces result. I think it reasonable to recognize the inherent risk and imprudence of setting any precise formula for making such determinations. Nor should my signing be viewed as any acknowledgement that the President's constitutional authority can be impermissibly infringed by statute, that congressional authorization would be required if and when the period specified in Section 5(b) of the War Powers Resolution might be deemed to have been triggered and the period had expired or that Section 6 of the Multinational Force in Lebanon Resolution may be interpreted to revise the President's constitutional authority to deploy United States armed forces."

Thus, President Reagan refused to concede that congressional authorization is required before the President constitutionally can deploy the United States Armed Forces in situations like those in Central America, Grenada, Lebanon, and the Persian Gulf.

Still, of all the provisions of the War Powers Resolution, the most debated provision has been Section 5(c), which allows Congress, by concurrent resolution, to require the President to remove troops engaged in the hostilities abroad. A concurrent resolution does not require the President's signature, nor is it subject to veto. The power of Congress to have the last word—the so-called legislative veto—has often been challenged and finally was held unconstitutional in Immigration and Naturalization Service v. Chadha. The reasoning of that decision apparently invalidates Section 5(c) of the War Powers Resolution. The Senate subsequently sought to bring that section within constitutional limits by providing that any congressional action requiring the President to withdraw United States forces engaged in hostilities abroad must follow certain priority procedures that do not constitute a legislative veto.

Whether Congress is willing and able to reassert its proper constitutional role in deciding when to use the war powers remains to be seen. Its attempt to do so in the War Powers Resolution seems, at least in part, to have failed. The resolution is an overbroad delegation of the war power of Congress that essentially writes the President a blank check. Unfortunately, court challenges to such flagrantly unconstitutional delegations of the war power encounter substantial practical roadblocks. Both supporters and opponents of the War Powers Resolution agree that its constitutionality is not likely to be adjudicated. Those difficulties, however, should not obscure the clear status of the law: the Supreme Court has never held that Congress may delegate the power to initiate war to the President. Even the dictum in the Curtiss-

Wright case said nothing of the sort. And the dictum in Curtiss–Wright has neither [progenitors] nor progeny.

The rule against the delegation of legislative power is our only legal guarantee of the continuance of republican government. The Roman republic perished through delegation, and Ulpian wrote its epitaph, "What pleases the prince has the force of law, since by a royal law established concerning his sovereignty the people confers all its sovereignty and power upon him."

————

Michael Glennon's article, immediately below, addresses the questions: What is the record of the War Powers Resolution? What are its prospects for resolving the problems relating to balancing the need for quick and efficient presidential action in time of emergency and the danger of an "Imperial Presidency?"

MICHAEL GLENNON, THE WAR POWERS RESOLUTION: SAD RECORD, DISMAL PROMISE

17 Loy.L.A.L.Rev. 656, 658–59, 661, 664–65, 670 (1984) (fns. omitted).*

* * *

[Rep. Zablocki's] first principal conclusion—that "predictions that the Resolution would weaken the nation's ability to react to foreign policy crises have proven unwarranted"—is difficult to quarrel with. Arguments to the contrary are for the most part unsupported and unsupportable assertions resting upon the major premise that anything and everything done by a President to halt the international communist conspiracy must perforce be constitutional.

These reflexive proponents of unfettered Presidential discretion fundamentally misapprehend the separation of powers concept. In place of the "divisiveness" engendered by the War Powers Resolution they would substitute an "iron demand" of "cooperation" between Congress and the President—a cooperation that is, upon analysis, the cooperation of a valet with his master. Brandeis, Corwin, and other boat-rockers presumably are among those who would, if given the chance, have played into the hands of Hanoi and Moscow. "[C]ooperation should always be the goal." Whether one branch should play war-powers manservant to the other is perhaps an issue that could be argued either way, but it should suffice at this point to note that the question seems to have been ventilated and resolved in 1789. * * *

Representative Zablocki is correct in his first conclusion only because he is quite wrong in his second—the Resolution has not hampered the President's ability to react to foreign policy crises precisely because it has *not* served to "restore the balance in the rights and responsibilities of the Congress and the President in the decision to commit troops." To the contrary, it has proven virtually ineffectual in achieving that statutorily-stated objective. Zablocki observes that "there has been more non-

* Reprinted with the permission of Loyola L.A.L.Rev.

compliance than compliance" by the executive branch. Although I am not certain that compliance or noncompliance can be neatly quantified, I quite agree that the record of executive branch adherence to the requirements of the Resolution has been dismal, and I am thus somewhat nonplussed by Zablocki's effusive assessment—set forth after a well-documented recounting of "halfhearted" consultation, inadequate reporting, and overall footdragging—that the product is "excellent," "workable" and that its "credibility * * * has never been higher." If credibility means the likelihood of compliance by future Presidents who, all things considered, would prefer to forget it, it seems to me that those chief executives will be on firmer ground than ever.

* * *

[The] failure of the Resolution's sponsors to articulate lucidly the reasons for its validity is disappointing because there exists a persuasive case for its validity. The argument is, in the sheerest outline, that the "fixed" powers approach to presidential power taken by the Supreme Court in *Curtiss–Wright, Pink,* and *Belmont* has given way to the very different "fluctuating" powers approach set forth initially by Chief Justice Marshall in *Little v. Barreme,* reiterated by Justice Jackson in *Steel Seizure Case,* and formally adopted by Justice Rehnquist in *Dames & Moore v. Regan.* Under the latter approach, the scope of the President's power is a function of the concurrence or non-concurrence of the Congress; once Congress acts, its negative provides "the rule of the case." That analytical framework, it seems to me, provides a general foundation for the congressional mandate of consultation and reporting as well as the imposition of a time limit upon the use of the armed forces in hostilities—all of which, in the absence of a statement by the Congress, might fall within a "zone of twilight."

* * *

* * * [A] reason for half-hearted compliance by the Executive is that fuller compliance has not been demanded—either legally by the Resolution, or politically by members of Congress. It vastly understates the problem to describe it * * * simply as a matter of "tepid congressional oversight." To cast the issue as one of oversight is to suggest that the need is merely for more hearings that generate more information. The problem has not been a lack of information, but Congress' failure to *act* on information—to act, specifically, by removing ambiguities in the Resolution and, more importantly, by living up to its responsibilities under the role it carved out for itself under the Resolution. At least three ambiguities have undermined [its] proper operation.

The Resolution should be amended to set forth a definition of "hostilities." In the absence of such a definition, officials of the executive branch and members of Congress engaged in a running argument whether United States military activities in Lebanon constituted "hostilities." When ten marines died in a twenty-day period after having been fired upon regularly by hostile forces, it seemed utterly disingenuous to claim, as the Reagan administration did, that the hostilities test was not met. Nonetheless, the term is not self-defining, and because the Resolution provides no guidance as to its meaning, a gradual escalation of hostilities can generate serious confusion as to the date on which the time limit is triggered. Similarly, there is no clear indication in the Resolution whether a variety of different activities are intended to fall within the "hostilities" test, such as exposure to minefields, missile attack, chemical or biological agents, or neutron rays. If Congress is serious about removing uncertainty and closing the door to semantic circumvention by the executive branch, it must define the term "hostilities."

Second, * * * consultation, time after time, has been perfunctory at best. This is true largely because the Executive has been allowed, time after time, to get away with perfunctory consultation. Aside from raising a political stink when such failure occurs—which congressional leaders have been loathe to do for fear of being mistakenly seen by the public as somehow critical of a military initiative—a Congress truly serious about consultation would amend the Resolution to specify precisely who is to be consulted, to make clear that "in every possible instance" does not include instances that present alleged security problems, and perhaps, to prohibit certain uses of the armed forces in the absence of genuine consultation.

Third, and most important, is the vagueness of the reporting requirement, which has led to the Resolution's virtual unraveling. Although the Executive's record here is clearly at odds with the Resolution's spirit, there is an argument to be made that presidential reports have complied with its letter. The reason is that there is in fact not one reporting requirement set forth in the Resolution, but three. Only one—that required by section 4(a)(1)—triggers the sixty-day time limit; those required by sections 4(a)(2) and 4(a)(3) are merely informational (although in the original House version of the Resolution they too triggered the time limitations). The problem arises in that the three situations overlap: facts that would require a report under section 4(a)(1) might also require a report under one of the two succeeding paragraphs, and the Resolution contains no requirement that the President specify which of the three reports he is submitting. Only the *Mayaguez* report (submitted after the military operations had terminated because they lasted less than forty-eight hours) referred expressly to section 4(a)(1). Consequently, the other reports effectively left unanswered the critical question: had the sixty-day time limit been triggered?

* * *

But these and other modifications of the Resolution will not, in themselves, "insure that the collective judgment of both the Congress and the President will apply to the introduction of United States Armed Forces into hostilities * * * [I]t has become clear that the Resolution's sponsors were naive to believe that any law could achieve that objective. The most that a statute can do, however artfully drawn, is to facilitate the efforts of individual members of Congress to carry out their responsibilities under the Constitution. To do that requires understanding, and it also requires courage: it demands an insight into the delicacy with which our separated powers are balanced, and the fortitude to stand up to those who would equate criticism with lack of patriotism. For a Congress comprised of such members, no War Powers Resolution would be necessary; for a Congress without them, no War Powers Resolution will be sufficient.

———

Any judicial role? *What articles of the Constitution are relevant?* Consider the following review by Carl Landauer of Franck's Book, Political Questions/Judicial Answers, 87 A.J.I.L. 465 (1993): "Thomas Franck's new book provides an elegant and at times emotional argument against the use of the political question doctrine by U.S. courts to abstain from deciding cases that touch upon foreign policy. Troubled by the resulting lacuna in the rule of law, Franck writes: 'Judicial deference ignores the evident truth that in our system a law that is not enforceable by adjudicatory process is no law at all.' Accordingly, a 'foreign policy exempt from judicial review is tantamount to governance by men and women emancipated from the bonds of law'."

Franck begins by tracing the political question doctrine back to what he calls a "Faustian pact" entered into by John Marshall. Franck believes that in order to assert the Court's power of judicial review over other important realms, Marshall traded away its ability to decide cases in the realm of foreign policy. In essence, Marshall adopted a line of British case law segregating the foreign policy realm as being nonjusticiable as a "relatively inexpensive 'giveback' to throw to the political branches and the states". Franck then chronicles the development of Marshall's trade-off into a matter of orthodoxy for the federal judiciary, finding its crystallized form in Justice Sutherland's dicta in *Curtiss–Wright* in 1936. But, Franck notes, despite repeated invocation of the doctrine, many of the courts invoking it seemed not to have taken its teaching entirely to heart, for they would make pious references to the doctrine while nevertheless deciding the case on the merits or, after abstaining from adjudication, feel free to explain how the case should be decided on the merits. In all this, Franck discerns "a powerful whiff of hypocrisy." In essence, he sees a result-oriented judiciary intent on confirming the foreign policy decisions of the Executive, whether doing it on the merits or by judicial restraint in the particular case.

Having undercut the intellectual integrity of the courts voicing the political question doctrine, Franck concentrates his criticism on the rationales given for relying on it. To those who believe that judges are not competent to deal with the factual aspects of foreign affairs cases, Franck responds that foreign policy cases would not create especially difficult evidentiary problems for our "sophisticated federal judicial system". To those who believe that issues in foreign affairs create problems of applicable legal standards, Franck answers that courts are well practiced in dealing with vague areas of law. To those who believe that courts cannot interfere with foreign policy because the stakes are too high, Franck answers that most uses of the political question doctrine are not "in the midst of military hostilities, the one circumstance in which some form of judicial reticence might seem warranted", and he adds that the real harm to the national interest results from the refusal to apply legal standards to those conducting our foreign policy. To those who believe that the judiciary is in no position to confront the

President, he insists that "judicial legitimacy depends on a willingness to challenge, when it is not justified to accommodate, political authority".

After these point-by-point responses to the federal judges who have used the political question doctrine in the realm of foreign affairs, Franck turns to the good news: the judges who refuse to dismiss foreign policy cases as nonjusticiable. Yet, despite the narrowing numbers of judges directly applying the political question doctrine, Franck points out that those who find foreign policy cases justiciable remain respectful enough to the doctrine to contrive some way to appear not to be directly violating it. Nevertheless, the list of cases in which the political question doctrine was not adopted is, for Franck, a source of encouragement. But Franck is encouraged, more than by this rather uneven record, by the German judiciary, which provides for him a usable model of a judiciary that, while giving German foreign-policy makers a good deal of latitude, refuses to allow foreign policy to be made outside the rule of law. And, after suggesting several strategies for judges in the United States similarly to provide room for the foreign-policy makers within the rule of law, Franck concludes with the moral force of his opening: "To make the law's writ inoperable at the water's edge is nothing less than an exercise in unilateral moral disarmament. It is a strategy urgently in need of judicial review".

* * *

WORMUTH & FIRMAGE, TO CHAIN THE DOG OF WAR
pp. 302–303 (1989).*

"Why the recent drift away from collegial determination of foreign policy direction by the President and Congress? One cause may be the modern technology of war. It has been suggested that nuclear weapons capable of continental destruction borne by missiles minutes from our shores make it essential that we be able to decide for war instantaneously, by one person, without debate or restraint."

However, it is [wrong] to equate collegiality with lack of effective, immediate response. Congress in the past has proven that it can quickly deliberate when required. One day after President Eisenhower asked Congress for authority to use American armed forces to protect Taiwan from attack by mainland China, the chairman of the House Rules Committee called up the resolution under a closed rule permitting only two hours of debate and no amendment. The House passed the resolution that same day.

But the belief that speed is essential in the event of a nuclear attack may be challenged. Precipitous action in response to an attack does not prevent or even mitigate the destruction we nevertheless suffer from the nuclear strike upon us. Even if we are obliterated by a massive salvo, we presumably can still respond by whatever remains of land-based

* Reprinted with the permission of the University of Illinois Press.

missiles of our own, plus submarine and air-launched missiles. Unless we plan to strike first, there is no situation beyond self-defense, which exists in any event in the President if we are under sudden attack, under which must we respond with alacrity.

Contrarily, with the evidence we now have of genocidal pandemic following nuclear war, with human society destroyed and human life in the balance, modern technology demands all the more our adherence to every institution we possess that ensures debate and reflection, negotiation, conciliation, and peaceful resolution of disputes. The founders' prescription that Congress possess the sole war power to chain the dog of war remains essential still.

FIRMAGE, BOOK REVIEW—ESSAY
59 G.W.L.Rev. 1684, at 1685–1688 (1991).*

The spectacular success of the American military in the war against Iraq not only obliterated the forces of President Saddam Hussein, but now threatens the same fate for those institutions and inclinations favoring peace and against war. The thoroughness of Iraq's defeat and the dispatch of its accomplishment, coupled with the unpredictably low number of Allied casualties, combined to produce unparalleled euphoria and nationalistic ardor. This spirit, exploited by politicians attempting to accomplish their own purposes in such a climate, seems to be leading toward a rash of nonsequiturs in the guise of conclusions regarding the efficacy of the military option to be drawn from this short but savage conflict.

The event in this portion of history that deserves our sympathetic attention is the ending of the Cold War. The collapse of the Berlin Wall in November 1989 saw the end of nearly a century of war, physical and mental. World War I initiated a form of war both global and total. Civilian populations became the primary victims of a war affecting the entire world. A system of world governance and society ended forever. The resulting forces of inflation, depression, war guilt, reparations, and dislocation inevitably produced World War II, an aftershock predictable in its consequence if not in its particularity and severity.

But the hatreds engendered by war that normally abate with its end instead were continued into a Cold War between the two nations that emerged as superpower rivals. Almost every conflict—decolonization, civil war, or local dispute—was perceived as involving this bipolar struggle between the USSR and the United States. Paradoxically, even while threatening to create violence and destruction on a scale never before known, the existence of nuclear weaponry helped in detering overt and massive violence between the superpowers. This corrosive rivalry, however, resulted in proxy wars and superpower intervention on opposing sides of civil wars throughout Asia, Africa, and Latin America. In addition, covert actions—too often covert from congressional approval and oversight, if not from the Soviet Union—were a characteristic of this time. Such violence, unacknowledged and often illegitimate, remains a corrosive element incongruous with principles of open debate and the rule of law within a democratic state.

* Reprinted with the permission of the University of Illinois Press.

Finally, may we have the opportunity to address impelling problems: the prevention of war, particularly nuclear war; the end of the arms race, nuclear and conventional; severely decreasing military spending, not only in the United States, but also in scores of nations throughout the world forced by peculiar logic to devote enormous sums for building large military forces whose main function more realistically seems to be the preservation of the incumbent regime from internal opposition rather than as a protection against external aggression. The war against Iraq could not be considered of the same historic importance if its geopolitical consequence—the replacement of a brutal Iraqi aggressor dictator in Kuwait in favor of the more benign, if medieval, Arabian oligarchy that had ruled this emirate—were the criterion. The national elation that has followed seemingly painless and decisive victory, however, has obscured the truly historic changes sweeping Eastern Europe and the Soviet Union, not only from the view of the American people but from the White House and congressional leadership.

Impelling reasons exist to question supposed lessons learned from the success of American arms. Our inclination both to objectify and personalize evil makes no more sense now than it did before the Allied victory. Even elimination of Saddam Hussein, standing alone, would produce no assurance that Iraqi alternatives for leadership will be less threatening to American interests than before. Iraq is in chaos and threatens to become fragmented beyond repair—another Lebanon. Shiite fundamentalist leadership, with Iranian influence, is not obviously in our best interest. Hussein's disappearance [would stop] far short of insuring stability in the Middle East as General Noriega's capture was from resolving drug traffic. We have moved through a dreary procession of devil figures in American mythology; from the Ayatollah Khomeini in Iran, General Noriega in Panama, Libya's Muammar Qadhafi to Hussein, without significantly affecting the real challenges that still must be met in this hemisphere or in the Middle East: preserving American interests abroad while respecting local sovereignty; guaranteeing Israeli borders and security; establishing and maintaining normal relations between the Arab states and Israel; and doing justice for Palestinian interests in the Middle East, including their possession of a homeland.

The real costs of the Gulf War are not yet visible to the American people: Iraqi casualties approaching mass slaughter, the country itself bombed into a preindustrial age, facing mass starvation and pandemic disease; Arab and Islamic hatred that will affect our relations for decades to come; an environmental disaster on a world scale never before known; [and] * * * a potentially disastrous weakening of our internal restraints against war, restraints presuming that peace is the norm and war the aberration, requiring anyone proposing war to bear an enormous burden of persuasion with the American people in national debate and consideration. In its place are we poised to bestow the war power on an American Caesar rather than to preserve and strengthen the constitutional decision to secure the peace by lodging the decision for war or peace within Congress—the democratic branch that must pay for the war and answer to the people for breaking the peace? Nationalistic euphoria surely will lead to a form of national hubris, corporate ego inflation, followed by mistakes in judgment in the form of foreign adventurism, then meeting our own nemesis in whatever form—unless we abide by our own structural checks designed to avoid this very phenomenon.

Our war with Iraq was preceded by a healthy national debate culminating in the most impressive example of responsible congressional debate on the decision for war since the Second World War. But the seeming conclusiveness, the quick success, and the modest number of Allied casualties in the Gulf War have combined to give this decision for war an aura of wisdom and popularity with the people that undermines the perceived vision of those who opposed offensive action at that time before economic sanctions reasonably could be expected to work against Iraq.

Yet all the reasons for an institutional bias in favor of peace and against war remain. War represents the failure of diplomatic and peaceful means of dispute resolution in favor of savagery, distinguished only by a gossamer thin cloak of respectability because the violence is done by nation-state actors.

The conclusion that war, with all its violence, is a decisive and final resolver of the problems leading to war is almost always an illusion. Despite American success on the battlefield, the Iraqi war almost inevitably will turn out to be *no* exception to this rule. Most of the political and economic factors that led to the dispute still remain unresolved. Since the end of the war, Kurdish and Shiite minorities in Iraq have suffered enormous hardship, Saddam Hussein remains in power and continues his ruthless regime, and Kuwait is no closer to democracy than it was prior to August 1990. Ultimately, war only creates enormous suffering as well as economic and environmental dislocation. *Query*: Have the assumptions in this article turned out to be true?

1. "OPERATION JUST CAUSE"— THE PANAMA INVASION

One could place the discussion of the invasion of Panama under the rubric of unilateral self defense, humanitarian intervention, or even under expansion of jurisdiction for the * * * purpose of curtailing drug trafficking. These were all justifications made by the U.S. Government. Consider the following questions as you read: Was the invasion justified by the claim of unilateral self-defense? Was it justified on the basis of regional self-defense and the promotion of regional security? Could it be justified as a "police action" in the basic sense of the term, to "capture a criminal?" Ultimately with some 26,000 U.S. military, the U.S. forces met early resistance and later sniper fire, but within just 3–4 days, all resistance ended. There were at least 400 Panamanian deaths (mainly civilian) and only 23 U.S. fatalities. Judge Hoeveler, in *U.S. v. Noriega,* noted: "[a]lthough the motives behind the military action are open to speculation, the stated goals of the invasion were to protect American lives, support democracy, preserve the Panama Canal Treaties, and bring Noriega to the United States to stand trial for narcotics offenses."

The United States has long had an interest in Panama, since it participated in its creation as it seceded from Colombia in 1903. The U.S. Navy held a presence off-shore, to be sure that Colombia would submit to dismemberment. The U.S. and Panama signed a treaty within a few weeks granting the U.S. expansive rights to the area which is now the Canal Zone. The latter Panama Canal Treaties (effective 1979) allow the gradual return of the Zone and the Canal to the control of Panama, to culminate in 1999.

The Invasion Of Panama:

As East Berliners celebrated their new freedom, the U.S. executive branch was planning an invasion of tiny Panama. Once the invasion was underway, the executive branch justified the surprise attack on various grounds: self-defense, protection of American citizens, defending democracy, protecting implementation of the Panama Canal Treaties, and combatting drug trafficking.

For years Noriega had been coddled by United States officials. The United States long had been aware of Noriega's illicit dealings, but chose to ignore them as long as Noriega remained a "stabilizing" source in the region. According to Panamanian Vice–President Arias, the United States government redefined Noriega as an adversary only after his regime became a "source of instability rather than stability." The executive branch suddenly reversed itself and began to treat Noriega as an enemy. Initially, economic isolation was employed. President Reagan declared a national emergency under the National Emergencies Act and the International Emergency Economic Powers Act [EEPA] on April 8, 1988. Then in May 1989, recently-elected President Bush deployed an additional two thousand combat troops to the canal zone, ostensibly to protect American lives. Predictably, tension and hostilities escalated and President Bush ordered Operation Just Cause, the code name for the Panamanian invasion, on December 20.

Could the invasion of Panama be justified under international and constitutional law? Can any legal definition of self-defense justify or excuse the invasion of Panama? The most fundamental principles of international law call for respect for the territorial integrity and sovereignty of another state. Does the fact that a state is governed by a corrupt tyrant and dictator justify invasion by another state? Did our own actions cause the threats and danger for United States citizens and the Panama Canal? We determined that our national interests would be served best if General Noriega were removed. We then invaded the country—at great cost to Panamanians. Does any principle of international law justify this action?

The invasion falls under the category of acts that are denied to the Executive under the War Clause, so congressional approval is required *before* any military action can occur. President Bush made the decision to invade unilaterally and only notified Congress after initiation of action. At no point prior to or during Operation Just Cause was congressional approval sought by the President.

The War Clause was drafted to demand congressional authorization for acts of war taken by the United States Government except in response to sudden attack on the United States. Therefore, the War Clause must apply to full scale invasions such as Operation Just Cause. First, the United States realistically was not threatened at any time. The Panamanian Assembly's "state of war" proclamation on December 15, 1989, was never more than a mouse that roared. [In fact, it was a domestic statement aimed at triggering domestic authority to Noriega]. Second, there was no "sudden" turn of events that required the President to act immediately without time to consult Congress. Both an attack on the United States and a degree of surprise are necessary prerequisites to an executive military response and neither were present at the beginning of Operation Just Cause. On the contrary, Operation Just Cause was a carefully planned and executed offensive, without congressional approval, against the forces of General Noriega.

Operation Just Cause also failed the "fluctuating powers" test governing the delegation of power in foreign relations. Under the test, when Congress has made its intention clear, then it is the will of Congress that controls. Congress has expressed its will regarding unauthorized executive military action on numerous occasions. The War Powers Resolution of 1973, the Hughes–Ryan Amendment to the Foreign Assistance Act of 1974, the Intelligence Authorization Act for Fiscal Year 1981, and the Boland Amendments establish a record of congressional intent; namely, no offensive military activity shall be planned and staged without the knowledge and authorization of the Congress.

The initial deployment of two thousand troops in May 1989 also should have triggered the sixty-day provision under section 5(b) of the War Powers Resolution. Under the Resolution, any introduction of United States troops into "imminent hostilities" *automatically* engages the sixty-day provision. As the House Report on the Resolution stated, the term "hostilities" also "encompasses a state of confrontation in which no shots have been fired but where there is clear and present danger of armed conflict." The House Report further defined imminent hostilities as situations "in which there is a clear potential * * * for actual armed conflict."

Did the act of introducing combat troops into a nation that is being intimidated politically, economically, and militarily create a potential for armed conflict? Can the troop reinforcement of May 1989 be seen as a planned prologue to invasion? Was the "clear and present danger of armed conflict" recognized by the executive branch? Is that precisely what was intended? Did combat troop reinforcement in May 1989 constitute introduction of United States forces into "imminent hostilities," according to both the language and intent of the War Powers Resolution?

Congress should have pressed the War Powers Resolution upon the President in May 1989 for three reasons. First, the situation in Panama had deteriorated to the point where the probability of armed confrontation was clear. Second, by triggering the clock of the War Powers Resolution, Congress would have forced the President to explain his intentions concerning military activity in Panama. This would have allowed Congress to participate in the decision on whether to initiate Operation Just Cause, thus satisfying not only the War Powers Resolution, but also the constitutional war power and foreign relations power. Third, it would have provided valuably needed precedent to increase the functional credibility of the War Powers Resolution. The last reason is vital. Every time Congress allows unauthorized executive action to go unchallenged by the War Powers Resolution—even in situations where Congress agrees with the action taken—the lack of action further weakens this already troubled Resolution.

Report to Congress, President George Bush (December 21, 1989): The White House, Washington, DC, December 21, 1989, to Hon. Thomas S. Foley, *Speaker of the House of Representatives, Washington, DC.*

Dear Mr. Speaker: On December 15, 1989, at the instigation of Manuel Noriega, the illegitimate Panamanian National Assembly declared that a state of war existed between the Republic of Panama and the United States. At the same time, Noriega gave a highly inflammatory anti-American speech. A series of vicious and brutal acts directed at U.S. personnel and dependents followed these events.

On December 16, 1989, a U.S. Marine officer was killed without justification by Panama Defense Forces (PDF) personnel. Other elements of the PDF beat a U.S. Naval officer and unlawfully detained, physically abused, and threatened the officer's wife. These acts of violence are directly attributable to Noriega's dictatorship, which created a climate of aggression that places American lives and interests in peril.

These and other events over the past two years have made it clear that the lives and welfare of American citizens in Panama were increasingly at risk, and that the continued safe operation of the Panama Canal and the integrity of the Canal Treaties would be in serious jeopardy if such lawlessness were allowed to continue.

Under these circumstances, I ordered the deployment of approximately 11,000 additional U.S. forces to Panama. In conjunction with the 13,000 U.S. Forces already present, military operations were initiated on December 20, 1989, to protect American lives, to defend democracy in Panama, to apprehend Noriega and bring him to trial on the drug-related charges for which he was indicted in 1988, and to ensure the integrity of the Panama Canal Treaties.

In the early morning of December 20, 1989, the democratically elected Panamanian leadership announced formation of a government, assumed power in a formal swearing-in ceremony, and welcomed the assistance of U.S. Armed Forces in removing the illegitimate Noriega regime. The deployment of U.S. Forces is an exercise of the right of self-defense recognized in Article 51 of the United Nations charter and was necessary to protect American lives in imminent danger and to fulfill our responsibilities under the Panama Canal Treaties. It was welcomed by the democratically elected government of Panama. The military operations were ordered pursuant to my constitutional authority with respect to the conduct of foreign relations and as Commander in Chief.

In accordance with my desire that Congress be fully informed on this matter, and consistent with the War Powers Resolution, I am providing this report on the deployment of U.S. Armed Forces to Panama. Although most organized opposition has ceased, it is not possible at this time to predict the precise scope and duration of the military operations or how long the temporary increase of U.S. Forces in Panama will be required. Nevertheless, our objectives are clear and largely have been accomplished. Our additional Forces will remain in Panama only so long as their presence is required.

Sincerely,
George Bush.

————

Did the invasion fit within any of the exceptions to Article 51 of the U.N. Charter? Was safeguarding U.S. nationals a valid justification either as a * * * form of self-defense or humanitarian intervention? Was apprehending General Noriega a valid justification in international law? Insuring the integrity of the Panama Canal Treaties? The restoration of democracy or protecting human rights in Panama?

————

ABRAHAM D. SOFAER (LEGAL ADVISER, U.S. DEPT. OF STATE AT THE TIME), THE LEGALITY OF THE UNITED STATES ACTION IN PANAMA

29 Colum.J.Trans.L. 281 (1991) (fns. omitted).*

V. The United States Action was Necessary and Proportionate

President Bush reasonably concluded that Operation Just Cause was both necessary and proportionate under international law. By December 20, 1989, Noriega had declared as his objective "only one territory and only one flag," and had repudiated the right of the United States to protect the Canal. He regarded Panama as being in a state of war with the United States, having crossed the line from harassment to homicide in the escalation of hostilities. The United States had attempted to negotiate Noriega's voluntary surrender of power, had protested both Noriega's violations of the Canal Treaties and his violence against U.S. forces, and had invoked all available forms of diplomatic and economic sanctions. All these efforts failed. Under these circumstances, ousting Noriega was a legitimate and necessary foreign policy objective, only that result could end the attacks on U.S. nationals, preserve U.S. (and Panamanian) rights under the Canal Treaties, restore the legitimate, democratic government selected by the people of Panama and end Noriega's alleged involvement in international drug violations.

* Reprinted with the permission of the Columb.J.Trans.L.

Because the objective of removing Noriega from authority in Panama is justifiable under international law, the substantial military action designed to achieve that result was fully warranted. The Joint Chiefs of Staff recommended, and the President adopted, a plan designed to employ a swift, overpowering force, on the belief that far fewer casualties would result than if any less intensive effort were implemented. United States diplomats and military officials on the scene emphatically concurred in this strategy, as did the democratically elected Panamanian leadership. Without total victory, the PDF or Noriega, or both, would have utilized their massive store of weapons to make democratic government impossible. A protracted operation could have been a tactical disaster, and would have exposed U.S. civilians to continuing danger.

International law, and international lawyers, should avoid utilizing the doctrine of proportionality as a vehicle for second-guessing tactical judgments as to what form a military action should take to achieve a legitimate objective. The military judgment President Bush accepted was reasonable in light of the continuing danger that otherwise would have existed for U.S. forces, for U.S. Canal rights and for President Endara's capacity to govern. U.S. forces were ordered to act in accordance with the laws of armed conflict, and the United States chose to provide all captured PDF members with prisoner-of-war protections under the Geneva Convention.

* * *

L. HENKIN, THE INVASION OF PANAMA UNDER INTERNATIONAL LAW: A GROSS VIOLATION

29 Colum.J.Trans.L. (1991).

* * *

III. The Legal Adviser's Justifications

The Legal Adviser's address offers no new legal justification for the invasion of Panama but places different emphasis on those originally published, making some more explicit and less ambiguous and, in my view, more radical, more clearly erroneous in law, and more damaging to the cause of maintaining international order through international law.

To begin, the Legal Adviser strikes at the explicit language and clear meaning of Article 2(4) of the Charter which prohibits "the use of force against the territorial integrity or political independence of any state." Rather than offering a narrow interpretation of key terms, his argument concludes that the action in Panama "cannot *be viewed* as having been *intended* to *compromise* the territorial integrity or political independence of Panama." If military invasion and toppling an incumbent government is not a use of force against the territorial integrity and political independence of another state, what is? What the United States did, and intended to do, was to violate—not merely "compromise"—the territorial integrity of Panama and its political independence as asserted by its incumbent government. The Legal Adviser invokes "the cooperation and support" of Endara as lending "substantial weight" to the legitimacy of the U.S. action. That Endara controlled no Panamanian territory and exercised no governmental powers, we are told, did not deprive his consent "of legal significance." In my view, that consent has no legal significance for justifying the U.S. invasion.

The Legal Adviser would extend and expand a small exception for "humanitarian intervention" to justify not merely using minimal force to protect or extricate hostages, but a full-scale invasion to overthrow a government. The right of "humanitarian intervention" is claimed as a justification for such an invasion even though few U.S. citizens were in fact threatened and they could have been extricated or protected without armed invasion. The Legal Advisor would extend "humanitarian intervention," not only to justify the use of force to save lives, but also to overthrow undemocratic governments. There is no basis in law for such radical exceptions to Article 2(4).

The Legal Adviser's principal blow at the law of the Charter lies in his interpretation of Article 51. The United States has long rejected claims by other states of a right to act in self-defense in the absence of an armed attack. During the Suez Canal Crisis in 1957 the United States rejected such a justification by its closest NATO allies. Before the Reagan Administration, the United States was careful not to justify its own resorts to force as acts in self-defense when there had been no armed attack. Even the Reagan Administration did not claim the right of self-defense in the absence of an armed attack, though it sought to stretch the concept of armed attack to justify its uses of force against Nicaragua and its bombing of Libya in response to terrorist activities attributed to Libya's government. Now the Legal Adviser explicitly declares that it is *not* the U.S. position that the right of self-defense applies only in response to armed attack. His claim contradicts a longstanding U.S. position and the established view of international law.

Recognizing that even when force is permissible in self-defense it is limited by requirements of necessity and proportionality, the Legal Adviser declares that the U.S. action was "necessary and proportionate." In my view, international law would conclude that the invasion was not "necessary" for any lawful purpose, and that invasion by 24,000 troops—inflicting several hundred casualties and much property damage, and overthrowing an incumbent government—was out of any proportion to the attacks on U.S. personnel cited, to the desire to bring Noriega to trial, or to anything else in the circumstances that might remotely contribute to a right to use force in self-defense. We are told, however, that "international law * * * should avoid utilizing the doctrine of proportionality as a vehicle for second-guessing tactical judgments as to what form a military action should take to achieve a legitimate objective." What, then, is left of the doctrine of proportionality?

The Legal Adviser also invokes the Panama Canal Treaties as authorizing the U.S. invasion. To support that conclusion he cites the Senate Report declaring that the Treaties would authorize U.S. action, "not only in connection with external threats to the Canal, but also with respect to internal threats." Indeed, under the Treaties, both the United States and the Government of Panama have the right to defend the Canal against internal threats, for example by terrorists. But there was no hint that the United States could defend the Canal against the Government of Panama, and surely there was no suggestion that the United States could replace one government of Panama with another in order to defend the Canal.

No government, in Panama or anywhere else, would conclude a treaty that would authorize what the United States did in Panama. Even if Panama and the United States had concluded such a treaty, it would be void: such a treaty would violate the U.N. Charter, which by its terms is to prevail over any inconsistent treaties. It would violate the principles of Article 2(4) of the Charter which are *jus cogens*.

In summary, to justify the U.S. action the Legal Adviser would:

— eviscerate Article 2(4) prohibiting "the use of force against the territorial independence or political integrity" of another state;

— expand "humanitarian intervention" to permit any state to invade another to impose the invading state's view and version of democracy;

— excise the requirement of an armed attack to justify the use of force in self-defense, and in effect accept the view that the use of force is permitted whenever a state concludes that it is the victim of various forms of "aggression" against its "vital interests" as it defines them, or that it has "just cause";

— render virtually meaningless the requirement of proportionality by insisting that the U.S. action in this case was proportionate and that international law cannot "second guess" the state using force as to what is proportional; and

— distort the clear meaning of an important treaty to render it one that no government of Panama would have concluded and giving it a meaning that will doubtless be disavowed by future governments of Panama.

In the end, the Legal Adviser has felt compelled to assert that "the threat or use of force is not inherently wrong." I disagree profoundly. His view is surely not international law. It was not the U.S. view of the law, and was not U.S. policy for at least 35 years after World War II. I deeply regret hearing that it is U.S. policy now. I profoundly hope it will not be U.S. policy tomorrow.

Additionally, the Legal Adviser has struck a different kind of blow at international law. He has suggested that we must treat international law as "common law." If by that he means that, like common law, international law develops in response to changing conditions, perceptions or values, his analogy is unexceptionable. His perception of international law as common law, however, implies something else. It implies that the United States—and therefore every other country—is entitled to decide for itself what the law is; that it can take any action it sees fit—including the use of armed force against other countries—and declare it permissible.

Customary international law indeed has important similarities to the common law, but there are essential differences between them. To invoke an analogy between them to justify the invasion of Panama misconceives the character of international law and the workings and processes of the international political system. To invoke it here may misconceive also the character, workings and processes of the common law. The common law grew, developed and changed in response to new experiences and growing understanding. Slowly and infrequently, society, speaking through perceptive judges, nudged the law along if it no longer fit new needs in new circumstances. But an individual who deviated from what had been long established as common law in the hope of changing it did so at the peril of being held to be in violation, and usually paid for it.

Customary international law, and even the interpretation of a treaty, may also change in response to new needs or new insights. A state might knowingly deviate from what had been established law (or established interpretation of a treaty) in the hope of changing the law. But that state does so at its peril. It does so at the peril that it will not succeed in changing the law and will be adjudged to have violated the law. It does so at the peril that it may succeed in destroying or eroding established law, to its later deep regret.

If the invasion of Panama, and the legal arguments to justify it, were designed to erode or modify established law, they have been rejected by the large majority of the states and of the legal community—"the judges" of the "international common law." If the Panama invasion and the attempts to justify it sought to change the law—whether to permit the use of force where there has been no armed attack but to defend *soi disant* "vital interests," to permit the use of force to impose more legitimate governments or to capture thugs—we can only hope that the attempt to effect such changes in the law will not succeed. The United States, I am deeply persuaded, will regret it if such a change in the "common law" occurs, and will itself seek to prevent that change.

Indeed, the history of the common law rejects its use as an analogy to justify the U.S. invasion of Panama. When the common law proved inadequate, when society could not tolerate the law's ambiguities and uncertainties and its dependence on imperfect institutions, the law was codified, made more clear, more firm, leaving less room for violators and for reliance on an imperfect judiciary. So too, some fifty years ago, the common (customary) international law may have allowed every state to decide for itself whether it was justified in using force to defend its "vital interests," or in what it considered a "just cause." Such claims have been advanced by every invader since law began; recently they have been repeated by Hitler, Stalin, and lesser invaders in the twentieth century. Because the "common law" on the use of force failed, the law was codified, establishing clearer, firmer prohibitions, designed to leave few loopholes and little room for distortion. To press for law that would justify the invasion of Panama in the terms invoked by the Bush Administration is radical and reactionary. It would push back the law where it was, long ago, as if the Second World War had not been fought and the United Nations Charter had not been written.

IV. Conclusion

With regret, I conclude that the invasion of Panama by the United States was a clear violation of international law as embodied in the principal norm of the U.N. Charter on which the world, under the leadership of the United States, built the new international order after World War II. The United States did not have even a color of justification for this invasion.

———

More questions: What do you think about the importance that President Bush and Legal Adviser Sofaer seemed to put on Noriega's "Declaration of War?" Was Noriega talking to us or to his own "Legislature and people?" Professor Alfred P. Rubin answered in the New York Times that Noriega's statement was aimed at the Panamanian Parliament to function as a means to trigger a "state of emergency" or to declare martial law.

The heavy fire-power and sheer size of the U.S. military force led to substantial loss of life and property. Claims for compensation were rejected by the U.S. and law suits followed. See, Semmelman, re Noriega, Non-self-executing treaty aspects of two CCA, cert. denied Cases v. U.G. as to the Panama Invasion, 87 A.J.I.L. 288 (1993).

R. WEDGWOOD REPORT, THE USE OF ARMED FORCE IN INTERNATIONAL AFFAIRS: THE CASE OF PANAMA

In the Record of the Association of the Bar of the City
of New York 604; 607–609; 692–93 (1992).*

[The Report is original, as Professor Wedgwood was able to persuade the Department of Defense to release contemporaneous documents and was able to conduct interviews in Panama. She argues that there was a significant problem of violence against American troops in Panama (the harassment of American ground personnel and the repeated attacks on the Araijan Tank Farm) that had to be addressed. Nevertheless, the Report severely criticizes the rationale used to justify the use of force. These included the Noriega declaration of a state of war on the 20th anniversary of the restoration of Torrijos to power, and the incident in front of the Commandancia on December 16, 1989. In addition, the Report clearly raises serious questions about the invasion—the availability of alternative remedies and proportionality. Brief portions of the Report follow].

The United States invasion of Panama in December 1989 has escaped serious scrutiny. The President asserted in the days immediate-

* Reprinted with the permission of Ruth Wedgwood and the Association of the Bar of the City of New York.

ly following that the use of force to overthrow the Noriega regime was necessary to safeguard Americans in Panama, advance democracy, fight drugs, and protect the integrity of the Panama Canal Treaties, but no further mustering of the factual record was put forward. Neither Congress nor the press took up the burden of exploring the facts.

Panama, like other incidents of the use of armed force, will help to shape the customary law of force and the working law of the United Nations Charter. Hence, it is important to seek to understand what happened in fact. Truncated official explanations after the event may not fully reflect the circumstances that internally were seen as warranting the use of force; explaining the landscape of decision may modify the precedential meaning of the action. Law is also formed by the *opinio juris* of statesmen, scholars, and, in a democracy, citizens. We must assess our decisions to use force in the harsh light of the facts, including alternative courses of action that were not pursued, to assure United States actions are consistent with the law we ask others to live by.

Following the invasion of Panama, this Association began a study of the American decision to use force in Panama. The task was undertaken by the Association's Committee on International Arms Control and Security Affairs and Committee on International Law. In the summer of 1990, three members travelled to Panama to interview officials of the United States Department of Defense Southern Command and of the new Endara government, Panamanian businessmen, civic groups and journalists, and, in several cases where access was possible, members of the prior Noriega regime. Interviews have also been conducted in the United States with officials of the United States Department of State, Department of Defense, and Central Intelligence Agency. At the request of the Association of the Bar, pertinent documents were newly released by the Department of Defense concerning the situation of American forces in Panama and events immediately prior to the invasion. Many of these new documents are set out in the Appendices to this Report, to allow public discussion and debate.

Our report sets forth some of the circumstances that should give pause to both critics and defenders of the United States' use of armed force in Panama in 1989. Section I recalls the history of relations between the United States and the Republic of Panama, the rise of Noriega, his abuse of power, and the events leading to the invasion. Section II addresses the central question of self-defense. Can the invasion be justified as an exercise of the United States' right of self-defense under the United Nations Charter? Here, the factual record discloses two keen surprises. The problem of violence faced by American armed service personnel and civilians in Panama was long-standing and was more serious than generally reported in the press. But equally surprising is the United States' extended failure to implement other available methods for thwarting the police brutality faced by Americans in Panama. This passivity undermines the claim of self-defense as a ground for the invasion. The use of force in international affairs is governed by requirements of necessity and proportionality; the United States' action remains vulnerable under these standards. In addition, the events of December 15 and 16, 1989, immediately before the President's decision to launch an invasion, prove upon examination to be ambiguous. These complicating circumstances were not aired to the public before American forces were deployed. Section III addresses other arguments proffered for the use of force: democracy, the drug war, and the integrity of the Panama Canal Treaties, and the facts pertaining to these rationales.

It is our conclusion that the legality of the Panama invasion under existing standards of international law has not been established on the developed factual record. We recognize that decisions in foreign policy are intricate and difficult, and that others may take a different view on the legality of the invasion. Indeed, it is one of the purposes of this study to make facts available for long term debate and assessment of the American decision. Nonetheless, in the light of our extended study of the record, we believe it is important to report our present assessment.

* * *

V. The Place of International Law in American Politics

We conclude that the United States invasion of Panama lacks clear support under international law, on the facts developed in our study. The problem of harassment faced by American military personnel and their dependents in Panama was significant. But the United States has not addressed in any public forum why the problem could not have been met by other prudent measures, including housing troops on U.S. defense sites, early withdrawal of military dependents and other American civilians from the area of confrontation, and providing escorts outside defense sites.

The events of December 15 and 16, 1989, offered as the immediate reason for a decision to invade, are far less clear than some supposed at the time. An adequate system of national security decision-making would allow an assessment of the circumstances of events before force is committed, rather than learning of the reasons to doubt after the eggs are broken. In our dislike for Noriega, we as Americans also have not adequately assessed how our own actions may have been in tension with treaty commitments under the Panama Canal Treaties, contributing to the escalation of events in Panama. And perhaps most important, national security decision-making has not provided any process for the weighing of civilian casualties in assessing proportionality.

We do not find the claim of proportionate and necessary self-defense as a justification for the Panama invasion to be established on the facts available to us. The supplementary rationales of democracy, fighting drugs, and the integrity of the Panama Canal Treaties face the additional problems noted above. The purpose served by closely parsing the factual background and legal rationale of the United States invasion of Panama is not to criticize any Administration or decision-maker. Rather, it is to contribute to the public debate concerning the use of force in international affairs. A President may be constrained by his reading of current public attitudes; if a President expects personal or political criticism for restraint in using force, this will influence the course of events. Military force will be used soberly only where the public, the press, the Congress, and the Executive are each fluent with the standards of international law. Legal rules help form the political morality of decision-makers and the political landscape in which they act.

U.S. v. NORIEGA

United States District Court, S.D.Fla.1990.
746 F.Supp. 1506 (for the immunity aspects of the case, see ch. 12).

HOEVELER, District Judge.

This cause comes before the Court on the several motions of Defendants Noriega and Del Cid to dismiss for lack of jurisdiction the indictment which charges them with various narcotics-related offenses. * * *

On February 14, 1988, a federal grand jury sitting in Miami, Florida returned a twelve-count indictment charging General Manuel Antonio Noriega with participating in an international conspiracy to import cocaine and materials used in producing cocaine into and out of the United States. Noriega is alleged to have exploited his official position as head of the intelligence branch of the Panamanian National Guard, and then as Commander-in-Chief of the Panamanian Defense Forces, to receive payoffs in return for assisting and protecting international drug traffickers, including various members of the Medellin Cartel, in conducting narcotics and money laundering operations in Panama.

Specifically, the indictment charges that General Noriega protected cocaine shipments from Colombia through Panama to the United States; arranged for the trans-shipment and sale to the Medellin Cartel of ether and acetone, including such chemicals previously seized by the Panamanian Defense Forces; provided refuge and a base for continued operations for the members of the Medellin Cartel after the Colombian government's crackdown on drug traffickers following the murder of the Colombian Minister of Justice, Lara–Bonilla; agreed to protect a cocaine laboratory in Darien Province, Panama; and assured the safe passage of millions of dollars of narcotic proceeds from the United States into Panamanian banks. Noriega also allegedly traveled to Havana, Cuba and met with Cuban president Fidel Castro, who, according to the indictment, mediated a dispute between Noriega and the Cartel caused by the Panamanian troops' seizure of a drug laboratory that Noriega was paid to protect. All of these activities were allegedly undertaken for General Noriega's own personal profit. Defendant Del Cid, in addition to being an officer in the Panamanian Defense Forces, was General Noriega's personal secretary. He is charged with acting as liaison, courier, and emissary for Noriega in his transactions with Cartel members and other drug traffickers.

Because of the activities alleged, Defendants are charged with engaging in a pattern of racketeering activity, in violation of the RICO statutes, 18 U.S.C. §§ 1962(c) and 1962(d); conspiracy to distribute and import cocaine into the United States, in violation of 21 U.S.C. § 963;

and distributing and aiding and abetting the distribution of cocaine, intending that it be imported into the United States, in violation of 21 U.S.C. § 959 and 18 U.S.C. § 2 [among other charges]. * * *

* * *

In the interval between the time the indictment was issued and Defendants were arrested, relations between the United States and General Noriega deteriorated considerably. Shortly after charges against Noriega were brought, the General delivered a widely publicized speech in which he brought a machete crashing down on a podium while denouncing the United States. On December 15, 1989, Noriega declared that a "state of war" existed between Panama and the United States. Tensions between the two countries further increased the next day, when U.S. military forces in Panama were put on alert after Panamanian troops shot and killed an American soldier, wounded another, and beat a Navy couple. Three days later, on December 20, 1989, President Bush ordered U.S. troops into combat in Panama City on a mission whose stated goals were to safeguard American lives, restore democracy, preserve the Panama Canal treaties, and seize General Noriega to face federal drug charges in the United States. Before U.S. troops were engaged, American officials arranged a ceremony in which Guillermo Endara was sworn in as president and recognized by the United States as the legitimate head of the government of Panama. Endara was reported to have won the Panamanian presidential election held several months earlier, the results of which were nullified and disregarded by General Noriega. * * *

* * * [General Noriega] successfully eluded American forces for several days, prompting the United States government to offer a one million dollar bounty for his capture. Eventually, the General took sanctuary in the Papal Nunciature in Panama City, where he apparently hoped to be granted political asylum. Noriega's presence in the Papal Nunciature touched off a diplomatic impasse and a round of intense negotiations involving several countries. Vatican officials initially refused to turn Noriega over. While he was still ensconced in the nunciature, American troops stationed outside pelted the building with loud rock-and-roll music blasted through loudspeakers. The music was played continuously for three days until church authorities protested the action as offensive. After an eleven-day standoff, Noriega finally surrendered to American forces, apparently under pressure from the papal nuncio and influenced by a threatening crowd of about 15,000 angry Panamanian citizens who had gathered outside the residence. On January 3, 1990, two weeks after the invasion began, Noriega walked out of the Papal Nunciature and surrendered himself to U.S. military officials waiting outside. He was flown by helicopter to Howard Air Force Base, where he was ushered into a plane bound for Florida and formally arrested by agents of the Drug Enforcement Agency. * * *

As is evident from the unusual factual background underlying this case, the Court is presented with several issues of first impression. This is the first time that a leader or de facto leader of a sovereign nation has been forcibly brought to the United States to face criminal charges. The fact that General Noriega's apprehension occurred in the course of a military action only further underscores the complexity of the issues involved. In addition to Defendant Noriega's motion to dismiss based on lack of jurisdiction over the offense and sovereign immunity, Defendants Noriega and Del Cid argue that they are prisoners of war pursuant to the Geneva Convention. This status, Defendants maintain, deprives the Court of jurisdiction to proceed with the case. Noriega contends that the military action which brought about his arrest is "shocking to the conscience", and that due process considerations require the Court to divest itself of jurisdiction over his person. Noriega also asserts that the invasion occurred in violation of international law. Finally, Noriega argues that, even in the absence of constitutional or treaty violations, the Court should dismiss the indictment pursuant to its supervisory powers so as to prevent the judicial system from being party to and tainted by the government's alleged misconduct in arresting Noriega.

* * *

VI. Illegal Arrest

Noriega also moves to dismiss the indictment on the ground that the manner in which he was brought before this Court—as a result of the United States government's invasion of Panama—is "shocking to the conscience and in violation of the laws and norms of humanity." He argues that the Court should therefore divest itself of jurisdiction over his person. In support of this claim, Noriega alleges that the invasion of Panama violated the Due Process Clause of the Fifth Amendment of the United States Constitution, as well as international law. Alternatively, he argues that even in the absence of constitutional or treaty violations, this Court should nevertheless exercise its supervisory authority and dismiss the indictment so as to prevent the Court from becoming a party to the government's alleged misconduct in bringing Noriega to trial.

A. The Fifth Amendment Due Process Argument

It is well settled that the manner by which a defendant is brought before the court normally does not affect the ability of the government to try him. The Ker–Frisbie doctrine, as this rule has come to be known, provides that a court is not deprived of jurisdiction to try a defendant on the ground that the defendant's presence before the court was procured by unlawful means.

* * * Noriega does not challenge the validity of the Ker–Frisbie rule but instead relies on what is commonly referred to as the Toscanino exception carved out by the Second Circuit. * * *

B. Violations of International Law

In addition to his due process claim, Noriega asserts that the invasion of Panama violated international treaties and principles of customary international law—specifically, Article 2(4) of the United Nations Charter, Article 20[17] of the O.A.S. Charter,[30] Articles 23(b)

---

30. Article 20[17] of the O.A.S. Charter provides that "[t]he territory of a State is inviolable; it may not be the object, even temporarily, of military occupation or of other measures of force taken by another State, directly or indirectly, on any grounds

and 25 of the Hague Convention, Article 3 of Geneva Convention I, and Article 6 of the Nuremberg Charter. Initially, it is important to note that individuals lack standing to assert violations of international treaties in the absence of a protest from the offended government. Moreover, the Ker–Frisbie doctrine establishes that violations of international law alone do not deprive a court of jurisdiction over a defendant in the absence of specific treaty language to that effect. To defeat the Court's personal jurisdiction, Noriega must therefore establish that the treaty in question is self-executing in the sense that it confers individual rights upon citizens of the signatory nations, and that it by its terms expresses "a self-imposed limitation on the jurisdiction of the United States and hence on its courts." United States v. Postal, supra.

As a general principle of international law, individuals have no standing to challenge violations of international treaties in the absence of a protest by the sovereign involved. * * * The rationale behind this rule is that treaties are "designed to protect the sovereign interests of nations, and it is up to the offended nations to determine whether a violation of sovereign interests occurred and requires redress." U.S. v. Zabanoh * * * (under international law, "individual rights are only derivative through the states"). Consistent with that principle, a treaty will be construed as creating enforceable private rights only if it expressly or impliedly provides a private right of action.

No such rights are created in the sections of the U.N. Charter, O.A.S. Charter, and Hague Convention cited by Noriega. Rather, those provisions set forth broad general principles governing the conduct of nations toward each other and do not by their terms speak to individual or private rights. *See* Frolova v. USSR (articles phrased in "broad generalities" constitute "declarations of principles, not a code of legal rights"); Tel–Oren (Bork, J., concurring) (Articles 1 and 2 of the United Nations Charter "contain general 'purposes and principles,' some of which state mere aspirations and none of which can be sensibly thought to have been intended to be judicially enforceable at the behest of individuals." * * * Lujan v. Gengler (individual may not invoke Article 2(4) of the U.N. Charter or Article 20[17] of the O.A.S. Charter if the sovereign state involved does not protest). * * * Thus, under the applicable international law, Noriega lacks standing to challenge violations of these treaties in the absence of a protest by the Panamanian government that the invasion of Panama and subsequent arrest of Noriega violated that country's territorial sovereignty.

It can perhaps be argued that reliance on the above body of law, under the unusual circumstances of this case, is a form of legal bootstrapping. Noriega, it can be asserted, is the government of Panama or at least its de facto head of state, and as such he is the appropriate person to protest alleged treaty violations; to permit removal of him and his associates from power and reject his complaint because a new and friendly government is installed, he can further urge, turns the doctrine of sovereign standing on its head. This argument is not without force,

whatever. No territorial acquisitions or special advantages obtained either by force or by other means of coercion shall be recognized." 2 U.S.T. 2394, 2420.

yet there are more persuasive answers in response. First * * * the United States has consistently refused to recognize the Noriega regime as Panama's legitimate government, a fact which considerably undermines Noriega's position. Second, Noriega nullified the results of the Panamanian presidential election held shortly before the alleged treaty violations occurred. The suggestion that his removal from power somehow robs the true government of the opportunity to object under the applicable treaties is therefore weak indeed. Finally, there is no provision or suggestion in the treaties cited which would permit the Court to ignore the absence of complaint or demand from the present duly constituted government of Panama. The current government of the Republic of Panama led by Guillermo Endara is therefore the appropriate entity to object to treaty violations. In light of Noriega's lack of standing to object, this Court therefore does not reach the question of whether these treaties were violated by the military action in Panama. * * *

      * * *

Finally, Defendant cites Article 6 of the Nuremberg Charter, which proscribes war crimes, crimes against peace, and crimes against humanity. The Nuremberg Charter sets forth the procedures by which the Nuremberg Tribunal, established by the Allied powers after the Second World War, conducted the trials and punishment of major war criminals of the European Axis. The Government maintains that the principles laid down at Nuremberg were developed solely for the prosecution of World War II war criminals, and have no application to the conduct of U.S. military forces in Panama. The Court cannot agree. As Justice Robert H. Jackson, the United States Chief of Counsel at Nuremberg, stated: "If certain acts in violation of treaties are crimes, they are crimes whether the United States does them or whether Germany does them, and we are not prepared to lay down a rule of criminal conduct against others which we would not be willing to have invoked against us." Nonetheless, Defendant fails to establish how the Nuremberg Charter or its possible violation, assuming any, has any application to the instant prosecution. As stated above, the Ker–Frisbie doctrine makes clear that violations of treaties or customary international law alone do not deprive the court of jurisdiction over the defendant in the absence of limiting language to that effect. * * * Defendant has not cited any language in the Nuremberg Charter, nor in any of the above treaties, which limits the authority of the United States to arrest foreign nationals or to assume jurisdiction over their crimes. The reason is apparent; the Nuremberg Charter, as is the case with the other treaties, is addressed to the conduct of war and international aggression. It has no effect on the ability of sovereign states to enforce their laws, and thus has no application to the prosecution of Defendant for alleged narcotics violations. "The violation of international law, if any, may be redressed by other remedies, and does not depend upon the granting of what amounts to an effective immunity from criminal prosecution to safeguard individuals against police or armed forces misconduct." United States v. Cadena * * * The Court therefore refrains from reaching the merits of Defendant's claim under the Nuremberg Charter.

C. Supervisory Authority

Having determined that Defendant Noriega fails to state a valid defense based on due process and international law principles, this Court's inquiry is nonetheless unfinished, as Defendant Noriega alternatively bases his motion on the inherent supervisory power of the Court. Noriega alleges that, by asserting jurisdiction over him, this Court would thereby sanction and become party to the Government's alleged misconduct in invading Panama and bringing Noriega to trial. * * *

* * *

* * * Noriega argues that his arrest and presence before the Court was secured as a result of deliberate and indiscriminate atrocities committed by the United States in the course of its invasion of Panama, and that such conduct "shocking to the conscience" calls for an exercise of the Court's inherent supervisory authority resulting in dismissal of the indictment. In response, the Government argues that, even pursuant to the Court's inherent supervisory authority, Noriega may not seek dismissal of the indictment based on alleged violations of the rights of third parties—in this case, the rights of individual Panamanians or of the Panamanian state. The Government's position thus seems to be that a defendant's own constitutional or statutory rights must be violated in order to trigger the exercise of a court's supervisory power. This stance blurs the critical distinction between the use of supervisory authority on the one hand and the courts' rulings based on violations of constitutional and statutory law on the other. Since use of supervisory authority presents an independent body of law and does not depend on the existence of a constitutional or statutory violation, the fact that a defendant's own such rights have not been violated is not decisive. * * *

* * * In a government of laws, existence of the government will be imperilled if its fails to observe the law scrupulously. Our government is the potent, the omnipresent teacher. For good or for ill, it teaches the whole people by its example. Crime is contagious. If the government becomes a lawbreaker, it breeds contempt for law; it invites every man to become a law unto himself; it invites anarchy. * * * This Court may someday have occasion to apply Justice Brandeis' wise words, but this is not that day, for we are confronted not with the above hypothetical but rather a military war in which innocent lives were unfortunately lost in the pursuit of foreign policy objectives. Although the motives behind the military action are open to speculation, the stated goals of the invasion were to protect American lives, support democracy, preserve the Panama Canal Treaties, and bring Noriega to stand trial for narcotics offenses. Because the President ordered Noriega arrested "in the course of carrying out the military operations in Panama," the capture of Noriega was incident to the broader conduct of foreign policy. While the Government's asserted rationales for the invasion are not beyond challenge and need not be blindly accepted by this Court, counsel for Noriega have offered no evidence to the contrary and the evidence they have offered in fact bolsters the conclusion that the invasion was primarily an exercise in foreign policy. * * *

That foreign policy objectives rather than just law enforcement goals are implicated radically changes the Court's consideration of the government conduct complained of and, consequently, its willingness to exercise supervisory power. For the question then posed is whether a court may, under the guise of its supervisory authority, condemn armed conflict as "shocking to the conscience." Any such declaration not only runs squarely into the political question doctrine, which precludes courts from resolving issues more properly committed to the political branches, but would indeed constitute unprecedented judicial interference in the conduct of foreign policy. * * *

* * *

Noriega does not, and legally cannot, allege that President Bush exceeded his powers as Commander-in-Chief in ordering the invasion of Panama. Rather, he asks this Court to find that the deaths of innocent civilians and destruction of private property is "shocking to the conscience and in violation of the laws and norms of humanity." At bottom, then, Noriega's complaint is a challenge to the very morality of war itself. This is a political question in its most paradigmatic and pristine form. It raises the specter of judicial management and control of foreign policy and challenges in a most sweeping fashion the wisdom, propriety, and morality of sending armed forces into combat—a decision which is constitutionally committed to the executive and legislative branches and hence beyond judicial review. Questions such as under what circumstances armed conflict is immoral, or whether it is always so, are not ones for the courts, but must be resolved by the political branches entrusted by the Constitution with the awesome responsibility of committing this country to battle. * * *

In view of the above findings and observations, it is the Order of this Court that the several motions presented by Defendants relating to this Court's jurisdiction as well as that suggesting dismissal under supervisory authority be and each is DENIED.

SECTION B.   COLLECTIVE MEASURES BY REGIONAL ORGANIZATIONS

1.   SOVIET MISSILES IN CUBA
THE SOVIET THREAT TO THE AMERICAS, ADDRESS BY PRESIDENT KENNEDY
47 United States Department of State Bulletin 715 (1962).

* * *

Neither the United States nor the world community of nations can tolerate deliberate deception and offensive threats on the part of any nation, large or small. We no longer live in a world where only the actual firing of weapons represents a sufficient challenge to a nation's security to constitute maximum peril. Nuclear weapons are so destructive and ballistic missiles are so swift that any substantially increased possibility of their use or any sudden change in their deployment may well be regarded as a definite threat to peace.

For many years both the Soviet Union and the United States, recognizing this fact, have deployed strategic nuclear weapons with great care, never upsetting the precarious status quo which insured that these weapons would not be used in the absence of some vital challenge. Our own strategic missiles have never been transferred to the territory of any other nation under a cloak of secrecy and deception; and our history, unlike that of the Soviets since the end of World War II, demonstrates that we have no desire to dominate or conquer any other nation or impose our system upon its people. Nevertheless, American citizens have become adjusted to living daily on the bull's eye of Soviet missiles located inside the U.S.S.R. or in submarines.

In that sense missiles in Cuba add to an already clear and present danger—although it should be noted the nations of Latin America have never previously been subjected to a potential nuclear threat.

* * *

Acting, therefore, in the defense of our own security and of the entire Western Hemisphere, and under the authority entrusted to me by the Constitution as endorsed by the resolution of the Congress, I have directed that the following initial steps be taken immediately:

First: To halt this offensive buildup, a strict quarantine on all offensive military equipment under shipment to Cuba is being initiated. All ships of any kind bound for Cuba from whatever nation or port will, if found to contain cargoes of offensive weapons, be turned back. This quarantine will be extended, if needed, to other types of cargo and carriers. We are not at this time, however, denying the necessities of life as the Soviets attempted to do in their Berlin blockade of 1948.

Second: I have directed the continued and increased close surveillance of Cuba and its military buildup. The Foreign Ministers of the OAS [Organization of American States] in their communiqué of October 3 rejected secrecy on such matters in this hemisphere. Should these offensive military preparations continue, thus increasing the threat to the hemisphere, further action will be justified. I have directed the Armed Forces to prepare for any eventualities; and I trust that, in the interest of both the Cuban people and the Soviet technicians at the sites, the hazards to all concerned of continuing this threat will be recognized.

Third: It shall be the policy of this nation to regard any nuclear missile launched from Cuba against any nation in the Western Hemisphere as an attack by the Soviet Union on the United States, requiring a full retaliatory response upon the Soviet Union.

Fourth: As a necessary military precaution I have reinforced our base at Guantanamo, evacuated today the dependents of our personnel there, and ordered additional military units to be on a standby alert.

Fifth: We are calling tonight for an immediate meeting of the Organ of Consultation, under the Organization of American States, to consider this threat to hemispheric security and to invoke articles 6 and 8 of the Rio Treaty in support of all necessary action. The United Nations Charter allows for regional security arrangements—and the nations of this hemisphere decided long ago against the military presence of outside powers. Our other allies around the world have also been alerted.

Sixth: Under the Charter of the United Nations, we are asking tonight that an emergency meeting of the Security Council be convoked without delay to take action against this latest Soviet threat to world peace. Our resolution will call for the prompt dismantling and withdrawal of all offensive weapons in Cuba, under the supervision of U.N. observers, before the quarantine can be lifted.

Seventh and finally: I call upon Chairman Khrushchev to halt and eliminate this clandestine, reckless, and provocative threat to world peace and to stable relations between our two nations. * * *

This nation is prepared to present its case against the Soviet threat to peace, and our own proposals for a peaceful world, at any time and in any forum—in the OAS, in the United Nations, or in any other meeting that could be useful—without limiting our freedom of action.

    * * *

Study the Inter–American Treaty of Reciprocal Assistance of September 2, 1947, 62 Stat. 1681, 21 U.N.T.S. 77. Also read the Charter of the Organization of American States

---

RESOLUTION OF COUNCIL OF THE ORGANIZATION OF AMERICAN STATES, MEETING AS THE PROVISIONAL ORGAN OF CONSULTATION, OCTOBER 23, 1962

47 United States Department of State Bulletin 722 (1962).

Whereas, The Inter–American Treaty of Reciprocal Assistance of 1947 (Rio Treaty) recognizes the obligation of the American Republics to "provide for effective reciprocal assistance to meet armed attacks against any American state and in order to deal with threats of aggression against any of them,"

    * * *

The Council of the Organization of American States, Meeting as the Provisional Organ of Consultation, Resolves:

1. To call for the immediate dismantling and withdrawal from Cuba of all missiles and other weapons with any offensive capability;

2. To recommend that the member states, in accordance with Articles 6 and 8 of the Inter–American Treaty of Reciprocal Assistance, take all measures, individually and collectively, including the use of armed force, which they may deem necessary to ensure that the Government of Cuba cannot continue to receive from the Sino–Soviet powers military material and related supplies which may threaten the peace and

security of the Continent and to prevent the missiles in Cuba with offensive capability from ever becoming an active threat to the peace and security of the Continent;

3. To inform the Security Council of the United Nations of this resolution in accordance with Article 54 of the Charter of the United Nations and to express the hope that the Security Council will, in accordance with the draft resolution introduced by the United States, dispatch United Nations observers to Cuba at the earliest moment;

4. To continue to serve provisionally as Organ of Consultation and to request the Member States to keep the Organ of Consultation duly informed of measures taken by them in accordance with paragraph two of this resolution.

UNITED STATES PROCLAMATION
INTERDICTION OF THE DELIVERY OF OFFENSIVE WEAPONS TO CUBA

47 United States Department of State Bulletin 717 (1962).

Whereas the peace of the world and the security of the United States and of all American States are endangered by reason of the establishment by the Sino–Soviet powers of an offensive military capability in Cuba, including bases for ballistic missiles with a potential range covering most of North and South America;

Whereas by a Joint Resolution passed by the Congress of the United States and approved on October 3, 1962, it was declared that the United States is determined to prevent by whatever means may be necessary, including the use of arms, the Marxist–Leninist regime in Cuba from extending, by force or the threat of force, its aggressive or subversive activities to any part of this hemisphere, and to prevent in Cuba the creation or use of an externally supported military capability endangering the security of the United States; and

Whereas the Organ of Consultation of the American Republics meeting in Washington on October 23, 1962, recommended that the Member States, in accordance with Articles 6 and 8 of the Inter-American Treaty of Reciprocal Assistance, take all measures, individually and collectively, including the use of armed force, which they may deem necessary to ensure that the Government of Cuba cannot continue to receive from the Sino–Soviet powers military material and related supplies which may threaten the peace and security of the Continent and to prevent the missiles in Cuba with offensive capability from ever becoming an active threat to the peace and security of the Continent:

Now, Therefore, I, John F. Kennedy, President of the United States of America, acting under and by virtue of the authority conferred upon me by the Constitution and statutes of the United States, in accordance with the aforementioned resolutions of the United States Congress and of the Organ of Consultation of the American Republics, and to defend the security of the United States, do hereby proclaim that the forces under my command are ordered, beginning at 2:00 p.m. Greenwich time October 24, 1962, to interdict, subject to the instructions herein contained, the delivery of offensive weapons and associated materiel to Cuba. For the purposes of this Proclamation, the following are declared to be prohibited materiel: Surface-to-surface missiles; bomber aircraft; bombs, air-to-surface rockets and guided missiles; warheads for any of the above weapons; mechanical or electronic equipment to support or operate the above items; and any other classes of materiel hereafter designated by the Secretary of Defense for the purpose of effectuating this Proclamation.

To enforce this order, the Secretary of Defense shall take appropriate measures to prevent the delivery of prohibited materiel to Cuba, employing the land, sea and air forces of the United States in cooperation with any forces that may be made available by other American States. The Secretary of Defense may make such regulations and issue such directives as he deems necessary to ensure the effectiveness of this order, including the designation, within a reasonable distance of Cuba, of prohibited or restricted zones and of prescribed routes.

Any vessel or craft which may be proceeding toward Cuba may be intercepted and may be directed to identify itself, its cargo, equipment and stores and its ports of call, to stop, to lie to, to submit to visit and search, or to proceed as directed. Any vessel or craft which fails or refuses to respond to or comply with directions shall be subject to being taken into custody. Any vessel or craft which it is believed is en route to Cuba and may be carrying prohibited materiel or may itself constitute such materiel shall, whenever possible, be directed to proceed to another destination of its own choice and shall be taken into custody if it fails or refuses to obey such directions. All vessels or craft taken into custody shall be sent into a port of the United States for appropriate disposition.

In carrying out this order, force shall not be used except in case of failure or refusal to comply with directions, or with regulations or directives of the Secretary of Defense issued hereunder, after reasonable efforts have been made to communicate them to the vessel or craft, or in case of self-defense. In any case, force shall be used only to the extent necessary. [The Proclamation was signed by President Kennedy at 7:06 P.M., October 23, 1962.]

MEEKER, DEFENSIVE QUARANTINE AND THE LAW

57 American Journal of International Law 515, 523 (1963.) *

Charter Limitation on the "Threat or Use of Force"

Before leaving the Charter of the United Nations it is relevant also to consider Article 2, paragraph 4, which provides: "All Members shall refrain in their international relations from the threat or use of force

* Reprinted with the permission of the American Society of International Law.

against the territorial integrity or political independence of any state, or in any other manner inconsistent with the Purposes of the United Nations." It was recognized that the defensive quarantine was dependent, ultimately, upon the use of naval forces for its effectiveness. Accordingly, there was acknowledged to be a threat, and potentially a use, of armed force. However, it did not follow that this must contravene Article 2, paragraph 4.

In considering the obligations imposed on Members by that article, it should be noted that not all threats or uses of force are prohibited; only those which are inconsistent with the purposes of the United Nations are covered by Article 2, paragraph 4. The presence of the word "other" in the concluding clause of the paragraph makes this clear. Even assuming that the measures taken could be considered to impinge upon the territorial integrity or political independence of some state or states, they would not be contrary to Article 2, paragraph 4, as long as they were not inconsistent with the purposes of the United Nations. The defensive quarantine, as indicated earlier, was considered to be in accordance with Chapter VIII of the Charter.

It is clear that collective action for peace and security which the Security Council may take under Chapter VII does not contravene Article 2, paragraph 4. It is also clear that individual or collective self-defense against armed attack, in accordance with Article 51, does not violate the Charter. Here it may be noted that the United States, in adopting the defensive quarantine of Cuba, did not seek to justify it as a measure required to meet an "armed attack" within the meaning of Article 51. Nor did the United States seek to sustain its action on the ground that Article 51 is not an all-inclusive statement of the right of self-defense and that the quarantine was a measure of self-defense open to any country to take individually for its own defense in a case other than "armed attack." Indeed, as shown by President Kennedy's television address of October 22 and by other statements of the Government, reliance was not placed on either contention, and the United States took no position on either of these issues.

The quarantine was based on a collective judgment and recommendation of the American Republics made under the Rio Treaty. It was considered not to contravene Article 2, paragraph 4, because it was a measure adopted by a regional organization in conformity with the provisions of Chapter 8 of the Charter. The purposes of the Organization and its activities were considered to be consistent with the purposes and principles of the United Nations as provided in Article 52. This being the case, the quarantine would no more violate Article 2, paragraph 4, than measures voted by the Council under Chapter 7, by the General Assembly under Articles 10 and 11, or taken by United Nations Members in conformity with Article 51.

Finally, in relation to the Charter limitation on threat or use of force, it should be noted that the quarantine itself was a carefully limited measure proportionate to the threat and designed solely to prevent any further build-up of strategic missile bases in Cuba.

* * *

Was the Cuban quarantine authorized by the Security Council? The author, Deputy Legal Adviser, Department of State, addresses the question of the conformity of the Cuban quarantine to Article 53(1) of the charter: "But no enforcement action shall be taken under regional arrangements or by regional agencies without the authorization of the Security Council * * *." The first two of his three arguments were: (1) Authorization need not be prior authorization and (2) it need not be express. "The Council did not see fit to take any action in derogation of the quarantine. Although a resolution condemning the quarantine was laid before the Council by the Soviet Union, the Council subsequently, by general consent, refrained from acting upon it and instead chose to promote the cause of a negotiated settlement, with the assistance of the Secretary General." 57 AJIL at 522. Argument (3) was that, in any event, the action was not enforcement action: "As understood by the United States, 'enforcement action' means obligatory action involving the use of armed force. Thus 'enforcement action,' as the phrase appears in Article 53(1), should not be taken to comprehend action of a regional organization which is only recommendatory to the members of the organization." Is this sound? Or did the coercion exerted by the quarantine on the Soviets and Cuba render it enforcement action? The deputy legal adviser found support for the United States' definition of enforcement action in the advisory opinion of the International Court of Justice in *Certain Expenses.*

CHAYES,[a] THE LEGAL CASE FOR U.S. ACTION ON CUBA

47 United States Department of State Bulletin 763, 765 (1962).

Some have asked whether we should not first have gone to the Security Council before taking other action to meet the Soviet threat in Cuba. And I suppose that in the original conception of the United Nations, it was thought that the Security Council would be the agency for dealing with situations of this kind. However, the drafters of the charter demonstrated their wisdom by making Security Council responsibility for dealing with threats to the peace "primary" and not "exclusive." For events since 1945 have demonstrated that the Security Council, like our own electoral college, was not a viable institution. The veto has made it substantially useless in keeping the peace.

The withering away of the Security Council has led to a search for alternative peacekeeping institutions. In the United Nations itself the

a. Legal Adviser, Department of State, during the Cuban missile crisis.

General Assembly and the Secretary–General have filled the void. Regional organizations are another obvious candidate.

* * *

2. REVOLT IN THE DOMINICAN REPUBLIC

Although not in perfect compliance with the United Nations Charter, the handling of the Cuban missile crisis by the United States was thought by some observers to be a moderate response to a large provocation, crafted as an approximation of the Charter plan. Unilateral action by the United States was avoided, in favor of multilateral action. To that extent, the Charter's call was heeded for collective, rather than parochial, responses to inflammatory situations. Can the same be said for the United States' response to the disintegration of public order in the Dominican Republic?

The United States Government justified its invasion of the Dominican Republic, after the April 24, 1965 revolt, on the basis of self-defense, defense of an international organization, and humanitarian intervention. "We landed troops in the Dominican Republic in order to preserve the lives of foreign nationals—nationals of the United States and many other countries. We continued our military presence in the Dominican Republic for the additional purpose of preserving the capacity of the OAS to function in the manner intended by the OAS Charter—to achieve peace and justice through securing a cease-fire and through reestablishing orderly political processes within which Dominicans could choose their own government, free from outside interference." * * * Meeker, *The Dominican Situation in the Perspective of International Law,* 53 Dept.St. Bull. 60 (1965).

Threat of a communist takeover. There is more than a slight suggestion in the statement of the basis for U.S. military action in the Dominican Republic that even unilateral use of force is lawful in aid of the preservation of democratic values. Compare the statement of the International Court of Justice in the case of *Nicaragua v. U.S.* [1986] I.C.J.Rep. 14, 109: 207. * * * The United States authorities have on some occasions clearly stated their grounds for intervening in the affairs of a foreign State for reasons connected with, for example, the domestic policies of that country, its ideology, the level of its armaments, or the direction of its foreign policy. But these were statements of international policy, and not an assertion of rules of existing international law.

209. The Court therefore finds that no such general right of intervention, in support of an opposition within another State, exists in contemporary international law. The Court concludes that acts constituting a breach of the customary principle of non-intervention will also, if they directly or indirectly involve the use of force, constitute a breach of the principle of non-use of force in international relations.

_____

3. DISINTEGRATION OF POLITICAL AUTHORITY IN GRENADA

Military forces from the United States, Barbados, and Jamaica landed in Grenada in October 1983 under circumstances described by Kenneth W. Dam, Deputy Secretary of State. Dam explained that the invasion was necessary because of the civil strife and the collapse of government in Grenada, which included the murder of Maurice Bishop and the members of his cabinet in a violent struggle for power and attempted coup. "The disintegration of political authority * * * had created a dynamic that made further violence likely and that spread uncertainty and fear * * *" Secretary Dam explained that the invasion occurred as a response to a request for assistance by the Governor–General and by the OECS (the Organization of Eastern Caribbean States). The purpose of the invasion was to restore order and human rights and to secure and evacuate endangered U.S. nationals on the island. Secretary Dam explained that the legal authority for the invasion included the request for assistance by the Governor–General, Articles 3, 4, and 8, of the OECS Charter (which concern local and external threats to peace and security), Articles 22 and 28 of the OAS Charter and Article 52 of the U.N. Charter, which "recognize the competence of regional security bodies in insuring regional peace and stability." Dam, *Statement on Grenada,* 78 A.J.I.L. 200 (1984).

Test the regional arrangement justification against the United Nations Charter; and against the Cuban missile crisis precedent. Was the United States action in Grenada on firm legal ground as a regional arrangement? What about the other justifications?

JOYNER, REFLECTION ON THE LAWFULNESS OF INVASION

78 American Journal of International Law 131 (1984).*

* * *

An especially intriguing facet of the entire diplomatic episode—and a second espoused legal justification as well—is that the United States was invited by at least five members of the Organization of Eastern Caribbean States (OECS) to intervene militarily into Grenada. Created in 1981, the OECS contains within its charter a quasi-collective security provision. Article 8 provides in relevant part:

> The Defence and Security Committee shall have responsibility for coordinating the efforts of Member States for collective defence and the preservation of peace and security against external aggression and for the development of close ties among the Member States of the Organisation in matters of external defence and security, including measures to combat the activities of mercenaries, operating with or without the support of internal or national elements, in the

* (Reprinted with the permission of the American Society of Int'l Law).

exercise of the inherent right of individual or collective self-defence recognised by Article 51 of the Charter.

While "collective defence" as such is called for in the Treaty, nowhere is there stipulated the option to invite outside assistance against a member state. Further, it is difficult to fathom how a treaty among seven small states could legally promote an invasion by the United States against one of its own members at the behest of the others. To be sure, considerable doubt also exists about whether the invasion of Grenada is consistent with the original intent of the signers, or for that matter, those specified treaty provisions relating to "external defence" and "arrangements for collective security against external aggression."

Several reasons rebut the use of this Treaty to legitimize U.S. intervention in Grenada. First, the United States is not a party to the Treaty and therefore legally lies outside the ambit of its concerns. (Interestingly enough, neither are Barbados and Jamaica, which also participated in the invasion.) Second, Article 8 specifically deals with "collective defence and the preservation of peace and security against external aggression." No external aggressor existed: Grenada, the state in question, was a Treaty member. In addition, the OECS Treaty makes no mention of any collective security or defensive measures to be taken against a member of the organization, should such an occasion arise. There is, in short, no provision for military action in instances other than those involving "external aggression, including mercenary aggression," and such a case was absent in the October 1983 Grenada episode.

A third contention concerns the procedure used for decision making under the OECS provisions. Paragraph 5 stipulates that decisions and directives pertaining to defense and security must be consented to unanimously by the member states. This requirement obviously was not observed for the Grenada invasion. Reportedly, three of the OECS Treaty members—Grenada, St. Kitts–Nevis and Montserrat—did not vote. In any event, even if the other two had voted affirmatively, it remains difficult to imagine that Grenada would have voted in support of foreign military intervention into its domestic affairs.

Yet this very contention—that Grenada's own Government might have advocated or even sanctioned external intervention into its domestic affairs—was advanced by the United States Government as the basis for a third prominent legal justification of the Grenadan action. In testimony before the House Foreign Affairs Committee on November 2, 1983, Deputy Secretary of State Kenneth Dam revealed that the Governor–General of Grenada, Sir Paul Scoon, had confidentially transmitted "an appeal for action by the OECS and other regional states to restore order on the island." * * *

There is no question about the legality of an external intervention occasioned by an explicit invitation that has been genuinely proffered by the legitimate government of a state; that legality is well grounded in international law. However, one may question the precise legal character of the office of Governor–General and the concomitant legal authority that the Governor–General may appropriately exercise under Grenada's operative constitutional law. Put succinctly, was the Governor-

General alone constitutionally empowered to invite in foreign military forces? The political, legal and constitutional realities of Grenada in October 1983 strongly suggest that he was not.

* * *

As a regional matter, the OAS resolved: "[t]o call for the withdrawal of the foreign troops used for the military intervention * * *." OAS Doc.CP/Res. 534 (800/89).

CERNA, BOOK REVIEW.
87 A.J.I.L. 471, 472–73 (1993).*

* * *

Randelzhofer prepared the comment on both the prohibition on the use of force (Article 2(4)) and the self-defense exception (Article 51). I can only surmise that his categorical antiwar approach to Article 2(4). The "heart of the UN Charter," is a product of the German experience. The analysis rings of conviction as much as of scholarship: Modern warfare threatens the survival of civilization as we know it. Consequently, the prevention of war is the dominant problem in international politics. The intellectual response is the development of peace research as an academic discipline. Only since the beginning of the twentieth century has international law assumed the task of preventing war; the prohibition on the use of force is the most direct way to prevent war. The formulation of Article 2(4) is described as an "advance" compared to the Kellog–Briand Pact of 1928, which prohibited states from using war as a means for resolving their disputes, since it prohibits the use of force and even the threat thereof.

The approach of U.S. scholars to Article 2(4) is, in general, much less categorical. Randelzhofer states that U.S. scholars are more willing than others to consider the use of force for humanitarian intervention. Today, in the light of the Security Council's resolution of March 26, 1993, on the creation of a peacekeeping force in Somalia (UNOSOM II), under specific orders "to use all force necessary to accomplish its mission" (of disarming the people and feeding the starving) under chapter VII of the Charter, such a comment seems dated indeed.

That the approach of U.S. scholars, many of whom attempted to justify the repeated use of U.S. force as in Grenada and Panama, sought to carve exceptions to the general prohibition of Article 2(4). Professor Ermacora's analysis of Article 2(7), the prohibition of UN intervention in matters within the domestic jurisdiction of states, describes the historical evolution of the human rights exception to this prohibition. It is the generalized acceptance by the international community that human rights matters are no longer exclusively within the domestic jurisdiction

* Reprinted with the permission of the American Society of Int'l Law.

of the state that enabled the community to reach correctness on the collective use of force for humanitarian reasons in Somalia.

A poignant historical note is Randelzhofer's listing of "three exceptions to the prohibition on the use of force," the first being measures taken by a regional arrangement (under chapter VIII of the Charter) against an "enemy" state pursuant to Article 53(1), which do not need the authorization of the Security Council. An "enemy" state is defined in Article 53(2) as any state "which during the Second World War has been an enemy of any signatory of the present Charter." He points out that these articles demonstrate that the creation of the United Nations "was not a new beginning but a continuation of the victorious alliances of the Second World War." Today, however, he adds, this provision is moot, in light of the fact that the former "enemy" states became members of the United Nations.

Randelzhofer cites Professor Franck's provocative article in this Journal some twenty years ago, which argued that the prohibition on the use of force was a dead letter since chapter VII of the Charter, to which, he argued, it was linked, never functioned. For Randelzhofer, as for Professor Henkin in the exchange of views in the Journal at that time, the prohibition on the use of force does not depend upon the use of chapter VII. Since the end of the Cold War and the Persian Gulf war of 1991, chapter VII of the Charter is no longer a dead letter. Unfortunately, this Commentary is of little use with regard to the formerly dormant articles of the Charter, which are now being invoked at a dizzying rate. Chapter VII, and in particular, Articles 39, 41, 42 and those that follow, [are in a state of evolution].

The very nature of the United Nations is changing from the time when this Commentary was written. Professor Grewe, who writes that no one would have expected that "not peace-keeping, but economic development, dealing with the alleviation of poverty and hunger and attempting to raise the living standards of the populations of the Third World would become the principal tasks of the United Nations" (p. xxxv) (my translation). UN Secretary–General Boutros Boutros–Ghali recently stated at the inauguration of the new headquarters of the United Nations University in Tokyo (February 1993): "In all of 1987, the Security Council met 49 times. In 1992, it held 129 meetings. Acting under Chapter VII of the Charter, it imposed sanctions against several countries considered to pose threats to international peace and security." Further, he pointed out that "[t]he limited peace-keeping role of the past is being expanded into new political fields" and that "since 1988, 13 new peace-keeping operations have been organized." Peacekeeping, in terms of the budget and political priorities of the United Nations, has now become the number-one objective, as the UN Charter intended it to be, yet as it was unable to become during the Cold War period described in this Commentary.

* * *

SECTION C.   COLLECTIVE SELF–DEFENSE

1.   CZECHOSLOVAKIA: DEFENSE OF THE FORMER SOCIALIST COMMUNITY

The disintegration of the Soviet Union also saw the repudiation of the *Brezhnev Doctrine*.   The first pronouncement of the *Brezhnev Doctrine*, the Soviet analogue to the *Reagan Doctrine*, was precipitated during the Soviet intervention in Czechoslovakia.   President Reagan had said in 1985, "freedom movements arise and assert themselves.   They're doing so on almost every continent populated by man—in the hills of Afghanistan, in Angola, in Kampuchea, in Central America * * * They're our brothers, these freedom fighters, and we owe them our help."   [Reported in Reisman, *Allocating Competences to Use Coercion in the Post–Cold War World: Practices, Conditions, and Prospects, in Law and Force in the New International Order* 26, 24, n. 13 (Damrosch & Scheffer, eds. 1991).   Jean Kirkpatrick and Allan Gerson have noted that "[t]he Reagan Doctrine, as we understand it, is above all concerned with the moral legitimacy of U.S. support—including military support— for insurgencies under certain circumstances: where there are indigenous opponents to a government that is maintained by force, rather than popular consent; where such a government depends on arms supplied by the Soviet Union, the Soviet bloc, or other foreign sources; and where the people are denied a choice regarding their affiliations and future." Kirkpatrick & Gerson, *The Reagan Doctrine, Human Rights, and International Law,* in Right v. Might, supra, at 19, 20 (1991); see also, Halberstam, The Copenhagen Document: Intervention in Support of Democracy, 34 Harv.I.L.J. 163 (1993); Franck, The Emerging Right of Democratic Governance, 86 A.J.I.L. 46 (1992); Reisman, Coercion and Self–Determination: Construing Charter Article 2(4), 78 A.J.I.L. 642, 644–45 (1984); and Schachter, The Legality of Pro–Democratic Invasion, 78 A.J.I.L. 645 (1934) (rejects the Reisman argument).

The Brezhnev Doctrine, on the other hand, claimed the right to use force to protect any socialist regime.   The legality of the Soviet invasion of Czechoslovakia is measured against the provisions of the Charter. Article 2(1) of the Charter states as a principle: "The Organization is based on the principle of the sovereign equality of all its Members." Was that "Bourgeois Law?"   Were Poland, Hungary, Czechoslovakia, Bulgaria, Rumania and the three Soviet members of the United Nations a single unit, with one sovereignty?   Did the USSR purport to guarantee to every segment of that unit a socialist form of government?   By what right?   And, if so, how is that guarantee (if enforced by arms) consistent with the Charter?   Compare Article 4, section 4 of the United States Constitution: "The United States shall guarantee to every state in this Union a Republican Form of Government * * *."   Does the United States have the right to guarantee to each state in North America (Central America) (the Western Hemisphere) (the World) a non-communist form of government?

2.　THE SOVIET INTERVENTION IN AFGHANISTAN

Much like the U.S. tragedy in Vietnam, the former Soviet Union suffered along with its opponents' great trauma and division in its attempt to intervene in Afghanistan. This war may have been a significant factor in the ultimate demise of that once powerful empire.

3.　THE CLAIM OF COLLECTIVE SELF-DEFENSE IN SOUTH VIETNAM

THE LEGALITY OF UNITED STATES PARTICIPATION IN THE DEFENSE OF VIETNAM, MEMORANDUM PREPARED BY THE LEGAL ADVISER OF THE DEPARTMENT OF STATE

54 United States Department of State Bulletin 474 (1966).

The United States and South Vietnam Have the Right Under International Law to Participate in the Collective Defense of South Vietnam Against Armed Attack.

In response to requests from the Government of South Vietnam, the United States has been assisting that country in defending itself against armed attack from the Communist North. This attack has taken the forms of externally supported subversion, clandestine supply of arms, infiltration of armed personnel, and most recently the sending of regular units of the North Vietnamese army into the South.

International law has long recognized the right of individual and collective self-defense against armed attack. South Vietnam and the United States are engaging in such collective defense consistently with international law and with United States obligations under the United Nations Charter.

A.　South Vietnam Is Being Subjected to Armed Attack by Communist North Vietnam

The Geneva accords of 1954 established a demarcation line between North Vietnam and South Vietnam. They provided for withdrawals of military forces into the respective zones north and south of this line. The accords prohibited the use of either zone for the resumption of hostilities or to "further an aggressive policy." During the 5 years following the Geneva conference of 1954, the Hanoi regime developed a covert political-military organization in South Vietnam based on Communist cadres it had ordered to stay in the South, contrary to the provisions of the Geneva accords. The activities of this covert organization were directed toward the kidnapping and assassination of civilian officials—acts of terrorism that were perpetrated in increasing numbers. In the 3-year period from 1959 to 1961, the North Vietnam regime infiltrated an estimated 10,000 men into the South. It is estimated that 13,000 additional personnel were infiltrated in 1962, and, by the end of 1964, North Vietnam may well have moved over 40,000 armed and unarmed guerrillas into South Vietnam.

The International Control Commission reported in 1962 the findings of its Legal Committee:

* * * [T]here is evidence to show that arms, armed and un-armed personnel, munitions and other supplies have been sent from the Zone in the North to the Zone in the South with the objective of supporting, organizing and carrying out hostile activities, including armed attacks, directed against the Armed Forces and Administration of the Zone in the South.

* * * [T]here is evidence that the PAVN [People's Army of Viet Nam] has allowed the Zone in the North to be used for inciting, encouraging and supporting hostile activities in the Zone in the South, aimed at the overthrow of the Administration in the South.

Beginning in 1964, the Communists apparently exhausted their reservoir of Southerners who had gone North. Since then the greater number of men infiltrated into the South have been native-born North Vietnamese. Most recently, Hanoi has begun to infiltrate elements of the North Vietnamese army in increasingly larger numbers. Today, there is evidence that nine regiments of regular North Vietnamese forces are fighting in organized units in the South.

In the guerrilla war in Vietnam, the external aggression from the North is the critical military element of the insurgency, although it is unacknowledged by North Vietnam. In these circumstances, an "armed attack" is not as easily fixed by date and hour as in the case of traditional warfare. However, the infiltration of thousands of armed men clearly constitutes an "armed attack" under any reasonable definition. There may be some question as to the exact date at which North Vietnam's aggression grew into an "armed attack," but there can be no doubt that it had occurred before February 1965.

B. International Law Recognizes the Right of Individual and Collective Self–Defense Against Armed Attack

International law has traditionally recognized the right of self-defense against armed attack. This proposition has been asserted by writers on international law through the several centuries in which the modern law of nations has developed. The proposition has been acted on numerous times by governments throughout modern history. Today the principle of self-defense against armed attack is universally recognized and accepted.

The Charter of the United Nations, concluded at the end of World War II, imposed an important limitation on the use of force by United Nations members. Article 2, paragraph 4, provides: All Members shall refrain in their international relations from the threat or use of force against the territorial integrity or political independence of any state, or in any other manner inconsistent with the Purposes of the United Nations. In addition, the charter embodied a system of international peacekeeping through the organs of the United Nations. Article 24 summarizes these structural arrangements in stating that the United Nations members: * * * confer on the Security Council primary responsibility for the maintenance of international peace and security, and agree that in carrying out its duties under this responsibility the Security Council acts on their behalf.

However, the charter expressly states in article 51 that the remaining provisions of the charter—including the limitation of article 2, paragraph 4 and the creation of United Nations machinery to keep the peace—in no way diminish the inherent right of self-defense against armed attack. Article 51 provides:

> Nothing in the present Charter shall impair the inherent right of individual or collective self-defense if an armed attack occurs against a Member of the United Nations, until the Security Council has taken the measures necessary to maintain international peace and security. Measures taken by Members in the exercise of this right of self-defense shall be immediately reported to the Security Council and shall not in any way affect the authority and responsibility of the Security Council under the present Charter to take at any time such action as it deems necessary in order to maintain or restore international peace and security.

Thus, article 51 restates and preserves, for member states in the situations covered by the article, a long-recognized principle of international law. The article is a "saving clause" designed to make clear that no other provision in the charter shall be interpreted to impair the inherent right of self-defense referred to in article 51.

Three principal objections have been raised against the availability of the right of individual and collective self-defense in the case of Vietnam: (1) that this right applies only in the case of an armed attack on a United Nations member; (2) that it does not apply in the case of South Vietnam because the latter is not an independent sovereign state; and (3) that collective self-defense may be undertaken only by a regional organization operating under chapter 8 of the United Nations Charter.

* * *

H. Summary

The analysis set forth above shows that South Vietnam has the right in present circumstances to defend itself against armed attack from the North and to organize a collective self-defense with the participation of others. In response to requests from South Vietnam, the United States has been participating in that defense, both through military action within South Vietnam and actions taken directly against the aggressor in North Vietnam. This participation by the United States is in conformity with international law and is consistent with our obligations under the Charter of the United Nations.

* * *

WRIGHT, LEGAL ASPECTS OF THE VIETNAM SITUATION

60 American Journal of International Law 750, 755 (1966).[a]

The legal issues, clarification of which might contribute to a judgment of the validity of the diverse images of the Vietnam situation, may be stated as follows:

1.   Are the hostilities between North and South Vietnam international hostilities or civil strife, i.e., is Vietnam two states or one?

2.   Was the requirement for an election in 1956 dependent on the development of conditions assuring that the election would be free and fair?

3.   Was the requirement concerning elections in the resolutions of the Geneva Conference such an integral part of the Cease–Fire Agreement between France and the Democratic Republic of Vietnam (Ho Chi Minh) as to permit suspension of the cease-fire when the elections were frustrated?

4.   If it is assumed that the cease-fire line continued in operation, was North Vietnam guilty of "armed attacks" upon South Vietnam justifying the United States bombing attacks north of the cease-fire line, which began in February, 1965, as measures of "collective self-defense"?

* * *

1.   The evidence suggests that Vietnam is one state and that the hostilities of Ho Chi Minh's government against the Saigon Government would be civil strife within its domestic jurisdiction unless forbidden by the cease-fire Agreement.   During the hostilities between the "Democratic Republic of Vietnam" under Ho Chi Minh and France, supporting the "Republic of Vietnam" under Bao Dai from 1946 to 1954 and during the Geneva Conference, both sides regarded Vietnam as one state, the legal issue being whether it was an independent state or a "Free State" within the French Community.   When the hostilities ended with French defeat, large areas of the south were occupied by Ho Chi Minh's forces, the Viet–Minh, and areas in the north by forces of France and Bao Dai. The Cease–Fire Agreement of 1954 signed by representatives of France and the Democratic Republic of Vietnam provided for the withdrawal of these forces across the cease-fire line, substantially the 17th parallel, and very explicitly declared that this line was not an international boundary but a "provisional military demarcation line" and that the territories at each side were not states but "zones."   The final resolutions of the Conference declared that "the independence, unity and territorial integrity" of Vietnam should be respected, and provided that elections "shall" be held in July, 1956, to determine the government of Vietnam.   These resolutions did not constitute a formal treaty and were not signed by any of the delegates.   They were, however, accepted by all of the delegates except those of the United States and Bao Dai's Republic of Vietnam, both of whom made statements "noted" by the Conference.   In regard to the reservation by Bao Dai's representative, the Chairman at the final

a.   Reprinted with the permission of the American Society of International Law.

session of the Conference, Anthony Eden, said: We can not now amend our final act, which is the statement of the Conference as a whole, but the Declaration of the Representative of the State of Vietnam will be taken note of. It seems clear that the Conference recognized Vietnam as one state and provided that it should be united by one government in 1956.

* * *

Question. Article 51 of the Charter of the United Nations contemplates that a state can use force in individual or collective self-defense only until action is taken by the Security Council. The design of the charter apparently envisioned only temporary self-defense measures. But fighting in Vietnam continued for many years. Why did the Security Council not take action in this case?

4. THE CLAIM OF COLLECTIVE SELF-DEFENSE IN NICARAGUA

CASE CONCERNING MILITARY AND PARAMILITARY ACTIVITIES IN AND AGAINST NICARAGUA (NICARAGUA v. UNITED STATES OF AMERICA) [a]

International Court of Justice, 1986.
[1986] I.C.J. Reports 14.

1. On 9 April 1984 the Ambassador of the Republic of Nicaragua to the Netherlands filed in the Registry of the Court an Application instituting proceedings against the United States of America in respect of a dispute concerning responsibility for military and paramilitary activities in and against Nicaragua. In order to found the jurisdiction of the Court the Application relied on declarations made by the Parties accepting the compulsory jurisdiction of the Court under Article 36 of the Statute.

18. The dispute before the Court between Nicaragua and the United States concerns events in Nicaragua subsequent to the fall of the Government of President Anastasio Somoza Debayle in Nicaragua in July 1979, and activities of the Government of the United States in relation to Nicaragua since that time. Following the departure of President Somoza, a Junta of National Reconstruction and government installed by the body which had led the armed opposition to President Somoza, the Frente Sandinista de Liberación Nacional (FSLN). That body had initially an extensive share in the new government, described as a "democratic coalition", and as a result of later resignations and reshuffles, became almost its sole component. Certain opponents of the new Government, primarily supporters of the former Somoza Government and in particular ex-members of the National Guard, formed

---

a. The editors have made a substantial number of omissions in this very long opinion. The reader can keep track of the omissions by referring to the paragraph numbers.

themselves into irregular military forces, and commenced a policy of armed opposition, though initially on a limited scale.

19. The attitude of the United States Government to the "democratic coalition government" was at first favourable; and a programme of economic aid to Nicaragua was adopted. However by 1981 this attitude had changed. United States aid to Nicaragua was suspended in January 1981 and terminated in April 1981. According to the United States, the reason for this change of attitude was reports of involvement of the Government of Nicaragua in logistical support, including provision of arms, for guerrillas in El Salvador. There was however no interruption in diplomatic relations, which have continued to be maintained up to the present time. In September 1981, according to testimony called by Nicaragua, it was decided to plan and undertake activities directed against Nicaragua.

20. The armed opposition to the new Government in Nicaragua, which originally comprised various movements, subsequently became organized into two main groups: the Fuerza Democrática Nicaragüense (FDN) and the Alianza Revolucionaria Democrática (ARDE). The first of these grew from 1981 onwards into a trained fighting force, operating along the borders with Honduras; the second, formed in 1982, operated along the borders with Costa Rica. The precise extent to which, and manner in which, the United States Government contributed to bringing about these developments will be studied more closely later in the present Judgment. However, after an initial period in which the "covert" operations of United States personnel and persons in their pay were kept from becoming public knowledge, it was made clear, not only in the United States press, but also in Congress and in official statements by the President and high United States officials, that the United States Government had been giving support to the contras, a term employed to describe those fighting against the present Nicaraguan Government. In 1983 budgetary legislation enacted by the United States Congress made specific provision for funds to be used by United States intelligence agencies for supporting "directly or indirectly, military or paramilitary operations in Nicaragua". According to Nicaragua, the contras have caused it considerable material damage and widespread loss of life, and have also committed such acts as killing of prisoners, indiscriminate killing of civilians, torture, rape and kidnapping. It is contended by Nicaragua that the United States Government is effectively in control of the contras, that it devised their strategy and directed their tactics, and that the purpose of that Government was, from the beginning, to overthrow the Government of Nicaragua.

21. Nicaragua claims furthermore that certain military or paramilitary operations against it were carried out, not by the contras, who at the time claimed responsibility, but by persons in the pay of the United States Government, and under the direct command of United States personnel, who also participated to some extent in the operations. These operations will also be more closely examined below in order to determine their legal significance and the responsibility for them; they include the mining of certain Nicaraguan ports in early 1984, and attacks on ports, oil installations, a naval base, etc. Nicaragua has also

complained of overflights of its territory by United States aircraft, not only for purposes of intelligence-gathering and supply to the contras in the field, but also in order to intimidate the population.

22. In the economic field, Nicaragua claims that the United States has withdrawn its own aid to Nicaragua, drastically reduced the quota for imports of sugar from Nicaragua to the United States, and imposed a trade embargo; it has also used its influence in the Inter–American Development Bank and the International Bank for Reconstruction and Development to block the provision of loans to Nicaragua.

23. As a matter of law, Nicaragua claims, inter alia, that the United States has acted in violation of Article 2, paragraph 4, of the United Nations Charter, and of a customary international law obligation to refrain from the threat or use of force; that its actions amount to intervention in the internal affairs of Nicaragua, in breach of the Charter of the Organization of American States and of rules of customary international law forbidding intervention; and that the United States has acted in violation of the sovereignty of Nicaragua, and in violation of a number of other obligations established in general customary international law and in the inter-American system. The actions of the United States are also claimed by Nicaragua to be such as to defeat the object and purpose of a Treaty of Friendship, Commerce and Navigation concluded between the Parties in 1956, and to be in breach of provisions of that Treaty.

24. The United States has not filed any pleading on the merits of the case, and was not represented at the hearings devoted thereto. It did however make clear in its Counter–Memorial on the questions of jurisdiction and admissibility that "by providing, upon request, proportionate and appropriate assistance to third States not before the Court" it claims to be acting in reliance on the inherent right of self-defence "guaranteed * * * by Article 51, that is to say the right of collective self-defence.

81. The operations which Nicaragua attributes to the direct action of United States personnel or "UCLAs", in addition to the mining of ports, are apparently the following:

(i) 8 September 1983: an attack was made on Sandino international airport in Managua by a Cessna aircraft, which was shot down;

(ii) 13 September 1983: an underwater oil pipeline and part of the oil terminal at Puerto Sandino were blown up;

(iii) 2 October 1983: an attack was made on oil storage facilities at Benjamin Zeledon on the Atlantic coast, causing the loss of a large quantity of fuel;

(iv) 10 October 1983: an attack was made by air and sea on the port of Corinto, involving the destruction of five oil storage tanks, the loss of millions of gallons of fuel, and the evacuation of large numbers of the local population;

(v) 14 October 1983: the underwater oil pipeline at Puerto Sandino was again blown up;

(vi) 4/5 January 1984: an attack was made by speedboats and helicopters using rockets against the Potosi Naval Base;

(vii) 24/25 February 1984: an incident at El Bluff listed under this date appears to be the mine explosion already mentioned in paragraph 76;

(viii) 7 March 1984: an attack was made on oil and storage facility at San Juan del Sur by speedboats and helicopters;

(ix) 28/30 March 1984: clashes occurred at Puerto Sandino between speedboats, in the course of minelaying operations, and Nicaraguan patrol boats; intervention by a helicopter in support of the speedboats;

(x) 9 April 1984: a helicopter allegedly launched from a mother ship in international waters provided fire support for an ARDE attack on San Juan del Norte.

85. The Court considers that it should eliminate from further consideration under this heading the following items:

— the attack of 8 September 1983 on Managua airport (item (i)): this was claimed by the ARDE; a press report is to the effect that the ARDE purchased the aircraft from the CIA, but there is no evidence of CIA planning, or the involvement of any United States personnel or UCLAs;

— the attack on Benjamin Zeledon on 2 October 1983 (item (iii)): there is no evidence of the involvement of United States personnel or UCLAs;

— the incident of 24–25 February 1984 (item (vii)), already dealt with under the heading of the mining of ports.

86. On the other hand the Court finds the remaining incidents listed in paragraph 81 to be established. The general pattern followed by these attacks appears to the Court, on the basis of that evidence and of press reports quoting United States administration sources, to have been as follows. A "mother ship" was supplied (apparently leased) by the CIA; whether it was of United States registry does not appear. Speedboats, guns and ammunition were supplied by the United States administration, and the actual attacks were carried out by "UCLAs". Helicopters piloted by Nicaraguans and others piloted by United States nationals were also involved on some occasions. According to one report the pilots were United States civilians under contract to the CIA. Although it is not proved that any United States military personnel took a direct part in the operations, agents of the United States participated in the planning, direction, support and execution of the operations. The execution was the task rather of the "UCLAs", while United States nationals participated in the planning, direction and support. The imputability to the United States of these attacks appears therefore to the Court to be established.

87. Nicaragua complains of infringement of its airspace by United States military aircraft. Apart from a minor incident on 11 January 1984 involving a helicopter, as to which, according to a press report, it

was conceded by the United States that it was possible that the aircraft violated Nicaraguan airspace, this claim refers to overflights by aircraft at high altitude for intelligence reconnaissance purposes, or aircraft for supply purposes to the contras in the field, and aircraft producing "sonic booms". The Nicaraguan Memorial also mentions low-level reconnaissance flights by aircraft piloted by United States personnel in 1983, but the press report cited affords no evidence that these flights, along the Honduran border, involved any invasion of airspace. In addition Nicaragua has made a particular complaint of the activities of a United States SR–71 plane between 7 and 11 November 1984, which is said to have flown low over several Nicaraguan cities "producing loud sonic booms and shattering glass windows, to exert psychological pressure on the Nicaraguan Government and population".

91. The Court concludes that, as regards the high-altitude overflights for reconnaissance purposes, the statement admitting them made in the Security Council is limited to the period up to March 1982. However, not only is it entitled to take into account that the interest of the United States in "verifying reports of Nicaraguan intervention"— the justification offered in the Security Council for these flights—has not ceased or diminished since 1982, but the photographs attached to the 1984 Background Paper are evidence of at least sporadic overflights subsequently. It sees no reason therefore to doubt the assertion of Nicaragua that such flights have continued. The Court finds that the incidents of overflights causing "sonic booms" in November 1984 are to some extent a matter of public knowledge. As to overflights of aircraft for supply purposes, it appears from Nicaragua's evidence that these were carried out generally, if not exclusively, by the contras themselves, though using aircraft supplied to them by the United States. Whatever other responsibility the United States may have incurred in this latter respect, the only violations of Nicaraguan airspace which the Court finds imputable to the United States on the basis of the evidence before it are first of all, the high-altitude reconnaissance flights, and secondly the low-altitude flights of 7 to 11 November 1984, complained of as causing "sonic booms".

93. The Court must now examine in more detail the genesis, development and activities of the contra force, and the role of the United States in relation to it, in order to determine the legal significance of the conduct of the United States in this respect. According to Nicaragua, the United States "conceived, created and organized a mercenary army, the contra force". However, there is evidence to show that some armed opposition to the Government of Nicaragua existed in 1979–1980, even before any interference or support by the United States. Nicaragua dates the beginning of the activity of the United States to "shortly after" 9 March 1981, when, it was said, the President of the United States made a formal presidential finding authorizing the CIA to undertake "covert activities" directed against Nicaragua. * * *

107. To sum up, despite the secrecy which surrounded it, at least initially, the financial support given by the Government of the United States to the military and paramilitary activities of the contras in Nicaragua is a fully established fact. The legislative and executive

bodies of the respondent State have moreover, subsequent to the controversy which has been sparked off in the United States, openly admitted
the nature, volume and frequency of this support. Indeed, they clearly
take responsibility for it, this government aid having now become the
major element of United States foreign policy in the region. As to the
ways in which such financial support has been translated into practical
assistance, the Court has been able to reach a general finding.

109. What the Court has to determine at this point is whether or
not the relationship of the contras to the United States Government was
so much one of dependence on the one side and control on the other that
it would be right to equate the contras, for legal purposes, with an organ
of the United States Government, or as acting on behalf of that Government. Here it is relevant to note that in May 1983 the assessment of
the Intelligence Committee, in the Report referred to in paragraph 95
above, was that the contras "constitute[d] an independent force" and
that the "only element of control that could be exercised by the United
States" was "cessation of aid". Paradoxically this assessment serves to
underline, a contrario, the potential for control inherent in the degree of
the contras' dependence on aid. Yet despite the heavy subsidies and
other support provided to them by the United States, there is no clear
evidence of the United States having actually exercised such a degree of
control in all fields as to justify treating the contras as acting on its
behalf.

114. In this respect, the Court notes that according to Nicaragua,
the contras are no more than bands of mercenaries which have been
recruited, organized, paid and commanded by the Government of the
United States. This would mean that they have no real autonomy in
relation to that Government. Consequently, any offences which they
have committed would be imputable to the Government of the United
States, like those of any other forces placed under the latter's command.
In the view of Nicaragua, "stricto sensu, the military and paramilitary
attacks launched by the United States against Nicaragua do not constitute a case of civil strife. They are essentially the acts of the United
States." If such a finding of the imputability of the acts of the contras
to the United States were to be made, no question would arise of mere
complicity in those acts, or of incitement of the contras to commit them.

115. The Court has taken the view * * * that United States
participation, even if preponderant or decisive, in the financing, organizing, training, supplying and equipping of the contras, the selection of its
military or paramilitary targets, and the planning of the whole of its
operation, is still insufficient in itself, on the basis of the evidence in the
possession of the Court, for the purpose of attributing to the United
States the acts committed by the contras in the course of their military
or paramilitary operations in Nicaragua. All the forms of United States
participation mentioned above, and even the general control by the
respondent State over a force with a high degree of dependency on it,
would not in themselves mean, without further evidence, that the United
States directed or enforced the perpetration of the acts contrary to
human rights and humanitarian law alleged by the applicant State.
Such acts could well be committed by members of the contras without

the control of the United States. For this conduct to give rise to legal responsibility of the United States, it would in principle have to be proved that that State had effective control of the military or paramilitary operations in the course of which the alleged violations were committed.

116. The Court does not consider that the assistance given by the United States to the contras warrants the conclusion that these forces are subject to the United States to such an extent that any acts they have committed are imputable to that State. It takes the view that the contras remain responsible for their acts, and that the United States is not responsible for the acts of the contras, but for its own conduct vis-à-vis Nicaragua, including conduct related to the acts of the contras. What the Court has to investigate is not the complaints relating to alleged violations of humanitarian law by the contras, regarded by Nicaragua as imputable to the United States, but rather unlawful acts for which the United States may be responsible directly in connection with the activities of the contras. The lawfulness or otherwise of such acts of the United States is a question different from the violations of humanitarian law of which the contras may or may not have been guilty. It is for this reason that the Court does not have to determine whether the violations of humanitarian law attributed to the contras were in fact committed by them. At the same time, the question whether the United States Government was, or must have been, aware at the relevant time that allegations of breaches of humanitarian law were being made against the contras is relevant to an assessment of the lawfulness of the action of the United States. In this respect, the material facts are primarily those connected with the issue in 1983 of a manual of psychological operations.

122. The Court concludes that in 1983 an agency of the United States Government supplied to the FDN a manual on psychological guerrilla warfare which, while expressly discouraging indiscriminate violence against civilians, considered the possible necessity of shooting civilians who were attempting to leave a town; and advised the "neutralization" for propaganda purposes of local judges, officials or notables after the semblance of trial in the presence of the population. The text supplied to the contras also advised the use of professional criminals to perform unspecified "jobs", and the use of provocation at mass demonstrations to produce violence on the part of the authorities so as to make "martyrs".

126. The Court has before it, in the Counter–Memorial on jurisdiction and admissibility filed by the United States, the assertion that the United States, pursuant to the inherent right of individual and collective self-defence, and in accordance with the Inter–American Treaty of Reciprocal Assistance, has responded to requests from El Salvador, Honduras and Costa Rica, for assistance in their self-defence against aggression by Nicaragua. The Court has therefore to ascertain, so far as possible, the facts on which this claim is or may be based, in order to determine whether collective self-defence constitutes a justification of the activities of the United States here complained of. * * *

127. Nicaragua claims that the references made by the United States to the justification of collective self-defence are merely "pretexts" for the activities of the United States. It has alleged that the true motive for the conduct of the United States is unrelated to the support which it accuses Nicaragua of giving to the armed opposition in El Salvador, and that the real objectives of United States policy are to impose its will upon Nicaragua and force it to comply with United States demands. In the Court's view, however, if Nicaragua has been giving support to the armed opposition in El Salvador, and if this constitutes an armed attack on El Salvador and the other appropriate conditions are met, collective self-defence could be legally invoked by the United States, even though there may be the possibility of an additional motive, one perhaps even more decisive for the United States, drawn from the political orientation of the present Nicaraguan Government. The existence of an additional motive, other than that officially proclaimed by the United States, could not deprive the latter of its right to resort to collective self-defence. The conclusion to be drawn is that special caution is called for in considering the allegations of the United States concerning conduct by Nicaragua which may provide a sufficient basis for self-defence.

152. The Court finds, in short, that support for the armed opposition in El Salvador from Nicaraguan territory was a fact up to the early months of 1981. While the Court does not possess full proof that there was aid, or as to its exact nature, its scale and its continuance until the early months of 1981, it cannot overlook a number of concordant indications, many of which were provided moreover by Nicaragua itself, from which it can reasonably infer the provision of a certain amount of aid from Nicaraguan territory. * * *

153. After the early months of 1981, evidence of military aid from or through Nicaragua remains very weak. This is so despite the deployment by the United States in the region of extensive technical resources for tracking, monitoring and intercepting air, sea and land traffic, described in evidence by Mr. MacMichael and its use of a range of intelligence and information sources in a political context where, the Government had declared and recognized surveillance of Nicaragua as a "high priority". The Court cannot conclude from this that no transborder traffic in arms existed, although it does not seem particularly unreasonable to believe that traffic of this kind, had it been persistent and on a significant scale, must inevitably have been discovered, in view of the magnitude of the resources used for that purpose. The Court merely takes note that the allegations of arms-trafficking are not solidly established; it has not been able to satisfy itself that any continuing flow on a significant scale took place after the early months of 1981.

160. On the basis of the foregoing, the Court is satisfied that, between July 1979, the date of the fall of the Somoza régime in Nicaragua, and the early months of 1981, an intermittent flow of arms was routed via the territory of Nicaragua to the armed opposition in El Salvador. On the other hand, the evidence is insufficient to satisfy the Court that, since the early months of 1981, assistance has continued to reach the Salvadorian armed opposition from the territory of Nicaragua

on any significant scale, or that the Government of Nicaragua was responsible for any flow of arms at either period.

164.   The Court, while not as fully informed on the question as it would wish to be, therefore considers as established the fact that certain transborder military incursions into the territory of Honduras and Costa Rica are imputable to the Government of Nicaragua. The Court is also aware that the FDN operates along the Nicaraguan border with Honduras, and the ARDE operates along the border with Costa Rica.

* * *

172.   The Court has now to turn its attention to the question of the law applicable to the present dispute. In formulating its view on the significance of the United States multilateral treaty reservation, the Court has reached the conclusion that it must refrain from applying the multilateral treaties invoked by Nicaragua in support of its claims, without prejudice either to other treaties or to the other sources of law enumerated in Article 38 of the Statute. The first stage in its determination of the law actually to be applied to this dispute is to ascertain the consequences of the exclusion of the applicability of the multilateral treaties for the definition of the content of the customary international law which remains applicable.

[The United States had pleaded that its reservation to the compulsory jurisdiction of the court precluded application of multilateral treaties, such as the United Nations Charter, unless all parties to the treaties affected by the decision were parties to the case. Accepting that defense, the court nevertheless held that the United States' actions could be judged under customary international law.]

179.   It will therefore be clear that customary international law continues to exist and to apply, separately from international treaty law, even where the two categories of law have an identical content. Consequently, in ascertaining the content of the customary international law applicable to the present dispute, the Court must satisfy itself that the Parties are bound by the customary rules in question; but the Court is in no way bound to uphold these rules only in so far as they differ from the treaty rules which it is prevented by the United States reservation from applying in the present dispute.

180.   The United States however presented a further argument, during the proceedings devoted to the question of jurisdiction and admissibility, in support of its contention that the multilateral treaty reservation debars the Court from considering the Nicaraguan claims based on customary international law. The United States observed that the multilateral treaties in question contain legal standards specifically agreed between the Parties to govern their mutual rights and obligations, and that the conduct of the Parties will continue to be governed by these treaties, irrespective of what the Court may decide on the customary law issue, because of the principle of pacta sunt servanda. Accordingly, in the contention of the United States, the Court cannot properly adjudicate the mutual rights and obligations of the two States when reference to their treaty rights and obligations is barred; the

Court would be adjudicating those rights and obligations by standards other than those to which the Parties have agreed to conduct themselves in their actual international relations.

181.   The question raised by this argument is whether the provisions of the multilateral treaties in question, particularly the United Nations Charter, diverge from the relevant rules of customary international law to such an extent that a judgment of the Court as to the rights and obligations of the parties under customary law, disregarding the content of the multilateral treaties binding on the parties, would be a wholly academic exercise, and not "susceptible of any compliance or execution whatever." The Court does not consider that this is the case. On the question of the use of force, the United States itself argues for a complete identity of the relevant rules of customary international law with the provisions of the Charter. The Court has not accepted this extreme contention, having found that on a number of points the areas governed by the two sources of law do not exactly overlap, and the substantive rules in which they are framed are not identical in content * * *. However, so far from having constituted a marked departure from a customary international law which still exists unmodified, the Charter gave expression in this field to principles already present in customary international law, and that law has in the subsequent four decades developed under the influence of the Charter, to such an extent that a number of rules contained in the Charter have acquired a status independent of it. The essential consideration is that both the Charter and the customary international law flow from a common fundamental principle outlawing the use of force in international relations. * * *

193.   The general rule prohibiting force allows for certain exceptions. In view of the arguments advanced by the United States to justify the acts of which it is accused by Nicaragua, the Court must express a view on the content of the right of self-defence, and more particularly the right of collective self-defence. First, with regard to the existence of this right, it notes that in the language of Article 51 of the United Nations Charter, the inherent right (or "droit naturel") which any State possesses in the event of an armed attack, covers both collective and individual self-defence. Thus, the Charter itself testifies to the existence of the right of collective self-defence in customary international law. Moreover, just as the wording of certain General Assembly declarations adopted by States demonstrates their recognition of the principle of the prohibition of force as definitely a matter of customary international law, some of the wording in those declarations operates similarly in respect of the right of self-defence (both collective and individual). Thus, in the declaration * * * on the Principles of International Law concerning Friendly Relations and Cooperation among States in accordance with the Charter of the United Nations, the reference to the prohibition of force is followed by a paragraph stating that: "nothing in the foregoing paragraphs shall be construed as enlarging or diminishing in any way the scope of the provisions of the Charter concerning cases in which the use of force is lawful". This resolution demonstrates that the States represented in the General Assembly regard the exception to the prohibition

of force constituted by the right of individual or collective self-defence as already a matter of customary international law.

194. With regard to the characteristics governing the right of self-defence, since the Parties consider the existence of this right to be established as a matter of customary international law, they have concentrated on the conditions governing its use. In view of the circumstances in which the dispute has arisen, reliance is placed by the Parties only on the right of self-defence in the case of an armed attack which has already occurred, and the issue of the lawfulness of a response to the imminent threat of armed attack has not been raised. Accordingly the Court expresses no view on that issue. The Parties also agree in holding that whether the response to the attack is lawful depends on observance of the criteria of the necessity and the proportionality of the measures taken in self-defence. Since the existence of the right of collective self-defence is established in customary international law, the Court must define the specific conditions which may have to be met for its exercise, in addition to the conditions of necessity and proportionality to which the Parties have referred.

195. In the case of individual self-defence, the exercise of this right is subject to the State concerned having been the victim of an armed attack. Reliance on collective self-defence of course does not remove the need for this. There appears now to be general agreement on the nature of the acts which can be treated as constituting armed attacks. In particular, it may be considered to be agreed that an armed attack must be understood as including not merely action by regular armed forces across an international border, but also "the sending by or on behalf of a State of armed bands, groups, irregulars or mercenaries, which carry out acts of armed force against another State of such gravity as to amount to" (inter alia) an actual armed attack conducted by regular forces, "or its substantial involvement therein". This description, contained in Article 3, paragraph (g), of the Definition of Aggression annexed to G.A. resolution 3314(29), may be taken to reflect customary international law. The Court sees no reason to deny that, in customary law, the prohibition of armed attacks may apply to the sending by a State of armed bands to the territory of another State, if such an operation, because of its scale and effects, would have been classified as an armed attack rather than as a mere frontier incident had it been carried out by regular armed forces. But the Court does not believe that the concept of "armed attack" includes not only acts by armed bands where such acts occur on a significant scale but also assistance to rebels in the form of the provision of weapons or logistical or other support. Such assistance may be regarded as a threat or use of force, or amount to intervention in the internal or external affairs of other States. It is also clear that it is the State which is the victim of an armed attack which must form and declare the view that it has been so attacked. There is no rule in customary international law permitting another State to exercise the right of collective self-defence on the basis of its own assessment of the situation. Where collective self-defence is invoked, it is to be expected that the State for whose benefit this right is used will have declared itself to be the victim of an armed attack.

199. At all events, the Court finds that in customary international law, whether of a general kind or that particular to the inter-American legal system, there is no rule permitting the exercise of collective self-defence in the absence of a request by the State which regards itself as the victim of an armed attack. The Court concludes that the requirement of a request by the State which is the victim of the alleged attack is additional to the requirement that such a State should have declared itself to have been attacked.

200. At this point, the Court may consider whether in customary international law there is any requirement corresponding to that found in the treaty law of the United Nations Charter, by which the State claiming to use the right of individual or collective self-defence must report to an international body, empowered to determine the conformity with international law of the measures which the State is seeking to justify on that basis. Thus Article 51 of the United Nations Charter requires that measures taken by States in exercise of this right of self-defence must be "immediately reported" to the Security Council. * * * [A] principle enshrined in a treaty, if reflected in customary international law, may well be so unencumbered with the conditions and modalities surrounding it in the treaty. Whatever influence the Charter may have had on customary international law in these matters, it is clear that in customary international law it is not a condition of the lawfulness of the use of force in self-defence that a procedure so closely dependent on the content of a treaty commitment and of the institutions established by it, should have been followed. On the other hand, if self-defence is advanced as a justification for measures which would otherwise be in breach both of the principle of customary international law and of that contained in the Charter, it is to be expected that the conditions of the Charter should be respected. Thus for the purpose of enquiry into the customary law position, the absence of a report may be one of the factors indicating whether the State in question was itself convinced that it was acting in self-defence.

201. To justify certain activities involving the use of force, the United States has relied solely on the exercise of its right of collective self-defence. However the Court, having regard particularly to the non-participation of the United States in the merits phase, considers that it should enquire whether customary international law, applicable to the present dispute, may contain other rules which may exclude the unlawfulness of such activities. It does not, however, see any need to reopen the question of the conditions governing the exercise of the right of individual self-defence, which have already been examined in connection with collective self-defence. On the other hand, the Court must enquire whether there is any justification for the activities in question, to be found not in the right of collective self-defence against an armed attack, but in the right to take counter-measures in response to conduct of Nicaragua which is not alleged to constitute an armed attack. It will examine this point in connection with an analysis of the principle of non-intervention in customary international law.

210. When dealing with the rule of the prohibition of the use of force, the Court considered the exception to it constituted by the exercise

of the right of collective self-defence in the event of armed attack. Similarly, it must now consider the following question: if one State acts towards another State in breach of the principle of non-intervention, may a third State lawfully take such action by way of counter-measures against the first State as would otherwise constitute an intervention in its internal affairs? A right to act in this way in the case of intervention would be analogous to the right of collective self-defence in the case of an armed attack, but both the act which gives rise to the reaction, and that reaction itself, would in principle be less grave. Since the Court is here dealing with a dispute in which a wrongful use of force is alleged, it has primarily to consider whether a State has a right to respond to intervention with intervention going so far as to justify a use of force in reaction to measures which do not constitute an armed attack but may nevertheless involve a use of force. The question is itself undeniably relevant from the theoretical viewpoint. However, since the Court is bound to confine its decision to those points of law which are essential to the settlement of the dispute before it, it is not for the Court here to determine what direct reactions are lawfully open to a State which considers itself the victim of another State's acts of intervention, possibly involving the use of force. Hence it has not to determine whether, in the event of Nicaragua's having committed any such acts against El Salvador, the latter was lawfully entitled to take any particular counter-measure. It might however be suggested that, in such a situation, the United States might have been permitted to intervene in Nicaragua in the exercise of some right analogous to the right of collective self-defence, one which might be resorted to in a case of intervention short of armed attack.

211. The Court has recalled above that for one State to use force against another, on the ground that that State has committed a wrongful act of force against a third State, is regarded as lawful, by way of exception, only when the wrongful act provoking the response was an armed attack. Thus the lawfulness of the use of force by a State in response to a wrongful act of which it has not itself been the victim is not admitted when this wrongful act is not an armed attack. In the view of the Court, under international law in force today—whether customary international law or that of the United Nations system— States do not have a right of "collective" armed response to acts which do not constitute an "armed attack". Furthermore, the Court has to recall that the United States itself is relying on the "inherent right of self-defence," but apparently does not claim that any such right exists as would, in respect of intervention, operate in the same way as the right of collective self-defence in respect of an armed attack. In the discharge of its duty under Article 53 of the Statute, the Court has nevertheless had to consider whether such a right might exist; but in doing so it may take note of the absence of any such claim by the United States as an indication of opinio juris.

212. The Court should now mention the principle of respect for State sovereignty, which in international law is of course closely linked with the principles of the prohibition of the use of force and of non-intervention. The basic legal concept of State sovereignty in customary

international law, expressed in, inter alia, Article 2, paragraph 1, of the United Nations Charter, extends to the internal waters and territorial sea of every State and to the air space above its territory. As to superjacent air space, the 1944 Chicago Convention on Civil Aviation (Art. 1) reproduces the established principle of the complete and exclusive sovereignty of a State over the air space above its territory. That convention, in conjunction with the 1958 Geneva Convention on the Territorial Sea, further specifies that the sovereignty of the coastal State extends to the territorial sea and to the air space above it, as does the United Nations Convention on the Law of the Sea adopted on 10 December 1982. The Court has no doubt that these prescriptions of treaty-law merely respond to firmly established and longstanding tenets of customary international law.

213. The duty of every State to respect the territorial sovereignty of others is to be considered for the appraisal to be made of the facts relating to the mining which occurred along Nicaragua's coasts. The legal rules in the light of which these acts of mining should be judged depend upon where they took place. The laying of mines within the ports of another State is governed by the law relating to internal waters, which are subject to the sovereignty of the coastal State. The position is similar as regards mines placed in the territorial sea. It is the sovereignty of the coastal State which is affected in such cases. It is also by virtue of its sovereignty that the coastal State may regulate access to its ports.

214. It is true that in order to enjoy access to ports, foreign vessels possess a customary right of innocent passage in territorial waters for the purposes of entering or leaving internal waters; Article 18, paragraph 1(b), of the UN Convention on the Law of the Sea of 10 December 1982, does no more than codify customary international law on this point. Since freedom of navigation is guaranteed, first in the exclusive economic zones which may exist beyond territorial waters (Art. 58 of the Convention), and secondly, beyond territorial waters and on the high seas (Art. 87), it follows that any State which enjoys a right of access to ports for its ships also enjoys all the freedom necessary for maritime navigation. It may therefore be said that, if this right of access to the port is hindered by the laying of mines by another State, what is infringed is the freedom of communications and of maritime commerce. It is certain that interference with navigation in these areas prejudices both the sovereignty of the coastal State over its internal waters and the right of free access enjoyed by foreign ships.

[The court found (paragraphs 227 and 228) that the United States had violated the prohibition against the use of force by mining Nicaraguan waters, attacking Nicaraguan ports, air installations and naval base, and arming and training the contras. It found further that those acts were not justified as collective self-defense (paragraphs 229–238). Nicaragua's arms supplies to El Salvador did not amount to armed attack; the court found it "difficult to decide" whether Nicaraguan border incursions into Honduras and Costa Rica amounted to armed attack. And, at no relevant time had El Salvador, Honduras or Costa Rica requested U.S. aid in collective self-defense.]

292. For these reasons, THE COURT, (1) By eleven votes to four, Decides that in adjudicating the dispute brought before it by the Application filed by the Republic of Nicaragua on 9 April 1984, the Court is required to apply the "multilateral treaty reservation" contained in proviso (c) to the declaration of acceptance of jurisdiction made under Article 36, paragraph 2, of the Statute of the Court by the Government of the United States of America deposited on 26 August 1946;

(2) By twelve votes to three, Rejects the justification of collective self-defence maintained by the United States in connection with the military and paramilitary activities in and against Nicaragua the subject of this case;

(3) By twelve votes to three, Decides that the United States, by training, arming, equipping, financing and supplying the contra forces or otherwise encouraging, supporting and aiding military and paramilitary activities in and against Nicaragua, has acted, against the Republic of Nicaragua, in breach of its obligation under customary international law not to intervene in the affairs of another State;

(4) By twelve votes to three, Decides that the United States, by certain attacks on Nicaraguan territory in 1983–1984, namely attacks on Puerto Sandino on 13 September and 14 October 1983; an attack on Corinto on 10 October 1983; an attack on Potosi Naval Base on 4/5 January 1984; an attack on San Juan del Sur on 7 March 1984; attacks on patrol boats at Puerto Sandino on 28 and 30 March 1984; and an attack on San Juan del Norte on 9 April 1984; and further by those acts of intervention referred to in subparagraph (3) hereof which involve the use of force, has acted, against the Republic of Nicaragua, in breach of its obligation under customary international law not to use force against another State;

(5) By twelve votes to three, Decides that the United States, by directing or authorizing overflights of Nicaraguan territory, and by the acts imputable to the United States referred to in subparagraph (4) hereof, has acted, against the Republic of Nicaragua, in breach of its obligation under customary international law not to violate the sovereignty of another State;

(6) By twelve votes to three, Decides that, by laying mines in the internal or territorial waters of the Republic of Nicaragua during the first months of 1984, the United States has acted, against the Republic of Nicaragua, in breach of its obligations under customary international law not to use force against another State, not to intervene in its affairs, not to violate its sovereignty and not to interrupt peaceful maritime commerce;

(7) By fourteen votes to one, Decides that, by the acts referred to in subparagraph (6) hereof, the United States has acted, against the Republic of Nicaragua, in breach of its obligations under Article XIX of the Treaty of Friendship, Commerce and Navigation between the United

States of America and the Republic of Nicaragua signed at Managua on 21 January 1956;

(8) By fourteen votes to one, Decides that the United States, by failing to make known the existence and location of the mines laid by it, referred to in subparagraph (6) hereof, has acted in breach of its obligations under customary international law in this respect;

(9) By fourteen votes to one, Finds that the United States, by producing in 1983 a manual entitled Operaciones sicologicas en guerra de guerrillas, and disseminating it to contra forces, has encouraged the commission by them of acts contrary to general principles of humanitarian law; but does not find a basis for concluding that any such acts which may have been committed are imputable to the United States of America as acts of the United States of America;

(10) By twelve votes to three, Decides that the United States, by the attacks on Nicaraguan territory referred to in subparagraph (4) hereof, and by declaring a general embargo on trade with Nicaragua on 1 May 1985, has committed acts calculated to deprive of its object and purpose the Treaty of Friendship, Commerce and Navigation between the Parties signed at Managua on 21 January 1956;

(11) By twelve votes to three, Decides that the United States, by the attacks on Nicaraguan territory referred to in subparagraph (4) hereof, and by declaring a general embargo on trade with Nicaragua on 1 May 1985, has acted in breach of its obligations under Article XIX of the Treaty of Friendship, Commerce and Navigation between the Parties signed at Managua on 21 January 1956;

(12) By twelve votes to three, Decides that the United States is under a duty immediately to cease and to refrain from all such acts as may constitute breaches of the foregoing legal obligations;

(13) By twelve votes to three, Decides that the United States is under an obligation to make reparation to the Republic of Nicaragua for all injury caused to Nicaragua by the breaches of obligations under customary international law enumerated above;

(14) By fourteen votes to one, Decides that the United States is under an obligation to make reparation to the Republic of Nicaragua for all injury caused to Nicaragua by the breaches of the Treaty of Friendship, Commerce and Navigation between the Parties signed at Managua on 21 January 1956;

(15) By fourteen votes to one, Decides that the form and amount of such reparation, failing agreement between the Parties, will be settled by the Court, and reserves for this purpose the subsequent procedure in the case;

(16) Unanimously, Recalls to both Parties their obligation to seek a solution to their disputes by peaceful means in accordance with international law.

DISSENTING OPINION OF JUDGE SCHWEBEL

1. To say that I dissent from the Court's Judgment is to understate the depth of my differences with it. I agree with the Court's finding that the United States, by failing to make known the existence and location of the mines laid by it, acted in violation of customary interna-

tional law (in relation to the shipping of third States); I agree that the CIA's causing publication of a manual advocating acts in violation of the law of war is indefensible; and I agree with some other elements of the Judgment as well. Nevertheless, in my view the Judgment misperceives and misconstrues essential facts—not so much the facts concerning the actions of the United States of which Nicaragua complains as the facts concerning the actions of Nicaragua of which the United States complains. It misconceives and misapplies the law—not in all respects, on some of which the whole Court is agreed, but in paramount respects: particularly in its interpretation of what is an "armed attack" within the meaning of the United Nations Charter and customary international law; in its appearing to justify foreign intervention in furtherance of "the process of decolonization"; and in nearly all of its holdings as to which Party to this case has acted in violation of its international responsibilities and which, because it has acted defensively, has not. For reasons which, because of its further examination of questions of jurisdiction, are even clearer today than when it rendered its Judgment of 26 November 1984, this Judgment asserts a jurisdiction which in my view the Court properly lacks, and it adjudges a vital question which, I believe, is not justiciable. And, I am profoundly pained to say, I dissent from this Judgment because I believe that, in effect, it adopts the false testimony of representatives of the Government of the Republic of Nicaragua on a matter which, in my view, is essential to the disposition of this case and which, on any view, is material to its disposition. The effect of the Court's treatment of that false testimony upon the validity of the Judgment is a question which only others can decide.

160. In today's Judgment, the Court acknowledges that the views of the parties to a case as to the law applicable to their dispute are very material, particularly when their views are concordant. The Court also does not deny that the Parties to this case agree on the definition of the acts which may constitute an armed attack. Nevertheless, on the critical question of whether a State's assistance to foreign armed irregulars who seek to overthrow the government of another State may be tantamount to an armed attack by the former State upon the latter, the Court arrives at a conclusion which is discordant with the agreed views of both Parties.

161. The Court's conclusion is inconsonant with generally accepted doctrine, law and practice as well. The Court's conclusion is inconsistent with the views of Professor Brownlie which Nicaragua's Memorial quotes that a "use of force" may comprise not merely an organized armed attack by a State's regular forces but the giving of "aid to groups of insurgents on the territory of another State". It is inconsistent with his conclusion that a general campaign by irregulars with the complicity of the government of the State from which they operate may constitute an "armed attack". It is inconsistent with what Nicaragua's Memorial describes as "a substantially unanimous modern view concerning indirect use of force * * * ". It is inconsistent with the position which the United States has maintained since 1947 that one State's support of guerrillas operating against another is tantamount to an armed attack against the latter's territorial integrity and political independence. It is

inconsistent with what Nicaragua rightly observes is a consistent practice of the United Nations holding that "substantial involvement" in the
activities of armed insurgent groups is a violation of "the prohibition on
the use of force in Article 2(4)". It is inconsistent with repeated
declarations of the UN expressive of the international legal duty of
States to refrain from fomenting civil strife—a form of aggression which
the General Assembly has denominated as among "the gravest of all
crimes against peace and security * * * ". It is inconsistent with the
terms of the "Friendly Relations" Declaration, which the Court treats as
an authoritative expression of customary international law—a declaration which, in its interpretation of Article 2, paragraph 4, of the Charter,
holds that, "Every State has the duty to refrain from organizing,
instigating, assisting or participating in acts of civil strife or terrorist
acts in another State * * * when the acts * * * involve a threat or use of
force". It is inconsistent with the conclusion of Judge Lachs that
"indirect means of attacking States were barred" by this Declaration. It
is inconsistent with the conclusion of Judge Jiménez de Aréchaga that
this Declaration, "an important interstitial development of some of the
implications of Article 2(4)", deals with indirect aggression, including
the support given by a government to acts of civil strife in another State.
Such acts, he points out, "may involve the use of force and States should
not be permitted to do indirectly what they are precluded by the Charter
from doing directly * * * ". The Court's conclusion is inconsistent with
the terms and intent of the UN Definition of Aggression on which both
Nicaragua and the Court rely.

* * *

[Judge Schwebel's 136 page opinion is accompanied by a factual
appendix of 133 pages. Other opinions by members of the court are
omitted.]

———

General Questions: Do you believe that the U.S. bombing of
Cambodia was justified? What theory would you apply to justify it? If
it were justified, were the Soviet attacks on refugee camps in Pakistan
during the Afganistan War also justified? Were those camps being used
as training and support bases for the Afgan rebels? By the same
rationale, was Nicaragua justified in attacking Honduras, because the
Contras were camped there? * * * Can you establish any distinctions
among these situations and justifications?

DOCUMENT ON INTEGRATED NATO DEFENSE
Bonn June 10, 1982.

We, the representatives of those members of the North Atlantic
Alliance taking part in its integrated defence structure, hereby set out
our detailed positions on defence.

Pursuant to the principles set out in the Programme for Peace and
Freedom, we agree that, in accordance with current NATO defence

plans, and within the context of NATO strategy and its triad of forces, we will continue to strengthen NATO's defence posture, with special regard to conventional forces. Efforts of our nations in support of the decisions reached at Washington in 1978 have led to improved defensive capabilities. Notwithstanding this progress, it is clear, as documented in the recently published comparison of NATO and Warsaw Pact forces, that continuing efforts are essential to Alliance security. Against this background, we will:

• Fulfill to the greatest extent possible the NATO Force Goals for the next six years, including measures to improve the readiness of the standing forces and the readiness and mobilization capability of reserve forces. Note was taken of the recently concluded agreement between the United States and the Federal Republic of Germany for wartime host nation support.

• Continue to implement measures identified in the Long Term Defence Programme designed to enhance our overall defence capabilities.

• Continue to improve NATO planning procedures and explore other ways of achieving greater effectiveness in the application of national resources to defence, especially in the conventional field. In that regard, we will continue to give due attention to fair burden-sharing and to possibilities for developing areas of practical co-operation from which we can all benefit.

• Explore ways to take full advantage both technically and economically of emerging technologies, especially to improve conventional defence, and take steps necessary to restrict the transfer of militarily relevant technology to the Warsaw Pact.

Noting that developments beyond the NATO area may threaten our vital interests, we reaffirm the need to consult with a view to sharing assessments and identifying common objectives, taking full account of the effect on NATO security and defence capability, as well as of the national interests of member countries. Recognising that the policies which nations adopt in this field are a matter for national decision, we agree to examine collectively in the appropriate NATO bodies the requirements which may arise for the defence of the NATO area as a result of deployments by individual member states outside that area. Steps which may be taken by individual Allies in the light of such consultations to facilitate possible military deployments beyond the NATO area can represent an important contribution to security.

Queries: Can Congress sitting in 1994 commit the U.S. to war under a treaty such as NATO in 1995? In 2000? Does the existence of Nuclear Weapons make a difference in your answer? See, Wormuth & Firmage, To Chain the Dog of War, Ch. 13, pp. 200–223, supra (2d ed., 1989); Jane E. Stromseth, Rethinking War Powers: Congress, the President, and the United Nations, 81 Geo.L.J. 597 (1993).

SECTION D. UNILATERAL SELF–DEFENSE

The easy cases, and some questions. State A sends infantry, tanks and airplanes across the border of its neighbor, State B, with the purpose of removing its government and substituting one of its own choosing, or to occupy State B and thereafter incorporate it into State A, or to take control of a portion of State B containing oil or some other natural resource it covets. State B responds with military force to defeat State A's forces and to send them back across the border. On these simple facts alone, so familiar to the founders of the United Nations in 1945, State B's action is an exercise in self defense against an armed attack and clearly falls within the rubric of the inherent right of self-defense recognized and preserved as among United Nations members by Article 51 of the United Nations Charter. What provocations less than the use of force such as that attributed to State A in the example just given justify a responsive unilateral use of armed force by a state today? How far does the right of self-defense encompass a state's going beyond its own border to use force against an adversary?

We saw in Chapter 11 (involving individual responsibility and the permissible uses of force in the conduct of war) that retaliatory acts (sometimes called reprisals) are permitted in the give and take of warfare, acts of violence that might otherwise be unlawful but are not so considered if committed to force an adversary to comply with the laws of war. But how far, if at all, are retaliatory uses of force (reprisals) outside the context of an ongoing war permitted by the Charter, or by customary international law? The Declaration on Principles of International Law Concerning Friendly Relations and Co-operation Among States in Accordance with the Charter of the United Nations (see the Doc. Suppl.) provides: "States have a duty to refrain from acts of reprisal involving the use of force." This statement appears as an elucidation of Article 2(4) of the Charter, but the Declaration, in its General Part, also states that nothing therein "shall be construed as prejudicing in any manner the provisions of the Charter or the rights and duties of Member States under the Charter." Does that invite states nevertheless to resort to reprisals, but now under the rubric of Article 51 and the inherent right of self defense? Indeed, what is meant by the term: self defense?

1. ISRAELI RAID ON TUNISIA
SECURITY COUNCIL CONDEMNATION
22 UN Chronicle Nos. 10/11 (1985), p. 3.

The Security Council has vigorously condemned Israel's "act of armed aggression" against Tunisian territory in flagrant violation of the United Nations Charter, international law and norms of conduct, and demanded that Israel "refrain from perpetrating such acts of aggression or from the threat to do so". The Council also urgently requested United Nations Member States to take measures to dissuade Israel from resorting to such acts against the sovereignty and territorial integrity of all States. In adopting resolution 573 (1985) on 4 October, the Council considered that Tunisia had "the right to appropriate reparations as a result of the loss of human life and material damage which it has suffered and for which Israel has claimed responsibility". The vote on the text was 14 in favour to none against, with 1 abstention (United States).

The Council met following a Tunisian complaint against Israel which stated that on 1 October, six Israeli military aircraft had bombed the civilian locality at Borj–Cedria, called Hammam–Plage, situated in the southern suburbs of Tunis. The action resulted in 68 civilian dead and nearly 100 wounded, as well as wide-scale material damage and destruction, Tunisia reported.

The attack was directed against "an exclusively residential urban area which traditionally has been home to Tunisian families and a small number of Palestinian civilians who had to flee from Lebanon following the invasion of that country by the Israeli army", Tunisia stated.

Forty-six speakers participated in four Council meetings held on the complaint on 3, 4 and 7 October. Beji Caid Essebsi, Minister for Foreign Affairs of Tunisia, said any attempt to justify Israel's "act of terrorism", any "indulgence shown to its perpetrators, no matter what the pretext, can only encourage aggression and set the seal of approval on the aggressor". The "crime" was particularly "reprehensible" because it aimed at jeopardizing efforts to bring about a peaceful, just and lasting settlement of the Palestinian problem on the basis of Charter principles and relevant United Nations resolutions.

The hospitality extended by Tunisia to the Palestinian leadership fell within that framework. The headquarters of the "so-called Force 17"—which had been blamed for the attack on three Israeli civilians at Larnaca, Cyprus—were not in Tunisia. It was only the political Palestinian leadership that had been extended Tunisian hospitality. In any case, no act of terrorism had been committed from Tunisia, and no Tunisian had ever been involved in any such act.

* * *

Benjamin Netanyahu (Israel) said that for the past year, the PLO headquarters in Tunisia had initiated, planned, organized and launched hundreds of "terrorist" attacks against Israel, against Israeli targets outside Israel, and against Jews everywhere. More than 600 such attacks had killed or severely wounded more than 75 Israelis, the PLO's "designated targets". The "butchery" of three Israelis at Larnaca, Cyprus, had been perpetrated by "Force 17", Yasser Arafat's personal bodyguard unit, which occupied the PLO headquarters in Tunisia. The target of Israel's strike were those headquarters and its action was "a legitimate act of self-defence" in response to "terrorism". Any civilian casualties, were the result of the "deliberate PLO tactic * * * of planting its bases among civilians". Tunisia was strong enough to stop the "terrorists" but it "knowingly harboured the PLO and allowed it complete freedom of action in planning, training, organizing and launching murderous attacks from its soil". The Israeli action was directed against the "terrorist killers" and not against their host country. Nevertheless, the host country did bear considerable responsibility.

* * *

Claude de Kemoularia (France) condemned the Israeli attack, which was an "inadmissible" violation of international law. France was concerned at the "disastrous consequences" the attack would have on the efforts to bring about a resumption of the peace process. All parties to the conflict should replace the "language of violence and reprisals" with a spirit of dialogue which alone could make possible an overall settlement. Ole Bierring (Denmark) also condemned the Israeli action, which had violated Tunisia's sovereignty and territorial integrity and represented a further stage in the continuing violence and counter-violence in the Middle East. While Denmark condemned acts of terrorism against Israelis, it did not believe that they justified "such action".

* * *

Carlos Alzamora (Peru) rejected Israel's act of aggression against Tunisia's sovereignty and territorial integrity. "By virtue of its timing, the characteristics of the attack and its inevitable political consequences", the air raid took on "special and ominous gravity". It was "a new and disproportionate application of the principle of an eye for an eye, carried out with arrogant disregard of others".

* * *

Sir John Thomson (United Kingdom) said the Israeli raid was an "outrage". Although his country condemned any "terrorist" act anywhere by whomsoever committed, it could not accept as valid Israel's reasons for its action of "arbitrary and disproportionate" violence. Even if there had been "demonstrable responsibility" by the PLO for the Larnaca killings, that would not have justified the Israeli retaliation.

* * *

Vernon Walters (United States) said the resolution "disproportionately" placed all blame for the latest spiral of violence in the Middle East "onto only one set of shoulders", while it did not hold at fault those responsible for the "terrorist" acts which had provoked it. A State subjected to continuing "terrorist" attacks should be able to respond with appropriate use of force to defend itself against further attacks. Each State should take appropriate steps to prevent persons or groups within its territory from perpetrating "terrorist" acts. The "incident" was not an obstacle to peace, but an impetus for the peace process and "renewed efforts towards its successful completion".

* * *

2. UNITED STATES RAID ON LIBYA

On April 14, 1986, the United States bombed Tripoli, Libya, hitting a residential suburb and killing both military personnel and civilians. One of the targets bombed was the complex where Colonel Qadafi was supposed to be residing. Qadafi was not killed, but his infant daughter and at least 300 civilians were killed. The U.S. argued self-defense. *Do any of the legal standards of self-defense fit?*

VETO OF RESOLUTION OF CONDEMNATION

23 UN Chronicle No. 4 (1986), p. 46.

Three permanent members of the Security Council—the United States, the United Kingdom and France—on 21 April cast vetoes against a draft resolution by which the Council would have condemned "the armed attack" by the United States against the Libyan cities of Tripoli and Benghazi "in violation of the Charter and the norms of international conduct". The Council would have also called on the United States to "refrain forthwith from any attacks or threats thereof".

The text also called on the Council to condemn "all terrorist activities, whether perpetrated by individuals, groups or States", and called on all parties to "refrain from resorting to force, to exercise restraint in this critical situation, and to resolve their differences by peaceful means in keeping with the Charter". The Secretary–General would have been asked to take all appropriate steps to restore and ensure peace in the Central Mediterranean and to keep the Council regularly informed of the implementation of the resolution.

The vote on the draft (S/18016/Rev. 1) was 9 to 5, with 1 abstention. Australia and Denmark, two nonpermanent Council members, joined the three Western Powers in casting negative votes. Venezuela abstained. Voting for the draft were Bulgaria, China, Congo, Ghana, Madagascar, Thailand, Trinidad and Tobago, USSR and the United Arab Emirates.

Vetoes: The United States rejected the draft as "totally unacceptable". Its assumption that the essential problem before the Council stemmed from actions of the United States armed forces against Libya was false, contradicted by irrefutable evidence and by the "long and tragic list of countries which have suffered brutality after brutality at the hands of Libyan terrorism". The real issue before the Council, the United States said, was not dealt with by the draft: Libya's "blatant, unrepentant and continuing use of force" in violation of the Charter.

For the Council to endorse such an "erroneous and deficient" text would be to mock the commitment of the United Nations to oppose terrorism in all its forms as "criminal conduct that must be resisted and punished". The United States was "outraged" that the draft had not mentioned Libya's brutal, growing and increasingly violent "campaign of terror". The text would have equated the use of terrorism with an act of justified self-defence against terrorism. It would have condemned acts of the United States against Libya but ignored Libya's "undeniable use of terrorism". It would have created an "appearance of even-handedness, but not the reality". Nowhere in it had Libya been asked to refrain from its "murderous activities".

* * *

On 14 April, the United States, in a letter (S/17990) to the Secretary–General, said that it had exercised its right of self-defence by responding to "an ongoing pattern of attacks by the Government of Libya". It said it had also "exercised great care in restricting its military response to terrorist-related targets". Every possible precaution had been taken to avoid civilian casualties and to limit collateral damage, the United States said. Its objective had been to destroy facilities used to carry out Libya's "hostile policy of international terrorism and to discourage Libyan terrorist attacks in the future."

* * *

Mr. Azzarouk (Libyan Arab Jamahiriya) on 15 April said the United States, using 33 aircraft, had perpetrated a "barbaric, savage" air raid against Libyan civilian targets in Benghazi and Tripoli. The act was "completely unjustified and unprovoked". The raid had taken place with the "blessing and support of certain States, first and foremost the United Kingdom, which had provided the logistics". A "number of European countries" had helped co-ordinate the carefully conceived and executed raid. Civilian airports and aircraft, schools, houses, foreign missions and a centre for the handicapped had been damaged. Fragmentation bombs had been used.

Ali Treiki (Libyan Arab Jamahiriya) on 18 April said that in Tripoli and Benghazi dozens of children, women and the elderly had fallen victim to "America's so-called civilization" and had been buried. The American Administration should permit a Security Council delegation to see for itself that all targets had been civilian. The United States had "fallen prey to the arrogance and madness of power" and wanted to become "the world's policeman". Any party that did not agree to become its "vassal and agent" was considered "an outlaw, a terrorist, a communist and a devil". The United States record was one of "colonialism, treachery and aggression".

The fault of Colonel Qaddafi and the Libyan revolution was that they had expelled Americans and their bases from Libya, had ended the American oil monopoly in Libya, and had helped the persecuted elsewhere. The United States had rejected all dialogue with Libya and wished to impose conditions. Libyans would fight to the finish in defence of their land, their dignity, their independence and their waters. Libyans condemned terrorism. They supported Palestinians and Namibians. The presence of foreign fleets and foreign bases in the Mediterranean area must be eliminated.

On 21 April, Mr. Treiki said that while Libya was proud of the international community's support, it denounced the United States' "dangerous policies" and its desire to paralyse the United Nations.

Vernon Walters (United States) on 15 April referred to a "series of carefully planned air strikes" by the United States against "terrorist-related targets in Libya". That "self-defence" had become necessary after the failure of repeated and protracted efforts to deter Libya from ongoing attacks against the United States in violation of the Charter. There was "direct, precise and irrefutable" evidence that Libya was responsible for the bombing in West Berlin on 5 April that had resulted in the deaths of a United States Army sergeant and a young Turkish woman and injury to 230 other people, among them 50 American military personnel. In the light of that "reprehensible act of violence", the latest in an ongoing pattern of attacks by Libya, and of "clear evidence that Libya was planning a multitude of future attacks", the United States was compelled to exercise its right of self-defence, he stated. The "scourge of Libyan terrorism" was not a problem for the United States alone; it threatened all members of the civilized world community. Colonel Qaddafi had made terrorism an integral part of his foreign policy. Libyan attacks were "concerted violence directed against the values, the interests and the democratic institutions of all freedom-loving States".

On 21 April, Mr. Walters said that Colonel Qaddafi had launched murderous attacks against American citizens, had fired at American ships, and was plotting "yet more deadly atrocities". How many Americans and innocents must be killed before the United States' right to respond was recognized? he asked.[a]

* * *

Andres Aguilar (Venezuela) rejected the use of violence to resolve differences between nations; that included both armed action and violence carried out by individuals or groups of individuals. Venezuela also rejected any breach of the foundations of the system to which all States owed respect. The use of military force was not the most appropriate way to fight terrorism. Violence bred violence, and sometimes the spiral of violence went far beyond what had been foreseen initially. Both parties should co-operate with the Security Council and the United Nations in general in seeking appropriate ways to end their dispute. The adoption of the draft would not have encouraged a solution by peaceful means nor alleviated tension in the region. It did not take duly into account the background of the problem in all its aspects, nor did it establish the necessary link between the crucial issues that had led to that conflict.

Sir John Thomson (United Kingdom) said it appeared that state-directed terrorism was the main policy of the Qaddafi Government. No one was safe from "Colonel Qaddafi's murderers". The United States had the inherent right of self-defence. The United Kingdom and many of its friends in Europe and the Arab world had had direct experience of Libyan terrorism. It was in their interest that effective measures be taken to end that menace so that no State would feel obliged to have

a. Mr. Walters' address to the Council, giving in detail the U.S. indictment against Libya, is reported in 80 AJIL 633 (1986).

recourse to armed force as a last resort in defence of its citizens or of its territory. Colonel Qaddafi had sought "to drape his nefarious activities in the colours of Arab and Palestinian nationalism"; in fact those activities did nothing but harm to the Arab and Palestinian causes. The central issue before the Council was terrorism. All should shun Colonel Qaddafi; none should act as if they were his accomplices. The Council should deal resolutely with countries which were the home of state-sponsored terrorism.

Pascal Gayama (Congo) said that the United States had reacted in "a brutal and surprisingly emotional manner" in what it had said was the only way to deal with what it called the "only source of terrorism in the world"—Colonel Qaddafi and Libya. The United States' "dangerous conduct" had unforeseeable consequences. By violating Libya's territorial integrity and sovereignty in "a flagrant and premeditated manner" with the additional "avowed intention" of removing its Head of State—"as in the worst of terrorist acts"—the United States had displayed a political irresponsibility that was difficult to understand from a great Power and permanent Council member.

* * *

Claude de Kemoularia (France) categorically condemned the intolerable escalation of terrorism, and shared the "legitimate indignation" of the United States and the United Kingdom concerning "the odious attacks" perpetrated against their nationals. France affirmed its solidarity with all countries' victims of "barbaric acts, which spread blind terror and in no way serve the political causes that their perpetrators claim to defend". States victims of such acts should join together in the fight against a threat affecting all of them. Determined, tenacious and patient efforts were needed, combining national measures with greater international cooperation. He appealed for reason, adding that there were serious risks of escalation in the present situation, and everything must be done to ensure that the chain of violence was broken.

* * *

Condemnation in the General Assembly. On November 20, 1986, the General Assembly, in Resolution 41/38, condemned the United States attack on Libya as "a violation of the United Nations Charter and international law," by a vote of 79 in favor to 28 against, with 33 abstentions. 24 UN Chronicle 1 (1987), p. 73.

President Reagan claimed that the bombings were "a series of strikes against the headquarters, terrorists facilities, and military assets that support * * * Qadafi's subversive activities * * *." Pres.Stmt., April 14, 1986, U.S. Dept.St.Docs. No. 24.

* * *

Two other incidents are related to the Libyan bombing: (1) the U.S. commandeered an Egyptian Airliner, forced it down in Sicily, and captured those whom it felt were responsible for the Achille Lauro incident; and (2) The U.S. request for the extradition of the Libyans allegedly involved in the downing of Pan Am flight 103, over Lockerbie, Scotland has resulted in protracted conflict with Libya. For discussion of this, see, Ch. 11, on individual responsibility and the latter part of this chapter on Terrorism. On the Egyptian Airliner incident and its legality, consider the material in this Chapter's section, Action Against Terrorism. See also, Schachter, In Defense of International Rules on the Use of Force, 53 U.Chi.L.Rev. 113, 139–40 (1986).

SECTION E.   ANTICIPATORY SELF–DEFENSE

1. *A bit of History:* Hugo Grotius, in 1625, noted that force could be used to forestall an attack, although it required a "present danger" which is "imminent in a point of time." He provided that the attack "may be anticipated." "It [is] lawful to kill him who is preparing to kill * * * " [Grotius, Di Jure Belli ac Pacis Ch. 1 (1625). Similarly, Emerich de Vattel wrote: "The safest plan is to prevent evil, where that is possible. A Nation has the right to resist the injury against the aggressor. It may even anticipate the other's design, being careful, however, not to act upon vague and doubtful suspicious, lest it should run the risk of becoming itself the aggressor." E. de Vattel, The Law of Nations IV (1758). Both warned of the danger of abusing this "right." See, Beres, Perspective: After the Gulf War: Israel, Preemption, and Anticipatory Self–Defense, 13 Hous.J.I.L. 259, 263–64 (1991).

2.   THE SIX DAY WAR
SITUATION IN THE MIDDLE EAST
4 UN Monthly Chronicle, July 1967, p. 3, at 8.

Meeting of June 5; Following the outbreak of hostilities in the Middle East, the Security Council met in emergency session.

The Council had a letter from the representative of the United Arab Republic which stated that Israel had "committed a treacherous premeditated aggression" against his country that morning, launching attacks in the Gaza Strip, Sinai, and several airports in Cairo, the Suez Canal area, and other localities. Preliminary reports, it was stated, indicated that 23 Israeli planes had been shot down and several pilots captured. The letter went on to say that the United Arab Republic, "in repelling this aggression * * * had decided to defend itself by all means in accordance with Article 51 of the Charter of the United Nations".

The Secretary–General, U THANT, in his statement, said the United Nations had no means of ascertaining how the hostilities began. Reports coming in from the parties were conflicting, but all agreed that there was serious military action on land and in the air at a number of points which was spreading.

* * * [At a subsequent meeting of the Security Council, the spokesman for Israel delivered the following explanation of Israel's military action. Security Council, Off.Rec. 1358th Meeting].

198. Let us look again at the events which preceded the outbreak of fighting on 5 June. On 18 May, the Government of the United Arab Republic demanded the eviction of the United Nations Emergency Force which was deployed along the Gaza Strip and the Sinai desert and at Sharm el Sheikh at the entrance to the Gulf of Aqaba, and on that day UNEF ceased to exist. Was this an act which promoted peace? Was this an act which demonstrated peaceful intent? It was not; it was preparation for aggression. The Emergency Force had to be gotten out of the way so that the aggression on Israel could be prepared and mounted.

199. On 23 May, the United Arab Republic declared that the Strait of Tiran would be closed to Israel shipping and to ships of other nations carrying what were described as strategic goods, that is to say, anything which the United Arab Republic chose to define as strategic goods, to Israel's southernmost port of Eilat. Was this act of blockade a peaceful act? Did this re-imposition of the blockade demonstrate peaceful intent? It did not. This was a clear act of hostility and the exercise of an internationally rejected claim to belligerency. A blockade is a classical act of war.

200. During this time, that is, the last week of May, Egypt started a massive build-up of forces in the Sinai desert. Some 80,000 men were assembled, with hundreds of assault aircraft, a thousand tanks. These huge forces were deployed in an offensive position along the Sinai frontier with Israel, along the Gaza Strip and at the approaches to Eilat. The deployment of these forces was accompanied by a mounting crescendo of warlike propaganda from Cairo. A holy war was proclaimed by the religious authorities in the Egyptian capital, and the Egyptian people were urged to march forward in a jehad to destroy Israel. The Egyptian President naturally was foremost in inciting his people for the coming war. This is what he said before the Central Council of Arab Trade Unions on 26 May 1967:

> The Arab people want to fight. We have been waiting for the suitable day when we shall be completely ready, since if we enter a battle with Israel we should be confident of victory and should take strong measures. We do not speak idly. We have lately felt that our strength is sufficient and that if we enter into battle with Israel we shall, with God's help, be victorious. Therefore, we have now decided to take real steps. The battle will be a full-scale one, and our basic aim will be to destroy Israel.

201. What were we in Israel and what was the Security Council expected to make of these words? A call for peace, or a call for war?

202. On 30 May, President Nasser signed a military agreement with King Hussein of Jordan, and Jordan began to mobilize. On 4 June, a similar agreement was signed with Iraq, and Iraqi detachments began arriving in Jordan and in Egypt. Was this evidence of peaceful intent? Were these agreements in keeping with the Charter of the United

Nations? Were these aggressive movements of troops in accordance with solemn agreements which Egypt and Jordan had entered into with Israel in 1949 with the object of preventing all hostile acts and serving as a transition to permanent peace? They were clear evidence of a preparation for aggression.

203. While these military moves were going on in Egypt, Jordan and Iraq, Syria had also mobilized its forces to the last man, and 50,000 troops were poised aggressively on the heights which overlook Israel. We were surrounded. The armed ring was closed. All that the Arab forces were waiting for was the signal to start.

204. That signal was given on 5 June, when Egyptian planes in accordance with the plans contained in battle order 6/67 of Air Force and Air Defence Headquarters of the Eastern Area in Sinai, dated 26 May 1967, took off for their assigned targets in Israel, while at the same time an artillery barrage on Israel farming villages was opened from the Gaza Strip. Shortly afterwards, Jordan guns sited amid the holy places of the Holy City of Jerusalem started shelling the Israel capital, causing heavy casualties, and the Syrian artillery joined the devil's chorus in the north. The aggression had begun.

205. This is the record; this is what happened.

* * *

1. ***Territorial control.*** Israel's success in the Six Day War resulted in her military occupation of substantial territory: Sinai, the Gaza Strip, parts of Jerusalem, portions of Jordan on the West Bank of the Jordan River and the Syrian Golan Heights. History-making changes are in process as this book goes to print. Palestinian police forces have replaced Israeli soldiers in Jerico on the heels of the agreement between Israel and the P.L.O.

2. ***Questions.*** Was Israel's military action lawful under the Charter? Article 51 preserves "the inherent right of individual * * * self-defense if an armed attack occurs * * *." Was Israel's response to an attack that occurred or to a threatened attack? Was Israel acting in anticipatory self-defense? Is such action lawful under the Charter? Does the U.N. Charter allow anticipatory self-defense? If so, when and under what circumstances? Must an armed attack be imminent? What is "imminent," especially in the nuclear age?

3. ***Views of certain writers.*** Writing before there had been major tests of the meaning of the Charter, Stone observed in discussing Article 51: "Major troop concentrations on the border would presumably warrant anticipatory use of force * * *." Stone, Legal Controls of International Conflict 244, n. 8 (1954). Following the Cuban missile crisis and prior to the events in the Middle East in 1967, the publicists in the United States were deeply divided on anticipatory self-defense, at least as an abstract concept.

Wright: Finally it has been argued that the quarantine and the O.A.S. resolution were justified as measures of "individual or collective self-defense" permitted by Article 51 of the Charter. It is suggested that the term "armed attack," which alone justified such defense without prior United Nations authority, must be interpreted to include a serious threat of armed attack.[53] Reference has been made to the statement by Secretary of State Webster in the Caroline case, generally accepted prior to the Charter, that military defensive action was permissible in case of "an instant and overwhelming necessity," thus creating a limited right of preventive action; that such a construction is necessary in the nuclear age because to delay defensive action until an actual nuclear attack would be suicidal, and that the Charter supports this construction by forbidding "threat" as well as "use" of force in Article 2, paragraph 4.

These arguments are not convincing. It appears that the Charter intended to limit the traditional right of defense by states to actual armed attack, even though it forbade "threat of force" and authorized the Security Council to intervene to stop "threats to the peace." Professor, later judge, Jessup wrote in 1948:

> This restriction in Article 51 very definitely narrows the freedom of action which states had under international law. A case could be made out for self-defense in the traditional law where the injury was threatened but no attack had yet taken place. Under the Charter, alarming military preparations by a neighboring state would justify a resort to the Security Council, but would not justify resort to anticipatory force by the state which believed itself threatened.[54]

The obligation of states to refrain from threats to the peace under Article 2, paragraph 4, and the competence of the United Nations to take action in case of a threat to the peace under Article 39, were not intended to give a unilateral right of military self-defense in case of such threats. For that reason, self-defense against threats was excluded in Article 51, and states were explicitly obliged to submit disputes or situations which they think threaten peace, to the United Nations and to refrain from unilateral use of force. * * * The Cuban Quarantine, 57 Am.J.Int'l L., 546, 559 (1963).*

McDougal: The more important limitations imposed by the general community upon this customary right of self-defense have been, in conformity with the overriding policy it serves of minimizing coercion and violence across state lines, those of necessity and proportionality. The conditions of necessity required to be shown by the target state have never, however, been restricted to "actual armed attack"; imminence of attack of such high degree as to preclude effective resort by the intended victim to non-violent modalities of response has always been regarded as

---

53. The United States has not used this argument officially * * *.

54. Philip Jessup, A Modern Law of Nations 166 (New York, Macmillan, 1948). After an exhaustive discussion of "The Use of Force in Self–Defence," Ian Brownlie concludes that "the beginning of an armed attack is a condition precedent for resort to force in self-defence." 37 Brit.Yr.Bk. of Int.Law 266 (1962). * * *

* Reprinted with the permission of the American Society of International Law.

sufficient justification, and it is now generally recognized that a determination of imminence requires an appraisal of the total impact of an initiating state's coercive activities upon the target state's expectations about the costs of preserving its territorial integrity and political independence. Even the highly restrictive language of Secretary of State Webster in the Caroline case, specifying a "necessity of self defense, instant, overwhelming, leaving no choice of means and no moment for deliberation," did not require "actual armed attack," [4] and the understanding is now widespread that a test formulated in the previous century for a controversy between two friendly states is hardly relevant to contemporary controversies, involving high expectations of violence, between nuclear-armed protagonists. The requirement of proportionality, in further expression of the policy of minimizing coercion, stipulates that the responding use of the military instrument by the target state be limited in intensity and magnitude to what is reasonably necessary promptly to secure the permissible objectives of self-defense under the established conditions of necessity.

* * *

* * * The apparent purpose of the inept language of Article 51, commonly ascribed to the late Senator Vandenburg, was only that of accommodating regional organizations, as specifically envisioned for the inter-American system by the Act of Chapultepec, with the more comprehensive centralized system of collective security projected by the Charter. Similarly, nothing in the "plain and natural meaning" of the words of the Charter requires an interpretation that Article 51 restricts the customary right of self-defense. The proponents of such an interpretation substitute for the words "if an armed attack occurs" the very different words "if, and only if, an armed attack occurs." The Soviet–Cuban Quarantine and Self–Defense, 57 AJIL 597, 598 (1963).*

Henkin: * * * While there have been few challenges to Article 2, recurring crises, we have noted, have evoked suggestions for broader readings of the exception of Article 51. One that has been strongly urged is that in the day of nuclear weapons and the ever-present possibility of sudden devastation, nations cannot wait for an armed attack to occur. At least, it is urged, the Charter must now be read to permit "anticipatory self-defense"—the right to act in self-defense in anticipation of attack.

The argument has specious appeal, but is fundamentally unpersuasive. If the Charter originally permitted force in self-defense only if an armed attack occurs, today's weapons hardly argue for extending the exception. The original reasons for barring "anticipatory self-defense" in regard to "old-fashioned war" apply even more to the new war. The logic of the deterrent and the balance of terror

4. Mr. Webster to Mr. Fox, April 24, 1841, in 29 British and Foreign State Papers 1129, 1138 (1840–41). See also Jennings, "The Caroline and McLeod Cases," 32 A.J.I.L. 82 (1938).

* Reprinted with the permission of the American Society of International Law.

does not suggest that nations should be encouraged to preventive or even pre-emptive attack. The exception of Article 51 was limited to the situation "if an armed attack occurs," which is comparatively clear, objective, easy to prove, difficult to misinterpret or fabricate. To permit anticipation may virtually destroy the rule against the use of force, leaving it to every nation to claim anticipation and unleash the fury. Nations will not be prevented or deterred by the fear that later—if there is anyone left to judge—someone may determine that there had in fact been no threat of armed attack legitimately anticipated.

Proponents of anticipatory self-defense raise the specter of the all-out nuclear attack and of the obvious need to anticipate it. In fact, of course, for determining what the Charter means or should mean, the major nuclear attack and the pre-emptive strike are not the relevant concerns. A nation planning all-out attack will not be deterred by the Charter, though it may well talk "anticipatory self-defense" in its justification. Nor does one prescribe rules for the nation threatened with such an attack. If a nation is satisfied that another is about to obliterate it, it will not wait. But it has to make that decision on its own awesome responsibility. Anticipation in that case may have to be practiced; it need not be preached. The Charter need not make a principle of it; the law need not authorize or encourage it. But surely that extreme hypothetical case, beyond the realm of law, should not be used to justify new rules for situations that do not involve the impending mortal thrust. "Anticipatory self-defense" as a rule of law has meaning only in less extreme cases. There, anticipatory self-defense, it should be clear, becomes easily a euphemism for "preventive war." The United Nations Charter in the beginning did not authorize it. Attempts later, in relation to Suez and Sinai, to read the Charter as permitting anticipatory self-defense, were rejected. Nothing since, least of all the new weapons, suggests that international society would be better if the Charter were changed or read to authorize it. Force, Intervention and Neutrality in Contemporary International Law, Proceedings, ASIL 147, 150 (1963).*

4. *Is Article 51 an example of flawed draftsmanship?* Some have argued that Article 51 was not intended to be a comprehensive statement (or restatement) of the law of self-defense, that it was hastily drafted (without full consideration?) at the San Francisco conference as part of the compromise that brought the Latin American states into the organization by preserving, in part, their preference for regional arrangements. An example of draftsmanship at another constitutional convention that clarifies the question of anticipatory self-defense is contained in Article I, Section 10 of the U.S. Constitution: "No State shall, without the Consent of Congress * * * engage in War, unless actually invaded, or in such imminent Danger as will not admit of delay."

* Reprinted with the permission of the American Society of International Law.

5. ***Israeli disaffection with the United Nations.*** Since 1948, the year of Israel's accession to statehood, the Arab states, including Lebanon, have regarded themselves as being in a state of war with her. This state of war has never been officially terminated; the Arab states have on numerous occasions asserted its continuing existence in seeking to justify various anti-Israel measures taken by them (such as the blocking of the Suez Canal and the Tiran Strait to Israeli navigation). Blum, The Beirut Raid and the International Double Standard, 64 AJIL 73, 77 (1970).* The author further states:

> * * * One of the most disturbing aspects of the Middle East conflict—disturbing as much to the cause of "world order" as to the cause of Israel—is the fact that on no single occasion over the past fifteen years has Israel been able to get satisfaction from the political organs of the United Nations on her complaints against neighboring Arab states. The Soviet veto that has been made available to the Arabs, to block any decision by the Security Council which the latter regarded as unfavorable to them, ensured that such a decision, even if it received the requisite number of votes in the Council, would not be adopted. This fact was naturally taken into account by other members of the Security Council more favorably disposed to Israel, and largely conditioned the very tone and formulation of many a watered-down draft resolution concerning Israeli complaints, since it was realized that the submission of a draft resolution giving satisfaction to Israel was bound to become an exercise in futility. This pattern, in turn, led to a growing conviction in Israel, which United Nations practice never effectively disproved, that it was difficult, if not impossible, for her rights to be recognized by the United Nations. * * * (at 98)

---

3.   DESTRUCTION OF IRAQ'S NUCLEAR REACTOR

READ THE UNITED NATIONS, SECURITY COUNCIL RESOLUTION 487 (1981) OF JUNE 19, 1981, In the Doc. Supp. The Security Council "Strongly Condemned" The Israeli Attack on Iraq's Nuclear Reactor. Resolutions and Decisions of the Security Council 1981.

U.N.Sec. Council Off.Rec., 36th year, p. 10.

COUNCIL CONDEMNS ISRAEL'S AIR ATTACK ON IRAQI NUCLEAR REACTOR
18 UN Chronicle No. 8 (1981), p. 5.

* * *

The Council met to consider the complaint by Iraq, contained in its letter of 8 June (S/14509), asking for an immediate meeting of the

Council "to deal with a grave act of aggression committed by Israel against Iraq with far-reaching consequences for international peace and security".

The letter stated that on Sunday, 7 June, Israeli warplanes raided Baghdad. Their objective was to destroy the Iraq nuclear reactor installations. The letter also stated that Israel had admitted "this premeditated act of aggression".

In a further letter of 10 June (S/14514) Iraq emphasized that the 7 June act of aggression by Israel was not the first of its kind against Iraq. On 27 September 1980, two raids had been carried out on Baghdad which were also aimed at the nuclear installations. Due to military, political and moral considerations, the two raids were referred to in a Government communique without mentioning that Israel had perpetrated them. The Council also had before it a letter of 8 June from Israel (S/14510) stating that "on Sunday, 7 June 1981, the Israel Air Force launched a raid on the atomic reactor 'Ossirac', near Baghdad. Our pilots carried out their mission fully; the reactor was destroyed; all our aircraft returned safely to base".

The letter stated that Israel had taken that decision because for a long time it had been watching with growing concern the construction of that atomic reactor and that from sources whose reliability was beyond doubt, Israel had learned that the reactor was designed to produce atomic bombs and that the target would be Israel, as was announced by the ruler of Iraq.

* * *

Also included among the documents before the Council was a letter of 12 June from the Director–General of IAEA (S/14532) transmitting a resolution adopted on the same date by the Agency's Board of Governors in which, among other things, it strongly condemned Israel, recommended to the IAEA General Conference that it suspend Israel's privileges and rights of membership, urged Agency member States to provide emergency assistance to Iraq and reaffirmed the Board's confidence in the effectiveness of the Agency's safeguards system as a reliable means of verifying the peaceful use of a nuclear facility.

* * *

Saadoon Hammadi (Iraq), Minister for Foreign Affairs, said the motives behind the zionist campaign and aggression against Iraq were the desire to cover up Israel's possession of nuclear weapons and more importantly, the determination not to allow the Arab Nation to acquire the scientific or technical knowledge necessary for their development and progress. The more the Arabs advanced their scientific knowledge, the weaker were Israel's chances of maintaining their occupation of Arab territories and their denial of the inalienable rights of the Palestinian people.

It was evident that Israel's nuclear programme had been geared to military purposes from its very inception and that all sorts of illegal means had been employed for its enhancement, in total violation of internationally accepted standards.

Despite the repeated calls upon Israel to accede to the Non–Proliferation Treaty, it had bluntly refused to do so. Iraq, in contrast, by accepting the terms of the Treaty, had fully subscribed to those standards in its nuclear programme. As noted by the Director–General of IAEA, Iraq had accepted IAEA safeguards on all its nuclear activities. The last safeguard inspection at the Iraqi nuclear centre had taken place in January of this year and all nuclear material there was satisfactorily accounted for.

* * *

The attack carried out by Israel against Iraq was clearly an act of aggression in accordance with the provisions of the Charter, as expounded in the definition of aggression in Assembly resolution 3314 (29), adopted on 14 December 1974. The Israeli allegation that it had acted in legitimate self-defence was totally unfounded, in fact and in law.

The zionist act of aggression against Iraq constituted a qualitative change in the aggressor's policy in the area. It was a clear indication of the determination of the Zionists, after the failure of Camp David, to escalate their provocations with acts of armed aggression prior to launching a full-scale war in order to subjugate the Arab countries and to impose full zionist domination over the whole Middle East.

The Israeli attack was a clear-cut case of premeditated aggression. The elaborate preparations that had preceded the commission of that act were fully described by the Prime Minister of Israel and other Israeli leaders in their press conference held in Tel Aviv on 10 June. What was worse was that Mr. Begin had stated categorically at that press conference that, if Iraq tried to rebuild the reactor, Israel would do all it could to destroy it again.

Faced with this grave situation, the Security Council should reaffirm the right of all States to develop nuclear programmes for peaceful purposes. Mandatory sanctions in accordance with the provisions of Chapter VII of the Charter should be imposed upon Israel to remove the grave menace to international peace and security posed by its actions. Israeli lawlessness should be brought to an end.

* * *

Yehuda Z. Blum (Israel) said that in destroying the Iraqi nuclear reactor Israel had performed an elementary act of self-preservation, both morally and legally. In so doing, Israel was exercising its inherent right of self-defence as understood in general international law and as preserved in Article 51 of the United Nations Charter.

A threat of nuclear obliteration was being developed against Israel by one of its most implacable enemies. Israel had tried to have that threat halted by diplomatic means, but its efforts had borne no fruit. Ultimately left with no choice, Israel was obliged to remove that mortal danger. Ever since the establishment of the State of Israel over 33 years ago, Iraq had been conspiring to destroy it. Iraq had joined several other Arab States which attacked Israel the day after it became independent in 1948. But while other Arab States—Egypt, Lebanon, Jordan and Syria—had signed armistice agreements with Israel in 1949, Iraq had adamantly refused to do so. Instead, it fomented and supported the unrelenting Arab belligerency and terrorism against Israel. It also had taken part in the Arab wars against Israel in 1967 and 1973. And it had doggedly rejected any international measure or instrument which might imply even the most indirect recognition of Israel and its right to exist.

Since 1948, Iraq had declared itself to be in a state of war with Israel. Iraq had missed no opportunity to make it clear that it would not abide by international law in respect to Israel and that it reserved its freedom of action with regard to Israel. That perverse doctrine had found expression in the so-called National Charter of Iraq, proclaimed by its President, Saddam Hussein, in 1980, which committed Iraq in no uncertain terms to all-out warfare against Israel and enjoined other Arab States to participate in that war, using "all means and techniques".

Over and beyond the development of its conventional forces, Iraq had in recent years entered the nuclear armaments field, while at the same time piously appending its signature to international instruments specifically prohibiting it from doing so. A senior member of Iraq's Revolutionary Command Council had stated at a meeting of the Arab league in 1977 that "the Arabs must get an atom bomb".

* * *

Israel had learned from unimpeachable sources that following the expected delivery of two additional shipments of weapons-grade uranium, about 24 kilograms, the nuclear reactor would have been completed, and put into operation soon—and not later than the beginning of September 1981. Thirty-six kilograms of weapons-grade uranium in Iraq's possession would enable it to make a nuclear bomb.

Iraq already possessed aircraft capable of delivering nuclear warheads. In addition, it was involved in the development of a new surface-to-surface missile with an effective range of up to 3,000 kilometres, also capable of delivering a nuclear warhead.

Unlike Israel, Iraq had not embarked on its large-scale nuclear programme for reasons of pure research, despite its protestations to the contrary. And again unlike Israel, Iraq had not embarked upon its nuclear programme because it faced an energy crisis; it was blessed with abundant supplies of natural oil and was normally one of the largest oil suppliers in the Organization of Petroleum Exporting Countries.

Israel's decision, taken in *the exercise of its right of self-defence,* was one of the most agonizing it had ever had to make. The operation was launched on a Sunday, timed for late in the day on the assumption that persons working on the site would have left. Israel regretted the loss of life, which was minimal. (emphasis added).

* * *

Natarajan Krishnan (India) said that to invoke the right to self-defence to justify a long-premeditated act of aggression was a cynical attempt to confuse the issue. To cite Article 51 of the Charter in support of an indefensible action was a travesty of the very provisions of the Charter.

That Israel should have sought to present such arguments was an affront to the United Nations and the international community. It was Israel which had been making systematic efforts in the pursuit of nuclear-weapons capability. There was growing evidence to show that Israel might already have acquired such capability and a stockpile of nuclear weapons. Against that background, the development of nuclear energy for peaceful purposes by Iraq could not be deemed to be a threat to Israel. The sovereign right of a developing country to acquire and develop nuclear technology for peaceful purposes could not be denied or thwarted through discriminatory policies and practices and much less by naked aggression as committed by Israel.

The Security Council had the obligation to signal clearly to Israel that the international community would not tolerate its transgressions any more.

Sergio Correa Da Costa (Brazil) said his country joined other Member States in a clear condemnation of the aggression suffered by Iraq. The notion of "preventive aggression" was unacceptable under the legal system which bound all nations. Toleration of that notion would lead to the destruction of the United Nations and to the foundering of any hope of coexistence among States.

* * *

Jeane J. Kirkpatrick (United States) said that it was precisely because of the United States' deep involvement in efforts to promote peace in the Middle East that it was shocked by the Israeli air strike on the Iraqi nuclear facility and had promptly condemned that action, which reflected and exacerbated deeper antagonisms in the region.

However, although the United States had condemned Israel's act, it was necessary to take into account its context as well as its consequences. As President Reagan had stated in his press conference, one had to recognize that Israel had reason for concern in view of the past history of Iraq, which had never signed a cease-fire or recognized Israel as a nation, and had never joined in any peace effort. President Reagan had further stated that Israel might have sincerely believed it was a defensive move.

The strength of United States ties and commitment to Israel were well known and the Reagan administration was proud to call Israel a friend and ally. None the less, the United States believed the means Israel had chosen to quiet its fears about the purposes of Iraq's nuclear programme had hurt the peace and security of the area. Diplomatic means available to Israel had not been exhausted and the Israeli action had damaged the regional confidence that was essential for the peace process to go forward.

* * *

Mr. Blum (Israel) said that Iraq's nuclear activities had troubled many Governments and experts around the world. Israel had indicated some of the questions arising in that regard. If Iraq could not address itself to the questions raised, others had done so. They included three eminent

French nuclear scientists, who had made a serious examination of those and other disturbing questions related to Iraq's nuclear development programme. The analysis and conclusions of the three scientists were to be found in a comprehensive memorandum entitled Osirak et la proliferation des armes atomiques, which they had presented to the French Government and public in May of this year.

It was of great interest and relevance to compare their scientific findings and conclusions with the version presented to the Council, which alleged that two "hypotheses"—namely the diversion of enriched uranium and the production of plutonium for the manufacture of a nuclear weapon—were both groundless.

Concerning the uranium path, the scientists indicated that two options existed: (a) the use of fresh enriched uranium and (b) the use of slightly irradiated enriched uranium. Even assuming that the diversion of the enriched uranium were to be detected and that the supplier would immediately halt further deliveries of enriched uranium, the authors of the memorandum concluded that Iraq already possessed sufficient weapons-grade material to produce two nuclear bombs.

As regarded the production of plutonium, the French scientists observed that by introducing a blanket of natural uranium around the reactor core of the Iraqi nuclear reactor, Ossirac plutonium could be produced. After the chemical separation of the plutonium, the yield per annum would be sufficient for one nuclear bomb.

In the course of the debate much had been made of the fact that Iraq was a signatory to the nuclear Non–Proliferation Treaty and that its nuclear reactors had been inspected periodically by IAEA. The French scientists' memorandum included an extensive analysis of the Non–Proliferation Treaty safeguards system.

Among the more significant points made were, first, the country being inspected had to approve in advance the name of the individual inspector whom the IAEA wished to designate. The country being inspected could reject the inspector whom the Agency had nominated. In that regard, it should be noted that since 1976 only Soviet and Hungarian inspectors had inspected Ossirac.

The second point made by the French scientists was that the frequency of routine inspections was a function of the size of the reactor. For Ossirac that meant no more than three or four inspections a year.

Third, for routine inspections, advance notice was given.

Fourth, in principle, the possibility existed of unscheduled inspections, but in practice advance notice of three or four days was given, even for such unscheduled inspections.

Fifth, as to the stipulation that the inspectors must have access to everything relating to fissible material, they could only inspect what had been declared.

Sixth, the inspectors within the facility were always accompanied by representatives of the State concerned.

Seventh, the effectiveness of the safeguards measures depended on the cooperation of the country concerned. In that connexion, the authors of the memorandum observed that for IAEA and France, Iraq's good faith had been taken for granted and its assurances at face value, without any guarantees.

In addition, experience had shown that inspections could be blocked for a certain period without causing any reaction. On that point the authors of the memorandum recalled that on 7 November 1980 at the beginning of the Iran–Iraq war, Iraq had informed IAEA that the inspectors from the Agency could not at that time get to Baghdad to monitor the two reactors and that a well-informed French source had stated that this was a completely new situation which had not been foreseen in any international treaty.

* * *

[In] the debate, Sigvard Eklund, Director–General of IAEA, said:
* * *

The attack on the Iraqi nuclear centre was a serious development with far-reaching implications. Not since its establishment had IAEA been faced with a more serious matter than the implications of that development. The Agency's safeguards system was conceived as a basic element of the Non–Proliferation Treaty. The same system of safeguards was applied to facilities covered by the Tlatelolco Treaty and facilities under bilateral safeguards agreements with the Agency.

The Agency's safeguards system was the product of extensive international cooperation. Its basic principles and modus operandi had been devised and were constantly being upgraded by the foremost international experts in that field. The results of the application of the system were periodically reviewed by the Board of Governors and the General Conference and the system had not been found wanting. Its application was extremely wide. By the end of 1980 approximately 98 per cent of the nuclear facilities of which the Agency was aware outside the nuclear-weapon States were under Agency safeguards.

In fulfilling its responsibilities, the Agency had inspected the Iraqi reactors and had not found evidence of any activity not in accordance with the Non–Proliferation Treaty. Nevertheless, a country which was not a party to the Treaty had evidently not felt assured by the Agency's findings and by its ability to continue to discharge its safeguarding responsibilities effectively.

In the interest of its national security, as was stated by its leaders, it had felt motivated to take military action. From a point of principle, one could only conclude that it was the Agency's safeguards system that had also been attacked. That was a matter of grave concern to the Agency and had to be well pondered.

———

Questions: As you now look back, do you think that Israel was justified? Does Self–Defense work as a justification? Does the nuclear era cause a new approach to be required in relation to the issue of *"imminence"* of an armed attack?

SECTION F.   FURTHER STRAINS ON THE LIMITS OF CONVENTIONAL JUSTIFICATIONS

1.   NATIONAL LIBERATION MOVEMENTS

DECLARATION ON THE GRANTING OF INDEPENDENCE TO COLONIAL COUNTRIES AND PEOPLES [a]

General Assembly Resolution 1514 (15) of Dec. 14, 1960.
U.N.Gen.Ass.Off.Rec., 15th Sess., Supp. No. 16 (A/4684), p. 66.

* * *

1.   The subjection of peoples to alien subjugation, domination and exploitation constitutes a denial of fundamental human rights, is contrary to the Charter of the United Nations and is an impediment to the promotion of world peace and co-operation.

2.   All peoples have the right to self-determination; by virtue of that right they freely determine their political status and freely pursue their economic, social and cultural development.

4.   All armed action or repressive measures of all kinds directed against dependent peoples shall cease in order to enable them to exercise peacefully and freely their right to complete independence, and the integrity of their national territory shall be respected.

5.   Immediate steps shall be taken, in Trust and Non–Self–Governing Territories or all other territories which have not yet attained independence, to transfer all powers to the peoples of those territories, without any conditions or reservations, in accordance with their freely expressed will and desire, without any distinction as to race, creed or colour, to enable them to enjoy complete independence and freedom.

* * *

UNITED NATIONS, GENERAL ASSEMBLY RESOLUTION 3382 (30) OF NOVEMBER 10, 1975

U.N.Gen.Ass.Off.Rec., 30th Sess., Sup. No. 34 (A/10034), p. 84.

The General Assembly,

Recalling its [earlier] resolutions.   Reaffirming the importance of the universal realization of the right of peoples to self-determination, to national sovereignty and territorial integrity and of the speedy granting of independence to colonial countries and peoples as imperatives for the enjoyment of human rights,

* * *

---

a.   The complete text of the declaration is in the Documentary Supplement.

1. Reaffirms the legitimacy of the peoples' struggle for independence, territorial integrity and liberation from colonial and foreign domination and alien subjugation by all available means including armed struggle;

2. Welcomes the efforts by the Fact–Finding Commission of Inquiry and Conciliation of the Organization of African Unity to resolve amicably the current conflict in Angola;

3. Rejects any foreign interference in the internal affairs of Angola and of the Comoros;

4. Condemns the policies of those members of the North Atlantic Treaty Organization and those countries whose military, economic, sporting or political relations with the racist régimes of southern Africa and elsewhere encourage these régimes to persist in their suppression of the aspirations of peoples for self-determination and independence;

5. Strongly condemns all Governments which do not recognize the right to self-determination and independence of peoples under colonial and foreign domination and alien subjugation, notably the peoples of Africa and the Palestinian people;

6. Demands full respect for the basic human rights of all individuals detained or imprisoned as a result of their struggle for self-determination and independence, and strict respect for article 5 of the Universal Declaration of Human Rights under which no one shall be subjected to torture or to cruel, inhuman or degrading treatment, and their immediate release;

8. Notes with appreciation the material and other forms of assistance that peoples under colonial and alien régimes continue to receive from Governments, United Nations agencies and intergovernmental and non-governmental organizations and calls for a maximization of this assistance. * * *

2400th plenary meeting
10 November 1975

[The foregoing resolution was considered and approved in draft form by the third committee of the General Assembly and reported to the assembly, where it was adopted by a vote of 99 to 1, with 18 abstentions.

----

1. ***Assistance to liberation movements.*** Is lawful assistance to liberation movements limited to humanitarian aid? Is it lawful for states to provide military assistance (money and arms) to them? Is provision of such military assistance consistent with Article 2(4) of the charter? Or is there an exception from Article 2(4)'s prohibition in the case of wars of liberation waged against a colonial state by people in the colony? Does Article 1(2) of the charter, referring to self-determination of peoples, supply the answer to these questions?

2. ***United Nations declaration.*** Note the following provisions of the General Assembly's Declaration on Principles of International

Law Concerning Friendly Relations and Cooperation Among States in Accordance with the Charter of the United Nations, adopted in 1970:

* * *

By virtue of the principle of equal rights and self-determination of peoples enshrined in the Charter of the United Nations, all peoples have the right freely to determine, without external interference, their political status and to pursue their economic, social and cultural development, and every State has the duty to respect this right in accordance with the provisions of the Charter.

* * *

Every State has the duty to refrain from any forcible action which deprives peoples referred to above in the elaboration of the present principle of their right to self-determination and freedom and independence. In their actions against, and resistance to, such forcible action in pursuit of the exercise of their right to self-determination, such peoples are entitled to seek and to receive support in accordance with the purposes and principles of the Charter.

* * *

Nothing in the foregoing paragraphs shall be construed as authorizing or encouraging any action which would dismember or impair, totally or in part, the territorial integrity or political unity of sovereign and independent States conducting themselves in compliance with the principle of equal rights and self-determination of peoples as described above and thus possessed of a government representing the whole people belonging to the territory without distinction as to race, creed or colour.

Every State shall refrain from any action aimed at the partial or total disruption of the national unity and territorial integrity of any other State or country.

———

National liberation movements and the notion of self-determination, of course, are related. Heather Wilson writes: "One of the most controversial issues in international law since the end of World War II has been whether self-determination is a right in international law or simply a principle of political thought which has assumed great prominence in international affairs at various periods since the late eighteenth century." Wilson, *International Law and the Use of Force by National Liberation Movements* 55 (1988). The U.N., in specially constituted committees and the General Assembly has condemned terrorism and the illegal use of force, yet these bodies have exempted the use of force in exercise of "the inalienable right to self-determination and independence of all peoples under colonial and racist regimes and other forms of alien domination and the legitimacy of their struggle, in particular the struggle of national liberation movements, in accordance with the purposes and principles of the Charter and the relevant resolutions of the organs of the United Nations." Report of the Ad Hoc Committee on International Terrorism, U.N. GAOR, 28th Sess.Supp. No. 28, at 1, U.N.Doc. A/9028 (1973); Resolution on the Definition of Aggression, art. 7, G.A.Res. 3314, U.N. GAOR, 29th Sess., Supp. No. 31, at 144, U.N.Doc. A/9631 (1975), reprinted in 13 I.L.M. 710, 714 (1974) (in Doc.Supp.). See also, Beres, Prosecuting Iraqi War Crimes: Allied and Israeli Rights Under International Law, 16 Hast.Int'l & Comp.L.Rev. 41 (1992). *See,* Firmage, The "War of National Liberation" and the Third World, Ch. 13, in Law and Civil War in the Modern World p. 304 (Moore ed. 1974).

The notion that national liberation movements have authority to use force for purposes of self-determination challenges the traditional rule that states alone may legitimately use force. Heather Wilson, Use of Force, supra at 91. Is this "special status" accorded to "national liberation movements" and the sanctioning of their use of force in contravention of the principles of the U.N. Charter? Halberstam, Book Review, *A Mandate for Terror: The United Nations and the PLO,* 86 A.J.I.L. 424 (1992). Or is it promoting those principles? Judith Gardam notes that, "article 1(4) of [Protocol I of the Geneva Convention] * * * treats some wars of self-determination as international for the purposes of applying the law of armed conflict. During the negotiation of Protocol I, the majority of states took the legal position that article 1(4) was merely a recognition of the existing situation in international law. A minority of states, however, chose to couch their arguments for the extension of Protocol I in very controversial and emotive concepts, particularly that of the just war * * *. The adverse implication for civilians is that acknowledging these wars as just implicitly legitimizes lesser standards in the armed pursuit of self-determination * * * [T]he ends will justify the means * * * [Victims categorized as being] in opposition to persons exercising their right of self-determination will not be entitled to the protection of the humanitarian law of armed conflict." On the other hand, if the notion that article 1(4) represents existing international law, "[f]rom the point of view of armed conflict, * * * wars waged by such peoples to achieve the right of self-determination are wars between international entities and have the status of international wars. Thus, they should attract the application of the rules of armed conflict relative to international conflict." Gardam, *Noncombatant Immunity and the Gulf Conflict,* 32 Va.J.Int'l L. 813, 824–25, & n. 47 (1992).

LEGITIMACY OF SELF–DETERMINATION

Buchheit, Secession: The Legitimacy of Self–Determination 216–218 (1978).*

[W]e can draw several conclusions. First, secessionist activity is an irrepressible feature of the contemporary world scene, and the future, from all indications, will not see an abatement in the frequency of these claims. Second, many of these movements seek legal justification in the international doctrine of self-determination. Third, at the present time there is neither an international consensus regarding the status of secession within this doctrine nor (should it be conceded such a status) is

* Copyright 1978. Reprinted with the permission of Buchheit and Yale University Press.

there an accepted teaching regarding the nature of a legitimate secessionist movement. Fourth, by its present inability to distinguish legitimate from illegitimate claims to secessionist self-determination, the international community is seriously handicapped in its attempt to minimize instances of unwarranted third-party intervention in secessionist conflicts under the aegis of the "peremptory norm" of self-determination. Finally, aside from the immense cost of secessionist wars to the immediate parties, the danger of unrestrained intervention inevitably brings in its wake a possibility of escalation and the confrontation of major power blocs. One is left, therefore, with the disturbing result that situations involving a potentially serious threat to international world order, situations which are by their nature arguably unregulated by the general legal restrictions upon the international use of force, remain equally unfettered by any specific doctrines of international law.

There are several apparent solutions to this problem. It is possible for the world community to make an ex cathedra pronouncement that secession has no place within the doctrine of self-determination, thus embracing a limitation of this principle to cases of overseas colonization, interracial domination, or some other arbitrary category. This approach is, I believe, both dangerous and highly unrealistic. Such a transparently artificial restriction of the principle to the relatively "safe" context of European-style colonialism, when articulated by the very entities (independent States) liable to be inconvenienced by its further extension, is not likely to convince minority groups within established States that their claims have been adjudged illegitimate by an impartial collective verdict. They will therefore tend to disregard all opinions coming from that body, whether concerning the outbreak, conduct, or settlement of separatist conflicts, as hopelessly self-protective. The international community would thus effectively cast itself in a role similar to that occupied by the Holy Alliance during the last century in its goal of guarding monarchic supremacy against "anarchic" nationalism; that is, the role of an entrenched power bloc flailing against threats to its dominance arising from the dissatisfactions of its own constituents. At the very least, the community will have to abandon its fondness for decrying the evils perpetrated by colonial Powers unless it can discover a convincing method of distinguishing, in principle, these evil policies from the equivalent deportment of "alien" governors occupying a contiguous land mass.

* * *

[Another] solution, and the one that will be pursued here, seeks to maintain the underlying force of the self-determination principle and yet minimize the dangers to international peace and security by concentrating upon a method of ascertaining legitimate claims of this kind. Acknowledging that self-determination (insofar as it derives its strength from an innate urge to self-government coupled with a sense of the moral objections to alien domination resulting in exploitation, humiliation, and deprivation of human rights) is prima facie applicable to some but not all groups within independent States, the focus of attention ought to be on determining which groups are entitled to invoke the principle. Inevitably, this will involve an inquiry into the nature of the group, its situation within its governing State, its prospects for an independent existence, and the effect of its separation on the remaining population and the world community in general. Taken as a whole, these considerations would evolve standards by which the international community could ascertain instances of legitimate claims to separatist self-determination.

The probable benefits of this approach are significant. Most importantly, the international community would be given the chance to adjust its posture with regard to a particular separatist demand by virtue of its ability to distinguish the legal merits of the claim. This might permit a collective judgment, as was reached in the cases of Rhodesia and South Africa, concerning the proper scope of outside States' behavior toward the situation. In addition, the norms of nonintervention and proscription of force would again enjoy some protection under this scheme. Unless specifically prohibited by an authoritative international decision, of course, intervention on behalf of the "legitimate" party would still be possible and perhaps invited as enforcement of a community standard; but then, even in the halcyon days before the emergence of self-determination as a peremptory norm only a minority of jurists opposed *all* intervention.   * * *

A veiled dictum by the International Court of Justice? In the Nicaragua case, the court made the following reference to wars of national liberation:

> 206. However, before reaching a conclusion on the nature of prohibited intervention, the Court must be satisfied that State practice justifies it. There have been in recent years a number of instances of foreign intervention for the benefit of forces opposed to the government of another State. The Court is not here concerned with the process of decolonization; this question is not in issue in the present case. It has to consider whether there might be indications of a practice illustrative of belief in a kind of general right for States to intervene, directly or indirectly, with or without armed force, in support of an internal opposition in another State, whose cause appeared particularly worthy by reason of the political and moral values with which it was identified. For such a general right to come into existence would involve a fundamental modification of the customary law principle of non-intervention. (Nicaragua v. United States of America, [1986] I.C.J. Reports 14, 98.)

In his dissenting opinion, Judge Schwebel commented on this statement by the court:

> 178. The disturbing implications of the Court's construction of the scope of lawful counter-intervention are much magnified by another of the Court's apparent asides. In discussing the nature of prohibited intervention, the Court, in paragraph 206 of its Judgment, notes that there have been in recent years a number of

instances of foreign intervention for the benefit of forces opposed to the government of another State. It then interposes: "The Court is not here concerned with the process of decolonization; this question is not in issue in the present case." The Court goes on to consider whether States have a general right to intervene directly or indirectly, with or without armed force, in support of the internal opposition of another State whose cause appears particularly worthy by reason of the political and moral values with which it is identified. The Court rightly observes that for such a general right to come into existence would involve a fundamental modification of the customary law principle of non-intervention.

179. Yet the implication, or surely a possible implication, of the juxtaposition of the Court's statements is that the Court is of the view that there is or may be not a general but a particular right of intervention provided that it is in furtherance of "the process of decolonization". That is to say, by these statements, the Court may be understood as inferentially endorsing an exception to the prohibition against intervention, in favour of the legality of intervention in the promotion of so-called "wars of liberation", or, at any rate, some such wars, while condemning intervention of another political character.

180. In contemporary international law, the right of self-determination, freedom and independence of peoples is universally recognized; the right of peoples to struggle to achieve these ends is universally accepted; but what is *not* universally recognized and what is *not* universally accepted is any right of such peoples to foreign assistance or support which constitutes intervention. That is to say, it is lawful for a foreign State or movement to give to a people struggling for self-determination moral, political and humanitarian assistance; but it is not lawful for a foreign State or movement to intervene in that struggle with force or to provide arms, supplies and other logistical support in the prosecution of armed rebellion. This is true whether the struggle is or is proclaimed to be in pursuance of the process of decolonization or against colonial domination. Moreover, what entities are susceptible of decolonization is a matter of dispute in many cases. What is a colony, and who is the colonizer, are the subjects of sharply differing views. Examples of what may be contentiously characterized—though not necessarily unreasonably characterized—as colonies may be readily assembled. But for present purposes, it is enough to point out that the lack of beauty is in the eye of the beholder.

181. For reasons both of principle and practicality, leading States for years have gone on record in support of the considerations recalled in the previous paragraph. It is not to be expected that their view of the law, or the content of the law, will be influenced by an acknowledged and ambiguous *dictum* of the Court on a topic of which no trace can be found in the pleadings of the Parties. Perhaps the best that can be said of this unnecessary statement of the Court is that it can be read as taking no position on the legality of intervention in support of the process of decolonization, but as

merely referring to a phenomenon as to which positions in the international community differ. Even so, it is difficult to find justification for the Court raising so contentious a question, the more so when it acknowledges that that question is not in issue in the present case. (Nicaragua v. United States [*supra*]).

NATIONAL LIBERATION, SELF–DETERMINATION, AND TERRORISM

BIANCHI, REVIEW OF TERRORISMO INTERNAZIONALE E GARANZIE COLLETIVE

87 A.J.I.L. 175, 177 (1993).*

* * *

Evaluating current trends in state practice can be a difficult exercise. One should not overlook the fact that, to trace general rules of international law, a consistent and general pattern of state practice is needed. In fact, one confronts a sense of uneasiness when considering the obligation to abstain from financing or directing acts of terrorism as an obligation erga omnes in terms of positive law.[1] In fact, establishing the link between a state and terrorist activities allegedly sponsored by it is often difficult. What amounts to state sponsorship remains murky. For example, can one maintain that financing a national liberation movement suspected of being involved in terrorist attacks or training its members would trigger the international responsibility of a state? It is worth noting that not even in the 1988 Rome Convention on Maritime Terrorism, a fairly sophisticated legal instrument, is mention made of state-sponsored terrorism. The absence of any such provision is not a cause for optimism about the existence or emergence of states' opinio juris. For a long time, political strains and ideological confrontation have prevented the achievement of consensus on a clear-cut distinction between terrorist acts and belligerent acts of national liberation movements. This difficulty has also overshadowed the prospects for achieving a generally accepted definition of terrorism.

Different considerations apply with respect to the punishment of individual terrorists. In this area, state practice shows a much higher degree of acceptance of the legal obligation to apprehend and prosecute those guilty of terrorist acts. Not only do extradition treaties often provide for exceptions to the political offense exemption in case of terrorist acts, but also the trend in recent practice is to invoke the universality principle in jurisdictional claims related to individual terrorist activities. One can hope that in the near future the overwhelming political condemnation of terrorism will be converted into peremptory

---

* Reprinted with the permission of the American Society of Int'l Law.

1. In 1990, however, the International Law Commission adopted, in the framework of a Draft Code of Crimes against the Peace and Security of Mankind, an article (Art. 16, International Terrorism) that expressly condemns such conduct.

legal terms so as to dissipate Judge Edwards's and Judge Bork's doubts about the status of terrorism in international law.

See also, the excellent article by N. Berman, "But the Alternative is Despair": European Nationalism and the Modernist Renewal of International Law, 106 Harv.L.Rev. 1792 (1993).

2. ACTION AGAINST TERRORISM

a. Rescue of Hostages

SUMMARY ACCOUNT OF ENTEBBE INCIDENT
McDowell, Introductory Note [a]
15 International Legal Materials 1224 (1976).*

An Air France airplane that left Israel for France with over 250 passengers and a crew of 12 aboard was hijacked by terrorists on June 28, 1976, after a stopover in Athens. The hijackers forced the plane to land first at Benghazi in Libya, and then at Entebbe Airport in Uganda. Acting for the Popular Front for the Liberation of Palestine, the hijackers demanded the release of some 153 terrorists jailed in Israel, West Germany, France, Switzerland, and Kenya. On June 30 the hijackers released 47 non-Israeli passengers, and the following day released an additional 100. The remaining 104 passengers and crew were held hostage in Uganda until rescued by an Israeli military commando unit on July 3 and taken to Israel. Reports indicated that in the rescue operation three of the hostages, one Israeli soldier, seven of the terrorists, and a number of Ugandan soldiers were killed. There were conflicting opinions on whether the Government of Uganda acted to protect the hostages and negotiate for their release, or was directly implicated in collaborating with the terrorists.

On July 9, the Security Council of the United Nations began consideration of a complaint by the Prime Minister of Mauritius, current chairman of the Organization of African Unity, which referred to the "act of aggression" by Israel against the Republic of Uganda. See U.N. Doc. S/12126. On July 12, two draft resolutions were introduced—one by the United Kingdom and the United States, the other by Tanzania, Libya, and Benin.

The U.K.–U.S. resolution, inter alia, condemned hijacking and called on states to prevent and punish all such terrorist acts, while reaffirming the need to respect the sovereignty and territorial integrity of all states.

The Tanzania–Libya–Benin draft condemned Israel's violation of Uganda's sovereignty and territorial integrity and demanded that Israel meet Uganda's claims for full compensation for damage and destruction.

When the Security Council voted on the U.K.–U.S. draft resolution on July 14, the resolution lacked the 9 affirmative votes required for adoption. The vote was 6 in favor (U.S., U.K., France, Italy, Japan,

---

a. The note serves as an introduction to materials concerning the incident.

* Reprinted with the permission of the American Society of International Law from materials published at 15 I.L.M. 1224 under the general title "United Nations: Security Council Debate and Draft Resolution Concerning the Operation to Rescue Hijacked Hostages at the Entebbe Airport."

Sweden), with 2 abstentions (Panama, Romania), and 7 countries not participating in the vote (Benin, the People's Republic of China, Guyana, Libya, Pakistan, Tanzania, and the U.S.S.R.).

The Tanzania–Libya–Benin draft was not pressed to a vote, but in a statement by the Tanzanian delegate * * * the co-sponsors reserved the right to revive consideration of it "at an appropriate moment."

EXCERPTS FROM UNITED NATIONS SECURITY COUNCIL DEBATE ON THE ENTEBBE INCIDENT

13 UN Monthly Chronicle, Aug.–Sept. 1976, p. 15.

* * *

* * * Kurt WALDHEIM, Secretary–General of the U.N., said he had issued a statement on 8 July immediately after his return from Africa in which he had given a detailed account of the role he had played in efforts to secure the release of the hostages at Entebbe.

The case before the Council raised a number of complex issues because, in this instance, the response of one State to the results of an act of hijacking involved an action affecting another sovereign State. In reply to a specific question, he had said: "I have not got all the details, but it seems to be clear that Israeli aircraft have landed in Entebbe and this constitutes a serious violation of the sovereignty of a State Member of the United Nations." The Secretary–General said he felt it was his obligation to uphold the principle of the territorial integrity and sovereignty of every State.

However, that was not the only element involved in considering cases of the kind which the Council was discussing. That was particularly true when the world community was required to deal with unprecedented problems arising from acts of international terrorism, which Mr. Waldheim said he had consistently condemned and which raised many issues of a humanitarian, moral, legal and political character for which, at the present time, no commonly agreed rules or solutions existed.

It was hoped that the Council would find a way to point the world community in a constructive direction so that it might be spared a repetition of the human tragedies of the past and the type of conflict between States which the Council would now be considering.

* * *

Percy HAYNES (Guyana) said the action taken by Israel against Uganda was nothing but naked and brutal aggression. Guyana strongly condemned Israel for its aggression against the black African country of Uganda.

It was being argued that the principle of sovereignty was subordinate to the principle of human freedom and that Israel had the right, whenever it chose, to violate the sovereignty of other States in order to secure the freedom of its own citizens. That was nothing but a modern-day version of gun-boat diplomacy.

Those who, like Israel, sought to give legitimacy to the violation of the sovereignty of other States were making many small States, whose faith in and commitment to international law were unshakable, hostage to the dictates of naked power.

* * *

Kaj SUNDBERG (Sweden) said the drama was started by an abhorrent act of terrorism perpetrated by a group of extremist Palestinian Arabs and Europeans. There was no excuse for that criminal act.

The world must react vigorously against terrorist acts and take all possible protective measures. New efforts must be undertaken to achieve broad international agreement to combat terrorism, in the form of generally recognized standards of international conduct. The international community must work towards general recognition of the clear obligation resting on every State to do everything in its power, where necessary in collaboration with other States, to prevent acts of terrorism and, even more, to refrain from any action which might facilitate the perpetration of such acts.

Any State where hijackers landed with hostages must be prepared to shoulder the heavy responsibility of protecting all victims under circumstances which were bound to be difficult and delicate.

The Israeli action being considered involved an infringement of the national sovereignty and territorial integrity of Uganda. At the same time, Sweden was aware of the terrible pressures to which the Israeli Government and people were subjected, faced with this unprecedented act of international piracy and viewing the increasing threat to the lives of so many of their compatriots.

Sweden, although unable to reconcile the Israeli action with the strict rules of the Charter, did not find it possible to join in a condemnation in such a case.

* * *

Mr. SCRANTON (United States) said the United States reaffirmed the principle of territorial sovereignty in Africa. In addition to that principle, the United States was deeply concerned over the problem of air piracy and the callous and pernicious use of innocent people as hostages to promote political ends. The Council could not forget that the Israeli operation in Uganda would never have come about had the hijacking of the Air France flight from Athens not taken place.

Israel's action in rescuing the hostages necessarily involved a temporary breach of the territorial integrity of Uganda. Normally, such a breach would be impermissible under the Charter. However, there was a well established right to use limited force for the protection of one's own nationals from an imminent threat of injury or death in a situation where the State in whose territory they were located was either unwilling or unable to protect them. The right, flowing from the right of self-defence, was limited to such use of force as was necessary and appropriate to protect threatened nationals from injury.

The requirements of that right to protect nationals were clearly met in the Entebbe case. Israel had good reason to believe that at the time it acted Israeli nationals were in imminent danger of execution by the hijackers. In addition, there was substantial evidence that the Government of Uganda cooperated with and aided the hijackers. The ease and success of the Israeli effort to free the hostages suggested that the Ugandan authorities could have overpowered the hijackers and released the hostages if they had really had the desire to do so.

* * *

Under such circumstances, the Government of Israel invoked one of the most remarkable rescue missions in history, a combination of guts and brains that had seldom, if ever, been surpassed. It was justified because innocent decent people had a right to live and be rescued from terrorists who recognized no law and who were ready to kill if their demands were not met.

* * *

Mikhail KHARLAMOV (USSR) said that the flight carried out, the material destruction wrought, the substantial number of Ugandans killed were all regarded by Israel as a measure which was just or at least justified. But there existed no laws in the world, no moral or international laws, which could justify such action.

However much the representative of Israel might have tried to refute the irrefutable, the armed action against Uganda was an act of direct, flagrant aggression and an outright violation of the Charter, especially of Article 2, ¶ 4, which stated: "All Members shall refrain in their international relations from the threat or use of force against the territorial integrity or political independence of any State, or in any other manner inconsistent with the purposes of the United Nations."

The Soviet Union consistently opposed acts of terrorism, and was prepared to do its part in order to end that phenomenon. But one could not replace one matter with another. The Council was considering not the matter of international terrorism but an attack on Uganda, the killing of Ugandans, the destruction of Entebbe Airport, and other material destruction inflicted by the Israeli action against that State.

There was a gap between individual acts of terrorism and an attack by one State—in this case Israel—against another. Therefore a policy approved by a State could not be exceptional, even in the case in question.

The Council must condemn in the most vigorous manner the Israeli aggression against the sovereignty and territorial integrity of Uganda and compel Israel to recompense Uganda for the material damage done in connection with the attack. In addition, the Council must extend a serious warning to Israel that such acts of aggression would not go unpunished in future.

* * *

Isao ABE (Japan) said international terrorism, whatever form it might take, constituted an abhorrent crime against mankind and must be denounced in the strongest terms by the world community. The countries in the world must take effective measures to prevent and eliminate such a crime against humanity, and they were required to cooperate fully with each other in attaining that goal.

The Air France hijacking was terminated in an extraordinary circumstance—military action by a State within the territory of another State. Although the motives as well as the circumstances which led Israel to take such action were presented in detail, nevertheless there was an act of violation by Israel of the sovereignty of Uganda.

Japan reserved its opinion as to whether the Israeli military action had or had not met the conditions required for the exercise of the right of self-defence recognized under international law, as the Israeli representative contended.

* * *

———

The raid on Entebbe continues to provide a precedent to justify rescue attempts.

Iranian Hostage Rescue Attempt: In 1980, President Carter sent a small, specially-trained unit to rescue the hostages who were still in the former Embassy compound in Tehran. Three of the helicopters, however, developed problems and the mission was aborted. The President gave the Chairman of the Joint Chiefs of Staff authority, once the mission had begun, to do what was "necessary" to accomplish the mission, while keeping civilian casualties to a minimum. What do you think would have happened if the troops had made it into Tehran, but had become trapped or engaged in a protracted conflict and then were threatened with capture or death? Did the mission comply with international law? If so, what was its justification? If not, why not? Did the mission comply with U.S. constitutional law? President Carter did "Report" to Congress on April 26, 1980, after the mission was terminated. See Louis Henkin, Use of Force: Law and U.S. Policy, in Right v. Might, supra, at 31, 41–42 (recognizing a limited right to intervene, if and when the territorial state cannot or will not do so).

Rescuing nationals—Liberia: Day, Legal Considerations in Noncombatant Evacuation Operations, 40 Naval L.Rev. 45 (1992), writes: "On August 5, 1990, a reinforced rifle company of Marines arrive at the U.S. Embassy in Monrovia. Their mission was to provide additional security for the U.S. Embassy and to evacuate U.S. nationals, in response to threats made by * * * a leader of one of the rebel factions in the insurrection * * * there." The U.S. claimed self-defense as the justification for the intervention to save U.S. nationals, citing the Israeli raid on Entebbe. The rationale was based on concepts of humanitarian intervention, which had developed despite the U.N. charter's severe limitation on a state's unilateral prerogatives to use force. The Security Council was unable to act. Is the proper basis for justifying this type of action self-defense or humanitarian intervention? See, Schachter, International Law in Theory and Practice (1991).

b. Arrest of Terrorists

TERRORISTS SEIZE CRUISE SHIP IN MEDITERRANEAN

United States Department of State Bulletin, December 1985, p. 74.

WHITE HOUSE STATEMENT, OCT. 10, 1985

At the President's direction, U.S. military forces intercepted an aircraft over international airspace that was transporting the Achille Lauro terrorists. The aircraft was diverted to the airbase at Sigonella, Italy. In cooperation with the Government of Italy, the terrorists were then taken into Italian custody for appropriate legal proceedings.

Earlier today, upon learning that the terrorists would be flown from Egypt to their freedom, the President directed that U.S. forces intercept the aircraft and escort it to a location where the terrorists could be apprehended by those with appropriate jurisdiction. U.S. F–14 aircraft, flying from the carrier Saratoga, detected the aircraft in international airspace and intercepted it. They instructed it to follow them and escorted it to the military airbase at Sigonella, Italy. This operation was conducted without firing a shot. The aircraft landed with Italian consent and was surrounded by American and Italian troops. The terrorists aboard were taken into custody by Italian authorities. The Egyptian aircraft, with its crew and other personnel on board, is returning to Egypt.

We have been assured by the Government of Italy that the terrorists will be subject to full due process of law. For our part, we intend to pursue prompt extradition to the United States of those involved in the crime. This action affirms our determination to see that terrorists are apprehended, prosecuted, and punished.

This episode also reflects our close cooperation with an exemplary ally and close friend—Italy—in combatting international terrorism. The American Government and people are grateful to Prime Minister Craxi, his government, and the Italian people for their help.

We are also grateful to the government of Tunisia for its refusal to permit the aircraft transporting the terrorists to land in Tunis.

Finally, we must at this point note our gratitude to the government of Egypt for its efforts to end this dangerous crisis without additional loss of life. We strongly disagreed with the Government of Egypt, however, on disposition of the terrorists.

From the onset, the U.S. Government made clear to all the governments involved our firm opposition to negotiations with the terrorists or concessions to them. We also made clear our expectation that the terrorists would be brought to justice.

We were, therefore, deeply distressed to learn that those responsible for the death of Leon Klinghoffer might be permitted to go free. We said yesterday that we were determined to see justice done and that we would use every appropriate means to that end.

The decision on ending the hijacking was an independent one by the Government of Egypt. When we were consulted, we advised strongly against any arrangements which would permit the terrorists to escape justice. Since the time the terrorists were taken off the ship, we have continued intensive contacts with the Government of Egypt to pursue that point.

The United States wants to emphasize the fundamental and durable interests that the United States and Egypt share, interests which transcend this difficult incident. These have been trying times for both our governments. We will do all we can to ensure that the basic U.S.–Egyptian relationship—in which both our countries have taken so much pride for so long—remains unaffected.

In closing, the President wants to emphasize once again that the international scourge of terrorism can only be stamped out if each member of the community of civilized nations meets its responsibility squarely—passing up no opportunity to apprehend, prosecute, and punish terrorists wherever they may be found. We cannot tolerate terrorism in any form. We will continue to take every appropriate measure available to us to deal with these dastardly deeds. There can be no asylum for terrorism or terrorists.

     *   *   *

"THIS WEEK WITH DAVID BRINKLEY," OCT. 13, 1985

Abraham D. Sofaer,
Department of State Legal Adviser

     *   *   *

"Q. What about the Egyptians' charge that this was piracy, that what our F–14s were doing was, in effect, no different * * * from what the terrorists have done?"

"A. That's completely inaccurate because, first of all, this was not an intercept of an Egyptian target. It's like a murderer hailing a taxi, and then the taxi company pretending that they were the target of the police arrest. The fact is, the pirates in the airplane were the target of the intercept, and they happened to be in a civilian Egyptian airliner. We have had the most excellent relations with the Egyptian military, and we did not view this as directed against them at all."

Notes & Questions: Did Legal Adviser Sofaer's explanation of the interception make any sense legally? Is Egypt a taxi? Was the interception of the Egyptian Airliner a precursor to the executive participation in the abduction of Alvarez–Machain, supra? Was it a violation of Egyptian sovereignty? Was it a simple arrest? If it was not a violation of Egyptian sovereignty, as the Reagan Administration claimed, what was it? What was its justification? Did Egypt invite the interception? If not, does international law provide justification for a nation to commandeer another nation's airliners? Was it an "official hijacking" prompted by a "just cause?" What "just cause" can justify hijacking? Which do we accept? How about others? Do the treaties on hijacking (Montreal, Chicago, Tokyo), to which we are a party, provide a justification? Can you meaningfully distinguish the U.S. action against the Egyptian airliner and an abduction of U.S. officials or agents who are considered to have violated the criminal laws of other regimes? See discussion of U.S. v. Alvarez–Machain, in Chapters 1 and 3, supra; and discussion of U.S. v. Fawaz Yuniz, in Chapter 3, supra.

CHRISTOPHER JOYNER & WAYNE ROTHBAUM, LIBYA AND THE AERIAL INCIDENT AT LOCKERBIE: WHAT LESSONS FOR INTERNATIONAL EXTRADITION LAW?

14 Mich.J.Int'l L. 222 excerpts from 222–224 (1993) (footnotes deleted).*

* * * At 6:56 P.M. EST, at the altitude of 31,000 feet, the Maid of the Seas made its last contact with ground control. Seven minutes later, the green cross-hair at air traffic control split into five bright blips as Pan Am Flight 103 exploded in midair. Her fiery skeleton, laden with the bodies of passengers and crew, rained down on the people of Lockerbie, Scotland. Within the hour, 243 passengers, 16 crew members, and 11 townspeople were dead.

Nearly three years later, following extensive international investigations, the United States indicted two Libyan intelligence officers in November 1991 for the bombing of Pan Am Flight 103. The Libyan response to informal extradition claims was not unexpected: the government refused to surrender the officers on the grounds that such an act constituted direct interference in Libya's internal affairs.

In January 1992, and again in March 1992, the United Nations Security Council responded to the Libyan position with two resolutions: the first urged the government of Colonel Muammar el-Qadhafi to cooperate with the international investigation of the bombing; the second imposed sanctions on Libya for its failure to comply with the Security Council's requests. Taken together as legal prescriptions, the Security Council's actions marked the first time that the United Nations had ever demanded extradition of nationals of one State to face trial in a second State, despite the existence of international legal principles supporting Libya's position to refuse extradition of its nationals.

The U.N. Security Council resolutions in the Lockerbie case represent a salient, albeit as yet unconsummated, step toward strengthening the international extradition process for dealing with alleged terrorist acts. In the past, international fugitives who committed unlawful acts abroad often found sanctuary behind the political veils of customary and

* Reprinted by permission Michigan Journal of Int'l Law.

codified law, evading extradition with the shield of State sovereignty. The lack of a universally accepted rule of law has left extradition to bilateral treaties and acts of reciprocity and comity, which provide only malleable standards that States can interpret and reinterpret to serve their needs. * * *

———

Notes: Libya, for its part, has denied any involvement in the incident and has claimed that Libya is the actual victim of terrorism, recalling the downing of a Libyan civil airplane over Sinai in 1973 and the 1986 U.S. bombing of Tripoli. Libya did offer to enter into talks with the U.S., France, and the U.K. and to submit the dispute to Libyan judges who were also investigating the bombing. See, League of Arab States—Libya: Resolution and Statements Regarding Investigations of Aerial Incidents, 31 I.L.M. 724 (1992). In addition, there have been reports that the Libyans have attempted to compromise, offering to accept trial in Switzerland or some other "neutral" country, or even to accept responsibility in exchange for termination of sanctions and other remedies being sought. * * *

Kidnapping Terrorists: Does a notion akin to anticipatory self-defense apply to allow an exception against state-sponsored kidnapping? Some commentators have argued that self-protection, the protective principle of jurisdiction, and the defensive use of force combine to create this exception. See, discussion of this issue in relation to the Alvarez–Machain Case, supra, in Chapters 1 and 3, supra and in Michael Glennon, Agora: State–Sponsored Abduction: A Comment on United States v. Alvarez–Machain, 86 A.J.I.L. 746, 748–49 (1992).

* * *

SECTION G.   USE OF STATE COERCION SHORT OF MILITARY FORCE

For discussion of this subject in relation to International Organizations, see Chapter 16, supra.

FIRMAGE, ROGUE PRESIDENTS

11 Geo. Mason L.Rev. 79, 86–94 (1988) * (fns. omitted).

"The existence of nuclear weaponry and the threat of the use of such weaponry in general war have discouraged all-out war between the two giants who emerged from World War II. However, the intensity of the ideological and geopolitical rivalry between them resulted in war nevertheless, albeit covert war. By extra-constitutional and illegal means, we initiated the fall of the legitimate government of the populist nationalist Mohammed Mossedegh in Iran and unseated the land-reforming government of Jacobo Arbenz Guzman of Guatemala. We experi-

* Reprinted with the permission of George Mason L.Rev.

enced disastrous failures in our attempts to prevent Baath Party control in Syria. We employed Sumatran pirates in our attempted coup against Sukarno in Indonesia for the sin of nonalignment. We carried on paramilitary operations in Tibet from the 1950s into the 1970s, prolonging and exacerbating the agonies of a subject people without the slightest hope of affecting the government of the People's Republic of China. We invaded Cuba at the Bay of Pigs, overthrew the government of Patrice Lumumba in the Congo and were complicit in his death. In Laos, the CIA secretly supported a right-wing faction in the military against the legitimate but neutralist government, forcing the incumbent into alliance with the Communists. In Vietnam we waged clandestine war under Kennedy before and during the time of our open involvement, bombing supply lines of the Viet Minh, dropping toxic chemicals and defoliants. We made league with Southeast Asian drug ringleaders and have a country awash with heroin and marijuana to show for it. After 1968 Nixon escalated secret warfare across the Vietnamese border into Cambodia. Hundreds of cross-border operations occurred in 1967 and 1968 and over one thousand during the next two years. B 52 carpet-bombing commenced in 1969. Pentagon records were falsified to indicate that the raids occurred in South Vietnam. Our support of the Kurds of Kurdistan at the urging of the Shah of Iran in his dispute with Iraq ended in Kurdish disaster when we abandoned them after the Shah made temporary peace with Iraq.

In Chile we were successful in ending a century of democratic tradition by our covert operations that aided in the overthrow and murder of Salvador Allende Gossens and the earlier assassination of the commander of the Chilean armed forces, a Constitutionalist who vigorously opposed any coup who was killed as he resisted being kidnapped. General Augusto Pinochet, chief of staff, led the coup that overthrew and killed Allende.

After the hey day of CIA covert war in Vietnam, Laos, and Cambodia, a rapid decline in covert actions occurred under Presidents Ford and Carter. By 1980 covert action received less than five percent of the CIA's budget. Under the Reagan administration covert actions tripled in number. By the mid–1980s, covert action accounted for about one-third of the CIA's budget.

Within weeks of his inauguration, President Reagan prepared for war in Nicaragua by a presidential "finding" that authorized covert war. After creating the Contras from the remnants of former dictator Somoza's National Guard and arranging for their training from our own CIA or under Argentine trainers fresh from their own "dirty war" against their own countrymen, we sent the Contras into Nicaragua against "soft targets" such as power plants, schools, transportation, and people. This guaranteed a protracted war of attrition marked by terrorism and atrocity, disproportionate civilian casualties, and enormous suffering. In late 1983 and early 1984, before Congress temporarily turned off the money spigot with the Boland Amendment, Reagan and CIA Director Casey laid plans for alternative funding of the Contras. This was done through subterranean channels with aid from Brunei, Saudi Arabia, and Israel. Private funds were tapped in the United States, South Korea,

Taiwan, and Latin America. Primarily, however, governmental support continued under cover of private means used to distract the press and our own citizens. Old CIA hands and covert warriors from adventures in Laos, Vietnam, the Bay of Pigs, Guatemala, and Chile returned to take part in the sale of weapons to the Ayatollah Khomeini in Iran and to wage war in Nicaragua. Oliver North coordinated the gathering of money and armaments and the training and direction of the forces we created: the Contras.

What have we to show for all this? * * * We unleashed a ruthless militarist government and guerilla opposition which together have killed thousands of their own countrymen.

In Iran and throughout much of the Middle East, we are roundly hated. British and American interests are gone. Latin American movements toward economic and social reform and democratic government can hardly look to America for support. We have initiated coups against elected governments and supported ruthless military governments who wage war against their own people. Our efforts have exacerbated, if not precipitated, massive death and dislocation of millions of people in Asia. We are directly responsible for thousands of deaths and great suffering, including the dislocation of tens, if not hundreds, of thousands of people: Meo tribesmen from Laos and thousands from Cambodia, Vietnam, El Salvador, Guatemala and Chile.

In our own country, we pay a price. Our laws governing war and violence, found in the Constitution, in statutes of Congress, and in international law, are shredded by an administration driven by an intense ideological zealousness unmatched in this century.

We have created thousands of mercenaries, modern brigands, who fight for the highest bidder in Africa, Asia, and Latin America. Trained by the CIA or special forces, these men kill and corrupt for a fee.

Congressional control of the war power, to decide for war or peace, absent a sudden attack on our country, was meant by the framers to be complete. This control has been lost by congressional default as much as by presidential usurpation.

We are naive indeed if we believe that our domestic politics will not be affected by these methods and these practitioners of subversion. If our assurance of the righteousness of our goals is so complete that our means, however brutal, can be ignored, why should questions of law and morality stop the application to those in our own country who would obstruct our course? If, as Oliver North starkly stated, our allegiance is to the leader who shares the end vision rather than to the constitutional system of democratic means, why not apply the same tactics to those of our fellow citizens who stand in the way? The participation by CIA agents Howard Hunt and James McCord in Watergate points the way.

Our culture, already drenched with drugs, is subjected to new sources of cocaine and the criminal activity it spawns as sources in Laos and Thailand find their way here through the same murky channels that supply guns and money. Now we have as well Central American sources in Colombia, Costa Rica, Panama, and Nicaragua.

We have, indeed, suffered an appalling loss of virtue. How did we get here? By what failure of leadership do we find ourselves initiating and supporting war, massive death, and suffering?

The ferocity of our ideological struggle with the Soviets since World War II has blinded us to the dialectical relationship that always exists between ends and means. Perhaps the initiation of the Cold War with Russia so soon after the truly unique war against Hitler's Germany, coupled with the enormity of Stalin's crimes against his own people, seduced us into continuing our belief in a Manichaean world of moral black and white. We therefore continued O.S.S. activity, operating at the margin of law, through the CIA into a time of peace. World War II has been called the last just war. We came close, at least, to objective good and evil in opposition to each other in that war, which was characterized by naked aggression and war crimes including the greatest crime against humanity of all time, the Holocaust. Within this mental paradigm of absolutes we continued the crusade, blinded to the dialectic between ends and means.

With atomic and then hydrogen bombs in possession of an enemy who dominated Eastern Europe, then allied with a communist giant on the Asian continent, that we thought was behind much of the violence in the Third World, we felt we must act; yet, overt, acknowledged war was too dangerous.

A passage from the Doolittle Report of Covert Operations, commissioned by President Eisenhower, reveals the powerful ideological zealousness of the time: "Another important requirement is an aggressive covert psychological, political and paramilitary organization more effective * * * and, if necessary, more ruthless than that employed by the enemy * * *. There are no rules in such a game. Hitherto acceptable norms of human conduct do not apply."

Somehow we forgot, for a time, that such savage means—the world of car bombs and terrorism, paramilitary action, intentionally killing and maiming civilians, subverting legitimate government, corrupting mass media in other countries and in our own—would inevitably affect the end we sought: peace and justice in our own land.

Conclusions can be drawn and lessons learned from our experience with covert action since World War II. The first is an observation about the tension between a democratic society and covert operations. A democratic state is built on decisions made openly in public debate. This is a compelling necessity when questions of war and peace, life and death are at issue. Consensus, vital in the establishment and the conduct of foreign policy, cannot be achieved in secret. Consensus between the president and Congress can hardly occur when the Congress is deliberately kept ignorant of covert actions of the government. By nature and definition, covert actions cannot be preceded by public debate and public consensus. Nostalgic reminiscence of the Vandenburg era consensus by supporters of so-called "strong" presidential leadership in the conduct of foreign policy is understandable. And the goal, consensus between the political branches in the conduct of foreign policy, is desirable. However, the proponents of a strong presidential leadership in foreign policy must understand the relationship between covert action kept secret from the target of such action and covert action kept secret from Congress. Consensus between the political branches becomes impossible by definition. Covert action possesses limitations yet more devastating to real consensus. For consensus between the political branches in reality only mirrors consensus achieved among the electorate. The nature of covert action makes this impossible, at least before the fact.

By definition, debate, legitimization, and wisdom from the electorate are unavailable. Critical flaws that would be apparent in the light of day do not appear. No debate occurs within government generally. Congress plays almost no role: "notification" at best going to a select few, dangerously close to an "old boy" network of senior committee chairmen and party leadership. Even debate between the White House and the Departments of State and Defense may be dangerously limited or nonexistent. Crucial parts of the Iran–Nicaragua affair, for example, saw White House control over the operations of clandestine activity go directly from the National Security Council to the CIA, excluding or ignoring the advice of cabinet officers at State and Defense.

Even within the CIA, the "need to know" division between intelligence evaluation and clandestine operations may make the assessment of the former without any impact on decisions and operations of the latter. Treverton concludes, for example, that Allende in Chile was not toppled by a rogue elephant CIA that really believed that Allende was a threat to the United States. As his regime governed for a few years, CIA estimates as to the survival of democracy in Chile became more and more optimistic. Yet pressure from the Nixon White House on CIA operations was unrelenting, possessing a life of its own, powered by ideological zeal rather than political facts. Once on track, this operation ground to its conclusion, however brutal, self-defeating, and unnecessary, much like the disaster, one would think the obviously foreseeable disaster, at the Bay of Pigs. Failure at the Bay of Pigs cost hundreds of lives, crippled our influence in Latin America, and began a chain of events that almost led to nuclear war in the Cuban missile crisis. "Success" in Chile meant the death of thousands of Chileans and a few citizens of the United States under a bloodthirsty tyranny. It also meant the death of a century of democratic tradition in Chile, a commodity in short supply in Latin America. It is not obvious how our own national security was advanced.

Of course, there is not simply a failure of the system if constitutional checks are available but are ignored. In supplying large numbers of our most lethal weapons to Iranian fanatics and terrorists, if the CIA is directed by the president not to comply with the law and inform Congress, and the objections of the administration's most senior cabinet officers in State and Defense are ignored, we pass the point where law and government may help. No system can protect us entirely from fools.

Second are some conclusions of law. Our Constitution commits the war power, the power to decide for war or peace, entirely to the Congress, not to the president, with but one exception. If a sudden attack on our country occurs, we are at war and the president may act in self-defense with no authorization from Congress, but in every other circumstance, the power of war and peace is with Congress.

The war clause grants Congress alone the power "to declare War" and "grant Letters of Marque and Reprisal." The "Letters of Marque and Reprisal" clause of the constitutional empowerment of Congress covers the determination for acts of war, whether covert or overt.

The war clause in its completeness, then, grants all power to decide on war to Congress, only a response to sudden attacks on this country being excepted. This includes public or private war, declared or undeclared, fought with public forces or by mercenaries or other brigands operating under authority of the state. This includes individual acts of war or sustained hostilities.

No statute of Congress authorizes covert war or acts of war. The National Security Act of 1947, usually relied on by presidents for their illegal acts, makes no mention of covert action or paramilitary operations. While providing for intelligence acquisition and analysis, this statute authorized the CIA to "perform such other functions and duties related to intelligence affecting the national security as the National Security Council may from time to time direct." On its face, this is not authorization for any paramilitary action and is most certainly no authorization for covert actions, unrelated to the acquisition of intelligence.

The Hughes–Ryan Amendment forbids clandestine operations other than intelligence activity unless the president "finds" that such an operation is important to the national security and reports a description of the operation to Congress "in timely fashion." While it could be argued that this provision authorizes covert actions where the above specifications are met, the statutory language is in the negative, forbidding certain acts.

The commander in chief clause gives the president no power to commit forces of the United States to war or to acts of war when the nation is at peace. Only Congress is empowered to change this condition unless we are attacked. In any event, public forces of the United States would not usually be involved in covert activity. More often, CIA officers and contracted agents, not under the commander in chief clause, would be used.

International law has been flagrantly violated by several administrations since the end of the Second World War in the conduct of covert actions. International law calls on states to resolve disputes by peaceful means, demands the protection of noncombatants, places severe limitations on acts of reprisal, denies the right of political assassination, brands terrorism a violation of the laws of war, forbids torture and mutilation, calls on all states to extend recognition and peaceful relations to other states. These and many other provisions of law are violated as a matter of course by covert war.

The term "covert action" could be used to include at least three categories of activity. First, and clearly within presidential power under an authorizing statute of Congress, is the acquisition and interpretation of intelligence. Some of this activity will occur by covert means. Short of war and acts of war, or violence and illegality prohibited by international law and acts of Congress, this activity is within presidential power.

The second and most troubling area conceptually is covert action beyond intelligence gathering but short of war, acts of war, or violence and illegality prohibited by statutes of Congress and by international law. Such activities might include some degree of manipulation of another country's media, their electoral, and governmental processes, or their economy. As such covert action approaches acts of reprisal, acts of war, or violence threatening the property or the integrity of another state, Congress should authorize such action before the president possesses clear authority to act.

The third category is clearer, more serious, and is equally clearly within the war power of Congress. This includes covert war and acts of war, reprisals, and other acts of violence. These acts usually share one or both of two criteria: violence at such a level as to be forbidden by municipal and international law and direct intervention in another state designed to affect its sovereign autonomy. Such activity is prohibited from presidential undertaking without congressional authorization. Even with congressional sanction a large part of such activity is nevertheless prohibited by international law.

The president's approval of covert CIA activities directed at overthrowing the Nicaraguan government without full disclosure to Congress and without congressional empowerment and covert activities conducted by administration officials, with or without express presidential approval, raise serious constitutional, statutory, and political questions about the president's capacity to administer his office properly, as does the apparent "disinformation" campaign aimed at Mr. Khadafy of Libya. Consider, for example, the earlier covert mining of Nicaraguan harbors and now the Iran–Contra scandal in light of the following statement by James Iredell, a member of the Constitutional Convention in Philadelphia and later a Justice of the Supreme Court:

> [The President] must certainly be punishable for giving false information to the Senate. He is to regulate all intercourse with foreign powers, and it is his duty to impart to the Senate every material intelligence he receives. If it should appear he has not given them full information, but has concealed important intelligence which he ought to have communicated, and by that means induced them to enter into measures injurious to their country, and which they would not have consented to had the true state of things been disclosed to them—in this case, I ask whether, upon an impeachment for * * * such an account, the Senate would probably favor him.

Third are some philosophical conclusions. There is indeed a dialectic relationship between ends and means. Warlike means, however covert, will come back to haunt us in many ways. Most importantly, we are distinguished most realistically from our adversaries not by the ends we seek but by the limitations we are willing to place on the means we employ to obtain them. We all seek peace and security in a just state, however defined. Only a tyranny largely unaffected by a morality that places enormous value on human life could justify the initiation of murderous violence other than in the most compelling circumstances of self-defense when no choice of peaceful means are available. That simply is not the record of our own experience with covert actions.

Our system of constitutional government is violated by the means of covert war and acts of violence and war. No reformation of those murderous means seems possible that might change this conclusion.

Fidelity to our own process is a compromise that humans who lead make with each other and with those they lead as an institutional reflection of our common fallibility. Government itself is a recognition of such fallibility. Those who break this bond demonstrate an arrogance that makes them unsuitable for governmental responsibility.

Few goals of foreign policy are so valuable that we should do such violence to our system of government to achieve them. Our terrorists are not physically or spiritually distinguishable from their terrorists. The only thing that stops our terrorists from running away with the state is our deeply rooted constitutional system. This system is dominated almost entirely by the definition of means: the jurisprudence of due process of law and democratic government.

The Mafia reputedly began as a patriotic movement dedicated to Italian national unity. The Ku Klux Klan began, ostensibly at least, to temper Reconstructionist excess. Their choice of violent means, coupled with massive assurance of their own virtue and omniscience, led to a fatal perversion of their own essence.

Intelligence gathering in our imperfect world may well be necessary. But the huge majority of our intelligence comes through means both open and legal. The CIA and other parts of government read thousands of documents from other lands. Individuals, private and public actors, cross increasingly porous borders. Professional groups conduct exchanges and read each other's literature. Formal governmental relations provide vital contacts. Electronic devices, more exotic but not unambiguously illegal, allow us to see each other and hear each other almost without the capacity to interdict. Foreign operatives, "spies," see, hear, sniff.

This is enough. Our record of covert war and acts of war is one of short-term embarrassment and long-term disaster. The advantages we achieve are overwhelmed by the violence we do to others and to ourselves. No system of congressional oversight realistically can meet this challenge. If acts of violence and war are contemplated, let us debate this possibility in the open. I prefer the obvious risks this would entail, to the corruption of our government and our souls that is unavoidable in covert decisions to engage in covert war.

Is non-military coercion subject to the law? Is a state free to impose its will on that of another so long as it refrains from the grosser violations of state personality that are encompassed in physical, military force? Does Article 2(4) of the Charter of the United Nations proscribe only military force, or also coercions of different types? Is there an emerging law of non-intervention (or a developing body of general international law) that embraces such a proscription? For example, is an economically strong state guilty of illegal conduct if it uses its economic power to seek to force another state to do what it wishes: (a) as to internal non-economic matters, such as establishing honest and democratic governments; (b) as to alignment among power blocs in international relations; (c) as to economic conduct (i) of the same sort as that of the denial practiced by the powerful state (e.g., trade denial as a pressure for change in the trading policy of the pressured state) or (ii) of a different sort (e.g., denial of economic development assistance to induce settlement of a nationalization claim)?

CHARTER OF THE ORGANIZATION OF AMERICAN STATES

119 U.N.T.S. 3; 2 UST 2394; as amended February 27, 1967, 21 UST 607.

Article 19. "No State may use or encourage the use of coercive measures of an economic or political character in order to force the sovereign will of another State and obtain from it advantages of any kind."

ANNEX TO UNITED NATIONS GENERAL ASSEMBLY RESOLUTION 2625 (25) OF OCTOBER 24, 1970

U.N.Gen.Ass.Off.Rec. Annexes, 25th Sess., Supp. No. 28 (A/8028), pp. 122, 123.

Declaration on Principles of International Law Concerning Friendly Relations and Co-operation Among States in Accordance with the Charter of the United Nations

* * *

The principle concerning the duty not to intervene in matters within the domestic jurisdiction of any State, in accordance with the Charter.

No State or group of States has the right to intervene, directly or indirectly, for any reason whatever, in the internal or external affairs of any other State. Consequently, armed intervention and all other forms of interference or attempted threats against the personality of the State or against its political, economic and cultural elements, are in violation of international law.

No State may use or encourage the use of economic, political or any other type of measures to coerce another State in order to obtain from it the subordination of the exercise of its sovereign rights and to secure from it advantage of any kind. Also, no State shall organize, assist, foment, finance, incite or tolerate subversive, terrorist or armed activities directed towards the violent overthrow of the régime of another State, or interfere in civil strife in another State.

The use of force to deprive peoples of their national identity constitutes a violation of their inalienable rights and of the principle of nonintervention. Every State has an inalienable right to choose its political, economic, social and cultural systems, without interference in any form by another State. Nothing in the foregoing paragraphs shall be construed as affecting the relevant provisions of the Charter relating to the maintenance of international peace and security.

* * *

Chapter 18

THEORIES ABOUT INTERNATIONAL LAW

Section A.   Some Samples of Theoretical Outlooks.
Section B.   Monism & Dualism.
Section C.   Principles, Practice and Legitimacy.

1. *Is theory influential on outcomes under international law and on its development?* If you have taken these materials in the order in which we have arranged them, your study of this chapter comes after you have had experience with many of the major aspects of law in the international system. You will have begun to form your own ideas about the similarities and differences between the law you have studied here and the public law you study in other courses. For example: putting to one side the difference between the United States Supreme Court and the International Court of Justice as to authorization to decide, do you find these courts acting similarly or in sharply different ways in similar types of cases, i.e. where the Supreme Court is sitting in judgment upon the conflicting interests of two or more states of the Union.

We have put the theory material this far along for three reasons: (a) we wanted you to begin to grope toward theory on your own as you went along; (b) we wanted you to see from case study that so far as professional methodology and involvement go, international law calls upon the same range of skills as other systems of law do; (c) we wanted to avoid raising too many doubts and prospects before you had become more experienced in the subject matter.

Although underdeveloped, the international legal system has engendered extensive theoretical discussion. Why so much doctrine for so few rules and effective institutions to apply them? Is it because the scholars who have committed themselves to this field are creating theories and schools, casting their expectations and preferences as law simply because they have so little in the way of real law stuff to deal with? Do the materials which follow suggest that scholars are theorizing about reality or their dreams? Are they promoting the development of the law?

2. *Critical independence is indispensable.* International public law, more so than other bodies of law, tends to be presented in discrete doctrinal packages. Schools abound. Learned people encourage disciples. Deviation becomes intellectual heresy. Those who do not agree are dolts. Also, international law is often appealed to by advocates highly interested in particular outcomes. This is done either because international law is highly amorphous and hence susceptible to a wide range of assertion or because it becomes an argument of last resort. Sometimes these groups of distorters, the didactic scholars and the argumentative activists, combine forces. As a result there is claimed for

the international legal system a competence, a completeness and a virtue that it may not in fact possess. In this field the rule of caveat emptor is quite important for shoppers of doctrine.

In methodology, international public law traditionally has been somewhat old-fashioned by the most modern techniques of some domestic systems. It is too often highly exegetic, rigorously logical (even when there are errors in the logic), antiseptic and remote. Quantification technique as to events, things and attitudes of social groups barely exists. Even the schools that claim for themselves the utmost in realistic modernity are hardly scientific in any sense of association with modern scientific and engineering technology. Major propositions are largely supported by secondary authorities. In large part, perhaps, the generally backward methodological standard reflects the reality that, after all, the international legal system exists by consensus, and the world does not yet have a consensus as to what law is and how it should be used.

3. ***Basic jurisprudential problems.*** International law shares with domestic law certain basic problems. These are the relationship of law to justice, the essential nature of law, and the judicial process in relationship to other types of decision-making.

Beyond these, international law throws into issue other fundamental questions:

(1) Is international law law in terms of a generally accepted concept of law, whatever that concept is?

(2) If international law is law in some sense or other, what is its relationship to other congeries of law, such as natural law, critical legal theory, feminist jurisprudence, national law, international organizations law, regional systems law?

(3) Do international and domestic law form two separate legal systems (dualism) or are they each a part of one monolithic system (monism)?

4. ***Philosophy, for what purpose considered?*** What follows is intended to assist you in the development of your philosophic outlook about the legal element in the international system. This includes the development of cognition of both what international law is and what it ought to be or become. You will have been doing these cerebrations, subliminally perhaps, as you have gone through the preceding chapters. Your instructor may have chosen to begin with this part or to go to it immediately after Chapter 1. Our preferences as to sequence are stated in the preface to the first edition, but we recognize that it is more traditional to begin with subject matter of the sort here dealt with.

The history, nature and sources of international law are sometimes coupled as parts of a single item of information. In this book sources are dealt with in Chapter 1 and elsewhere. History and nature are very closely linked by a number of thinkers about international law, especially those writing up to World War II. For others, mainly contemporary scholars, history is not seen as having much to do with nature.

5. *The origins of international law.* What a majority of modern writers regard as international law began to differentiate from a universalistic public law in the West about 600 years ago. Politically, after the Roman city-state that became an empire withered away, segments of the old imperium began to see themselves as entities, not as mere extensions of a king's domain. These discrete new entities, despite Louis XIV's famous statement of identity between himself and the state, were incorporeal and distinct from any monarch. Certainly by the time of Ferdinand and Isabella—and probably at least one hundred years earlier—the nation-state as we know it today (territory, population, government) was in being in the West.

These entities soon evolved standards of conduct toward each other beyond the rules of etiquette between monarchs. Some of these were and still are standards of political propriety, such as diplomatic protocol, principles of international relations and comity. Other standards of conduct—always minimum ones—came to be thought of as creating rights and obligations for states, analogous to the rules (or norms) that states themselves imposed on persons within their jurisdiction, not as whim or caprice but as law. Specifically, the part of Roman law that pertained in the hey-day of Roman authority to controversies between non-Romans, the jus gentium, became a term used yesterday, and in some measure still, to refer to "customary international law."

The international law of today does not show distinct linkages to ancient Oriental and African practices. Even the modern descendants of very old Oriental cultures accept international law as the product of Western evolution. Ignorance and neglect in the West of the history of law and related institutions in the East constitute the most likely explanation of this omission. Scholars in some of the modern states that have evolved from the Oriental historical matrix sometimes chide the West for this inattention and threaten (usually mildly) to set the matter aright sometime. New states in Africa sometimes are heard in similar vein.

This fact makes the existing international legal system somewhat vulnerable to attacks on its universality by states not present at its creation. More often, however, the states that are not satisfied with the existing order attack specific rules or principles, not the system. Classical, scholarly Marxists, and many who are non-Marxist, deprecate the system of customary international law because it seems to them unavoidably to state, as law, rules and principles fostering the interests of the power elites asserting them. The socialist states of the former Second World, however, came in practice to accept the system and many of its most conventional rules and principles, while selectively seeking to deny status as law to other rules and principles because they are contradictory to national preferences including, but not limited to, ideological ones.

6. *Naturalists, positivists, the "new wave", and eclectics.* In the West international law was systematized by more or less scholarly writers (publicists), not power-wielding officials. The excerpt from Stone, *supra,* a modern publicist, refers to some of these. Vitoria (1480–1546) and Suarez (1548–1617) perceived that beyond individual states

there was a community of states governed as to their interactions by international rules. These rules were to be found by rational derivation from basic moral principles of divine origin. These Spaniards' concepts developed into a school of natural law, paralleling for international law an earlier jurisprudence about domestic secular law.

The school of scholastic naturalism was resisted by writers who recognized a legal community but said that its rules came either in whole or in part from state practice, not from God. Gentilis (1552–1608) seems to have been the first to dare say there was more earthliness than theology behind international law. Hugo Grotius (the latinized version of a Dutch name) was born in 1583, and if systematized international law has a single historical beginning it is in his De Jure Belli Ac Pacis, printed in 1625. Grotius served once as Sweden's ambassador, an interesting practice not long continued by states; and as a representative of fishing and sea-trading national interests he gave us, inter alia, the principle of the freedom of the seas as customary international law. Grotius is also type-cast as the first eclectic, because he accepted not only positive law—state practice—as a source of international law, but also natural law. But the natural law of Grotius was more secular than that of the Spanish scholastics, for it was based upon man's rationality— "the dictate of right reason"—rather than upon revelation, exegesis, and deduction of God's will.

A second school of naturalism, secular and rationalist, evolved and had some influence on the early recognition and reception of international law by courts in the United States. Thus, in finding vessels engaged in the slave trade subject to seizure by American privateers, Justice Story, on circuit, wrote:

> " * * * I think it may unequivocally be affirmed, that every doctrine that may be fairly deduced by correct reasoning from the rights and duties of nations, and the nature of moral obligation, may theoretically be said to exist in the law of nations; and unless it be relaxed or waived by the consent of nations, which may be evidenced by their general practice and customs, it may be enforced by a court of justice * * *." United States v. The Schooner La Jeune Eugenie, 26 F.Cas. 832, 846 (U.S.Cir.Ct., 1st Cir., 1822) (No. 15,551).

But at the Supreme Court commitment to positivism prevailed in a philosophically indistinguishable slave trade situation. Marshall let the slavers keep their "property" [sic]: " * * * This, [slavery], which was the usage of all, could not be pronounced repugnant to the law of nations * * *." The Antelope, 23 U.S. (10 Wheat.) 66 at 120 (1825). Why? The "usage of all [States]" is otherwise and controls. Generally speaking adherence to natural law, especially if of the second or rationalist variety, tends to be a form of idealism about law. Positivism tends to emphasize conduct-phenomenology, e.g. how many states accept that "x" is law, just or unjust?

The role of the writers. Idealism tends to transform into law decision-makers' preferences and down-grade the element of states' volition in accepting a rule or principle as one of law. There has long been in international law a pronounced emphasis on the distinction between the law that is and what ought to be the law. But in some legal philosophies about international law it is harder to discern the line of difference than in others, especially if the publicist is an eclectic, or policy-oriented.

Some modern American writers, for example, devote themselves to telling us how to make better systems, stressing structural and procedural arrangements as if these were the basic need or problem. Others, self-characterized as American philosophic neo-realists, are really so idealistic as to assume that American values are common goal values on the planet and that law is not normative but an argumentative variable in the power process by which authorized decisionmakers—lawyers, judges, diplomats, politicians—put these goal values into effect with authoritativeness. Others, just as seriously argue for deconstruction of the whole system. Recently theorists, including those who concentrate in feminist philosophy and critical legal theory, have begun to approach the subject of international law from different perspectives, some challenging the very nature and operation of international law. Perhaps at the central core are those who are essentially mild positivists—in the tradition of American pragmatism—who try to find out what the great weight of acceptance by states shows and to emphasize the norms stated in obligatory form in international agreements.

The writers—and now in the United States, the Restaters—have had, and continue to have, great influence on what judges—and even foreign offices—do in relationship to international law. In civil law countries, where doctrine, i.e. scholarly writing, is the primary influence on jurisprudence, i.e. case law, this is normal. In the common law world it is not normal for domestic law, but it is for international law. For today the judges' perceptions of customary international law are not their own but those of the writer or school they have chosen to follow, rejecting others. And the writers, as we have seen, vary widely in what they perceive. This is the basis of their power and their responsibility. Advocacy in any arena, national or international, as to what the relevant international law rule is requires the advocate to be very familiar with the literature, both that which can help his cause and that which might destroy it.

7. *Some questions and issues for you to come back to.* With the above guide, and with questions in mind such as those to follow, evaluate the messages of the excerpts from writings below. Is the writer an idealist or is he reality-oriented? In the historic scheme of differentiation, what label do you give the writer? To your mind does the writer help or hurt the cause of legal order in the world community? Why?

What is international law to you now? Is its existence considered by you to be proved, disproved or not proved? Do you see an identity or a difference between international law and law in the international system? Is international law merely an aspect of a science of international relations? If not, where do you draw lines between principles of international relations and principles of international law? On which side of a line do these fall: self-determination of peoples, nonintervention, equality of states, use of economic force? Can the "rules of international law" be ignored? Would Hitler have had one answer before and another after WWII? What would Saddam Hussein's answer be today? How about the leaders of the various factions in Bosnia. What do you think? Are these matters of pure power or is law involved? If so, how? As to the existence or not of international law, should it suffice to note, as then Professor (later judge of the International Court of Justice) Jessup did in 1940, that foreign ministries have legal staffs, that diplomatic correspondence is full of assertion and counterassertion as to the international law issues involved in a controversy, that this has been true for at least three centuries, and that, by inference, there are jobs of international lawyering? See Jessup, *The Reality of International Law,* 18 For.Aff. 244 (1940).

SECTION A. SOME SAMPLES OF THEORETICAL OUTLOOKS

---

1 AUSTIN, JURISPRUDENCE 177, 189 (1861)

* * * Speaking with greater precision, international law, or the law obtaining between nations, regards the conduct of sovereigns considered as related to one another.

And hence it inevitably follows, that the law obtaining between nations is not positive law: for every positive law is set by a given sovereign to a person or persons in a state of subjection to its author. As I have already intimated, the law obtaining between nations is law (improperly so called) set by general opinion. The duties which it imposes are enforced by moral sanctions: by fear on the part of nations, or by fear on the part of sovereigns, of provoking general hostility, and incurring its probable evils, in case they shall violate maxims generally received and respected.

* * *

* * * But if perfect or complete independence be of the essence of sovereign power, there is not in fact the human power to which the epithet sovereign will apply with propriety. Every government, let it be never so powerful, renders occasional obedience to commands of other governments. Every government defers frequently to those opinions and sentiments which are styled international law. And every government defers habitually to the opinions and sentiments of its own subjects. If it be not in a habit of obedience to the commands of a determinate party, a government has all the independence which a government can possibly enjoy.

PHILLIPSON, INTRODUCTION TO GENTILI, DE JURE BELLI LIBRI TRES (2 TRANS., CARNEGIE ENDOWMENT, 1933) 22A *

* * *

5.   Conception of the Law of Nations—Society of States—Civil Basis—Membership of the Society.   The law of nations, designated by Gentili ius gentium (the customary expression adapted from Roman Law) is that law which all nations or the greater part of them—"maior parsorbis"—agree upon.   It is the law of the society or community of states, of the "Societas gentium".   This is a concise and simple description, whereby the ambiguous Roman term is made to refer explicitly to international relations.   It is not, of course, an exact definition, as it involves, though unavoidably, a tautologism.   Indeed, no satisfactory definition had hitherto been formulated.   Grotius adopts substantially the conception of Gentili, when he says that the law of nations (ius gentium) is that law which has received obligatory force from the will of all nations or of many; whilst Vattel, like Gentili, verges on tautology in his statement that the law of nations (droit des gens) is the science of the rights and obligations which exist between nations.   Some writers emphasize in their definitions the origin of the law of nations, others the nature of the subject-matter, and others again lay stress on those concerned in and bound by it.   * * *

* * *

* * * Very frequently we find that Gentili appeals to the ius naturae in order to test the validity of a particular doctrine or the legitimacy of a certain practice; but usually he disregards the current vague metaphysico-legal significance of that term, and interprets it in the sense of humanity, justice, and the best common sense of mankind.   And throughout his exposition he insists on the positive juridical sanction quite as much as on the considerations of ethics or on the behests of divine law, and he is careful to discriminate between the work and objects of theologians and the sphere and functions of jurists.

The pioneer work of Gentili was in harmony with the larger movement of the sixteenth century which witnessed a transformation of society, the establishment of a new spirit and wider outlook, the decline of theocracy, and the rise of the modern State.   The political conceptions of the Middle Ages, which identified civil and ecclesiastical authority, were derived on the one hand from Greek and Roman doctrines, and on the other from Hebrew and Christian teaching.   Towards the end of the thirteenth century the temporal supremacy of the papacy began to be seriously opposed, especially in France, and its decline was further hastened on by the great schism.   The conciliar movement of the fifteenth century spread the theory that sovereign power was of the nature of a trust.   The Renaissance and the Reformation, two sides of

* Reprinted with the permission of the Carnegie Endowment for International Peace.

the same great intellectual and moral awakening, revived humanism, scientific curiosity, established a spirit of independence, political as well as spiritual, and a desire to find a more rational basis than the arbitrary theocratic for human society, and substituted civil for clerical authority, a society of territorial States resting on law and juridical sanction for a theocratic confederation subject to canon law. * * *

* * *

----

2 WOLFF, CLASSICS OF INTERNATIONAL LAW CARNEGIE ENDOWMENT 11, 19 (1934) *

§ 7.—Of the society established by nature among nations. Nature herself has established society among all nations and binds them to preserve society. For nature herself has established society among men and binds them to preserve it. Therefore, since this obligation, as coming from the law of nature, is necessary and immutable, it cannot be changed for the reason that nations have united into a state. Therefore society, which nature has established among individuals, still exists among nations and consequently, after states have been established in accordance with the law of nature and nations have arisen thereby, nature herself also must be said to have established society among all nations and bound them to preserve society.

* * *

§ 25.—Of the positive law of nations. That is called the positive law of nations which takes its origin from the will of nations. Therefore since it is plainly evident that the voluntary, the stipulative, and the customary law of nations take their origin from the will of nations, all that law is the positive law of nations. And since furthermore it is plain that the voluntary law of nations rests on the presumed consent of nations, the stipulative upon the express consent, the customary upon the tacit consent, since moreover in no other way is it conceived that a certain law can spring from the will of nations, the positive law of nations is either voluntary or stipulative or customary.

* * *

----

* Reprinted with the permission of the Carnegie Endowment for International Peace.

STONE, LEGAL CONTROLS OF INTERNATIONAL CONFLICT LIII (1954) **

* * * Is there an international law? In what sense, if any, are its rules binding? To whom are such rules (insofar they exist and bind) directed? Can international law be said to be the law of a society or a community? Nor have the new approaches yielded even substantially new answers to the old questions. John Austin's denial of the *legal* force of international law lacked, no doubt, the temperateness of Professor Corbett or the passionate cynicism of a Lundstedt; but there is little now said that he did not foreshadow a century ago. Today, as centuries ago, those who champion the cause of international law as "law", find its source of validity either in natural law, as did Vitoria and Suàrez, or in positive enactment, as did Gentili and Zouche, or in a mixture of the two as in Grotius. Even Kelsen's reduction of the relations between international law and international society to the identity of *legal order* and *legal community,* while apparently resolving a traditional perplexity into a mere verbal illusion, has proved to be a new evasion rather than a new solution. Its identification of the international legal order with the international legal community is achieved only by excluding from the notion of "society" the very reference to the world of existence which was the essential source of the exorcised perplexity. * * *

* * *

So, too, it may be striking that modern theories as opposed in temper as to those of Professors Lauterpacht, Lundstedt and Messner converge by different paths on the importance of recognising the role of the individual in international law. But these questions of the "Aye" or "No" of the international status of individuals are in themselves as old as the natural law of a Suàrez or a Grotius: and mere theory is unlikely to advance them further. What theory rather requires is a fuller understanding of the mediating, distorting or obstructing operation of State entities on human relations.

Such fuller new inquiries do not lend themselves to quick answers, nor at all to armchair answers. The need for long and arduous field research within the most inaccessible and dangerously controversial area of human relations is (it is believed) a basic reason for the modern stalemate in juristic thought concerning international law. If such needed inquiries are shunned, then theory is thrown back on such barren questions as whether the actual self-subordination of States to wider international association, functionally limited, warrants the use of the term "community" to describe such an international association. And since the degrees of such self-subordination are potentially infinite in number, ranging from the most transient association on the battlefield by way of a truce for burying the dead, through the intimate organic association (on paper) of a United Nations Organization, to the intimacy in fact of a successful federation such as that of the United States or the Commonwealth of Australia, such inquiries are as interminable as they are barren.

** © Julius Stone 1954. Reprinted with the permission of Julius Stone and Wm. W. Gaunt & Sons, Inc., Holmes Beach, Fla.

Insofar, therefore, as we are concerned with a "living" or "operative" international law, with "law in action" as distinct from "the books", the continuance of armchair debate whether international law is "law", will not advance understanding. Nor does it really advance matters to interpret "law in action", as do Dr. Schwarzenberger and others, to mean the law enounced or applied by tribunals or competent State organs, as distinct from the writings of publicists. So far as concerns the effects of international law *on men,* and *of men on law,* the law of tribunals and State organs may still be "law in the books" rather than "law in action". Nor has Professor Corbett's search for international "law in action", despite its courage and vigour, really faced the preliminary question, what "international law in action" may mean. It is, in the present view, impossible to study "law in action" without relating the law not merely to the supposed interests and conduct of States, but also (and above all) to those of the men and women of particular times and places. And if this be so, then it becomes apparent that the task of assessing the effect on human interests and human conduct of the interposition of State entities between the great aggregations of mankind, is an inescapable preliminary.

* * *

It is at least probable, that the magic circle of the unsolved classical problems will not be broken until we cease to assume that the categories, conceptions, and methods of municipal law are sufficient, or even necessarily relevant, either for testing the validity of international law or for understanding its actual operation. Certainly our plight seems to cry out for insights which the classical problems, even when clothed in twentieth century philosophical garb, fail to yield. Such an escape from the classical magic circle might also release intellectual energy for tasks more fruitful than those which now engage them.

KELSEN, THE PURE THEORY OF LAW [a]

51 Law Quarterly Review 517 (1935).*

* * *

28. The law, or the legal order, is a system of legal norms. The first question we have to answer, therefore, is this: What constitutes the unity in diversity of legal norms? Why does a particular legal norm belong to a particular legal order? A multiplicity of norms constitutes a unity, a system, an order, when validity can be traced back to its final source in a single norm. This basic norm constitutes the unity in diversity of all the norms which make up the system. That a norm belongs to a particular order is only to be determined by tracing back its validity to the basic norm constituting the order. According to the

---

a. The late Professor Albert A. Ehrenzweig, one time a student of Kelsen, always said the correct translation is "the theory of pure law."

* Reprinted with the permission of Stevens & Sons, Ltd., London.

nature of the basic norm, i.e. the sovereign principle of validity, we may distinguish two different kinds of orders, or normative systems. In the first such system the norms are valid by virtue of their content, which has a directly evident quality compelling recognition.   * * *

29.   With legal norms the case is different. These are not valid by virtue of their content. Any content whatsoever can be legal; there is no human behaviour which could not function as the content of a legal norm. A norm becomes a legal norm only because it has been constituted in a particular fashion, born of a definite procedure and a definite rule. Law is valid only as positive law, that is, statute (constituted) law. Therefore the basic norm of law can only be the fundamental rule, according to which the legal norms are to be produced; it is the fundamental condition of law-making. The individual norms of the legal system are not to be derived from the basic norm by a process of logical deduction. They must be constituted by an act of will, not deduced by an act of thought. If we trace back a single legal norm to its source in the basic norm, we do so by showing that the procedure by which it was set up conformed to the requirements of the basic norm. Thus, if we ask why a particular act of compulsion—the fact, for instance, that one man has deprived another of his freedom by imprisoning him—is an act of law and belongs to a particular legal order, the answer is, that this act was prescribed by a certain individual norm, a judicial decision. If we ask, further, why this individual norm is valid, the answer is, that it was constituted according to the penal statute book. If we inquire as to the validity of the penal statute book, we are confronted by the State's constitution, which has prescribed rules and procedure for the creation of the penal statute book by a competent authority. If, further, we ask as to the validity of the constitution, on which repose all the laws and the acts which they have sanctioned, we come probably to a still older constitution and finally to an historically original one, set up by some single usurper or by some kind of corporate body. It is the fundamental presupposition of our recognition of the legal order founded on this constitution that which the original authors declared to be their will should be regarded as valid norm. Compulsion is to be exercised according to the method and conditions prescribed by the first constitutional authority, or its delegated power. This is the schematic formulation of the basic norm of a legal order.

30.   The Pure Theory of Law operates with this basic norm as with an hypothesis. Presupposed that it is valid, then the legal order which rests on it is valid also. Only under this presupposition can we systematize as law (i.e. arrange as a system of norms) the empirical material which presents itself for legal recognition. On the composition of this material (acts) will depend also on the particular content of the basic norm. This norm is only an expression for the necessary presupposition of all positivistic constructions of legal material. In formulating the basic norm, the Pure Theory of Law in no way considers itself as inaugurating a new scientific method of jurisprudence. It is only trying to make conscious in the minds of jurists what they are doing when, in seeking to understand their subject, they reject a validity founded on natural law, yet affirm the positive law, not as a mere factual assembly

of motives, but as a valid order, as norm. With the theory of the basic norm, the Pure Theory of Law is only trying to elucidate, by an analysis of the actual procedure, the transcendental-logical conditions of the historic methods of positive legal knowledge.

31. Just as the nature of law, and of the community which it constitutes, stands most clearly revealed when its very existence is threatened, so the significance of the basic norm emerges most clearly when the legal order undergoes not legal change, but revolution or substitution. In an hitherto monarchic State a number of men attempt to overthrow by force the legitimate monarchic government and to set up a republican form in its place. If in this they are successful, that is, the old government ceases and the new begins to be effective, in that the behaviour of the men and women, for whom the order claims to be valid, conforms in the main no longer to the old but to the new order, then this latter is operated as a legal order, the acts which it performs are declared legal, the conditions which it proscribes, illegal. A new basic norm is presupposed—no longer that which delegated legislative authority to the monarch, but one which delegates such authority to the revolutionary government. Had the attempt been a failure, had the new order, that is, remained ineffective, in that behaviour did not conform to it, then the acts of the new government become not constitutional but criminal (high treason), not legislation but delict, and this on the ground of the validity of the old order, which presupposed a basic norm delegating legislative power to the monarch.

If we ask what, then, determines the content of the basic norm, we find, on analysing judicial decisions back to their first premises, the following answer: The content of the basic norm is determined by the condition of fact out of which the order emerges, given that to the order there corresponds, amongst the human beings to whom it refers, a substantial measure of actual behaviour.

This gives us the content of a positive legal norm. (It is not, of course, a norm of a State's legal order, but a norm of international law, which, as a legal order superior to that of the individual States, legally determines their sphere of jurisdiction.) * * *

     * * *

DeVISSCHER, THEORY AND REALITY IN PUBLIC INTERNATIONAL LAW 404 (1968) *

It was doubtless inevitable that a long period of war on a world scale and of unexampled political tensions should have a profound influence on the direction of thought in the field of international law. The descriptive methods of voluntarist positivism in vogue at the beginning of the century, like those derived exclusively from formal logic, are

* Translated by P.E. Corbett (copyright © 1968 by Princeton University Press). Re- printed with the permission of the transla- tor and the Princeton University Press.

everywhere in retreat. Contemporary legal thought is intensely alive to the need of a new set of values in the foundations of positive international law. From now on it refuses to see in that law merely a technical order without moral inspiration or teleological direction.

The legal thought of today seeks in the direct observation of international life a new field of study. This is not a matter, as there is a tendency to say, of reconstructing international law on a foundation of sociology, but of scrutinizing the *raison d'être* of norms, restoring the contract between the normative apparatus and the underlying realities, and thus sifting through a more broadly informed criticism the rules and practices of international law perceived in the living process of application. In this renewed study the man of law will confront without methodological prejudice realities which at times are ill-adapted to his formal categories. He will not forget, however, that the observation of international life, though it never consists in the mere collection of raw facts, provides only the data for legal elaboration; that legal elaboration has its proper function, which is to select from these data only those which are adapted to social ends and which a complex of characteristics (external prominence, generality, regularity) makes fit material for his particular technique. So understood, enquiries into international relations promise to be fruitful. Properly conducted, they will have a vivifying influence; they will re-establish international law in the plenitude of its ends and its efficacity.

Even now this new orientation is apparent on the plane of doctrinal studies. We can find it again in the jurisprudence of the International Court of Justice, in the work of codification going on under the auspices of the United Nations, in the creative effort of international organizations. Everywhere is felt the need to reinvigorate legal technique, to free it from prefabricated categories by associating it more closely with the study of a social milieu in accelerated evolution.

From this realization flow new demands. One is fundamental and moral; in a crisis of human values it insists upon respect for these at the heart of every organized society. There are others, more contingent in character, because tied to the present forms of the distribution of power among nations: such is that demand of effectivity which we have so often encountered and which, in a still primitive order of relations, has a more prominent place than anywhere else.

The study of power, both in its distribution and in its action, has had a large part in our discussion. The reason is that, more than any other, it reveals the tensions and the convergences that characterize the present relations between the political fact and the law. Belonging as it does both to the internal and to the international order, the action of the State is at the center of international relations and is for the moment their most salient feature. It compels the man of law to penetrate beyond the formal manifestations of power into its intimate springs and to do his share towards endowing power with an organization adapted to the common international good.

The problem of the future is that of the transformations of power. There are many signs that the structure of international relations is on the eve of profound changes. Territory, which since the end of the middle ages has provided the firmest base for these relations and ensured their stability, has no longer the same significance. It is all too clear that the existence of atomic weapons, of long-range rockets of increasing accuracy, rob frontiers of their traditional role as bulwarks of power and security. It is not less evident that some of the pacific activities of States cannot go on without more or less serious repercussions in neighboring countries. Consequently some scientific and technological operations (nuclear experiments, diversion and pollution of waters) call for international regulation. Similarly, an economy of international dimensions can no longer conform to political and legal conceptions allied with a configuration of close-walled national units. Association, even integration, are the new forms of power-distribution that force themselves upon States in search of wider markets.

Some of these structural transformations are partially in effect and in course of development. Others are scarcely visible on the horizon. The man of law owes it to himself to watch them; he will go surety for them only in so far as they seem to him factors of progress. No more than any other form of organization do federal structures have value in themselves: like the others they may become the instrument of political or economic antagonisms that divide peoples. The redistribution of power can be efficacious only when based upon solid realities; it can be beneficent only if it guarantees order and peace.

KAPLAN AND KATZENBACH, THE POLITICAL FOUNDATIONS OF INTERNATIONAL LAW 5 (1961) *

No one can observe the international political system without being aware that order does exist, and that this order is related in important ways to formal and authoritative rules, that is, to a body of law and to a process of law-government. These rules are sustained by the genuine interests which nations have in restraining certain forms of international conduct, even though these constraints must apply to their own conduct as well as to that of other states. To understand the substance and limits of such constraining rules, it is necessary to examine the interests which support them in the international system, the means by which they are made effective, and the functions they perform. * * *

* * *

* Copyright © 1961 by Dr. Morton A. Kaplan and John Wiley & Sons. Reprinted by permission.

International Law as "Law:" Sometimes international law is viewed as a rather strange breed of law to which the term "law" is applied only by courtesy if at all. A number of great legal philosophers—Hobbes, Pufendorf, Bentham, and Austin are examples—have all doubted the legal character of international law, and the charges and counter charges which pervade the international community today seem to provide empirical support for their view. Clearly some definitions of law would exclude international law. Disputes, for example, are not routinely decided by an international judiciary, and there exists no coercive agency of formal international status which can effectively enforce the law. Rules do not emanate from any single "sovereign." Indeed, the legal order is not primarily vertical, or hierarchical, as it normally is in domestic government. Rather it is structured horizontally, composed predominantly of formally equal centers of legal authority called "states." We have only the beginnings of supranational authority in the United Nations and in various regional organizations.

* * *

Now, in spite of the differences in terminology and the fact that a critic may get considerable political mileage from invoking the accusation that international law has been flouted, processes in the international and domestic arenas are in some respects comparable. The particular decision disposes of the case and enters into the body of available precedent, whether that decision is persuasive or not. The focus of critical attention is to undercut its status as a norm to be invoked by others in similar circumstances, and it is to this end that some continue to call it a violation of international law. The more arbitrary it can be made to appear, the more radical the innovation, the more it can be related to selfish objectives of a particular state, and the more it offends widely shared and deeply felt values, the less persuasive it will be as precedent for others.

* * *

Doubts about a law-system which lacks judge and sheriff have, we think misleadingly, been frequently expressed as a theory of international law which describes it as a "voluntary" system based on the "consent" of "sovereign" states. It does not require much insight into law-politics to see a parallel between this theory and the consent theory of domestic government. Whatever the moral appeal of the consent theory at both levels (it represents a dislike for coercion), states "consent" to international prescriptions in the same sense that individuals "consent" to existing laws. They recognize the general need for a system of order, they regard the bulk of existing regulation as either desirable or at least tolerable, and they accept what remains because they have to—because they lack the ability to change it. The more intolerable a regulation is, the more pressure there is to seek a change by any means possible.

The point is not, of course, that legal institutions in the international community are adequate to contemporary affairs. Obviously they are not. But these institutions, such as they are, exist and contribute to international order. They will continue until some political combination has the capability to create new institutions more consonant with order and, we can at least hope, with a decent regard for human values. This creative process is presently taking place, on both a universal scale (the United Nations complex) and, perhaps more successfully, in a variety of regional and functional organizations such as NATO and the European Communities.

The authors recognize the merits of criticisms that distinguished observers such as George Kennan have made regarding too great a reliance upon legal processes. American foreign policy has often been formulated without sufficient attention to the role of force and of national interests. We do not wish to encourage naiveté of the sort he describes as "legal idealism," a reliance upon abstract rules that are institutionally unsupported. We concede that nations often do act in partisan ways in support of immediate political objectives. But we contend that much of international conduct is doctrinally consonant with normative standards, even though inconsistent with particular immediate interests, and that long-term self-interest can and does provide political support for internationally lawful conduct.

    * * *

———

Question. At this stage of your study are you willing to accept international law as law? Why or why not? In retrospect, does Chapter 1 have a positive, negative, or neutral influence on your attitude? If you do not consider at this point that international law is law, what is the minimum required to make it law?

    * * *

SCHACTER, PHILIP JESSUP'S LIFE AND IDEAS

80 American Journal of International Law 878, 890 (1986).*

Jessup's Ideas on International Law

In his long, productive life, Jessup expressed himself on virtually all of the major issues of contemporary international law. He did so mainly in articles, lectures and AJIL editorials, many of which were collected and published in books. He never produced a comprehensive treatise or a grand theory. Typically, he addressed specific current issues and that led him often into fundamentals. He felt impelled to rebut the skeptics who questioned the reality of international law and the nationalists who construed the country's interests in a narrow way. Jessup's responses to them were essentially pragmatic. He stressed the essential role of rules in the day-to-day business of world affairs; he pointed to the costs of disorder and conflict in the absence of law; he sought to show how law furthered the shared interests of states. In the same vein, he dealt with the meaning of rules and concepts, pointing out always how the issues bore on the interests of the governments and peoples concerned.

* Reprinted with the permission of the American Society of International Law.

His concern with the function of rules is evident particularly in his judicial opinions such as those in Barcelona Traction and the North Sea Continental Shelf Cases and in his writings on state responsibility.

Jessup's practicality led him to make numerous suggestions to improve the process of conflict resolution and the efficacy of international law. He did not disdain small, concrete proposals involving procedural changes or institutional arrangements. Broadly speaking, he was an incrementalist and he tended to be skeptical of grand projects to change the existing order. Experience rather than theory was his guide. * * *

However, his pragmatism was also imbued with a distinct teleological element. Like Elihu Root, his early mentor, Jessup saw the main trends of international society as part of an evolutionary development toward a more organized and effective legal order. The main features of that order could be briefly summarized as follows: recognition of the interest of the international community; protection of the basic rights of individuals; the prohibition of armed force except in self-defense; recourse to judicial procedures or conciliation for dispute settlement; the extension of international regulation and administration in areas of interdependence, global and regional. For Jessup, these ends appeared almost axiomatic. They described the direction in which the world had to move in its enlightened self-interest. The optimism of an earlier age and Jessup's own buoyant spirit are reflected in this outlook.

Jessup's theoretical assumptions were implicit in his analysis of specific issues. They could be characterized as a sophisticated blend of positivism, idealism and pragmatism. He was always careful to distinguish positive law—the *lex lata* —from proposed or predicted future law. At the same time, he was mindful that positive law included principles and concepts that expressed basic values and that these "received ideals" were authoritative guides in construing and extending existing rules. In this manner, his approach transcended strict positivism. It is well exemplified in The Modern Law of Nations. Concepts as general as the freedom of the seas, pacta sunt servanda, sovereign equality, the obligations of peaceful settlement, self-determination, equitable sharing, are among those persuasively used to infuse values into concrete decisions. Like a good practitioner, Jessup believed a stronger case for a new rule can be made by linking it to an established principle. He was also aware that broadly stated policies in legal instruments must be construed with regard to the consensus of the community on which their authority ultimately depends. The fact that social ends are plural and often conflict impressed him with the necessity for balancing competing considerations in reaching particular decisions.

* * *

Related to Jessup's conception of the international community was his notion of "transnational law," a term he did not invent but which was developed and popularized in his Storrs lectures of 1956. With that notion, Jessup sought to show the growing legal complexity of an interdependent world. The international legal realm could no longer be compartmentalized in its two classic divisions of public international law, applicable only to relations among states, and private international law, governing choice of law and enforcement of national judgments in cases involving nationals of two or more states. The legal rules and process applicable to situations that cut across national lines must now be sought in both public and private international law and, to a significant degree, in new bodies of law that do not fit into either traditional division. As examples of the latter, Jessup cited the growing areas of European Community law, maritime law, international administrative law, war crimes, the law of economic development and the rules applicable to multinational enterprises.

* * *

————

McDOUGAL, LASSWELL, REISMAN, THEORIES ABOUT INTERNATIONAL LAW: PROLOGUE TO A CONFIGURATIVE JURISPRUDENCE

8 Virginia Journal of International Law 188, 195 (1968).*

* * * The indispensable function of jurisprudence is to delimit a frame of reference appropriate to the study of the interrelations of law and community process and to specify in detail the intellectual tasks by which such study can be made and applied to the solution of the exigent problems it reveals. A jurisprudence of international law which would be relevant to the needs both of specialists in decision and of all who would understand and affect the processes in which they live must, accordingly, comprise a configurative approach, having at least three major characteristics:

1. It must be contextual, i.e., it must perceive all features of the social process of immediate concern in relation to the manifold of events comprising the relevant whole.

2. It must be problem-oriented.

3. It must be multi-method.

A jurisprudence aspiring to relevance must be contextual because the comprehensiveness and realism with which an observer conceives his major focus of attention—how he locates law in the community which it affects and is affected by—will determine how he conceives every detailed part of his study, his framing of problems, and his choice of tools for inquiry. It is only by a configurative examination of the larger context that an observer can be assured of extending his inquiry to all relevant variables and of being able to appraise the aggregate consequences of alternatives in decision. A relevant jurisprudence must be problem-oriented if it is to facilitate performance of the various intellectual tasks which confront all who are interested in the study of the interrelations of law and society, to avoid sterile inquiry into meaningless questions, and to contribute as creatively as possible to our institutions of public order in ways that promise to extricate us from the continuing destructive anarchy of our times. A relevant jurisprudence

* Reprinted with the permission of the Virginia Journal of International Law.

must be multi-method in order to promote mastery over all the necessary intellectual skills, to encourage the employment of strategies in the management of both authority and control, and to insure rationality of choice among alternatives in recommendation and decision.

It may require emphasis that a contextual, problem-oriented, multi-method jurisprudence of international law must provide for the systematic and disciplined performance of a series of distinguishable, but interrelated intellectual tasks. The appropriate specification of a comprehensive set of intellectual tasks, or skills, is important because it is the range of tasks performed, as well as the quality of performance which determines the relevance of inquiry for policy. The most deliberate attempts to clarify general community policy which do not at the same time systematically pursue other tasks, such as the description of past trends in decision and the analysis of factors affecting decision, may achieve only Utopian exercises. The description of past trends in decision, which is not guided by policy priorities and explicitly related to social processes, affords a most meager basis for drawing upon the wisdom of the past. The scientific study of factors affecting decision, which is not oriented by reference to problems in basic community policy, may be of no more than incidental relevance, despite enormous cost. The effort to predict future trends in decision by the mere extrapolation of past trends, without considering whether the factors that affect decision will remain the same, may produce destructive illusion rather than genuine forecast. In confusion about the character of, and appropriate procedures for, the different relevant intellectual tasks, the creativity in the invention and evaluation of policy alternatives, which is indispensable to rational decision, may be lost. The more specific intellectual tasks, for which a policy-relevant jurisprudence must make provision in theory and procedures, must thus include at least:

1. Clarification of the goals of decision;

2. Description of the trends toward or away from the realization of these goals;

3. Analysis of the constellation of conditioning factors that appear to have affected past decision;

4. Projection of probable future developments, assuming no influence by the observer;

5. Formulation of particular alternatives and strategies that contribute, at minimum net cost and risk, to the realization of preferred goals.

Adequate and sufficiently detailed performance of these various tasks in reference to the past, present and future of the various relevant social and decision processes of the world community must obviously require a comprehensive analytic framework which can bring into view the principal features of decision. A "conventional" analysis in terms of government organs and of the technical doctrines employed by officials, an effective technique for certain problems, is on the whole, inappropriate for the study of international decision. Conventional usage must yield to "functional" analysis if comprehensive and realistic orientation is to be achieved. No dependable relationship exists between a structure that is called "governmental" in a particular body politic and the facts of authority and control on the global scale. Analysts of comparative government are well aware of the discrepancy between convention and functional fact for the understanding of the legal and political process at the national or sub-national level, since it is not unusual to discover, for example, that the authority formally provided in a written constitutional charter may be ignored, or totally redefined by unwritten practice. Similarly, when the international arena is examined, the presumed congruence of formal and actual authority of intergovernmental organizations may or may not be sustained by the concurrence of expectations necessary to justify a claim of actual constitutive authority. On a wide range of matters, the principal nation-states may—and do—continue to perceive one another as unilaterally making the critical decisions, for which they accept, and reciprocally enforce, a substantial measure of responsibility.

The comprehensive analytic framework required must, accordingly, include a conceptual technique for delineating the relevant aspects for power and policy of any interpersonal interaction. This technique may be sought by first locating the decision—that is, choosing the phase at which a sequence of interactions appears to culminate in choices enforced by sanctions and deprivation or indulgence. The culminating phase may be organized or unorganized; for example, it may be a formal agreement or a fight, a vote or a combination of unilateral assertion and passive acquiescence. The questions that must be raised in an appropriate phase analysis cover the outcome, pre-outcome and post-outcome dimensions of the whole sequence:

1. Who acted or participated in roles of varying significance in the process which culminated in the decision? (*Participants*)

2. What were the significant perspectives of the participants? With whom were they identified? What value demands were they pursuing, with what expectations? (*Perspectives*)

3. Where and under what conditions were the participants interacting? (*Situations*)

4. What effective means for the achievement of their objectives were at the disposal of the different participants? (*Base Values*)

5. In what manner were these means or base values manipulated? (*Strategies*)

6. What was the immediate result—value allocation—of the process of interaction? (*Outcomes*)

7. What are the effects, of differing duration, of the outcome and process? (*Effects*)

It would, thus, appear that the goal criteria appropriate for the creation of a relevant jurisprudence of international law are entirely comparable to those which experience has demonstrated to be appropriate for national law. For the better appraisal of the potential contributions to a viable jurisprudence of our vast legacy of inherited theories about international law, it may be helpful to make more fully explicit certain goal criteria fashioned after those recommended today as appropriate for a jurisprudence of national law.

———

Questions about configurative jurisprudence. The founders of the Yale School of thought about international law have had influence on scholars and teachers, many of them their former students, both in the United States and to some extent abroad. The questions which follow are intended to focus your attention on your personal conception of international law.

What is the ideal professional training and experience for a decision-maker using configurative jurisprudence? Is law training in such jurisprudence enough? Is configurative jurisprudence advocated as a process or as a value-selection system? Or both? Is the lawyer's role expected to be the dominant one in the decision-making process? If so, is this in conformity with reality, considering that the vast majority of decisions about international law are made as a part of the foreign policy process in governments where, unlike in the United States, lawyers are treated as experts whose role is only to advise?

Jessup, whose views are discussed above, was a professor of international law, an ambassador, an undersecretary of state, and a judge on the International Court of Justice. The protagonists of configurative jurisprudence have not had much experience in non-legal roles in government operations. Do the different experience backgrounds of these lawyers and of Jessup give evidence of having influenced their respective philosophic outlooks about international law?

In other writings, the above three Yale School authors develop some fundamental attitudes that are identifiable in the excerpt under reference here. These include: (i) a rejection of norm-identification-application as the basic function of legal science and an emphasis on policy-choice processes; (ii) the ascription of a relatively low value to the ideal of universality as a goal of international law (such a goal would operate as a limiter of choice); (iii) strong emphasis in policy science of identifying and reinforcing by decision what are denominated as "common goal values", the most fundamental of which is that of human dignity. Are the above parts congruent, or are there inherent contradictions?

———

OLIVER, THE FUTURE OF IDEALISM IN INTERNATIONAL LAW: STRUCTURALISM, HUMANISM, AND SURVIVALISM

The Structure and Process of International Law: Essays in Legal Philosophy Doctrine and Theory 1207, 1208 (Macdonald & Johnston eds. 1983).*

* * *

* Copyright © 1983 Martinus Nijhoff Publishers, reproduced by permission of Kluwer Academic Publishers, Dordrecht, the Netherlands.

2. Idealism and the State of International Law Today

The thesis here is a simple one drawn from many examples in recent political and social history. When a situation or system decays—loses its effectiveness—it either dies or requires unusual social energy to revive it. Such unusual social energy requires mobilization of Purpose and Will. Such mobilization in our species requires an ethical, ennobling component. This component is Idealism, in some form.

It is all too evident that international law is in serious need of resuscitation today, not only in actual effectiveness but in the very expectation of its being able to be effective. Full proof of the degree of decline need not be offered here but the main point must be driven home, largely because it is so often denied or rejected by Idealists who, consciously or in a Freudian subconsciousness, will not face the facts that the *realpolitikers* are always willing to overstate. The truth of the matter is that, as every government international lawyer comes to realize, international legal structures and international legal rules are not in the practice of states treated as superior and ineluctable but as talking, arguing, and negotiating variables. It is always useful for a state to maintain credible "juridical cover" and to avoid—most but not all states think so—becoming an international scoff-law. The point here is not that law is a "variable in the power process" but that the value of fidelity to legal order is not an absolute value in international relations.

* * *

In any closed social system (a society), major value choices are political in their inception and legal order follows along to put these choices into effect. American international lawyers often tend to reverse this sequence, at least in terms of their own sense of mission, importance, and assumed competence (both in the jurisdictional and the capacity meanings). On the whole, United States academic international law scholars tend to expect to lead too much as to the value-choice process, rather than being willing to be technicians-after-the-fact of choice. As a result, their legalistic prescriptions for good (improvement, change, better structure, better principles) make less than expected impact on the politicians, national and international, who are ultimately in charge of making the choices (exercises of will and purpose). Thus in today's world we have significant segments of international legal scholarship that are often blind to the deterioration of international law, erroneously confident of competence to fashion the key to growth of what in fact is a semi-moribund science, this to the exclusion of all other cures, and thus widely divergent and combative as to essentials and priorities.

* * *

5. Survivalism: Idealistic or Inescapably Realistic?

Earlier references in this paper have indicated that notions of an irreducible minimum of structural and normative legal order are not widely professed within the academic branch of specialization in international law nor explicitly articulated by official spokespersons for the international legal outlooks of states. It is not difficult to understand these reticences. To too many among the scholars, the facts of degradation in international legal order and the seriousness of the ensuing crisis have simply not penetrated individual universes of perception, busy as each is with cherished projects, determined activism, and the like, from which each derives a degree of optimism that shuts off the unsatisfactory or the unthinkable. Scholars who are also sensitive teachers find it necessary to assure students that what they are studying is real and significant, either or both for the future as well as for now. Some of these also engage in deliberate self-encouragement that understates reality.

Practitioners of international law do not often have time for wide-sweeping reflection, and foreign offices are not given to philosophic disquisitions of an evaluative or programmatic nature. Practitioners tend to live from incident to incident, from crisis to crisis. * * * Another reason that a bed-rock minima approach has not widely appealed is the fear or belief that an imprecise line divides such outlooks from non-expectant, anti-legal *realpolitik*. * * *

A final reason is that a program for an international law of survival brings one immediately to fundamental needs that so far law has failed to regulate: the use of force in fact to achieve national goals; the insufficiency and impotence of legal controls over the first use, in any posture, of nuclear, chemical and bacteriological weapons (and what of laser/maser?); compulsory peaceful settlement of disputes by legal processes and substantive rules; some degree of obligatory sharing of planetary resources on the basis of need, ability to assist, and managerial competence; abolishment of the rule of vested rights to the first exploiter of earth's remaining non-appropriated areas, the moon and other celestial bodies; the provision of more and more assured means for individuals to complain internationally against states, particularly the one to which, willy nilly, they owe "allegiance." In all these instances, there is so far a marked lack of Will–Purpose among states and people who influence states for genuine achievement. Yet without the development first of Will–Purpose in these areas, it is not assured that many of the specific activities in which legal idealists engage will bring effective improvement in planetary conditions. Under these circumstances, the most basic question becomes: how is Will–Purpose to be generated as to a particular line of action through legal structure and normative regulation thereunder? The ultimate pessimist will say, "only after cataclysm." A somewhat more expectant realist will express the hope that, at the very verge of destruction, awareness will come in the nick of time and the whole experience will breed a resolution to ensure a system under which the imminent catastrophy cannot threaten again.

There is some slight evidence that some would risk neither cataclysm nor the brink but wish to revive attention to the fundamentals as a place to begin to build order anew. Expectation and determination (effective Idealism) will become essential to such revival, for there is much frustration and pessimism to be combatted. * * *

In as much as the basic necessity is to develop Will–Purpose, it is desirable to start with the fundamentals, hard to solve though they may be, for it is the vast, planetary mind that must be reached, and there is wider truth in Dr. Johnson's observation as to concentrating the mind than the mere certainty of being hanged in the morning.   The notion held by many peoples that they and the states over them are unable to influence outcomes as to the fundamentals—or some of them—needs response, including raising the question whether significant segments of the developing world are acting responsibly in focusing on certain issues of importance to them to the disregard of those of a planetary dimension.

Survivalism is ensuring survival. But it cannot be achieved, as in a lifeboat, by non-idealistic realism. It requires an Idealism about which it will be more difficult to be idealistic than many would like, thus making the task of commitment harder and perhaps less rewarding in terms of personal professional success. The Idealism required ought to be widely communicated in acceptable form for effectiveness outside professional circles. Not all academic international lawyers need be involved, but more than presently are should be. Professional international practitioners ought all to be involved, and the academics and the practitioners ought to improve their collaborations with each other and with other relevant professional groups. Perhaps it is the Idealism of a Sancho Panza not a Quixote that is needed. One recalls that Sancho not only said the windmills were not monsters but that he eventually became an acceptable governor of the island!

The first needs are not the only ones; they only must be met before others can be assured.

———

1. ***Questions about "norms".*** Are law persons (scholars, judges, practitioners) qualified, strictly on the basis of their professional training, to work well in "non-rule" situations?

The "Yale School", represented by the excerpts beginning on p. 1405 rejects norm-oriented approaches to legal participation in decision-making. But it articulates principles. What is the difference between a principle and, in Kelsenian terms, a norm?

Kelsen says that legal science is qualified to identify norms, scale them as to authoritativeness, interpret them, and apply them, but that it is not qualified to deal with value choices that lie outside the legal order. Do you agree or disagree? Do lawyers as a class self-limit their qualifications to norm-oriented processes?

In the United States, can it plausibly be argued that the lawyer class is qualified to deal professionally and competently with domestic value choices? With foreign affairs value choices?

2. ***General legal philosophy and legal philosophy about international law.*** General theories about law have had and are having influences on outlooks about international law. Notions of divine and secular natural law are at home in international law. So would be sociological jurisprudence if chief protagonists of the various schools of sociological jurisprudence (Savigny, Pound, et al.) had been concerned very much about international law. In a very broad and inexact sense,

the Yale School adapts old-fashioned sociological jurisprudence to the international arena. The logical positivists too, beginning with that nemesis for international law, John Austin, have given it their attention. Kelsenian philosophy about international law is inherently positivistic in origin and outlook. In fact, a good case can be made that international legal positivism has had a definite influence on general legal philosophy.

The neo-realism movement in American jurisprudence of the twenties and thirties did, especially through Professor Walter Wheeler Cook of Yale, bring private international law into its ambit of attention; but the legal philosophers of this sector did not focus on international public law to any significant degree. Their attention was captured by the judicial process within the United States and the need for sharper analyses, in part through sharper nomenclature, in stating and using American law. Their influence on international public law, nonetheless, has come through limited degrees of adoption of their outlooks by American international legal thinkers. Just as American neo-realism has not died, but has been absorbed into American thinking about internal law, it has come into American methodology about international law, especially as to Hohfeldian nomenclature. (It is very useful in the analysis of international legal situations to know the difference between a right, a privilege, and a power, for instance—or a duty as differentiated from a liability.) Less influential on American international legal philosophy has been the neo-realists' focus on the fact that judges sometimes consciously, more often unconsciously, mask the true reasons for their decisions behind rationalistic use of precedents and analogistic rationales. The reason for this invites fascinating speculations. Perhaps the fact that international law is not wholly American has something to do with it. However, recent criticisms of the judicial stances and methodologies of members of the International Court of Justice in connection with Nicaragua v. United States may also mark a wider willingness to address the matter.

Recently, a new wave of skeptical examination of law and the realities of power, the Critical Legal Studies movement, has aroused contention, and even furor, by its views about internal American law and international law. The Critical Legal Studies movement although still far from making its way into American law outlooks in the way the older neo-realism has. In many ways, international law is a more vulnerable target for the movement's attacks than internal law, because international law has fewer committed defenders and is structurally more vulnerable. For instance, one element of the less than cohesive Critical Legal Studies movement is "deconstruction", a process borrowed from literary criticism, which focuses on texts and analyzes them to show inherently self-cancelling internal contradictions. International law, alas, for a good deconstructor, would be an easy target! On the other hand, the movement is very suspicious of the masking of naked power behind law.

CRITICAL LEGAL STUDIES AND FEMINIST APPROACHES TO INTERNATIONAL LAW

Law, in a broad sense, is indeterminate. Proponents of critical legal studies argue * * * that every legal problem accommodates more than one viable solution and that policy determines the choice of which solution is adopted. Thus, politics forms the major component of law. Is this insight new or original? Like in the realm of literary criticism, the analytical method of deconstruction is utilized to study law.

KRAMER, LEGAL THEORY, POLITICAL THEORY, AND DECONSTRUCTION

238–239; 254–255 (1991).

Deconstructive theory, as a result of anticipating countercritiques and noting its own problems of incoherence, will position itself to seize on problems of incoherence that ravage countercritiques. Its power is made perfect in weakness, its own weakness. Because all critiques become implicated in what they censure, and because careful deconstructionist writing will have stayed keenly alert to both the general dissemination of paradoxes by transference and the specific maelstroms of many of its own paradoxes, our anticipating the countercritiques by helping them with their work may be the most adroit way to gain some leverage in deconstructing countercritiques. Complacent parries will highlight their own weak spots by fastening upon weak spots that have been highlighted in a deconstructionist discourse. At that point, where a deliberate nondefense has become the best defense, battles will be less over (in)coherency and elegiac than over competing ways in which incoherence can articulate itself. * * *

* * *

* * * [a]rguments will be framed in a vocabulary of 'struggles', 'tactics', 'disruption', and 'subversion' rather than 'truth' * * * Critical and legal force at a particular juncture, not illusive veracity, is the touchstone that guides our choices * * * [a] process of choosing that is based on strategic factors will partake of no fewer problems than a logocentric pursuit of Truth. In a process of either broad type, we shall have to undergo a fatal disquietude * * * Critical power and tactical adroitness must serve as one's leading goals, but the game in which one is strategizing will go on endlessly. One must try—always with a considerable degree of failure to attend carefully to the blindness that will be entailed by each one of one's insights * * *. [What must be] constantly kept in mind is a near-paralyzing tentativeness.

KENNEDY, A NEW STREAM OF INTERNATIONAL
LAW SCHOLARSHIP

7 Wis.L.Rev. 1 (1988). *

* * *

My project * * * [is], quite literally, to redraw some rather familiar territory, returning to some of the most basic materials of public international law to describe them in a somewhat novel way. Overall, my aspiration is to begin releasing the discipline of public international law from a constellation of images of law, politics and the state which seemed characteristic of the field as late as 1980. My sense is that some aspects of my method may seem strange at first. Let me finish * * * with a few precautions and clarifications which may be helpful. * * * Think of a traditional piece of contemporary international law scholarship. It might contain one or more of three types of argument: theoretical or historical justification, doctrinal description or elaboration, and programmatic or institutional recommendations.

The theoretical and historical work, whether developed to support or criticize particular doctrinal and institutional analyses, works to support the project of the field as a whole—indeed, takes that project for granted to resolve the problems it sets forth for the scholar. In seeking to displace this set of problems, I have taken a somewhat different approach to questions in history and theory. I have not looked to them as sources for the authority or wisdom or content for international law doctrine. Rather, I have looked at the discipline's history, and its sense of history, for clues to its general argumentative practice. In other words, I have treated stories about history and theories about "international law" and "sovereignty" as if they were simply doctrines.

Doctrinal work, moreover, whether supportive or critical of particular doctrinal interpretations, generally begins with a sense both of doctrine's independent coherence and of doctrine's authoritative origin in history or theory and normative bite in the culture of sovereign behavior. Doctrine, as normally considered in international law scholarship, gets its energy and motivation from its origin in sovereign accord, in history, or in theory. And it has its effects outside the realm of law, in practice or thought. I have not considered doctrine in this way. I do not analyze the relationship between international legal materials and their political and interpretive milieu. I am not concerned about the context within which arguments are made and doctrines developed.

I focus rather upon the relationships among doctrines and arguments and upon their recurring rhetorical structure. I trace the references which one doctrine makes to another and the repetitions which characterize doctrinal materials widely dispersed through the field as a whole. Setting aside issues of origin and meaning to discuss international law internally, as a self-sufficient rhetoric, encourages an often implausible attribution of moods, desires and affect to the rhetoric of law. I often will speak as if one doctrine "sought independence" from

* Reprinted with the permission of the
Wisconsin L.Rev.

another or "seemed uneasy" about its coherence. It might be useful to think of this project as a look at public international law from the *inside*.

Programmatic and institutional scholarship in the international field is generally preoccupied either with establishing an institutional form—with the doctrinal pragmatics of constitutional structure—or with implementing the resolution of doctrine and the wisdom of theory in the terrain of inter-sovereign activity. Scholars worry about capturing the functional relationship between institutions and states and the details of institutional design on paper. The discipline considers problems of situated and practical management rather than normative authority and application. But I do not follow this invitation to harness modernity's tone to the realm of institutional life. My work on international institutions treats the patterns of constitutional establishment and implementation as histories and doctrines. I am concerned to understand institutional life, even the professional life of the international legal scholar, as the enactment of a set of rhetorical maneuvers, as the living forth of doctrine and historiography.

Taken together, this methodological reformulation seeks to unify the historical, theoretical, doctrinal and institutional projects of the discipline. My method is to begin by focusing on argumentative patterns—patterns of contradiction and resolution, of difference and homology—which are reasserted in the materials of international law history, doctrine, and institutional structure. The project thus begins with a certain unsettling of the stability of differences both within and among the materials about international legal history, doctrine and institutions. Within the legal world I describe, stability—between what are now simply terms in a debate—needs to be explained solely *within* the debate itself. This means, for example, that sociological explanations of doctrine will be set aside in favor of accounts anchored solely within the materials of doctrine. It also means that the sociological contexts of international law—its institutions and history—need be reconceptualized in rhetorical terms. To do so, I have sought to develop close, anthropology-like accounts of the relations in particular bureaucratic settings of doctrine and institutional structure.

* * * I will seek a single optic—a single structural pattern which could be followed throughout the discipline. In this sense perhaps my effort will be too linear, too logical, and indeed, I am somewhat dissatisfied with the structural repetitiveness, the flat logical demeanor of my results. Perhaps it is only a way to begin the project of redrawing the discipline.

Later, * * *, it may be useful to think more systematically about ways to reinvigorate the project's specificity—by discussing its relationship to the margins of legal culture, to women, to the religious, to the impoverished, to the violent, to the sexual. One way of understanding this critical move to substance is as an attempt to reawaken—or capture, or, less kindly, exploit—the exotic margins of establishment culture. Indeed, the central contemporary reorientation of the relationship between law and politics—the claim that law is a restatement of its imaginary relationship to society—has been developed by bringing the margin (society) into the core of law, rather than trying to stabilize and relate one to the other.

I want to question the stability of both, and I think this desire might be responsible for political difficulties much contemporary critical legal scholarship has encountered with the left, the right and the center of legal academia. Without anchor, my vision might be pursued equally well by pushing law to the limit ("completing" the project of liberalism, finally enforcing rights, etc.) or by pushing society to the limit ("deconstructing" and historicizing liberalism, disaggregating rights, completing the project of the market). In this, of course, it refers us back to our image of law's origin and to the procedures of social transaction.

Nevertheless, most recently, I have been working to anchor this effort in a broader margin, for it seems that the entire rhetorical apparatus I have been contemplating—all of law and society—however fuzzy and uncertain, exists within and against another set of margins—a margin composed of things thought of as perversion, faith, eros, terror, chaos, tyranny, war, etc. These things are excluded from, distanced from international public culture exactly as society or political economy seemed to be distanced from law. They are treated as at once frightening and fascinating. And most importantly, they are treated as *real* things, capable of signification within public culture. * * *, I will reach out to these margins along what might be thought of as a rhetorical final frontier. * * *

Thinking about things this way suggests that we approach international law, institutions and even the state somewhat differently. When thinking about international law, we can set aside the obsession with its authority and independence. We can ease off the desire to demonstrate and enhance international law's normative drive and enforceability. To the extent "rights"—more rights, new rights, rights enforcement—has been the mechanism by which we imagine international law able to touch sovereign power, they might come to seem less central, less compelling, simply less interesting. The law of force would not be interesting as a system of weaponry rights, but as a vocabulary for state violence. The law of asylum would not be interesting as a struggle for the rights of refugees, but as a language of exclusion and difference.

ONUF, BOOK REVIEW: INTERNATIONAL LEGAL STRUCTURE
By David Kennedy, 83 A.J.I.L. 630 (1989).*

David Kennedy has undertaken a remarkable project—nothing less than a reconsideration of the development of international legal doctrine over several centuries.

* * *

What now can we say about the era after 1980, Kennedy's own? Obviously, it must depart from, or self-consciously repudiate, the hall-

* Reprinted with the permission of the American Society of Int'l Law.

marks of modernity. If modern authors disappear from their texts, it is because they want readers to think of those texts as transparent media. Thus, he argues, "Modern theory builds space for complacency in an expansive humility." After modernity, against this complacency, must come acknowledgment that texts are decisive. Modern texts work on behalf of proceduralized authority by employing the rhetorical strategy of self-effacement. Against this strategy must come a rhetoric of challenge and exposure.

The problem for a rhetoric against modernity is to find its proper voice. The voice of rectitude is primitive—too passionate for a modern, knowing world. The scornful voice is self-defeating, the voice of revolutionary abandonment unconvincing, the nostalgic voice meretricious, the Aquarian voice naive. The late modern voice of accommodation to criticism is escapist. Kennedy's own voice is unsure; his reticence lacks the "self-assurance" he finds in modernity's "theoretical structure of false humility." Kennedy's sensitivity to rhetoric effectively denies him a proper voice with which to confront modernity and launch a new era. Instead, he occupies a vantage point after modernity from which to look back on past eras. This is his stance in *International Legal Structure*. His long view permits him to see the structure of each era. More specifically, because these are eras in the development of doctrine, his focus is "upon the relationships among doctrines and arguments and upon their recurring rhetorical structure". "Structure" does not refer to some meta-textual, orienting feature of social reality, as the term usually connotes. Kennedy's interest is not "the relationship between international legal materials and their political and interpretive milieu". Nor is it "the meaning and distinctiveness of public international law doctrine". If rhetorical structure is all that counts, then we may be forgiven the inference that it alone grants law and society their meaning and distinctiveness. For Kennedy to say as much would be a greater challenge to modernity's smug conceits than he ever permits himself.

* * *

———

Feminist philosophers and lawyers have begun to approach international law from their own various perspectives. See Chapter 10 for feminist approaches to international human rights law. Consider the following overviews and perspectives.

KAREN ENGLE, INTERNATIONAL HUMAN RIGHTS AND FEMINISM: WHEN DISCOURSES MEET

13 Mich.J.I.L. 517, 518–21 (1982). *

In recent years, legal scholars have been embroiled in an intense debate about rights that has touched almost every area of domestic law. Controversy about the role and utility of rights discourse has been

* Reprinted with the permission of Mich. J.Int'l L.

especially fierce in areas generally identified with popular struggles, such as civil rights for minorities and women.

Surprisingly, international law has not been a target of rights critics. Even international human rights law, with its near total reliance on rights discourse and its intimate relationship with nongovernmental organizations and popular struggles, has remained largely untouched by the rights debate.

In this article, I bring some of the issues identified and discussed in domestic law into public international law, through an analysis of that area of human rights law pertaining to women. Although I am inspired by the domestic debate, my purpose here is not specifically to critique or defend rights. Rather, I explore the various ways that advocates of international women's rights have deployed, and at the same time critiqued, existing rights frameworks in order to achieve change for women. In doing so, I analyze the multiple roles that rights discourse plays in the advocacy of women's rights internationally.

The literature on women's human rights is a particularly rich site for an analysis of rights discourse deployment, because in this literature two different, and sometimes competing, models of rights converge. Although it might seem that international human rights law would naturally incorporate women's rights, since women are human, women's rights advocates have suggested that such incorporation cannot be assumed. While some maintain that women's rights are already included in international human rights law, others argue that the international human rights régime will have to change before it can take women into account. In either case, women's rights discourse is generally positioned at the periphery of human rights discourse, both challenging and defending the dominant human rights model as it attempts to fit its causes into that model. In this arena, filled with rights enumeration and rights talk, possibilities for conflicts between competing rights ensue. Examining how different women's rights advocates deal with those potential conflicts sheds light both on international rights discourse and on feminist approaches to law.

* * *

Feminists form one of the groups that has attempted to expand human rights, urging it to better encompass women's rights. Through their work, they have not only identified those international legal instruments that include provisions prohibiting sex discrimination, but they have also helped establish international legal instruments that pertain specifically to women's rights. Using the number of such instruments as a measure of progress, it would appear feminists' work has paid off: in 1986, Natalie Hevener identified twenty-two international documents relating to the status of women. Much of the work of women's rights advocates was realized during the United Nations Decade for Women, with the creation of the 1979 Convention on the Elimination of All Forms of Discrimination Against Women (Women's Convention). Although that Convention has only been open for signature since 1980, it already has been ratified by as many States as have ratified the International Covenant on Civil and Political Rights, and the International Covenant on Economic, Social and Cultural Rights.

As the number of legal instruments has increased, so has the scholarly literature on women's human rights. Before the Women's Convention, only a few works had been written about women's rights, but since then the number of works has skyrocketed.[11] Some of those written since the Women's Convention focus specifically on that Convention, while others deal generally with women's human rights. The Women's Convention, then, has both generated and reflected a renewed interest in women's human rights, as much as it has been the actual subject of discourse.

This article examines in detail much of the literature that has emerged on women's human rights since 1979,[12] identifying three broad approaches taken by women's human rights advocates. I have labeled these approaches doctrinalist, institutionalist, and external critique. Each represents a particular feminist approach to law as well as a specific approach to human rights discourse.

Regardless of the approaches they take, women's human rights advocates confront a difficult task in attempting to secure women's place in the international human rights framework. Explicitly or implicitly, they challenge traditional notions of human rights for failing to take women into account adequately. At the same time, though, they rely on international legal instruments and human rights law and language as vehicles for achieving women's equality. Thus, a tension emerges, an ambivalence about whether and how women's rights can become a part of human rights. This tension manifests itself through the approaches the advocates take.

Two approaches, doctrinal and institutional, work within the field of international human rights and use language internal to that discourse. Their proponents are, for the most part, liberal feminists who generally believe in the effectiveness of human rights legal doctrine and institutions. Advocates who take a third approach pose what I consider external critiques. They approach human rights discourse as feminists, generally radical or cultural feminists, who are troubled by the existence of a system that claims to protect the rights of all human beings while systematically excluding one-half of the human race.

Those taking the first two approaches advocate women's rights by interpreting and sometimes criticizing the existing doctrinal and institutional framework. Doctrinalists generally describe a specific problem

---

11. For a comprehensive bibliography of works dealing with international law regarding the status of women, see Rebecca J. Cook, Women's International Human Rights: A Bibliography, 24 N.Y.U.J.Int'l L. & Pol'y (forthcoming 1992); Rebecca J. Cook, Bibliography: The International Right to Nondiscrimination on the Basis of Sex, 14 Yale J.Int'l L. 161, 163–81 (1989).

12. The articles and books I examine comprise much of the English language literature in this area that does more than merely describe the provisions of international legal instruments that apply to women. The authors represent a variety of disciplines and several different countries. As I have explored this area I have been surprised by the lack of communication between people writing in this discipline. Few of the authors react to others who have written about similar problems before them.

facing women in some or all parts of the world and then show doctrinally how the problem constitutes an international human rights violation. Institutionalists critically examine international legal institutions that are created to enforce human rights. They study both mainstream human rights institutions and specialized women's institutions to determine whether and how they protect women's human rights.

I consider both of these approaches positivist since they generally rely on international legal doctrine and institutions to make their arguments.[15] Doctrinalists and institutionalists do not see themselves as approaching human rights law with any preconceptions about what rights should be derived from the instruments or enforced by the institutions. Doctrinalists, for example, extract particular rights from documents as if, were it not for the documents, the rights might not exist at all. The positive nature of the work of both groups evinces a general approach to human rights that sees women's rights as a normal part of human rights law and discourse, readily assimilable to the human rights model.

Those who take the third approach, rather than working within human rights discourse in its present form, critique the human rights framework either for being male-defined or -deployed, or for being based on inherently male concepts. These external critics aim to have what they see as women's human rights achieved, regardless of whether those rights exist in positive law. In doing so, they raise difficult questions about whether women's needs and rights can fit into the existing definition and conception of human rights. Thus, they are less likely than doctrinalists and institutionalists to see women's rights as assimilable to the human rights model. The views of external critics range from those who think human rights theory will only be fully consistent after it incorporates women's rights to those who think human rights theory must change and be reconceptualized in order to address successfully women's concerns.

The primary distinction between the first two approaches and the third approach, then, is that the first two assume and act upon the belief that women's rights have and can be assimilated to the human rights structure. The third approach, on the other hand, questions whether assimilation to the structure as it exists is possible. Advocates who take this latter approach tend to believe that the structure itself will have to change in order to accommodate women's rights.

---

15. I do not use positivism here in the way it is often used in public international law discourse. That is, by calling the approaches positivist, I do not mean to suggest that the advocates see doctrine and institutions as mere products of sovereign consent. To the extent, however, that they believe that international law is authoritative and that States are bound by it, particularly those States that have signed or ratified specific documents, their views are more traditionally positivist.

I primarily use the term positivism to highlight these advocates' use of positive law as the starting point from which they derive rights. I also use positivism to contrast the suggestion that rights only exist by virtue of their embodiment in particular documents with a theory of rights that relies on natural law for its basis. *But see* Martti Koskenniemi, From Apology to Utopia: The Structure of International Legal Argument 106–17 (1987) (discussing various meanings of positivism and displaying how in 19th century public international legal discourse—the "golden age of positivism"—those considered positivists commonly relied on naturalist notions and vice versa).

Whether their approach be assimilation or accommodation, all advocates encounter difficulties with making women's rights a part of human rights. Some of the difficulties are with human rights generally, while others are specific to women's rights. The recognition of these difficulties, however, does not lead any of the advocates to abandon human rights law or rhetoric. None of the advocates suggests that including women's rights would fundamentally disrupt the human rights régime. And none openly explores the possibility that women's rights and human rights might be incommensurable.

* * *

FERNANDO R. TESÓN, FEMINISM AND INTERNATIONAL LAW: A REPLY

33 Va.J.Int'l L. 647, 647–57; 664–68; 672; 677–684 (1993).*

* * *

Until recently international law had not undergone a sustained feminist critique. This gap is now slowly being filled; a notable contribution to that effort is a recent article by Hilary Charlesworth, Christine Chinkin, and Shelley Wright.

This Essay presents a reply to the Charlesworth–Chinkin–Wright critique. Although much of this reply engages more general issues in feminist theory, it would be impossible, within the scope of this work, to address every important political, cultural, biological, epistemological, and metaphysical issue raised by the various feminist critiques of traditional jurisprudence. I therefore confine the analysis to arguments directly relevant to international law, focusing on the analogies and contrasts between the differing feminist approaches to international law and the Kantian theory of international law defended in my previous writings.

The feminist critique of international law contains many disparate strands of theory that must be disentangled. A central difficulty with the article by Charlesworth and her associates is that it conflates divergent arguments from very different (and often irreconcilable) camps within feminist theory. The most important such mismatch is between liberal and radical feminism, which coexist in uneasy tension throughout the article. Much of the analysis in this essay is therefore devoted to separating, analyzing, and ultimately evaluating these interwoven but uncongenial threads of feminist thought.

In examining the liberal and radical feminist approaches to international law, as manifested in the Charlesworth article, I distinguish three different levels of criticism. The first level concerns the *processes* of international lawmaking, the second addresses the *content* of international law, and the third attempts to derive a critical theory from the (purported) "nature" or "inherent qualities" of liberal international

* Reprinted with the permission of Fernando Tesón and the Virginia J. Int'l L.

legal institutions. These critiques are treated differently, in complex ways, by radical and liberal feminism. Yet on all three critical dimensions, my conclusion is the same: although *liberal* feminism has important things to say about international law and relations, radical feminism is inconsistent both with the facts and with a view of international law rooted in human rights and respect for persons.

* * *

Liberal, or Kantian, international legal theory is founded on the idea of the individual as rational and autonomous. Liberal theorists regard individuals as capable of rational choices, possessed of inherent dignity, and worthy of respect. Liberal states in international relations, or members of the liberal alliance, are those nation-states with democratically elected officials, where human rights are generally respected. Liberal internationalism assumes a right to democratic governance, and holds that a state may not discriminate against individuals, including women. This principle is, of course, a centerpiece of the international law of human rights. A corollary of the Kantian thesis is that illegitimate governments may not be embraced as members of the liberal alliance.

Liberal feminists rely on liberal principles of domestic and international law to end abuses against women. Very succinctly, liberal feminism is the view that women are unjustly treated, that their rights are violated, and that political reform is needed to improve their situation, thereby allowing them to exercise autonomous choices and enjoy full equal status as free citizens in a liberal democracy. The governing international principles are the imperatives of human rights, nondiscrimination, and equal opportunity for women, as envisioned in articles 1(3), 8, and 55 of the United Nations Charter. When a state discriminates or deprives women of these human rights, it commits an injustice, a violation of international human rights law for which it is responsible.

Radical feminists agree with liberal feminists that the situation of women must be improved. They believe, however, that liberal institutions are themselves but tools of gender oppression, and that women are exploited by men in even the least suspecting ways. Radical feminists believe that existing states are hierarchically structured according to gender, and that gender hierarchy necessarily infects the process of legal reasoning itself. Radical feminists hold that the "actual choices" of women only *seem* to be autonomous and free; in reality they are *socially* determined. Human beings are not, as liberals would have it, separate, rational entities capable of individual decision-making, but rather beings to some degree defined and determined by their social—and particularly gender—relationships. Under radical feminist theory, no woman is truly free, not even in the "freest" of societies.

III. THREE FEMINIST CRITIQUES OF INTERNATIONAL LAW

In light of the differences in feminist theory it will be convenient to set forth three feminist critiques of international law, and the central claim associated with each: (A) the *processes* of international lawmaking exclude women; (B) the *content* of international law privileges men to the detriment of women; and (C) international law, as a patriarchal institution, *inherently* oppresses women, marginalizes their interests, and submerges their experiences and perspectives.

* * *

Feminists criticize the international lawmaking process for depriving women of the access and opportunity to take part in lawmaking in two important ways. First, feminists argue that women are *underrepresented* in international relations, that is, in high positions in international organizations, in diplomatic services, and as heads of state and government. Second, they contend that because of this underrepresentation, the *creation* of international law is reserved almost exclusively to men. Women are thus effectively prevented from participating in the processes of international lawmaking.

Central to the claim of exclusion is the fact that women are underrepresented in international relations. There is no doubt that there are relatively few women heads of state, diplomats, or international organizations officials. Is this state of things, however, an injustice? And how can the statistical underrepresentation (whether or not it is an injustice) be redressed? It is useful, in addressing these issues, to distinguish, first, between legitimate and illegitimate governments, and second, between governments and international organizations.

Let us consider first the case of illegitimate, undemocratic governments. Plainly, it does not make sense to criticize a dictator, say, for not appointing enough women to his government or diplomatic corps. To do so would constitute a contextual *category* mistake: blaming a dictator who has taken and held power by means of torture and murder for not appointing a woman as ambassador to the United Nations is like blaming a burglar ransacking our home at gunpoint for not having asked our permission to use the telephone. The normative context of a burglary is one in which it does not make sense to insist on compliance with the norms of courtesy. Likewise, the normative context of a tyrannical state is one in which it does not make sense to ask the tyrant to appoint more women (or men, or blacks, or Catholics).

In such a case, the government is illegitimate in the first place, so its appointments are morally invalid regardless of the sex of the appointees. If an illegitimate government consists of a group of men systematically excluding women, this is of course an injustice, but it is one that is subordinated to the greater injustice of tyranny, which by definition includes the illegitimacy of origin and the violation of human rights. It is true that discriminating against women aggravates the injustice of tyranny; it therefore makes sense to put pressure on all governments to refrain from sexist practices. The analysis, however, does not work the other way round: tyranny is not cured by the tyrant's celebration of diversity, as it were. Even in cases where human rights abuses (other than exclusion from government) are primarily directed at women, suggesting that what we need is more women as international representatives of dictators is absurd on its face. The only remedy, here as elsewhere, is to get rid of the tyrants and secure human rights.

Put differently, in a tyrannical state the *agency* relationship between people and government, the vertical social contract, has broken down * * *. Therefore, the tyrant cannot legitimately address the question of the sex of his political appointees because he does not represent anybody. The women he decides to appoint to office to achieve gender balance are likewise blighted by the original illegitimacy. A partial reply to the complaint by Charlesworth and her associates about women being underrepresented in international relations, then, is that it is not sensible to start addressing that issue globally without addressing also the issue of democratic legitimacy.

More interesting is the case of full members of the liberal alliance, states with democratically elected officials where human rights are generally respected. Assuming a right to democratic governance, a state may not discriminate against women in their exercise of that right. The governing principle, then, is the imperative of nondiscrimination and equal opportunity for women, along the lines suggested by the pertinent international instruments, themselves inspired in articles 1(3), 8, and 55 of the U.N. Charter. * * *

Radical feminists, however, seem to believe that there is a global injustice even where, as a result of democratic elections held in independent, rights-respecting states, it is mostly men who are elected to government, or if in such states mostly men *traditionally* seek admission to the diplomatic service. An example is the discussion by Charlesworth and her associates of the Women's Convention. They strongly criticize the Convention for assuming that men and women should be treated alike, which is the liberal outlook. The Charlesworth view is that sexism is "a pervasive, structural problem." Further, it is male dominance which lies at the root of the structural problem and which must be addressed as a means to reach the structural issues. But what are the authors' suggestions? If we descend from the abstract slogan that liberal equality is just the men's measure of things, how do they suggest rewriting each of the rights recognized by the Convention to meet their concerns? Take article 7, for example, which directs states to eliminate all discrimination against women in the political and public life of the country. Would a radical feminist's rewriting of this article require states to appoint women, regardless of popular vote? Would it impose a 50% gender quota for elected positions, or force women who do not want to run for office to do so? These are not just rhetorical questions: given the radical feminists' rejection of rights discourse and formal political equality, it is difficult to imagine what a radical list of international women's rights would look like.

* * * [I]nternational law cannot go beyond mandating democratic governance and nondiscrimination in a general way. Local conditions will vary, and in states where women have been previously excluded from politics it may be permissible and desirable to adopt preferential electoral arrangements. Such measures, when properly tailored, do not do violence to the international law principle of nondiscrimination and the right of all citizens to participate in public life. * * *

* * *

In addition to criticizing the processes of international lawmaking, many feminists argue that the content of international law privileges men to the detriment of women. The claim that the content of international law favors the interests of men may incorporate either or both of the following arguments: first, international law rules in general are "gendered" to privilege men; and second, international rules such as sovereign equality and nonintervention protect states, and states are instrumental in disadvantaging or oppressing women. * * *

* * * I find little plausibility in the claim of some feminists that the specific content of international law rules systematically privileges men. Positive international law is a vast and heterogeneous system consisting of principles, rules, and standards of varying degrees of generality, many of a technical nature. Rules such as the principle of territoriality in criminal jurisdiction, or the rule that third states should in principle have access to the surplus of the entire allowable catch of fish in a coastal state's exclusive economic zone are not "thoroughly gendered" but, on the contrary, gender-neutral. It cannot be seriously maintained that such norms operate overtly or covertly to the detriment of women. The same can be said of the great bulk of international legal rules.

* * *

Feminists are correct, however, on their second claim that international law overprotects states and governments. International law, as traditionally understood, is formulated in exaggeratedly statist terms. Statism, the doctrine that state sovereignty is the foundational concept of international law, repudiates the central place accorded to the individual in any liberal normative theory; and, by extension, it often results in ignoring the rights and interests of women within states. This criticism is identical to the one made by the Kantian theory of international law.

* * *

[R]adical feminists also attack liberalism. Insofar as this attack is predicated on the perception that liberal philosophy and the liberal state oppress women, it must be met with a philosophical and political defense of the liberal vision. But if the feminist attack on liberalism is predicated on the belief that statism, as an assumption of international law, is necessarily entailed by liberalism, the answer is simply that this is a mistaken inference. Statism is at odds with liberalism. The human rights theory of international law (certainly the most liberal international legal theory) rejects statism because it protects illegitimate governments and is thus an illiberal theory of international law. The whole point of the liberal theory of international law is to challenge absolute sovereignty as an antiquated, authoritarian doctrine inhospitable to the aspirations of human rights and democratic legitimacy.

Liberal feminism and the Kantian theory of international law join in rejecting statism. Indeed, one of the most valuable contributions of feminist international legal theory is the attempt to disaggregate states, to pierce the sovereignty veil and inquire about real social relations, relations among individuals and between individuals and government within the state. This is also the thrust of the Kantian theory of international law.

* * *

Both radical and liberal feminists generally agree that the statist orientation of traditional international legal theory tends to the detriment of women. A truly liberal theory of international law, on the Kantian model, rejects statism as impermissibly solicitous of rights violations by states, and unresponsive to the justified claims of all persons, including women, to dignity and equal treatment. The rejection of statism entails scrutiny not only of the official acts of states, but also of their complicity and even omissions in the protection of human rights. The notion that liberalism entails statism is therefore misconceived; the logic of liberal internationalism requires that international law limit absolute sovereignty to improve the situation of women, insofar as women remain deprived of equal respect and dignity.

* * *

[Radical feminists claim] that international law is inherently oppressive of women. Some feminists argue that because current international law derives from European, male, liberal legalism, its very form and structure are inherently patriarchal and oppressive.

[Several] radical feminists argue that states are inherently patriarchal entities—again, bothering little with distinctions between liberal and illiberal governments. Perhaps radical feminists believe that the governments of liberal democracies are, to paraphrase Marx, mere committees to handle the interests of men. If an interest of men were to secure the continuing oppression of women, and if the state were now and forever a property of men, then the international law principles of sovereign equality and nonintervention would indeed operate systematically to the detriment of women. Of course, under these assumptions no truly legitimate state or government currently exists; all appear in this light as simply men's devices to perpetuate their domination of women. Under this view, states are patriarchal entities; governments (even formally democratic ones) represent the male élites of those entities; and international law abets this tyranny by securing the sovereignty of states. These assertions hold true—equally true—for all states.

It is significant, in this regard, that Charlesworth and her associates do not emphasize violations of women's rights by particular governments, even though in many countries women are *officially* discriminated against, and sometimes even horribly mutilated with official endorsement or complicity. This omission is related, I believe, to the inherent oppressiveness thesis. Identifying and opposing egregious human rights practices simply holds less *philosophic* interest for the radical feminist than unmasking patriarchal oppression as a pervasive (albeit often "invisible") evil. * * * Their obsession with male dominance leads [these] radical feminists to the grotesque proposition that the oppression of women is as serious in liberal democracies as in those societies that institutionally victimize and exclude women. For feminists to try to improve the condition of women in even the freest societies is a commendable goal, since liberal democracies are not free of sexist practices. This is very different, however, from claiming that liberal democracies and tyrannical states are morally equivalent in the way they treat women. Such an assertion not only perverts the facts; it does a disservice to the women's cause.

The sweeping radical thesis that states are inherently oppressive is not only politically counterproductive, but also philosophically untenable. The assertion that a social arrangement is unjust or oppressive is contingent; it depends not only on the theory of justice that is presupposed, but on the facts as well. "Oppression" does not follow from the definition of "state"; it is not therefore inherent in the social organization we know as the modern state. Oppression may be defined as occurring when an individual or a group unjustly prevents others from exercising choices, and this may or may not occur in a particular case. Viewing oppressiveness as a necessary rather than contingent property of states is undoubtedly an epistemological convenience for the radical; there is no need to bother with scrutinizing the political practices of *actual* states. Unfortunately, the product of this sort of inquiry can be nothing more than nominalism: metaphysics in, metaphysics out.

* * *

The inherent oppressiveness thesis is connected with a radical notion of social determinism; that notion, too, admits of no degree or gradation, and lies beyond dispute. For at least some radical feminists there may be a possible *future* world in which women will be emancisocieties (the Western liberal democracies) where most choices by women are apparently autonomous in the liberal sense, radical feminists insist either that such choices are not really autonomous because women have been socialized to make them, or that there is no such thing as autonomy anyway. Indeed, even consensual sexual intercourse is regarded by some of them as oppressive. Accordingly, every social fact is interpreted in the light of this premise, which is itself immune to challenge. Like Marxists before them, radical feminists see their theory of gender oppression and hierarchy confirmed in every single social event, for the good reason that no single fact counts as a counterexample. No improvement in women's condition counts. * * *

So the sweeping definition of the state as inherently oppressive of women is, in my view, factually false because there are or could be states where women are not oppressed, and morally irresponsible because it trivializes tyranny. States come in many moral shapes. In some states women are oppressed; in some others blacks are oppressed; whites are persecuted in a few; in yet other states members of a particular religion, speakers of a certain language, or foreigners may be mistreated; and in some states almost everyone is oppressed. The radical feminist's insistence on the inherent oppression of women by the state succeeds only in blurring the distinction between freedom and tyranny, * * *

* * * Radical feminists align liberal autonomy with a conception of the family as a Dantésque place where the physically stronger husband victimizes weaker family members. Calling wife abuse an instance of

"family autonomy" is as offensive as calling Saddam Hussein's genocide of the Kurds [or the Marsh Arabs] an instance of Iraqi "self-determination." Family autonomy is the least liberal part of the "liberal" theory that radical feminists believe they are challenging. * * * Genuine liberal theory refuses to tolerate a private domain in which the strong can victimize the weak with impunity.

* * *

Radical feminists * * * ignore, disparage, or assume away the actual choices of women when it is convenient for them to do so; for example, the choice of some women to stay in the home. Because radical feminists believe homemakers' choices to be degrading, they conclude that those are not real choices, but are rather forced by socialization. Leaving aside the disdain for family, motherhood, and heterosexuality associated with this claim, the form of argument itself is highly suspect. One cannot just pick those choices that one approves of ideologically as being "real" choices, and discount those that do not fit our preferred utopia as merely "apparent." From a Kantian standpoint, there is an imperative to respect people's rational, autonomous choices. If the individual's autonomy has been impaired by coercion or fraud, then of course it will not be a real choice in the Kantian sense. Absent coercion or fraud, however, the choice of a homemaker to devote herself to the family ought to be valued and honored.

* * *

IV.   CONCLUSION: DEFENDING THE LIBERAL VISION

Legal theory has been much enriched by feminist jurisprudence. Feminists have succeeded in drawing attention to areas where uncritically received legal theories and doctrines have resulted in injustices to women. International law should be no exception, and the contribution of Charlesworth and her associates will rightly force international lawyers to re-examine features of the international legal system that embody, actually or potentially, unjust treatment of women.

Much of the radical critique is commendably compatible with a committed liberal feminism. For example, radical feminists are correct to urge international organizations to try to achieve gender balance in their internal appointments. Radical feminists are also right in challenging statism and a notion of "family autonomy" that countenances state complicity or inaction in the face of mistreatment of women by private individuals. Privacy and state sovereignty must be wedded to democratic legitimacy and respect for individual human rights, including the rights of women. All of these goals are easily justified under the Kantian theory of international law.

Yet the basic assumptions of the radical feminist critique are untenable and must be rejected with the same energy and conviction that we reserve for the rejection of other illiberal theories and practices. Radical feminism exists at a remove from international reality because it exempts itself, by philosophical fiat, from critical examination and empirical verification. It wrongly assumes that *oppression* belongs to a category of thought accessible to pure philosophic speculation, and thus renders scrutiny of real human rights practices superfluous. Perhaps most ominously, radicalism "unprivileges" the imperatives of objectivity, placing the demands of intellectual integrity and responsible political dialogue on a normative par with other, more political agendas.

When we move from the philosophical domain to global political realities, there is even more reason to resist the radical feminist agenda. Radical feminists have joined other radicals in attacking liberalism; indeed, their whole case rests upon the supposed bankruptcy of liberal society, on the moral inadequacy of the kind of civil society mandated by the Kantian theory of international law. But is the oppression of women correlated to liberal practices? The answer is, emphatically, "no." The feminist claim that male domination is an inherent part of liberal discourse and that liberal institutions are therefore inevitably oppressive of women is both politically counterproductive and patently false.

The truth is that the situation of women is immeasurably better in liberal societies, Western or non-Western. The most sexist societies, in contrast, are those informed and controlled by *illiberal* theories and institutions. These societies are much more exclusive of women than liberal societies (and most of the Western societies are liberal). Thus, naive assertions such as that "decisionmaking processes in [non-Western] societies are every bit *as exclusive* of women as in Western societies" merely reflect the warped starting premise that free societies and tyrannical ones are, in some "deep" reality, morally equivalent. As we have seen, this sort of "depth" only obscures. The failure to reckon with the facts on record by those claiming to be concerned with the plight of women amounts to serious moral irresponsibility.

The situation of women in liberal societies plainly reveals that liberalism has not yet fulfilled its promise to women of equal dignity. Liberalism is an ideal only partially realized, and its progress can at times seem painfully slow. Yet notwithstanding its imperfections, liberalism remains the most humane and progressively transformative system of social organization known to our time. Its aspiration to universal human flourishing is worthy; its principles of respect, equal treatment, and human dignity are sound. The great, pervasive injustices of the present arise not from liberalism, but from illiberal alternatives, and, sometimes, from the lack of resolve to press the liberal vision to its ultimate resolution. Those who would dispirit that resolve, even while wrapped in banners of liberation, deserve our most wary and searching scrutiny.

SECTION B. MONISM & DUALISM

---

1 O'CONNELL, INTERNATIONAL LAW 38 (2D ED. 1970) *

The Theory of the Relationship: Monism and Dualism

Almost every case in a municipal court in which a rule of international law is asserted to govern the decision raises the problem of the

* Reprinted with the permission of Stevens & Sons, Ltd., London.

relationship of international law and municipal law; and in many cases before international tribunals it must also be disposed of when deciding the jurisdictional competence of a State to affect alien interests through its own internal legal order.

There are four possible attitudes towards the question:

(a) That international law has primacy over municipal law in both international and municipal decisions. This is the *monist* theory.

(b) That international law has primacy over municipal law in international decisions, and municipal law has primacy over international law in municipal decisions. This is the *dualist* theory.

(c) That municipal law has primacy over international law in both international and municipal decisions. This is a species of monism in reverse.

(d) That there should be no supposition of conflict between international law and municipal law.

(a) Monism

The monist position is an emanation of Kantian philosophy which favours a unitary conception of law. According to this view, since the capacities of States derive from the idea of law, the jurisdiction to exercise these capacities is granted by the law. It follows that the law to which jurisdictional reference must be made is independent of sovereignty and determinative of its limits. If a State exceeds the limits, its acts are invalid. This argument concedes to international law a broader and more fundamental competence than to municipal law. However, it tends to sidestep the point made by the dualists, namely, that a municipal court may be instructed to apply municipal law and not international law, and hence has no jurisdiction (using the term as descriptive of the capacity in municipal law to decide a case) to declare the relevant municipal law invalid. Hence, the characterisation of the jurisdictional excess as "invalid," or even merely "illegal" (if there is any difference between the terms), is of no meaning internally within the municipal law of the acting State. To this objection, the monist has only one answer, that this conflict of duties, owing to a defect in organisation, has been wrongly resolved.

* * *

(b) Dualism

The dualist position is associated with Hegelianism and has governed the judicial attitudes of States where this philosophy has prevailed. The common starting point is the proposition that law is an act of sovereign will, municipal law being differentiated from international law in that it is a manifestation of this will internally directed, as distinct from participation in a collective act of will by which the sovereign undertakes obligations with respect to other sovereigns. This results in a dualism of legal origin, of subjects and of subject matters. International law and municipal law are two quite different spheres of legal action, and theoretically there should be no point of conflict between them. Municipal law addresses itself to the subjects of sovereigns, international law to the sovereigns themselves. If the sovereign by an act of municipal law exceeds his competence in international law it does not follow that municipal law is void; it merely follows that the sovereign has violated international law. Anzilotti has explained the relationship between the dualist thesis and the alleged incapacity of the individual in international law as follows:

> A rule of international law is by its very nature absolutely unable to bind individuals, i.e., to confer upon them rights and duties. It is created by the collective will of States with the view of regulating their mutual relations; obviously it cannot therefore refer to an altogether different sphere of relations. If several States were to attempt the creation of rules regulating private relations, such an attempt, by the very nature of things, would not be a rule of international law, but a rule of uniform municipal law common to several States.

(c) Inverted monism

The theory that municipal law is in its nature superior to international law has never found favour in international tribunals, and is no more than an abstract possibility. It is associated with Bergbohm, whose almost pathological resentment against natural law led to an exaggerated emphasis on the State will. Unlike Austin, who would deny even the term "law" to international law and thereby avoid a potential collision of two systems, Bergbohm allows for international law as a manifestation of the "auto limitation" of the sovereign will. The State is superior to and antecedent to the international community, and remains the only law-making entity. Unlike Triepel, who would distinguish the State will as internally manifested from the State will as externally manifested, Bergbohm allows for only one manifestation, and international law is thus a derivation from municipal law.

(d) The theory of harmonisation

According to this view, neither the monist nor the dualist position can be accepted as sound. Each attempts to provide an answer, derived from a single theoretical premise, to two quite different questions. The first question is whether international law is "law" in the same sense as municipal law, i.e., whether both systems are concordant expressions of a unique metaphysical reality. The second question is whether a given tribunal is required by its constitution to apply a rule of international law or municipal law, or vice versa, or authorised to accord primacy to the one over the other. The resemblance between the two questions is only apparent; the lack of jurisdiction in a given tribunal to accord primacy to international law in the event of a conflict between it and municipal law has no relevance to the question whether municipal law does or does not derive its competence from the same basic juridical reality as international law. In some federal systems of law, a State court may be required to apply state legislation which a federal court would declare unconstitutional. The norms of reference are different but the systems are concordant.

The starting point in any legal order is man himself, considered in relation to his fellow man. Law, it has often been said, is life, and life is law. The individual does not live his life exclusively in the legal order of the State any more than he lives it exclusively in the international order. He falls within both jurisdictions because his life is lived in both. Here again, the comparison with a federal system is instructive. It follows that a monistic solution to the problem of the relationship of international law and municipal law fails because it would treat the one system as a derivation of the other, ignoring the physical, metaphysical and social realities which in fact detach them. The world has not yet reached that state of organisation where there is only one civitas maxima delegating specific jurisdiction to regional administrations.

But a dualist solution is equally deficient because it ignores the all-prevailing reality of the universum of human experience. States are the formal instruments of will for the crystallisation of law, but the impulse to the law derives from human behavior and has a human goal. Positive international law is not pure whim, but an expression of needs and convictions. If it were otherwise, international law and municipal law would be competitive regimes ill-suited to the solution of human problems. The correct position is that international law and municipal law are concordant bodies of doctrine, each autonomous in the sense that it is directed to a specific, and, to some extent, an exclusive area of human conduct, but harmonious in that in their totality the several rules aim at a basic human good.

Questions about monism and dualism. What do you think about this: are these terms descriptive merely of what a particular state does with international law in its own courts and agencies, or do they have direct relevance to the fundamental question whether international law is law? Review Chapters 1 and 14 and take a position as to whether the United States is properly classifiable as evidencing a monist or a dualist state philosophy. If a federal state has in its constitution a provision that rules of customary international law prevail over state of the union law and constitutions, is that federal state necessarily monist? If any state, federal or unitary, has in its constitution a provision that rules of customary international law prevail over any national law, is that state necessarily monist?

SECTION C. PRINCIPLES, PRACTICE
AND LEGITIMACY

A final question on theory. What do you see as the greatest need for the effectiveness of the international legal system today? Acceptance? Structure? Rule, scope and precision? Methodology? Essentiality? Commonality of values? Other?

FRANCK, LEGITIMACY IN THE INTERNATIONAL SYSTEM

82 A.J.I.L. 705 (1988) [a]

The surprising thing about international law is that nations ever obey its strictures or carry out its mandates. This observation is made not to register optimism that the half-empty glass is also half full, but to draw attention to a pregnant phenomenon: that most states observe systemic rules much of the time in their relations with other states. That they should do so is much more interesting than, say, the fact that most citizens usually obey their nation's laws, because the international system is organized in a voluntarist fashion, supported by so little coercive authority. This unenforced rule system can obligate states to profess, if not always to manifest, a significant level of day-to-day compliance even, at times, when that is not in their short-term self-interest. The element or paradox attracts our attention and challenges us to investigate it, perhaps in the hope of discovering a theory that can illuminate more generally the occurrence of voluntary normative compliance and even yield a prescription for enhancing aspects of world order. * * *

Legitimacy is used here to mean that quality of a rule *which derives from a perception on the part of those to whom it is addressed that it has come into being in accordance with right process.* Right process includes the notion of valid sources but also encompasses literary, socio-anthropological and philosophical insights. The elements of right process that will be discussed below are identified as affecting decisively the degree to which any rule is perceived as legitimate. * * *

A series of events connected with the role of the U.S. Navy in protecting U.S.-flagged vessels in the Persian Gulf serves to illustrate the paradoxical phenomenon of uncoerced compliance in a situation where the rule conflicts with perceived self-interest. Early in 1988, the Department of Defense became aware of a ship approaching the gulf with a load of Chinese-made Silkworm missiles en route to Iran. The Department believed the successful delivery of these potent weapons would increase materially the danger to both protected and protecting U.S. ships in the region. It therefore argued for permission to intercept the delivery. The Department of State countered that such a search and seizure on the high seas, under the universally recognized rules of war and neutrality, would constitute aggressive blockade, an act tantamount to a declaration of war against Iran. [If] the delivery ship and its cargo of missiles were allowed to pass. Deference to systemic rules had won out over tactical advantage in the internal struggle for control of U.S. policy.

Why should this have been so? In the absence of a world government and a global coercive power to enforce its laws, why did the U.S. Government, with its evident power to do as it wished, choose to "play

a. Reprinted by permission, American Society of International Law. Much of this material also appears in Franck, The   Power of Legitimacy Among Nations (New York, 1990).

by the rules" despite the considerable short-term strategic advantage to be gained by seizing the Silkworms before they could be delivered? Why did preeminent American power defer to the rules of the sanctionless system? At least part of the answer to this question, quietly given by the State Department to the Department of Defense, is that the international rules of neutrality have attained a high degree of recognized legitimacy and must not be violated lightly. Specifically, they are well understood, enjoy a long pedigree and are part of a consistent framework of rules—the *jus in bello*—governing and restraining the use of force in conflicts. To violate a set of rules of such widely recognized legitimacy, the State Department argued, would transform the U.S. posture in the gulf from that of a neutral to one of belligerency. That could end Washington's role as an honest broker seeking to promote peace negotiations. It would also undermine the carefully crafted historic "rules of the game" applicable to wars, rules that are widely perceived to be in the interest of all states. * * *

Four elements—the indicators of rule legitimacy in the community of states—are identified and studied in this essay. They are *determinacy, symbolic validation, coherence* and *adherence* (to a normative hierarchy). To the extent rules exhibit these properties, they appear to exert a strong pull on states to comply with their commands. To the extent these elements are not present, rules seem to be easier to avoid by a state tempted to pursue its short-term self-interest. This is not to say that the legitimacy of a rule can be deduced solely by counting how often it is obeyed or disobeyed. While its legitimacy may exert a powerful pull on state conduct, yet other pulls may be stronger in a particular circumstance. The chance to take a quick, decisive advantage may overcome the counterpull of even a highly legitimate rule. In such circumstances, legitimacy is indicated not by obedience, but by the discomfort disobedience induces in the violator. (Student demonstrations sometimes are a sensitive indicator of such discomfort.) The variable to watch is not compliance but the strength of the compliance pull, whether or not the rule achieves actual compliance in any one case.

Each rule has an inherent pull power that is independent of the circumstances in which it is exerted, and that varies from rule to rule. This pull power is its index of legitimacy. For example, the rule that makes it improper for one state to infiltrate spies into another state in the guise of diplomats is formally acknowledged by almost every state, yet it enjoys so low a degree of legitimacy as to exert virtually no pull towards compliance. As Schachter observes, "some 'laws,' though enacted properly, have so low a degree of probable compliance that they are treated as 'dead letters' and * * * some treaties, while properly concluded, are considered 'scraps of paper.'" By way of contrast, we have noted, the rules pertaining to belligerency and neutrality actually exerted a very high level of pull on Washington in connection with the Silkworm missile shipment in the Persian Gulf.

Perhaps the most self-evident of all characteristics making for legitimacy is textual *determinacy*. What is meant by this is the ability of the text to convey a clear message, to appear transparent in the sense that one can see through the language to the meaning. Obviously, rules with a readily ascertainable meaning have a better chance than those that do not to regulate the conduct of those to whom the rule is addressed or exert a compliance pull on their policymaking process. Those addressed will know precisely what is expected of them, which is a necessary first step towards compliance.

To illustrate the point, compare two textual formulations defining the boundary of the underwater continental shelf. The 1958 Convention places the shelf at "a depth of 200 meters or, beyond that limit, to where the depth of the superjacent waters admits of the exploitation of the natural resources of the said areas." The 1982 Convention on the Law of the Sea, on the other hand, is far more detailed and specific. It defines the shelf as "the natural prolongation of * * * land territory to the outer edge of the continental margin, or to a distance of 200 nautical miles from the baselines from which the breadth of the territorial sea is measured," but takes into account such specific factors as "the thickness of sedimentary rocks" and imposes an outermost limit that "shall not exceed 100 nautical miles from the 2,500 meter isoba," which, in turn, is a line connecting the points where the waters are 2,500 meters deep. The 1982 standard, despite its complexity, is far more determinate than the elastic standard in the 1958 Convention, which, in a sense, established no rule at all. Back in 1958, the parties simply covered their differences and uncertainties with a formula, whose content was left in abeyance pending further work by negotiators, courts, and administrators and by the evolution of customary state practice. The vagueness of the rule did permit a flexible response to further advances in technology, a benefit inherent in indeterminacy.

Indeterminacy, however, has costs. Indeterminate normative standards not only make it harder to know what conformity is expected, but also make it easier to justify noncompliance. Put conversely, the more determinate the standard, the more difficult it is to resist the pull of the rule to compliance and to justify noncompliance. Since few persons or states wish to be perceived as acting in obvious violation of a generally recognized rule of conduct, they may try to resolve the conflicts between the demands of a rule and their desire not to be fettered, by "interpreting" the rule permissively. A determinate rule is less elastic and thus less amenable to such evasive strategy than an indeterminate one. * * *

To summarize: the legitimacy of a rule is affected by its degree of determinacy. Its determinacy depends upon the clarity with which it is able to communicate its intent and to shape that intent into a specific situational command. This, in turn, can depend upon the literary structure of the rule, its ability to avoid *reductio ad absurdum* and the availability of a process for resolving ambiguities in its application. * * *

As determinacy is the linguistic or literary-structural component of legitimacy, so *symbolic validation, ritual* and *pedigree* provide its cultural and anthropological dimension. As with determinacy, so here, the legitimacy of the rule—its ability to exert pull to compliance and to command voluntary obedience—is to be examined in the light of its ability to communicate. In this instance, however, what is to be communicated is not so much content as *authority:* the authority of a rule, the authority of the originator of a validating communication and, at times, the authority bestowed on the recipient of the communication. The communication of authority, moreover, is symbolic rather than literal. We shall refer to these symbolically validating communications as cues.

All ritual is a form of symbolic validation, but the converse is not necessarily true. *Pedigree* is a different subset of cues that seek to enhance the compliance pull of rules or rule-making institutions by emphasizing their historical origins, their cultural or anthropological deep-rootedness. * * * Professor Schachter has observed that a body of rules produced by the UN legislative drafting body, the International Law Commission, will be more readily accepted by the nations "after [the Commission] has devoted a long period in careful study and consideration of precedent and practice." Moreover, the authority will be greater if the product is labeled *codification* —that is, the interpolation of rules from deep-rooted evidence of state practice—"than if it were presented as a 'development' (that is, as new law)," even though the Commission (as a subsidiary of the General Assembly) is equally empowered by the UN Charter to promote "the progressive development of international law and its codification." The compliance pull of a rule is enhanced by a demonstrable lineage. A new rule will have greater difficulty finding compliance, and even evidence of its good sense may not fully compensate for its lack of breeding. Nevertheless, a new rule may be taken more seriously if it arrives on the scene under the aegis of a particularly venerable sponsor such as a widely ratified multilateral convention, or a virtually unanimous decision of the International Court of Justice. * * *

* * * Symbols of pedigree and rituals are firmly imbedded in state diplomatic practice. The titles ("ambassador extraordinary and plenipotentiary"), prerogatives and immunities of ambassadors, consuls and others functioning in a representative capacity are among the oldest of symbols and rites associated with the conduct of international relations. The sending state, by the rituals of accreditation, endows its diplomats with pedigree. They become, in time-honored tradition, a symbolic reification of the nation ("full powers" or *plenipotentiary*), a role that is ritually endorsed by the receiving state's ceremony accepting the envoy's credentials. These ceremonies, incidentally, are as old as they are elaborate and are performed with as remarkably faithful uniformity in Communist citadels as in royal palaces. Once accredited and received, an ambassador *is* the embodiment of the nation. The status of ambassador, once conferred, carries with it inherent rights and duties that do not depend on the qualities of the person, or on the condition of relations between the sending and receiving states, or on the relative might of the sending state. To insult or harm this envoy, no matter how grievous the provocation, is to attack the sending state. Moreover, when an envoy, acting officially, agrees to something, the envoy's state is bound, usually even if the envoy acted without proper authorization. The host state normally is entitled to rely on the word of an ambassador as if his or her state were speaking.

The venerable ritual practices of diplomacy are almost universally observed, and the rules that govern diplomacy are widely recognized as imbued with a high degree of legitimacy, being both descriptive and predictive of nearly invariable state conduct and reflecting a strong sense of historically endowed obligation. When the rules are violated—as they have been by Iran and Libya in recent years—the international community tends to respond by rallying around the rule, as the Security Council and the International Court of Justice demonstrated when the Iranian regime encouraged the occupation of the U.S. Embassy in Tehran. Violations of the elaborate rules pertaining to embassies and immunities usually lead the victim state to terminate its diplomatic relations with the offender. The offended state—as Britain demonstrated after the St. James Square shooting—usually takes care not to retaliate by means that the rules do not permit.

Both determinacy and symbolic validation are connected to a further variable: coherence. The effect of incoherence on symbolic validation can be illustrated by reference to diplomatic practices pertaining to the ritual validation of governments and states. The most important act of pedigreeing in the international system is the deep-rooted, traditional act that endows a new government, or a new state, with symbolic status. When the endowing is done by individual governments, it is known as *recognition.* The symbolic conferral of status is also performed collectively through a global organization like the United Nations when the members vote to admit a new nation to membership, or when the General Assembly votes to accept the credentials of the delegates representing a new government.

These two forms of validation are important because they enhance the status of the validated entity; that is, the new state or government acquires legitimacy, which, in turn, carries entitlements and obligations equal to those of other such entities. Such symbolic validation cannot alter the empirically observable reality of power disparity among states and governments, nor, properly understood, does it give off that cue. It does, however, purport to restrict what powerful states legitimately may do with their advantage over the weak. It is a cue that prompts the Soviets, however reluctantly, to do a lot of explaining when they invade Afghanistan. The pedigreed statehood of Afghanistan, together with the determinacy of the rules against intervention by one state in the internal affairs of another, then combine to render those Soviet explanations essentially unacceptable, global scorn evidencing the inelastic determinacy of the applicable rules. * * *

To summarize: coherence, and thus legitimacy, must be understood in part as defined by factors derived from a notion of community. Rules become coherent when they are applied so as to preclude capricious checkerboarding. They preclude caprice when they are applied consistently or, if inconsistently applied, when they make distinctions based on underlying general principles that connect with an ascertainable purpose of the rules and with similar distinctions made throughout the rule system. The resultant skein of underlying principles is an aspect of community, which, in turn, confirms the status of the states that constitute the community. Validated membership in the community accords equal capacity for rights and obligations derived from its legitimate rule system.

By focusing on the connections between specific rules and general underlying principles, we have emphasized the horizontal aspect of our central notion of a community of legitimate rules. However, there are vertical aspects of this community that have even more significant impact on the legitimacy of rules. * * *

* * * A rule * * * is more likely to obligate if it is made within the procedural and institutional framework of an organized community than if it is strictly an ad hoc agreement between parties in the state of nature. The same rule is still more likely to obligate if it is made within the hierarchically structured procedural and constitutional framework of a sophisticated community rather than in a primitive community lacking such secondary rules about rules. * * * Of course, there *are* lawmaking institutions in the system. One has but to visit a highly structured multinational negotiation such as the decade-long Law of the Sea Conference of the 1970s to see a kind of incipient legislature at work. The Security Council, the decision-making bodies of the World Bank and, perhaps, the UN General Assembly also somewhat resemble the cabinets and legislatures of national governments, even if they are not so highly disciplined and empowered as the British Parliament, the French National Assembly or even the U.S. Congress. Moreover, there *are* courts in the international system: not only the International Court of Justice, the European Community Court and the regional human rights tribunals, but also a very active network of quasi-judicial committees and commissions, as well as arbitral tribunals established under such auspices as the Algiers agreement ending the Iran hostage crisis. Arbitrators regularly settle investment disputes under the auspices and procedures of the World Bank and the International Chamber of Commerce. Treaties and contracts create jurisdiction for these tribunals and establish rules of evidence and procedure.

The international system thus appears on close examination to be a more developed community than critics sometimes allege. It has an extensive network of horizontally coherent rules, rule-making institutions, and judicial and quasi-judicial bodies to apply the rules impartially. Many of the rules are sufficiently determinate for states to know what is required for compliance and most states obey them most of the time. Those that do not, tend to feel guilty and to lie about their conduct rather than defy the rules openly. The system also has means for changing, adapting and repealing rules.

Most nations, most of the time, are both rule conscious and rule abiding. Why this is so, rather than that it is so, is also relevant to an understanding of the degree to which an international community has developed in practice. This silent majority's sense of obligation derives primarily not from explicit consent to specific treaties or custom, but from *status*. Obligation is perceived to be owed *to a community of states as a necessary reciprocal incident of membership in the community.* Moreover, that community is defined by secondary rules of process as well as by primary rules of obligation: states perceive themselves to be participants in a structured process of continual interaction that is governed by secondary rules of process (sometimes called rules of recognition), of which the UN Charter is but the most obvious example. The Charter is a set of rules, but it is also about how rules are to be made by the various institutions established by the Charter and by the subsidiaries those institutions have created, such as the International Law and Human Rights Commissions. * * *

In the world of nations, each of these described conditions of a sophisticated community is observable today, even though imperfectly. This does not mean that its rules will never be disobeyed. It does mean, however, that it is usually possible to distinguish rule compliance from rule violation, and a valid rule or ruling from an invalid one. It also means that it is not necessary to await the millennium of Austinian-type world government to proceed with constructing—perfecting—a system of rules and institutions that will exhibit a powerful pull to compliance and a self-enforcing degree of legitimacy.

*

INDEX

The Text of many of the documents indexed appears in the Coursebook
or in the Documentary Supplement of this Coursebook

References are to pages

†

1–56662–135–6

90000

9 781566 621359